The DORLING KINDERSLEY ENCYCLOPEDIA *of* FISHING

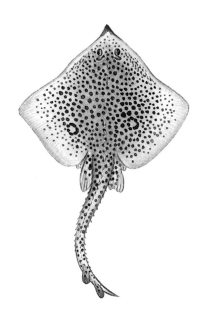

The DORLING KINDERSLEY ENCYCLOPEDIA *of* FISHING

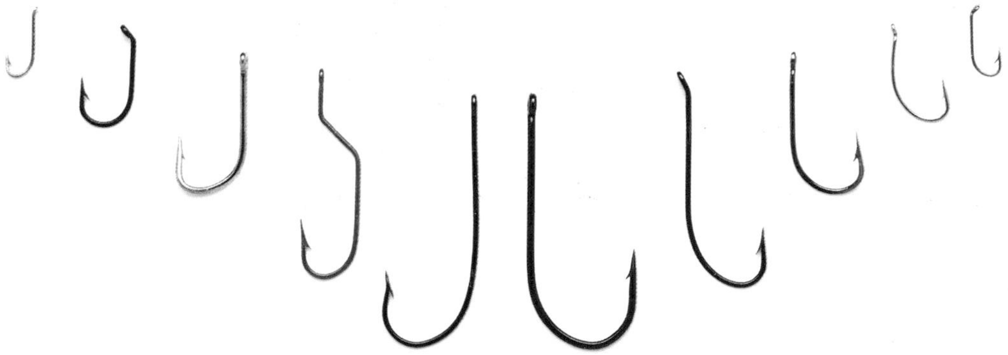

DORLING KINDERSLEY
London • New York • Stuttgart

A DORLING KINDERSLEY BOOK

Devised, designed, and edited for Dorling Kindersley by Bookbourne Limited
Editor: Ian Wood
Art Editor: Steve Leaning
Designer: Stuart John
Fish Species Illustrator: Colin Newman

Managing Editor: Krystyna Mayer
Managing Art Editor: Derek Coombes
Production Controller: Antony Heller
US Editor: Ray Rogers

Contributors: Peter Gathercole, Trevor Housby, Dennis Moss, Bruce Vaughan, Phill Williams

First American Edition, 1994
6 8 10 9 7 5
Published in the United States by
DK Publishing, Inc.,
95 Madison Avenue
New York, New York 10016

Library of Congress Cataloging-in-Publication Data

The Dorling Kindersley encyclopedia of fishing.—1st American ed.
p. cm.
Includes index.
ISBN 1-56458-492-5
1. Fishing—Encyclopedias.
2. Fishes—Encyclopedias.
SH411.E48 1994
799.1—dc20
93-28861
CIP

Typeset by Ace Filmsetting Limited, Somerset
Reproduced by J. Film Process, Singapore
Printed and bound in Italy by L.E.G.O.

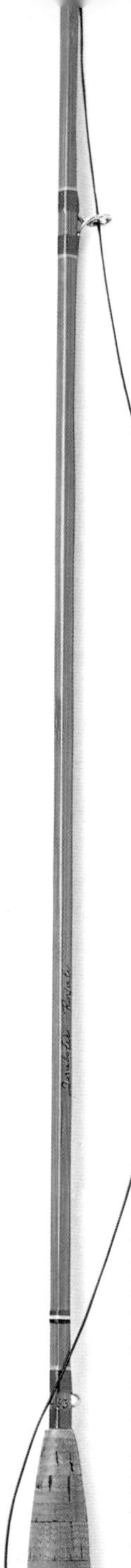

Contents

Species

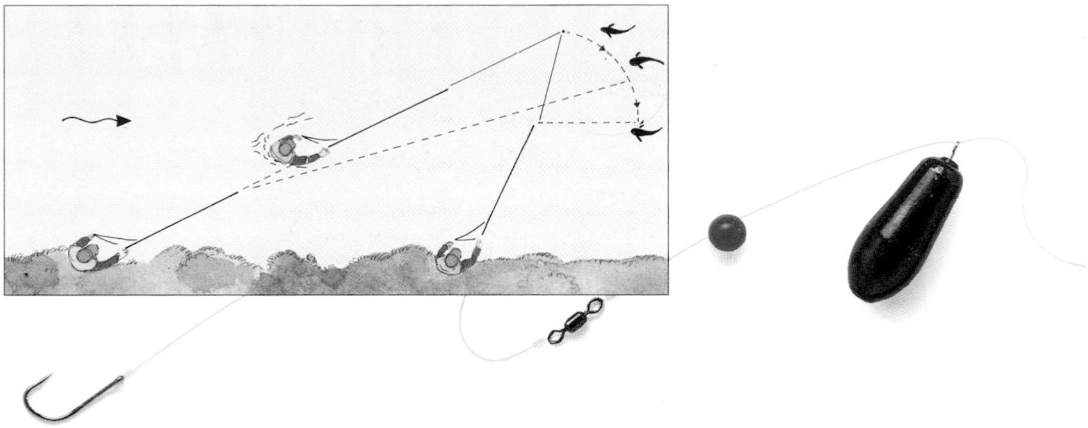

Techniques

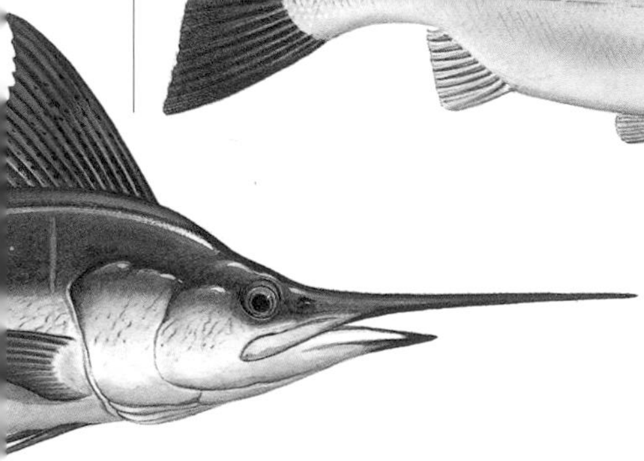

The Water

Appendices

FOREWORD

TREVOR HOUSBY
This book is dedicated to the memory of Trevor Housby, who died in August, 1993, shortly before it was completed.

As the amount of leisure time has increased during the course of the 20th century, so has the popularity of fishing, and with good reason: no other sport offers such a wide range of approaches, methodologies, and goals that appeal to so many people.

Fishing can mean dunking worms for catfish in a local pond or speed trolling for half-ton blue marlin 100 miles offshore. It can be a months-long cross-country bass fishing tournament or a quest for ultra-wary brown trout in a transparent mountain stream. Fishing can be a cerebral pursuit, a method of relaxation, a source of food, a contest of strength, or simply a fine way to spend a day outdoors. The choice is up to the angler.

There are many of us: more than 65 million in the United States alone, according to most recent surveys, plus millions more throughout the world. If you are joining these ranks, or are already part of them, *The Dorling Kindersley Encyclopedia of Fishing* was published for you.

Frank S. Golad
Almanac Editor, *Sports Afield*

INTRODUCTION

ANCIENT SPORT
The tranquility of freshwater angling is evoked by this old woodcut, which depicts an angler sitting at the edge of the water in the quiet early morning.

The development of angling techniques and tackle is a story of continuing advance, from the early days of simple fixed-line rods to the invention of the reel, and from then to the ever-improving modern tackle and methods of using it. This book describes typical examples of the latest rods, reels, and other essential items of tackle, tells you what baits to use in freshwater and in the sea, explains the basics of fly tying, and illustrates typical examples of the major categories of artificial fly. It also describes the major freshwater and marine fish species – which are depicted in beautiful full-color drawings – tells you how to catch them, and explains the secrets of "reading the water" to find out where the fish are.

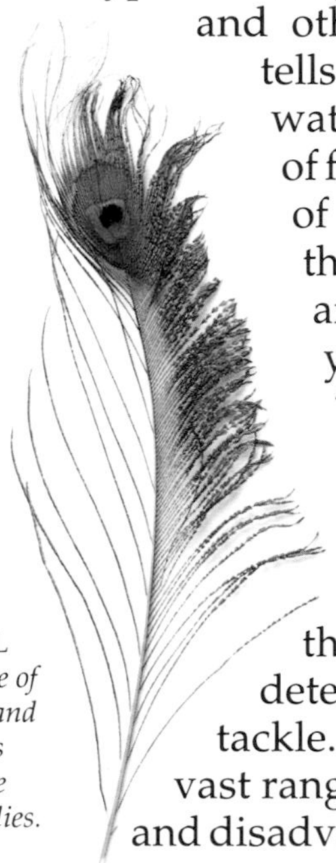

PEACOCK QUILL
Peacock quill is one of the many natural and synthetic materials that are used in the tying of artificial flies.

TACKLE

Good-quality tackle is as important to an angler as a well-tuned instrument is to a musician: the limits to your angling performance should be determined by your ability, not by any inadequacy of your tackle. This comprehensive chapter gives examples of the vast range of tackle on the market, discusses their advantages and disadvantages, and gives guidance on choosing basic outfits.

BAITS

You can have the best rods, reels, lines, and hooks in the world, but you will never catch fish unless you have good baits and know how to use them. This chapter tells you how to choose and use natural and processed baits for freshwater fishing, and how to mix and use

SEA FISHING
Saltwater anglers fish from beaches, rocks, piers, and harbor walls, and from private and charter boats. Here, anglers and crews are busy loading tackle, bait, and other supplies onto charter boats before setting off for a day's fishing.

freshwater chum. It describes the main types of artificial bait, including spinners, spoons, and plugs, and concludes with practical advice on the use of natural baits, chum, and lures in saltwater fishing. Flies, whether the natural insects or artificial patterns, are also baits, but because of their complexity they are described separately, in the following chapter.

SURFCASTING
Surf beaches are often exciting and very productive fishing venues. This angler is wading in the surf of Inch Beach, in County Kerry, Ireland, a wild Atlantic beach that is noted for its excellent bass fishing.

THE FLY

Fly fishing is one of the oldest forms of angling, and is known to have been practised in Macedonia as early as the 3rd century AD. Its age, complexity, and subtlety, and the fact that fishing on many of the best salmon and trout waters is beyond the financial reach of most anglers, have given it enormous prestige. But there is no doubt that catching a good-sized fish on an artificial fly, especially a fly that you have tied yourself, is an immensely rewarding experience. This experience is now available to everyone, thanks to the extensive stocking of reservoirs and other public waters with popular gamefish species such as brown trout and rainbow trout.

BOAT FISHING
Fishing from a small boat, whether on a pond or a large river, allows you to cover water that is beyond the casting range of anglers fishing from the bank or wading in the shallow margins.

This chapter describes the natural insects that form an important part of the diet of salmon, trout, bass, and other gamefish and also discusses and illustrates the different types of artificial fly, how they are tied, and how they are used.

SPECIES

There are thousands upon thousands of different fish species in the world, of which comparatively few are sought by anglers. But even this small minority of species is numbered in hundreds, and this chapter describes nearly 250 of them, from little freshwater fish such as dace and sunfish to ocean giants such as marlin and tuna. Each species is accurately illustrated in full color to make identification easy, and the accompanying text gives details of distribution, habitat, food, and size, and suggests techniques, tackle, and bait for catching them. The basic anatomy of fish is also described, with cutaway drawings to indicate the principal internal organs and the basic skeletal structure. The main differences between bony fish and cartilaginous fish are described, and there are details of important features such as types of scale, the functions of the lateral line, and how fish "breathe" with their gills.

WILD TROUT
Wild trout, such as these fine browns, tend to be warier and wilier than their hatchery-bred cousins, and can therefore be much harder to catch.

TECHNIQUES

In general, there is no single, foolproof method of catching a particular species in a particular water at any given time, and experienced anglers need little encouragement to argue for hours over the best technique to use. However, such arguments are usually about variations on the basic techniques and tackle rigs, and you need to learn these before you can begin to modify them in the light of personal experience and preference. In this chapter, you will find concise, easy-to-follow descriptions of a wide range of angling techniques, from pole fishing to big-game fishing.

LURES
Fishing with artificial lures, such as plugs and spinners, is an effective and enjoyable way to catch pike, perch, bass, and other predatory species.

THE WATER

There is a lot more to successful angling than acquiring the right tackle and learning how to use it. The best anglers are also good naturalists, who learn the habits of fish, and study currents, tidal flows, bankside vegetation, submerged weeds, the underwater topography, and a host of other natural and artificial underwater features that indicate where the fish are likely to be and what they will be feeding on. You can build up an enormous store of useful knowledge while you are fishing, simply by observing what is going on in and around the water, and noting how the movements and feeding habits of the fish vary with the time of day, the weather, and the light conditions. If you are a freshwater angler, studying your favourite fishing water during the closed season will help you to understand it better, and provide you with information that can be put to good use when the next season opens. This chapter gives an insight into the underwater world and its inhabitants, and tells you how to find the best fishing spots.

HANDLING FISH
Always handle fish with care, and return them promptly to the water if you are not keeping them for the table. Hold them securely but gently, and remove hooks carefully to minimize damage. When returning them, support them in the water until they have recovered their strength and are ready to swim off. Never leave discarded hooks, line, or other tackle on the bank or shore or in the water, where they will be a danger to birds and other forms of wildlife.

READING THE WATER
Experienced anglers who spend time studying the water in which they fish can read it like a map. They know where the fish are likely to be at a particular time, and can therefore usually avoid the frustration of fishing an unproductive stretch of water.

TACKLE

THE PRODUCTION OF FISHING TACKLE is one of the world's oldest industries, one that can trace its origins back to prehistoric times. The earliest known fishing implements were harpoons and small lengths of bone, antler, stone, or shell, pointed at each end, that were concealed within bait and fished on handlines. These were in use in Asia Minor during the Middle Stone Age (*c.* 12,000 to 9000 BC), and the first curved fish hooks, made of bone, appeared toward the end of that period. The first metal hooks, made of copper, were produced about 5000 BC, and since then the development of hooks has continued alongside that of metallurgy. The production of rods and reels is also an ancient craft. The Macedonians were using short rods to fish simple flies by the 3rd century AD, and the Chinese were probably using rod-and-reel combinations at around the same time.

Today, the manufacture of fishing tackle is a diverse, worldwide, and innovative industry, and its products are under continuous development. New styles and trends in angling are quickly catered for, and tackle manufacturers are among the first to exploit new alloys and composite materials. This chapter describes typical examples of the vast range of tackle now available to anglers, but these are of necessity just a small sample.

TACKLE CHOICE
Good-quality, well-balanced tackle is a pleasure to use and will improve your chances of landing a good catch.

Basic Tackle

When you are buying a basic outfit, always remember that having expensive tackle will not in itself guarantee that you will catch large numbers of fish. Additionally, if you are a newcomer to the sport, it is unlikely that you will be able to realize the full potential of your tackle anyway. It is far better to begin with a reliable but inexpensive outfit, and upgrade it as your angling skills develop.

Saltwater Fishing

In shore fishing, especially from a beach, the ability to cast long distances is important, but do not be misled into thinking that distance casting with high-performance tackle catches all the fish. Many species move into very shallow water, and if a beach slopes steeply, deep, fish-holding water may be quite close to the shore and easily covered with an inexpensive, relatively soft-actioned rod. For boat work, there is no single outfit that will cover every eventuality. For example, you cannot cast every distance with a basic boat rod, and a supple-tipped uptide rod cannot cope with the rigors of wreck fishing. Buy tackle appropriate to your intended style of fishing.

Shore fishing
In general, fishing from rocks or piers calls for less casting than fishing from an open beach, so the rods used need not be quite as refined in their design. What is needed is strong, reliable tackle, for beating heavy ground and subduing large fish from positions where your freedom of movement is restricted. This means having an outfit with plenty of backbone for pulling free from snags, steering fish away from obstacles, and lifting fish from the water with the rod. Comparatively short rods, well-made reels with high gear ratios, and strong, abrasion-resistant lines form the basis of shore-fishing kit.

Beach fishing
Because most beaches slope relatively gently, the deep, fish-holding water is usually further out than is the case on a rocky shore, and there is more need to place the baits a long way out. As a result, beach fishing tackle is generally lighter and more suited to distance casting than that used for rocky-shore fishing, but it should also be strong enough to deal with mixed or broken ground. However, rods designed primarily for casting are very stiff and demand a high level of skill, so until you have acquired that skill, use softer tackle that matches your ability, and fish close in for shallow-water species.

Boat fishing
To get the most out of boat fishing, you need at least two different rods plus suitable reels. The first rod should be a 2.1 m (7 ft), 13.6 kg (30 lb) class boat rod which, although too heavy for some aspects of boat work and a shade too light for others, will cope with most situations. The second, for casting out from the boat, should be a 9 to 10 ft (2.7 to 3 m) rod able to cast weights of up to 8 oz (227 g). In addition to these, it is worth having a 12 lb (5.4 kg) class boat rod or a 2 to 4 oz (57 to 113 g) uptider for light inshore work, or a 50 lb (22.7 kg) class boat rod for deep-water work and wreck fishing.

Big-game fishing
Big-game fishing is not a cheap pursuit, and specialist big-game tackle is expensive. However, most big-game charter boats will provide the tackle if required, and standard boat and casting tackle can be used when drift fishing for the smaller big-game species. Trolling requires a short, stiff rod to set the hook, and a heavy-duty reel with a smooth-acting drag mechanism (preferably a lever drag) and a large line capacity. A 30 to 50 lb (13.6 to 22.7 kg) class standup rod, with a 30- to 50-class lever drag reel, is adequate for all but the largest fish, for which 80 or 130 lb (36.3 or 59 kg) class tackle is advisable.

Shore Tackle
Rod: 11 ft (3.4 m) baitcaster.
Reel: baitcaster with two retrieve speeds.
Line: 20 to 40 lb (9.1 to 18.1 kg) mono.
Hooks: bait holder, in sizes from 1 to 8/0.
Terminal tackle: disposable sinkers, small bank sinkers, bullet sinkers; 30 to 60 lb (13.6 to 27.2 kg) leader mono; strong swivels; beads; line stops; selection of sliding floats.
Landing tackle: wherever access allows, use a gaff. When fishing a vertical drop, take a drop net.
Bait: crab, mackerel, squid, and worms.

Beach Tackle
Rod: 12 ft (3.7 m) surf.
Reel: baitcaster or large-capacity spinning.
Line: 12 to 18 lb (5.4 to 8.2 kg) mono.
Hooks: Aberdeens, in sizes 1 to 4/0.
Terminal tackle: bank and pyramid sinkers weighing from 2 to 6 oz (57 to 170 g); shock leader mono to 70 lb (31.8 kg); 20 to 40 lb (9.1 to 18.1 kg) leader mono; oval split rings; swivels; beads; selection of line stops.
Landing tackle: landing net or gaff.
Bait: crab, mackerel, squid, and worms.

Boat Tackle
Rods: a 7 ft (2.1 m), 30 lb (13.6 kg) class boat rod, and a 9 to 10 ft (2.7 to 3 m) uptide rod able to cast weights of up to about 8 oz (227 g).
Reels: baitcasters.
Line: 18 to 50 lb (8.2 to 22.7 kg) mono.
Hooks: bait holder, in sizes from 1 to 8/0.
Terminal tackle: selection of sinkers; 40 to 60 lb (18.1 to 27.2 kg) leader mono; strong swivels; beads.
Landing tackle: charter boats usually provide this.
Bait: crab, mackerel, squid, worms; mackerel feathers or Hokkai lures.

Big-Game Tackle
Rod: 30 to 50 lb (13.6 to 22.7 kg) class standup.
Reel: lever-drag baitcaster, 30- to 50-class.
Line: 30 to 50 lb (13.6 to 22.7 kg) big game.
Hooks: forged hooks rigged with suitable lures; wide-gap livebait hooks.
Terminal tackle: 100 to 200 lb (45.4 to 91 kg) mono and braided wire leaders; crimps; link swivels.
Landing tackle: the boat will supply this.
Bait: range of suitably rigged trolling lures to suit species sought; live and dead baits caught from or supplied by the boat.

Freshwater Fishing

The species of fish that live in freshwater are many and various, and many different methods of catching them have been developed. Some, particularly the non-predatory species, are fished for with natural or processed baits. These baits are sometimes fished on a freeline – the most natural presentation of all – but more usually they are presented beneath a float or on a weighted line that takes them down to the river or lake bottom. Predatory species can be fished for with natural baits, but they will also take artificial baits, or lures. Lures are very effective, and they have the added advantage of being more convenient to use than natural baits. Some are designed to imitate the prey of particular species, others simply to trigger the predators' aggressive instincts, and these principles are also used in the creation of artificial fly patterns. Trout, salmon, and many other freshwater species are taken by fly fishing, which is claimed by its countless devotees to be one of the most enjoyable of all forms of angling.

Lure fishing
Lure fishing is the pursuit of predatory species by casting and retrieving artificial baits, or lures, and it is the action of the lure on the retrieve that makes it attractive to fish. When lures are fished with a baitcaster reel, the technique is known as baitcasting; when a spinning or spincasting reel is used, it is known as spinning. Whichever type of reel is used, its slipping clutch or drag mechanism must be smooth-running, and the rod must be fitted with ceramic guides to prevent wear: as many as several thousand casts may be made in the course of a single lure-fishing session.

Lure-fishing rods include some of the shortest used in angling, and an ultralight baitcasting rod can be as short as 4½ ft (1.4 m). These little rods are ideal for use in confined areas, for example where dense bankside vegetation and overhanging trees make casting with a long rod difficult or impossible.

Bait fishing
In freshwater, almost all fishing with natural or processed baits is done with float or leger tackle. Floats are undoubtedly the most sensitive devices there are for detecting bites, and just about every species of freshwater fish can be caught on some form of float rig.

Floats consist of two basic types: those attached to the line by the top and the bottom and designed mainly for river work, and those attached by the bottom end only, which can be used on both still and moving water.

In legering, baits are presented on the bottom of the river or lake, anchored by a weight or weights attached to the line. Although it is not as sensitive as float fishing, legering is a very good method of presenting baits to bottom-feeding fish, and it is often more effective than float fishing, for instance when fishing in swiftly flowing streams or at extreme range on large stillwaters.

Pole fishing
In pole fishing there is no reel: the line is attached to the pole tip either directly or via a length of shock-absorbing elastic. Because there is no running line, control of the terminal tackle is very precise. Fishing with a pole is one of the oldest forms of angling, and poles were in use for centuries before the reel was invented. The traditional cane pole is still around, but pole technology was revolutionized by the introduction of glass fiber poles in the 1960s. These have since been largely replaced by carbon fiber poles, either telescopic or take-apart, which are extremely light and strong, and easy to handle despite being anything up to 56 ft (17 m) in length.

Poles are always fished in conjunction with floats, and because they are most often used to catch small fish, a great variety of small and highly sensitive pole floats have been developed to show up the most delicate of bites.

Fly fishing
Many species can be taken on an artificial fly, but most freshwater fly fishing is for the members of the salmon family and for largemouth and smallmouth bass.

The main categories of artificial fly are dry flies, wet flies, and nymphs. Dry flies are fished on the surface of the water, while wet flies and nymphs are fished submerged. Dry-fly fishing is probably the most visually exciting way to catch trout and salmon, but its use is restricted to the warm months of the year, when the fish are feeding on insects at or near the surface.

The most important skill you need for successful fly fishing is an ability to cast well, and the best way to learn casting is to take lessons from a properly qualified instructor. Casting a fly is enjoyable in itself, and it is worth learning how to do it properly in a variety of styles to suit different weather and water conditions.

Lure Tackle

Rod: 7 to 9 ft (2.1 to 2.7 m) spinning or baitcasting rod with a medium to stiff action.
Reel: spinning or small baitcaster.
Line: 8 to 10 lb (3.6 to 4.54 kg) mono.
Hooks: already on lures (usually trebles).
Terminal tackle: wire leaders; swivels; anti-kink vanes; weights for fishing buoyant baits just off bottom in snaggy waters.
Landing tackle: landing net, or glove for lifting out sharp-toothed species.
Bait: spinners, spoons, and plugs to suit quarry.

Bait Tackle

Rod: 12 ft (3.7 m) float or 10 ft (3 m) leger; or an 11 ft (3.4 m) Avon rod for both float fishing and legering.
Reel: spinning.
Line: 3 lb (1.36 kg) mono for float fishing, 6 lb (2.7 kg) mono for legering.
Hooks: sizes 12 to 26 for float fishing, sizes 2 to 12 for legering.
Terminal tackle: split shot; swimfeeders and weights for legering; selection of stick, round, and oblong floats for float fishing.
Landing tackle: landing net.
Bait: maggots, bread, worms, hempseed.

Pole Tackle

Pole: carbon fiber, about 16 to 23 ft (5 to 7 m) long.
Line: mono, 8 to 12 oz (227 to 340 g) for very small fish, stronger pro rata for bigger, heavier species.
Hooks: spade-ended, in sizes 16 to 26 fine-wire for small fish, and sizes 10 to 16 medium-wire for larger fish.
Terminal tackle: bristle, bung, and quill floats; split shot; olivettes (BB shot); selection of ready-made rigs.
Landing tackle: fine-mesh pan net with a long but stiff telescopic handle.
Bait: maggots, bloodworms, bread, hempseed.

Fly Tackle

Rod: 10 ft (3 m), #6/7 medium-action fly rod.
Reel: lightweight fly reel taking a #6/7 line and 50 yds (46 m) backing.
Fly lines: floating, neutral density, medium-sinking, fast-sinking.
Leaders: 2 to 5 lb (910 g to 2.27 kg) for dry fly, 6 lb (2.7 kg) for wet fly, 7 to 12 lb (3.2 to 5.4 kg) for lures.
Landing tackle: folding or landing net.
Flies: selection of dry, wet, nymph, and lure patterns to suit species sought, style of fishing, water conditions, and season.

The Rod

Until the middle of the 19th century, rods were made of woods such as hazel, ash, hickory, and greenheart, but in the 1840s both William Blacker in England and Samuel Phillippe in Pennsylvania began fashioning rods from split cane, which is bamboo split lengthwise into strips and glued together. Split cane rods proved lighter, more flexible, and more durable than wooden rods, and cane was to remain the most popular rod material for over a hundred years. It is still used today for expensive, hand-built fly rods, but since the late 1940s its use has rapidly declined in the face of strong competition from man-made materials. Tubular steel and aluminum were its first challengers, but were quickly superseded by fiberglass, itself now eclipsed by even newer materials, including boron, Kevlar, and, most successful of all, carbon fiber (graphite).

Rod Components

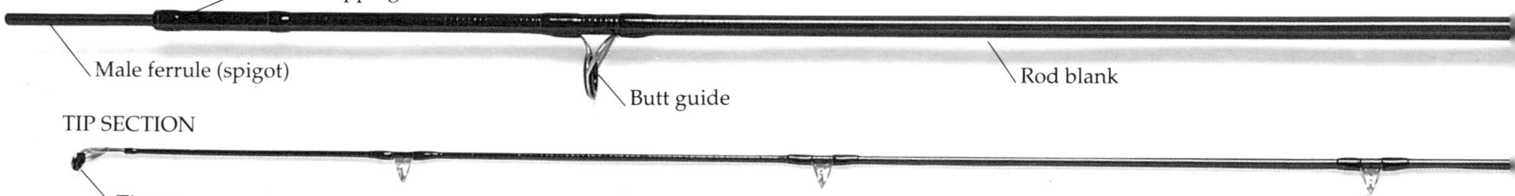

Rod Guides

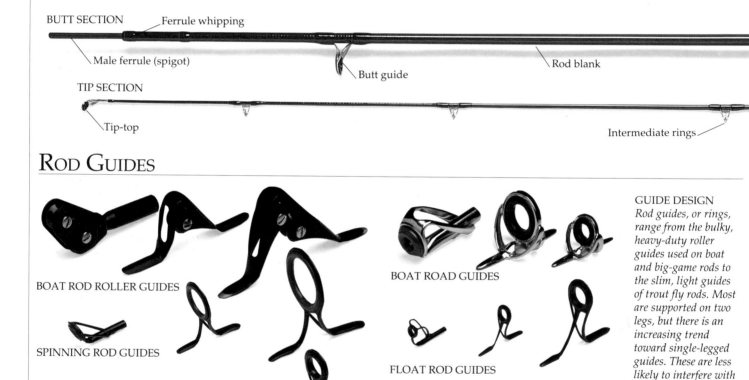

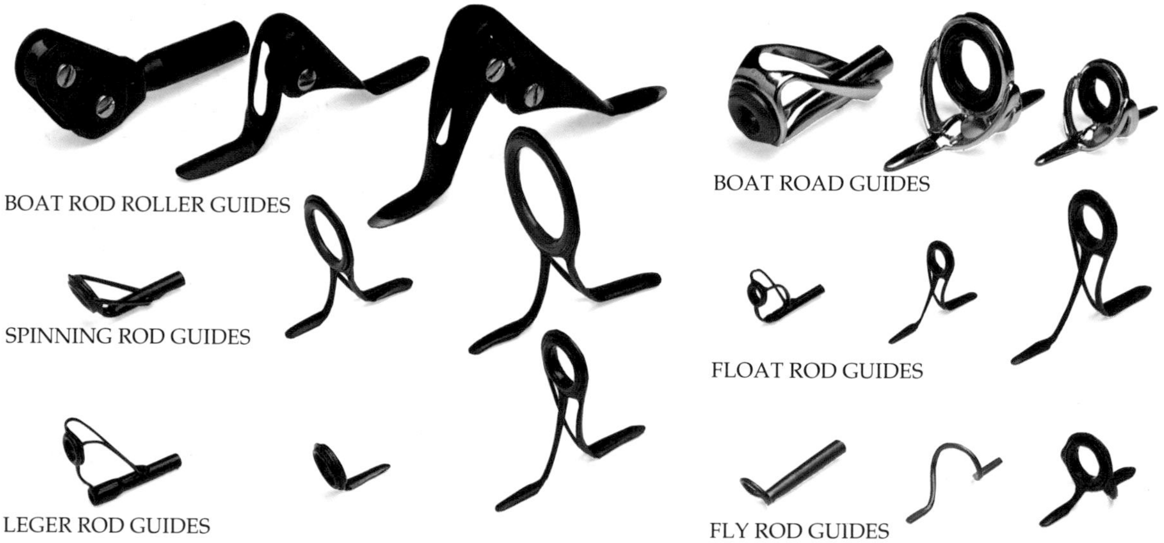

GUIDE DESIGN
Rod guides, or rings, range from the bulky, heavy-duty roller guides used on boat and big-game rods to the slim, light guides of trout fly rods. Most are supported on two legs, but there is an increasing trend toward single-legged guides. These are less likely to interfere with the action of the rod, and because of improvements in ring technology they are just as strong as two-legged guides.

Beachcasting, spinning, and leger rod guides
Generally, all three types of rod are fitted with circular guides, most of which are lined to reduce wear (of both line and guide) and friction. On standard leger rods the tip guide is often threaded to take a screw-in tip, while on rods with spliced-in quivertips the fine tip is normally ringed with lined, single-legged guides. Some boat rods sport roller guides throughout, or roller butt and tip guides with low-bridge intermediates. Rollers cut down resistance to the passage of line and minimize guide wear, particularly when wire line is being used.

Float rod guides
The most important task of float rod guides is to keep the line away from the blank. This is particularly important in wet weather, when line is all too ready to stick to the rod, inhibiting the flow of line from the spool and ultimately the presentation of the bait. For this reason, float rods use standoff guides, usually hard chrome and lined with durable, low-friction materials such as aluminum oxide or silicon carbide.

Fly rod guides
In the past, trout fly rods were always fitted with stainless steel or hard chrome guides: circular, bridge-type tip and butt guides, with snake intermediates – pieces of twisted wire whipped down at both ends. Snake guides are still in use today, but many rods are now fitted with ceramic-lined guides, usually two-legged butt guides (to withstand the rigors of heavy casting) plus single-legged intermediates. Light salmon rods generally have a similar guide configuration, but those for heavy-duty work usually have two-legged intermediate guides.

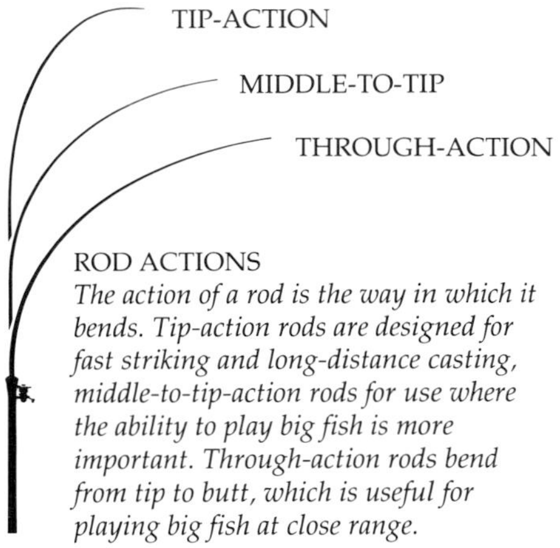

ROD ACTIONS

The action of a rod is the way in which it bends. Tip-action rods are designed for fast striking and long-distance casting, middle-to-tip-action rods for use where the ability to play big fish is more important. Through-action rods bend from tip to butt, which is useful for playing big fish at close range.

GLOSSARY OF TERMS

AFTMA scale A method of classifying fly lines according to their weight and other characteristics, devised by the American Fishing Tackle Manufacturers Association (AFTMA). Fly rods are classified by the AFTMA number of the line they are designed to cast (the higher the AFTMA number, the heavier the line).

Blank The basic rod minus its fittings such as guides, reel seat, and ferrules.

Butt The handle section of the rod.

Line class Boat rods are classified by the breaking strain of the line with which they should be used, for example a 30 lb (13.6 kg) class rod with 30 lb (13.6 kg) line.

Reel seat Device for fixing reel to rod.

Taper The change in the diameter and wall thickness of the rod from tip to butt. The taper of a rod has a direct effect on its action.

Test curve This gives an indication of the power a rod possesses. It is the amount of force that is needed to pull the tip end of the rod around until it is at a right angle to the butt end.

Winch fitting The reel seat.

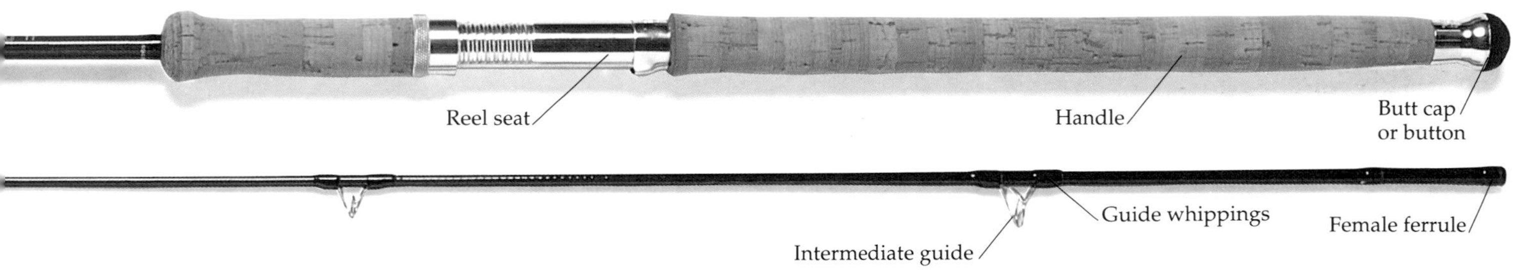

REEL SEATS

SLIDING RINGS

This simple method of siting the reel has the advantage of flexibility in positioning, but its drawback is that it is not very secure.

FIXED BUTT CAP/SLIDING RING

This is not a very secure fitting, but it is often used on the shorter fly rods, where it is desirable to keep weight to the minimum.

UPLOCK/DOWNLOCK

In this version of the screw winch, the reel foot locates either in a recess in the cork handle (uplocking) or in a fixed butt cap (downlocking).

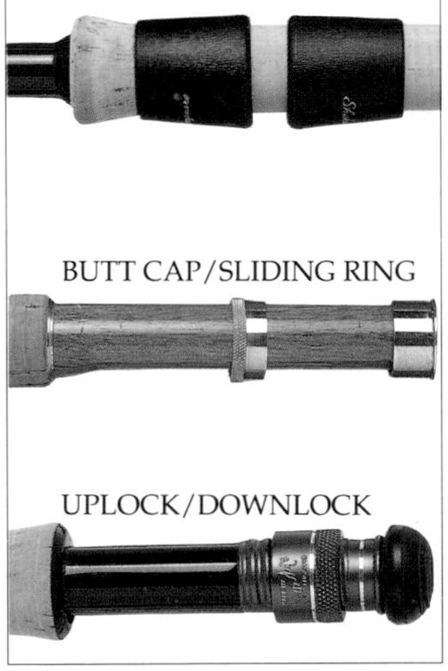

SLIDING RINGS

BUTT CAP/SLIDING RING

UPLOCK/DOWNLOCK

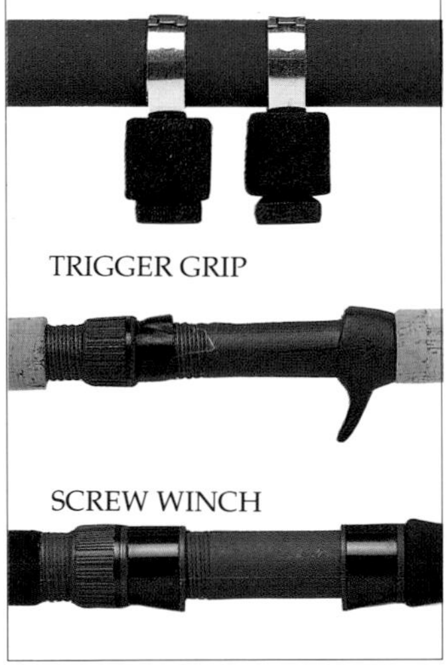

COASTERS

TRIGGER GRIP

SCREW WINCH

COASTERS

Like sliding rings, coasters have the advantage of flexible reel positioning, but with the additional security of a pair of locking rings.

TRIGGER GRIP

Designed for baitcasting reels that sit on top of the handle, the trigger forms a comfortable grip for the forefinger of the rod hand.

SCREW WINCH

The twin locking rings make for a very secure fixing, but there is no choice of positioning on the handle to suit the individual angler.

FERRULES

Ferrules are the components that join the sections of a rod together. Most are overfit ferrules, in which the upper (female) section fits straight over the spigot of the lower (male) section. The spigot is usually a cylindrical length of carbon fiber, of smaller diameter than the blank, at the tip of the lower section. Two-piece brass ferrules are used on cane rods, and a typical boat rod has a one-piece blank joined to the handle by a combined ferrule and reel seat.

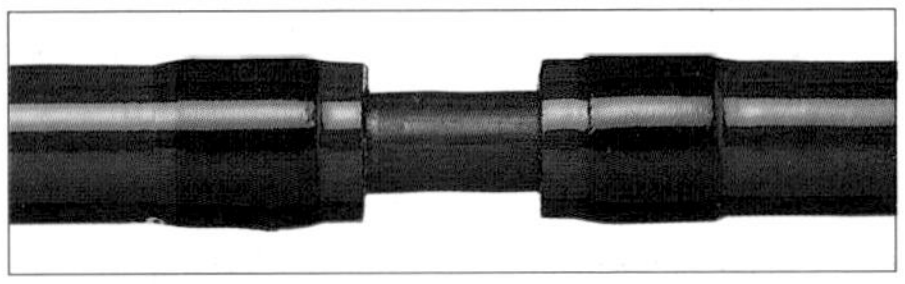

SPIGOT FERRULE

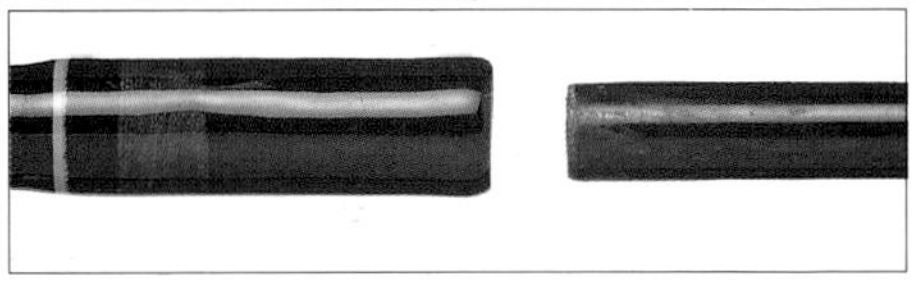

OVERFIT FERRULE

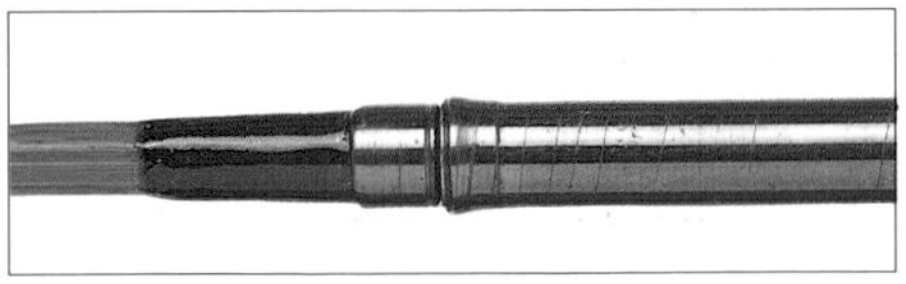

BRASS FERRULE

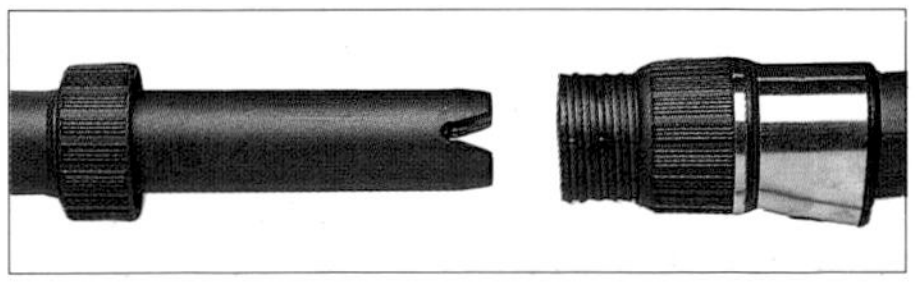

COMBINED FERRULE/REEL SEAT

Spinning Rods

Spinning rods are designed to cast artificial lures of all types. They need to be as light as possible because they may well be in use for many hours at a time, and should be fitted with guides of the highest quality because many hundreds, if not thousands, of casts may be made during a single fishing session. For general spinning, a rod with a medium action is best. Such a rod will bend progressively from the tip into the middle section, leaving latent power nearer the handle to come into play should a big fish be hooked. Anglers specializing in fishing surface lures need a stiff, tip-actioned rod for best results, because this type will impart the most life into the lures. One-piece rods, generally under 7 ft (2.1 m) long, are often known as baitcasters. These are designed for use with a small baitcaster reel seated on top of the rod rather than with a spinning reel positioned below it.

SHIMANO CANIS CS80D-T
This is an 8 ft (2.4 m), two-piece rod, with a forefinger trigger on the reel seat for a secure and comfortable grip of both rod and reel. It is designed to be used in conjunction with small plugs, and is particularly suitable for salmon and steelhead fishing. The recommended lure weights for this rod are ⅜ to ¾ oz (10 to 20 g), and these should be fished on 8 to 12 lb (3.6 to 5.4 kg) lines.

SHIMANO CANIS CS80D-T

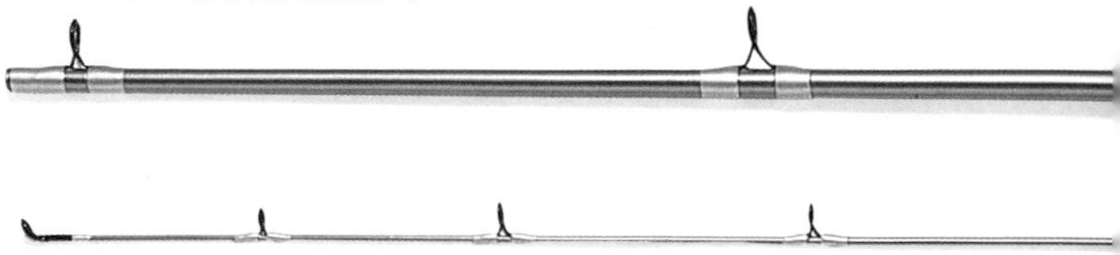

SHIMANO CONVERGENCE CV70H2

DAIWA OSPREY AWS10M

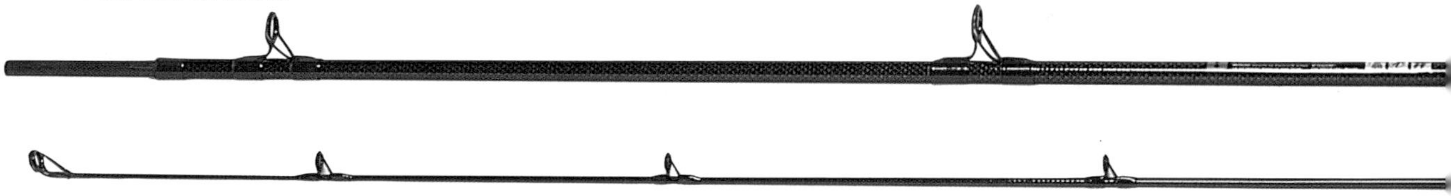

SOUTH BEND PROFESSIONAL

HARDY FAVOURITE
This 8½ ft (2.6 m) rod from the long-established Hardy Favourite range is ideal for medium spinning conditions, and equally at home with a spinning reel or a light baitcaster. Weighing 7 oz (198 g), it is designed to cast weights up to 1¼ oz (35 g) on 6 to 12 lb (2.7 to 5.4 kg) line.

HARDY FAVOURITE

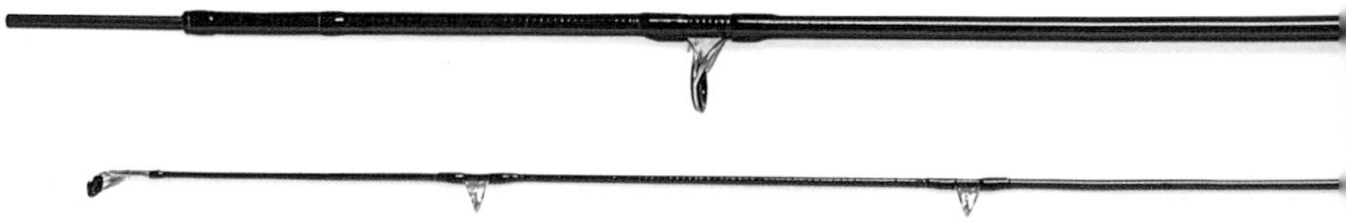

DAIWA OSPREY AWS9S

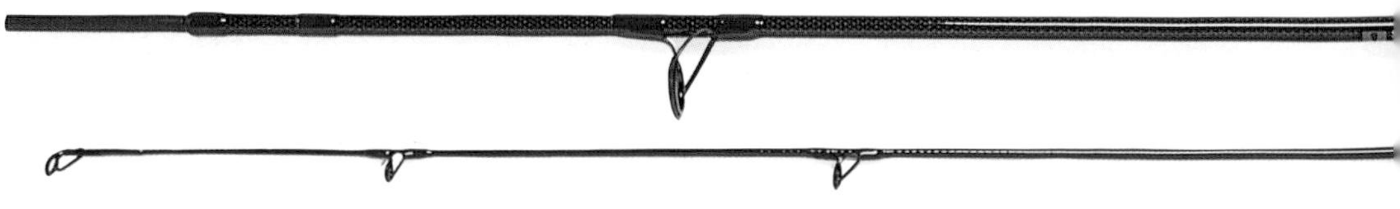

DAIWA OSPREY AWS9S
This 9 ft (2.7 m), two-piece rod is whipped with Fuji SiC (silicon carbide) guides and used with a spinning reel. It is at its best when casting artificials weighing from ¼ to 1 oz (7 to 30 g).

SHIMANO CONVERGENCE CV70H2

The Convergence CV70H2 is a 7 ft (2.1 m) baitcasting rod with a snappy action. The blank material has a high carbon content, and the rod is at its best when casting plugs, spoons, and spinners in the ¾ to 2 oz (20 to 60 g) weight range. It sports a comfortable forefinger trigger on the reel seat, is lined throughout with hard-wearing, three-legged Fuji guides, and is suitable for use with 12 to 25 lb (5.4 to 11.3 kg) lines.

DAIWA OSPREY AWS10M

A construction process combining carbon cloth with 24-strand amorphous metal braid and silicon carbide whiskers produces an extremely light rod, weighing only 10 oz (283 g), with plenty of power. Made in two sections, this 10 ft (3 m) rod is fitted with a forefinger trigger and screw winch reel fitting. It is designed for use with a baitcaster reel, and for casting lures in the ⅜ to 1¾ oz (10 to 50 g) weight range.

SOUTH BEND PROFESSIONAL

The South Bend Professional is a 5½ ft (1.7 m), one-piece baitcasting rod with a medium action and a short, but comfortable, pistol-grip handle with forefinger trigger. The best performance of this light, compact piece of tackle is achieved when it is used with a small baitcaster reel filled with 10 to 20 lb (4.54 to 9.1 kg) monofilament line and casting plugs and spinners weighing about ¼ to ¾ oz (7 to 20 g).

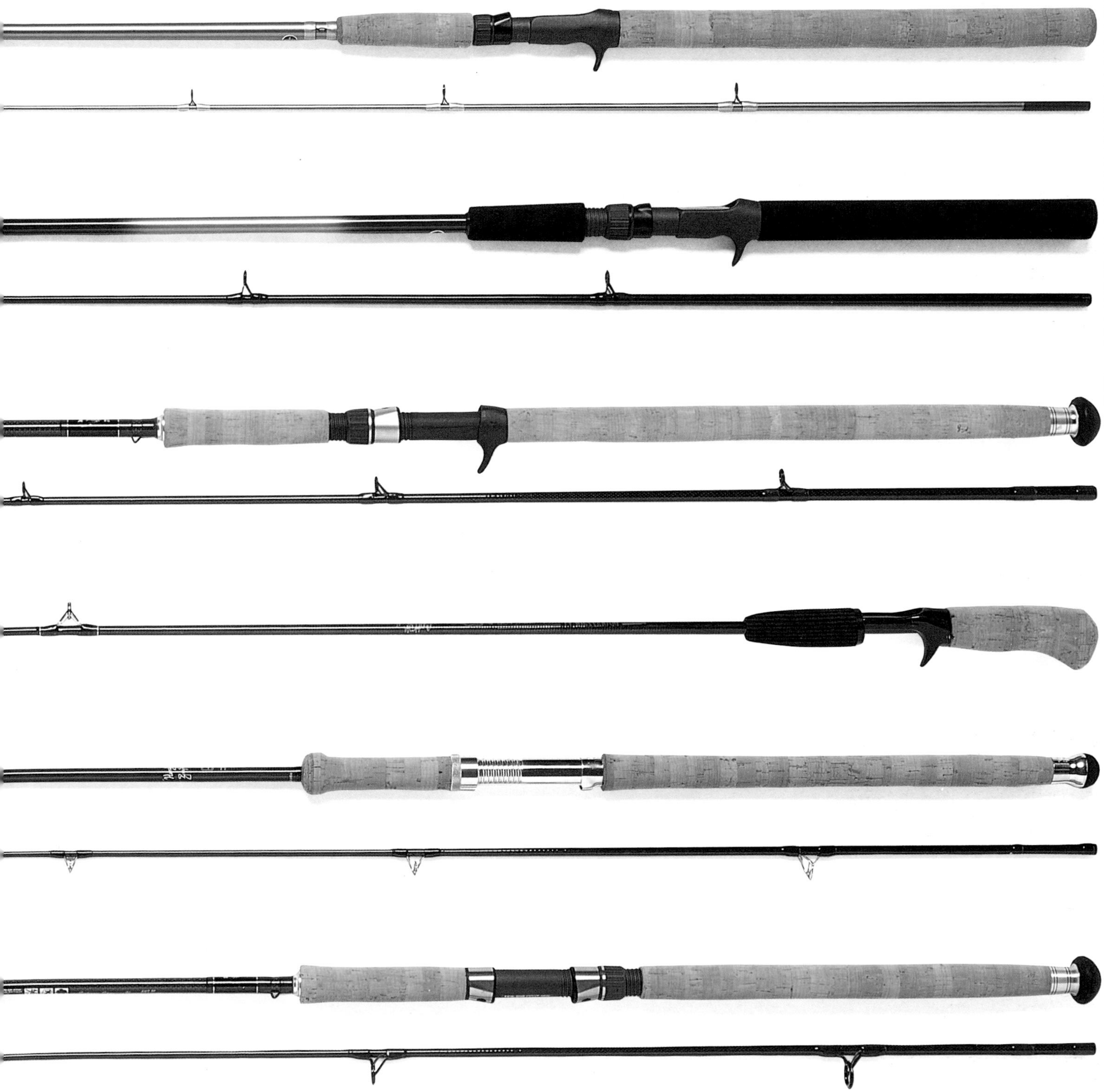

Leger Rods

Leger rods can be separated into two basic types. The first is the standard rod, generally between 9 and 10 ft (2.7 and 3 m) in length, with a threaded tip ring to take a swingtip or quivertip but also suitable for touch legering. The action of standard rods ranges from soft to stiff. A soft action is best when a swingtip is to be used, because steady, looping casts and a progressive lifting of the rod on the strike are called for if tangling around the rod tip is to be avoided. The second leger rod type is that with a spliced-in quivertip. Although most commonly used on rivers, rods with spliced-in quivertips can be fished on stillwaters. They are particularly useful for the pursuit of shy or wary fish.

SHIMANO TWIN POWER HEAVY FEEDER

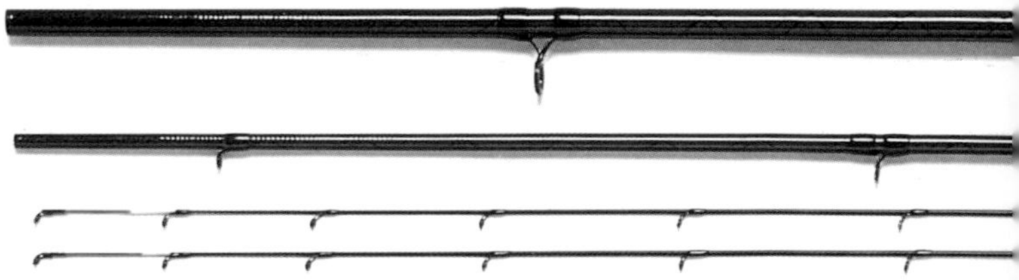

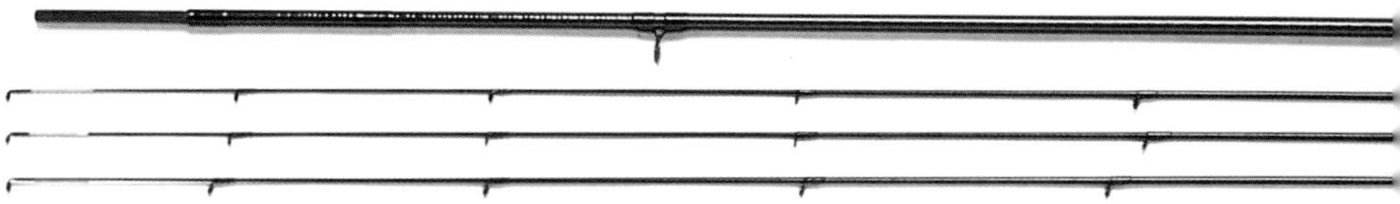

DAIWA AWL9QT CANAL

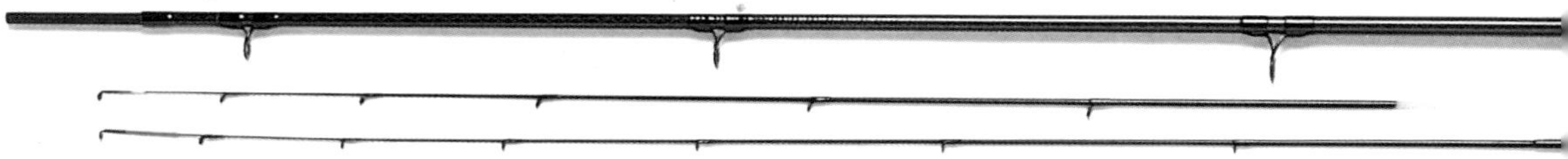

HARDY RICHARD WALKER CARP NO. 1

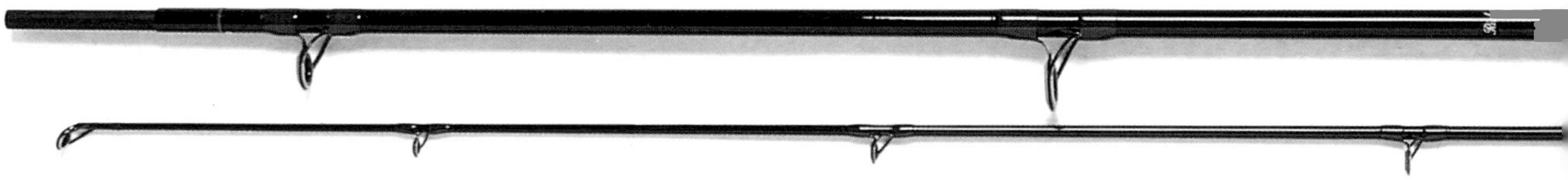

RYOBI JOHN WILSON AVON/QUIVERTIP

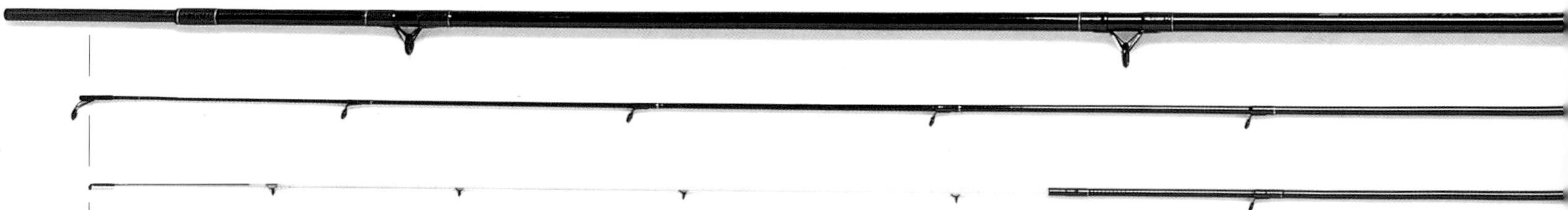

SHAKESPEARE CLUBMASTER TWIN-TIP

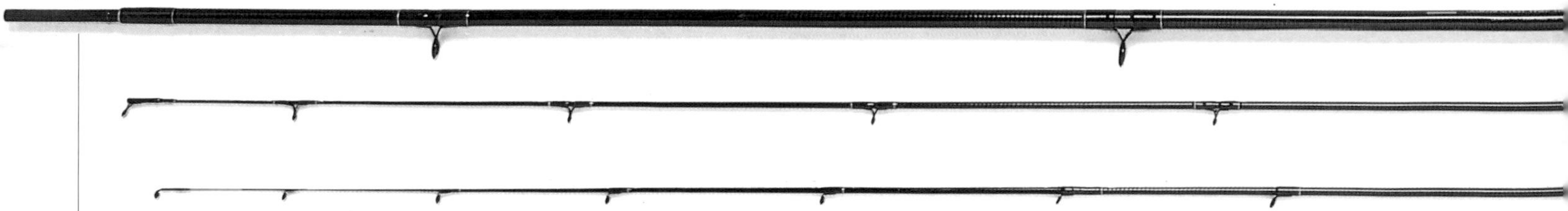

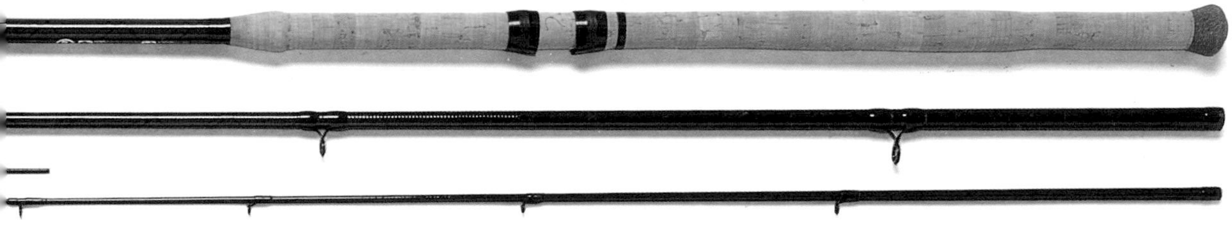

SHIMANO TWIN POWER HEAVY FEEDER

This powerful 12 ft (3.7 m) graphite rod, designed for use with heavy crankbaits on big waters, is capable of casting weights of 2 to 3½ oz (60 to 100 g) up to 60 yds (55 m). It comes with two tips and the handle is fully covered in cork.

DAIWA AWL11QT MULTI-QUIVER

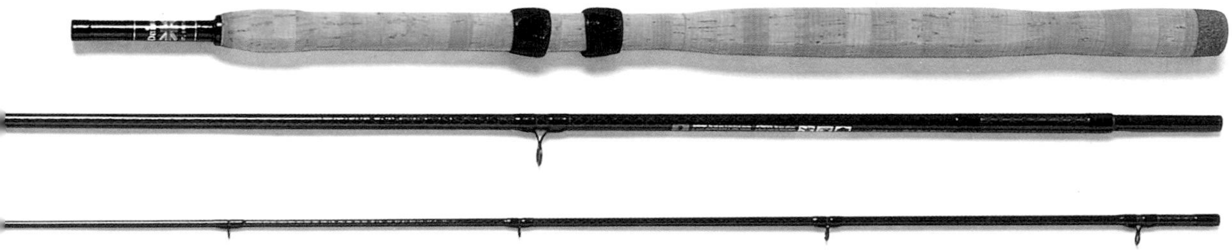

DAIWA AWL11QT MULTI-QUIVER

This 11 ft (3.4 m), light to medium rod comes complete with three push-in quivertips (light, medium, and heavy) to cover a wide range of fishing situations. It is capable of casting lures a long way, but it will not pull the hook out of a fish at close range.

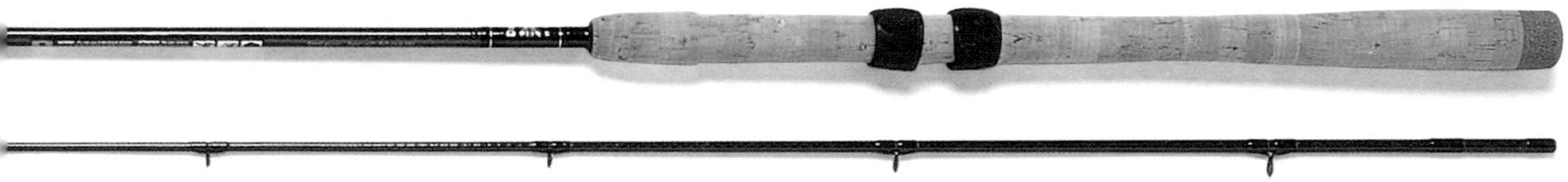

DAIWA AWL9QT CANAL

This 9 ft (2.7 m) rod was developed for drain or canal fishing, and has two push-in quivertips, one soft and one extra soft, for indicating the tiniest, most delicate bites.

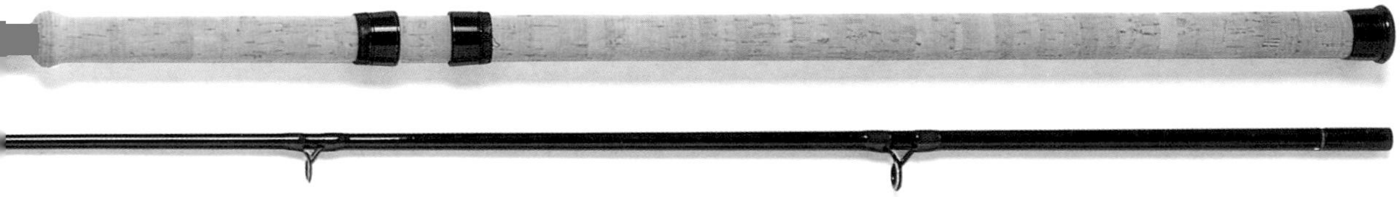

HARDY RICHARD WALKER CARP NO. 1

The Richard Walker Carp No. 1 is a two-piece, 10 ft (3 m) rod made on a fiberglass blank. Its test curve is 1½ lb (680 g), making it suitable for 6 to 10 lb (2.7 to 4.54 kg) lines.

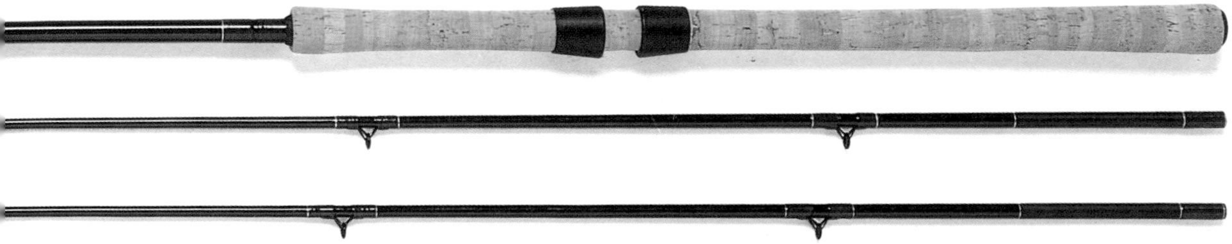

RYOBI JOHN WILSON AVON/QUIVERTIP

Avons are standard leger rods, usually 11 or 12 ft (3.4 or 3.7 m) long, designed for powerful fish in fast rivers. The Ryobi John Wilson Avon/Quivertip has two top sections, one an Avon, the other with a spliced-in quivertip.

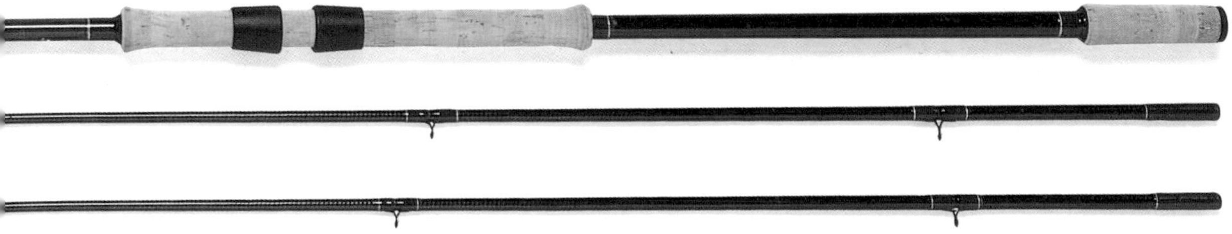

SHAKESPEARE CLUBMASTER TWIN-TIP

This versatile 11 ft (3.4 m) feeder rod has two top sections, one with a spliced-in quivertip, the other a standard top with threaded tip ring for attaching a quivertip, springtip, or swingtip. The carbon blank is fitted with lined guides to reduce wear.

FLOAT RODS

Most float rods (including those termed match rods) are made of carbon fiber. As a general rule, the greater the percentage of carbon there is in the blank, the better the rod will perform. Rods 12 to 13 ft (3.7 to 4 m) in length will meet most float-fishing requirements, while longer rods, of 14 to 15 ft (4.3 to 4.6 m), are better for fishing very deep swims. Even longer rods, of up to 20 ft (6.1 m) or more, are used in the "Bolognese method" of fishing (so called because it originated in Italy), which is a recent arrival on the match-fishing scene. Their benefit is seen as giving superior float control, as with a pole, but with the advantage of a running line. Select a rod with a sensitive tip action when after small fish, and one with a through action when fishing for bigger fish such as tench and small carp. Float rod handles should be no longer than about 24 in (60 cm) and around ⅞ to 1 in (2.2 to 2.5 cm) in diameter.

SHIMANO DIAFLASH MATCH 360

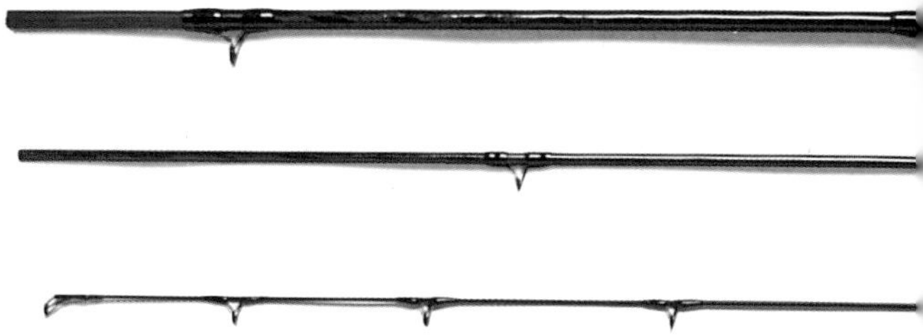

SHIMANO POWER LOOP MATCH 450

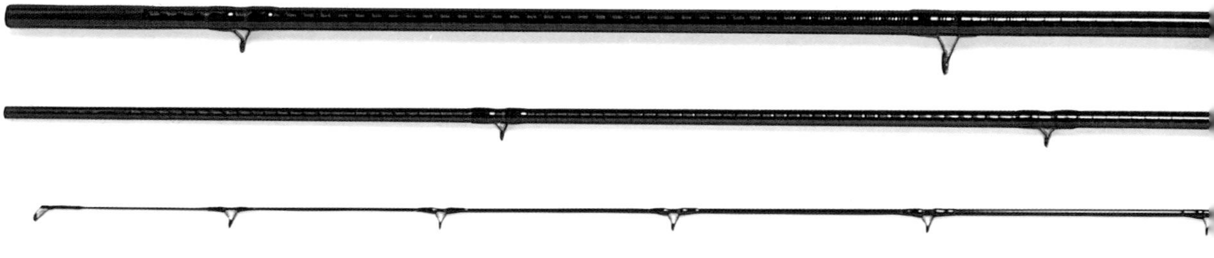

DAIWA TDCM14LD

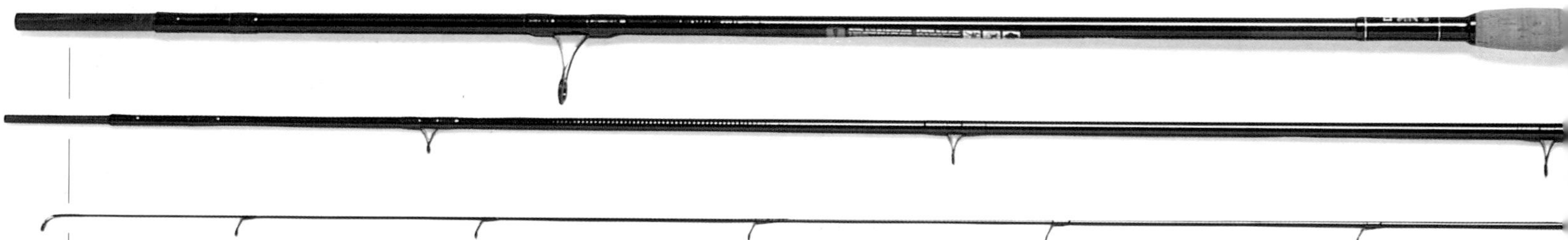

SHIMANO DIAFLASH 390H

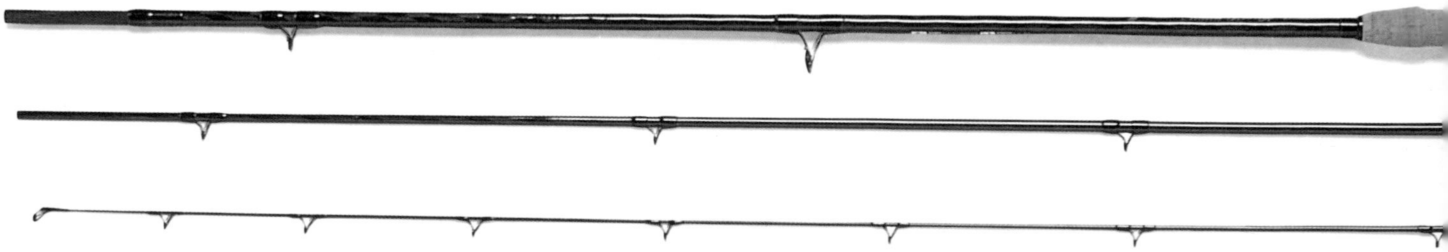

DAIWA TDCM13W

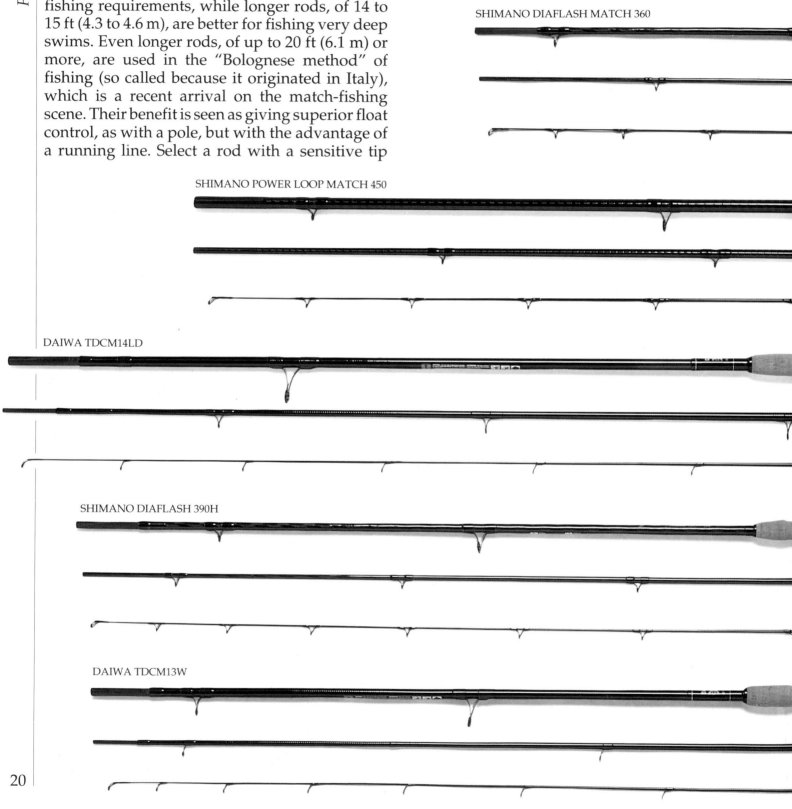

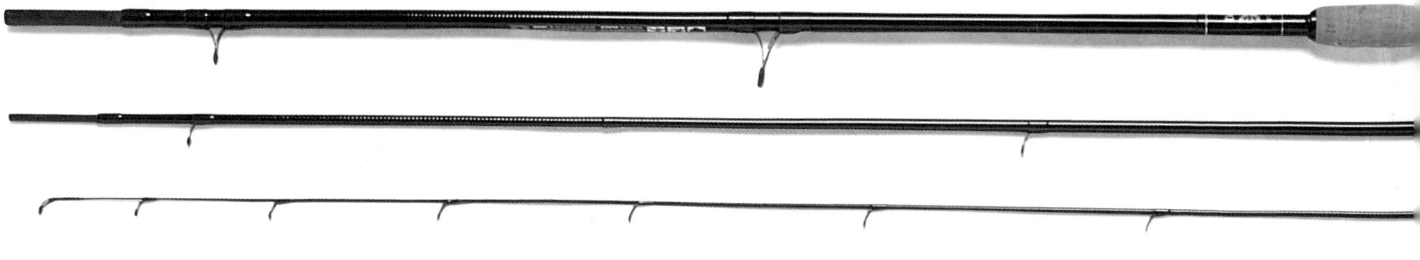

SHIMANO DIAFLASH MATCH 360

The Match 360, a beautifully balanced 12 ft (3.7 m) tournament rod, is considered to be one of the better models currently available for general float work. Manufactured from high-quality carbon fiber, it is extremely light and slim and possesses a crisp action with rapid tip recovery. It is ringed throughout with Fuji guides lined with hard-wearing silicon carbide (SiC), has a slim, 2 ft (60 cm) cork handle, and is suitable for both bait and jig fishing.

SHIMANO POWER LOOP MATCH 450

This 15 ft (4.6 m) rod is aimed at the float angler who wants a longer rod at a competitive price. It is a versatile rod, suitable for a variety of float-fishing situations, but is especially useful for fishing at long range and in deepwater swims, where its extra length and good line pickup ability will score. Finished in an attractive reddish brown, it has a comfortable cork handle and is whipped with guides lined with hard-wearing aluminum oxide.

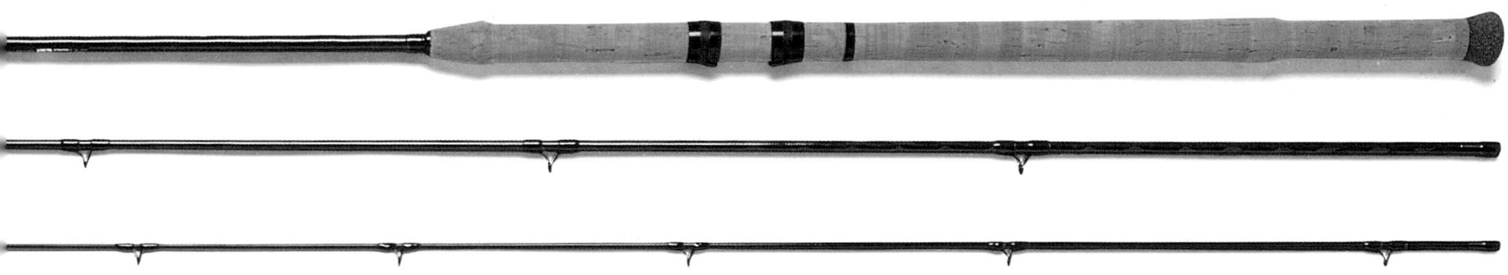

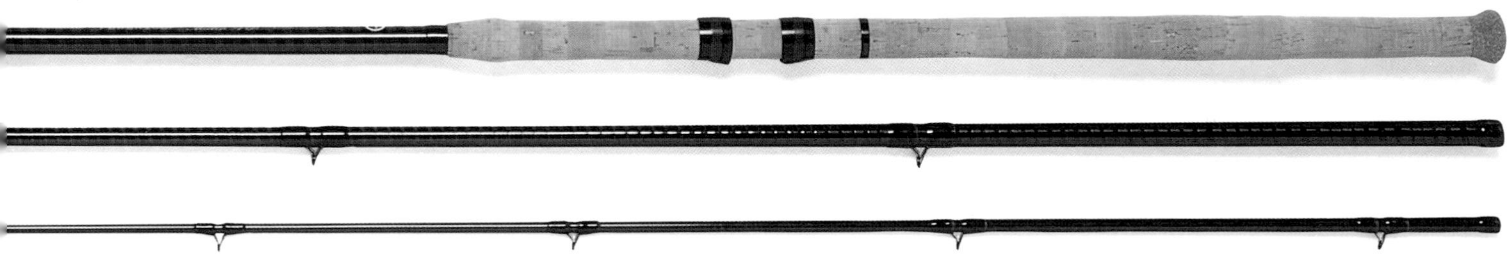

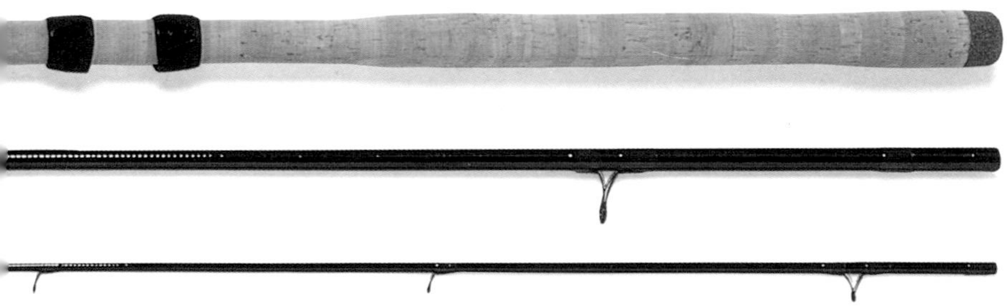

DAIWA TDCM14LD

This 14 ft (4.3 m) rod is designed for long-range or deepwater float fishing with 2½ to 4 lb (1.1 to 1.8 kg) reel lines and hook links down to 1½ lb (680 g). When fishing outsize jigs at range, however, it is advisable to use a shock leader of 6 to 8 lb (2.7 to 3.6 kg) mono between the reel line and hook link. A shock leader absorbs the stress of casting heavy terminal tackle, which can break a relatively light reel line; it should be twice the length of the rod plus a few turns around the reel spool.

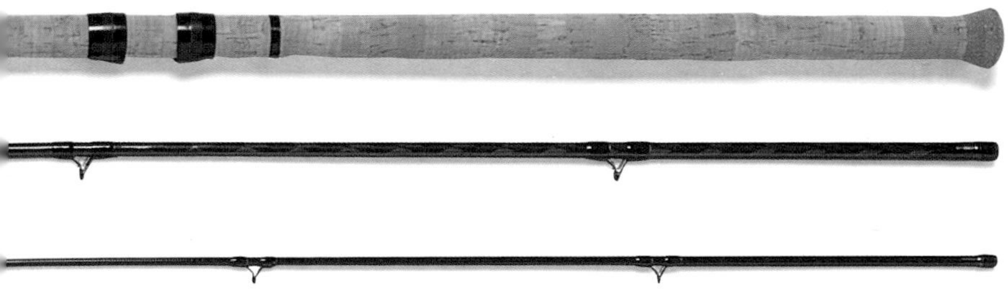

SHIMANO DIAFLASH 390H

The 390H is similar to the Diaflash 360 but longer, at 13 ft (4 m), and with a heavier action, and is designed for use by those anglers wishing to use stronger lines for bigger fish. It features the same lined guides and slim, short handle of the other models in the Diaflash range.

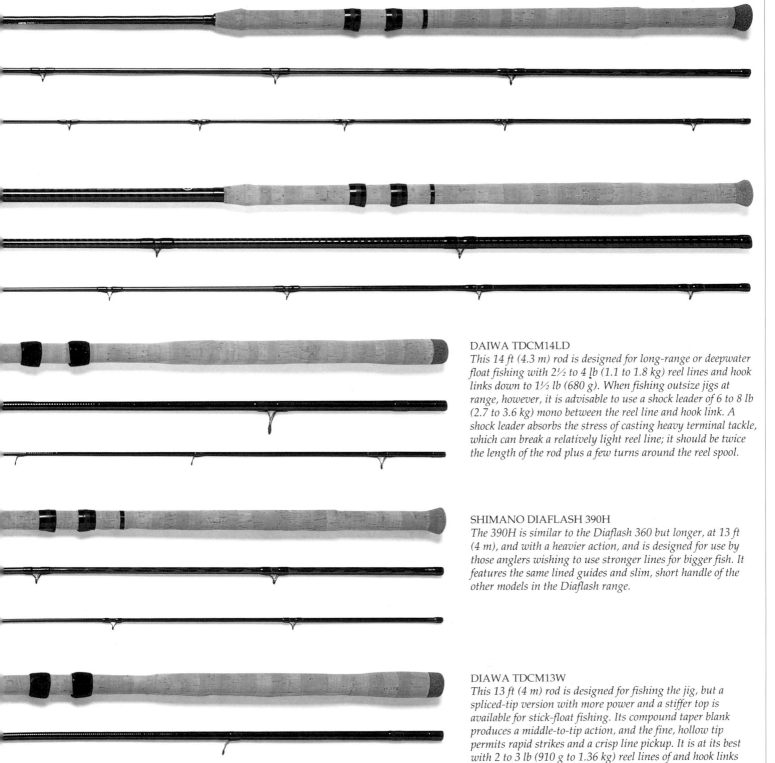

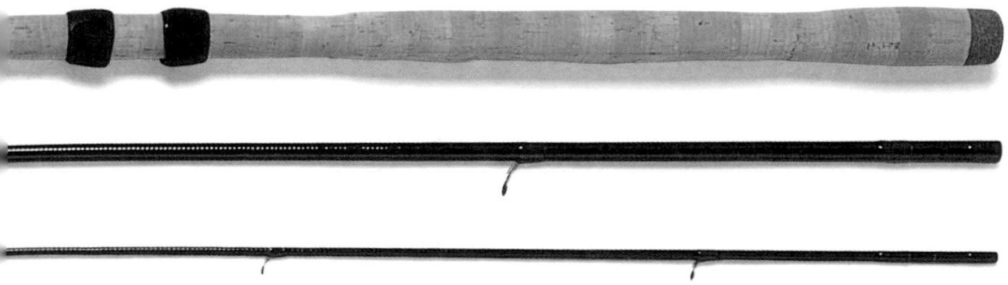

DIAWA TDCM13W

This 13 ft (4 m) rod is designed for fishing the jig, but a spliced-tip version with more power and a stiffer top is available for stick-float fishing. Its compound taper blank produces a middle-to-tip action, and the fine, hollow tip permits rapid strikes and a crisp line pickup. It is at its best with 2 to 3 lb (910 g to 1.36 kg) reel lines of and hook links down to 1 lb (454 g).

FLY RODS 1

For fly fishing, it is vital to use a reel and line that match the rating of your rod, and your chosen rod should be suitable not only for the style of fishing but also for the prevailing conditions. For example, it is no use expecting a 6 ft (1.8 m) midge rod to perform properly when casting into a strong wind on a big lake. When choosing a fly rod, consider carefully what you expect from it.

PARTRIDGE DUNNERDALE #4

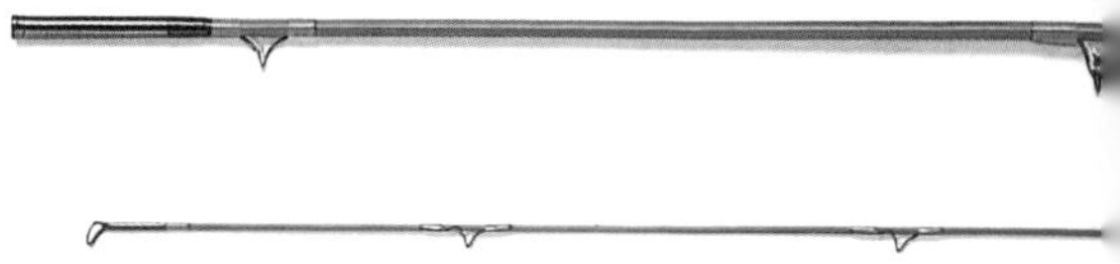

ORVIS ONE-WEIGHT #1

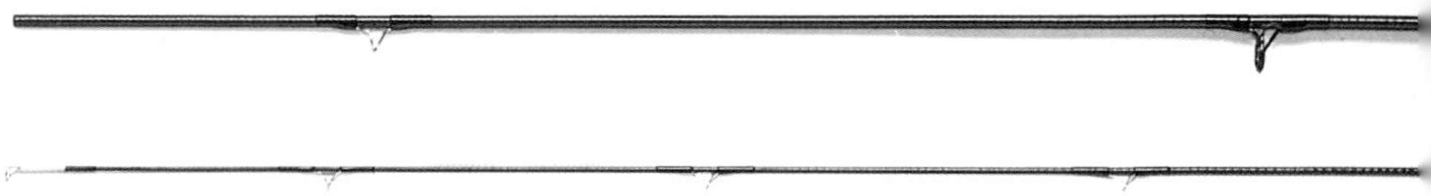

RYOBI CHALLENGE LOCH STYLE #5/7
This 11 ft (3.4 m) carbon fiber rod takes #5 to #7 lines, and is ideal for fishing from a drifting boat with floating or intermediate lines. Its length allows the angler to lift the bob fly and hold it on the surface away from the fish-scaring boat.

RYOBI CHALLENGE LOCH STYLE #5/7

SAGE GFL 796 RPL #7
A blend of lightness and power makes this 9½ ft (2.9 m) carbon fiber rod a good all-arounder for bank fishing on large stillwaters and rivers. It is ideal for large trout, summer salmon, and steelhead. It has a ceramic butt guide, and the snake intermediates and tip ring are hard chrome.

SAGE GFL 796 RPL #7

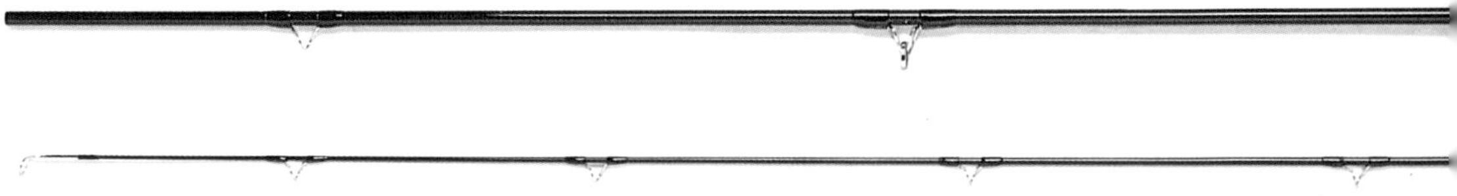

BERKLEY ACCUFLEX SERIES 1 #7/9

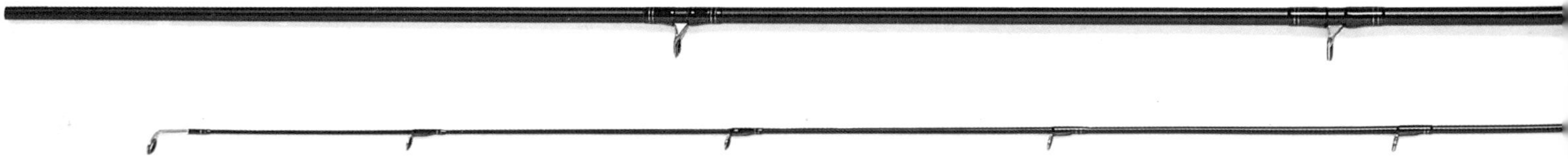

BERKLEY ACCUFLEX SERIES 1 #7/9
The Accuflex Series 1 is a 10½ ft (3.2 m), two-piece carbon fiber rod for #7 to #9 lines. The cork handle has an uplocking screw-winch reel seat and extended fighting butt, and the non-flash satin finish will not scare fish in bright weather. It is ideal for sunkline work from a drifting boat and for species such as sea trout, summer salmon, and steelhead.

HARDY SOVEREIGN #5/6

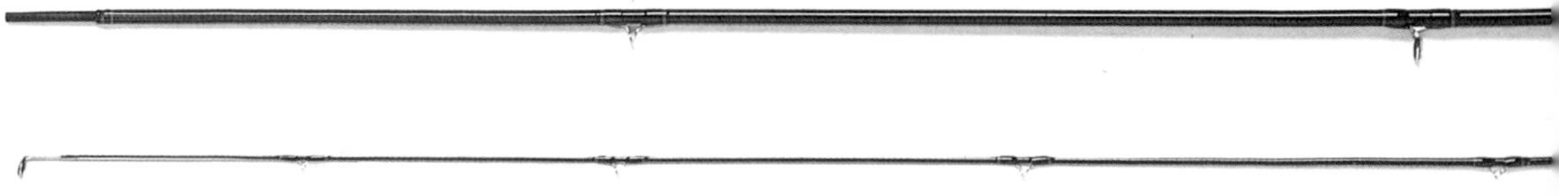

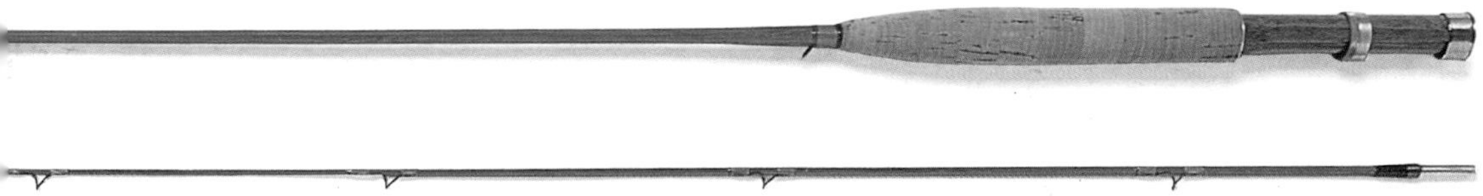

PARTRIDGE DUNNERDALE #4
This is a 6 ft (1.8 m) split cane rod with a progressive action, and matched to a #4 DT floating line it is ideal for fishing dry flies and nymphs on streams and small rivers. Cane has a slower action than carbon fiber, and projects a wider loop of line, which permits better judgement of the cast.

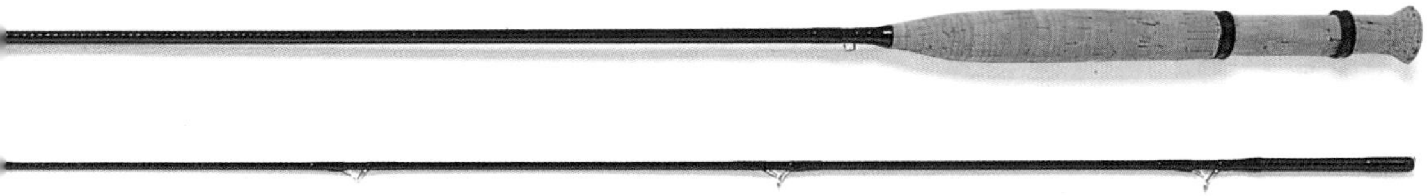

ORVIS ONE-WEIGHT #1
At 7½ ft (2.3 m) and weighing just 1¾ oz (50 g), this is a two-piece carbon fiber rod with a superfine grip, taking a #1 line, and is designed for fishing light lines on small rivers and streams. This is a specialist tool, not recommended for beginners or for anglers looking for a general-purpose fly rod.

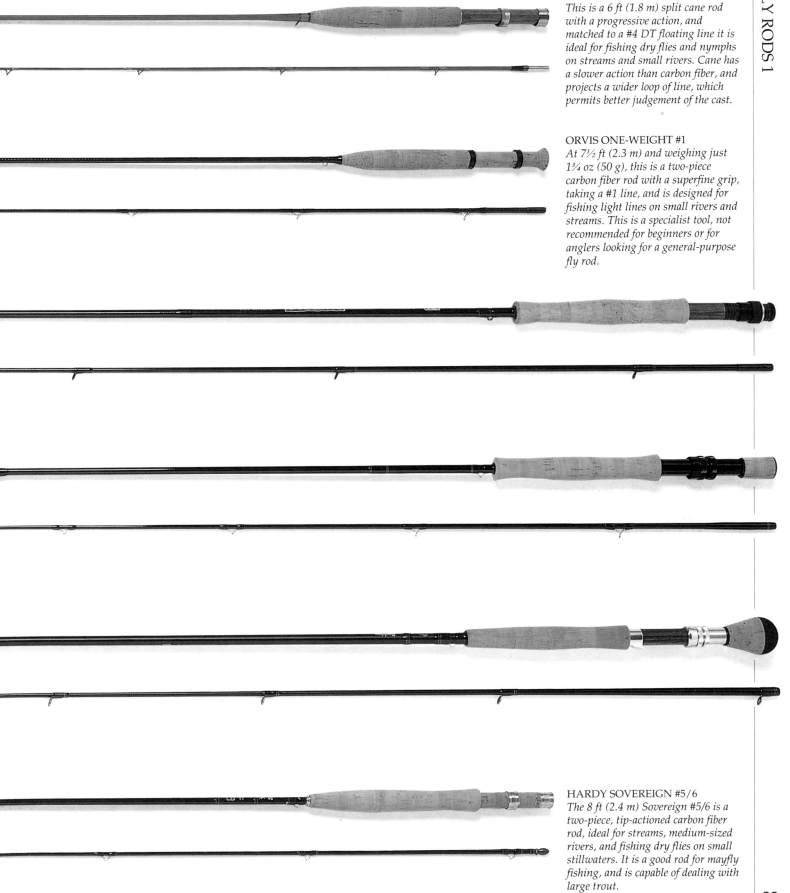

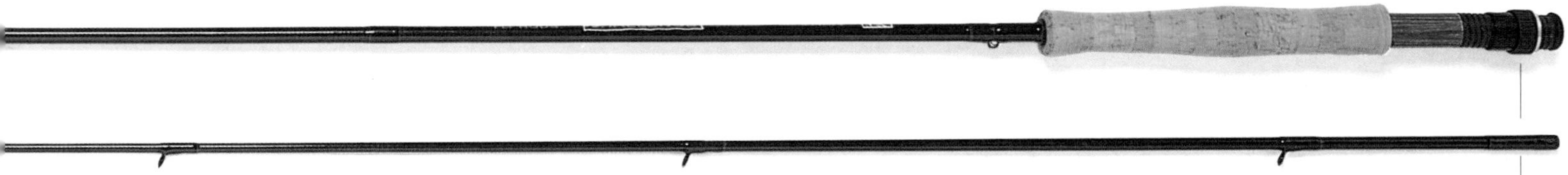

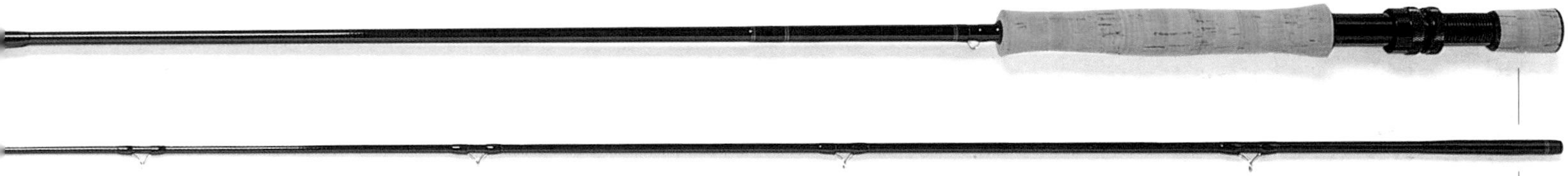

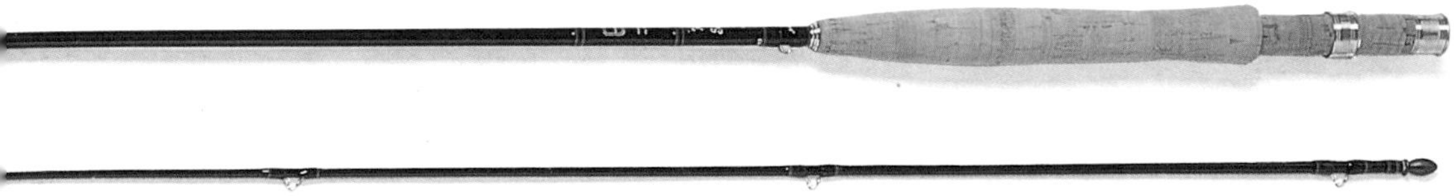

HARDY SOVEREIGN #5/6
The 8 ft (2.4 m) Sovereign #5/6 is a two-piece, tip-actioned carbon fiber rod, ideal for streams, medium-sized rivers, and fishing dry flies on small stillwaters. It is a good rod for mayfly fishing, and is capable of dealing with large trout.

Fly Rods 2

This selection of rods is from the heavier end of the fly-rod range. The models described may appear similar, but each is designed for a specific application and there is little overlap between them. However, they are all designed for heavy lines and are suitable for salmon and steelhead, big trout on large stillwaters and rivers, and for saltwater fly fishing.

HARDY FAVOURITE SALMON #9

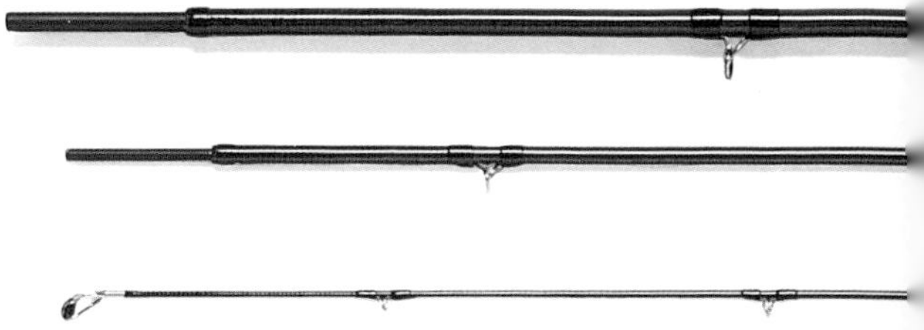

SHIMANO TWIN POWER SALMON FLY #9/11

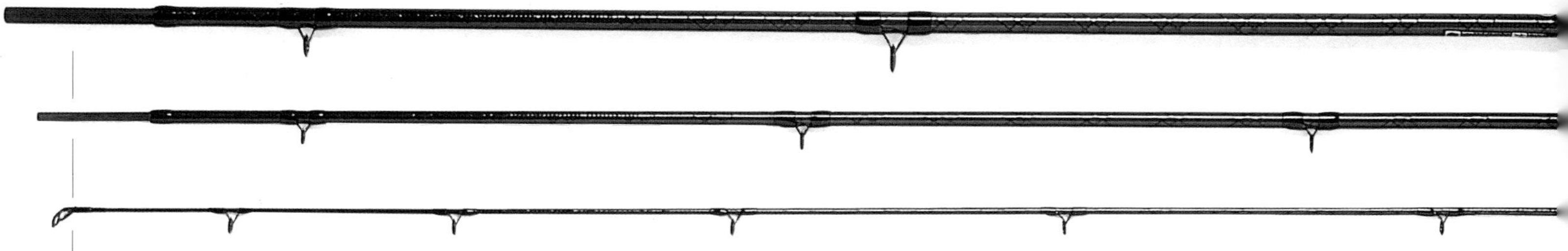

SHIMANO TWIN POWER SALMON FLY #9/11
At 15 ft (4.6 m), this is the longest of the Twin Power salmon rods. It is fine for late spring and summer fishing with light flies on #10 floating or intermediate lines, but lacks the power required for early spring and fall fishing with heavy flies and sinking lines.

DAIWA AUTUMN GOLD CWF17 #11/13

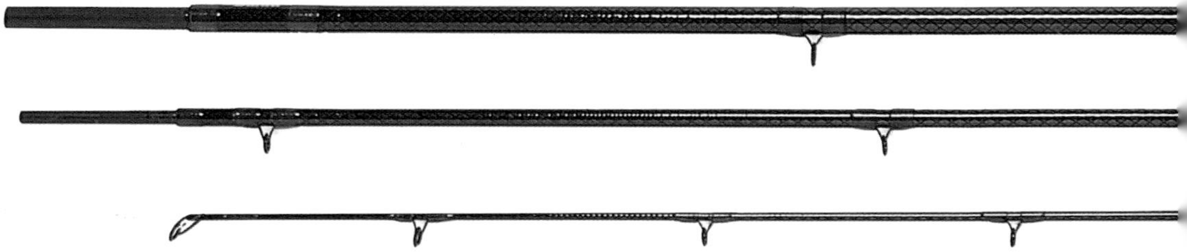

DAIWA AUTUMN GOLD CWF17 #11/13
The CWF17 is a four-piece, 17 ft (5.2 m), double-handed salmon rod built on a carbon fiber blank. It is a powerful rod, which makes it very suitable for fishing in the early spring, and in fall, when heavy lines and large tube flies or Waddingtons are called for.

SAGE GFL 996 RPL #9

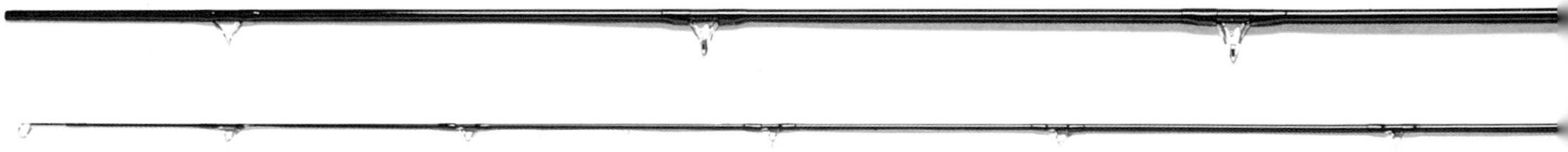

ORVIS RESERVOIR #8

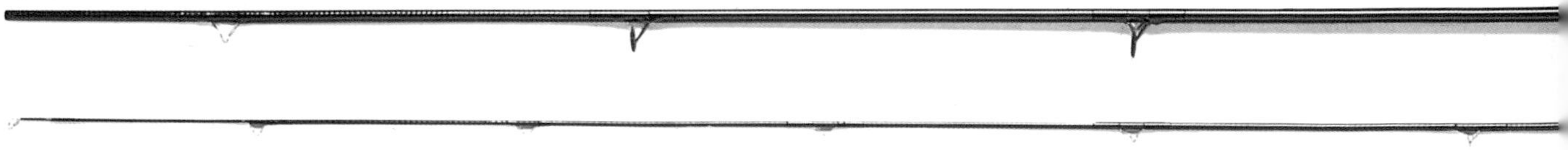

SAGE GFL 7100 RPL #7

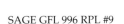

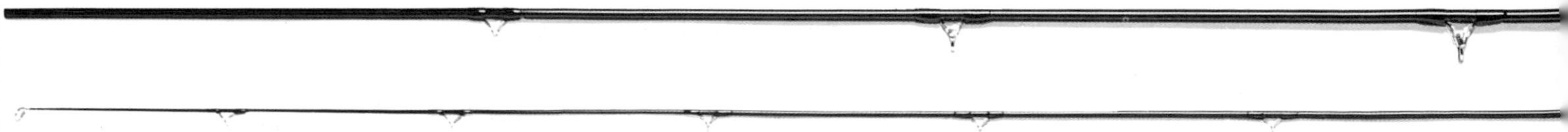

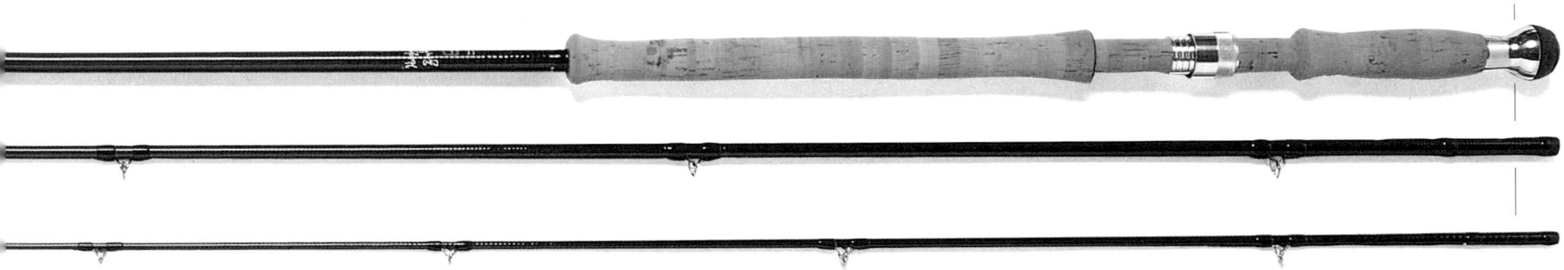

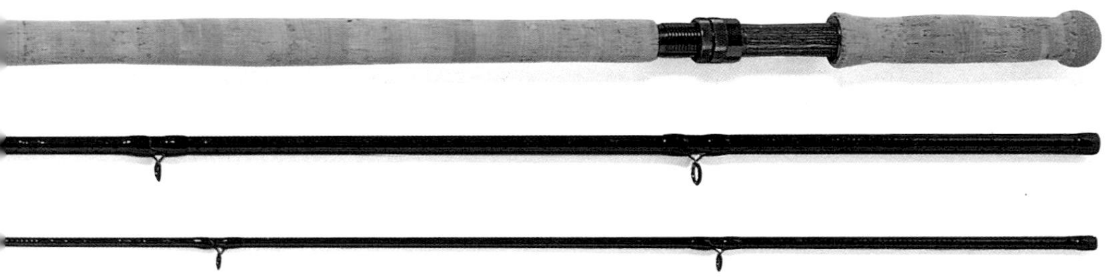

HARDY FAVOURITE SALMON #9

This light 12½ ft (3.8 m), double-handed carbon fiber rod, with a middle-to-tip action, is a good choice for summer salmon fishing with floating or intermediate lines. It is whipped with aluminum oxide butt and tip guides and hard chrome intermediates, and has a long handle with an uplocking reel seat.

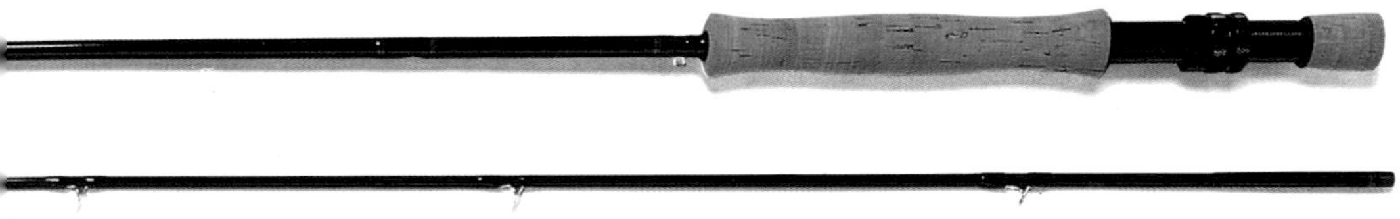

SAGE GFL 996 RPL #9

This is a powerful 9½ ft (2.9 m), two-piece rod, weighing just 3⅞ oz (110 g). It is excellent for casting long distances with WF lines and shooting heads, and for bank fishing on large stillwaters, with big streamers and hairwings. It is a good rod for steelhead, bonefish, and salmon.

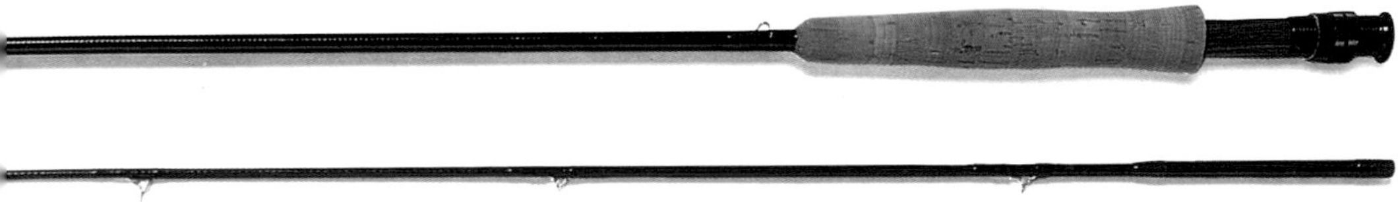

ORVIS RESERVOIR #8

The two-piece, 9½ ft (2.9 m) Orvis Reservoir #8 is a good choice of rod for bank fishing on large lakes and reservoirs, where both distance and accuracy can be very important. It is ideal for large trout, including sea trout, and for steelhead and summer salmon.

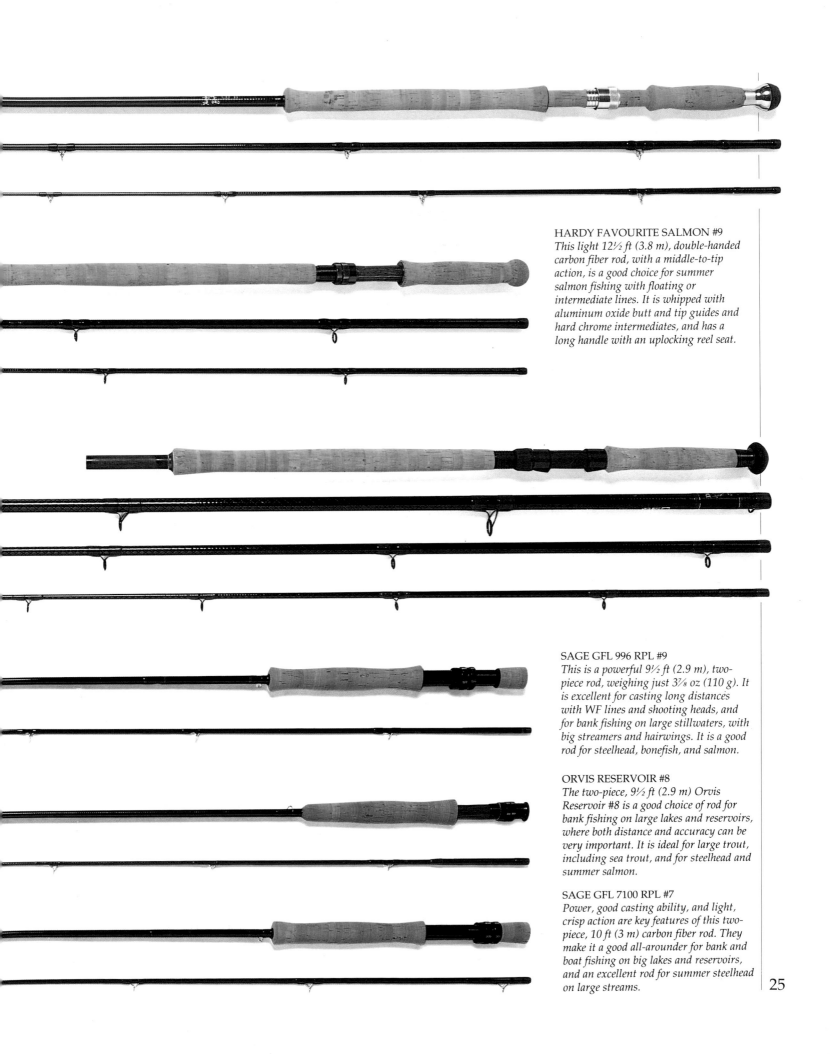

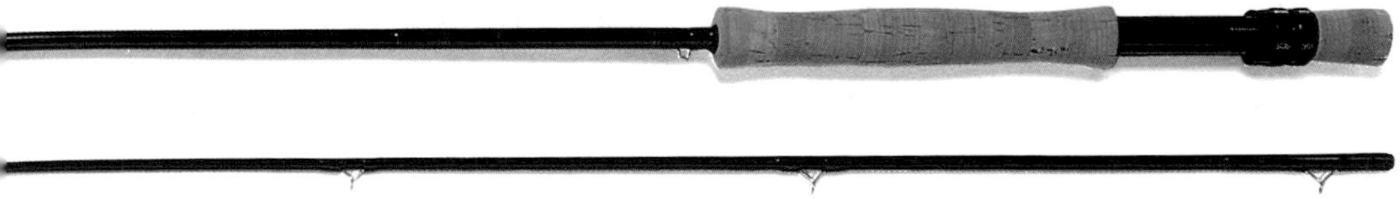

SAGE GFL 7100 RPL #7

Power, good casting ability, and light, crisp action are key features of this two-piece, 10 ft (3 m) carbon fiber rod. They make it a good all-arounder for bank and boat fishing on big lakes and reservoirs, and an excellent rod for summer steelhead on large streams.

Poles & Whips

Poles and whips enable the terminal tackle to be controlled with tremendous accuracy and great delicacy, and allow baits to be lowered into places to which it would be difficult, if not impossible, to cast. Instead of having a reel and running line, a pole has a fixed line attached to its tip, which is either a "flick" tip or an "elasticated" tip. On flick-tip poles, the line is tied directly to a ring or nylon loop whipped to the tip, while on elasticated-tip poles it is attached to a short length of elastic running through the tip section and anchored within the section below it. Poles can be up to 56 ft (17 m) long, and are used for tackling medium-range to distant swims; whips are very light, slim, and short poles, usually less than 20 ft (6 m) long, and used for close-in work. Poles are either telescopic or have several take-apart sections, while whips are usually telescopic.

GARBOLINO VECTRA 13 ft (4.0 m)

GARBOLINO COUNTESS 23 ft (6.90 m)

GARBOLINO SPIRIT 31 ft (9.30 m)

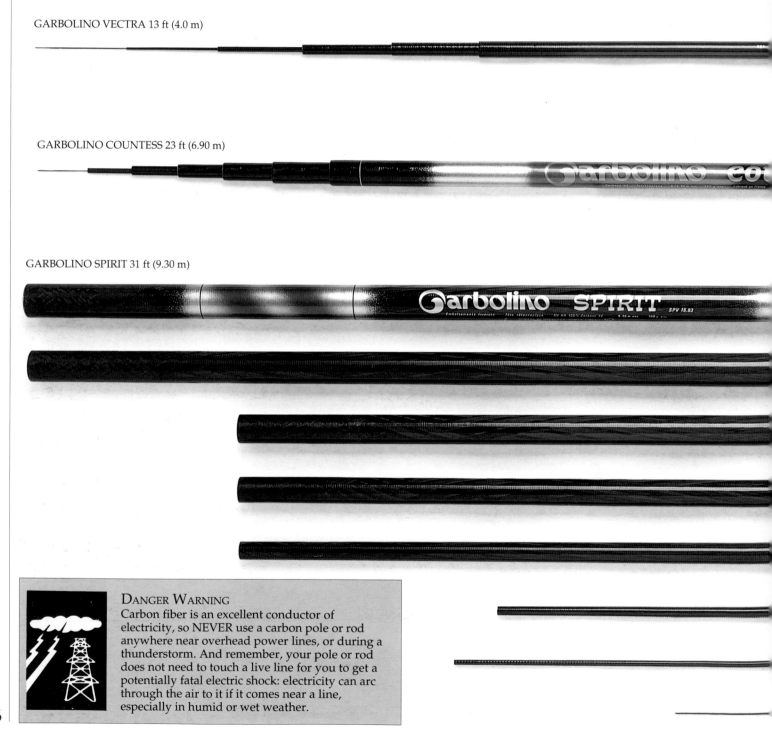

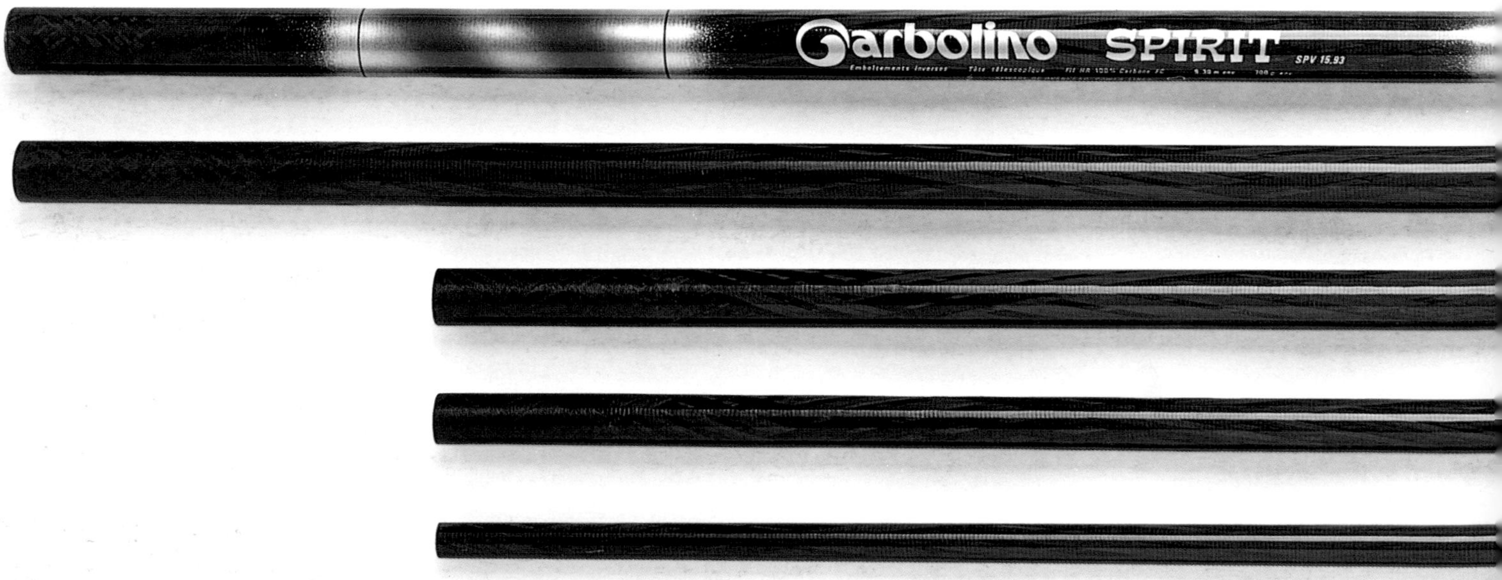

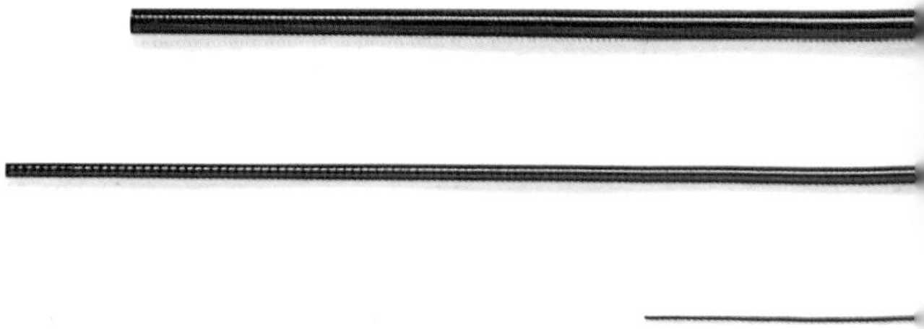

Danger Warning

Carbon fiber is an excellent conductor of electricity, so NEVER use a carbon pole or rod anywhere near overhead power lines, or during a thunderstorm. And remember, your pole or rod does not need to touch a live line for you to get a potentially fatal electric shock: electricity can arc through the air to it if it comes near a line, especially in humid or wet weather.

GARBOLINO VECTRA 13 ft (4.0 m)
The Vectra range of telescopic whips, available in 20 in (50 cm) size increments, are made of carbon fiber reinforced with Kevlar and combine strength and a fast action with delicacy and lightness: the 13 ft (4.0 m) version weighs only about 3.5 oz (100 g). Whips such as this are ideal for close-range fishing for small species such as bream, perch, and rudd, especially when fishing into difficult spots, such as gaps in weedbeds close to overhanging trees. When held supported on the forearm, they can be used comfortably for quite long periods.

GARBOLINO COUNTESS 23 ft (6.90 m)
Poles really come into their own in running water because they permit the float and bait to be held back gently. A float fished out in the flow on rod-and-reel tackle tends to lurch slightly off line each time it is checked, but this does not happen with pole presentation because the pole tip is above and just upstream of the float. The Countess 23 ft (6.90 m) pole is designed specifically for use on rivers where good bait presentation is of utmost importance. It is telescopic, with seven sections, and is made of carbon fiber and weighs just 10 oz (280 g).

GARBOLINO SPIRIT 31 ft (9.30 m)
In addition to offering precise control over float tackle in running water, a pole allows you to fish baits overdepth far more effectively than you can with rod and reel. This is because it gives you a very high level of control over the terminal tackle, and the more rigid the pole, the higher that level will be. In general, take-apart poles are more rigid than telescopic models, and the Spirit 31 ft (9.30 m) carbon take-apart pole is exceptionally stiff, slim, and light, weighing about 26 oz (730 g). A 36 ft (11 m) model is also available, which weighs 33 oz (930 g).

Boat Rods

Boat fishing can be hard work for the angler and punishing for the tackle, so a boat rod needs to be tough, well made, and able to withstand a fair amount of use. A compromise between power and flexibility is a must, however, because all power with no "give" kills the action, overwhelming small to average-sized fish, and without that vital "soft cushion" there is a risk of losing big fish. Boat rods are built to IGFA test curve ratings from 12 through to 120 lb (5.4 to 54 kg), with 20 lb (9.1 kg) and 30 lb (13.6 kg) the most popular, and they should be used with lines of the same rating. Another option is the uptide rod, which has a longer casting butt and a long, soft tip to cast the weight and play fish without risk to the obligatory light line.

CONOFLEX INTEGRA UPTIDE
Uptide rods are used from boats to cast a grip weight that holds the bait away from the scare area in shallow water. Optimum lengths are 9 to 10 ft (2.7 to 3 m). The Integra offers three tips, including a 3 oz (85 g) tip for light tide work. It also has a telescopic butt, which reduces to a more comfortable standard boat length after casting.

CONOFLEX INTEGRA UPTIDE

SHIMANO TWIN POWER UPTIDE 1028

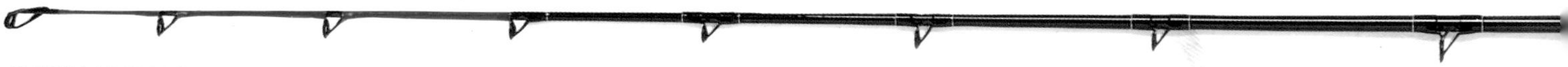

DAIWA TDB 12/30

DRENNAN 30-POUND BOAT ROD

SHAKESPEARE PRO-MAX 50-POUND BOAT ROD

PULLEN STANDUP ROD

SHIMANO TWIN POWER UPTIDE 1028
The current trend with uptide rods is to make them around 10 ft (3 m) long and capable of throwing a wide range of weight sizes. In this respect, the Twin Power Uptide 1028 is without doubt a market leader. It is gentle enough to feel good handling even the smallest codling, yet has enough power to subdue a small shark.

DAIWA TDB 12/30
Rods covering a range of IGFA ratings rarely work really well, but Daiwa's Amorphous Whisker TDB 12/30 is an exception. With the right reel and line, it can be rated at 12, 20, or 30 lb (5.4, 9.1, or 13.6 kg). Some individually rated rods may well outperform it, but it is an excellent compromise rod when used with a suitably balanced reel and line combination.

DRENNAN 30-POUND BOAT ROD
Most boat fishing situations, apart from shark or heavy wreck fishing, are handled readily with a 30 lb (13.6 kg) class rod, making it the number-one choice for multi-purpose use. At 8 ft (2.4 m) in length, with an easy-actioned tip and power in reserve, the Drennan 30 boat rod offers across-the-board fishing pleasure.

SHAKESPEARE PRO-MAX 50-POUND
Shakespeare's 50 lb (22.7 kg) class Pro-Max is intended for the bigger end of the boat fishing range, designed to work very heavy weights and subdue large fish. Its action is stiffened by the carbon in the blank, enabling it to deliver more power at an earlier stage in the taper, and the gimballed butt offers extra leverage when used with a butt pad.

PULLEN STANDUP ROD
Standup fishing is a technique for beating big fish quickly by standing on the boat deck and using body weight as opposed to arm strength. Standup rods are short, powerful, and have roller guides, a very long butt, and a low reel position to maximize leverage. A 30 to 50 lb (13.6 to 22.7 kg) class Pullen Standup Rod would suit most situations.

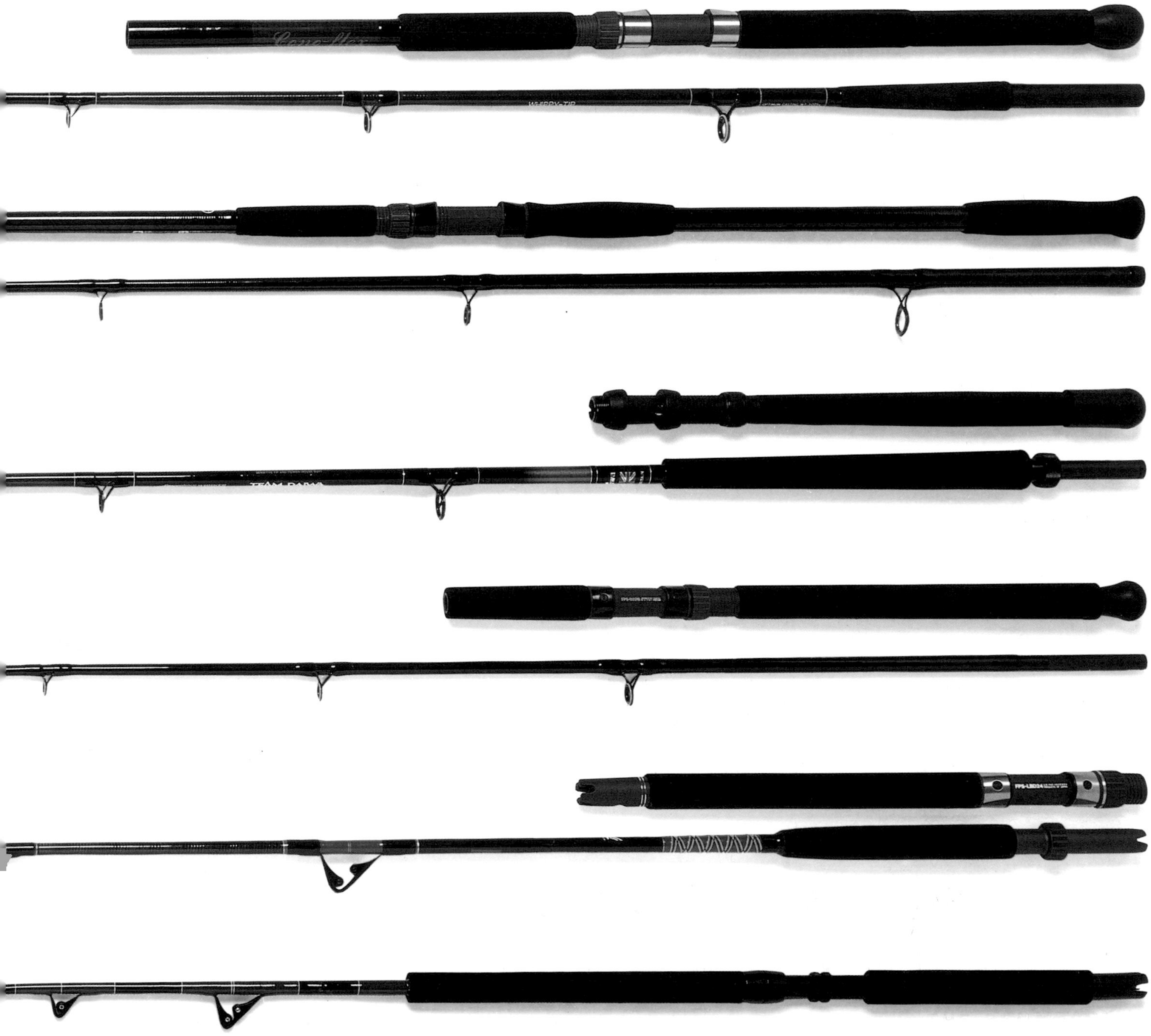

Surf & Shore Rods

Shore-rod design is probably the most complex aspect of sea-rod production. With so many tapers, lengths, materials, and layup thicknesses to choose from to get the required action, blank design has become a highly technical art. To make things worse for the designer, there is no such thing as an optimum action, length, or power rating unless related to a particular individual. Because anglers differ in casting style, stature, and strength, buying a rod thus becomes rather like buying a suit: either you have one made, or, like most people, you buy off the rack and ignore any minor shortcomings. The secret is to try before you buy. The rods shown here are representative of the wide range available, but your individual casting requirements may well dictate a different choice.

SHAKESPEARE INTERNATIONAL EQUALIZER CARP
The best way to enjoy surf fishing for species such as bluefish and flounder is with a rod such as the International Equalizer. A length of around 11 ft (3.4 m) gives ease of casting and is good for playing a lively fish at close range, while a 2 to 2½ lb (910 g to 1.1 kg) test curve lets the fish know who's boss.

CENTURY LONG E-ZEE MATCH

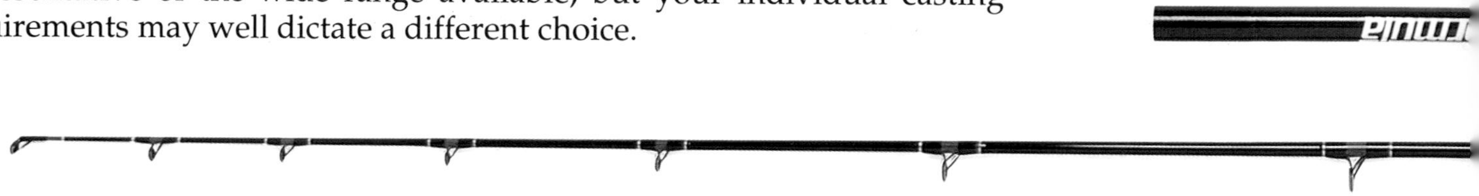

SHAKESPEARE HURRICANE BASS MASTER

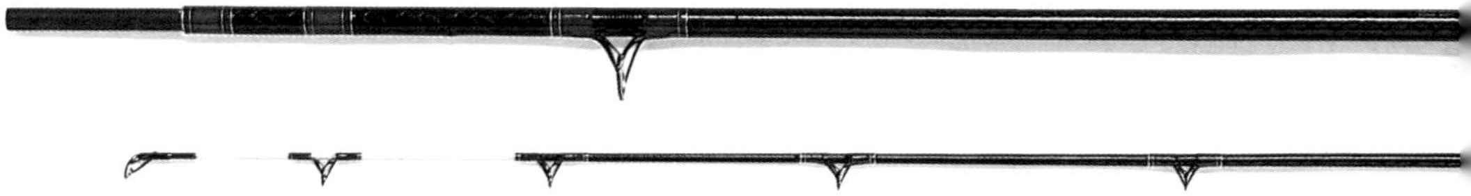

DAIWA PMB122M

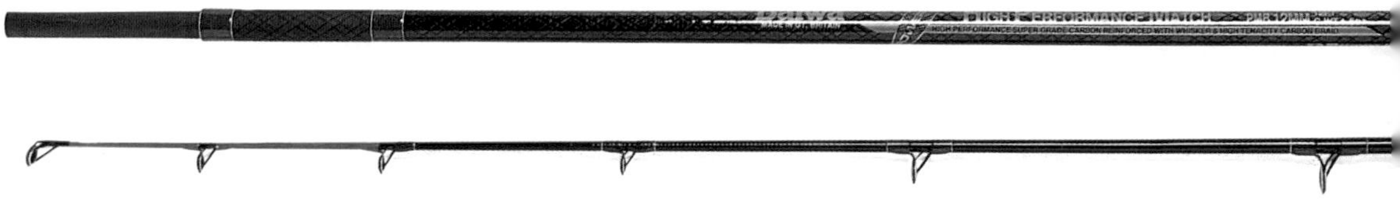

DAIWA AWB129PM

CENTURY FORMULA ONE

SHAKESPEARE HURRICANE BASS MASTER
When fishing from the shore, you often need to use weights of only 2 oz (57 g) or so placed at close to medium range. In such situations, the best rod to use is one with a soft, tippy action and good reserves of mid-blank power, such as the 11½ ft (3.5 m) Hurricane Bass Master. It is a superb example of a rod that enables you to feel a hooked fish and be in tune with its every move, without losing control.

DAIWA PMB122M
The pendulum style of casting requires stiff rods, which need immense amounts of body power from the angler to wind them up to their maximum. Only anglers favoring this casting style should choose power-casting rods such as the Daiwa Powermesh Beach (PMB) range. The PMB122M is a formidable rod, designed for casting weights in the 4 to 6 oz (113 to 170 g) range, and its coaster reel grips permit fine tuning of its overall balance.

CENTURY FORMULA ONE
Rods exceeding 13 ft (4 m) in length are currently regarded as the optimum distance-casting tools, and Century has invested much effort in creating rods for this particular corner of the market. The slow taper and stiffish action of its Formula One make it a pendulum caster's rod that is a good choice for heavy-ground work with a large-capacity reel.

SHAKESPEARE INTERNATIONAL EQUALIZER CARP

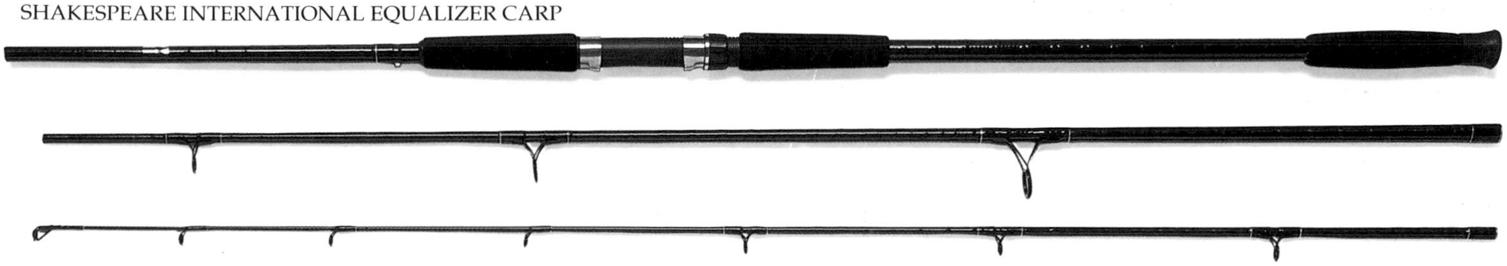

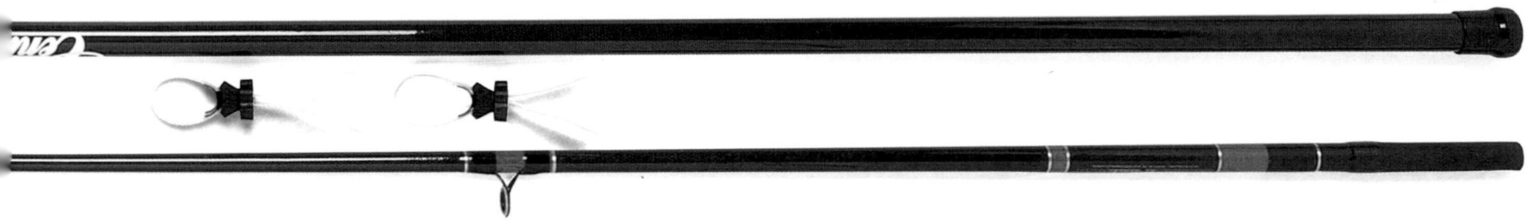

CENTURY LONG E-ZEE MATCH

Because of its soft, tippy action, the Long E-zee Match is more of an angler's rod than a casting-tournament machine. But it is still a powerful rod and is capable, in the right hands, of throwing a 5 oz (142 g) weight a couple of hundred yards. Its light-walled blank gives it excellent sensitivity and bite detection, and it is an excellent choice of rod for the non-specialist beach angler.

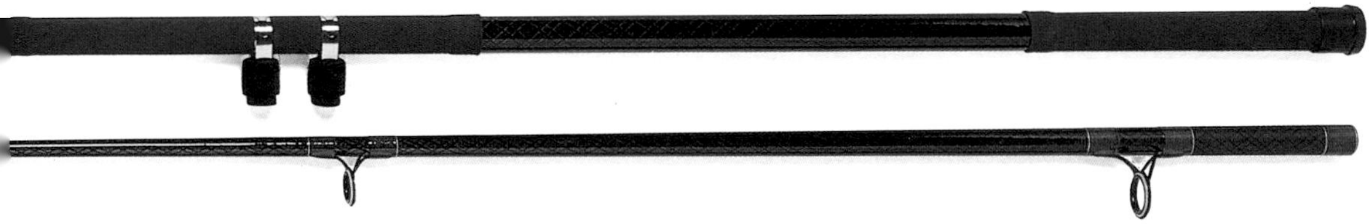

DAIWA AWB129PM

Part of the Team Daiwa Amorphous Whisker range of power casting rods, this rod can handle 8 oz (227 g) weights to cope with difficult fishing conditions. The overall stiffness of the blank is moderated at the tip by the inclusion of fiberglass, which has a softening effect that enhances bite detection. This is an angler's rod designed for ultra-long-distance work, not a caster's rod that can also be used to fish.

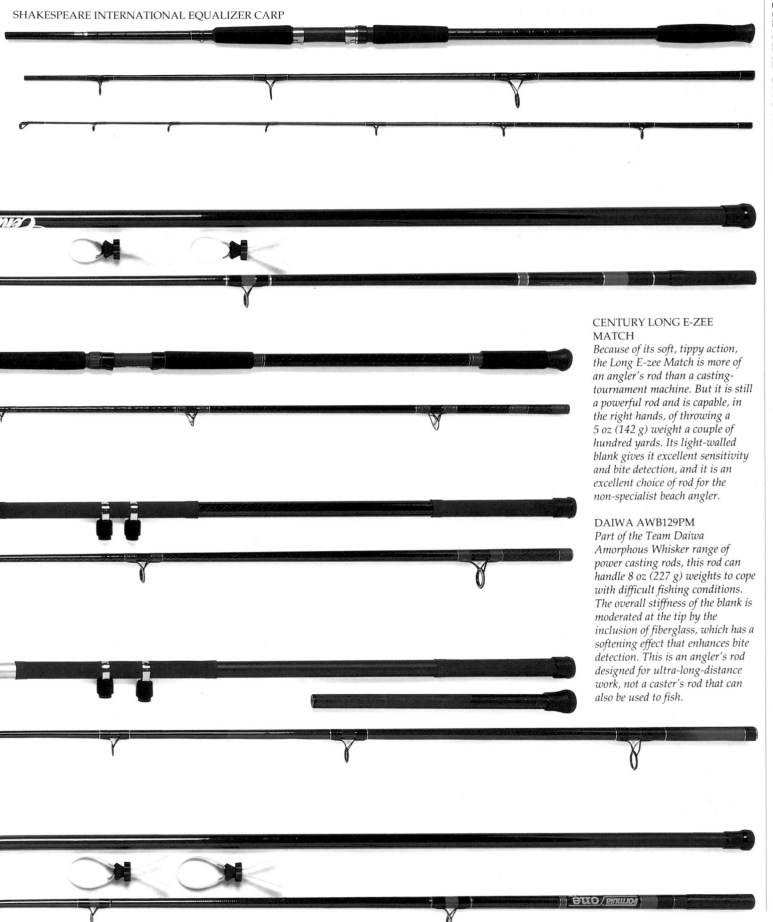

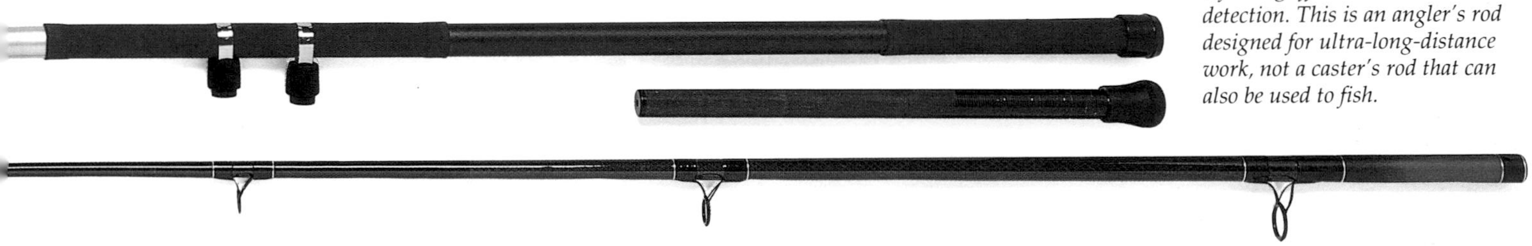

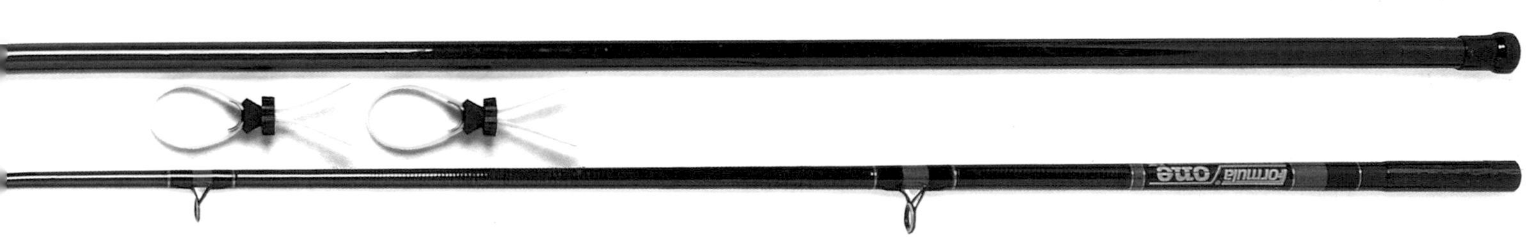

The Reel

The reel is primarily a line reservoir that enables the angler to fish at a greater range than is possible with a line fixed to the rod tip, which was the only method available to the earliest anglers. The reel has evolved into several different forms, with two distinct types of spool: the revolving spool and the spinning spool. The oldest and simplest form of revolving-spool reel is the centerpin, in which the line is carried on a simple flanged spool that revolves on a steel axle; this reel was once close to extinction but is now showing signs of making a comeback. Fly reels and baitcasters are more complex forms of revolving-spool reel. In a spinning reel, the spool does not revolve, and the line is retrieved and wound onto it by a rotating arm, called the bail arm.

ADCOCK STANTON CENTERPIN REEL
The spool of this centerpin runs on ball bearings, which give it an exceptionally smooth and sensitive action.

Evolution of the Reel

ALCOCK-STANLEY SPINNING REEL
S. Alcock & Company produced this early spinning reel in 1926.

It is likely that the first fishing reel was invented by the Chinese in about the 3rd century AD. Reels of the centerpin type entered common use in the West during the 18th century. The first baitcaster reel was produced by George Snyder, a Kentucky watchmaker, in 1810, about a century before the advent of the spinning reel. The first patent on a spinning reel was obtained in Britain by Alfred Holden Illingworth, of Yorkshire, who apparently got his inspiration from the bobbins operating in a Lancashire cotton mill early in this century. The rapidly increasing availability of the spinning reel during the 1940s and 1950s revolutionized freshwater fishing, for it gave every angler the opportunity to cast and fish at much greater range than ever before.

Glossary of Terms

Anti-reverse A mechanism that prevents the spools of baitcasters and spinning reels from turning backward and thus releasing line.
Bail arm The wire arm on a spinning reel that picks up the line and guides it onto the spool.
Check or ratchet A device that varies the tension at which line is pulled from a fly reel by a running fish.
Drag/slipping clutch A mechanism on baitcasters and spinning reels that allows hooked fish to take line from the spool at a preset tension.
Foot The part of the reel that attaches to the rod handle.
Gear ratio The number of times the spool or bail arm of a reel rotates for each turn of the handle.
Level wind Fitted on baitcasters to spread line evenly across the spool.
Line guard Found on centerpin and fly reels, this prevents line from tangling around the drum or the handle.
Rotor The part of a spinning reel on which the spool sits.

Types of Reel

Fly reel
The two most common types of fly reel are the single action and the multiplier. The spool of a single-action reel revolves once for each turn of the handle, while that of a multiplier makes several turns. A third type, the automatic, has a clockwork mechanism, which turns the spool when a lever is operated. Fly reel check mechanisms are either simple ratchets or more sophisticated drag systems.

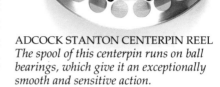

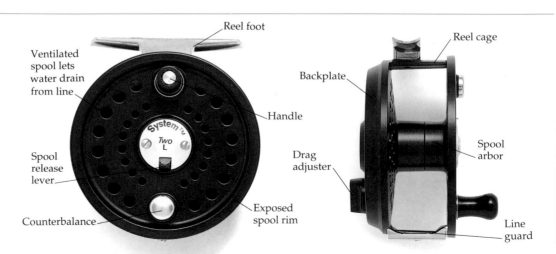

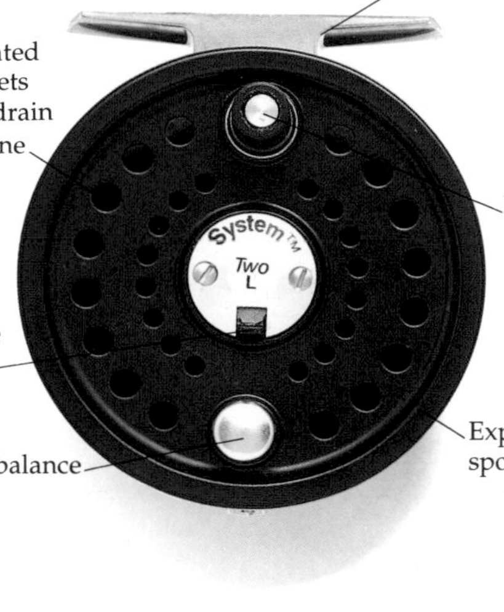

Baitcaster
A baitcaster is basically a geared version of the centerpin. Baitcasters are used for a wide variety of techniques, from freshwater baitcasting to surfcasting and blue-water big-game fishing. Most have a free-spool facility, which allows the spool to rotate without resistance for casting, mechanical or magnetic brakes, a drag system, and often a level-wind mechanism for even line lay. Baitcasters fit on top of the rod.

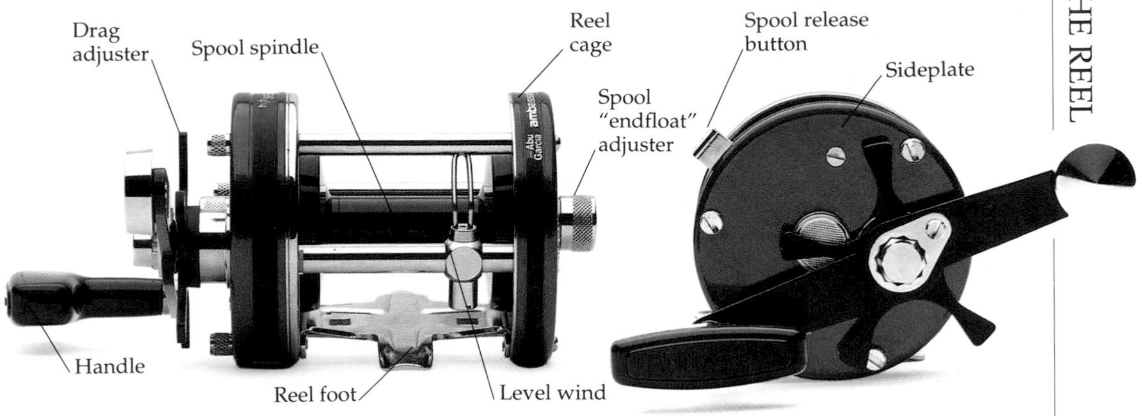

Spinning reel
This type of reel is so named because the spool does not revolve to recover line: the line is wound around it by a rotating bail arm. The spool does rotate, under tension from a slipping clutch, to give line to a running fish, and an anti-reverse system prevents the handle from backwinding while the spool rotates. This reel is very versatile and, within reason, will handle most freshwater fishing except fly fishing.

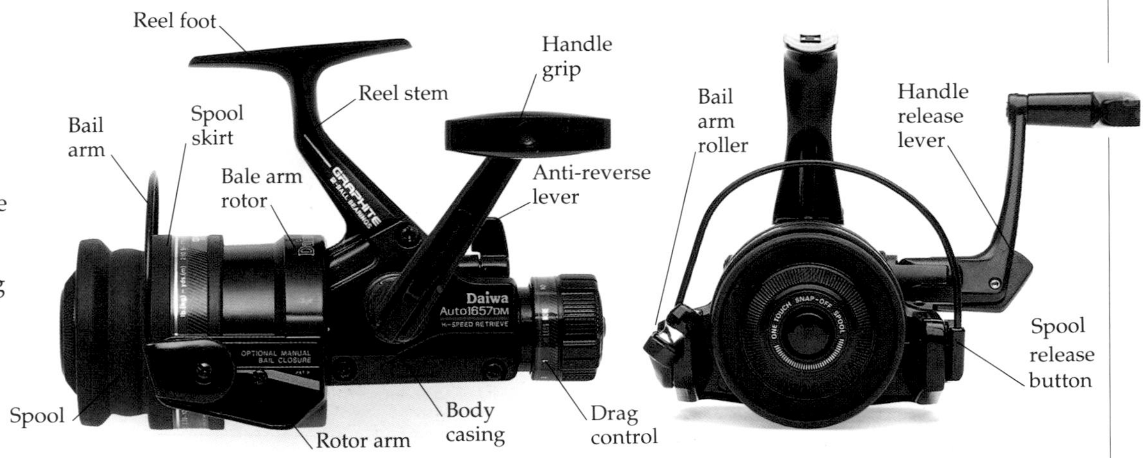

Closed-face reel
This is a spinning reel with an enclosed front face. The line passes through a hole in the center of the face and is wound onto the spool by a pickup pin. The pin is freed for casting by finger pressure on the front face or on a rear-mounted button. A very efficient light-line reel, especially for float fishing, because the enclosed spool gives good line control when fishing in windy weather.

Spincaster
This is a rugged version of the closed-face reel, suitable for 5 to 20 lb (2.27 to 9.1 kg) lines. Most spincasters are mounted on top of the rod but some, like the Zebco shown here, are fitted beneath it. Line is released by a pushbutton, by pressure on the front face, or by a lever (which allows "feathering" of the cast to prevent the lure from overshooting). The bell housing virtually eliminates line coil problems.

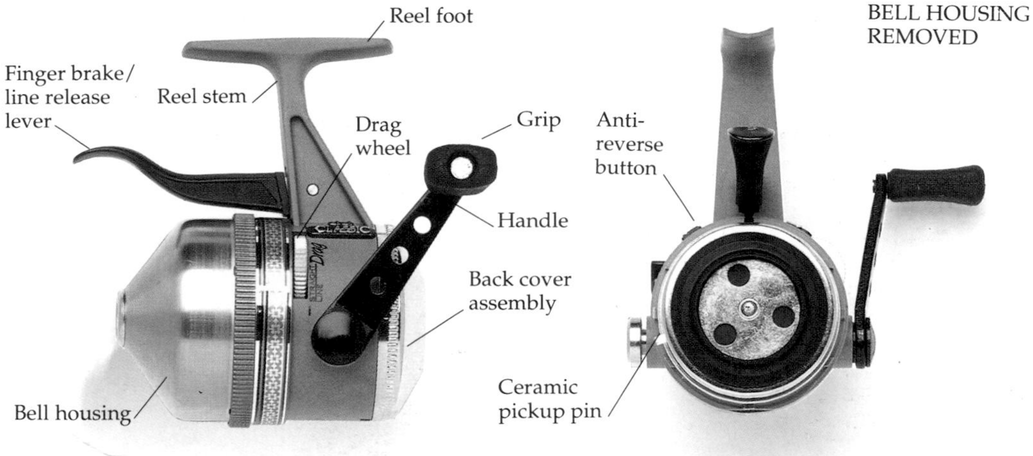

Spinning Reels 1

Unlike fly reels and baitcaster reels, which have revolving spools, the spinning reel has a static spool, onto which line is wound by a rotating bail arm made of wire. To ensure that line is laid on evenly, the spool oscillates (moves backward and forward) on a rotor as the reel handle is turned. Good-sized fish, when hooked, can be prevented from breaking the line by use of the adjustable slipping clutch. This mechanism allows running or lunging fish to take line from the spool at a preset level of tension or resistance. This tension should be adjusted so that the line is released from the spool at a little below the breaking strain of the line, thus making a hooked fish fight for every inch of line it takes. On most spinning reels, the reel is prevented from winding backward when the spool is turning and giving line by an anti-reverse mechanism. On some reels this mechanism is silent, but on others a clicking noise can be heard while winding.

General-purpose Reels

RYOBI PROTARGET 2000M *(right)*
The 2000M is a lightweight reel of an ideal size for both float fishing and light legering, with a high gear ratio of 6.1:1 that ensures a rapid retrieve. Its line capacity is 100 yds (91 m) of 3 lb (1.36 kg) mono, and it has three ball bearings for smooth and reliable operation.

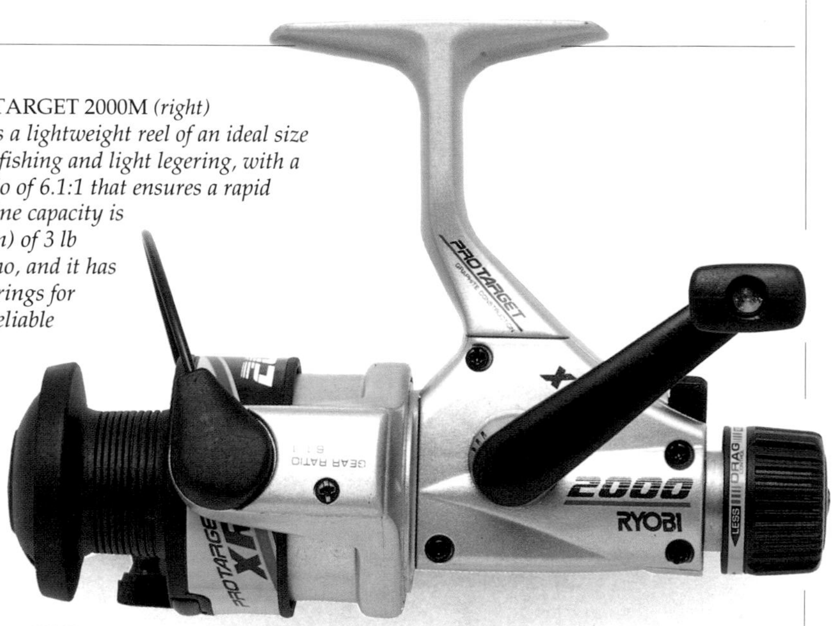

SHIMANO AERO GTM2000 *(below)*
This high-speed reel has a gear ratio of 6.2:1 and is supplied with three spools, one deep, one shallow, and one match (ultra-shallow). Its effective line-laying system and long, tapered spool enable light baits to be cast long distances, which is ideal for situations in which a gentle presentation is vital for success.

MITCHELL EXCELLENCE 60 *(right)*
The Excellence 60 is a rear-drag version of the world-famous Mitchell 300. It comes complete with two spools, one shallow, one deep; line capacities are 100 yds (91 m) of 6 lb (2.7 kg) mono (shallow spool), and 200 yds (182 m) of 10 lb (4.54 kg) mono (deep spool).

DAIWA TD1650DF *(right)*
This is a top-of-the-line long-cast reel with a long-stroke spool oscillation, giving excellent line lay and consistent casting. It has a line capacity of 220 yds (200 m) of 10 lb (4.54 kg) mono, and a gear ratio of 5.2:1.

DAIWA HARRIER AUTO 1657DM *(below)*
The Harrier Auto series are the only match reels available with a bail arm that can be opened by a dab of the finger then closed either the same way or automatically by a turn of the reel handle. Line capacity is 110 yds (100 m) of 2 lb (910 g) line, the gear ratio 5.4:1.

SHAKESPEARE PRESIDENT DELUXE 2510/030 *(above)*
This reel sports many features, including brass gears, stainless steel ball bearings, a ceramic line roller, and a long, tapered spool for easy long-distance casting with light rigs. It has a line capacity of 164 yds (150 m) of 6 lb (2.7 kg) mono, and a gear ratio of 5.2:1.

SHAKESPEARE SIGMA SLS 2500/035 *(left)*
The Sigma is a lightweight, carbon-bodied reel with an extended spool for improved casting performance. It has a gear ratio of 5.6:1 and is supplied with two spools, one deep, one match. The deep spool will take 262 yds (240 m) of 6 lb (2.7 kg) mono, the match 110 yds (100 m) of 2½ lb (1.1 kg) line.

Spinning Reels 2

A variety of speeds of retrieve are available in spinning reels; a few reels even have two, one fast, the other slow. Most have gear ratios of between 3:1 and 4:1, which give retrieval rates of about 15 to 20 in (40 to 50 cm) of line wound onto the reel spool for each revolution of the handle. For high-speed work, such as occurs in saltwater fishing, a reel with the rapid retrieval rate offered by a high gear ratio is best. A ratio of 6:1 will see about 30 in (75 cm) of line retrieved for every turn of the handle. A rapid retrieve is also an advantage if you want to crank lures rapidly through clear water. Whatever the gear ratio of a spinning reel, it will operate at its most efficient when fully loaded with line. Half-filled spools make casting any distance difficult, because the line encounters excessive friction as it rubs against the underside and lip of the spool.

Specialist Reels

SHIMANO AERO GTM3000 *(left)*
This high-speed reel is a perfect size for use with a crankbait and comes with three spools (deep, semi-deep, and shallow). Line capacity is 250 yds (230 m) of 10 lb (4.54 kg) mono (semi-deep spool), gear ratio 6.2:1.

SHIMANO BAITRUNNER AERO 3500 *(above)*
The Aero 3500 features a long, coned spool for greater casting distance, a gear ratio of 4.7:1, and a line capacity of 280 yds (256 m) of 10 lb (4.54 kg) mono. The lever-operated Baitrunner facility allows fish to take line without the angler having to open the bail arm, while turning the reel handle engages the preset clutch.

SHIMANO BAITRUNNER AERO GT4500 *(left)*
One of the most popular specialist reels in use today for long-distance fishing, the Aero GT4500 possesses all the features of the standard Aero reels plus a trio of ball bearings for a very smooth retrieve. It has a gear ratio of 4.7:1 and a line capacity of 320 yds (293 m) of 12 lb (5.4 kg) mono, and is supplied with two spools.

BROWNING 8512 *(left)*
This reel has a long carbon fiber spool (it is supplied with two) for medium-range specialist fishing. Its capacity is 220 yds (200 m) of 8 lb (3.6 kg) mono, and an oscillating winding mechanism on a worm shaft produces excellent line lay. The gear ratio is 4.6:1.

BROWNING 9512 *(below)*
The 9512 is aimed at the specialist angler fishing at medium range. It features three ball bearings for smooth and durable operation and is supplied with three spools. The gear ratio and line capacity are the same as those of the 8512.

DAIWA BR2050 *(left)*
Designed for medium-range fishing, this reel has a line capacity of 295 yds (270 m) of 10 lb (4.54 kg) mono. The gear ratio is 4.9:1, and the long, coned spool and even, crossover line lay permit good casting distance and accuracy.

ABU CARDINAL GOLD MAX 4 *(right)*
This reel, designed for close- to medium-range bass and pike fishing, has a line capacity of 230 yds (210 m) of 8 lb (3.6 kg) mono and a gear ratio of 5:1. It is fitted with five ball bearings to give reliable, super-smooth operation.

CLOSED-FACE REELS

The closed-face reel is a variant of the spinning. The front of the reel is shrouded by a casing through which the line emerges, and line retrieval is by means of a pin that guides the line onto the spool. Pressing a spring-loaded button retracts the pin, leaving the line free for casting. This design eliminates the common problem associated with fine lines, which is that they blow about on windy days, constantly tangling around the reel spool, rotor, or bail arm with potentially disastrous results. They are at their best when fitted with light lines.

ABU GARCIA 507 MK II GOLD MAX *(above)*
Designed for competition fishing at the highest level, the 507 Mk II contains no drag system; instead, big fish are played by backwinding the handle. The extra-wide spool and dual-geared oscillation system produces a criss-cross line lay on the retrieve, eliminating the possibility of coils of line bedding into gaps between the coils beneath them. This line bedding, a traditional problem with closed-face reels, inhibits subsequent casts and float control. The reel has a gear ratio of 3.23:1.

D.A.M. QUICK POWER CFP *(above)*
The Quick Power CFP is fitted with a disk brake, adjustable drag, and low gearing (3.5:1) to enable big fish to be played sensitively yet with power. The reel also possesses a quick-release bell (rotor) fitted with two hard-chromed steel pins for quick line pickup.

D.A.M. QUICK CFM MATCH *(right)*
Designed for tournament fishing, this reel features a fast retrieve (gear ratio 4.2:1) and has no drag system: fish are played by backwinding. It has two revolving, hard-chromed pickup pins for fast line take-up, and the bell has a quick-release mechanism for rapid access to the spool.

ABU GARCIA 1044 ABUMATIC *(left)*
The 1044 is very well engineered, with brass gearing (ratio 3.9:1) and a stainless steel pinion gear for smooth operation. Its drag system is designed to reduce the risk of fish hooked on light lines being lost if they suddenly surge off: winding the handle back one quarter of a turn reduces the braking power by up to 75 percent.

DAIWA HARRIER 123M *(above)*
With its carbon fiber body and lack of drag, the Harrier 123M is extremely light in weight. It comes with two spools, and with its high gear ratio of 4.1:1 it is aimed specifically at the tournament angler. It is a simple reel, yet one with the right features to ensure that it is up to the demands of the open match circuit.

DAIWA HARRIER 125M *(left)*
This reel is very popular with tournament anglers. It has a high gear ratio (4.1:1) for rapid line retrieval, and the line is wound onto the spool in a cross-weave pattern to minimize the danger of bedding-in and subsequent poor line release. The reel comes complete with two spools, and has a rear drag control for those who prefer to play fish off the clutch rather than by backwinding.

Baitcasting Reels

Baitcasting reels are specifically designed to be both easy to use and comfortable to operate for long periods. Many are fitted with a level-wind mechanism, which spreads the retrieved line evenly across the spool, and big and hard-running fish being played are allowed to take line by an adjustable drag system. Tangles during casting (caused by the spool overrunning) have been eliminated by adjustable magnetic braking systems, which slow down the speed at which the spool rotates, and newer-generation baitcasting reels are fitted with a thumb bar to enable rapid casting. Clamping the thumb onto the spool prior to casting automatically depresses the bar, which in turn disengages the spool.

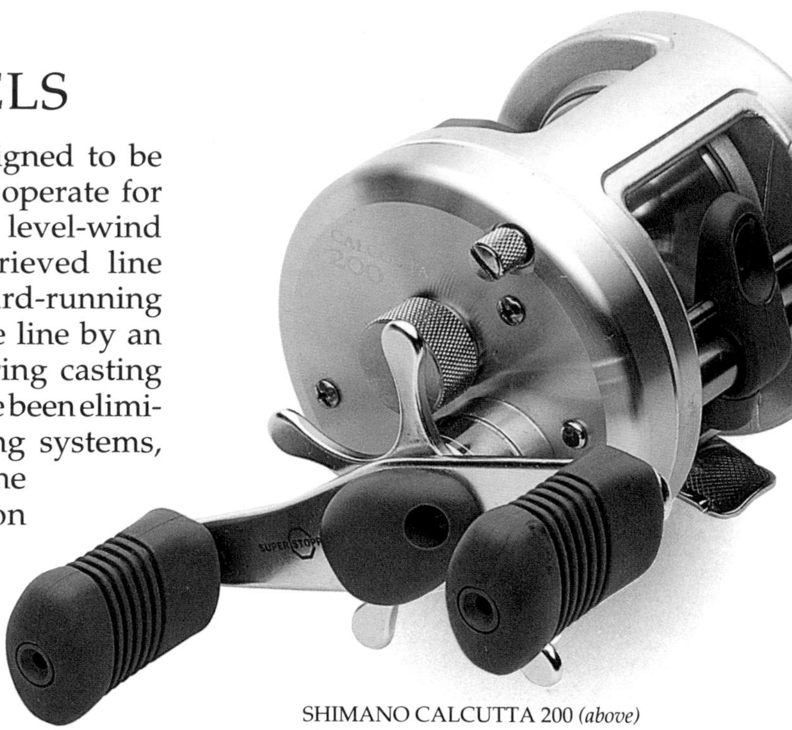

SHIMANO CALCUTTA 200 *(above)*
The Calcutta 200 has a one-piece, anodized aluminum body and aluminum spool, and a line capacity of 230 yds (210 m) of 8 lb (3.6 kg) mono or 120 yds (110 m) of 14 lb (6.4 kg) line. It features a recessed foot to give a low profile on the rod, ball bearings for smooth running and durability, "Quickfire" thumb bar casting system, and a hard-wearing ceramic line guide on the level-wind mechanism.

SILSTAR NOVA 20 *(above)*
The sideplates and frame of the Nova 20 are made of a lightweight blend of carbon fiber and titanium, and the level wind is fitted with an aluminum oxide line roller to reduce line wear. The Nova also features a thumb bar to disengage the spool, a star drag, and a magnetic braking system. The gear ratio is 5:1, and the line capacity is 270 yds (247 m) of 12 lb (5.4 kg) mono or 225 yds (206 m) of 15 lb (6.8 kg) line.

ABU GARCIA AMBASSADEUR 1022 *(below)*
This reel features a gear ratio of 4.7:1, a level wind, two braking systems (one mechanical, the other magnetic), and a thumb bar. The spool is released for casting by flicking the thumb bar, and re-engaged for retrieving either by turning the reel handle or by using the "flipping trigger," which permits instant striking.

RYOBI LX4 *(below)*
Streamlined shaping and lightweight construction make this an excellent reel to use with many of today's pencil-thin baitcasting rods. It has a line capacity of 200 yds (182 m) of 10 lb (4.54 kg) mono, and it has a level wind, a star drag, a thumb bar for rapid casting, and adjustable magnetic braking to eliminate overruns during casting.

SHIMANO BANTAM CITICA 200 *(above)*
The Citica has a high gear ratio (5:1) for rapid line retrieval, while trouble-free casting is aided by a magnetically controlled casting system. The line capacity is 210 yds (192 m) of 10 lb (4.54 kg) mono or 140 yds (128 m) of 14 lb (6.4 kg) line, and the weight has been kept to a minimum by the use of carbon fiber for the body and aluminum for the spool.

SHIMANO BANTAM CURADO 200 *(below)*
This is a reel with a very rapid rate of retrieve, having a gear ratio of 6:1. Four stainless steel ball bearings and one roller bearing ensure silky-smooth operation and long-term reliability, and line capacity is 210 yds (192 m) of 10 lb (4.54 kg) mono or 140 yds (128 m) of 14 lb (6.4 kg) line.

RYOBI LR-130 *(above)*
The LR-130 has a gear ratio of 4.2:1, and its line capacity is 180 yds (165 m) of 10 lb (4.54 kg) mono. Its level wind disengages for improved distance casting, and it also features a thumb bar and a handle drag, with which the spool drag setting can be altered quickly and accurately by simply turning the reel handle backward.

FLY REELS 1

Whether you are content with a well-made, budget-priced reel or insist on a leading brand from the top end of the market, the most important thing to consider when buying a reel is how you are going to be using it. For instance, a lightweight, narrow, small-diameter, caged-drum reel will not be robust enough for large salmon, steelhead, or sea bass, or capable of holding the heavy lines required. This selection of small-capacity, single-action, geared, and disk-braked models is ideal for trout, sea trout, and small salmon on light, single-handed rods.

LEEDA/3M SYSTEM TWO 67L *(above)*
This aluminum alloy reel has a counterbalanced spool with an exposed rim, a stainless steel spindle, and a fully adjustable disk brake. It takes WF7F line plus 60 yds (55 m) backing.

ORVIS BATTENKILL
5/6 3⅛ in (7.9 cm) *(right)*
This cast aluminum reel will take #5 or #6 lines plus 100 yds (91 m) backing. It has a counterbalanced spool, bronze bushings, and an exposed rim for fingertip control.

HARDY PERFECT
3⅛ in (7.9 cm) *(below)*
First introduced in 1891 (see page 45), *Hardy Perfect reels are machined to very close tolerances, and the interchangeable spools are mounted on ball bearings. They are available in left- and right-hand versions.*

LEEDA LC80 *(below)*
The LC80 is a light reel with a graphite outer frame and a wide, interchangeable plastic spool. It has a capacity of DT6 plus 75 yds (69 m) backing, and there is a useful line clip on the backplate to hold the loose end of the leader.

HARDY LRH LIGHTWEIGHT *(above)*
This aluminum alloy reel has an adjustable compensating check, interchangeable spools, and a caged drum, and converts to left- or right-hand wind. It is an ideal reel for all-around trout fishing, and its capacity is DT5F plus 40 yds (37 m) backing.

SHAKESPEARE SPEEDEX
3½ in (8.9 cm) *(above)*
The 2:1 gear ratio of the Speedex gives rapid line retrieval, and an adjustable drag provides resistance to running fish. It is available with narrow or wide spools; the narrow spool takes DT6F plus 25 yds (23 m) backing, the wide spool DT7F plus 75 yds (69 m) backing.

HARDY MARQUIS 2/3
2 9/16 in (6.5 cm) *(above)*
This little aluminum reel is designed for use on small streams with #2 or #3 lines. It has a reversible nickel silver lineguard, interchangeable spools, and an exposed rim, and converts to left- or right-hand wind.

ORVIS CFO III 3 in (7.6 cm) *(above)*
The CFO III has a similar specification to the CFO 123 but its larger size makes it more versatile, and it is popular with stillwater boat-fishing enthusiasts using short rods. Its capacity is WF6F plus 50 yds (46 m) backing.

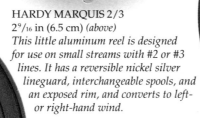

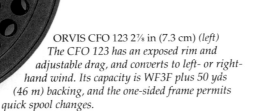

ORVIS CFO 123 2⅞ in (7.3 cm) *(left)*
The CFO 123 has an exposed rim and adjustable drag, and converts to left- or right-hand wind. Its capacity is WF3F plus 50 yds (46 m) backing, and the one-sided frame permits quick spool changes.

Fly Reels 2

These reels are suitable for the heavier end of fly fishing, such as steelhead, salmon, large trout, and sea trout fishing, and for saltwater fly fishing. They are capable of holding the heavy lines and ample backing that are so necessary for large, hard-running fish, and most feature exposed rims, which are essential for controlling big fish. In addition, their large diameters allow quick line recovery and also limit line memory – the tendency of line to remain coiled when stripped from the reel – because the line is wound on in larger coils. Line memory can be a problem with small-diameter reels.

ORVIS CFO VI 4 in (10 cm) *(above)*
This reel is similar to the CFO 123 (see page 43) *but larger and with a caged drum; capacity is DT11F plus 150 yds (137 m) backing. It is ideal for steelhead and salmon, but unsuitable for bonefish or estuary sea trout because it is not designed for saltwater fishing.*

ORVIS BATTENKILL DISK 8/9
3$\frac{3}{8}$ in (8.6 cm) *(right)*
This reel is similar to the Battenkill 5/6 model (see page 42) *but it is larger and has a Teflon disk drag. This drag is normally audible, but it can be switched to silent running if preferred. The wide, lightweight drum reel has good capacity for its diameter, and can take WF9F plus 170 yds (155 m) backing.*

HARDY OCEAN PRINCE *(below)*
The Ocean Prince is a heavy reel ideal for salmon, tarpon, and bonefish, and has a multi-plate clutch, strong, adjustable, anti-reverse drag, interchangeable spools, and exposed rim control. It converts to right- or left-hand wind and its capacity is DT10F plus 150 yds (137 m) backing.

LEEDA MAGNUM 140D *(below)*
The 140D is a full-cage reel with adjustable disk drag, exposed rim, counterbalanced interchangeable spools, and a capacity of DT10F plus 140 yds (128 m) backing. It is ideal for shooting-head work, steelhead, and salmon.

SHAKESPEARE PFLUEGER MEDALIST 4 in (10 cm) *(right)*
This large-capacity reel is ideal for shooting-head work and for heavy sunk-line fishing. It is often used by anglers fishing deep stillwaters with a lead-cored trolling line for fry-feeding brown and rainbow trout.

HARDY MARQUIS 8/9 MULTIPLIER
3⅝ in (9.2 cm) *(below)*
This reel is similar to the Marquis 2/3 (see page 43) *but is larger and geared for rapid line retrieval; capacity WF8F plus 50 yds (46 m) backing. It is ideal for trout, sea trout, steelhead, and salmon fishing with single-handed rods.*

LEEDA/3M SYSTEM TWO
1011 *(left)*
With its fully adjustable disk brake, exposed rim, and capacity of DT10 plus 110 yds (100 m) backing, this reel is ideal for large trout, sea trout, steelhead, and salmon.

HARDY PERFECT *(right)*
The Perfect was first introduced by Hardy in 1891 and then later dropped from their range. It was reintroduced during the 1970s because of the resurgence of interest created by angler/author Hugh Falkus, who professed it to be the ultimate sea trout reel. The older reels are much sought after by collectors. It is ideal for large trout, sea trout, steelhead, and salmon.

SHAKESPEARE REVOLUTIONARY CASSETTE FLY 4 in (10 cm) *(above)*
This unusual reel from Shakespeare has the line spooled onto a plastic cassette, which is then loaded onto the spool proper. Its disk brake, cageless design, and counterbalanced spool offer generous line capacity and make it a good reel for fast-running gamefish.

Boat Reels

To cope with the rigors of boat angling, a baitcaster reel must be strong and well-engineered with an adequate spool capacity for its intended use. The gearing should be precise and robust, and the drag mechanism should be smooth and reliable to minimize the risk of line breakage when you are playing a large, free-running fish. Boat reel drag mechanisms are adjusted either by turning a star-shaped knob (star drag) or by moving a lever (lever drag) – pushing the lever forward increases the drag tension, and pulling it back reduces it. The lever drag, once found only on large, expensive reels designed for big-game fishing, is now used on many smaller models. The advantage of the lever drag over the star drag is that it allows you to increase the drag tension more gradually and precisely.

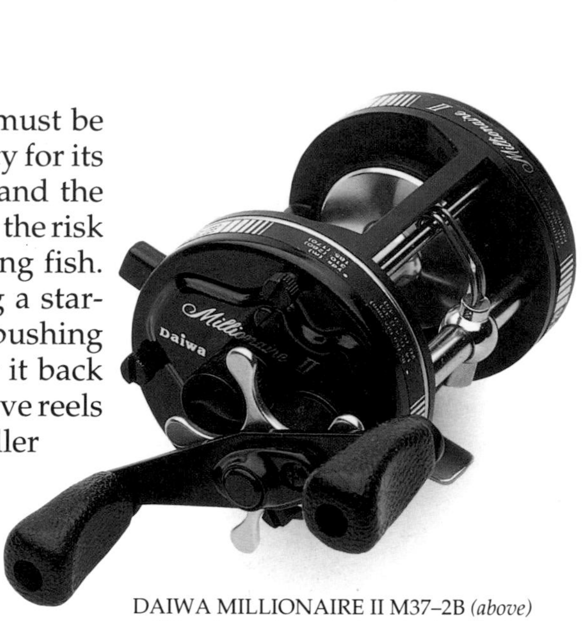

DAIWA MILLIONAIRE II M37–2B *(above)*
Millionaire reels are designed primarily for surfcasting, but they are also excellent as light to medium boat reels. The M37–2B has a spool capacity of 370 yds (340 m) of 12 lb (5.4 kg) line, and its two stainless-steel ball bearings ensure smooth spool rotation under pressure and at speed. It is an ideal light surf reel, perfect for light-line pollack fishing, shallow-water redfish, fast-moving bass, and some of the smaller pelagic gamefish such as dolphin.

SHIMANO TRITON 100G *(right)*
Shimano has played a large part in popularizing the lever drag outside of the big-game scene, and the drag application on the Triton 100G is wonderfully smooth and precise. This small baitcaster has a carbon/titanium body and a spool capacity of 250 yds (230 m) of 17 lb (7.7 kg) mono line. It is a perfect reel for basic boat work, but is not suitable for surf fishing because lever drag reels do not cast well.

ABU GARCIA AMBASSADEUR 7000 C SYNCRO *(above)*
A spool capacity of 250 yds (230 m) of 35 lb (15.9 kg) mono line makes this reel ideal for all light to medium work, and its centrifugal braking prevents overruns when casting heavy lures. When playing troublesome fish, you can remove up to 75 percent of the drag simply by backwinding; full drag is reapplied automatically when the handle is cranked. Unfortunately, it comes with a level wind, but conversion kits are available.

ABU GARCIA AMBASSADEUR 10000 C *(left)*
This high-quality, heavy-duty reel is designed for both beach work and boat fishing, including trolling. The gear ratio of 4.2:1 is shifted down automatically to 2.5:1 when a big fish is being played and the reel is heavily loaded, giving a slower but more powerful retrieve.

PENN INTERNATIONAL II 30 SW *(left)*
Reels with two-speed retrieves help anglers beat the biggest fish on the lightest tackle. The Penn International II 30 SW features a 3.8:1 gear ratio for regular retrieval work, and 1.8:1 for when the pressure is really on. A ratio of less than 2:1 might seem too low to be useful, but when a big fish is proving difficult, using too high a ratio can result in failure. It is like riding a bicycle uphill: get the gearing right, and you will progress with relative ease.

SHAKESPEARE FULMAR 400 *(right)*
Lever-drag reels have rightly earned themselves the reputation of being the first choice for heavy boat-fishing work. They also have a reputation for being expensive, but the Fulmar 400, with its 3:1 gear ratio, carbon/titanium construction, aluminum spool, and capacity for 500 yds (460 m) of 50 lb (22.7 kg) mono line, is both reliable and reasonably priced. It is a perfect reel for heavy-duty wreck fishing and for middle-range gamefish work.

PENN INTERNATIONAL 50 *(left)*
The biggest jobs in the boat-fishing world require reels that have earned themselves the biggest reputations. On the big-game scene, that usually means Penn reels. Penn makes larger reels than the International 50 – up to 130 class – but it has the capacity, power, and quality of construction to handle almost any big fish. Its spool capacity is 600 yds (550 m) of 50 lb (22.7 kg) mono line, the gear ratio is 3:1, and its lever drag is the smoothest anyone could desire.

SURF & SHORE REELS

Surf and shore reels, like shore rods, have great demands placed on them by the rugged nature of fishing from the shore. This has lead to much innovation in their design and manufacture, but so far it has not proved possible to combine the best features of each main type (baitcaster, spinning and sidecaster) into one super-reel. The baitcaster, in theory more robust and capable of casting greater distances, is not as easily mastered as the spinning reel, which in turn is better suited to light spinning and float work than the baitcaster. The third option, the Alvey Sidecast, is a cross between a centerpin and a spinning reel. It has some undoubted benefits but also, like the other types, has its drawbacks.

ABU GARCIA AMBASSADEUR 9000 CL *(above)*
The robust, high-capacity 9000 CL is ideal for the tougher jobs along the shore, such as fishing in heavy kelp, and for dealing with powerful fish. Good casting ability is combined with a two-speed retrieve: low for playing fish and high for skipping fast over snags.

ABU GARCIA AMBASSADEUR 7000 *(right)*
The precision of the Ambassadeur 7000 revolutionized casting and distance fishing, and its design has not changed in two decades because it has not needed to. It is still the best casting and fishing option for general shore angling.

ABU GARCIA AMBASSADEUR 6500 C SPECIAL *(left)*
The 6500 C puts proven Abu Garcia technology into arguably the smallest practical package for medium to heavy shore use. A tournament casting favorite with real angling ability.

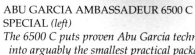

DAIWA MILLIONAIRE TOURNAMENT 7HT *(right)*
The 7HT's 5:1 gear ratio, its lack of level wind and top bar, and its special foot to suit coaster clamps, make it a superb distance-caster's reel. It is also very good for long-range beach fishing.

ABU GARCIA CARDINAL C5 *(right)*
The Cardinal C5, with its skirted spool and rear drag, typifies the sort of middle-range spinning reel that is so valuable for pelagic species such as bass and bonito. It is also useful for light legering over snaggy terrain.

DAIWA PM9000H *(below)*
A good, heavy-duty spinning reel requires a skirted, coned spool; automatic and manual bail arm operation; a powerful, rear-operated drag; anti-reverse; and fast line retrieval. Such features are found on the PM9000H, which is suitable for most shore work involving long, easy casting for small to medium-sized fish.

ALVEY SIDECAST 60 A-5 *(right)*
An Alvey Sidecast is a type of centerpin with a two-position spool. For casting, the spool is positioned with its axle parallel to the rod, and the line spills freely over the rim as with a spinning reel. On the retrieve, the spool is aligned with the rod and the line is wound on as with a standard centerpin. An Alvey casts well and offers tremendous direct power, but slow line uptake makes it less suitable for work where other reels can cope.

Lines, Crimps, Beads, & Swivels

Although they are small and seem insignificant, leader (or trace) lines, crimps, beads, swivels, and the like are as important as rods and reels because, along with hooks and lures, they constitute the tackle that fish come directly into contact with. Unless they perform correctly and reliably, perfect bait presentation (without which the bait, no matter how good, loses some of its appeal to fish) will be difficult, as will the successful playing and landing of a hooked fish. Similar considerations apply to the reel line, whether it be monofilament, braided fiber (such as braided Dacron), or wire. An outfit can only be as strong and reliable as its weakest link, which is often the line. Look after it and change it regularly, and always use line that is of the correct type and breaking strain (the load or weight that a line can take before it breaks) for its intended application.

Monofilament

For bait and lure fishing, monofilament nylon (mono) far outsells every other line material combined, and it is also used as backing for fly lines, which are usually made of coated Dacron *(see page 52)*. It is cheap, reliable, the only line that can be distance cast, and a virtual must for freshwater fishing. However, there are disadvantages to consider. Different brands stretch to varying degrees. This can be helpful in cushioning violent movement from big fish, but it also cushions the bite and strike in deep water. Other drawbacks of mono are that it is weakened by knotting, its breaking strain is reduced when it is wet, and exposure to the ultraviolet light in sunlight will weaken it. In general, mono line should be changed at least once per year.

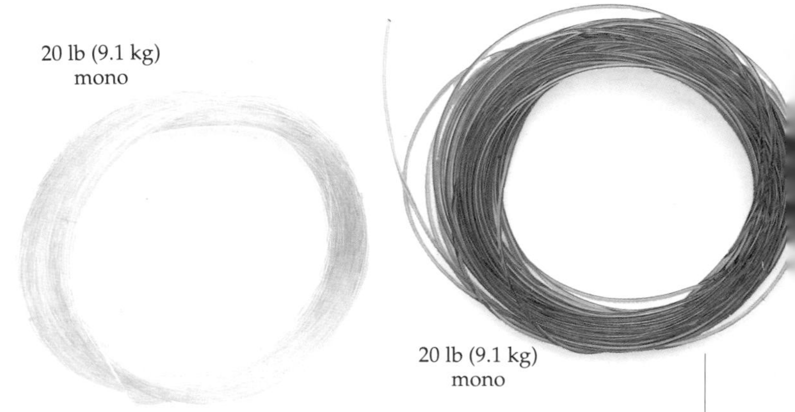

Braided Line

Once extremely popular, braided Dacron line has fallen from favor as a result of monofilament improvement and competition from wire. This is a pity, because it has useful attributes such as specified breaking strain control for IGFA line class records, excellent knot strength, and no deterioration over time. On the downside, it chafes easily, offers no cushion for bullying lively fish, and has a low breaking strain for its diameter. Its big advantage is its lack of stretch, which is vital in deep water and helpful for trotting float-fished baits *(see page 223)*, where mono might mask the strike. Otherwise, it is used mainly for trolling, float fishing for sharks, and sea fishing in deep water with not much tide.

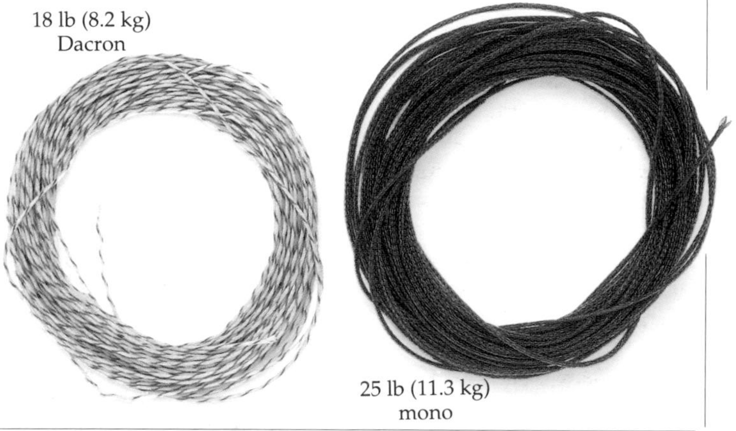

Wire Line

Wire line comes in three forms: single-strand stainless steel, braided or twisted multi-strand steel, and single-strand Monel (an alloy based on copper and nickel). It is an excellent choice for sea fishing in deep water where tides run particularly hard, because it does not stretch and has a high breaking strain for its diameter. This means instant bite detection at any depth, positive striking, and the ability to hold bottom with a fraction of the additional weight that is required by other lines. Its drawbacks are that it requires a narrow, deep-spooled baitcaster reel without a level wind, a rod with roller guides (at least a roller tip), and a monofilament weak link at the end. It cannot be cast, hooks can be ripped out easily because it has no cushioning stretchiness, and care must be taken to avoid cut hands.

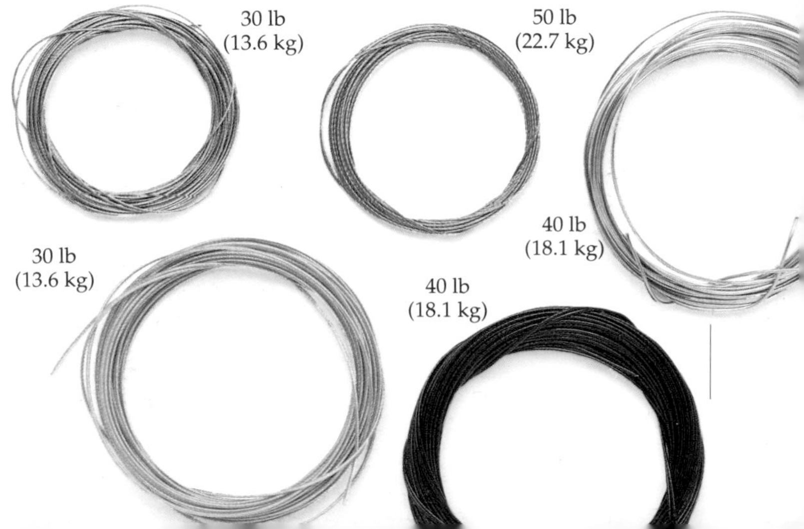

Leader Line

When fishing in freshwater for pike and other species with sharp teeth and strong jaws, a strong leader (trace) between the reel line and the hook or lure is essential. Freshwater leaders should be uncoated braided wire or, for deadbait trolling, single-strand wire. In saltwater, plain mono is adequate for small to medium-sized fish without teeth, but for large fish, or those with sharp teeth, use longliner's nylon or wire. Generally speaking, plain monos from 40 lb (18.1 kg) upward make the best leaders for boat fishing; anything lighter tends to present the bait poorly. Use nylon of 150 lb (68 kg) for heavy wreck and reef fishing, and at least 200 lb (91 kg) nylon for giant tuna and billfish.

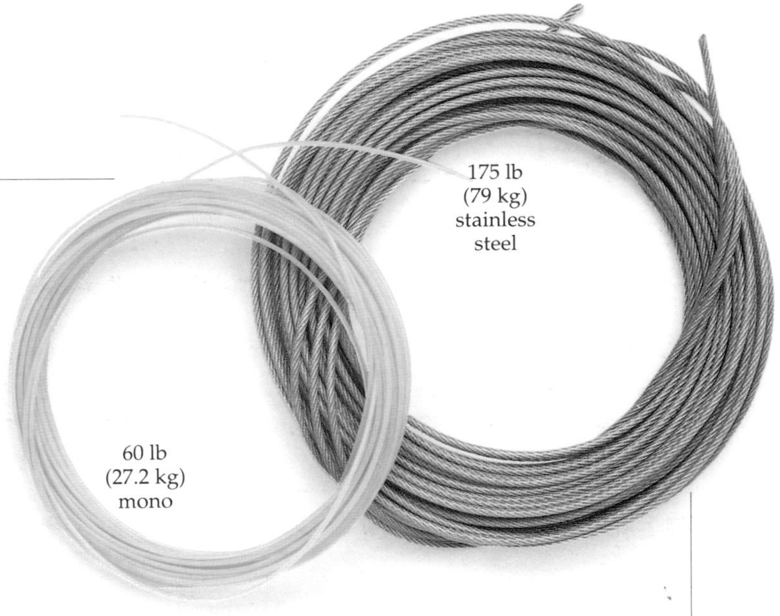

Crimps & Beads

Wire line and heavy-guage mono are joined to other lines and to swivels by means of crimps, which are small metal sleeves. For example, to fix a swivel to a wire line, a crimp is slipped over the end of the line, which is then looped through the eye of the swivel and back into the crimp. Then the crimp is squeezed tight with crimping pliers. Beads are used to protect knots from sliding booms and to act as buffers ahead of fixed stops.

CRIMPS

BEADS

COIL CRIMP *(right)*
Coil crimp is springy, spiral stainless steel wire. Short lengths of it can be wound onto the line to replace stop knots and plastic stoppers that are superglued into position for fixing droppers and booms in place. They can be repositioned quickly or removed for reuse.

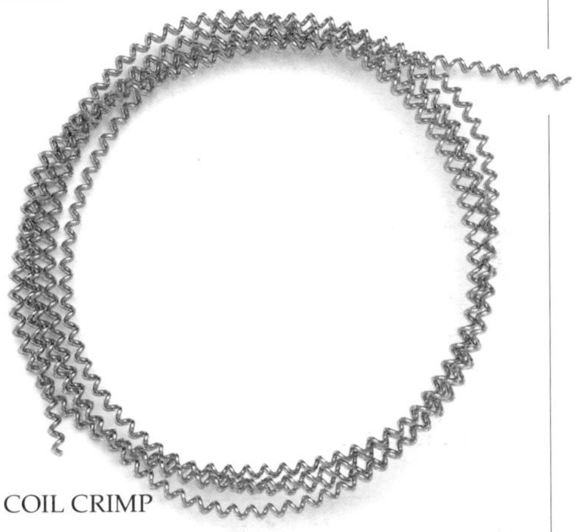

COIL CRIMP

Swivels

Every terminal rig, no matter how simple, should ideally contain at least one swivel to prevent twists in the line, and using a swivel is the perfect way to attach a leader or a dropper to the reel line. Even the best brands are cheap, so go for the quality names such as Berkley, Mustad, Drennan, and Sampo; unbranded imitations are generally unreliable and can refuse to turn under stress.

BARREL SWIVELS
Barrel swivels are the best choice for general-purpose work. Their design almost guarantees long-term reliability.

BALL-BEARING SWIVELS
These offer superb, freely rotating twist correction, which is essential for all trolling work.

THREE-WAY SWIVELS
These were once popular for linking in droppers, but standoff booms terminating in barrel swivels are now generally preferred.

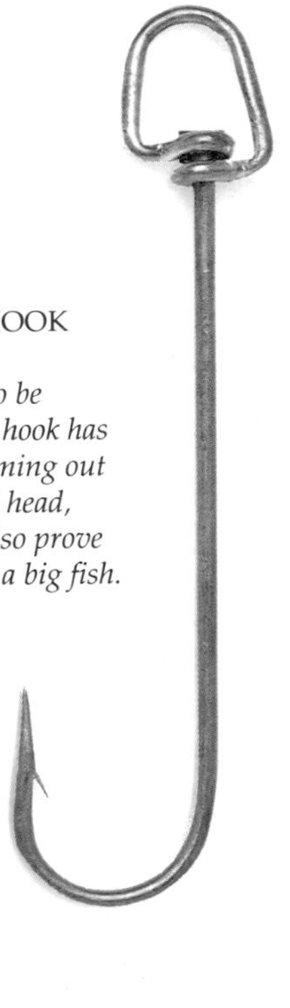

CONGER HOOK SWIVEL
This is not to be trusted. The hook has a habit of coming out of the swivel head, which can also prove too weak for a big fish.

LINK SWIVELS

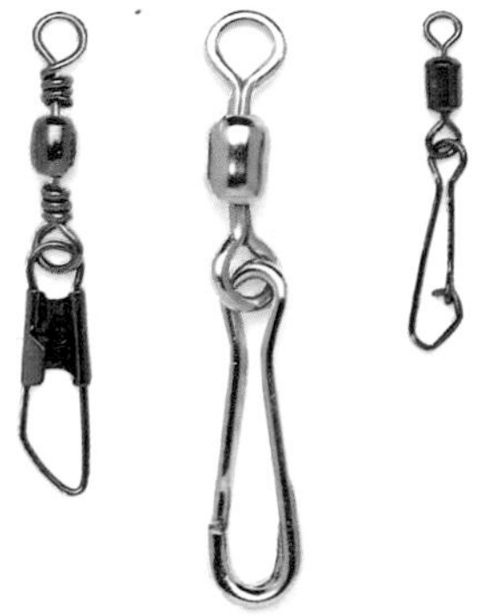

SNAP SWIVELS
A snap swivel is a swivel with a quick-release link to which the terminal tackle is attached. Several types of link are available, but they all allow easy changing of terminal tackle, either to unhook fish while continuing fishing, or to replace a kinked or damaged leader.

SAMPO SWIVELS

BIG-GAME SWIVEL
Reliable, heavy-duty ball bearing swivels, such as those made by Sampo and Berkley, are essential for the prolonged, tackle-testing battles with exceptionally large fish that are typical of big-game fishing.

Fly Lines & Leaders

Most artificial flies are small and weigh next to nothing, and the casting weight needed to carry them out onto the water is provided by the fly line. The fly is joined to the fly line via a braided or solid leader, and the fly line in turn is attached to a length of braided or solid backing line. The backing provides a reserve of line for playing big, fast-running fish, and, by partly filling the reel spool, it ensures that the fly line coils are of large circumference. These big coils are less likely than small ones to tangle as they are pulled off the reel. Fly lines are made from materials such as braided nylon, braided Dacron, and PVC, and coated with a variety of polymers such as polyurethane and PTFE.

LINE COLOR
Most floating lines are pale in color, but sinking lines are usually produced in darker hues.

The AFTMA System

Formulated by the American Fishing Tackle Manufacturers Association (AFTMA), this system uses a code of letters and numbers to describe the characteristics of a fly line. The first letters of the code indicate the line's profile or shape, the number that follows indicates its weight, and the last letter (or two letters) signifies its density. The number assigned to a fly line *(see right)* depends on the weight, in grains, of the first 30 ft (9.1 m) of the line, excluding any level tip. AFTMA numbers are also assigned to fly rods, and the number of the line should match that of the rod with which it is used.

AFTMA Line Weight Numbers

AFTMA number	Weight in grains	Weight range
1	60	54–66
2	80	74–86
3	100	94–106
4	120	114–126
5	140	134–146
6	160	152–168
7	185	177–193
8	210	202–218
9	240	230–250
10	280	270–290
11	330	318–342
12	380	368–392
13	430	418–442
14	480	468–492

AFTMA Fly Line Profiles

Anatomy of a Fly Line (double taper)

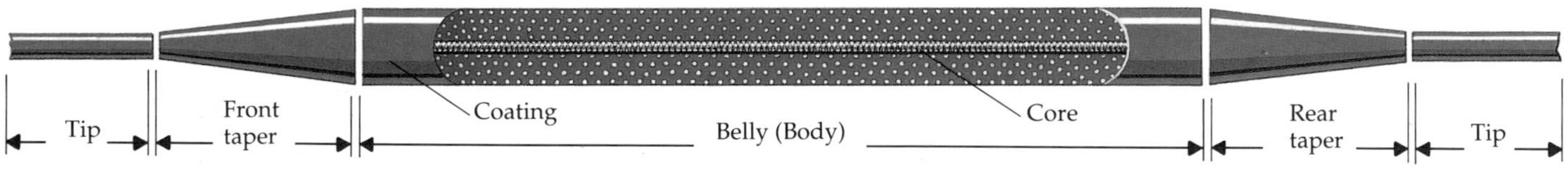

The fly line profiles, or tapers, in common use today are the double taper, the weight forward, and the shooting head or shooting taper. The level line, which is the same diameter throughout its length, is difficult to cast and is now seldom used. Double-taper lines are designed to present flies gently at close to medium distance and are easy to cast. Weight-forward lines are intended for medium to long-distance casting, and once the tip and belly of the line have been cast, the thin running line shoots easily through the rod guides. A well-designed weight-forward line will present a fly just as delicately as a double taper. Shooting heads consist of short lengths of fly line, backed by fine braided or flat solid monofilament, which produce little resistance when pulled through the rod guides, and are used for casting prodigious distances on lakes or in saltwater.

DOUBLE TAPER

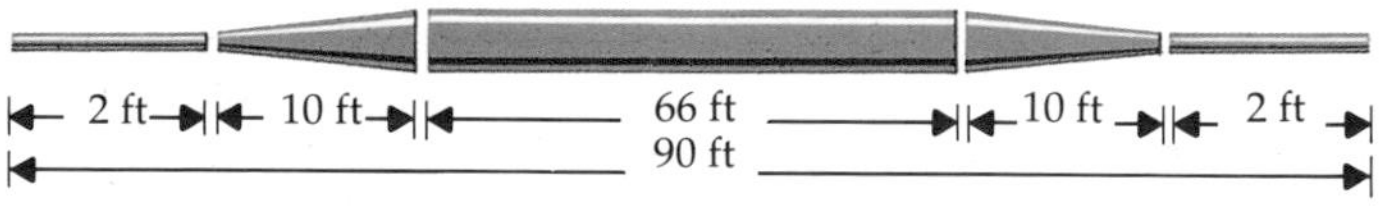

WEIGHT FORWARD

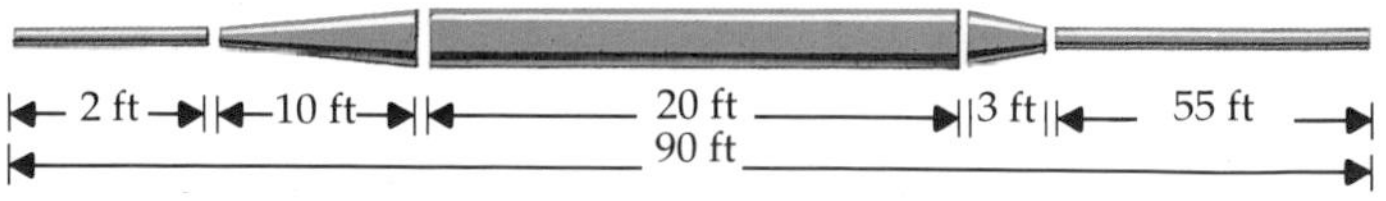

SHOOTING TAPER

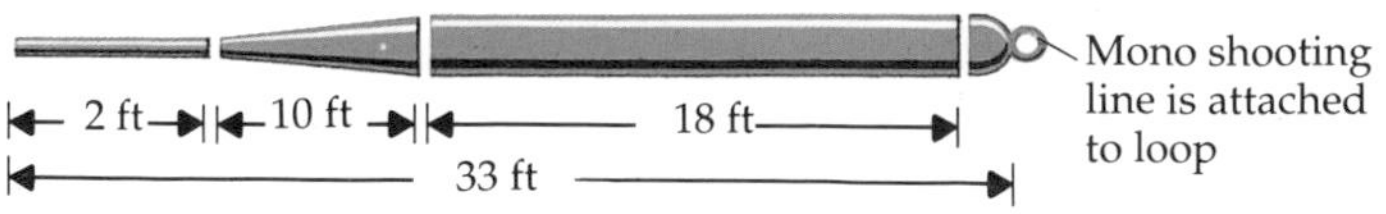

AFTMA Fly Line Symbols

In the AFTMA system of fly line classification, the letters preceding the weight number (DT, WF, or SH – or sometimes L, for level line) indicate the taper of the line. The letter or letters that come after the weight number (such as F, ND, I, S, FS, and VFS) signify the density, or function, of the line, that is, whether the line floats, sinks, or has an intermediate or neutral density and thus sinks very slowly.

For example, a fly line described as DT9F is one that has a double taper, is of weight number 9, and floats, while a number 7 line with a weight-forward taper and a neutral density is described as WF7ND.

Fly Line Symbols

DT	Double taper
WF	Weight forward
SH	Shooting head
F	Floating
ND	Neutral density
I	Intermediate
S	Sinking
FS	Fast sinking
VFS	Very fast sinking

Line Densities

Fly lines are made in a variety of densities, and the density of a line determines whether it will float or sink. Those with the lowest densities are floating lines, and those with the highest are the very fast sinkers. However, the descriptions given to individual lines are not always a reliable guide to their performance, and one manufacturer's fast-sinking line might sink at the same rate as another's very fast sinker.

To give a more accurate indication of how their sinking fly lines perform, many manufacturers publish their sinking rates. These are given in centimeters per second or inches per second, or as the depth to which the line will sink after a specified period of time. The only problem with this is that different parts of a line may sink at different speeds, and sinking rates may be influenced by many factors. For example, water temperature and wind speed (with attendant current) both affect the rate at which a line will sink.

Airflo DI Line Sinking Rates

Depth attained after 30 seconds

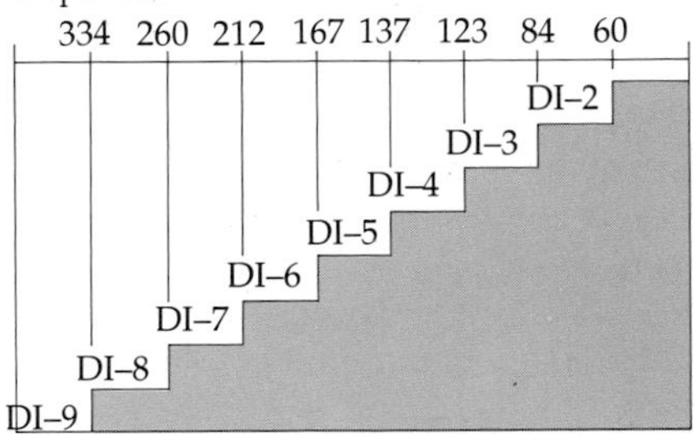

SINKING RATES *(above)*
This is an example of a manufacturer's sinking rate data, in this case for Airflo's DI range. The depths are stated in inches.

Leaders

The leader is the length of nylon or monofilament that connects the fly line to the fly. To ensure a good turnover during casting, it should taper from the fly line down, with the butt section (that closest to the fly line) being at least a third of the fly line's thickness. When surface fishing, use a long leader to put a good distance between the thick, colored fly line and the fly. This distance is usually not so important when you are using sinking lines.

ROMAN MOSER BRAIDED LEADERS

LEADER DENSITIES
The high-density braided leaders now available allow unleaded or very small flies to be fished deep without the need for a sinking fly line.

Braided leaders

These leaders are made of nylon braid that tapers continuously throughout its length and is very supple. They are produced in a range of floating and sinking versions, and because of their excellent turnover they are a great aid to good fly presentation. With some braided leaders, the butt end fits over the tip of the fly line and is held in place by a piece of silicone tubing, while others are joined to the fly line by loops. The fly is attached to a braided leader by a short length of mono called a tippet.

Monofilament leaders

Commercially made mono leaders consist either of a continuous, tapering length of nylon, or of lengths of progressively smaller diameters and lower breaking strains knotted together. The knotless leaders are stronger and less likely to pick up weeds than the knotted versions, but they do have the drawback that each time the fly is changed, the tip of the leader becomes thicker. Eventually, the entire leader has to be changed or a finer tip section attached.

AIRFLO BRAIDED LEADERS

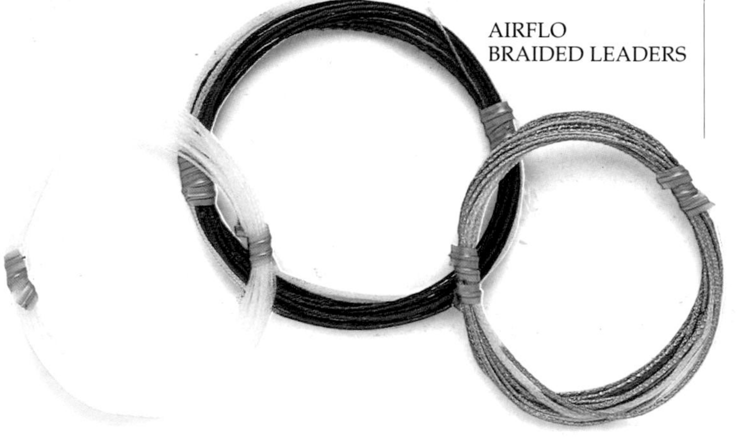

Hooks 1

Hooks are essential if unglamorous items of tackle. Although their functions are simple, their design is often complex and subtle, and there are innumerable patterns, sizes, and finishes on the market. These have evolved in response to the requirements of the different styles and methods of fishing; the varied sizes, mouth shapes, teeth, and lips of fish; and the baits needed to tempt them. As a result, it is essential to match your choice to your intended method of fishing and the species you intend to catch when buying your hooks. In this respect, as with any other tackle purchase, the advice of a reputable dealer will prove invaluable.

HOOK CHOICE
Always use a hook large enough to cope with the fish you intend to catch.

Hook Types

There are three basic types of hook, the single, the double, and the treble. The range of hooks is enormous, but without doubt the most popular type is the single in its many guises, from the small spade-end hooks used by tournament fishermen to the large stainless steel hooks used by big-game anglers. Double hooks are used chiefly for fly fishing, but some, such as the Whichway, are used for pike fishing. With its three points, the treble hook offers great hooking potential and is used mainly for plugs and spoons, pike rigs, and salmon flies (either long-shank trebles or tube flies).

SINGLE HOOK

DOUBLE HOOK

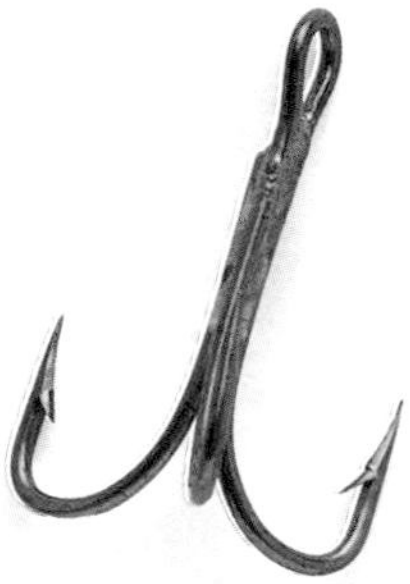

TREBLE HOOK

Parts of a Hook

The component parts of a typical hook are the eye, shank, bend, point, barb, throat, and gap (or gape). Hooks are made of high-carbon steel, usually with a corrosion-resistant finish, or of stainless steel.

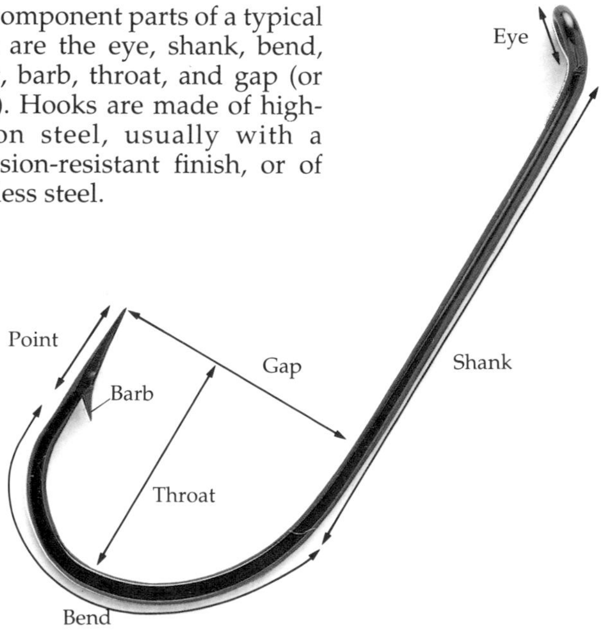

Hook Sizes

Hook sizes are denoted by numbers, but the number allocated to a particular size of hook may vary from one manufacturer to another. The smallest hook size is the 30, and, as an approximate guide, hooks from size 30 up to size 1 are used for freshwater fishing, and hooks 1/0 up to 16/0 for saltwater fishing. Japanese hooks tend to be a size smaller than European hooks, and importers compensate for this by moving the hooks down one size, so a Japanese size 6 becomes a size 8.

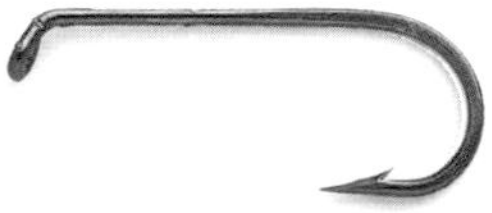

EUROPEAN SIZE 8
Forged heavy wire, round bend

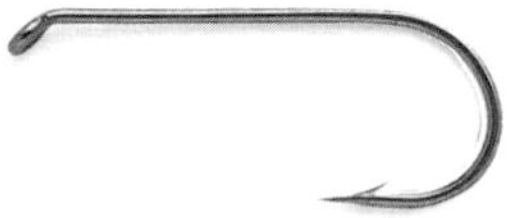

JAPANESE SIZE 6
Medium wire, round bend

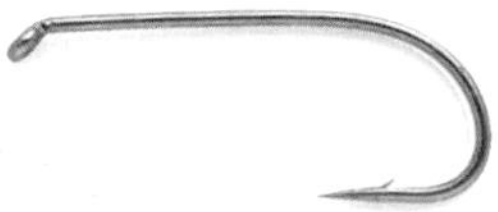

JAPANESE SIZE 6
Medium wire, sproat bend

Wire Gauges

The diameter, or gauge, of the wire from which a hook is made depends on the hook's pattern and size, but manufacturers now offer a choice of gauges for each pattern and size of hook. Fine-wire hooks are used for light-line fishing and dry flies, and medium-wire hooks for general fishing and most wet flies. Heavy wires are used for very strong hooks for big-game fishing, freshwater fishing for large fish, and heavy flies such as salmon flies and wet flies that are required to sink rapidly through the water.

HEAVY GAUGE

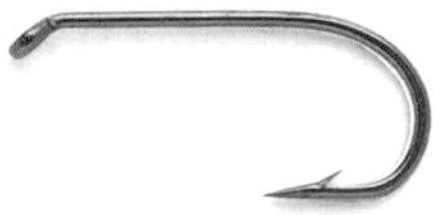

MEDIUM GAUGE

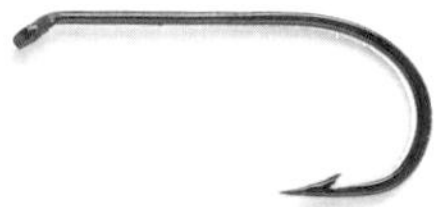

FINE GAUGE

Hook Eyes

Hook eyes come in many different shapes and sizes, and some hooks have spade ends instead of eyes. Flattened shanks were once very popular for hooks tied to nylon, but the labor-intensive whipping and varnishing required is no longer commercially viable when competing with whipped spade-end hooks. Similarly, tapered ball eyes are more expensive to produce than straight-wire ball eyes and are falling out of favor with manufacturers. Ringed eyes are very popular with freshwater and sea anglers for bait fishing, and the angle-eyed hooks are popular with fly anglers. When buying a hook, always check that the end of the wire used for forming the eye butts up against the shank; any hook with a gap at the eye should be discarded. A spade-end hook should have no sharp edges at the front of the spade that could cut the nylon when it is pulled tight.

BALL EYE
This is a round eye formed from straight wire, and is the most popular type of eye.

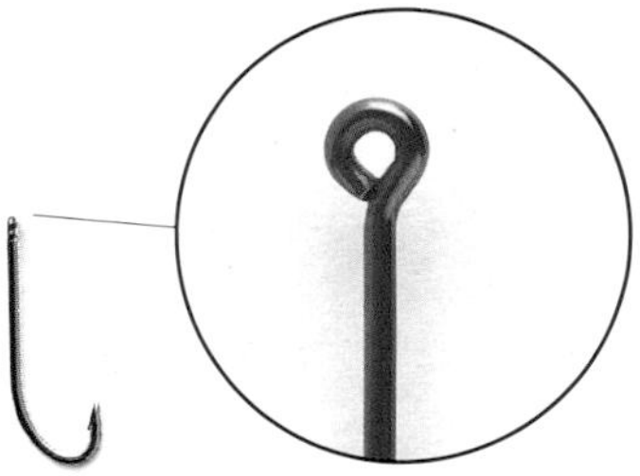

TAPERED EYE
The wire is tapered where it meets the shank, giving a neat, unobtrusive eye.

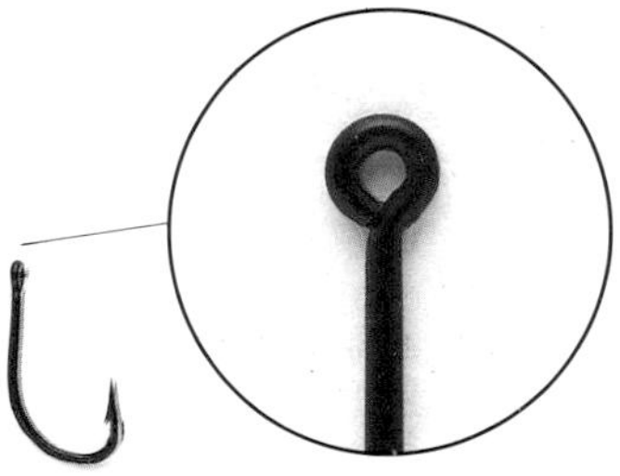

SPADE END
The spade end is formed by flattening the end of the wire.

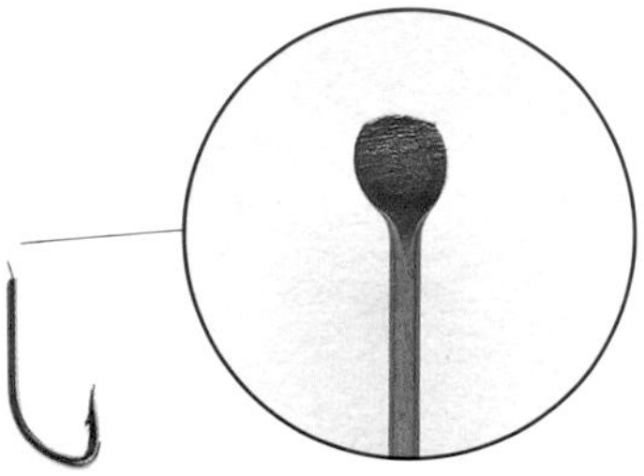

LOOPED EYE
This very strong eye is used on traditional single salmon hooks.

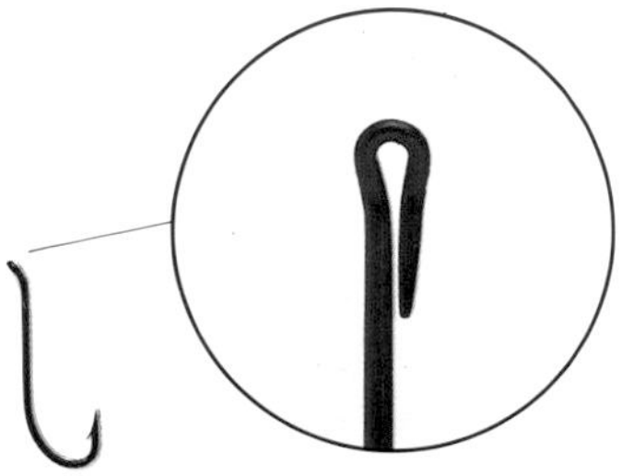

NEEDLE EYE
The needle eye is used on treble hooks, especially those for tube flies.

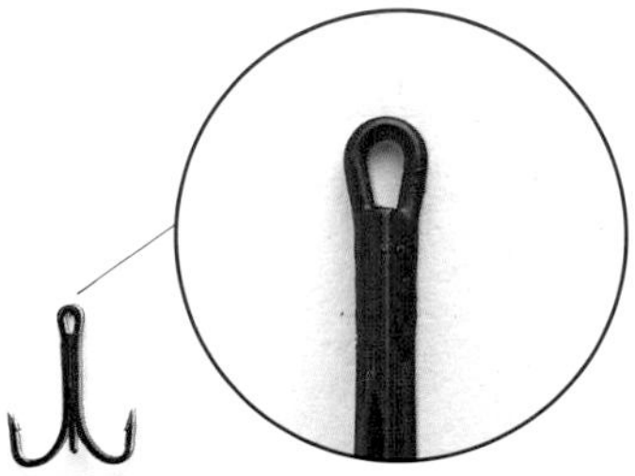

SWIVEL EYE
This is used on strong hooks for big game and large sea fish.

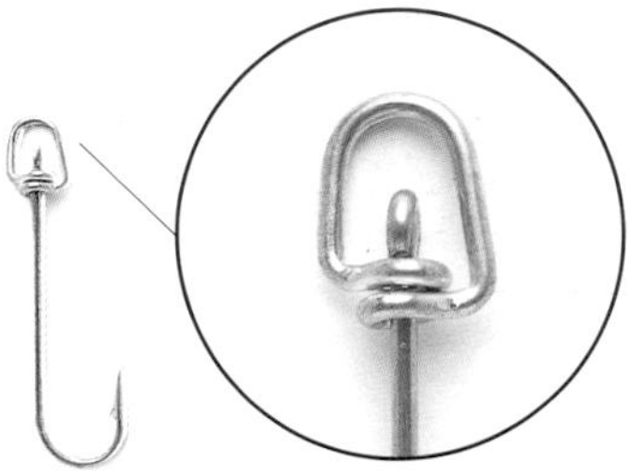

Angled eyes
Eyes are formed either straight (in line with the hook) or angled toward or away from the point. The eye of a turned-up eye hook is angled away from the point for good clearance between the shank and the point. The turned-down eye hook has its eye angled towards the point to give better penetration on the strike.

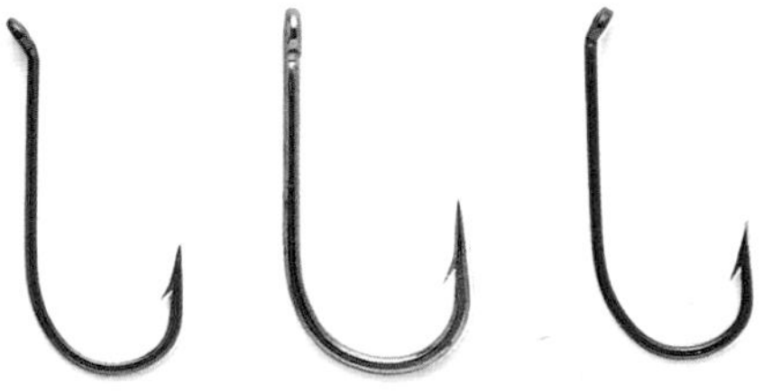

TURNED-UP RINGED TURNED-DOWN

GUT EYES
Gut eyes, now obsolete, were formed from gut whipped to the shank before a fly was tied.

Hook Shanks

Hooks designed for bait fishing vary less in shape and in shank length than hooks designed for fly fishing, which have to cater for the huge number of different sizes and patterns of fly. Hooks with short or standard-length shanks are used for freshwater bait fishing, but saltwater hooks tend to have long shanks, to accommodate the larger baits used and to protect leaders from the teeth of many species of sea fish. Many large hooks, especially saltwater patterns, have forged shanks and bends. Forging involves hammering the wire of the hook, after it has been shaped, to give it a flattened cross-section. This makes the hook much stronger than one of the same size with an unforged, round cross-section.

STANDARD SHANK
In a standard-shanked hook, of whatever size, there is a fixed ratio of shank length to gap width.

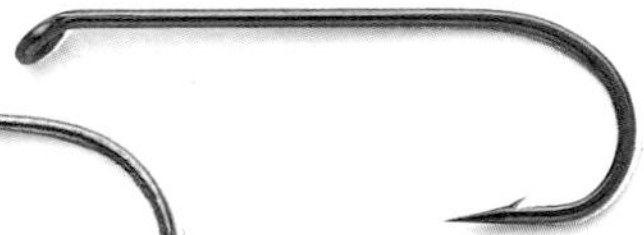

LONG SHANK
A 2X long-shanked hook has a shank the same length as that of a standard hook two sizes larger.

SHORT SHANK
A 2X short-shanked hook has a shank the same length as that of a standard hook two sizes smaller.

HOOK CROSS-SECTIONS

ROUND WIRE FORGED WIRE

CURVED SHANK
This shank gives a natural shape to the body of a fly, and is ideal for sedge pupa, midge, and grub patterns.

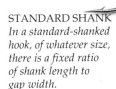

BAIT HOLDER
The slices (barbs) cut into the shank help to hold soft saltwater baits firmly in place on the hook.

Hooks 2

Hook Bends

The shape of the bend is an important distinguishing factor between one hook pattern and another, and as with other features of hooks, such as shank length and eye, a large number of different forms have evolved over the years. The shape of a bend is largely dictated by the intended use of the hook, but in general, a smoothly rounded bend is stronger than one that is sharply angled, while angled bends allow the hook point to penetrate deeper. Some bends are at their best when used for a particular style or method of fishing, but others are more versatile. The Sproat, for example, is an ideal bend for traditional flies, emergers, and dry flies, while the Kirby is suitable not only for freshwater and saltwater bait fishing but also for fly hooks.

CRYSTAL BEND
The crystal is a popular bend for freshwater bait fishing, particularly in small sizes.

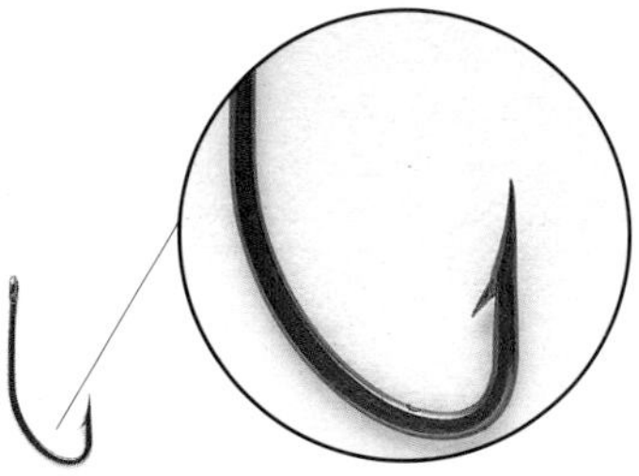

ROUND BEND
Round bends are used with offset points for bait angling, straight points for fly fishing.

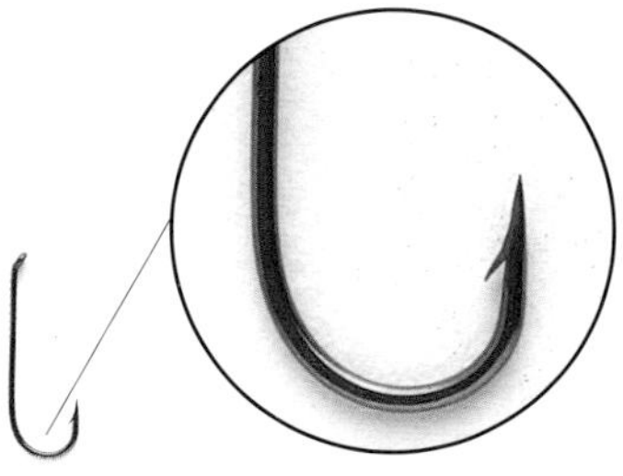

SPROAT
The Sproat is a good fly hook bend. The front angle is not as sharp as that of the crystal.

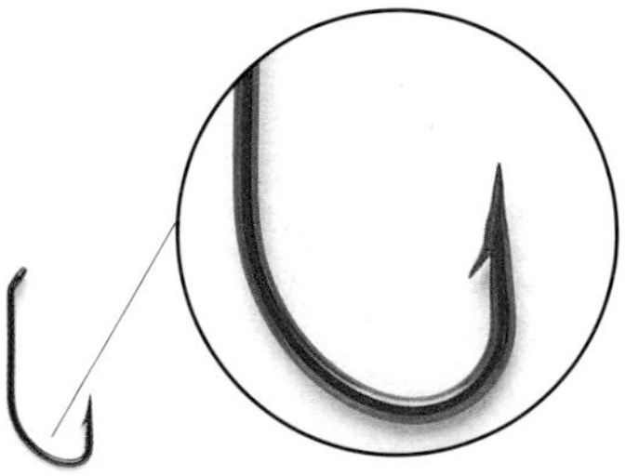

ABERDEEN
This is a round-bend, fine-wire sea hook with a long shank. It is a good bait hook.

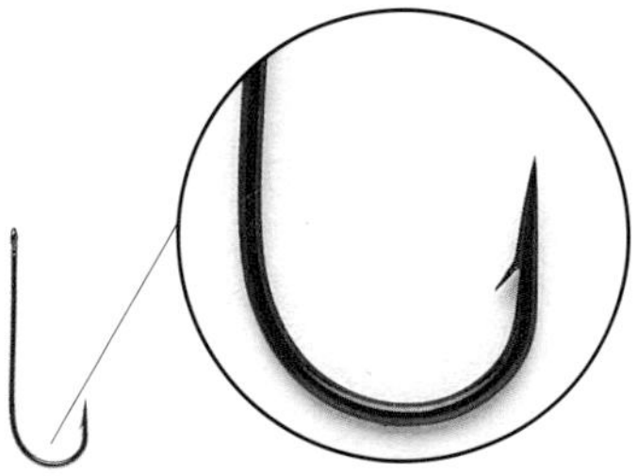

LIMERICK
The Limerick is widely used for freshwater and saltwater hooks and for salmon hooks.

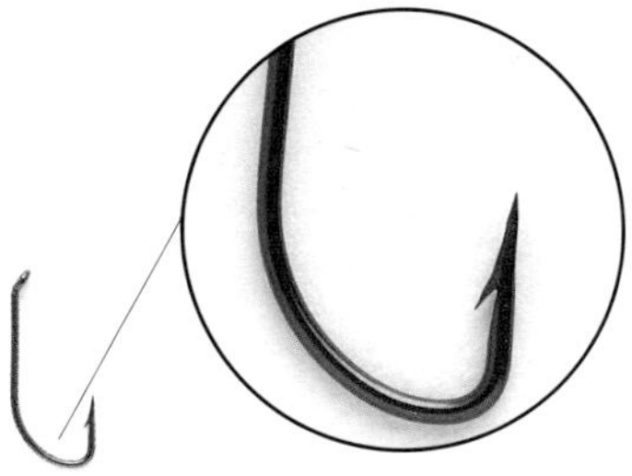

KIRBY
This is a slightly less rounded, more angular version of the ordinary round bend.

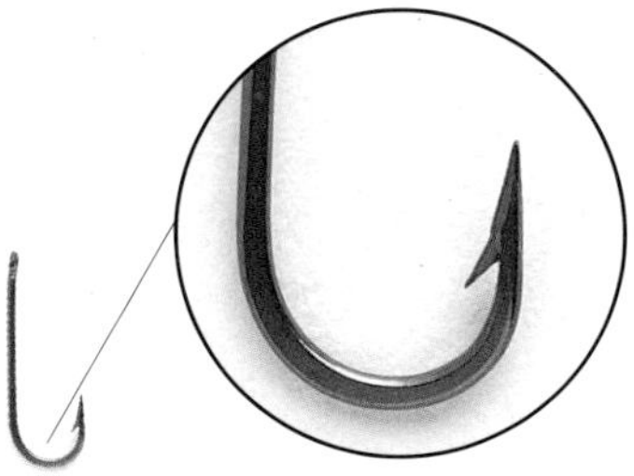

WIDEBEND
This long bend is designed for humpbacked flies such as shrimp and bug patterns.

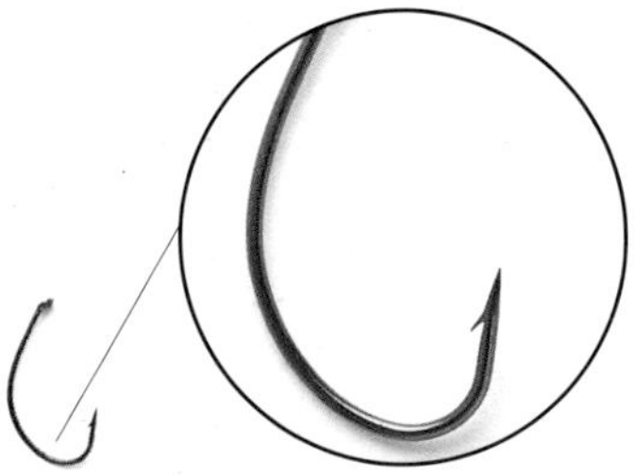

CINCINNATI BASS
This has a slightly curved shank and a straight point, and is ideal for emerger and dry-fly patterns.

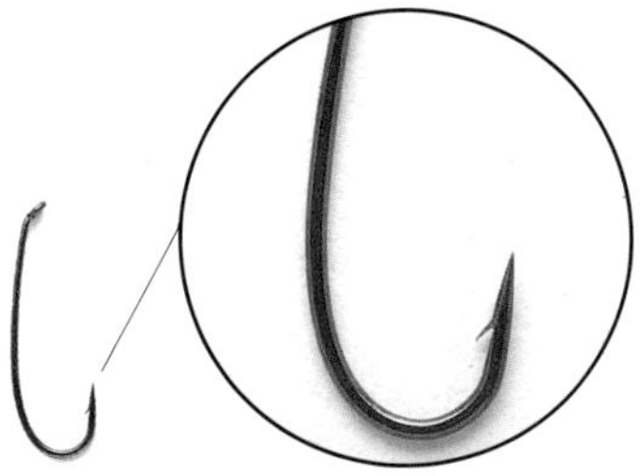

O'SHAUGNESSY
The O'Shaughnessy is a classic and very strong bend for heavy sea fish, including big-game species.

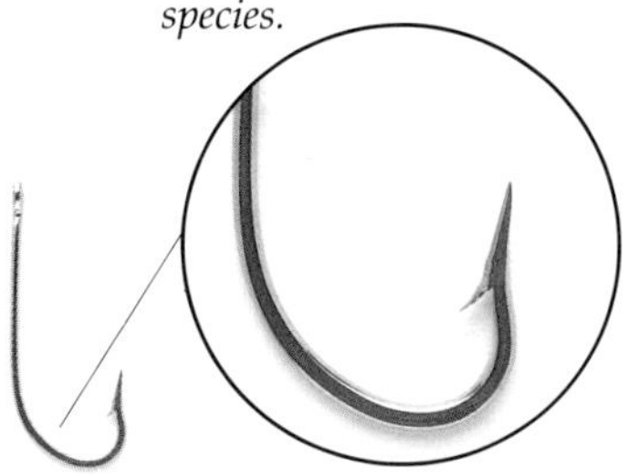

O'SHAUGHNESSY HEAVY
A modern bend, used with an offset point, for freshwater and saltwater bait fishing.

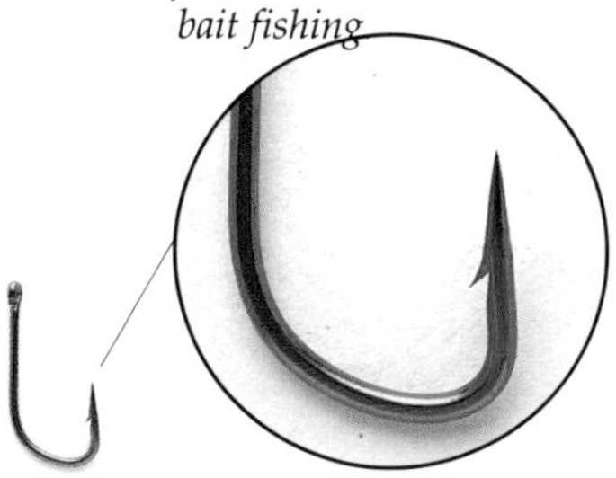

Hook Shapes

The overall shape of a hook is its style of bend, point, shank, and eye. Freshwater bait hooks tend to have offset points with short or standard straight shanks, and are either eyed or spade end. The "weedless" hook has a spring-loaded wire guard that shields the point to prevent it snagging in weeds. For saltwater bait fishing, the hooks are eyed and usually have longer shanks than those used for freshwater work. The very popular O'Shaughnessy, Kirby, and Aberdeen patterns are good examples of saltwater bait hooks. The majority of fly anglers use turned-up eye or turned-down eye hooks with straight points, straight shanks of various lengths, and a variety of bends.

CENTRAL-DRAUGHT SHANK

MIDGE HOOK

KEEL HOOK

SALMON SINGLE

TERRESTRIAL HOOK

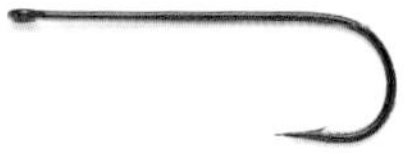

ABERDEEN

PIGGYBACK

BEAKED

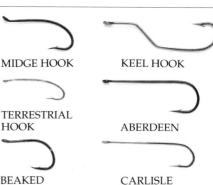

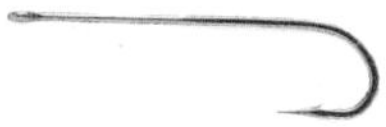

CARLISLE

Hook Points

Hook points vary with the different patterns and from manufacturer to manufacturer; cut hollow and superior points, for example, are typical of the Mustad range of hooks. Most hooks have cut or knife-edge points because these are easier to mass-produce than ground points. The outer edge of the hollow point is straight, while the inner line between the point and the tip of the barb is curved. With the superior point this arrangement is reversed and the outer edge is slightly curved while the inner edge is straight. A Dublin point, found on many salmon hooks, has features of both, and the point curves away from the shank. Some of the best and strongest points, however, are the ground and chemically sharpened needle points with fine-cut barbs that are produced in Japan.

BARBLESS
A point without a barb allows easy unhooking so is ideal for catch-and-release fishing.

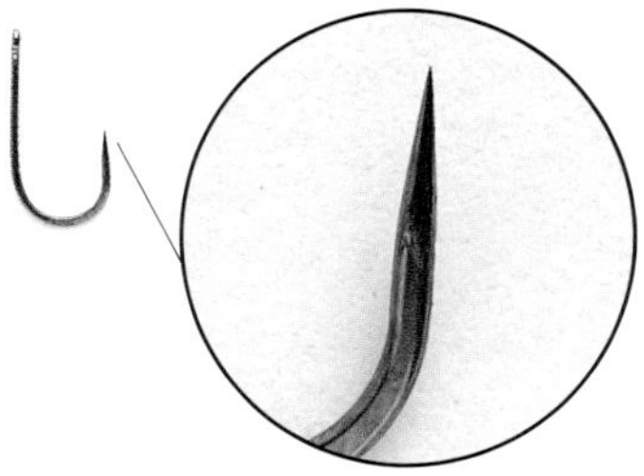

HOLLOW POINT
This cut point is used on many of the wide range of hooks produced by Mustad of Norway.

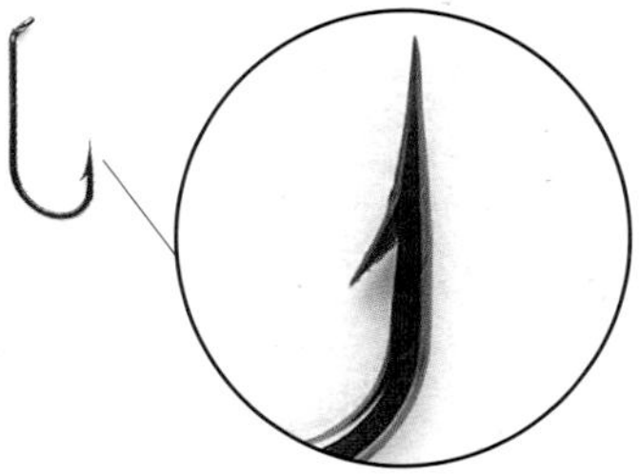

DUBLIN
This point originated in Dublin and is used on salmon "irons" and game fishing hooks.

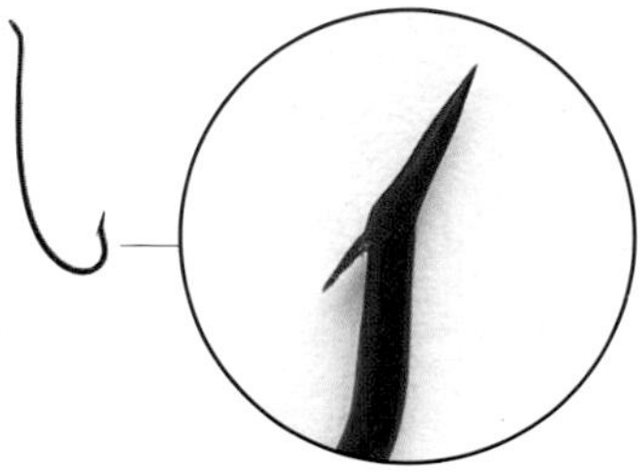

ARROWPOINT
The arrowpoint does not penetrate as easily as a standard barbless point, but it is claimed to hold fish better.

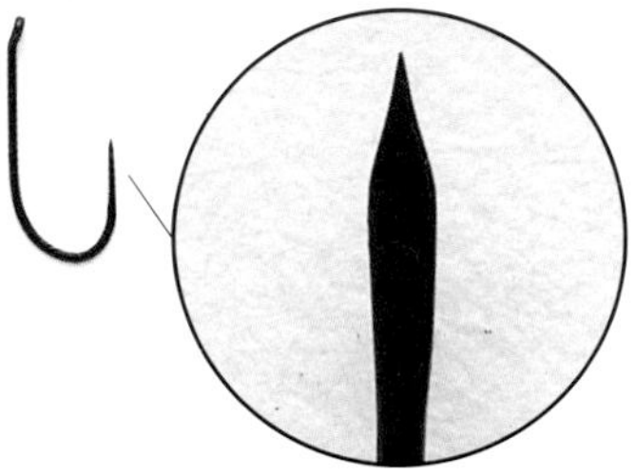

BEAKED
This ground, chemically sharpened point is strong, and penetrates well, because its barb is not deeply cut.

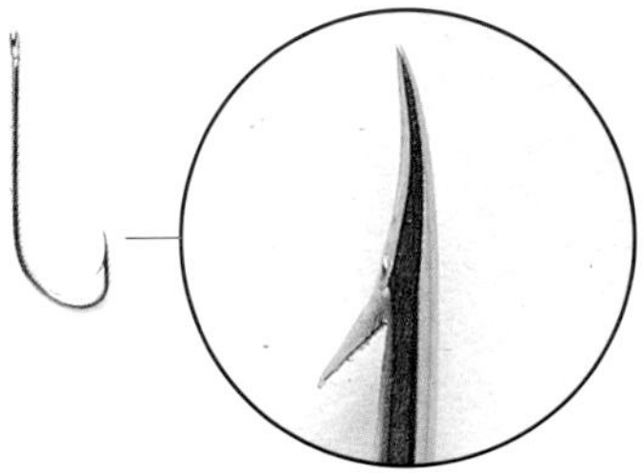

FALKUS OUTBARB
The barbs of this treble are on the outsides of the points. It has excellent fish-holding properties.

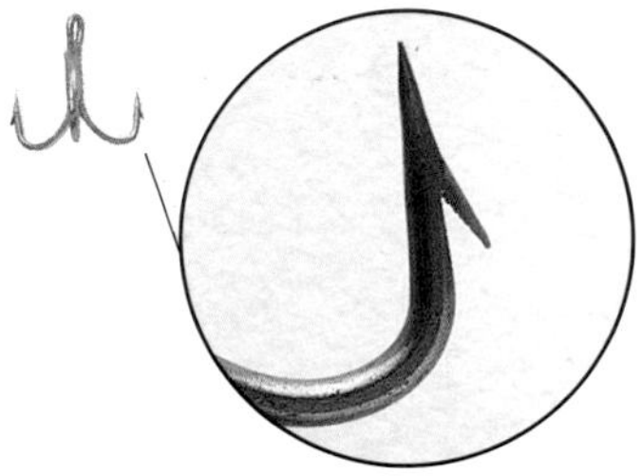

Offset Points

Hook points not only vary in shape but also are either straight or offset. To determine whether a point is straight or offset, check the alignment of the point to the shank. If the point is straight, it will be in line with the shank. An offset point will point either to the left, which is known as kirbed, or to the right, which is reversed. Straight points are ideal for fly fishing, but offset points are better for bait fishing. The most popular offset is the reversed, because most anglers are right-handed: for them, it is easier to bait a hook with a reversed point than one with a kirbed point, because the point is angled upward when the hook is held in the right hand.

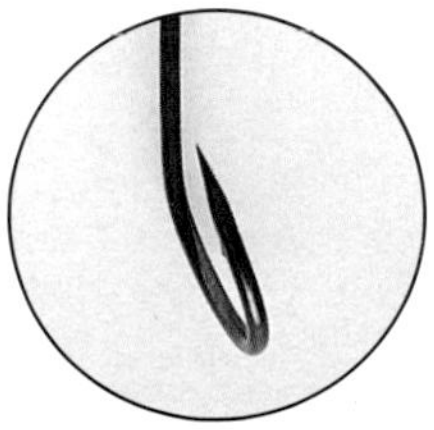

OFFSET LEFT/ KIRBED

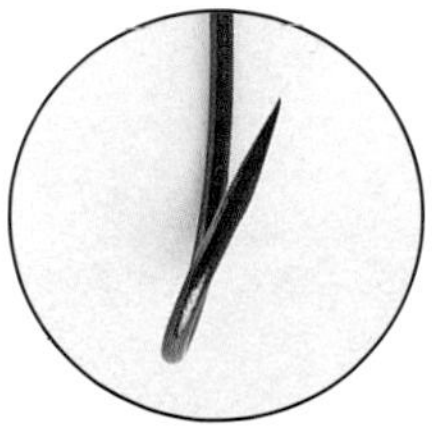

OFFSET/RIGHT REVERSED

Hook Faults

UNFORMED EYES

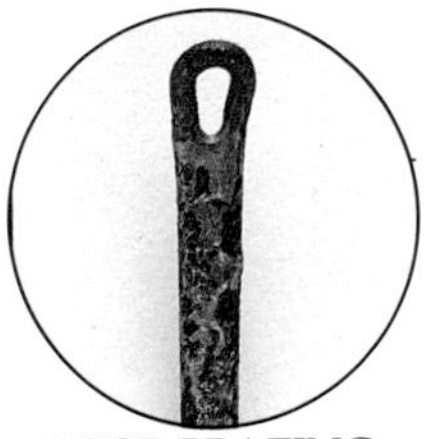

POOR BRAZING

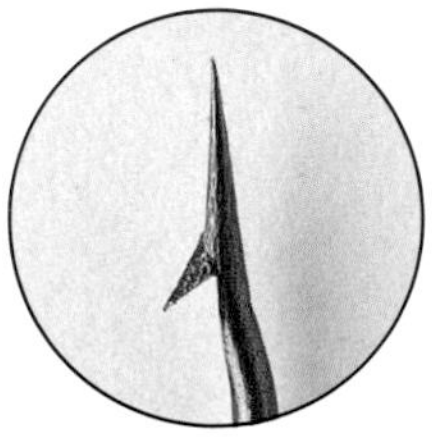

OVERCUT BARB

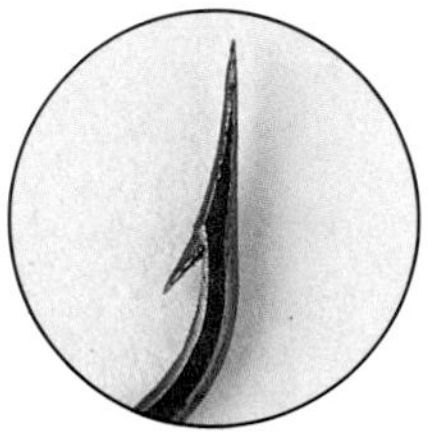

OVERLONG POINT

Common hook faults include unformed eyes, poor brazing, overcut barbs, poor temper, and overlong points. Most will be obvious, but poor temper may be difficult to detect. Carefully hook the point behind your thumbnail and pull the hook to open the bend. An under-tempered hook will bend out easily and not spring back when released; an overtempered hook will snap.

Hook Finishes

Hooks come in a variety of colored and corrosion-resistant finishes for different styles of fishing. The traditional black japanned finish is still used on some patterns, particularly salmon hooks, but the most unobtrusive color is bronze, and most hooks are now coated with a bronze finish. Some saltwater hooks are made of stainless steel, which is left uncoated because it is almost totally resistant to the corrosive properties of seawater. Other saltwater hooks are sometimes colored silver so that they attract fish to the bait.

JAPANNED

NIFLOR

GOLD

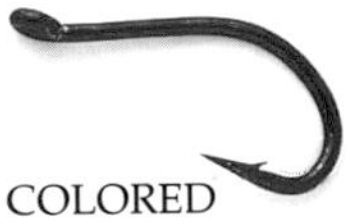

COLORED

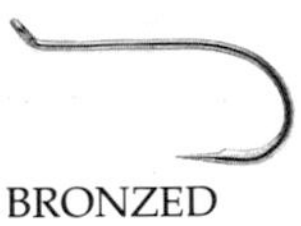

BRONZED

SILVERED

Freshwater Weights

The great many sizes and designs of weight are used to perform a variety of functions, from cocking a float to anchoring a bait. In the past, almost all weights were made of lead, but in many countries the use of lead weights has been banned or restricted for environmental reasons. In the United Kingdom, for example, all weights weighing up to 1 oz (28 g) and split shot between sizes 6 and SSG (swan shot, also known as buck shot) must be made of non-toxic materials, so weights in the affected sizes are usually steel, zinc, or brass, and split shot is made of tungsten or heavy alloys.

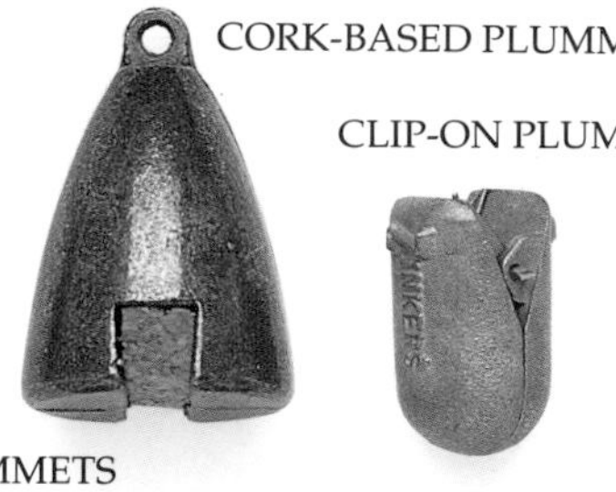

CORK-BASED PLUMMET

CLIP-ON PLUMMET

PLUMMETS
These are used in float fishing to find the depth of the swim. With a cork-based plummet, the line is threaded through an eye and the hook embedded in a cork strip at the base; a clip-on plummet has spring-loaded jaws that clamp over the hook.

SSG (SWAN SHOT)

AA

BB

No. 1

No. 4

No. 8

No. 10

No. 12

SPLIT SHOT
Split shot are versatile weights, being used in float fishing to lock eyed floats in position, to cock floats, and to add weight to rigs. They also are used to lock larger weights in position and to weight light rigs. They are available in a range of sizes from swan, or buck, shot (SSG) – so called because this size is used in shotgun cartridges when swans or bucks are the shooters' quarry – down to "dust" shot (sizes from 8 down to 12). As a rule of thumb, two split shot of any one size are roughly equal in weight to one shot of the size above (see page 222). *Always use a finger and thumb, never your teeth, to close shot over the line. Never slide them along the line when altering their position: this causes abrasion and frictional heat that can damage and weaken the line. Open them up with a thumbnail and then reposition them.*

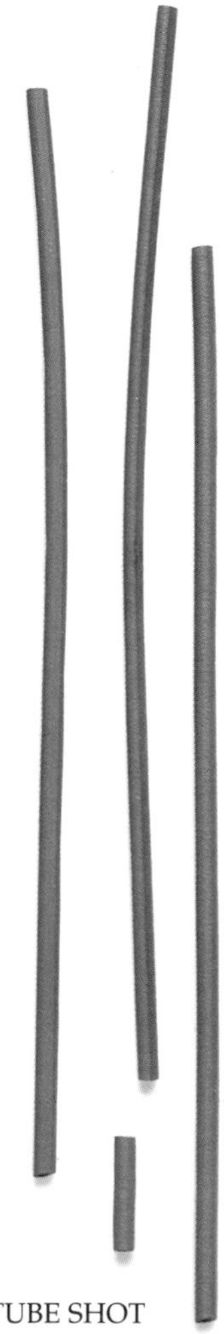

TUBE SHOT
These thin, flexible tubes, made of polymer and tungsten, are less likely to snag than shot, and are a good alternative when seed baits are being used: fish often nibble at the shot instead of the bait. They are cut to length with scissors, threaded on the line, and locked in place with tiny shot.

LEADED WIRE
Like tube shot, leaded wire is a good alternative to split shot when float fishing with seed baits. To cock the float, the wire can be twisted directly around its base, or wound around a matchstick then threaded onto the line beneath the float and held in place by a small shot.

PUTTY WEIGHT
This heavy, puttylike material was an early alternative to lead shot, but its use declined when satisfactory non-lead shot was developed. It is now used mainly by carp anglers as a casting weight and to balance the weight of baits for improved presentation.

OLIVETTES
These tiny, streamlined weights originated in France, and are used in pole fishing. The smallest, the size 4/0, weighs 0.003 oz (0.081 g); the largest, size 12, weighs 0.106 oz (3 g).

BULLET SINKERS
A bullet sinker is used to present a moving bait. It will roll freely through a fast-flowing swim, pulling the bait toward fish holding station in the flow.

HILLMAN
This is used in spinning to take the lure down farther in deep or swift-flowing water, and to help reduce line twist. This weight should be clipped to the eye of the swivel to which the main line tied.

BARREL
The barrel weight is designed to roll slowly along the bed of a river to present a moving bait. The line is threaded through the weight's hollow body.

COFFIN WEIGHTS
The coffin weight was designed for presenting static baits in running water. Its flattened shape and sharp edges ensure that it sits tight on the bottom, digging itself into gravel or silt. The line is threaded into a hole drilled down the center of the weight.

DISK WEIGHTS
These flattened, almost circular weights will keep baits static in fast-flowing swims. Being flat, a disk weight offers little resistance to the current flowing over it when it is lying on the riverbed, while its large surface area gives it a good grip on the bottom. It is attached to the rig by a swivel, which minimizes the risk of tangling during casting.

SPHERICAL BOMB
This is often used on bottom rigs. It should be attached by a short link of weak line, so that if a hooked fish runs into a snag such as thick weeds, the weight will break off. Without the weak link, the reel line may break first, leaving the fish tethered to the snag and condemned to a lingering death.

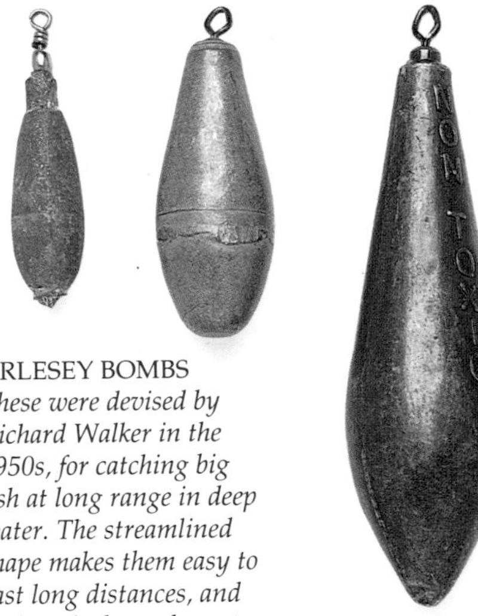

ARLESEY BOMBS
These were devised by Richard Walker in the 1950s, for catching big fish at long range in deep water. The streamlined shape makes them easy to cast long distances, and their swivel attachments reduce the risk of tangling. They are available in sizes ranging from ⅛ oz (3.5 g) to 4 oz (113 g), and some incorporate a screw-in swivel that allows the size of weight being used on a rig to be changed rapidly.

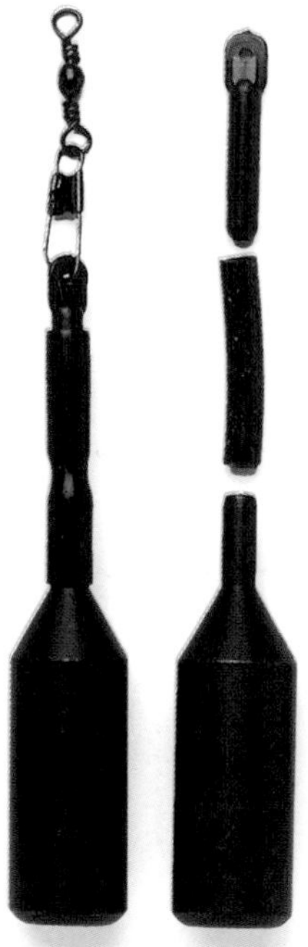

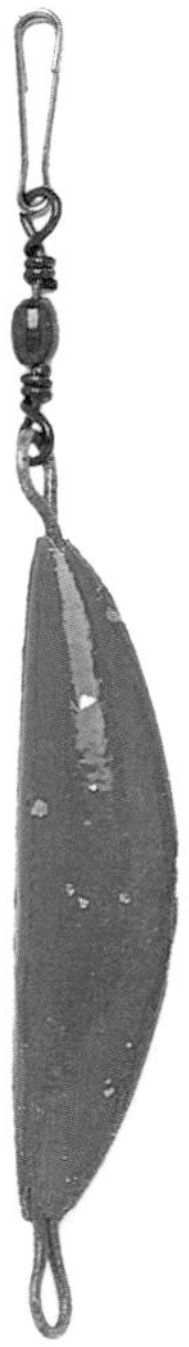

BUZZ BOMB *(right)*
The buzz bomb is a variation of the Arlesey bomb incorporating fins that reduce wobble during flight. It can be cast with consistent accuracy over distances of about 100 yds (90 m) or more.

BOTTLE WEIGHTS
This clever design allows the weight on the line to be changed quickly. A piece of silicone rubber tubing is attached to the line by a snaplock swivel, and a bottle-shaped weight is inserted into its lower end. The weight can be changed simply by pulling it out of the silicone tubing and replacing it with one that is the same size but either lighter or heavier.

WYE
Like the Hillman weight, the Wye is used in spinning to add weight to a lure and to overcome the problem of line twist produced by a revolving lure. Many anglers prefer it to the spiral weight, also used in spinning, which has a tendency to fall off the line. Its shape is not as aerodynamic as that of the spiral, but it casts well enough.

SPIRAL WEIGHT
This is used on spinning rigs to add weight and prevent line twists. It is attached to the reel line above the swivel that joins the line to the lure or leader. The line is wrapped tightly around the body of the weight (in the spiral channel) and through the spirals of wire at each end. The aerodynamic shape of the weight gives good casting distance.

FLAT-BOTTOMED WEIGHT
This type of weight is used mainly in carp fishing. Its flattened shape helps it to rise quickly from the bed and plane through the water when retrieved, and makes it less prone to snagging.

TROLLING WEIGHT *(right)*
Trolling weights can weigh up to 3 lb (1.36 kg), and are used to get the bait down quickly in deep water. They are simply lowered into the water, so a streamlined shape is not necessary.

Saltwater Weights & Booms

Sea angling often involves coping with strong tidal currents, deep waters, and long casting distances. To avoid problems, make sure you have enough weight on the line to get the bait down and hold it in position, and use standoff booms to prevent leaders (traces) from tangling. In addition, you can minimize the risk of damage to baits during long-distance casting by using devices such as impact shields and bait clips.

EXTENDED-NOSE BREAKAWAY

Weights

In general, a weight or sinker is anything an angler cares to put on the end of a line to take it to the bottom. For example, shore anglers fishing heavy ground, where there is a high risk of snagging, often use cheap, expendable sinkers such as old sparkplugs instead of specially made weights. It is, however, usually best to use a weight that has been designed for use in the prevailing conditions and for the type of fishing intended.

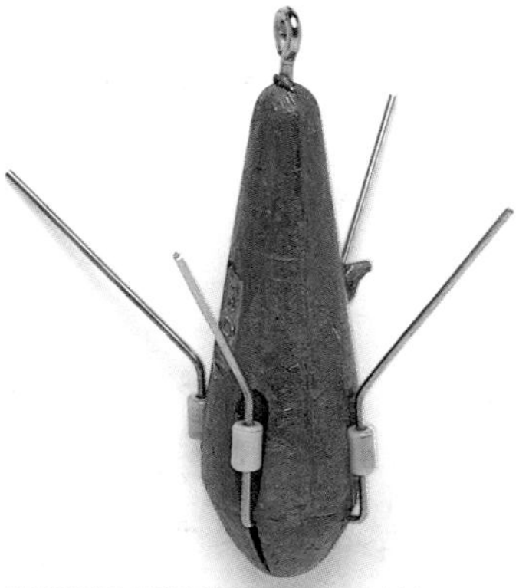

STANDARD BREAKAWAY

BREAKAWAY ADAPTER

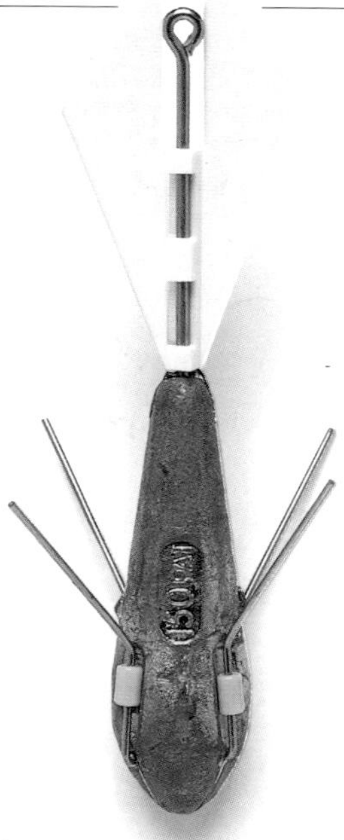

LONG-TAILED BREAKAWAY (with clip-on lifter)

BREAKAWAY SINKERS
The wires of a breakaway sinker dig into the seabed to anchor the bait. They are clipped against the sinker body, and on the retrieve they spring free and trail behind for a snagless return. The extended-nose and long-tailed versions give good grip at short range or in deep water, making them suitable for surf fishing; the plastic breakaway adapter can be used in tandem with a standard breakaway for increased grip.

Booms

Nylon leaders tend to tangle, and baits dropped from a boat often spiral as they fall, wrapping their leaders around the main line. Mounting the leaders on carefully spaced booms will reduce these problems. Droppers (short leaders) suspended from booms spaced above the weight are good for shore fishing when large numbers of small fish are sought, because they present multiple baits in the best possible way.

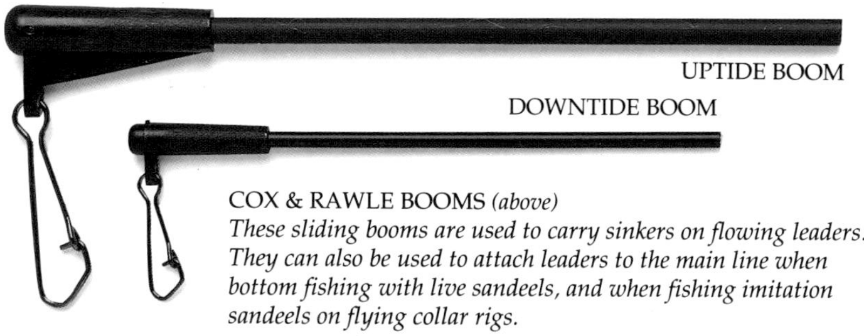

UPTIDE BOOM

DOWNTIDE BOOM

COX & RAWLE BOOMS *(above)*
These sliding booms are used to carry sinkers on flowing leaders. They can also be used to attach leaders to the main line when bottom fishing with live sandeels, and when fishing imitation sandeels on flying collar rigs.

RELAY CLIP
This is attached to the rig to help hold the bait in place and to prevent it breaking apart during casting.

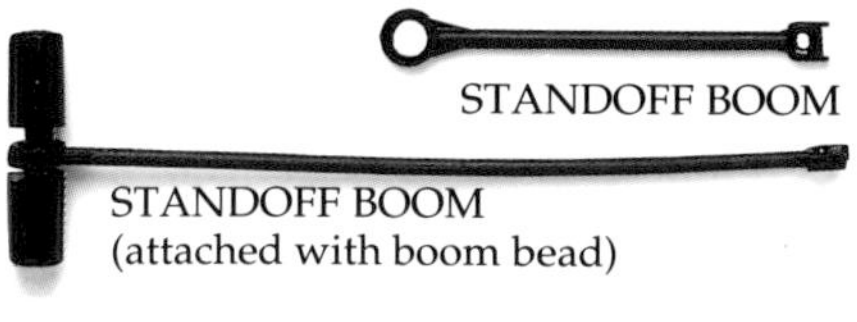

STANDOFF BOOM

STANDOFF BOOM (attached with boom bead)

COX & RAWLE STANDOFF BOOMS *(left)*
These are excellent standoff pivoting booms, some requiring beads and stoppers to position them on the line, and others with built-in locking fixtures. They are useful for shore angling, and for boat work when small fish are expected.

BREAKAWAY BOOMS *(right)*
These booms, attached to the line by beads, are used as flying collar booms and as dropper booms. When bottom drifting, however, they can get choked with sand, which can stop them from sliding.

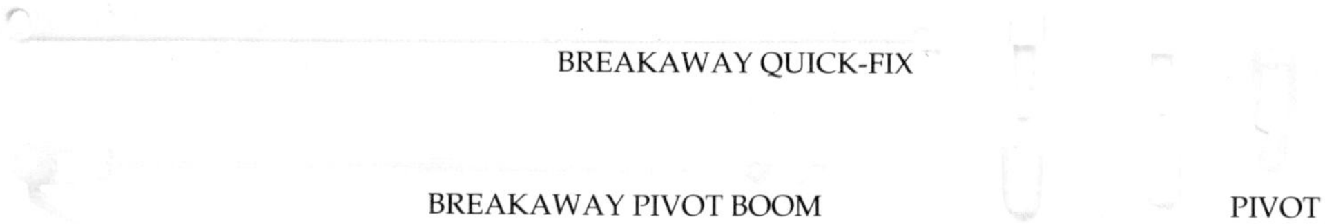

BREAKAWAY QUICK-FIX

BREAKAWAY PIVOT BOOM

BOOM BEADS

PIVOT BEAD

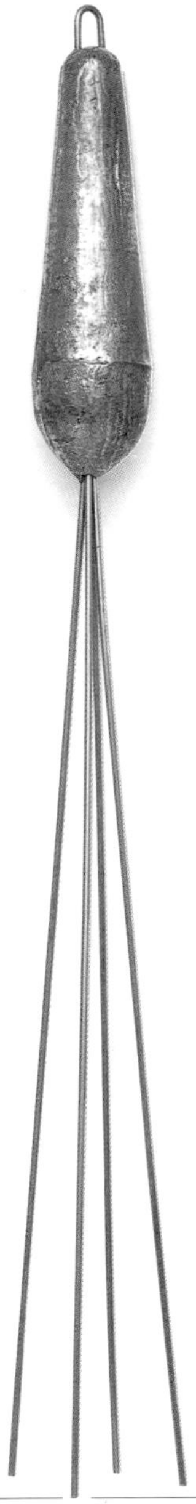

SPIRAL WEIGHT
This is designed for use with cast or trolled lures. Because the line is simply wrapped around it, its position can be altered quickly and easily. It can also be used to sink slowly trolled livebaits.

SURF WEIGHT *(left)*
This is favored by surf fishermen because its long nose wires give exceptional grip in fierce currents. The wires dig into the bed to anchor the bait, but pull out easily when a fish picks it up, and they spring readily out of snags.

WYE
The streamlined shape of this lure-fishing weight makes it ideal for distance-casting spinners and rubber eels, and for getting them down deep.

TORPEDO
Because of its flat sides, this beach sinker is less likely to roll in the current than rounded weights.

ROUND BOMB
This is ideal for slow downrigger trolling. It can also be used for bottom fishing, but it tends to roll.

PIERCED BALL
This is used for weighting slider float tackle and for helping to get large deadbaits down when freelining.

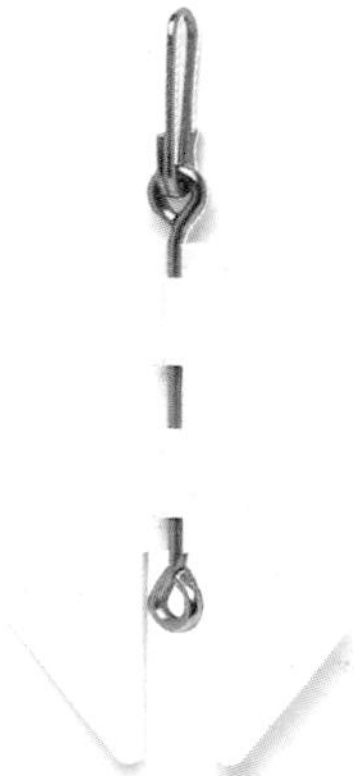

WEIGHT LIFTER
On a fast retrieve with the rod held high, this plastic vane rises in the water. This helps to lift the sinker clear of heavy snags close to your feet.

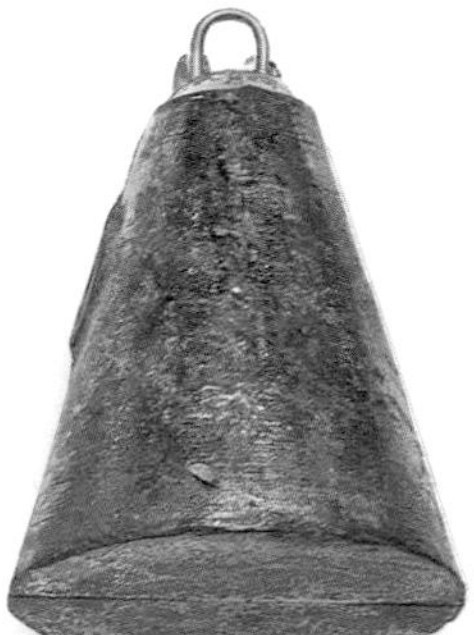

BELL WEIGHT
This can be used from an anchored boat, but is not the best shape for drift fishing.

BOMB
The bomb is the best shape for beating snags and tide, and good for working a constantly moving bait from the beach.

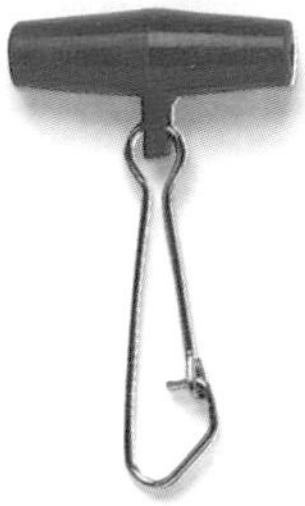

SLIDING LINK
Attaching a flowing leader to the main line by a sliding link allows it to move without taking the sinker with it, which could cause a fish to drop the bait.

WATCH WEIGHT
This is a useful grip sinker for short-range beach work and drift fishing over banks.

PLASTIC BOOM

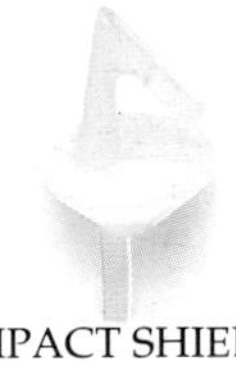

IMPACT SHIELD
This is similar to the bait clip but offers even more protection to the bait. As well as holding the bait securely during casting, it shields it from impact damage when it hits the water.

PLASTIC BOOMS
These are plastic versions of the French boom. Some types have three or four "teeth", around which the line is wrapped to hold them in place, and others have eyelets, through which the line is threaded, and are locked in place with swivels or beads.

PLASTIC BOOM

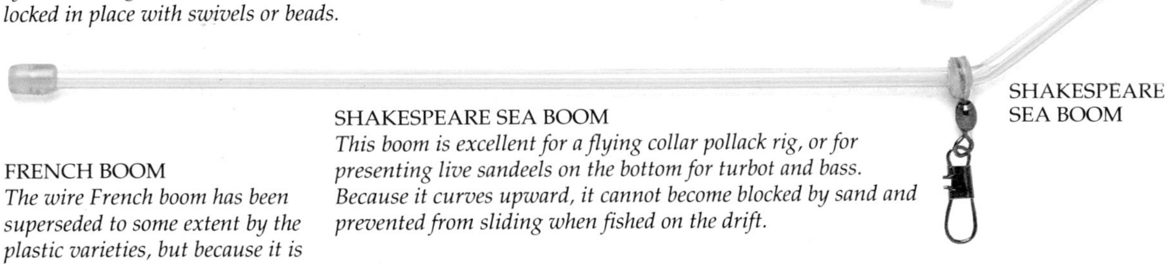

SHAKESPEARE SEA BOOM

SHAKESPEARE SEA BOOM
This boom is excellent for a flying collar pollack rig, or for presenting live sandeels on the bottom for turbot and bass. Because it curves upward, it cannot become blocked by sand and prevented from sliding when fished on the drift.

FRENCH BOOM
The wire French boom has been superseded to some extent by the plastic varieties, but because it is stronger for direct leader tying it is still widely used by wreck anglers for flying collar rigs.

FRENCH BOOM

Floats

Floats are extremely sensitive and versatile bite indicators, and much more pleasing to watch than a rod tip. Although they are available in a staggeringly wide variety of materials, shapes, sizes, and colors, all floats have been designed to perform specific tasks.

BALSAS
These floats, made entirely of balsa wood, are superior to stick floats in windy conditions and fast-flowing swims. Fish them close in and attach them top and bottom to the line. They tend to lift out of the water if held back too hard, due to the inherent buoyancy of the balsa wood.

LOAFERS
Made either from hollow plastic or balsa, loafers are very buoyant and designed to fish swift, turbulent waters. They should be attached top and bottom.

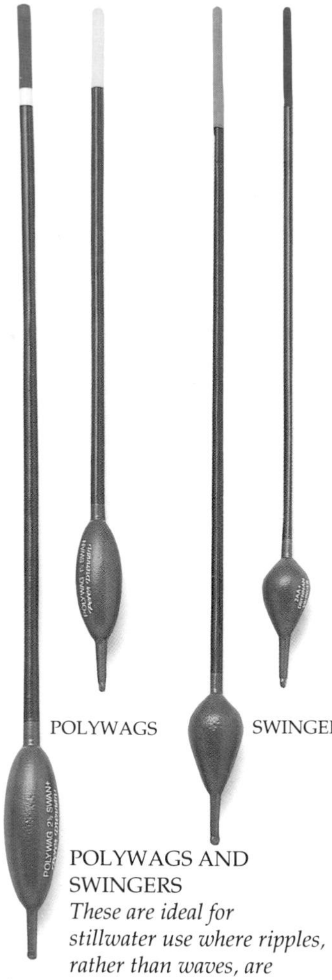

POLYWAGS

SWINGERS

POLYWAGS AND SWINGERS
These are ideal for stillwater use where ripples, rather than waves, are being created on the surface by the wind. Both patterns are fished bottom-end only, and a short distance beyond the rod tip.

DRIFTBEATERS
The ideal floats for stillwater fishing in strong winds, when there are big waves on the water. They are fished bottom-end only.

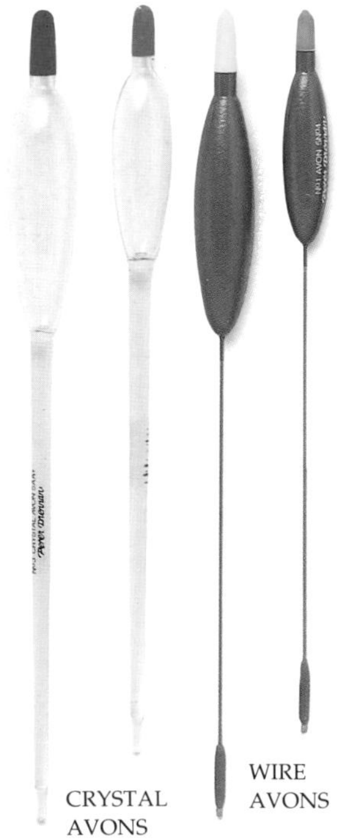

CRYSTAL AVONS

WIRE AVONS

AVONS
These floats, attached top and bottom, can present baits in quite turbulent streams and be fished at longer range than stick floats.

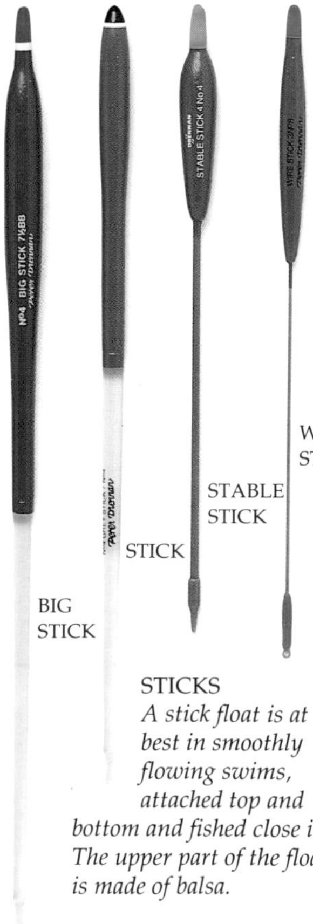

BIG STICK

STICK

STABLE STICK

WIRE STICK

STICKS
A stick float is at its best in smoothly flowing swims, attached top and bottom and fished close in. The upper part of the float is made of balsa.

ONIONS
These floats are designed for use in stillwaters, in all but the strongest of winds, and in swims at fairly close range (up to several rod lengths).

BLUES

GRAYS

DARTS

BLUES, GRAYS, AND DARTS
These are fished bottom-end only and are at their best on stillwaters and canals.

GIANTS

CANAL

INSERT

BODIED

CRYSTALS

Crystals are made of clear plastic, and designed for use in clear, shallow water where wary fish might regard the arrival in the swim of a solid-colored float as highly suspicious and a sign of danger. They are equally effective on still and slow-flowing waters.

PEACOCKS

Quills taken from the tail feathers of peacocks make superb floats. The quills are long and straight, very light, and completely waterproof. Floats made from the thicker ends of quills are buoyant in turbulent water and easily visible at a distance, while those produced from the thinner ends will be more sensitive to delicate bites.

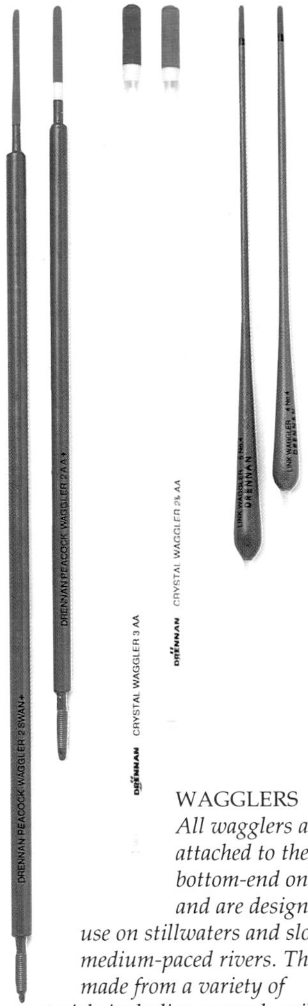

WAGGLERS

All wagglers are attached to the line bottom-end only, and are designed for use on stillwaters and slow- to medium-paced rivers. They are made from a variety of materials including peacock quill, sarcandas reed, plastic, and balsa.

LOADED

These floats have weighted bases. Their increased weight means that they can be cast greater distances and do not need shotted lines.

ZOOMERS

The zoomer was developed by tournament anglers for catching wary fish in shallow swims at long distances. It consists of a cane stem with a big balsa body and a brass stem insert at the base. It should be attached top and bottom, and is at its best in light winds on wide rivers and stillwaters.

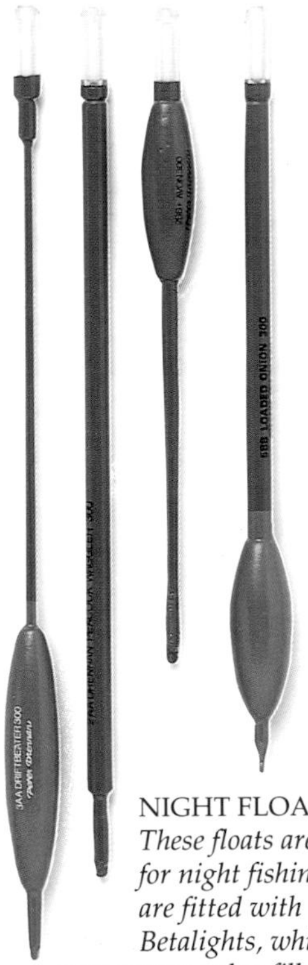

NIGHT FLOATS

These floats are used for night fishing. They are fitted with Betalights, which are transparent tubes filled with a luminous gas. They will glow for 20 to 30 years.

POLE FLOATS

Floats for pole fishing tend to be small, often with thin bristle tops, to show up the most delicate of bites.

PIKE FLOATS

Most pike floats are built for slider fishing, being either hollow or fitted with eyes. Some, equipped with a dartlike vane above the tip, are designed to catch the wind and take the bait long distances from the bank, to predatory fish lying beyond casting range.

Bite Indicators & Rod Rests

Bite indicators are used primarily in legering, where there is no float to indicate that a fish has taken the bait. Bites can be indicated simply by movement of the rod tip, but often this is not sensitive enough and some other form of indication is needed. This can be a swingtip, springtip, or quivertip fitted to the rod tip, or a device such as a bobbin or electronic alarm that indicates any movement of the line. Rod rests are used when it is not necessary to hold the rod all of the time, for instance when bites are expected to be infrequent, and when two rods are in use at the same time.

DROP-OFF ARM *(left)*
This was developed for pike fishing. The end with the indicator ball clips to the line and the hinged end is attached to the rear rod rest. When a bite occurs, the line pulls free and the end with the ball drops down.

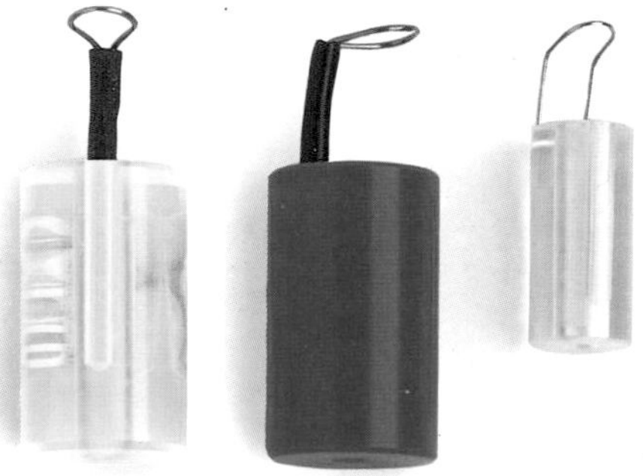

BOBBINS *(right)*
A bobbin is attached to the line between the reel and the butt ring. If a fish takes the bait and moves away, the bobbin climbs toward the rod; if the fish moves toward the bank, the bobbin drops toward the ground.

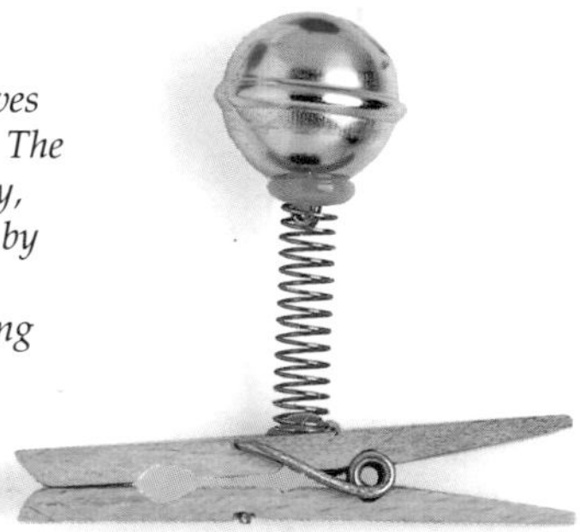

BELL *(right)*
A bell clipped to the rod tip gives an audible indication of a bite. The use of bells has declined greatly, but they are occasionally used by freshwater anglers and more commonly by sea anglers fishing from beaches and piers.

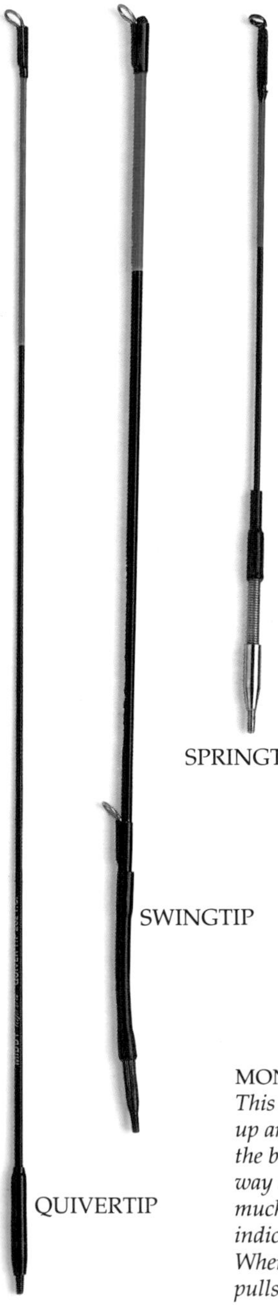

SPRINGTIP

SWINGTIP

QUIVERTIP

ELECTRONIC ALARM *(left)*
An electronic bite alarm sounds an audible warning when a fish takes the bait. The line is passed over a sensitive antenna, or a flanged wheel, which triggers the alarm when the line is pulled by a taking fish. The type shown here is designed to be screwed to a bankstick in place of a front rod rest.

SWINGTIP, SPRINGTIP, AND QUIVERTIP *(right)*
These screw into the threaded tip rings found on most leger rods. The swingtip hangs at an angle and indicates bites by lifting or dropping back. The springtip is similar, but has a sprung base. This holds it in line with the rod but acts like a hinge when a bite occurs, allowing the tip to swing down. A quivertip acts as a sensitive extension of the rod tip.

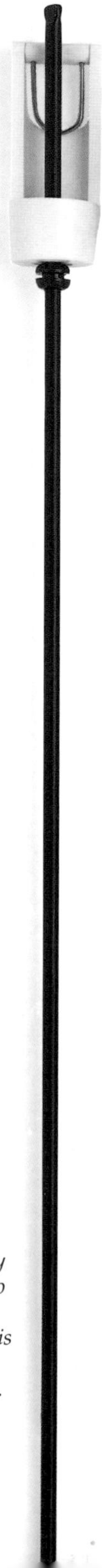

MONKEY CLIMBER *(right)*
This is a bobbin that slides freely up and down a shaft pushed into the bank. It is used in the same way as an ordinary bobbin, but is much less likely to give false indications in windy conditions. When a strike is made, the line pulls out of the bobbin clip.

BANKSTICK *(below)*
This is a spiked metal rod with a threaded top to take a screw-on rod rest head or electronic bite alarm. Most are 2 to 3 ft (60 to 90 cm) long, but telescopic models that extend to 4 ft (1.2 m) are also available.

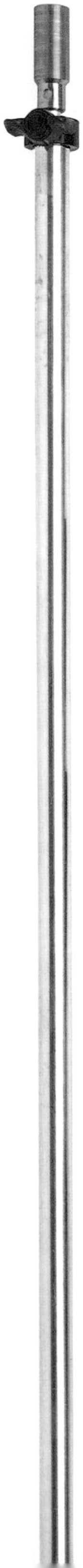

T-BAR *(left)*
T-bars double the rod-holding capacity of a pair of banksticks. Instead of screwing a rod rest head onto each bankstick, a T-bar is screwed on and a rod rest is fitted to each end of it.

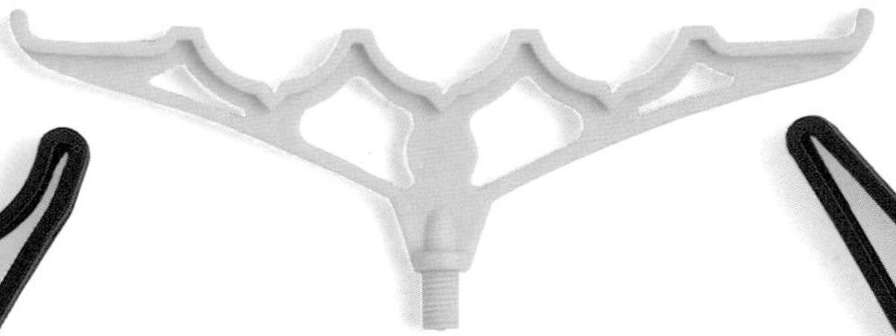

ROD REST HEADS
Rod rests consist of rest heads screwed onto banksticks, and are normally used in pairs, one supporting the rod ahead of the reel, and the other supporting the rod butt. The rest heads are available in a variety of shapes and sizes to suit different angling styles.

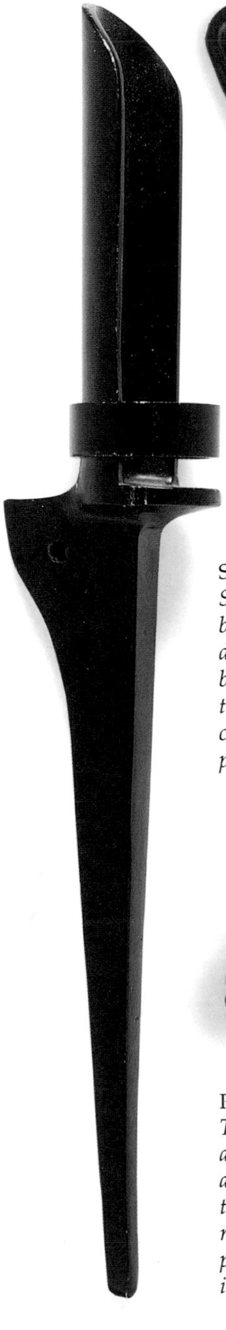

SANDSPIKE *(left)*
Sandspikes, or monopods, are used by beach anglers to hold their rods upright during the often lengthy intervals between bites. They hold either one or two rods, and have sharp points that can be driven deep into the sand to provide stability.

TRIPOD *(right)*
Tripod rod rests, especially those with adjustable telescopic legs, are very stable. They are available with single or double rest heads, and are widely used by shore anglers fishing from pebble beaches and harbor walls.

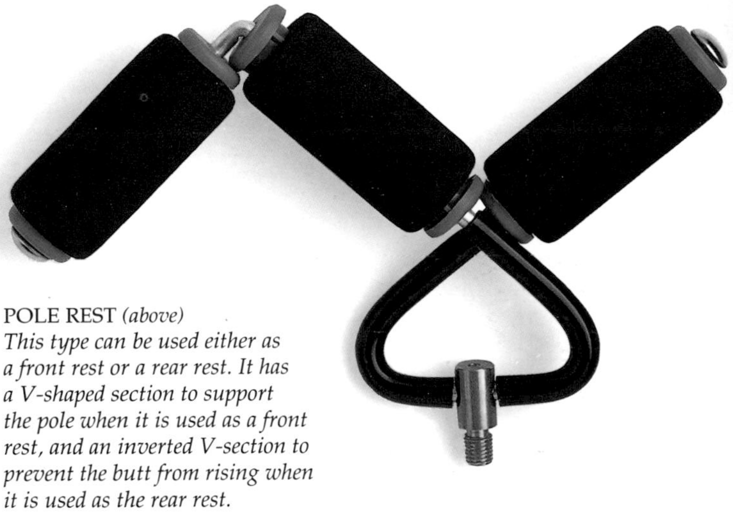

POLE REST *(above)*
This type can be used either as a front rest or a rear rest. It has a V-shaped section to support the pole when it is used as a front rest, and an inverted V-section to prevent the butt from rising when it is used as the rear rest.

Landing Tackle

After being hooked and played out, a fish should be landed as quickly as possible. If it is too big to be swung to the bank or boat, or gently lifted from the water by hand, it can be landed in a net or lifted out with a tailer or gaff. Landing nets vary in size and design from the shallow, fine-meshed "pan" nets with long handles that are used to land small fish, to the large nets used by specialist anglers to engulf the biggest fish they are likely to encounter. Tailers and gaffs are used mainly for salmon and saltwater fish. A tailer is a running noose of braided wire, attached to a handle, which is slipped over the "wrist" of the fish's tail, and the gaff is a metal hook that is impaled in the body of the fish. The use of a gaff is now illegal on many waters.

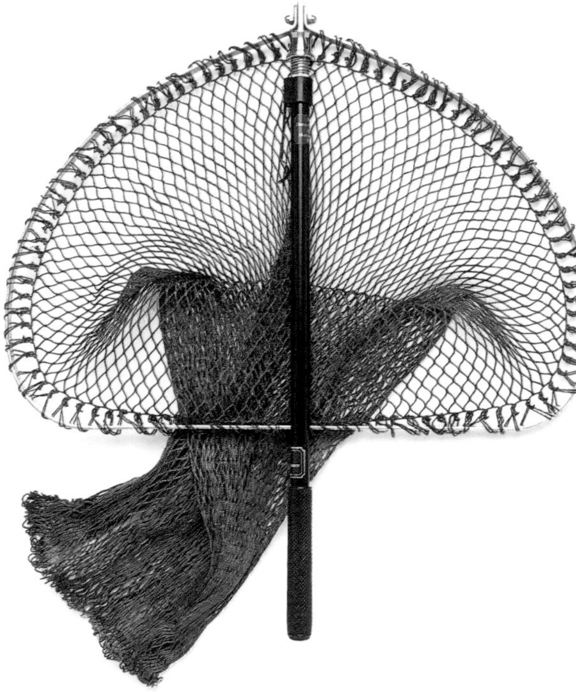

HARDY TROUT NET *(above)*
The bow-shaped frame of this net folds back over the telescopic handle when not in use, but can be brought quickly into action with one hand. It is ideal for both stillwater and river trouting, and can be carried clipped to a vest.

STEADE-FAST TRIANGULAR SPECIMEN NET *(below)*
This 42 in (107 cm) landing net has two rigid arms of solid fiberglass, mounted on a nylon spreader block and connected at their tips by a nylon cord. The nylon mesh is deep, soft, and knotless, and can accommodate large fish such as heavyweight carp, pike, and catfish.

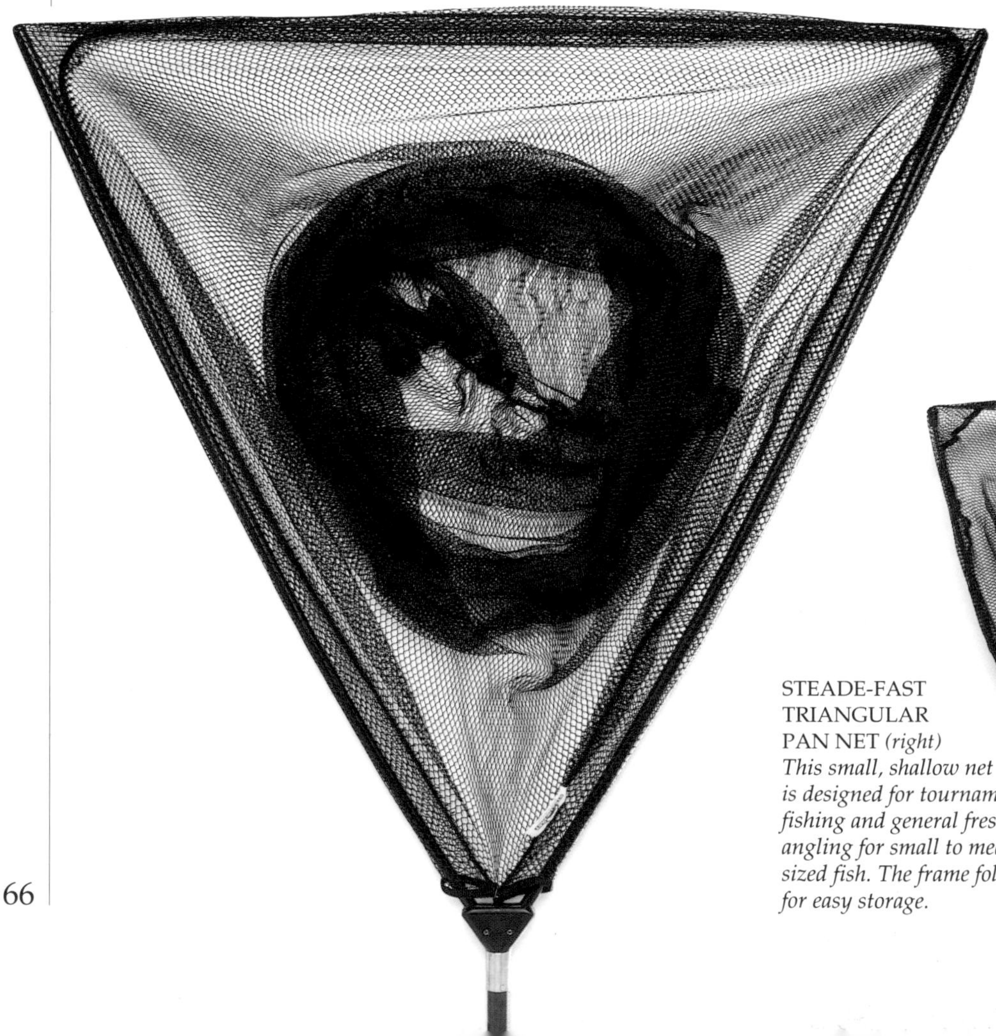

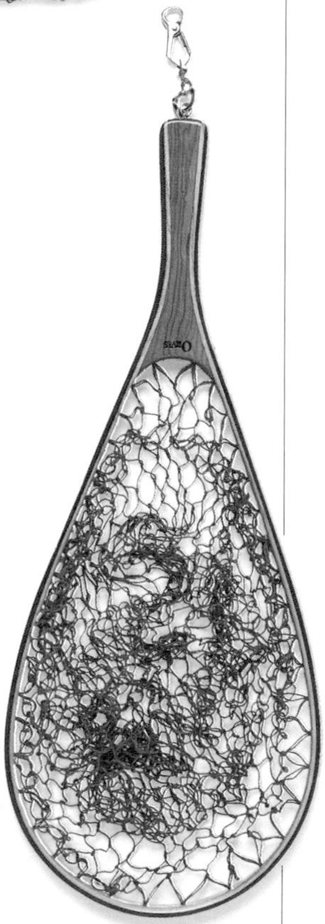

ORVIS MADISON TROUT NET *(right)*
This compact net is popular with anglers who fish by wading or from float tubes, allowing the hooked fish to be brought close to hand. It has a laminated wood frame and Dacron mesh.

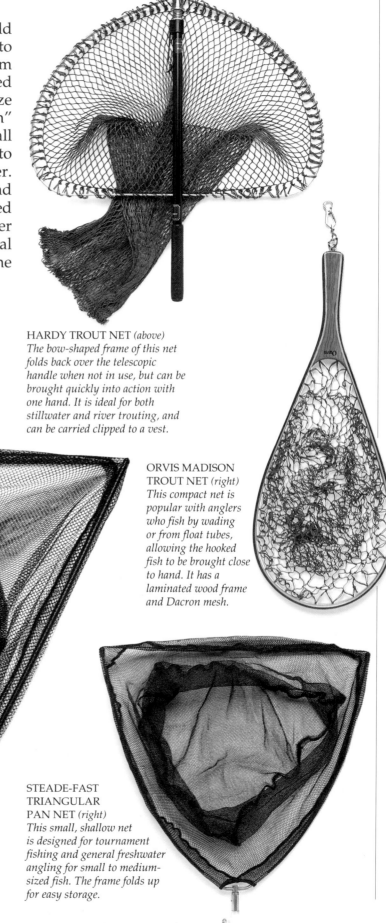

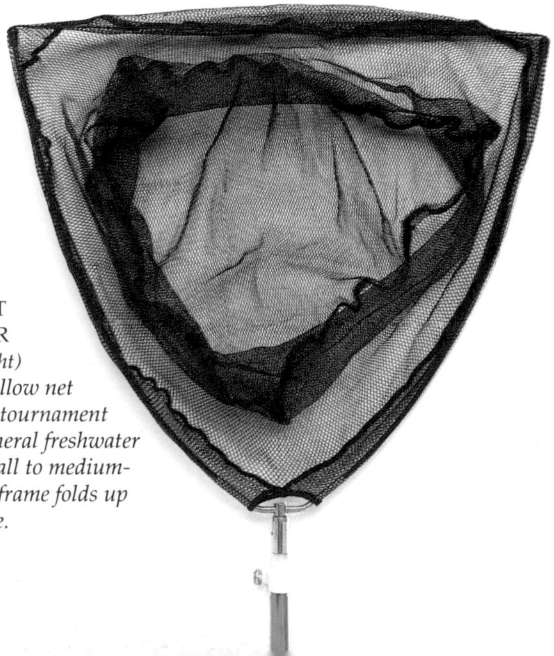

STEADE-FAST TRIANGULAR PAN NET *(right)*
This small, shallow net is designed for tournament fishing and general freshwater angling for small to medium-sized fish. The frame folds up for easy storage.

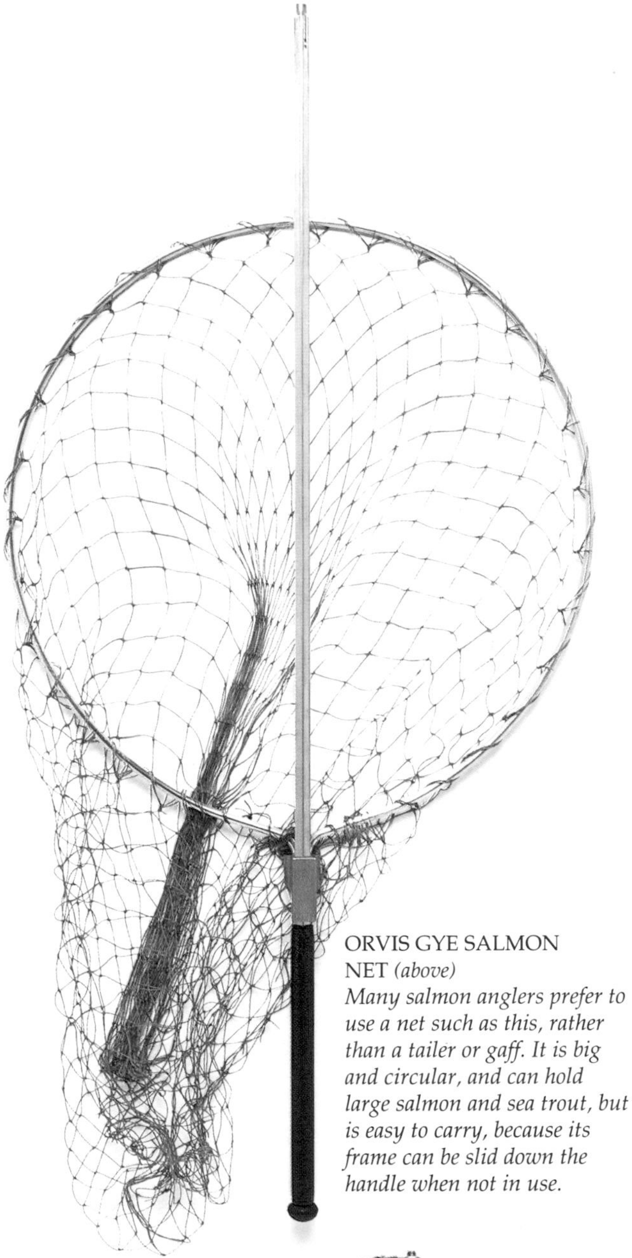

ORVIS GYE SALMON NET *(above)*
Many salmon anglers prefer to use a net such as this, rather than a tailer or gaff. It is big and circular, and can hold large salmon and sea trout, but is easy to carry, because its frame can be slid down the handle when not in use.

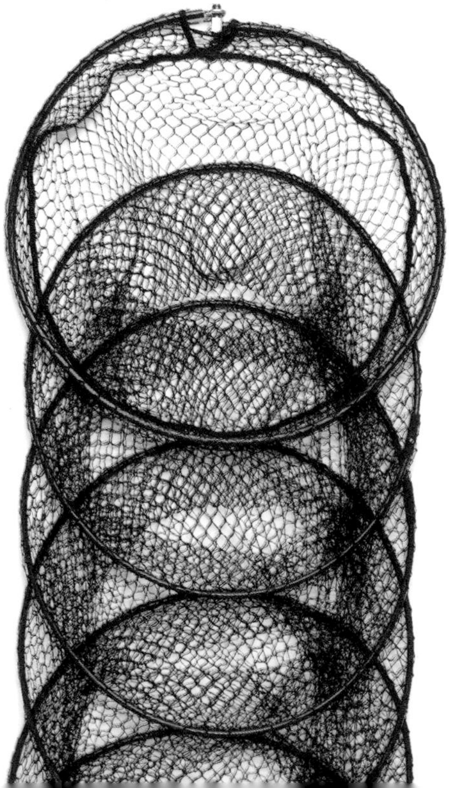

STEADE-FAST KEEPNET *(right)*
Keepnets are long nets, anchored to the bank and submerged in the water, in which caught fish can be retained alive until the end of the fishing session, when they are weighed, measured, and perhaps photographed, then released. This model is available in 8 ft and 10 ft (2.4 m and 3 m) versions, both with 18 in (45 cm) diameter rings.

HARDY TELESCOPIC TAILER EXTENDED

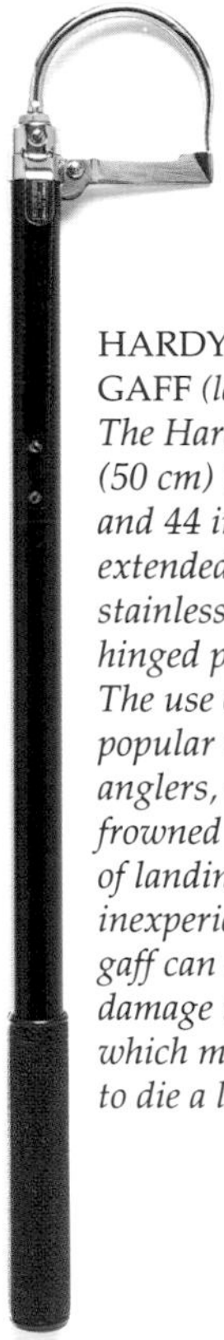

HARDY TELESCOPIC GAFF FOLDED

HARDY TELESCOPIC GAFF *(left)*
The Hardy gaff is 20 in (50 cm) long when folded and 44 in (112 cm) fully extended, and the hook is stainless steel with a hinged point protector. The use of gaffs, once very popular with salmon anglers, is now generally frowned upon as a method of landing salmon. In inexperienced hands, a gaff can cause serious damage to a hooked fish, which might then escape to die a lingering death.

HARDY TELESCOPIC TAILER *(right)*
This tailer has a wrist strap to prevent it from being pulled out of the hand and an anti-swivel pin to prevent the loop from swinging away from the fish. It is 32 in (81 cm) long when folded, 40 in (102 cm) when fully extended.

HARDY TELESCOPIC TAILER FOLDED

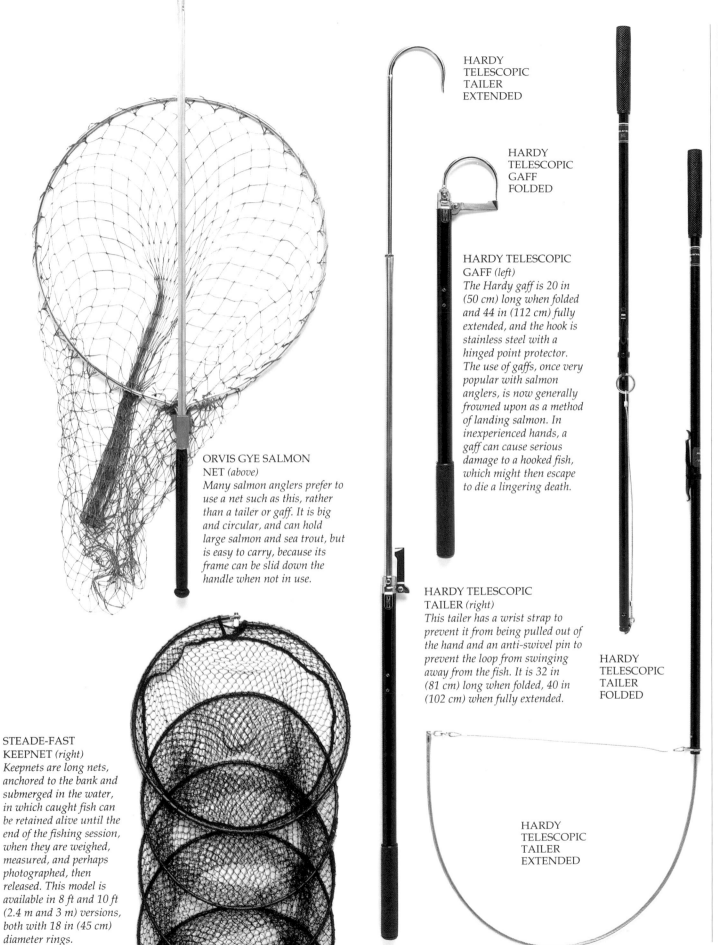

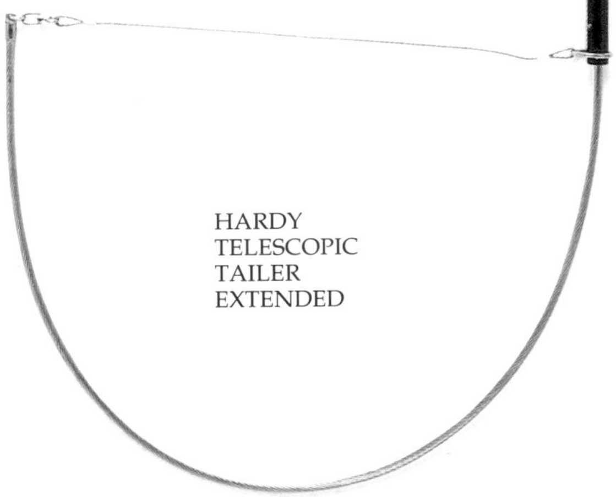

HARDY TELESCOPIC TAILER EXTENDED

TACKLE BOXES

Tackle boxes fall into two broad categories: the small type, in which you can carry a selection of lures, flies, floats, or other small items when you are actually fishing, and the large, capacious type, in which you can store all your small tackle when it is not in use. Many anglers use improvised tackle boxes, adapted from containers ranging from cigar boxes to toolboxes, but in general there is no substitute for a specially made storage system. Wooden tackle boxes look nice, but are heavy and need to be cared for, so most anglers choose plastic or aluminum boxes, which are light, strong, and water resistant.

SEAT BOXES

These are large tackle boxes that double as seats. They are used mainly by freshwater anglers who fish with float or leger tackle and spend long periods fishing one swim. Most have two sections, one large and deep for storing bulky items such as chum, and one with drawers that take small items such as floats, sinkers, rigs, and hooks.

SHAKESPEARE/SNOWBEE SPECIMEN TACKLE BOX *(right)*
This is a good example of the cantilever type of tackle box, which offers good storage capacity, gives easy access to the contents when opened out, and is compact when closed. It is made in two-tone green plastic, and has three trays with movable dividers so that the compartment sizes can be adjusted to suit individual requirements. It is also available in one-, two-, and six-tray versions.

FOX BOX *(below)*
This plastic fly box will hold up to 66 dry flies, and its rubberized lining will not retain moisture, which could rust their hooks. The clips are designed to hold the flies securely without crushing their delicate hackles.

WOODEN FLOAT BOX *(below)*
Made of varnished hardwood, this simple, three-tray float box has foam strip inserts, in which you can cut slits to hold the ends of the floats.

RICHARD WHEATLEY FLY BOX MODEL 4607F *(right)*
The lid of this tough aluminum fly box is lined with closed-cell plastic foam, into which wet flies and nymphs can be hooked, and its base contains 16 dry-fly compartments with individual, spring-loaded plastic lids.

RICHARD WHEATLEY TUBE-FLY BOX *(right)*
Tube flies require special boxes for proper storage. Some tube-fly boxes have a row of needles over which the flies are slipped, but this one has bullet-shaped indentations to hold up to 28 of them. The loose treble hooks can be stuck into the foam lining.

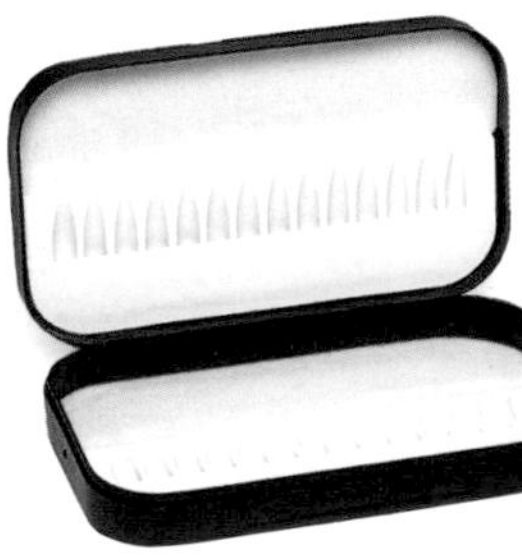

FLY-TYING MATERIALS CASE *(below)*
This type of box is used by fly fishers who tie flies at the waterside to match the insects that the fish are feeding on. The model shown here has a hardwood block, which clips to the side to provide a base for a fly vise, and materials can be stored in both the base and the lid.

SHAKESPEARE/SNOWBEE LURE BOX *(right)*
The upright dividers in this box have slots in their top edges to take the hooks of plugs, spinners, and spoons. Hanging lures by their hooks prevents tangling, and the divider positions are adjustable to cope with lures of different sizes.

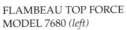

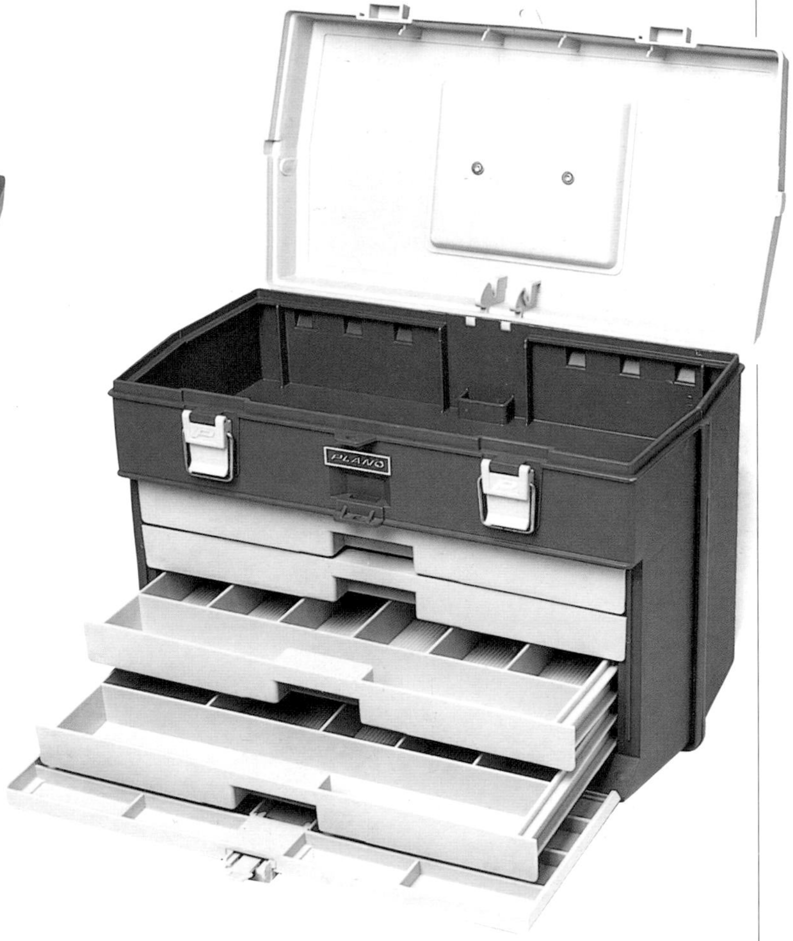

FLAMBEAU TOP FORCE MODEL 7680 *(left)*
This briefcase-size tackle/lure box has a hinged top lid, and a fixed tackle tray with a sliding drawer in the base. In addition, the front face of the lid is hinged to permit access to the drawer without opening the whole lid.

PLANO 757 *(above)*
The Plano 757 is one of the largest tackle chests on the market, and is best used as a base from which to load smaller tackle boxes for use at the waterside. It is ideal for long fishing trips when you need a lot of gear: leave it in the car, or in your hotel room, tent, or cabin. If you are boat fishing, take it on the boat with you.

FOOTWEAR

Good footwear is an essential part of any angler's equipment. Whichever type you choose, it should give a secure grip on slippery surfaces, and be both comfortable and suitable for the prevailing conditions. For example, lightweight boots are excellent during the warm summer months, but in cold winter weather you need boots with thick, insulated soles to keep your feet warm. Similarly, waders with lightweight uppers that can be folded down, transforming them into boots for walking to and from the water, are ideal for summer use. But when wading for salmon or trout in the springtime, when the water can be extremely cold, you need thick, thermally insulated waders.

TYPES OF SOLE

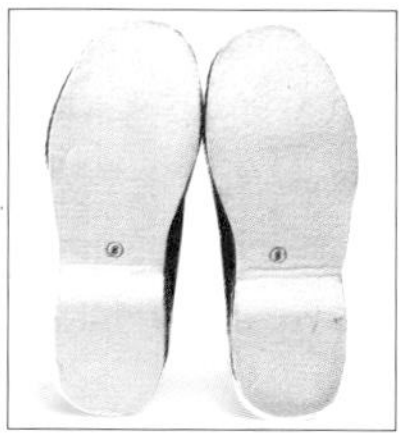

Felt soles
Felt soles provide the best grip of all on wet, slippery surfaces, and have the advantage of being quiet, so you can wade without scaring fish.

Studded soles
These are excellent for walking across wet grass or mud banks, but are noisy and do not give as much grip as felt soles do on slippery underwater stones.

Rubber soles
Rubber soles are usually cheaper than felt or studded soles. They give reasonably good grip on grass or mud but are less effective on rocks.

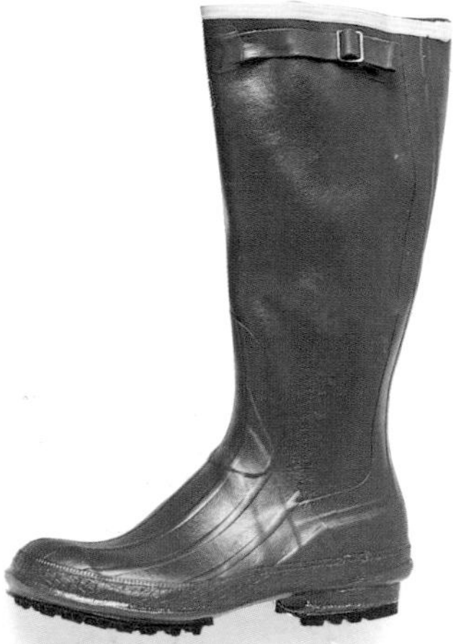

AIR-GRIP KNEE BOOTS *(left)*
These fully waterproof, knee-length boots are 17 in (43 cm) high and made of nylon-lined rubber. The cushioned soles provide insulation and comfort, and the top straps can be tightened for a snug fit to stop stones, leaves, and other debris from getting in.

SKEE-TEX INSULATED KNEE BOOTS *(above)*
Insulated knee boots such as these are widely used by winter anglers who choose to sit on the bank and fish in one swim all day. The thick, insulated soles prevent cold from creeping up into the boot and chilling the feet, and because the insulation is so good, a pair of ordinary socks is sufficient to keep feet warm.

EDINGTON WELLY-WADERS *(left)*
These boots have thin, lightweight wader uppers that can be folded down to below the knee when not required. They can thus be used both as waders and as boots for walking along the bank. The wader uppers should be kept away from snags such as thorns and barbed wire.

ORVIS GREEN MOUNTAIN THIGH BOOTS *(above)*
These rubber thigh boots have non-slip felt soles, and wader uppers made of lightweight, laminated PVC. In warm weather, the uppers can be folded down and held in clips to allow air to circulate around the legs.

ORVIS LIGHTWEIGHT
BOOT-FOOT CHEST WADERS *(below)*
These waders, made of nylon with all the seams sealed, weigh only 12 oz (340 g) and can be rolled up very small to tuck into the corner of a tackle bag until needed. They are ideal for use in warm weather, and highly resistant to punctures and abrasion.

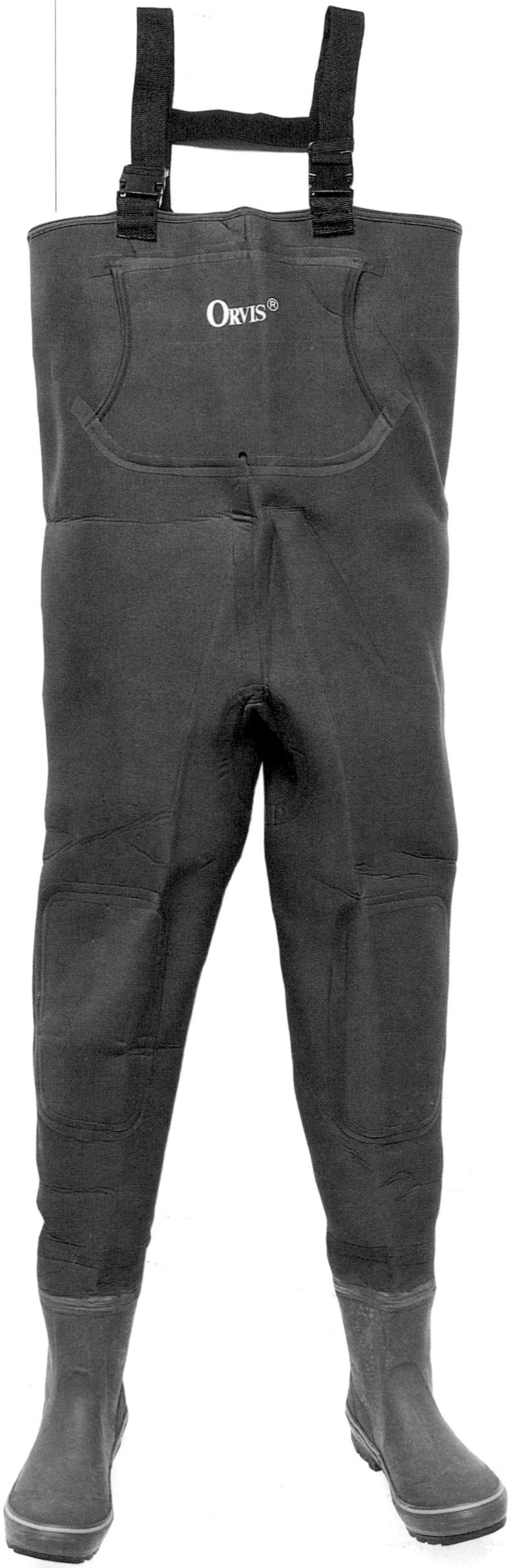

ORVIS GUIDEWEIGHT
STOCKING-FOOT CHEST WADERS *(above)*
Made of nylon and thick neoprene foam, these waders provide comfort and warmth even in icy waters, such as those endured by early-spring salmon anglers. They feature reinforced knees, a handwarmer pocket, and quick-release buckles, and all the seams are sealed. Unlike boot-foot waders, which are a combination of boots and waders, stocking-foot waders do not have tough soles and must be worn with wading shoes.

ORVIS GRAVEL GUARDS *(above)*
Gravel guards are fixed around the tops of ordinary boots, in effect making them higher, and prevent stones from getting inside. Stones inside boots are uncomfortable, and if they are not removed they may cut into the soles.

ORVIS LIGHTWEIGHT
WADING SHOES *(below)*
The molded, one-piece heel and sole design of these shoes, and their felt covering, provide excellent stability when wading on slippery river-beds. In addition, foam-padded insoles, hard toes, and padded ankle collars give good protection on rough ground.

ORVIS GRIP STABIL-ICERS
FITTED TO BOOT

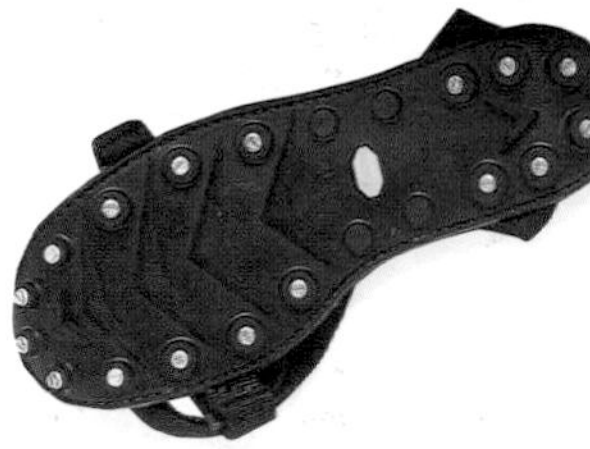

ORVIS GRIP STABIL-ICERS
(above)
These are fitted to the soles of boots, boot-foot waders, or wading shoes to give extra grip when walking on ice or slopes of wet grass or mud. They are also reasonably effective on slippery rocks.

VESTS & JACKETS

The great advantage of fishing vests is that an array of small but essential items of tackle can be carried in their multiple pockets. This makes them very useful in any form of angling where mobility is important, including fly fishing, lure fishing, and stalking freshwater fish such as bass. Most vests are short, so that they do not trail on the water during wading, but longer-length designs are also available for anglers who usually fish from the bank. These keep the lower back area covered, and so in cool weather they are more comfortable to wear than short vests.

Jackets made of traditional materials, such as waxed cotton, are still available, but most are made of lightweight, waterproof, synthetic fabrics *(see page 74)*. These jackets "breathe" to prevent condensation from building up inside them, need no reproofing, are fully washable, and can be rolled up and tucked away in a corner of a tackle bag, to be forgotten until the rain comes. Some have detachable linings, and can be used comfortably all year.

STEADE-FAST BAIT SMOCK *(above)*
Designed for tournament fishing, the Steade-fast bait smock is light and supple for ample freedom of movement, and has adjustable, quick-release side fastenings for easy fitting and removal. There are two bait pockets, the larger sporting a rain flap to ensure that its contents remain dry in bad weather, and three other pockets designed to carry a range of terminal tackle and rigs.

WYCHWOOD FOUR SEASONS *(right)*
This multi-pocketed vest is designed for use in cool weather. It is made of a polyester/cotton mix with a fleecy lining, and is cut long to ensure that the small of the back is protected from drafts in cold winds. Its features include a rugged two-way zipper that can be opened from the bottom to prevent constriction when sitting in a boat, pockets in a variety of sizes, a scissors retainer, and two landing net rings.

ORVIS SUPER TAC-L-PAK *(below)*
This vest is virtually a wearable tackle bag, with no less than 35 pockets to carry almost everything an angler might need, from a pair of scissors to a set of lightweight rain gear. Made of a tough polyester/cotton mix, it features a yoke collar for good weight distribution, wide-cut shoulders, and oversize armholes, and it is cut short for deep wading.

SHAKESPEARE SAFETY VEST *(below)*
This light, comfortable fly-fishing vest doubles as a buoyancy aid should a mishap occur while boat fishing or walking the bank. It can be inflated instantly by pulling a toggle to activate a replaceable carbon dioxide cartridge, and can also be inflated by mouth. It has numerous pockets, a D-ring for scissors, and a loop to carry a landing net.

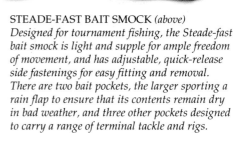

MUSTO HIGHLANDS JACKET *(right)*
The Highlands jacket has a waterproof Gore-Tex liner between its polyester/cotton outer shell and its inner lining, and can be cleaned in a domestic washing machine. It has a two-way zipper for comfort when sitting down, plenty of generously cut pockets, and a built-in waterproof flap to sit on. A hood and a zip-in vest are available as extras.

NOMAD ⅝ RANGER *(above)*
This five-eighths-length jacket has a stretch cord and toggles at the waist, so that its weight is carried on the hips rather than the shoulders, and its sleeves are generously cut to give unrestricted movement when casting. It is machine washable and has plenty of pockets, a permanently attached hood, two handwarmer pockets, a double storm flap, and a two-slider main zipper.

HARDY WAXED WADING JACKET *(below)*
Designed primarily for use with chest waders, this waist-length jacket has generously cut sleeves for easy casting and features breast pockets and internal pockets. It is made of waxed Egyptian cotton, with a smart tartan lining, and is fully waterproof, but like all waxed clothing it eventually needs reproofing to prevent water from seeping through it.

Rain Gear

In the past, the big drawback of most waterproof clothing was that perspiration would condense inside it, making it uncomfortable to wear. The fabrics tended to be heavy, were often difficult to clean, and required regular reproofing, often with waxes that would leave marks on car seats. These problems have been eliminated by the use of new fabrics and proofing processes, and modern rain gear is comfortable to wear and easy to care for. The use of "breathable" fabrics, which have microscopic pores that prevent water from getting in but allow water vapor to escape, has solved the condensation problem, and clothing made from these fabrics is light, washable, needs no reproofing, and does not stain car seats.

ORVIS EASY-ON-AND-OFF OVERTROUSERS *(below)*
These lightweight, waterproof overtrousers can be rolled up and tucked away in a pocket or bag until needed, and the zippers at the bottoms of the legs allow you to put them on or take them off without removing your shoes. Made of nylon waterproofed with polyurethane, they are ideal for bank fishing on showery days and for boat fishing in choppy water. They are also thornproof, so they will protect your trousers if you are pushing through high bankside vegetation when stalking fish.

WYCHWOOD ONE-PIECE THERMAL SUIT *(above)*
This light, fully waterproof, one-piece suit has a heat-retaining thermal lining, and is also breathable to prevent condensation. It has a high, protective collar and a zip-on hood, and is ideal for static fishing in cold weather.

WYCHWOOD THERMAL BIB & BRACE *(below)*
In the cooler months of the year, a cold draft in the small of the back can be most uncomfortable and spoil a day's fishing. A bib and brace eliminates this problem, and when teamed with a jacket is more versatile than a one-piece suit. The Wychwood Thermal Bib & Brace is made of a lightweight, thermally lined polyester/cotton mix that has been made fully waterproof and breathable. It has ample pocket space and its two side zippers make it easy to put on and take off.

MAINSTREAM SURVIVAL FLOTATION SUIT *(above)*
This is an insulated and waterproof, but not breathable, one-piece suit designed for use at sea. As well as providing protection from spray and the weather, it acts as a buoyancy aid should the wearer be unfortunate enough to fall in (but is not an alternative to a lifejacket). It is produced in a bright red material for maximum visibility. Velcro straps at the ends of the sleeves and legs allow wrists and ankles to be kept snug, and a simple hood, permanently attached, folds up and tucks inside the collar.

Hats, Gloves, & Sunglasses

A suitable hat will keep your head dry in wet weather, cool in summer, and (probably most importantly) warm in winter: in cold weather, you can lose 30 percent or more of your body heat through your head if it is not covered.

A pair of warm gloves or mittens, preferably waterproof, should always be a part of your outfit in inclement winter weather. Having cold and aching fingers can be very uncomfortable, and makes it difficult to set up your tackle and to use it properly. Gloves are also useful when handling sharp-toothed or sharp-spined fish.

Polarized sunglasses cut out reflected glare from the surface, which helps you to spot fish more easily in clear water. They can also protect your eyes from badly cast hooks – whether your own or someone else's – especially when fly fishing.

SHAKESPEARE OPTI-SHIELDS
The frames of these polarized sunglasses are shaped to provide top shade, and the tinted side panels offer extra protection from miscast flies.

ASSET NIGHT VISION GLASSES
These glasses give enhanced contrast in poor light conditions, which makes them a useful form of eye protection when fly fishing at dusk.

ASSET HALF-EYE MAGNIFIERS
Available in a range of magnification strengths, these are useful when you are performing intricate tasks such as tying on flies at the waterside.

ORVIS NEOPRENE GLOVES
Neoprene is an excellent glove material, providing both warmth and resistance to water. These neoprene gloves are nylon lined to make them easy to take off and pull on, and have adjustable Velcro closures at the wrist to ensure a snug fit.

DAIWA SHOWERPROOF SPLIT-PALM MITTENS
The split-palm design of these fully lined mittens permits the end sections to be folded back to expose the fingers. This is useful when setting up tackle and when sensitive control is required, for instance during casting.

GUL NEOPRENE GLOVES
These gloves are designed to keep hands warm and dry in the foulest of weather. They are also supple and flexible, allowing the freedom of movement that is essential when, for example, you are tying knots or unhooking lively fish.

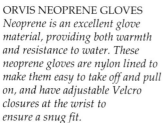

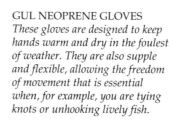

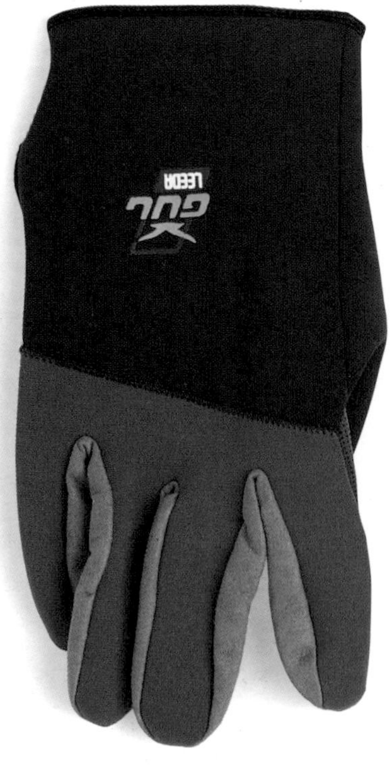

DAIWA THERMAL FINGERLESS MITTS
Fingerless mitts keep hands warm but leave fingers free for detailed tasks such as controlling the line as it leaves the reel, and making up or adjusting terminal rigs. These Daiwa mitts have elasticated wrists for a snug, draft-free fit.

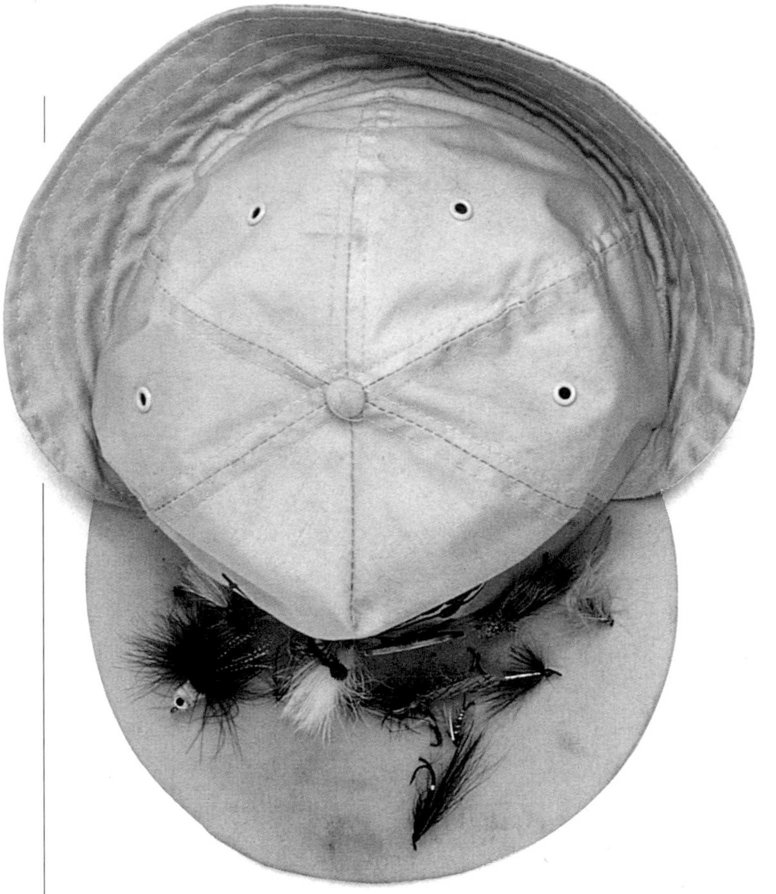

UP-DOWNER *(left)*
This lightweight hat is similar in style to those that were worn by the French Foreign Legion in North Africa, having a large visor to shade the eyes and a back-flap to cover the nape of the neck. It gives excellent sun protection in hot weather, and has become popular with American fishing guides.

SHAKESPEARE SUN VISOR
The Shakespeare sun visor has a tinted plastic peak and a lined, elasticated headband that acts as a sweatband on hot days. A sun visor leaves the top of the head exposed to any cooling breeze that might blow, but a cap is preferable in very hot weather because it shields the head from the sun.

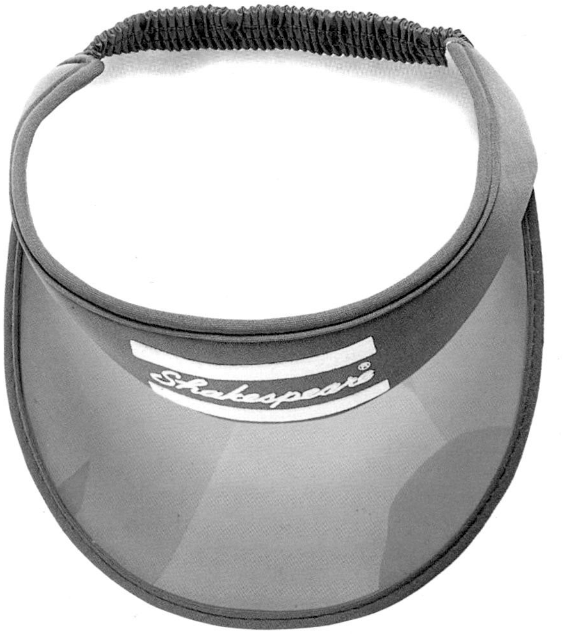

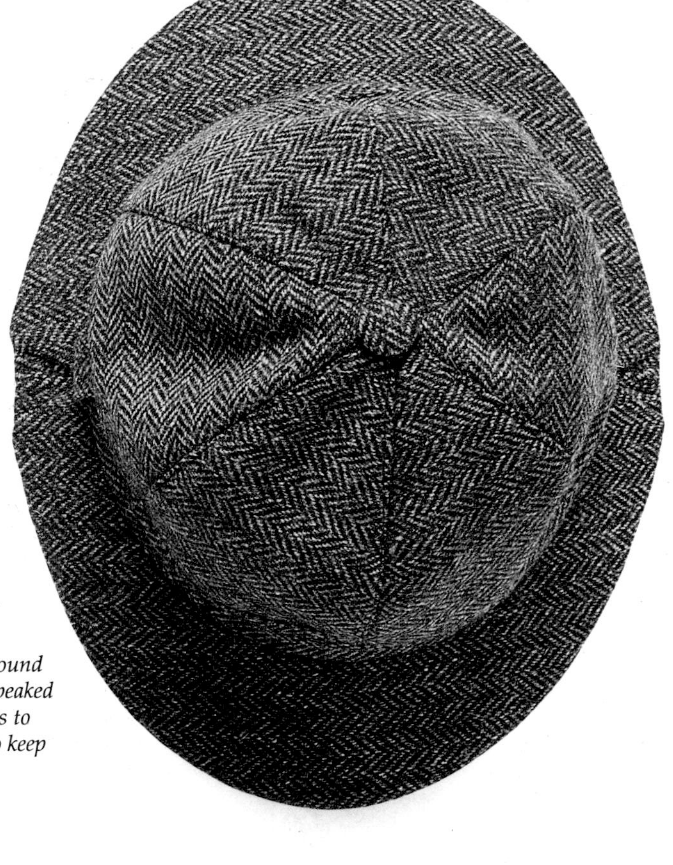

DAIWA BASEBALL CAP *(above)*
This nylon cap is available in either a full cloth style or a half-mesh version that provides better ventilation for the back of the head. A large peak shields the face from the sun, and an adjustable, press-studded strap at the back ensures that the cap will fit all head sizes.

DEERSTALKER
The deerstalker is a traditional type of tweed hat, made either with a rigid rim all the way around or peaked front and back. The peaked versions usually have side flaps to cover the ears for warmth or to keep biting midges at bay.

Accessories

In addition to basic gear such as rods, reels, lines, and hooks, there are a number of items of tackle, broadly categorized as accessories, that every well-equipped angler should have. These include equipment for unhooking fish, weighing them, and dispatching and cleaning those retained for eating. Additional accessories, not described here but worth considering, include padded unhooking mats, a pair of binoculars for watching for signs of fish activity, and a compass. The last should be considered essential by any angler who wishes to explore some remote hill lake or a stream far off the beaten track, and cannot afford the luxury of a GPS (Global Positioning System) receiver.

HARDY PIN-ON RETRACTOR *(below)*
This contains a spring-loaded spool of cord carrying a snaplock swivel. Items such as scissors can be clipped to the swivel, where they hang out of the way until needed.

SHAKESPEARE KNOT-TYING TOOL *(left)*
This is useful if you do not have nimble fingers, and when cold weather makes knot-tying difficult.

HARDY POCKET THERMOMETER *(right)*
A thermometer helps you to find the areas of a water that are likely to be holding fish, such as cool spots in hot weather and warm ones in cold weather. Tie it to a line, lower or cast it into the water, and leave it there for a few minutes to get an accurate reading.

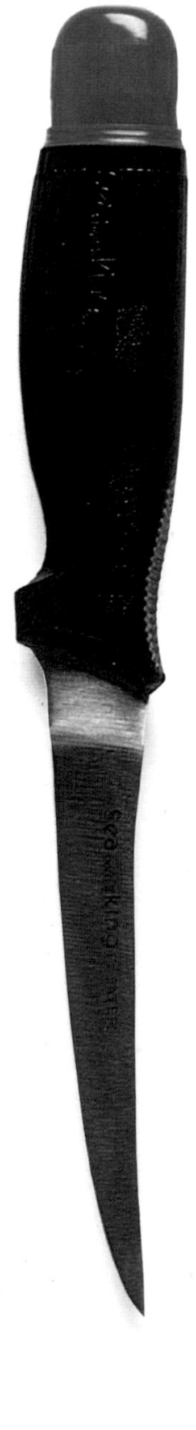

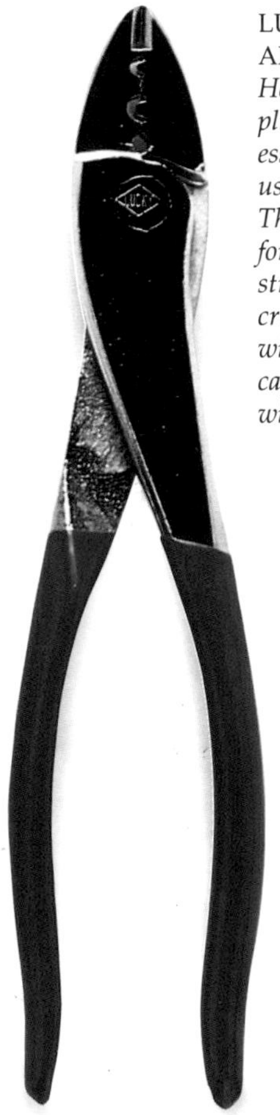

LUCKY TOOLS ANGLING PLIERS
Heavy-duty angling pliers such as these are essential when you are using wire line or leaders. They have long handles for good leverage, their strong jaws make crimping easy, and their wirecutter blades are capable of cutting heavy wire line.

DAIWA HEADLAMP LIGHT *(right)*
Anglers who fish at night, such as beach anglers, find lights of this type very useful because they are worn strapped to the forehead, leaving the hands free to handle the tackle. The model shown here is powered by a battery pack that clips to your belt.

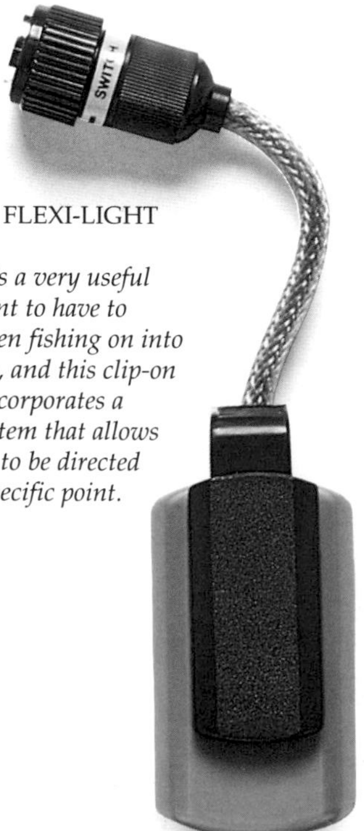

DAIWA FLEXI-LIGHT *(right)*
A lamp is a very useful implement to have to hand when fishing on into darkness, and this clip-on model incorporates a flexible stem that allows the light to be directed onto a specific point.

DAIWA SEA KING FILLET KNIFE *(left)*
Fish that are to be retained for the table should be gutted with a sharp filleting knife, such as this one, as soon after capture as possible.

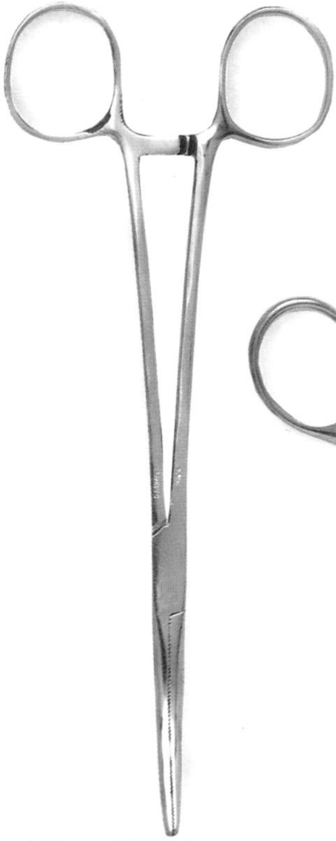

HARDY ARTERY FORCEPS *(above)*
These are an excellent tool for removing hooks of about size 10 upward, especially from sharp-toothed fish such as pike. The finer wire of smaller hooks is easily bent by forceps, and these hooks are best removed with a disgorger.

HARDY SCISSOR PLIERS *(left)*
This versatile tool has many uses, such as pinching on split shot, debarbing hooks for barbless fishing, and (using the cutting blades) cutting through monofilament and light wire.

HARDY PRIEST *(left)*
Using a priest is a humane way of dispatching fish that are to be retained for eating. The weighted head should be brought down smartly on the skull of the fish at least twice.

HARDY SPRING BALANCE *(below)*
Using a spring balance is a convenient method of weighing fish. This balance is calibrated in kilograms and pounds, and has a micrometer adjustment for accurate zeroing.

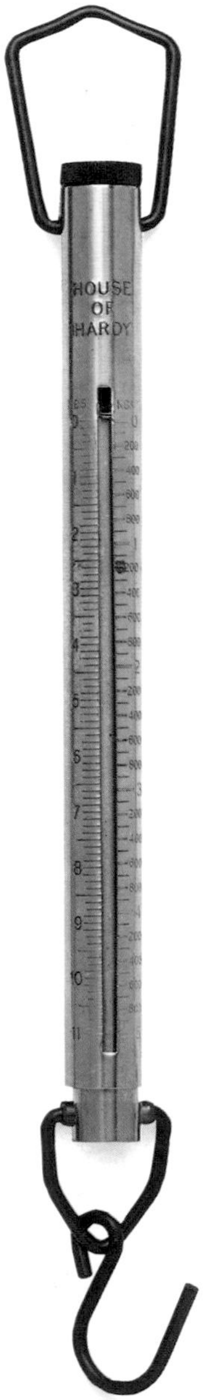

HARDY HOOK SHARPENER *(left)*
Hook sharpeners can improve the points of mechanically sharpened hooks, but chemically etched points to not need further sharpening.

HUFF FISHING FLY ROD BUTT GRIP *(left)*
This 20 in (50 cm) aluminum spike is designed to hold your fly rod so that it does not get stepped on when you are resting or changing your terminal tackle. The rod butt sits in a cup, and a spring clip at the top of the grip holds the rod upright.

NICAN ENTERPRISES UNI-LOADA *(left)*
The onerous task of loading line onto a reel is made easier if you use a line spool holder such as this. This tool is adjustable so that line spools can be aligned correctly for loading either spinning or baitcaster reels, and it can cope with all but the largest bulk line spools.

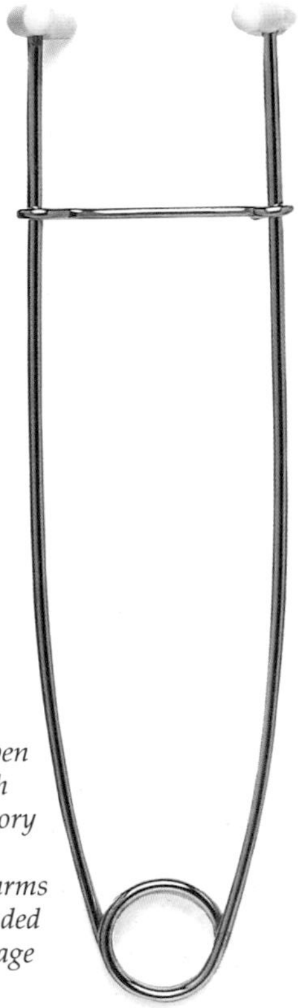

SHAKESPEARE PIKE GAG *(right)*
A gag is used to hold open the sharp-toothed mouth of a pike or other predatory fish while it is being unhooked. The sprung arms of this model are ball-ended so that they do not damage the mouth of the fish.

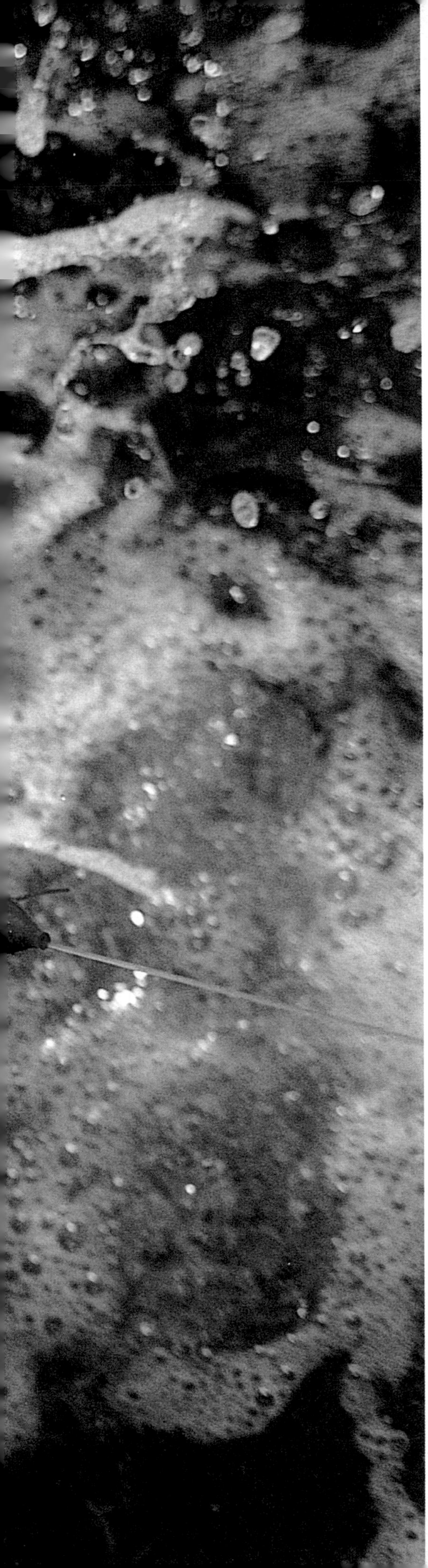

BAIT

USING A SUITABLE BAIT is one of the secrets of successful angling, whether you are fishing for panfish on a small pond or marlin on a tropical ocean. But the variety of baits used by today's anglers is huge, and choosing the right one requires a good knowledge not only of the diet and feeding habits of your chosen quarry but also of the range of baits that have proved effective in luring it. Baits can be divided into naturals, artificials, and processed baits, but the essential function of all of them is to fool fish into taking the hook.

Naturals are whole or cut items of the natural diet of the quarry, and are therefore inherently attractive to it. Most can be collected easily and free of charge from the water, its banks, or the shore; some, such as worms and minnows, are available from tackle dealers. Artificials, such as plugs and spinners, either mimic natural food items, such as small fish, or are designed to incite fish to grab them out of aggression, curiosity, or hunger. Their benefits include their ease of use and the fact that they can be used time and time again. Processed baits, such as cheese and bread, although edible, are obviously not part of any wild fish's natural diet. For fish, their attraction lies in their smell and taste, and for anglers, in their convenience and proven effectiveness.

This chapter describes the most effective and widely used baits for both freshwater and saltwater species.

THE RIGHT BAIT
Using a bait that will tempt your quarry into taking the hook is one of the secrets of angling success.

Natural Baits

Most natural baits cost nothing and often have the additional benefit of being part of the diet of the fish you are seeking. For example, earthworms (usually called nightcrawlers) will tempt almost every freshwater fish worth catching, and water-based fauna that make good baits include freshwater shrimp and caddis grubs. Never collect more naturals than you think you will need, and always return any that are unused.

Maggots & Casters

The type of maggot most often used as bait is the larva of the bluebottle fly, a proven catcher of fish of all species. Maggots are usually sold in their natural white or dyed bronze, although they can be changed to any color with a suitable liquid dye. The main places to use these dyed maggots are waters where the fish have been subjected to a lot of angling pressure and become wary of the white or bronze varieties.

Anglers fishing for small fish will often use other varieties of maggot, such as squatts (housefly larvae) and pinkies (greenbottle fly larvae). These are smaller and lighter than bluebottle maggots and are particularly good for fishing on the drop.

Casters (pupated maggots) are an excellent bait for most species and tend to attract bigger fish. They are good where fish have become maggot-shy, and are very effective when fished as a hookbait over a bed of hempseed. They become darker in color and lighter in weight as they age, and old, floating casters are a splendid bait for surface-feeding species such as rudd.

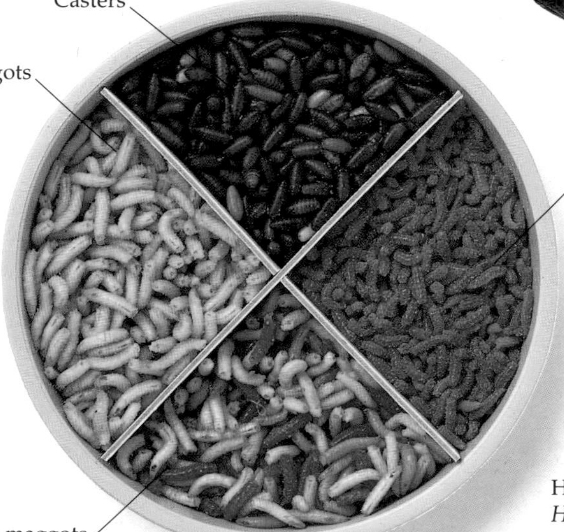

HOOKING MAGGOTS (*above*)
Hook a maggot through the blunt end and as lightly as possible to ensure that it remains livelier for longer. Use maggots singly on hook sizes 16 to 18, or in bunches on a size 12. When fish are proving wary, it can pay to hook maggots halfway along their bodies. This will make them sink horizontally, and therefore more slowly and naturally.

HOOKING CASTERS (*right*)
To hook a single caster, pierce the thick end and push the hook in, completely burying it inside. Use hook sizes 14 to 18. Casters can also be presented singly, or in twos or threes, by lightly hooking them through their blunt ends.

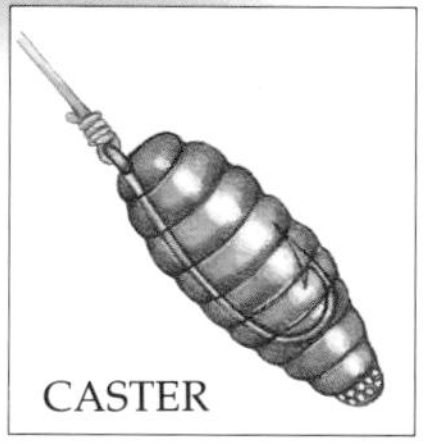

Worms & Slugs

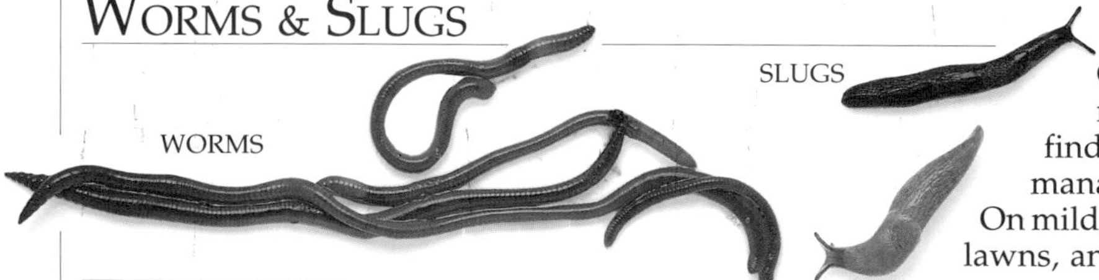

Carp, tench, and chub will gulp down a whole nightcrawler in seconds, while smaller species find a smaller worm, such as an angleworm, more manageable. Slugs are adored by chub, carp, and roach. On mild, damp nights, nightcrawlers can be collected from lawns, and slugs emerge from many garden areas; angleworms and redworms can be found in compost heaps.

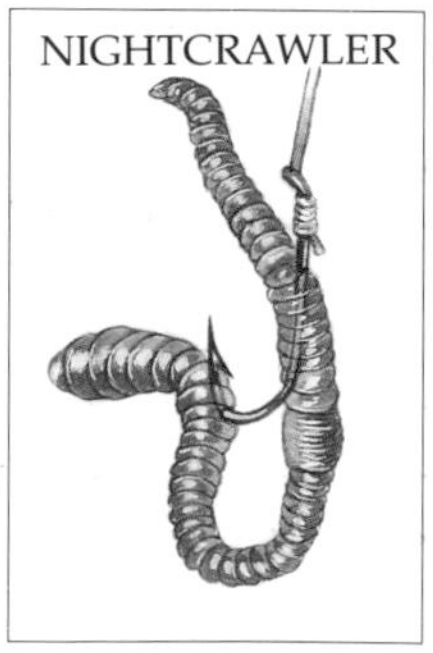

HOOKING WORMS
When using worms, either thread the hook a good way through the body, or hook it twice, top and bottom, to prevent it from flying off during casting or being torn off by a lunging fish. Use hook sizes 4 to 8 for nightcrawlers, and 10 to 14 for worm sections or angleworms. Lightly hook small worms once when fish are confident, but thread the hook some way through the body when fish are only plucking tentatively at the bait.

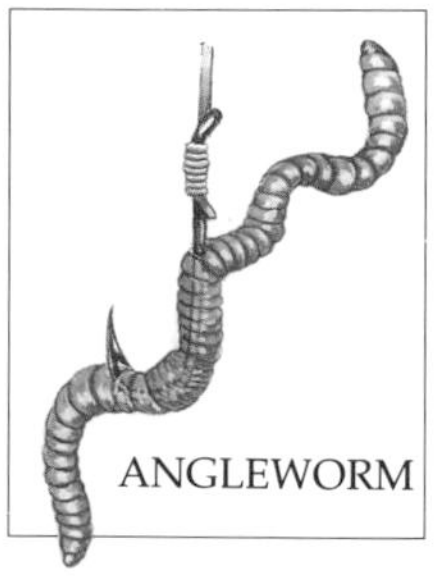

HOOKING SLUGS
Use a big hook, size 2 or 4, and nick it gently through the body. A slug's weight enables it to be cast a long way, and because of its tough skin, more than one fish can be caught on it.

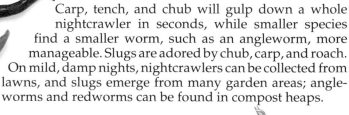

Fish

MACKEREL

HERRING

SARDINE

Many fish species include other fish in their diet. Pike, for instance, will eat just about any fish bait offered to them, although some are undoubtedly preferred: herring, sprat, smelt, sardine, mackerel, trout, and grayling are all good pike baits, as is freshwater eel. Where pike become used to certain fish baits, try painting these baits with liquid dyes to make them different.

Other freshwater species regularly taken on fish baits include catfish, perch, zander, bass, muskellunge, and trout, and in recent years some big chub have fallen to deadbaits intended for pike.

Fish baits can be freelined or legered static, trotted beneath a float, or spun or wobbled like an artificial lure. Being relatively soft-fleshed, sea fish tend not to last too long when continually cast out and retrieved. Freshwater baits are preferable for this, and none are better than small trout.

HOOKING FISH
Fish deadbaits on a pair of semibarbless trebles, size 8 or 10. Set the upleader treble in the tail root and the other no more than 3 in (8 cm) from it, with both facing the tail. For spinning, set the upleader treble in the mouth, the other in the flank.

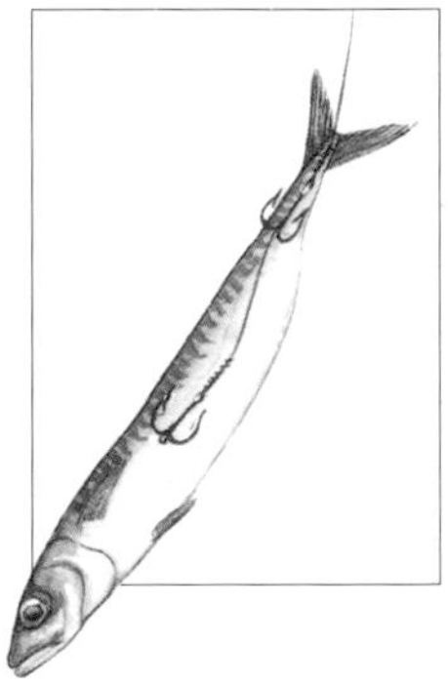

Shrimps & Prawns

These baits, when peeled, are excellent for catching just about every freshwater species. Unpeeled, they are best known as salmon baits, but they will also account for catfish, chub, bass, barbel, carp, tench, and crappies. They can be used raw or boiled, and are readily available canned, frozen, or fresh from most supermarkets.

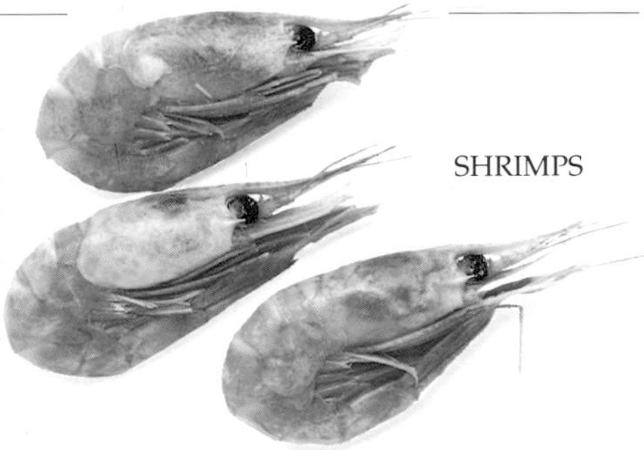

SHRIMPS

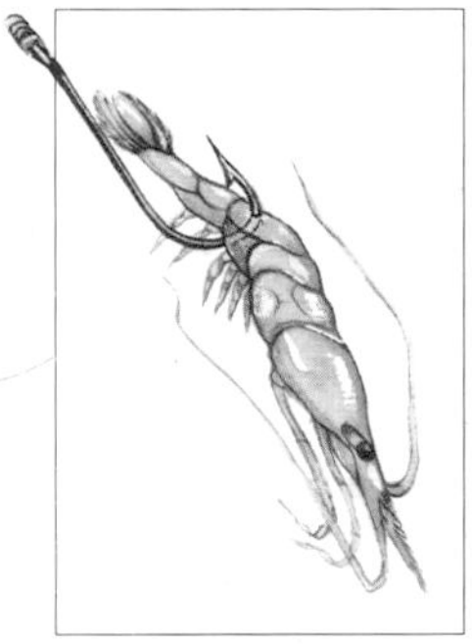

HOOKING PRAWNS
Peeled prawns are best presented singly on a size 8 or 10 hook pushed through the thick end of the tail. Mount unpeeled prawns on a size 2 or 4 hook, threaded through the tail or through and out of the underside of the body.

Mussels

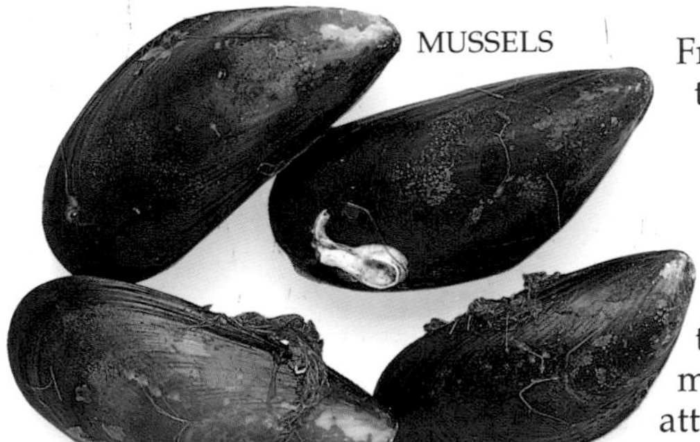

MUSSELS

Freshwater mussels are a traditional tench bait but will also be eaten by carp, bream, eels, and catfish. They are found in the margins of muddy stillwaters and are best collected by gently raking the bed. Open the shells with a thick-bladed knife, then cut through the area of thick meat, or "foot," where the mussel is attached to its shell.

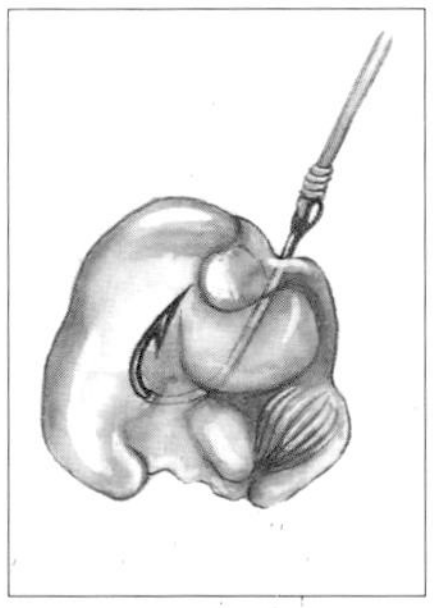

HOOKING MUSSELS
For close to medium casting, use a size 2 or 4 hook passed through the meaty foot. For fishing at a greater distance, also lash the softer part of the flesh to the hook shank with elastic thread.

Eels

Freshwater eels are a fine pike bait and can be used whole, if small, or in sections. They are tough-skinned, which often allows several fish to be caught on the same bait, and can be cast a long way. Eels up to 12 in (30 cm) long make good baits for wobbling, while smaller eels and cut sections are generally fished on a freeline or legered.

CUT EEL

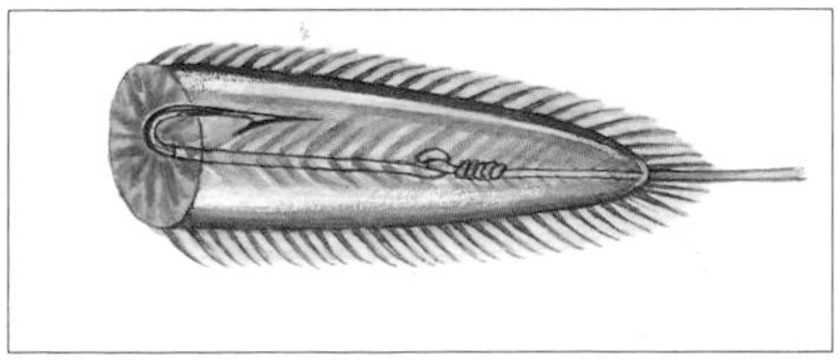

HOOKING EELS
For wobbling and legering, mount an eel or eel portion on a standard snap tackle of two size 8 or 10 semibarbless trebles on a 20 in (50 cm) wire trace. Small sections of eel can be fished on a large single hook threaded through the flesh with only part of the bend and point visible.

Processed Baits

Most of the large number of processed baits are common foodstuffs such as bread, cheese, meat, and vegetables, and while most are very unlikely to feature naturally in the diets of fish, they are nonetheless eaten when offered. In addition to these household foods, there is one group of processed baits that is produced exclusively for fishing: the high-protein (HP) baits. These were originally developed for carp fishing but are now widely used for many other non-predatory species, such as tench.

HOOKING CORN
Use size 10 or 12 for a single kernel and up to a size 4 for a bunch.

Cheese

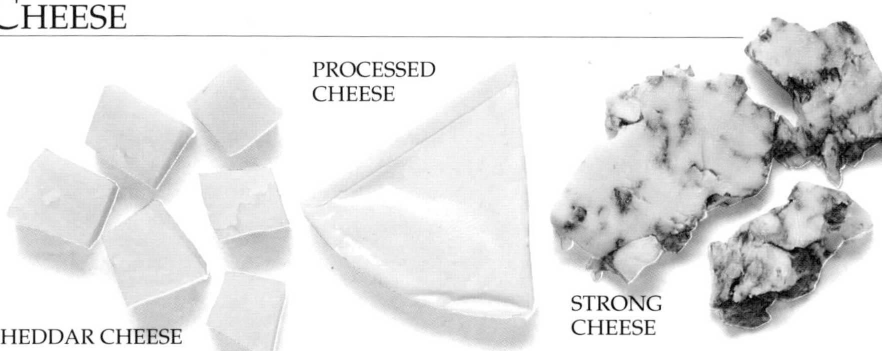

In summer, cheese can be used straight from the pack. However, cold water hardens cheeses such as cheddar, so in winter grate these and mix them into a stiff paste with breadcrumbs and a sprinkling of water and cooking oil.

HOOKING CHEESE
For large baits, such as for carp or chub, use a size 4; for small ones use a 10. Bury the hook point inside the cheese.

Sweet Corn

Available either canned or frozen, corn is liked by many species. The kernels are relatively tough-skinned, enabling them to be cast a fair distance without flying off the hook. They are also fairly dense and sink quite quickly to the bottom, which is useful on rivers. On waters where corn has been used extensively, it can still be an effective bait if you liven it up with a tiny amount of edible flavoring such as clove oil, or dye it a different color.

Bread

Bread provides a number of different baits that can be fished in a variety of ways. The crust can be trotted, legered, or even freelined, on lakes for carp and rudd and on rivers for roach and chub. A chunk of bread can be used both as a hookbait and as a groundbait. For the hook, use a chunk from a really fresh loaf because it will stay on longer. It can also be turned into dough for balls by mixing with water then kneading in a porous cloth.

HOOKING A BREAD CHUNK
Use hook sizes 4 to 14, depending on the size of fish you are after. Fold the chunk around the hook, then squeeze it together to ensure it stays on.

Meat & Biscuits

Canned pork and ham, cut into small cubes, are fine bait for chub and barbel. Canned cat food is liked by carp and catfish: mix it into a paste with breadcrumbs, then shape it into small balls. Dog biscuits are a good surface bait for carp, and can be turned into a paste bait by grinding them up with eggs and cornmeal.

HOOKING MEAT
Use a hook size 4 to 8, threaded carefully through the meat so that the point shows, and secure the bait with a piece of leaf.

Potatoes & Carrots

POTATO CUBES WHOLE POTATO CARROT RINGS WHOLE CARROTS

Small potatoes are a traditional and effective bait for carp and other cyprinids if the water is chummed to allow the fish to become accustomed to them. (To chum, throw about a handful of bait into it at the same time every day for a few days before you fish it.) Parboil them to soften them, or use canned boiled potatoes. Carrots, boiled and sliced, are taken by many cyprinids. As with potatoes, chumming is necessary when using carrots.

HOOKING POTATOES
Thread the line through the potato with a needle, attach the hook (size 2 to 8), and pull it inside.

Peas, Beans, & Pasta

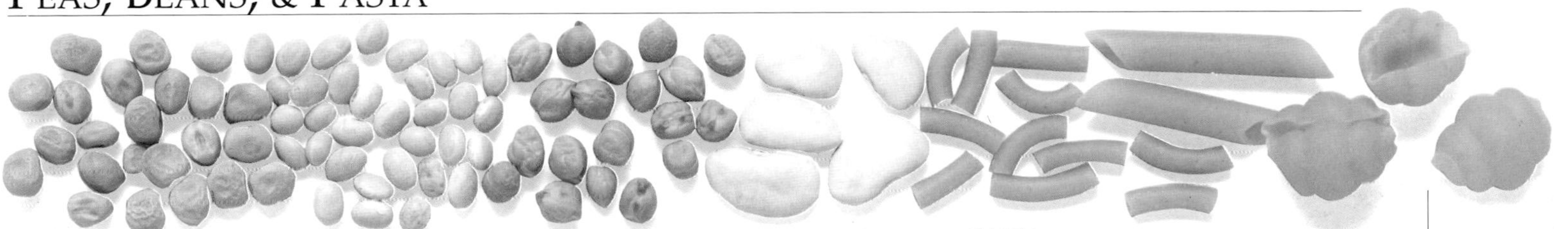

DRIED PEAS NAVY BEANS CHICK PEAS LIMA BEANS PASTA

Fresh and dried peas, beans, and other small "particle" baits have all been used to catch carp since the early 1970s. Mass chumming of these baits will, in the right place, also work for chub, tench, barbel, and roach. All dried peas and beans must be boiled to soften them before use, but do not allow them to become mushy. Pasta, if boiled until soft, and chummed, will take many fish; macaroni is a tried and tested chub bait but nowadays little is used.

HOOKING PEAS AND BEANS
Use hook sizes 8 to 12. Round baits are simply threaded onto the hook; mount oval beans lengthwise.

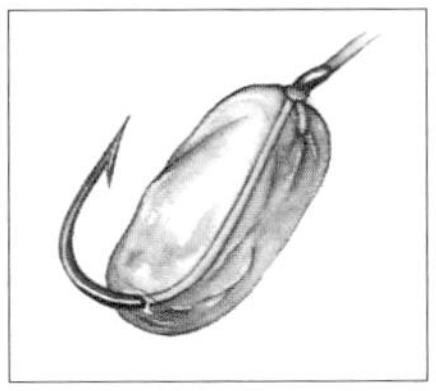

Seeds & Grains

RICE GRAIN RAW VETCHES PROCESSED HEMP COOKED VETCHES PEANUTS

Many seeds and grains make excellent particle baits, but all must be boiled to soften them before use, because fish cannot digest them uncooked. The most widely used seed is hemp, which sends many cyprinid species into a feeding frenzy. It is often used as groundbait, with the bigger vetch, a reddish brown berry, fished on the hook. Boiled peanuts have proved to be a very effective bait for carp, and corn, wheat, and barley (all boiled) are good roach baits. Boiled rice is useful for supplementing a meager supply of maggots.

HOOKING SEEDS AND GRAINS
Most seeds and grains are simply pushed onto the hook (size 6 to 14). Boiled hemp splits, and the hook is inserted into the split.

High-Protein (HP) Baits

HP baits are made of milk proteins, eggs, animal proteins, soy flour, wheatgerm, colorings, and flavorings. The mixture is either used as a paste or rolled into balls and boiled, producing "boilies." These have a thin skin that is impervious to the attentions of small nuisance fish. Most boilies produced are sinkers, but floaters are also made.

BOILIES

HOOKING BOILIES
Use a hook size 2 to 8 and ensure that the hook point and gap are not impeded, or use a hair rig or a boilie bayonet.

Freshwater Chum

Chum is a bait or mixture of baits introduced into the water to draw fish to the vicinity of the baited hook, and to keep them feeding in the area long enough for them to notice and take the hookbait. The key to successful chumming is to use a bait that will attract the species you are after, and to use enough to hold their attention without offering them so much food that they are likely to miss or ignore the hookbait.

Using Chum

Chum can be used both in rivers and in stillwaters. In rivers with moderate or swift currents, and in waters where bottom-feeding species are the quarry, use balls of stiff, heavy, bread-based chum that sink quickly to the bottom before breaking up.

In still or slow-moving waters, and for fish feeding in the upper layers, use the lighter, finer type of chum known as cloudbait. This is made of finely crushed dried breadcrumbs, dampened with water and squeezed into small balls immediately before use. When they are thrown into the water, the balls break up into a slowly sinking cloud of tiny bread particles.

The effectiveness of cloudbait can be enhanced by mixing a little powdered milk with the crumbs before forming them into balls.

Mixing chum

When mixing chum, the first step is to prepare the base. For a fast-sinking chum, soak stale bread in cold water for at least half an hour (do not use warm water because it makes the bread go slimy). Then pour away the water in which it was standing, and remove some of the water it has soaked up by gently squeezing it – the more you squeeze, the firmer the mixture will be. Mash the wet bread into a smooth paste consisting of tiny particles of crumbs and crust with no lumps. Stiffen the paste with bran or a coarse cereal meal, such as corn meal.

This mixture can be formed into balls, preferably with the addition of hookbait samples such as maggots or cut worms, and perhaps something to enhance their flavor. For example, many members of the carp family have a sweet tooth, and find chum laced with small amounts of sweet flavorings highly palatable.

Chum Bases

The simplest bases for chum are soaked, mashed-up stale bread, and bread that has been heated in an oven to dry it and then crushed into crumbs. Both can be used alone or mixed with hookbaits and other additives. Many anglers consider that brown bread makes a more effective chum than white.

Commercial chum and additives

Commercially made chums need little or no preparation, and many are formulated specifically for particular species or fishing methods. Additives, either liquid or powder, add color, flavor, and scent to baits and chums and revitalize their attractiveness when fish have become suspicious of them. These additives should be used sparingly, because too high a concentration of additives in a bait will usually repel fish rather than attract them.

Slingshots

A good way to deliver balls of chum into distant swims is to use a slingshot, preferably one designed specifically for the task. To prevent the balls from breaking up in flight, form them from a stiff chum mixture and make the firing action as smooth as possible. For consistent accuracy when chumming at long range, aim toward a feature on the far bank, such as a tree, and pull the slingshot pouch back the same distance on each firing. When you are using a slingshot, always hold it at arm's length and chest height. This will ensure that if the elastic breaks and flies back, it will not injure your eyes.

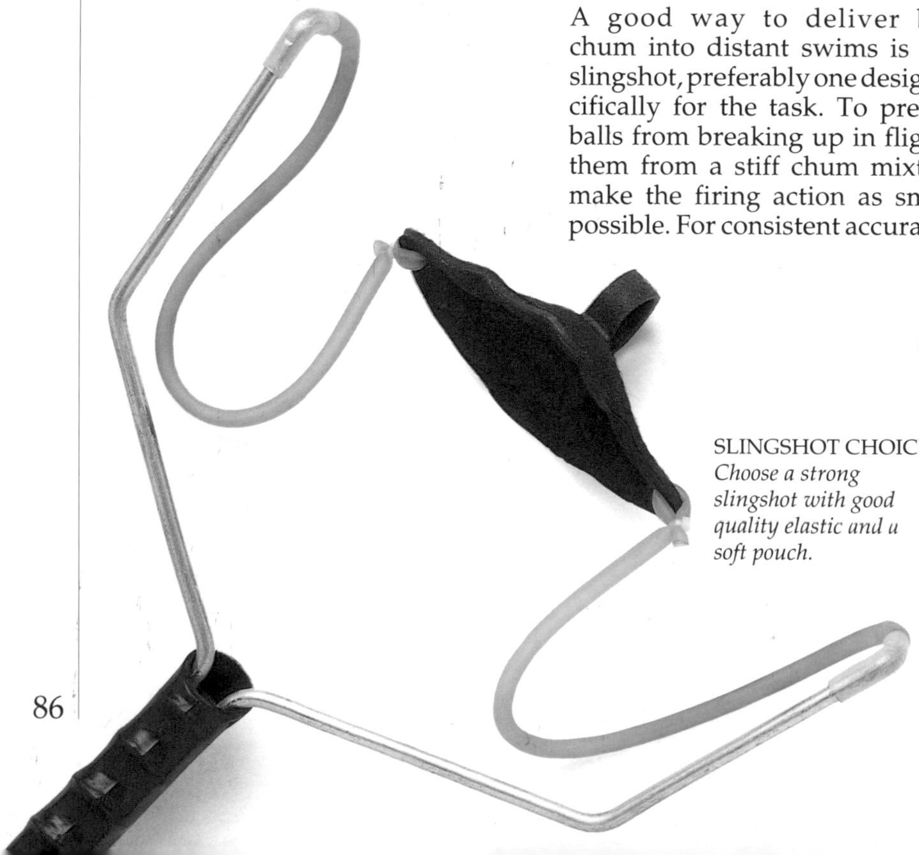

SLINGSHOT CHOICE
Choose a strong slingshot with good quality elastic and a soft pouch.

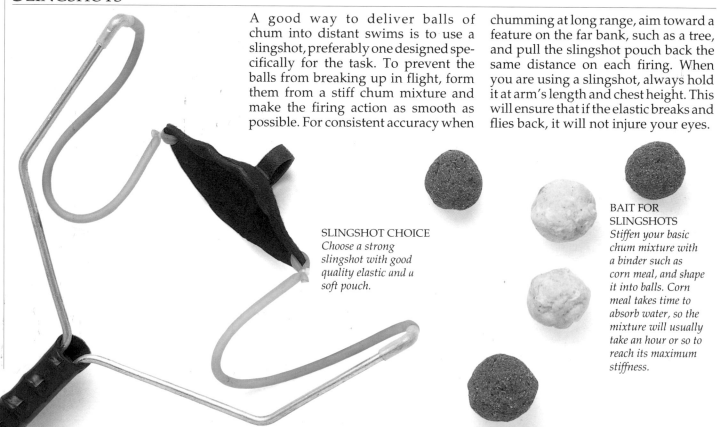

BAIT FOR SLINGSHOTS
Stiffen your basic chum mixture with a binder such as corn meal, and shape it into balls. Corn meal takes time to absorb water, so the mixture will usually take an hour or so to reach its maximum stiffness.

CRANKBAITS

Crankbaits, or swimfeeders, are widely used in legering for presenting either chum or samples of the hookbait close to the baited hook, and are attached to the terminal tackle in place of the leger weight. Most are simple perforated plastic or wire-mesh cylinders, and are weighted to aid casting and to ensure that they remain on the bed of the lake or river after their contents have been released. This weighting can take the form of a weight or weights at the base of the feeder, or may be a metal strip running along one side.

Open-ended feeders
Open-ended feeders are plastic tubes, open at both ends and usually perforated to hasten the inflow of water, thus speeding up dispersal of the bait contained inside. They are usually weighted with strips of lead, folded over and stapled at either end. Because the weight is not adjustable, these feeders are produced in a range of different sizes with different widths of lead strip.

Open-ended feeders are generally used with chum, although they can also be filled with hookbait samples, held inside by a plug of chum at each end. They are particularly suitable for bream and other species that roam in big schools and need large quantities of bait to hold them in a swim.

Blockend feeders
As their name suggests, these feeders are blocked (closed) at each end by caps. On some models, both caps are removable, while on others only the top cap can be taken off for the feeder to be filled with bait.

They are normally used with maggots, earthworms, or hempseed; the plastic tube is liberally perforated to allow the maggots and worms to crawl out and the static hemp to be washed out by the water. The release of bait can be slowed by winding insulating tape around part of the feeder to seal some of the holes.

The position of the weight on blockend feeders varies. On some, it is located below the base, on others in one of the end caps, while on others flat lead strip is used. Most blockends are tubular, but some are oval in cross-section to hold bottom in fast water.

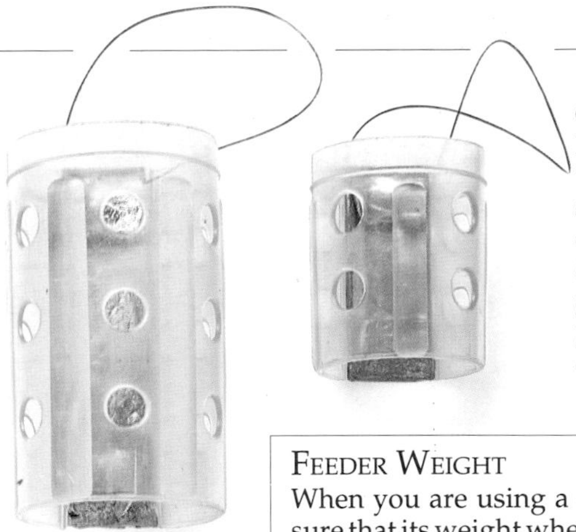

OPEN-ENDED FEEDERS
These are used with straight or bait-laced chum, or samples of hookbait held in by plugs of chum pushed firmly into each end.

> **FEEDER WEIGHT**
> When you are using a crankbait, make sure that its weight when filled with bait is not too great for the rod and line you are using.

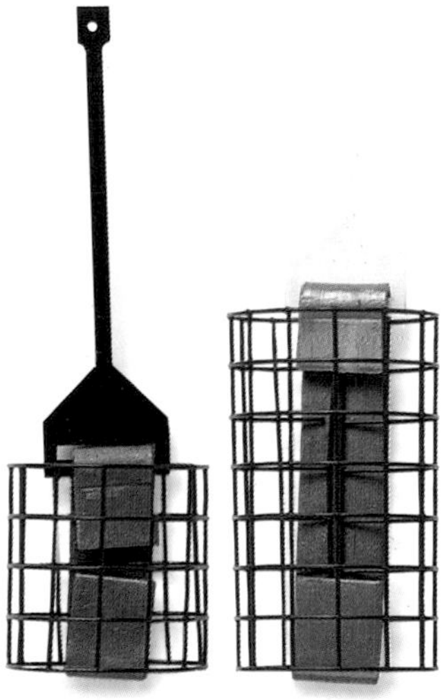

WIRE CAGE FEEDERS
These are made of wire mesh and filled quickly and easily by simply pushing them into chum.

DAIWA HARRIER FEEDERS
The aerodynamic shape of these feeders permits accurate, long-range casting and helps them to rise quickly to the surface for a rapid retrieve. Slots instead of holes speed up the inflow of water and therefore bait release.

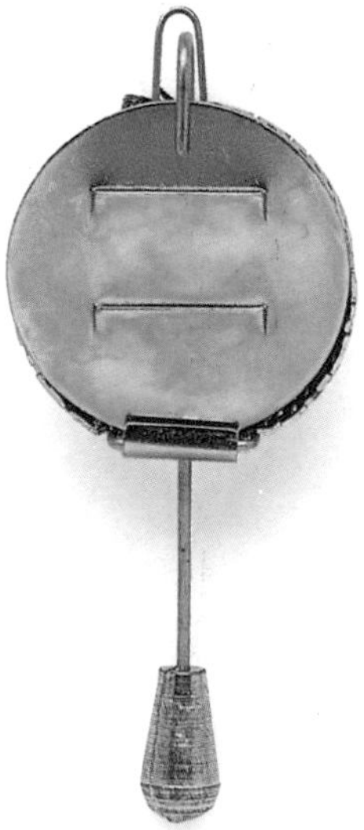

BAIT DROPPER
The hinged front face of the bait dropper opens to release the bait when the weighted plunger hits bottom. It is sometimes cast out and retrieved on a separate rod and line.

DRENNAN FLAT BLOCKEND
This feeder has a flattened shape (rather like that of a hip flask) and lead strip weight to help it stay in place on the bottom in fast-flowing water.

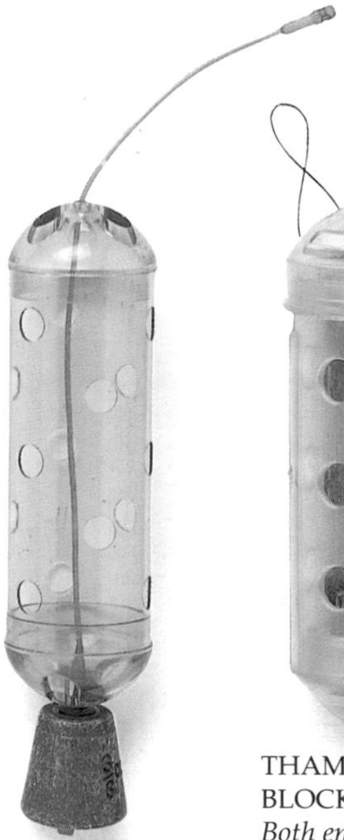

DRENNAN FEEDERLINK
The Feederlink has a removable top cap, and interchangeable weights that are clipped onto the base.

THAMESLEY BLOCKEND
Both end caps of this versatile feeder are removable. This facility enables it to be quickly and easily converted from a blockend to an open-ended feeder.

Spinners & Spoons

Spinners and spoons are artificial baits designed to provoke a response from predatory fish as they pass through their line of vision, either because the fish are hungry or because they are defending their territory. They can be made of a variety of materials and come fitted with single or treble hooks.

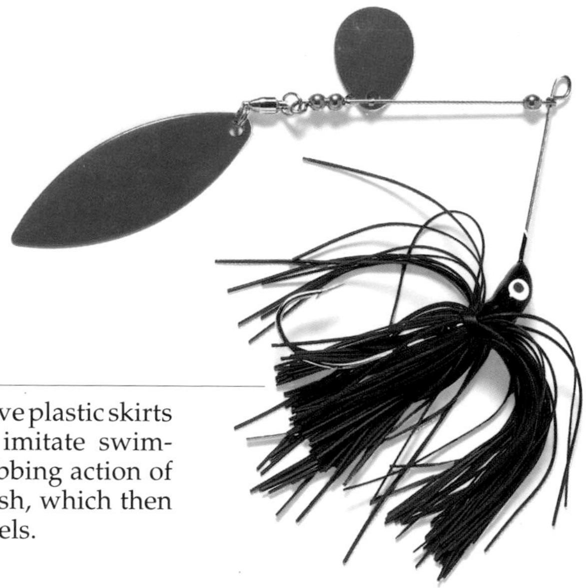

Spinners

On a spinner, a vane or blade rotates around a central bar as the lure is retrieved. Some have lifelike worms or fish of soft rubber that encourage fish to hang on after grabbing the lure. Others, including buzz baits, have plastic skirts over their hooks that imitate swimming crayfish: the throbbing action of the blade attracts the fish, which then lunge at the plastic tassels.

LIL' HUSTLER SPOILER *(above)*
A spinner bait. Being virtually weedless, it is at its best when worked in fish-holding vegetation. Fish it shallow on a continuous retrieve or by sink and draw.

SPRAT (DEVON MINNOW)
Made in both floating and sinking versions for a variety of water conditions, this is a traditional salmon and trout lure that takes many other species.

TEASER *(above)*
An in-line spinner bait, best fished at a medium to fast pace. Its sleek, aerodynamic shape ensures that it casts well.

GOLD WING *(above)*
A buzz bait, at its best when retrieved on or just under the surface. Virtually weedless, it can be fished among lily pads where pike often lurk.

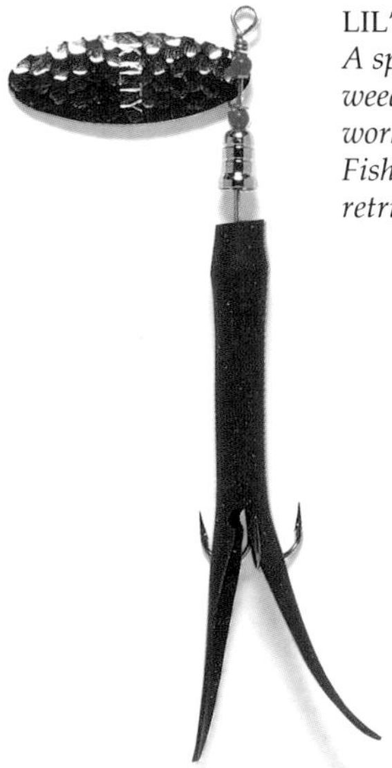

FLYING CONDOM
This unique lure produces a tremendously heavy throbbing action on the retrieve, and it has proved highly effective for many species including salmon, bass, pike, and perch.

SNAGLESS SALLY *(left)*
Fitted with a double-pronged weed guard, this lure can be cast right into and pulled through dense fish-holding weedbeds without fear of snagging.

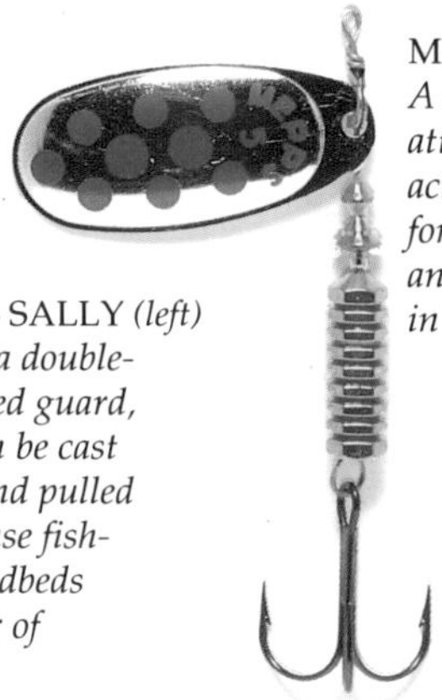

MEPPS COMET *(left)*
A small lure with an attractive fluttering action that works well for trout, chub, pike, and perch. It fishes best in lakes or slow rivers.

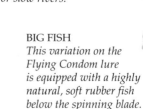

BIG FISH
This variation on the Flying Condom lure is equipped with a highly natural, soft rubber fish below the spinning blade.

SPOONS

Spoons wobble through the water in a fishlike manner, and are often trolled behind boats as well as being cast and retrieved. Most are oval, and cast well due to their all-metal construction. Their action depends on the style of retrieve: winding in erratically can give the impression of a fish in distress, while twitching the rod tip when winding in gives extra "life" to the lure.

ABU ATOM
The Atom's rippled finish catches and reflects light as it is pulled through the water. It has an irregular action and is particularly good for pike in clear water.

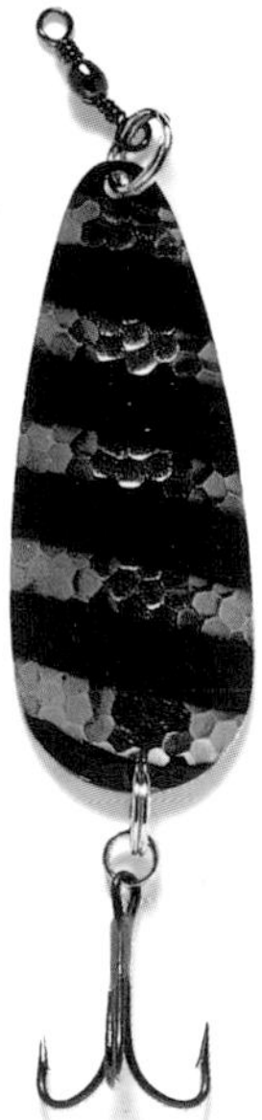

ATLANTIC
This is a well-proven spoon for pike and other predatory fish. It is at its most effective when fished very slowly, just off the bottom, in lakes and gravel pits.

CISCO
A lure with a realistic action, designed for salmon, trout, and pike. Equally at home trolled, even up to 8 mph (13 km/h), or fished from the bank, where sink-and-draw is recommended.

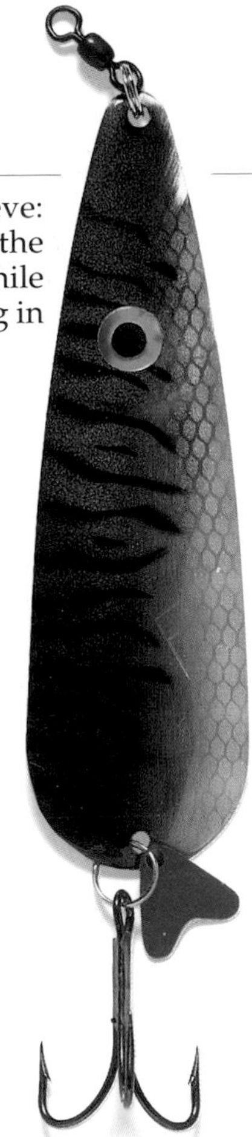

HERON
A king-sized spoon designed specifically for big pike, this is perfect for distance casting on large, deep waters as well as for trolling or downrigging.

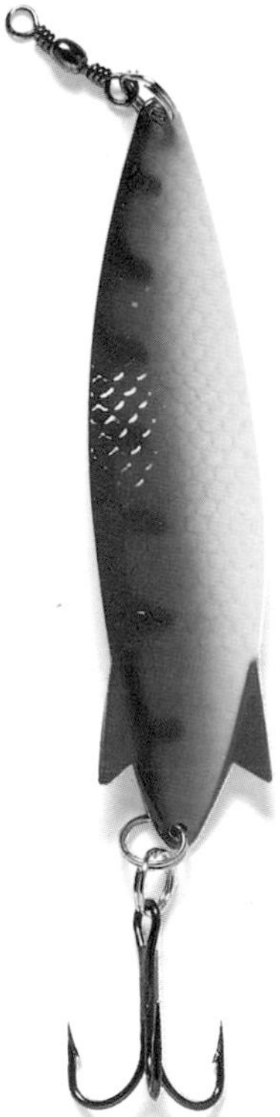

ABU TOBY SALMO
A highly effective gamefish lure that imitates the movement of a small fish as it twists and turns on its way through the water. The Salmo is a good lure to use in moving water.

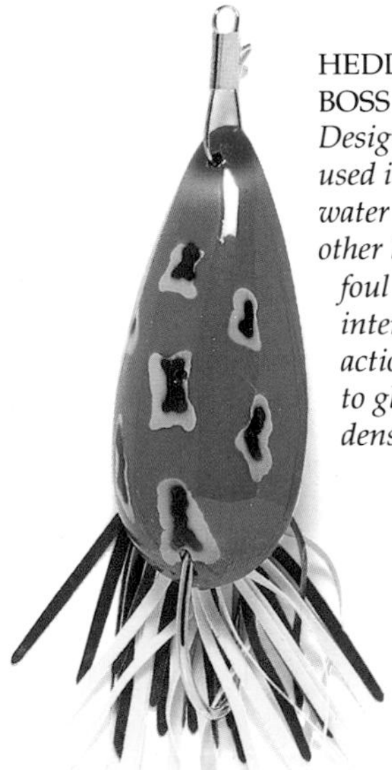

HEDDON MOSS BOSS *(left)*
Designed to be used in weedy water where other lures can foul up. Its interesting action helps it to glide over dense weed.

ABU GLIMMY
An excellent pike and salmon lure with an undulating swing produced by its double-curve profile. Surfaces rapidly when retrieved at speed.

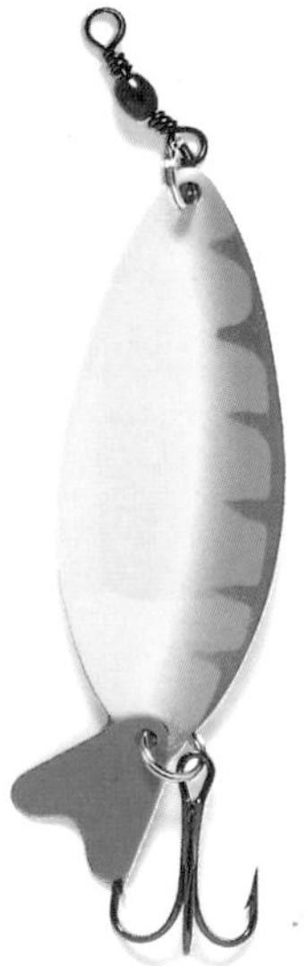

ABU STOR-ÖRINGEN
A lively big brother to the Lill-Öringen, this is a productive lure for salmon and zander. Displaces a lot of water during the retrieve.

KILTY KERRYMAN
This Irish salmon lure has also proved to be an enticer of pike. Its fluttering action often produces hard takes.

ABU LILL-ÖRINGEN *(below)*
This is a small, streamlined, and lightweight spoon, good for fishing near the surface or in shallow water.

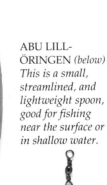

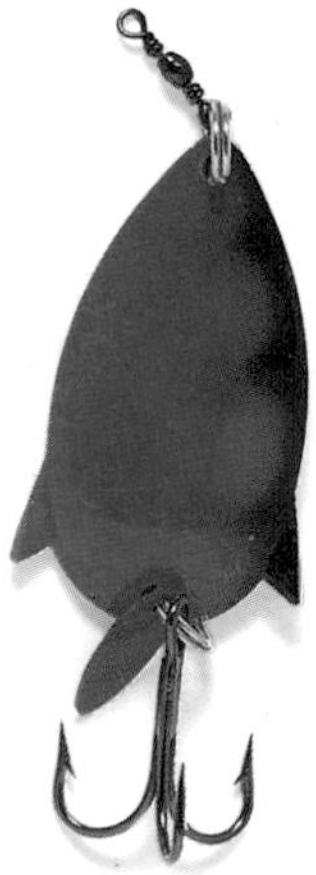

TOBY FAT
The elliptical shape and double curve of this spoon induce a lively but undulating action. A good lure for long casts. Retrieve slowly for best results.

Plugs

Plugs are made of materials such as wood, plastic, and metal, and designed to either float, dive below the surface, or sink when retrieved. Floating plugs are fished across the surface, and they often have features that create extra fish-attracting surface disturbance, such as propellers or plastic skirts. Floating plugs that dive when cranked in are very versatile, because the speed of retrieve determines how deep they dive, allowing a great variety of depths to be explored. The diving action is produced by an angled vane or lip at the head, and some plugs contain balls that rattle to enhance their attractiveness. Sinking plugs are made in a variety of densities to fish at different depths.

Floating Plugs

SPUTTERBUG *(right)*
This lure has a big-bladed propeller at the front that gurgles and splutters through the water on the retrieve, and a skirt at the rear that pulsates.

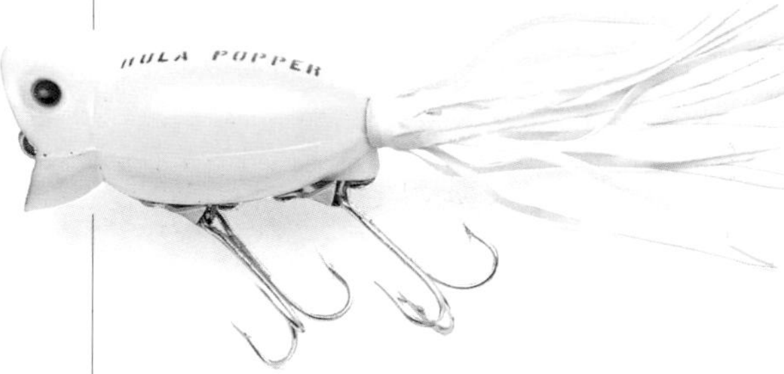

HULA POPPER *(above)*
A surface worker in which all the action has to be produced by the rod tip. The tassel skirt ripples through the water.

HEDDON TORPEDO *(right)*
The propeller churns up the water, while the disturbance caused by the blunt head creates additional fish-attracting vibrations.

BILL LEWIS SLAPSTICK *(left)*
This lure features hollow chambers containing rattling ball bearings. Action is created by twitching or flicking the rod tip on the retrieve.

Floating/Diving Plugs

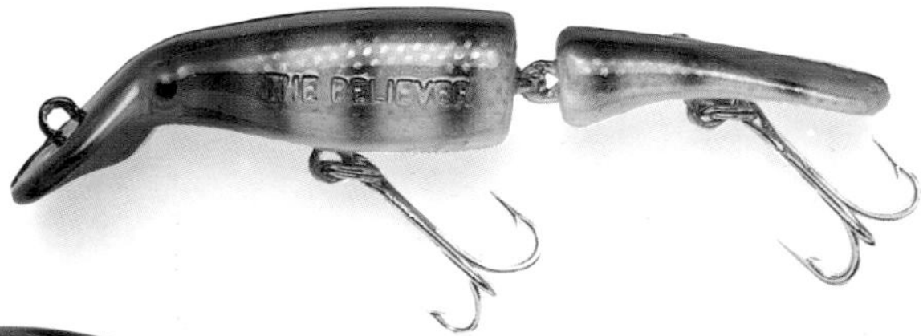

JOINTED BELIEVER *(right)*
The jointed body gives this plug lifelike motion, and the depth to which it dives depends on which of the two nose rings is used.

RIVER RUNNER *(above)*
This plug has a two-position, spoon-shaped lip. The position of the lip, which is set before the lure is cast, determines the depth to which the lure dives when it is retrieved.

CORADO CONQUEROR *(below)*
A floating diver from Poland. Its wobbling action becomes more exaggerated as the retrieve is quickened, and the largest models will dive down to about 12 ft (3.7 m) when they are cranked in hard.

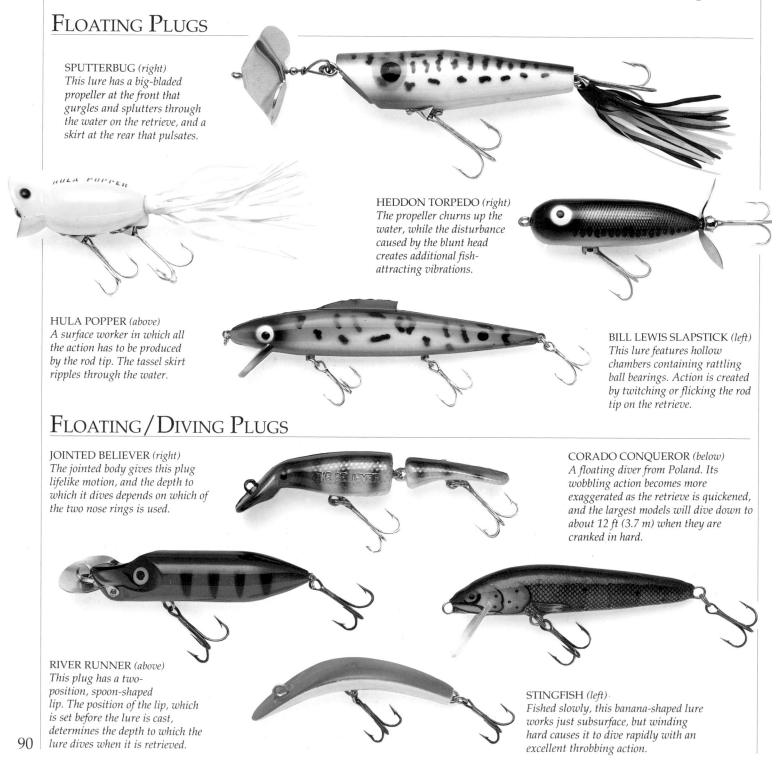

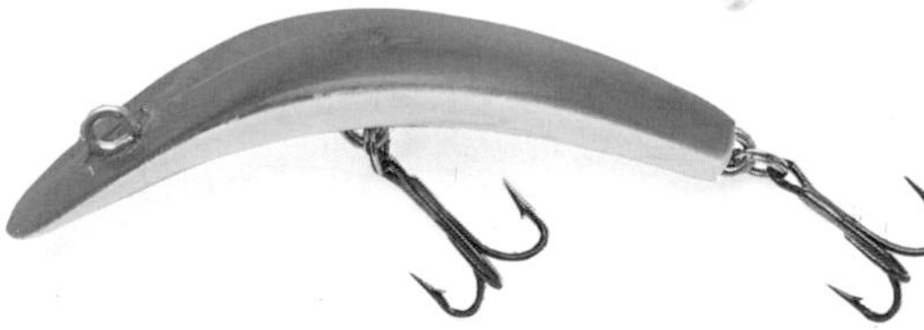

STINGFISH *(left)*
Fished slowly, this banana-shaped lure works just subsurface, but winding hard causes it to dive rapidly with an excellent throbbing action.

Sinking Plugs

SMITHWICK DEVIL'S HORSE *(right)*
This wooden lure can be cast and retrieved or trolled. Its twin propellers churn up the water, creating a disturbance similar to the thrashing of an injured baitfish.

LEROY BROWN *(below)*
A lifelike vibrating lure with a busy, wobbling action that is a very effective fish attractor.

SHIMMY *(right)*
A darting lure with a built-in wriggle. This slow-sinking plug is designed to be fished sink-and-draw at varying speeds of retrieve.

CORDELL RATT'L SPOT *(above)*
The shiny finish of this lure makes it more easily visible in poor light, and its vibrating action is enhanced by rattling ball bearings that are housed inside the body.

JOINTED WIGGLER *(left)*
A heavy, fast-sinking plug from Canada that is excellent for fishing large stillwaters and deep, swift-flowing rivers.

Deep-Diving Plugs

BAGLEY DIVING BANG-O-B *(right)*
A large, tough, hardwood trolling lure with a big lip that will take it down to depths of 20 to 30 ft (6 to 9 m). It can be used for marine species as well as for freshwater fish.

THE HUNTER *(below)*
A pike lure designed to be fished slowly just off the bottom, especially in winter when the fish are lying deep and torpid.

HEDDON MAGNUM HELLBENDER *(above)*
This classic lure will dive rapidly down to 35 ft (11 m) when trolled. Effective along deep banks, marginal ledges, and drop-offs.

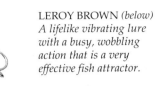

BAGLEY DEEP DIVING 5 *(left)*
A tough lure made of balsa reinforced with hardwood. Designed for use in the deeper parts of lakes and reservoirs and in powerful rivers.

Natural Baits

In addition to fish baits, such as cut or whole mackerel and herring, the saltwater angler has a wide range of natural baits to choose from. There are probably more species of fish reliant on non-fish meals than species regularly eating other fish, so the broader the range of natural baits used, the greater the chances of angling success. Fresh, good-quality bait has no equal, but it must be kept cool and moist at all times during storage, and should, if possible, be presented naturally when used.

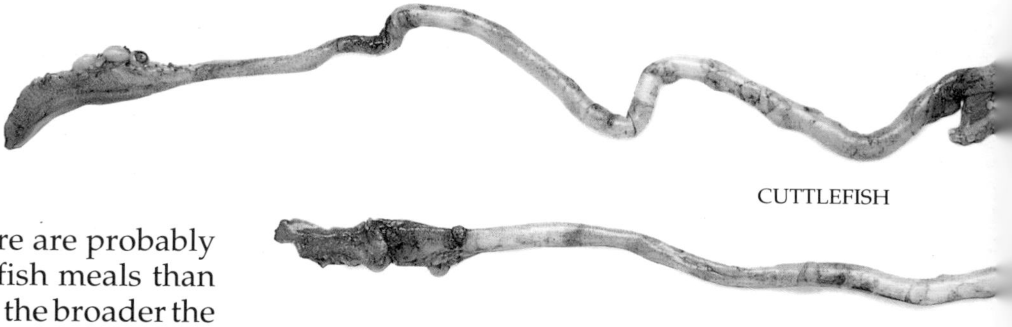

CUTTLEFISH

SQUID

Sandworms

Anglers classify the various species of sandworm (*Nereis* spp.) by color and size. Red sandworms can be dug from shellfish beds and stone patches in estuaries, and kept for up to a week if loosely wrapped in damp newspaper and refrigerated. King sandworms are the largest reds, used in portions or whole for stingrays, pollack, and similar large predators. Smaller reds are popular general-purpose baits, while tiny harbor sandworms, dug from estuarine mud, are much loved by flounders and mullet. White sandworms, the favorite bait of tournament anglers, are found on clean sands.

KING SANDWORM

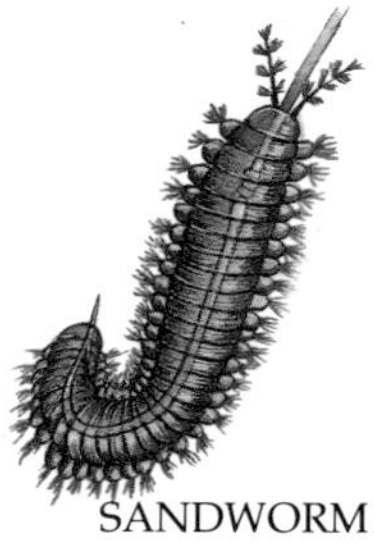

SANDWORM

HOOKING SANDWORMS

Feed the worm up the shank until the hook is full, or push it up onto the trace leaving nothing hanging free for fish to tug at. Beware of the nippers at the head end when handling sandworms.

Lugworms

There are two common species of lugworm (*Arenicola* spp.), and both leave telltale heaps of debris at their burrow entrances. Brown lug can be dug from the middle shore sands. They will keep for a few days if loosely wrapped in damp newspaper and put in a refrigerator, or they can be kept in tanks. The larger black lug live beneath the lower shore and can be frozen. Many species of fish find them irresistible.

LUGWORM

HOOKING LUGWORMS

To hook a lugworm, carefully thread the hook through the head and the center of the body, taking care not to burst the worm. Nip off any surplus tail that might give small fish a starting point for tearing the bait from the hook.

BROWN LUGWORM

Sandeels

SANDEELS

The various sandeel species (family Ammodytidae) are small, elongate, gregarious fish that form vast schools for protection and also burrow into the sand to escape predation. They are a major link in the marine food chain – most predatory fish feed on them and some, such as sandbank turbot and bass, are almost reliant on them. They are netted in areas of strong tidal activity (which seem to attract them) or dug from surf beaches, and kept in aerated tubs.

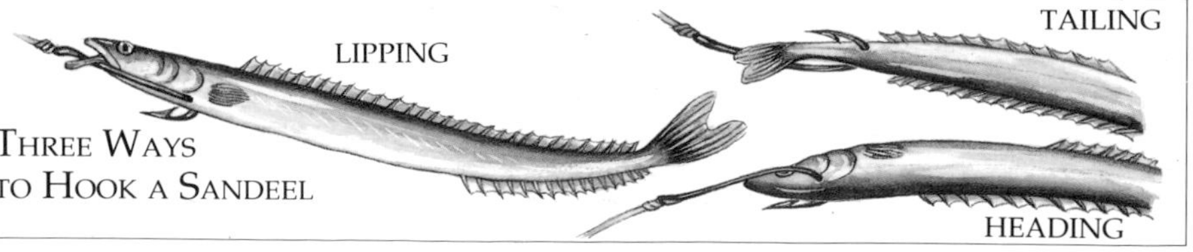

THREE WAYS TO HOOK A SANDEEL

HOOKING SANDEELS

To be at their most effective as a bait, sandeels must be alive and swimming and fished on the drift. The most natural presentation is lipping, with the point also nicked into the skin under the gill cover. Heading and tailing can also be used but appear less natural.

Squid and Cuttlefish

Squid and cuttlefish are cephalopods, tentacled mollusks with small internal shells. They are highly intelligent and active predators in their own right, but, either strip-cut or whole, they make excellent baits for a very wide range of species. If they have a fault it is their lack of fish-attracting scent, but fish will take them avidly once they find them. Small squid are available from retail fish outlets, cuttlefish and large squid from inshore fishing boats.

CUTTLEFISH HEAD

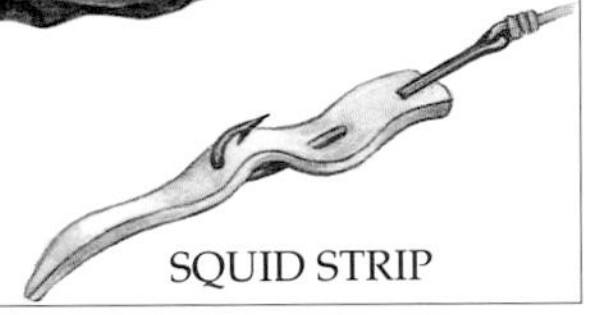

SQUID STRIP

HOOKING SQUID *(left)*
Cut open, remove guts and outer skin, then strip-cut the flesh. Insert the hook through twice; the flesh is tough, so bait hanging beyond the hook is not a problem.

HOOKING CUTTLEFISH
Prepare and hook as for squid. The head, on a big hook, is good for conger and cod. The entire body, and cut or whole tentacles, can also be used.

Octopus

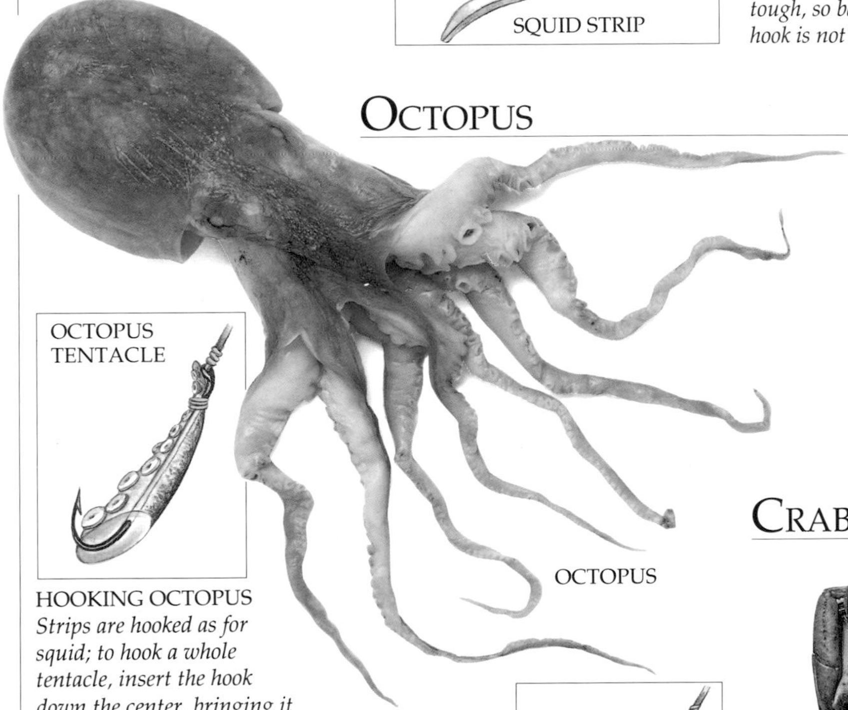

OCTOPUS

Octopus are more common in inshore waters than many people realize, and are taken on rod and line in some areas. Like squid and cuttlefish, they are predatory cephalopods, and as baits they are prepared and used in much the same way; small ones can be used whole. Long strips of octopus flesh, when fished fluttering in the tide, will attract fish by their visual appeal. When using long strips, give a taking fish enough time to get the whole bait down before striking to set the hook.

OCTOPUS TENTACLE

HOOKING OCTOPUS
Strips are hooked as for squid; to hook a whole tentacle, insert the hook down the center, bringing it out a shank's length down.

Razor Clams

Several species of razor clam (*Ensis* spp. and *Solen* spp.) inhabit the sands of the extreme lower shore. Razor clams move too quickly to be dug up, so are either speared or coaxed from the sand by squirting a strong salt solution into their keyhole-shaped burrow apertures. They appeal to many fish, including those usually taken on fish strips. Take care not to damage the flesh when taking it from the shell, and remove the tough foot, which fish dislike.

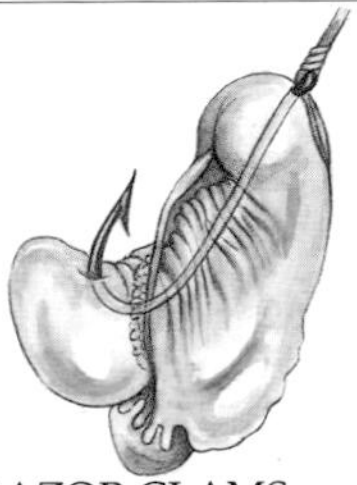

RAZOR CLAMS

HOOKING RAZOR CLAMS
Cut a suitably firm section of flesh, and pass the hook through it as many times as possible because it is soft and tears easily.

RAZOR CLAM

Crabs

PEELER CRABS

As crabs grow, they shed their shells and grow larger ones. At such times, the crab crawls out, then takes on water to expand a soft, wrinkled outer skin that hardens in a few days to form the new shell. Crabs about to shed are called peelers; those without hard shells, softshells. Both make excellent baits for a wide range of fish, but the peeler is the more effective.

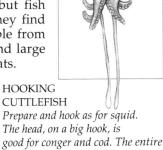

PEELER CRAB

HOOKING CRABS
Peel fully, then cut into halves. Pile these onto the hook and bind in place with thread. Appearance is unimportant: the appeal lies in the smell.

SALTWATER CHUMMING

Saltwater chumming, also known as groundbaiting or swimfeeding, is a very effective means of attracting fish into the vicinity of a baited hook, and of delaying the passage of passing fish so that you can place baits in front of them. It can also be used to give fish a taste for whatever bait you intend to put on your hook, and to encourage them to feed when they otherwise might not. The secret lies in using measured amounts appropriate to the species and the prevailing conditions, and in using enough to tempt the fish without feeding them so much that they have no appetite for the hookbait.

GROUND CHUM *(above)*
The best ground chum is made from stale mackerel mixed with bran and pilchard oil. Some anglers mince the mackerel, but this produces particles of uniform size that will disperse in a uniform manner, which fails to exploit the technique's full potential. It is far better to pulp the fish in a tub or bucket with a block of wood. This gives a variety of particle sizes, which will sink to different depths, and some of them will not wash out of the bag but stay there to draw fish right up to the boat.

GROUND CHUM

This is a very effective particulate mixture, based on the flesh of oily fish, that is released into the water and carried along by the tide to create a long, continuous slick of particles, blood, and body juices. The heavier particles sink, making the slick three-dimensional, and the baits are set at appropriate depths within it. For pelagic fish, such as sharks, it is normally used when drift fishing but can also be used from an anchored boat.

When fishing at anchor for bottom-feeding fish, some anglers tie a mesh bag full of minced mackerel to the anchor in the belief that the ensuing trail will pass beneath the boat, but this will not always be the case. On a dying tide with a stiff breeze cutting across it, the boat will be pushed out of line, and fish following the slick through to its source will not pass beneath it. It is better to hang the bag over the stern on a short, weighted rope.

USING GROUND CHUM *(left)*
The mixture is packed in a mesh bag and hung over the side of the boat. It should be shaken and topped up regularly to maintain the consistency of the slick.

BAIT DROPPERS

Bait droppers are lowered on a rope, or by rod and line, to place large portions of bait on the seabed. These attract sharks and other large predators, and draw territorial species such as conger from their lairs. Because a strong tide will tend to disperse the bait portions away from the hookbaits, this technique works best on neap tides.

A bait dropper usually consists of a weighted plastic tube with a flap that opens when the dropper hits the bottom. A cheaper alternative is a plastic bag with a sinker tied inside one corner. On a fast drop, water pressure keeps the bag closed around its contents, which are released by raising the rod tip a couple of times when the sinker has touched the bottom.

LOWERING DROPPERS *(left)*
Lower a custom-made dropper carefully so as not to trigger the flap prematurely.

BAITS FOR DROPPERS *(above)*
When using a dropper, choose a bait or baits that are likely to attract the species of fish you hope to catch. Suitable baits to use in droppers include large pieces of fish or squid, whole or cut worms, whole or crushed shellfish, and broken crabs; you can also use pulped or minced fish.

BIG-GAME CHUMMING

CHUMMING FOR SHARKS
Cruising sharks can be attracted toward the baited hooks by chumming – dropping chopped stale fish and squid into the water. Oily fish, such as mackerel and herring, are the most effective.

Big-game chumming can take a number of forms, but all are intended either to draw fish toward the hooks or to stir them into a feeding frenzy.

Ground chum and bait droppers are good ways of attracting fish to the baited hooks when fishing with natural baits. Another method is to drop chum chunks (small pieces of fish) into the water, but to be effective this needs one person to be constantly cutting and dropping the chunks.

When trolling with natural baits, one way of attracting fish up from the depths is to space twenty link swivels along a length of mono, then clip a live pilchard to each. This rig is trailed astern, and more live pilchard are thrown in loose to form a school with those on the links. If you are trolling lures, you can create the impression of a small school of fish by using multiple lures or by trailing a team of teaser lures. These are hookless lures designed simply to attract species such as marlin and sailfish into the vicinity of the hooked lures.

SHORE CHUMMING

Rock and pier anglers cannot normally reach the areas where fish are feeding, but they can draw feeding fish within casting range by chumming with shirvy. When this paste is put into deep water, such as that below rock ledges, it is carried out to sea by the tide, creating a scent trail that will entice fish right up to the shore. Mullet and bass are among the species readily attracted by shirvy, and conger respond well to a bag of ground chum hung over a harbor wall at night.

Fish also gather to feed on bits of fish washed from the decks of trawlers, and on refuse from pier restaurants and moored boats.

USING SHIRVY
When using shirvy, it is essential to create a continuous slick to keep the fish moving inshore. You can do this by putting it into a mesh bag and lowering it into the sea, or by throwing in small amounts with an old serving spoon. The slick makes an oily line on the surface, showing where the baits should be placed. When this fades, throw in another spoonful.

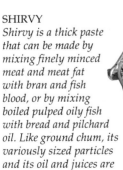

SHIRVY
Shirvy is a thick paste that can be made by mixing finely minced meat and meat fat with bran and fish blood, or by mixing boiled pulped oily fish with bread and pilchard oil. Like ground chum, its variously sized particles and its oil and juices are carried along by the tide to form a three-dimensional slick.

LURES

Artificial lures, used alone or in conjunction with natural baits, will take most species of saltwater gamefish. As in freshwater fishing, the size and type of lure to use depends mainly on the species you intend to catch and the style of fishing you are going to employ, such as trolling or spinning. There are thousands of different lures on the market, but if you equip yourself with a small range of each of the basic patterns you will have a selection to cover most of your normal fishing requirements.

TROLLING FEATHER (*above*)
This is a loose lure, one that is threaded onto the line before the hook is attached. This allows it to be used with your personal choice of hook and leader. It can be used weightless and skipping the surface, lightly weighted with a trolling weight, or sent deeper on a downrigger.

FEATHERS (*above*)
When feathers are strung out on short droppers above a sinker, there are few fish they cannot catch. The original versions, devised for mackerel fishing, were simply bunches of feathers, sometimes dyed, whipped to the shank of a hook. These are still used, but bright synthetic materials are increasingly popular. For mackerel, they should be worked up and down repeatedly at all levels until the school has been located.

PLASTIC SQUID (*below*)
Known informally as "muppets," these lures first proved their value in wreck fishing. They are very attractive to cod, but will take many other species, including ling and pollack, and are especially effective when baited. Like feathers, they are put onto short droppers above a sinker or pirk, but they are fished only at the bottom. The dropper is passed through a small hole in the head of the lure, then a bead is added to prevent it from sliding down over the hook.

SALTWATER FLIES (*above*)
Small saltwater fish, such as shad, mackerel, and bass, can be taken on many freshwater fly patterns, including the Dog Nobbler. Streamers and bucktails, some based on freshwater flies and others designed specifically for saltwater species, are used for fish such as tarpon, sharks, and sailfish.

MARLIN LURE (*above*)
This large plastic lure is one of many on the market that are similar in appearance and action to the original Kona Head design. The Kona Head, which originated in Hawaii, is a big-fish trolling lure with a big reputation. It is one of the standard big-game lures and will take a wide range of species including marlin, tuna, dolphinfish, and bonito.

LARGE SQUID (*above*)
The large version of the plastic squid is often used in conjunction with a trolled deadbait, or as an additional skirt for another lure, when fishing for open-ocean gamefish such as marlin. On its own, with a big single hook, a large plastic squid is a good trolling lure for species such as sailfish.

SPOONS (*right*)
The fixed-hook spoon is designed specifically to attract fish to within detection range of a natural bait, which induces the fish to take the hook. The metal blade wobbles as it moves through the water, sending out eyecatching glints of light that attract species such as cod, snapper, and grouper.

SPINNER (*above*)
In saltwater, as in freshwater, a spinner is fished by casting and retrieving. Spinners can be used with light spinning tackle for small species such as bass, barracuda, and jack.

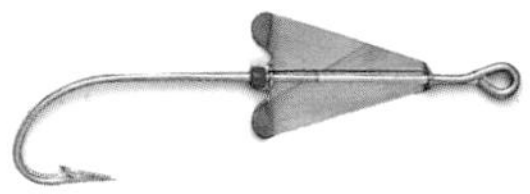

MACKEREL SPINNER (*above*)
This spinner has a blade that rotates like a propeller when the lure is retrieved or trolled. It is an excellent lure for mackerel and most small predatory species.

TWO-TAILED EEL (*below*)
This version of the rubber sandeel has two tails to give it a lively, attractive action when worked through the water. When fished on a flying collar rig (see page 249) *it is good for pollack, bass, and cod.*

ATTRACTOR SPOON (*above*)
A small attractor spoon is a useful flatfish lure when the water is clear and long drifts over clean ground are possible. When mounted just above a baited hook on a long leader, and fished along the bottom, it glints and stirs up puffs of sand as it rotates.

TROLLING LURE (*above*)
There are many variations on this basic theme, which is essentially a loose lure with a plastic skirt and a drilled head that allows it to be rigged to personal taste. Skirts are made of turkey marabou, feathers, or plastic, and colored to imitate a particular baitfish or to trigger an aggressive response from predatory fish.

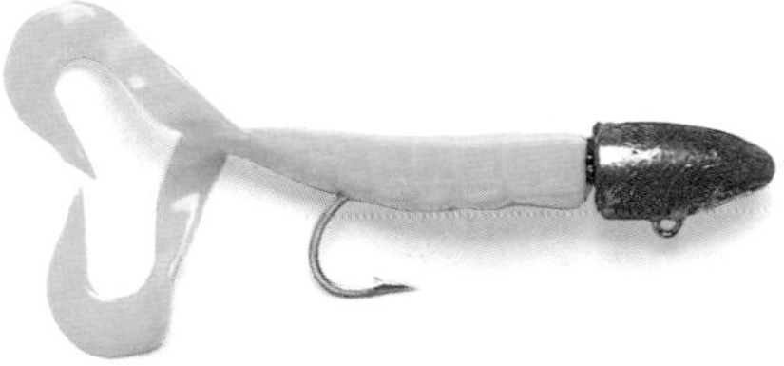

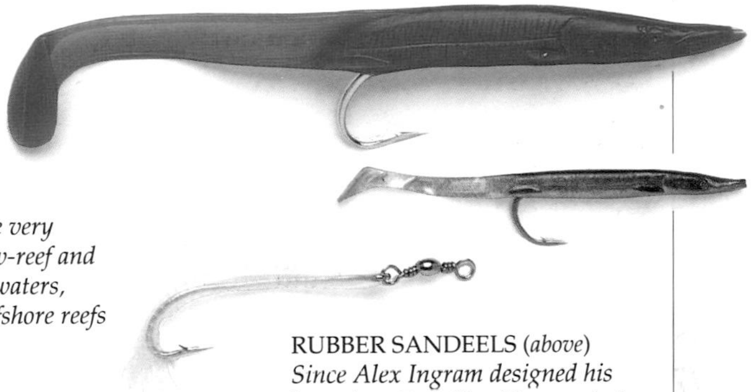

PLUGS (*below*)
In warm waters, slowly trolled plugs are very effective lures for a wide range of shallow-reef and open-ocean species. In cooler temperate waters, bass that are hunting around shallow offshore reefs will take them without hesitation.

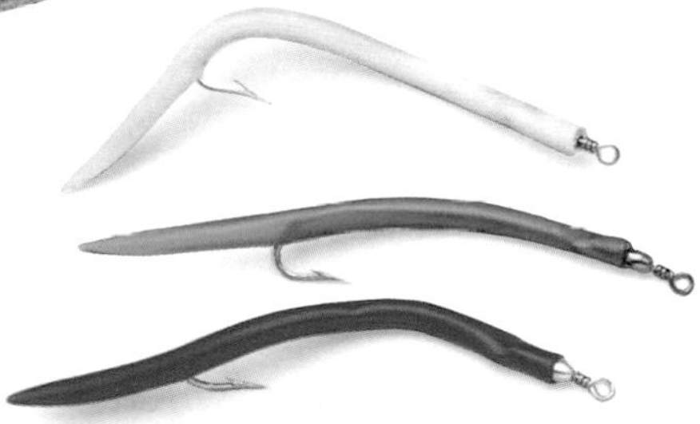

PLASTIC EELS (*above*)
These simple but effective jigging lures are made of lengths of colored plastic tube, crimped to swivels attached to long, twisted-shanked hooks. The lures are fished on short droppers above the sinker, which is bounced along the bottom. Plastic eels are excellent lures for cod, striped bass, and pollack.

RUBBER SANDEELS (*above*)
Since Alex Ingram designed his legendary Redgill rubber sandeel, imitations, which are reputedly the sincerest form of flattery, have been legion. The leader passes down the body via the mouth to the hook, which appears from the vent. The tail is thin, flat, and flexible, with an angled end, and provides a lifelike swimming action and enticing vibrations that few fish can resist. Most species will take rubber sandeels, and they are fished on long leaders, retrieved slowly from bottom to top, for free-swimming species such as pollack and bass.

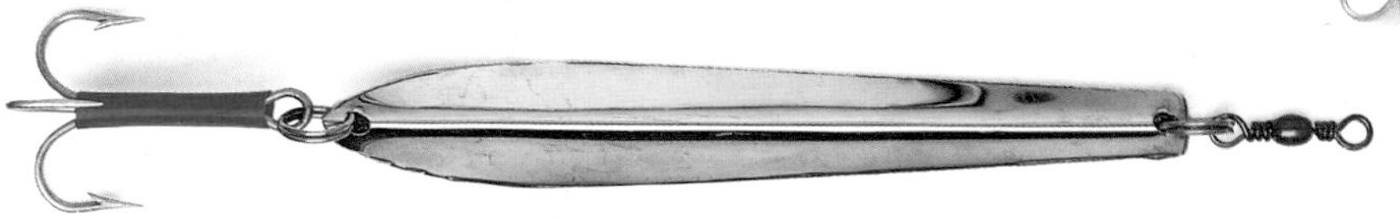

PIRKS (*above and right*)
These metal jigging lures were developed from cod lures used by commercial handliners. They range in size from tiny lures weighing as little as 1 oz (28 g), which are used to catch baitfish, to huge slabs of metal weighing 2 lb (910 g) or more for use in deep water with strong currents. Pirks are used unbaited for cod, bluefish, and pollack, and baited for ling and halibut.

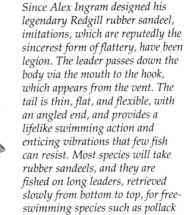

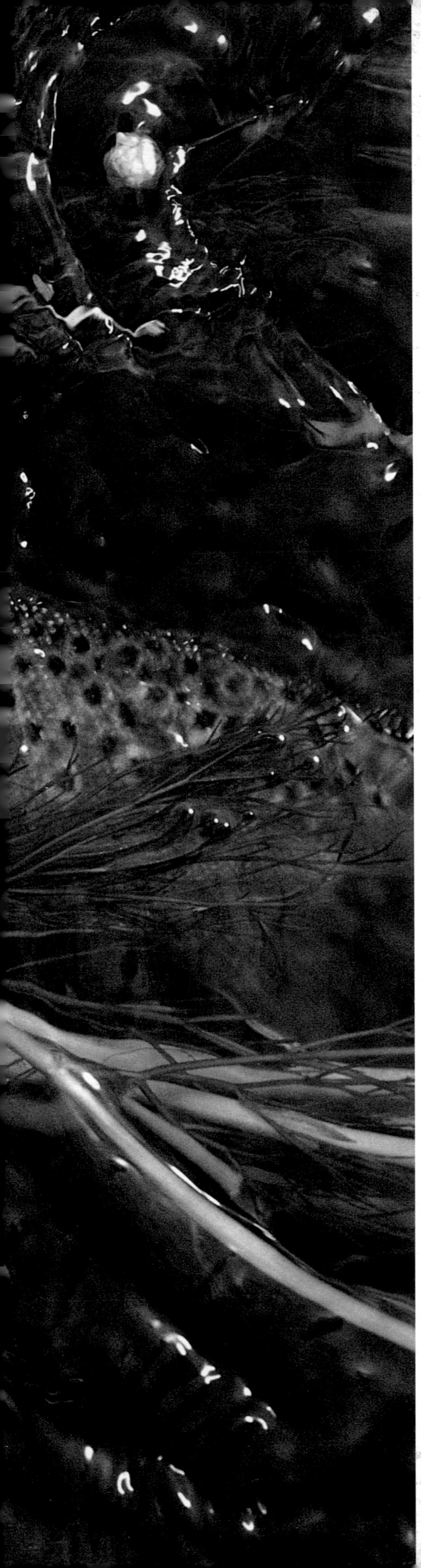

THE FLY

THE CAPTURE, ON ARTIFICIAL FLY, of a fish instilled with all the cunning that evolution bestows, is to many the ultimate angling challenge. Where other methods, such as fishing with a natural bait, may be more effective, fly fishing offers an experience that has tested the angler's skill for many hundreds of years.

Today, except where local fishing rules dictate, our choice of fly is extremely wide but essentially practical. We simply choose the most effective for the prevailing conditions, be it a large streamer or a tiny dry fly. Many new materials, including man-made products, ensure that the development of the artificial fly carries on at a pace more rapid than at any time in its history.

This chapter looks at the various fly classifications, from the gaudiest of attractors to the most delicate of imitative patterns. The major fly groups, including streamers, hairwings, nymphs, wet flies, and dry flies, are all covered, and effective examples are illustrated. The groups include patterns that appeal to a wide range of species, from trout and salmon to pike, bass, and grayling. The link between artifice and nature is also covered, with a review of the main prey items and insect groups that are so important to the angler intent on an imitative approach. This craft of mimicry is further illustrated by an outline of fly tying and the relevant tools and materials.

FLY PATTERNS
The earliest flies were tied to catch the brown trout, but today there are patterns designed for a wide range of freshwater and saltwater species.

NATURALS 1

For the fly fisher intent on an imitative approach, a comprehensive knowledge of the fish's prey is extremely important. Even for the less dedicated, a basic understanding of it provides an important insight into the way that a fish will respond to an artificial fly. There are seven main groups of creatures of interest to the fly fisher and imitated or suggested by artificial flies: mayflies (Ephemeroptera); caddis flies (Trichoptera); stoneflies (Plecoptera); chironomids or non-biting midges (Diptera); damselflies and dragonflies (Odonata); crustaceans and fish; and terrestrials, creatures that find their way inadvertently onto the water.

FEEDING TROUT
Brown trout will take full advantage of whatever food is available. Try to use a fly pattern that corresponds to the naturals that the fish are feeding on at the time.

MAYFLIES

The order Ephemeroptera encompasses the up-wing flies and olives that are among the most important insects to the fly fisher. They are called "up-wing" because they fold their wings vertically when at rest, as a butterfly does.

The life cycle begins with the egg hatching into a larva or nymph. This is the longest-lived stage, which (depending on the species) feeds on detritus, small organisms, or algae until fully developed. Once mature, it rises to the water's surface, emerging as the subimago, or dun. Although winged, it is not yet sexually mature, and it must cast its skin one more time to become the imago, or spinner. Its task then is simply to reproduce.

The largest of all the up-wings are the mayflies, genus *Ephemera*, which measure 1 in (2.5 cm) or so in body length. Although the mayflies are the largest of the group, smaller species, including the medium olive, blue-winged olive, iron blue, and spurwings, have longer seasons and are taken more often by fish. Some, such as *Caenis*, are so small that imitations are tied on hooks as tiny as size 24.

FEMALE MAYFLY SPINNER
The imago, or spinner, of the mayfly Ephemera danica *is a handsome creature with sparkling, dark-veined wings. After mating, the female returns to the water to lay her eggs. With this task accomplished, her life is over, and she falls spent upon the water's surface. The trout are quick to take advantage.*

FEMALE MAYFLY DUN
The subimago, or dun, of the mayfly emerges toward mid-day, when it may elicit a spectacular rise of fish.

GREENWELL'S GLORY
This, perhaps the most famous of all up-wing imitations, was devised in 1854 by Canon Greenwell and James Wright to tempt large brown trout on Scotland's River Tweed.

POND OLIVE NYMPH
This has the typical profile of nymphs of the family Baetidae, which also includes the medium olive and large dark olive. They are all basically olive in color, well camouflaged to avoid detection by predators, and because of their ability to move quickly when necessary are called "agile darters."

OLIVE NYMPH
This is a simple, general tying to suggest a wide range of up-wing nymphs. It uses a pale olive fur body plus dark pheasant tail fibers to mimic the coloration of the natural close to emergence. It should be fished dead-drift or with a slow retrieve.

Caddis Flies

Caddis or sedge flies are to be found on both still and running water, and their life cycle includes larval, pupal, and adult stages. They are mothlike insects belonging to the order Trichoptera, which means "hairy-winged"; caddis flies have hairs on their wings, whereas the wings of moths are covered in tiny, dustlike scales.

The larva is soft bodied, and many species build protective cases from stones, sand, weeds, even small snail shells. There are also caseless caddis fly larvae, however, and these include species of *Hydropsyche* and *Rhyacophila*. The larva is an active creature with a pair of specially adapted, hair-fringed legs that enable it to swim strongly.

When pupation occurs, even the caseless species build a protective case, which is usually anchored to a large rock. When fully developed, the pupa uses its strong jaws to cut itself free of its case. It then rises to the surface, at which point its skin splits along the thorax and the adult emerges. The adult has four wings, which lie along the body when at rest, and these give the caddis its typical roof-winged profile.

CADDIS LARVA CASES
The protective cases built by the larvae of many caddis species are bonded together by a tough material that is secreted by the creatures.

CADDIS PUPA
This imitation of a medium-sized caddis pupa mimics the natural's curved body and antennae.

ADULT SEDGE
The adult sedge has long antennae and four wings. Species range in size from ¼ in (6 mm) up to 1½ in (38 mm) in the case of the great red sedge Phryganea grandis.

Fish & Crustaceans

The diet of trout and bass is not restricted to insects; various baitfish also make up a proportion of their diet. Many not only provide a substantial meal but are to be found in convenient, tightly packed schools, just there for the taking. Silvery-flanked species such as minnows and some panfish are very important on stillwaters, where trout can go into a veritable feeding frenzy as they charge into the schools. On rivers, minnows and small bottom-dwelling species are the selected prey.

Crustaceans, too, rank high on the dietary list. Most numerous are the freshwater shrimps, such as *Gammarus*, which are bottom-dwelling creatures ranging in length from ¼ in (6 mm) to ¾ in (18 mm) and varying in color from a pale, washed-out olive to a rusty brown. Imitations should reflect this if they are to be effective. Another common food item, the water scud (*Asellus*), is similar in size to a freshwater shrimp. This crustacean is most often found in stillwaters, where it occurs in prolific numbers, living and feeding in the bottom detritus.

MILLER'S THUMB
Sculpins such as the miller's thumb are heavily preyed upon, particularly by large brown trout.

FRESHWATER SHRIMP
The freshwater shrimp, Gammarus, *forms an important part of the diet of both stillwater and river trout. Imitations should be well weighted, and similar in color to the naturals.*

WATER SCUD
This dull, insignificant-looking creature inhabits many lakes and slow rivers in huge numbers.

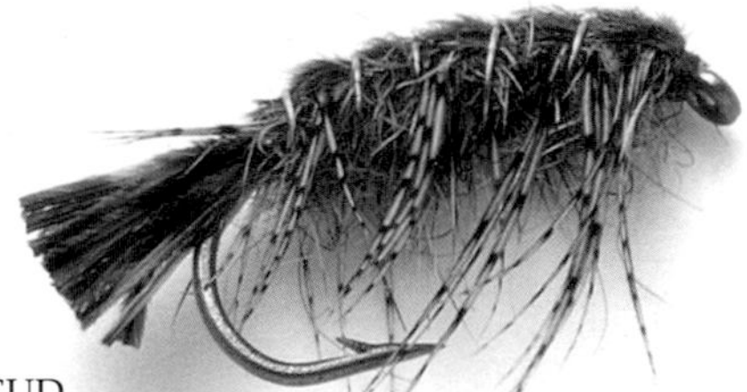

SCUD
Hare fur, brown partridge, and dark turkey tail make an effective copy of the natural.

NATURALS 2

DAMSELFLIES & DRAGONFLIES

Summer would not really be the same without the sight of these large predatory insects darting around marginal vegetation as they quarter their territories. Both belong to the order Odonata but are grouped into suborders, the damselflies being Zygoptera while the dragonflies are Anisoptera.

Both suborders have an aquatic nymphal stage, which is also predatory and feeds on tiny aquatic creatures. The adults of damselflies may be distinguished from adult dragonflies by their slimmer bodies and by the way they fold their wings along their bodies when at rest; the dragonflies hold their wings out horizontally. Both nymphs and adults are taken by fish such as bass and trout, and good imitations can prove very successful when cast around weedbeds and partly submerged timber.

DAMSELFLY NYMPH *(left)*
The damselfly nymph may be distinguished from the dragonfly nymph by its much slimmer appearance and the three leaflike gills on the tip of the abdomen. It comes in a wide range of shades of olive and brown to mimic its habitat.

DAMSELFLY
A dry damselfly imitation can prove effective in summer, when trout and bass leap to take the natural insects.

COMMON BLUE DAMSELFLY *(below)*
The common blue damselfly, Enallagma cyathigerum, *is a well-known sight around lakes. When mature, the nymph climbs free of the water, its skin splits along the back, and the adult emerges.*

STONEFLIES

Stoneflies, which are insects of the order Plecoptera, are creatures of stony or gravel-bottomed rivers. On these waters, particularly in their nymphal form, they form an important part of the diet of trout and other fish.

Most species are brown or black, but a few are much brighter, notably the aptly named Yellow Sally. At rest, the hard, shiny, heavily veined wings are held flat along the top of the body. The aquatic nymphal stage (or creeper) of the stonefly is an active creature, scuttling over the rocks that are its habitat. When mature, it clambers free of the water, usually onto marginal rock. The skin along the back of the thorax splits and the adult emerges.

Although trout will take the female returning to lay her eggs, the nymph is the most important stage to the fly fisher. A heavily weighted nymph imitation, allowed to drift just off the bottom, can prove very effective during high water conditions.

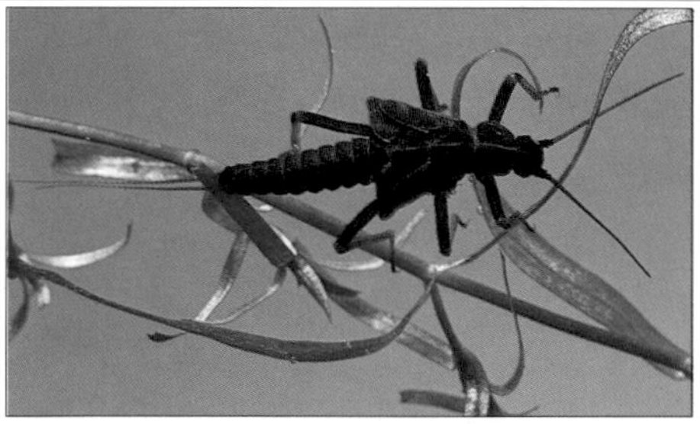

STONEFLY NYMPH
The stonefly nymph differs from the nymphs of up-winged flies in having two tails rather than three.

DRY STONEFLY
When female stoneflies return to lay their eggs, flopping along on the water's surface, trout feeding on them will often take a dry imitation of the correct size.

ADULT STONEFLY
Stoneflies vary in length from less than ¼ in (6 mm), in the case of small species such as needle flies, to the 2 in (5 cm) of the Pteronarcys *species. Although they are capable of flight, many stoneflies are happy to crawl through bankside cover.*

CHIRONOMIDS

The various species of chironomid, or non-biting midge, belonging to the genus *Chironomus* make up a very large proportion of the stillwater trout's diet. The life cycle begins when the egg hatches into a small, wormlike larva that burrows into the bottom mud. Chironomid larvae vary in color from pale olive and brown to the vivid blood-red of the *Chironomus plumosus* larva, known as the bloodworm. The bloodworm receives its color from hemoglobin, a substance that enables it to thrive in the black, oxygen-poor mud of lakebeds.

When the larvae pupate, the pupae remain within their mud burrows until fully developed, a period that can be as little as 36 hours. Then they rise to the surface to transform into adults, where they are at the mercy of the trout, which take them in truly prodigious quantities. The pupae are taken not only as they rise but also at the very point of emergence as adults.

ADULT CHIRONOMID
The adults of the chironomids have slim bodies and two wings, and range in size from the merest wisp up to ½ in (12 mm) or more. They vary in color from black and brown to bright green.

MIDGE PUPA
Imitations of chironomid pupae should mimic the bulbous-thoraxed profiles of the naturals.

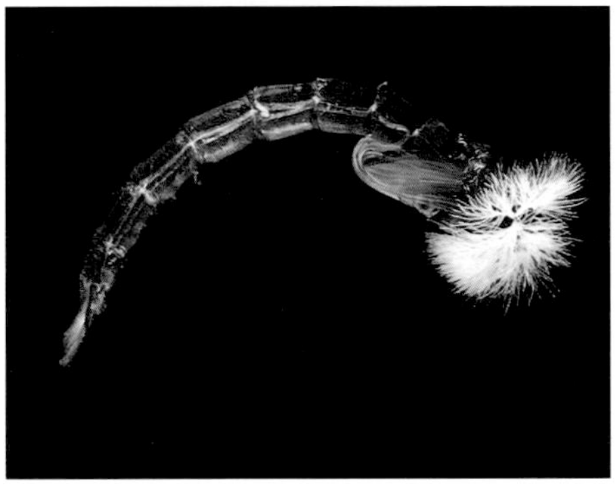

CHIRONOMID PUPA
Although varying in size, all chironomid pupae have slim abdomens, bulbous thoraxes, and white breathing filaments. Black is the most common color.

TERRESTRIALS

Not all creatures that find themselves engulfed by large predatory fish are aquatic: many are terrestrials, which are non-aquatic insects and other life forms that are carried or fall onto the water's surface. Many, such as spiders, beetles, hoverflies, ants, and aphids, are blown onto the water by the wind. On large, windswept expanses of water, it is common for winged insects to be blown out over the surface. Many of them succumb to the waves, or are simply weak fliers that have to touch down on the water.

The large, gangling-legged crane fly is one such insect. Also known as the daddy longlegs, it is usually at its most numerous during the damp days of autumn, when it can produce a confident rise of feeding fish. Earlier in the year, the hawthorn fly and related species can find their way onto rivers and lakes with similar results.

Terrestrials make up a large part of the diet of many fish, including trout, in rainfed rivers. The water in this type of river is often deficient in nutrients, resulting in a poor aquatic biomass. In such waters the trout are opportunist feeders, quick to snap up caterpillars, beetles, and indeed any unfortunate small creature that happens to fall from bankside vegetation.

CRANE FLY
To be effective, imitations of the crane fly, or daddy longlegs, should always include the long, trailing legs of the natural.

HAWTHORN FLY
This large, jet-black fly is on the wing during late spring, when the long-legged males hover in small swarms around bankside vegetation.

BLACK ANT
This pattern is useful during the sultry days of late summer, when swarms of flying ants often appear.

GUM BEETLE
The iridescent gum beetle is very popular with Australian brown and rainbow trout.

The Artificial Fly

The artificial fly is the link between the fly fisherman and the fish, and designing it offers the angler the challenge of creating the illusion of a delicate insect or other small creature from a handful of inanimate objects. The fly and the skill of presentation then come together to seduce the fish into taking that fly, either from aggression or from the belief that it is a living creature. It is this pitting of the angler's abilities against the natural guile of the fish that gives fly fishing its special appeal.

ORANGE BUSTARD

GOLDEN DRAKE

FLY HISTORY
The first stirrings of modern fly design began in 1676 with Charles Cotton's chapter in The Compleat Angler *listing 65 effective fly patterns. The creation of new patterns reached its peak in the late 19th and early 20th centuries.*

Attractors & Deceivers

Artificial flies fall into two main groups: attractors and deceivers. Attractors are usually gaudy, bright creations designed to stimulate a predatory fish's aggression; they suggest nothing edible but provoke a predatory response. Orange and yellow are favorite colors for attractor flies. Deceivers are intended to fool the fish into mistaking them for natural food items, such as nymphs, crustaceans, or small fish. This group includes dry flies, nymphs, and some wet-fly patterns, particularly those that are direct imitations of a fish's food. Deceivers are usually subtle in coloration, mimicking the hues of the naturals.

ATTRACTOR

DECEIVER

Types of Fly

WINGED WET FLY

WINGED DRY FLY

NYMPH

HAIRWING

Wet flies
Wet flies are effective on a wide range of water types, from rivers and streams to vast, windswept lakes, but all have one thing in common: they are fished beneath the water's surface. Some wet flies are subtly colored deceivers, while the more gaudy types of dressing work as attractors.

Wet-fly types vary from simple spider patterns, with merely a few turns of hackle at the eye, to intricate dressings with hackles both along the hook and at the throat, plus a wing. Many of the winged wet flies used for stillwater boat fishing are of this latter type.

Another type, palmers, have rough, dubbed bodies with hackles running the entire length.

Dry flies
The dry fly is designed to float on the water's surface. To prevent it from sinking, water-repellent hackles are wound around the hook to distribute the weight over the surface. The hackles also simulate the legs and "buzz" of an aquatic or terrestrial insect trapped on the water.

Most dry flies are deceivers, and many patterns are designed to imitate specific insects; examples include the Blue Winged Olive, Grannom, and Crane Fly. Others, such as the Wickham's Fancy and the Adams, are more general designs that are intended just to look edible.

Dry flies may be simply hackled, or tied with wings, depending on the level of imitation required.

Nymphs
A nymph is the immature stage of certain aquatic insects such as mayflies and damselflies. Imitations of this stage are likewise termed nymphs, and the term is also applied to wingless patterns that suggest the larval and pupal stages of insects. Natural nymphs have somber hues, so the artificials are similarly colored. Browns, olives, and greens are especially effective, as are mottled shades.

Emergers
Emergers are tied to imitate that stage of an aquatic insect's life when it actually emerges, at the water's surface, from its nymphal or pupal skin. While trapped on the surface, emerging insects are particularly vulnerable to fish predation.

Streamers and hairwings
Streamer and hairwing flies, which are generally large and tied on long-shanked hooks, include the majority of salmon and steelhead patterns. The difference between streamers and hairwings is simply that the wings of streamers are tied with feathers, such as marabou or rooster hackles, while those of hairwings are tied with hair, including bucktail.

Like wet flies, streamers and hairwings may be brightly colored attractors or more subtle deceivers, and many have an imitative role. For example, some are tied to imitate the small fish that are eaten by predators such as trout and pike. These patterns often incorporate white and silver materials.

Parts of a Fly

The head
The head is normally the last part of the fly to be tied, and usually consists of turns of tying thread that hold in place the wing, the hackle, and the loose ends of both rib and body materials. Because it secures these other components it is the weak point of the fly, and therefore it is important that the thread is finished off correctly and that the bare turns are well protected. The head is protected by coats of varnish, which are applied with either the tip of a fine needle or a specially designed applicator. When colored threads are used, clear varnish gives the best results, though for streamers and other large flies, two or three coats of black or red varnish produce a smooth, glossy effect.

The wing
In both dry and wet flies the wing often suggests that of a natural insect, but may be added simply to provide movement. This is particularly the case in those wet flies and streamers that use mobile wing materials, such as rooster hackles, to give "life" to the fly. Many feathers and furs are used to produce fly wings, one of the most popular materials being slips taken from the primary feathers of game birds. Duck feathers are especially useful, and the smoky shades of mallard and teal closely match the wing coloration of many species of mayfly.

The tail
In dry flies the tail not only acts in an imitative way, suggesting that of the natural, but also, by becoming trapped on the surface of the water, it balances the fly and helps it to float. In wet flies and streamers the tail is usually decorative rather than functional; often brightly colored, it is added to give the fly extra fish-attracting allure.

Rooster hackle fibers are often used for imitative tails, while for a brighter effect, wool, fluorescent floss, hair, and golden pheasant toppings and tippets are all very popular. Highly mobile materials are also widely used; marabou, dyed in a variety of colors, gives a wonderfully sinuous action to a wide range of large nymphs and lead-headed patterns.

Hooks
Fly hooks range from the tiny midge-sized models to giant long-shanks, with single, double, or treble points, depending on their use. Worldwide, singles are by far the most popular for all types of fly.

The hackle
Hackles, in their various forms, are the basis of the vast majority of fly patterns. Although a range of feathers may be used, it is those taken from the necks or "capes" of domestic poultry that provide the hackle on over 90 percent of artificial flies. The diversity of colors and stiffnesses, found in both male and female plumage, has shaped the whole development of wet flies and dry flies throughout their history.

In dry flies, it is inevitably the stiffer-fibered, more water-repellent rooster hackles that provide the flotation. The softer hen hackle is preferred for wet flies and streamers, where its ability to become rapidly waterlogged is a prime factor. Soft hackles also work better in the water, providing movement and a semblance of life to what is an otherwise dead object.

Where softness and mobility are the prerequisite, rather than the ability to float, other types of feather may be used. Feathers from species such as grouse, snipe, partridge, and mallard are all effective examples; their coloration mimics superbly that of many natural nymphs and pupae.

The body
The body of a fly covers the bulk of the hook and provides the substance of a pattern. A wide range of materials is used, from somber furs to flashy metallic products. On imitative patterns, or those that merely suggest a living creature, fur (or a man-made substitute) gives a wonderful shaggy effect, especially when teased out. Smoother effects are produced by floss, flat metal tinsel, or Lurex. Mylar tubing, with its scaly appearance, is particularly good for imitations of small fish. Feather fiber also gives an interesting texture: goose, turkey, and cock pheasant tail are effective examples.

Detached body
The detached body is the only type that is not formed around the hook: it is created out of plastic, deer hair, or feather and secured to the hook at one end only, projecting back over the bend. Its advantages, even on a large fly, are that it is light and it allows the use of a much smaller hook.

The rib
The function of a rib is threefold. First, it mimics the segmentation of the body of an insect or small crustacean. Second, if made from a sparkling material, such as metal tinsel or Lurex, it adds extra flash to a pattern, or, on more imitative dressings, it is used to suggest the gases trapped within an emerging insect's skin. Third, a tough material (metal wire for example) adds to the durability of the fly, holding a delicate body in place or protecting it from the ravages of a predatory fish.

Traditionally, wire and metal twists were used to rib all types of fly. Plain wire is still very popular, and now comes in a variety of colors. While metals are fine for patterns intended to sink, their weight is a disadvantage on flies intended to sit on or in the surface. Here, lighter materials are better. Nylon monofilament is a robust alternative, while Lurex, although more delicate, works superbly on emerger-style patterns. Colored, translucent plastic strands produce a very lifelike segmented effect on nymph and pupa imitations.

Fly-Tying Equipment

Before you can begin tying your own flies, you need to obtain the basic tools and materials. For tools, a vise, scissors, hackle pliers, and a bobbin holder are all that are really necessary at first, and the other tools can be purchased as you gain experience. The most difficult decision is what to choose from the dazzling array of furs and feathers available. The best solution to this is to take a look at three or four of your favorite patterns, make a note of all the ingredients, and then use this as your shopping list.

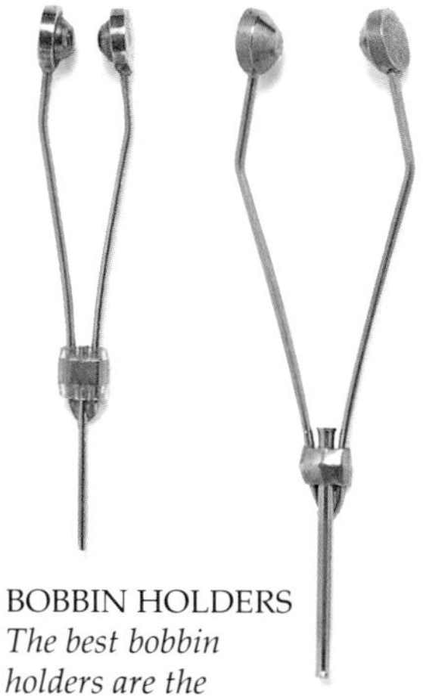

BOBBIN HOLDERS
The best bobbin holders are the spigot type, where the bobbin is held by sprung metal arms. The thread is fed off through a tube.

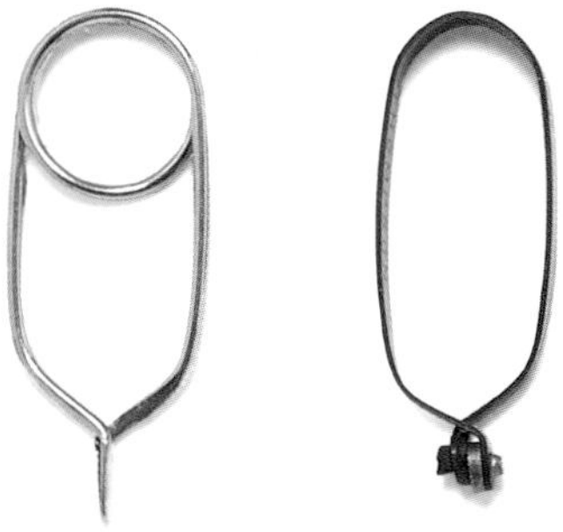

HACKLE PLIERS
Hackle pliers are used to wind hackles, chenille, and other materials. The simplest and best are made of sprung metal, with either smooth metal or rubber-covered jaws to prevent them cutting the hackle material.

DUBBING NEEDLE
A fine, sharp needle has many uses, such as dividing wing slips or picking out dubbed body material to create a ragged effect. You can buy a specially made dubbing needle or use a large sewing needle.

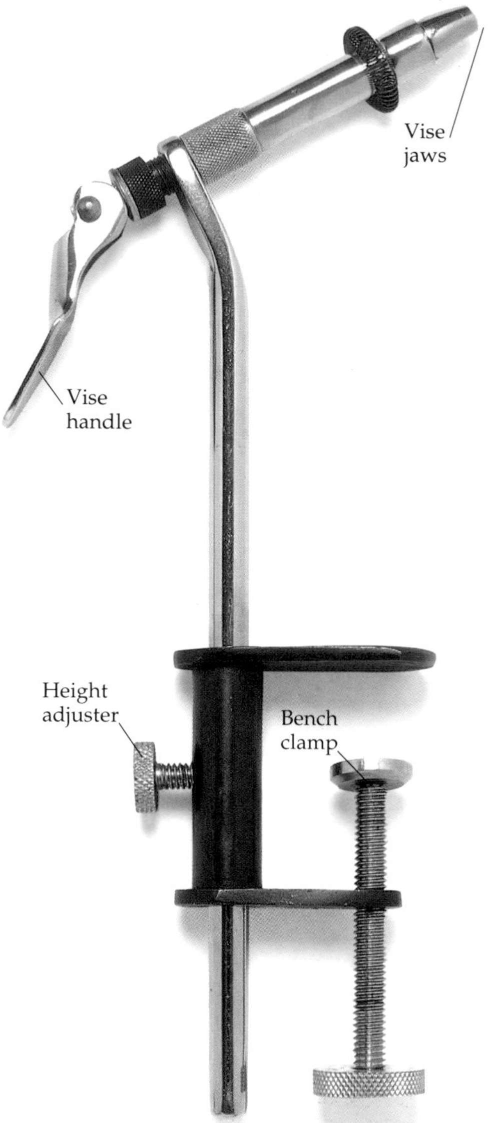

VISE
Of all the tools used by the fly tier, the vise is certainly the most important. It is the means by which the hook is held stationary while all the threads and materials are added to produce the finished fly. The hook is held between a pair of metal jaws, which can be adjusted to accommodate a wide range of hook sizes and diameters of wire. Various types of vise are available. Some have simple screw-tightened jaws, while on others the jaws are spring loaded or, as in the type shown here, are operated by a single cam lever. Whichever type of mechanism is used, the mark of a good vise is that it holds the hook securely, allowing no movement.

SHARP-NOSED SCISSORS
Scissors, with either straight or curved blades, are extremely important to the fly tier. The base of the jaws is used to cut tough materials, leaving the tips sharp enough for precise trimming.

HAIR STACKER
Producing a neat hairwing with all the tips even is not easy: all too often the hairs remain staggered. Using a hair stacker enables you to get the tips neatly aligned.

WHIP FINISH TOOL
The whip finish tool is very useful if you find the hand whip finish difficult, or when materials are very close to the eye of the hook. The standard tool has two wire arms over which the thread is looped.

DUBBING TWISTER
Looping the dubbing produces some interesting effects. This tool uses sprung metal arms to hold the loop open, and its weight helps you to spin the thread.

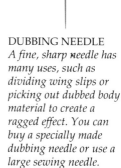

BOBBIN THREADER
Using this simple tool makes it much easier to feed thread through the thin tube of a spigot bobbin holder.

PHEASANT FEATHERS

The feathers of many species of pheasant are used for tying flies, especially the center tails of both sexes of the ring-necked pheasant. The most colorful pheasant feathers are used for salmon patterns.

CAPES

The hackles from the capes of domestic poultry form the basis of most flies. The soft hackles of hens are good for wet flies, while the more water-repellent rooster hackles are used for dry flies.

TEAL WINGS

The primary feathers of a number of duck species, including teal, offer pale gray shades that mimic those found in the wings of many natural up-winged flies.

DUCK FEATHERS

Among the most popular duck feathers used in fly tying are bronze and speckled gray mallard feathers and the barred black-and-white feathers of the teal and pintail. The striking black-and-white and speckled, lemon feathers of the wood duck are also used.

SQUIRREL TAIL

Although the gray, white, and black tail hair of the gray squirrel may be used in its natural state, bleaching it and then dyeing it with pure colors vastly increases its versatility as a fly material.

MARABOU

Once obtained from the marabou stork, this highly mobile feather now comes from the domestic white turkey.

PEACOCK HERL

The herl (barbs) of the male peacock's eye feather produce sparkling, bulbous bodies and thoraxes.

TYING THREAD

Fly-tying thread was originally made of natural silk, but today silk has been almost entirely superseded by man-made fibers, such as nylon, which are much stronger and also rotproof. Tying threads are sold in many colors, either plain or pre-waxed.

RAYON FLOSS

Like tying thread, floss was originally made from silk. Today, fibers such as rayon are used to make multi-stranded, rotproof floss that spreads and flattens as it is wound, helping to produce a neat body.

TINSEL

Tinsel gives sparkle to the fly and protects delicate body materials.

WOOL

Natural or man-made wool is used to make tails, or wound or teased out and dubbed to form fat, "buggy" fly bodies.

VARNISH

Varnish is used to protect the bare threads at the eye of the hook. Clear or colored varnish may be used, but for bonding materials in place, an adhesive varnish with a vinyl base is much better.

MYLAR TUBING

This sparkling, metallic-finish tubing has a wonderful scale-effect surface, perfect for producing the bodies of fish fry imitations.

POLYPROPYLENE FLOSS

This light, water-repellent material is ideal for both bodies and for the wings of dry flies that imitate "spent" naturals.

Fly-Tying Basics 1

The ability to tie flies is one of the fly fisher's greatest assets, and fly tying is also a source of considerable pleasure in itself. Tying flies allows the individual angler to develop new and effective patterns, or to make subtle adjustments to an established dressing to increase its fish-catching potential. To the angler-entomologist it is an indispensable skill: to watch a fish taking a particular insect, then to construct an imitation good enough to fool that fish into taking it, elicits a sense of satisfaction rarely found elsewhere in angling.

FLY TYING
The pleasures of fly fishing are greatly enhanced when you use flies that you have tied yourself.

Starting Off & Whip Finishing

There is obviously little point in beginning to tie a fly if you do not know how to start off the tying thread. What may not be so obvious is that it is equally important to learn how to finish the fly securely: without a robust finish, the fly will simply fall apart during fishing. Starting the thread off properly allows you to build a neat, strong bed to which you will attach the rest of the materials; neatness and strength are the secret of constructing a tidy, robust fly. The whip finish is the most secure way of finishing a fly. It entails winding a loop of thread over itself repeatedly then pulling it tight, and bedding the loose end beneath turns of thread produces a firm finish that will take a good deal of punishment.

Starting off

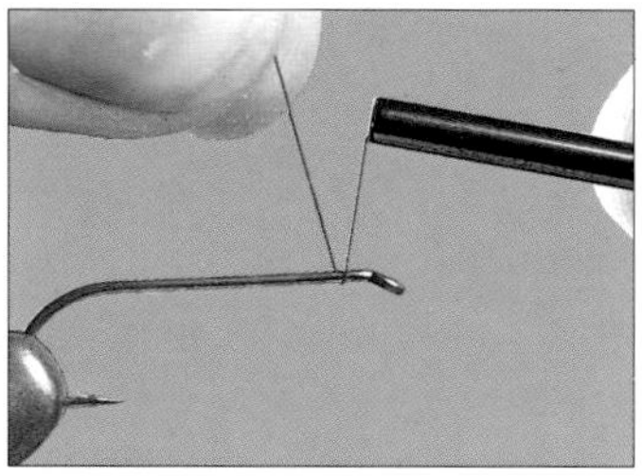

1 Fix the hook securely in a vise. Next, loop the thread beneath the hook, forming an upright V-shape.

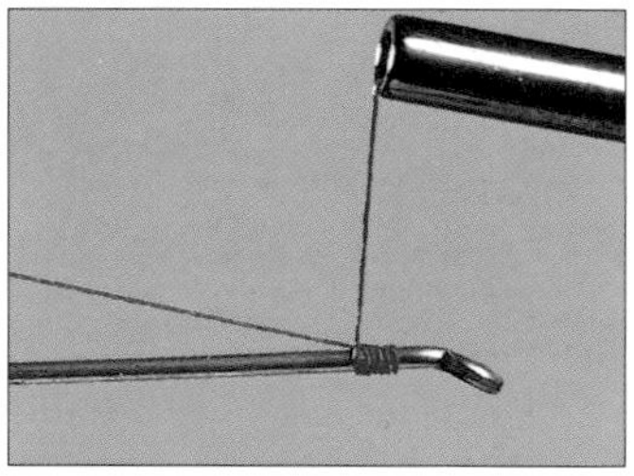

2 Hold the loose end of thread taut and wind the bobbin end over it. Wind until the loose end is trapped.

Whip finishing by hand

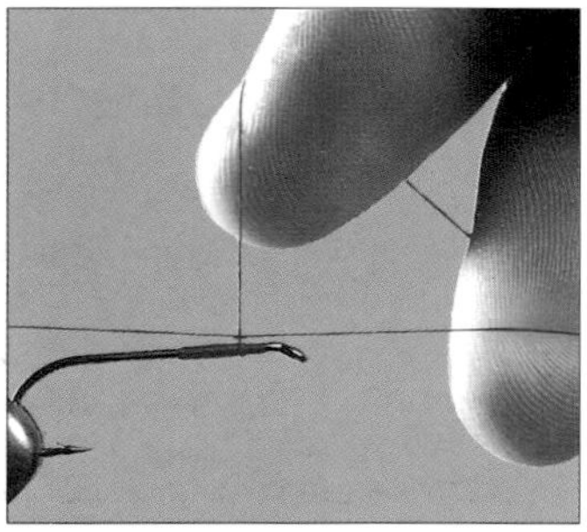

1 When the fly is complete, form a figure-4-shaped loop over the first two fingers of your right hand.

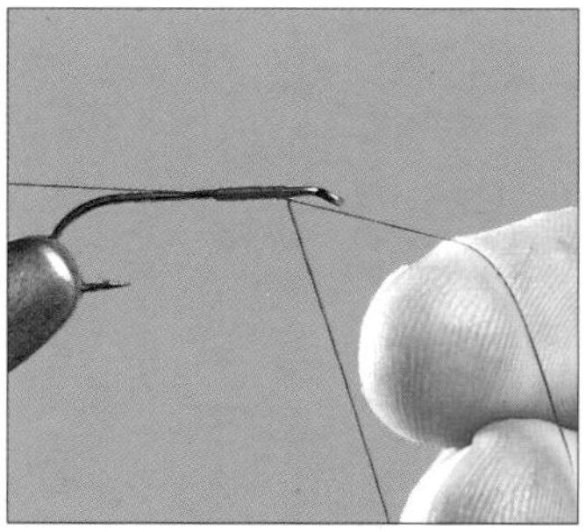

2 Flip the fingers around, bringing them beneath the hook. This takes the vertical strand over the loose end.

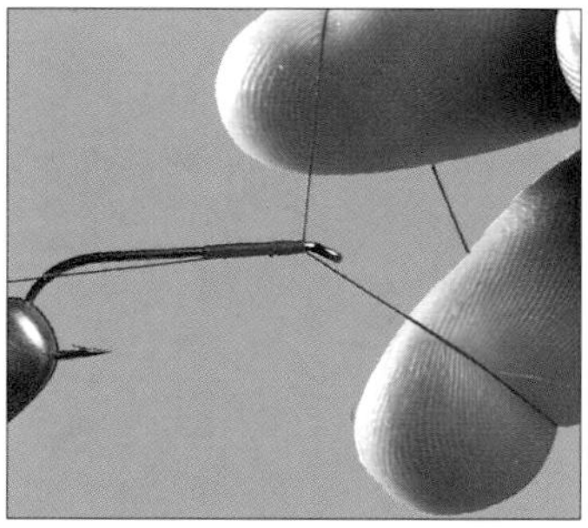

3 Repeat four or five times, ensuring that the loop is wound neatly over the loose end lying back along the hook.

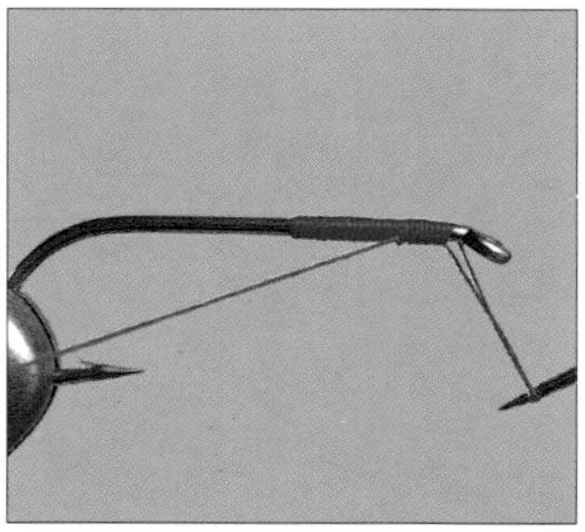

4 Slip the thread off the fingers, draw the loop tight, and insert a dubbing needle into it to retain tension.

Using a whip finish tool

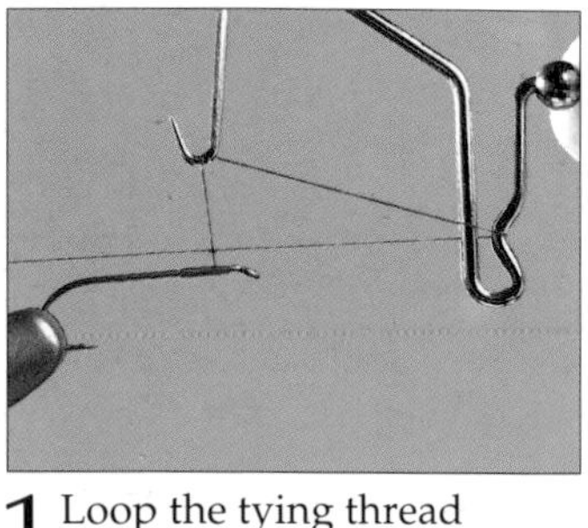

1 Loop the tying thread around the two prongs of the whip finish tool. Then bring the thread back to form a figure-4 shape.

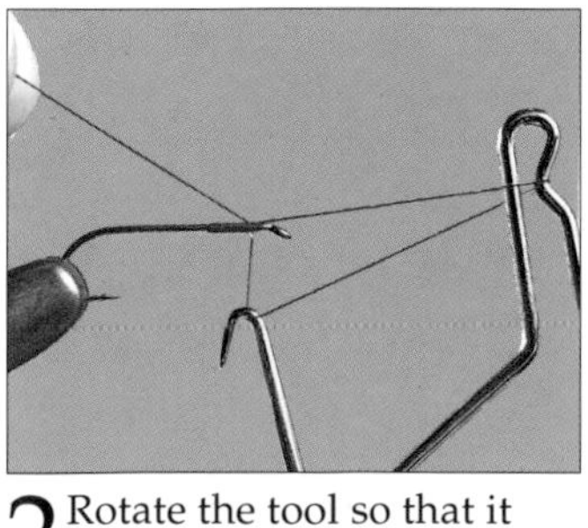

2 Rotate the tool so that it falls beneath the hook, trapping the loose end. This movement forms the first turn of the whip finish.

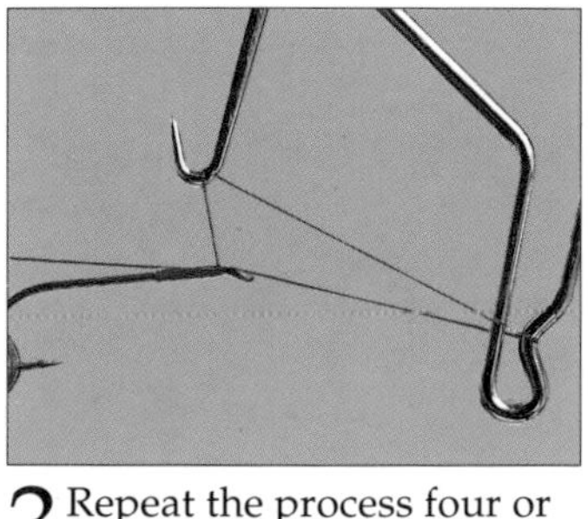

3 Repeat the process four or five times. When you are happy with the number of turns, slip the thread off the lower prong of the tool.

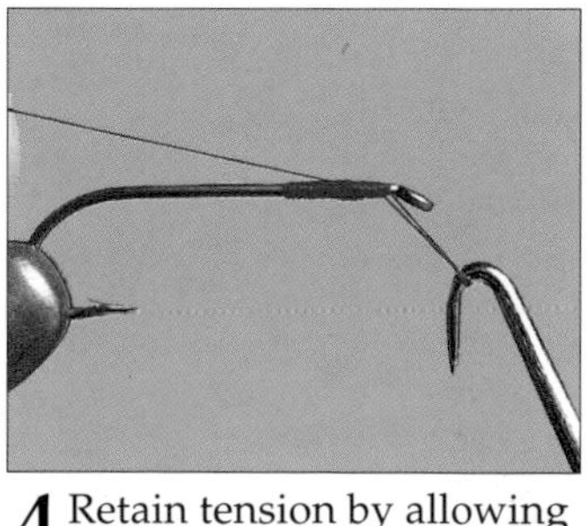

4 Retain tension by allowing the thread to catch on the hooked prong. Steadily pull the loose end of the thread to draw the loop tight.

TAILS

A tail may represent that of a natural insect, impart movement to a fly, or just add a flash of color. The materials used for tails range from rooster hackle fibers to fluorescent floss, and on traditional wet-fly patterns, the black and gold banding of the golden pheasant tippet feather produces a striking effect.

Tying a tail

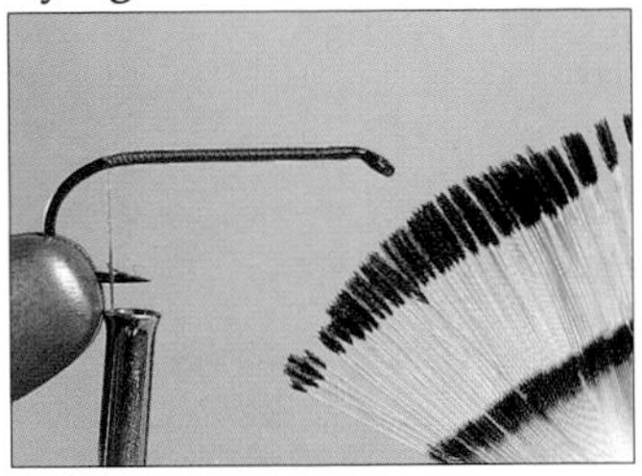

1 Tie the thread to the hook shank opposite the barb. Select a well-marked golden pheasant tippet feather.

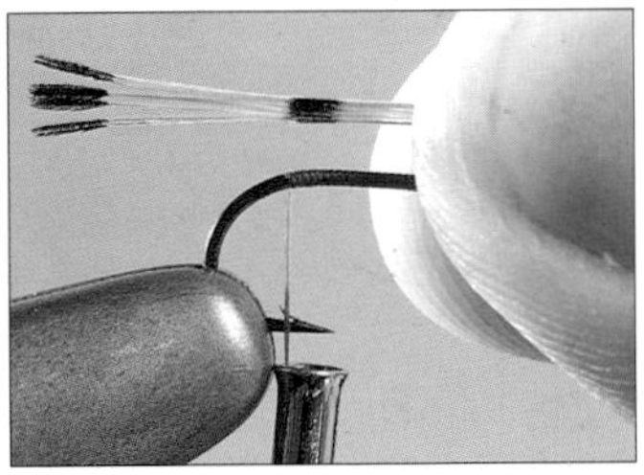

2 Remove five or six fibers from the feather. Offer the bunch up to the hook, extending it beyond the bend.

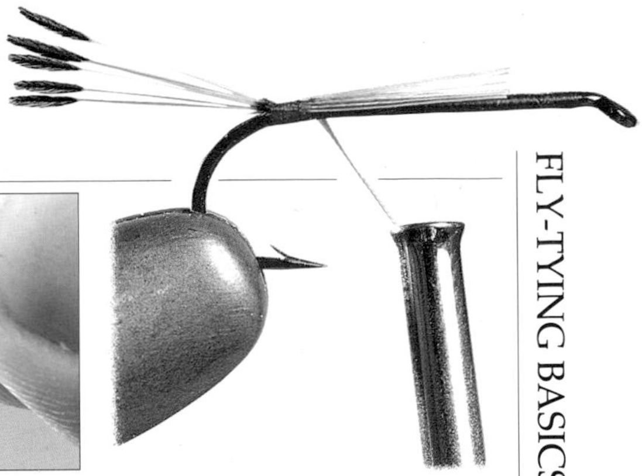

3 Catch in the tail with turns of thread, ensuring it does not twist. The tail should be about half the hook's length.

BODIES

Bodies come in many shapes and sizes, from the slimness of flat tinsel to the ragged effect of dubbed fur. In most patterns, the main task of the body is to provide the substance of the fly.

Most bodies, except those that are detached or of Mylar tubing, are actually wound around the hook shank. Take care to ensure that each turn is as close to the next one as possible, with no gaps.

Tying a tinsel body

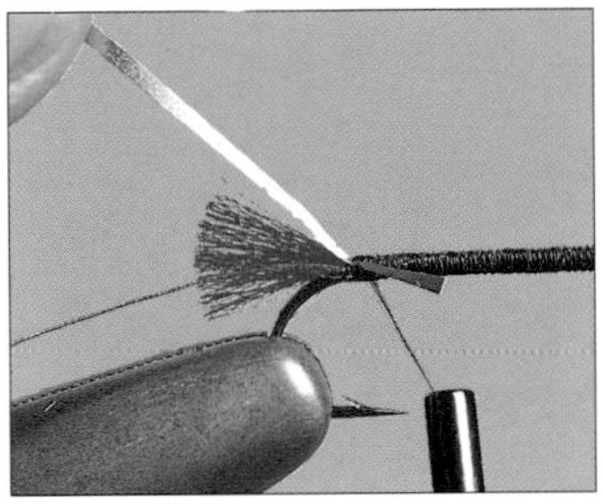

1 Ensure that an even bed has been formed, then cut the tip of the tinsel to a thin "scallop" and catch it in.

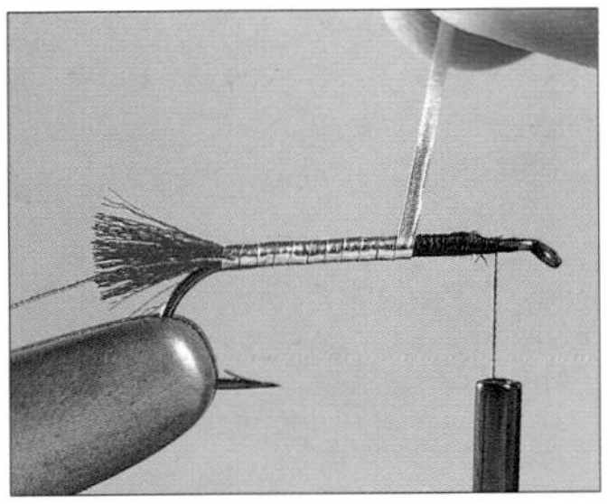

2 Take the tying thread to just short of the eye. Wind the tinsel up the body in tight, closely butted turns.

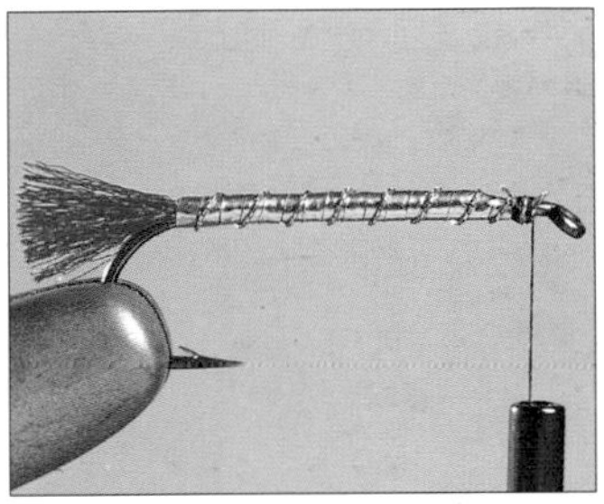

3 Secure the loose end with turns of thread; remove excess tinsel. Wind rib over the body in an open spiral.

Dubbing a body

1 With the rib caught in, offer a small pinch of dubbing up to prewaxed thread. Ensure that the spread is even.

2 Gently twist the dubbing between forefinger and thumb into an even rope. Wind over hook in close turns.

3 Finish the body just short of the eye. Wind the rib, then tease out the fibers of fur with a dubbing needle.

RIBS

The rib provides sparkle and adds strength, whether it is bedding into a soft body or protecting a delicate body or hackle. The perfect rib forms a neat, open spiral, running the length of the body. Colored wires and tinsel are the traditional materials, but nylon monofilament is ideal for ribbing dry flies. Lurex and Crystal Hair both give a superb, non-tarnish sparkle effect.

Tying a rib

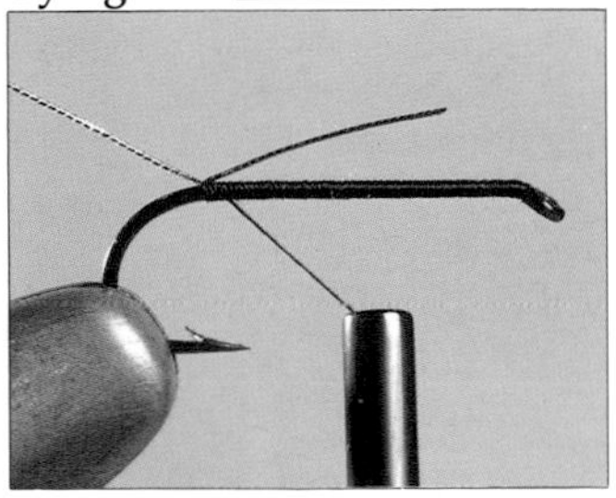

1 Run the tying thread down the hook to a point opposite the barb. There, catch in the ribbing material with several turns of thread.

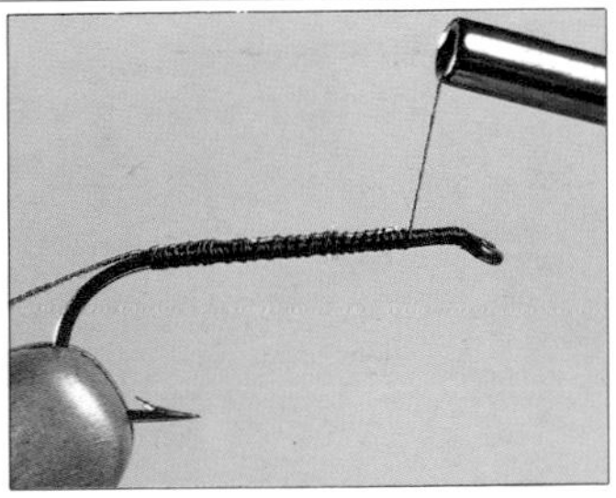

2 Allow the waste end of the ribbing to lie along almost the full length of the hook shank to produce an even underbody.

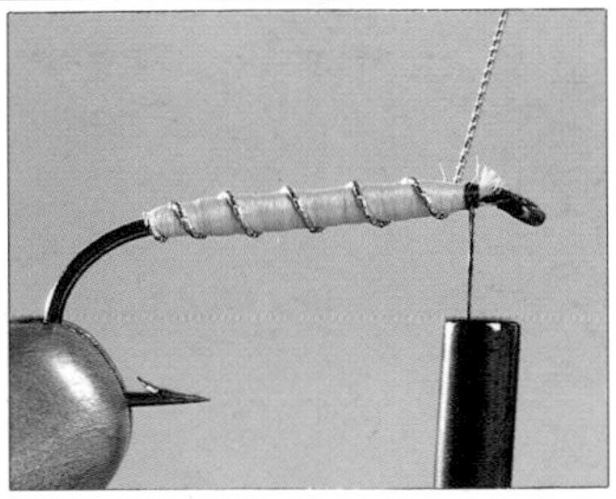

3 Add the body material. Then wind the ribbing material firmly around and along the body so that it forms a neat, open spiral.

Fly-Tying Basics 2

Hackles

The exact function of a hackle depends on the type of fly it is tied on. In wet flies, nymphs, streamers, and in fact any pattern that is fished subsurface, the hackle represents the legs of a nymph or the twitching fins of a small fish. In dry flies and emergers, the hackle is used to suggest the legs and wings of an insect and also to keep the fly afloat. Palmered flies not only have a hackle at the head but also one wound along the body. This produces a dense "bumble" effect, providing great floatability in dry flies and a superb action in wet flies.

Most hackles are made of feathers, but various types of hair may also be adapted into a hackle: rabbit, hare, and squirrel may all be spun in a dubbing loop, then wound over the hook to form a thorax-cum-hackle. It is a technique that lends itself particularly well to nymph and pupa imitations.

Wet-fly hackle

1 Catch in the hackle feather just behind the eye. Make four full turns, using hackle pliers, then secure the tip.

2 Stroke the hackle fibers beneath the hook, fastening them in place with turns of tying thread.

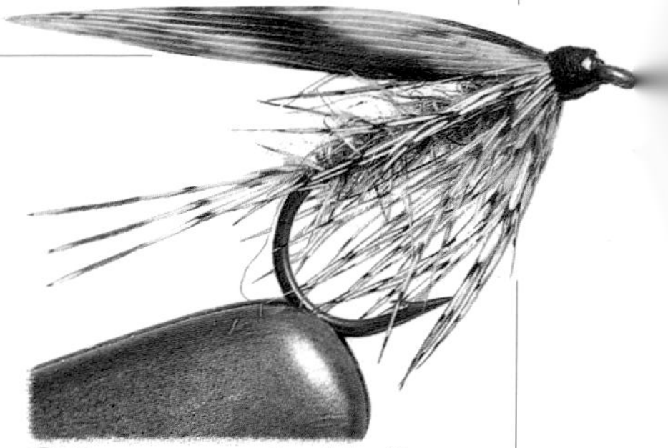

3 Remove any hackle fibers still above the hook or not lying back properly. Finally, add a wing and a whip finish.

Dubbing-loop hackle

1 With the body covering the rear two-thirds of the hook, insert a pinch of hare's fur into a loop of tying thread.

2 Take hold of the loop with a pair of hackle pliers and twist it until the fur spins into a fluffy rope.

3 Wind the fur over the hook up to the eye; trim the thorax top and sides, but leave some hairs beneath the hook.

Dry-fly hackle

1 With the body complete, prepare a rooster hackle by stripping the butt, leaving a short, bare stem.

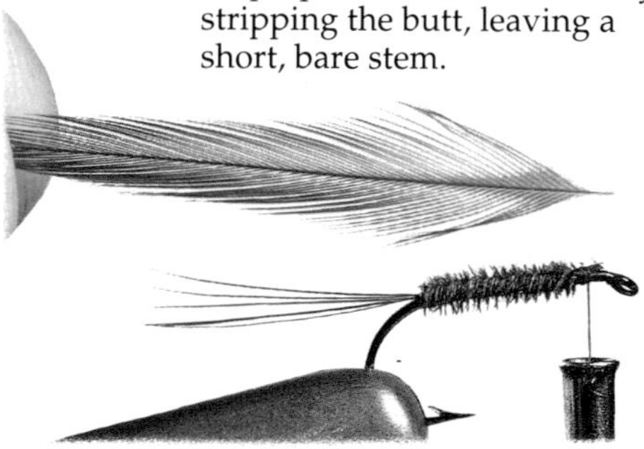

2 Catch in the hackle and take hold of the tip with a pair of hackle pliers. Make three or four full turns.

3 Ensure that the turns are butted together. Secure the hackle tip, remove the waste end, and tie a whip finish.

Palmered hackle

1 With body in place, strip the butt of a rooster hackle, leaving a short, bare stem. Catch in the hackle.

2 Using pliers, wind the hackle down the body to the bend. Ensure each turn is evenly spaced.

3 Wind the ribbing material up through the hackle in the opposite spiral. This will fix the hackle in place.

4 Remove excess hackle at the bend and ribbing at the eye. Add a slightly longer-fibered hackle at the eye.

Wings

Wings can give movement to a fly or, when used in a more imitative role, suggest those of a real insect. In streamers, the traditional wing material is rooster hackle, taken either from the neck or saddle of the bird, but dyed turkey marabou, with its superb, pulsating action, is now the firm favorite. Hairwings use a variety of hair types to provide their profile and to create a stiff, robust appearance well suited to fast water.

Imitative wet-fly and dry-fly wings may be tied in a variety of positions, such as paired, split, or advanced, depending on the insect stage being copied. Paired slips of duck primary feather are the most widely used, but other materials, including hackle points, polypropylene yarn, feather fiber, and even hair, all have their place.

Hackle-point wing

1 With tail and body complete, select two well-marked hackle points with fibers the same length as the hook gap.

2 Remove the base fibers from the bottom of each hackle, leaving two points approximately the same length as the hook shank.

3 Catch the hackle points in by their bare stems and bring them to a vertical position with a few turns of tying thread.

Feather wing

1 With body and hackle in place, remove two equal-sized slips from duck primaries taken from opposite sides of the bird.

2 Place the slips together, curves inward, so the curves cancel each other out. Secure the wing with several turns of thread.

3 With the wing in place, remove the excess stubs of feather before building up a neat head and finally adding a whip finish.

Single wing case

1 When the tail and body are complete, catch in a slip of feather fiber at the rear of the thorax position.

2 Add the thorax (here it is dubbed fur) then stretch the fiber over the back, securing it at the eye.

Hair wing

1 Leaving a space behind the eye, take a small bunch of hair, removing broken hairs before judging for length.

2 With the hair projecting slightly past the bend, fix it in position with locking turns of thread around the base.

Heads

The head may simply be the finishing point of a fly or it may have an extra function: it can be weighted to make the fly sink, or else made buoyant to enable the fly to be "waked" through the water's surface. The Muddler, with its buoyant deer-hair head, is a famous example of this latter group.

Muddler head

1 With body and wing in place, offer up a bunch of deer hair to the hook shank, securing it in place with two loose turns of thread.

2 Pull the thread tight. This makes the hair flare and spin. Add further bunches, if required, and then carefully trim the hair to shape.

3 Using a sharp pair of scissors, clip the hair into a neat bullet shape. Allow a ruff of hair tips to remain as a sort of hackle.

SIMPLE HEAD

DRY FLIES

The term "dry fly" covers a vast and structurally diverse range of patterns, from the merest speck intended to imitate a midge right up to something as bulky as a large caddis fly, mayfly, or dragonfly imitation. The main prerequisite of all dry flies is that they should float on or in the surface, and so they are tied with various light or water-repellent materials. Rooster hackles are the most often-used aid to flotation, but other materials such as deer hair and polypropylene are also used to good effect.

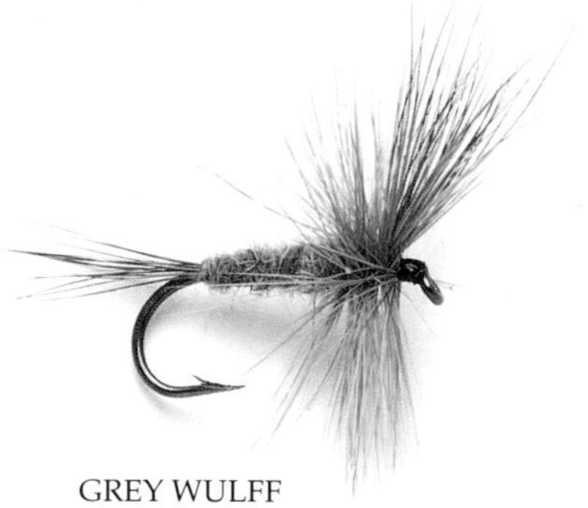

GREY WULFF
This is one of a series of large, well-hackled patterns, devised by the late Lee Wulff, which ride high even in fast-flowing or broken water. This version is a representation of the mayfly Ephemera danica.

IRON BLUE *(right)*
This imitates a number of small, dark, up-winged flies of the genus Baetis, *including* B. muticus. *This hackled pattern is effective during the naturals' main emergence periods of early summer and autumn.*

LETORT HOPPER
Pennsylvania's Letort River gives its name to this simple grasshopper imitation. As in many other imitations of this chunky terrestrial, deer body hair is used for the head and overwing to give the required buoyancy.

DADDY LONGLEGS
The daddy longlegs, or crane fly, is a large, gangling terrestrial and is common in late summer and early autumn. Imitations fished dry or wet often produce better-than-average fish.

TRAUN-WING CADDIS
Traun River Products manufactures meshed, lifelike wing material, which mimics the veining of a caddis fly's wing. Used in conjunction with softer materials, it produces good imitations of many caddis species.

CUT-WING GREEN DRAKE
This pattern uses shaped mallard breast feathers to imitate the wings of a mayfly dun or green drake. The realistic profile makes the fly effective even when the trout have seen everything else.

POLY-WING SPINNER
The water-repellent properties of polypropylene are put to good use here, where the material forms the wing of a small imitation of a spent spinner.

GODDARD SEDGE
This highly buoyant imitation of an adult caddis, devised by John Goddard, is made almost entirely of deer hair. It works well on both stillwaters and streams.

HUMPY
The Humpy uses the buoyancy of deer body hair to keep it riding high even in fast, broken water. It is an excellent general pattern that will take anything from trout in small streams to salmon on wide, powerful rivers.

IRRESISTIBLE
The Irresistible, dressed in a range of sizes, is a truly adaptable pattern that will take trout from small, broken streams and even salmon and steelhead. The key to its effectiveness is the body of spun and clipped deer hair, which produces an almost unsinkable fly.

ADAMS
The Adams has gradually become the most widely used up-winged dun pattern. Its gray fur body, grizzle hackle-point wings, and mixed grizzle and brown hackle give the subtle coloration of a freshly emerged olive dun. It may be tied on hooks ranging in size from a 10 right down to a 24.

BLACK KLINKHAMMER

Hans van Klinken, of the Netherlands, devised this novel variation on the parachute hackle theme. It is tied large on an emerger hook to give it the bent effect typical of an emerging chironomid.

COMPARA-DUN

The easily tied Compara-dun, which was devised by American fly tiers Al Caucci and Bob Nastasi, offers a very lifelike profile of a newly emerged olive dun mayfly.

TROTH CADDIS

Al Troth is the originator of this very effective imitation of an adult caddis fly. It uses a wing of bleached elk hock to create the correct silhouette and make it very buoyant, and is effective on both still and running water.

DUCK'S DUN

Cul de canard feathers, which are taken from around the preen glands of ducks such as mallard, make effective wings for up-wing imitations. The Duck's Dun suggests a wide range of species including the blue-winged olive, medium olive, and lake olive.

EPHEMERELLA SPINNER

This imitates the spent imago or spinner of up-wings of the genus Ephemerella*, such as the blue-winged olive. Its hackle suggests the insect's wings trapped in the surface of the water.*

HARE'S FACE MIDGE

Charles Jardine devised this fine representation of an adult chironomid midge. It uses the sandy fur from a hare's mask to suggest the shading of the natural, plus a wing of cul de canard feather for good visibility.

HAWTHORN FLY

This is a specific imitation of the hawthorn fly Bibio marci*, a terrestrial that gathers in small swarms around bankside vegetation in middle to late spring. Imitations should mimic the size, color, and trailing legs of the natural.*

CLARET HOPPER

The Hopper series has taken the stillwater fishing scene by storm. Dry-fly fishing was once seldom considered an effective technique on lakes and reservoirs, but the Hopper, with its devastating effectiveness even in calm conditions, has changed all that.

GINGER QUILL

This traditional pattern imitates the dun of small to medium-sized olives or up-wings. A strand of peacock eye feather represents segmentation, and slips of gray mallard or starling primary imitate the wing coloration of the natural. Similar patterns include Olive Quill and Red Quill.

THORAX MAYFLY

The speckled, lemon feathers from wood duck are used to mimic the wing color and markings in this imitation of the larger mayfly species such as Ephemera danica.

BEACON BEIGE

This fly, popularized by fly tier Peter Deane, is one of the best general imitations of an olive dun. It uses a mixed hackle of grizzle and brown to give a lifelike "buzz," and the body is of stripped peacock quill.

DAVE'S HOPPER

The Dave in this instance is American fly tier Dave Whitlock, an angler who has put his name to many very effective trout and bass patterns. This wonderful imitation of a grasshopper uses knotted slips of turkey feather to imitate the large jumping legs of the natural.

Wet Flies

The wet fly is designed to fish below the water's surface. In order to accomplish this, many wet flies are tied slim, with wing and hackle swept back to minimize water resistance. Exceptions to this include the palmers, which are dense, bushy-hackled flies created for use on large natural waters. These are designed to make an attractive disturbance in the water's surface as they are retrieved. Other winged wet-fly patterns are tied as general attractors or as the suggestion of an adult insect.

DARK CAHILL
This is the dark member of a pair of patterns created by American fly tier Dan Cahill. With its dark gray body and lemon wood-duck wing it is a fair representation of a number of darker medium-sized species of Ephemeroptera, including members of the genus Stenonema. *It may be fished upstream or in the classic down-and-across style.*

INVICTA
The Invicta, created back in the late 19th century by James Ogden, is as popular today as ever. With its yellow seal-fur substitute body and palmered brown hackle, it makes a fair imitation of an emerging sedge pupa.

PARTRIDGE AND ORANGE
The best known of the Partridge series, and an excellent fly for rough-stream trout and grayling. In this variation, the body is of fur instead of the silk of the original version.

OLIVE BUMBLE
The doyen of Irish fly tiers, T. Kingsmill Moore, created this as part of a range of bumbles designed for the wild conditions found on large Irish waters. It is a big, bushy representation of a mayfly.

MALLARD AND CLARET
A traditional wet-fly pattern, and the most popular and enduring of a large series with bodies and hackles of various colors. The wing of the Mallard and Claret comes from the shoulder feathers of the drake mallard, and the body is of seal-fur substitute. Good for brown trout and sea trout.

BUTCHER
A fly with a long pedigree dating back at least 150 years, when it was known as Moon's Fly. Its name was changed to Butcher in the early 19th century. A fine pattern for both stillwater and river, and good for sea trout.

DUNKELD
Originally the Dunkeld was a fully dressed salmon fly with a married wing. This much-simplified version is an effective attractor pattern for trout, and it works well when fished on the point of a three-fly cast.

SOLDIER PALMER
Although this pattern should really be known as the Red Palmer, it is the dressing most stillwater trout fishers recognize as the Soldier Palmer. A superb top-dropper pattern for fishing the drift, it works well throughout the season and particularly during early summer. An indispensable pattern.

BREADCRUST
Not an imitation of a piece of bread, but a general hackled wet-fly-cum-nymph. Seal-fur substitute or wool is used to build the succulent body, which is ribbed with a stripped brown rooster hackle stem. It provides a fair imitation of a caddis pupa.

DARK WATCHETT
This version of the Dark Watchett, by T. E. Pritt, is a traditional soft-hackled fly that has proved very effective on trout streams.

OLIVE QUILL
A wet-fly member of the popular Quill series, all of which use stripped peacock quill to give the body a striking segmented effect. This version suggests a medium-sized olive such as a lake olive or a large dark olive. Good on both lakes and rivers.

TEAL, BLUE, AND SILVER
With its barred wing and silver body, this member of the Teal series is a fine representation of a small fish. Good for stillwater and river trout, and large versions (up to a size 2 hook) are excellent for night fishing for sea trout.

BIBIO
This highly effective pattern is a good general representation of a number of terrestrials of the Bibionidae family, especially the heather fly, whose red legs are imitated by the brighter central section.

MARCH BROWN
An effective imitation of the natural March brown, Rhithrogena germanica, *this is a very edible-looking fly that works well even on trout that have never seen the natural. It may also be tied in a silver-bodied version.*

SOOTY OLIVE
The lake olives (Cloeon simile) *that hatch from the large limestone loughs of western Ireland are of a particularly dark hue. This pattern uses a dark olive seal-fur substitute body and a brown mallard wing to mimic their coloration. A great fly for early season.*

ROYAL COACHMAN
This definitive American pattern is the gaudy cousin of the Coachman. This, the wet-fly version, is a derivative of John Haily's 1878 dry fly and has spawned a whole range of variants including streamers and hairwings. The wings may vary, but all have the same red central body section, butted on either side with peacock herl. It often works when nothing else will.

GREEN PETER
The Green Peter (Phryganea varia) *is a beautiful caddis species. The imitation is effective even when there are no naturals in evidence, and is a good point fly.*

GOSLING *(right)*
The Gosling is the epitome of the Irish stillwater fly. It is tied to represent the dun of the mayfly Ephemera danica, *which is distributed throughout Europe and hatches in impressive numbers from limestone lakes. It uses an orange rooster hackle, overwound with one of speckled gray mallard flank, to suggest the wings. The color match is hardly perfect, but it certainly does work.*

OAKHAM ORANGE
During the warmer summer months, stillwater rainbows experience what can only be described as "orange madness". As the water warms they become more and more willing to chase bright flies, and little could be brighter than hot orange. This palmered fly, with its tag of fluorescent orange floss, is a very effective pattern either on a floating line or fished slightly deeper.

DOOBRY
The Scottish angler and fly tier, Stan Headley, devised the Doobry for fishing in clear water on overcast days or in colored water in brighter conditions. It is very successful in peaty water, where its combination of black, orange, and gold not only looks very good, but also catches fish.

KATE MCLAREN
A somber, heavily hackled pattern, this fly is named after the wife of Charles McLaren, a truly great sea-trout angler. It is a very effective pattern on large lakes, taking brown trout, sea trout, and salmon, and works well as a top-dropper fly.

NYMPHS

Although the word "nymph" refers to the larval stages of a number of aquatic insect species, to the fly fisher it has become a far more general term. Along with the true nymphs, it includes insect pupae, small crustaceans, and even general patterns used to suggest something small and edible. The diversity of flies classified as nymphs is truly astounding, ranging from tiny imitations of larval up-wings and midge pupae to the veritable giants that mimic creatures as different as dragonfly and stonefly nymphs.

SUSPENDER BUZZER
This Brian Leadbetter pattern imitates the chironomid pupa at the point of emergence. It uses a thorax of buoyant, closed-cell foam to keep the fly floating in the water's surface.

DISTRESSED DAMSEL
The long, mobile tail of olive marabou adds a wonderful sinuous action to this oversized imitation of a damselfly nymph. Devised by Charles Jardine, it works well on small stillwater trout, either fished blind on a slow-sinking or intermediate line, or cast to individual fish.

FOX-SQUIRREL NYMPH
This effective general nymph pattern was devised by Dave Whitlock and suggests a wide range of naturals such as stonefly nymphs and caddis larvae. It is constructed almost entirely from fox-squirrel fur.

GOLDEN STONE
The nymphs or creepers of the stonefly species vary widely in size and color. This dressing mimics the medium to large, golden types, and should be heavily weighted to fish hard along the riverbed.

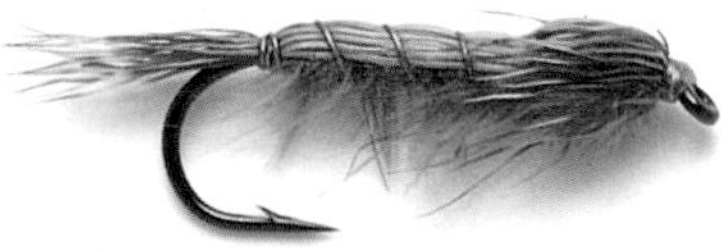

MARABOU NYMPH
Mobile turkey marabou works well in both tails and wings, and it may also be dubbed to produce an effect that is especially good for nymph imitations. The Marabou Nymph is one such pattern, and the buoyant back of deer hair makes it a very slow-sinking fly.

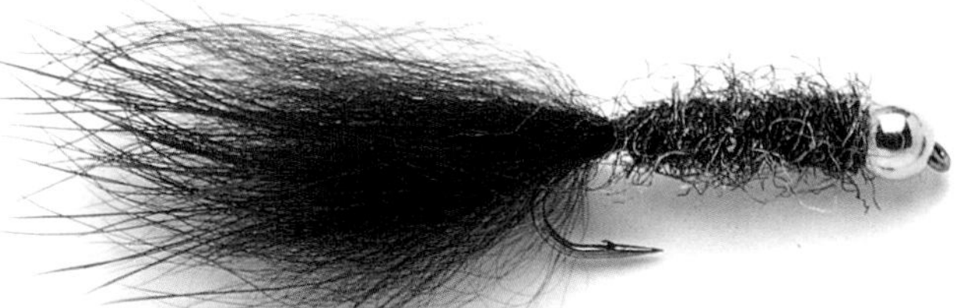

GOLD-HEAD DAMSEL
This effective pattern resembles a damselfly nymph, and has a gold bead at the head plus a tail of dyed olive arctic fox. The weighted bead and highly mobile tail impart a ducking, diving action to the fly that trout find irresistible. This olive form works particularly well when the natural damselfly nymphs are in abundance, but it will take fish throughout the season.

CASUAL DRESS
The Casual Dress, a highly effective general nymph pattern, was devised in the early Sixties by E. H. (Polly) Rosborough for fishing the Upper Big Deschutes in Oregon. It is made almost entirely from muskrat fur; even the thorax-hackle consists of spun muskrat, and the only exception is the ruff of black ostrich herl at the head. It is a very good suggestion of medium to large stonefly nymphs, and may be fished weighted.

DRAGONFLY NYMPH
Large, sluggish dragonfly nymphs form an important part of the diet of trout and bass in late summer. This pattern incorporates lead eyes to help work the pattern along the lakebed. Fish it around sunken timber and weedbeds.

GE NYMPH
This Charles Jardine pattern suggests a general range of up-wing or ephemerid nymphs, hence GE for "general ephemerid." It is tied in many sizes, from 20 to 10, mimicking the Baetidae and other nymphs of similar form.

LONGSHANK PHEASANT TAIL
A much smaller version of this fly is used on rivers and streams, but this large, heavy nymph is a useful addition to the stillwater angler's armory. It works best when fished from midwater down, and is often weighted.

OLIVE FLASHBACK
This is part of a range of patterns that have a strip of pearl Lurex along the back to impart sparkle. The Lurex mimics the effect created by subcutaneous gases trapped within a nymph about to change into an adult.

WOOLY WORM
The Wooly Worm is an easily dressed pattern that has the appearance of a hairy caterpillar but is used more as a general bottom-grubbing nymph. It is tied in various natural colors including olives and browns.

JORGENSEN'S FUR THORAX PUPA
The Fur Thorax Pupa is Poul Jorgensen's superb caddis pupa imitation. The interesting part of this fly is that, by spinning in a dubbing loop, hare, rabbit, or squirrel fur is used to form a very lifelike combined thorax and hackle.

WALKER'S MAYFLY NYMPH
Richard Walker was without doubt one of the greatest contemporary designers of trout flies, with many well-thought-out patterns to his credit. His Mayfly Nymph is one of the best; observing the natural mayfly, he noted that it was not olive, as some authorities stated, but a pale ivory.

TRUE-TO-LIFE MIDGE PUPA
This is a highly lifelike imitation of the pupal stage of the non-biting midge, or chironomid. It includes the most important features of the natural, including the bulbous thorax, slim body, and breathing filaments.

LARGE DARK STONE
This imitates many of the largest stonefly nymphs, particularly the darker types such as Pteronarcys californica. *Since it is fished in fast water it should be tied with a heavily weighted underbody.*

PHEASANT TAIL NYMPH
All of the great many versions of this pattern use the glossy chestnut tail feather fibers of the cock ring-necked pheasant.

THE GOLDHEAD
Hans van Klinken originated this novel but highly effective bottom-grubbing pattern. It is a very good suggestion of a cased caddis fly, and uses a combination of a weighted underbody and a gold bead at the head to allow it to be bumped along the riverbed.

FOUR WATER FAVOURITE
This variation of the Hare's Ear nymph is a specific stillwater pattern developed by Gordon Fraser, and uses a small tuft of rabbit fur in the tail to provide extra movement. It should be tied weighted, using either a weighted underbody or a gold bead.

EMERGENT PUPA
This is part of a range developed by Gary LaFontaine to imitate the various stages of the caddis pupa. It uses a man-made material, Antron, to give a sparkling layer over the duller dubbed body. The Antron is added as a loose sheath so that it traps bubbles of air, giving a great impression of life. The pattern is dressed in a range of colors including brown and amber.

CASED CADDIS
This Bob Carnill dressing is a great early-season fly, imitating the cased caddis larva as it trundles along the bottom. Its weighted underbody helps it fish deep and slow.

SHRIMP
This is a specific imitation of the freshwater shrimp Gammarus pulex. *The natural tends to skulk along the bottom among stones and weeds, so the imitation should be fished similarly.*

BIRD'S STONEFLY NYMPH
This very good suggestion of the larger species of stonefly nymph was created by Calvert T. Bird. It is not as obviously lifelike as some imitations, but Bird's philosophy of producing a fly that is suggestive of something for the trout to eat, rather than an exact imitation of a natural, has produced a classic pattern.

Salmon & Steelhead Flies

With a few exceptions, migratory salmonids cease feeding as they return to freshwater to spawn, but salmon and steelhead can be tempted or provoked into taking a general attractor pattern or an impression of something that they were feeding upon in the open ocean. Shrimp or prawn patterns are very effective, but curiously few dressings are produced to imitate sandeels or other baitfish. Often, however, a salmon will succumb to something as nondescript as a tiny black hairwing, having totally ignored a whole procession of larger, more colorful patterns.

SILVER RAT
The Rat series of patterns has proved extremely effective for Atlantic salmon throughout their range. The silver version uses gray fox guard hairs for the wing and has a soft grizzle hackle. It is a truly universal fly and a great favorite on Canadian rivers such as the Restigouche and Matapedia.

SILVER DOCTOR *(right)*
The Silver Doctor is one of the fully dressed patterns much loved by salmon anglers of the 19th and early 20th centuries. The dressings of these patterns are extremely complicated, and the original dressings included strips of dyed swan feather, married together, plus exotic plumage such as Indian crow, blue chatterer, and toucan, many of which materials are no longer available.

BLACK BRAHAN
This fly is ideal for salmon in early summer, when the water is at a reasonable level. A good fly at both dawn and dusk, its only sparkle comes from the red (or sometimes green) Lurex body.

EGG-SUCKING LEECH
This large, dark pattern suggests the big leeches that feed on the eggs of Pacific salmon. The weighted head and the pulsating body and tail of dyed black rabbit fur give this pattern a superb action, and salmon, steelhead, and rainbows find it very attractive, attacking it with gusto.

ALLY'S SHRIMP
Alistair Gowans created this pattern to simulate the translucent, shrimplike crustaceans he had observed in a trawler catch. The pattern has proved successful for salmon on large rivers.

TEENY NYMPH
Jim Teeny rates among the very best of salmon and steelhead anglers, and any pattern of his design is worth a second look. The Teeny Nymph is not really a nymph at all, but it is a very effective pattern. It uses natural or dyed pheasant tail for the body.

GENERAL PRACTITIONER
This was developed in the early Fifties by Esmond Drury as an imitation of a prawn, for use where the natural is banned. It consists of golden-pheasant body feathers and orange fur, and has proved effective on a wide range of waters in Britain, Canada, and Iceland.

SPARKLE SHRIMP
A direct imitation of a shrimp, the Sparkle Shrimp uses a strip of pearl Lurex tied as a shell back to add extra fish attraction. It has proved a good fly for Pacific salmon.

CHARTREUSE STREAMER
Steelhead and Pacific salmon find chartreuse a very attractive color, and this pattern works well in colored water even when fished near the bottom. Its mobile tail and weighted bead chain eyes give a superb action.

PURPLE ZONKER
The strip of rabbit fur used for the wing gives the Purple Zonker great movement, which is attractive to steelhead and salmon. However, although purple is a good color to use during dull conditions or when light levels are low, it can either prove very effective or actually spook the fish.

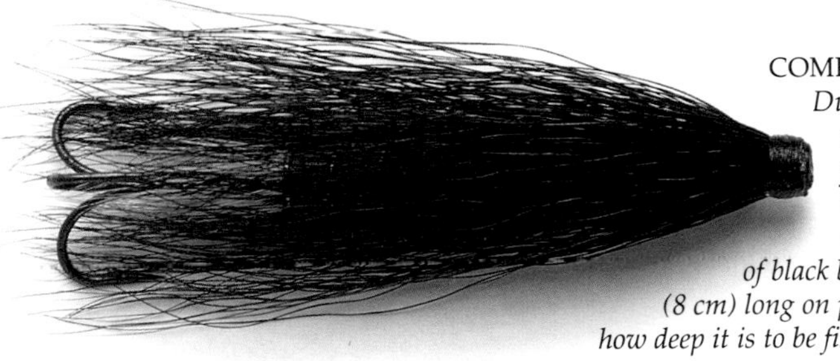

COMET
During the early season, when the water is cold, tube flies offer the fly fisher a lure large enough to tempt what can be very dour fish. The Comet is a dark fly that has a wing of black bucktail, and may be tied up to 3 in (8 cm) long on plastic or brass tubes, depending on how deep it is to be fished.

GREEN HIGHLANDER
This is the hairwing version of the famous fully dressed Green Highlander pattern, and mixes various colors of bucktail to form the wing, rather than feathers as in the original. This method is used to update many traditional patterns.

WILLIE GUNN *(right)*
The Willie Gunn is named after the Sutherland Estate's head keeper on the River Brora in Scotland, and its wing is a mixture of yellow, red, and black bucktail. This tube-fly version may be tied on plastic or metal tubing, and works well in high or cold water.

SPRUCE
The Spruce was originally designed for sea-run cutthroat trout and rainbows, but it has also proved to be very successful for steelhead. It has become one of the most popular West Coast streamer patterns.

TWO-EGG SPERM FLY *(below)*
Egg flies are effective patterns for steelhead and salmon, and this fly develops the idea by imitating two salmon eggs in tandem. Fluorescent orange chenille mimics the roe being shed, and a white turkey marabou wing imitates the flow of sperm over them.

UMPQUA SPECIAL
This classic pattern was developed by Don Hunter in the Thirties to tempt the steelhead of Oregon's Umpqua River. It is a bright fly, ideal for colored water where the red-and-white combination of the hair wing is particularly deadly for steelhead. It is tied in a range of sizes, most commonly on up-eyed salmon hooks sizes 2 to 8.

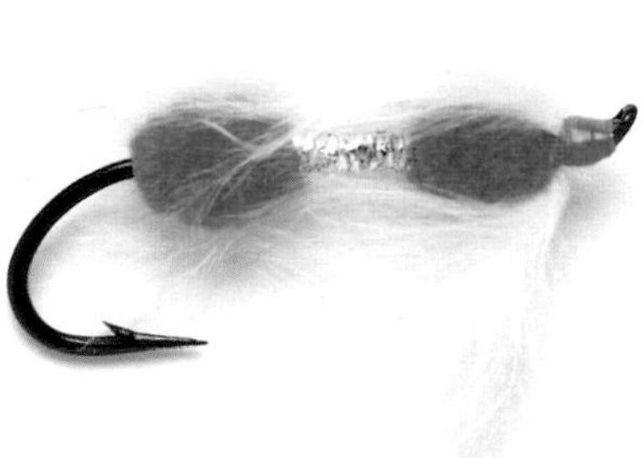

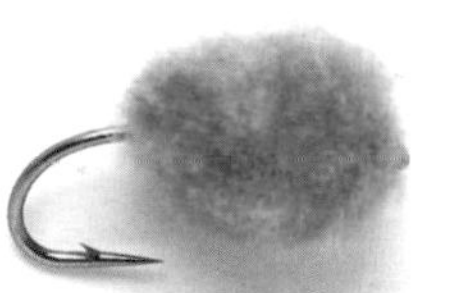

EGG FLY
This is one of the simplest of all flies, being formed from a clipped ball of Glo-Bug yarn. It is extremely effective for steelhead, Pacific salmon, and rainbow trout, and it should be weighted and fished dead-drift to imitate the movement of real eggs.

Streamers & Hairwings

Streamers and hairwings differ in one obvious way: the wing of the streamer is made of feather, while that of the hairwing is made of hair. Most streamers and hairwings are large and usually dressed on long-shank hooks, and tend to be attractors or suggestive of something alive and edible for a predatory fish. The major exceptions are the imitations of coarse fish or baitfish, which include representations of species such as miller's thumbs, sculpins, or more active schooling fish such as perch or minnows.

ORANGE BOOBY
This is the lure version of Gordon Fraser's original Booby nymph. All Boobies have buoyant eyes of closed-cell foam, and this buoyancy plus a turkey marabou tail gives a tremendous action. Fish it on a fast-sinking line and an ultra-short leader.

GOLDIE
Black, gold, and yellow is an effective color combination where brown trout are concerned, and Bob Church used it when he devised this pattern to tempt big stillwater browns. It may be tied on a single hook or as a tandem, and is a good fly for sea trout as well as browns.

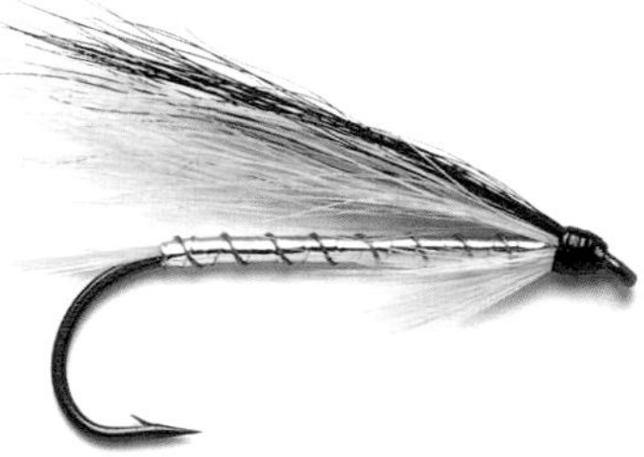

BLACK GHOST
This is a typical streamer, using pairs of rooster hackle back-to-back for the wing. A good general pattern for trout and steelhead on both rivers and stillwaters, and an effective fry imitation.

DAHLBERG DIVER
This Muddler variation, created by Larry Dahlberg of Minnesota, is designed to dive by means of an angled vane trimmed from the collar of the head. It has terrific action, popping along the surface as well as diving at each pull of the retrieve. A great pattern for big trout and bass.

THUNDER CREEK MINNOW
This was designed by Keith Fulsher as a specific imitation of a range of small baitfish species. It offers a slim profile using brown and white bucktail, tied forward and then drawn back and secured along the hook, to provide it with the all-important countershading.

JAFFA
This orange mini-lure, tied with dyed turkey marabou, is very effective for stillwater rainbows in high summer, and is tied to fall within the size limit for international-rules fly-fishing competitions.

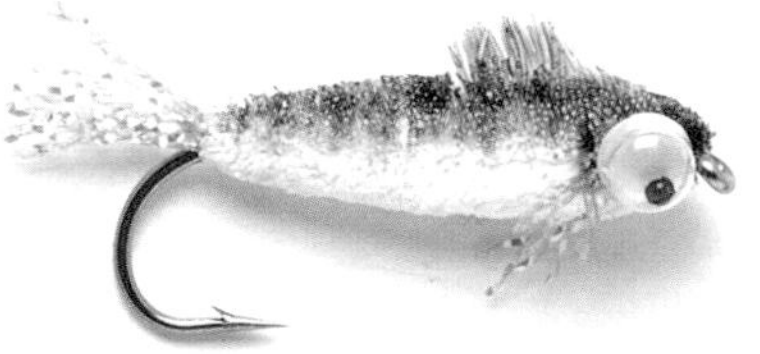

FLOATING FRY
When small baitfish are dying off, trout often take them rather than chase a more elusive meal, and an imitation designed to float can prove extremely effective. Deer hair is the perfect material for this type of buoyant pattern.

MUDDLER MINNOW
This is the original Don Gapen dressing, tied with a wing and tail of oak turkey and a head of deer body hair to imitate a small sculpin. From this pattern has developed the vast range of Muddlers we have today.

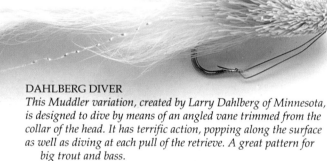

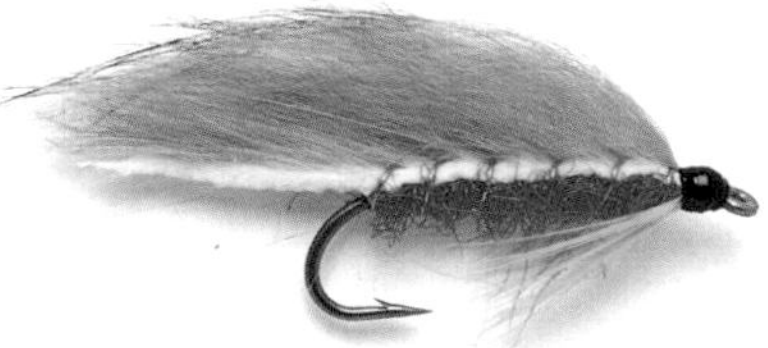

RABBIT
This effective Australian pattern uses a small strip of rabbit fur to produce a highly mobile wing. The body color may be varied to give a wide range of patterns of an impressionistic nature.

WOOLLY BUGGER
Tied in a variety of sizes and colors, this big streamer is used as a general bottom-grubbing pattern, as an imitation of a leech, and as a general representation of large nymphs such as those of stoneflies and dragonflies.

TIN HEAD
Flies with weighted heads and long, mobile tails are much in vogue on the British stillwater scene. The Tin Heads come in a variety of tail, body, and head color combinations. These include olive with a silver head, and black with a grizzle hackle and either a red or a fluorescent green head.

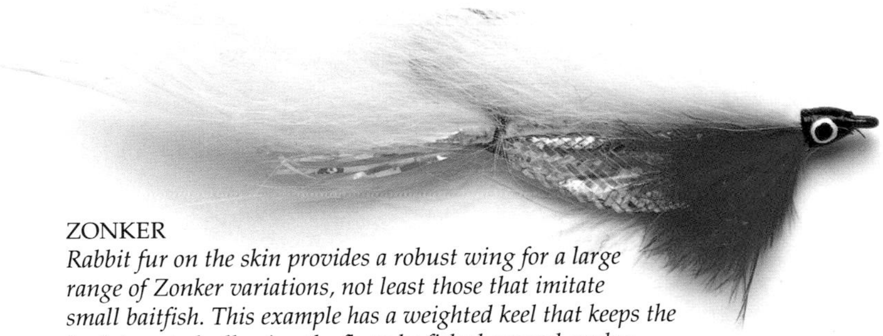

ZONKER
Rabbit fur on the skin provides a robust wing for a large range of Zonker variations, not least those that imitate small baitfish. This example has a weighted keel that keeps the hook inverted, allowing the fly to be fished around sunken timber and weedbeds without snagging.

MINKIE
This pattern is similar to the Zonker, but uses mink fur rather than the more mundane rabbit. It is tied weighted or plain and with or without a Muddler head, and is excellent as a fry imitation fished in slow draws or with a figure-eight retrieve.

WHITE TANDEM
Trout will at times concentrate on quite large fish fry, sometimes as large as 6 in (15 cm), to the exclusion of all other food forms. It is then important to use a pattern similar in size to the prey fish, and by joining two long-shank hooks together in tandem, a large, lightweight, and easily cast streamer is created.

PINK NASTY
Pink is a curious color, sometimes proving almost totally ineffective, but often triggering a response in the fish that no other color will. Gordon Fraser is responsible for this garish pattern, which combines striking fluorescent pink with a mobile tail.

BADGER MATUKA
The idea of binding the hackle wing of a streamer along the top of the hook shank originated in New Zealand. It is a technique that makes for a very robust wing resembling an elongated dorsal fin.

SOFT HACKLE STREAMER
American fly tier Jack Gartside came up with the idea of using a marabou feather as a hackle rather than as a bunched wing or tail. This simple but very effective turkey marabou tying works as a general attractor or fry imitation.

VIVA
Black and green is a very effective color combination for a stillwater trout fly, especially when fished slowly in the early season. This Viva is a compact hairwing version of the Victor Furse original.

SPECIES

A SPECIES OF FISH (or any other organism) is a genetically distinct group, consisting of related individuals that resemble each other in appearance and behavior, and can breed among themselves but not – with some exceptions – with other species. Closely related species are grouped together into genera, and related genera are grouped into families.

Because the common names of fish can vary greatly from one region or country to another, biologists refer to them by their scientific names to avoid confusion. The scientific name of a species consists of two words, usually derived from Latin; the first of these defines the genus, and the second identifies the species. The brown trout, *Salmo trutta*, is thus the species *trutta* of the genus *Salmo*. It is also described as a salmonid, because it belongs to the Salmonidae family, which includes the salmon, trout, and char.

There are about 22,000 known species of fish, of which relatively few are of interest to anglers. This chapter gives brief descriptions of major sporting species, together with notes on the sort of techniques, tackle, and bait that may be used to catch them. They are grouped, as far as is practical, into freshwater and saltwater species, and arranged within these groups alphabetically by family name.

THE ANGLER'S QUARRY
The fish pursued by anglers range from small species that feed mainly on insects to voracious predators such as pike and shark.

Anatomy

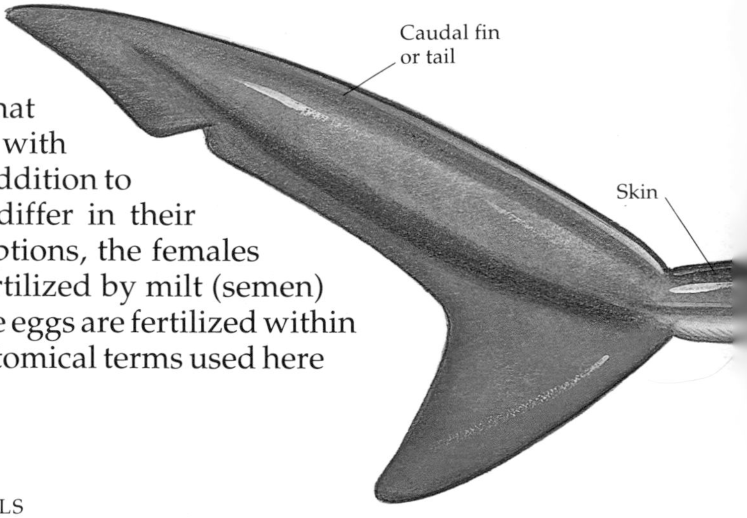

Fish can be divided broadly into two groups: those that have skeletons made of bone (the bony fish) and those with skeletons made of cartilage (the cartilaginous fish). In addition to having different skeletal materials, the two groups differ in their means of reproduction. In bony fish, with a few exceptions, the females discharge their eggs into the water, where they are fertilized by milt (semen) from the males. In cartilaginous fish, as in mammals, the eggs are fertilized within the bodies of the females. (Brief explanations of the anatomical terms used here are given in the glossary on pages 280–281.)

Bony Fish (Osteichthyes)

A typical bony fish has two sets of paired fins (pectoral and pelvic) and a set of vertical fins (dorsal, anal, and tail). The four gill openings on each side of the head are covered by flattened bones, of which the operculum is the largest, and most species possess a gas-filled swim bladder. By altering the amount of gas (usually oxygen) in this bladder, a bony fish can adjust its buoyancy and maintain its chosen depth in the water without constantly swimming. Cartilaginous fish *(see opposite)* lack swim bladders and must keep swimming or sink to the bottom.

Gills

A fish "breathes" by drawing water into its mouth, then forcing it through its gill chambers and out via the gill slits. Inside the gill chambers, delicate filaments absorb oxygen from the water and pass it into the blood, and remove carbon dioxide from the blood and then discharge it into the water.

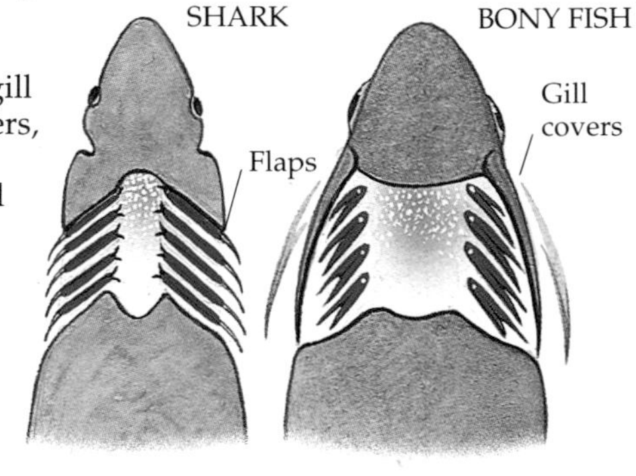

ANATOMY OF A BONY FISH

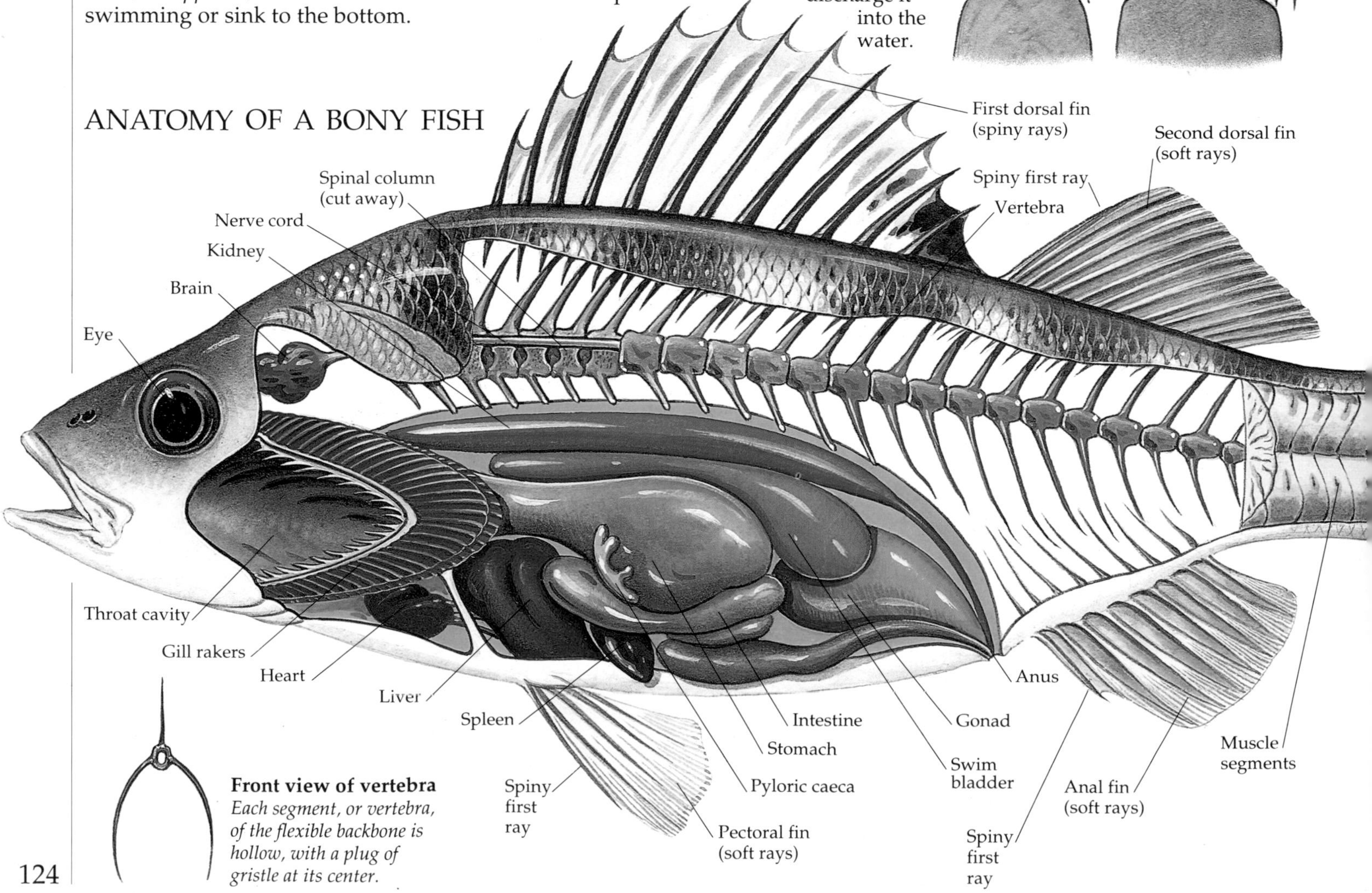

Front view of vertebra
Each segment, or vertebra, of the flexible backbone is hollow, with a plug of gristle at its center.

ANATOMY OF A CARTILAGINOUS FISH

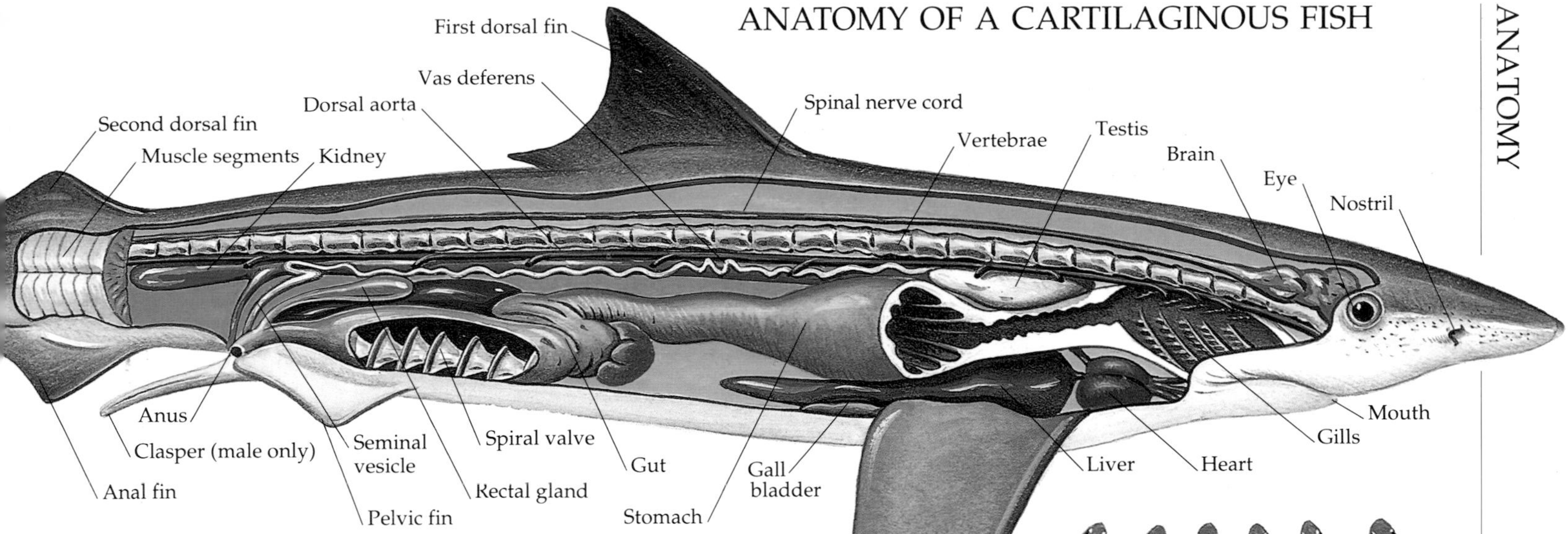

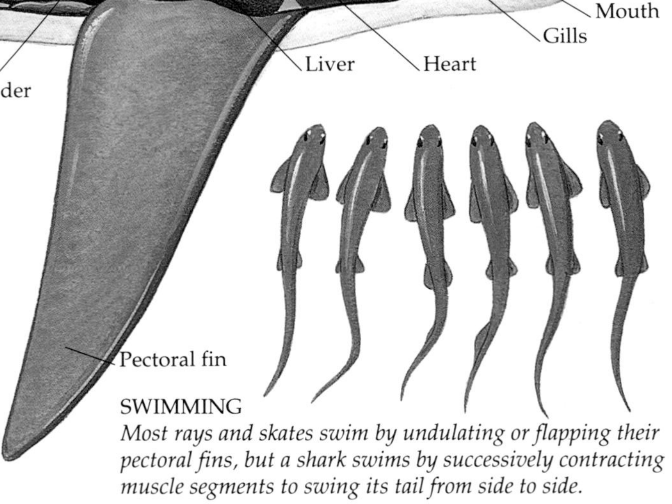

SWIMMING

Most rays and skates swim by undulating or flapping their pectoral fins, but a shark swims by successively contracting muscle segments to swing its tail from side to side.

Cartilaginous Fish (Chondrichthyes)

These are primarily marine species and include the rays, skates, and sharks. Most rays and skates have flattened bodies and elongated, winglike pectoral fins, and their mouths and gill openings are on their undersides. A shark has the same basic fin arrangement as a bony fish, but its gill openings are simple slits and its digestive tract contains a spiral valve. This increases the surface area available for the absorption of food.

Lateral Line

The lateral line running along each side of the body is a canal lined with sensory organs. These detect vibrations and changes in temperature and pressure, and help the fish to maintain its balance.

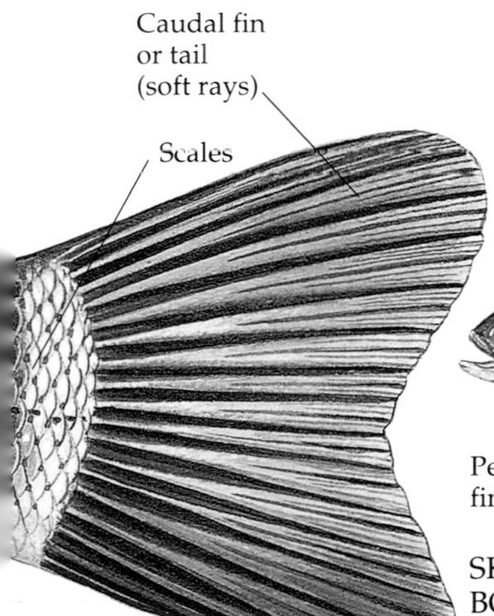

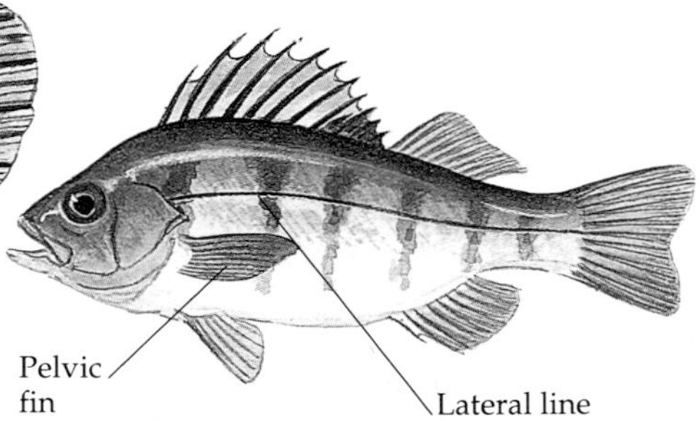

SKULL OF A BONY FISH

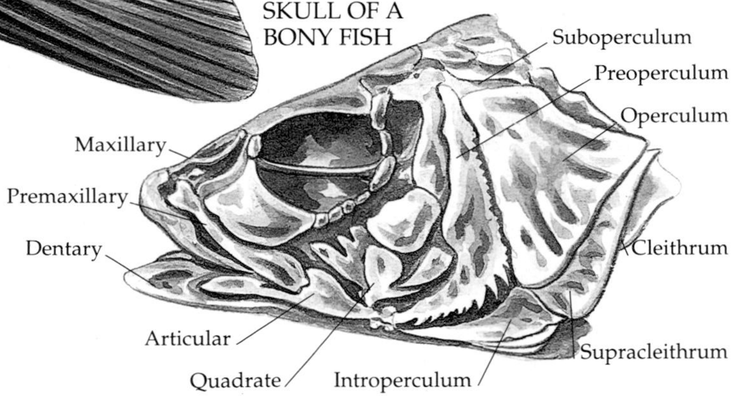

Scales

The scales of most bony fish are either cycloid (with smooth rear edges) or ctenoid (with serrated rear edges). The scales are usually layered in rows, like roof tiles. Scales lost through injury are soon replaced, but often they do not grow back in the same pattern as existing scales.

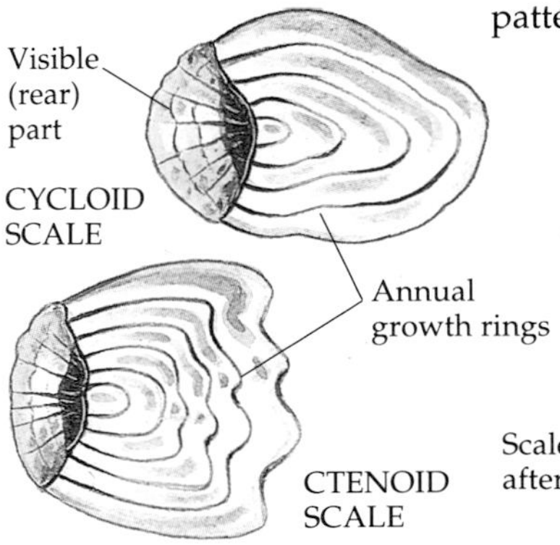

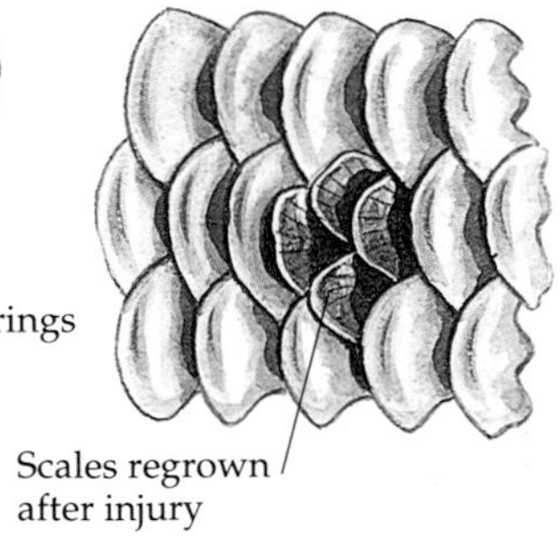

Shark Scales

Sharks have tiny, pointed scales called placoid scales.

SPOTTED DOGFISH

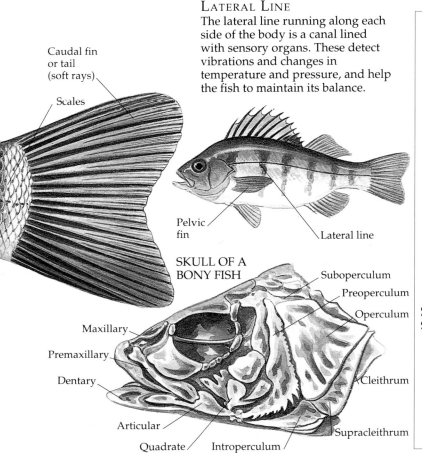

SMOOTHHOUND

CENTRARCHIDAE

BLACK BASS

The species collectively known as black bass include two of the most important sporting species in North America: the smallmouth bass and the largemouth bass. Black bass are the largest members of the Centrarchidae family, which also includes the bluegill, the crappies, and the sunfish *(see page 128)*.

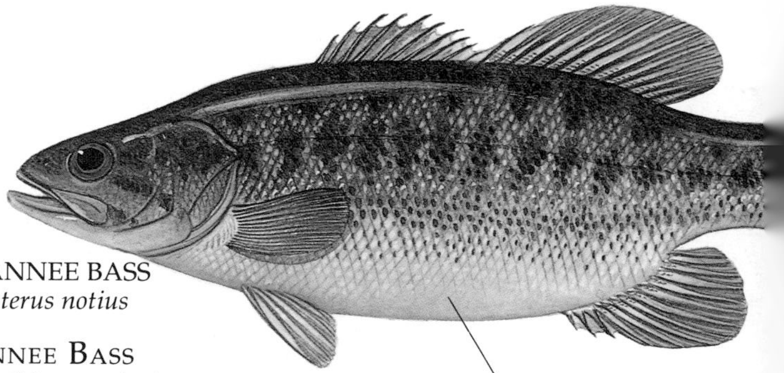

SUWANNEE BASS
Micropterus notius

SUWANNEE BASS

This small bass, which rarely exceeds 12 oz (340 g), is found in the Suwannee and Ochlockonee river drainages of Florida and Georgia. Its overall coloration is brownish, with dark markings along the back and sides; the adult male has blue cheeks, breast, and belly.

SPOTTED BASS

This bass gets its name from the rows of small, dark spots on its pale flanks and belly. It is found mainly in the Ohio and Mississippi river systems and has two localized subspecies, the Alabama spotted bass and the Wichita spotted bass, *Micropterus punctulatus henshalli* and *M. p. wichitae*. It grows to about 5 lb (2.27 kg).

GUADALUPE BASS

The Guadalupe bass is similar to the spotted bass, but has distinctive dark bars along each side and is smaller, seldom reaching 1 lb (454 g). Its range is restricted to the Guadalupe, Colorado, Brazos, San Antonio, and Nueces river systems of central Texas.

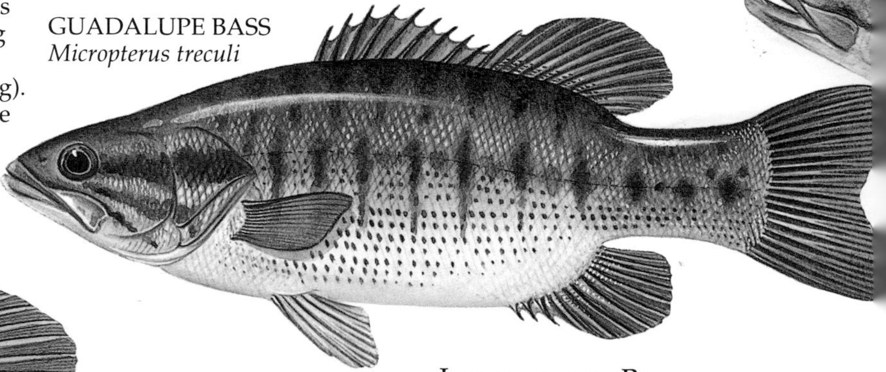

GUADALUPE BASS
Micropterus treculi

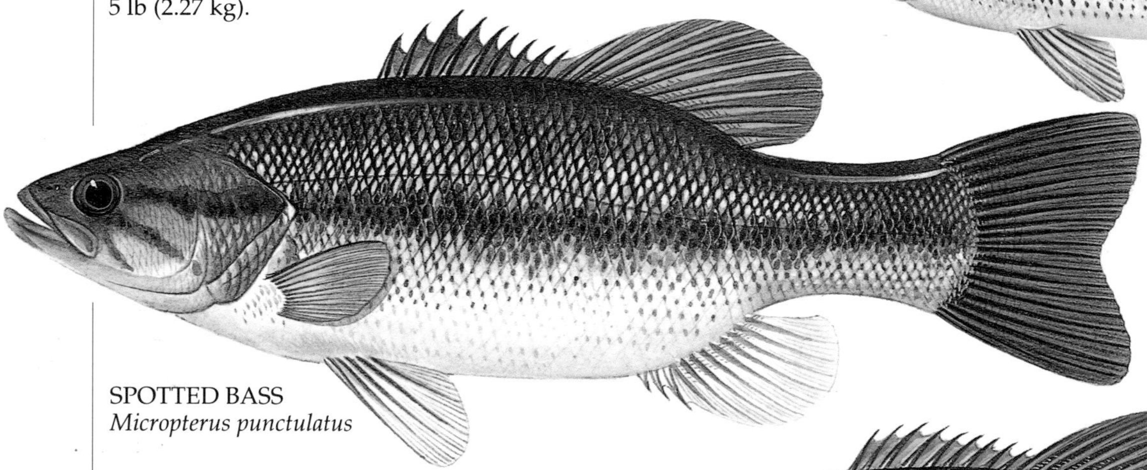

SPOTTED BASS
Micropterus punctulatus

LARGEMOUTH BASS

The largemouth bass is so named because its upper jaw extends to behind its eye; that of the smallmouth bass does not extend beyond the eye. The northern largemouth seldom exceeds 10 lb (4.54 kg), but the southern subspecies, the Florida largemouth *(M. s. floridanus)*, can reach more than 20 lb (9.1 kg).

REDEYE BASS

The red eyes and white-tipped orange caudal (tail) fin of the redeye bass make it easy to distinguish from other bass; young redeyes also have brick-red dorsal and anal fins. The redeye is one of the smaller bass species, and although it can exceed 8 lb (3.6 kg) it usually does not grow to more than about 1 lb (454 g).

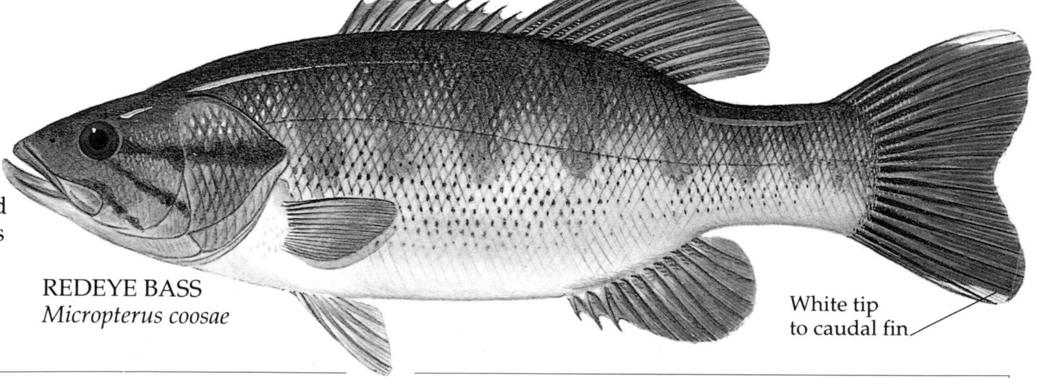

REDEYE BASS
Micropterus coosae

FISHING NOTES

Techniques

Spinning or baitcasting with artificial lures, fly fishing, and trolling with livebaits will all prove successful.

Tackle

For lure fishing, try a 5½ to 7 ft (1.7 m to 2.1 m) spinning or baitcasting rod and a spinning or baitcaster reel with 6 to 10 lb (2.7 to 4.54 kg) mono line. A good rod to use for fly fishing is a 7 to 9 ft (2.1 to 2.7 m) bass fly rod with a fast taper, fitted with a single-action fly reel carrying a floating #7 to #9 line with a 6 to 8 lb (2.7 to 3.6 kg) leader. For trolling, use a 9 or 10 ft (2.7 or 3 m) stiff-action rod with a 2½ lb (1.1 kg) test curve, and a baitcaster reel with 10 to 20 lb (4.5 to 9.1 kg) mono line, a nylon or Dacron leader, and hook sizes 2/0 to 5/0. Use weedless hooks in very dense cover.

Bait

Black bass, being active predators that feed on a wide variety of creatures, can be tempted to strike at practically any kind of bait, either artificial or natural. Artificials such as spinners, spoons, crankbaits, surface plugs, and plastic worms are particularly effective. For fly fishing, bass bugs, streamers, and bucktails have all proved their worth; for trolling, try worms, crayfish, leeches, and minnows.

Smallmouth Bass

The hard-fighting smallmouth is the most highly regarded black bass. It is slightly larger than the northern largemouth, reaching a maximum of about 12 lb (5.4 kg), and it prefers clear lakes and streams with rocky or gravel bottoms. The largemouth favors weedy, mud-bottomed waters.

SMALLMOUTH BASS
Micropterus dolomieui

Distribution

Smallmouth: from North Dakota to Quebec, Oklahoma, and Alabama; also widely introduced elsewhere.
Largemouth: from Minnesota to Quebec and south to the Gulf; widely introduced elsewhere.
Spotted: Mississippi basin from southern Ohio to the Gulf; introduced elsewhere.
Guadalupe: central Texas.
Suwannee: Florida and Georgia.
Redeye: Alabama, Georgia, South Carolina; introduced elsewhere.

LARGEMOUTH BASS
Micropterus salmoides

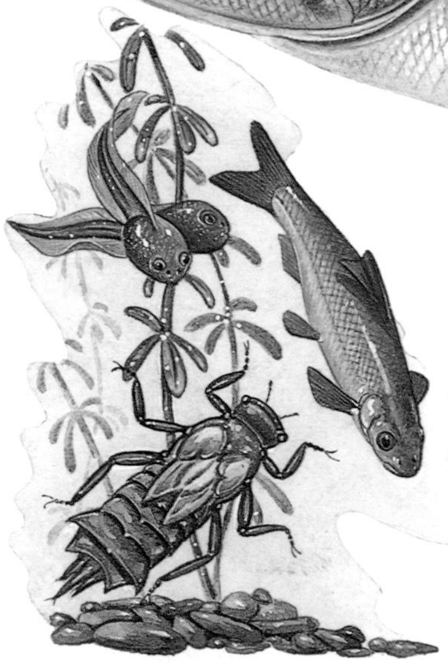

Feeding

All the black bass are active predators. When young, they feed at first on tiny crustaceans, insects and their larvae, worms, and tadpoles, but they soon progress to larger prey such as fish, crayfish, and frogs. The largest bass will even take small waterfowl.

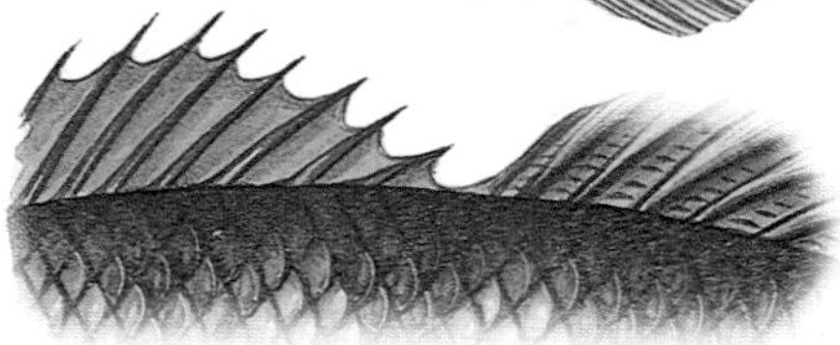

LARGEMOUTH BASS

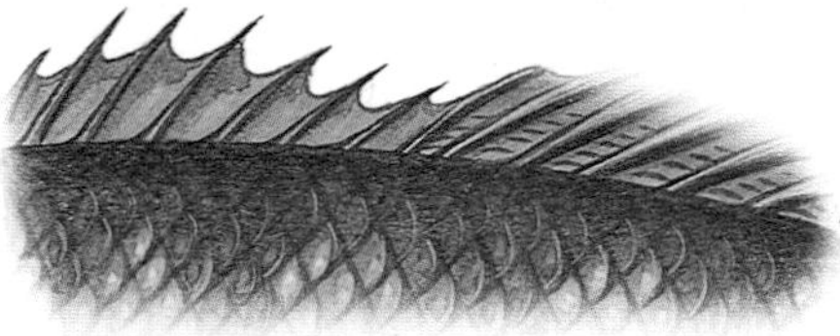

SMALLMOUTH BASS

Dorsal fins

In addition to the different lengths of their upper jaws, largemouth and smallmouth bass have different dorsal fin structures. The spiny first dorsal fin of the largemouth bass is highest at its midpoint and is almost separated from the soft-rayed second dorsal. The smallmouth bass has a somewhat flatter first dorsal fin, which is connected to the second dorsal, and the second dorsal has a patch of scales at its base.

Size comparison

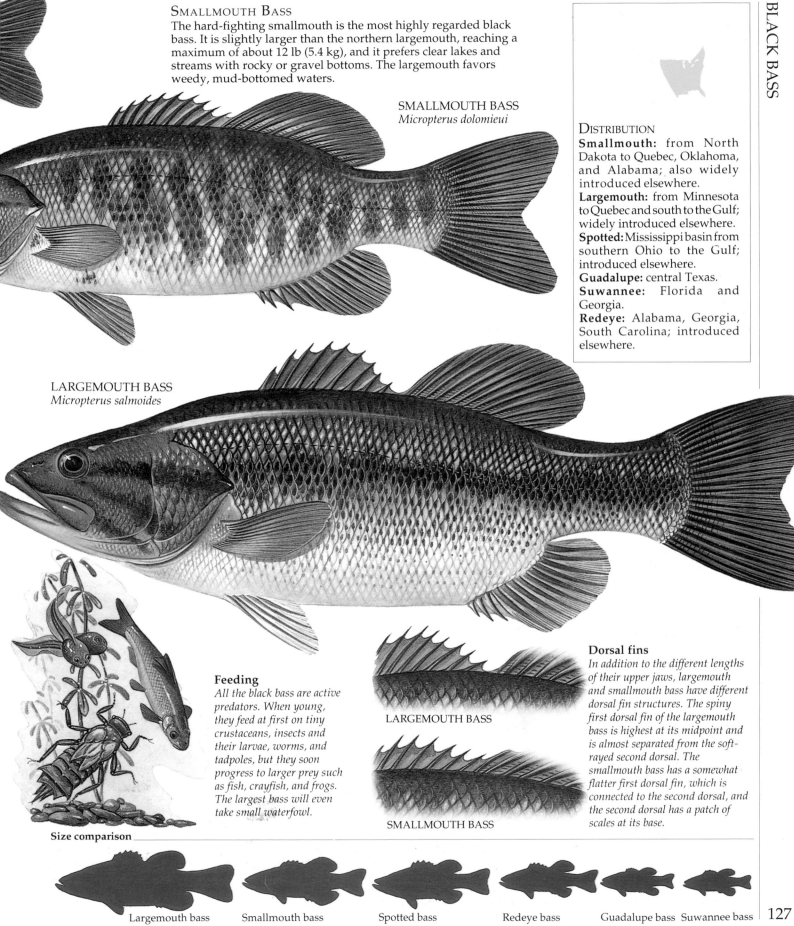

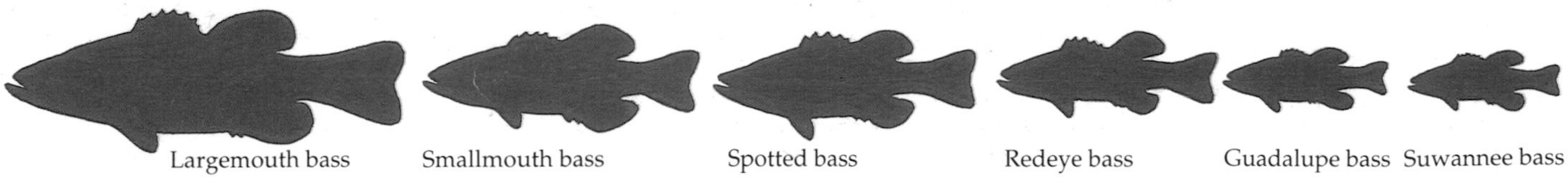

CENTRARCHIDAE

Bluegill, Crappies, Pumpkinseed, & Sunfish

These small relatives of the black bass are among the most popular American panfish, which are fish that are too small to be considered true gamefish but still provide considerable angling (and eating) pleasure. The range of each of these species has been considerably extended by widespread stocking programs.

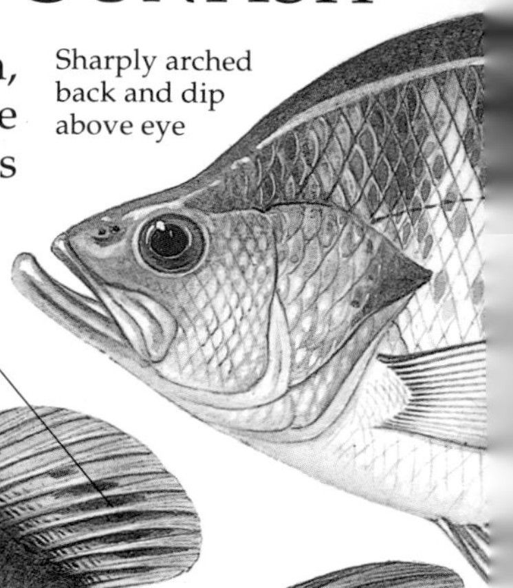

Pumpkinseed

This attractive little fish lives among the weeds in lakes, ponds, and quiet river pools. Its maximum weight is about 1 lb 1 oz (482 g), but most individuals are much smaller.

Bluegill

This the most widely distributed panfish, and probably the most fished-for species in North America. It prefers quiet, weedy waters and averages about 4 oz (113g), although it can grow to over 4 lb (1.8 kg).

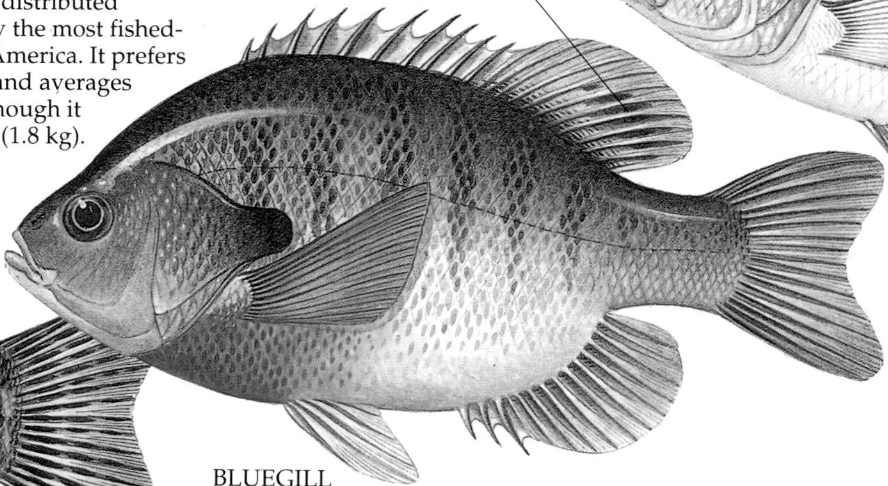

BLUEGILL
Lepomis macrochirus

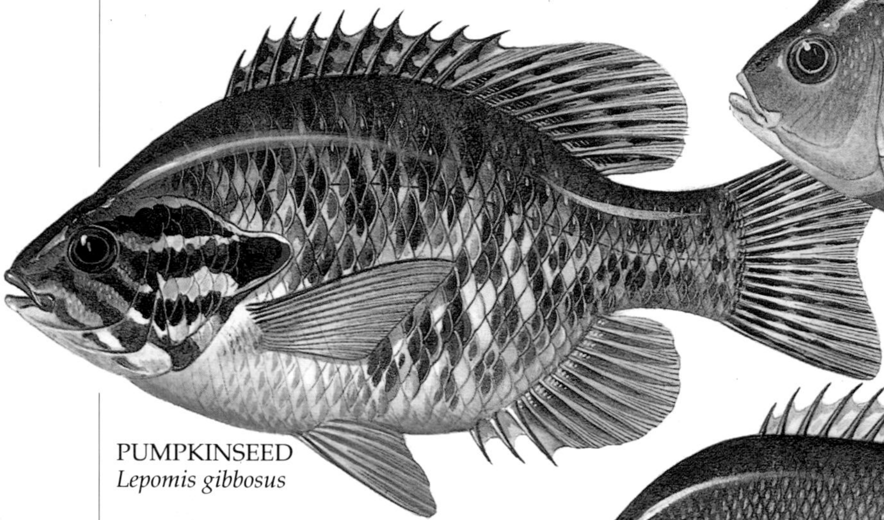

PUMPKINSEED
Lepomis gibbosus

Redbreast Sunfish

The redbreast sunfish, which reaches a maximum weight of about 1 lb (454 g), is most abundant in the creeks and small to medium-sized rivers of the Atlantic Slope. It is also sometimes found in ponds and lake margins.

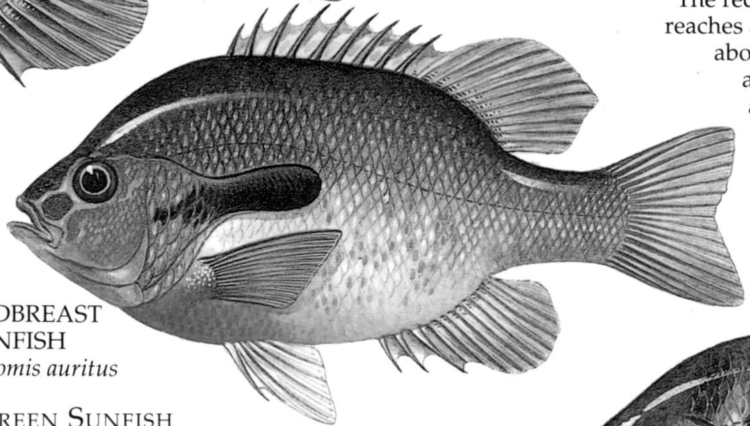

REDBREAST SUNFISH
Lepomis auritus

Gill covers
Sunfish of the genus Lepomis *can be identified by examining the shape and markings of their gill covers.*

Green Sunfish

The green sunfish has a more elongated body than most other sunfish, and the upper jaw of its large mouth extends back to below the midpoint of the eye. Like the redbreast sunfish, it is primarily a stream fish but is also found in stillwaters. It can attain a weight of over 2 lb (910 g).

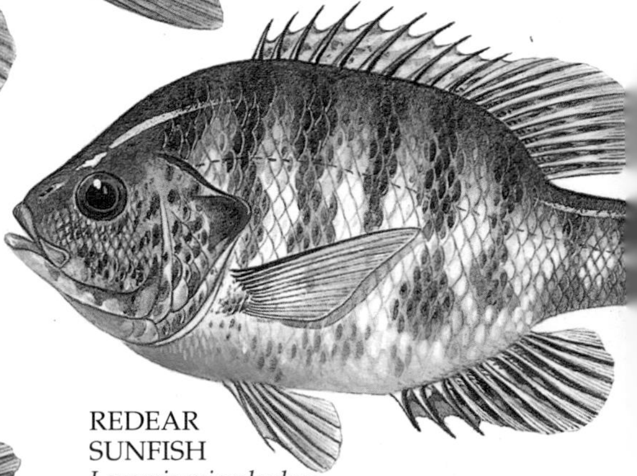

REDEAR SUNFISH
Lepomis microlophus

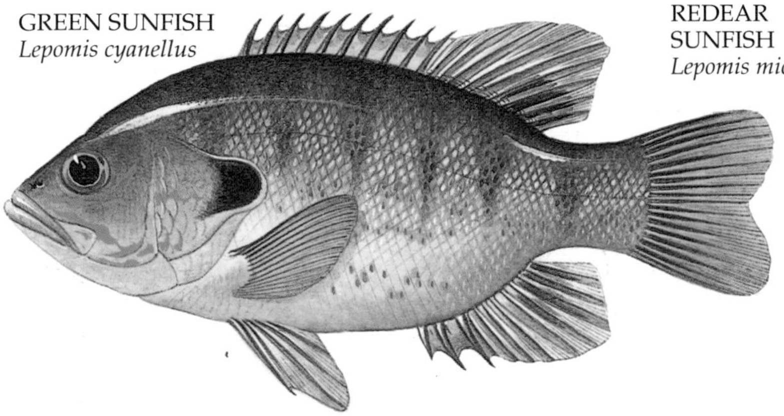

GREEN SUNFISH
Lepomis cyanellus

Redear Sunfish

The plump redear sunfish is also called the "shellcracker", because its diet includes snails and clams, which it crushes up with powerful grinding teeth. It can grow to over 4 lb 12 oz (2.15 kg).

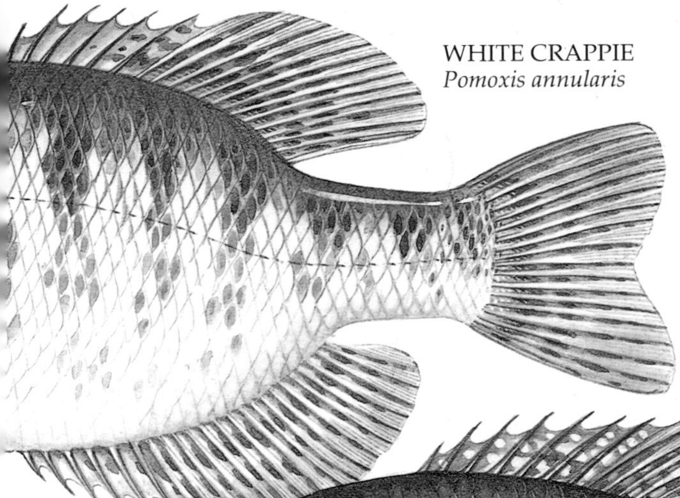

WHITE CRAPPIE
Pomoxis annularis

White Crappie

The white crappie is generally a little larger than the closely related black crappie, and its overall coloration is usually paler. The most reliable way to distinguish between the two is to count the spines in the first dorsal fin: the white crappie has six, while the black crappie has seven or eight. The white crappie usually reaches 1 lb to 1 lb 8 oz (454 to 680 g), but it can grow to over 5 lb (2.27 kg).

Distribution

Pumpkinseed: the Dakotas and Iowa to the Atlantic drainages.
Bluegill: from the Great Lakes to the Gulf and New Mexico; widely introduced elsewhere.
Redbreast sunfish: the Atlantic drainages.
Green sunfish: From the Great Lakes to Texas.
Redear sunfish: Indiana to the Gulf; introduced elsewhere.
Crappies: eastern North America from southern Canada to the Gulf; widely introduced.
Rock bass: From Manitoba to New England and northern Alabama.

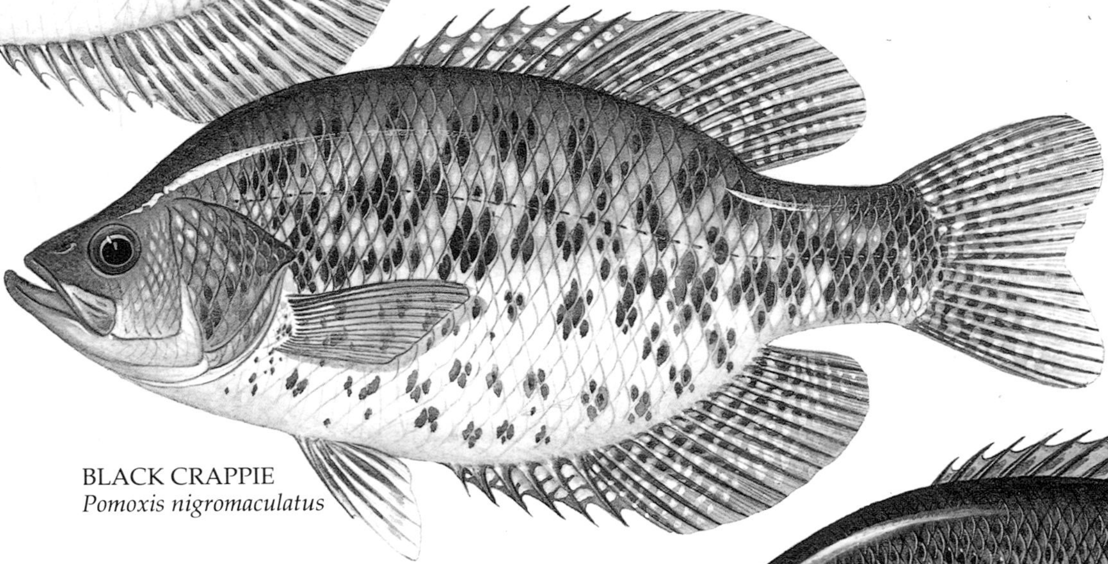

BLACK CRAPPIE
Pomoxis nigromaculatus

Black Crappie

The black crappie is often found together with the white, and both species are widely distributed in ponds, lakes, and rivers, although the black tends to prefer larger, clearer waters than those tolerated by the white. Its average weight is in the 12 oz to 1 lb 8 oz (340 to 680 g) range, with a maximum of up to 5 lb (2.27 kg).

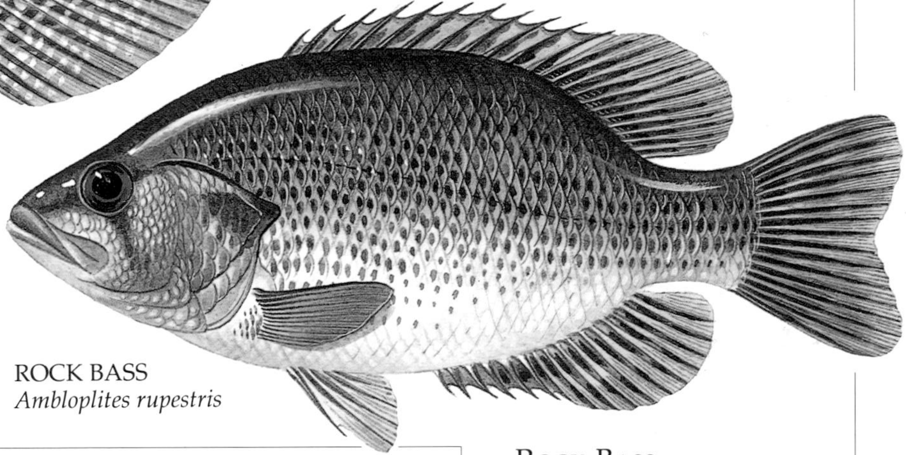

ROCK BASS
Ambloplites rupestris

Fishing Notes

Techniques
Float fishing, fly fishing, and baitcasting, all with light tackle.

Tackle
For float fishing, a 10 to 14 ft (3 to 4.3 m) pole, 6 to 15 lb (2.7 to 6.8 kg) mono line, and a small jig or livebait fished below a small float; or a 6 to 7 ft (1.8 to 2.1 m) ultralight spinning rod with a spinning reel, 3 lb (1.36 kg) mono line, and a small float. Use hook sizes 10 to 14, and weight the rig with suitable split shot about 12 in (30 cm) from the hook. For fly fishing, use a fly rod up to 4 oz (113 g) in weight, with matching reel and line. When baitcasting, use a 4½ to 6 ft (1.4 to 1.8 m) rod, a baitcasting reel, and 2 to 4 lb (910 g to 1.8 kg) line.

Bait
Small minnows, worms, grubs, and jigs for float fishing; tiny wet flies, nymphs, and dry flies for fly fishing; miniature spinners and crankbaits for baitcasting.

Rock Bass

The mottled, dark olive rock bass has distinctive red eyes and a large mouth, and there is usually a white or gold margin to the dark spot on its gill cover. It is most common in clear, rocky streams and is also found in lake margins where the bottom is rocky and there is ample vegetation. Its maximum weight is about 1.36 kg (3 lb), but it typically weighs around 227 g (8 oz).

Size comparison

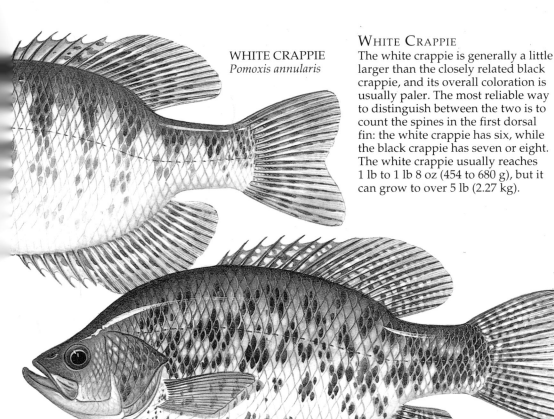

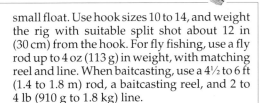

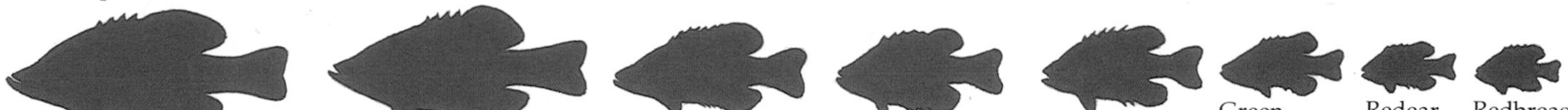

CYPRINIDAE

Barbel, Tench, & Asp

The tench is a very popular angling species in its native Eurasian waters and has been introduced into North America and Australia. It is mainly a stillwater species, although it also inhabits the lower reaches of rivers. The asp is found in large lakes and, like barbel, in the middle reaches of clean rivers where the current is relatively fast and the water well oxygenated. Asp and barbel are often found together in those areas of Europe where their ranges overlap, asp in midwater and barbel on the bottom.

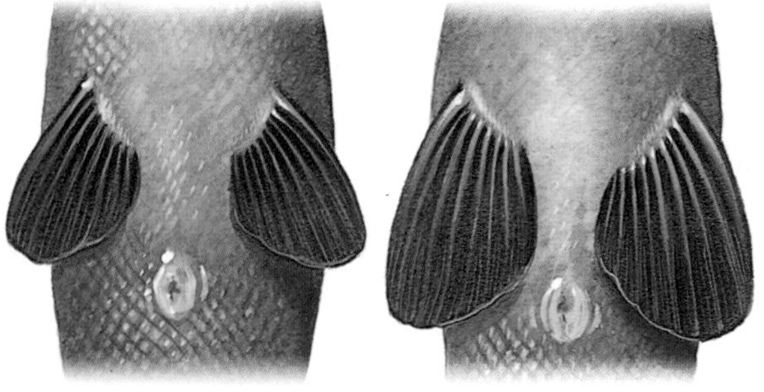

Male and female tench
The sex of a tench can be determined from its pelvic fins. Those of the male are much longer and broader than those of the female, and they extend to beyond the anal vent.

Tench

The tiny scales of the tench are covered with a layer of protective slime and set flat against its thick-set body, making it appear almost scaleless. The fins are smoothly rounded, and the wrist of the barely forked tail is distinctively thick. Large individuals of up to 18 lb 12 oz (8.5 kg) have been reported, but the tench is slow-growing, and the usual maximum is about 4 lb (1.8 kg).

Golden Tench
The rare golden variety of tench is stocked as an ornamental fish in private ponds and park lakes. It has an orange or yellow body with scattered black markings, and its pink-tinged fins are less rounded than those of the common tench.

Spawning male asp
At spawning time the male asp develops numerous tough, wartlike lumps (tubercles) on its head, which help it to fend off rivals. Asp spawn in spring over gravel beds.

Asp

The slender, streamlined body of the predatory asp gives it the speed and agility it needs to capture its food, which is primarily small midwater and near-surface fish. A popular angling species that fights strongly when hooked, it favors deep water and is often found in dam pools. Asp average about 7 lb 11 oz (3.5 kg), but can reach a maximum of around 26 lb 7 oz (12 kg).

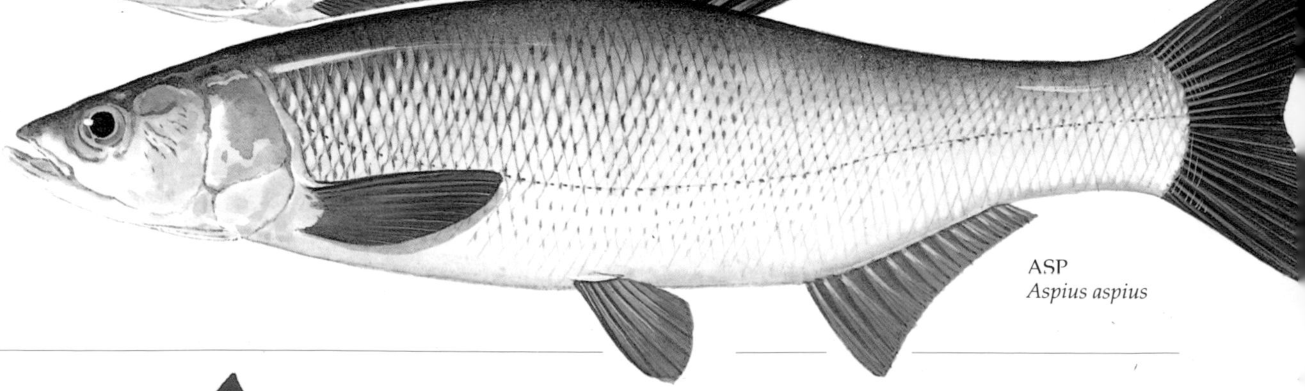

Natural food
Tench and barbel have a varied diet that includes plants, insects, mollusks, and crustaceans. When young, the asp eats insects and small crustaceans, but as an adult it preys on small fish such as bleak.

Size comparison

Southern Barbel

The southern or Mediterranean barbel inhabits fast-flowing upland rivers and streams in southern Europe. It is much smaller than the common barbel, averaging only about 9 oz (250 g).

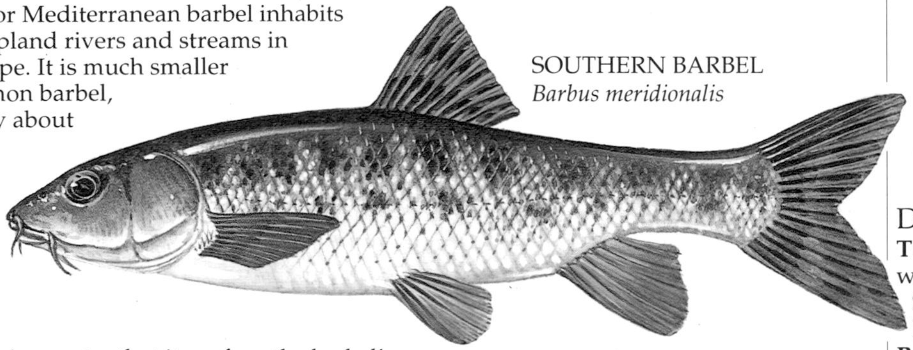

SOUTHERN BARBEL
Barbus meridionalis

Distribution

Tench: throughout Europe with the exception of northern Scandinavia; introduced into North America and Australia.
Barbel: from southern England and Wales to southern Europe.
Southern barbel: northern Spain, southern France, and northern Italy; Danube basin.
Asp: from eastern Holland east through northern and central Europe to the Caspian Sea.

Barbel

In the fast-flowing water that it prefers, the barbel's streamlined, flat-bellied body helps it to stay close to the river bed, where it feeds. When hooked, it will use its considerable strength and stamina fully and fight hard until it is exhausted, and its power is comparable with that of a salmon of similar weight. It usually grows to about 5 lb (2.27 kg), but it can reach a maximum of around 16 lb (7.3 kg).

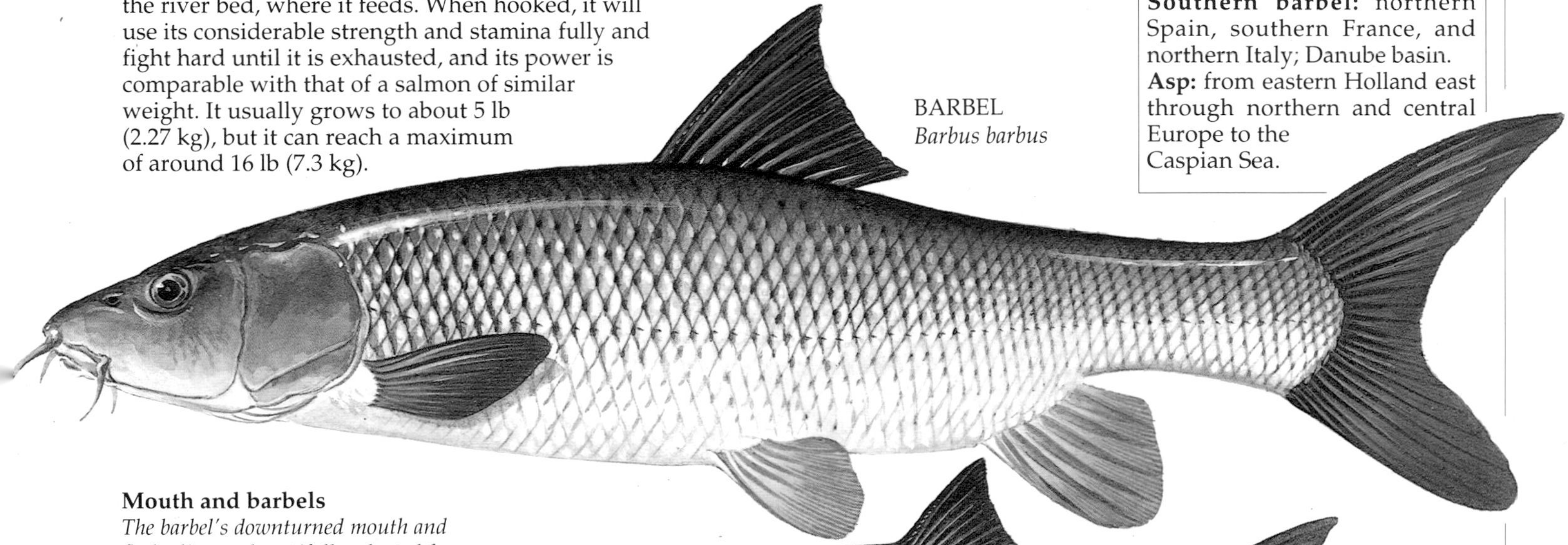

BARBEL
Barbus barbus

Mouth and barbels
The barbel's downturned mouth and fleshy lips are beautifully adapted for bottom feeding. The four barbels (or barbules) that give the fish its name carry a large number of taste and touch cells, and act like external tongues with which the fish can examine potential food items.

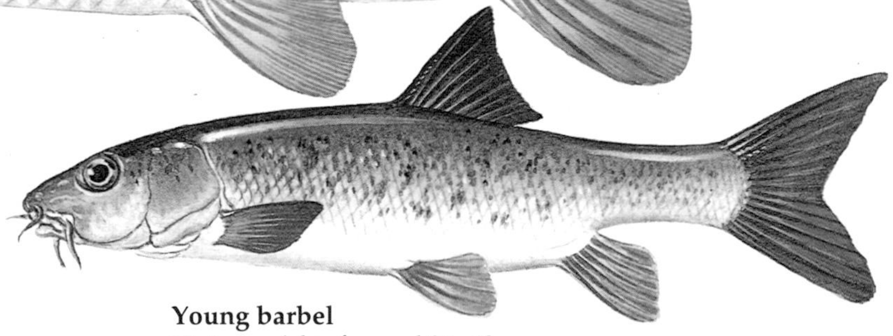

Young barbel
Up to a weight of around 8 to 12 oz (227 to 340 g) and a length of 6 to 8 in (15 to 20 cm), young barbel often have speckled flanks, and their overall coloration tends to be more olive-green than that of their parents.

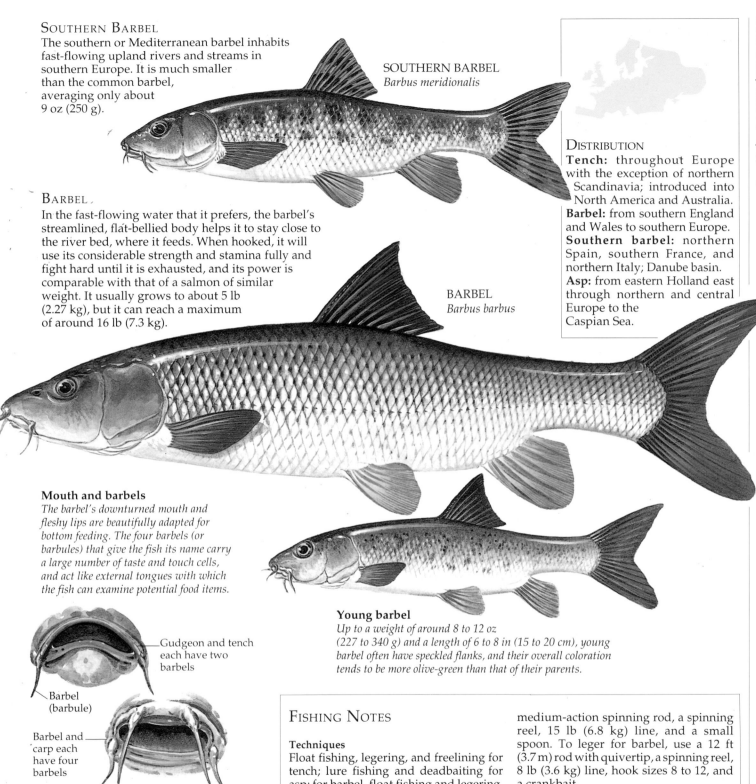

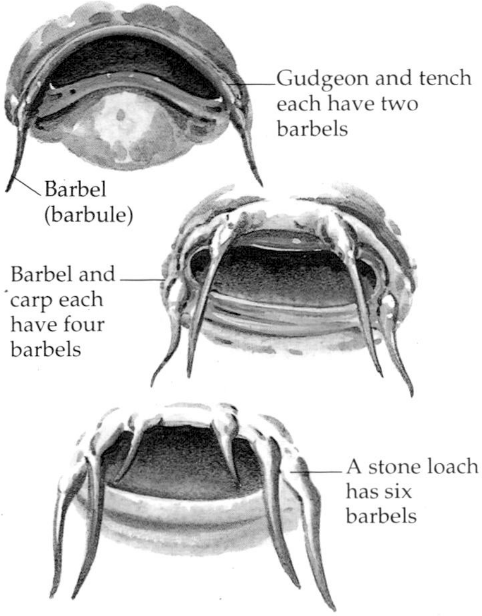
Gudgeon and tench each have two barbels
Barbel (barbule)
Barbel and carp each have four barbels
A stone loach has six barbels

Identification
Count the barbels to distinguish young barbel and carp from similar fish.

Fishing Notes

Techniques
Float fishing, legering, and freelining for tench; lure fishing and deadbaiting for asp; for barbel, float fishing and legering, especially legering with a crankbait.

Tackle
When float fishing for tench, use a 12 ft (3.7 m) medium-action rod, a spinning reel, 10 lb (4.54 kg) line, and hook sizes 6 or 8. To leger for tench, try a 12 ft (3.7 m) Avon rod with a spinning reel, 7 lb (3.2 kg) line, size 6 to 12 hook, and a crankbait. For asp, try a 9 ft (2.7 m) medium-action spinning rod, a spinning reel, 15 lb (6.8 kg) line, and a small spoon. To leger for barbel, use a 12 ft (3.7 m) rod with quivertip, a spinning reel, 8 lb (3.6 kg) line, hook sizes 8 to 12, and a crankbait.

Bait
Good tench baits include bread, maggots, corn, worms, meat, and small boilies. Asp can be taken on spoons, especially if a small piece of red wool is tied to the hook to provide extra attraction, and on small fish baits such as bleak. For barbel, try maggots, meat, vetches, corn, worms, bread, and cheese.

BREAM, NASE, & VIMBA

These European members of the carp family are all primarily bottom-feeders. Bream are widely distributed in stillwaters, canals, and deep, slow-flowing rivers; the nase prefers the faster-flowing waters of the middle reaches of rivers; and the vimba is found in the middle and lower reaches of large, slow rivers. The most widespread of these species, and the most popular with anglers, is the bronze bream.

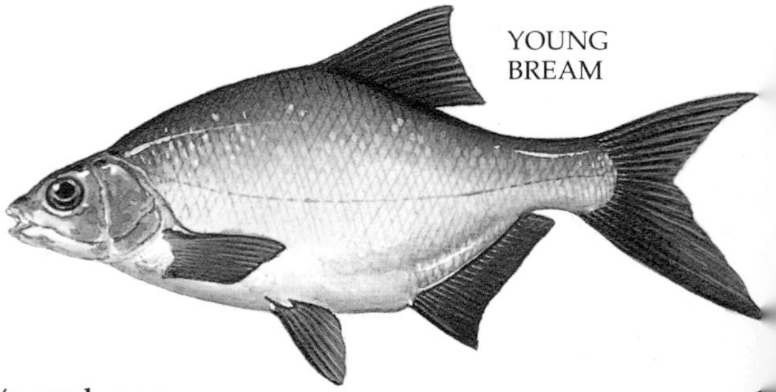

YOUNG BREAM

Young bream
When young, bronze bream are silvery with black fins. In Britain, these little fish are known as tinplate bream or skimmers.

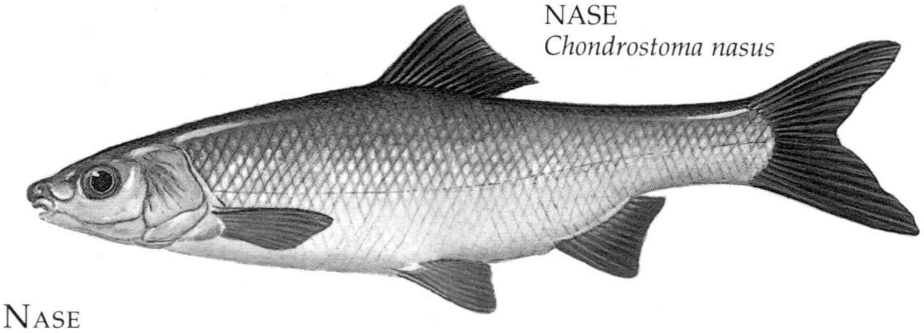

NASE
Chondrostoma nasus

NASE

The silvery, slender-bodied nase has red-tinged fins and a smallish head with a noticeably protuberant snout. It feeds on algae and diatoms, which it scrapes from rocks and stones with its hard, horny lower lip, and can reach a maximum weight of about 4 lb (1.8 kg). The toxostome, or soiffe (*Chondrostoma toxostoma*), is similar to the nase, but smaller.

Roach/bream hybrids
Where spawning schools of bream and roach (see page 137) *occur in the same waters, roach/bream hybrids are common. To identify a hybrid, count the number of rays in the anal fin: a roach has 9 to 12, a bream has 23 to 29, and a hybrid 14 to 19.*

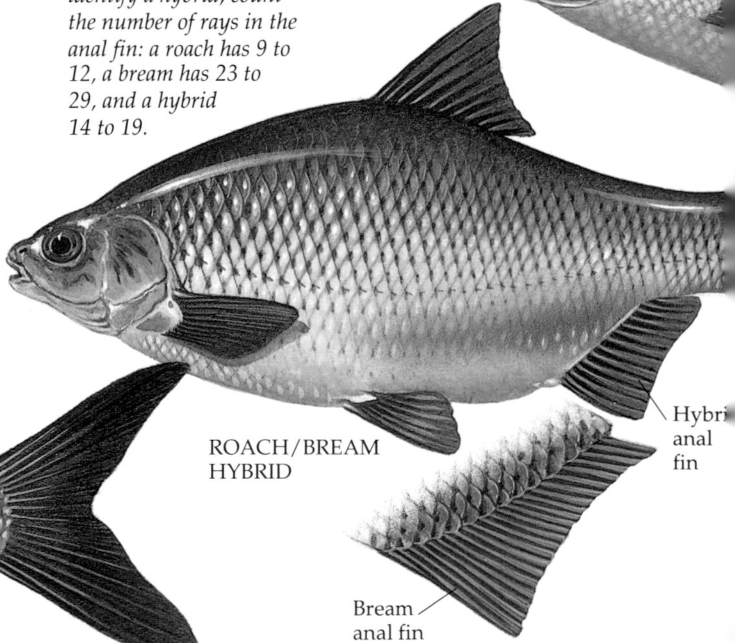

ROACH/BREAM HYBRID

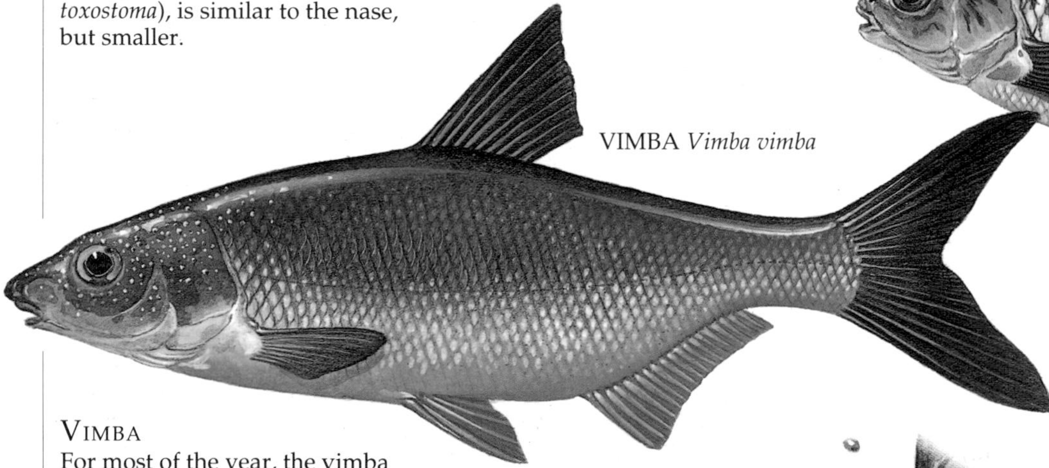

VIMBA *Vimba vimba*

VIMBA

For most of the year, the vimba (known in Germany as the Zährte) has silvery sides and a blue-gray back, but at spawning time (in early summer) the male becomes very dark on the back with an orange-red belly. The vimba's staple diet consists of worms, mollusks, and crustaceans, and its weight ranges from around 2 lb (910 g) to 6 lb 10 oz (3 kg).

Feeding bream
When feeding, a bream upends itself and its mouth protrudes down to suck in worms, mollusks, crustaceans, and insect larvae. A school of feeding bream will betray its presence by stirring up clouds of silt from the bottom.

SILVER BREAM
Blicca bjoerkna

Size comparison

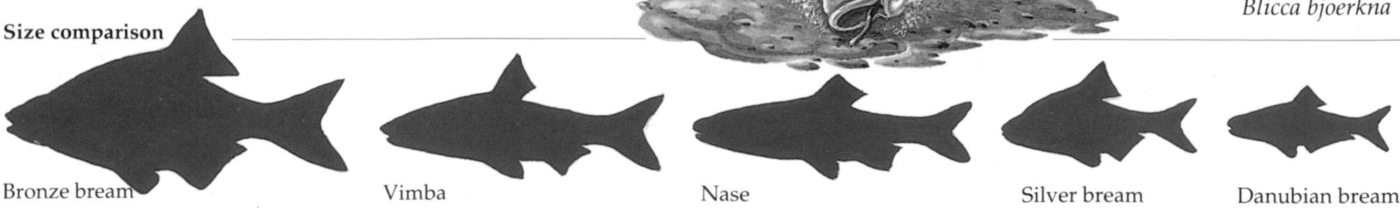

Bronze bream Vimba Nase Silver bream Danubian bream

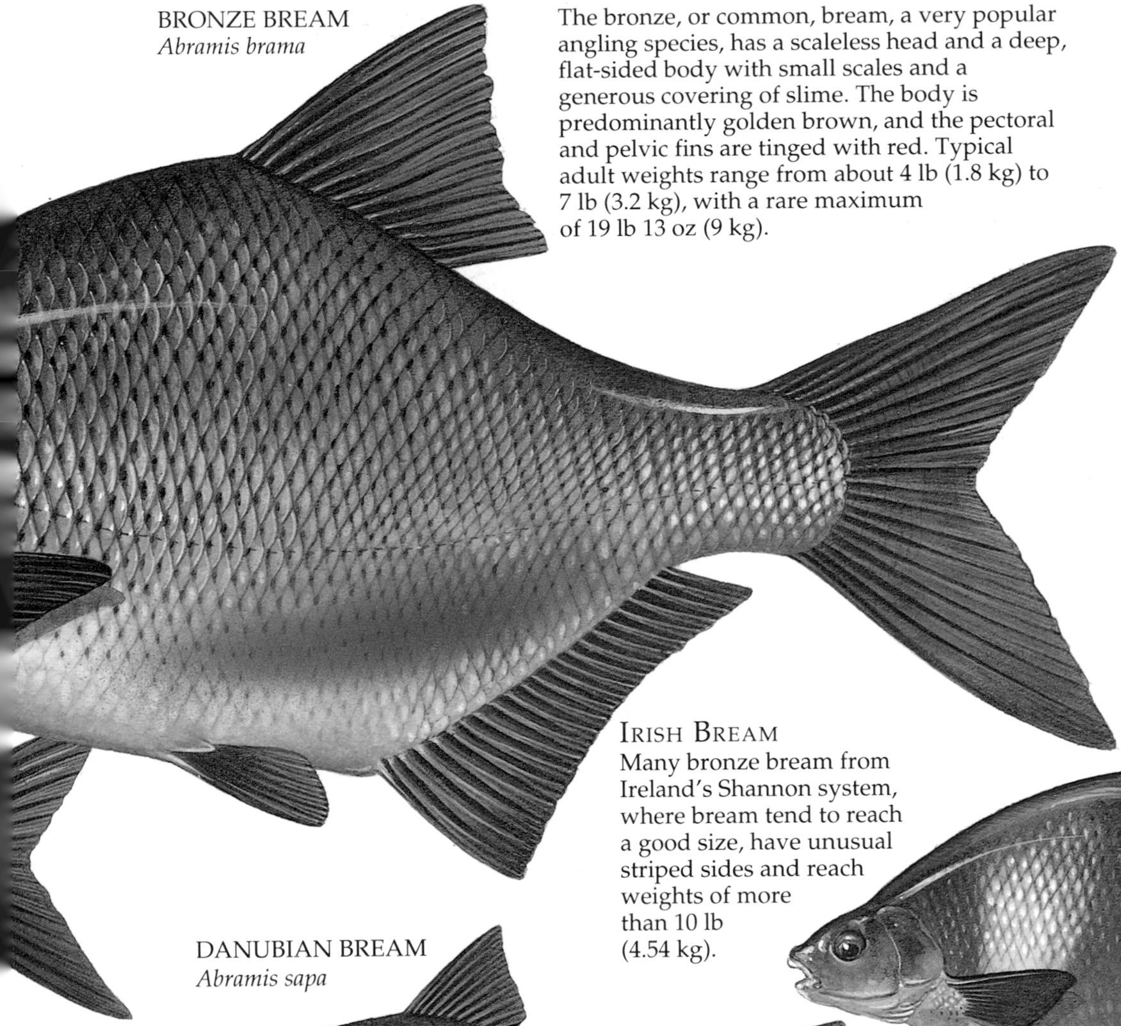

BRONZE BREAM
Abramis brama

Bronze Bream

The bronze, or common, bream, a very popular angling species, has a scaleless head and a deep, flat-sided body with small scales and a generous covering of slime. The body is predominantly golden brown, and the pectoral and pelvic fins are tinged with red. Typical adult weights range from about 4 lb (1.8 kg) to 7 lb (3.2 kg), with a rare maximum of 19 lb 13 oz (9 kg).

Distribution

Bronze bream: from Ireland east through most of northern, central, and southern Europe to the Urals and into parts of central Asia.
Silver bream: from eastern England to the Caspian, except northern Scandinavia, Spain, Portugal, and Italy.
Danubian bream: Danube and Volga basins.
Nase: from France to western Russia and the Caspian.
Vimba: from the Baltic Sea through northern, central, and eastern Europe.

Irish Bream

Many bronze bream from Ireland's Shannon system, where bream tend to reach a good size, have unusual striped sides and reach weights of more than 10 lb (4.54 kg).

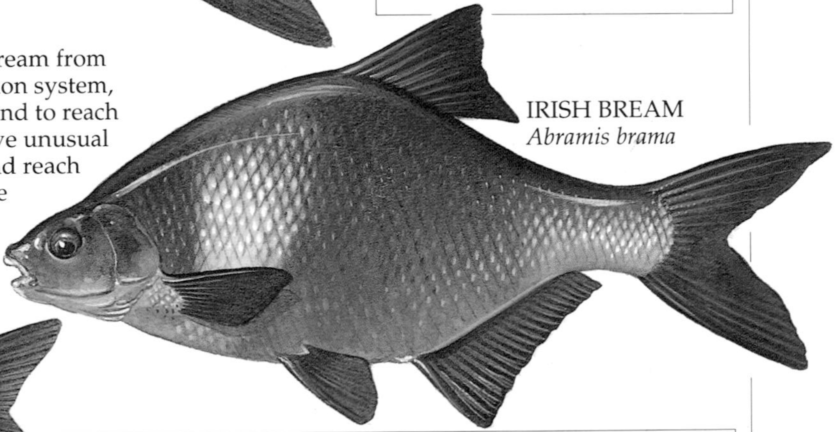

IRISH BREAM
Abramis brama

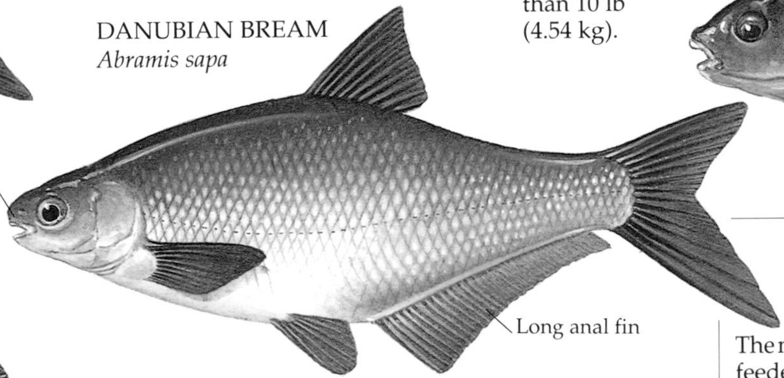

DANUBIAN BREAM
Abramis sapa

Danubian Bream

The Danubian, or whiteye, bream is a small, silvery fish, weighing only some 1 lb 12 oz (800 g), with a blunt snout and long anal fin. It is found in the Danube basin and rivers feeding the Black, Caspian, and Aral Seas.

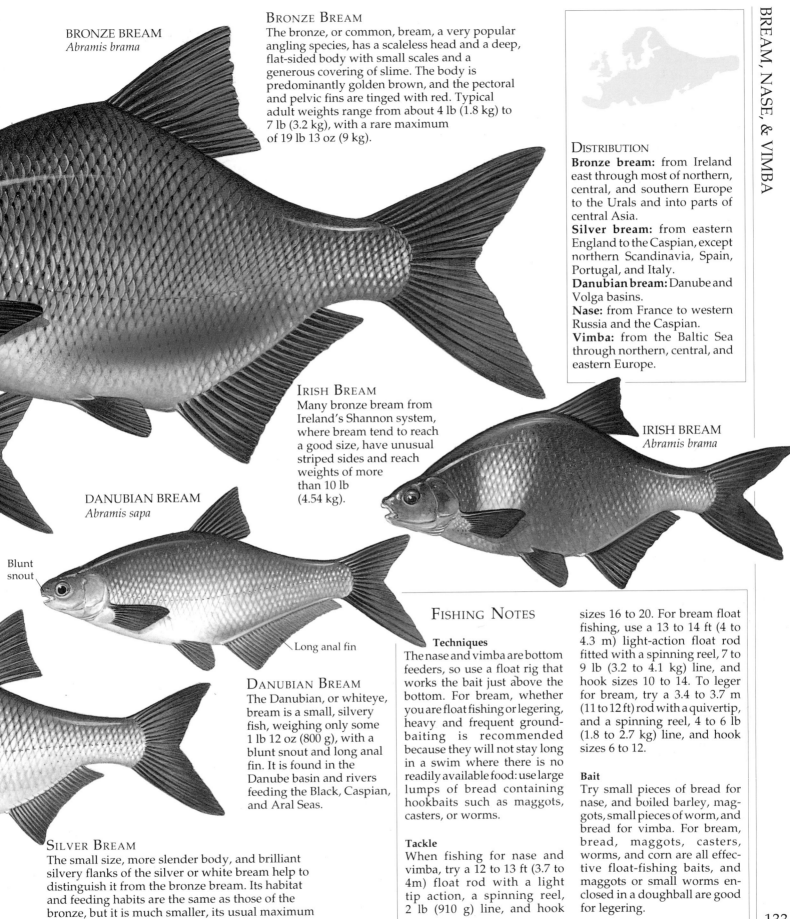

Silver Bream

The small size, more slender body, and brilliant silvery flanks of the silver or white bream help to distinguish it from the bronze bream. Its habitat and feeding habits are the same as those of the bronze, but it is much smaller, its usual maximum weight being only 1 lb (454 g).

Fishing Notes

Techniques

The nase and vimba are bottom feeders, so use a float rig that works the bait just above the bottom. For bream, whether you are float fishing or legering, heavy and frequent groundbaiting is recommended because they will not stay long in a swim where there is no readily available food: use large lumps of bread containing hookbaits such as maggots, casters, or worms.

Tackle

When fishing for nase and vimba, try a 12 to 13 ft (3.7 to 4m) float rod with a light tip action, a spinning reel, 2 lb (910 g) line, and hook sizes 16 to 20. For bream float fishing, use a 13 to 14 ft (4 to 4.3 m) light-action float rod fitted with a spinning reel, 7 to 9 lb (3.2 to 4.1 kg) line, and hook sizes 10 to 14. To leger for bream, try a 3.4 to 3.7 m (11 to 12 ft) rod with a quivertip, and a spinning reel, 4 to 6 lb (1.8 to 2.7 kg) line, and hook sizes 6 to 12.

Bait

Try small pieces of bread for nase, and boiled barley, maggots, small pieces of worm, and bread for vimba. For bream, bread, maggots, casters, worms, and corn are all effective float-fishing baits, and maggots or small worms enclosed in a doughball are good for legering.

CYPRINIDAE

CARP

The wild carp was being farmed for food in Asia by about 400 BC. Since then, selective breeding on eastern European fish farms has produced a number of variants such as the common, leather, and mirror forms. These and the wild carp have spread throughout Europe both naturally and by introduction, and have been introduced elsewhere, including North America and Australia.

FISHING NOTES

Techniques
Float fishing, legering, and freelining for common carp; float fishing for crucian.

Tackle
For common carp float fishing, use a 12 ft (3.7 m), 1½ lb (680 g) test curve rod with a spinning reel, 8 lb (3.6 kg) line, and hook sizes 8 to 12. Legering calls for heavier tackle, for instance a 12 ft (3.7 m), 2 lb (910 g) test curve rod with a spinning reel, 12 lb (5.4 kg) line, and hook sizes 6 to 10. For crucian carp, use a 13 ft (4 m) light-action rod with a spinning reel, 1½ to 2½ lb (680 g to 1.1 kg) line, and hook sizes 12 to 18.

Bait
The range of baits used by carp fishermen is enormous and constantly growing. It extends from simple, traditional baits, such as bread, worms, and maggots, through luncheon meat, sweet corn, and potatoes, to the numerous commercially prepared baits such as boilies, and bait additives such as meat-, spice-, and aromatic fruit-flavored oils.

WILD CARP

The wild carp is a strong, slow-growing fish with a scaleless head and a fully scaled body. Smaller and less deep-bodied than the common carp, its average weight is 2 to 5 lb (910 g to 2.27 kg) and it seldom exceeds 20 lb (9.1 kg).

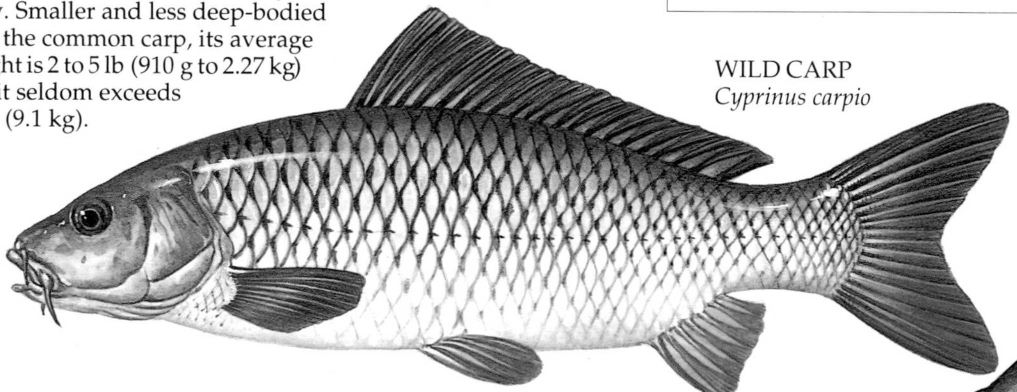

WILD CARP
Cyprinus carpio

Breeding
Wild and common carp spawn in late spring and early summer, when the water temperature exceeds 64°F (18°C). The eggs are laid in shallow water that has abundant dense vegetation and good exposure to sunlight, and are attached to the leaves and stems of water plants. They hatch in five to eight days, the hatchlings initially remaining attached to the plants. The young fish grow very quickly.

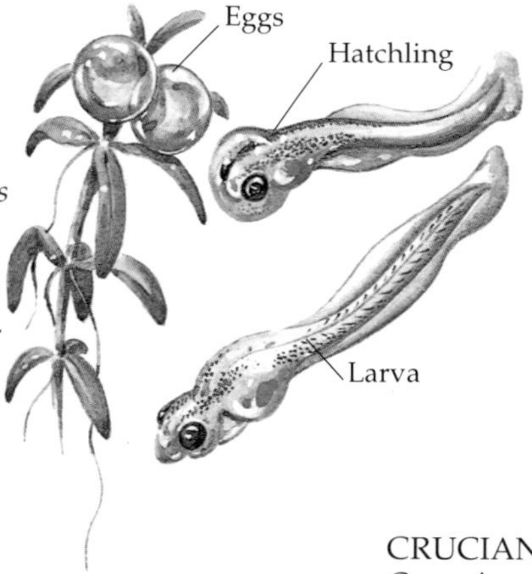

Feeding
The common carp feeds at the surface, on the bottom, or in midwater on plants, algae, snails, worms, insect larvae, shrimps, mussels, and many other organisms. It opens its mouth wide and sucks its food in like a vacuum cleaner, and often rummages through the bottom detritus, sending up clouds of silt and uprooting plants.

CRUCIAN CARP

This small, deep-bodied carp is more closely related to the goldfish than to the wild carp, but will interbreed with both species. It averages about 9 oz (255 g), but can exceed 5 lb 8 oz (2.5 kg), and it will tolerate a wide range of temperatures, low oxygen levels, acidity, and dense vegetation.

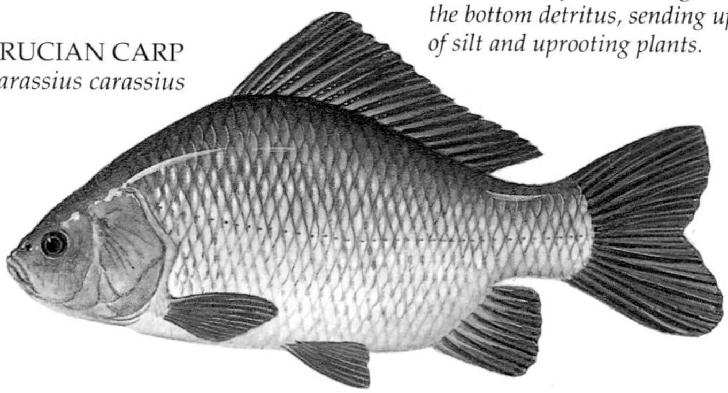

CRUCIAN CARP
Carassius carassius

Size comparison

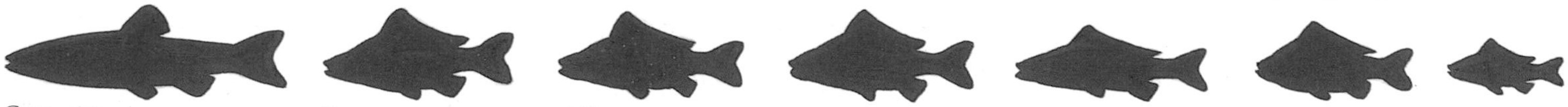

Grass Carp

The wide mouth of the grass carp is superbly adapted for feeding on plants, and because of its huge appetite it has been introduced into many canals, ponds, and drains in Europe and North America for weed clearance. Its growth rate is very rapid, and in warm waters it can reach 77 lb (35 kg).

GRASS CARP
Ctenopharyngodon idella

Distribution

Common carp: through most of Eurasia; North America, South Africa, India, Australia, and New Zealand.
Crucian, grass, and goldfish: native to Eurasia and widely introduced elsewhere.

GOLDFISH
Carassius auratus

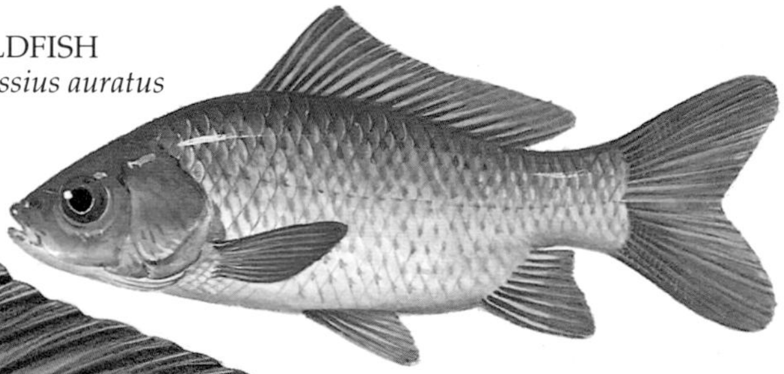

Goldfish

Within a few generations of release into the wild, the domestic goldfish reverts to its natural carplike coloration and can grow to a weight of about 6lb 10 oz (3 kg).

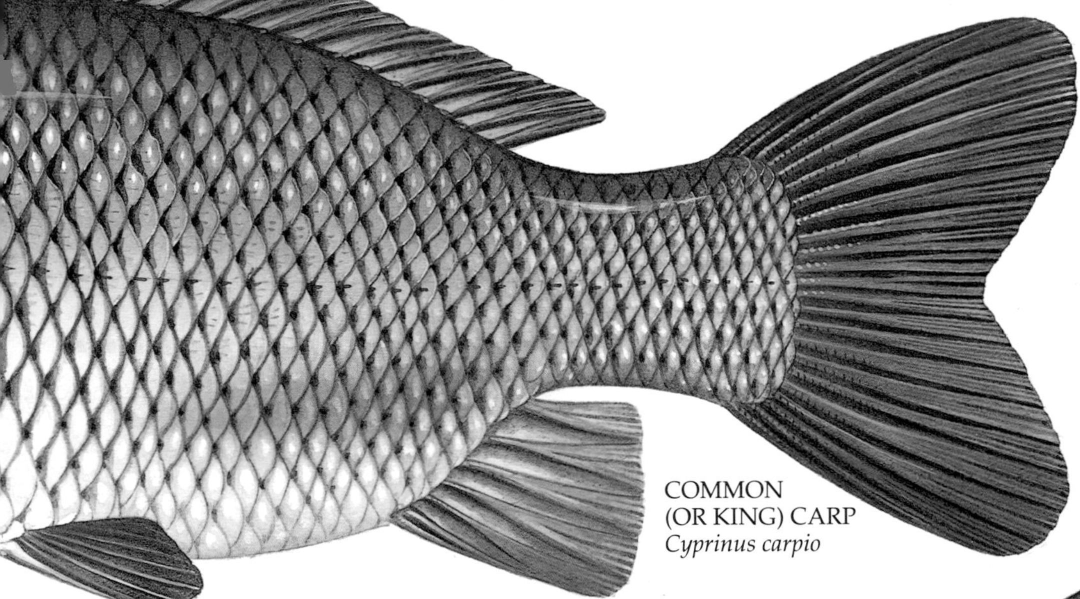

COMMON (OR KING) CARP
Cyprinus carpio

Common (or King) Carp

The heavy, deep-bodied common, or king, carp, together with its leather and mirror varieties, is the result of centuries of selective breeding by fish farms. Like the wild carp from which it derives, the common carp has a scaleless head and a fully scaled body, and its coloration is variable. It can reach a weight of 80 lb (36 kg) and a length of about 5 ft (1.5 m).

Mirror carp scale
The scales of the mirror carp are much larger than those of the common carp. A typical mirror carp scale might be 2 in (5 cm) long and 1.2 in (3 cm) wide, compared with a length of 1.2 in (3 cm) and a width of 1 in (2.5 cm) for a scale of a similar-sized common carp.

MIRROR CARP
Cyprinus carpio

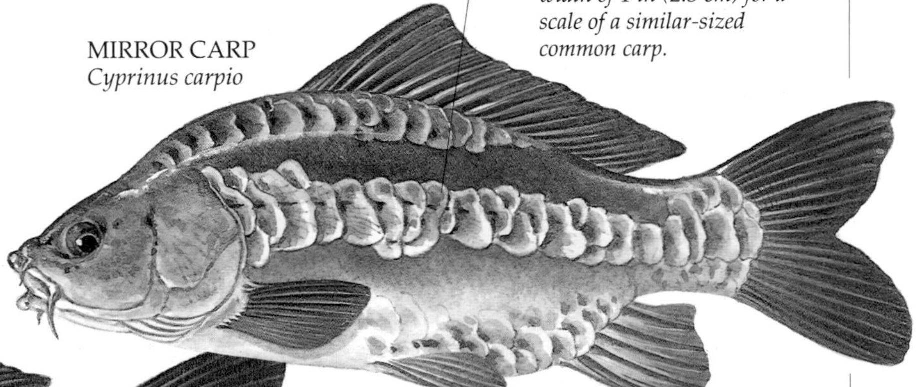

Leather Carp

The scaleless or almost-scaleless leather carp is a variety of common carp. Any scales that are present are large and few in number, and usually near the fins and tail. Like the common and mirror varieties, it has been introduced around the world.

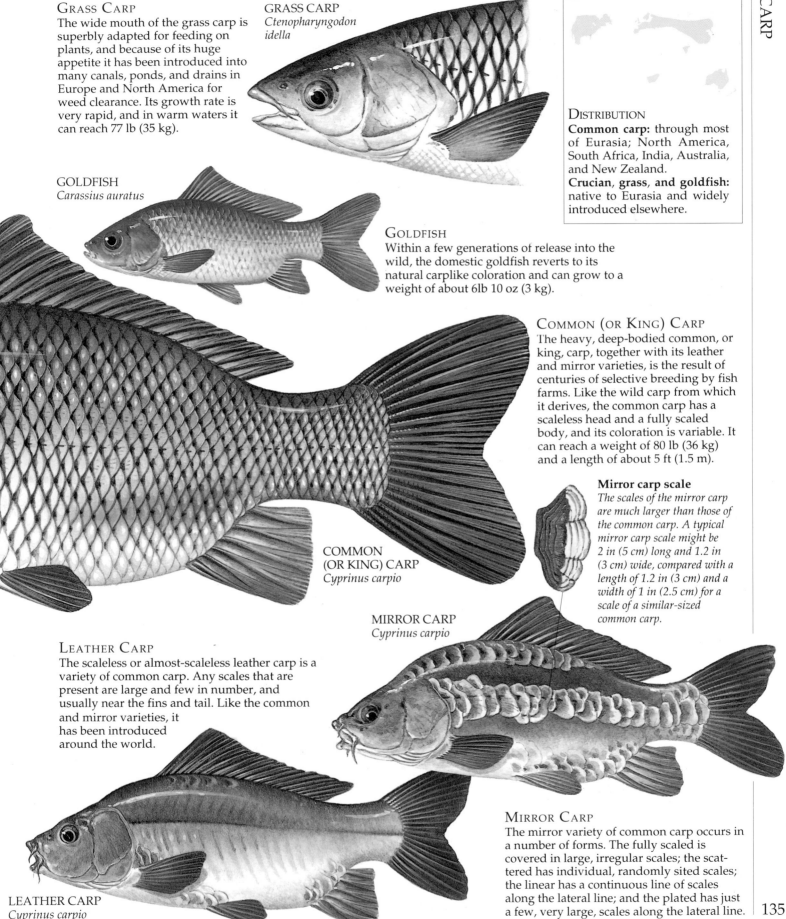

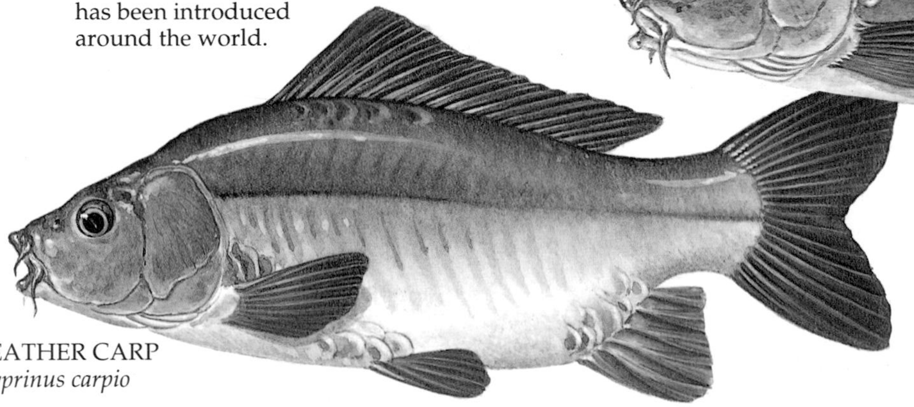

LEATHER CARP
Cyprinus carpio

Mirror Carp

The mirror variety of common carp occurs in a number of forms. The fully scaled is covered in large, irregular scales; the scattered has individual, randomly sited scales; the linear has a continuous line of scales along the lateral line; and the plated has just a few, very large, scales along the lateral line.

CYPRINIDAE

Chub, Dace, Roach, & Rudd

These popular angling species are widespread in the rivers and stillwaters of Europe. Chub and dace prefer moderate to fast flows of clean water, but they are also found in slow lowland rivers and sometimes in lakes. Roach and rudd thrive in canals, slow-flowing rivers, and stillwaters where there is plenty of vegetation. The roach has been introduced into Australia, where it is found in Victoria and southern New South Wales, and the rudd has been introduced into the northeastern United States, where there are breeding populations in Maine and in the lower Hudson basin in New York.

Chub food
Young chub eat mostly insect larvae and aquatic invertebrates. Adults will take anything edible that comes their way, opening their large, wide mouths to engulf small fish, frogs, crayfish, and small water voles, and snapping up berries that fall from overhanging trees and bushes.

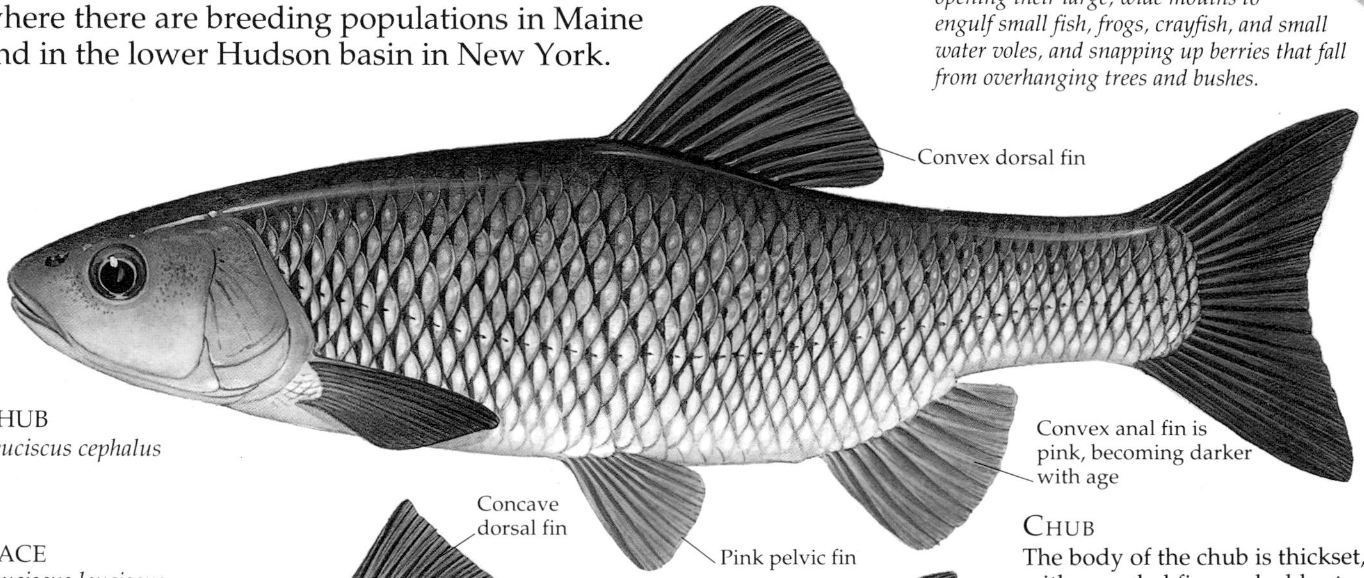

CHUB
Leuciscus cephalus

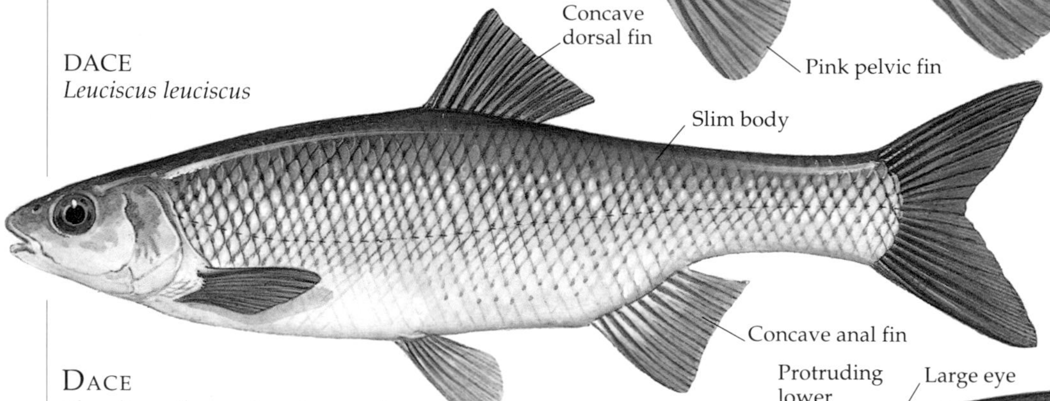

DACE
Leuciscus leuciscus

Chub

The body of the chub is thickset, with rounded fins and a blunt snout, and the dark edges of its scales give its back and sides an attractive, latticed appearance. In British waters the maximum weight is probably about 12 lb (5.4 kg), but in mainland Europe it can reach 16 lb (7.26 kg).

Dace

The slim, silvery dace is one of the smallest species to be of serious angling interest: its maximum weight is only about 1 lb 5 oz (600 g), and a fish of 6 to 8 oz (170 to 227 g) would be a good catch. It feeds on insects, crustaceans, and plants.

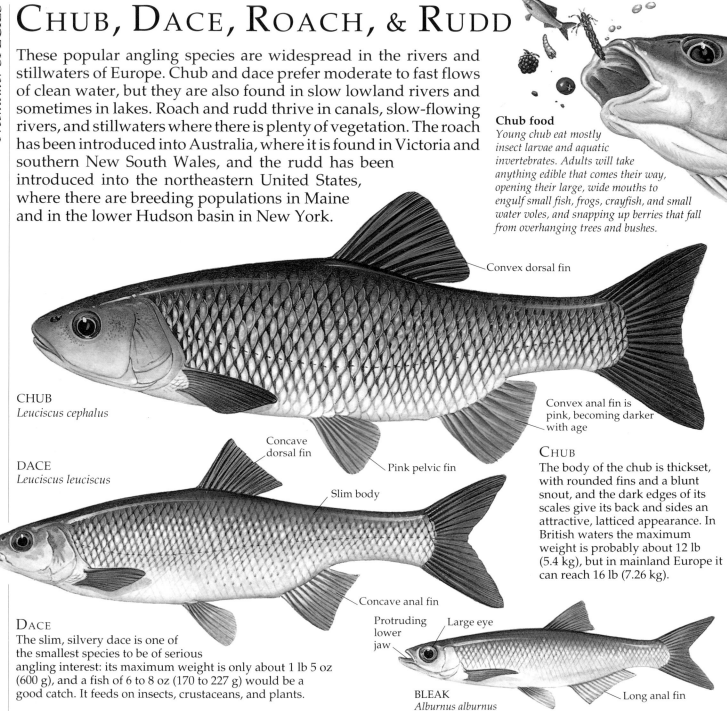

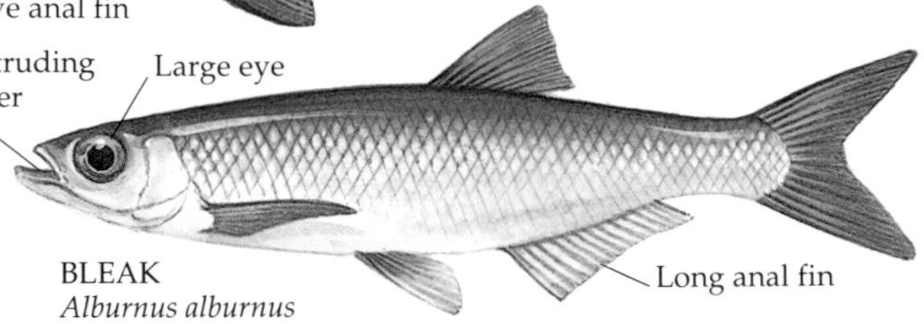

BLEAK
Alburnus alburnus

Fishing Notes

Techniques
Float fishing and legering are the most usual techniques for these species, but fly fishing is an enjoyable alternative.

Tackle
To leger for chub, use a 12 ft (3.7 m) rod with a built-in quivertip, and a spinning reel, 5 lb (2.27 kg) line, hook sizes 8 to 16, and a suitable blockend crankbait. For float fishing, try a 12 to 13 ft (3.7 to 4 m) rod with a spinning reel, 3 lb (1.36 kg) line, and hook sizes 14 to 20. To float fish for dace, use a 12 ft (3.7 m) rod with a light tip action, a spinning reel, 2 lb (910 g) line, and hook sizes 16 to 20. To float fish for roach or rudd, try a 12 ft (3.7 m) rod with a light action, a spinning reel, 2½ lb (1.1 kg) line, and hook sizes 14 to 20. When legering for roach or rudd, use a 10 to 12 ft (3 to 3.7 m) rod with quivertip, a spinning reel, 2½ to 4 lb (1.36 to 1.8 kg) line, and hook sizes 10 to 16.

Bait
For all these species, good float fishing or legering baits include maggots, casters, bread, and worms, and large slugs are especially effective for chub. These species can also be taken on fly tackle, using either wet or dry flies.

Chub, dace, or bleak?
Young chub are similar in size and general appearance to dace and bleak, but each has its own distinguishing features. The chub has convex dorsal and anal fins, and its pelvic and anal fins are pink. In comparison, the grayish dorsal fin and pale, yellowish anal fins of the dace are concave, and the grayish, concave anal fin of the bleak is much longer than that of either the chub or the dace. The bleak also has a protruding lower jaw and large, prominent eyes.

Danubian Roach

This relatively slender-bodied roach has a small head and large, silvery scales, and occurs as two subspecies: *Rutilus pigus pigus* of the Po basin in northern Italy, and *R. p. virgo* of the Danube basin. It can reach a weight of 2 lb 3 oz (1 kg) or more, but most are much smaller.

DANUBIAN ROACH
Rutilus pigus

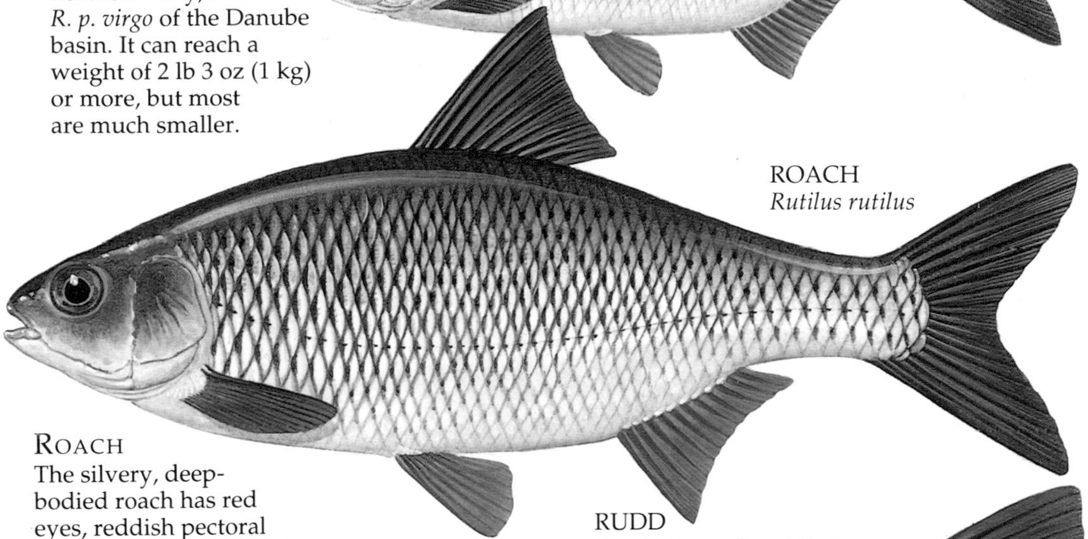

ROACH
Rutilus rutilus

Roach

The silvery, deep-bodied roach has red eyes, reddish pectoral fins, red pelvic and anal fins, and dusky dorsal and tail fins. It is the most popular angling species in Europe, mainly because it is extremely common and catching it requires skill. It reaches about 4 lb (1.8 kg), and often hybridizes with bream *(see page 132).*

Distribution

Chub: Europe, except Ireland, the snowbelt of Scandinavia, and southern Italy.
Dace: from Ireland to Siberia, but not south of the Pyrenees and the Alps.
Roach: Europe from Ireland to the Urals, but not found in the Scandinavian snowbelt or south of the Pyrenees and the Alps; has been introduced into Australia.
Rudd: Europe from Ireland to the Urals and from southern Sweden to northern Italy and Greece; introduced into the northeastern United States.

RUDD
Scardinius erythrophthalmus

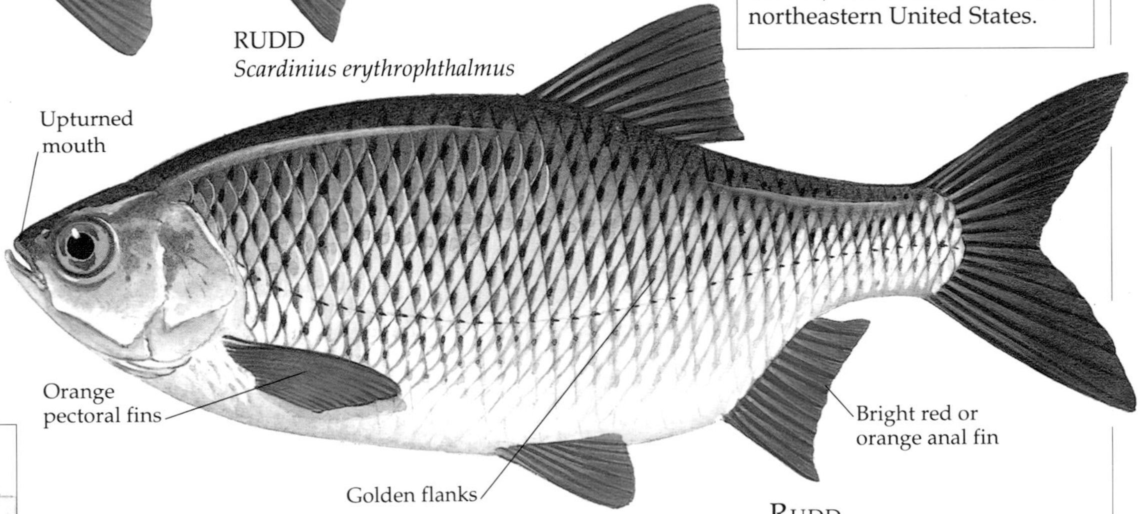

Rudd

The deep-bodied rudd grows to a maximum weight of about 4 lb 7 oz (2 kg), slightly more than that of the roach. Because it takes much of its food at or near the surface, it is more easily located than the deeper-feeding roach, and this makes it somewhat easier to catch. However, the older, larger individuals often lie deep and feed at the bottom, so bottom fishing may catch bigger (if fewer) rudd than fishing near the surface.

Feeding rudd and roach
The rudd's upturned mouth is adapted for surface feeding on food such as insects, plants, and fish fry. The roach has a similar diet but is less of a surface feeder.

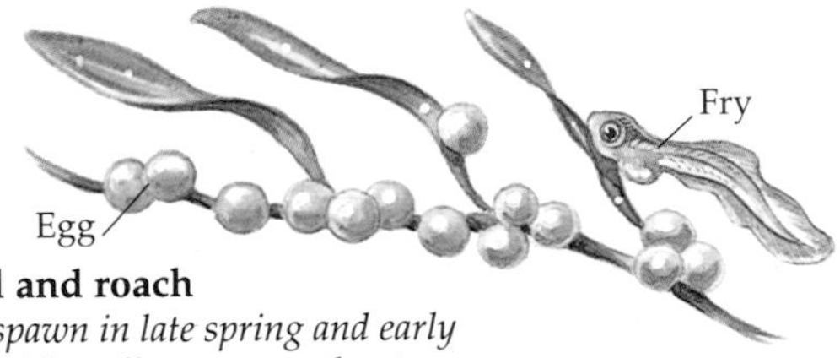

Breeding rudd and roach
Rudd and roach spawn in late spring and early summer, laying sticky yellow eggs on the stems and leaves of aquatic plants. Rudd eggs hatch in 8 to 15 days and roach eggs in 9 to 12 days; on average, fish of both species take nine or ten years to reach a weight of 1 lb 2 oz (500 g).

Size comparison

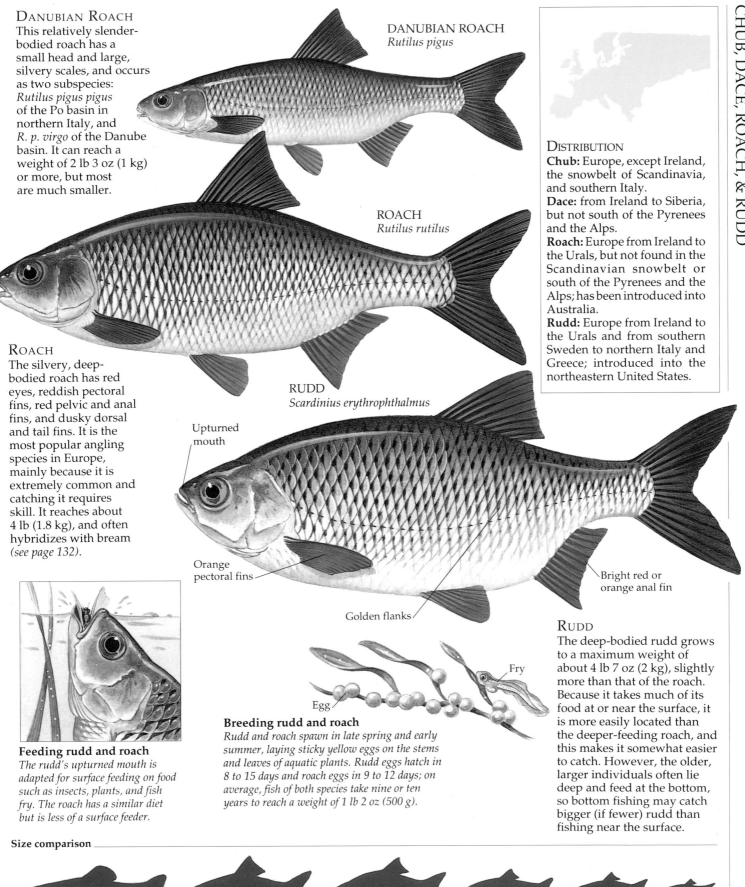

ESOCIDAE

Pike, Pickerel, & Muskellunge

The members of the pike family are voracious predators, disliked and even feared by some anglers but greatly admired by others because of their size and the tenacious fight they put up when hooked. They inhabit rivers, streams, and stillwaters with clear water but with plenty of vegetation in which to lurk in wait for their prey. The pike itself, known in North America as the northern pike, is one of the few freshwater species native to both Eurasia and North America. Pickerel and muskellunge are purely North American species.

REDFIN PICKEREL
Esox americanus americanus

GRASS PICKEREL
Esox americanus vermiculatus

CHAIN PICKEREL
Esox niger

Pickerel

The chain pickerel averages only 2 lb (910 g) but has been known to reach 9 lb 6 oz (4.25 kg). Despite being relatively small, it provides good sport on light tackle, as do the even smaller grass and redfin pickerels, which are less than half its size. Apart from the difference in their sizes, the chain pickerel can be distinguished from the grass and redfin by its markings. The chain pickerel has a distinctive dark, chainlike pattern on its sides, while the grass and redfin are both marked with dark bars; the redfin, as its name implies, also has red fins.

Muskellunge

The mighty muskellunge is a powerful, fast-growing fish that can reach a length of 12 in (30 cm) in only four months and grows to 6 ft (1.83 m) or more. Its maximum weight is at least 70 lb (31.75 kg), and weights in excess of 100 lb (45 kg) have been reported. The most visible difference between the muskellunge and the northern pike is in their markings: the "muskie" has dark bars or blotches on its sides, while the pike has a series of pale bars and spots.

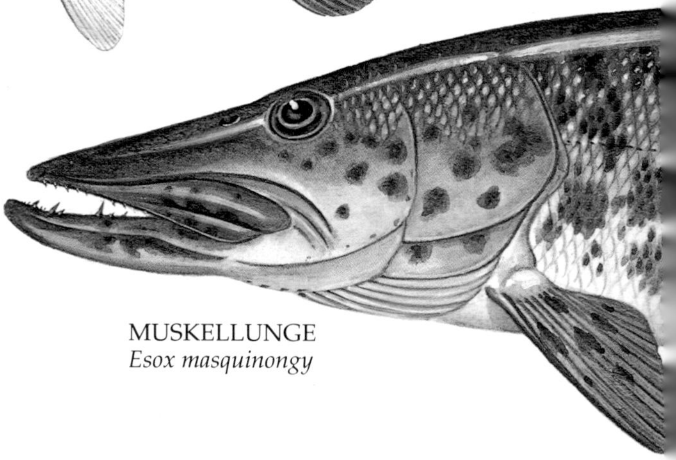

MUSKELLUNGE
Esox masquinongy

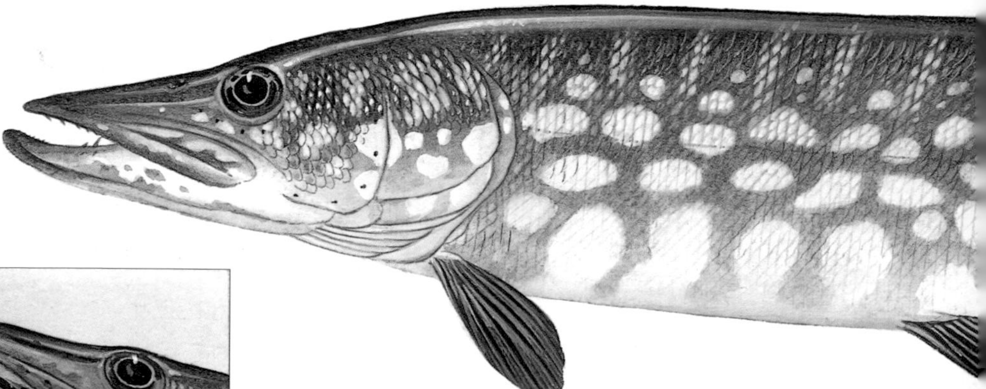

FEEDING
The principal food of the pike family is fish, including smaller fish of their own kind. They are, however, great opportunists and will take any available small prey including frogs, snakes, crayfish, rodents, and ducklings. Their markings provide excellent camouflage as they hide among the weeds, waiting to pounce on passing fish, which they swallow head first.

Fishing Notes

Techniques
These active predators are usually caught by spinning, baitcasting, and trolling, using lures, deadbaits, and livebaits. Fish for them from the bank, or use a boat to reach weedbeds that are otherwise inaccessible.

Tackle
For pickerel, try a 5½ ft (1.7 m) baitcaster with a baitcaster reel or a 6 to 7 ft (1.8 to 2.1 m) spinning rod with a spinning reel; use 6 to 8 lb (2.7 to 3.6 kg) line with a short wire leader. When lure fishing from the bank or a boat for pike or muskellunge, try a 6 to 9 ft (1.8 to 2.7 m) spinning or baitcasting rod with a baitcaster or a spinning reel, 10 to 15 lb (4.54 to 6.8 kg) line, and a 20 lb (9.1 kg) wire leader. When you are downrigger trolling for pike or muskellunge, use a 6 to 7 ft (1.8 to 2.1 m) fast-taper rod with a baitcaster reel, 15 to 20 lb (6.8 to 9.1 kg) line, and a 25 lb (11.3 kg) wire leader.

Bait
Small spinners and spoons are ideal baits for pickerel. For pike and muskellunge, use large spinners, spoons, and plugs, cut fish baits (especially herring, mackerel, and eel), and whole minnows.

Distribution

Pike: northern Europe south to the Pyrenees, east to Siberia; Labrador west to Alaska, south to Pennsylvania, Missouri, and Nebraska.
Muskellunge: Great Lakes region, Mississippi basin, Atlantic drainages south to Georgia and Virginia.
Chain pickerel: Atlantic drainages from Nova Scotia to Florida, Mississippi basin from Missouri south.
Redfin pickerel: Atlantic drainages.
Grass pickerel: Mississippi basin and Great Lakes.

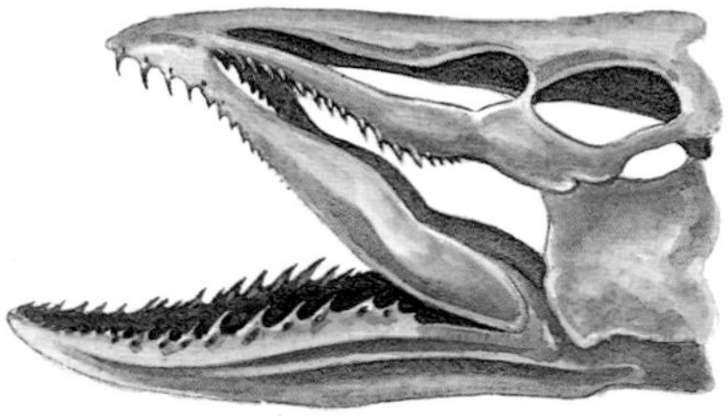

Jaws
The members of the pike family have abundant sharp teeth and very complex skull and jaw structures. These enable them to seize and swallow relatively large fish and other prey; the pike, for example, tends to select prey that is 10 to 25 percent of its own body weight.

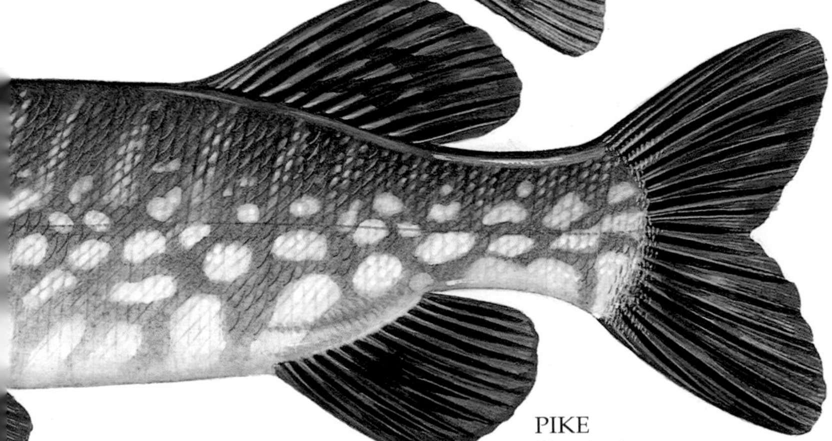

PIKE
Esox lucius

Northern Pike

Like the other members of the family, the pike is an aggressive, solitary hunter, and its torpedo-shaped body is built for short bursts of acceleration rather than sustained speed. It is usually found in or near weedbeds that provide it with cover, but in large lakes it ventures into open water to feed on salmon, trout, or other fish. Growth rates for pike vary enormously and are directly dependent on the available food supply, but an annual weight gain of 2 to 3 lb (910 g to 1.4 kg) is fairly typical. The maximum weight is thought to be about 75 lb (34 kg), but most are much smaller and a pike of 10 to 20 lb (4.54 to 9.1 kg) is a worthwhile catch.

Size comparison

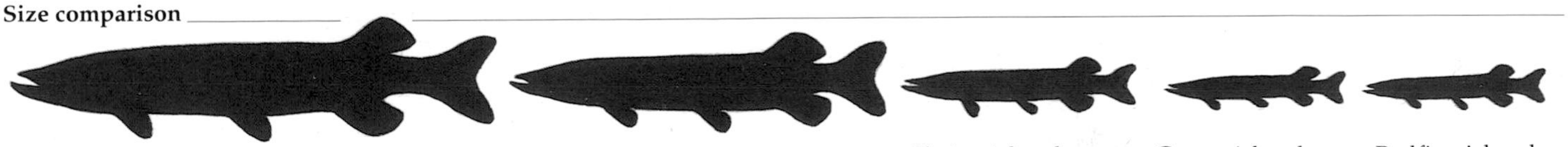

ICTALURIDAE

BULLHEAD

The North American bullhead and freshwater catfish *(see page 142)* are members of the Ictaluridae, which, with some 40 species, is the largest family of freshwater fish native to North America; some have been introduced into Europe and elsewhere. Bullhead are omnivorous, bottom-feeding fish, found mostly in still and slow-flowing waters and characterized by a scaleless body, four pairs of barbels, an adipose fin, and stiff, sharp spines at the leading edges of the pectoral and dorsal fins.

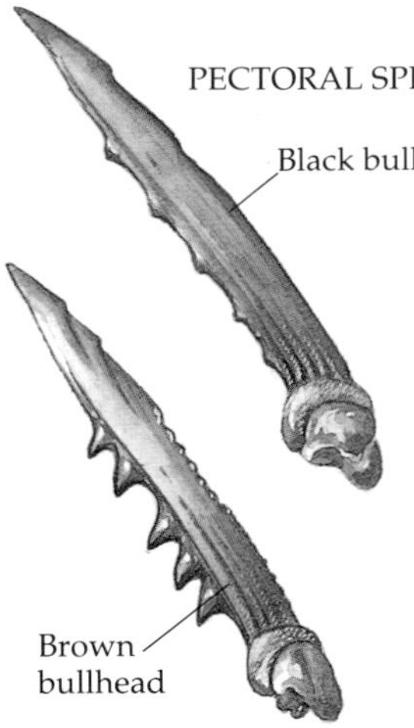

Pectoral spine comparison
The teeth on the black bullhead's pectoral spines are much smaller than those of the brown bullhead.

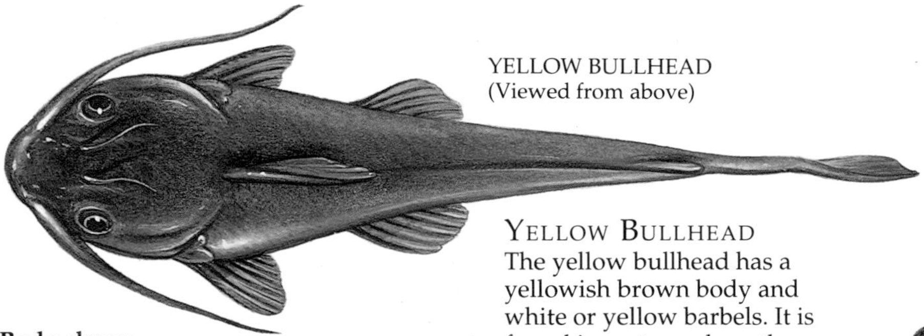

Body shape
Viewed from above, a bullhead has a large, bulbous head and broad "shoulders," and its body tapers sharply from the pectoral fins back to the tail.

YELLOW BULLHEAD

The yellow bullhead has a yellowish brown body and white or yellow barbels. It is found in waters where the bottom is soft, and will eat almost any available food, including plants, snails, insect larvae, small fish, and crayfish. It grows to a maximum weight of about 4 lb 4 oz (1.9 kg).

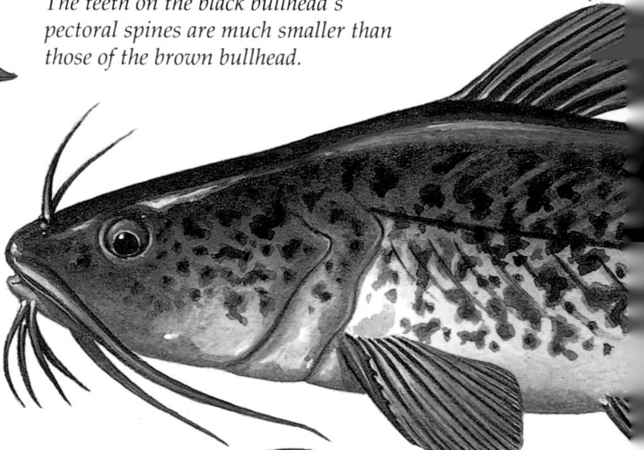

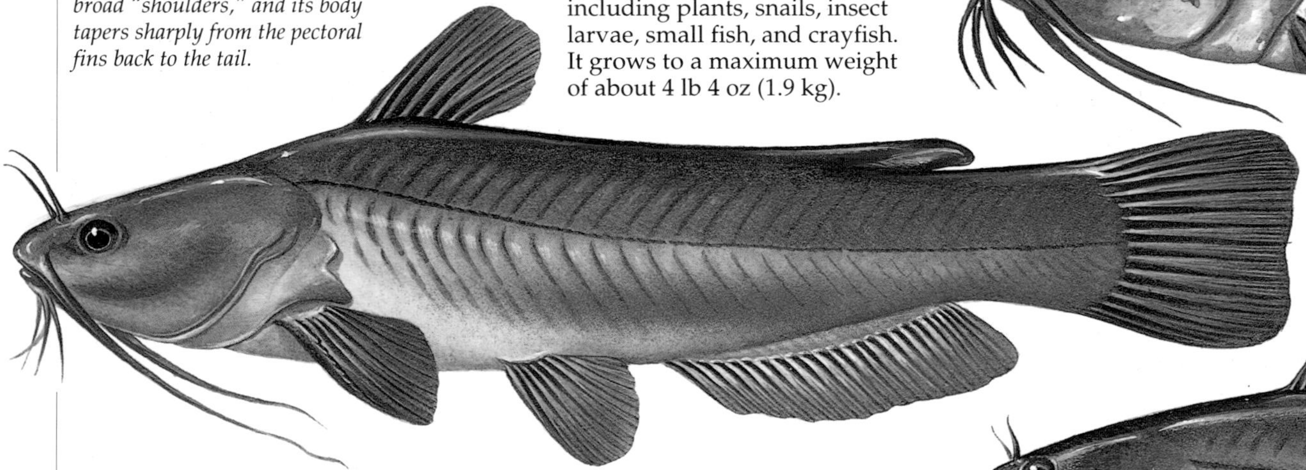

YELLOW BULLHEAD
Ameiurus natalis

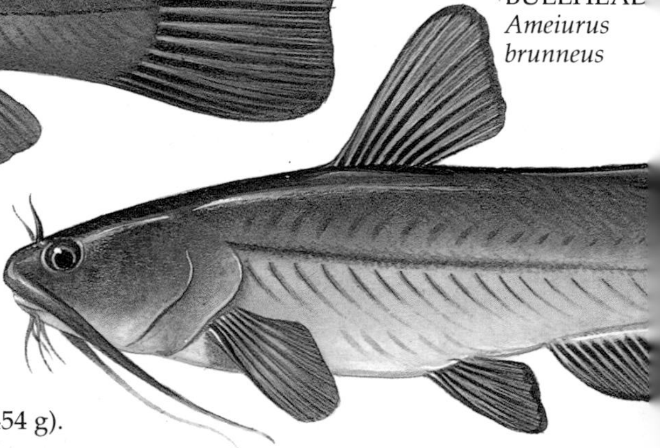

SNAIL BULLHEAD
Ameiurus brunneus

SPOTTED BULLHEAD

The pale spots on the dark body of the spotted bullhead make it easy to recognize. A small fish, its maximum weight is only about 1 lb (454 g).

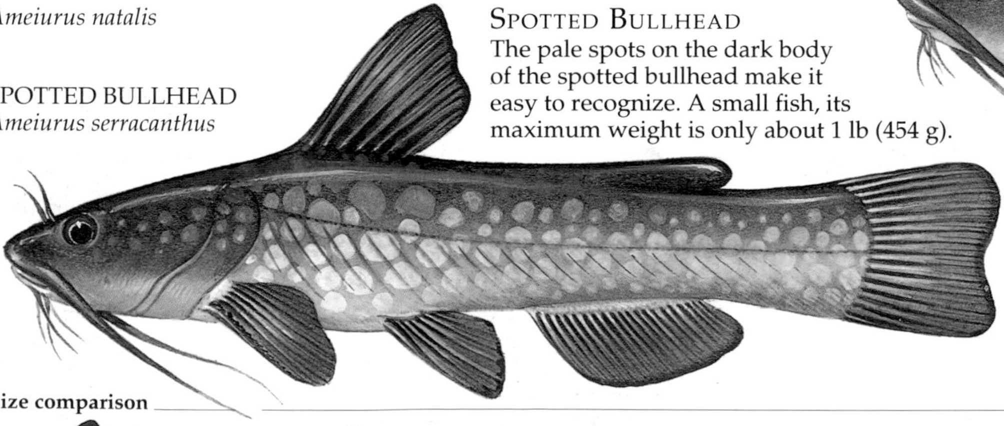

SPOTTED BULLHEAD
Ameiurus serracanthus

SNAIL BULLHEAD

The snail bullhead prefers the rocky runs and flowing pools of swift streams to muddy-bottomed stillwaters and sluggish streams. Its weight ranges from around 4 oz (113 g) up to about 1 lb (454 g).

Size comparison

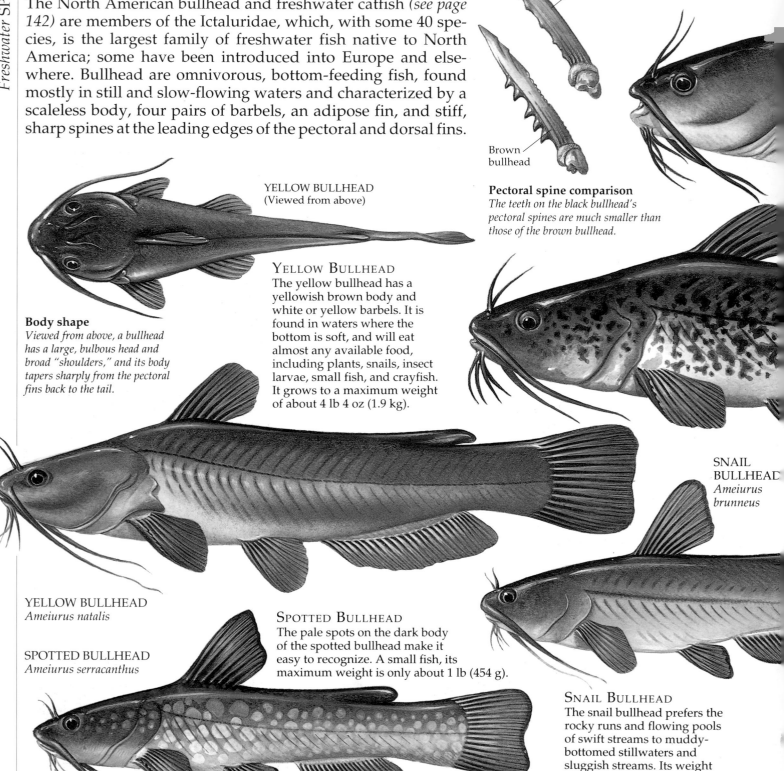

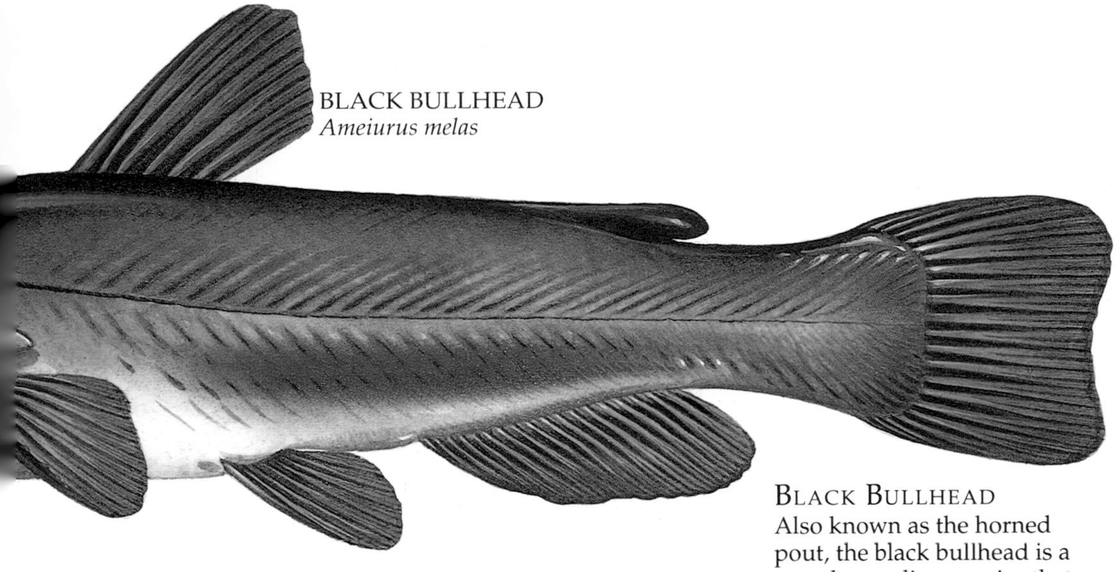

BLACK BULLHEAD
Ameiurus melas

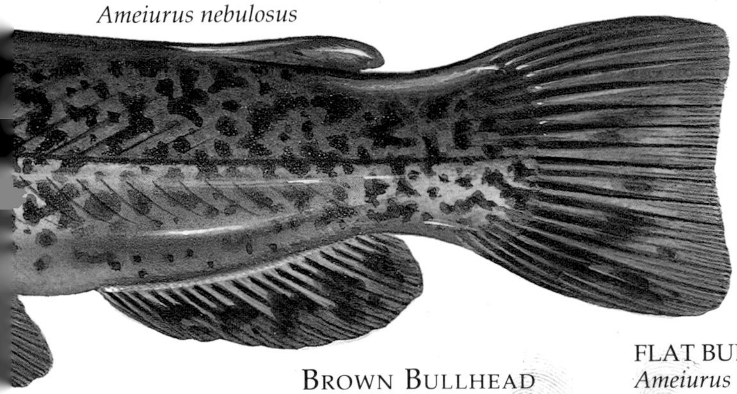

BROWN BULLHEAD
Ameiurus nebulosus

Black Bullhead

Also known as the horned pout, the black bullhead is a popular angling species that will tolerate very poor water quality. It is broadly similar in appearance to the brown bullhead, but lacks the mottled coloration and large pectoral-spine teeth of that species. The black is the largest of the bullheads, but although it can grow to about 8 lb (3.6 kg) it seldom exceeds 2 lb (910g).

Distribution

Black: from Montana east to the Great Lakes and south to the Gulf Slope drainages; introduced into Europe.
Brown: the Great Lakes and Maine south to Mexico and Florida; introduced into Europe and New Zealand.
Yellow: Dakotas to Atlantic and Gulf Slope drainages.
Spotted: Florida, Georgia, and Alabama.
Snail: southern Virginia to eastern Alabama and northern Florida.
Flat: Virginia to Georgia.

Flat Bullhead

In profile, the flat bullhead has a flattened head and relatively straight snout. Its coloration is a mottled yellow to dark brown, with a light belly, and it averages about 1 lb (454 g) with a maximum of 2 lb (910 g).

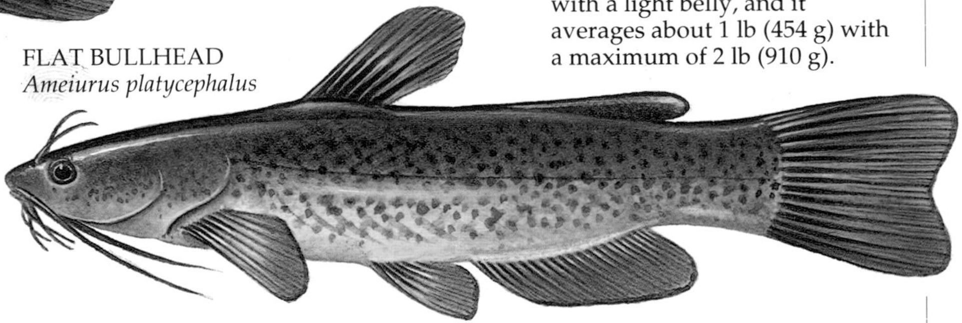

FLAT BULLHEAD
Ameiurus platycephalus

Brown Bullhead

The brown bullhead has a mottled coloration, and sharp teeth on its pectoral spines. Its maximum weight of around 5 lb 8 oz (2.5 kg) is less than that of the black, but its average of about 3 lb (1.36 kg) is slightly more. Both have been introduced into many European waters, with the brown now common in Holland and Germany and the black thriving in southern France.

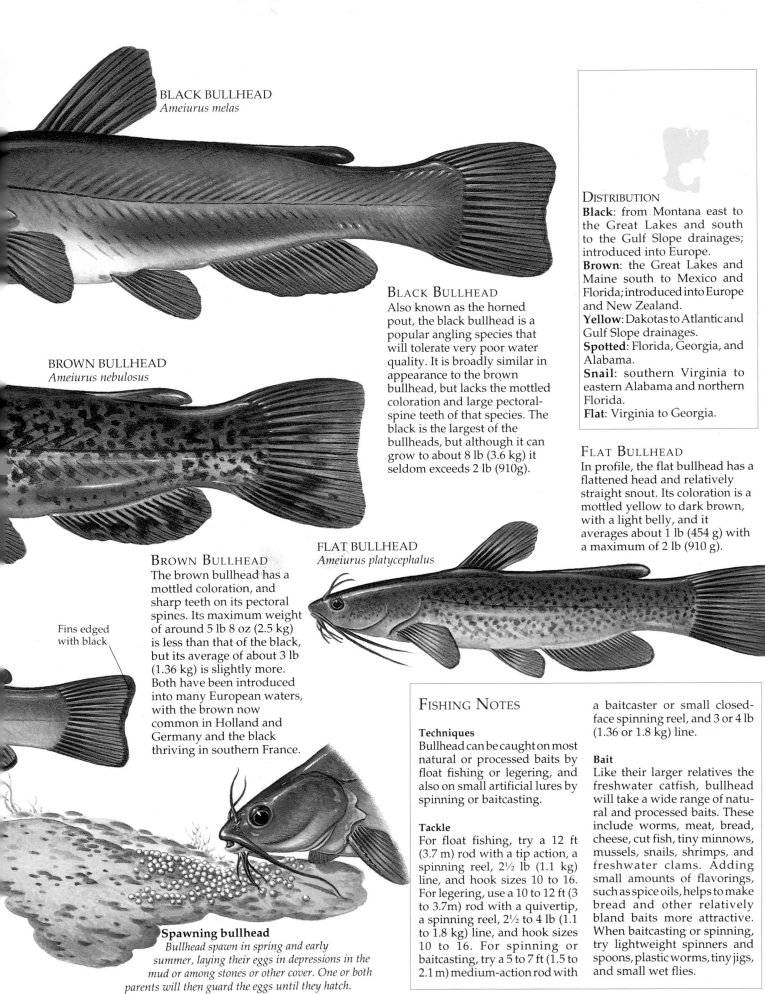

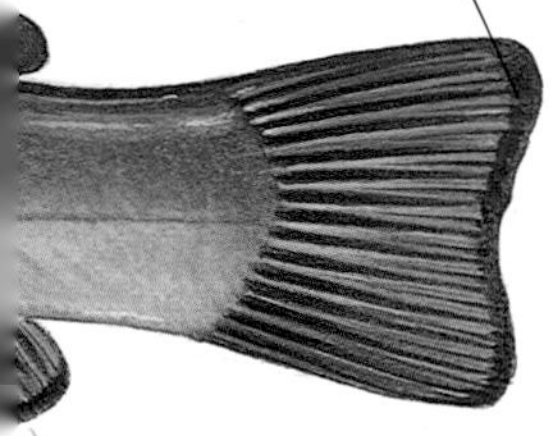

Spawning bullhead
Bullhead spawn in spring and early summer, laying their eggs in depressions in the mud or among stones or other cover. One or both parents will then guard the eggs until they hatch.

Fishing Notes

Techniques
Bullhead can be caught on most natural or processed baits by float fishing or legering, and also on small artificial lures by spinning or baitcasting.

Tackle
For float fishing, try a 12 ft (3.7 m) rod with a tip action, a spinning reel, 2½ lb (1.1 kg) line, and hook sizes 10 to 16. For legering, use a 10 to 12 ft (3 to 3.7m) rod with a quivertip, a spinning reel, 2½ to 4 lb (1.1 to 1.8 kg) line, and hook sizes 10 to 16. For spinning or baitcasting, try a 5 to 7 ft (1.5 to 2.1 m) medium-action rod with a baitcaster or small closed-face spinning reel, and 3 or 4 lb (1.36 or 1.8 kg) line.

Bait
Like their larger relatives the freshwater catfish, bullhead will take a wide range of natural and processed baits. These include worms, meat, bread, cheese, cut fish, tiny minnows, mussels, snails, shrimps, and freshwater clams. Adding small amounts of flavorings, such as spice oils, helps to make bread and other relatively bland baits more attractive. When baitcasting or spinning, try lightweight spinners and spoons, plastic worms, tiny jigs, and small wet flies.

ICTALURIDAE; SILURIDAE; PLOTOSIDAE

FRESHWATER CATFISH

Worldwide, there are over 30 families of freshwater and marine catfish, containing about 2,250 species. These families include the Ictaluridae of North America *(see also page 140)*, the Siluridae of Europe, and the Plotosidae of Australasia, all of which have scaleless bodies, broad heads, and "whiskers" around their mouths. They generally inhabit still or slow-flowing waters, and are most active at night and on cloudy days.

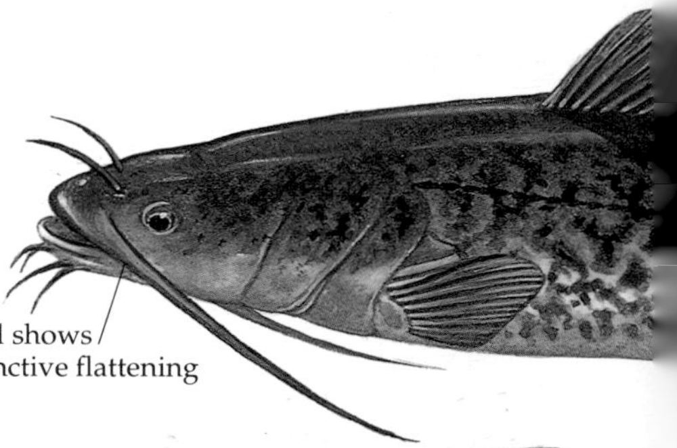

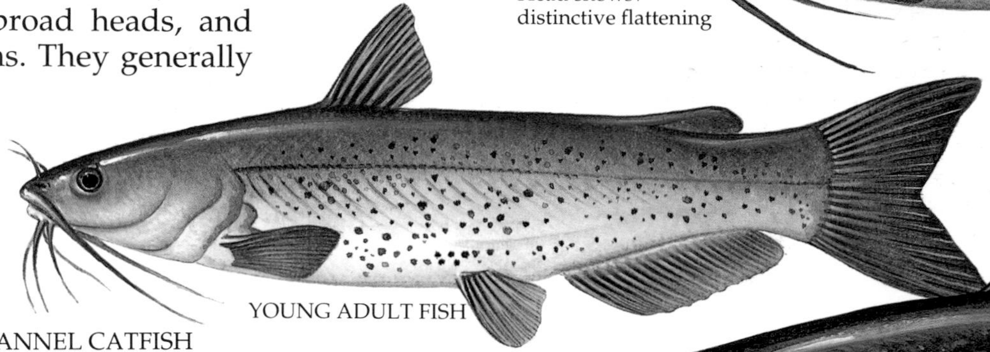

CHANNEL CATFISH
Ictalurus punctatus

CHANNEL CATFISH

The channel catfish, one of the larger North American catfish species, is the only one to have both spots and a deeply forked tail; the spots tend to fade in old, large fish. Its maximum size is about 60 lb (27 kg).

WHITE CATFISH

The coloration of the white catfish varies from white to silvery beige or blue, with a white belly. It is very popular as an angling and food fish, and usually grows to about 3 lb (1.36 kg) although it has been known to reach weights of over 17 lb (7.7 kg).

WELS

Also known as the Danubian catfish, the wels is native to central and eastern Europe but has been widely introduced into western European waters. The reason for these introductions is that the wels is one of the largest of all freshwater fish, reliably known to reach a length of 9 ft 10 in (3 m) and a weight of 441 lb (200 kg); individuals weighing over 700 lb (320 kg) have been reported.

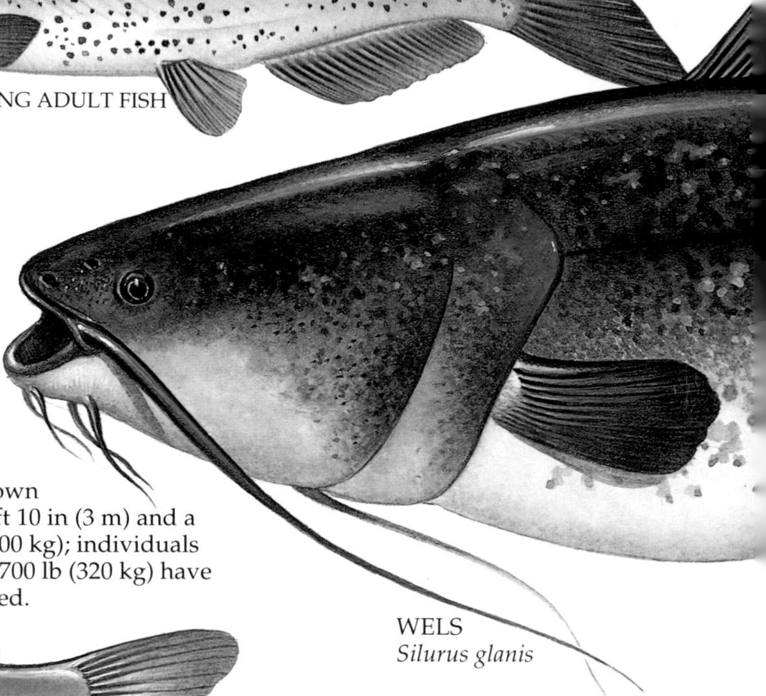

WELS
Silurus glanis

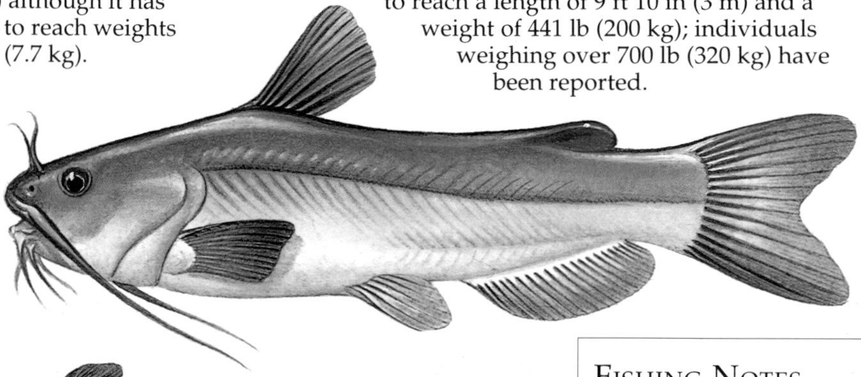

WHITE CATFISH
Ameiurus catus

TANDAN
Tandanus tandanus

TANDAN

The tandan is a member of the Plotosidae family, which comprises about 30 marine and freshwater species that are widely distributed throughout Australasia and the Indo-Pacific. It inhabits stillwaters and slow-flowing streams, typically reaching a weight of up to 4 lb 7 oz (2 kg) with a maximum of about 13 lb 4 oz (6 kg).

FISHING NOTES

Techniques
Freshwater catfish are usually taken on natural or processed baits by float fishing, legering, or freelining, but spinning with artificial lures is also effective, particularly for channel and blue catfish.

Tackle
Use a 9 to 10 ft (2.7 to 3m) rod, such as a heavy bass rod, with a spinning reel, 6 to 12 lb (2.7 to 5.4 kg) line, and hook sizes 6 to 1/0. To freeline for the larger species, such as the wels, use a 10 to 12 ft (3 to 3.7 m) rod with a powerful action, a spinning reel, 15 lb (6.8 kg) line, 20 lb (9.1 kg) Dacron leader, and hook sizes 4 to 2/0.

Bait
Freshwater catfish can be taken on practically any type of bait or lure, even a bare, shiny hook. Every catfish angler has a personal preference when it comes to a choice of bait, but the best results are said to come with "stink" baits. These baits include soured clams and ripened chicken entrails, beef liver, pig liver, and rabbit liver, coagulated blood, and even pieces of scented soap.

FLATHEAD CATFISH
Pylodictis olivaris

Flathead Catfish

The preferred habitat of the flathead is the deep, sluggish pools of large rivers, but it is also found in smaller streams and stillwaters. It averages about 4 lb (1.8 kg) but may reach 100 lb (45 kg).

Front view of a wels showing its very wide and flattened head

Whiskers
The barbels or "whiskers" around the mouth of a catfish are highly sensitive organs with which the fish can taste, smell, and feel its food. The wels has six whiskers, and the American catfish and the tandan have eight.

Distribution

Wels: southern Sweden to the Danube basin and Amu Darya; introduced into England, France, Spain, Italy.
Channel: Great Lakes to Gulf Slope drainages.
White: Atlantic and Gulf Slope drainages.
Flathead: lower Great Lakes, Mississippi basin, Gulf Slope drainages.
Blue: Mississippi basin, Gulf Slope drainages.
Tandan: Queensland, New South Wales, Victoria, and South Australia.

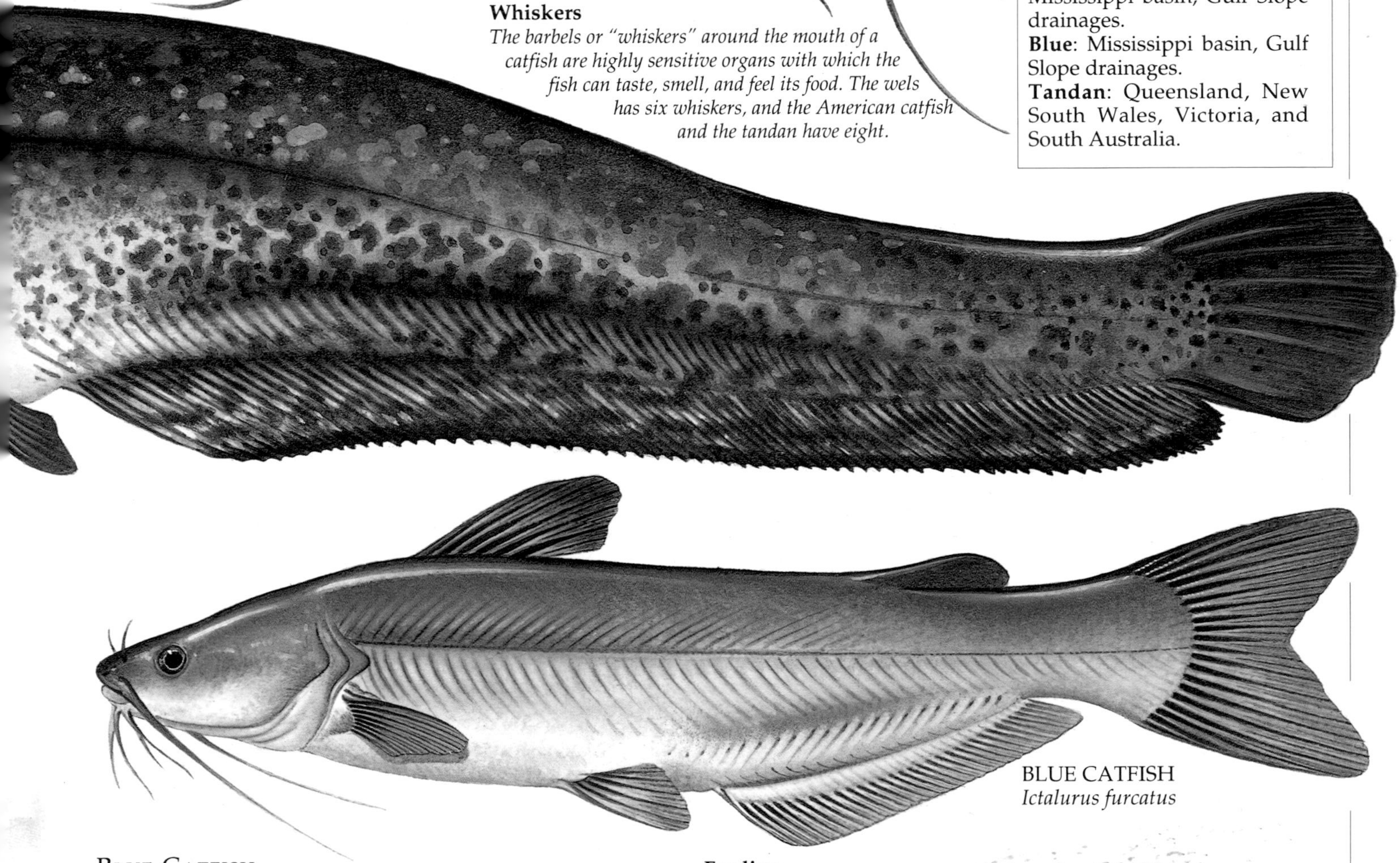

BLUE CATFISH
Ictalurus furcatus

Blue Catfish

The blue catfish is the largest North American catfish, averaging up to 50 lb (22.7 kg) and capable of exceeding 100 lb (45 kg). Unlike most catfish it prefers swift-flowing and relatively clear streams to slow, turbid waters, and is found over rock, sand, or gravel bottoms rather than mud or silt.

Feeding
Blue catfish feed mainly at night, when they move from deep water into shallow, swift-flowing rapids and chutes to hunt for fish and crayfish.

Size comparison

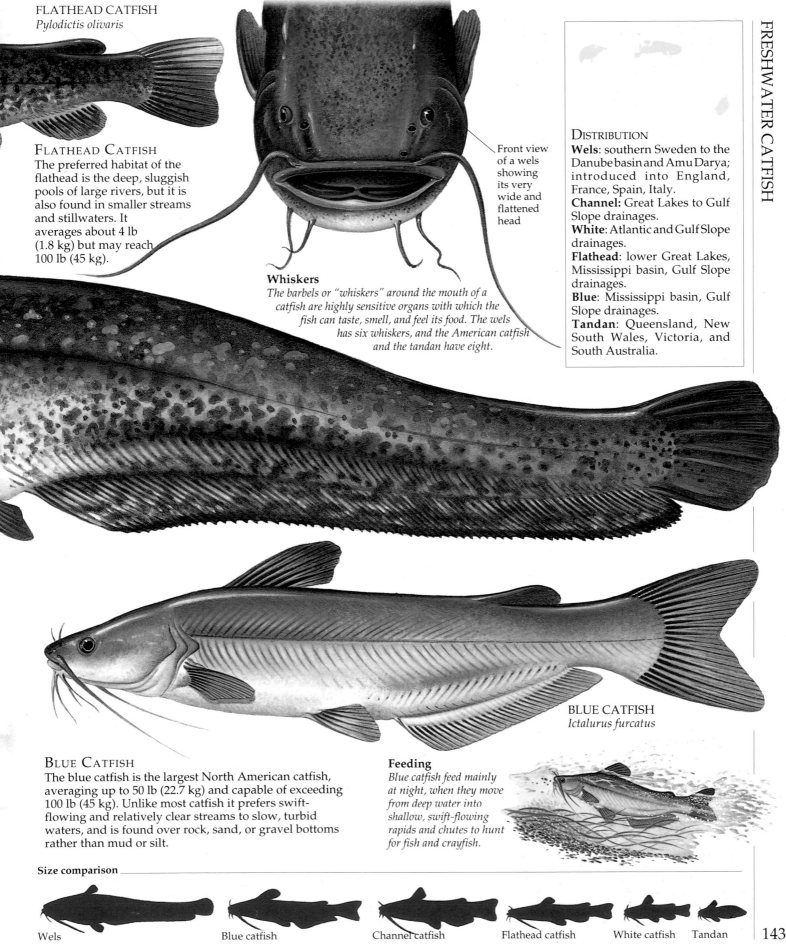

BASS & MURRAY COD

Until recently, these perchlike species were all classified as members of the Percichthyidae family, but those of the genus *Morone* are now considered to be a separate family, the Moronidae. Both families are widely distributed in temperate and tropical waters, some being exclusively freshwater fish, others exclusively marine, and some migrating from the sea into freshwater to spawn. They feed mainly on small fish, crustaceans, worms, and insects.

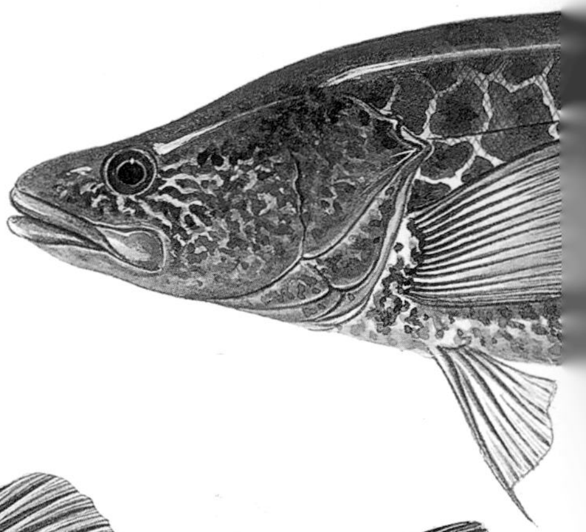

AUSTRALIAN BASS

This is one of the most important gamefish of the coastal rivers, estuaries, and lakes of southeastern Australia. It grows to a weight of 2 lb 3 oz (1 kg) or more, and spawns in estuaries during the winter. The eggs hatch in about three days, and by around three months of age, the young fish resemble small adults but are marked with faint vertical bars on the back and sides.

AUSTRALIAN BASS
Macquaria novemaculeata

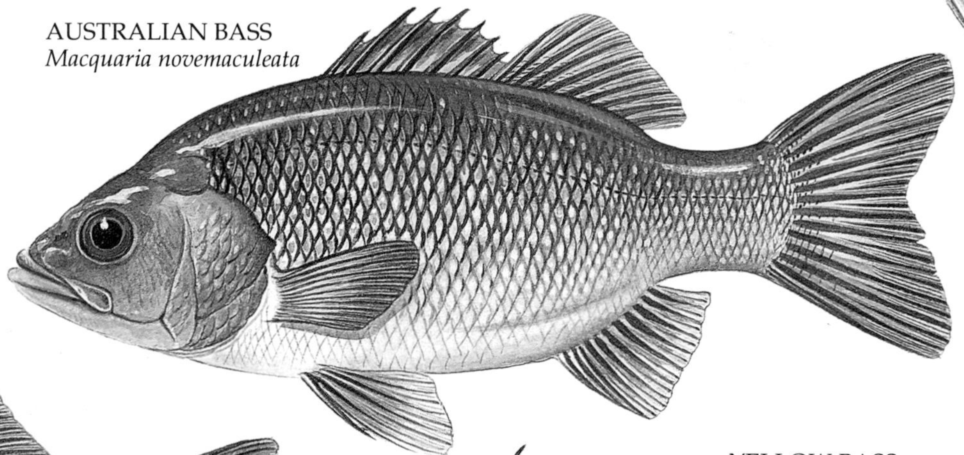

WHITE PERCH
Morone americana

YELLOW BASS
Morone mississippiensis

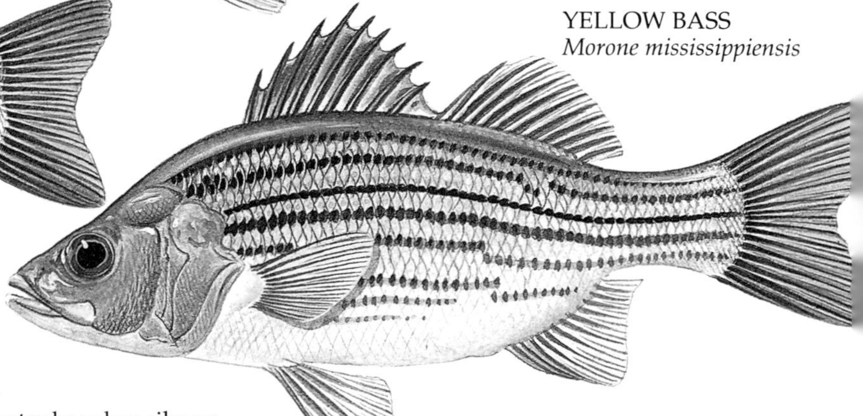

WHITE PERCH

The white perch can reach a weight of about 4 lb 12 oz (2.2 kg), but averages only about 1 lb (454 g). It is found in the Atlantic Slope drainages of northeastern North America, primarily in brackish water near the mouths of rivers. It is also found in the quiet pools of medium to large rivers, and close inshore in shallow coastal waters.

YELLOW BASS

This little freshwater bass has silvery yellow sides, and the lower stripes along them are broken and offset. It rarely exceeds 2 lb 3 oz (1 kg) and usually weighs only 4 to 12 oz (113 to 340 g), but despite its small size it offers good sport on light tackle.

WHITE BASS
Morone chrysops

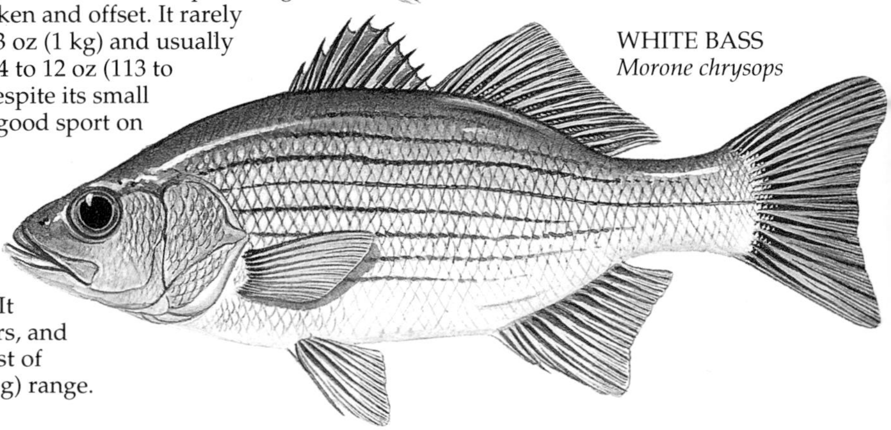

WHITE BASS

The white bass is very similar to the yellow bass, but its coloration is silvery white, the stripes along its sides are not broken and offset, and its lower jaw is more protuberant. It is found mainly in large, relatively clear waters, and although it grows to over 6 lb 10 oz (3 kg) most of those caught are in the 8 oz to 2 lb (227 to 910 g) range.

Size comparison

Striped bass | Murray cod | European sea bass | Spotted sea bass | Australian bass | Yellow bass | White bass | White perch

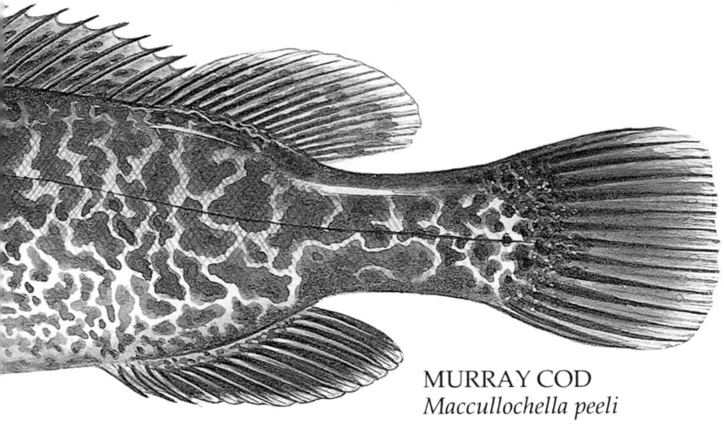

MURRAY COD
Maccullochella peeli

Murray Cod

With a maximum length of 6 ft (1.8 m) and a weight of up to 250 lb (113.5 kg), the Murray cod is the largest Australian freshwater fish. Its preferred habitat is deep holes in muddy, slow-flowing water, and it is fished for commercially as well as for sport. It is widely distributed through the Murray-Darling River system, and has been introduced into many lakes in New South Wales and Victoria.

Distribution

Australian bass, Murray cod: Queensland to Victoria.
White perch: from Quebec to South Carolina.
Yellow bass: from Montana and Wisconsin south to the Gulf of Mexico.
White bass: Manitoba and Quebec to the Gulf.
Spotted sea bass: western France to North Africa.
European sea bass: southern Norway to the Black Sea.

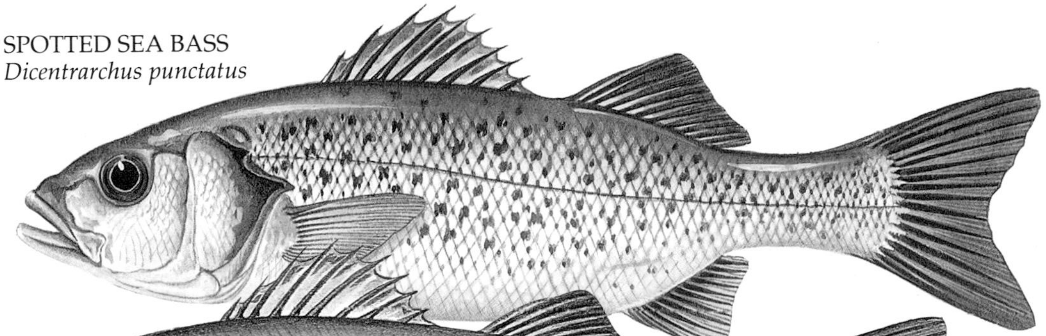

SPOTTED SEA BASS
Dicentrarchus punctatus

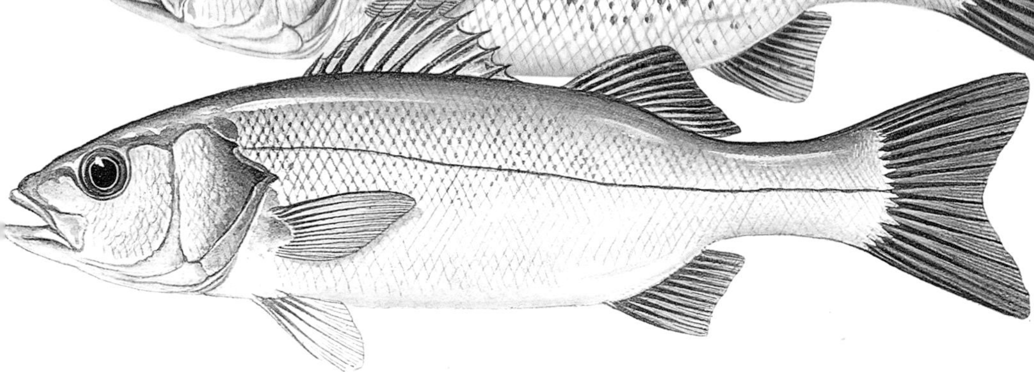

EUROPEAN SEA BASS
Dicentrarchus labrax

Spotted Sea Bass

The spotted sea bass is similar in size and habits to the European sea bass, from which it may be distinguished by its spotted sides. Its range overlaps that of the European sea bass, but it is not found as far north.

European Sea Bass

The European sea bass is found in coastal waters and the brackish water of estuaries, and reaches a weight of about 19 lb (8.6 kg). It spawns in the sea in spring and early summer, and young fish often have spots on their sides like those of the spotted bass; these spots fade and disappear as the fish mature.

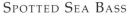

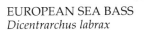

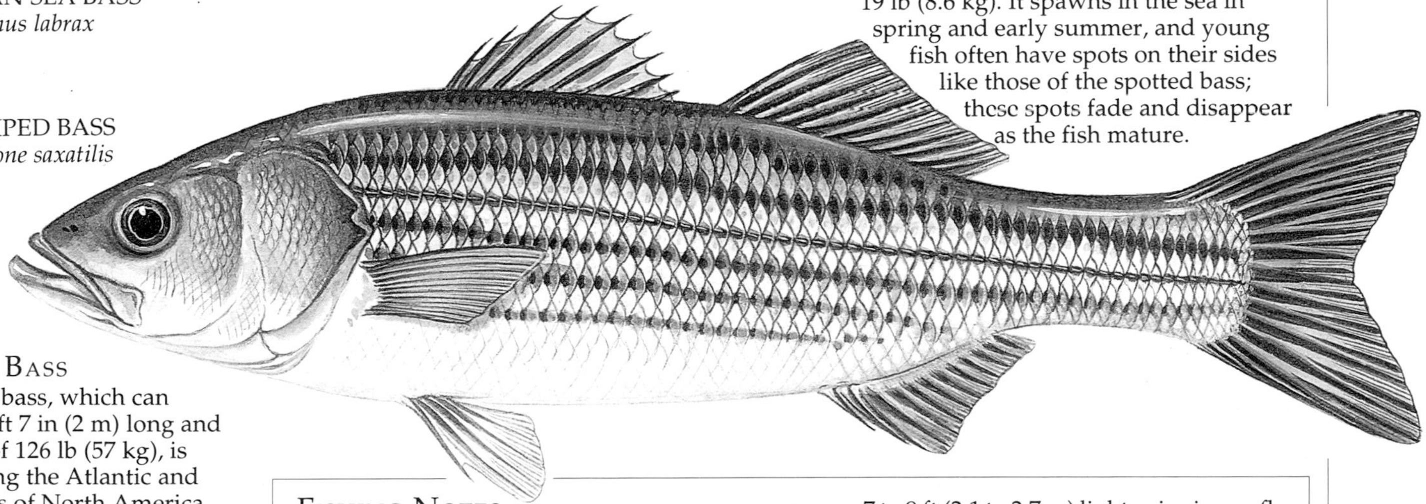

STRIPED BASS
Morone saxatilis

Striped Bass

This large bass, which can grow to 6 ft 7 in (2 m) long and a weight of 126 lb (57 kg), is found along the Atlantic and Gulf coasts of North America, and was introduced into the Pacific coastal waters in 1886. It migrates into freshwater to spawn during late spring and early summer, and there are a number of landlocked, lake-dwelling populations. It will readily take baits such as mullet, sandeels, squid, crabs, clams, worms, and lures, and is fished for commercially as well as for sport.

Fishing Notes

Techniques
In freshwater, try spinning or trolling for striped bass and Murray cod, and spinning or fly fishing for the smaller species. In saltwater, try surfcasting, trolling, or uptide fishing.

Tackle
For freshwater striped bass and Murray cod, use a heavy spinning rod with 20 to 40 lb (9.1 to 18.1 kg) line. For the smaller freshwater fish, use a 7 to 9 ft (2.1 to 2.7 m) light spinning or fly rod. For striped bass in saltwater, try a 30 lb (13.6 kg) class boat rod for trolling and a 12 ft (3.7 m) rod for surfcasting; when fishing for the smaller species in saltwater, use an 11 ft (3.4 m) light surfcasting rod or a 12 lb (5.4 kg) class uptide rod.

Bait
These fish are all active predators, and will therefore take most suitably sized natural baits or artificial lures.

Australian Perch & Grunters

The Macquarie, golden, and estuary perches are members of the Percichthyidae family *(see page 144)*, while the jungle perch belongs to the Kuhliidae, a small family of fish that are similar to the Centrarchidae of North America *(see pages 126–9)*. The silver perch and sooty grunter are members of the Teraponidae (grunter) family, which consists of about 45 Indo-Pacific marine and freshwater species.

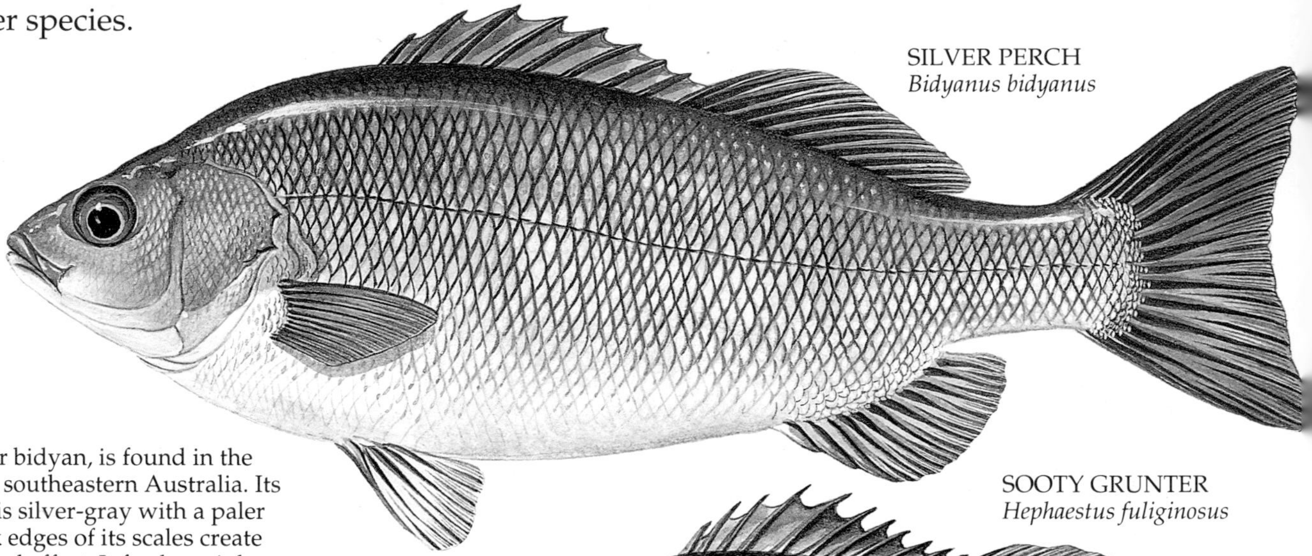

SILVER PERCH
Bidyanus bidyanus

Silver Perch

The silver perch, or bidyan, is found in the rivers and lakes of southeastern Australia. Its overall coloration is silver-gray with a paler belly, and the dark edges of its scales create an attractive, latticed effect. It feeds mainly on insects, worms, and mollusks and grows to a maximum weight of about 3 lb 5 oz (1.5 kg). Its flesh is tasty, so it is fished for commercially as well as being a popular angling species.

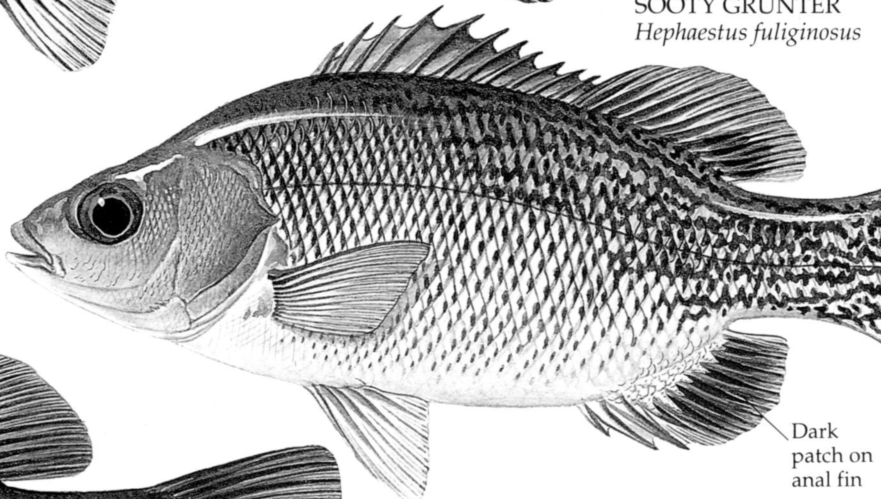

SOOTY GRUNTER
Hephaestus fuliginosus

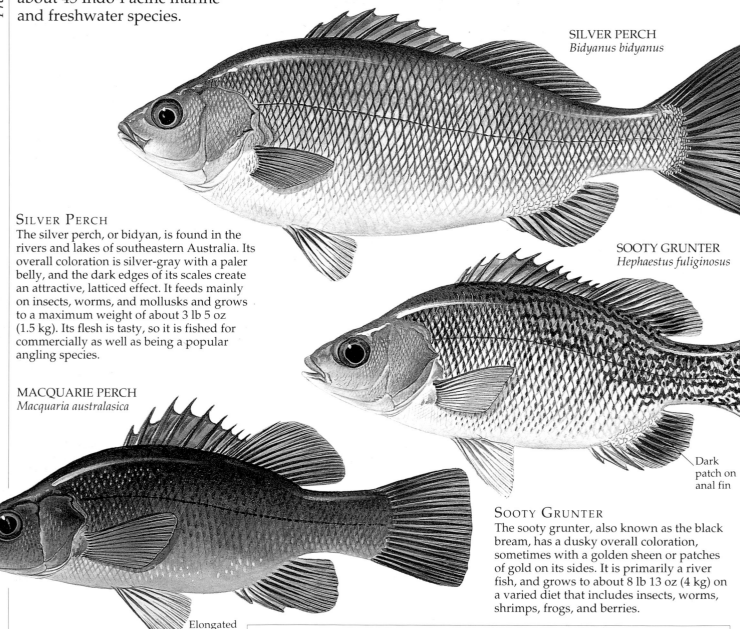

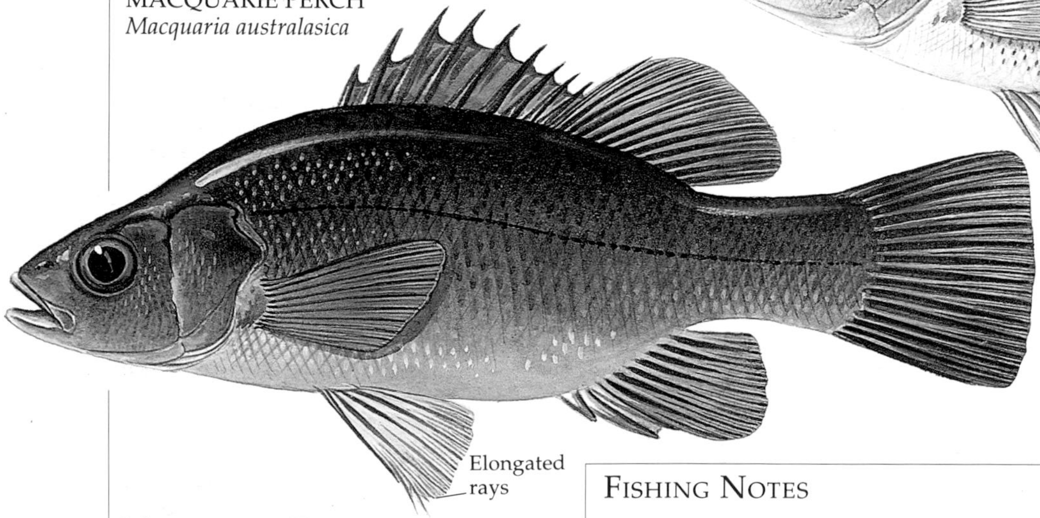

MACQUARIE PERCH
Macquaria australasica

Sooty Grunter

The sooty grunter, also known as the black bream, has a dusky overall coloration, sometimes with a golden sheen or patches of gold on its sides. It is primarily a river fish, and grows to about 8 lb 13 oz (4 kg) on a varied diet that includes insects, worms, shrimps, frogs, and berries.

Macquarie Perch

The color of the Macquarie perch varies from greenish brown to almost black, with a pale, sometimes yellowish, belly. It occurs in cool rivers and deep lakes, and has been introduced into reservoirs. Its diet consists mainly of insects, mollusks, and crustaceans, and it reaches a weight of around 3 lb 5 oz (1.5 kg). It spawns in spring and early summer.

Fishing Notes

Techniques

Spinning or baitcasting with artificial lures, fly fishing, and trolling with livebaits will all prove successful.

Tackle

For lure fishing, try a 2.1 m (7 ft) spinning or baitcasting rod, a spinning or baitcaster reel and 6 lb (2.7 kg) mono line. For fly fishing, use a 9 ft (2.7 m) rod with a fast taper, a fly reel, and a floating #7 to #9 line with a 6 lb (2.7 kg) leader. For trolling, use a 9 ft (2.7 m) stiff-action rod with a 2½ lb (1.1 kg) test curve, and a baitcaster reel with 10 to 20 lb (4.54 to 9.1 kg) mono line, a nylon or Dacron leader attached by a swivel, and hook sizes 2/0 to 5/0.

Bait

These fish will take a wide range of lures and flies, and trolled natural baits such as worms, minnows, and crayfish.

JUNGLE PERCH
Kuhlia rupestris

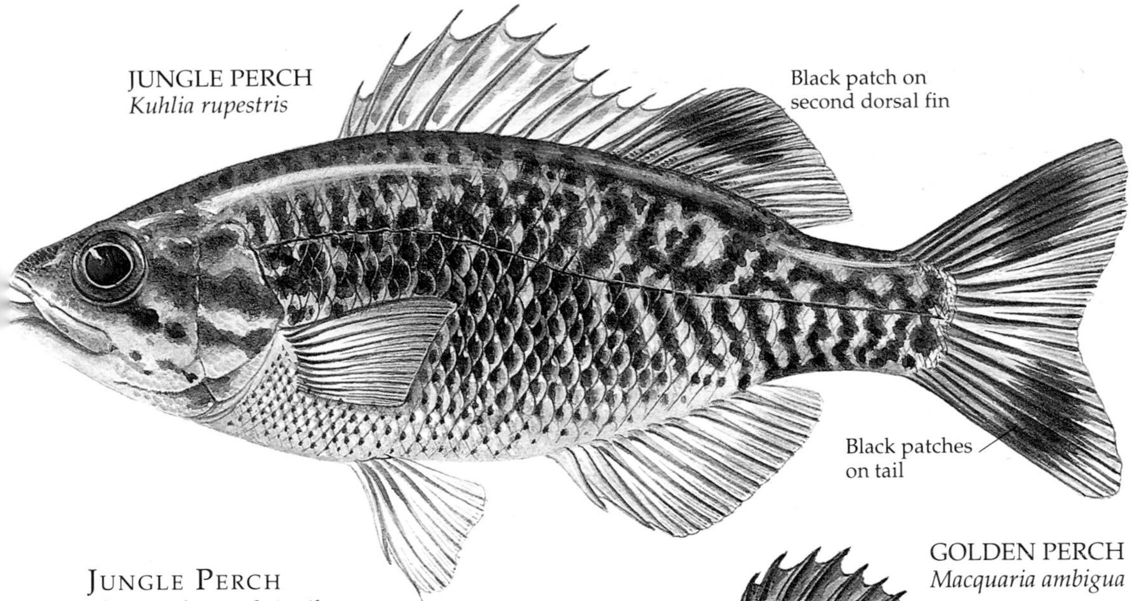

DISTRIBUTION
Silver perch: Victoria, New South Wales, Queensland.
Sooty grunter: Northern Territory and Queensland.
Macquarie perch: New South Wales and Victoria.
Jungle perch: Queensland.
Golden perch: South Australia, Victoria, New South Wales, Queensland, and Northern Territory.
Estuary perch: New South Wales, Victoria, and South Australia.

Jungle Perch

The jungle perch is silvery with distinctive reddish brown markings, and there are black patches on the second dorsal fin and each lobe of the tail fin. It lives in clear, fast-flowing streams, feeding on insects, fish, and crayfish, and its maximum weight is about 6 lb 10 oz (3 kg). It is found in the coastal streams of eastern Queensland, and occurs widely elsewhere in the tropical Indo-Pacific region.

GOLDEN PERCH
Macquaria ambigua

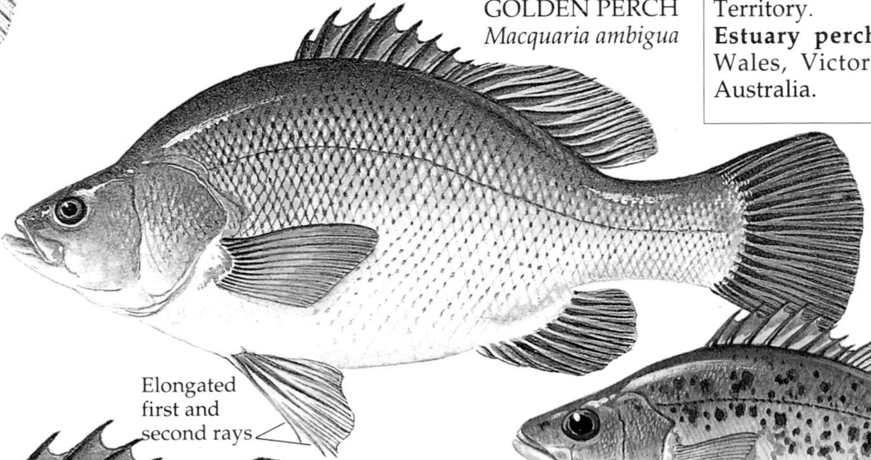

Young golden perch
The juvenile golden perch has a slender body and is heavily spotted.

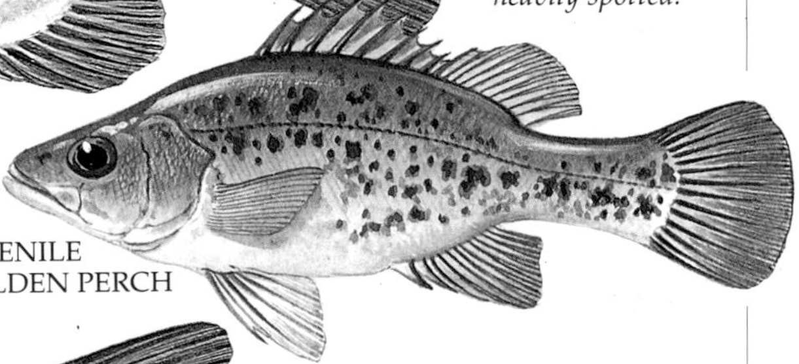

JUVENILE GOLDEN PERCH

ESTUARY PERCH
Macquaria colonorum

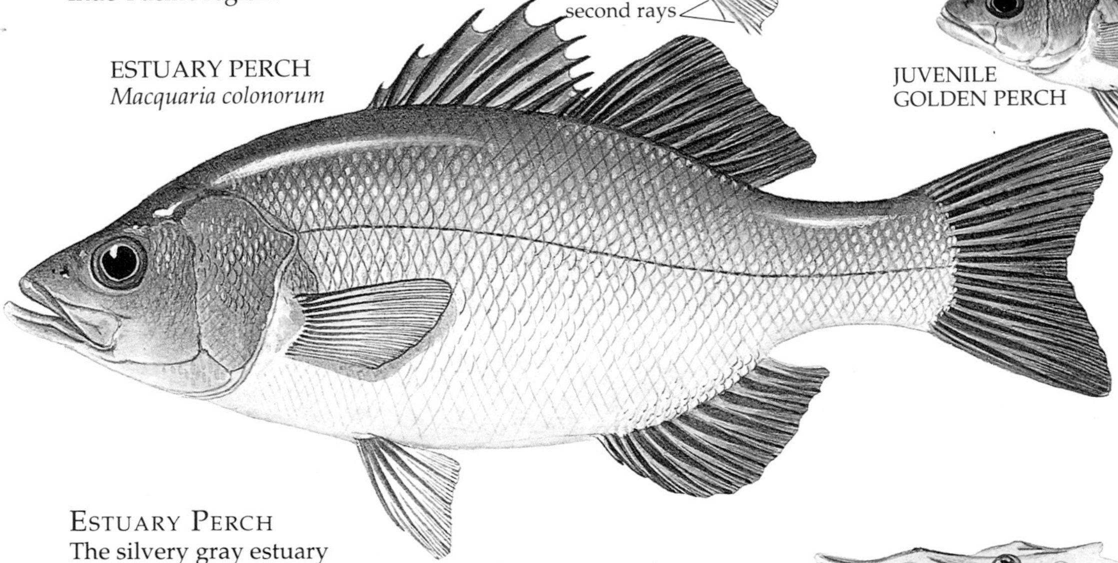

Golden Perch

This is one of the largest Australian perch, having a maximum weight of around 50 lb 11 oz (23 kg). It is widely distributed through the Murray-Darling system and elsewhere, and its preferred habitat is muddy, slow-moving water. It feeds on shrimps and crayfish, and its coloration varies from olive green to yellow, with a pale, yellowish belly.

Estuary Perch

The silvery gray estuary perch is found in the coastal streams and estuaries, and some lakes, of southeastern Australia. It feeds on fish, crustaceans, mollusks, and worms, and can grow to a weight of 22 lb (10 kg). Spawning takes place in the saltwater reaches of estuaries, and occurs in winter in New South Wales but not until early summer in Victoria. The eggs float on the surface, and hatch within three days.

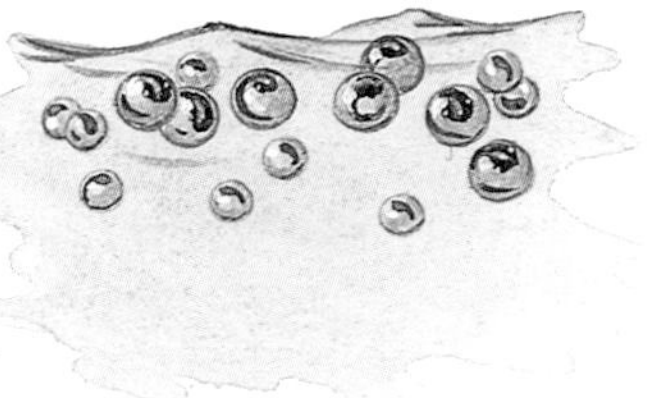

Estuary perch spawning
Each female lays many hundreds of thousands of eggs, which float to the surface and are eaten by fish and other marine predators. Only a tiny number become adults.

Size comparison

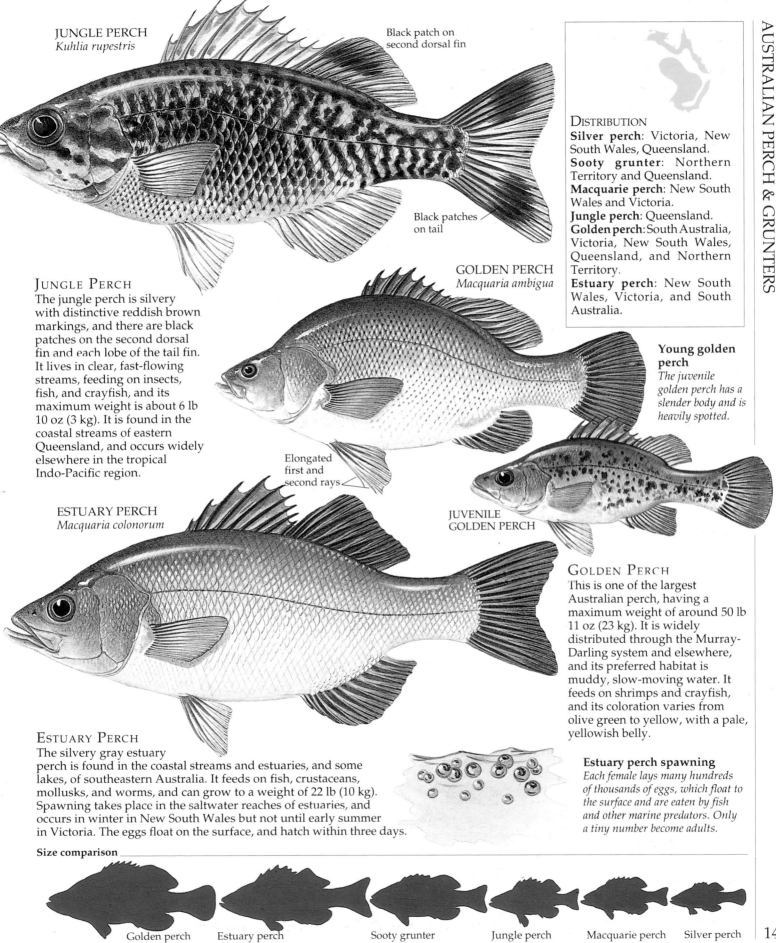

PERCIDAE

PERCH, SAUGER, WALLEYE, & ZANDER

The Percidae is a large and diverse family of fish consisting of perch and related species. These are characterized by their long, slender bodies and their two dorsal fins, separate in some species but joined in others, with the first dorsal having spines and the second having soft rays. The members of the Percidae are found both in streams and in stillwaters. The small species and the young of the large ones feed on insect larvae and other invertebrates; the adults of the large species are fish-eaters.

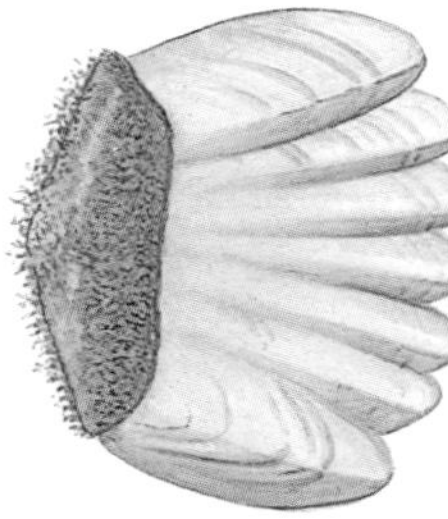

Perch scales
Perch feel rough to the touch because they have ctenoid scales – scales that have fine teeth on their exposed edges. Smooth scales with no teeth, such as those of the carp family, are called cycloid scales.

Perch eggs
The European perch and the yellow perch both spawn in spring and lay their eggs in long, lacelike ribbons. These are deposited on stones, or woven among water plants and tree roots, in the shallows of still or slow-flowing waters.

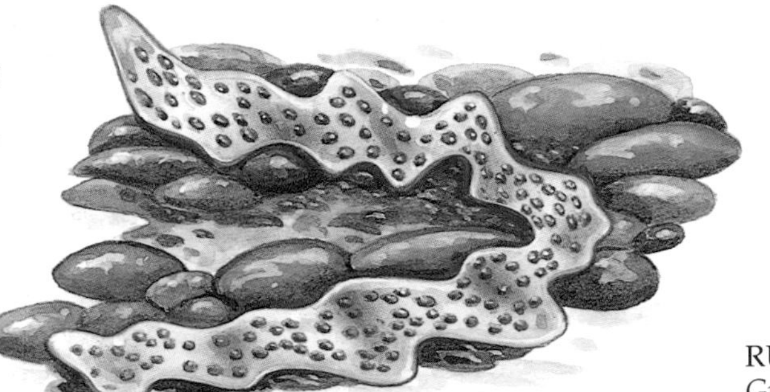

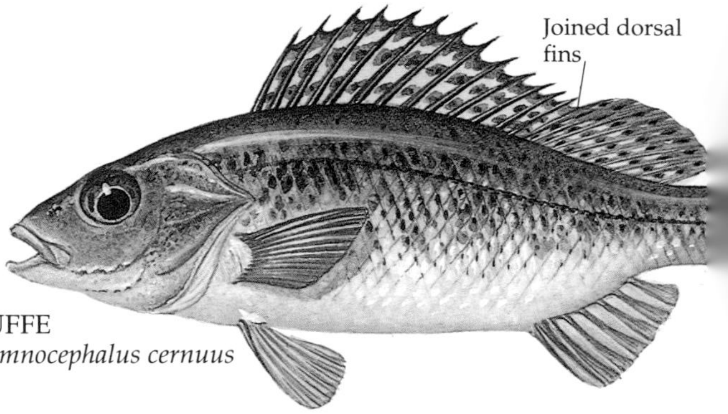

RUFFE
Gymnocephalus cernuus

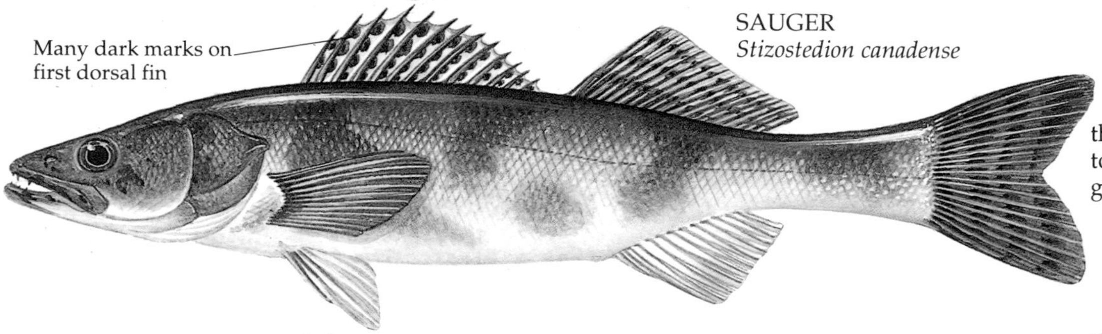

SAUGER
Stizostedion canadense

RUFFE

The diminutive ruffe, or pope, is one of the smallest of the perch family to be of interest to anglers as a quarry. It usually grows to about 6 oz (170 g), but can reach 1 lb 10 oz (750 g).

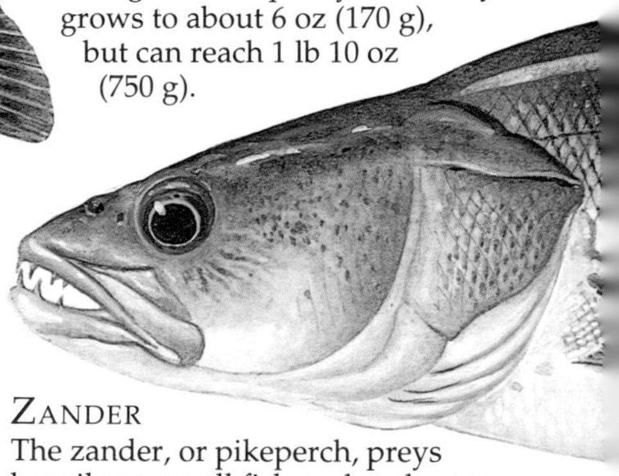

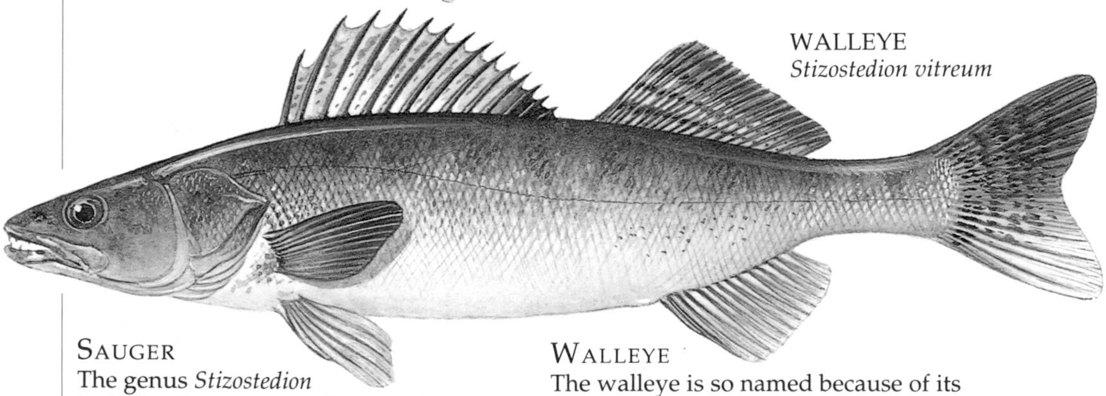

WALLEYE
Stizostedion vitreum

SAUGER

The genus *Stizostedion* includes the sauger, walleye, and zander, collectively known as pikeperch, which have only slight genetic differences and are very similar in appearance and habits. Like all pikeperch, the sauger is a predator; it can reach a maximum weight of more than 8 lb (3.6 kg).

WALLEYE

The walleye is so named because of its large, glassy eyes, which are distinctive in daylight and glow at night when a light is shone on them, like the eyes of a cat. It is the largest of the North American perches, typically reaching 3 lb (1.36 kg) with a maximum of 25 lb (11.3 kg), and is a prized food fish as well as being a favorite quarry of anglers.

ZANDER

The zander, or pikeperch, preys heavily on small fish such as bream, ruffe, and roach, and can reach a weight of over 26 lb 8 oz (12 kg). It was originally found in the Danube and other waters of northern and central Europe, but it has been introduced as far west as England and its range is slowly spreading. Some introductions have been controversial, with the zander being blamed for drastic reductions in local fish populations, but in many waters the introductions seem to have caused no major problems.

Size comparison

YELLOW PERCH
Perca flavescens

EUROPEAN PERCH
Perca fluviatilis

DISTRIBUTION

Sauger, walleye: Northwest Territories east to Quebec, southeast to Alabama.
Zander: northern and central Europe; also introduced into western Europe and England.
Volga zander: river systems entering the northern Black and Caspian Seas.
Ruffe: eastern England to Asia; introduced into Scotland and the Great Lakes.
European perch: from Ireland to Siberia; has been introduced into Australia.
Yellow perch: found from the Northwest Territories to the Atlantic drainages as far south as South Carolina.

YELLOW PERCH

The North American yellow perch is very similar to the European perch in appearance and habits, and the two species are closely related. Like all the large members of the Percidae, they make excellent eating and are among the tastiest of freshwater fish.

EUROPEAN PERCH

This perch is widespread in stillwaters and slow-flowing lowland rivers throughout Europe. It is a schooling fish that feeds on insects and small fish, including perch fry, and in some waters of the European mainland it can attain a weight of up to 14 lb (6.5 kg).

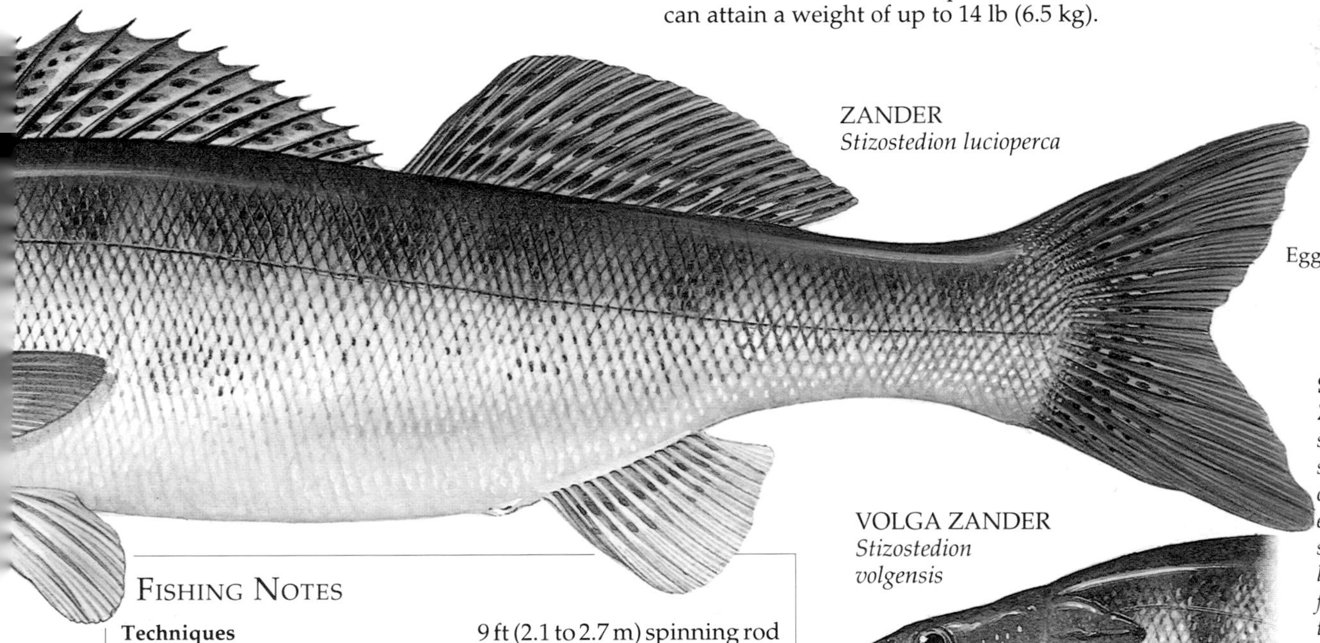

ZANDER
Stizostedion lucioperca

Spawning zander
Zander spawn in spring and early summer, laying clumps of pale yellow eggs on plants or on sand and stones. The larvae hatch after a few days and live on their yolk sacs until their teeth develop and they can feed themselves. Young zander feed on small prey, such as insect larvae and fish fry.

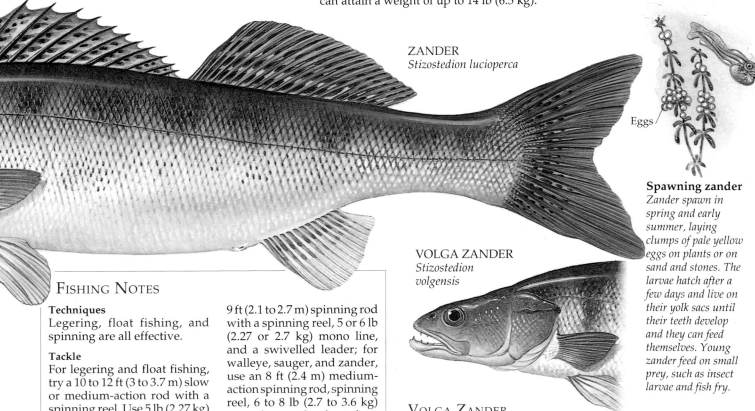

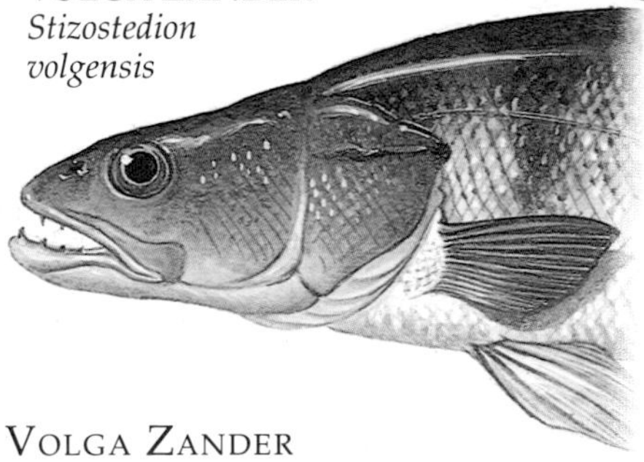

VOLGA ZANDER
Stizostedion volgensis

FISHING NOTES

Techniques
Legering, float fishing, and spinning are all effective.

Tackle
For legering and float fishing, try a 10 to 12 ft (3 to 3.7 m) slow or medium-action rod with a spinning reel. Use 5 lb (2.27 kg) mono line and hook sizes 4 to 10 for ruffe and perch, and 6 to 10 lb (2.7 to 4.54 kg) mono with a 20 in (50 cm) wire leader and size 10 treble hook for walleye, sauger, and zander. When spinning, for perch use a 7 to 9 ft (2.1 to 2.7 m) spinning rod with a spinning reel, 5 or 6 lb (2.27 or 2.7 kg) mono line, and a swivelled leader; for walleye, sauger, and zander, use an 8 ft (2.4 m) medium-action spinning rod, spinning reel, 6 to 8 lb (2.7 to 3.6 kg) mono line, and a short, fine-wire leader.

Bait
Worms and maggots for perch, small fish for walleye, sauger, and zander. Spinning: spinners, spoons, jigs, plugs.

VOLGA ZANDER

The appearance of the Volga zander is similar to that of the zander, but the dark markings on its back are much more well defined. It is also generally smaller, and lacks the long fangs of the zander, although its mouth is well equipped with small, sharp teeth. The Volga zander is found in rivers flowing into the Caspian and Black seas, including the Volga itself and the Danube as far upstream as Vienna. It prefers open, deep water to vegetated areas, and grows to about 4 lb 6 oz (2 kg).

SALMONIDAE

CHAR

The most obvious difference between char (salmonids of the genus *Salvelinus*) and salmon and trout (genera *Salmo* and *Oncorhynchus*) lies in their coloration: char have light markings on a darker background; salmon and trout have dark markings on a lighter background. Char feed on invertebrates and small fish, and they are native to the cool waters of the northern parts of the Northern Hemisphere; they are all excellent angling species. Lake and brook trout have been widely introduced elsewhere.

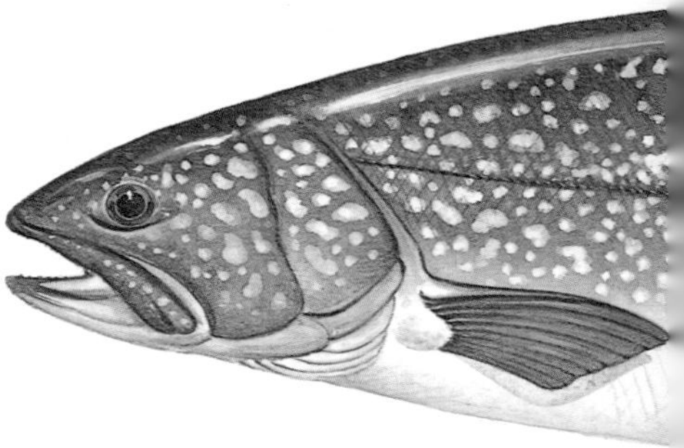

ARCTIC CHAR
Salvelinus alpinus

BREEDING MALE

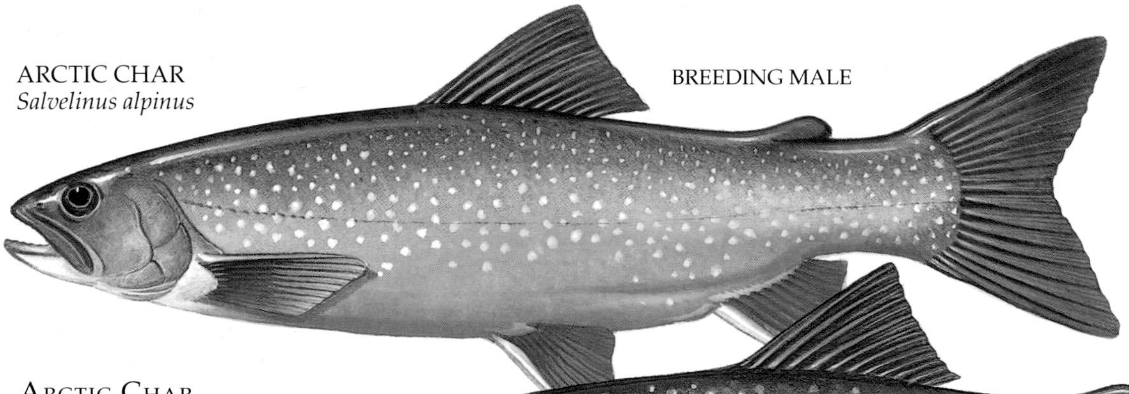

Breeding male char
In the breeding season the coloration of both sexes deepens, but that of the male becomes especially vibrant, with rich orange fins and a bright orange-red belly.

ARCTIC CHAR

Above latitude 64°N, all arctic char winter in coastal waters and move into rivers to spawn. Below that latitude, they also inhabit cold, deep lakes, and many of these lake populations have evolved into distinct varieties that vary greatly in size and coloration. The sea-run char, silver with reddish spots, grows to about 26 lb (12 kg); the lake char, typically greenish with red and white spots and an orange belly, reaches about 8 lb (3.6 kg).

CHAR PARR

Parr marks
In the parr stage of its life cycle, from a few months up to about two years of age, a char has the banded markings on its sides that are typical of young salmonids.

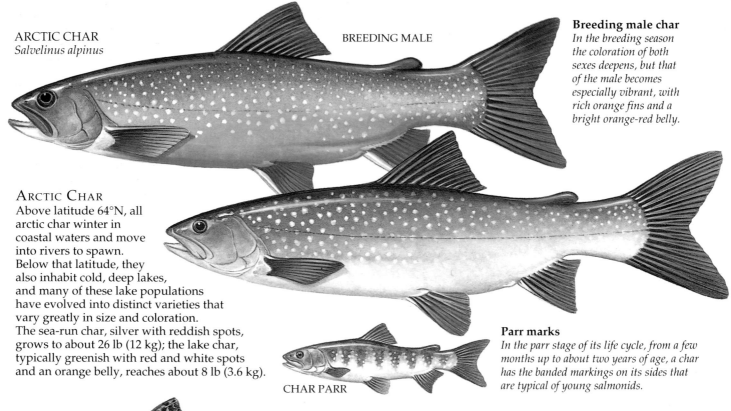

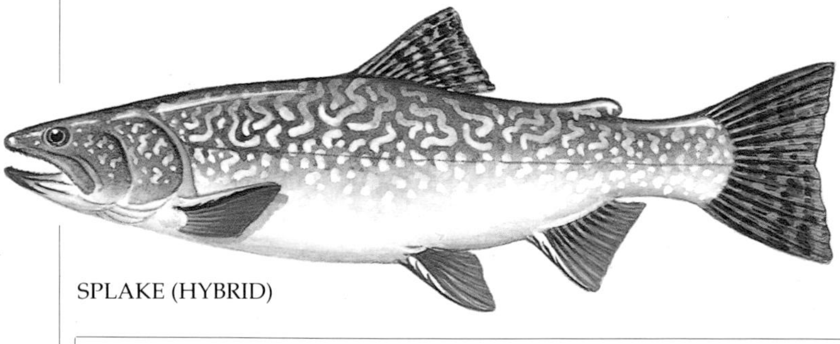

SPLAKE (HYBRID)

Hybrids
Hybridization among members of the Salmonidae family occurs both naturally and as a result of selective breeding by fish farms. Natural hybrids include Atlantic salmon × sea trout and rainbow × cutthroat; farmed crossbreeds include the splake (brook trout × lake trout), the tiger trout (brook × brown), and the cheetah trout (brook × rainbow).

FISHING NOTES

Techniques
Fly fishing, spinning and trolling for arctic char and lake trout; fly fishing and spinning for brook trout and Dolly Varden.

Tackle
For fly fishing use a 8 to 11 ft (2.4 to 3.4 m) fly rod with a fly reel, floating or sinking line as appropriate, and flies dressed on hook sizes 10 to 14. For spinning and for shallow trolling try a 9 ft (2.7 m), medium spinning rod with a spinning reel, and use 4 to 6 lb (1.8 to 2.7 kg) line for spinning and 10 to 15 lb (4.54 to 6.8 kg) line for shallow trolling work.

For deep trolling, use a 6ft (1.8m), fast-taper trolling rod with braided wire line; the rod should have hardened rings or roller guides to resist the abrasive action of the wire line.

Bait
For arctic char, use small, bright spinners or spoons, or wet-fly patterns that incorporate a flashy material such as gold or silver tinsel, for example Butcher or Mallard and Claret. Use large, trolled spoons or livebait for lake trout in deep water, and spoons, spinners, plugs, or streamer flies when the fish are close inshore. Brook trout and Dolly Varden may be taken on lures, dry flies, wet flies, and nymphs.

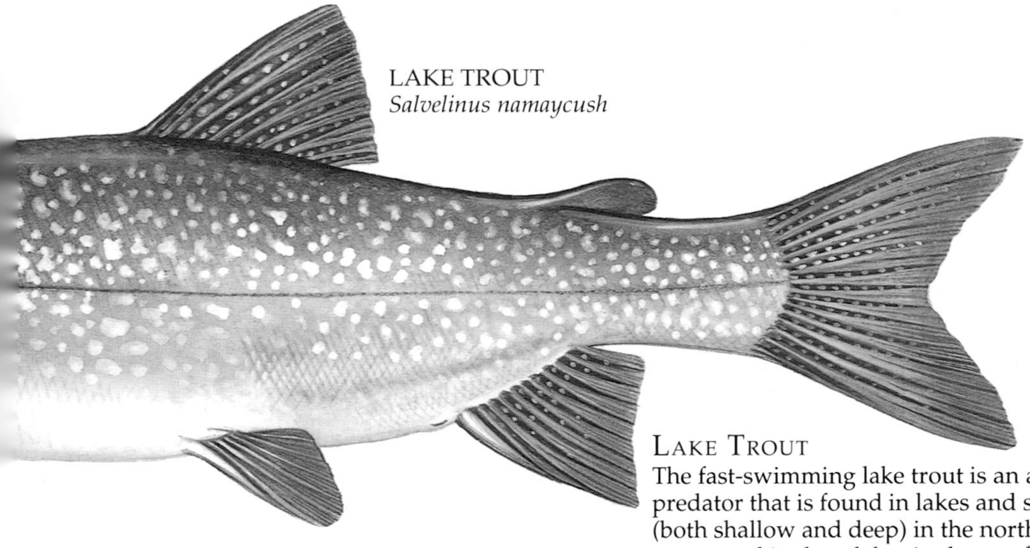

LAKE TROUT
Salvelinus namaycush

Lake Trout

The fast-swimming lake trout is an aggressive predator that is found in lakes and streams (both shallow and deep) in the north of its range, and in deep lakes in the south. It has a relatively slender, streamlined body with a deeply forked tail, and usually reaches a maximum of about 40 lb (18 kg), although it can grow to over 100 lb (45 kg).

Distribution

Arctic char: Alaska, northern Canada, and New England; Greenland, Iceland, northern Eurasia; cold lakes in Russia, Britain, Ireland, Scandinavia, and the Alps.
Lake trout: Alaska through Canada to New England; introduced into western USA, South America, Europe, and New Zealand.
Brook trout: northeastern North America; introduced elsewhere in North America and in South America, Europe, Asia, southern Africa, and Australasia.
Dolly Varden: western North America, eastern Asia.
Bull trout: southern Yukon to northern California.

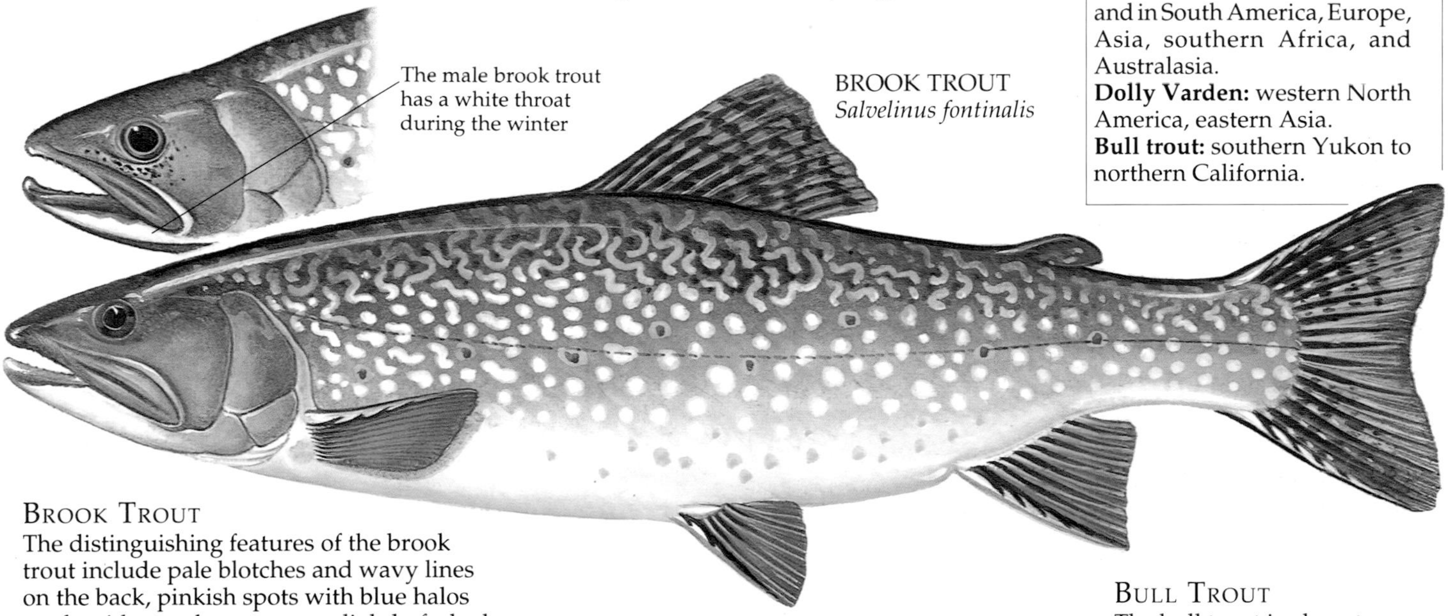

The male brook trout has a white throat during the winter

BROOK TROUT
Salvelinus fontinalis

Brook Trout

The distinguishing features of the brook trout include pale blotches and wavy lines on the back, pinkish spots with blue halos on the sides, and a square or slightly forked tail. It inhabits cool, well-oxygenated streams and lakes, and some northern populations are migratory. It has been known to reach 14 lb 8 oz (6.58 kg) but the usual maximum is about 10 lb (4.54 kg) and it rarely exceeds 5 lb (2.27 kg).

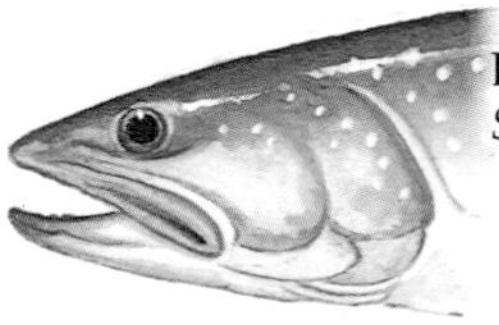

BULL TROUT
Salvelinus confluentus

Bull Trout

The bull trout is almost identical to the Dolly Varden, but its head is slightly longer and flatter. It lives in deep, cold rivers and lakes, and rarely migrates to the sea.

Dolly Varden

In freshwater, the Dolly Varden is similar in appearance to the arctic char, and can reach a weight of 8 lb (3.6 kg). Its migratory form, when in the sea, is silvery and steel blue with cream and pink spots.

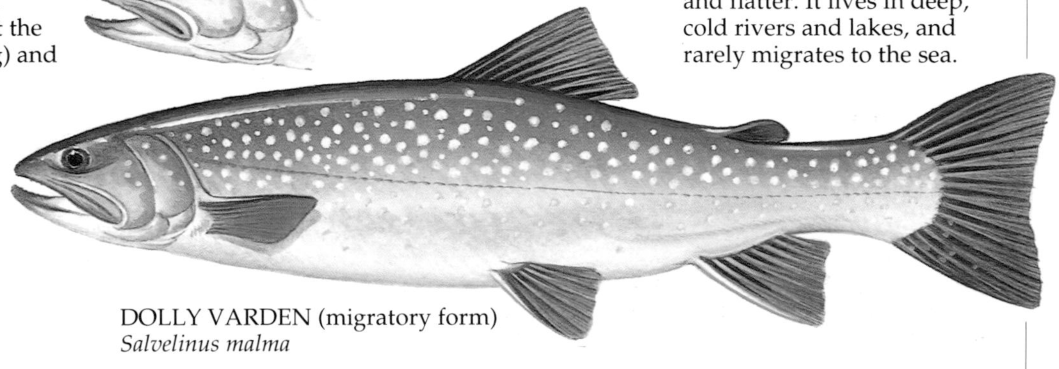

DOLLY VARDEN (migratory form)
Salvelinus malma

Size comparison

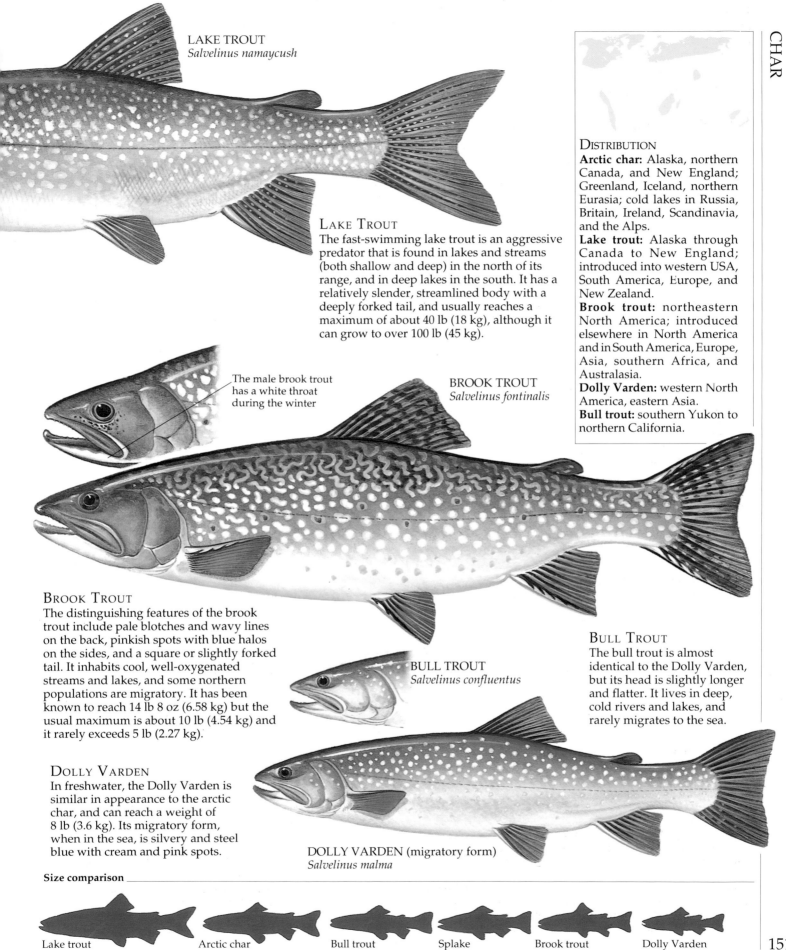

SALMON

Salmon are some of the most important commercial and sport fish in the world. All begin their lives in freshwater and most migrate to the sea to mature, returning to freshwater to spawn. The principal exceptions are the landlocked varieties of the Atlantic and sockeye salmon, and two Eurasian landlocked species, the huchen (*Hucho hucho*) and the taimen (*Hucho taimen*). The huchen, a fish of the Danube basin, is now a protected species in many of its native waters but has been introduced successfully into some French rivers; the taimen is common in the Volga basin and Siberia.

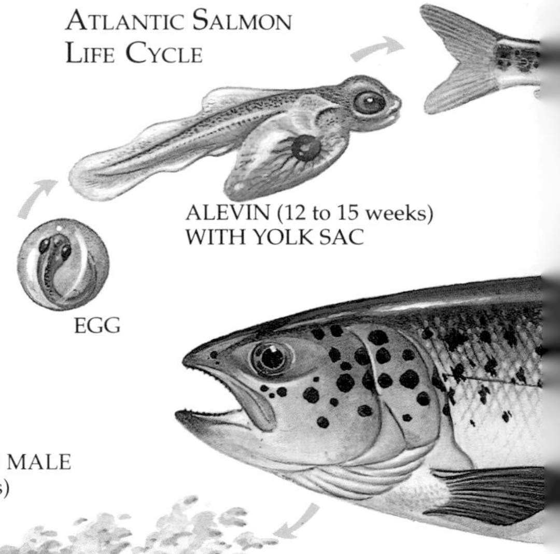

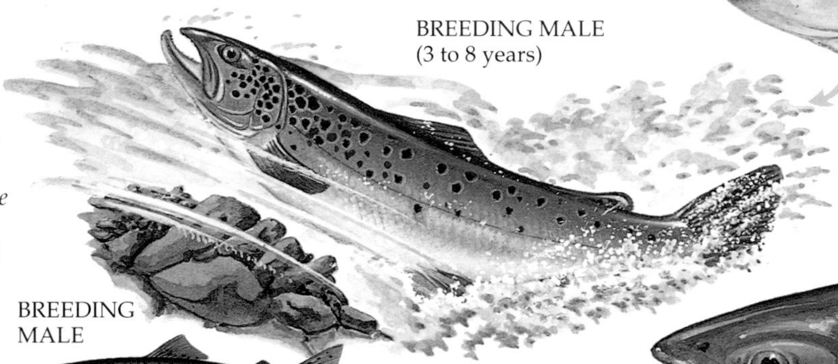

Life cycles
The life cycles of all the salmon species are broadly similar. The main differences are that the Pacific species die after spawning but many Atlantic salmon spawn more than once; the landlocked species do not migrate to the sea but mature in freshwater; and there are some differences in timing. The eggs are laid in redds (nests) scooped out of gravel by the female, and take from 70 to 200 days to hatch.

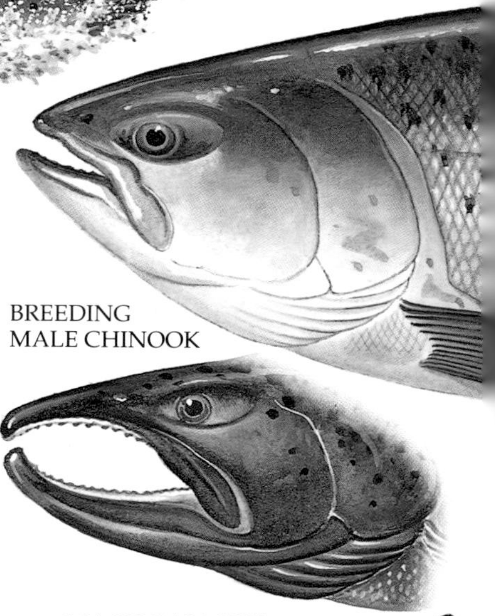

Coloration
The coloration of a salmon changes when it is ready to breed, and the male develops a hook (kype) on its lower jaw.

COHO SALMON

The coho or silver salmon is an important sport fish both in its native waters and those to which it has been introduced, such as the Great Lakes. It is similar to the chinook, but has white gums rather than black, less extensive spotting on the tail, and is smaller, reaching a maximum of around 33 lb (15 kg).

FISHING NOTES

Techniques
The Atlantic salmon is fished for in freshwater. The most usual technique is fly fishing, but it is also taken on spoons, plugs, and natural baits on waters (and at times of the year) where these methods are permitted. Pacific salmon, of which the chinook and coho are the most important species for the sport fisherman, are usually taken by trolling just offshore and in estuaries, but they are also caught by fly fishing and spinning (as are the landlocked varieties) when they move into freshwater to spawn.

Tackle
Fly tackle for freshwater salmon fishing is typically a 12 to 16 ft (3.7 to 4.9 m) rod, a fly reel, and weight-forward fly line. For spinning and bait fishing, try a heavy 10 ft (3 m) spinning rod with a baitcaster reel and 15 to 20 lb (6.8 to 9.1 kg) line. The usual saltwater rig for chinook and coho is a boat or trolling rod with a star-drag baitcaster reel and 20 to 45 lb (9.1 to 20.4 kg) line.

Bait
In freshwater, use flies, lures, worms, or prawns. In saltwater, use streamers, lures, or fish baits.

MASU SALMON

The relatively small and stocky masu, or cherry salmon, is an Asian species with both migratory and freshwater forms. It reaches maturity in three or four years, growing to about 10 lb (4.54 kg), and is fished for commercially as well as for sport.

PINK SALMON

Because of the distinctively humped back of the spawning male, the pink salmon is also known as the humpback or humpy. It is the most abundant of the Pacific species and is of considerable commercial importance, but it is a small fish, usually averaging 3 to 5 lb (1.36 to 2.27 kg) with a maximum of 12 lb (5.4 kg).

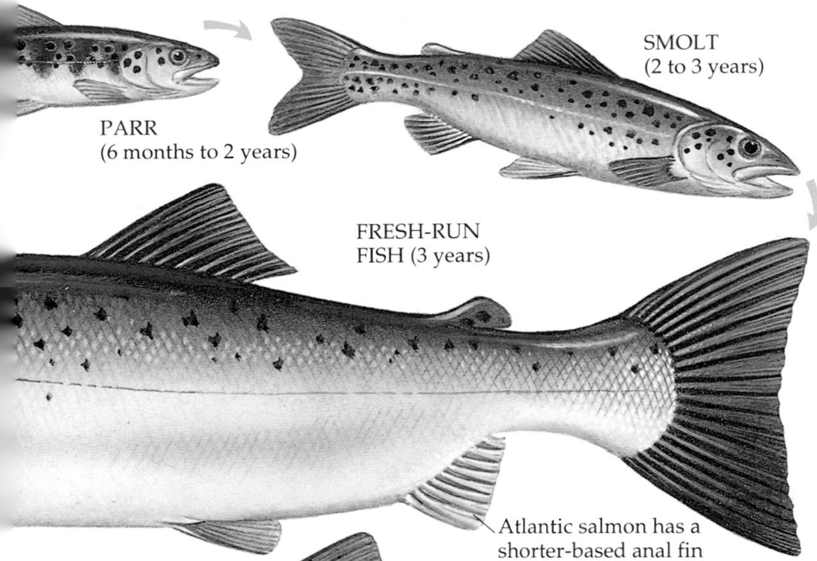
PARR
(6 months to 2 years)
SMOLT
(2 to 3 years)
FRESH-RUN
FISH (3 years)
Atlantic salmon has a shorter-based anal fin with fewer rays than the Pacific species

Atlantic Salmon

The Atlantic salmon is highly prized because of its size, its tasty flesh, and the expertise needed to catch it: it does not feed when it returns to freshwater, so inducing it to take a fly, lure, or bait calls for great skill. At sea, it feeds mainly on crustaceans, and the size it reaches depends on how long it stays in the sea. A fish that has spent one winter at sea, known as a grilse or jack, will weigh up to 9 lb (4.1 kg), while a three-sea-winter fish can exceed 70 lb (31.75 kg).

Distribution

Atlantic salmon: Europe from the Arctic to Portugal, and North America from Quebec to Connecticut; landlocked form (the ouananiche or Sebago salmon): northeast United States, eastern Canada. Also introduced into Australia, New Zealand and Argentina.
Coho, chinook, pink, chum, sockeye, kokanee: Alaska to California; northeast Asia; introduced elsewhere.
Masu: northeast Asia.

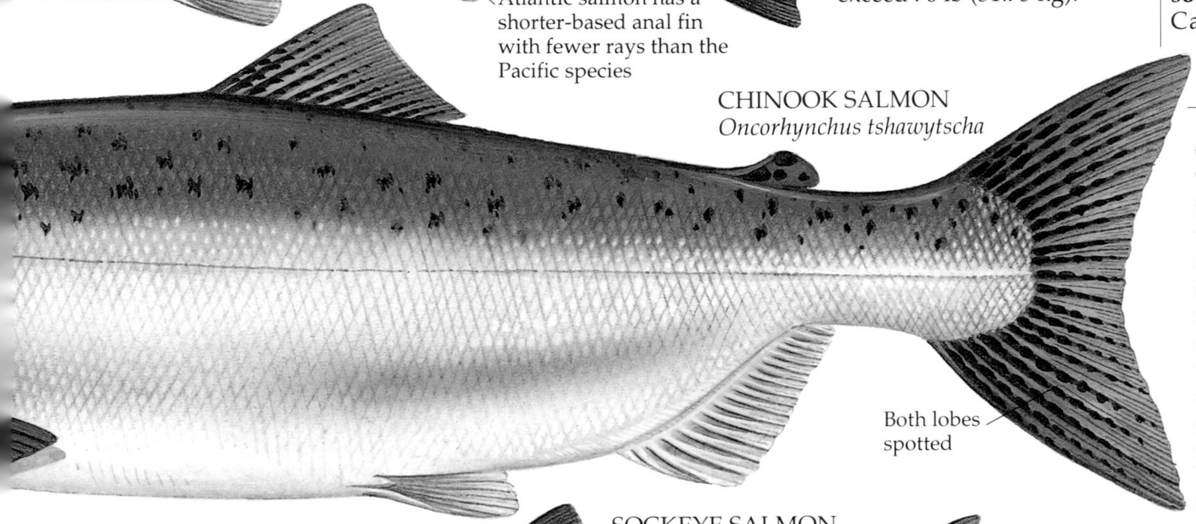
Both lobes spotted

CHINOOK SALMON
Oncorhynchus tshawytscha

Chinook Salmon

The largest Pacific salmon is the chinook or king salmon, which averages 10 to 15 lb (4.54 to 6.8 kg) with a maximum of 120 lb (54 kg) or more. Like most salmon, it does not feed when it runs upriver to spawn but relies on stored energy reserves to sustain it during what may be a long and arduous journey. For example, chinook that spawn in Teslin Lake, Yukon, travel over 2,400 miles (3,860 km) up the Yukon and Teslin Rivers to get there.

Very fine speckles

SOCKEYE SALMON
Oncorhynchus nerka

BREEDING MALE SOCKEYE

BREEDING MALE MASU

Sockeye Salmon

The migratory sockeye or red salmon will rarely take a lure or bait and so is of only minor interest to anglers. The landlocked form, however, which is known as the kokanee, is a very popular angling species that readily takes lures, flies, and baits. The sockeye can reach 15 lb (6.8 kg), but the kokanee seldom exceeds 5 lb (2.27 kg).

Chum Salmon

Although it is not highly regarded as a gamefish, the chum salmon can provide good sport on light saltwater tackle. Sea-run chum and sockeye are very similar, but the chum is generally larger, averaging about 10 to 15 lb (4.54 to 6.8 kg) with a maximum of 33 lb (15 kg), and has white-tipped lower fins.

Dark tip to caudal fin

CHUM SALMON
Oncorhynchus keta

Size comparison

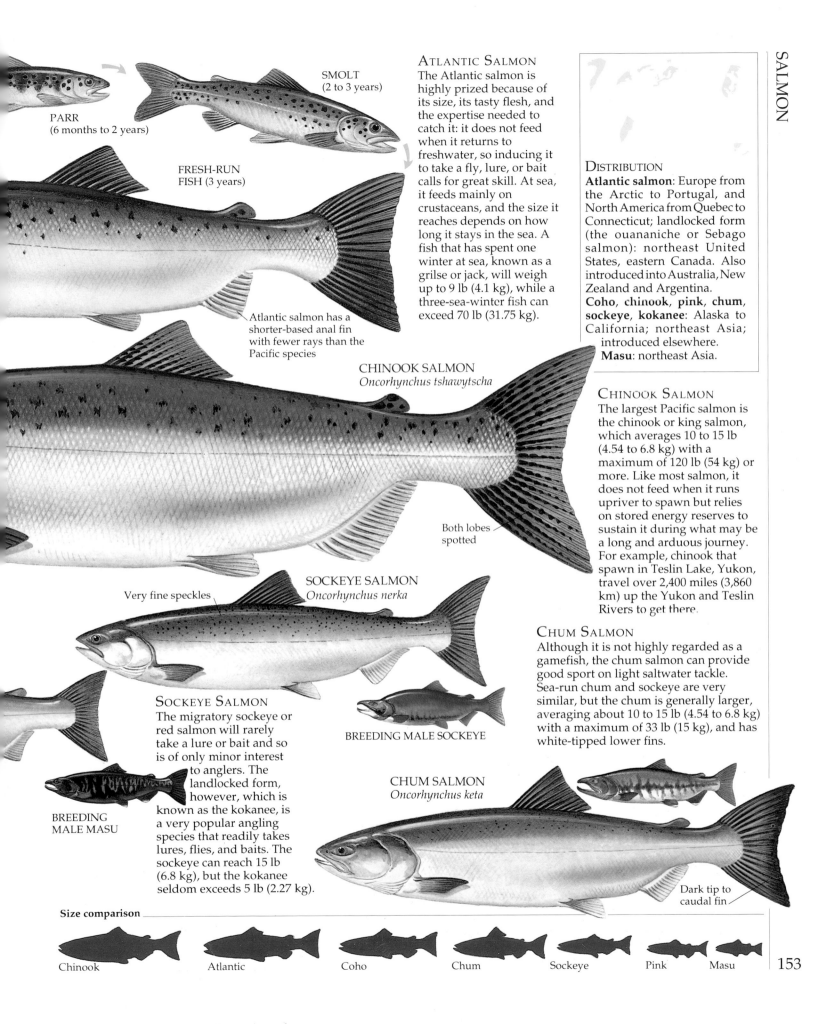

Chinook
Atlantic
Coho
Chum
Sockeye
Pink
Masu

SALMONIDAE

TROUT

The brown trout and the rainbow trout are two of the world's most important gamefish species, and because of the high-quality sport they offer their distribution has been increased by extensive introduction programs. The cutthroat trout, despite its qualities as a gamefish, has not been widely introduced beyond its natural range for a number of reasons, such as its tendency to hybridize with the rainbow trout. Trout thrive in cool, clean streams and lakes and feed mainly on insects, insect larvae, crustaceans, and fish. When at sea, the migratory forms eat fish and crustaceans.

Rainbow Trout

The rainbow trout varies greatly in appearance and size, and there are many different races and subspecies such as the Kamloops, Shasta, and Kern River rainbows. Most, however, have a pink stripe along the lateral line and small black speckles on the sides, back, upper fins, and tail. In North America, rainbows weighing more than 50 lb (22.7 kg) have been recorded, but the usual maximum in European waters is only around 24 lb (11 kg).

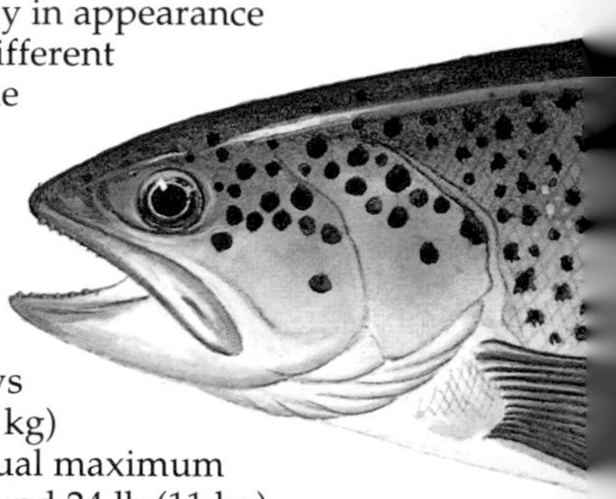

Steelhead

Steelhead are rainbow trout that migrate to sea before returning to rivers to spawn, or live in lakes and move into streams to spawn. Fresh-run steelhead are silvery, but their coloration soon changes to resemble that of non-migratory rainbows.

SEA TROUT
Migratory form of brown trout

BROWN TROUT
Salmo trutta

Sea Trout

The sea trout, the silvery migratory form of the brown trout, enters the sea at about two years old but returns to rivers to spawn. A large sea trout resembles an Atlantic salmon *(see page 152)*, but its tail has a thicker "wrist" and is more squared-off.

Brown Trout

The brown trout is highly variable in appearance and size, and these variations are caused by environmental and genetic factors. In general, the body is brownish and sprinkled with black and red spots, and its weight ranges from under 1 lb (454 g) in small streams to over 30 lb (13.6 kg) in large waters.

Fishing Notes

Techniques
Trout are taken on natural baits and on spinners, but fly fishing is without any doubt the preeminent trout-fishing technique.

Tackle
For fly fishing, use a 6 to 11 ft (1.8 to 3.4 m) fly rod, a fly reel, and floating or sinking line as appropriate. To fish for trout with naturals, such as worms, use a 7 to 10 ft (2.1 to 3 m) medium-action rod with a spinning reel, 4 to 8 lb (1.8 to 3.6 kg) line, and hook sizes 6 to 14. For spinning with artificial lures, try a 7 to 9 ft (2.1 to 2.7 m) spinning rod with a spinning reel and 4 to 8 lb (1.8 to 3.6 kg) line.

Bait
For fly fishing, use whichever pattern is appropriate for the water, the style of fishing, and the prevailing conditions. For spinning, use small spinners, spoons, and plugs. Suitable naturals for trout include larvae and worms.

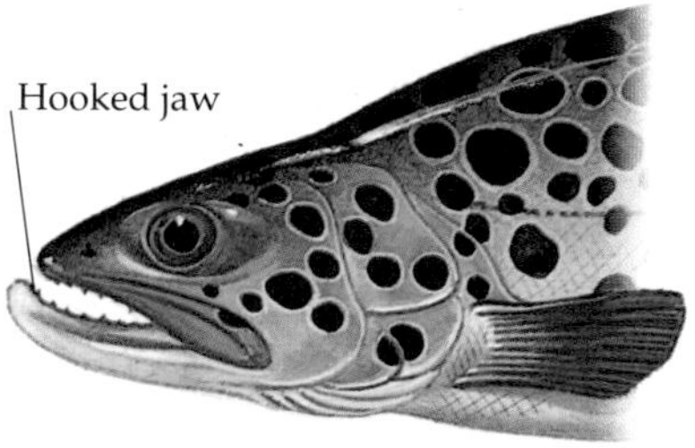

Cannibal trout
Although all brown trout are carnivorous, large individuals will even eat smaller members of their own species. These cannibal trout, which develop a distinctly hooked lower jaw, lurk in deep water waiting to pounce on their prey as it swims past.

RAINBOW TROUT
Oncorhynchus mykiss

STEELHEAD
Migratory form of rainbow trout

Distribution

Brown: Norway to North Africa and Ireland to Russia; introduced into North and South America, Australia, New Zealand, Africa, India.
Rainbow: from Alaska to California, and northeast Asia; introduced elsewhere in North America, and into Europe, South America, Australia, New Zealand, Africa, India.
Cutthroat: Alaska to New Mexico; introduced elsewhere.
Golden: California; introduced into over 300 mountain waters elsewhere in North America.

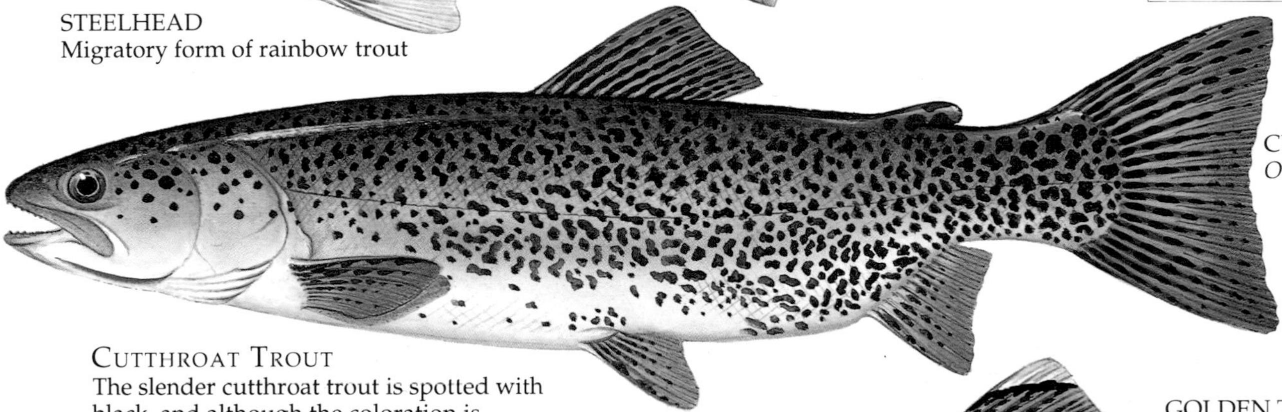

CUTTHROAT TROUT
Oncorhynchus clarki

Cutthroat Trout

The slender cutthroat trout is spotted with black, and although the coloration is otherwise very variable there is always a red "cutthroat" mark under the lower jaw, and sometimes a faint coppery line along the side. The migratory coastal cutthroat has a green back and silvery or olive sides. Cutthroat of over 40 lb (18 kg) have been recorded, but the usual maximum is about 5 lb (2.27kg).

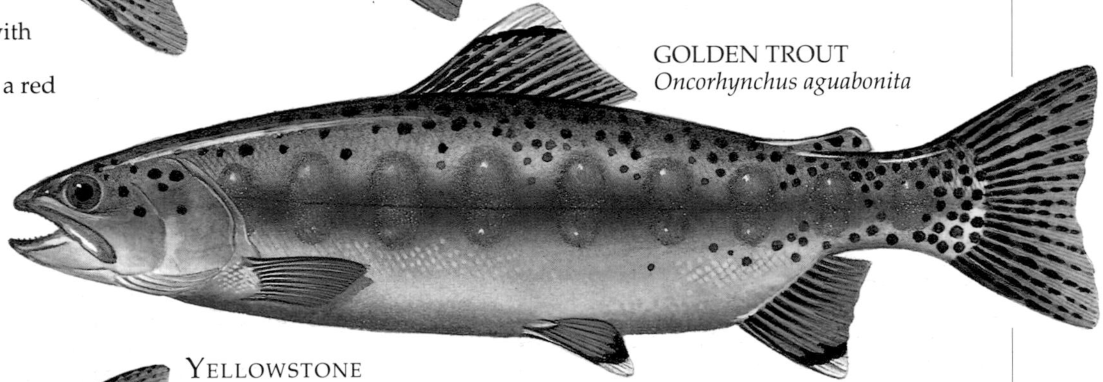

GOLDEN TROUT
Oncorhynchus aguabonita

YELLOWSTONE CUTTHROAT
Oncorhynchus clarki lewisi

Yellowstone Cutthroat

Many of the local forms of the principal trout species, such as the Yellowstone variety of cutthroat, are sufficiently distinct to be classifiable as subspecies. The Yellowstone is sparsely spotted, with red-tinged gill covers.

Golden Trout

The beautiful golden trout is native to the high-altitude headwaters of the Kern River in the Sierra Nevada Mountains, California. It retains its parr marks *(see page 150)* all its life, and its maximum weight ranges from about 1 lb (454 g) in streams to around 11 lb (5 kg) in lakes.

Size comparison

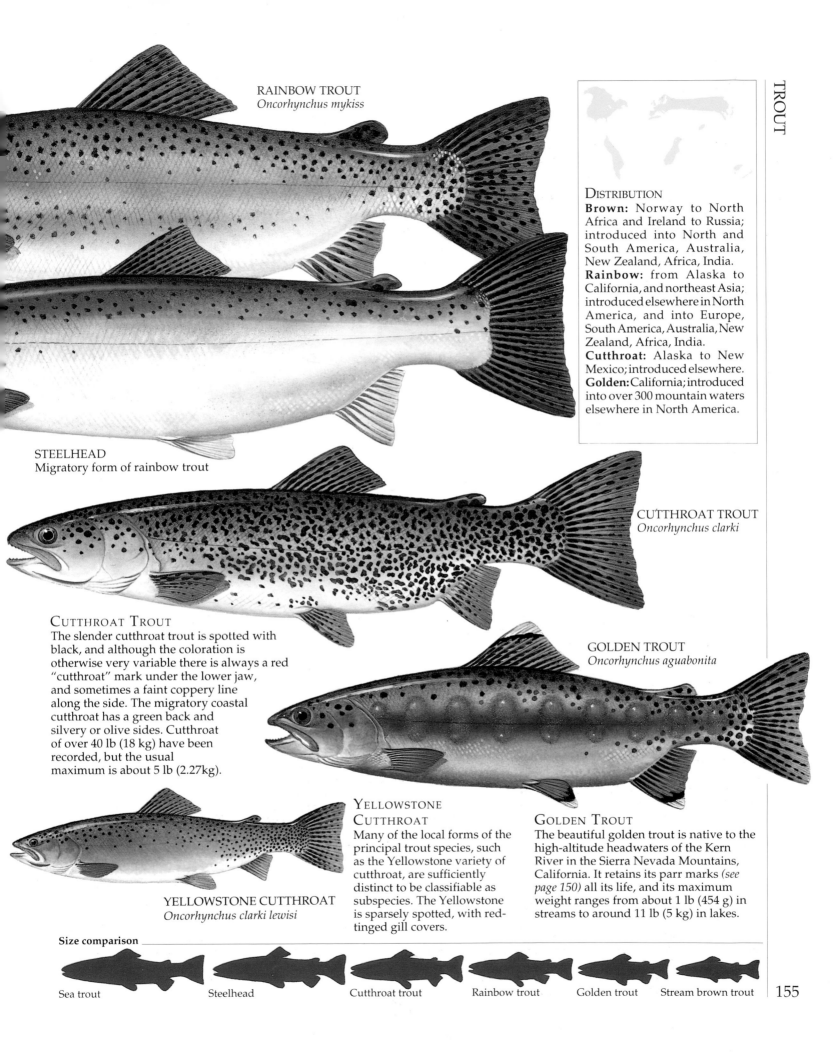

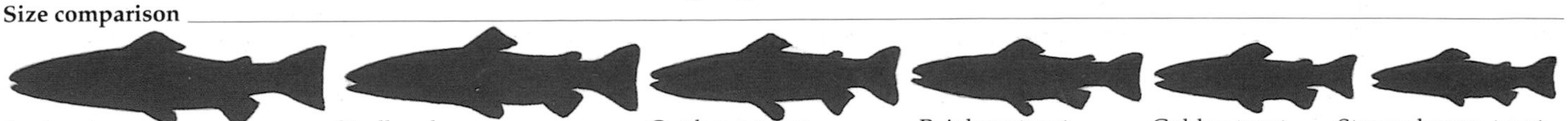

Sea trout | Steelhead | Cutthroat trout | Rainbow trout | Golden trout | Stream brown trout

Whitefish & Grayling

Whitefish and grayling are widely distributed in the colder lakes and streams of the Northern Hemisphere. Grayling are popular angling species, as are several of the whitefish, but many whitefish species are threatened with extinction *(see page 279)* and it is illegal to fish for them in many countries and on certain waters. Grayling feed mainly on bottom-dwelling creatures such as insect larvae, crustaceans, and worms, but will also take insects at the surface. The whitefish's diet ranges from plankton to fish.

Inconnu

The large, powerful inconnu, or sheefish, is the only predatory whitefish in North America. Its average weight is about 5 lb (2.27 kg), but it can live for over 20 years and has been known to reach weights of up to 55 lb (25 kg). Most inconnu live in the estuaries and lower reaches of rivers and migrate upstream to spawn, but there are some non-migratory lake populations. The young fish feed on plankton at first, and then on small, bottom-dwelling creatures before becoming predatory during their second year.

INCONNU
Stenodus leucichthys

EUROPEAN WHITEFISH
Coregonus sp.

European Whitefish

In Europe, the many whitefish species, subspecies, races, and local variants have yet to be classified definitively. In general, they are at best of minor interest to anglers, but many are netted commercially because of their tasty flesh. Common names include vendace, houting, powan, and schelly; they are slender, silvery fish that range in size from about 1 lb (454 g) *(Coregonus albula)* to around 11 lb (5 kg) *(C. pallasi)*.

Cisco

Because of its herringlike size, shape, and general appearance, the cisco is also known as the lake herring. Despite being a small fish, rarely exceeding 2 lb (910 g), it is popular with anglers because it will readily take a wide range of lures and baits, including flies.

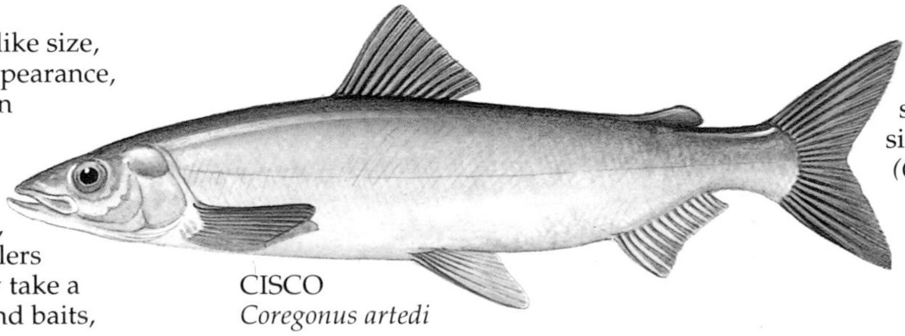

CISCO
Coregonus artedi

Size comparison

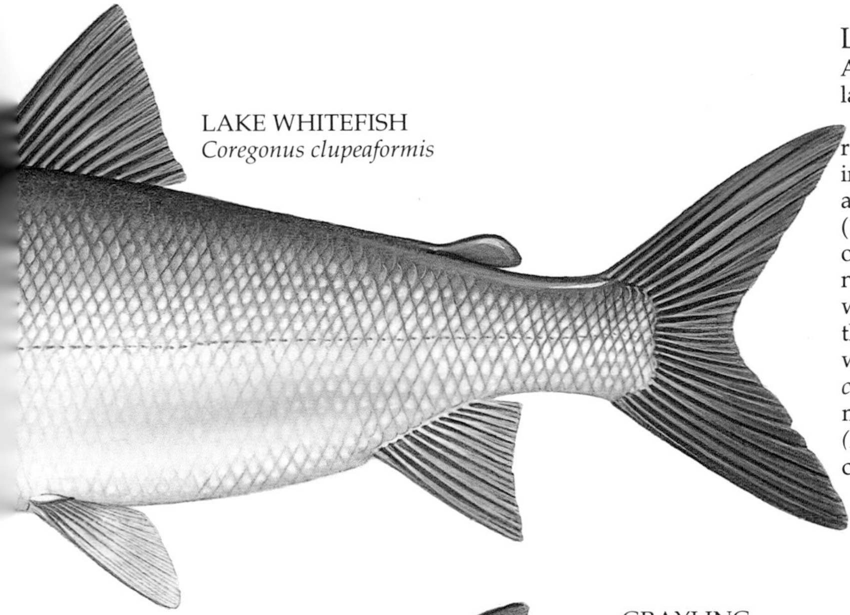

LAKE WHITEFISH
Coregonus clupeaformis

Lake Whitefish

Although it is primarily a lake-dwelling species, the lake whitefish also enters rivers. It feeds mainly on insects and crustaceans, and averages about 3 lb (1.4 kg); larger specimens, of up to 20 lb (9.1 kg), are now rare. The lake whitefish, together with the cisco, the round whitefish *(Prosopium cylindraceum)* and the mountain whitefish *(P. williamsoni),* is commercially important as well as being a popular angling species.

Distribution

Lake whitefish: throughout Alaska, Canada, and northern United States.
Inconnu: Alaska, northwest Canada, northeast Asia.
Cisco: northern Canada to the Great Lakes and upper Mississippi basins.
European whitefish: a few lakes in Britain and Ireland; cool lakes, rivers, and coastal waters of mainland Europe and northern Asia.
European grayling: England and Wales to the Black Sea.
American grayling: Alaska to Hudson Bay; Montana; the northeast of Asia.

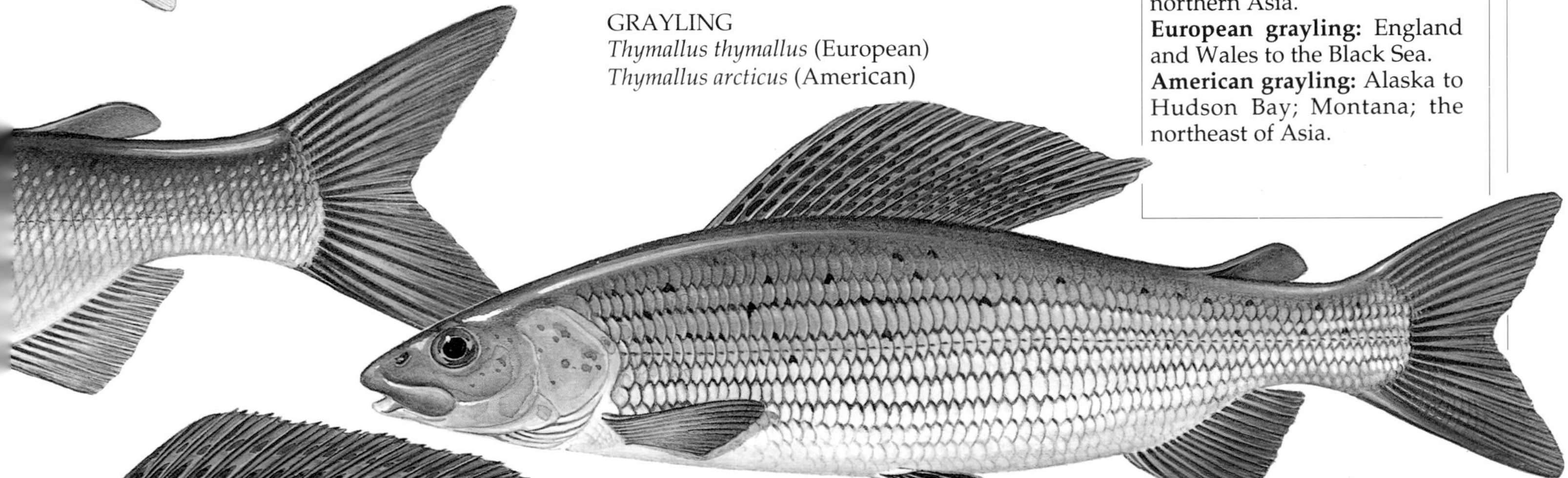

GRAYLING
Thymallus thymallus (European)
Thymallus arcticus (American)

Grayling dorsal fin
The huge, rounded, and sail-like dorsal fin of the grayling develops a more intense coloration in the breeding season. When a pair of grayling are spawning, the male curls his dorsal fin over the female.

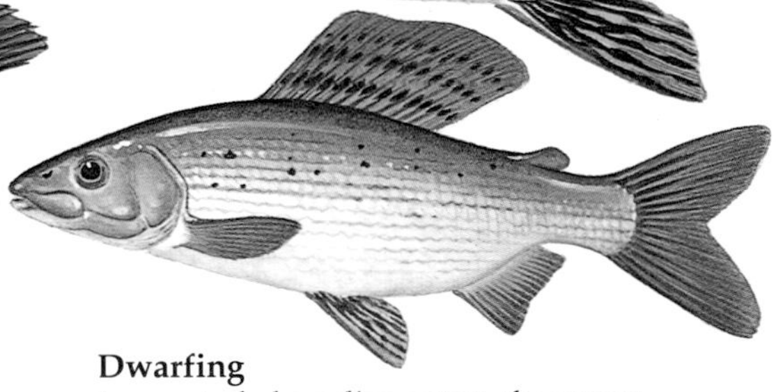

Dwarfing
In overstocked grayling waters, the amount of food available to each fish is limited, and small, deep-bodied individuals are common.

Grayling

The European grayling and the American, or arctic, grayling are very similar, and nowadays are usually classified separately from the Salmonidae in a family of their own, the Thymallidae. Like the brown trout, grayling are found in cool, clean, well-oxygenated streams, and they also occur in lakes, especially in North America. Grayling are relatively small, with a maximum weight of about 6 lb (2.7 kg).

FISHING NOTES

Techniques

Whitefish and grayling are taken by fly fishing, by spinning with artificial baits, and also by float fishing or legering with natural baits.

Tackle

For fly fishing, try an 8 to 9 ft (2.4 to 2.7 m) medium-action fly rod with a fly reel and #5 to #7 line. For float fishing or legering, try a 11 to 13 ft (3.4 to 4 m) rod with a spinning reel, 2 to 3 lb (910 g to 1.36 kg) line, and hook sizes 10 to 16. For spinning, use an ultralight rod for grayling and cisco, and a medium-action rod for inconnu and lake whitefish.

Bait

Use imitative dry flies, wet flies, and nymphs for grayling, streamers for inconnu, and dry flies for cisco and lake whitefish. When spinning, use small, bright spinners and spoons. Natural baits for grayling include maggots and small worms; lake whitefish can be taken on cut fish.

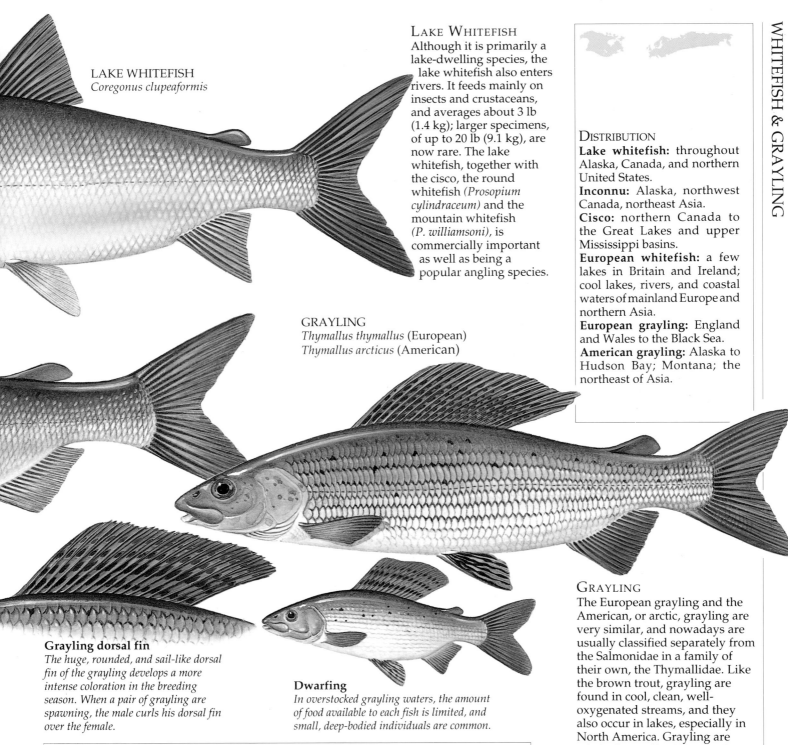

Breeding grayling
Grayling spawn in gravelly shallows in spring and early summer, lake fish entering streams to spawn. The hatchlings lurk among stones, living off their yolk sacs.

ALBULIDAE; ELOPIDAE; POMATOMIDAE

Bonefish, Bluefish, & Tarpon

These fish haunt the shallow coastal waters of the tropical and warm-temperate regions of the world, and are among the most exciting and popular marine sports species. The food of bonefish (the Albulidae) and tarpon (the Elopidae) consists mainly of crustaceans and small fish, but the bluefish (a member of the Pomatomidae) is a savage predator that will eat virtually anything edible that crosses its path.

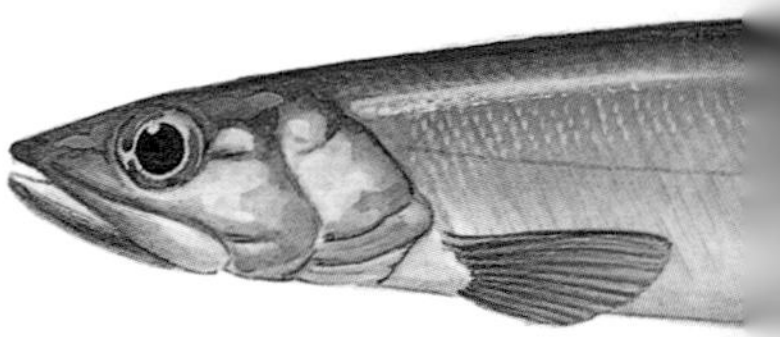

Bonefish

The bonefish is a bottom feeder that grubs in the mud or sand for food such as shrimps and crabs. In very shallow water, the tails of feeding bonefish often break the surface, betraying their presence to stalking anglers who wade the mudflats in pursuit of them. Adult bonefish typically weigh up to 10 lb (4.54 kg) but can reach 19 lb (8.6 kg).

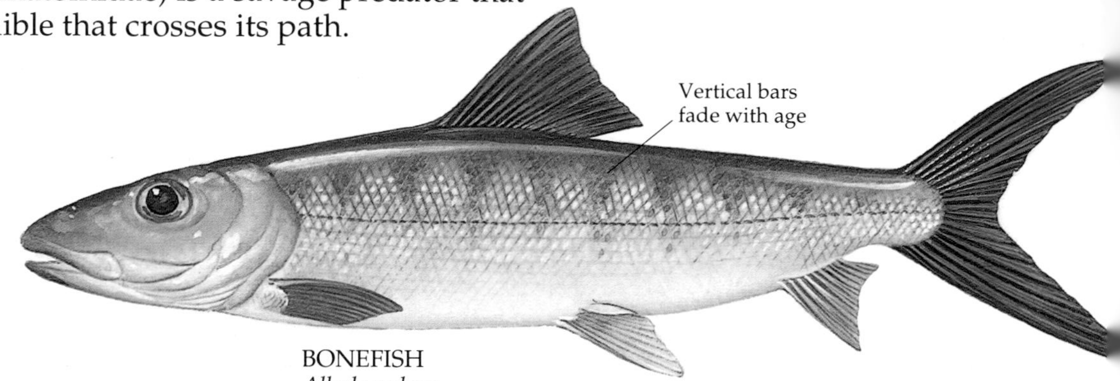

BONEFISH
Albula vulpes

BLUEFISH
Pomatomus saltatrix

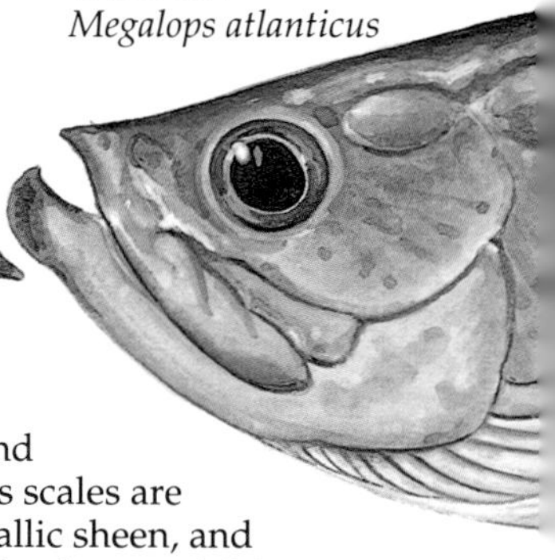

TARPON
Megalops atlanticus

Bluefish

The highly migratory bluefish can grow to over 50 lb (23 kg), and travels in huge schools that go into a feeding frenzy when they encounter schools of prey fish such as herring or menhaden. They have been known to come close inshore and attack bathers, and their sharp, prominent, triangular teeth can inflict painful wounds. They should be handled with care when caught, especially when they are being unhooked.

Tarpon

The large, silvery tarpon is usually caught in tidal creeks, estuaries, mangrove swamps, and lagoons, and can sometimes be taken offshore. Its scales are large and tough, with a bright, metallic sheen, and the last ray of the dorsal fin is greatly elongated. Most tarpon landed by anglers weigh between 20 and 80 lb (9.1 and 36.3 kg), but the maximum weight is much higher and individuals of over 300 lb (136 kg) have been reported.

Fishing Notes

Techniques

The usual techniques are trolling for bluefish, and spinning and fly fishing for bonefish and tarpon.

Tackle

For bluefish, use a 20 lb (9.1 kg) class boat rod with a 4/0 baitcaster, 20 lb (9.1 kg) nylon or Dacron line, a trolling weight, a wire terminal leader, and hook sizes 4/0 to 6/0. When spinning for bonefish and tarpon, try a 6½ to 7 ft (2 to 2.1 m) medium-action rod and spinning reel. Use 8 lb (3.6 kg) mono line with a mono leader for bonefish, and 15 lb (6.8 kg) mono line with a short wire leader for tarpon. Suitable fly tackle for bonefish and tarpon would be a 9 to 10 ft (2.7 to 3 m) saltwater fly rod and a 4 in (10 cm) reel, with 8 lb (3.6 kg) backing for bonefish and 27 lb (12.2 kg) backing for tarpon; hook sizes are 6 to 1/0 for bonefish, 2 to 5/0 for tarpon.

Bait

Bluefish are usually taken on plugs or baitfish. For bonefish, spin with small leadhead lures and use shrimp imitator patterns, bucktails, and small imitation marabou streamers for fly fishing. For tarpon, spin with medium-sized plugs, and use yellow or orange splayed-wing streamers for fly fishing.

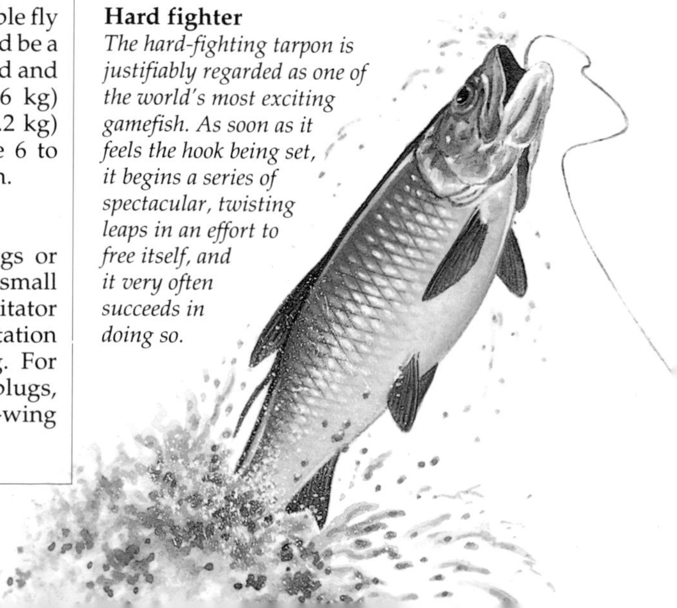

Hard fighter
The hard-fighting tarpon is justifiably regarded as one of the world's most exciting gamefish. As soon as it feels the hook being set, it begins a series of spectacular, twisting leaps in an effort to free itself, and it very often succeeds in doing so.

LADYFISH

This slender, fine-scaled fish is usually found in shallow, warm-temperate or tropical waters with mud or sand bottoms. It is generally fished for on light tackle, and despite also being commonly known as the tenpounder it usually weighs no more than about 5 lb (2.27 kg), although it can occasionally reach around 15 lb (6.8 kg).

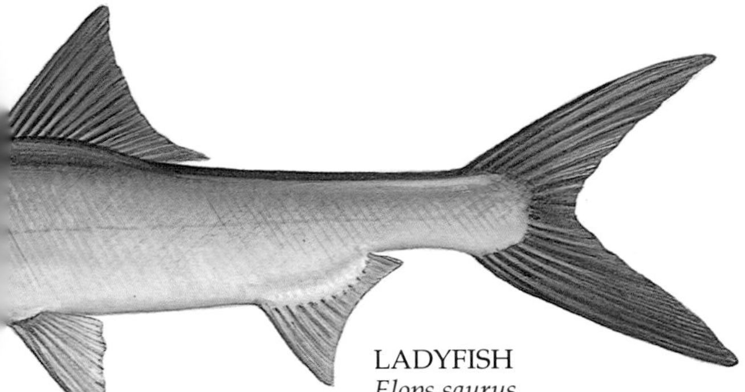

LADYFISH
Elops saurus

Bonefish larva
The larva of the bonefish is similar to that of an eel, with a small head and a transparent body. As it matures it shrinks in size and begins to resemble a tiny adult bonefish, and then grows to its full size.

BONEFISH LARVA

Elongated rays

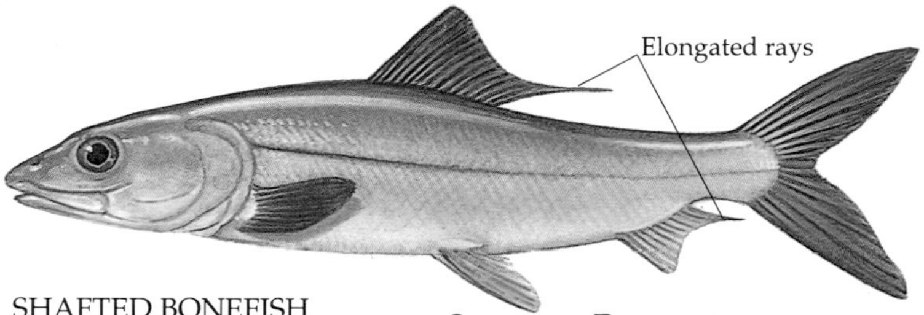

SHAFTED BONEFISH
Albula nemoptera

SHAFTED BONEFISH

The shafted, or longfin, bonefish resembles the bonefish (to which it is closely related) but grows to only half its size, and has distinctively elongated last rays in its dorsal and anal fins. Its habits are generally similar to those of the bonefish.

DISTRIBUTION

Bonefish: worldwide in tropical coastal waters.
Shafted bonefish: tropical coastal waters of Central and South America.
Bluefish: temperate to tropical coastal waters of the Atlantic and Indian Oceans; absent from European waters.
Tarpon: western Atlantic, Gulf of Mexico, the Caribbean, the west coast of Central America, and coast of northwest Africa.
Ladyfish: mainly Florida and the Caribbean.
Oxeye tarpon: Indo-Pacific.

The oxeye tarpon, like its Atlantic cousin, has an elongated dorsal fin ray

Caudal peduncle ends in double V shape

OXEYE TARPON

Also known as the oxeye herring, this Indo-Pacific fish is very like its Atlantic relative, the tarpon, but is smaller and rarely grows to more than 40 lb (18 kg). Like the tarpon, it ventures into creeks and estuaries and it fights hard when hooked.

Lower fins lighter than those of larger tarpon

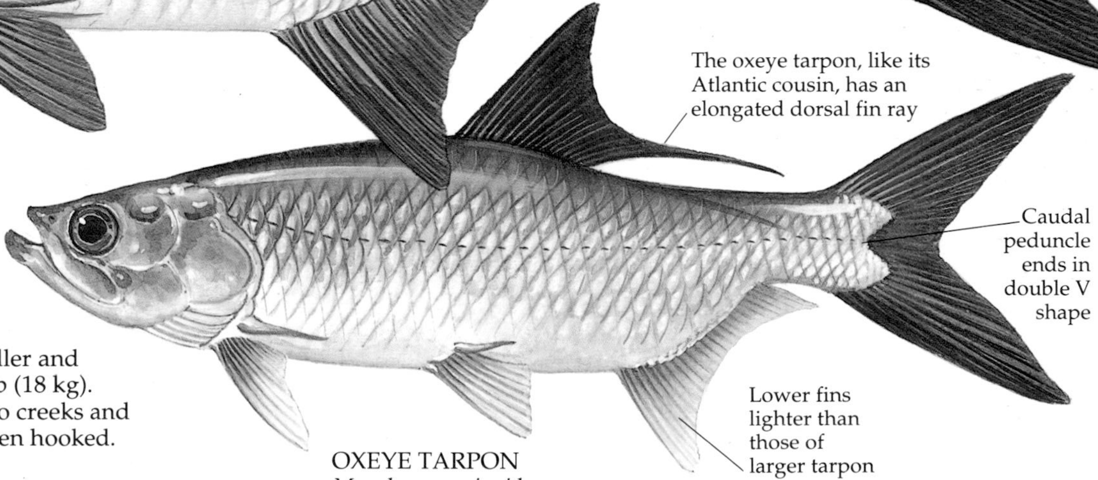

OXEYE TARPON
Megalops cyprinoides

Size comparison

Tarpon Oxeye tarpon Bluefish Bonefish Ladyfish Shafted bonefish

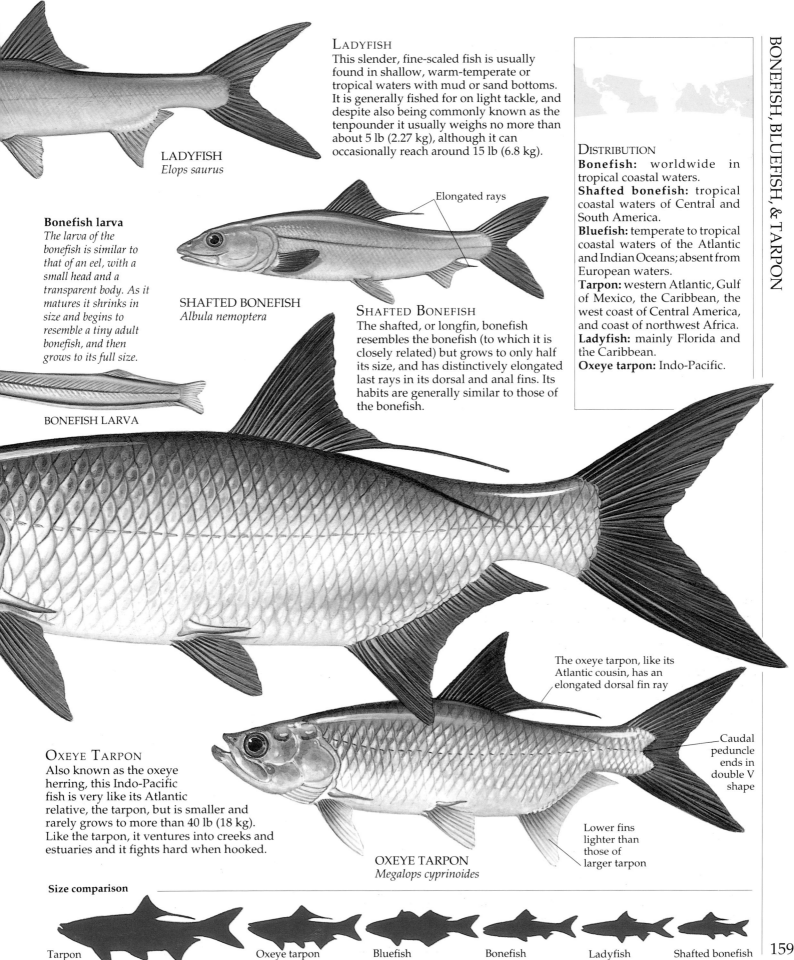

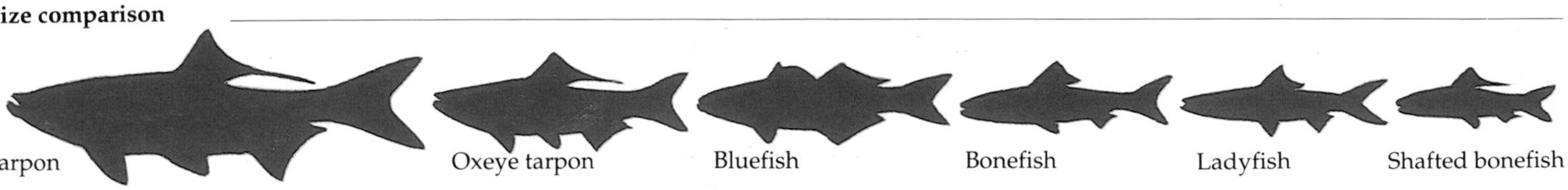

ANGUILLIDAE; CONGRIDAE; MURAENIDAE

EELS

There are more than 20 families of eel, including the Muraenidae (morays) and Congridae (congers), and all but one of them consist of exclusively saltwater fish. The exception is the family Anguillidae, which includes the American, European, and longfinned eels, all of which mature in freshwater and travel to the sea to spawn. The American and European eels travel to the Sargasso Sea, an area in the North Atlantic; the longfinned eel and the other Australasian species of Anguillidae migrate to the Indian Ocean.

CONGER
Conger conger

MORAY

The European moray *Muraena helena*, found in the eastern Atlantic and the Mediterranean, is one of the more than 80 species of moray. All are notoriously short-tempered and quick to use their razor-sharp teeth when they feel threatened. They are rarely fished for, but are sometimes hooked when other species are being sought. *M. helena* can reach 4 ft 3 in (1.3 m) but is usually much smaller.

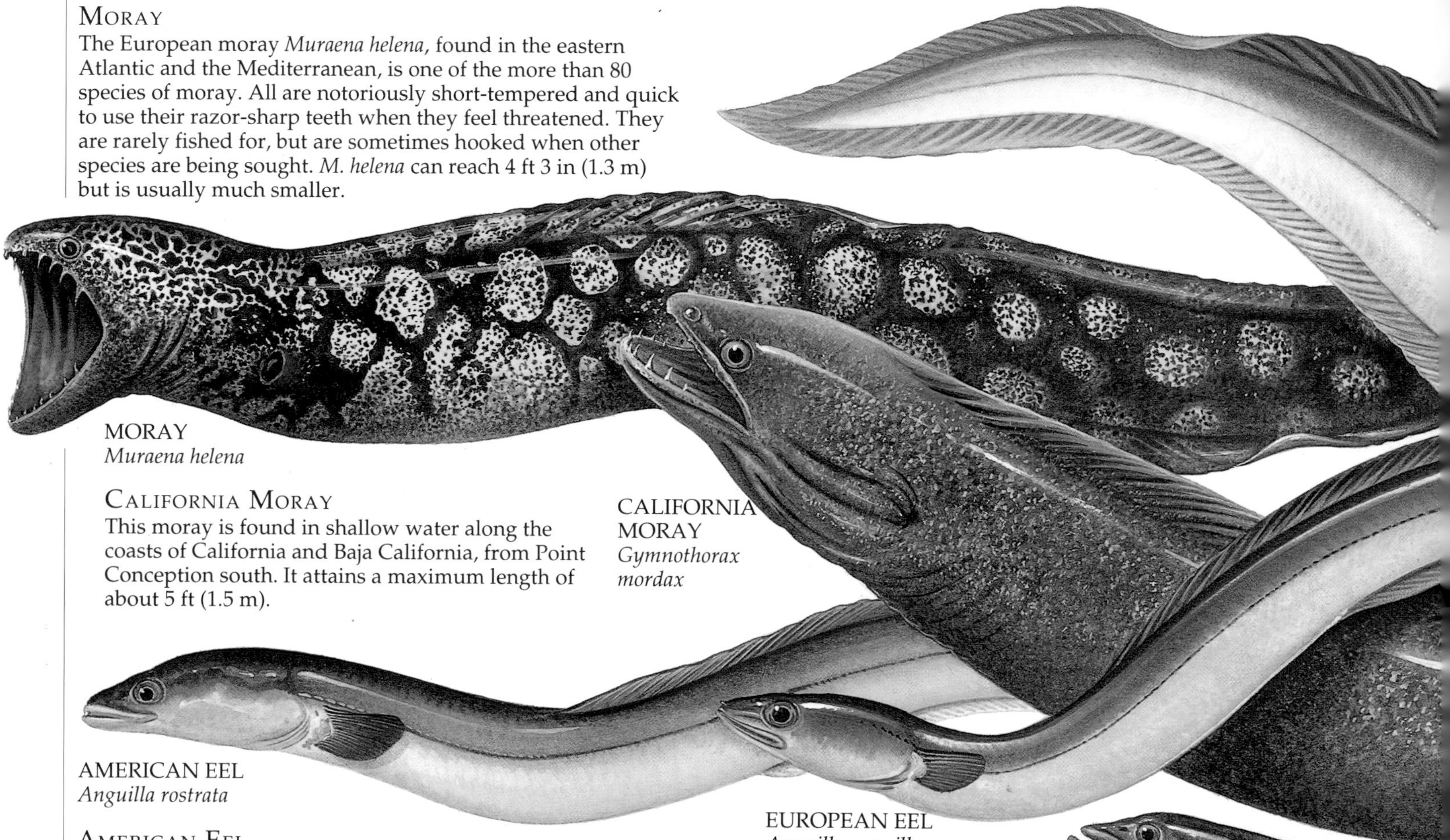

MORAY
Muraena helena

CALIFORNIA MORAY
Gymnothorax mordax

AMERICAN EEL
Anguilla rostrata

EUROPEAN EEL
Anguilla anguilla

CALIFORNIA MORAY

This moray is found in shallow water along the coasts of California and Baja California, from Point Conception south. It attains a maximum length of about 5 ft (1.5 m).

AMERICAN EEL

Adult American eels usually spend several years in freshwater, the males staying near the mouths of rivers and the females traveling far upstream. The females grow to 3 ft 3 in (1 m) or more and a weight of over 11 lb (5 kg), but the males are much smaller, generally around 1 ft (30 cm) in length.

EUROPEAN EEL

The European eel is very similar to its American counterpart, and the two may be a single species. After spawning, the adults die; the journey to freshwater takes young American eels about a year, and young European eels three or four years.

LONG-FINNED EEL
Anguilla reinhardtii

LONGFINNED EEL

This is one of a number of freshwater eels found in Australasia. Like the American and European eels, it migrates to the sea to spawn, possibly in the Coral Sea. It grows to 31 lb (14 kg).

Eel larvae
In the early stages of their development, eel larvae are strange, transparent, leaflike creatures called leptocephali. Later, they become elvers, miniature versions of their parents, and it is as elvers that freshwater eels arrive in rivers.

EARLY STAGE

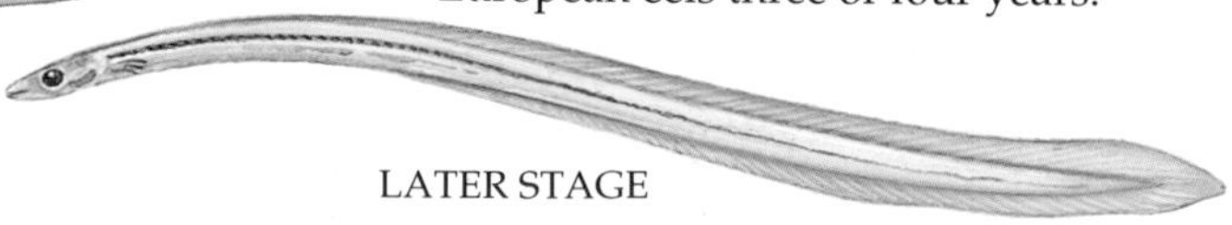

LATER STAGE

Size comparison

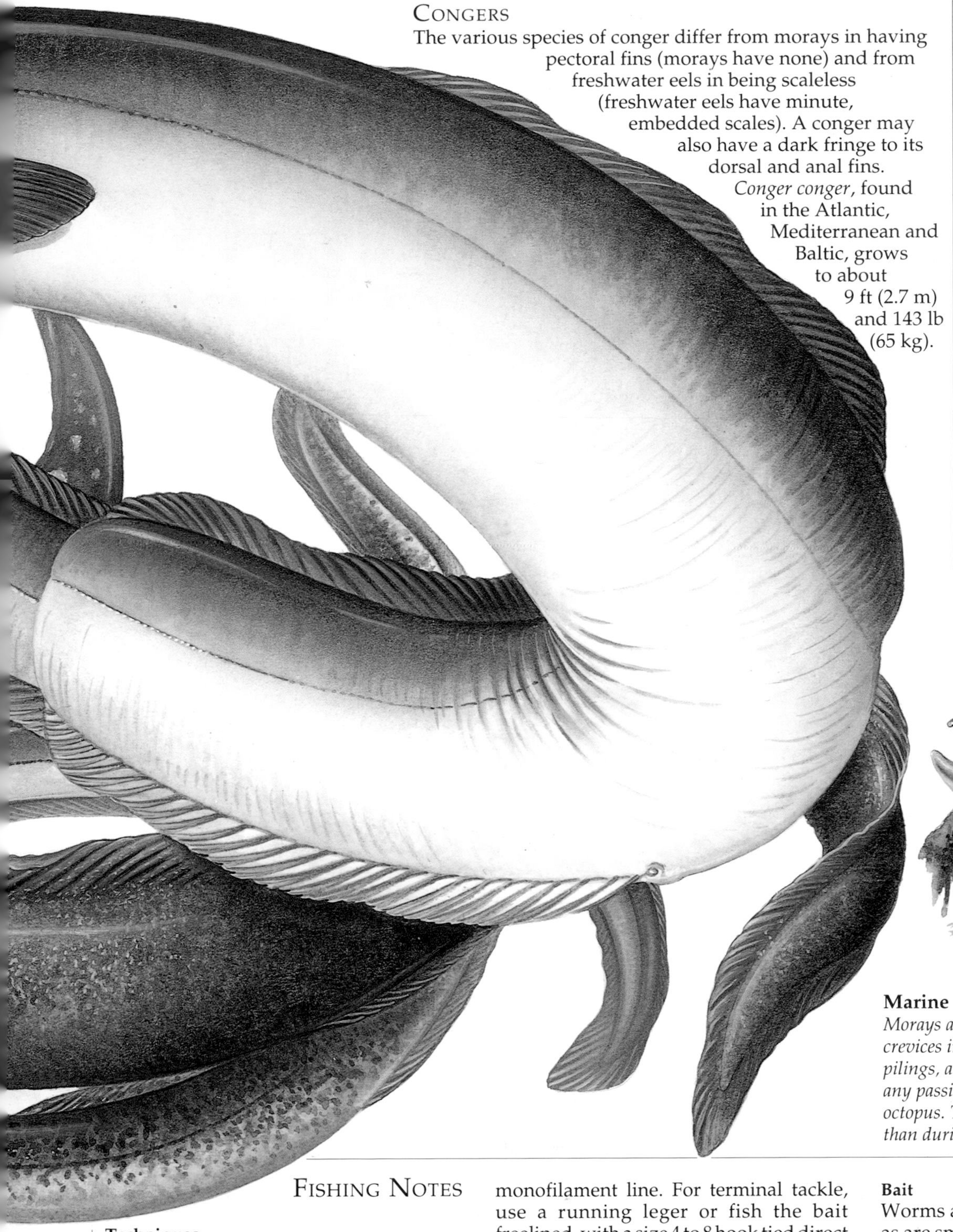

Congers

The various species of conger differ from morays in having pectoral fins (morays have none) and from freshwater eels in being scaleless (freshwater eels have minute, embedded scales). A conger may also have a dark fringe to its dorsal and anal fins. *Conger conger*, found in the Atlantic, Mediterranean and Baltic, grows to about 9 ft (2.7 m) and 143 lb (65 kg).

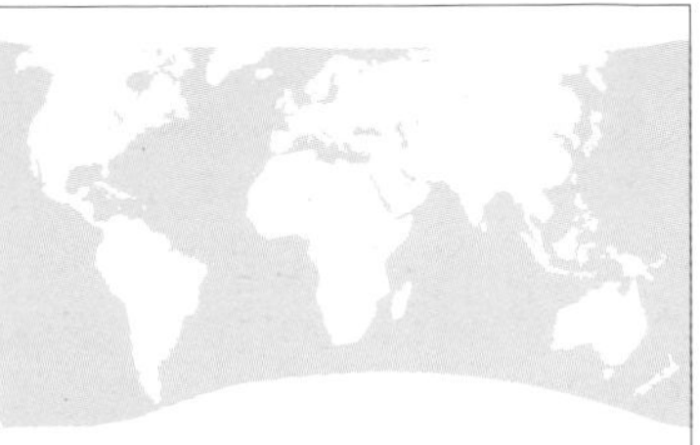

Distribution

Morays: worldwide in subtropical and tropical waters; some species found in warm-temperate waters.
California moray: southern California and Baja California.
American eel: eastern North America, the Caribbean, and northeastern South America.
European eel: from Iceland and Norway to the Mediterranean.
Longfinned eel: Tasmania and eastern Australia.
Congers: most temperate and tropical waters.

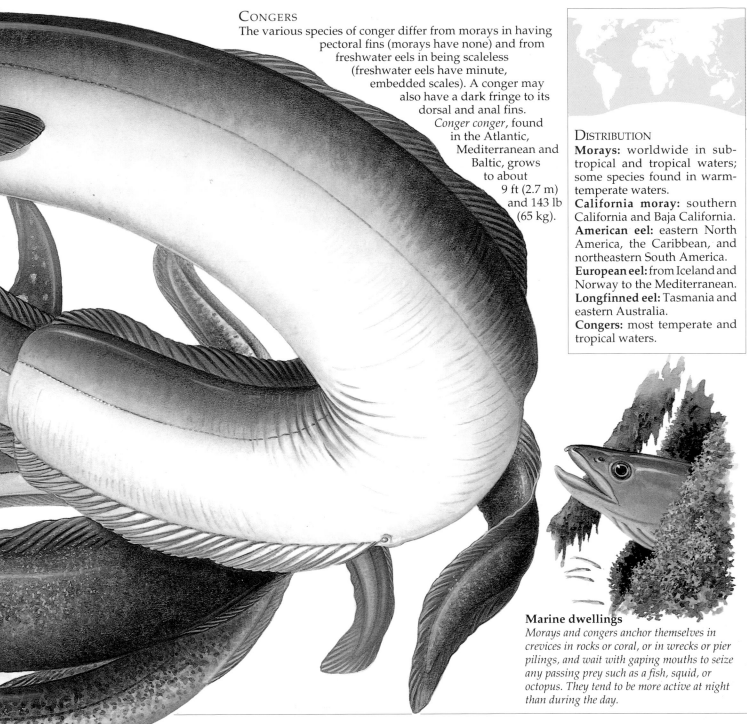

Marine dwellings
Morays and congers anchor themselves in crevices in rocks or coral, or in wrecks or pier pilings, and wait with gaping mouths to seize any passing prey such as a fish, squid, or octopus. They tend to be more active at night than during the day.

Fishing Notes

Techniques

The migratory eels are usually fished for in freshwater, by legering. Marine eels (conger and moray) are taken by fishing with natural baits from rocky shores, piers, jetties, and sea walls, and from boats over rocks and wrecks.

Tackle

For migratory eels, use a 10 to 12 ft (3 to 3.7 m), 2 lb (910 g) test curve, carp or pike rod, with a spinning reel, and 5 lb (2.27 kg) monofilament line. For terminal tackle, use a running leger or fish the bait freelined, with a size 4 to 8 hook tied direct to the line. When fishing from the shore for marine eels, use a 20 to 50 lb (9.1 to 22.7 kg) class surfcasting rod, a 4/0 baitcaster reel, 30 to 35 lb (13.6 to 15.9 kg) line, a running leger wire leader, a pear- or pyramid-shaped weight, and a 6/0 hook. To fish from a boat for marine eels, try a 50 lb (22.7 kg) boat rod, 8/0 baitcaster reel, and 50 to 60 lb (22.7 to 27.2 kg) line. Use a wire leader, a size 8/0 hook, and a pear- or pyramid-shaped weight.

Bait

Worms are good bait for freshwater eels, as are small, dead fish. Fish baits are very effective for large eels, and they should be whole, about 5 in (13 cm) long, and punctured so that they sink. Pungent baits such as fish liver and smoked fish are also effective, and it is worth using an oily, smelly, non-floating groundbait to attract eels into the swim you are going to fish.

The marine eels can be caught on large natural baits, such as whole or cut fish, squid, and cuttlefish, and these baits should be fished on the bottom.

ARIIDAE; SPHYRAENIDAE

SEA CATFISH & BARRACUDA

The Ariidae family of sea catfish consists of about 80 species, widely distributed around the world in warm coastal waters and estuaries, and also (in the tropics) in freshwater. When caught, a sea catfish must be handled carefully, because the dorsal and pectoral fins have sharp spines that can inflict painful wounds. Barracuda belong to the Sphyraenidae family, which contains about 20 species. They are all fierce predators that feed voraciously on small, schooling species, and because they are attracted to their quarry by sight rather than smell they tend to concentrate on bright, silvery colored prey.

Mouth brooding
In most species of sea catfish, the male keeps the marble-sized fertilized eggs in his mouth until they hatch, which can take up to a month.

HARDHEAD CATFISH

The hardhead catfish, also called the sea catfish, is common in coastal and brackish waters from Massachusetts to Mexico. It has four barbels on its chin and two on its upper jaw, and can reach a weight of 12 lb (5.4 kg) although it usually does not exceed 2 lb (910 g). Several related species are found in the coastal waters, rivers, and lakes of northern Australia, including the blue catfish or salmon catfish *(Arius graeffei)*.

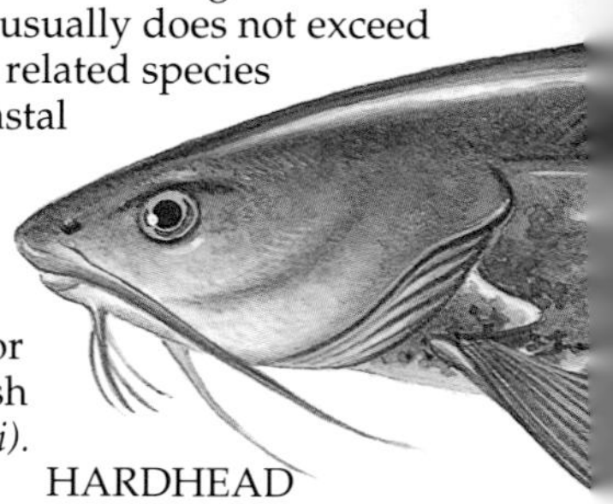

HARDHEAD CATFISH
Arius felis

GUAGUANCHE

Like other barracuda, the guaguanche has a slender, cigar-shaped body, two widely separated dorsal fins, and a protruding lower jaw; it is identifiable by the yellow stripe along its lateral line. It is found on both sides of the Atlantic, and grows to a length of about 2 ft (60 cm).

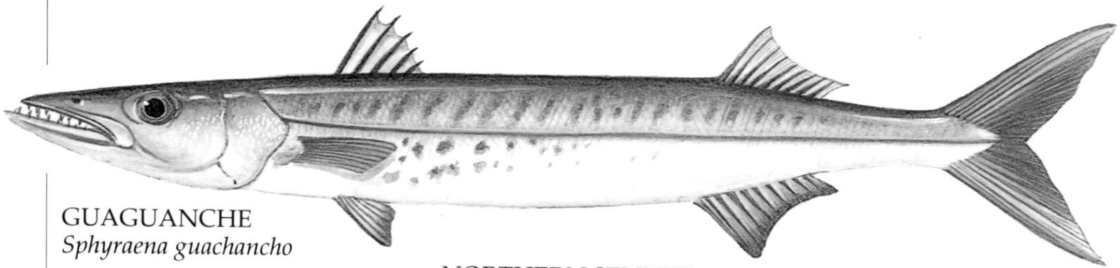

GUAGUANCHE
Sphyraena guachancho

GREAT BARRACUDA
Sphyraena barracuda

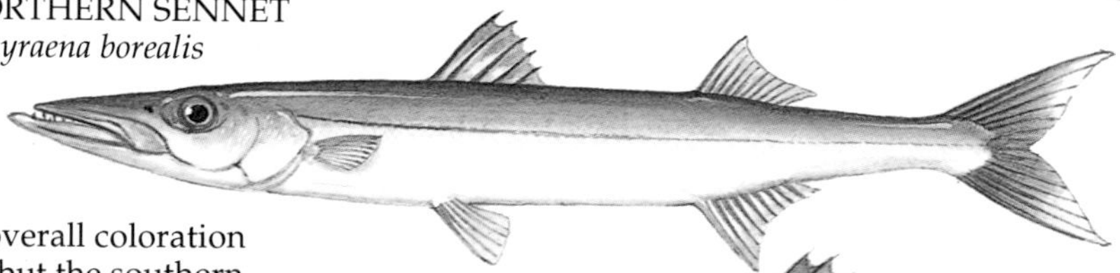

NORTHERN SENNET
Sphyraena borealis

SENNETS

The northern sennet and southern sennet are almost identical, and may in fact be a single species. These little barracuda have the same overall coloration and both grow to about 18 in (45 cm), but the southern sennet has fewer scales on its lateral line (107 to 116 as opposed to 118 to 135) and its eyes are larger. The northern sennet is found from New England to Florida and the Gulf of Mexico, and the southern sennet from Florida to Uruguay. In the eastern Atlantic and the Mediterranean, barracuda are represented by the European barracuda *(Sphyraena sphyraena)*.

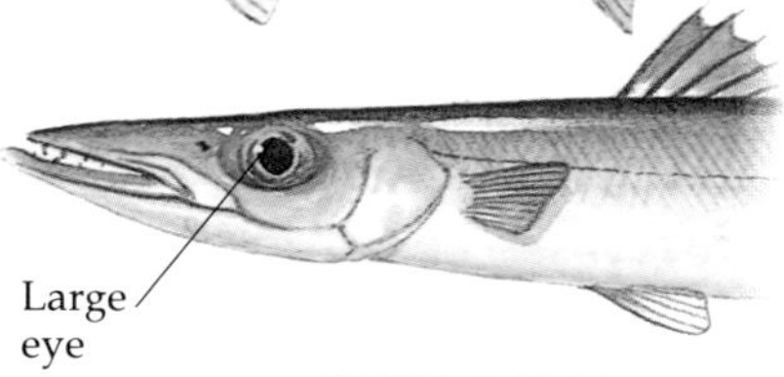

SOUTHERN SENNET
Sphyraena picudilla

PACIFIC BARRACUDA
Sphyraena argentea

FISHING NOTES

Techniques
Catfish are caught by bottom fishing from the shore or piers. For barracuda fishing try trolling, or spinning from a boat or from the shore.

Tackle
For catfish, try an 11 or 12 ft (3.4 or 3.7 m) medium-action rod, with a spinning reel, 7 to 15 lb (3.2 to 6.8 kg) mono line, size 4 to 6/0 hook, and a 1 oz (28 g) weight. To troll for barracuda, use a 12 to 30 lb (5.4 to 13.6 kg) class boat rod with a baitcaster reel, 12 to 30 lb (5.4 to 13.6 kg) nylon line with a wire leader, a size 4/0 to 8/0 hook, and a banana-shaped trolling weight. Spinning calls for a medium spinning rod with a spinning reel, 12 to 30 lb (5.4 to 13.6 kg) nylon line with a wire leader, and hook sizes 4/0 to 8/0.

Bait
Cut fish and livebaits such as sandworms are ideal for catfish, which can also be taken on jigs and plugs. For barracuda, use bright, flashy spinners, wooden plugs, strips of fish, and whole fish such as sardines, anchovies, and queenfish.

Barracuda in shallows
Barracuda are often found in shallow water, where their natural curiosity leads them to follow (and sometimes attack) swimmers.

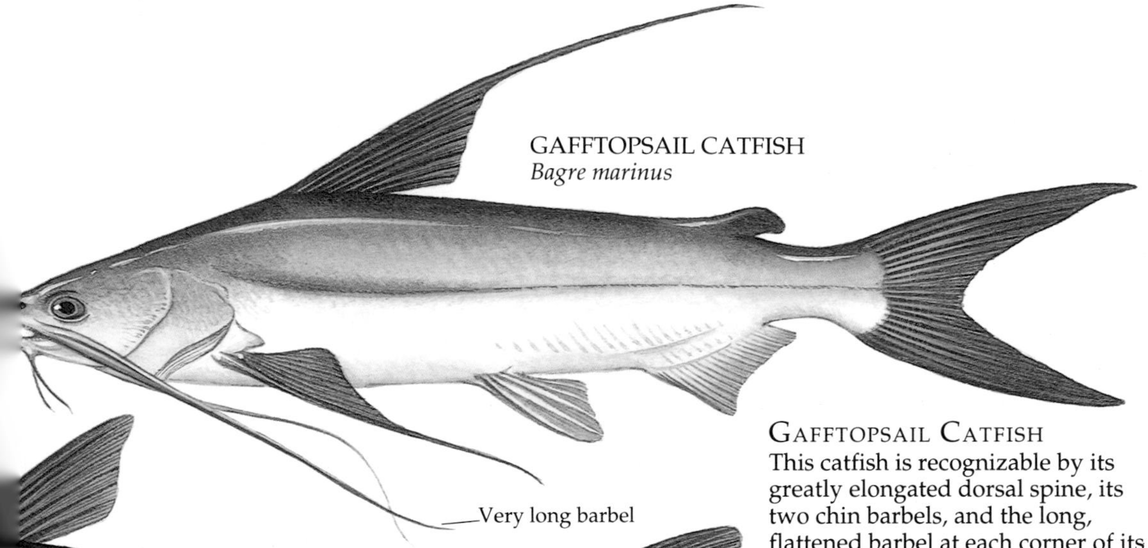

Gafftopsail Catfish

This catfish is recognizable by its greatly elongated dorsal spine, its two chin barbels, and the long, flattened barbel at each corner of its mouth. Its range overlaps that of the hardhead catfish, but it is less common, and its maximum weight is around 5 lb 8 oz (2.5 kg). The gafftopsail and the hardhead are both bottom feeders, taking a variety of small prey including blue crab, and are commonly caught from piers and jetties.

Distribution

Hardhead catfish: western Atlantic and Gulf of Mexico.
Gafftopsail catfish: from Massachusetts to Venezuela.
Guaguanche: warm-temperate and tropical Atlantic waters.
Northern sennet: from New England to Florida and the Gulf of Mexico.
Southern sennet: Florida to Uruguay; Bermuda, Bahamas.
Great barracuda: tropical and temperate Atlantic waters, and the Mediterranean and Black Seas.
Pacific barracuda: Pacific coast of North America.

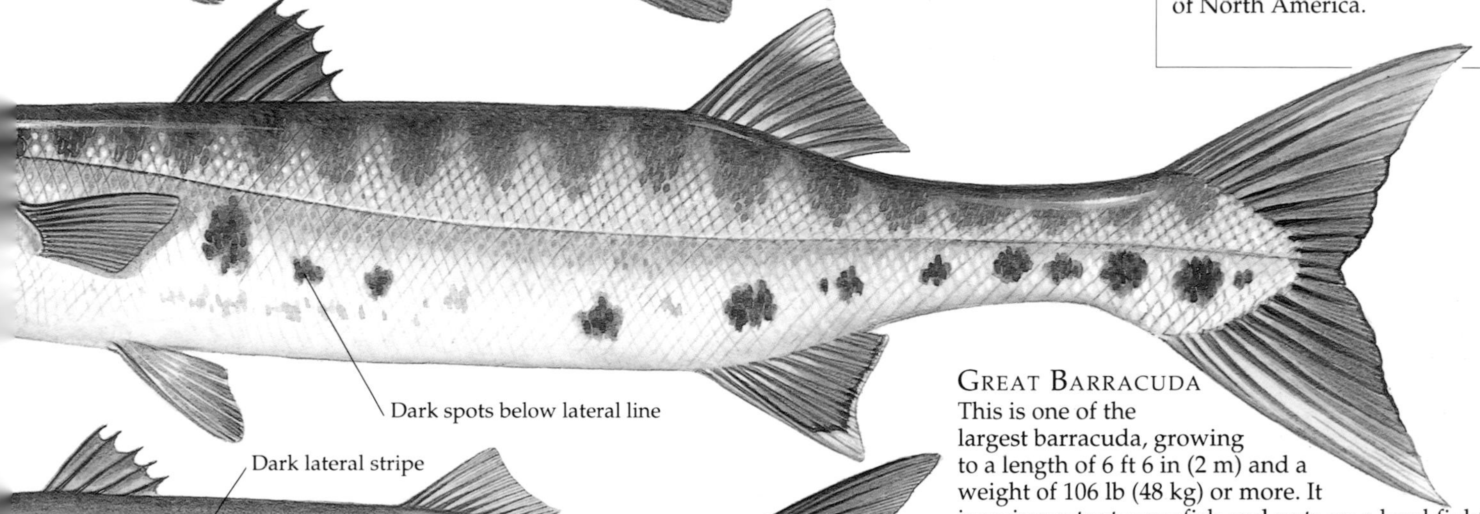

Great Barracuda

This is one of the largest barracuda, growing to a length of 6 ft 6 in (2 m) and a weight of 106 lb (48 kg) or more. It is an important gamefish and puts up a hard fight when hooked, making extremely fast runs and often leaping from the water, but it has little stamina and soon tires. Small individuals are found close inshore, where they may be taken on light tackle fished from the shore or a boat, but larger fish usually stay in deeper water and are fished for by trolling with medium-heavy tackle.

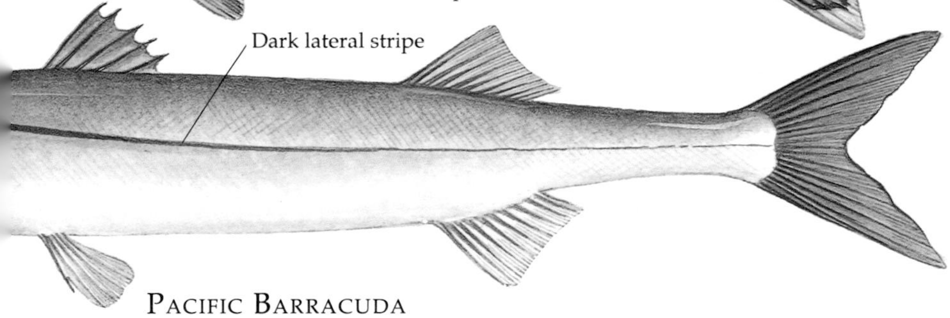

Pacific Barracuda

This barracuda is found from the Gulf of Alaska to Baja California, but it is not common north of Point Conception, California. Also known as the California barracuda, it has a distinctive black stripe along its lateral line and grows to about 18 lb (8.2 kg). The Mexican barracuda *(Sphyraena ensis)* is similar, but has dark bars along its sides. Other barracudas of the Indo-Pacific region include the shortfin barracuda *(S. novae-hollandiae)*, the golden barracuda *(S. flavicauda)*, and the striped barracuda *(S. obtustata)*.

Barracuda jaws
The powerful jaws of a barracuda are equipped with large canine teeth that seize and grip its prey, and small, very sharp teeth that cut it to ribbons.

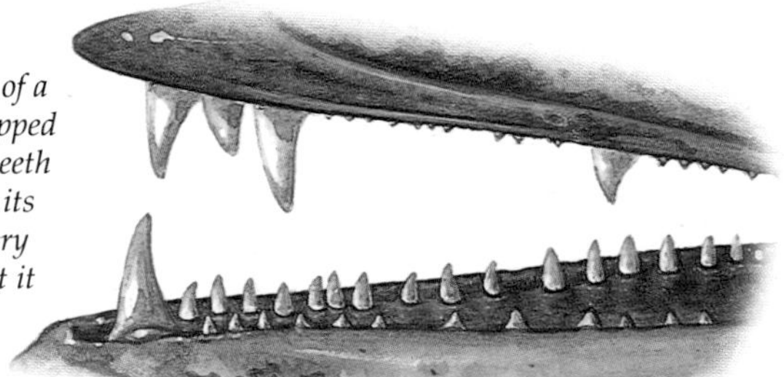

Size comparison

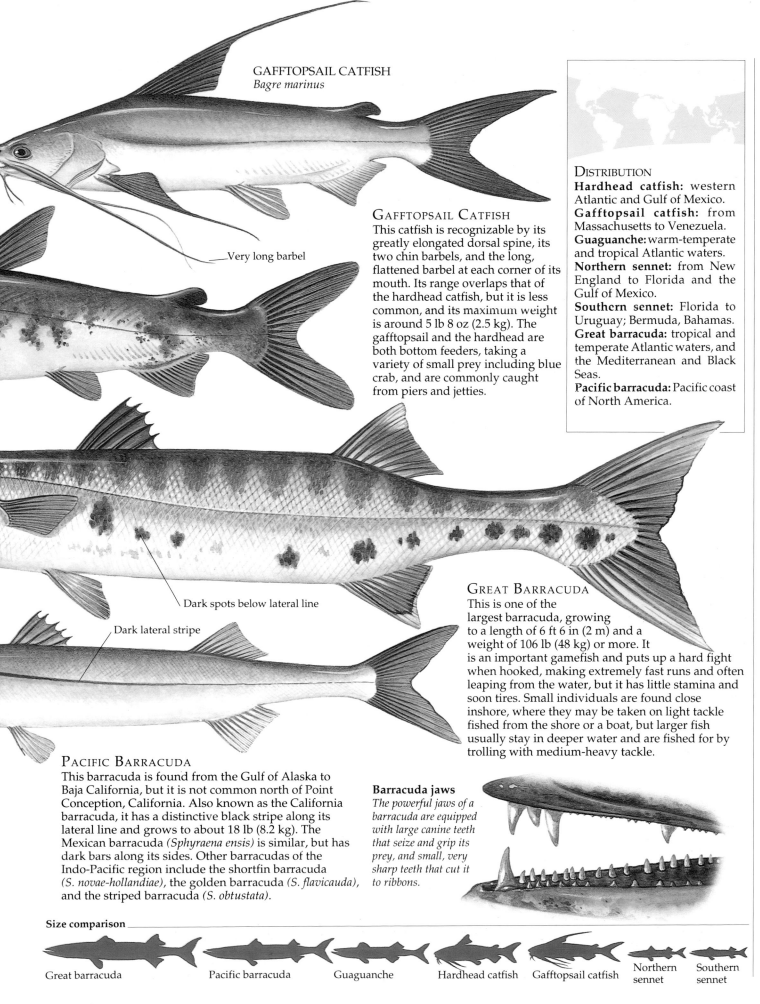

AMBERJACK & JACK

The Carangidae is a large family of predatory marine fish, and has over 200 members including amberjack, jack, and pompano *(see page 166)*. They have streamlined bodies with deeply forked tails, the spiny and soft parts of their dorsal fins are separate, and they feed on fish and invertebrates such as squid. Their flesh is tasty, but you should seek local advice before eating any you catch because they can be a source of ciguatera, a distressing type of food poisoning that can be fatal.

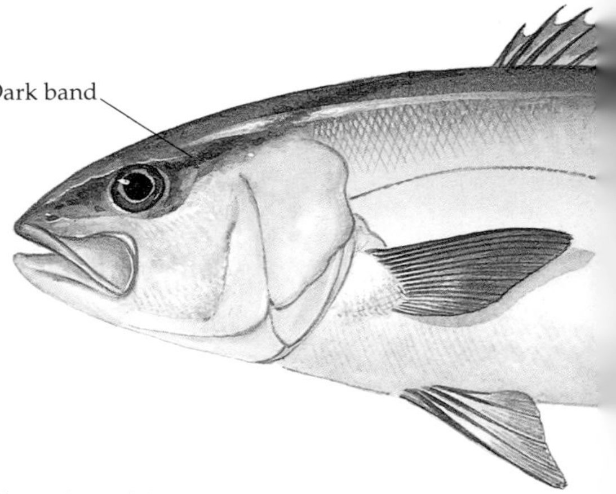

ALMACO JACK

The almaco jack is distributed worldwide in warm waters and grows to a weight of 126 lb (57 kg) or more. It is similar to the greater amberjack and the yellowtail, but the dark bands through its eyes are more pronounced, and the front lobe of its soft dorsal fin is longer and sickle-shaped. The almaco jack of the eastern Pacific is sometimes classified as a separate species, the Pacific amberjack (*Seriola colburni*).

ALMACO JACK
Seriola rivoliana

Schooling fish
Young fish of the Carangidae family often form small schools beneath floating objects such as jellyfish. Older fish of most species roam the seas in large, fast-swimming schools, but the oldest, largest fish tend to be solitary. The carangids are widely distributed in temperate and tropical seas, and are usually at their most abundant in inshore waters.

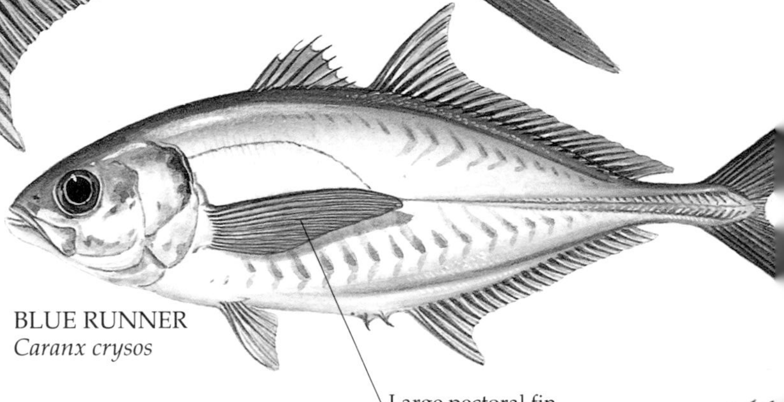

BLUE RUNNER
Caranx crysos

BLUE RUNNER

The blue runner is a small Atlantic jack, very closely related to the Pacific green jack (*Caranx caballus*). It grows to over 8 lb (3.6 kg) but averages less than 1 lb (454 g); like most carangids, its flesh is tasty and it is fished for commercially. It is a popular angling species, and makes a very good bait for big-game fish.

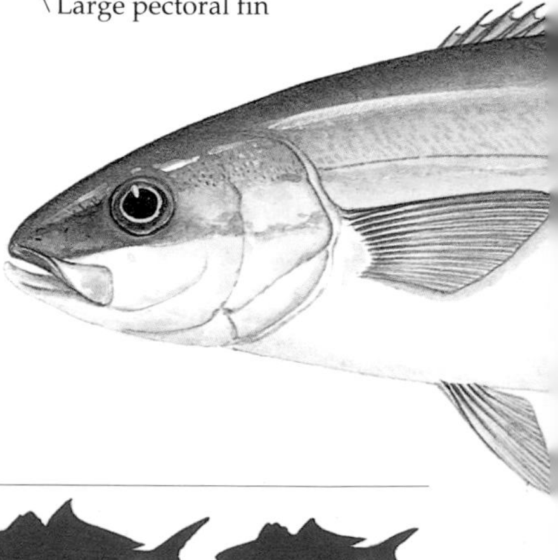

Size comparison

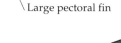

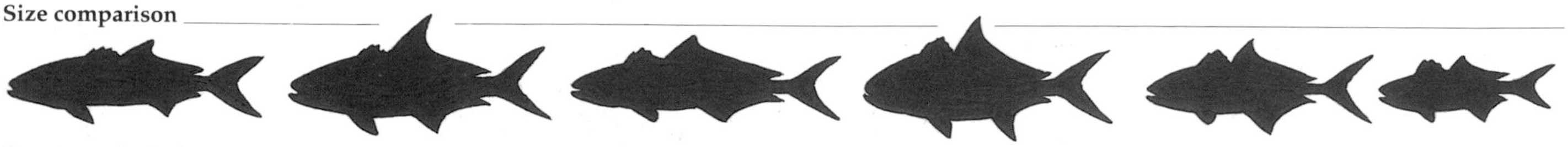

Greater Amberjack

This fish is widely distributed in warm waters and is the largest amberjack in the Atlantic, averaging about 15 lb (6.8 kg) but capable of exceeding 176 lb (80 kg). Its overall coloration is silvery, and there is often a broad, yellow or coppery stripe along each side. The dark bands that run from its upper jaw through its eyes meet at the point where the dorsal fin begins, forming an inverted V-shape.

Distribution

Almaco jack: most tropical and warm-temperate waters.
Blue runner: tropical and warm-temperate Atlantic.
Greater amberjack: most tropical and warm-temperate waters.
Lesser amberjack: western Atlantic from Massachusetts south to Brazil.
Crevalle jack: most tropical and warm-temperate waters.
California yellowtail: eastern Pacific from British Columbia south to Chile.

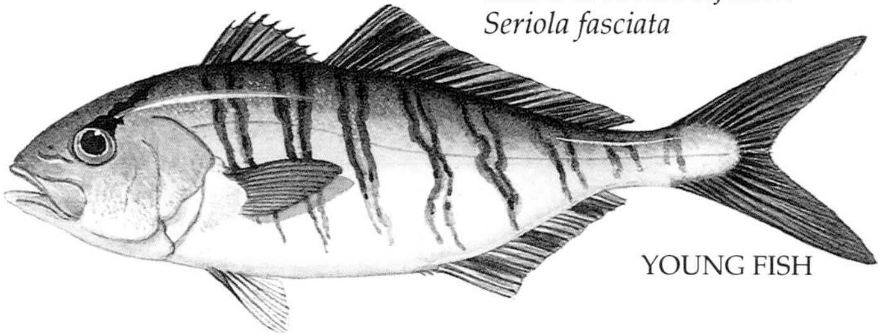

Lesser Amberjack

The adult lesser amberjack is similar in appearance to the greater amberjack, but the dark bands on its head converge well in front of the first dorsal fin. The lesser amberjack is a relatively small fish, reaching a maximum weight of only about 10 lb (4.54 kg). It is found in the warm waters of the western Atlantic.

Young lesser amberjack
The young of the lesser amberjack are distinctively marked with several broad, dark brown bands, usually separated by paler areas. These dark bands fade as the fish mature.

Crevalle Jack

The hard-fighting crevalle jack is widely distributed in warm waters, and is found both inshore and in the open ocean. It averages under 2 lb (910 g), but can reach 55 lb (25 kg). The crevalle jack found in the Pacific is often regarded as a separate species, *Caranx caninus*; other Pacific and Indo-Pacific members of the genus *Caranx* include the trevally (*Caranx georgianus*), the ulua (*C. stellatus*), and the pauu'u (*C. ignobilis*).

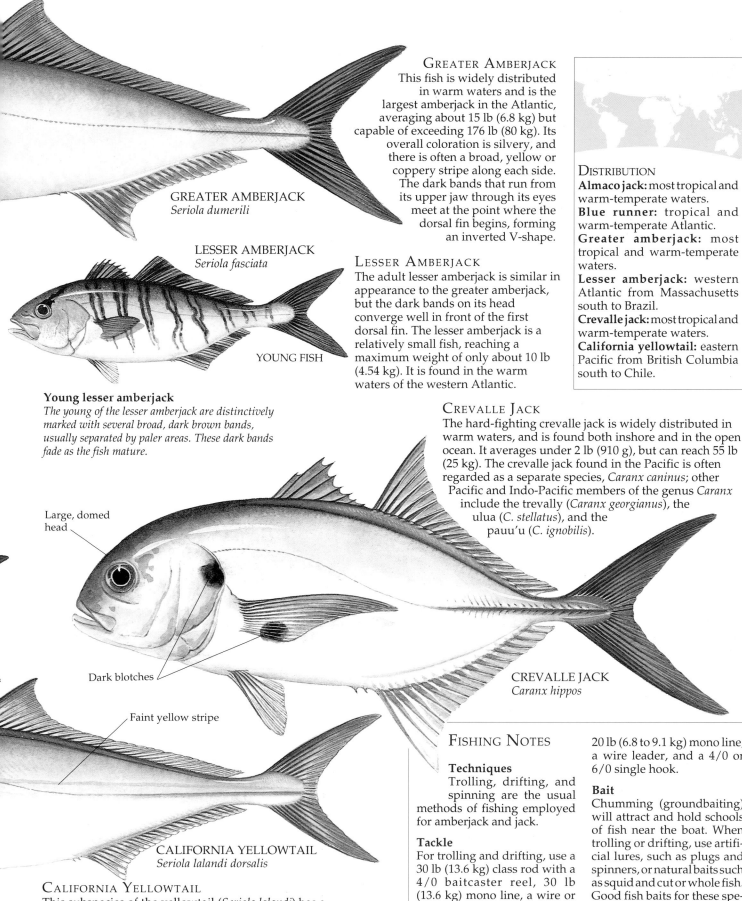

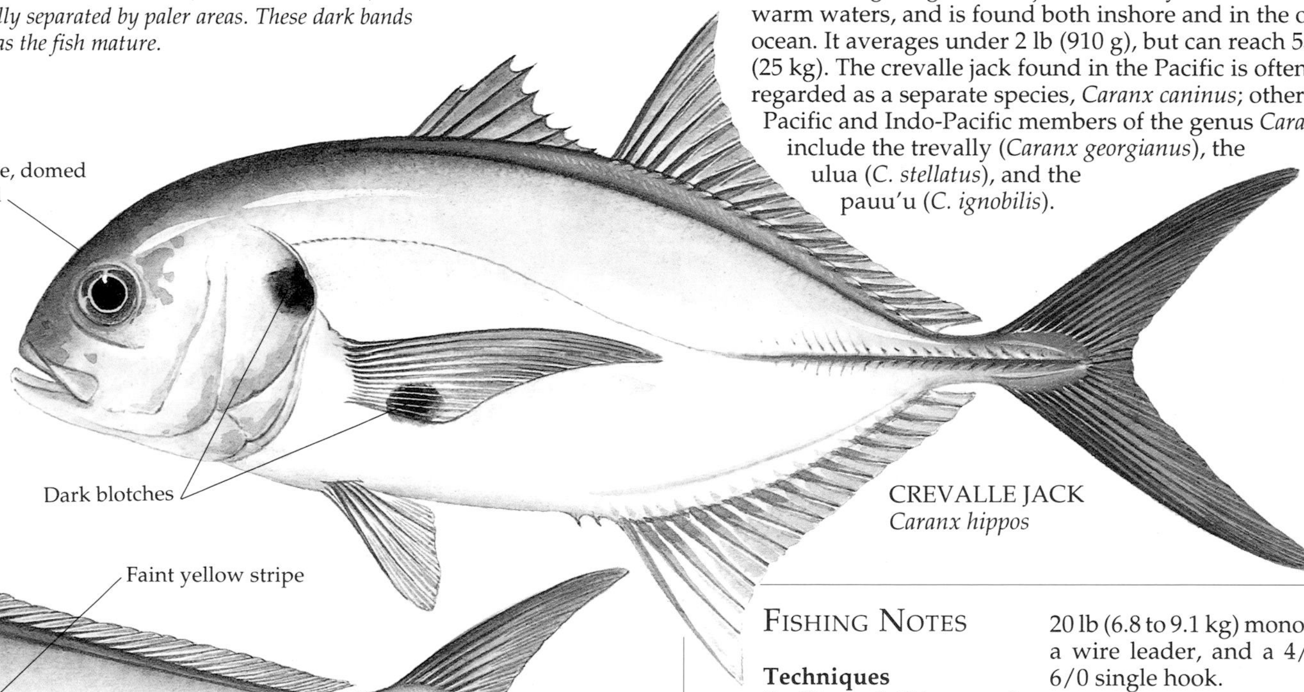

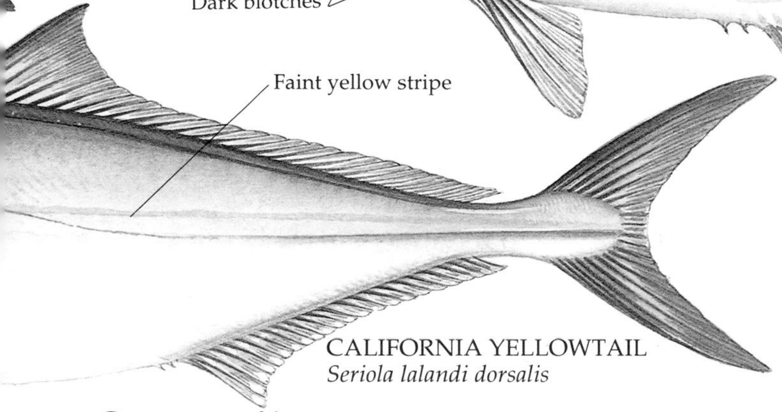

California Yellowtail

This subspecies of the yellowtail (*Seriola lalandi*) has a maximum weight of about 80 lb (36 kg), and is one of the most highly prized gamefish of the Pacific coast of North America. The closely related southern yellowtail, *S. grandis*, which is abundant in Australian and New Zealand waters, can reach a weight of 114 lb 10 oz (52 kg).

Fishing Notes

Techniques
Trolling, drifting, and spinning are the usual methods of fishing employed for amberjack and jack.

Tackle
For trolling and drifting, use a 30 lb (13.6 kg) class rod with a 4/0 baitcaster reel, 30 lb (13.6 kg) mono line, a wire or heavy mono leader, and a 6/0 or 8/0 single hook. For spinning, use a heavy spinning rod with a large spinning reel, 15 to 20 lb (6.8 to 9.1 kg) mono line, a wire leader, and a 4/0 or 6/0 single hook.

Bait
Chumming (groundbaiting) will attract and hold schools of fish near the boat. When trolling or drifting, use artificial lures, such as plugs and spinners, or natural baits such as squid and cut or whole fish. Good fish baits for these species include mullet, pinfish, sardines, and anchovies. For spinning, use plugs, spinners, or spoons.

CARANGIDAE; NEMATISTIIDAE

POMPANO, JACKMACKEREL, & ROOSTERFISH

The jackmackerel and the four species of pompano shown here (including the permit) are members of the Carangidae family, which also includes the amberjack and jack *(see page 164)*. The roosterfish is sometimes classified as a member of the Carangidae, but is usually placed in a separate family, the Nematistiidae. Pompano have deep, almost diamond-shaped bodies, while the jackmackerel and roosterfish are more elongated and streamlined. All except the African pompano venture close inshore, often into very shallow water within easy reach of shore anglers, and they offer good sport on light tackle.

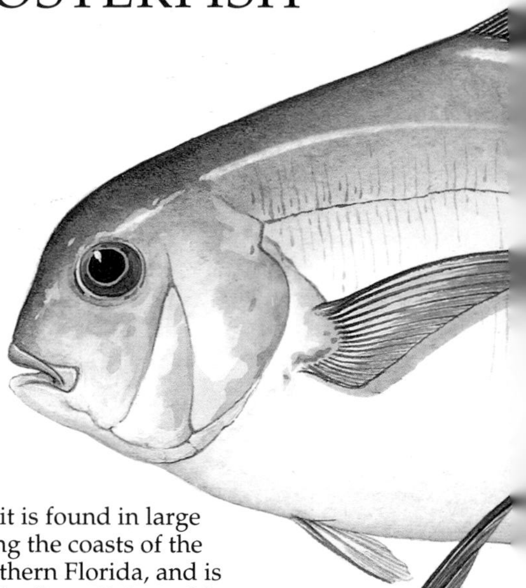

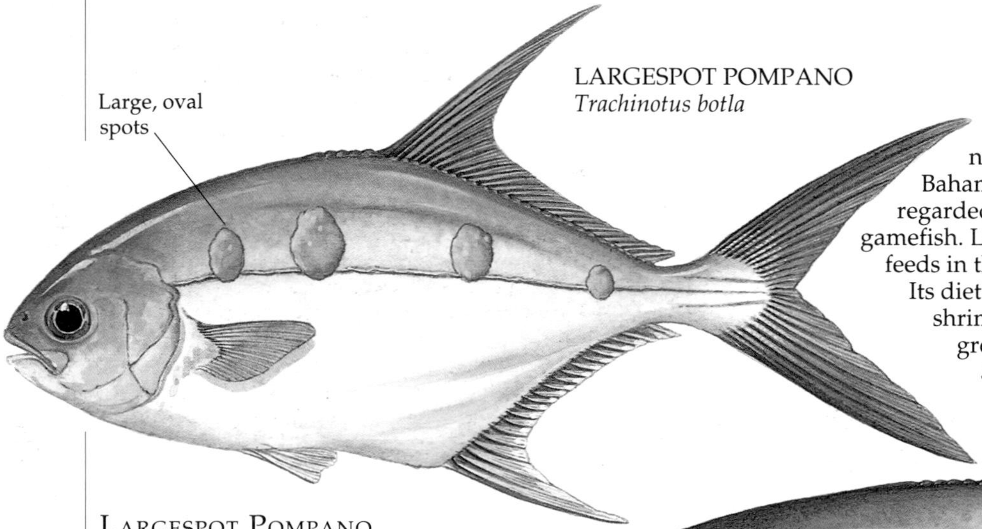

LARGESPOT POMPANO
Trachinotus botla

PERMIT

The permit is found in large numbers along the coasts of the Bahamas and southern Florida, and is regarded as one of the finest light-tackle gamefish. Like the bonefish *(see page 158)*, it feeds in the shallow waters of coral flats. Its diet includes crabs, mollusks, shrimps, and sea urchins, and it grows to a weight of over 51 lb (23 kg).

JUVENILE PERMIT

LARGESPOT POMPANO

The largespot pompano is widely distributed in coastal waters of the Indian Ocean from Africa to Australia. It is found in the surf zones of sandy beaches, and when feeding it will often swim on its side so that it can move into very shallow water. It grows to a weight of more than 4 lb 6 oz (2 kg).

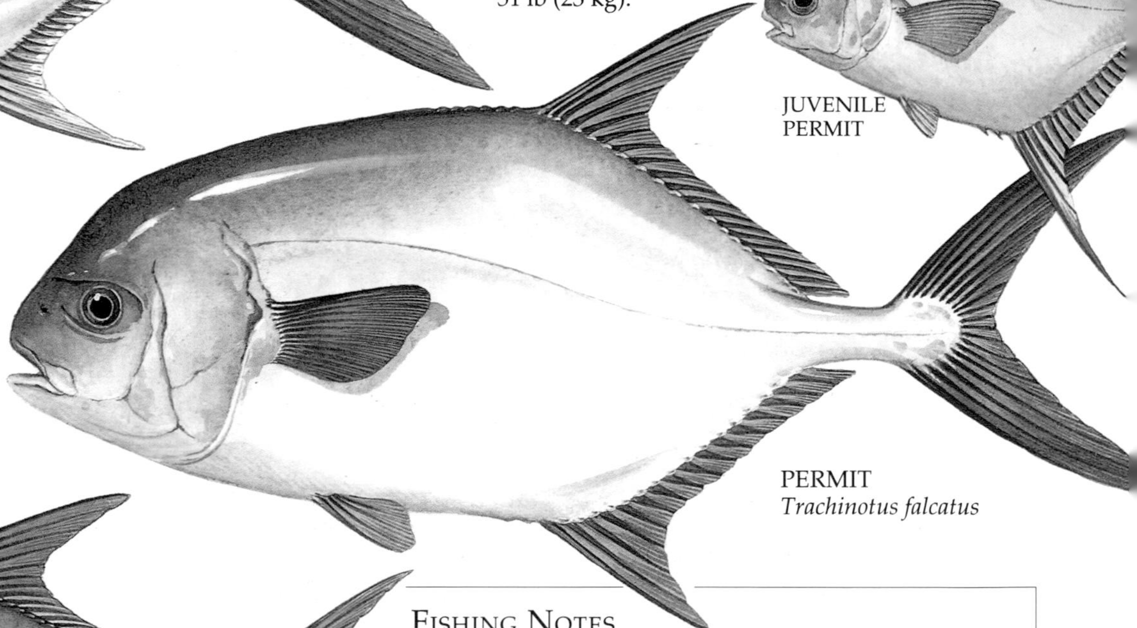

PERMIT
Trachinotus falcatus

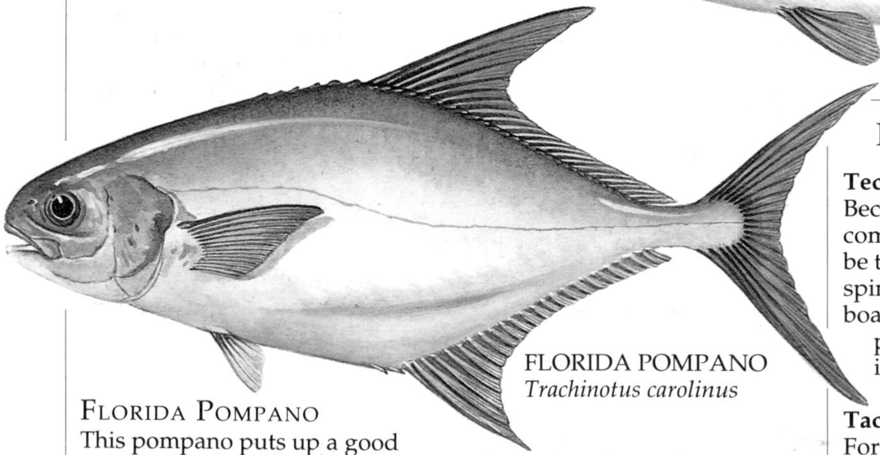

FLORIDA POMPANO
Trachinotus carolinus

FLORIDA POMPANO

This pompano puts up a good fight on light tackle, and is renowned for its fine-tasting flesh. Like the permit, it enters very shallow water, and is taken from beaches, piers, jetties, bridges, and drifting or anchored boats. It averages 2 lb (910 g), with a maximum weight of 8 lb (3.6 kg).

FISHING NOTES

Techniques

Because most of these species come close inshore, they can be taken by surfcasting or by spinning from the shore or a boat. The African pompano prefers deeper water and is caught by trolling.

Tackle

For surfcasting, try a 12 ft (3.7 m) rod that is capable of handling 3 to 5 oz (85 to 142 g) sinkers. For spinning and trolling, try a 6½ to 8 ft (2 to 2.4 m) medium spinning rod with 6 to 12 lb (2.7 to 5.4 kg) mono line, a short, 20 lb (9.1 kg) mono leader, and hook sizes 2 to 2/0.

Bait

The usual baits are crabs, clams, sand fleas, small bucktails, and jigs; anchovies are an excellent bait for jackmackerel.

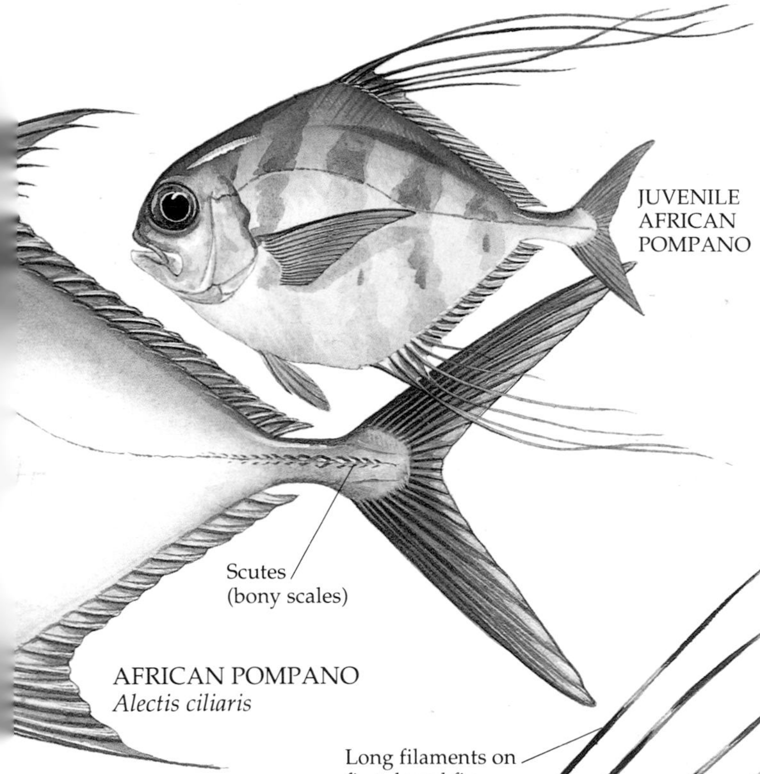

AFRICAN POMPANO
Alectis ciliaris

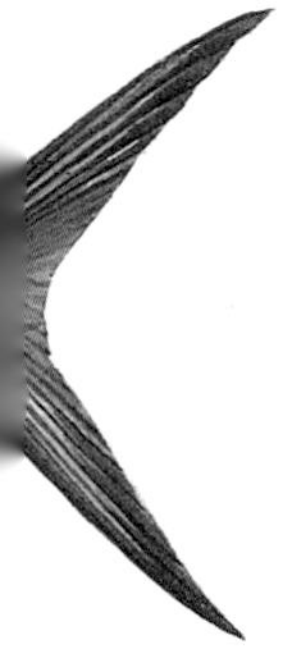

African Pompano

The African pompano is found in many warm-temperate waters, and is distributed worldwide in tropical seas. Its preferred habitat is around rocky reefs in deep water, and it can grow to a weight of around 40 lb (18 kg). Young African pompano, known as threadfish, have very deep bodies and long, threadlike dorsal and anal fin rays.

Distribution
Permit, Florida pompano: warm-temperate and tropical western Atlantic.
African pompano: worldwide in tropical waters; warm-temperate Atlantic.
Largespot: Indian Ocean.
Roosterfish: Pacific from southern California to Peru.
Jackmackerel: Pacific from Alaska to Mexico.

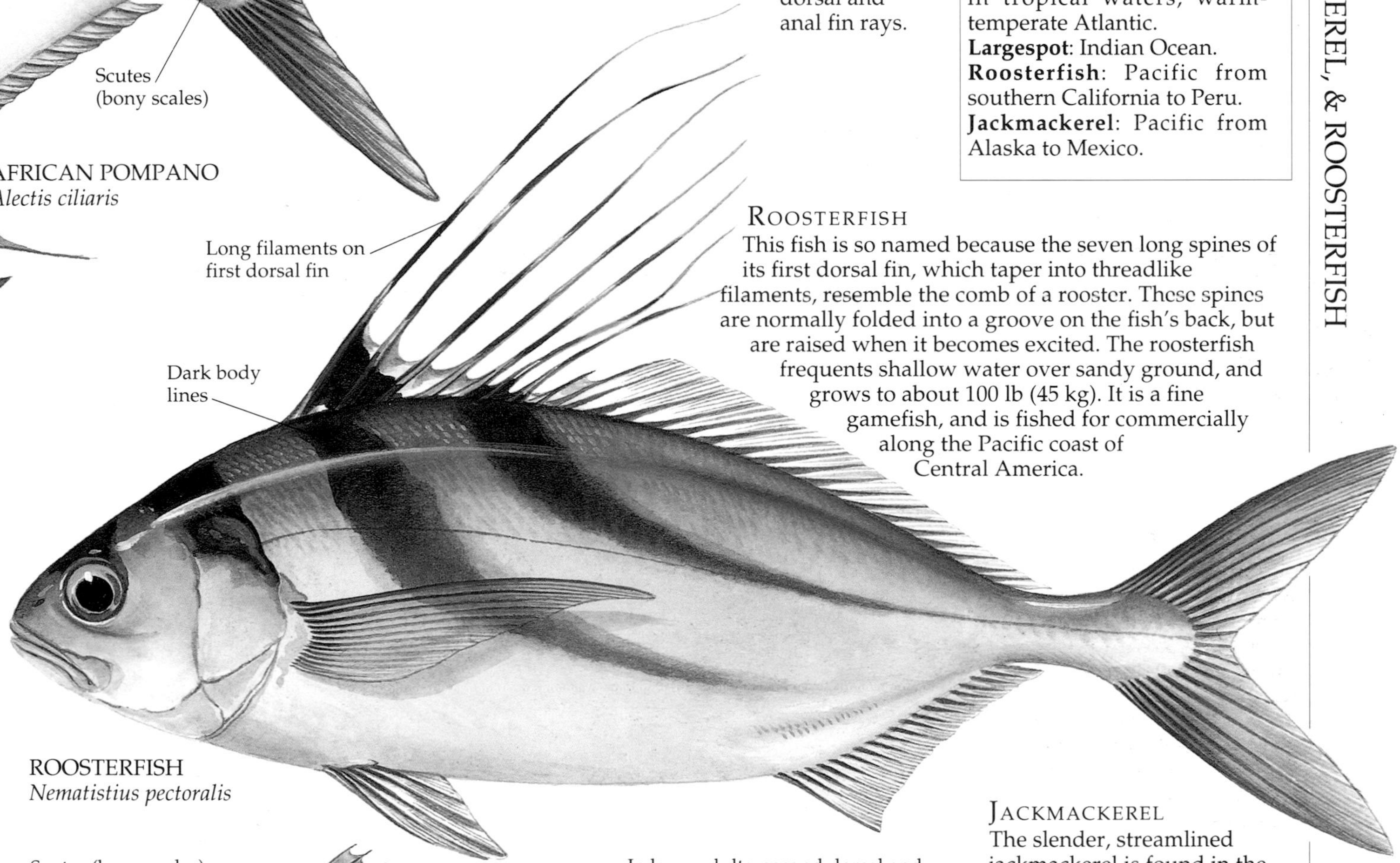

ROOSTERFISH
Nematistius pectoralis

Roosterfish

This fish is so named because the seven long spines of its first dorsal fin, which taper into threadlike filaments, resemble the comb of a rooster. These spines are normally folded into a groove on the fish's back, but are raised when it becomes excited. The roosterfish frequents shallow water over sandy ground, and grows to about 100 lb (45 kg). It is a fine gamefish, and is fished for commercially along the Pacific coast of Central America.

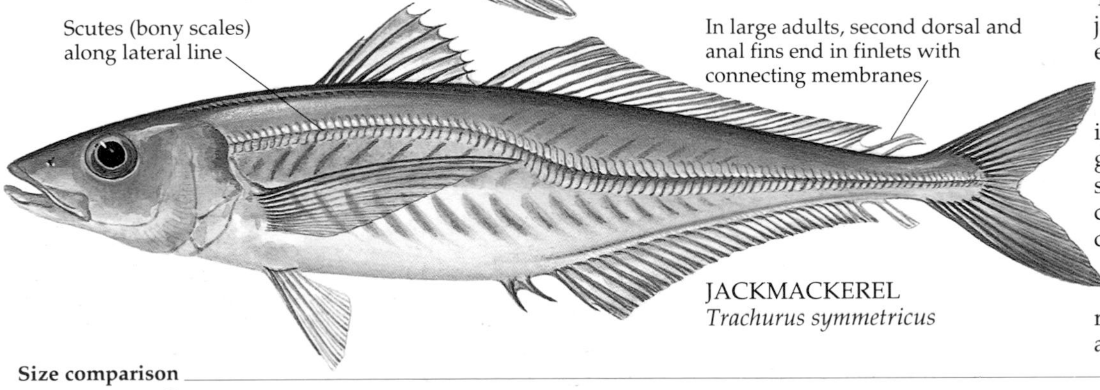

JACKMACKEREL
Trachurus symmetricus

Jackmackerel

The slender, streamlined jackmackerel is found in the eastern Pacific and is often abundant along the coast of California, where it is an important light-tackle gamefish. It often has a dark spot at the rear of the gill cover, and the lateral line is covered in bony scales called scutes. It is found both inshore and offshore, and reaches a maximum weight of about 5 lb (2.27 kg).

Size comparison

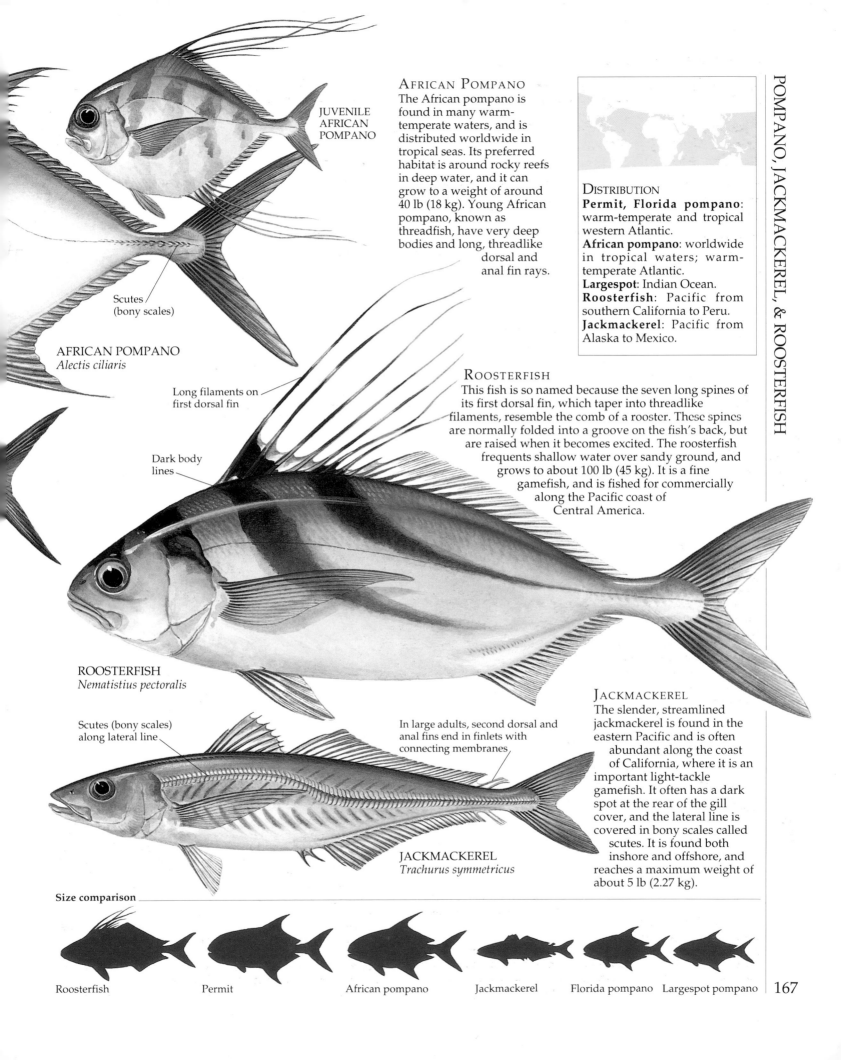

Cobia, Snook, & Barramundi

The cobia, the only member of the Rachycentridae family, is a prized gamefish. It is also fished for commercially for its fine flesh, which is often sold smoked. Snook and barramundi belong to the Centropomidae family, which contains about 30 species. Some of the Centropomidae are exclusively marine, others are marine but move into brackish water and even into rivers; some live in rivers and spawn in brackish estuaries, while a few are found only in freshwater.

TARPON SNOOK
Centropomus pectinatus

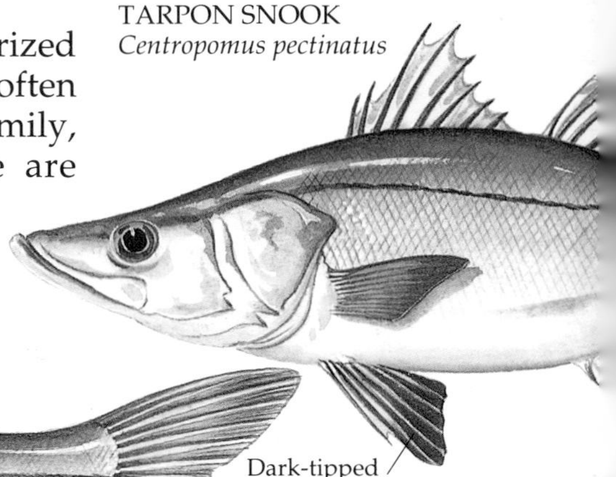

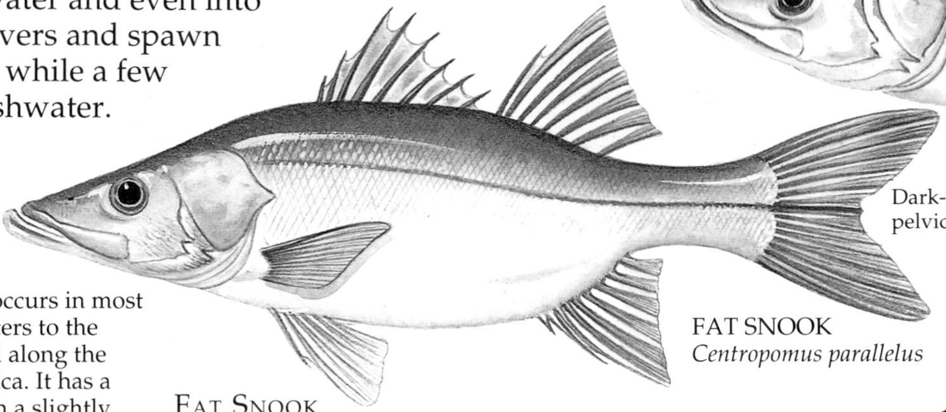

FAT SNOOK
Centropomus parallelus

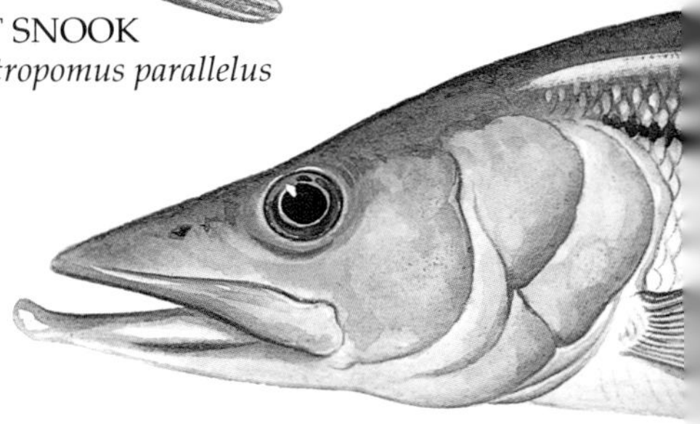

Cobia

This long, slim-bodied fish occurs in most warm seas, from coastal waters to the open ocean, but is not found along the Pacific coast of North America. It has a flat head, a large mouth with a slightly protruding lower jaw, and a first dorsal fin that consists of eight separate spines. Fish and crustaceans make up the bulk of its diet, and it grows to a weight of about 150 lb (68 kg). It is usually solitary but sometimes forms small schools.

Fat Snook

The fat snook is a small, rather deep-bodied fish that rarely exceeds about 3 lb (1.36 kg). The most reliable way to distinguish it from other small snook is to count the number of scales along the lateral line: the fat snook has 80 to 90, the tarpon snook 65 to 70, and the black about 60.

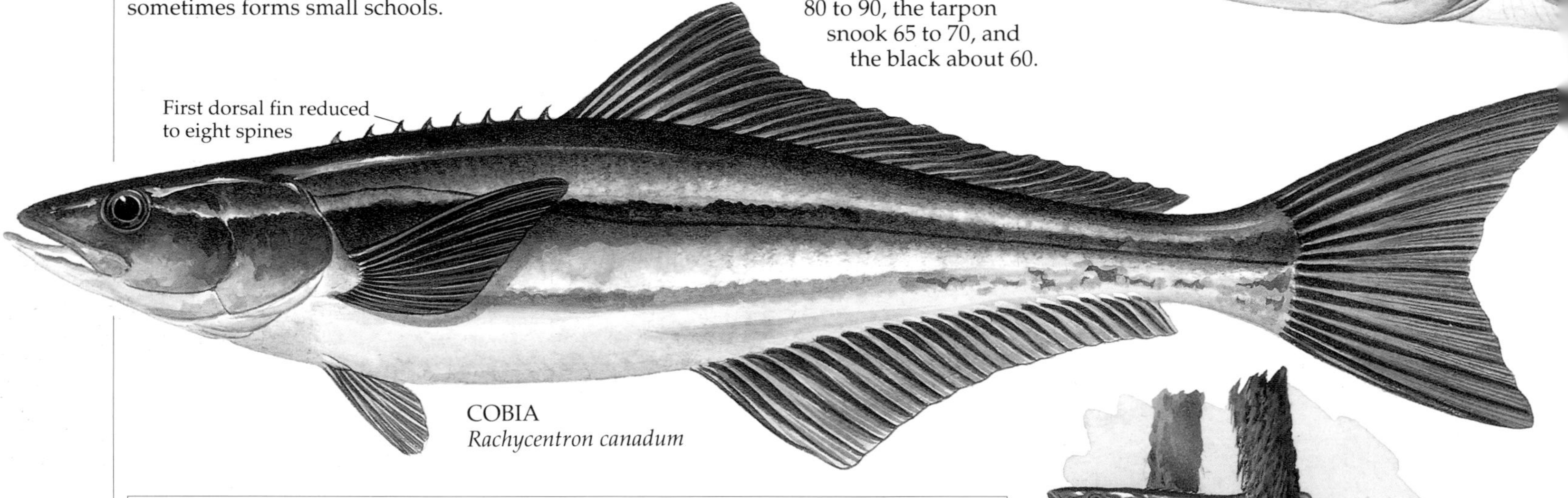

COBIA
Rachycentron canadum

Fishing Notes

Techniques
Cobia are usually taken by bottom fishing with lures or natural baits. Lure fishing is an effective technique for barramundi and for snook, which can also be taken on fly tackle.

Tackle
For cobia, use a heavy spinning rod with 15 to 20 lb (6.8 to 9.1 kg) mono line and a 3 ft (90 cm) leader of wire or 60 to 80 lb (27.2 to 36.3 kg) mono, and hook sizes 2/0 to 4/0. Try a 6 ft (1.8 m) surfcaster with 10 to 12 lb (4.54 to 5.4 kg) mono when lure fishing for snook, and a fast, 9 ft (2.7 m) tip-action rod for fly fishing. For barramundi, use a 9 to 10 ft (2.7 to 3 m) spinning rod with 20 to 30 lb (9.1 to 13.6 kg) mono line.

Bait
Good baits for cobia include natural baits such as fish, crabs, and shrimps, and artificials including large plugs with bright blue or silver finishes, and 1½ to 3 oz (42 to 85 g) jigs with yellow or white skirts. Try plugs, spoons, jigs, shrimps, streamer flies, and fish (especially mullet) for snook, and jointed, 6 in (15 cm) shallow-diving plugs for barramundi.

Cobia habitat
Cobia like to lurk in the cover of pilings and wrecks, and beneath buoys, floating wreckage, and other flotsam. They are also often found in the company of cruising sharks.

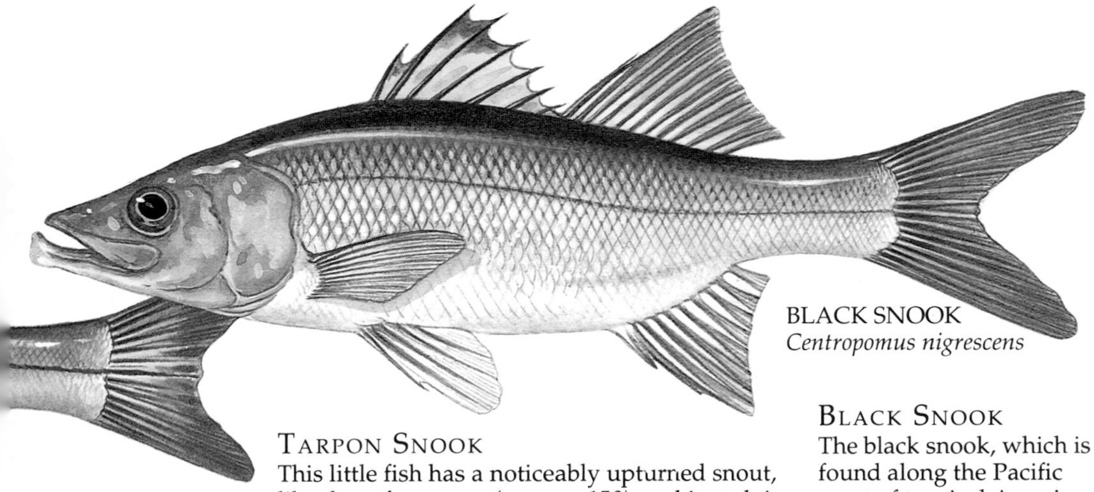

BLACK SNOOK
Centropomus nigrescens

Tarpon Snook

This little fish has a noticeably upturned snout, like that of a tarpon *(see page 158)*, and its pelvic fins are orange or orange-yellow with dark tips. Its preferred habitat is brackish, well-shaded lakes and lagoons, and its maximum weight is usually less than about 2 lb 3 oz (1 kg).

Black Snook

The black snook, which is found along the Pacific coast of tropical America, grows to a weight of over 3 lb (1.36 kg). It is common in shallow coastal waters and also occurs in brackish estuaries, the lower reaches of rivers and streams, and in coastal canals.

Distribution

Cobia: most warm seas, but not along the Pacific coast of North America.
Fat snook, tarpon snook: southern Florida and West Indies to Brazil.
Black snook: eastern Pacific from Baja California to Peru.
Snook: western Atlantic from South Carolina to Brazil.
Barramundi: Asian coastal regions and islands from the Persian Gulf to China, and around the northern half of the Australian coast.

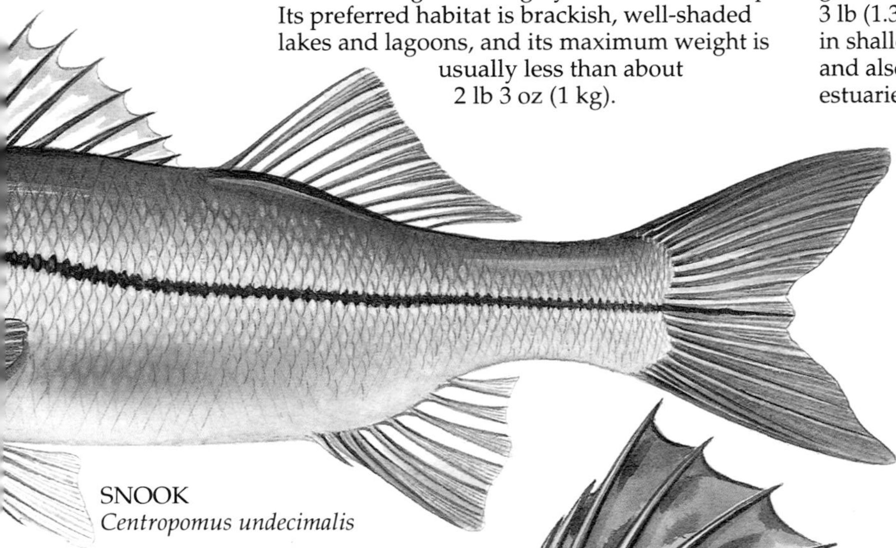

SNOOK
Centropomus undecimalis

Snook

This large, pikelike fish has a protruding lower jaw and a distinctive black lateral stripe that extends into its tail. It is an active predator, feeding on fish, shrimps, and crabs, and averages 5 to 8 lb (2.27 to 3.6 kg) with a maximum of over 53 lb (24 kg). Although it is usually found in shallow coastal waters, it also explores estuaries, mangrove swamps, and creeks, and sometimes travels well inland along rivers and canals. It should be handled with care when caught, because the edges of its gill covers are very sharp.

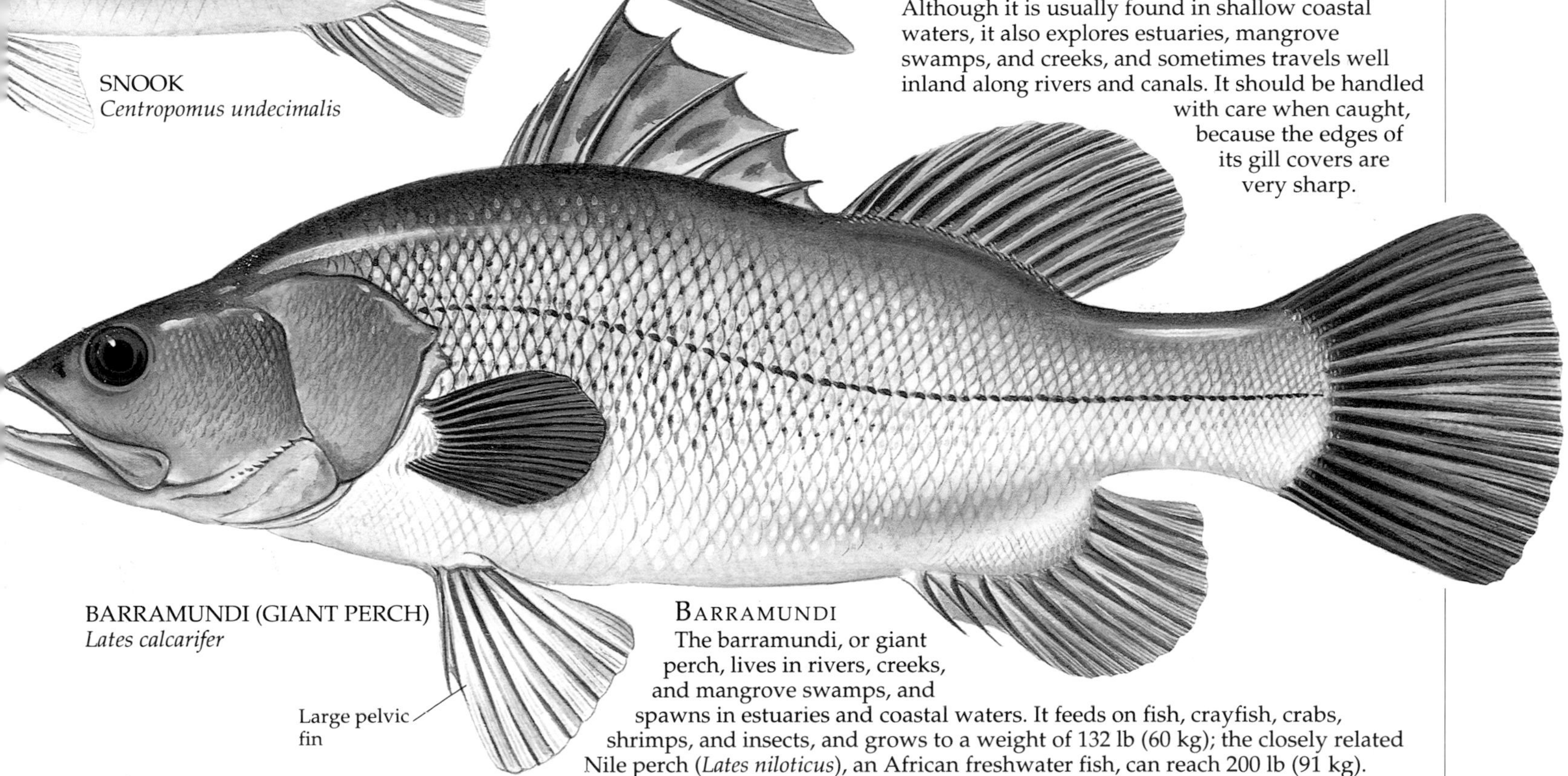

BARRAMUNDI (GIANT PERCH)
Lates calcarifer

Barramundi

The barramundi, or giant perch, lives in rivers, creeks, and mangrove swamps, and spawns in estuaries and coastal waters. It feeds on fish, crayfish, crabs, shrimps, and insects, and grows to a weight of 132 lb (60 kg); the closely related Nile perch (*Lates niloticus*), an African freshwater fish, can reach 200 lb (91 kg).

Size comparison

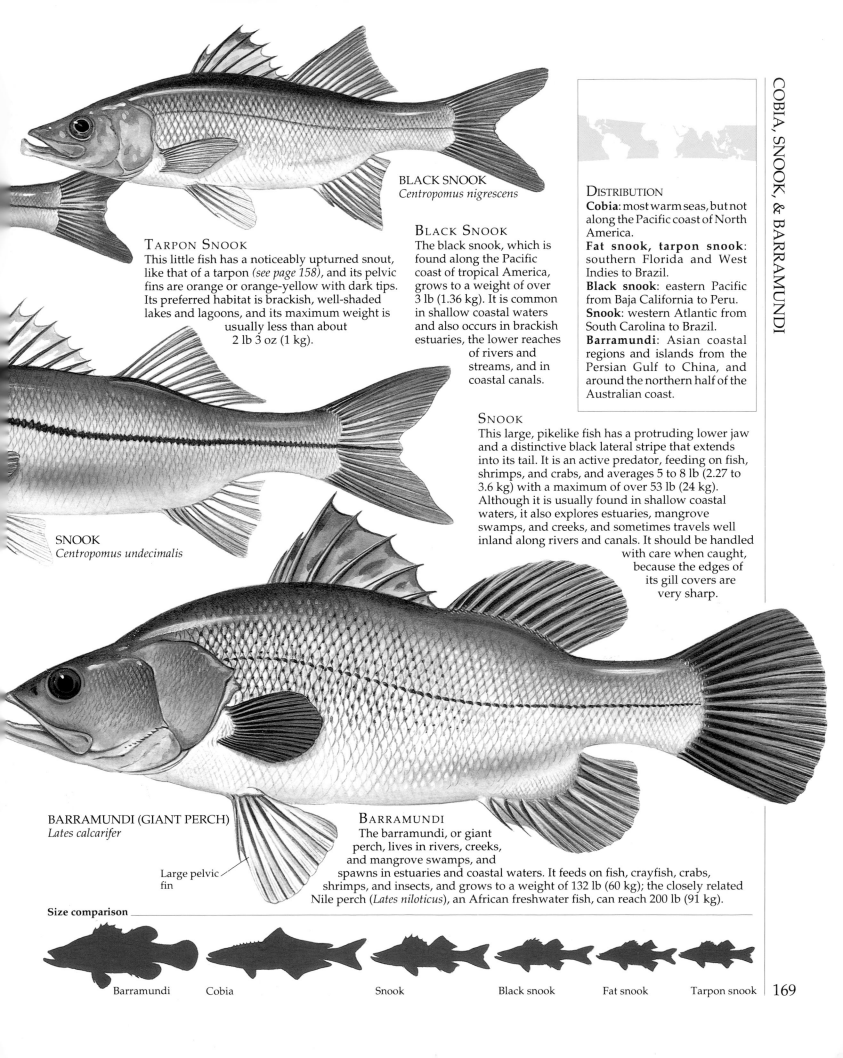

SURFPERCH

The Embiotocidae family consists of 21 species, of which two occur in Japan and Korea; the rest are found along the Pacific coast of North America, and all but one are marine species. The exception is the tule perch (*Hysterocarpus traski*), a freshwater fish that has a limited distribution in central California. Surfperch males use their anal fins to transfer sperm to the females, which give birth to live young. Their food includes algae, invertebrates, and fish, and they range in length from 4 to 18 in (10 to 45 cm).

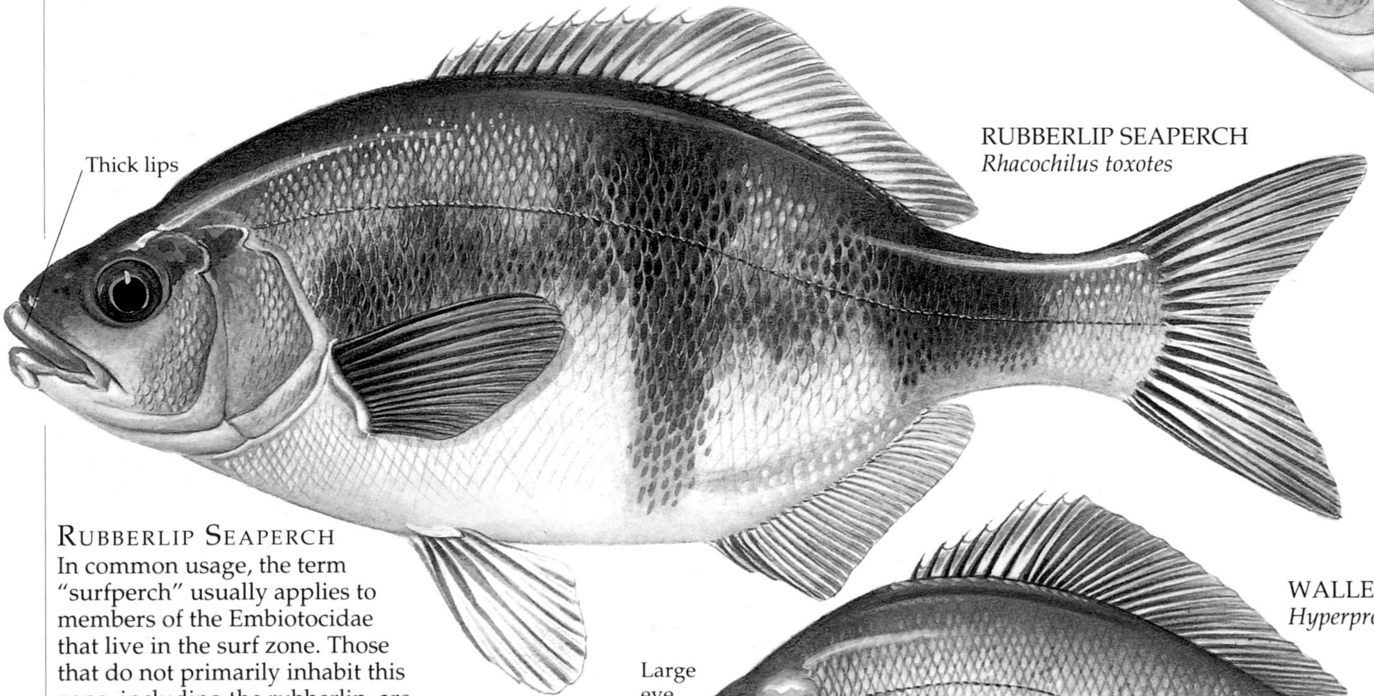

RUBBERLIP SEAPERCH
Rhacochilus toxotes

RUBBERLIP SEAPERCH

In common usage, the term "surfperch" usually applies to members of the Embiotocidae that live in the surf zone. Those that do not primarily inhabit this zone, including the rubberlip, are called "seaperch," and species with no distinct habitat are simply "perch." The rubberlip, which is found in rocky areas and around pilings, is the largest of the Embiotocidae and reaches a length of around 18 in (45 cm).

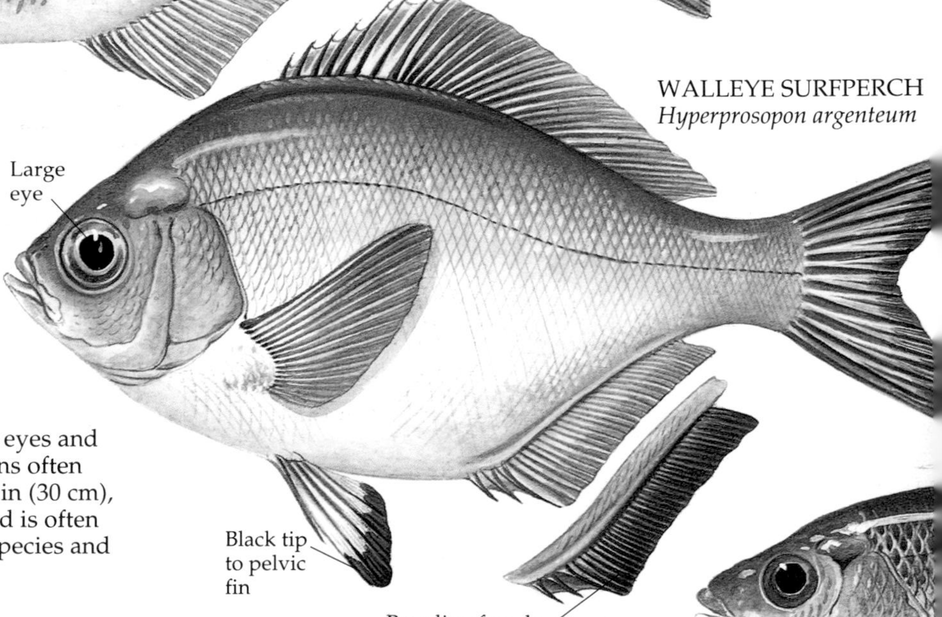

WALLEYE SURFPERCH
Hyperprosopon argenteum

WALLEYE SURFPERCH

The walleye surfperch is recognizable by its large eyes and its black-tipped pelvic fins, and its anal and tail fins often have dark edges. Its maximum length is about 12 in (30 cm), and it inhabits the surf zones of sandy beaches and is often found around piers. It is a very popular angling species and is of commercial importance.

SHINER PERCH

This little surfperch, which grows to about 7 in (18 cm), is abundant and easily caught from piers, which makes it very popular with young anglers. Its habitat ranges from shallow water, where it frequents weedbeds, pilings, and piers, to depths of about 480 ft (146 m), and it will also venture into brackish areas and sometimes into freshwater. There is often a dark spot above its upper lip.

FISHING NOTES

Techniques
Surfperch are usually caught by light surfcasting or by bottom fishing.

Tackle
For surfcasting, use a light surfcaster with a small baitcaster reel, 10 to 15 lb (4.54 to 6.8 kg) monofilament line, a size 1/0 hook (or smaller, depending on species sought), and a grip or bomb-shaped sinker. For bottom fishing, try a spinning rod or a 12 lb (5.4 kg) class boat rod, fitted with a spinning reel or small baitcaster reel, 10 to 15 lb (4.54 to 6.8 kg) monofilament line, a size 1/0 hook (or smaller), and a bomb-shaped sinker.

Bait
Surfperch baits include cut fish and crab, ghost shrimps, clams, and mussels.

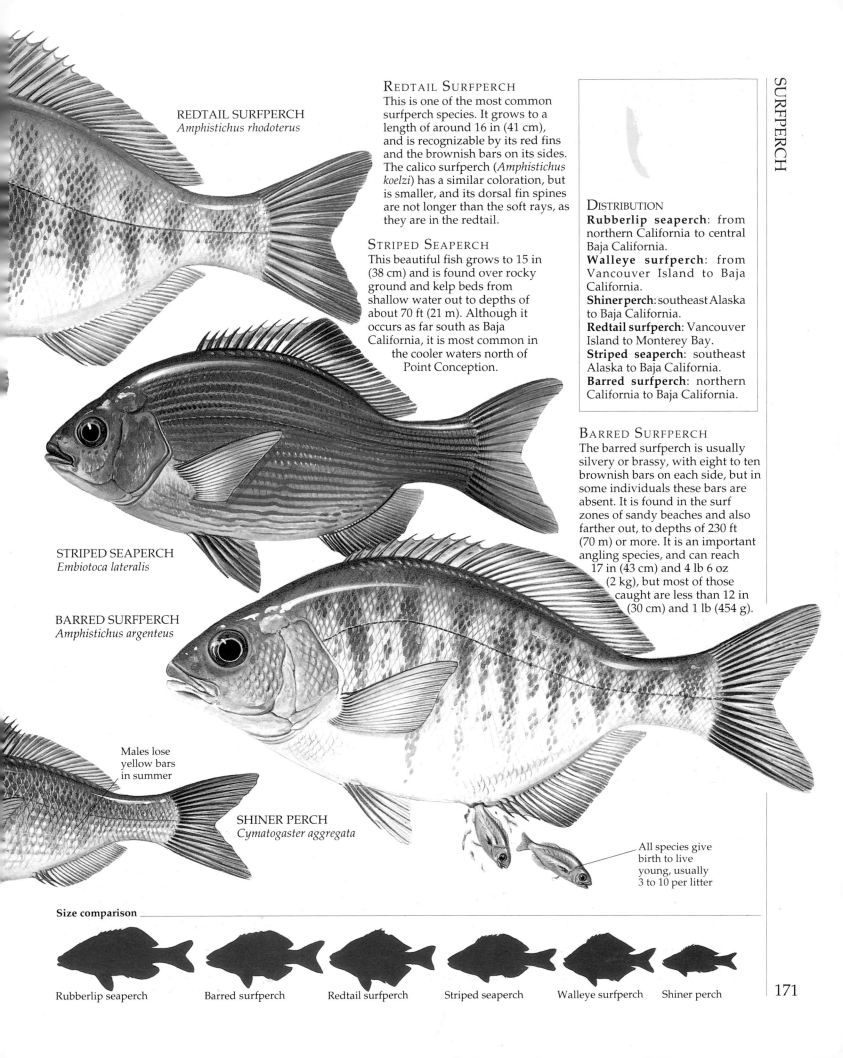

REDTAIL SURFPERCH
Amphistichus rhodoterus

Redtail Surfperch

This is one of the most common surfperch species. It grows to a length of around 16 in (41 cm), and is recognizable by its red fins and the brownish bars on its sides. The calico surfperch (*Amphistichus koelzi*) has a similar coloration, but is smaller, and its dorsal fin spines are not longer than the soft rays, as they are in the redtail.

Striped Seaperch

This beautiful fish grows to 15 in (38 cm) and is found over rocky ground and kelp beds from shallow water out to depths of about 70 ft (21 m). Although it occurs as far south as Baja California, it is most common in the cooler waters north of Point Conception.

Distribution

Rubberlip seaperch: from northern California to central Baja California.
Walleye surfperch: from Vancouver Island to Baja California.
Shiner perch: southeast Alaska to Baja California.
Redtail surfperch: Vancouver Island to Monterey Bay.
Striped seaperch: southeast Alaska to Baja California.
Barred surfperch: northern California to Baja California.

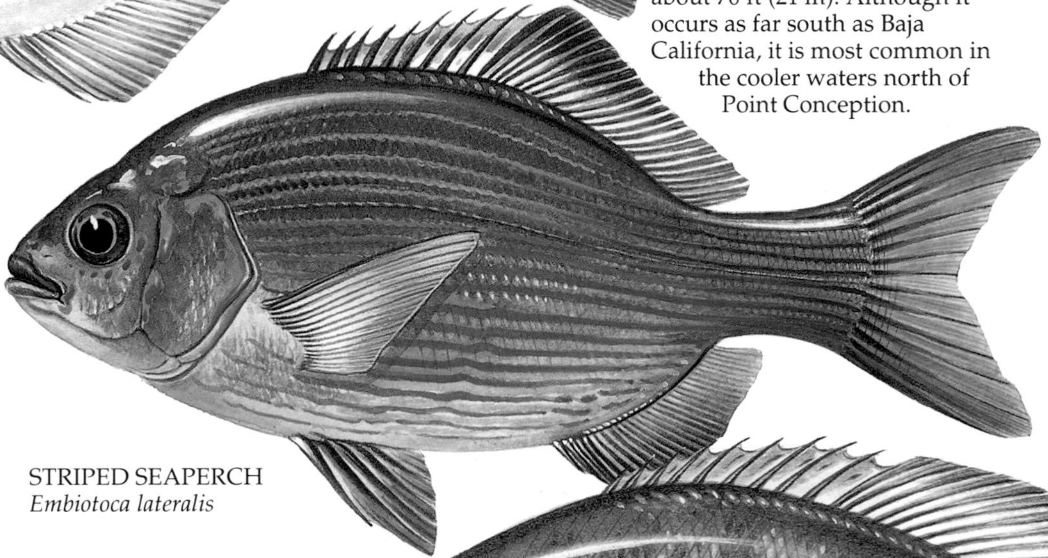

STRIPED SEAPERCH
Embiotoca lateralis

Barred Surfperch

The barred surfperch is usually silvery or brassy, with eight to ten brownish bars on each side, but in some individuals these bars are absent. It is found in the surf zones of sandy beaches and also farther out, to depths of 230 ft (70 m) or more. It is an important angling species, and can reach 17 in (43 cm) and 4 lb 6 oz (2 kg), but most of those caught are less than 12 in (30 cm) and 1 lb (454 g).

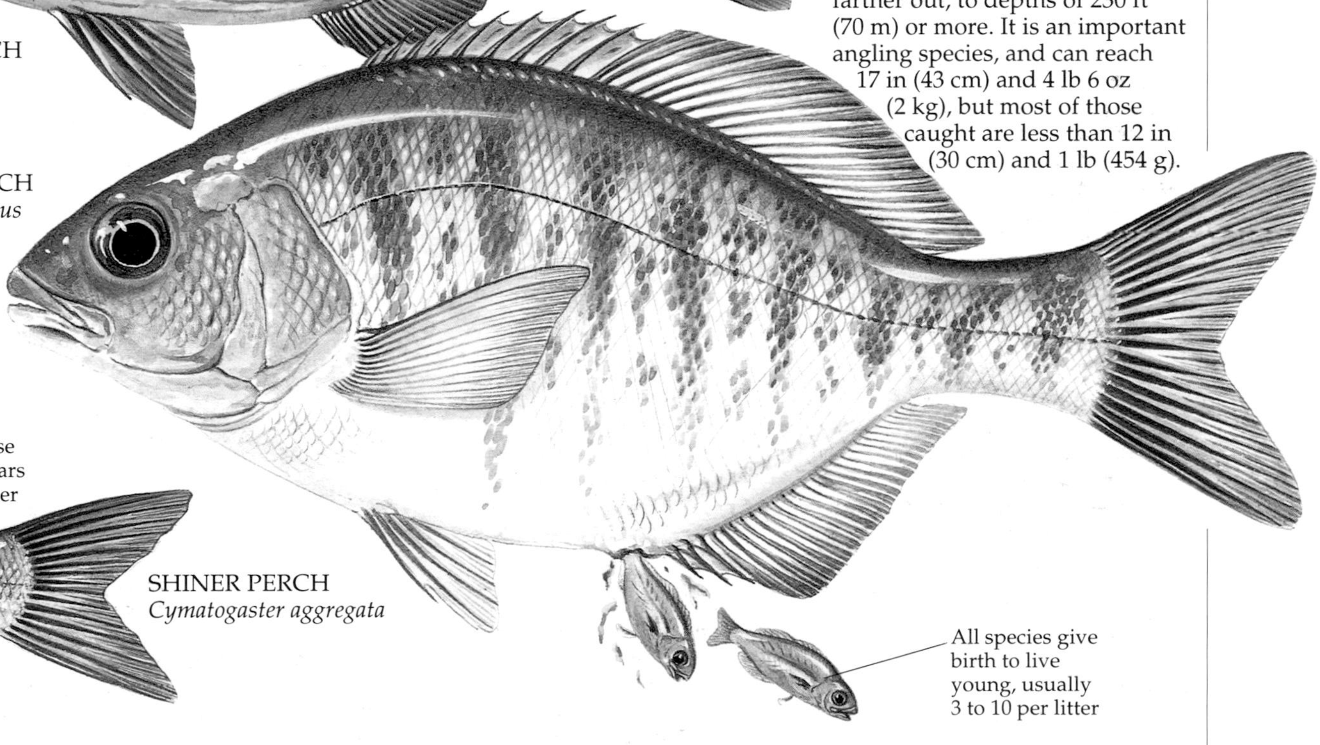
All species give birth to live young, usually 3 to 10 per litter

BARRED SURFPERCH
Amphistichus argenteus

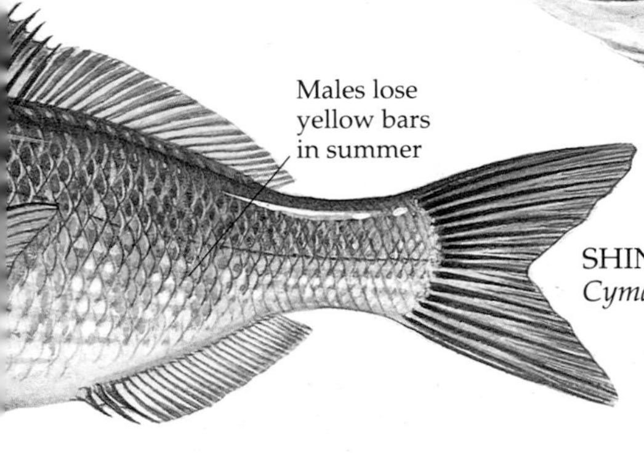
Males lose yellow bars in summer

SHINER PERCH
Cymatogaster aggregata

Size comparison

Rubberlip seaperch
Barred surfperch
Redtail surfperch
Striped seaperch
Walleye surfperch
Shiner perch

GADIDAE

COD, HAKE, LING, & BURBOT

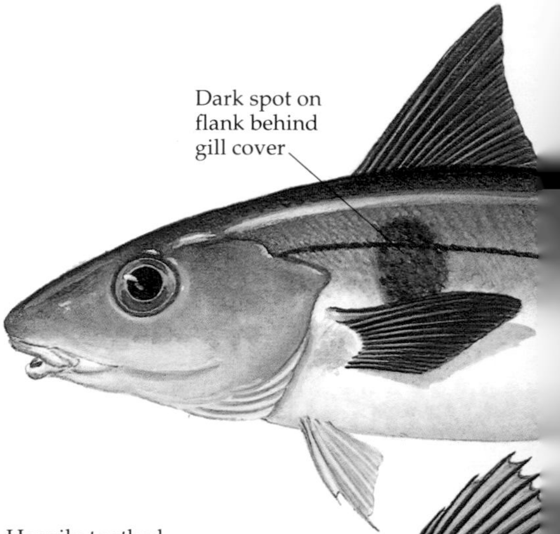

The members of the Gadidae, the codfish family, are distributed widely around the world, especially in the colder waters of the Northern Hemisphere. Most live at or near the bottom, feeding on fish and invertebrates, and many of them have great commercial importance as well as being popular quarry for sea anglers. Unfortunately, the commercial value of many species has led to serious overfishing in some areas, particularly the North Atlantic. As a result, there has been a serious decline in the numbers and sizes of these species.

EUROPEAN POLLACK

Like many other members of the Gadidae, such as the Atlantic cod, this fish has three dorsal and two anal fins. It is most easily identified by its protruding lower jaw and the distinct curve of its lateral line. Small European pollack are found over sandy bottoms, but the larger ones, which can reach a weight of about 29 lb (13 kg), prefer rocky ground.

AMERICAN POLLACK

The American pollack is similar to the European, but its upper and lower jaws are approximately the same size, and its lateral line is only slightly curved. Its maximum size is about 71 lb (32 kg), and the largest individuals are usually found in the vicinity of reefs.

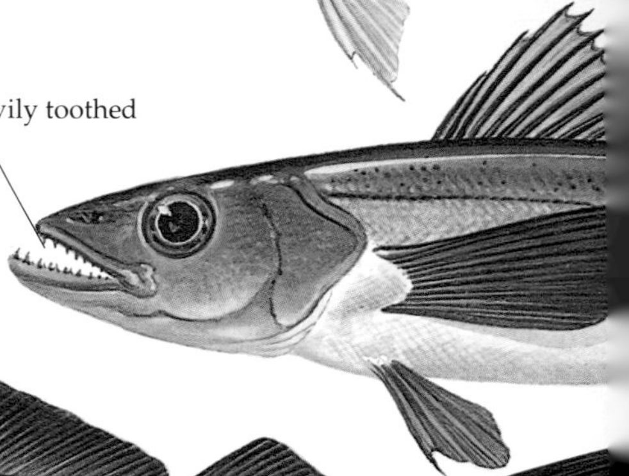

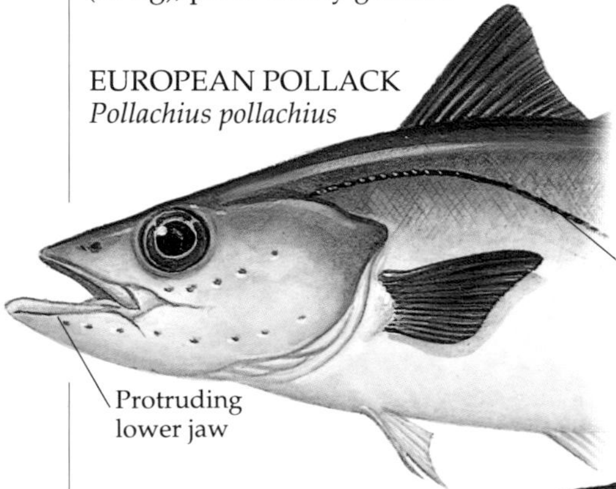

EUROPEAN POLLACK
Pollachius pollachius

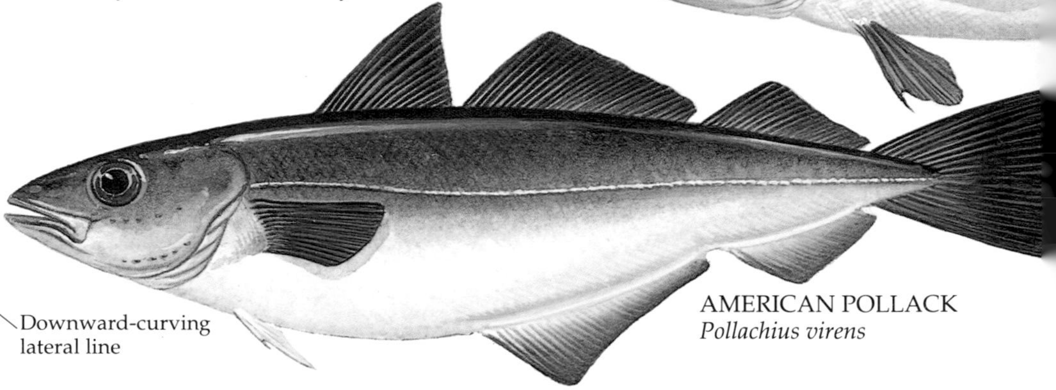

AMERICAN POLLACK
Pollachius virens

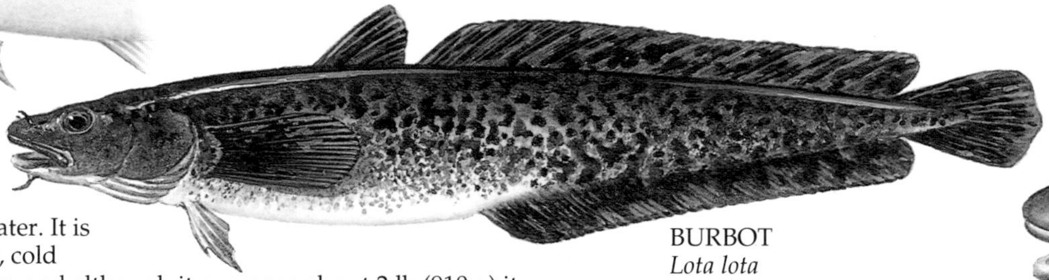

BURBOT
Lota lota

BURBOT

This is the only member of the codfish family that lives exclusively in freshwater. It is widely distributed in deep, cold waters in northern latitudes, and although it averages about 2 lb (910 g) it can grow much larger, and specimens weighing in at around 71 lb (32 kg) have been taken from European waters. It is probably now extinct in the British Isles.

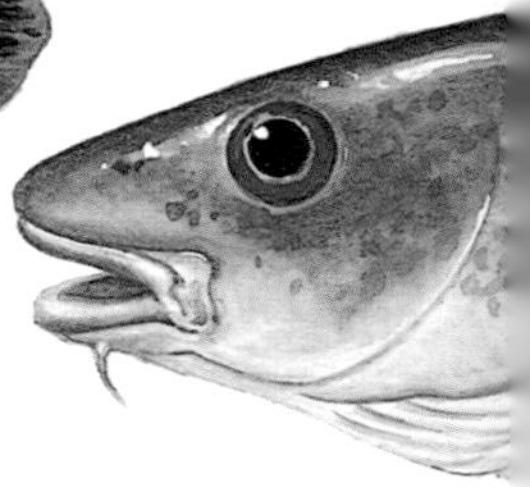

FISHING NOTES

Techniques
The marine codfish may be fished for from the shore by surfcasting or by fishing from rocks, piers, and jetties with natural baits, and from a boat with natural baits or by feathering, jigging (pirking), or using attractor spoons in conjunction with baited hooks. The burbot, the freshwater member of the codfish family, is a slow-moving fish that feeds mostly at night and may be caught by static legering in shallow water.

Tackle
When shore fishing for the marine species, try a 12 ft (3.7 m) surfcasting rod with a baitcaster reel, 30 lb (13.6 kg) nylon line, hook sizes 2/0 to 8/0, and a bomb-shaped or grip weight. To fish for the marine species from a boat, use a 30 lb (13.6 kg) class boat rod with a 4/0 to 6/0 baitcaster reel, 30 lb (13.6 kg) wire or nylon line, and hook sizes 2/0 to 8/0. When using natural baits and when feathering, use a bomb-shaped weight. For burbot, try a 10 to 12 ft (3 to 3.7 m) leger rod with a spinning reel, 6 lb (2.7 kg) mono line, and size 10 to 14 hook.

Bait
The wide range of effective natural baits for the marine species includes many invertebrates, such as mussels, lugworms, sandworms, razor clams, and squid. Fish baits, either cut or whole, are also worth trying, especially the oily fish such as herring, mackerel, sprat, and pilchard. Among the artificial baits, leadhead jigs, metal pirks, and plastic sandeels will get results, and a bunch of orange or white feather hackles on a 5/0 hook is excellent as a boat fishing lure. Burbot will take a bunch of large worms or a small fish.

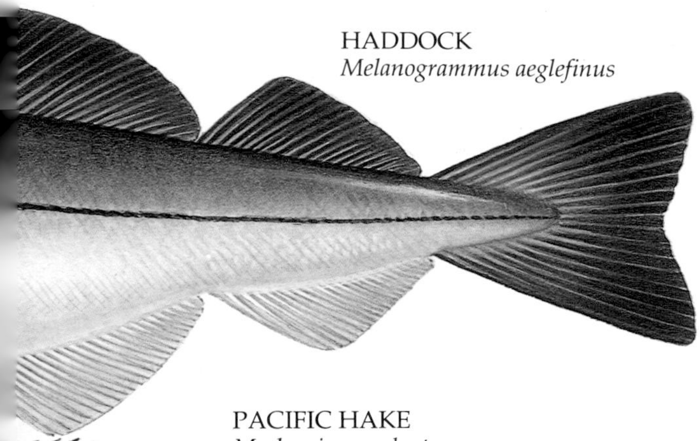

Haddock

The features that help to distinguish the haddock from other codfish are its high, pointed first dorsal fin, its black lateral line, and a dark "thumbprint" above its pectoral fin. In addition, its lower jaw, which carries a small barbel, is shorter than the upper. It travels in large schools, usually near the bottom at depths of 130 ft (40 m) or more, and averages less than 5 lb (2.27 kg) with a usual maximum of around 13 lb (6 kg).

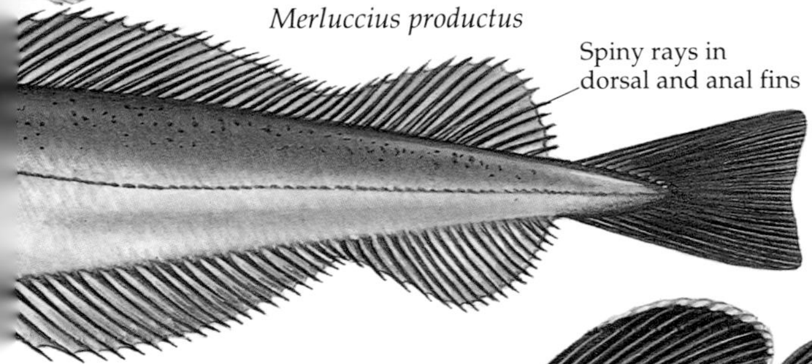

Pacific Hake

In all the many species of hake, the second and third dorsal fins are joined to form one long fin, as are the anal fins; in several species, such as the Pacific hake, these fins are notched or indented. The Pacific hake and its Atlantic cousin *(Merluccius merluccius)* reach weights of over 25 lb (11 kg).

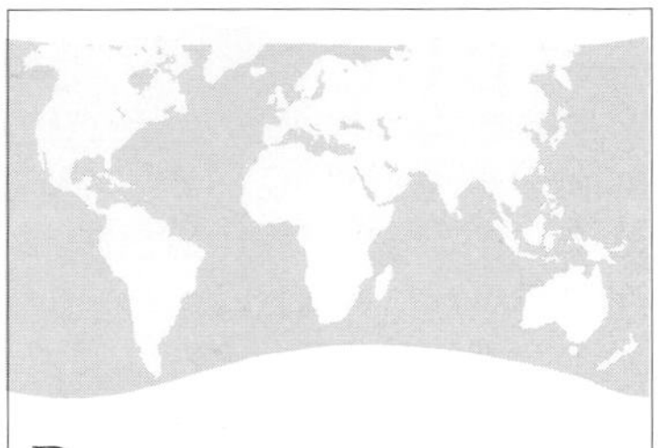

Distribution

European pollack: northeast Atlantic; Mediterranean.
American pollack: Atlantic.
Burbot: northern Eurasia, Alaska, Canada, the northern United States.
Haddock: North Atlantic.
Pacific hake: North Pacific; other hake occur elsewhere in the Pacific and the Atlantic.
Ling: northeast Atlantic.
Atlantic cod: North Atlantic; other varieties occur elsewhere in the Atlantic and the Pacific.

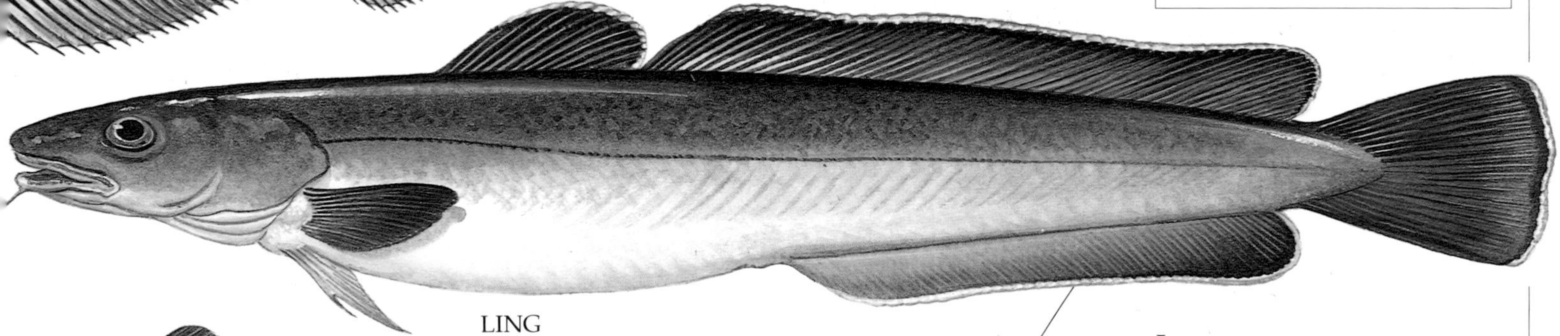

Ling

The ling, or white hake, is one of the larger members of the codfish family, growing to around 60 lb (27 kg), and is common around wrecks. The young spend the first few years of their lives in shallow water, and move into deeper water, usually of between 165 and 1,300 ft (50 and 400 m), as they mature. As a result, ling caught from the shore are generally smaller than those that are taken offshore.

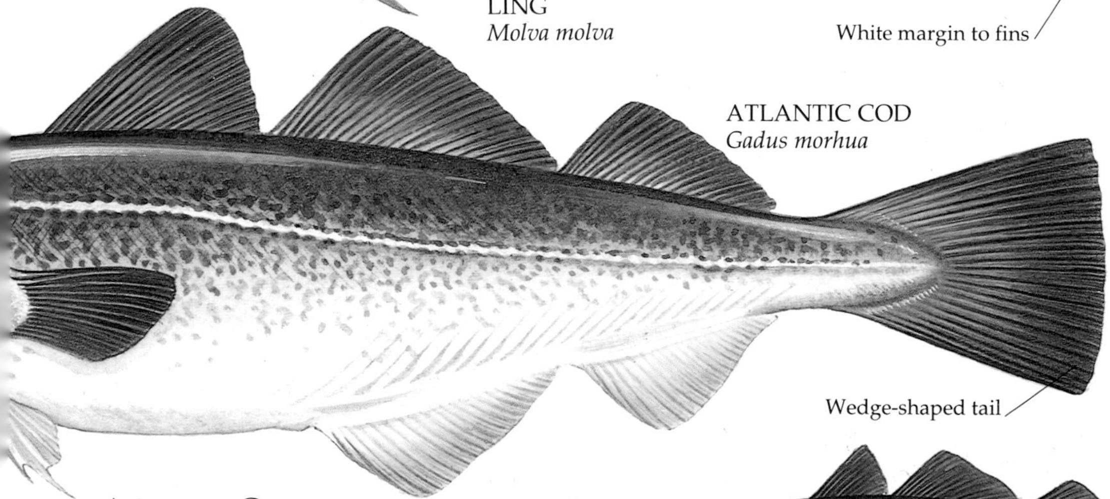

Atlantic Cod

The Atlantic cod has had immense commercial importance for hundreds of years, and European fishermen were working the cod-rich Grand Banks, off Newfoundland, long before Columbus reached America. It usually reaches about 10 lb (4.54 kg), but it can grow to over 100 lb (45 kg) and has been known to attain 211 lb (95.7 kg).

Red cod
The coloration of the cod varies considerably from one area to another. One of the most distinctive variations is the red cod, which is red-gold with a paler belly and is occasionally found in rocky waters that have abundant weed growth.

Size comparison

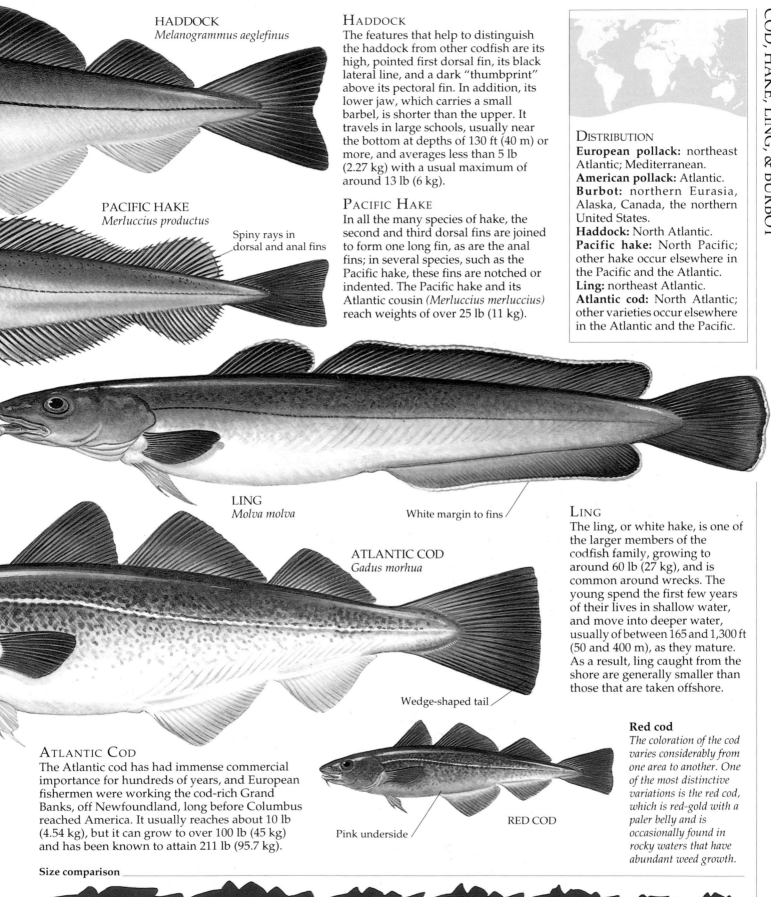

BILLFISH & SWORDFISH

Highly prized by big-game anglers, the spectacularly hard-fighting billfish and swordfish roam widely through the world's tropical and warm-temperate seas, occasionally venturing into higher latitudes in summer. In all of these huge, fast-swimming fish – marlin, spearfish, sailfish, and swordfish – the upper jaw is elongated into a "bill" or "sword."

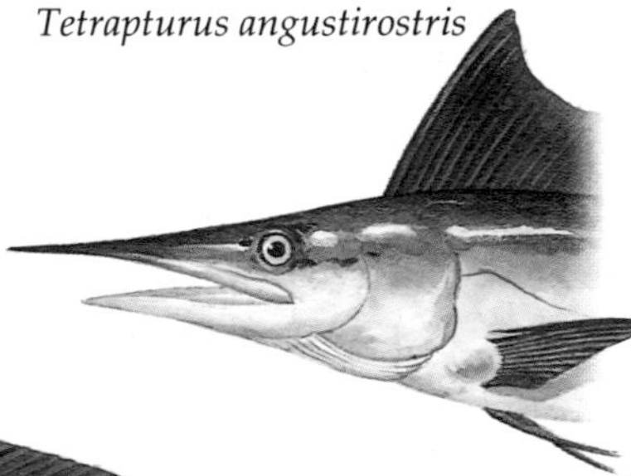

SHORTBILL SPEARFISH
Tetrapturus angustirostris

LONGBILL SPEARFISH
Tetrapturus pfluegeri

SPEARFISH

Spearfish are the smallest of the billfish, reaching 7 to 8 ft (2.1 to 2.4 m) and a weight of 90 to 115 lb (40 to 52 kg). The upper jaw of the shortbill (a Pacific species) is only about 50 percent longer than the lower, while in the longbill (an Atlantic fish) the upper jaw is at least twice the length of the lower. A third species of spearfish, *Tetrapturus belone,* is found in the Mediterranean. Spearfish are seldom found in coastal waters, except in areas that have steep drop-offs.

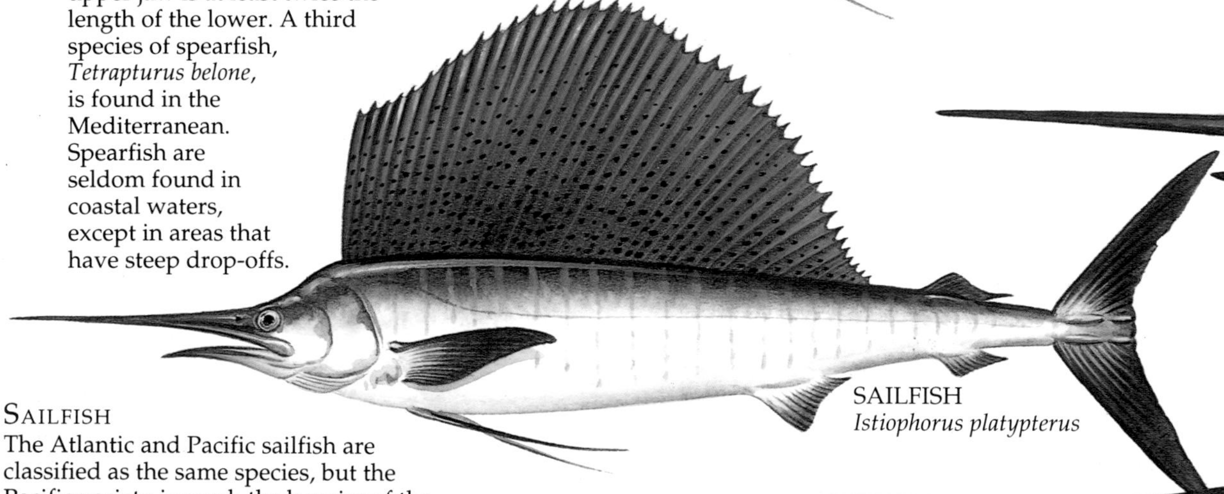

SAILFISH
Istiophorus platypterus

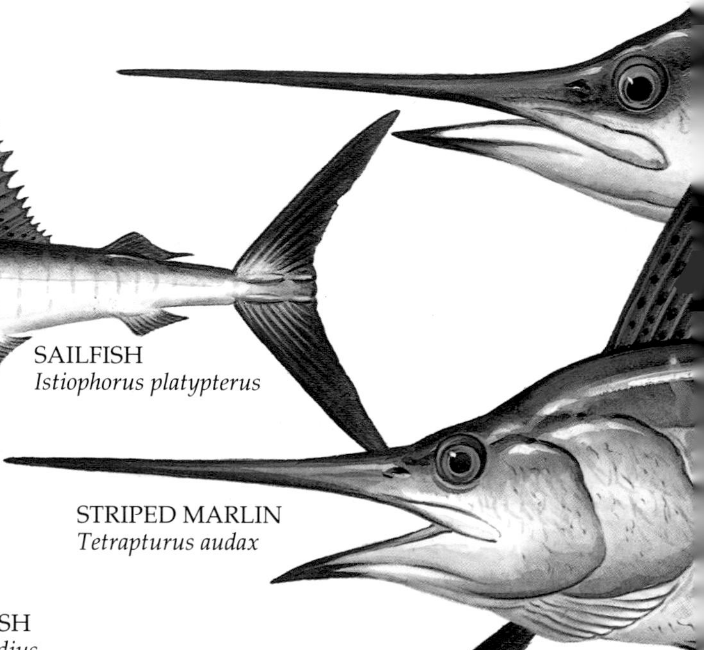

STRIPED MARLIN
Tetrapturus audax

SAILFISH

The Atlantic and Pacific sailfish are classified as the same species, but the Pacific variety is much the heavier of the two, growing to about 240 lb (110 kg) and 10 ft 10 in (3.3 m) as opposed to the 128 lb (58 kg) and 8 ft (2.4 m) of the Atlantic fish. A sailfish is easily recognizable by its long bill and huge, sail-like dorsal fin; the length of the longest ray of this fin is some 150 percent or more of the maximum depth of the body.

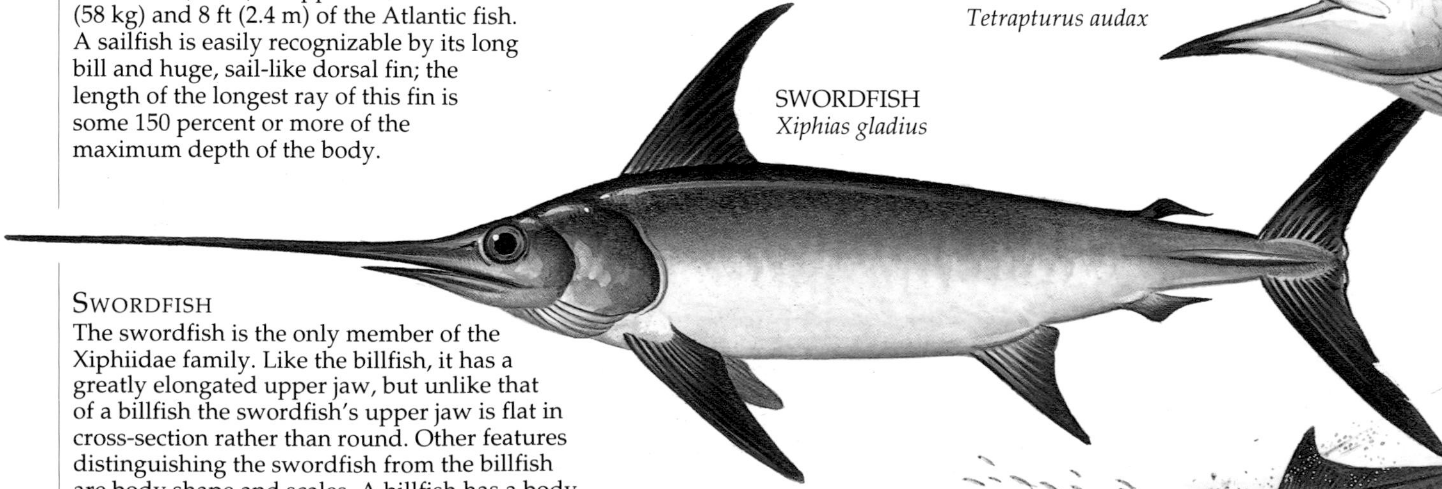

SWORDFISH
Xiphias gladius

SWORDFISH

The swordfish is the only member of the Xiphiidae family. Like the billfish, it has a greatly elongated upper jaw, but unlike that of a billfish the swordfish's upper jaw is flat in cross-section rather than round. Other features distinguishing the swordfish from the billfish are body shape and scales. A billfish has a body that is compressed in cross-section and has narrow, pointed scales; the body of a swordfish is nearly round, and the adult fish has no scales. In size, the swordfish is comparable to the largest billfish, reaching 15 ft (4.6 m) and weighing up to 1,300 lb (590 kg).

Natural food
Billfish and swordfish feed on fish (particularly tuna and herring), crustaceans, and squid. Once pursued, the quarry has little chance of escaping these powerful, fast-swimming predators.

Fishing Notes

Techniques
Trolling at or close to the surface is the usual technique for these species, but swordfish and blue marlin may also be taken by deep still-fishing using live or dead natural baits. In addition, the sailfish offers exciting sport to the saltwater fly fisherman. A billfish must be handled carefully when it is brought to the boat to be hauled on board or cut free, because the bill can inflict nasty wounds, and it is wise to wear gloves to protect your hands because the bill is very rough.

Tackle
For the smaller species, use a 20 to 50 lb (9.1 to 22.7 kg) class boat rod with a 20- to 50-class lever drag reel or a 6/0- or 7-class star drag reel. For larger fish use a 80 to 130 lb (36.3 to 59 kg) class rod with an 80- to 130-class lever drag or 12/0 or 14/0 star drag. Use 20 to 130 lb (9.1 to 59 kg) nylon or Dacron line with a heavy wire or nylon leader. Hooks should be flat-forged, 8/0 to 14/0. When fly fishing for sailfish, use a heavy fly rod with a suitable saltwater fly reel, a weight-forward #10 line with a 20 lb (9.1 kg) leader, and a streamer fly on a 2/0 to 5/0 hook.

Bait
Live or dead fish, such as mullet, mackerel, herring, and squid, and lures such as Kona Heads, feathered jigs, and plastic squids.

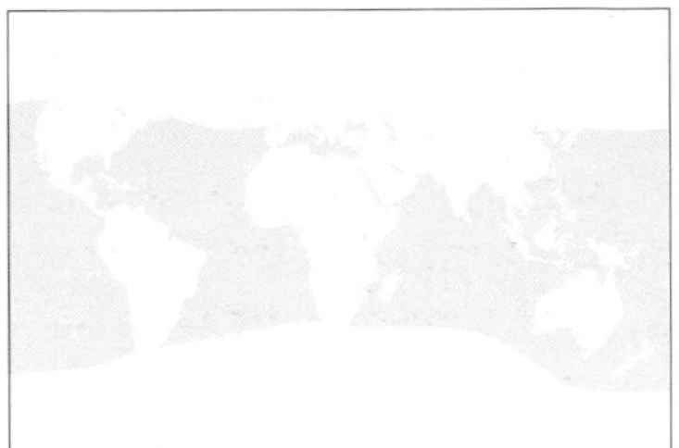

Distribution

Blue marlin, **sailfish** and **swordfish**: worldwide.
Black and **striped marlins**: Pacific and Indian Oceans.
Shortbill spearfish: Pacific.
White marlin, **longbill spearfish**: Atlantic.

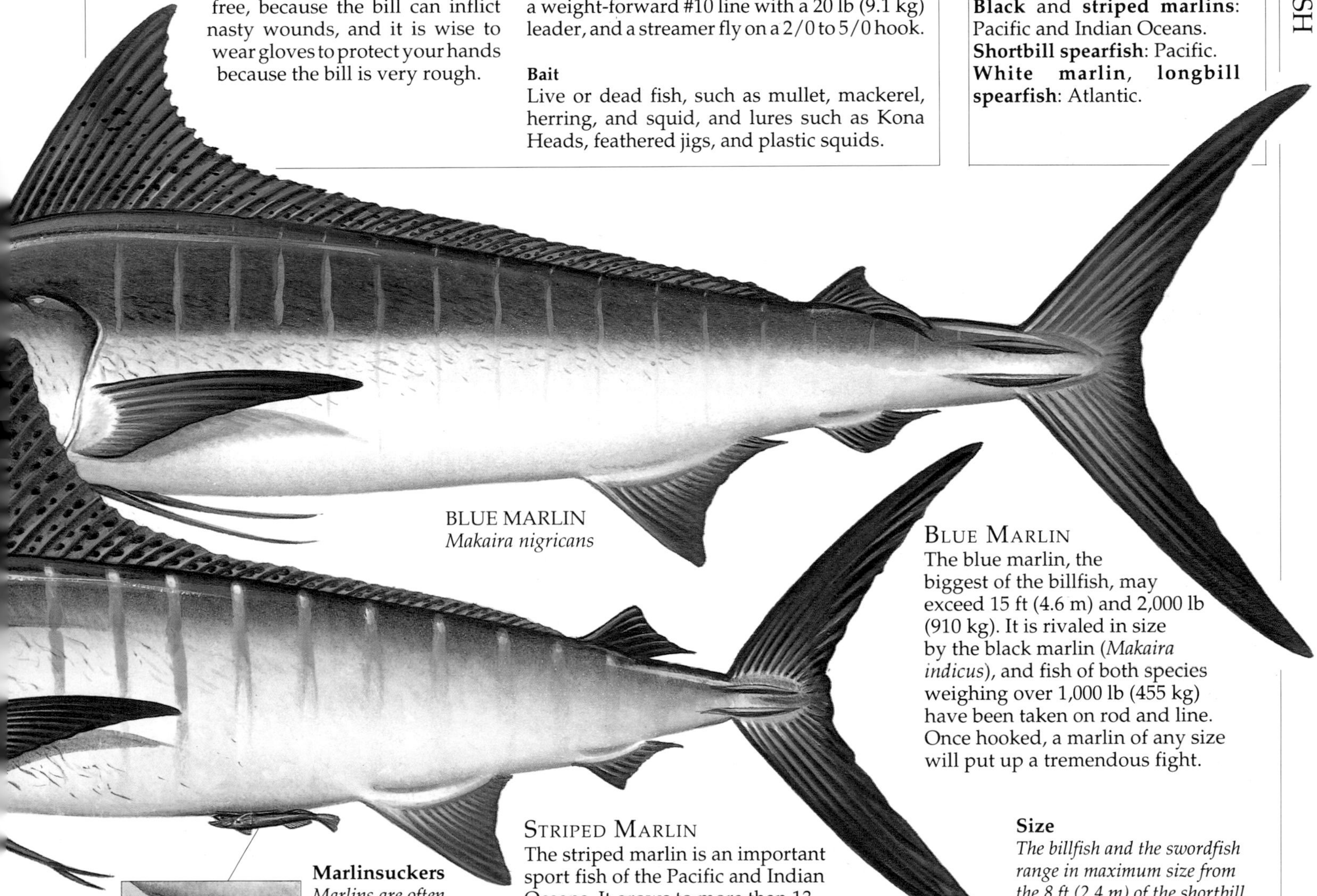

BLUE MARLIN
Makaira nigricans

Blue Marlin

The blue marlin, the biggest of the billfish, may exceed 15 ft (4.6 m) and 2,000 lb (910 kg). It is rivaled in size by the black marlin (*Makaira indicus*), and fish of both species weighing over 1,000 lb (455 kg) have been taken on rod and line. Once hooked, a marlin of any size will put up a tremendous fight.

Marlinsuckers
Marlins are often accompanied by remoras (suckers), which cling to their hosts with suction disks on the tops of their heads. They feed on scraps of the marlins' food.

Striped Marlin

The striped marlin is an important sport fish of the Pacific and Indian Oceans. It grows to more than 13 ft (4 m) and about 690 lb (313 kg), but in the waters accessible to anglers those caught are usually 200 to 250 lb (91 to 113 kg). Some of the best striped marlin fishing is to be found off the coasts of Chile and New Zealand, where fish in the 400 to 500 lb (180 to 227 kg) range have been taken.

Size
The billfish and the swordfish range in maximum size from the 8 ft (2.4 m) of the shortbill spearfish to the 15 ft (4.6 m) of the blue marlin.

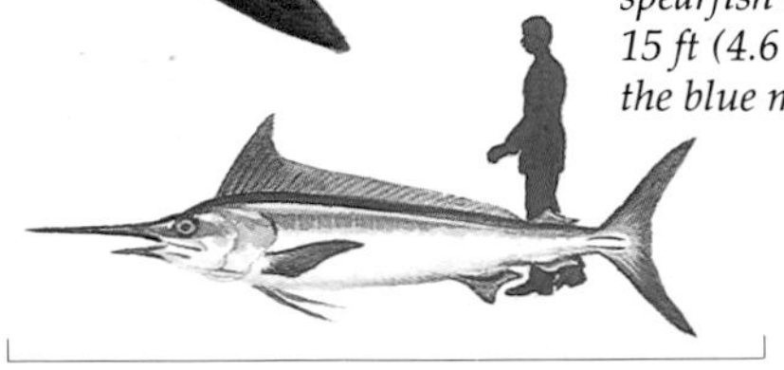

Size comparison

WRASSE & DOLPHINFISH

Wrasse belong to the Labridae family, which has more than 400 members distributed widely in coastal tropical and temperate waters. A typical wrasse has thick lips and strong teeth, which it uses to crush shellfish, and swims by flapping its pectoral fins rather than by using its tail. Wrasse range in size from small species about 4 in (10 cm) long up to the 7 ft 6 in (2.3 m) giant maori wrasse (*Cheilinus undulatus*) of Indo-Pacific waters. The dolphinfish is one of the two members of the Coryphaenidae family.

CALIFORNIA SHEEPHEAD

The coloration of the California sheephead varies with age and sex. Adult males are typically a striking black and red, but females are usually pinkish overall; both sexes have white throats. Young fish are red, with a dark spot on each fin. This wrasse is found along the coast of southern California, usually over rocky ground and kelp beds, at depths of about 10 to 180 ft (3 to 55 m). It grows to a maximum of around 3 ft (90 cm) and 36 lb 4 oz (16.4 kg).

SENORITA
Oxyjulis californica

SENORITA

This small, cigar-shaped fish inhabits kelp beds and rocky ground off the coast of southern California, and is best known to anglers as an expert bait stealer. It feeds on small invertebrates, and larger fish come to it to be cleaned of their parasites. Its maximum size is about 10 in (25 cm), and like many other small wrasse it buries itself in the sand at night.

FEMALE

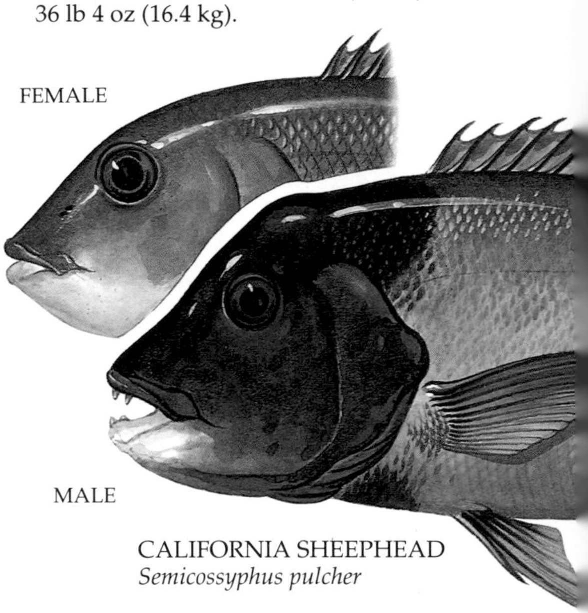

MALE

CALIFORNIA SHEEPHEAD
Semicossyphus pulcher

MALE

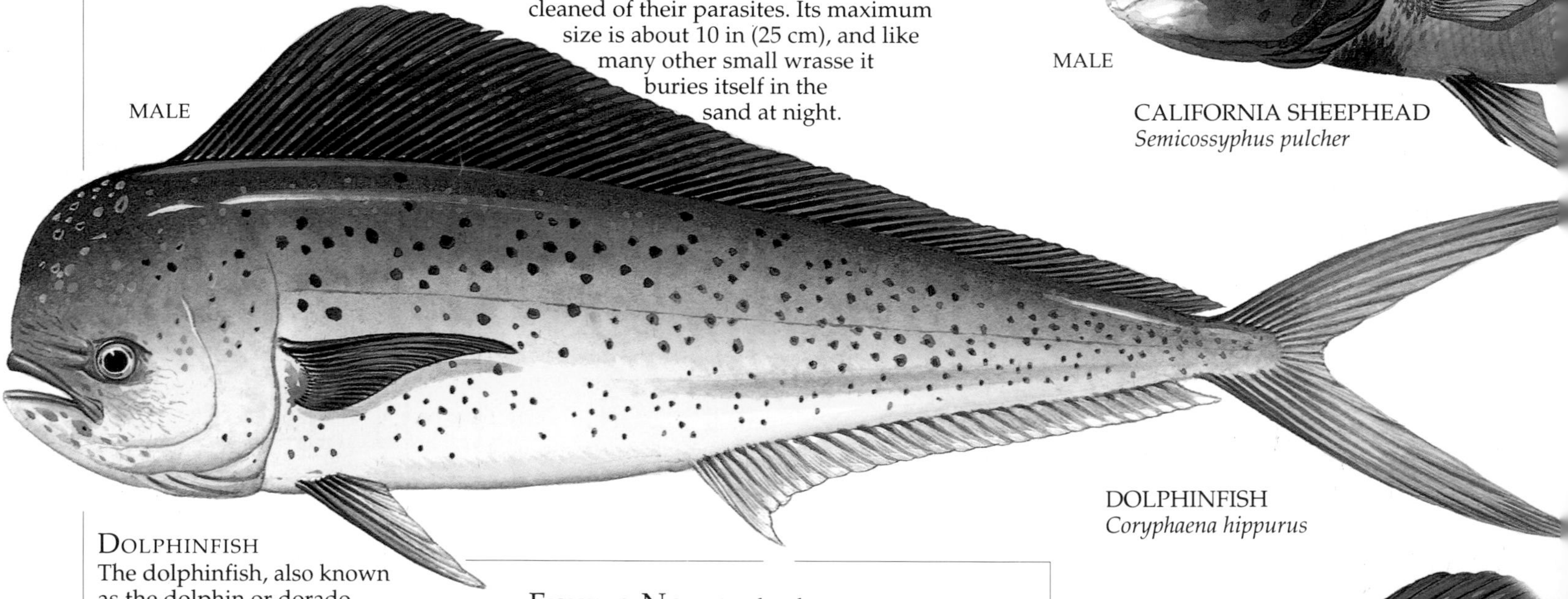

DOLPHINFISH
Coryphaena hippurus

DOLPHINFISH

The dolphinfish, also known as the dolphin or dorado, grows to about 88 lb (40 kg). Its diet consists mainly of fish (especially flying fish) plus squid and crustaceans, and it puts up a tremendous fight when hooked, making fast, powerful runs and leaping and tailwalking over the surface. The flesh of the dolphinfish is delicious, and is often sold under its Hawaiian name, *mahi mahi.* The much smaller pompano dolphin (*Coryphaena equisetis*), which resembles the female dolphinfish, reaches a weight of about 5 lb (2.27 kg).

FISHING NOTES

Techniques
Most wrasse are taken by bottom fishing from the shore or cliffs. The usual techniques for dolphinfish are drift fishing, trolling, and spinning.

Tackle
For wrasse, try a 10 to 12 ft (3 to 3.7 m) light surfcasting or heavy spinning rod with 12 to 15 lb (5.4 to 6.8 kg) mono line. Terminal tackle should be a size 1/0 or 2/0 hook on a paternoster or running leger, with the sinker attached by a sacrificial weak link. For dolphinfish, try a heavy spinning rod or a 20 lb (9.1 kg) class boat rod, with 20 lb (9.1 kg) mono line and a 4/0 hook.

Bait
Wrasse will take a wide range of natural baits, including worms, crabs, mollusks, and crustaceans, and dolphinfish take fish, plugs, and spoons.

FEMALE

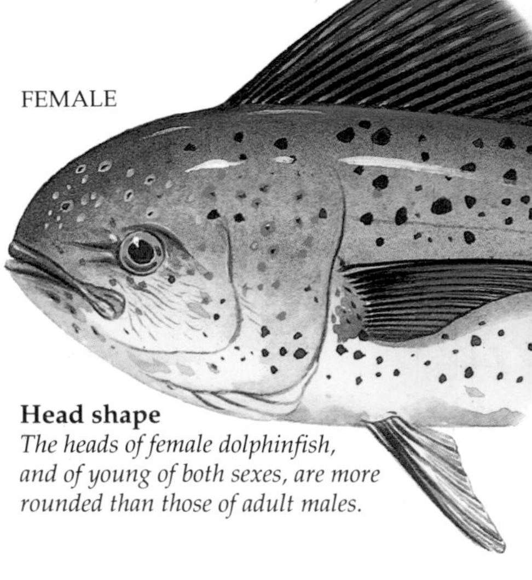

Head shape
The heads of female dolphinfish, and of young of both sexes, are more rounded than those of adult males.

TAUTOG
Tautoga onitis

Tautog

The tautog is a large, western Atlantic wrasse, found over rocky ground and around wrecks and pilings. Females and young fish are a pale olive or brownish gray, with dark mottles and blotches, but adult males are darker, with much less blotching. The tautog feeds mainly on mussels and other shellfish, and its average weight is about 3 lb (1.36 kg), with a maximum of around 24 lb (10.9 kg).

Distribution
California sheephead: eastern Pacific from Monterey Bay to the Gulf of California.
Senorita: eastern Pacific from northern California to central Baja California.
Dolphinfish: worldwide in open waters of tropical and warm-temperate seas.
Tautog: western Atlantic from Nova Scotia to South Carolina.
Cunner: western Atlantic from Newfoundland and Gulf of St. Lawrence to Chesapeake Bay.
Ballan wrasse: northeastern Atlantic from Scotland and southern Norway to Morocco.

BALLAN WRASSE
Labrus bergylta

Ballan Wrasse

The overall coloration of the ballan wrasse varies from reddish brown to dark green, with an abundant covering of small, pale spots. It inhabits kelp beds, rocky ground, and wrecks, in waters up to 66 ft (20 m) deep, and its maximum weight is about 9 lb 6 oz (4.25 kg).

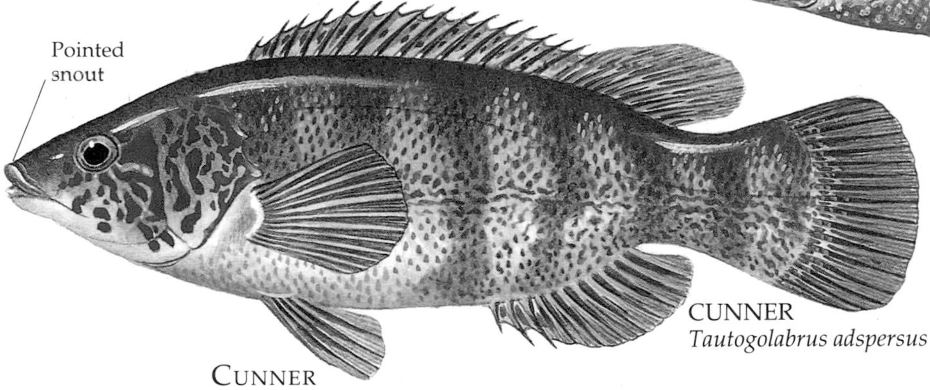

CUNNER
Tautogolabrus adspersus

Cunner

Like the tautog, the cunner is a western Atlantic species, and where their ranges overlap (from Maine to New Jersey) they are often found together. They are similar in overall appearance and habits, but the cunner is smaller and slimmer than the tautog, averaging only about 4 oz (113 g) with a maximum of 2 lb (910 g), and has a noticeably pointed snout.

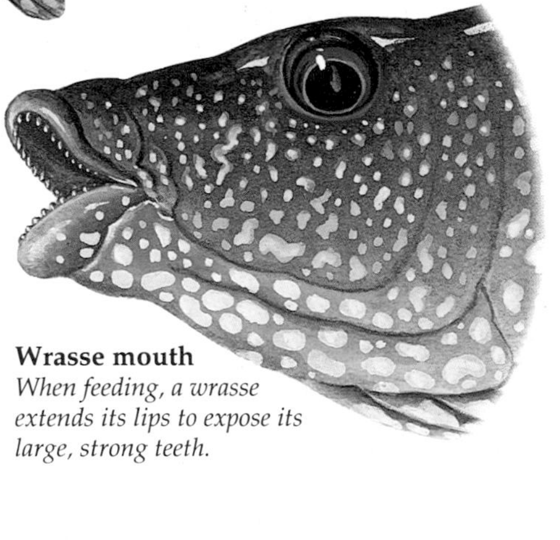

Wrasse mouth
When feeding, a wrasse extends its lips to expose its large, strong teeth.

Size comparison

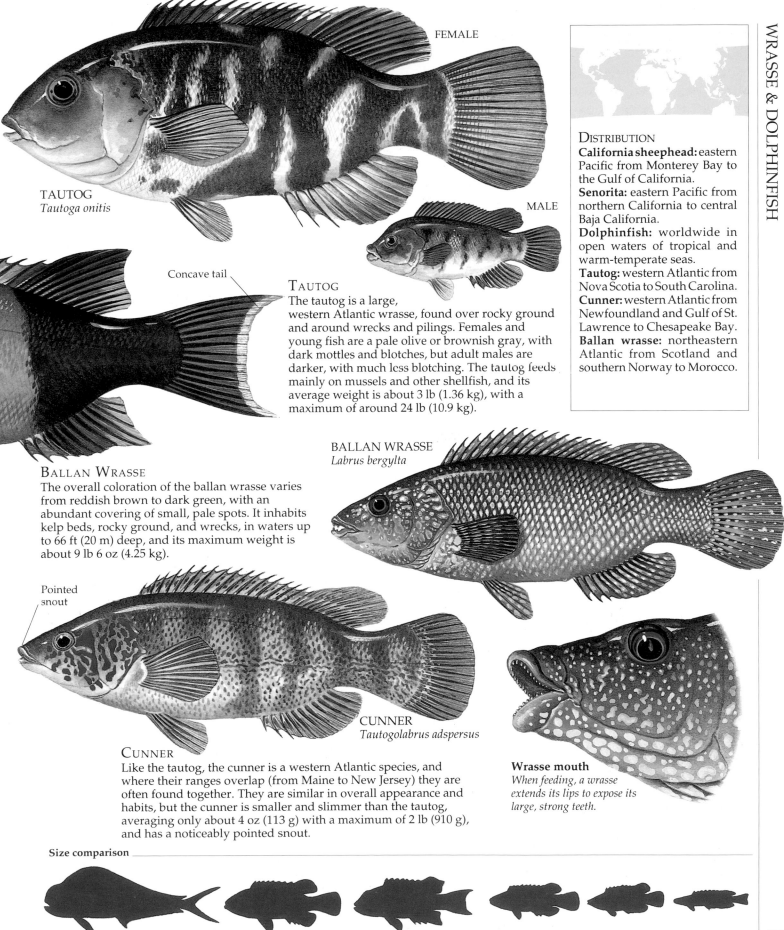

Snapper

Most of the 230 or so species of snapper that make up the Lutjanidae family are found in tropical seas, but a few also occur in warm-temperate waters. They are predatory fish, with sharp, conical teeth, including one or two large canine teeth on either side of the front of each jaw. These canine teeth help to distinguish the snappers from the groupers *(see page 200)*, many species of which are similar in overall appearance. Large numbers of snapper are taken in shallow coastal waters and over reefs by anglers and spearfishers, and some species are fished for commercially.

Mutton Snapper

This is one of the most common snappers in the Caribbean and the waters off southern Florida, and is found near coral heads, in shallow channels and tidal creeks, on coral flats, and in blue holes – deep, circular holes or pits in the seabed. Its coloration is variable, but there is a blue stripe beneath each eye and a small dark spot on each side. Adults usually weigh from 5 to 10 lb (2.27 to 4.54 kg), and the maximum weight is about 25 lb (11.3 kg).

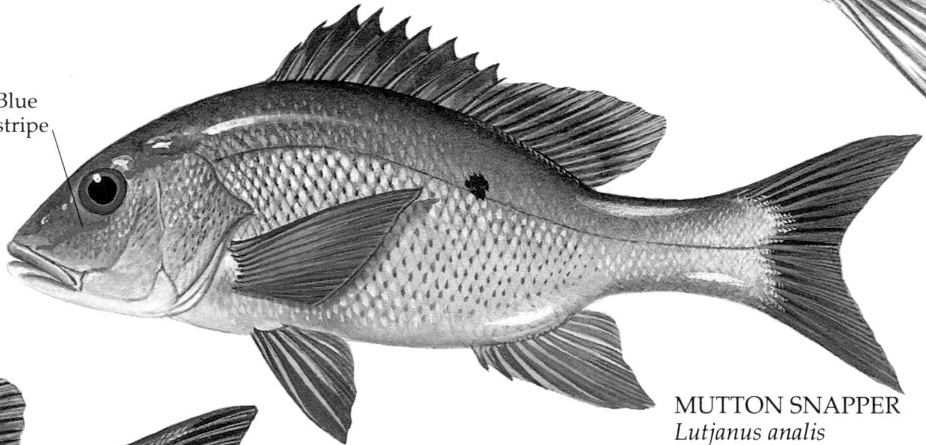

MUTTON SNAPPER
Lutjanus analis

Gray Snapper

The gray snapper, also known as the mangrove snapper, is found in the same waters as the mutton snapper and also occurs along the coast of tropical western Africa. It is most common along mangrove shores, but also lives over reefs, and grows to about 10 lb (4.54 kg). The overall coloration is grayish, sometimes tinged with red or copper, and there is often a dark stripe running from the snout through each eye.

GRAY SNAPPER
Lutjanus griseus

Lane Snapper

This little snapper is identifiable by its pink and yellow stripes, the black edge of its tail fin, and the large dark spot on each side between the dorsal fin and the lateral line. It is found in shallow water throughout the tropical west Atlantic, and although it usually weighs less than 1 lb (454 g), it is popular with anglers because it can be caught from piers and the shore and is good to eat.

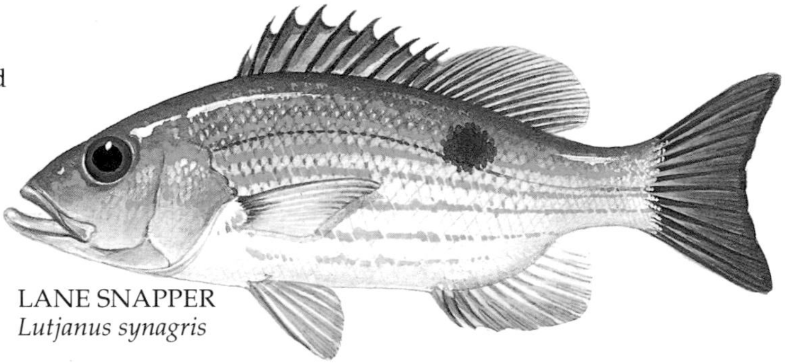

LANE SNAPPER
Lutjanus synagris

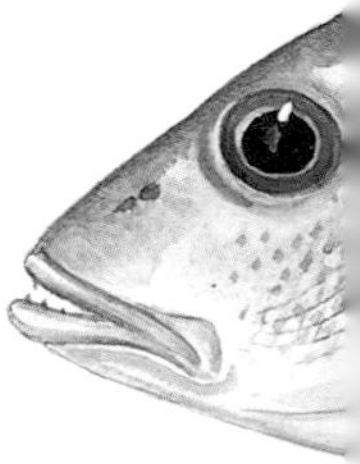

Fishing Notes

Techniques
Cubera, mutton snapper, and red snapper are taken by slow bottom trolling. Cubera and mutton snapper are also brought to the surface by chumming, and then taken by spinning with artificial lures. Spinning, with either artificial lures or natural baits, will take gray snapper, lane snapper, and river roman.

Tackle
For trolling, try a medium spinning rod with a spinning reel, 15 to 20 lb (6.8 to 9.1 kg) mono line, a 12 in (30 cm) wire or heavy mono leader, and a size 2/0 hook. For spinning, use a light or medium spinning rod with a baitcaster reel, 15 to 20 lb (6.8 to 9.1 kg) mono line, a 12 in (30 cm) wire or heavy mono leader (use transparent mono for gray snapper), and a size 2/0 treble hook.

Bait
Good natural baits for cubera, mutton, red, and lane snapper include shrimp and cut fish such as mullet. Artificial lures used for cubera snapper, mutton snapper, and river roman include bucktails, feathers, and jigs, and plugs with a flashy, silvery finish. These often work best when fished with a jerky retrieve. The best bait to use when fishing for gray snapper is live shrimp.

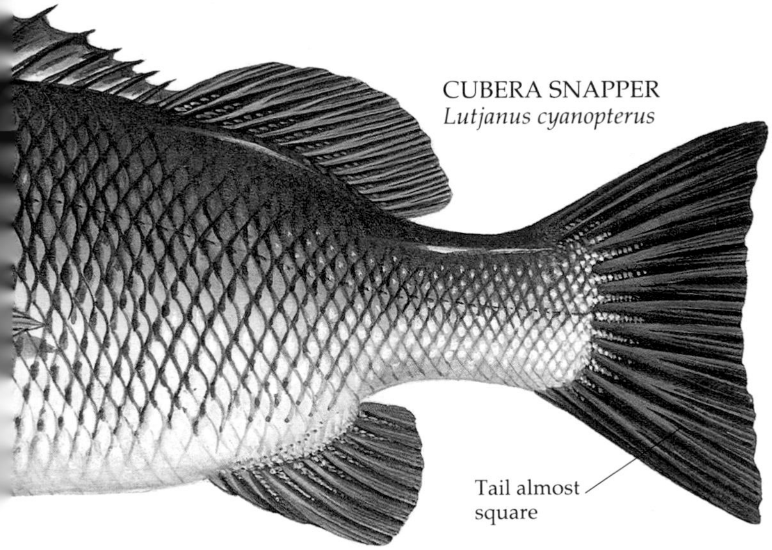

CUBERA SNAPPER
Lutjanus cyanopterus

Cubera Snapper

The cubera snapper or Cuban snapper occurs in the tropical west Atlantic, usually along rocky ledges at depths of a yard or so down to about 180 ft (55 m). Young cubera and small adults also enter estuaries and the tidal reaches of streams and freshwater canals. The cubera snapper's overall coloration ranges from gray to purple-brown, and it can grow to a length of 5 ft (1.5 m) and a weight of over 126 lb (57 kg), making it easily the largest Atlantic snapper. Small cubera are good to eat but can cause ciguatera poisoning (*see page 164*).

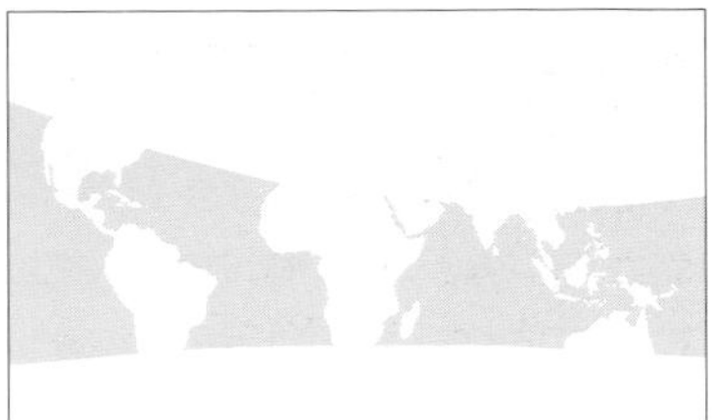

Distribution

Mutton snapper: from Massachusetts to Brazil.
Gray snapper: Massachusetts to Brazil; west Africa.
Lane snapper: North Carolina to Brazil.
Cubera snapper: southern Florida to Brazil.
Red snapper: North Carolina to Yucatan (Mexico).
River roman: Indo-Pacific, including tropical Australia.

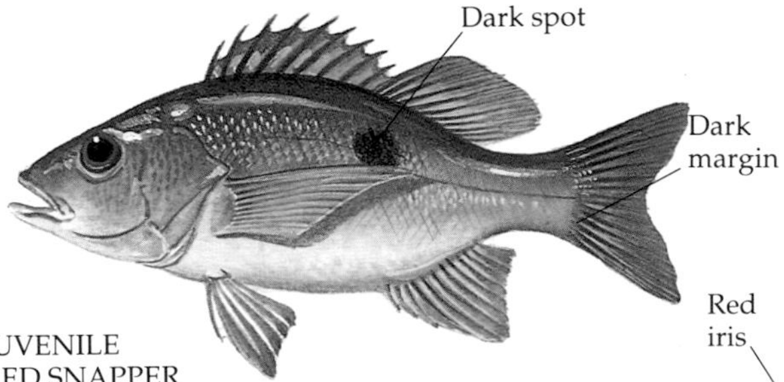

JUVENILE RED SNAPPER

Juvenile red snapper
Up to a length of about 10 in (25 cm), a juvenile red snapper has a dark spot on each side, on or just above the lateral line. In addition, there is often a dark margin along the rear edge of the tail fin. These features fade as the fish matures, and are usually very faint or absent in adults.

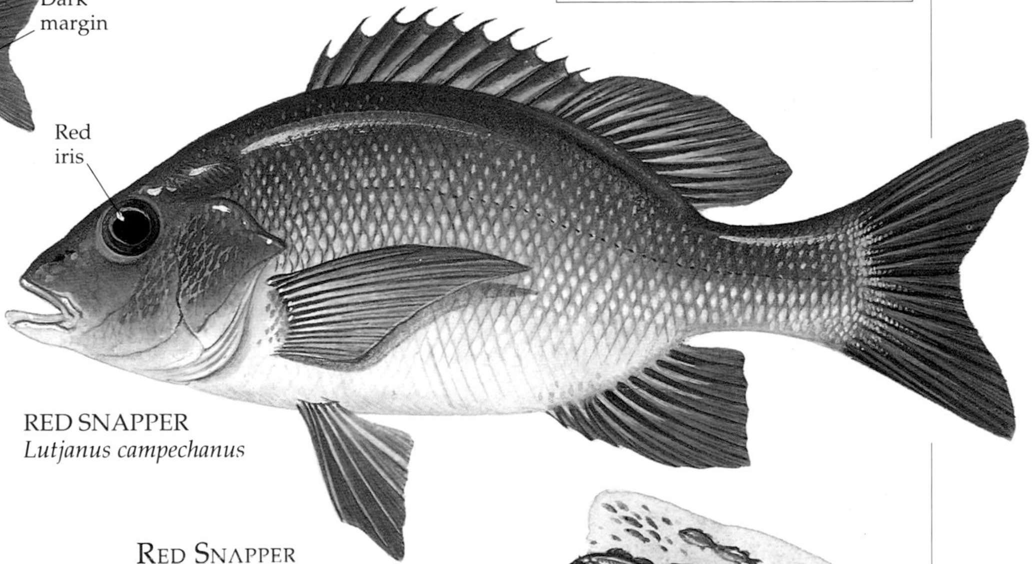

RED SNAPPER
Lutjanus campechanus

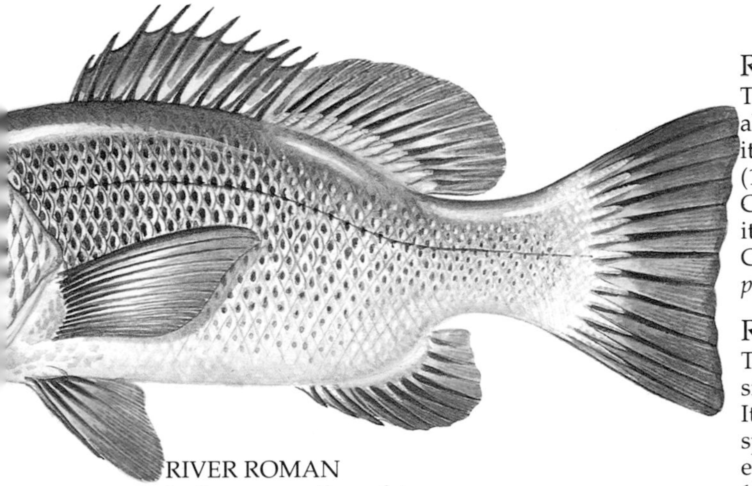

RIVER ROMAN
Lutjanus argentimaculatus

Red Snapper

This snapper occurs at depths of about 120 to 600 ft (37 to 183 m), and its maximum weight is about 35 lb (16 kg). It is found from North Carolina to Mexico, and in the south its range overlaps that of the similar Caribbean red snapper (*Lutjanus purpureus*).

River Roman

The river roman, also known as the silver jack, is an Indo-Pacific species. It inhabits coral reefs as an adult, but spawns and matures in mangrove estuaries to a weight of about 8 lb 13 oz (4 kg). Like most snappers, its coloration tends to vary with age, size, and habitat.

Red snapper schools
The red snapper forms large schools that swim close to the bottom over rocky ground. These schools are easily detected by sonar.

Size comparison

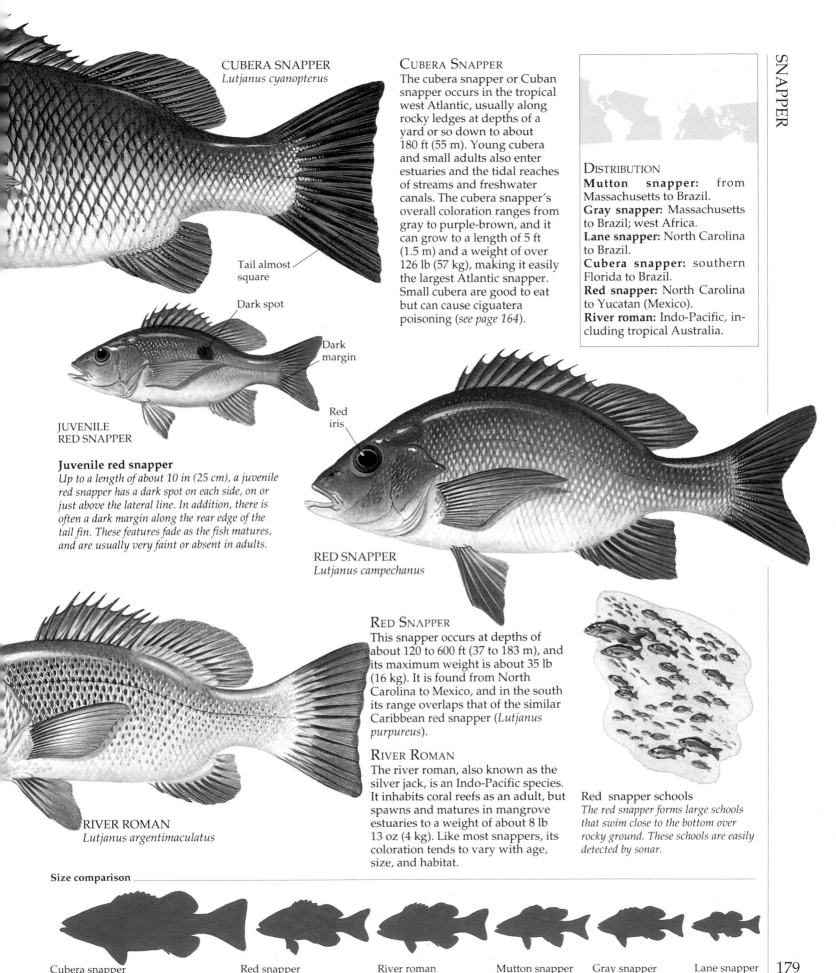

MULLET

There are about 70 species of mullet in the Mugilidae family, distributed worldwide in temperate and tropical waters. Most live close to the shore and often move into estuaries and rivers, and some, including the Australian mullet, inhabit freshwater. They are primarily bottom-feeders, living on algae, organic detritus, and small, mud-dwelling organisms, and are fished commercially as well as by anglers. The red mullet belongs to the Mullidae family (the goatfish), which consists of over 50 species widely distributed in warm waters.

STRIPED MULLET

This is one of the largest and most widely distributed of the mullet family, reaching a weight of about 15 lb (6.8 kg) and occurring in most warm seas. It is the only species of mullet found along the Pacific coast of North America. Its stripes are formed by horizontal rows of small dark spots, and there is a dark patch at the base of each pectoral fin. The origin of the second dorsal fin is in line with that of the anal fin.

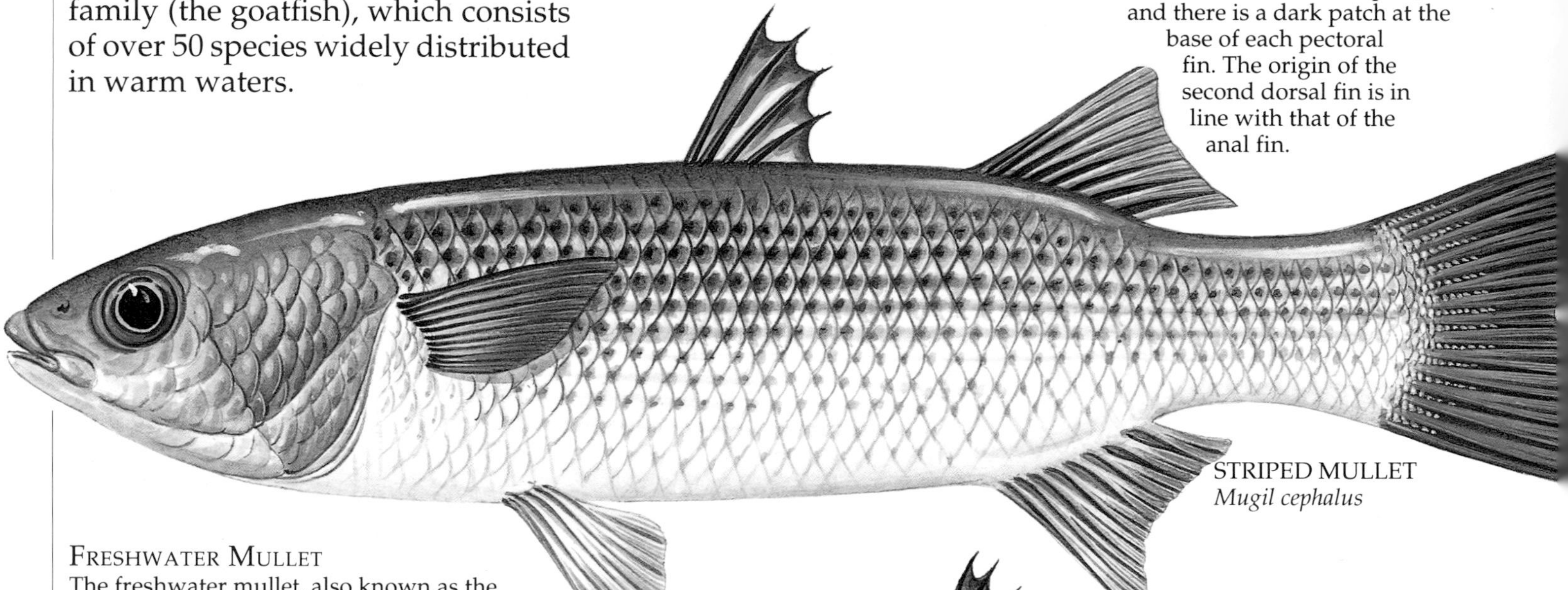

STRIPED MULLET
Mugil cephalus

FRESHWATER MULLET

The freshwater mullet, also known as the pinkeye, lives in the coastal rivers of southeast Australia, and migrates downstream to estuaries to spawn. It usually grows to about 16 in (40 cm), but can reach twice that length and a weight of 16 lb 8 oz (7.5 kg). Like marine mullet, it feeds mainly on algae and detritus.

FRESHWATER MULLET
Myxus petardi

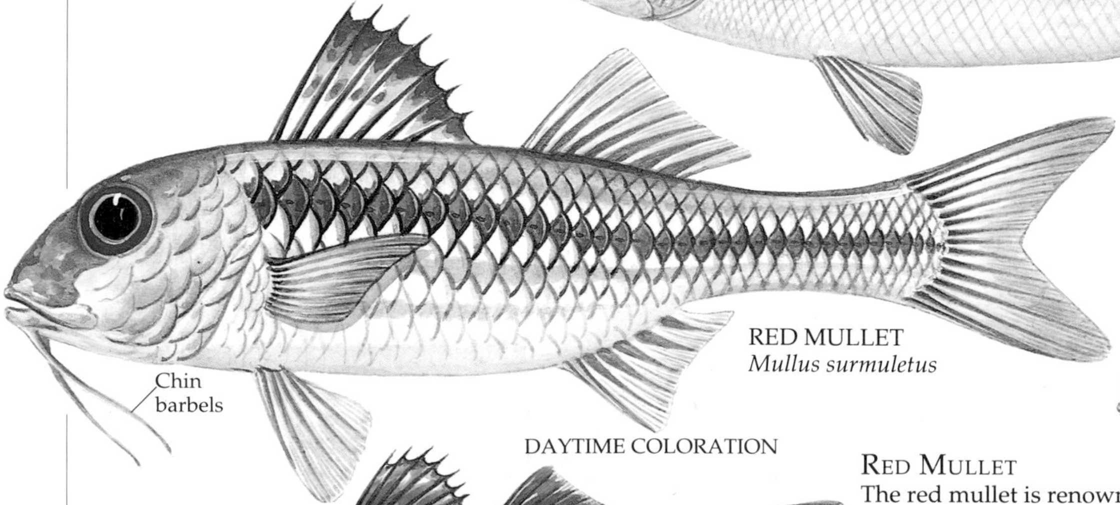

RED MULLET
Mullus surmuletus

DAYTIME COLORATION

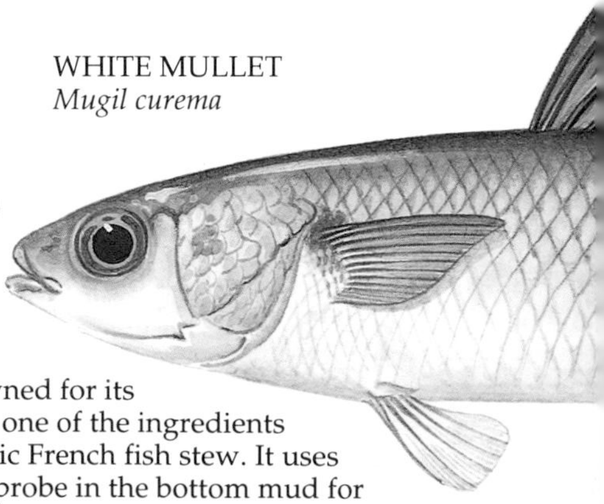

WHITE MULLET
Mugil curema

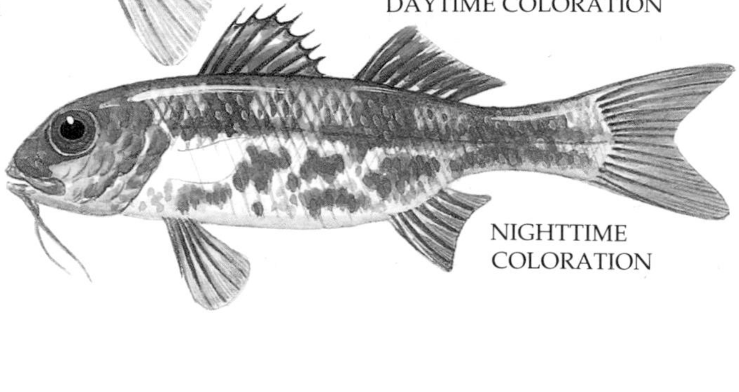

NIGHTTIME COLORATION

RED MULLET

The red mullet is renowned for its fine-tasting flesh and is one of the ingredients of *bouillabaisse*, the classic French fish stew. It uses its long chin barbels to probe in the bottom mud for its food, which is mainly worms, mollusks, and crustaceans, and at night its coloration changes from striped to mottled and barred. Its maximum weight is about 3 lb 10 oz (1.64 kg).

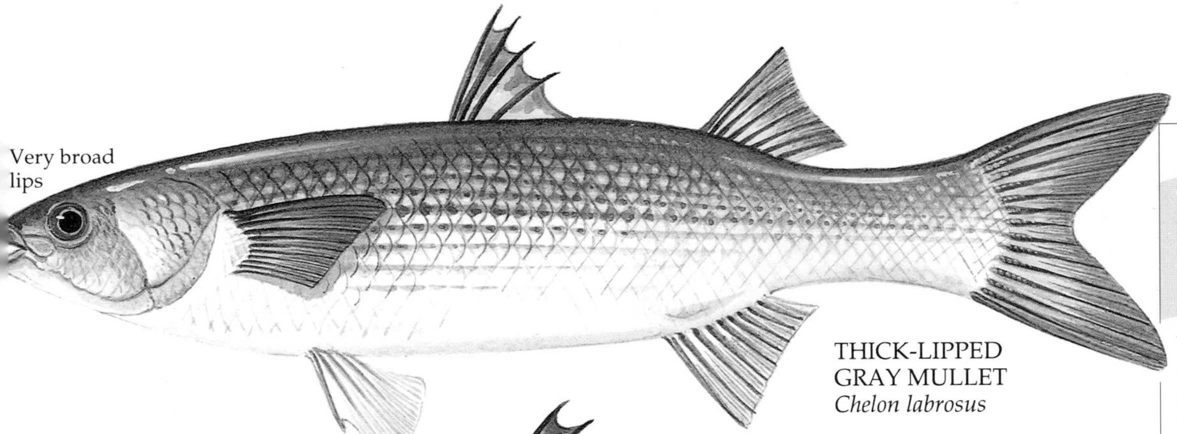

THICK-LIPPED GRAY MULLET
Chelon labrosus

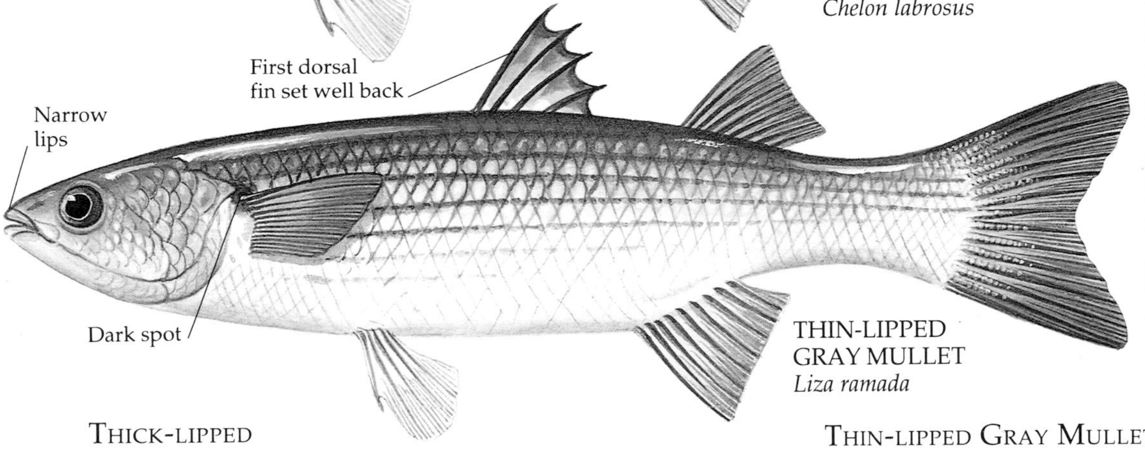

THIN-LIPPED GRAY MULLET
Liza ramada

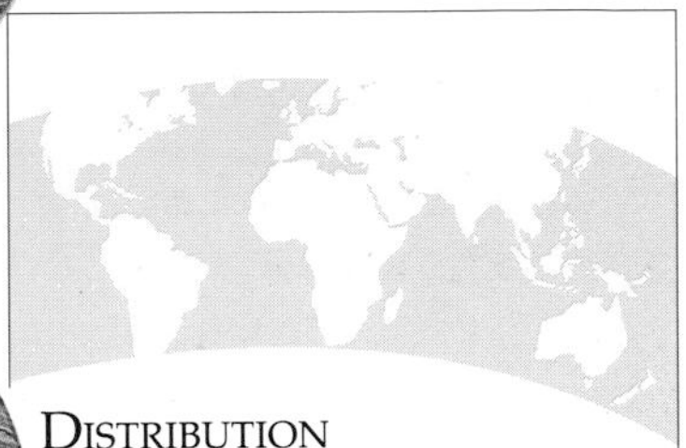

Distribution

Striped: almost worldwide in warm waters.
Freshwater: Burnett River, Queensland, to Georges River, New South Wales.
Red: Mediterranean; eastern Atlantic from southern Norway to the Canary Islands.
Thick-lipped, thin-lipped, golden: Mediterranean; eastern Atlantic from southern Norway to the Canary Islands.
White: warm-temperate and tropical Atlantic; eastern Pacific from Mexico to Chile.

Thick-lipped Gray Mullet

The large lips of this European mullet help to distinguish it from the very similar thin-lipped gray mullet, which is found in the same waters where their ranges overlap. The thick-lipped gray mullet, which forms small schools that cruise near the surface, is found close inshore and enters harbors and estuaries. Its maximum weight is around 14 lb (6.4 kg).

Thin-lipped Gray Mullet

In addition to having thinner lips than the thick-lipped gray mullet, this fish has a dark spot at the base of each pectoral fin and its first dorsal fin is set further back. Its habits are similar to those of the thick-lipped gray, but it is more likely to enter freshwater and is the most abundant mullet in European estuaries. It grows to a maximum of about 7 lb (3.2 kg).

Golden Mullet

The golden mullet, sometimes called the golden gray mullet, resembles the thin-lipped gray but has an overall bronze hue and golden blotches on its cheeks. It is also smaller, with a maximum weight of under 3 lb (1.36 kg).

GOLDEN MULLET
Liza aurata

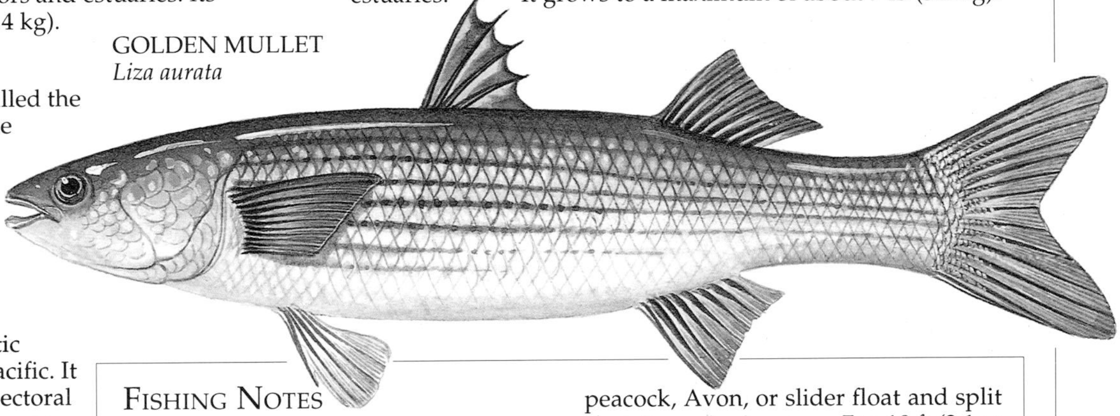

White Mullet

This mullet is found in warm Atlantic waters and in the tropical eastern Pacific. It has a dark spot at the base of each pectoral fin, and often one or two gold patches on each side of its head. It usually grows to a weight of about 3 lb (1.36 kg).

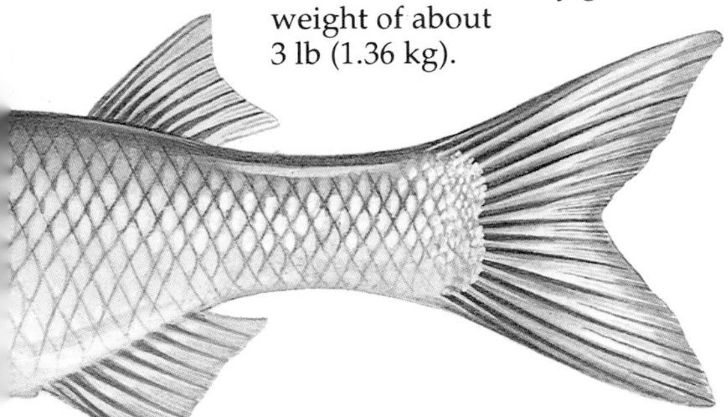

Fishing Notes

Techniques
Float fishing, spinning, or freelining. These fish have soft, relatively small mouths and are easily spooked, so light tackle, delicate bait presentation, and a careful approach are required.

Tackle
Use a 10 to 12 ft (3 to 3.7 m) float rod for float fishing and freelining, with a spinning reel, 5 lb (2.27 kg) mono line, and hook sizes 6 to 16; for float fishing, use a peacock, Avon, or slider float and split shot. For spinning, try a 7 to 10 ft (2.1 to 3 m) light spinning rod with a spinning reel, 5 lb (2.27 kg) mono line, and size 10 treble hook.

Bait
Mullet will take a wide range of small, soft, natural and processed baits, including small or cut worms, maggots, banana, corn, cut fish, bread, cheese, peas, minced meat, and pasta. For spinning, use tiny spoons and spinners, baited with a small or cut sandworm.

Size comparison

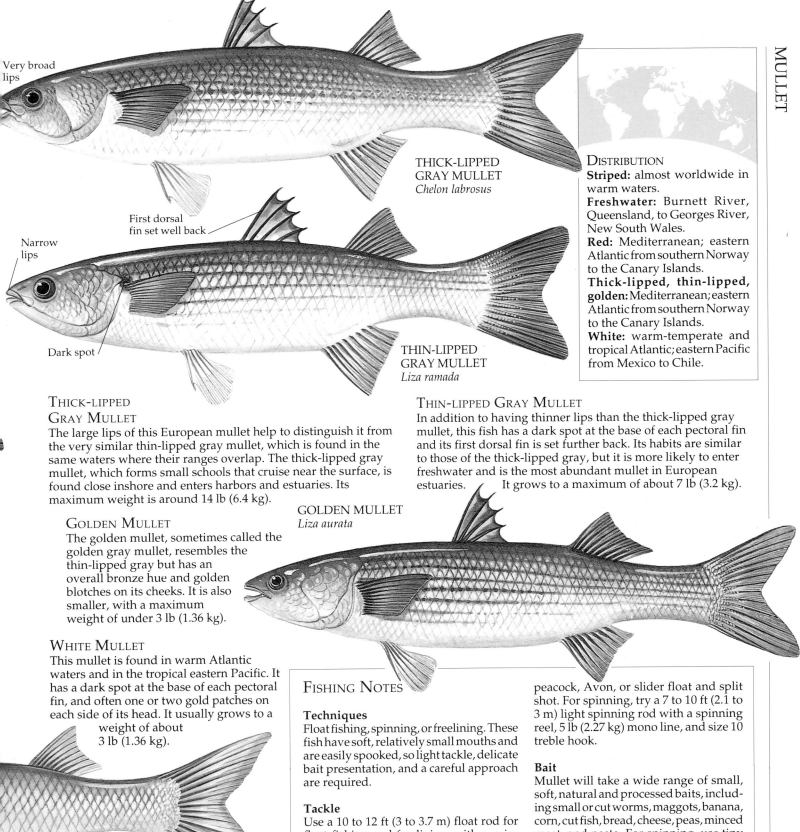

PLEURONECTIDAE; BOTHIDAE; SOLEIDAE

FLATFISH

For a few days after hatching from the egg, the larva of a flatfish resembles that of any other fish, but then it begins to change into the compressed, asymmetrical shape that makes flatfish superbly adapted to a bottom-hugging life. There are over 500 species, the main families being the Pleuronectidae or righteyed flatfish, in which both eyes are on the right side of the body; the Bothidae or lefteyed flatfish, in which both eyes are on the left; and the Soleidae or sole family, which contains mostly righteyed species.

PACIFIC HALIBUT

This huge, righteyed flatfish and its Atlantic counterpart *(Hippoglossus hippoglossus)* are among the largest fish in the sea, probably capable of exceeding 800 lb (360 kg). However, most caught by anglers are young fish weighing less than 10 lb (4.54 kg), the largest adults being found in very deep water.

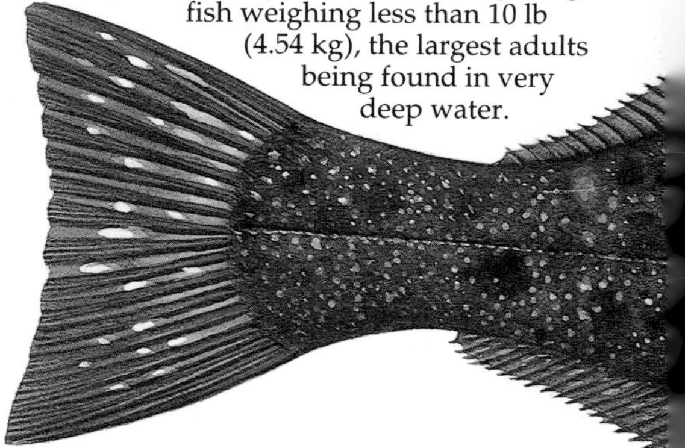

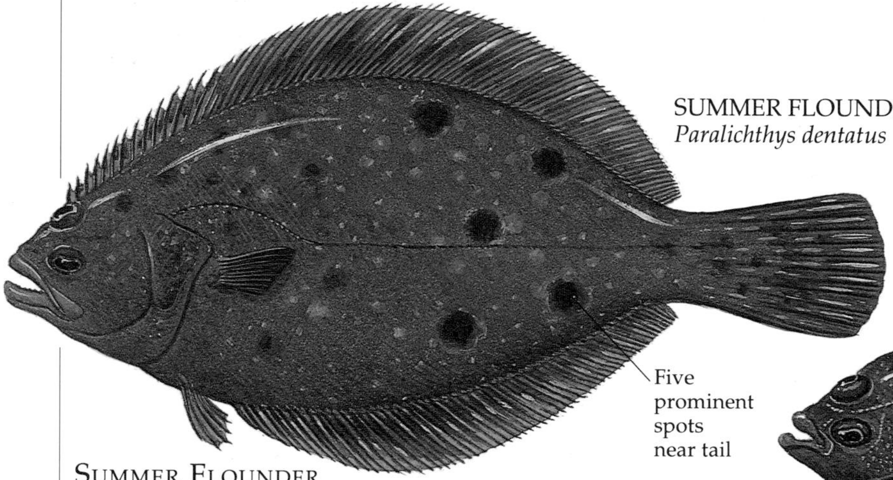

SUMMER FLOUNDER
Paralichthys dentatus

SUMMER FLOUNDER

This lefteyed flatfish reaches a weight of 26 lb (12 kg) and is usually marked with numerous ocelli (rimmed spots), of which five near the tail are large and prominent. It is found along the Atlantic coast of the United States, and from the Carolinas south its range overlaps that of the southern flounder *(Paralichthys lethostigma)*, which is often marked with spots but not with ocelli.

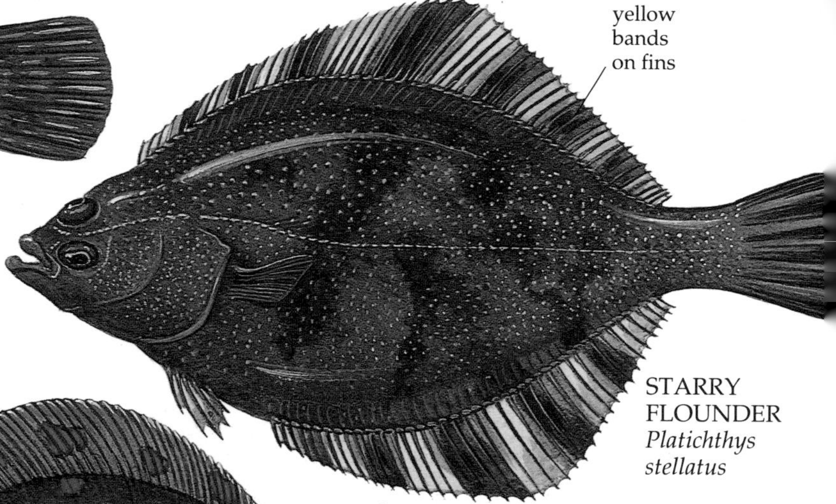

STARRY FLOUNDER
Platichthys stellatus

STARRY FLOUNDER

This flatfish, which can be righteyed or lefteyed, is common on the Pacific coast of North America. Its fins are marked with black and yellow bands, and the upper side of its body has patches of shiny, star-shaped scales. It grows to 20 lb (9.1 kg), and hybridizes with the English sole *(Parophrys vetulus)* to produce the "hybrid sole."

SOLE

The sole, a common flatfish of the eastern Atlantic and the Mediterranean, is brown with dark patches on its upper side and creamy white below. It spends the day buried in the sand, feeding at night in midwater, and grows to 6 lb 10 oz (3 kg).

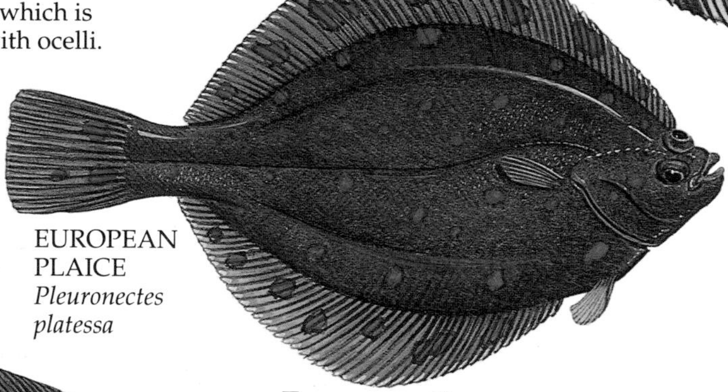

EUROPEAN PLAICE
Pleuronectes platessa

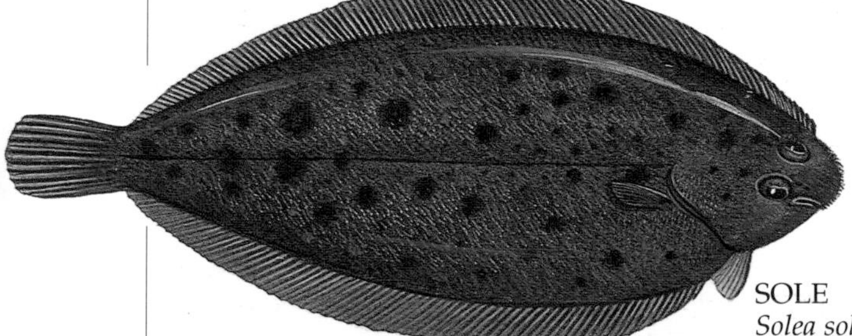

SOLE
Solea solea

EUROPEAN PLAICE

The righteyed European plaice is found in the eastern Atlantic from the tidal shallows out to depths of about 650 ft (200 m). It is marked with bold red or orange spots and grows to a weight of over 10 lb (4.54 kg). The American plaice *(Hippoglossoides platessoides)* is similar, but lacks the red spotting and reaches 14 lb (6.4 kg).

Eggs and larvae
Female flatfish lay up to 500,000 eggs. These float in the water, as do the symmetrically shaped larvae.

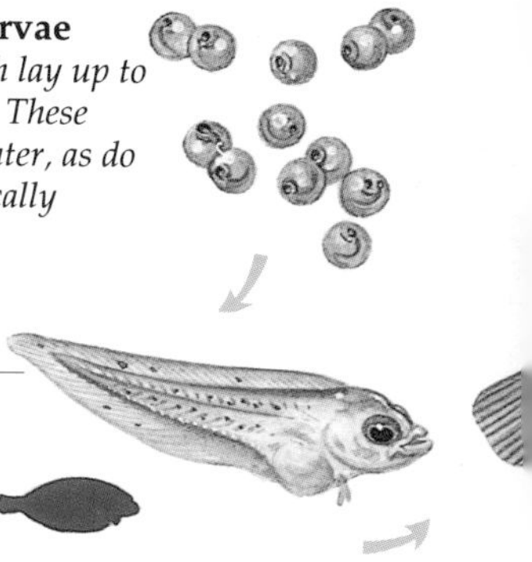

Size comparison

PACIFIC HALIBUT
Hippoglossus stenolepis

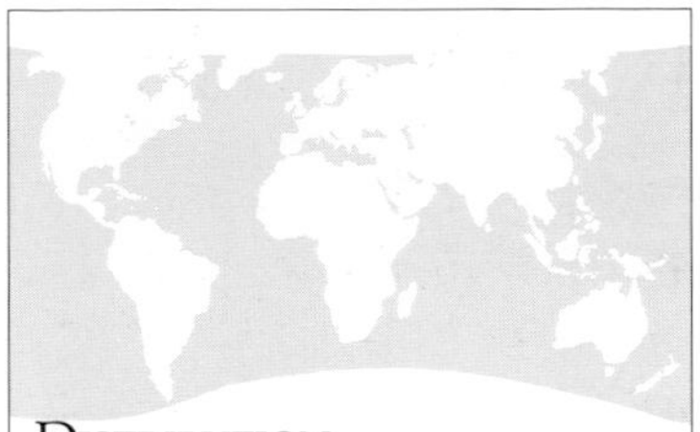

DISTRIBUTION
Pacific halibut: North Pacific.
Starry flounder: North Pacific.
Summer flounder: western Atlantic from about Maine to northern Florida.
Plaice: North Atlantic and western Mediterranean.
Sole: Norway to Morocco and the Mediterranean.
Turbot: from Norway to the Black Sea.
Winter flounder: western Atlantic from Labrador south to Georgia.

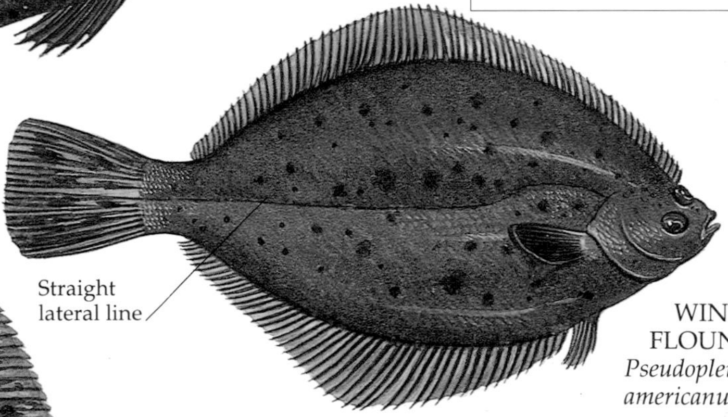

WINTER
FLOUNDER
Pseudopleuronectes americanus

TURBOT
Scophthalmus maximus

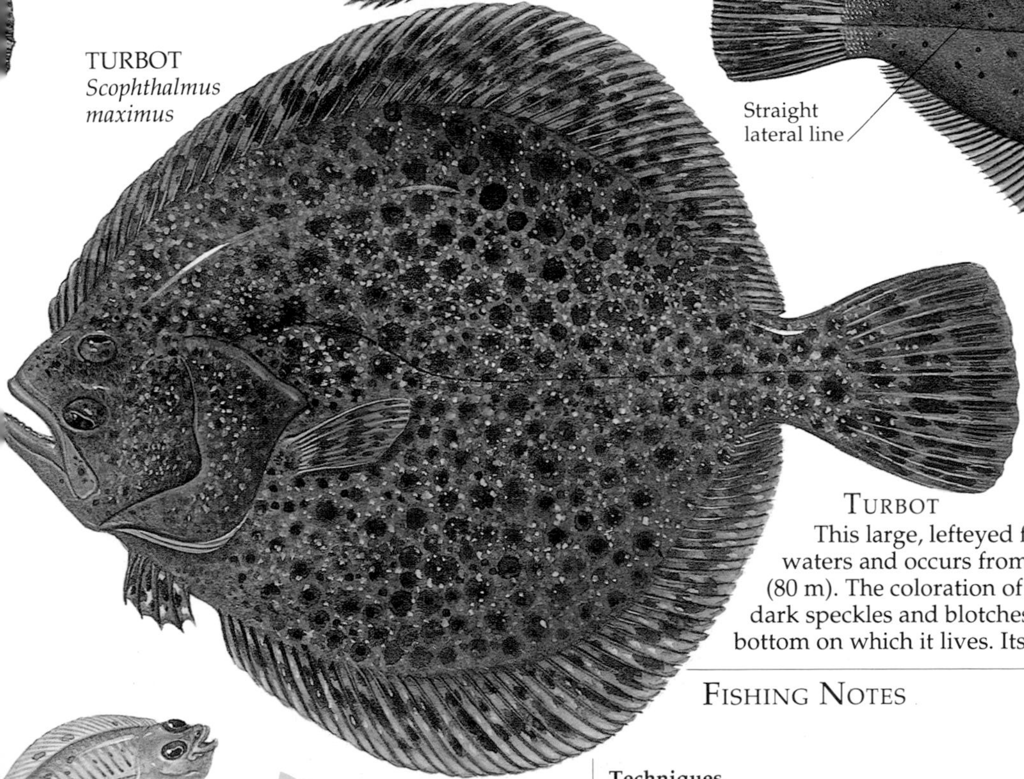

WINTER FLOUNDER

The winter flounder is one of the most common flatfish of the western Atlantic. It is a valuable commercial species and a popular gamefish, capable of reaching 8 lb (3.6 kg) and occurring from the tidal shallows out to depths of about 400 ft (120 m) or more. Its coloration and markings are very variable.

TURBOT

This large, lefteyed flatfish is widely distributed in European waters and occurs from near the shoreline to depths of up to 260 ft (80 m). The coloration of its upper side is typically light brown with dark speckles and blotches, and generally matches the color of the bottom on which it lives. Its maximum weight is about 33 lb (15 kg).

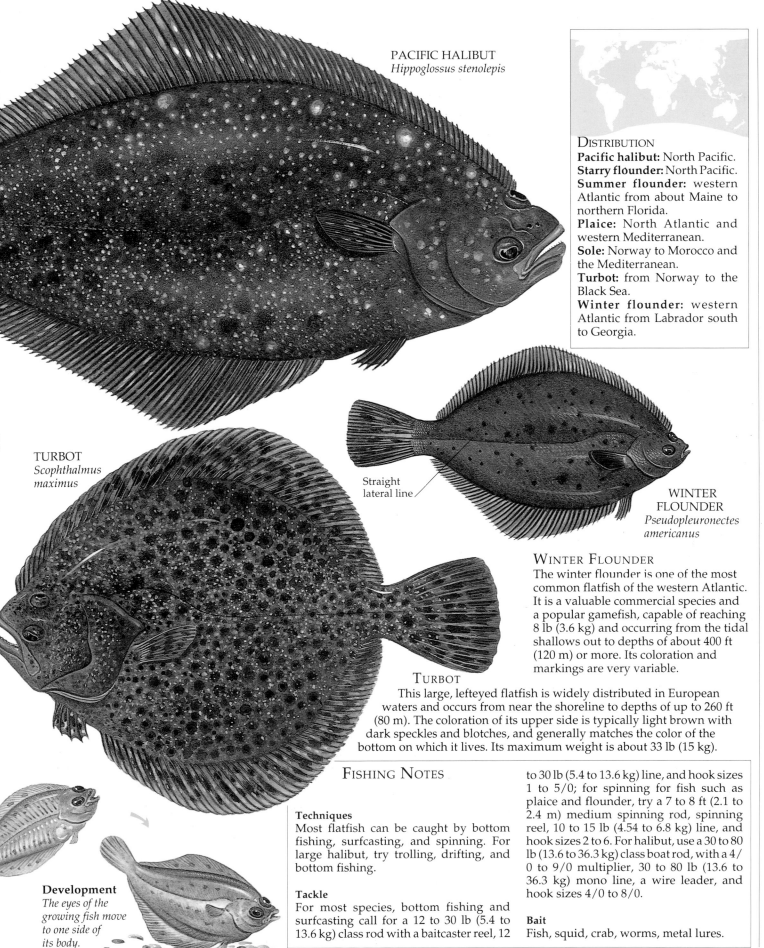

Development
The eyes of the growing fish move to one side of its body.

FISHING NOTES

Techniques
Most flatfish can be caught by bottom fishing, surfcasting, and spinning. For large halibut, try trolling, drifting, and bottom fishing.

Tackle
For most species, bottom fishing and surfcasting call for a 12 to 30 lb (5.4 to 13.6 kg) class rod with a baitcaster reel, 12 to 30 lb (5.4 to 13.6 kg) line, and hook sizes 1 to 5/0; for spinning for fish such as plaice and flounder, try a 7 to 8 ft (2.1 to 2.4 m) medium spinning rod, spinning reel, 10 to 15 lb (4.54 to 6.8 kg) line, and hook sizes 2 to 6. For halibut, use a 30 to 80 lb (13.6 to 36.3 kg) class boat rod, with a 4/0 to 9/0 multiplier, 30 to 80 lb (13.6 to 36.3 kg) mono line, a wire leader, and hook sizes 4/0 to 8/0.

Bait
Fish, squid, crab, worms, metal lures.

ORDER RAJIFORMES

Rays

The order Rajiformes consists of eight families of cartilaginous fish and includes the rays, mantas, sawfish, and skates *(see page 186)*. These fish are characterized by flattened bodies and wide, often winglike, pectoral fins; their mouths and gill openings are on the undersides and their eyes on the upper. In most families, the eggs are fertilized and hatch within the body of the female; the exception is the Rajidae, in which the internally fertilized eggs are laid before hatching.

Manta

The mantas or devil rays belong to the Mobulidae family, which contains about a dozen species. These range in size from the Australian mobula *(Mobula diabola)*, which measures about 2 ft (60 cm) across its wings, to the manta *(Manta birostris)*, which reaches 22 ft (6.7 m) across the wings and a weight of 4,000 lb (1,820 kg). Despite its tremendous size, the manta is a generally harmless fish that feeds on small fish and crustaceans, which it steers into its mouth with its cephalic fins, the pair of "horns" on its head. Mantas cruise between midwater and the surface, and frequently leap into the air, perhaps to rid themselves of parasites or maybe just for fun.

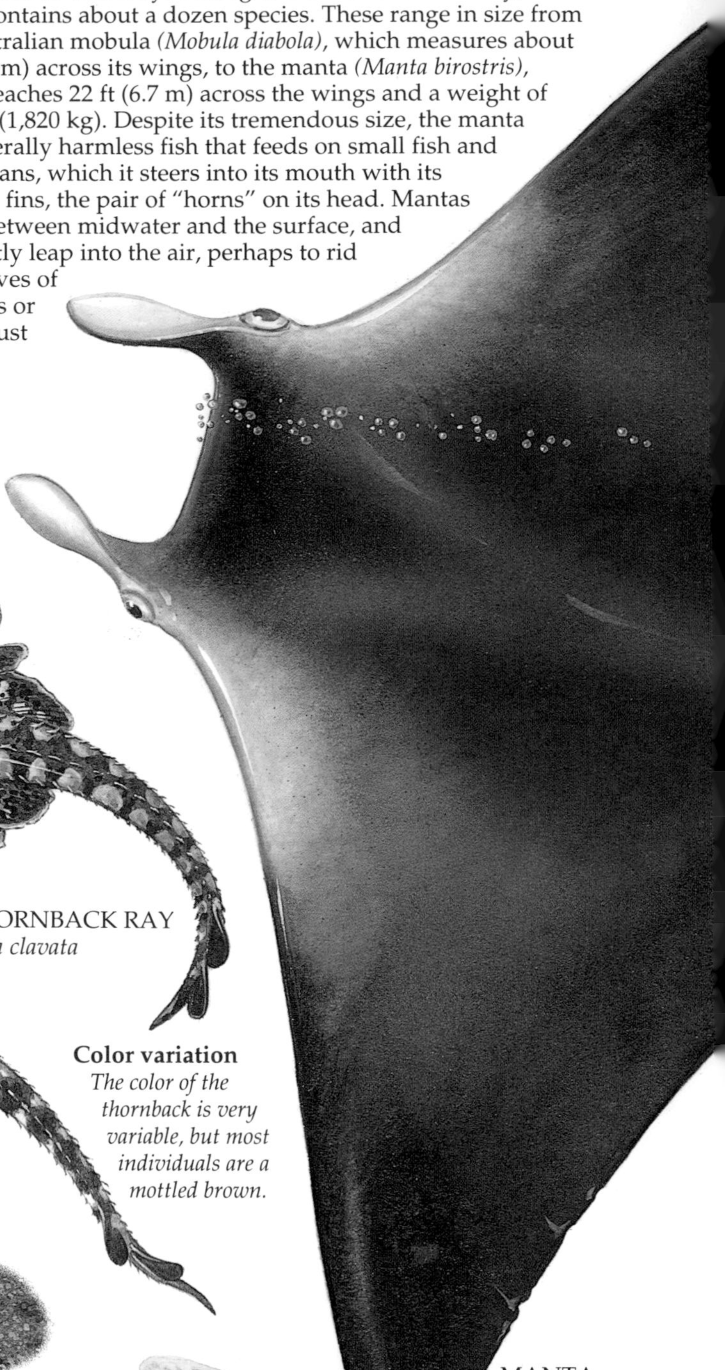

MANTA
Manta birostris

Thornback Ray

The thornback is the most common ray in European waters. A member of the Rajidae family, it is a bottom-dweller found at depths of about 30 to 200 ft (10 to 60 m), and gets its name from the numerous thorny spines on its tail, back, and pectoral fins. Young thornbacks live in shallow water and feed on small crustaceans, and as they grow they move into deeper water and begin feeding on larger prey including crabs and fish. They grow to about 40 lb (18 kg).

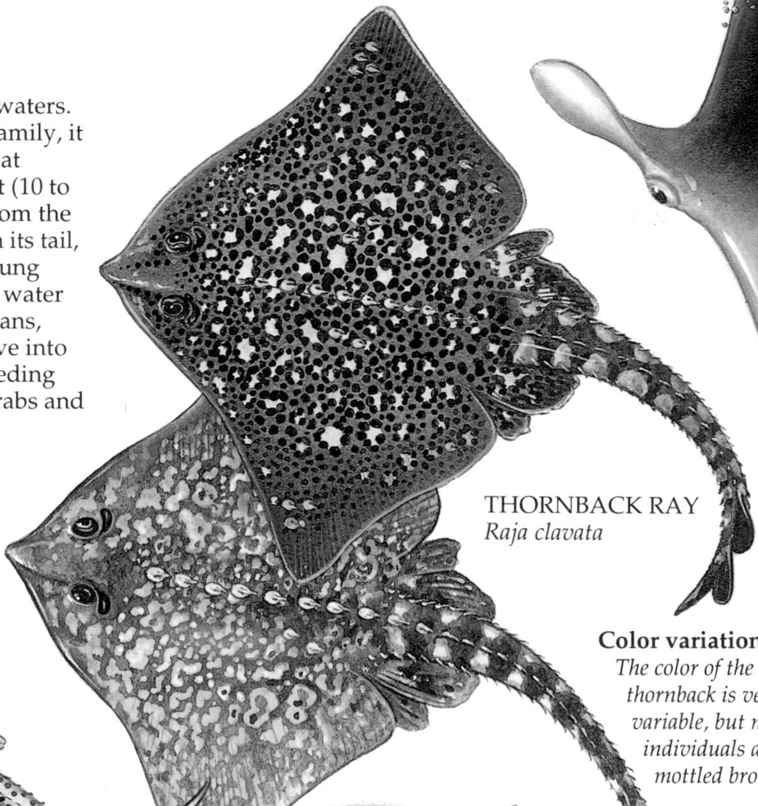

THORNBACK RAY
Raja clavata

Color variation
The color of the thornback is very variable, but most individuals are a mottled brown.

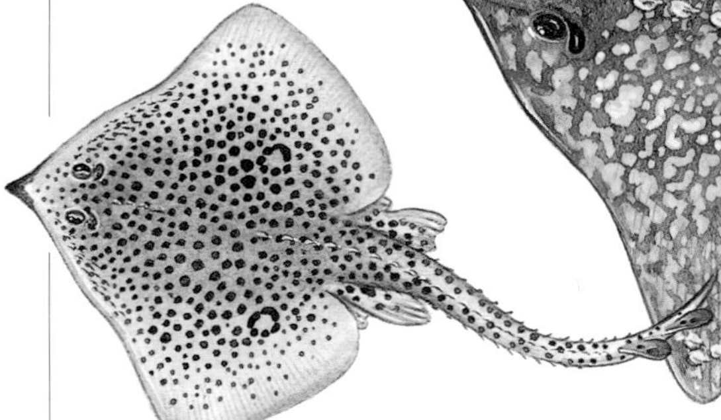

SPOTTED RAY
Raja montagui

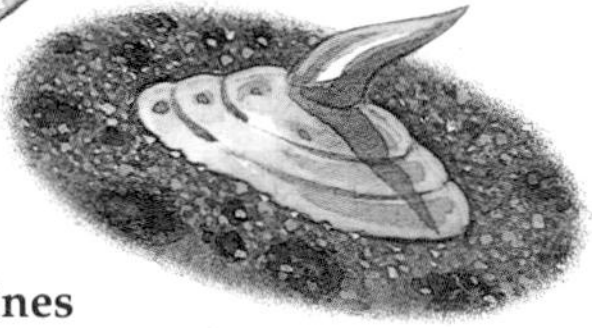

Spines
The thorny spines of the thornback and many other species have a strong, buttonlike base.

Spotted Ray

Like the thornback, the spotted ray is a European member of the Rajidae family. It lives in deeper water than the thornback, preferring depths of about 200 to 400 ft (60 to 120 m), and is a smaller fish, with a maximum weight of around 8 lb 6 oz (3.8 kg). Its diet consists mainly of crustaceans but it will also take small fish.

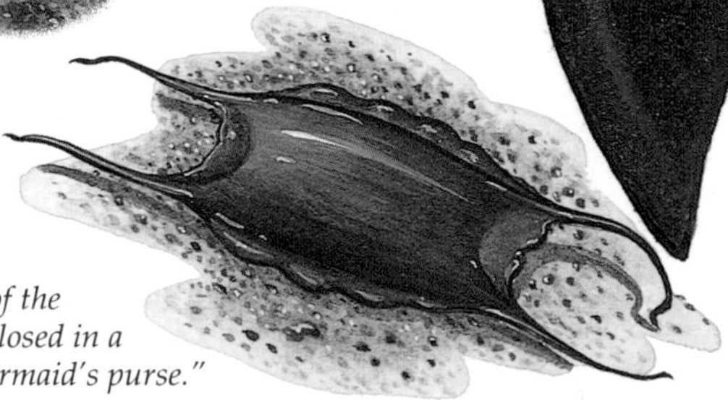

Egg cases
The eggs laid by members of the Rajidae family are each enclosed in a tough case known as a "mermaid's purse."

Size comparison

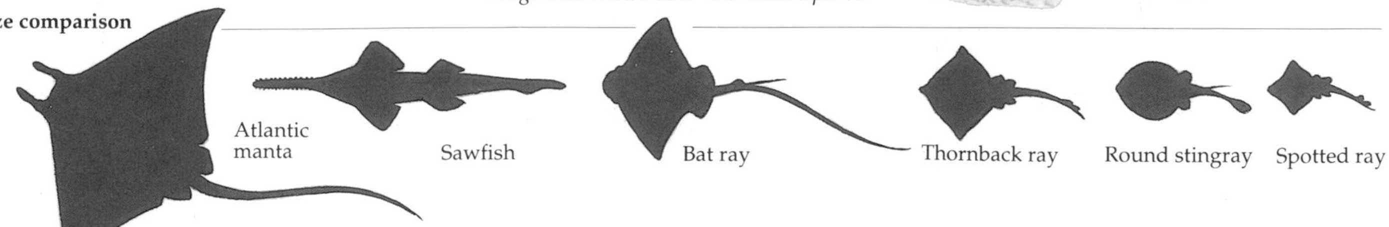

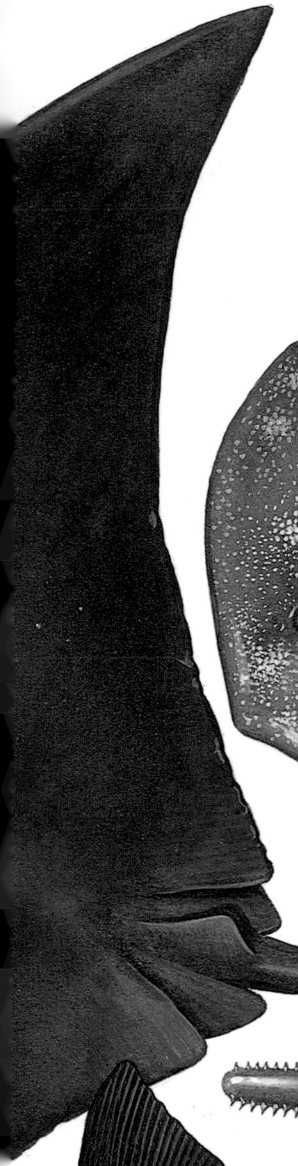

Round Stingray

The stingrays, members of the Dasyatidae family, have one or more venomous spines on their whiplike tails. Any wounds inflicted by the spines must get prompt medical attention because they can be fatal. The round stingray, measuring about 1 ft 10 in (56 cm) across the wings, is one of the smaller species; the Atlantic roughtail stingray *(Dasyatis centroura)* can be 7 ft (2.1 m) across.

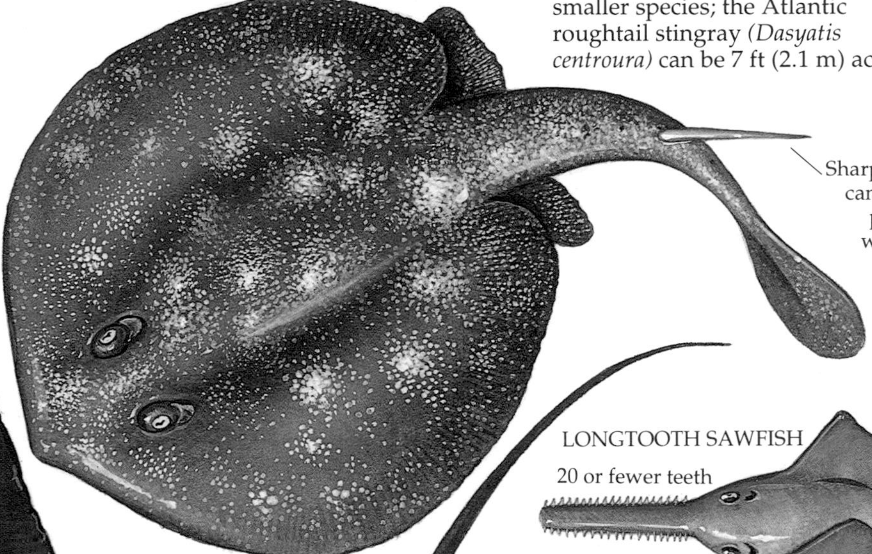

ROUND STINGRAY
Urolophus halleri

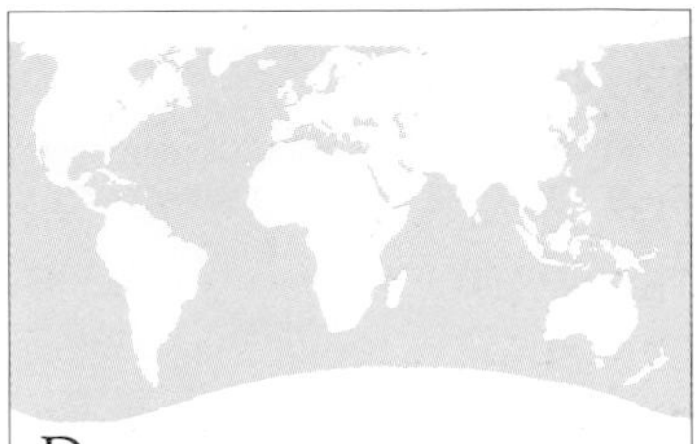

Distribution

Manta: worldwide in warm-temperate and tropical waters.
Thornback ray: from Iceland to the Black Sea.
Spotted ray: from Scotland to the western Mediterranean.
Round stingray: from northern California to Panama.
Smalltooth sawfish: Mediterranean and warm-temperate and tropical Atlantic.
Bat ray: from Oregon to the Gulf of California.

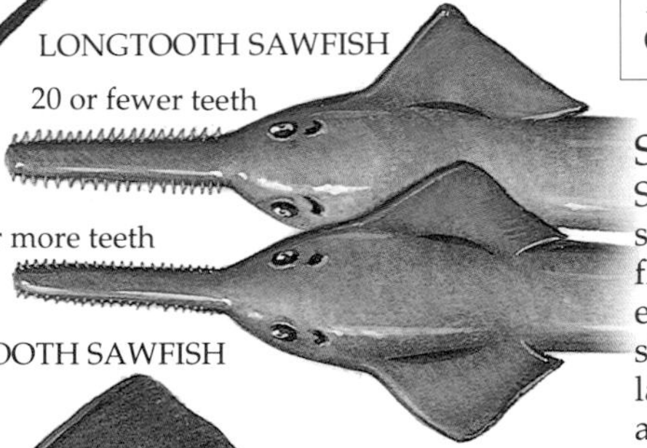

Sawfish

Sawfish (the Pristidae) are sharklike rays with elongated, flattened snouts that are equipped with rows of strong, sharp teeth along each side. The largetooth sawfish *(Pristis pristis)* and the smalltooth sawfish *(P. pectinata)* are Atlantic species that can reach weights of up to 800 lb (360 kg). Sawfish are also found in freshwater; for example, the largetooth sawfish is found 470 miles (750 km) up the Amazon.

SMALLTOOTH SAWFISH
Pristis pectinata

Bat Ray

The bat ray is a member of the Myliobatidae, the eagle ray family, which consists of about 30 species. They are large, free-swimming rays with distinct heads and very long tails, and feed on the bottom on shellfish and crustaceans. The bat ray grows to about 6 ft (1.8 m) across the wings.

BAT RAY
Myliobatis californica

Fishing Notes

Techniques
Most rays live or feed on the bottom, so bottom fishing is the best technique. Manta usually feed at midwater or close to the surface, and are sometimes taken by trolling; they can be very dangerous and difficult to handle when hooked.

Tackle
For the thornback and spotted rays and the round stingray, use a heavy shore rod or a 20 lb (9.1 kg) class boat rod, with a 4/0 to 6/0 baitcaster, 25 lb (11.3 kg) mono line and a 30 lb (13.6 kg) mono leader, size 2/0 to 4/0 hook, and a bomb-shaped weight. For sawfish and manta, try an 80 to 130 lb (36.3 to 59 kg) class rod with 80 to 130 lb (36.3 to 59 kg) mono line and a heavy wire or nylon leader, and size 8/0 to 14/0 hook.

Bait
Peeler crab, sandworms, and strips of fish such as mackerel.

ORDER RAJIFORMES

SKATES

The skates are members of the Rajidae *(see also page 184)*, which contains over a hundred species and is the largest family within the order Rajiformes. Most skates are a mottled brownish color with whitish undersides, and their tails are relatively thick, rather than whiplike. Skates usually rest on the bottom during the day, lying partly buried in sand or mud, and become active at night to feed on shellfish, crustaceans, and sometimes small fish. They swim by making smooth undulations of their pectoral fins.

BIG SKATE
Raja binoculata

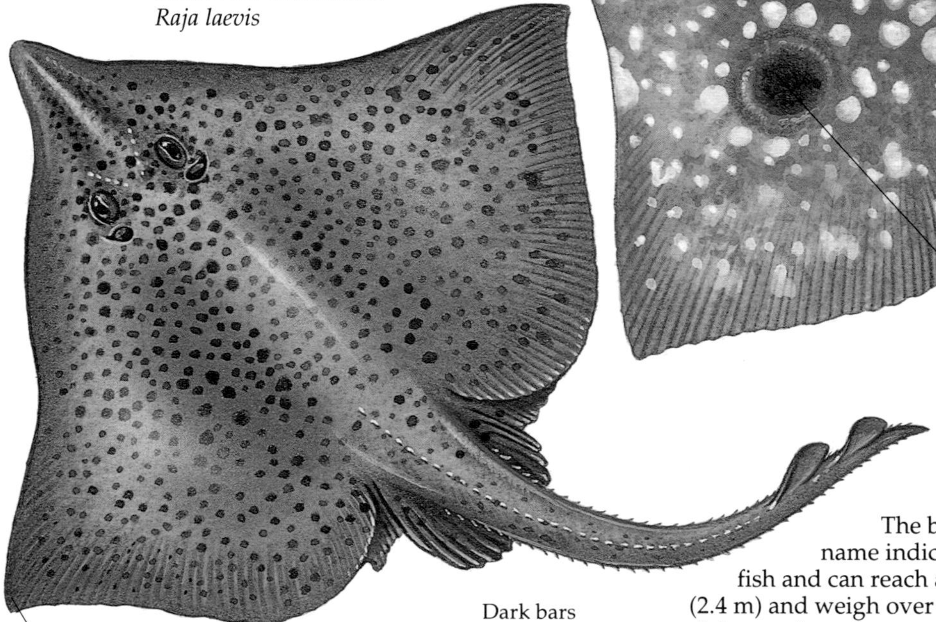

BARNDOOR SKATE
Raja laevis

BARNDOOR SKATE

This large, aggressive skate of the northwestern Atlantic grows to a length of around 5 ft (1.5 m) and a weight of 40 lb (18 kg). It is found from the tidal shallows out to depths of 1,410 ft (430 m), and will sometimes enter brackish water. It has a noticeably pointed snout, large, black pores on its underside, and a smooth skin. Its wings (pectoral fins) have concave leading edges and sharply angled corners. It feeds mainly on large crustaceans, mollusks, and fish such as herring, and it will readily take a baited hook.

BIG SKATE

The big skate, as its name indicates, is a large fish and can reach a length of 8 ft (2.4 m) and weigh over 200 lb (91 kg). It has a triangular snout, and there is a large eyespot on the upper surface of each wing. The big skate is found at depths of 10 to 360 ft (3 to 110 m) along the Pacific coast of North America, and the southern part of its range overlaps that of the California skate *(Raja inornata)*. This skate is much smaller, about 2 ft 6 in (76 cm) long, with a sharply pointed snout and usually no eyespots.

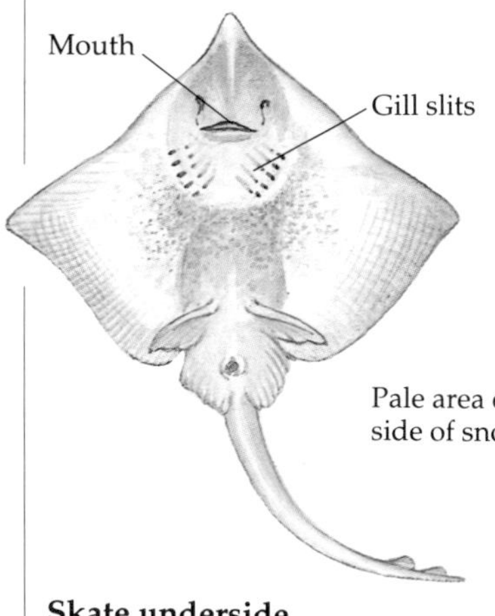

Skate underside
The underside of a skate is usually a pale, whitish color. The mouth is just below the snout, and just above the two sets of five gill slits.

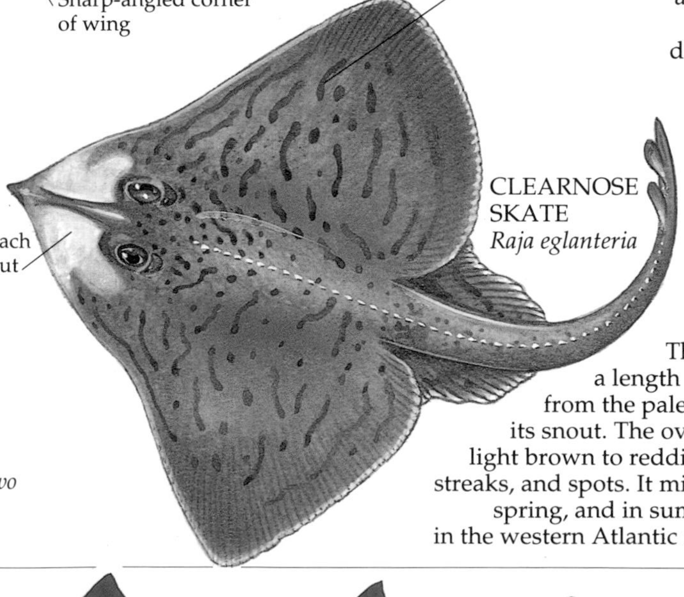

CLEARNOSE SKATE
Raja eglanteria

CLEARNOSE SKATE

The clearnose skate, which grows to a length of about 3 ft (90 cm), gets its name from the pale, translucent areas at either side of its snout. The overall coloration of its upper side is light brown to reddish brown, marked with dark bars, streaks, and spots. It migrates inshore to breed during the spring, and in summer it is the most abundant skate in the western Atlantic from Long Island to the Carolinas.

Size comparison

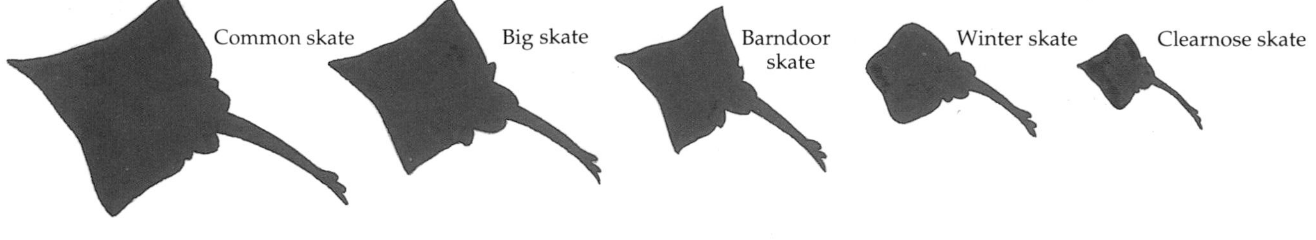

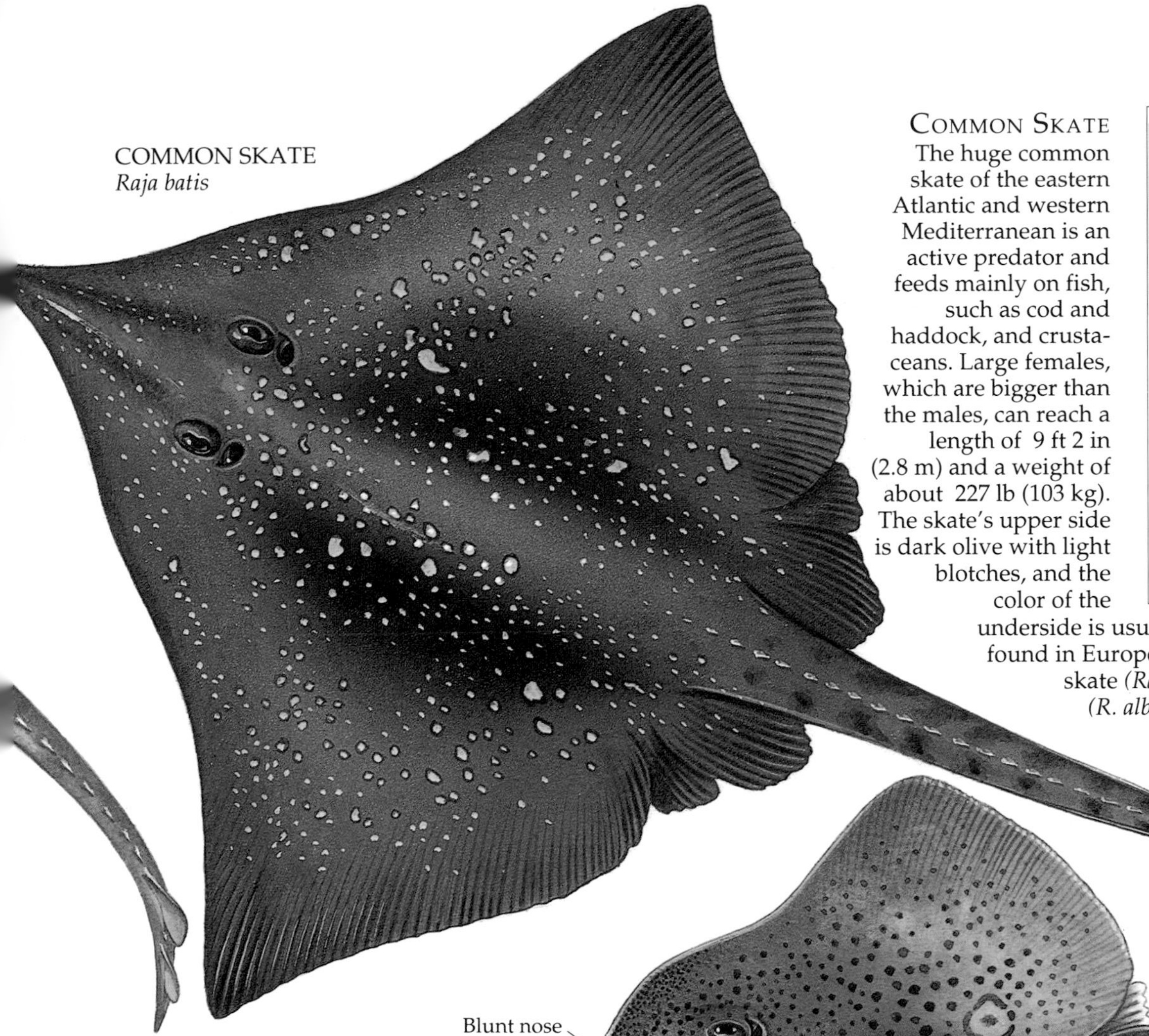

COMMON SKATE
Raja batis

Common Skate

The huge common skate of the eastern Atlantic and western Mediterranean is an active predator and feeds mainly on fish, such as cod and haddock, and crustaceans. Large females, which are bigger than the males, can reach a length of 9 ft 2 in (2.8 m) and a weight of about 227 lb (103 kg). The skate's upper side is dark olive with light blotches, and the color of the underside is usually a pale blue-gray. Other skates found in European waters include the long-nosed skate *(Raja oxyrinchus)* and the white skate *(R. alba)*. The long-nosed skate is similar in color to the common skate, but has a long, thin snout and the leading edges of its wings are more concave.

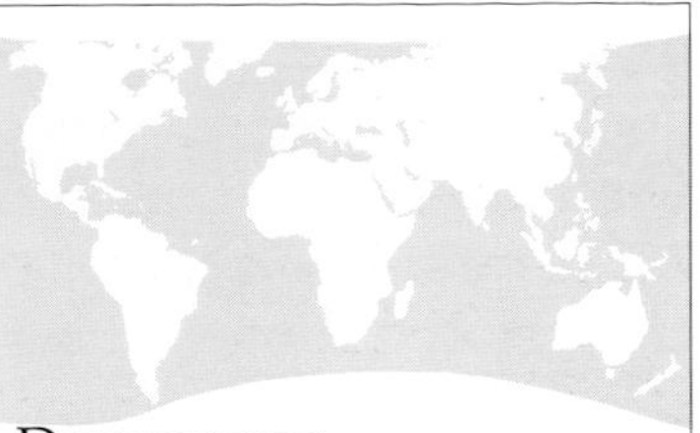

DISTRIBUTION
Barndoor skate, winter skate: from Newfoundland south to North Carolina.
Big skate: from the Bering Sea to Baja California.
Clearnose skate: from New England to the Gulf of Mexico.
Common skate: Iceland to Madeira; the Mediterranean.

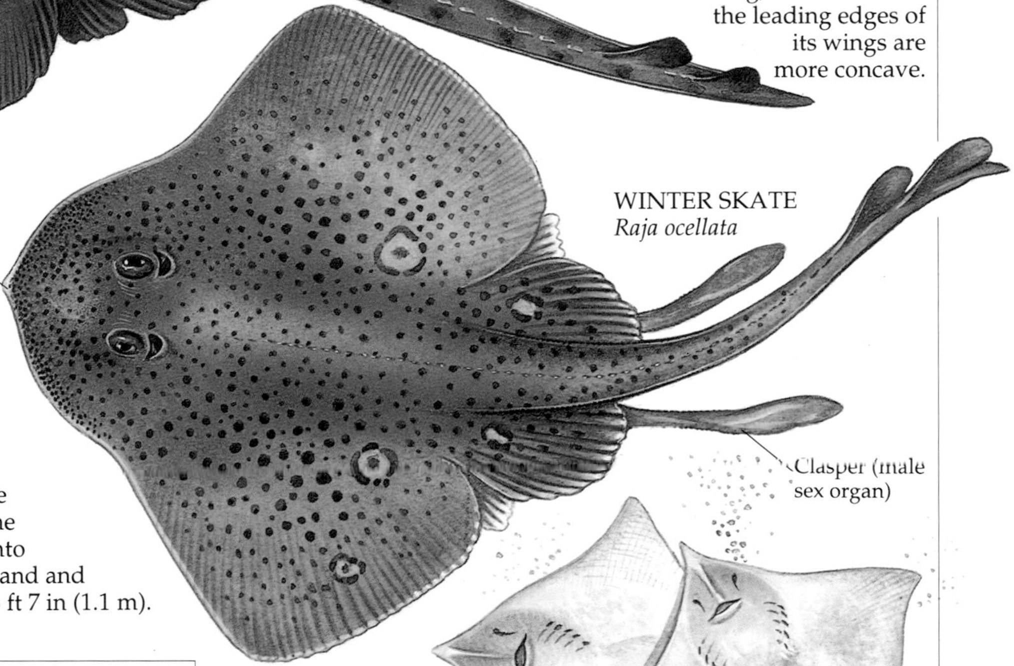

WINTER SKATE
Raja ocellata

Winter Skate

The winter skate usually has one to four eyespots on each wing, but these are sometimes absent. A winter skate with no eyespots closely resembles the little skate *(Raja erinacea)*, and the only reliable way to distinguish between the two is to count the rows of teeth in the upper jaw: the winter skate has at least 72, the little skate fewer than 66. The winter skate is so named because it migrates into inshore waters, principally between New England and New Jersey, in winter. It grows to a length of 3 ft 7 in (1.1 m).

Fishing Notes

Techniques
Bottom fishing from a boat is the usual method for skate.

Tackle
Use a 6½ to 7 ft (2 to 2.1 m), 50 lb (22.7 kg) class boat rod with a 4/0 to 6/0 baitcaster reel, 50 lb (22.7 kg) mono line and a 100 lb (45.4 kg) wire leader, size 6/0 to 8/0 brazed eye hooks, and a pyramid-shaped weight. Use a butt socket or full harness to help you exert maximum leverage on the rod when fighting the fish, and to make the fight less tiring for you: it can take a lot of effort to dislodge a skate from the bottom, and big skate have been known to fight hard for up to an hour.

Bait
Most skate are caught on fresh fish. Mackerel is particularly effective, but almost any common fish will do, and large strips of cuttlefish and squid are also good skate baits. Small fish can be used whole, because skate have big mouths and readily gulp them down.

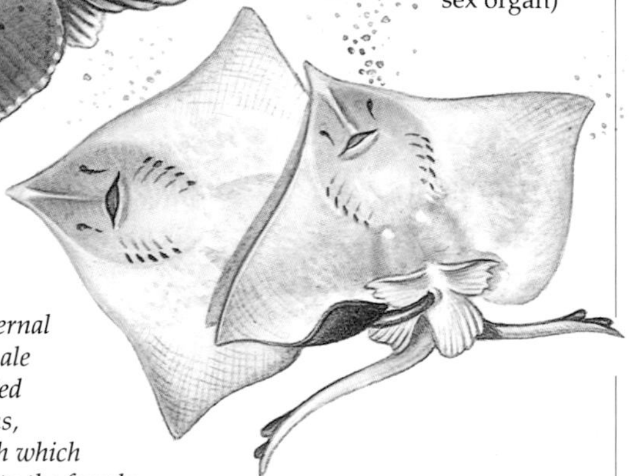

Mating
Skates breed by internal fertilization. The male has a pair of modified pelvic fin extensions, called claspers, with which he inserts sperm into the female.

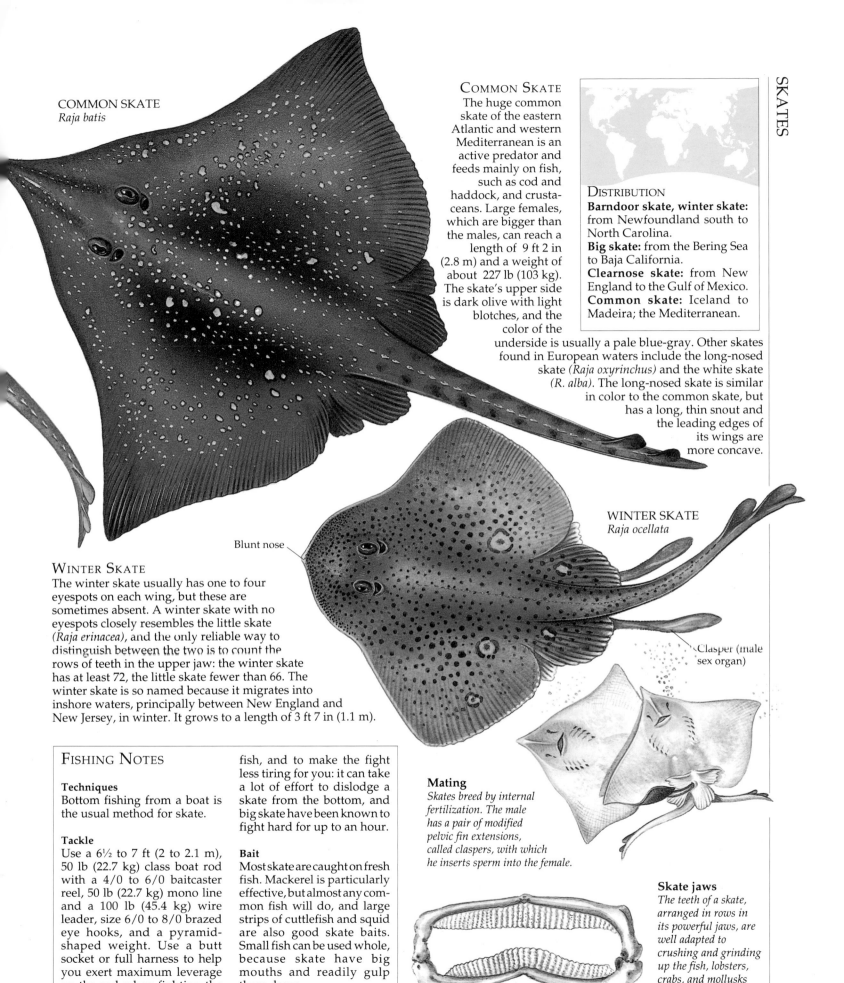

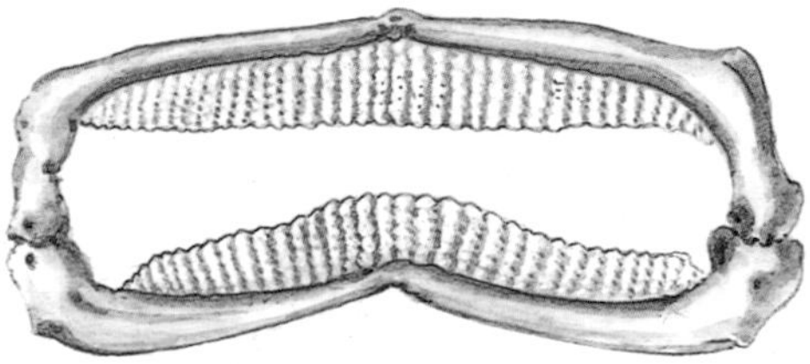

Skate jaws
The teeth of a skate, arranged in rows in its powerful jaws, are well adapted to crushing and grinding up the fish, lobsters, crabs, and mollusks that it feeds on.

Drum & Kahawai

The widely distributed Sciaenidae (drum) family consists of over 200 tropical and warm-temperate marine species – including drum, croaker, seatrout, seabass, and weakfish – plus the freshwater drum (*Aplodinotus grunniens*) of North America. Many species can make drumming sounds by contracting muscles on the walls of their swim bladders (gas-filled bladders that help to give them buoyancy). The kahawai, one of the two members of the Arripidae family, is also known as the Australian salmon because its juveniles bear a superficial resemblance to the Atlantic salmon.

Black Drum

The black drum grows to a weight of over 115 lb (52 kg), and its deep body is marked with four or five dark bars on each side. It is a bottom feeder, and uses the barbels on its chin to help it locate the crustaceans and mollusks that make up the bulk of its diet. It is an important gamefish, commonly caught from the shore and piers.

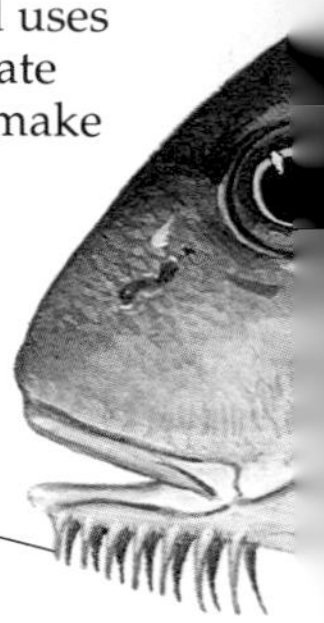

Red Drum

This large drum, also known as the redfish or channel bass, has a reddish overall coloration and one or more dark spots at the base of the tail. Its body is not as deep as that of the black drum, and it lacks chin barbels. It feeds at the bottom on crustaceans and mollusks and also takes small fish, especially mullet. The usual adult weight is under 40 lb (18 kg) but it can reach about 95 lb (43 kg).

RED DRUM
Sciaenops ocellatus

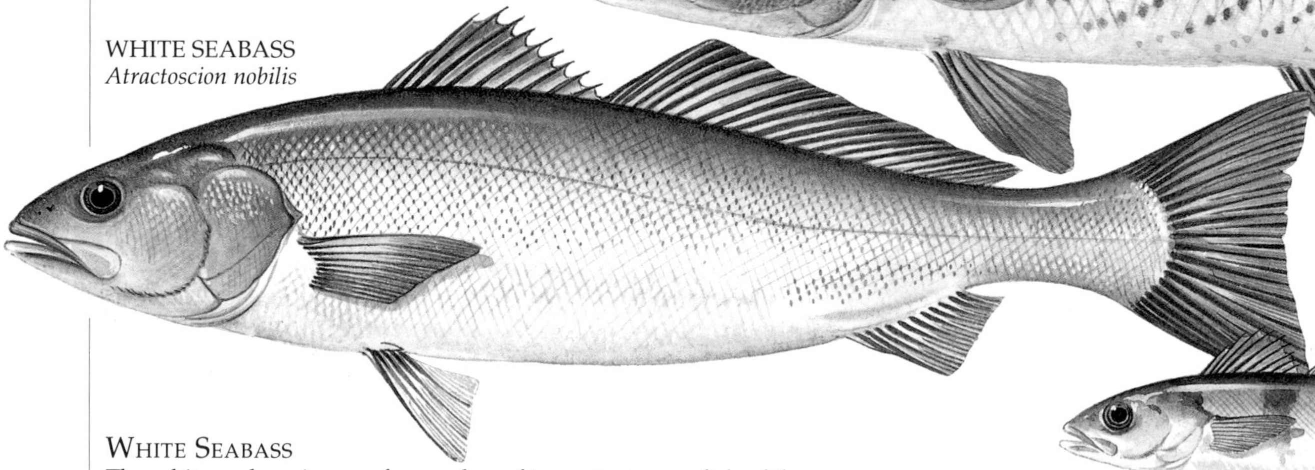

WHITE SEABASS
Atractoscion nobilis

JUVENILE
WHITE SEABASS

White Seabass

The white seabass is one of a number of important gamefish of the drum family found along the Pacific coast of North America. Others include the white croaker (*see opposite page*), the California corbina (*Menticirrhus undulatus*), the spotfin croaker (*Roncador stearnsii*), and the yellowfin croaker (*Umbrina roncador*). The white seabass is found over rocks, near kelp, and in the surf zone, feeding on fish and squid and growing to about 90 lb (41 kg).

Kahawai

The two members of the Arripidae family, the kahawai and the ruff (*Arripis georgianus*), are related to the Sciaenidae and resemble them in overall appearance. During the summer, kahawai form huge schools that cruise inshore near the surface, feeding on small fish and krill. Its average weight is 3 to 10 lb (1.36 to 4.54 kg), with a maximum of around 16 lb (7.3 kg).

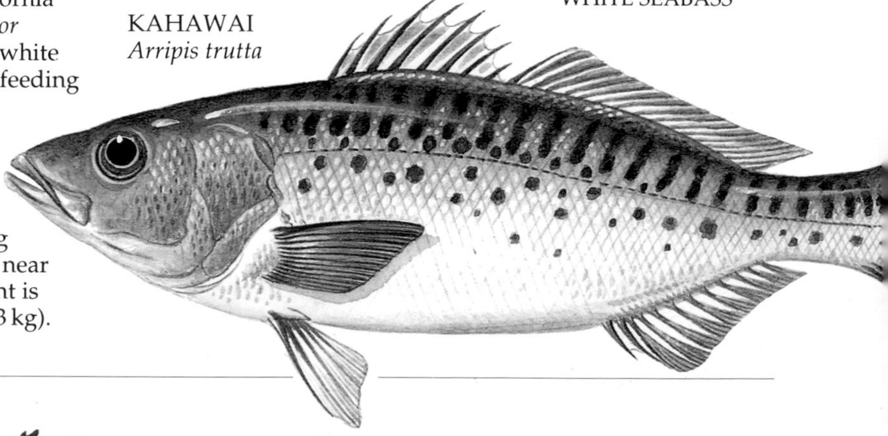

KAHAWAI
Arripis trutta

Size comparison

BLACK DRUM
Pogonias cromis

DISTRIBUTION
Black drum: Nova Scotia to Mexico; Brazil and Argentina.
Red drum: Massachusetts to northern Mexico.
White seabass: Alaska to the Gulf of California.
Kahawai: southern Australia (Perth to Sydney), New Zealand.
Spotted seatrout: New York to the Gulf of Mexico.
Weakfish: Nova Scotia to northern Florida.
White croaker: from British Columbia to Baja California.

SPOTTED SEATROUT
Cynoscion nebulosus

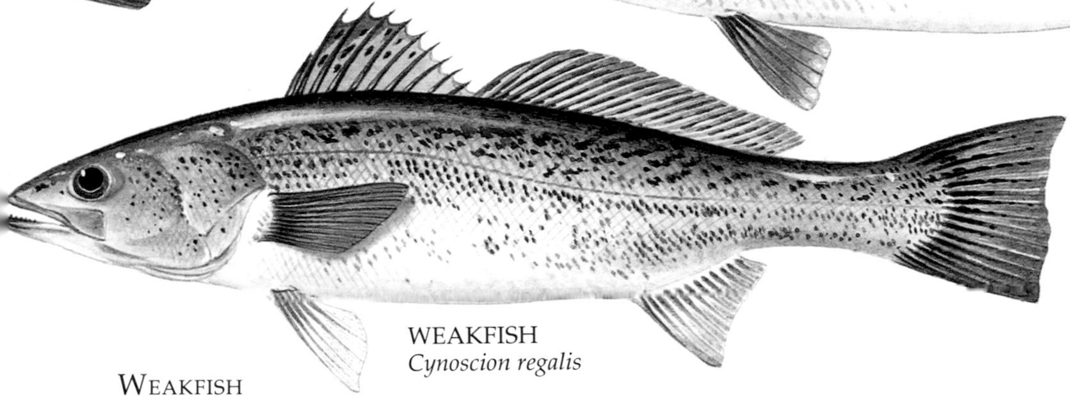

WEAKFISH
Cynoscion regalis

Spotted Seatrout

The spotted seatrout, which grows to about 16 lb (7.3 kg), is a very popular western Atlantic gamefish and, because of its delicate flesh, it is an important commercial species. It is attractively marked with numerous small black spots, which make it easily distinguishable from the unspotted, and smaller, sand seatrout (*Cynoscion arenarius*) and silver seatrout (*Cynoscion nothus*).

Weakfish

The weakfish is so named because its mouth is soft and tears easily when hooked. It forms small schools in shallow water over sandy ground, and feeds at the bottom on worms, crustaceans, and mollusks, and in midwater and at the surface on small fish. Weakfish weighing over 19 lb (8.6 kg) have been caught, but the average size is declining and a weight of over 6 lb (2.7 kg) is rare.

WHITE CROAKER
Genyonemus lineatus

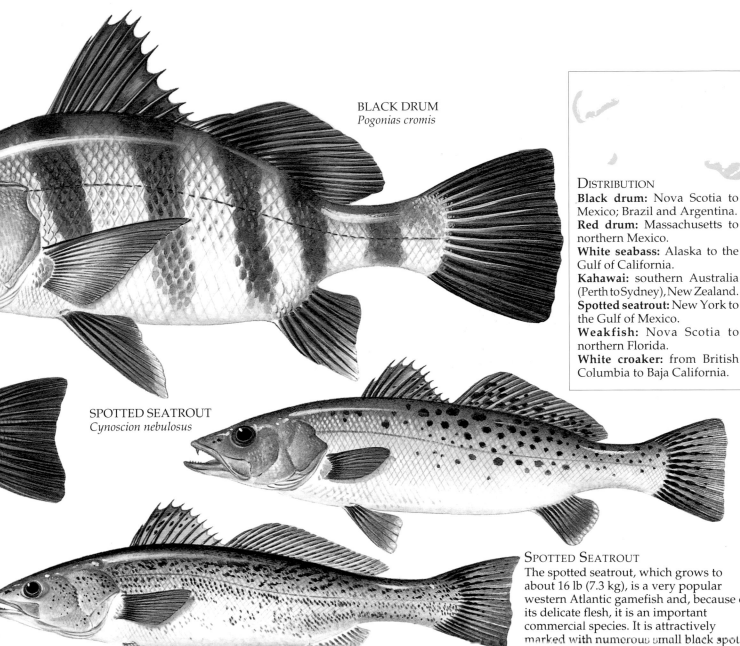

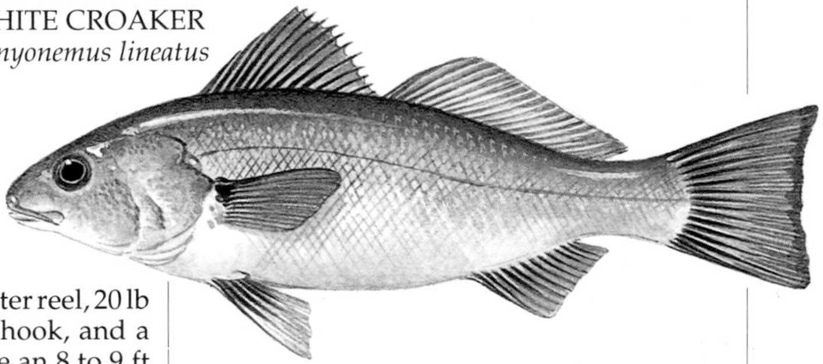

White Croaker

The white croaker is most reliably distinguished from other species of drum found along the Pacific coast of North America by the number of spines in its first dorsal fin: the white croaker has 12 to 16, the others 11 or fewer. It is found from close inshore to depths of 600 ft (183 m), and grows to about 1 lb (454 g).

Fishing Notes

Techniques
These fish are taken by a number of methods, the most usual being bottom fishing, surfcasting, and spinning.

Tackle
For bottom fishing, try a 30 lb (13.6 kg) class boat rod with a size 4/0 baitcaster reel, 30 lb (13.6 kg) mono line, size 4/0 hook, and a bomb-shaped sinker. When surfcasting, use a 12 ft (3.7 m) surfcasting rod with a spinning or baitcaster reel, 20 lb (9.1 kg) mono line, size 4/0 hook, and a grip sinker. For spinning, use an 8 to 9 ft (2.4 to 2.7 m) spinning rod with a spinning reel, 15 to 20 lb (6.8 to 9.1 kg) mono line, and size 1/0 to 4/0 hook.

Bait
Good baits include shrimp, fish, crab, clams, mussels, worms, and most types of artificial lure.

SCOMBRIDAE

MACKEREL

The Scombridae family consists of about 45 species and includes the many species of mackerel plus tuna, bonito, and wahoo. The typical scombrid is a fast-swimming predator with a beautifully streamlined, spindle-shaped body and a large, deeply forked or lunate (crescent-shaped) tail. Many scombrids are able to fold some of their fins into slots in their bodies to make them more streamlined and enable them to swim faster. The bluefin tuna, for example *(see page 193)*, withdraws its pectoral, pelvic, and first dorsal fins in this way when traveling at speed.

CHUB MACKEREL

The chub mackerel or Pacific mackerel can reach a weight of 6 lb 5 oz (2.9 kg) but usually does not exceed 2 lb 3 oz (1 kg). It occurs in temperate and subtropical waters worldwide but its distribution is uneven, and there are minor differences between the Atlantic and Pacific varieties. Both, however, have widely separated first and second dorsal fins and about 30 wavy, dark bars on the back. This species is a very important commercial fish, especially in the Pacific region, and is found in large schools in inshore waters.

ATLANTIC MACKEREL
Scomber scombrus

ATLANTIC MACKEREL

The Atlantic mackerel is very similar to the chub mackerel, but has fewer (20 to 23) dark bars on its back and lacks the dusky spotting on the flanks that is present in the Atlantic form of the chub mackerel. Some individuals, known as "scribble" mackerel, have dark, wormlike markings on their backs instead of bars. The Atlantic mackerel forms large schools, which can often be seen close inshore, feeding voraciously on small fish, and although it can grow to around 7 lb 8 oz (3.4 kg) the usual adult weight is about 1 lb 8 oz (680 g).

Jack mackerel

The jack mackerel or scad (Trachurus trachurus) *is not a mackerel but a member of the Carangidae* (see page 164). *It has a distinctive row of scutes (bony scales) along its lateral line.*

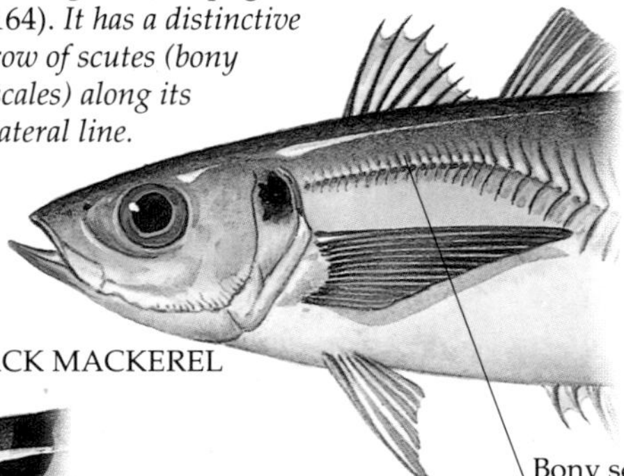

JACK MACKEREL

CERO

The orange and yellow stripes and spots along its side help to distinguish the cero from the somewhat similar king and Spanish mackerel. The species is found in the warmer parts of the western Atlantic and in the Caribbean, and although most of those caught are in the 5 to 10 lb (2.27 to 4.54 kg) range its maximum weight is thought to be about 35 lb (16 kg).

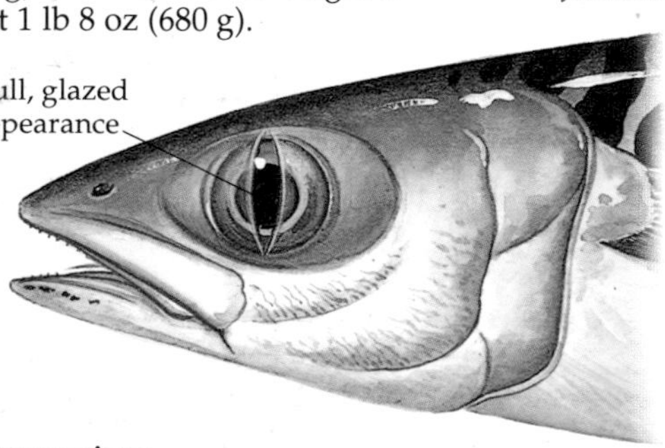

EYELIDS
Fish of the genus Scomber, *including the Atlantic and chub mackerels, are easily identified by their unusual eyelids. These are translucent membranes covering the front and rear margins of each eye, giving the eyes a dull appearance. These fish also have only five dorsal and anal finlets.*

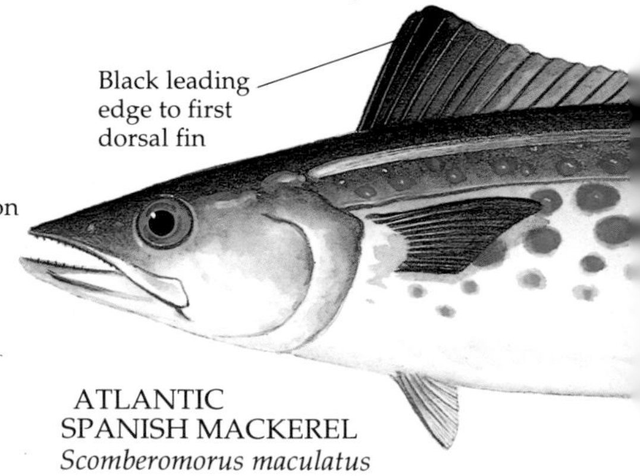

ATLANTIC SPANISH MACKEREL
Scomberomorus maculatus

Size comparison

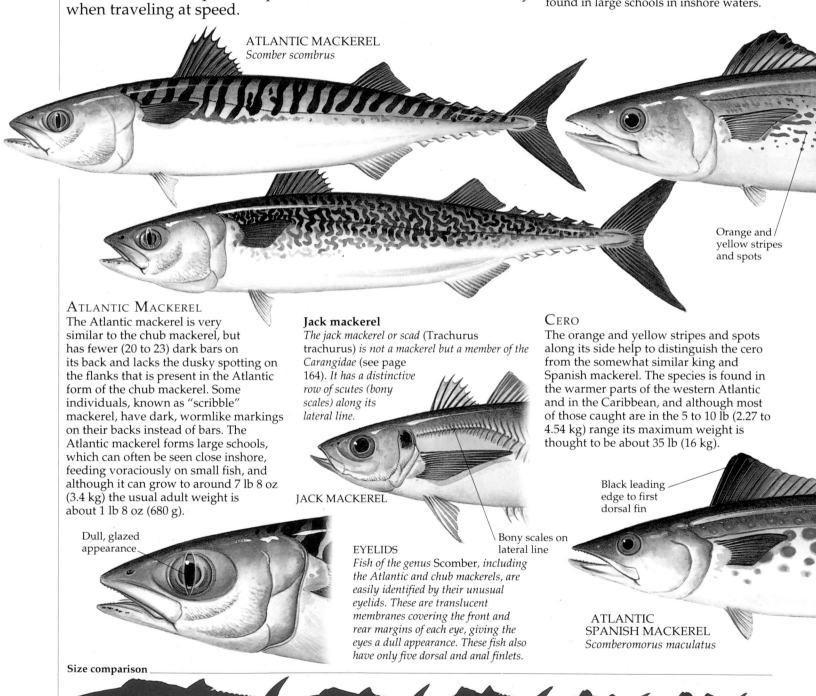

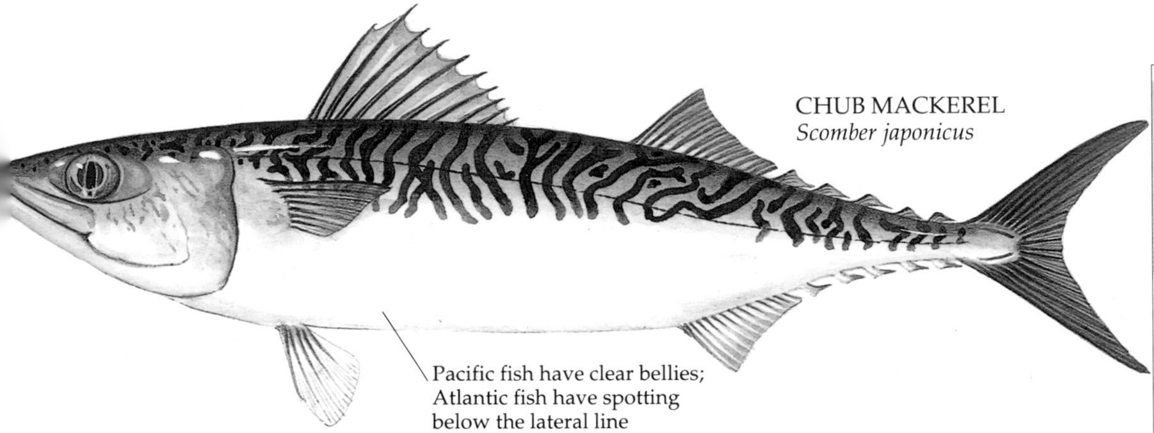
CHUB MACKEREL
Scomber japonicus
Pacific fish have clear bellies; Atlantic fish have spotting below the lateral line

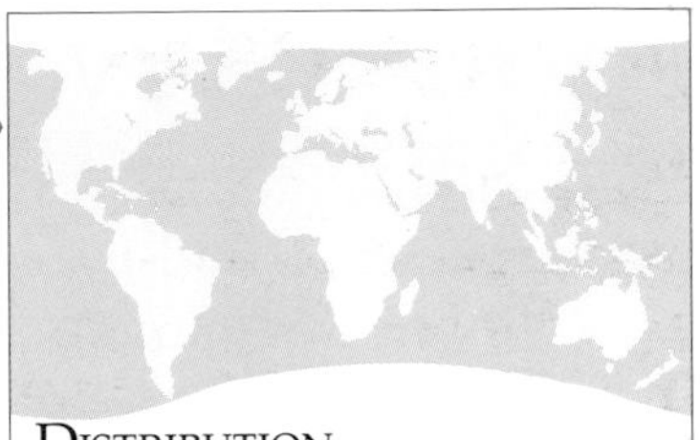

DISTRIBUTION
Chub mackerel: worldwide in temperate and tropical seas.
Atlantic mackerel: Atlantic, Mediterranean, Black Sea.
Horse mackerel: Atlantic, Mediterranean.
Cero and king mackerel: the western Atlantic from about Massachusetts to Brazil.
Atlantic Spanish mackerel: warm-temperate and tropical Atlantic waters; related species found in the Atlantic, Pacific, and Indian Oceans.

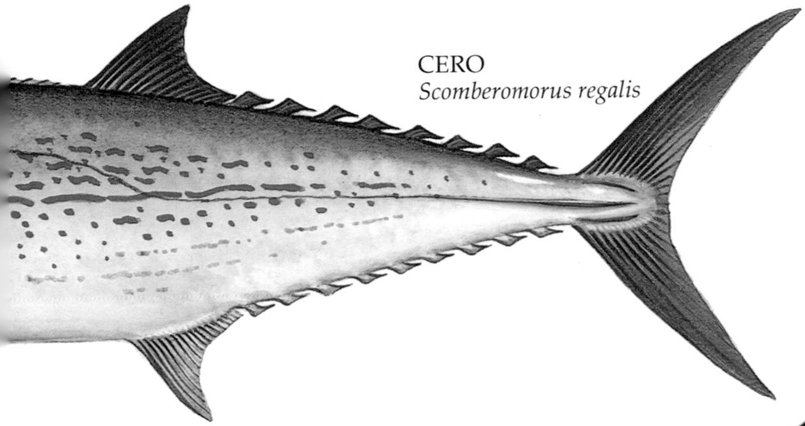
CERO
Scomberomorus regalis

KING MACKEREL

This is one of the largest mackerel and perhaps the most popular with anglers, who appreciate it for its size, the strong fight it puts up, and its tasty flesh. It averages only about 10 lb (4.54 kg), but it can grow much larger and individuals weighing around 100 lb (45.4 kg) have been netted by commercial fishermen. Huge schools of king mackerel gather in the Caribbean in the spring and migrate northward to the Gulf of Mexico. The fish in these schools are in the 7 to 25 lb (3 to 11 kg) range; larger fish tend to be more solitary.

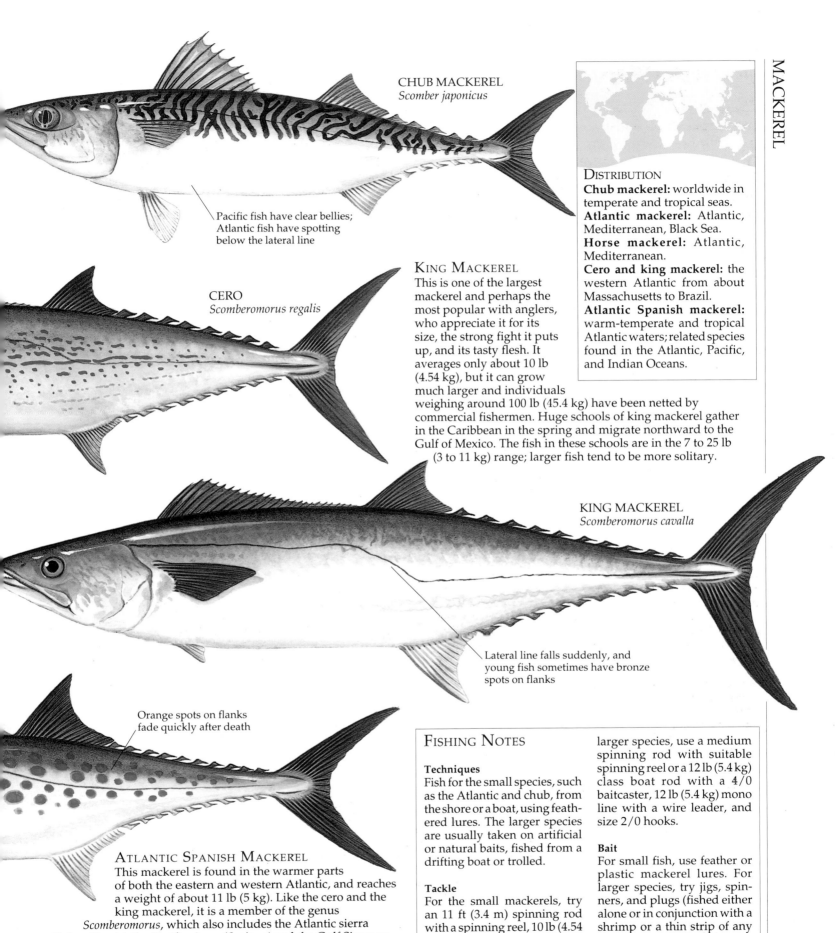

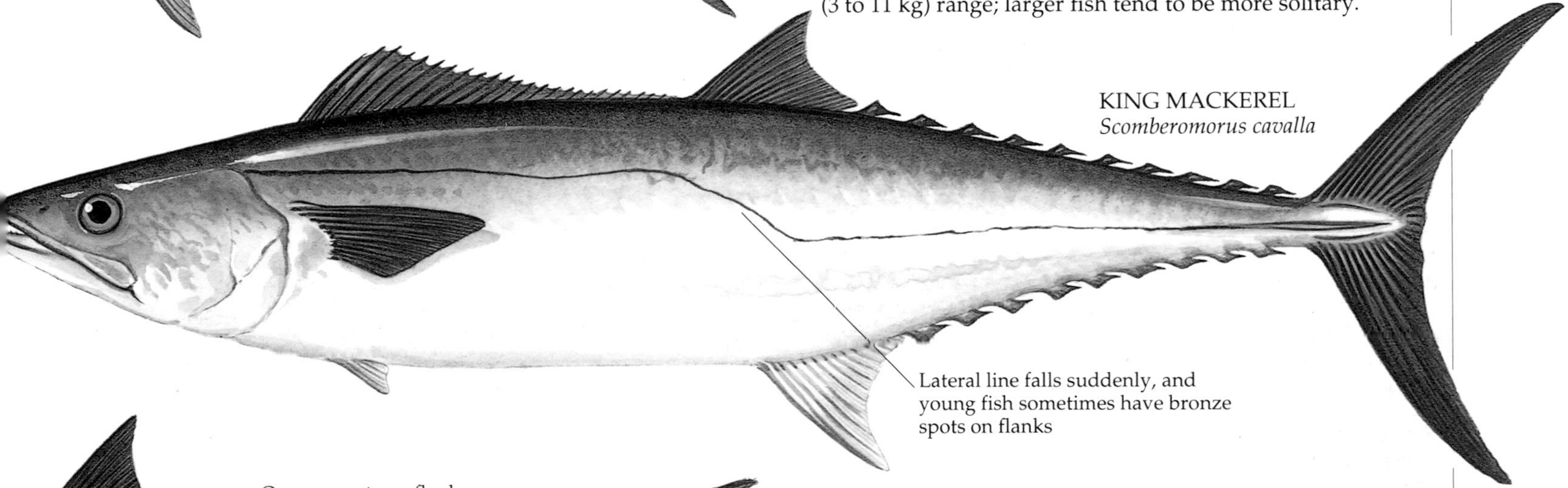
KING MACKEREL
Scomberomorus cavalla
Lateral line falls suddenly, and young fish sometimes have bronze spots on flanks

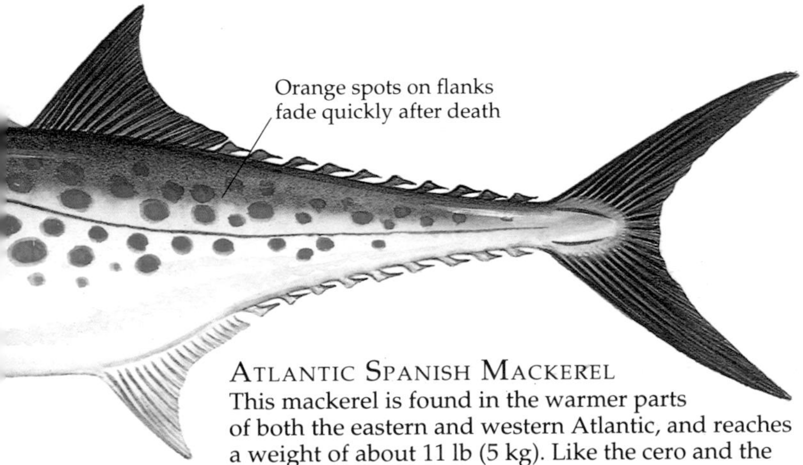
Orange spots on flanks fade quickly after death

ATLANTIC SPANISH MACKEREL

This mackerel is found in the warmer parts of both the eastern and western Atlantic, and reaches a weight of about 11 lb (5 kg). Like the cero and the king mackerel, it is a member of the genus *Scomberomorus*, which also includes the Atlantic sierra *(S. brasiliensis)*, the Pacific sierra *(S. sierra)* and the Gulf Sierra or Monterey Spanish mackerel *(S. concolor)*, both of which are Pacific species; and the Indo-Pacific mackerels *S. commerson* and *S. guttatus*, which are very common in Australian waters.

FISHING NOTES

Techniques
Fish for the small species, such as the Atlantic and chub, from the shore or a boat, using feathered lures. The larger species are usually taken on artificial or natural baits, fished from a drifting boat or trolled.

Tackle
For the small mackerels, try an 11 ft (3.4 m) spinning rod with a spinning reel, 10 lb (4.54 kg) line, a team of four lures with 1/0 hooks, and a 2 oz (57 g) bomb sinker. For the larger species, use a medium spinning rod with suitable spinning reel or a 12 lb (5.4 kg) class boat rod with a 4/0 baitcaster, 12 lb (5.4 kg) mono line with a wire leader, and size 2/0 hooks.

Bait
For small fish, use feather or plastic mackerel lures. For larger species, try jigs, spinners, and plugs (fished either alone or in conjunction with a shrimp or a thin strip of any common baitfish), and cut or whole baitfish such as mullet and balao.

SCOMBRIDAE

Tuna & Wahoo

These members of the Scombridae family are widespread in temperate and tropical waters, and have considerable commercial importance as well as being important gamefish. The commercial value of tuna led to them being fished for with enormous driftnets, especially in the Pacific, but use of these nets has been restricted by international agreements because they took a heavy toll not only of tuna but also of unsought-for species including dolphins, sunfish, billfish, and Ray's bream.

Albacore

Because of its very long pectoral fins, which extend beyond the front of the anal fin, the albacore is also known as the longfin tuna. These fins help to distinguish the albacore from other tuna such as the bluefin. The Atlantic and the Pacific albacore were once considered to be separate species but are now known to be identical, and reach weights of around 95 lb (43 kg).

Blackfin Tuna

The blackfin of the western Atlantic is one of the smaller tuna, averaging less than 10 lb (4.54 kg) with a maximum of about 42 lb (19 kg). It is renowned more for its delicious flesh than for its sporting qualities, and large numbers are taken by blue marlin as well as by commercial fishermen.

BLACKFIN TUNA
Thunnus atlanticus

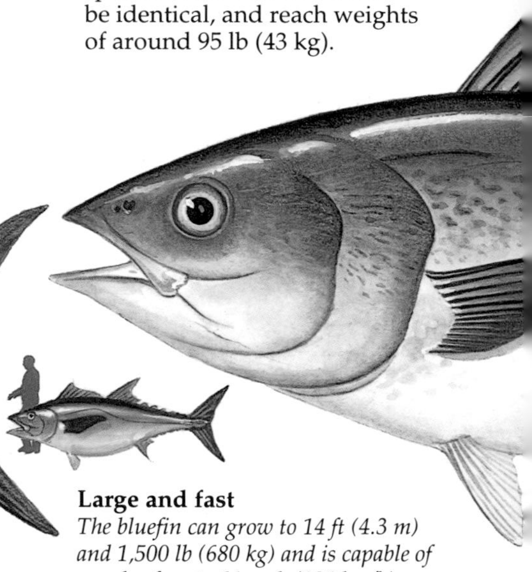

Large and fast
The bluefin can grow to 14 ft (4.3 m) and 1,500 lb (680 kg) and is capable of speeds of up to 64 mph (104 km/h).

Little Tunny

The little tunny of the Atlantic and the Mediterranean is a popular gamefish, occurring in large schools close to the shore. It is very similar to the skipjack tuna and the other species of *Euthynnus* found in the Pacific, and grows to a maximum of about 26 lb (12 kg); most of those caught are, however, much smaller.

LITTLE TUNNY
Euthynnus alletteratus

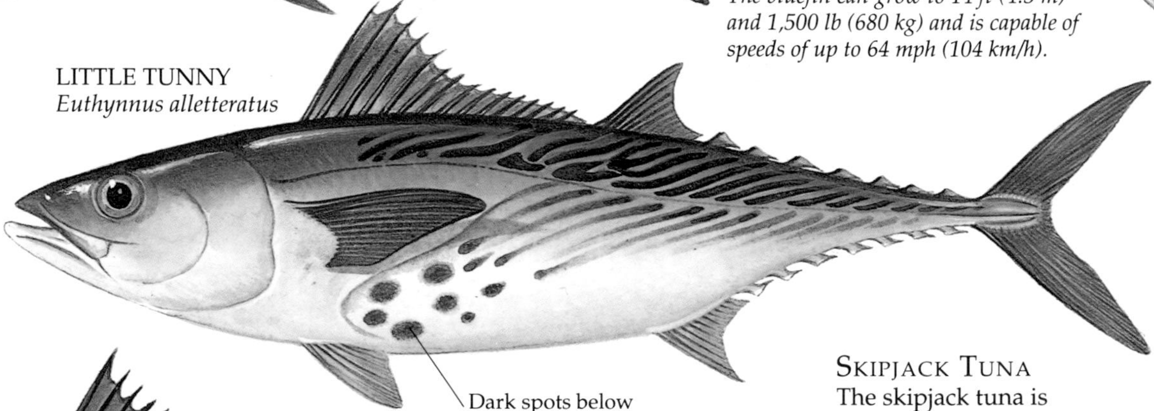

Skipjack Tuna

The skipjack tuna is found in most temperate and tropical oceans and can reach a weight of 77 lb (35 kg). Two very similar species occur in the Pacific: the wavyback skipjack or kawakawa *(Euthynnus affinis)* and the black skipjack *(E. lineatus)*.

SKIPJACK TUNA
Euthynnus pelamis

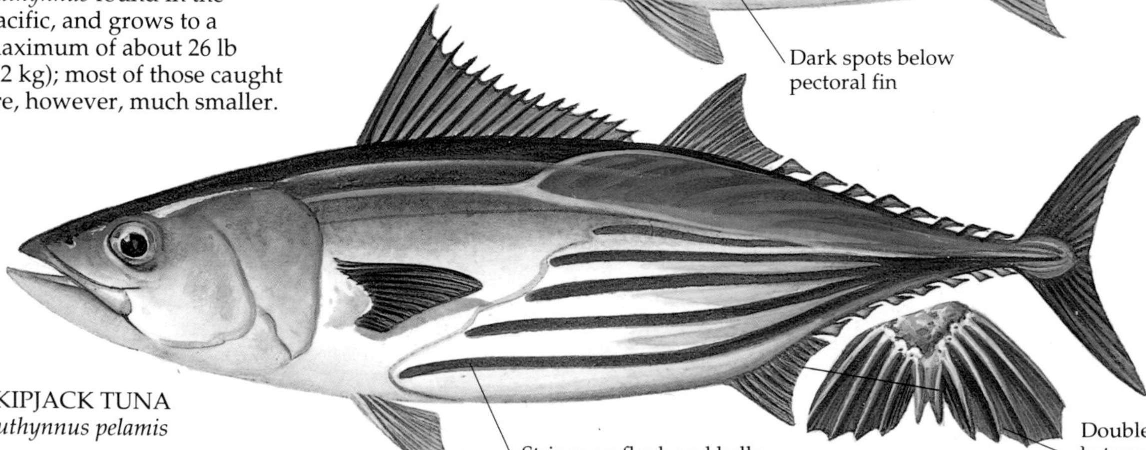

Size comparison

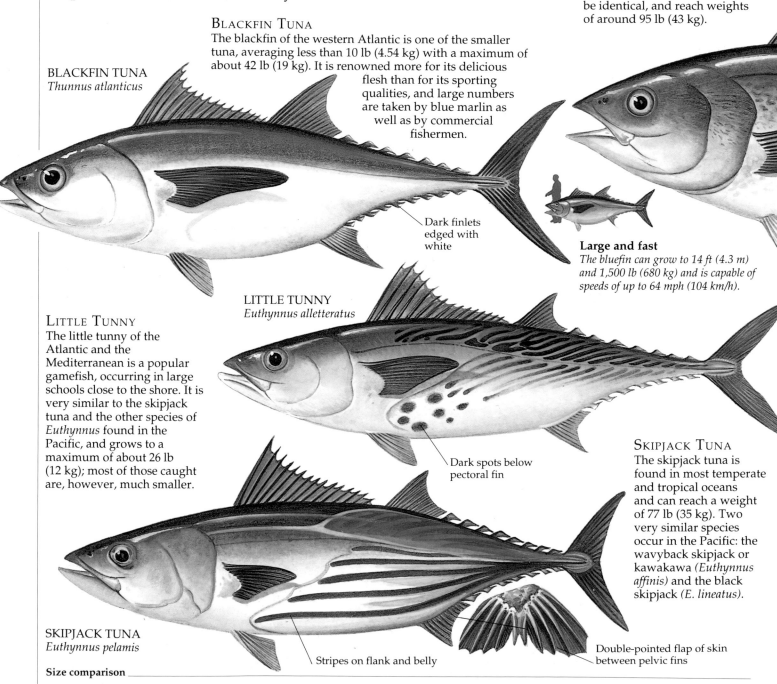

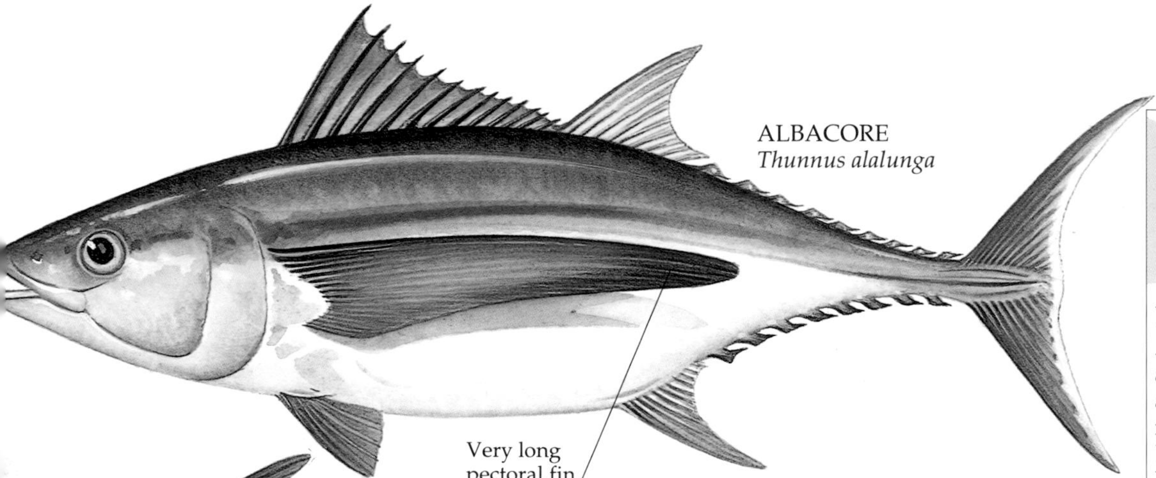

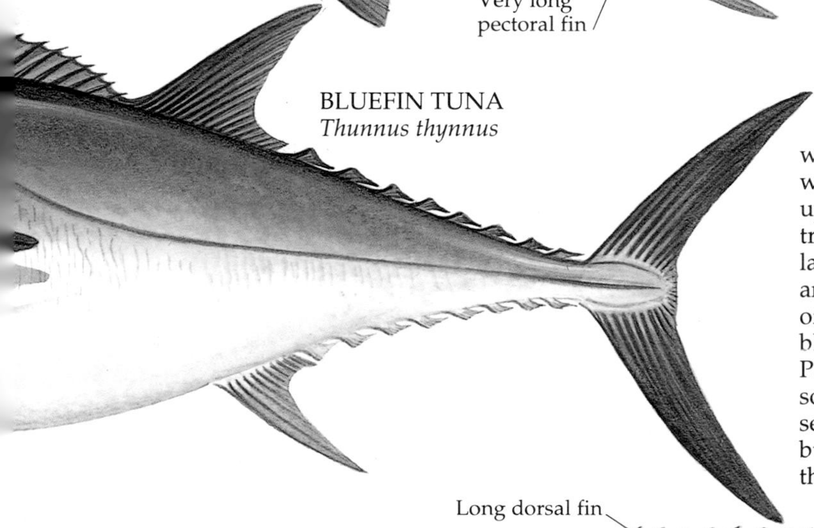

Bluefin Tuna

The bluefin is a highly migratory fish, which is found in subtropical seas during winter and moves into cooler waters in summer. Bluefin of up to about 100 lb (45 kg) travel in huge schools, but larger fish form smaller schools and the biggest individuals are often solitary. North Atlantic bluefin and those found in the Pacific and Indian Oceans are sometimes classified as separate species or subspecies, but the differences between them are very slight.

Distribution

Albacore: in most temperate and tropical waters; more abundant in the Pacific than in the Atlantic.
Blackfin tuna: Atlantic from Massachusetts to Brazil.
Little tunny: warm-temperate and tropical Atlantic waters and the Mediterranean.
Skipjack tuna, bluefin tuna: worldwide in temperate and tropical waters.
Wahoo: most warm-temperate and tropical waters.

Finlets
One of the distinctive features of the members of the Scombridae, including the wahoo, is the presence of delicate, soft-rayed finlets between the tail, dorsal, and anal fins.

Wahoo

The long, slender-bodied wahoo makes tremendous runs with abrupt changes of direction when hooked, sometimes leaping from the water, and this makes it one of the most exciting fish to catch. Its long, heavily toothed jaws form a beaklike snout, and its first dorsal fin is long, low, and spiny. The average weight is about 15 to 20 lb (6.8 to 9 kg), but it can grow to 183 lb (83 kg) and a length of 6 ft 11 in (2.1 m).

Fishing Notes

Techniques
Trolling with lures and drift fishing with natural baits are the usual methods of fishing for tuna, little tunny, and albacore. When fishing for wahoo, try trolling with lures and natural baits, and drift fishing with natural baits. Wahoo are usually taken on flatlines that are fished quite near to the boat, rather than lines on outriggers.

Tackle
For tuna, use an 80 to 130 lb (36.3 to 59 kg) class rod with full roller rings, a lever drag multiplier, and 80 to 130 lb (36.3 to 59 kg) nylon line with a 400 to 600 lb (181 to 272 kg) nylon leader. Use hook sizes 10/0 to 12/0, flat for trolling and offset for drifting. For wahoo, use a 30 to 50 lb (13.6 to 22.7 kg) class rod with a 6/0 star drag or 30- to 50-class baitcaster reel, 30 to 50 lb (13.6 to 22.7 kg) nylon line with a heavy wire leader, and a flat hook size 5/0 to 10/0.

Bait
Use a Kona Head lure when trolling for tuna, and try live mackerel or dead herring when drifting. When trolling for wahoo, use a Kona Head or other large artificial, or try a natural bait, such as a whole mullet or balao, mounted for trolling. For drift fishing, use a live baitfish on hook sizes 5/0 to 8/0.

HEAD OF WAHOO

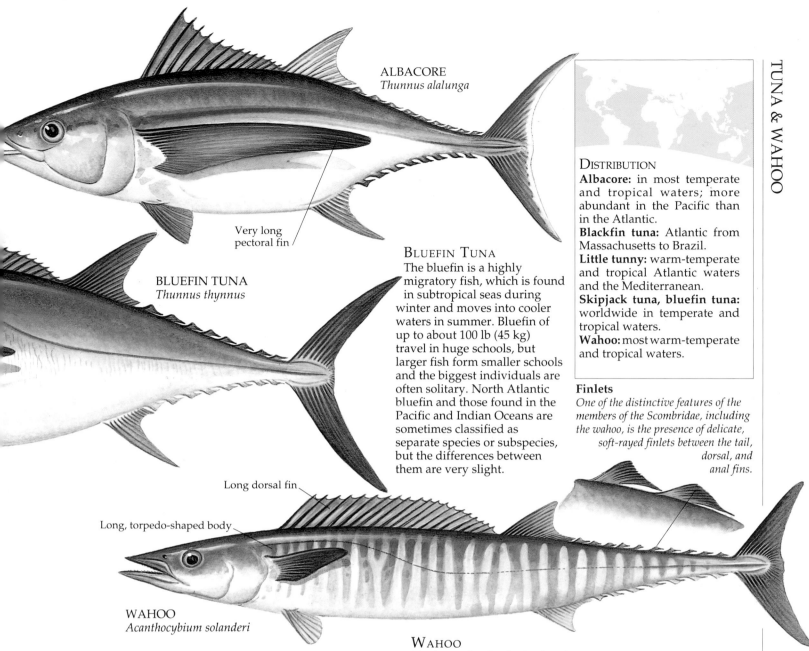

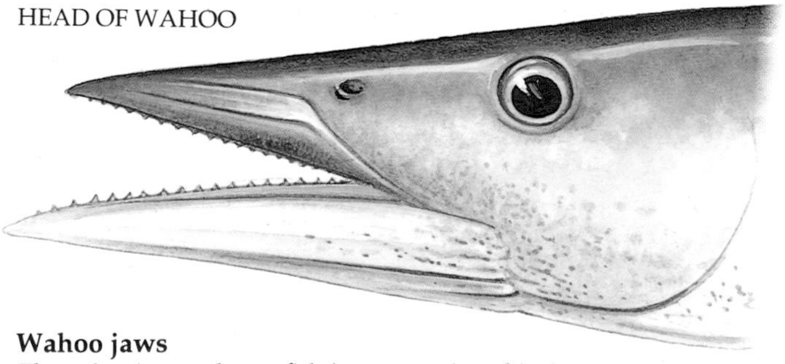

Wahoo jaws
The wahoo is a predatory fish (as are tuna), and its jaws contain rows of flat-sided, razor-sharp teeth that enable it to rip into squid and schools of baitfish. An unusual feature of the wahoo is that both its jaws are movable.

Bonito & Shad

Bonito, like mackerel and tuna *(see pages 190–193)*, belong to the Scombridae family. They are fast-swimming predators that feed on squid and small schooling fish, including mackerel, taken just below the surface. Shad, fish of the genus *Alosa*, are members of the herring family, the Clupeidae. They are marine fish that spawn in freshwater (some species also have landlocked populations), and differ from most other herring species in having a "keel" or "sawbelly," a ridge of sharp-edged scales along the belly.

Pacific Bonito

The Pacific bonito is a medium-sized fish that averages less than 12 lb (5.4 kg) but can grow to over 24 lb (11 kg). The northern and southern populations of the eastern Pacific are regarded as separate subspecies. Those north of Baja California are classified as *Sarda chiliensis lineolata*, and those off Peru and Chile as *S. c. chiliensis*. The striped bonito, *S. orientalis*, occurs from Baja to Peru, and in the western Pacific.

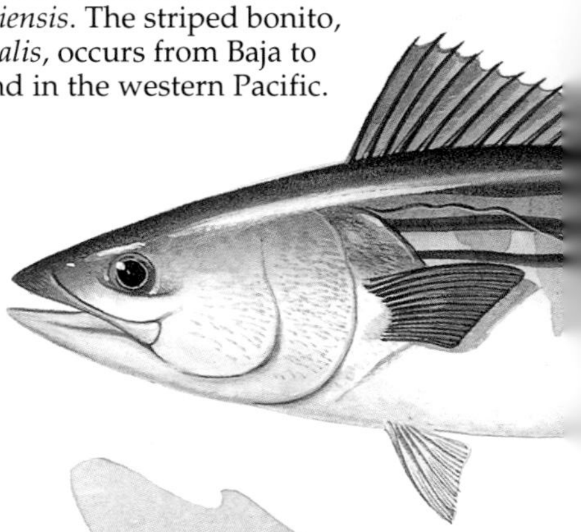

TWAITE SHAD
Alosa fallax

Twaite Shad

This shad differs from the Atlantic herring (*Clupea harengus*) in having a notch in its upper jaw, into which the lower jaw fits, a keel of sharp scales along its belly, and often has dark blotches along each side. Its maximum weight is about 3 lb 2 oz (1.4 kg).

ALLIS SHAD
Alosa alosa

Allis Shad

The allis shad is similar to the twaite shad, but its keel is more pronounced and there may be a single dark blotch on each side, just behind the gill cover. It is also larger, reaching a weight of 6 lb (2.7 kg). Populations of both species have been severely depleted, mainly by pollution and damming of their spawning rivers.

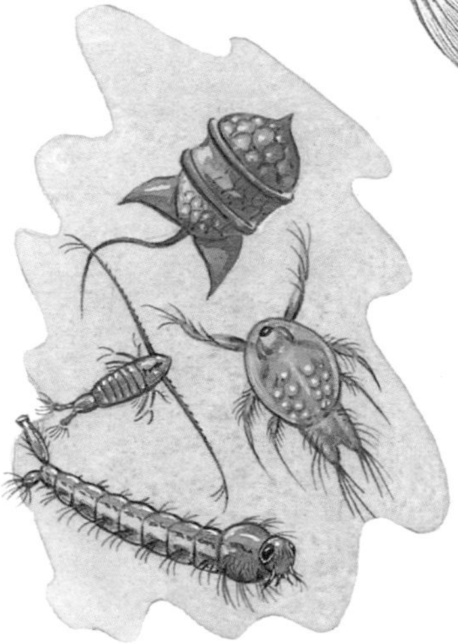

Shad diet
The diet of shad consists mainly of plankton, both animal and plant, plus insect larvae and copepods (tiny crustaceans). Skipjack herring and twaite, allis, and hickory shad also feed on small fish.

American Shad

The American shad, which is capable of reaching a weight of over 12 lb (5.5 kg), has a large, dark spot behind each gill cover and usually one or two rows of dark spots along each side. It feeds almost entirely on plankton, and the adults have no jaw teeth.

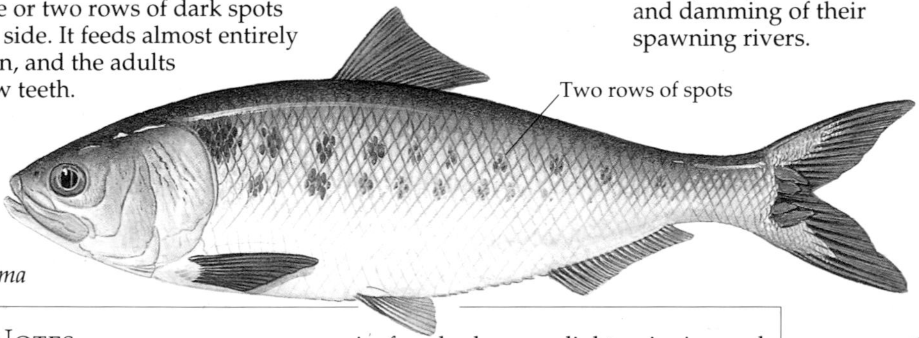

AMERICAN SHAD
Alosa sapidissima

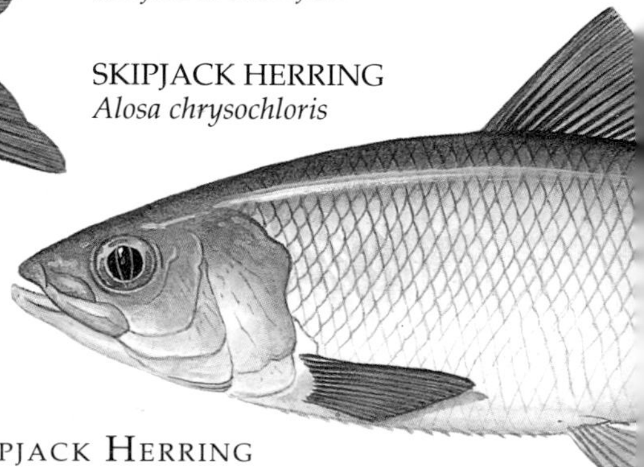

SKIPJACK HERRING
Alosa chrysochloris

Skipjack Herring

The skipjack herring is also known as the river herring, and when in freshwater it prefers the open water of medium to large rivers and stillwaters. It is very similar to the hickory shad, but its flanks have a brassy tinge and no dark spots. Its maximum weight is about 3 lb 8 oz (1.6 kg).

Fishing Notes

Techniques
Trolling and spinning for bonito, spinning and fly fishing for shad.

Tackle
To troll for bonito, use a 12 lb (5.4 kg) class boat rod with a size 2/0 baitcaster reel, 12 lb (5.4 kg) mono line, and a size 2/0 hook. When spinning for bonito, try a light spinning rod with a spinning reel, 12 lb (5.4 kg) line, and size 2/0 hook. To spin for shad, use a light spinning rod with a spinning reel, 8 lb (3.6 kg) mono line, and small lures with treble hooks. For fly fishing, try a 9 ft (2.7 m) trout rod, weight-forward floating line, and flies tied on size 6 to 8 hooks.

Bait
For bonito, good baits include plugs, spoons, plastic squid, and whole or cut squid and fish. For shad, try small spinners and bar spoons, and small, white-colored flies.

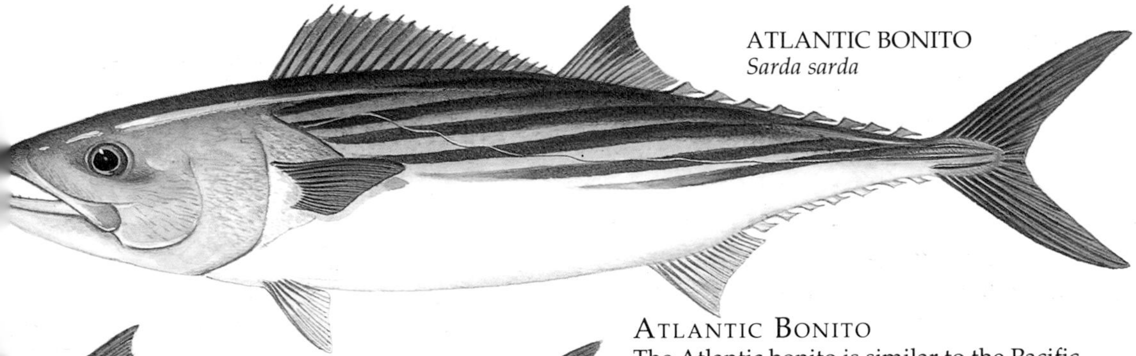

Atlantic Bonito

The Atlantic bonito is similar to the Pacific bonito, but the stripes on its sides are more oblique, and it has 20 to 23 spines in its first dorsal fin, whereas its Pacific counterpart has 17 to 19. When feeding, it develops a yellow stripe along each side of its back and a series of dark, vertical bars down each side. These fade when it stops feeding. It travels in schools at depths between about 165 ft (50 m) and the surface, and its average weight is 3 lb (1.36 kg) with a maximum of around 19 lb (8.6 kg).

Distribution

Pacific bonito: Pacific Ocean.
Twaite shad and allis shad: western European waters.
American shad: from about Newfoundland to northern Florida; Siberia to Mexico.
Skipjack herring: Mississippi basin and Gulf Slope.
Atlantic bonito: Atlantic and Mediterranean.
Australian bonito: southwest Pacific and Tasman Sea.
Hickory shad: from Maine to Florida.
Alewife: Great Lakes; from Labrador to South Carolina.

Australian Bonito

This bonito is found in the southwest Pacific, in the waters off Norfolk Island, southeast Australia, and New Zealand. The stripes on its sides are almost horizontal, rather than oblique like those of the Atlantic and Pacific species, and they are also present along the belly. It grows to a maximum weight of about 22 lb (10 kg).

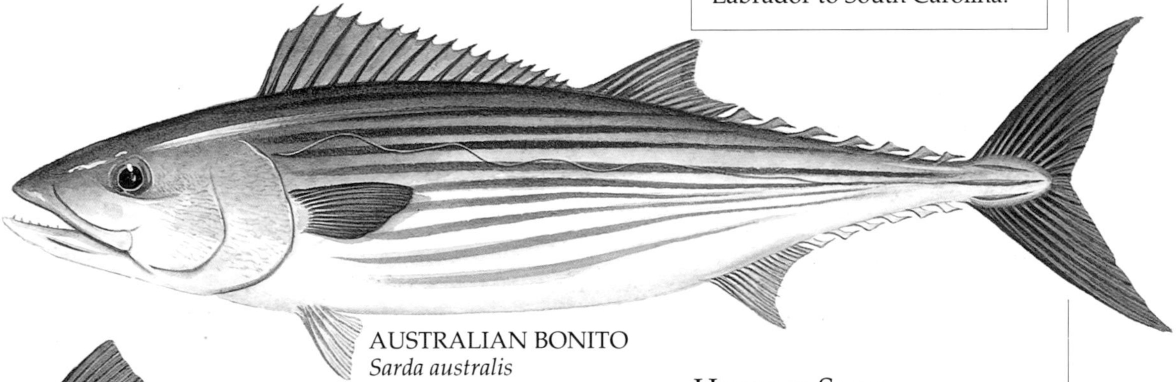

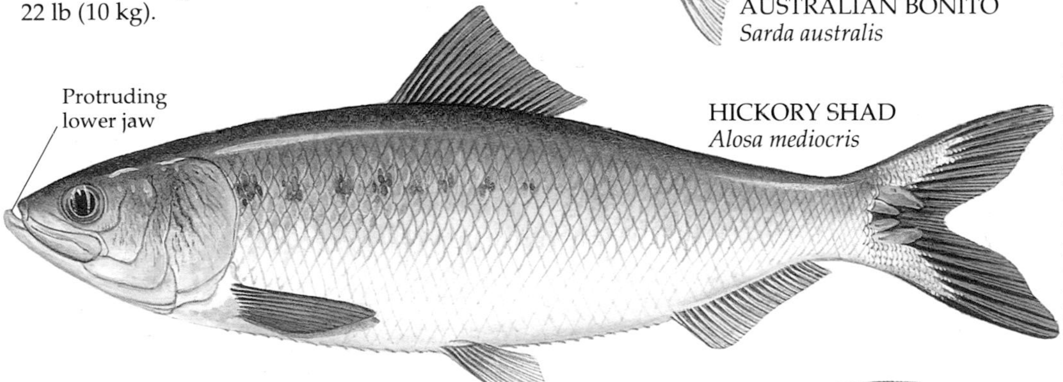

Hickory Shad

This large shad has a protruding lower jaw, a dark spot behind each gill cover, and a row of dusky blotches along each side. Its usual maximum weight is about 2 lb 8 oz (1.1 kg), but it can reach 5 lb (2.27 kg). Fish make up a large part of the diets of hickory shad and skipjack herring, so they will take a lure more readily than other North American shad.

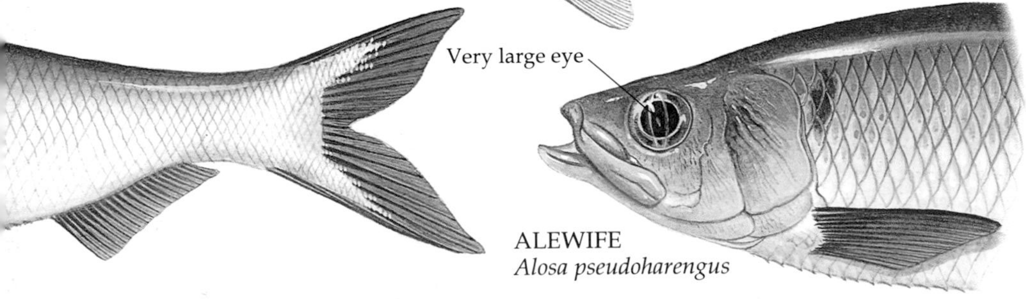

Alewife

The alewife can grow to 8 oz (227 g) in saltwater, but the landlocked form is much smaller. It has large eyes (greater in diameter than the length of its snout), a prominent keel, and a small, dark spot behind each gill cover. The blueback herring (*Alosa aestivalis*) is similar in size and overall appearance, but its back is bluish and its eyes are smaller.

Size comparison

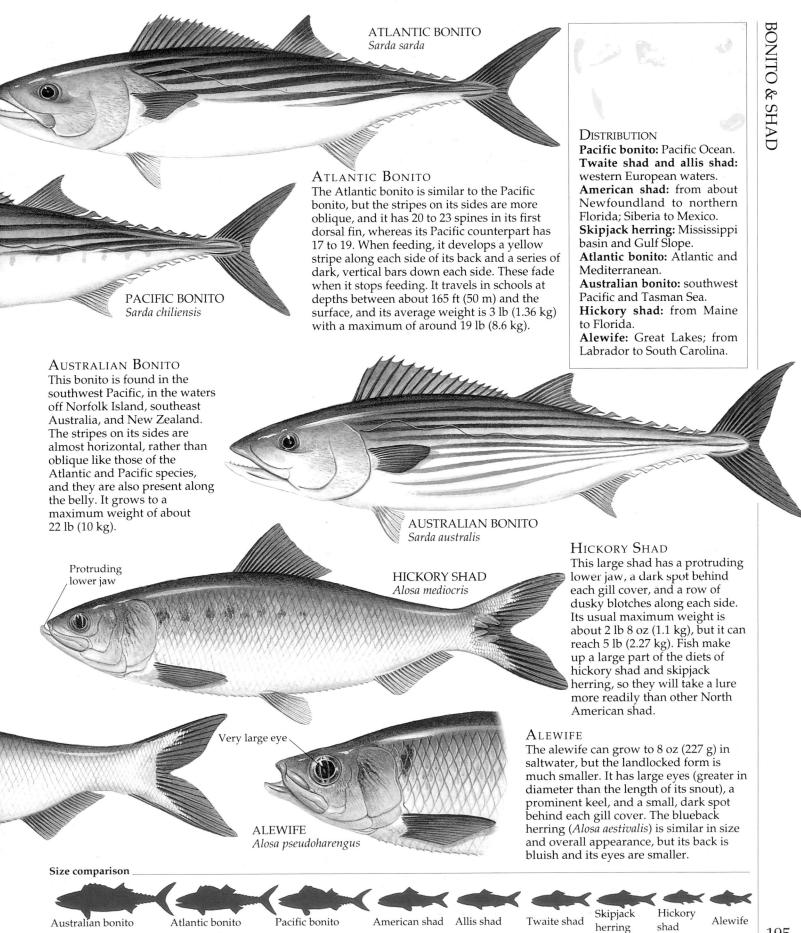

SUBCLASS SELACHII

SHARKS 1

The sharks are a very ancient group of fish, characterized by cartilaginous skeletons, skins covered in tiny, thornlike scales called placoid scales, five to seven gill slits, and powerful jaws equipped with rows of strong, sharp teeth. There are about 300 species, distributed widely throughout the world's seas but particularly in tropical waters, and although most are marine some enter estuaries, rivers, and creeks. They range in size from about 2 ft (60 cm) in length up to at least 60 ft (18 m); those shown here are among the smaller species, up to 11 ft 6 in (3.5 m) long.

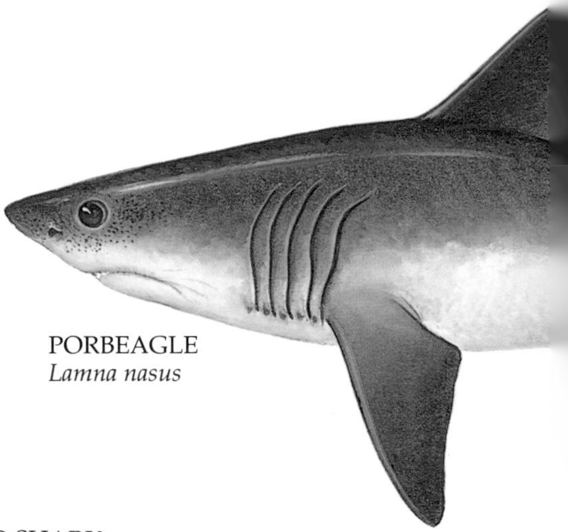

PORBEAGLE
Lamna nasus

LEOPARD SHARK

This distinctively patterned shark occurs close inshore along the Pacific coast of the United States, and is especially common in the shallow bays of California. It is usually found in shallow, sandy-bottomed waters less than 12 ft (3.7 m) deep. Males grow to a length of 5 ft (1.5 m), and females reach 7 ft (2.1 m) and 71 lb (32 kg).

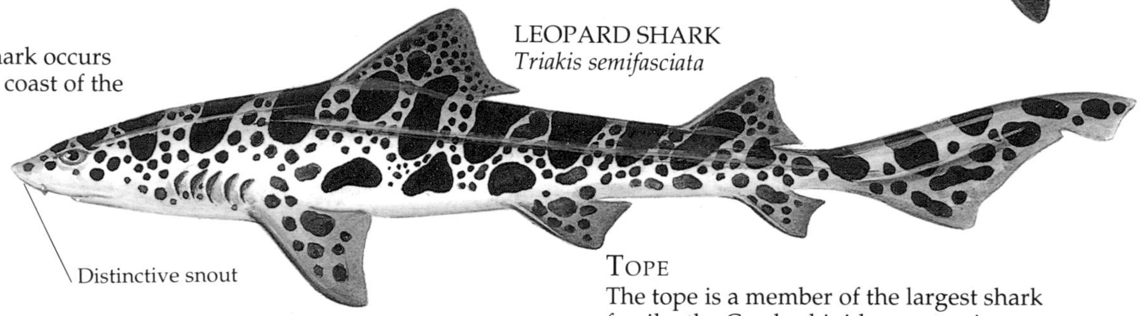

LEOPARD SHARK
Triakis semifasciata

TOPE

The tope is a member of the largest shark family, the Carcharhinidae or requiem sharks. It has a slender body and prominent snout, long pectoral fins, and a strong tail fin with a large lower lobe. It is found inshore in depths of about 10 ft (3 m) or more, and can attain a length of 5 ft 6 in (1.68 m) and a weight of 75 lb (34 kg). It feeds mainly on fish, such as cod, and also takes squid.

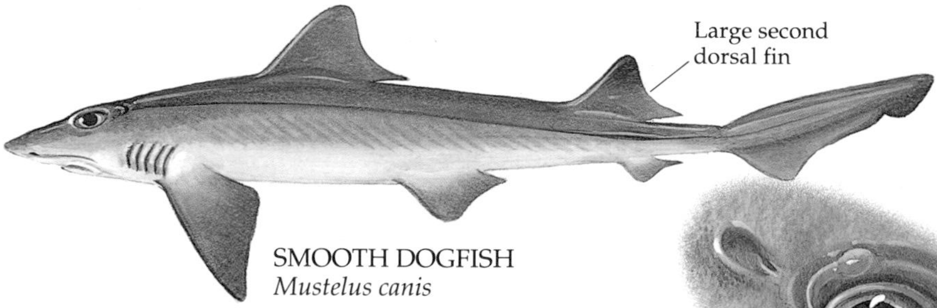

SMOOTH DOGFISH
Mustelus canis

SMOOTH DOGFISH

This very common, bottom-dwelling shark of the western Atlantic is usually found at depths of about 30 to 1,200 ft (9 to 360 m) and will sometimes enter freshwater. It has long pectoral fins and a large second dorsal fin that is almost the same size as the first, and there is a spiracle (a round opening that is the remnant of a first gill slit) behind each eye. It grows to about 5 ft (1.5 m).

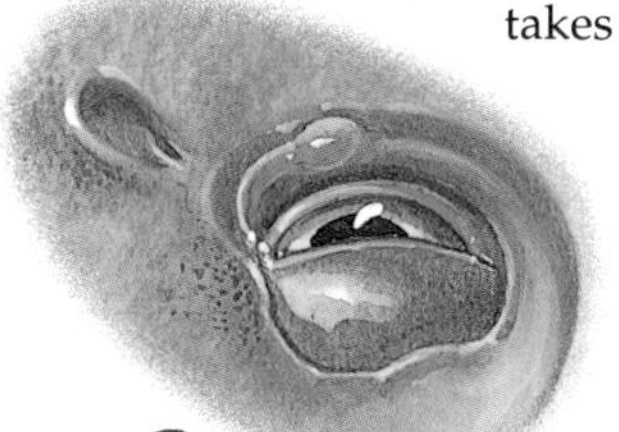

Tope eyes
The eyes of the tope and most other requiem sharks have translucent membranes (nictitating membranes) that can be drawn across for protection.

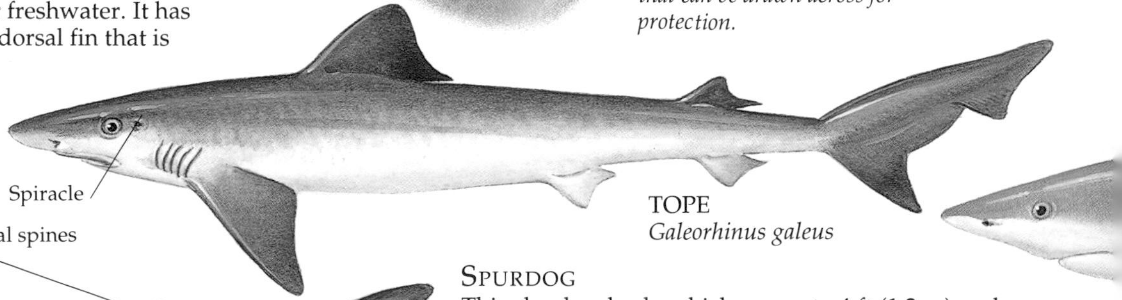

TOPE
Galeorhinus galeus

SPURDOG
Squalus acanthias

SPURDOG

This slender shark, which grows to 4 ft (1.2 m) and 21 lb (9.5 kg), is unusual in having a sharp spine at the leading edge of each dorsal fin. Like the tope, it has a large, strong tail, but it has no anal fin. It lives just above the bottom in depths of about 30 to 650 ft (10 to 200 m), and it has a very varied diet consisting of schooling fish, such as herring, plus invertebrates such as squid, jellyfish, and worms.

Size comparison

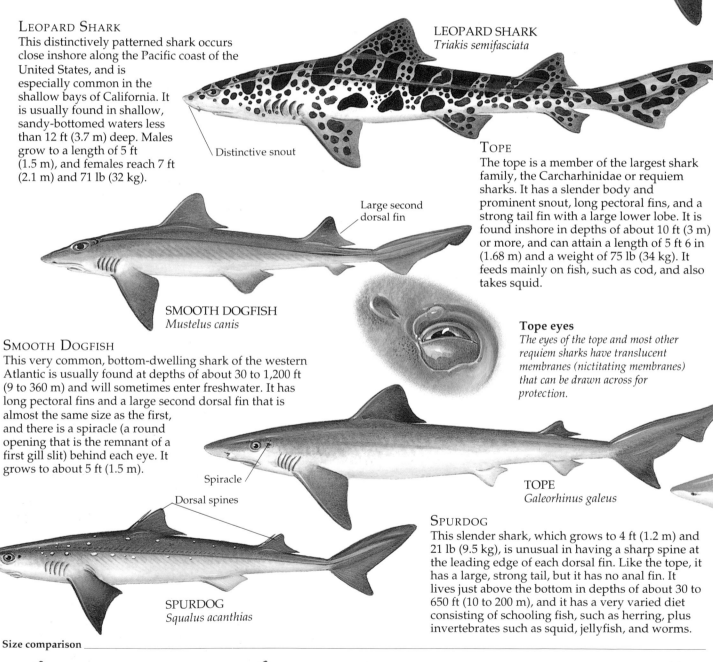

Porbeagle

The porbeagle is a heavy, thickset shark with a rounded snout, a large tail fin, and five prominent gill slits just ahead of each pectoral fin. It is found in the Atlantic and Mediterranean and belongs to the Lamnidae or mackerel shark family, which also includes the salmon shark *(Lamna ditropis)*, found in the Pacific, and the shortfin mako and white shark *(see page 198)*. The porbeagle lives near the surface and usually prefers deep, open water, but it will venture into water of less than 20 ft (6 m) and shore anglers have landed porbeagles weighing over 100 lb (45 kg). The maximum length of the porbeagle is about 10 ft (3 m), and it can weigh up to 500 lb (227 kg).

Porbeagle tooth
A porbeagle tooth has an additional point, or cusp, on each side of the main shaft.

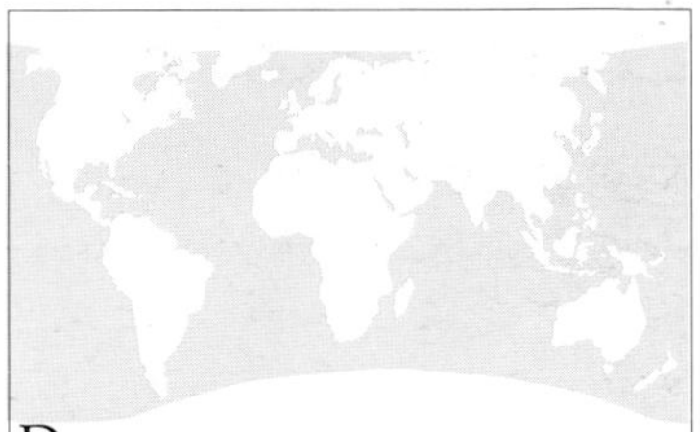

Distribution

Leopard shark: from Oregon to the Gulf of California.
Smooth dogfish: from the Bay of Fundy to Uruguay.
Tope: from Iceland to Morocco and the Mediterranean.
Spurdog: worldwide in cold and temperate waters.
Porbeagle: North Atlantic and the Mediterranean.
Sand tiger: most warm Atlantic waters.
Bull shark: worldwide in warm-temperate and tropical waters.
Spinner shark: subtropical and tropical Atlantic waters.

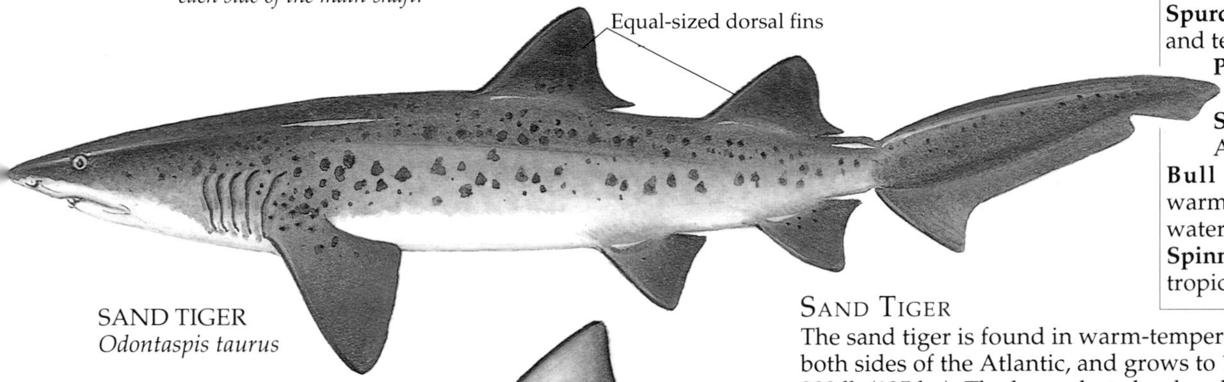

SAND TIGER
Odontaspis taurus

Sand Tiger

The sand tiger is found in warm-temperate coastal waters on both sides of the Atlantic, and grows to 10 ft 6 in (3.2 m) and 300 lb (135 kg). The larger but closely related gray nurse shark *(Odontaspis arenarius)* is abundant along the coasts of Australia and southern Africa. It grows to about 15 ft (4.6 m), and will readily attack swimmers and skindivers.

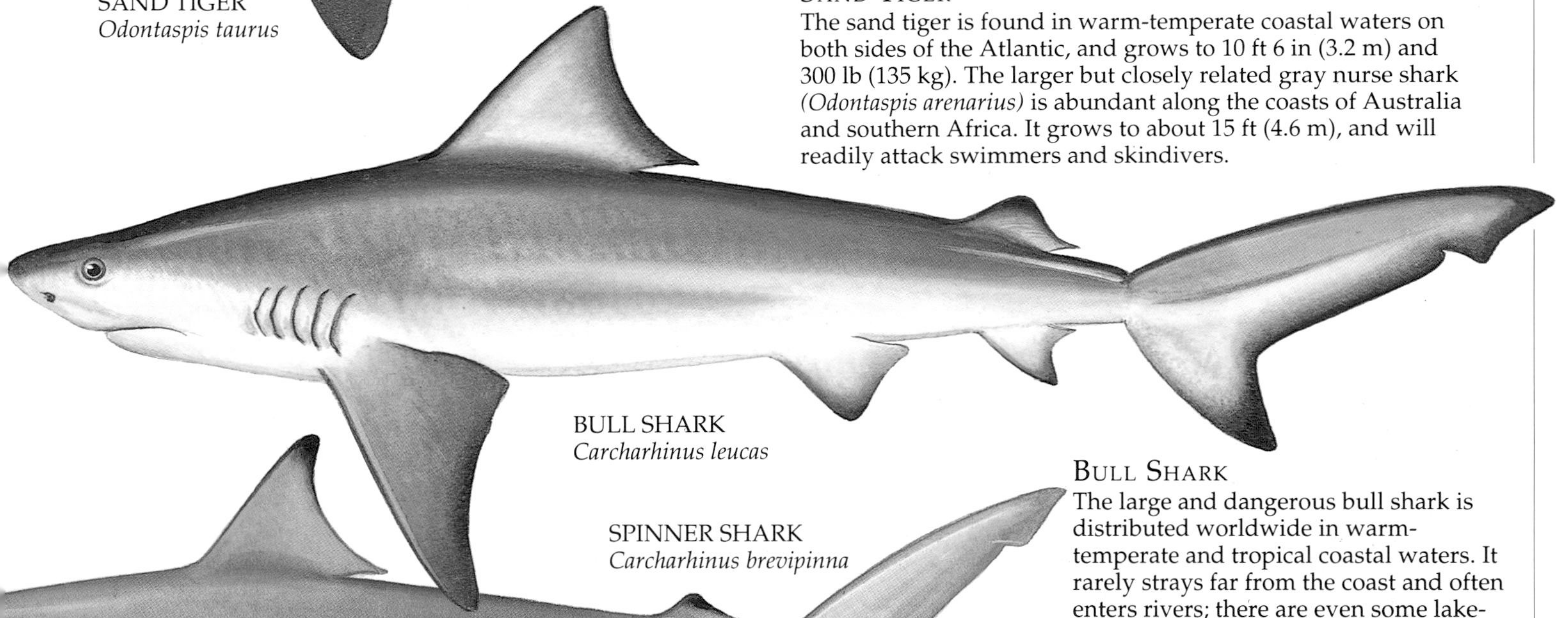

BULL SHARK
Carcharhinus leucas

Bull Shark

The large and dangerous bull shark is distributed worldwide in warm-temperate and tropical coastal waters. It rarely strays far from the coast and often enters rivers; there are even some lake-dwelling populations, most notably that in Lake Nicaragua. The bull shark grows to 11 ft 6 in (3.5 m) and 400 lb (180 kg), and has been known to attack swimmers.

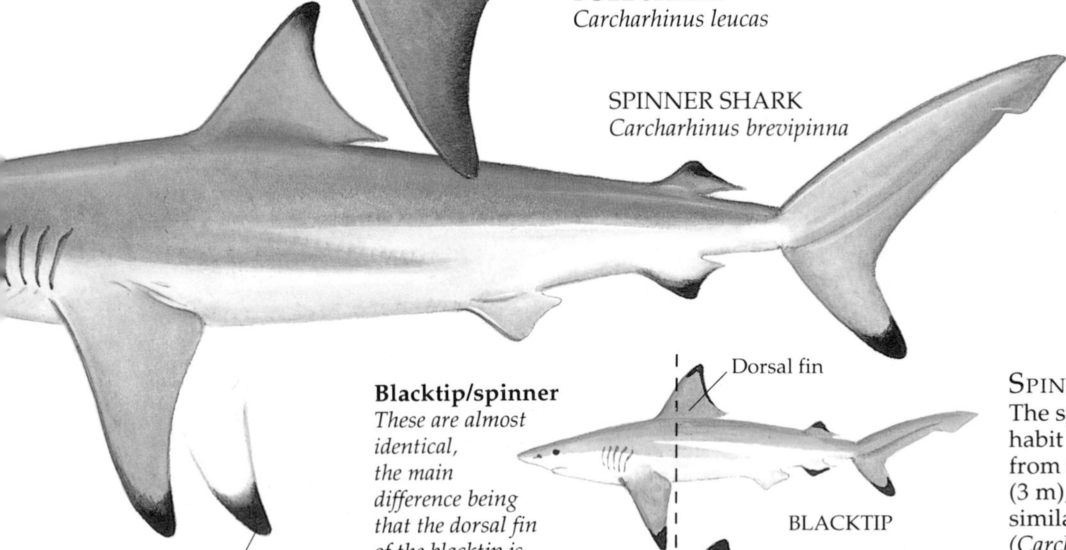

SPINNER SHARK
Carcharhinus brevipinna

Inside view of pectoral fin

Blacktip/spinner
These are almost identical, the main difference being that the dorsal fin of the blacktip is set farther forward.

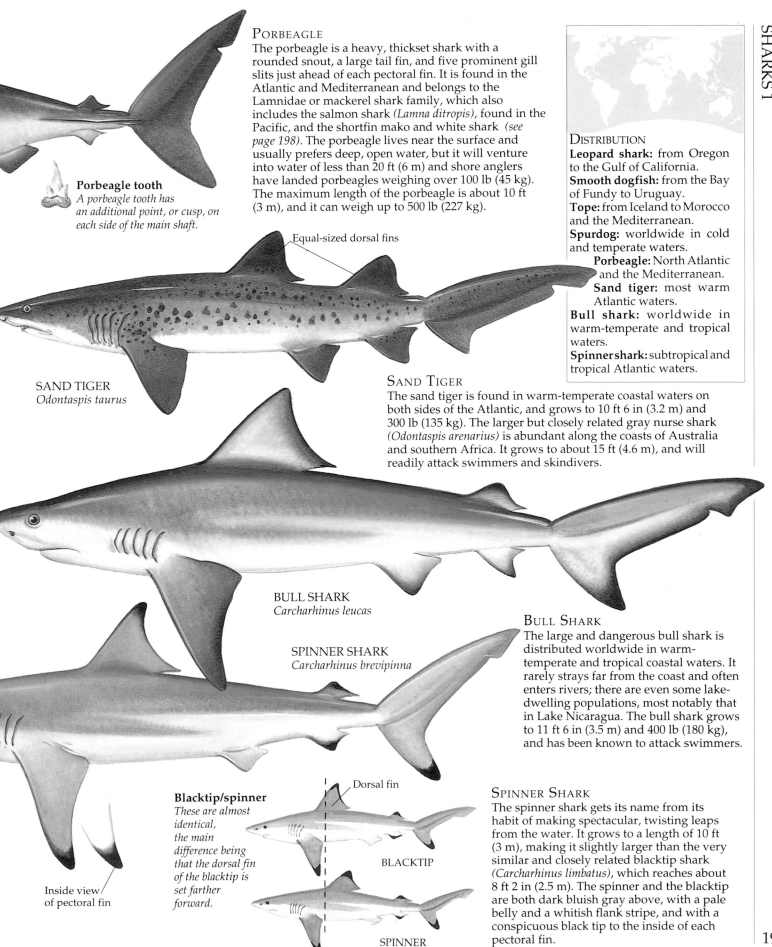

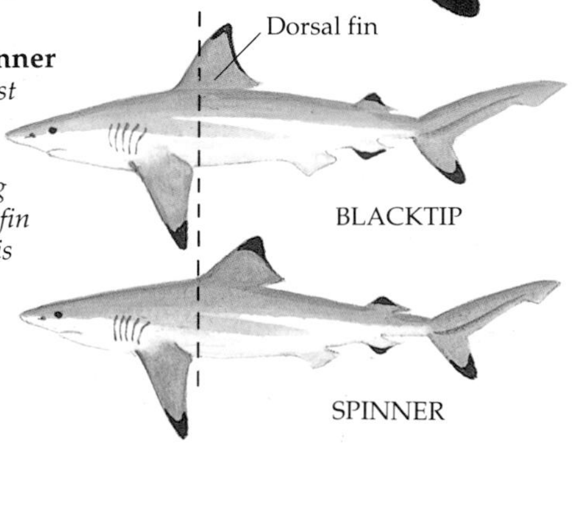

Spinner Shark

The spinner shark gets its name from its habit of making spectacular, twisting leaps from the water. It grows to a length of 10 ft (3 m), making it slightly larger than the very similar and closely related blacktip shark *(Carcharhinus limbatus)*, which reaches about 8 ft 2 in (2.5 m). The spinner and the blacktip are both dark bluish gray above, with a pale belly and a whitish flank stripe, and with a conspicuous black tip to the inside of each pectoral fin.

SUBCLASS SELACHII

SHARKS 2

The sharks shown here are representative of the larger species, and range in length from just under 13 ft (4 m) up to about 30 ft (9 m) or more. Not shown, because they are too big to be fished for, are the basking shark *(Cetorhinus maximus)* and whale shark *(Rhincodon typus)*, huge but generally placid sharks that feed mainly on plankton. The basking shark is the largest shark in temperate waters, possibly growing to 45 ft (13.7 m) and 44,000 lb (20,000 kg); the whale shark, found in tropical seas, is the world's largest fish and may exceed 50 ft (15.2 m) and 77,000 lb (35,000 kg). The largest verified specimens of these two sharks were a 40 ft 3 in (12.27 m) basking shark and a 41 ft 6 in (12.65 m) whale shark.

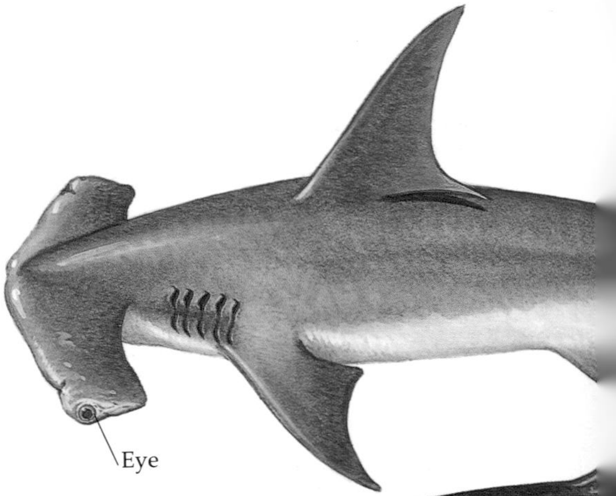

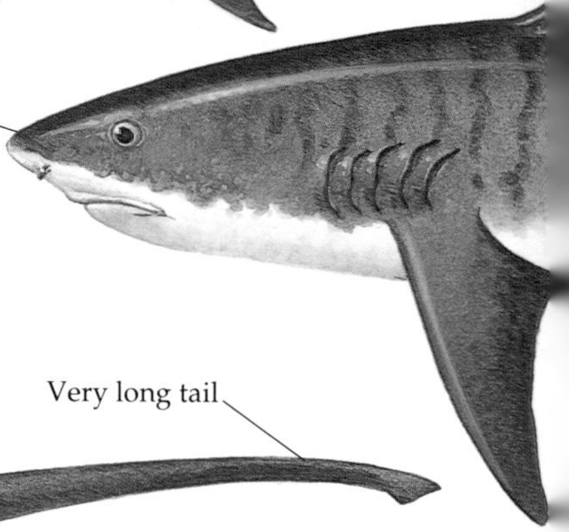

THRESHER SHARK

This warmwater shark is immediately recognizable by the exceptionally long upper lobe of its tail, which may be longer than its body. Threshers are found in the open ocean at depths from the surface down to 330 ft (100 m), and they grow to about 20 ft (6.1 m) and 1,000 lb (450 kg). They hunt in packs, using their tails to stun their prey.

THRESHER SHARK
Alopias vulpinus

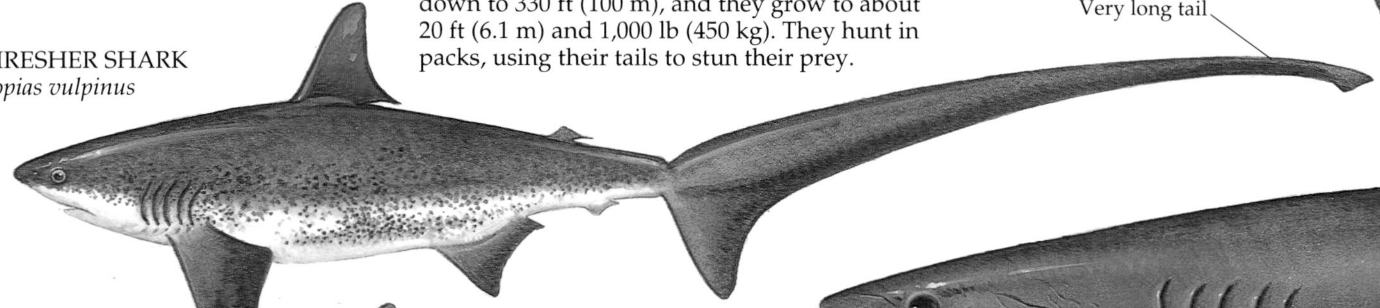

SHORTFIN MAKO
Isurus oxyrinchus

SHORTFIN MAKO

The shortfin mako, also known as the mako or bonito shark, is probably the fastest-swimming shark, capable of speed bursts of up to 46 mph (74 km/h). Its maximum size is about 12 ft 6 in (3.8 m) and 1,115 lb (506 kg), and it makes spectacular leaps when hooked.

White shark bite
When a white shark bites, it opens its huge jaws wide to expose its razor-sharp, serrated teeth, which can be up to 3 in (7.6 cm) long.

FISHING NOTES

Techniques
Trolling and drift fishing are the usual forms of shark fishing, but small sharks that venture into the inshore shallows are also taken by shore anglers, including saltwater fly fishers. Take care to avoid injury when handling sharks.

Tackle
When shore fishing for shark, try an 11 to 12 ft (3.4 to 3.7 m) rod with a baitcaster reel, 18 lb (8.2 kg) mono line with a wire leader, a 4 to 6 oz (113 to 170 g) weight, and hook sizes 4/0 to 6/0, or a medium to heavy saltwater fly outfit with a 12 in (30 cm) wire leader at the end of the tippet, and flies tied on 5/0 or 6/0 hooks. For trolling and drift fishing, the tackle depends on the size of shark you expect to catch. For example, a 20 lb (9.1 kg) class outfit should suffice for small species such as spurdog, but larger fish such as blue shark, porbeagle and mako require 50 to 80 lb (22.7 to 36.3 kg) class tackle.

Bait
Strips of fresh fish (such as mackerel or pollack) for small species, whole fish for the larger ones. For fly fishing, try white streamer flies.

SIXGILL SHARK

This large, bulky shark is identifiable by its single dorsal fin, which is set near the tail, and the six gill slits just ahead of each pectoral fin. The sixgill is found in temperate waters and lives at or near the bottom, the young in shallow water but the adults preferring depths of 250 ft (75 m) or more. It attains a size of at least 16 ft (4.9 m) and 1,300 lb (590 kg).

SMOOTH HAMMERHEAD
Sphyrna zygaena

Smooth Hammerhead

The odd-looking head of a hammerhead shark is flattened and extended to form a pair of hammerlike lobes with an eye at the tip of each lobe. There are about eight species of hammerhead, most of which are found in tropical and subtropical waters; the smooth hammerhead, however, is a fish of temperate to subtropical coastal waters. It is a large fish, with a maximum size of about 13 ft (4 m) and 900 lb (408 kg), and it can be a danger to swimmers and skindivers.

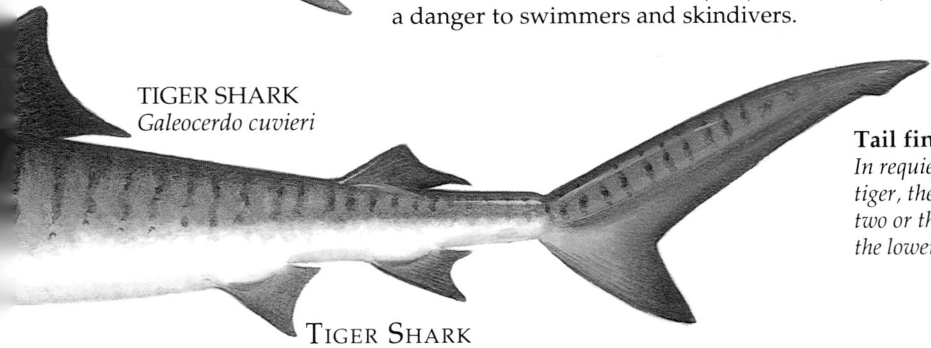

TIGER SHARK
Galeocerdo cuvieri

Tail fin
In requiem sharks, such as the tiger, the upper tail lobe is two or three times the size of the lower lobe.

Tiger Shark

This is a large and very dangerous shark, capable of reaching a length of 24 ft (7.3 m) and a weight of 6,800 lb (3,084 kg), that will attack just about anything that moves. It is abundant in warm seas, and is found in the shallow waters of bays and estuaries (where it often feeds at night) as well as offshore. It is a dark grayish color above with pale underparts, and younger fish have prominent, black, tigerlike markings that gradually fade with age and are sometimes absent from large adults.

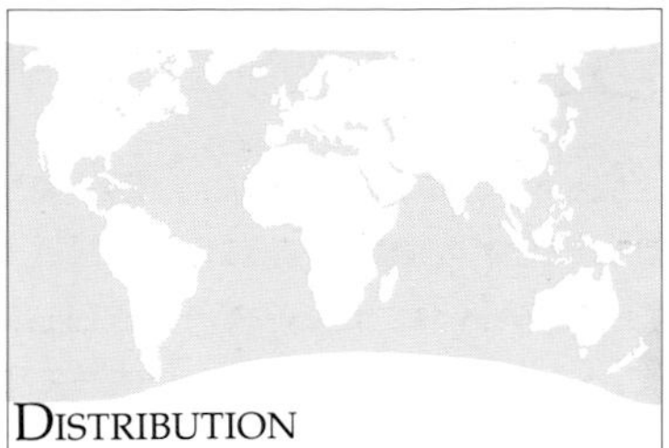

Distribution

Thresher shark, shortfin mako: worldwide in temperate and tropical waters.
Sixgill shark: worldwide in warm-temperate waters.
Smooth hammerhead: almost worldwide in subtropical and warm-temperate waters.
Tiger shark: almost worldwide in warm-temperate seas and tropical waters.
White shark, blue shark: worldwide in temperate and tropical waters.

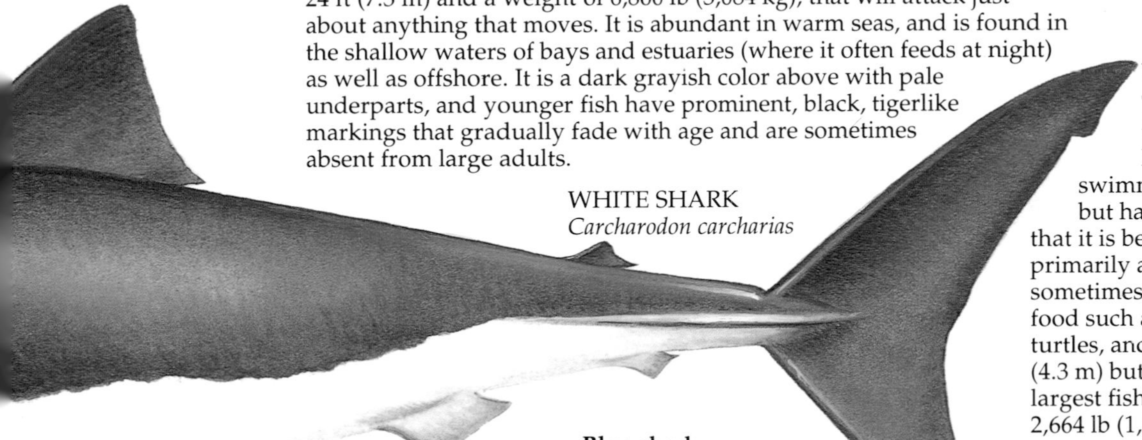

WHITE SHARK
Carcharodon carcharias

White Shark

This huge shark, also known as the great white shark or maneater, has been known to attack swimmers, skindivers, and even boats, but has itself been so mercilessly hunted that it is becoming endangered. It is primarily a fish of the deep ocean, but it sometimes enters shallow water in search of food such as seals. It also eats fish, shellfish, turtles, and seabirds, and averages 14 ft (4.3 m) but may reach over 36 ft (11 m). The largest fish ever caught by an angler was a 2,664 lb (1,208 kg) white shark, taken by Alf Dean at Denial Bay, South Australia, in 1959.

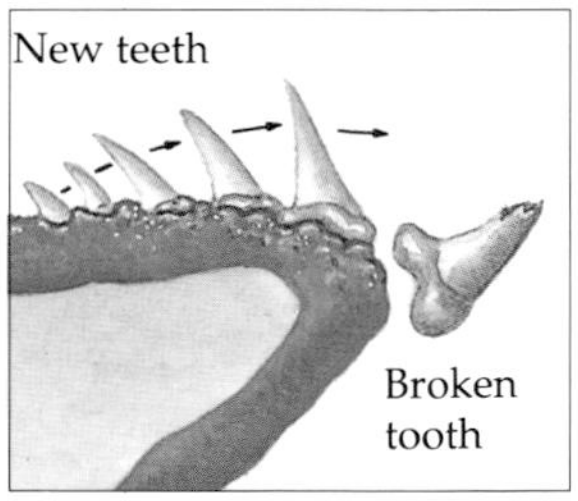

Shark teeth
Teeth are constantly breaking and falling out, only to be replaced by whole rows growing behind them in the gums.

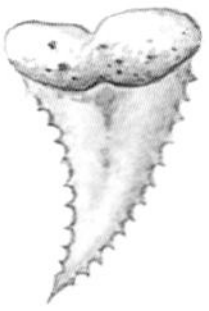

Blue shark teeth
The teeth of the blue shark are pointed, with serrated edges.

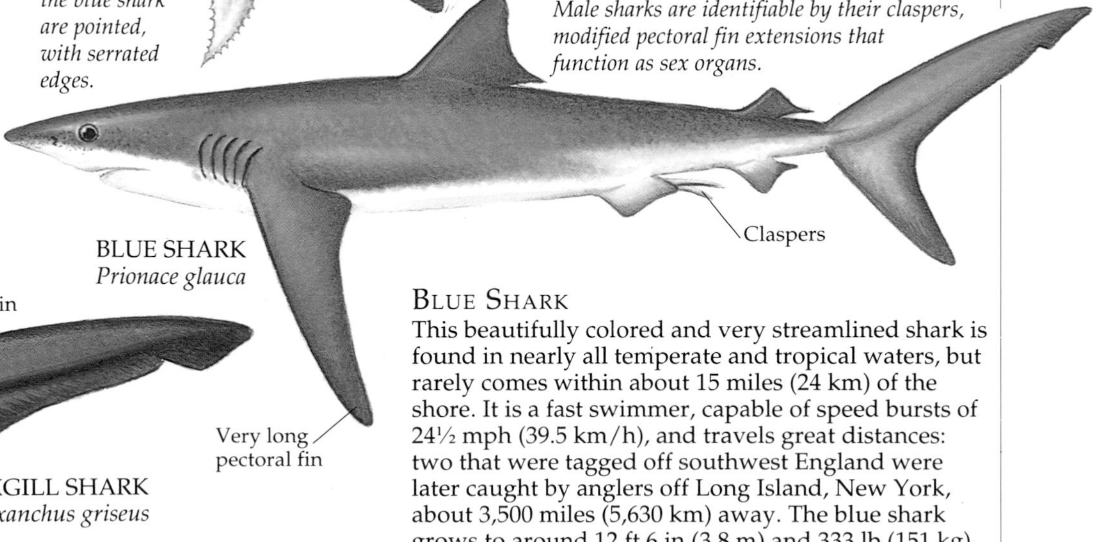

Claspers
Male sharks are identifiable by their claspers, modified pectoral fin extensions that function as sex organs.

BLUE SHARK
Prionace glauca

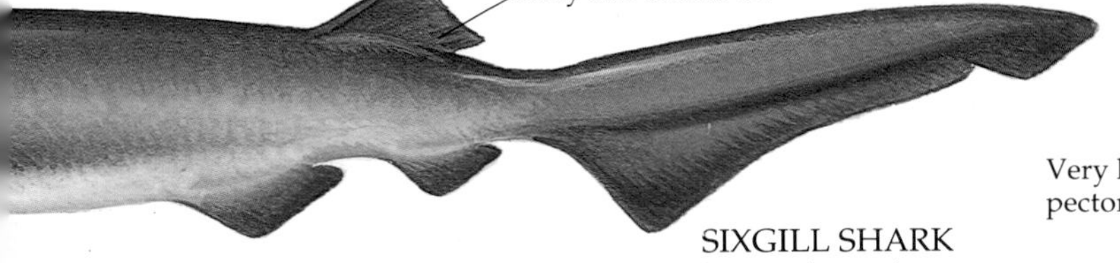

SIXGILL SHARK
Hexanchus griseus

Blue Shark

This beautifully colored and very streamlined shark is found in nearly all temperate and tropical waters, but rarely comes within about 15 miles (24 km) of the shore. It is a fast swimmer, capable of speed bursts of 24½ mph (39.5 km/h), and travels great distances: two that were tagged off southwest England were later caught by anglers off Long Island, New York, about 3,500 miles (5,630 km) away. The blue shark grows to around 12 ft 6 in (3.8 m) and 333 lb (151 kg).

Size comparison

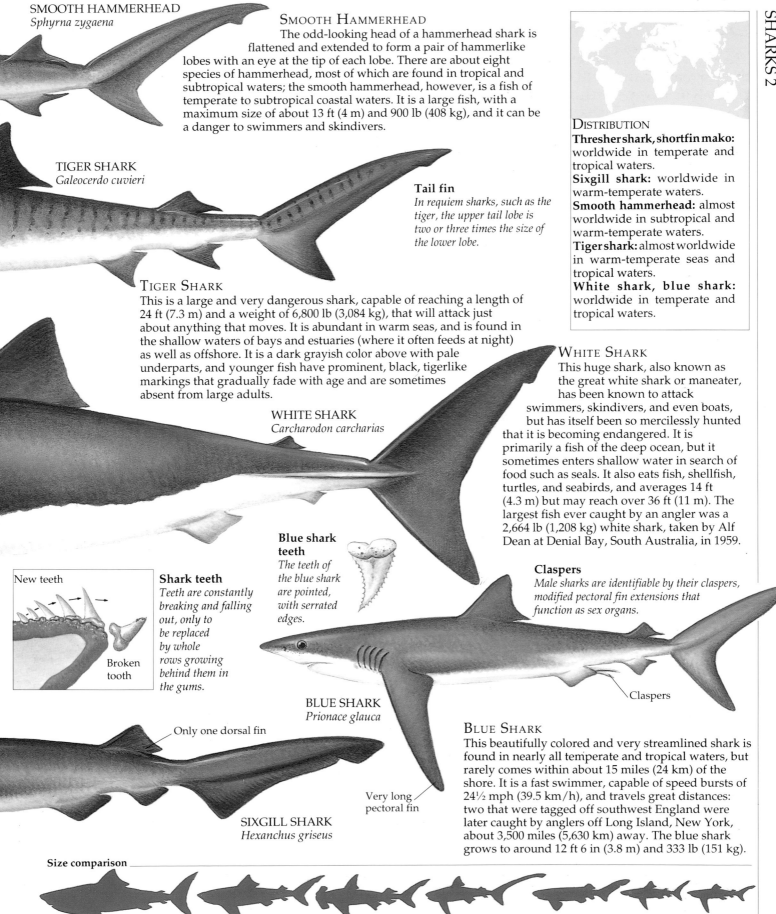

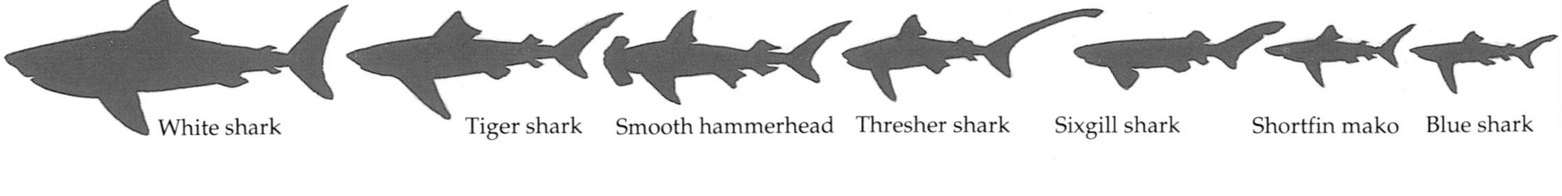

GROUPER

The Serranidae is a large and important family of fish, consisting of more than 375 species. These are mostly temperate and tropical marine fish, ranging in size from less than 12 in (30 cm) to about 12 ft (3.7 m), and are found near rocks, reefs, wrecks, and piers in coastal waters. The larger members of the family are robust, sharp-toothed, basslike fish, which live near the bottom and feed on fish, crustaceans, and shellfish. They tend to be solitary rather than schooling, except at spawning time, and the individuals of many species change sex as they grow: they mature and breed as females, and become males when they grow older and larger.

NASSAU GROUPER
Epinephelus striatus

YELLOWFIN GROUPER

This grouper has distinctive yellow tips to its pectoral fins, dark oval blotches on its head and body, and is speckled with small black spots. Its coloration is otherwise highly variable, but those in shallow water tend to be yellowish or green (yellow phase) and those in deep water red (red phase). Maximum weight is about 20 lb (9.1 kg).

RED PHASE

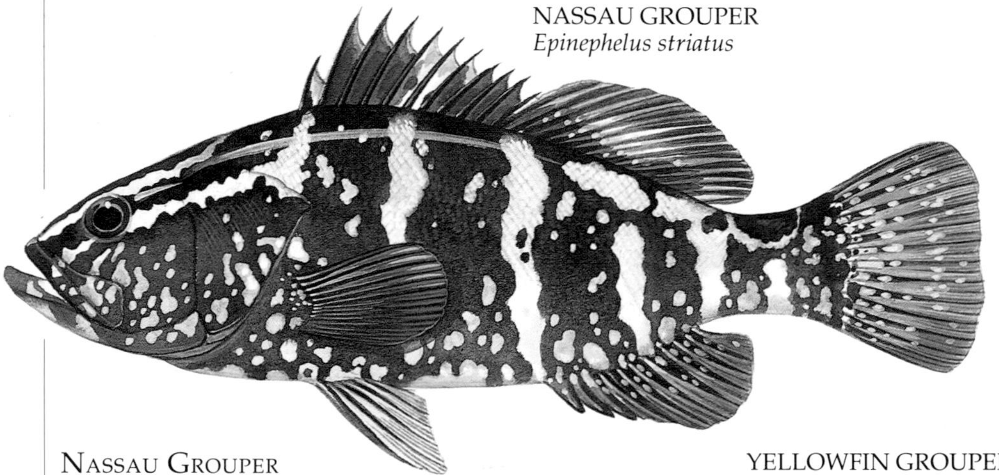

NASSAU GROUPER

The Nassau grouper is found over rocks, coral reefs, and weedbeds from shallow inshore waters out to depths of around 100 ft (30 m). Its maximum weight is about 55 lb (25 kg), and it is one of the most attractive groupers, having a variable, pale overall coloration marked with dark bars and light spots. It is an important commercial species, as are the red grouper, black grouper, and black seabass, and it fights hard when hooked.

YELLOWFIN GROUPER
Mycteroperca venenosa

YELLOW PHASE

FEMALE

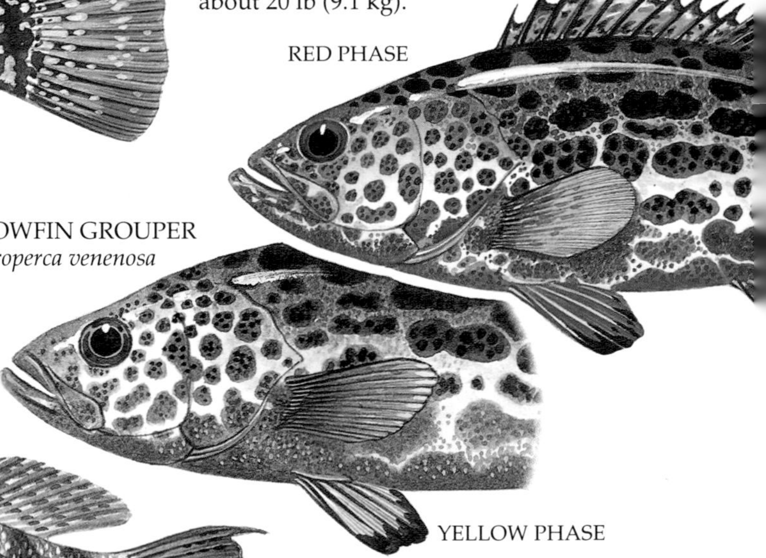

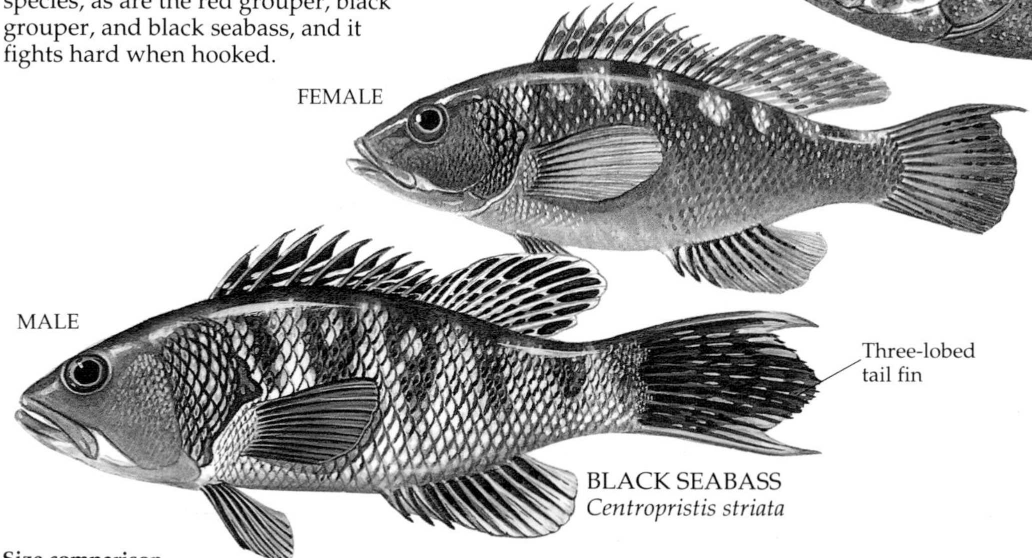

BLACK SEABASS

The black seabass has an average weight of around 1 lb 8 oz (680 g) and a maximum of 8 lb (3.6 kg), but despite its relatively small size it is one of the most popular marine gamefish along the Atlantic coast of the United States. It winters offshore and moves to inshore waters in spring and summer, when it enters sounds and bays where the bottom is hard and there are abundant shellfish. It is caught by bottom fishing from anchored boats, and from piers and docks.

MALE

Three-lobed tail fin

BLACK SEABASS
Centropristis striata

Size comparison

Jewfish Black grouper Red grouper Yellowfin grouper Nassau grouper Black seabass

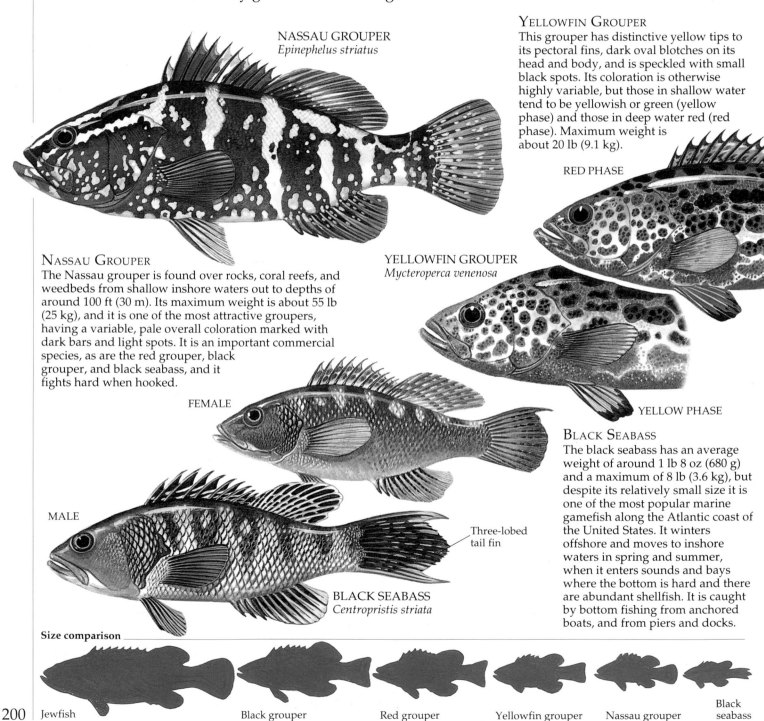

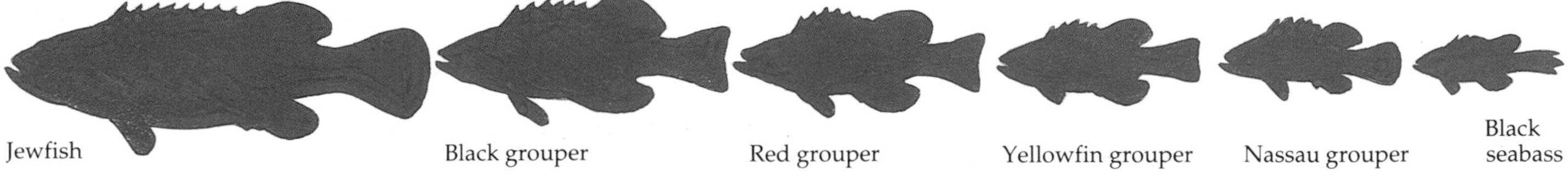

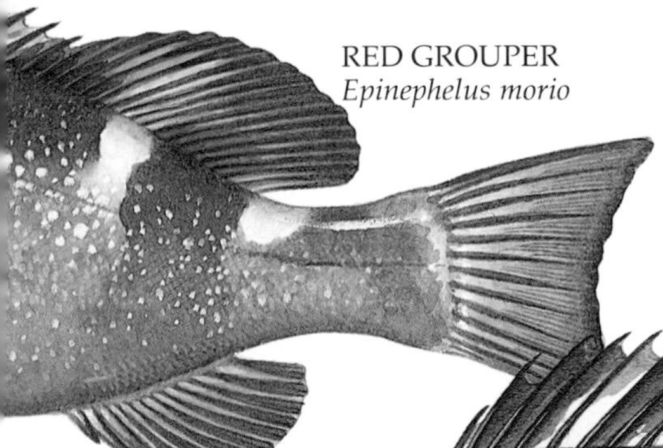

RED GROUPER
Epinephelus morio

Red Grouper

The red grouper inhabits rocky reefs at depths of 80 to 400 ft (24 to 120 m), but small individuals are sometimes found near the shore in shallow water. This grouper is recognizable by its blotched, reddish coloration, its squared-off tail, and the even top edge of its first dorsal fin; the lining of its mouth is orange or deep red. It can attain a weight of 50 lb (23 kg) or more, and fights hard when hooked on light tackle.

Distribution

Yellowfin grouper: Bermuda and Florida to Brazil.
Nassau grouper: Bermuda and North Carolina to Brazil.
Black seabass: from Maine to northeast Florida; eastern Gulf of Mexico.
Red grouper: Bermuda and Massachusetts to Brazil.
Black grouper: Bermuda and Massachusetts to Brazil.
Jewfish: Bermuda; Florida to Brazil; Pacific from the Gulf of California to Panama.

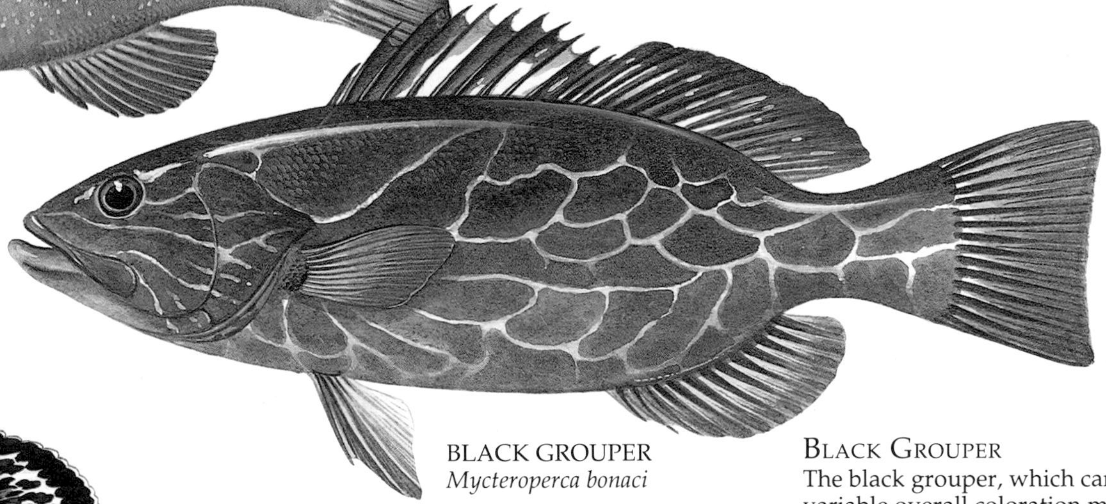

BLACK GROUPER
Mycteroperca bonaci

Black Grouper

The black grouper, which can weigh over 180 lb (82 kg), has a variable overall coloration marked with dark, rectangular blotches. The name "black grouper" is sometimes also used for the warsaw grouper (*Epinephelus nigritus*), which has a uniform dark brown coloration and grows to 580 lb (263 kg).

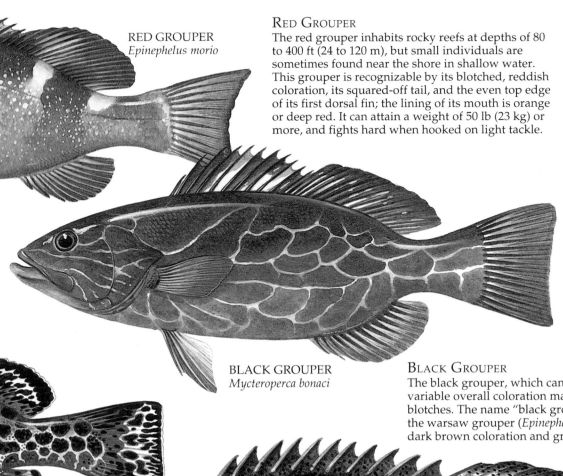

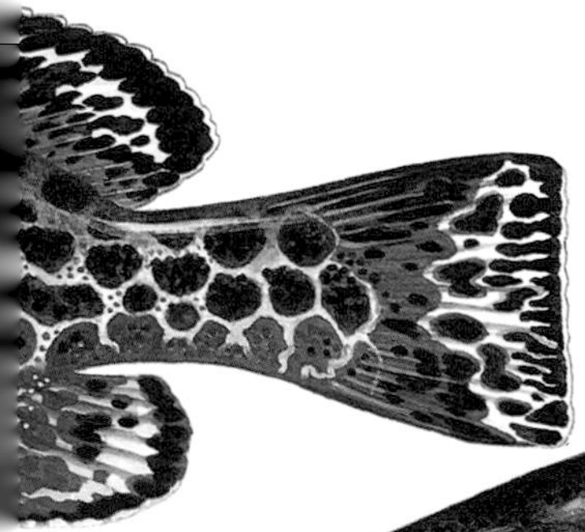

JEWFISH
Epinephelus itajara

Jewfish

This huge grouper is known to reach a length of 8 ft (2.4 m) and a weight of 680 lb (310 kg), and may grow to 1,000 lb (454 kg) or more. Despite its size, it lives in shallow water – usually no deeper than 100 ft (30 m) – and is found around rocky ledges, wrecks, and pilings. It is not a hard fighter, but its size and weight, and its habit of bolting into a hole when hooked, make it difficult to land. The Queensland grouper (*Promicrops lanceolatus*), an Indo-Pacific species, is even larger and can grow to 12 ft (3.7 m) and over 1,100 lb (500 kg).

Fishing Notes

Techniques
Bottom fishing and trolling, using natural or artificial baits, are effective methods for these species. Black seabass are also taken from jetties, docks, breakwaters, and piers on saltwater spinning gear and light, general-purpose tackle.

Tackle
For bottom fishing, use a 30 to 50 lb (13.6 to 22.7 kg) class boat rod with a 4/0 to 6/0 baitcaster reel and 30 to 50 lb (13.6 to 22.7 kg) mono line; terminal tackle should be a running leger with an 3 to 8 oz (85 to 227 g) pyramid- or bomb-shaped sinker and 2/0 to 6/0 hook. For trolling, try an 80 lb (36.3 kg) class rod with a 9/0 baitcaster reel, 80 lb (36.3 kg) mono line, a heavy wire leader and 10/0 hook.

Bait
Fish, squid, worms, shrimps, clams, and crab are good baits for bottom fishing. These natural baits can also be used for trolling, as can plugs, spinners, spoons, and feathers.

Porgy & Seabream

Porgy and seabream are among the 120 species that make up the Sparidae family. The Sparidae have a worldwide distribution in temperate and tropical waters, but are most abundant in warm coastal seas. Most are small to medium-sized fish but some are quite large; in African waters, some species of steenbras (or musselcracker), such as *Pagrus nasutus* and *Petrus repuestris*, can grow to well over 120 lb (54 kg).

Red Seabream

The red seabream has red fins and a reddish tinge to its silvery body, and there is a large dark spot behind each gill cover. It is found in depths of 160 to 1,000 ft (50 to 300 m), particularly near reefs and wrecks, and feeds mainly on fish but also takes shrimps, crabs, and squid. Its maximum weight is about 10 lb (4.54 kg).

Black Seabream

This seabream is silvery gray overall, with a darker back, and usually has six or seven dark vertical bars on each side. Its maximum weight is around 7 lb (3.2 kg). The gilthead (*Sparus aurata*) is somewhat similar, but has a golden stripe across its forehead.

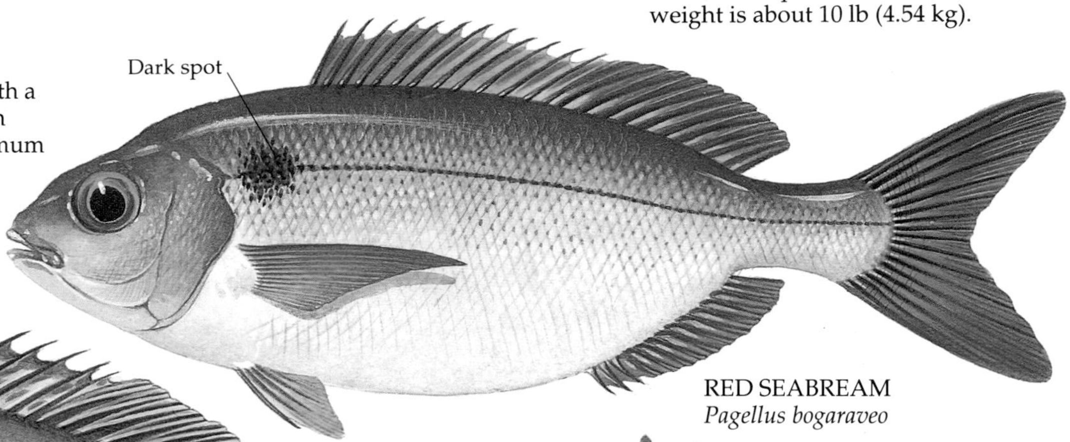

RED SEABREAM
Pagellus bogaraveo

BLACK SEABREAM
Spondyliosoma cantharus

Natural food
Fish make up the bulk of the red seabream's diet, but black seabream and most species of porgy feed mainly on mollusks and crustaceans.

Scup

This small porgy, which grows to about 4 lb (1.8 kg), is a dull silvery gray overall, often with faint dark bars on its sides and sometimes a blue stripe at the base of its dorsal fin. The front teeth are sharp and incisor-like. The closely related longspine porgy (*Stenotomus caprinus*) is found from North Carolina to Florida and in the Gulf of Mexico.

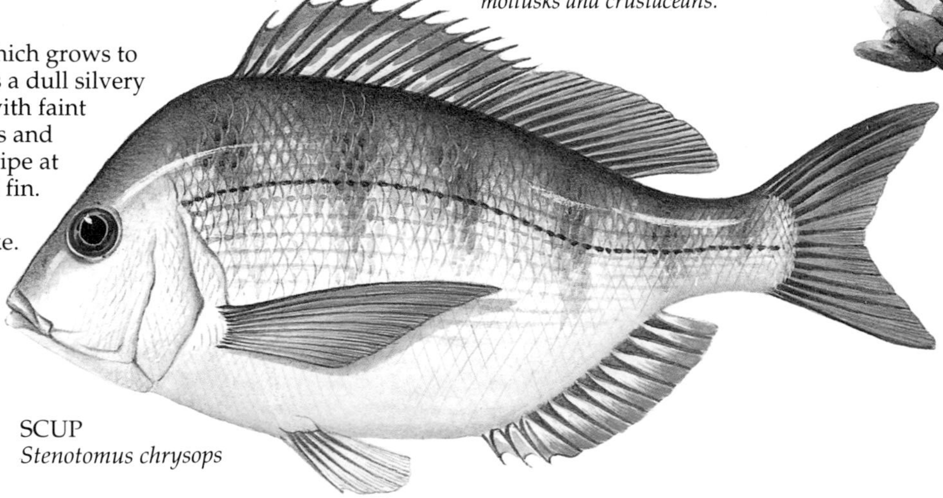

SCUP
Stenotomus chrysops

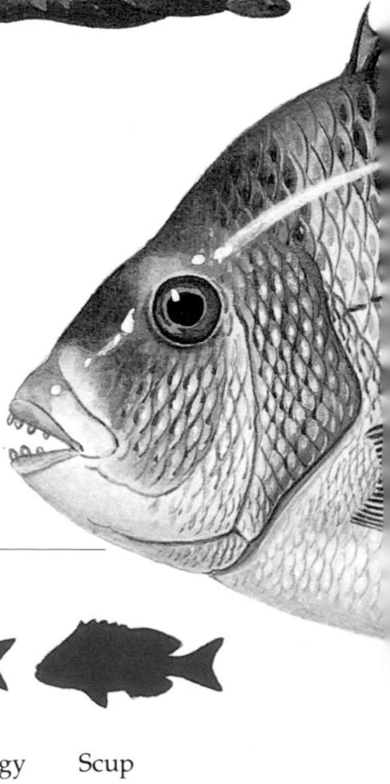

Size comparison

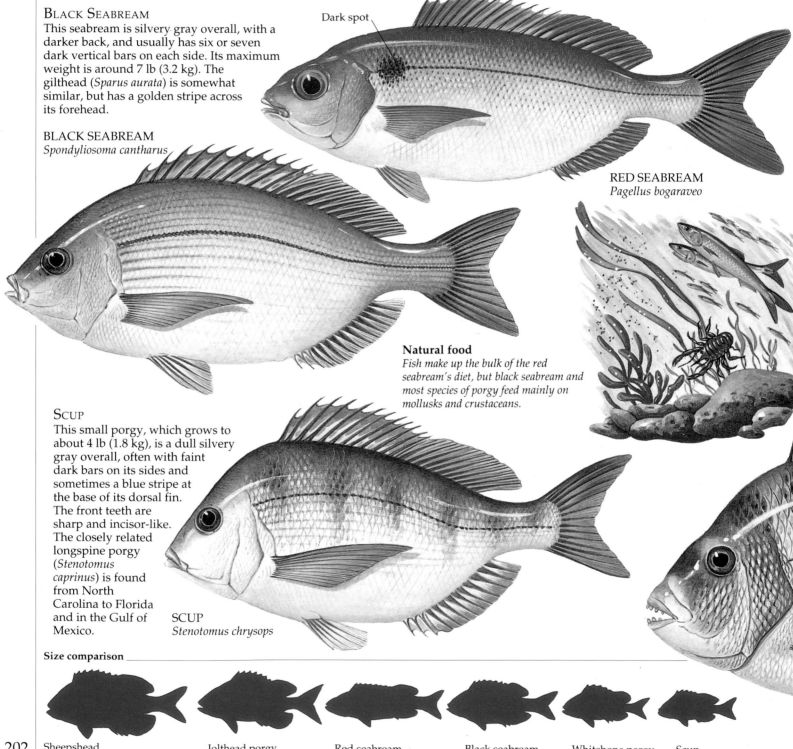

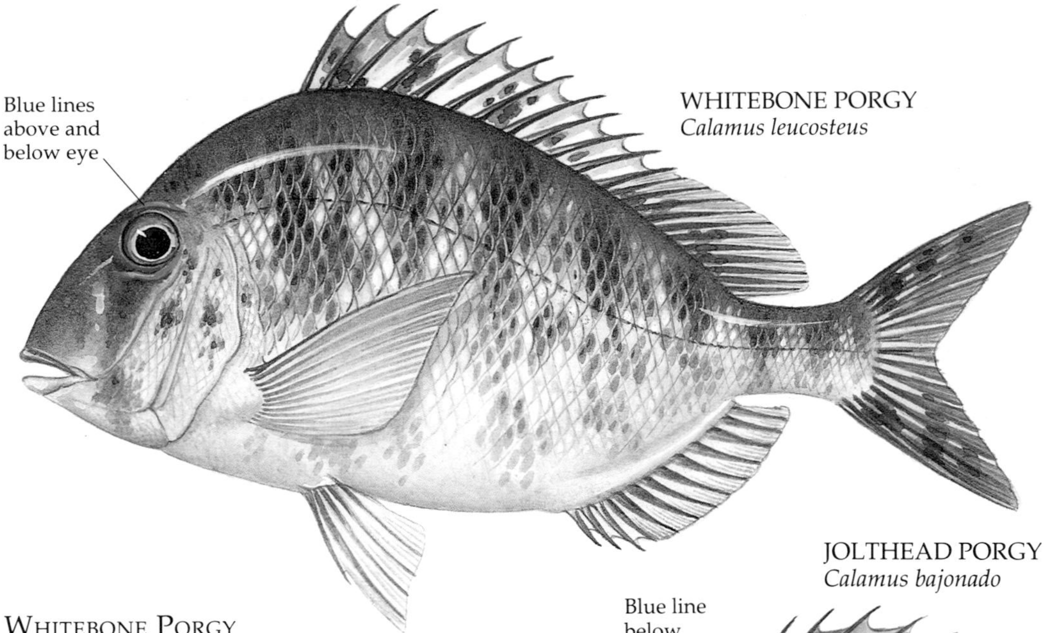

WHITEBONE PORGY
Calamus leucosteus

Distribution
Red seabream: from Norway to the Mediterranean and the Canary Islands.
Black seabream: Norway to the Mediterranean and Angola.
Scup: Nova Scotia to Florida.
Whitebone porgy: North Carolina to southern Florida; Gulf of Mexico.
Sheepshead: mainland coastal waters from Nova Scotia to the Gulf of Mexico and Brazil.
Jolthead porgy: New England and Bermuda to Brazil.

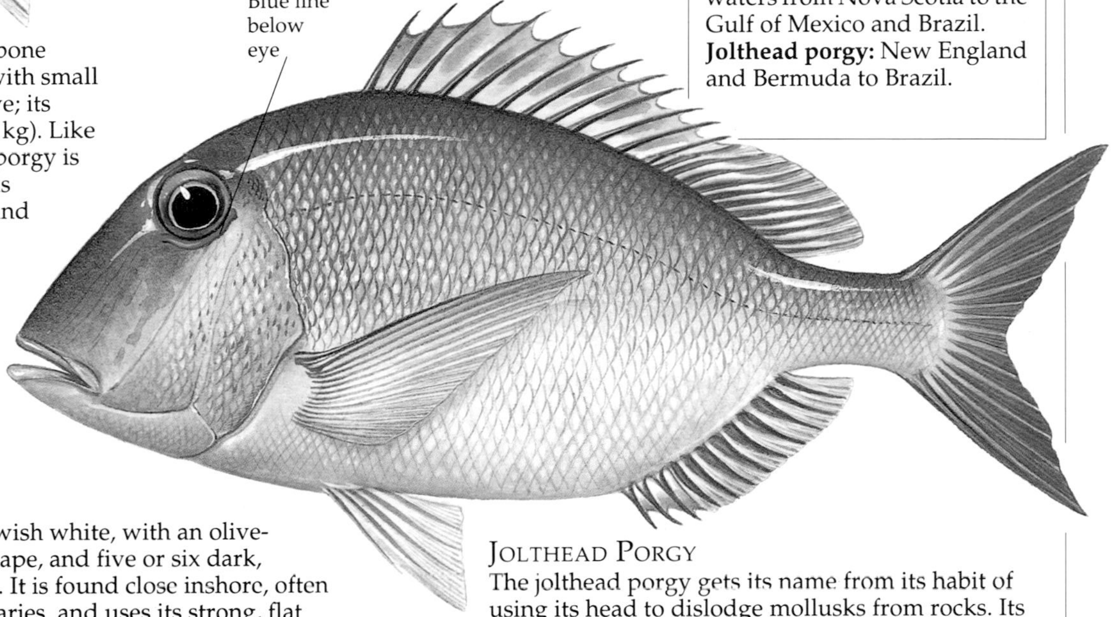

JOLTHEAD PORGY
Calamus bajonado

Whitebone Porgy

The overall coloration of the whitebone porgy is a blotched, bluish silver, with small blue lines above and below each eye; its maximum weight is about 4 lb (1.8 kg). Like the jolthead porgy, the whitebone porgy is one of a number of fish of the genus *Calamus* found in western Atlantic and Caribbean waters. Others include the sheepshead porgy (*C. penna*), grass porgy (*C. arctifrons*), and saucereye porgy (*C. calamus*). The Pacific porgy (*C. brachysomus*) occurs from Baja California to Peru, and sometimes along the coast of southern California.

Sheepshead

This large porgy is silvery to yellowish white, with an olive-brown back, a dark bar across its nape, and five or six dark, slightly diagonal bars on each side. It is found close inshore, often in the brackish zones of estuaries, and uses its strong, flat teeth to crush mollusks and crabs and to scrape barnacles from rocks and pilings. Its maximum weight is about 20 lb (9.1 kg). The red porgy (*Pagrus pagrus*) reaches a similar size and is found in relatively deep waters from New York to Argentina.

Jolthead Porgy

The jolthead porgy gets its name from its habit of using its head to dislodge mollusks from rocks. Its body is a metallic, silvery yellow with bluish overtones; there is a blue line below each eye, and an orange patch at each corner of the mouth. The maximum weight of the jolthead porgy is about 8 lb (3.6 kg), and its flesh is good to eat but may cause ciguatera poisoning (*see page 164*).

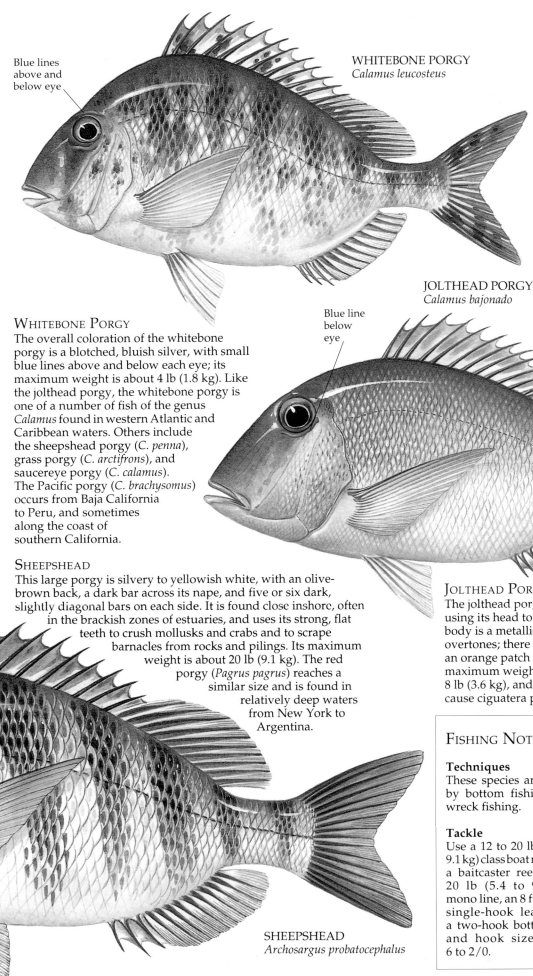

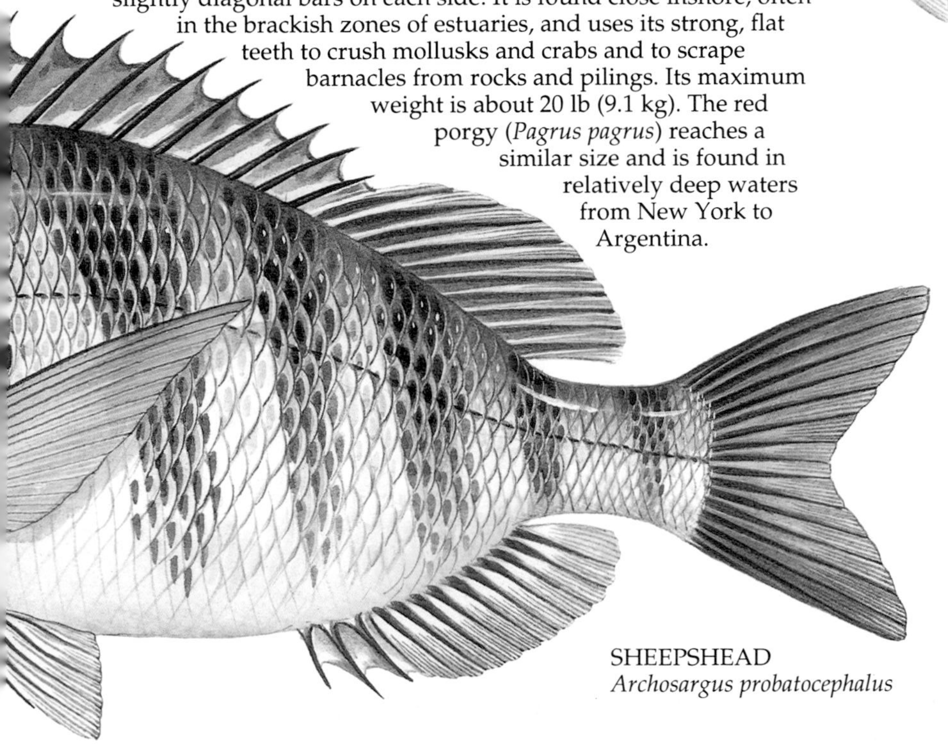

SHEEPSHEAD
Archosargus probatocephalus

Fishing Notes

Techniques
These species are taken by bottom fishing and wreck fishing.

Tackle
Use a 12 to 20 lb (5.4 to 9.1 kg) class boat rod with a baitcaster reel, 12 to 20 lb (5.4 to 9.1 kg) mono line, an 8 ft (2.4 m) single-hook leader or a two-hook bottom rig, and hook sizes from 6 to 2/0.

Bait
In general, porgy do not readily take artificial lures. Black and red seabream can be taken on mackerel feathers lowered to the bottom and retrieved in a jerky fashion, but, like porgy, they are best fished for with cut or whole natural baits. These include crab, shrimps, mussels, clams, worms, and sandeels, and strips of mackerel, cuttlefish, squid or octopus.

TECHNIQUES

THE BASIC TECHNIQUES of angling are easy to learn, but you could spend a lifetime and more mastering all the subtleties of any particular style. As a result, many experienced anglers tend to concentrate on one type of fishing, for example fly fishing, or on fishing for one particular species, such as bass or carp. While undoubtedly deriving great pleasure and satisfaction from their specialization, such anglers also deny themselves the variety and enjoyment offered by other kinds of fishing.

The predominant techniques used in a particular area depend as much, if not more, on the fish species sought after as on local custom and practice. For example, where the major freshwater quarry fish are predatory species, as is the case in much of North America, most fishing will be with artificial lures. But in parts of the world where non-predatory species provide the bulk of freshwater sport, as they do in Europe, the emphasis will be on fishing with hookbaits. This chapter covers the basic techniques of freshwater and saltwater angling, from pole fishing and legering to spinning and fly fishing, and from surfcasting and inshore boat fishing to big-game fishing. It also gives advice on setting up your tackle, and shows you how to tie the basic knots that join lines to reels, hooks and swivels to lines, and leaders to fly lines.

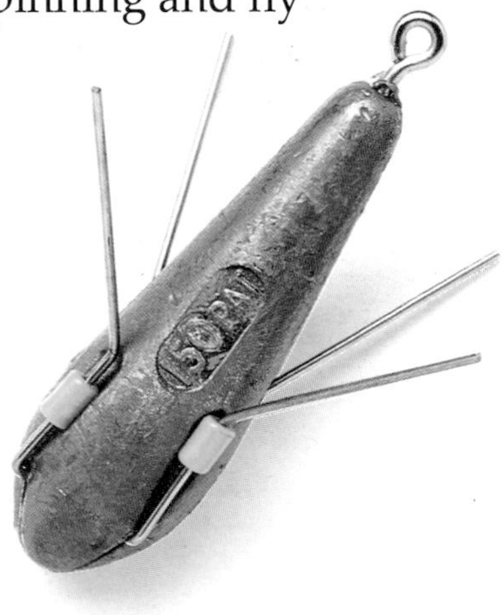

DEVELOPING SKILLS
Making the transition from hesitant beginner to skilled, confident, successful angler takes dedication and practice.

Setting Up Reels

For a reel to work at its optimum efficiency, the line must be wound onto it properly and the spool must be neither underfilled nor overfilled. When loading a reel with line, it is also worth giving some thought to how you are going to use it. For example, many spinning reel spools are deep with a big line capacity, but your style of fishing might require only a small proportion of the line to leave the reel. So instead of loading the spool with many hundreds of yards of high-quality and expensive mono, and actually using only, say, about a third of it, half-fill the spool with cheap nylon or even string and then attach a suitable length of your "working line" on top.

Spinning & Baitcaster Reels

When loading these, it is important to wind the line on correctly and fill the spool to the correct level and line profile (the shape the wound line forms on the spool). Incorrect winding twists the line, which can reduce casting distance and cause line tangles. To load a spinning reel, mount the spool of line in a spool holder and position it at right angles to the front of the reel. The coils of line should leave the spool in the same direction as the bail arm of the reel rotates. When loading a baitcaster, align the spool and reel so that the line runs straight from one to the other.

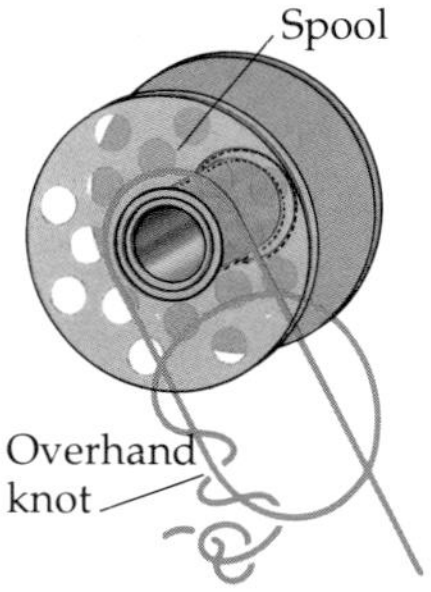

REEL KNOT
Wet both knots to avoid damage and improve binding before pulling tight.

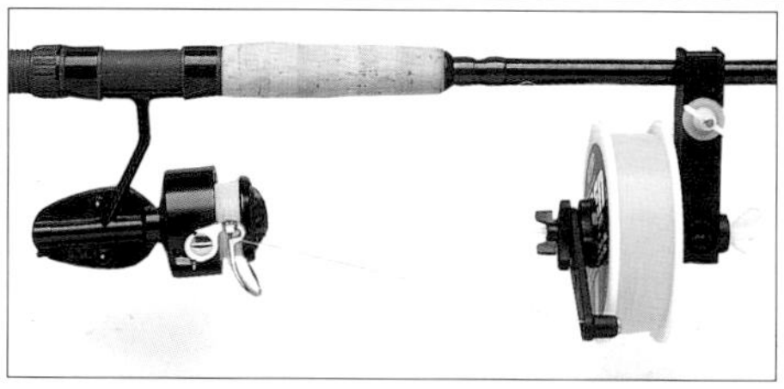

SPINNING REEL
Position the reel and line spool as shown, so that coils of line unwind from the spool and wind onto the reel in the same direction, without twisting.

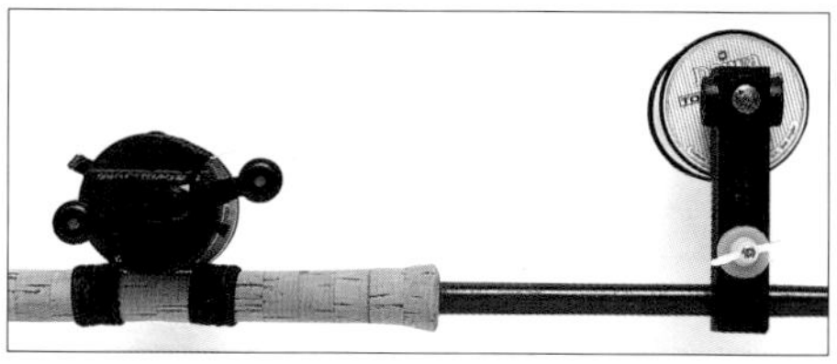

BAITCASTER REEL
Position the line spool in front of the reel and in the same plane, so that the line runs straight off the spool onto the reel.

Filling a baitcaster reel
In general, the spool of a baitcaster should be filled with line to within about 1⁄16 in (around 2 mm) of the flanges. However, some baitcasters run better when slightly underfilled, but the only way to determine the optimum line level of a particular reel is by trial and error.

A level spread of line across the spool is vital if good casting distance is to be achieved, and to avoid problems such as rough running and vibration during casting. Although levelwind mechanisms lay line evenly across the spool, they tend to feed the line on in a criss-cross fashion rather than in tight, closely packed turns. This can be a disadvantage in long-range fishing because it reduces the line capacity of the spool.

EVEN LOADING
An even spread of line will ensure that the reel runs smoothly. If the line profile is convex, concave, or irregular, it can throw the spool out of balance and cause wobbling or vibration during casting.

CORRECT LEVEL
When you find the line level that best suits your reel, mark it on the spool with a small dab of white enamel paint. This mark will show you how far to fill the spool when you load a new line.

Filling a spinning reel
The line profile of a correctly filled spinning reel is a smooth cone, tapering gently from the back of the spool to the front. The spool is full when the line at the front is about 1⁄16 in (around 2 mm) below the lip. This ensures that the line will flow freely over the lip during casting, but will not fall off in coils and tangle.

CORRECT PROFILE

Poor line profile
Overfilling the spool will produce a convex line profile, and create terrible problems during casting because coils of line will fall off and tangle. Underfilling limits casting distance by increasing the angle (and thus the friction) between line and the lip of the spool.

CONVEX PROFILE

Profile correction
A poor line profile, such as this concave shape, can be corrected by winding on some of the line by hand in the opposite profile to that produced by the reel. Then, when the reel is about a third filled by this manner, wind on the rest of the line by turning the reel handle.

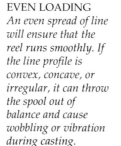

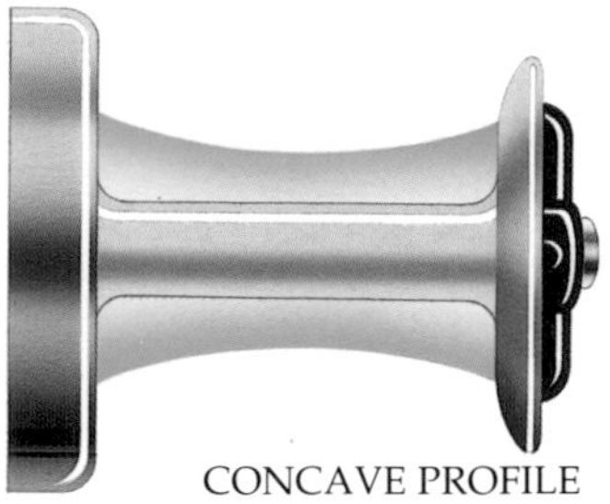

CONCAVE PROFILE

Loading a Fly Reel

The best way to load a fly reel is to use a linewinder, but if you do not have one, you will need a second, similarly sized reel. Wind the fly line onto the second reel, join the backing line to it, wind the backing onto the reel until it is full, and cut it to length. Then take the first reel, tie the free end of the backing line to it, and wind on the backing and fly line.

1

1 When using a linewinder, first wind the fly line onto the empty reel.

2 Next, wind on backing until reel is full. Cut to length, then wind the backing from the reel onto one side of the linewinder, and the fly line onto the other.

2

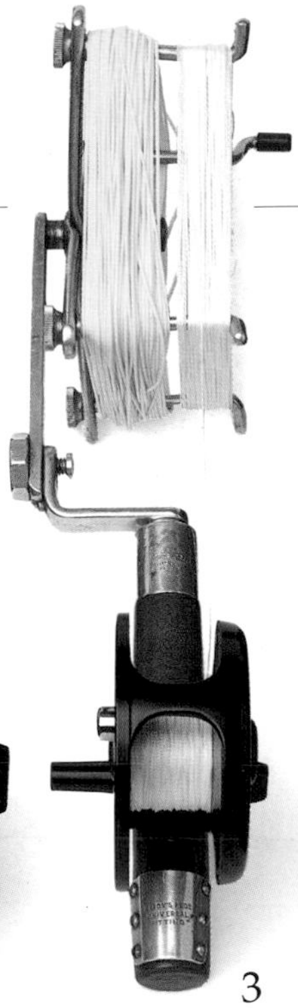

3

4

3 Tie the end of the backing to the reel, wind it on, and join the fly line to it. Wind the fly line on top of the backing.

4 Slightly underfill the reel: when in use the line will not wind on as tightly as it does when you load it on at home.

Joining Backing to Fly Line

Backing is made of materials such as braided Terylene, braided monofilament, and solid monofilament, both round and flattened. Joining braided backing to a fly line is easy, because it is hollow and the fly line is pushed up inside it and held in position with a sleeve. Solid mono should be tied to the fly line, using a knot such as the needle knot shown here. The flattened type must first be tapered to make it thin enough to go through the needle hole.

Braided mono to fly line

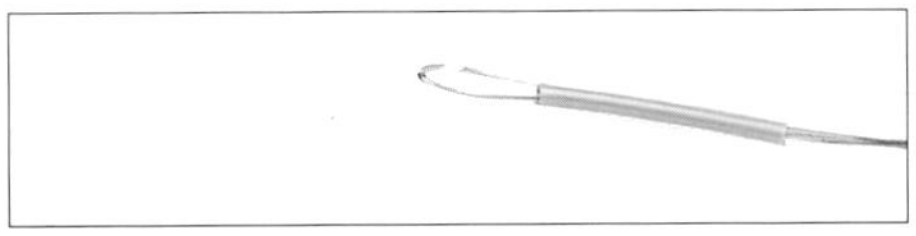

1 Use a looped length of mono to pull the braided line through a ½ in (12 mm) length of braid sleeve.

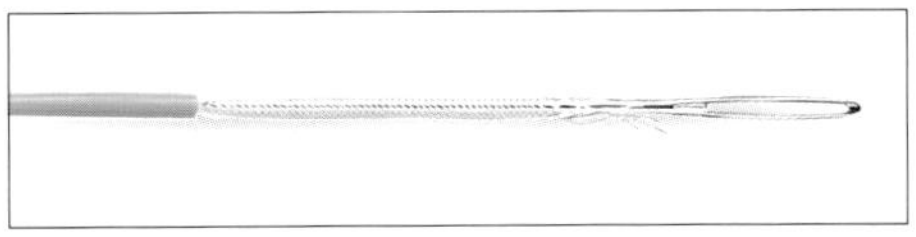

2 Open up the hollow center of the braid with a needle. Touch the braid ends lightly with a flame to prevent fraying.

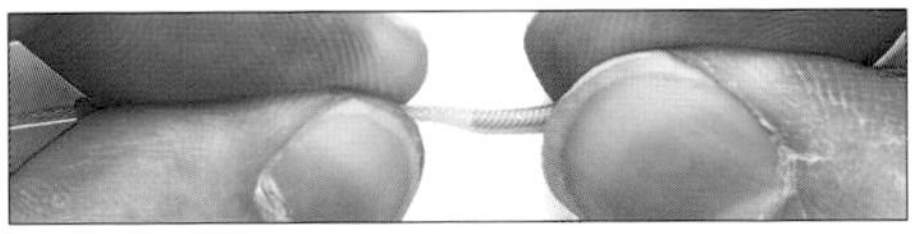

3 Insert the fly line tip into the hollow braid. Work the fly line into the braid a little at a time.

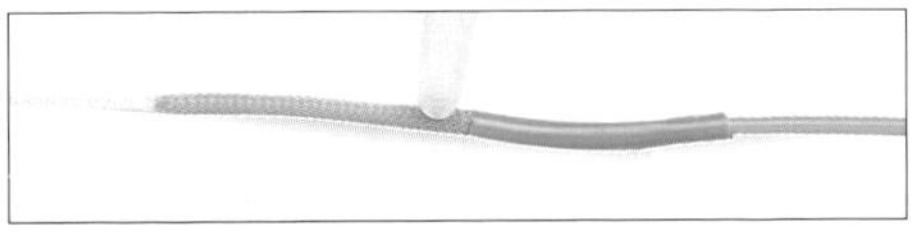

4 With 2 in (5 cm) of fly line inside the braid, slide the sleeve up the line to just overlap the braid; glue it in place.

Solid mono to fly line

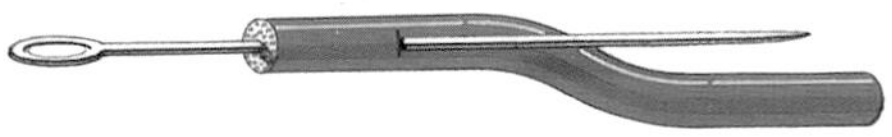

1 Push a needle into the end of the fly line and out through the side ¼ in (6 mm) from the tip. Heat needle until line starts to bend.

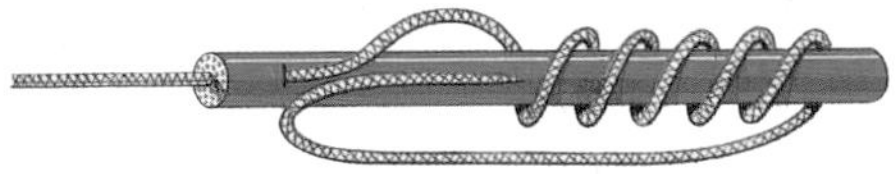

2 Remove needle when cool. Thread the mono through the fly line and five or six times around it. Bring end back and hold against line.

3 Unwind all the mono turns by winding the long loops in the direction shown, creating new, tight turns that trap the loose end.

B

A

4 Maintain grip on knot. Gently tighten by pulling alternately at points A and B. When knot is firm, pull mono tight.

Leader to Fly Line

Some fly lines are fitted with braided loops at their tips to which leaders can be attached quickly and easily. You can also buy ready-made loops for fixing to lines, or you can make your own from short lengths of braided mono.

Forming a braid loop

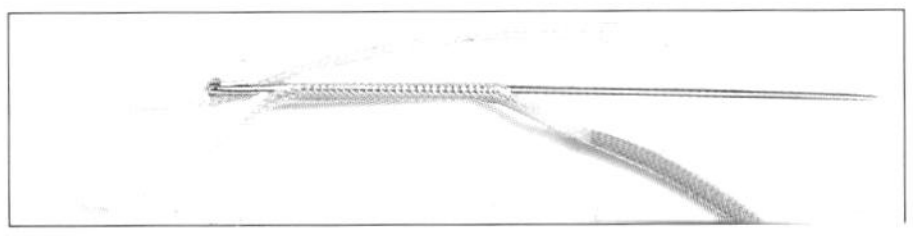

1 Push a large-eyed needle 1 in (2.5 cm) into the braid. Thread the braid through the needle eye.

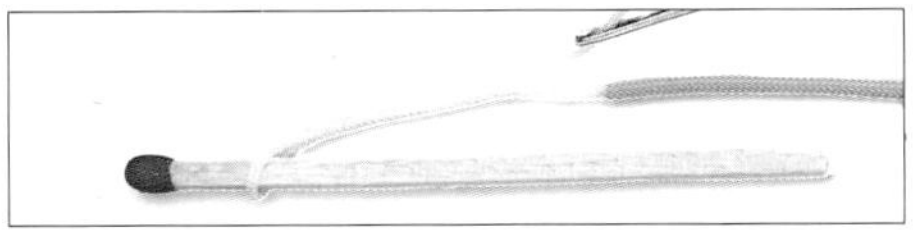

2 Pull needle through braid until loose end emerges. Use a matchstick to keep the loop from closing completely.

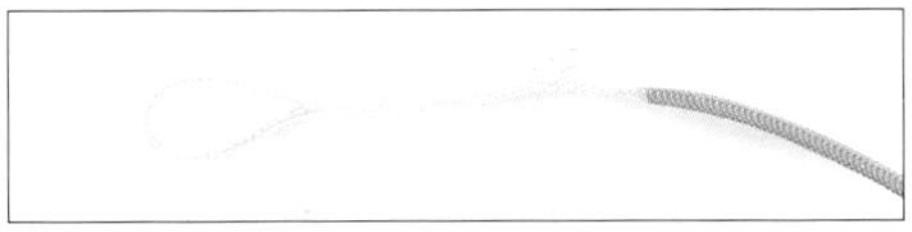

3 Adjust the loop to the required size and trim the loose end flush. Pull the loose end back inside the braid.

4 Secure the loop with a few drops of a waterproof superglue such as Krazyglue or Permabond 102.

Basic Knots

All anglers should learn how to tie secure knots. This is because there will usually be at least two knots in a fishing rig (one joining the line to the reel or pole, the other joining the hook or lure to the line) and every knot is a potential weak point. Before tightening a knot, wet it with water to reduce the friction that can damage the line, and when attaching a hook, lure, or fly to a line be careful not to impale a finger on the hook point. Trim all loose ends so that they do not snag in the rod rings.

Knots for Joining Line to Tackle

Clinch knot

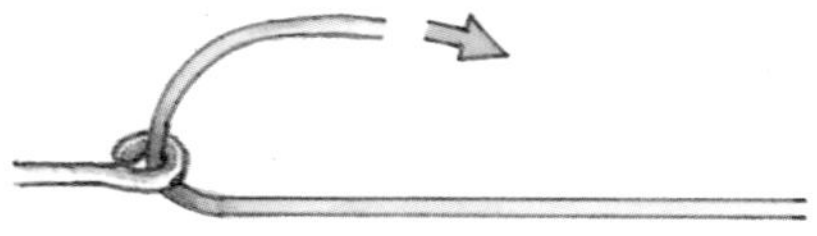

1 Pass the free end of the line through the eye of the hook.

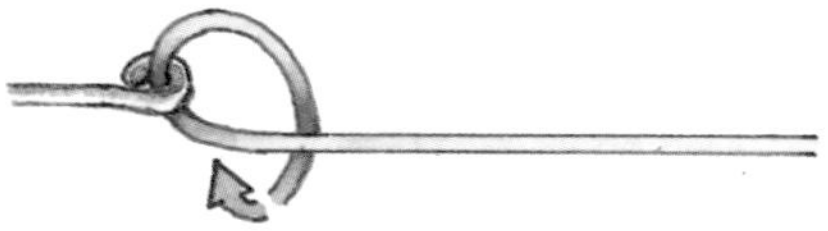

2 Take the free end back and tuck it under the line.

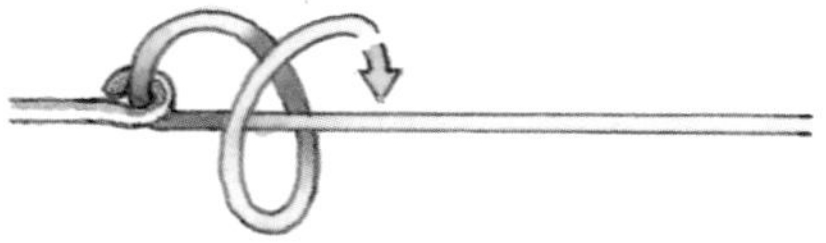

3 Bring the end back over the line to form a loop.

4 Continue looping the end around the line, making about four turns.

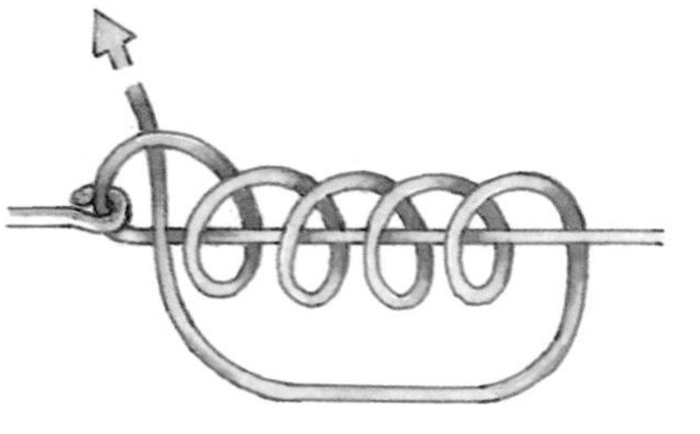

5 Bring the end back and pass it between the eye and the first loop.

6 Pull tight and trim off the end.

Spade end whip

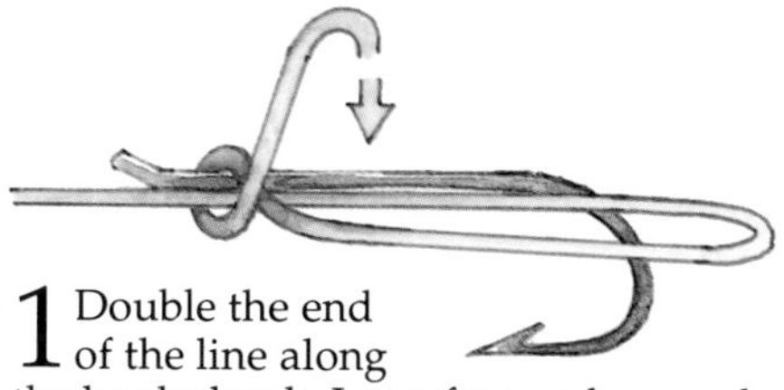

1 Double the end of the line along the hook shank. Loop free end around both line and hook.

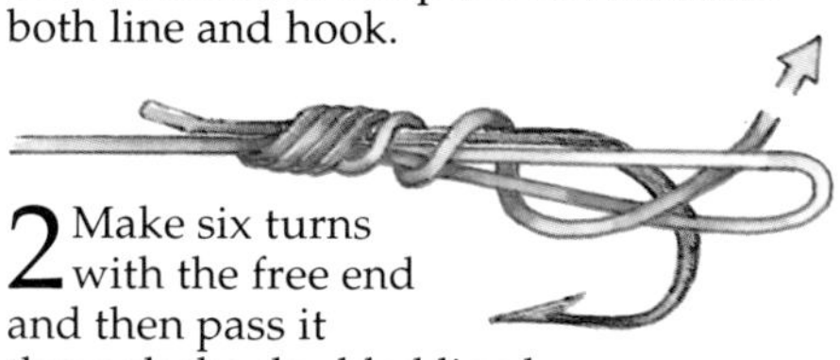

2 Make six turns with the free end and then pass it through the doubled line loop.

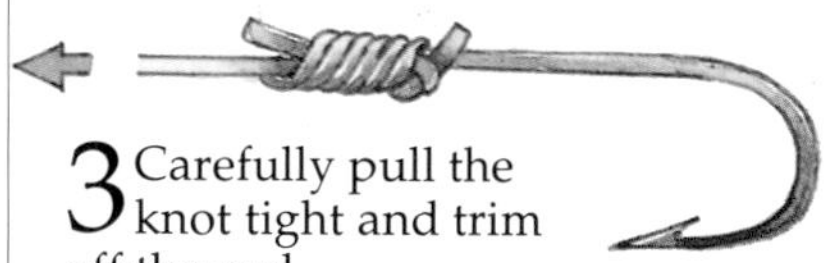

3 Carefully pull the knot tight and trim off the end.

Uni knot

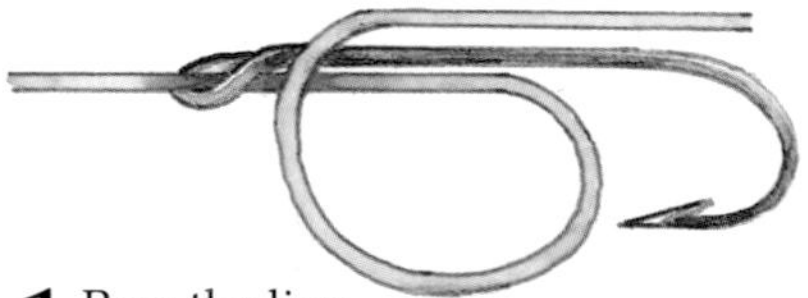

1 Pass the line through the eye of the hook and form a large loop alongside the hook shank.

2 Loop the free end of the line several times around the hook and the upper part of the loop, binding the two together. Then pass the end out through the loop and pull tight. Trim off the end.

Spool knot (arbor knot)

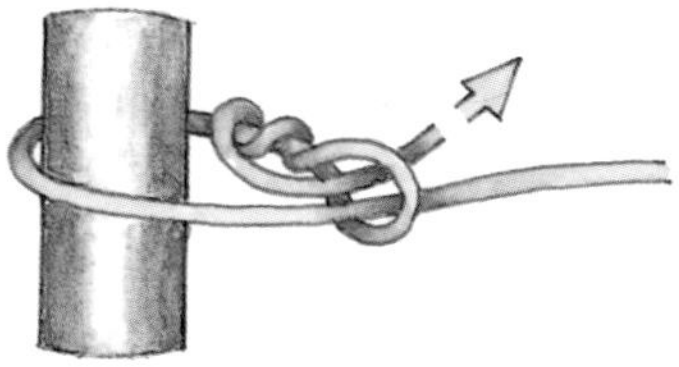

This simple knot is the most effective way to tie the line to the reel spool.

Palomar knot

1 To join a swivel (or a lure or large hook) to a line, double the end of the line and pass it through the eye.

2 Tie a single overhand knot in the doubled line.

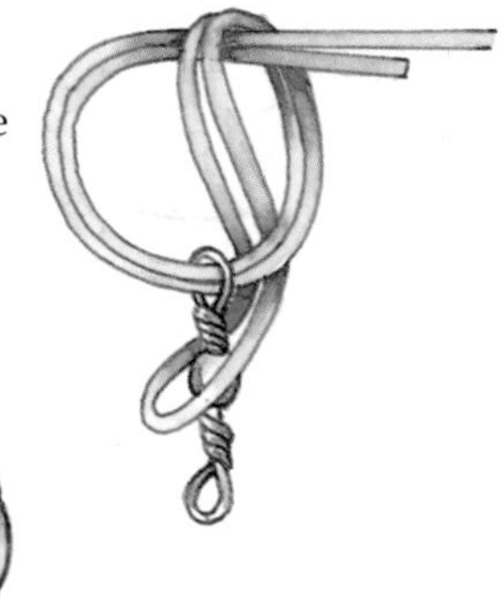

3 Pull the looped end over the swivel or hook.

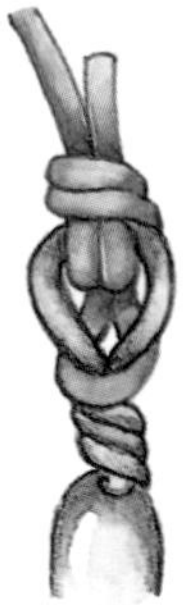

4 Pull knot tight and trim off end.

Knots for Forming Loops

Spider hitch

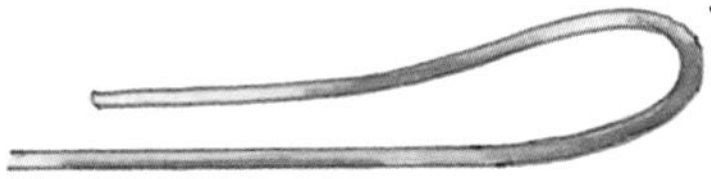

1 Double the end of the line back against itself.

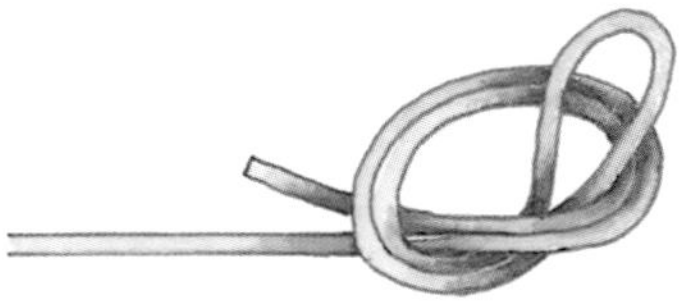

2 Tie an overhand knot in the doubled line.

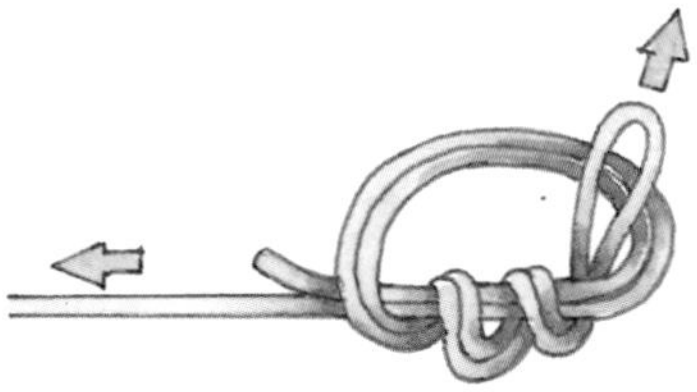

3 Tuck the doubled end through the loop again.

4 Pull the knot tight and trim off the end.

End loop

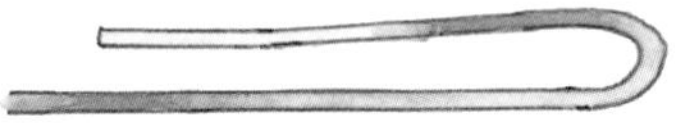

1 Double the end of the line back against itself.

2 Turn the doubled end once around the line.

3 Pass the looped end back through the turn.

4 Pull the knot tight and trim off the end.

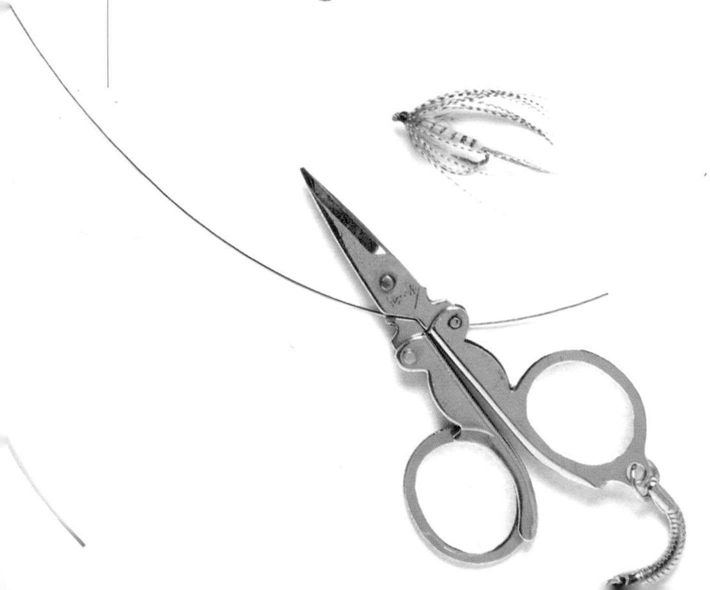

Knots for Joining Lines

Surgeon's knot

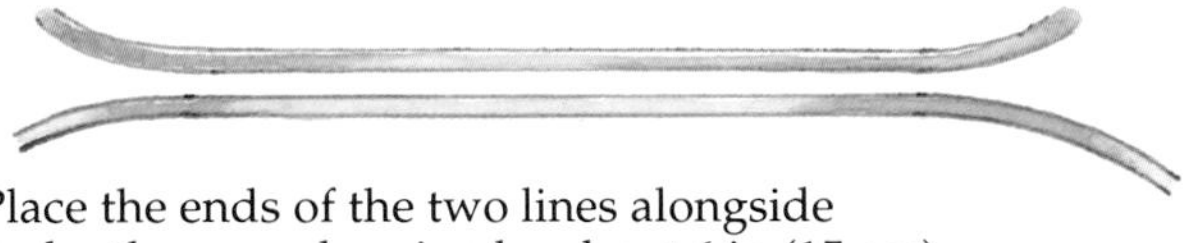

1 Place the ends of the two lines alongside each other, overlapping by about 6 in (15 cm).

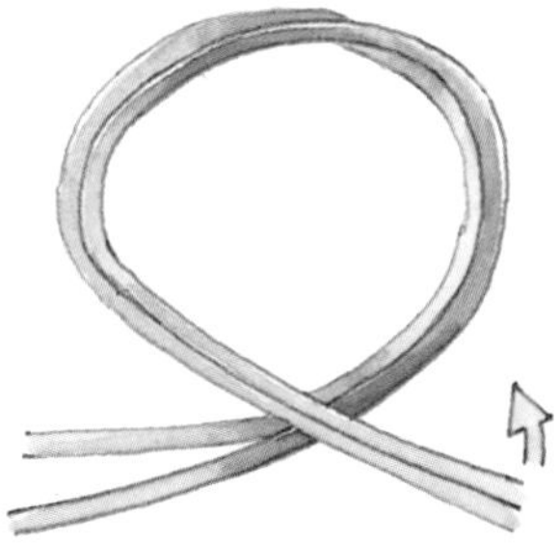

2 Hold the two lines together and form them into a wide loop.

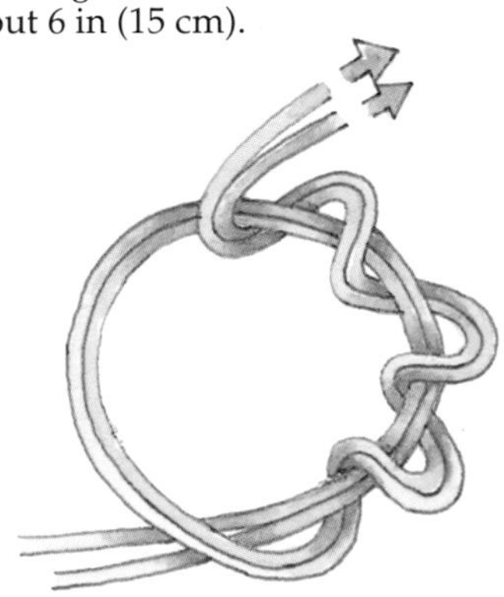

3 Keeping the two lines together, pass the ends through the loop four times.

4 Pull the lines to tighten the loop into a knot, and trim ends.

Blood knot

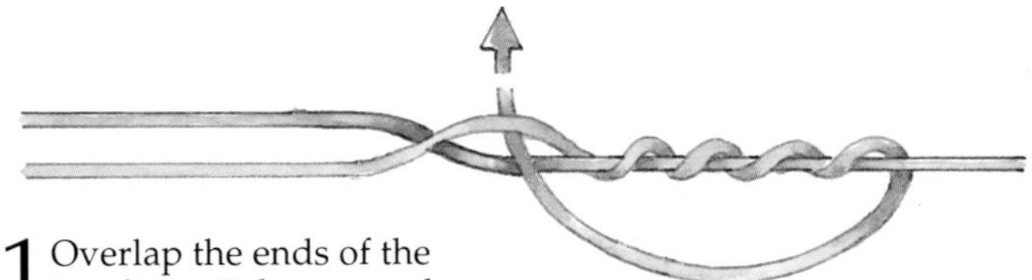

1 Overlap the ends of the two lines. Take one end and twist it four times around the other line. Then bring it back and pass it between the two lines.

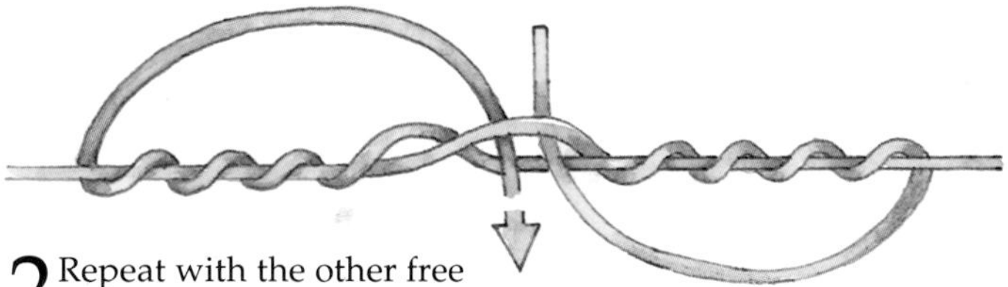

2 Repeat with the other free end, taking care that the first stage does not unravel.

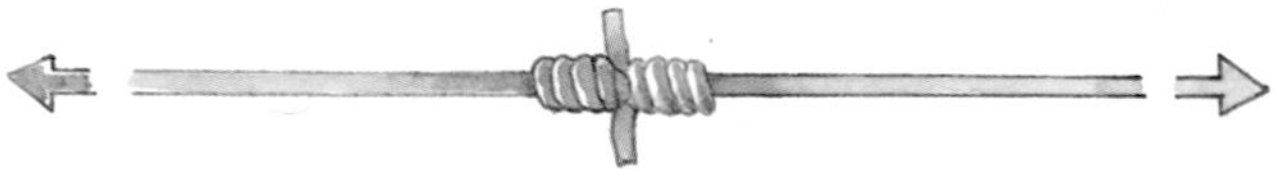

3 Wet the knot to lubricate it, then pull it tight and trim off the ends.

Playing & Landing

Playing a hooked fish successfully requires sound knowledge of your tackle, which must be well balanced in all respects. Before you start, set the reel clutch to slip when the rod has reached its "fighting curve," and check the setting occasionally through the day because use and temperature changes can affect the setting. The techniques shown here can be adapted directly for boat and seashore fishing, but fly fishing employs a different style of line control. When playing a fish on a fly reel, either use your free hand to pay out line under tension and to recover it, allowing it to fall in loose coils, or release line from the reel against the check mechanism or finger pressure on the spool rim, and recover it by winding in.

Reel Control

When using a spinning reel, engage the anti-reverse and brake the spool with your finger, or, on reels that allow it, let the handle backwind against pressure on the pick-up carrier base. With a baitcaster, control the spool with your thumb.

Control with anti-reverse "on"

Backwinding (anti-reverse "off")

Thumb pressure control

Playing

When a fish runs, apply firm pressure by keeping the rod well up, and if necessary increase drag by using one of the reel control methods. When the rod is in this position it is well placed to absorb any lunges the fish may make. Never allow the rod to point down the line, or a break is almost certain. Do not be afraid to let a fish run, because that is what tires it.

Keep the rod well up to exert maximum pressure on a running fish
Increase the pressure by slowing the spool with your finger

TIRING THE FISH
If you play the fish until it is completely exhausted, it is less likely that you will lose it during landing.

Using sidestrain
To turn a fish away from snags, lower the rod so that it is parallel to the surface and pointing in the direction of the run (but not down the line). In one firm movement, sweep the rod around hard in the opposite direction. This knocks the fish off balance, forcing it to turn toward the pull. Repeat until under control.

REPEATING SIDESTRAIN *(left)*
Sidestrain must be applied repeatedly because a hooked fish will make many runs.

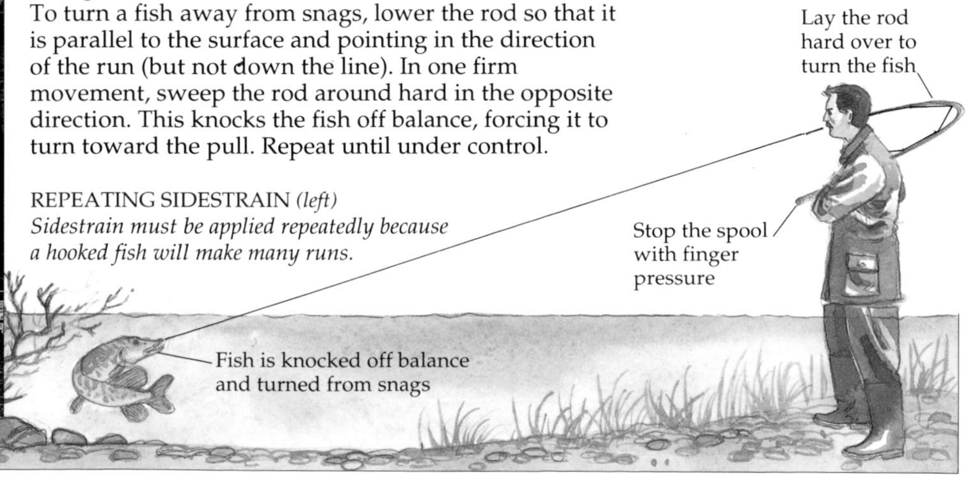
Lay the rod hard over to turn the fish
Stop the spool with finger pressure
Fish is knocked off balance and turned from snags

GAINING LINE
Each time you pump the rod you wind in more line, bringing the fish progressively closer to the net.

Pumping
When the fish reaches the end of a run and is tiring, lower the rod tip while reeling in line to maintain tension. With the rod at about 30°, clamp the spool to prevent line being drawn off and raise the rod smoothly to about 70°. This is "pumping." Hold the rod in this position to see if the fish will run again, and if it does not, repeat.

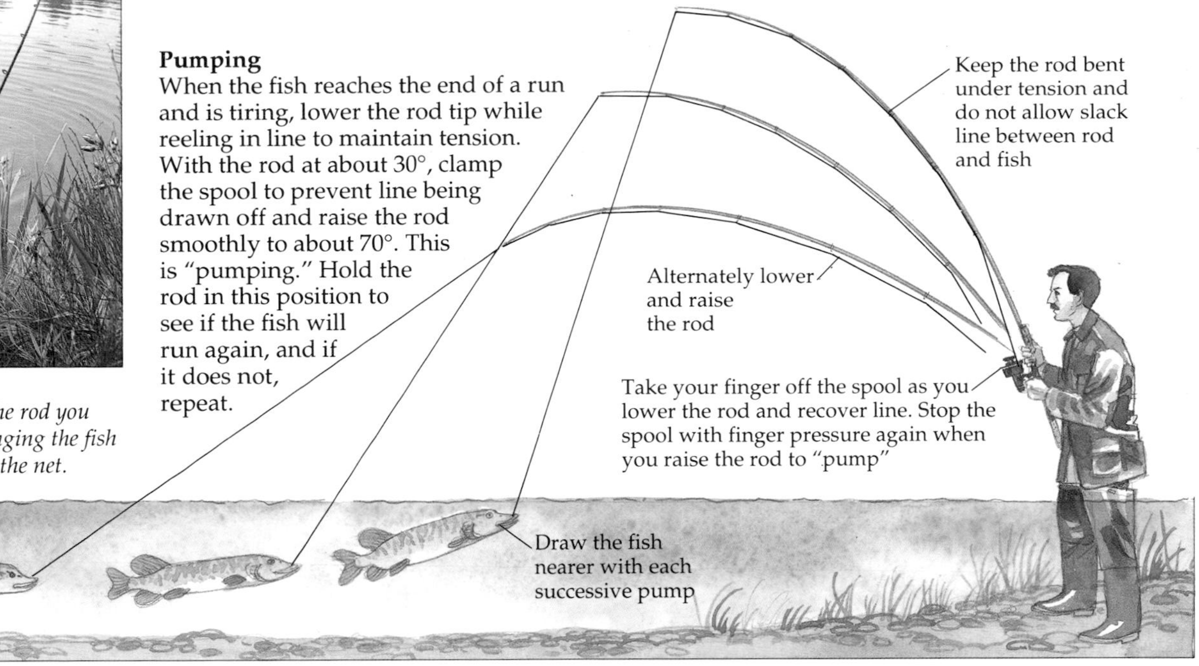
Keep the rod bent under tension and do not allow slack line between rod and fish
Alternately lower and raise the rod
Take your finger off the spool as you lower the rod and recover line. Stop the spool with finger pressure again when you raise the rod to "pump"
Draw the fish nearer with each successive pump

Landing

Beaching, tailing, lipping, netting, and even gaffing are all methods of landing fish, but not all are equally suitable. Tailing is an ideal method for Atlantic salmon but will end in disaster with sea trout. Lipping is suitable for the less "toothy" species. Beaching removes mucus from the scales, leaving a fish vulnerable to infection, so is not suitable if the fish is to be released. Gaffing is banned in many areas, because a mistimed stroke can allow a fish to escape but leave it badly injured and doomed to a painful death.

LIPPING A FISH
Grip the lower lip gently between your thumb and forefinger.

Lipping
A played-out fish can be lifted from the water to be unhooked, or held in the water for unhooking, by gripping its lower lip firmly but gently between thumb and forefinger. This is not suitable for fish with sharp teeth, such as pike. For these, gently slip the fingers of a gloved hand into one gill casing, clamp down with your thumb, and carefully lift the fish out or unhook it in the water.

NETTING FROM THE BANK
Keep the net low in the water so that you do not drag the fish against the rim. If the fish is heavy, lift the net out of the water by grasping the rim; lifting it by the handle could bend the rim.

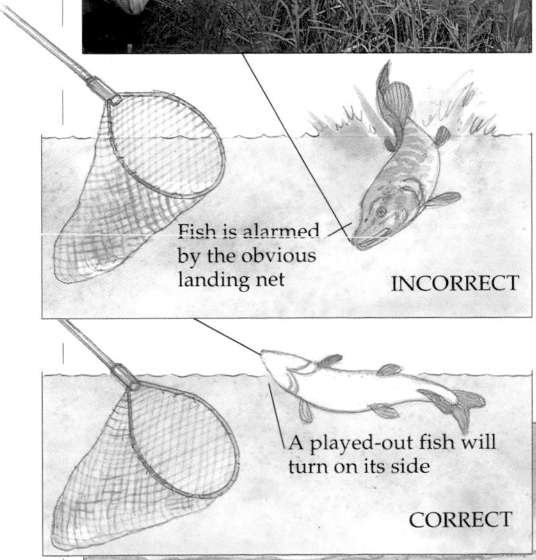
Fish is alarmed by the obvious landing net
INCORRECT
A played-out fish will turn on its side
CORRECT

NETTING
Never attempt to net a lively fish by lunging wildly at it. When the fish is played out, it should be drawn over a fully submerged net with a single, smooth action of the rod.

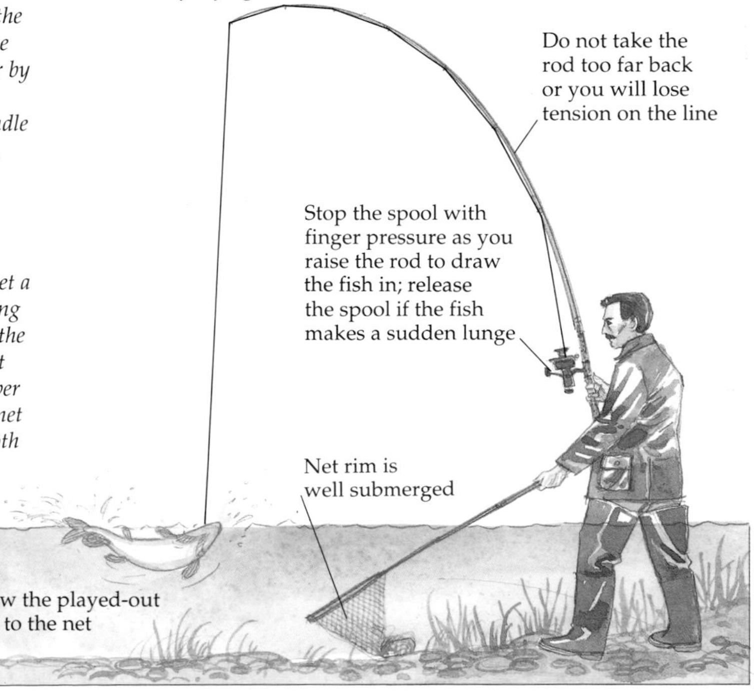
Do not take the rod too far back or you will lose tension on the line
Stop the spool with finger pressure as you raise the rod to draw the fish in; release the spool if the fish makes a sudden lunge
Net rim is well submerged
Draw the played-out fish to the net

Basic Casting

Over the years, the design and construction of both spinning and baitcaster reels have been greatly improved to provide trouble-free casting and fishing for everyone. However, to get the best from any reel, you must learn how to cast properly, and practise your casting until you have eliminated any faults in your technique. Skill is more important than strength, and when you acquire it, you will be able to place your baits where you want them with consistent accuracy. The basic technique shown here is that of casting a lure with a spinning reel, but it can also be used for casting float and leger rigs and, with the appropriate reel and line control methods, with baitcaster and closed-face reels. The techniques of fly casting and surfcasting are different, and details of these are given on pages 232–35 and 250–51 respectively.

Reel Control

SPINNING REEL

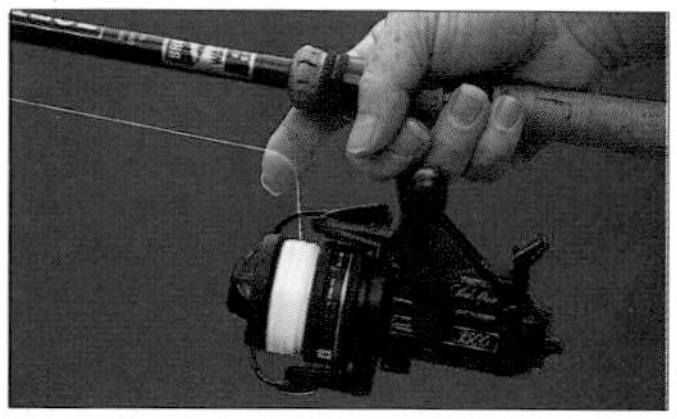

First open the bail arm. Then hook the line over the pad of the index finger of your rod hand, to take the weight of the terminal tackle and prevent it from stripping line from the reel. For extra support, press the line against the rod handle.

BAITCASTER

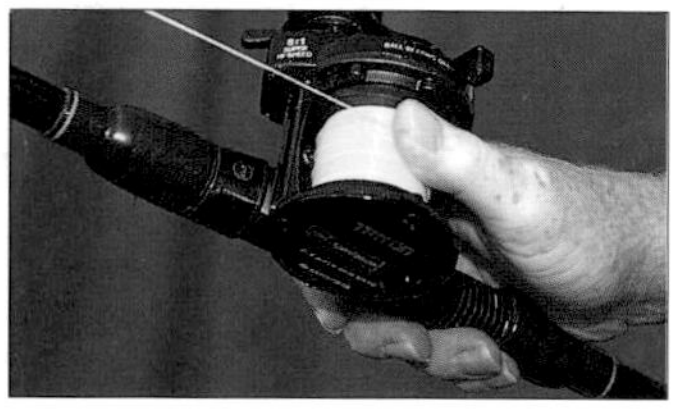

With a baitcaster, clamp the thumb of your rod hand hard on the spool to stop it turning, and put the reel into free-spool mode. With most baitcasters, clamping your thumb onto the spool depresses a bar that disengages it.

CLOSED-FACE/SPINCASTER

On these reels, the line passes through a hole or slot in the front casing and is guided onto the fixed spool by a steel pin. When you want to release the line at the end of a cast, you simply press a button on the reel to retract the pin.

The Overhead Cast

With the bail arm open, support the line on your index finger with the lure about 12 to 18 in (30 to 45 cm) below the rod tip. Hold the rod at the 2:00 position and in line with the spot at which you want the lure to land **(A)**.

Lift the rod briskly but smoothly toward the 12:00 position by raising your forearm and cocking your wrist back **(B)**. At the start of the lift, the inertia of the rod tip and the weight of the lure will cause the tip to droop.

Stop the rod at the 12:00 position **(C)**. The tip will straighten, and then bend behind you as it is pulled back by the still-traveling lure. You will feel a pull on the rod tip as the lure reaches the limit of its travel.

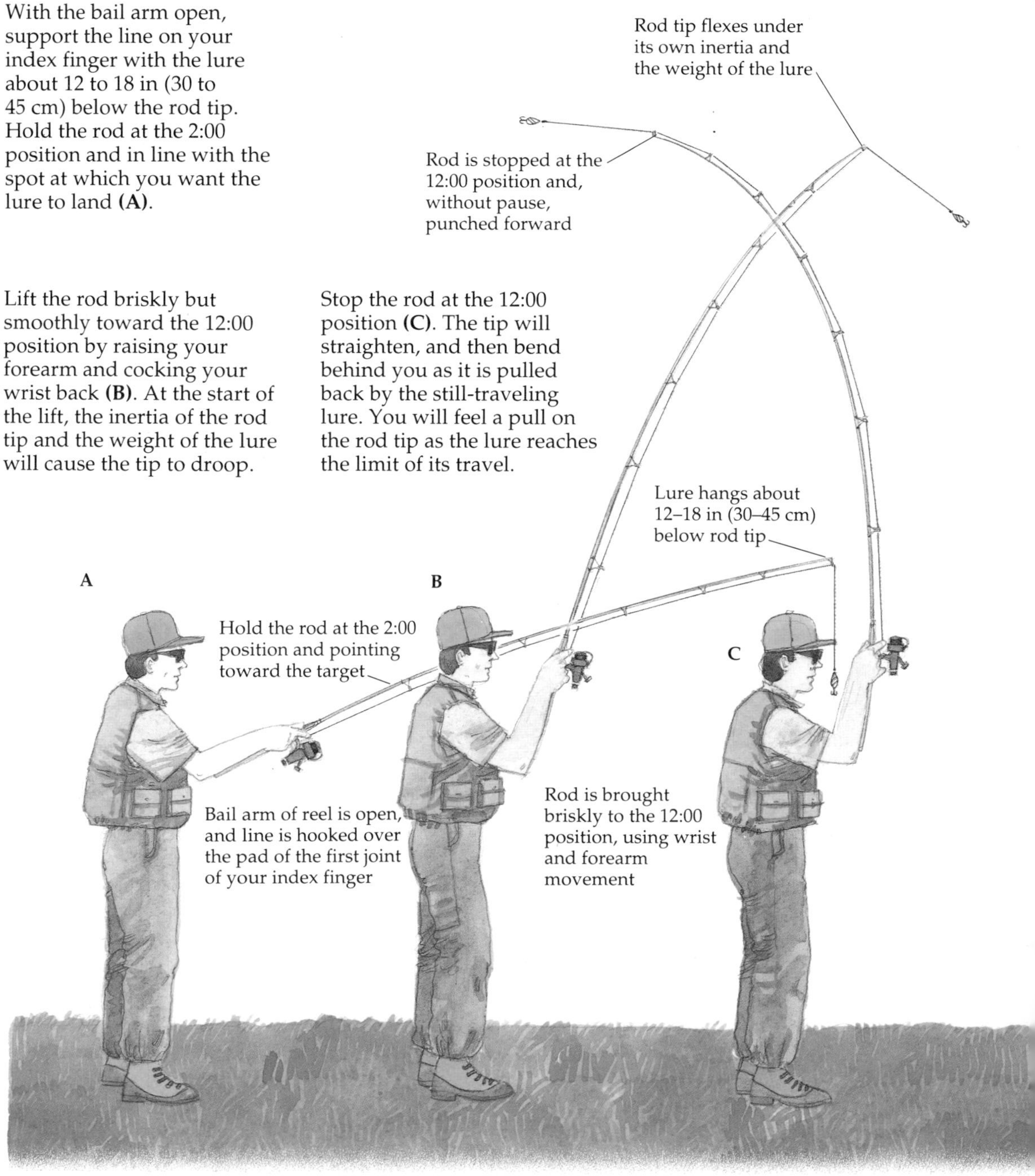

Rod tip flexes under its own inertia and the weight of the lure
Rod is stopped at the 12:00 position and, without pause, punched forward
Lure hangs about 12–18 in (30–45 cm) below rod tip
A
B
C
Hold the rod at the 2:00 position and pointing toward the target
Bail arm of reel is open, and line is hooked over the pad of the first joint of your index finger
Rod is brought briskly to the 12:00 position, using wrist and forearm movement

LURE FLIGHT
When casting, always pick a target spot in the water and aim to land your lure (or other terminal tackle) in it. After releasing the line, follow the path of the lure with the rod tip so that the line flows freely through the tip ring. The lure should travel in a gentle arc toward the water.

Common Casting Faults

The lure overshoots
- Too much power in the cast
- Line release not slowed by feathering the spool

The lure falls short
- Lure too light
- Line was released too early during the cast
- Rod held too high after line was released

The lure lands too hard
- Lure was released with the rod at too low an angle and failed to describe a gentle arc through the air

The cast is inaccurate
- The lure went off course because rod was allowed to move from side to side as the forward cast was made

THE CLOCK FACE
Clock face positions are used to describe the rod movements during casting, and make it easy to remember the position of the rod at various stages of the cast.

When you feel the pull on the tip, the rod is under maximum load and storing energy like a spring **(D)**. Immediately punch the rod forward. This action, plus the energy released by the rod as it straightens, will throw the lure rapidly forward.

Stop the movement of the rod at about the 2:00 position, and at the same time straighten your index finger to release the line **(E)**. The lure will shoot forward in an arc toward the water, stripping line from the reel.

As the lure falls, follow its descent with the rod tip **(F)**. When it lands, put your index finger on the spool rim to stop the line, and turn the reel handle to close the bail arm and keep a tight line between the lure and the rod.

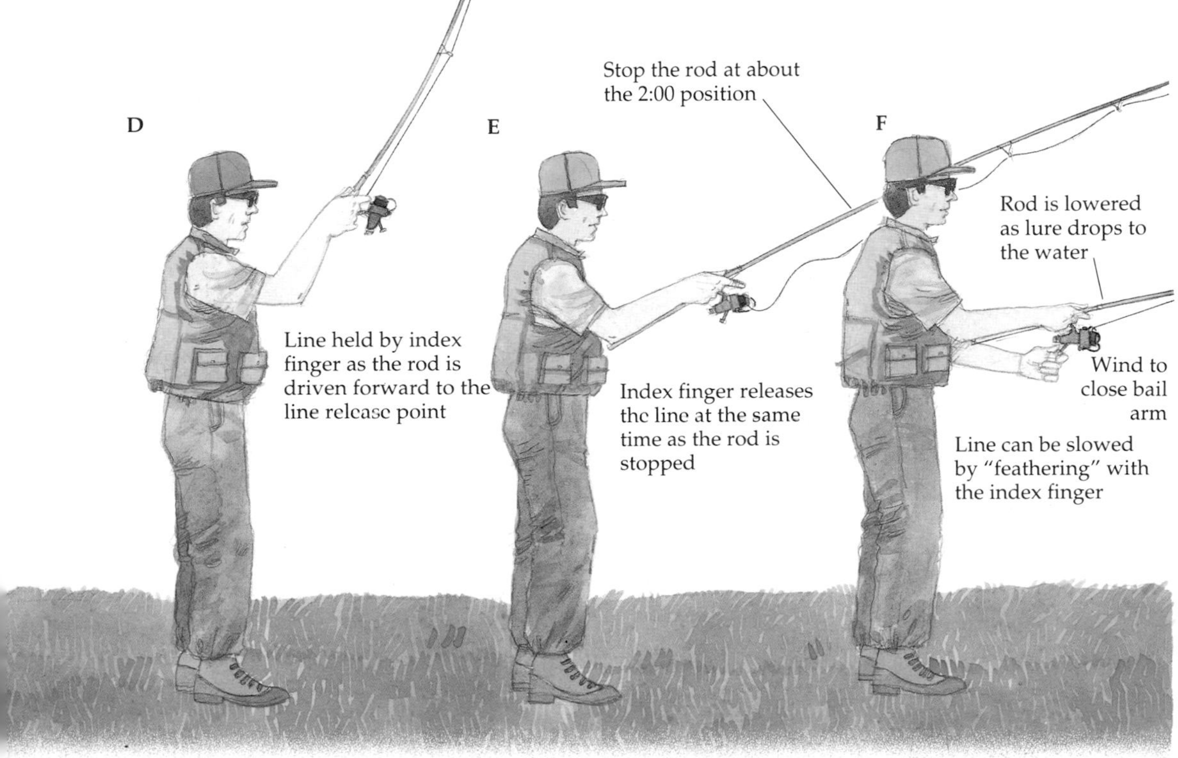
Rod under maximum load
D
Line held by index finger as the rod is driven forward to the line release point
E
Stop the rod at about the 2:00 position
Index finger releases the line at the same time as the rod is stopped
F
Rod is lowered as lure drops to the water
Wind to close bail arm
Line can be slowed by "feathering" with the index finger

Line Control

SPINNING REEL

To prevent the lure from overshooting the target, and to achieve a gentle landing, slow its flight by gently dabbing or touching the lip of the spool with the tip of your index finger. This "feathering" acts as a brake on the line.

BAITCASTER

To slow down a bait fished on a baitcaster, apply gentle thumb pressure to the revolving spool (but beware of friction burns). Overruns are rare with modern reels because they have magnetic braking systems.

CLOSED-FACE/SPINCASTER

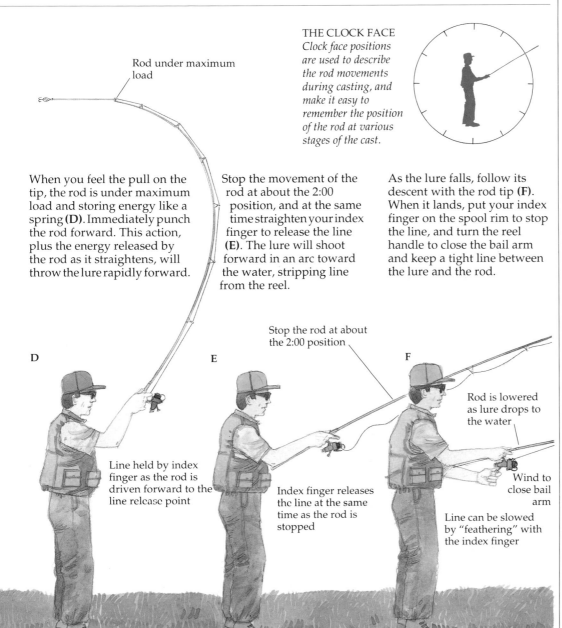

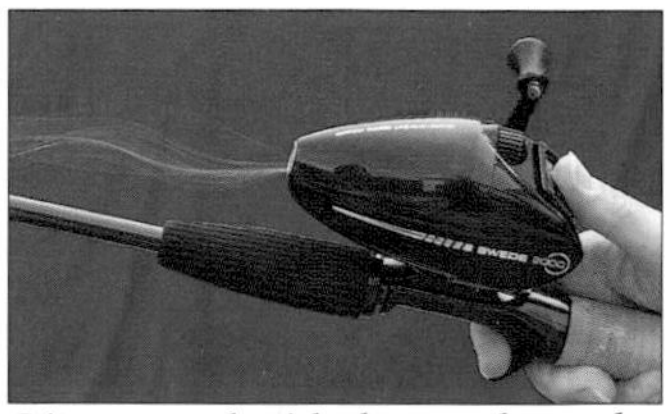

Line control with these reels can be difficult, because the spool is shrouded and finger pressure on the lip is not possible. Slow the line by gently squeezing it between the index finger and thumb of your free hand as it emerges from the casing.

LURE FISHING – SPINNING

The relative ease of use of spinning tackle accounts for spinning being one of the most popular forms of fishing worldwide. When correctly loaded with a full spool of line, spinning reels allow long, effortless casts to be made and the angler often has to do no more than crank the handle to make the lure fish attractively. Obviously, the skilled practitioner will outfish the tyro, but spinning offers the beginner the best chance of comparatively easy success. Spinners are so termed because at least part of the lure revolves. Usually, there is a rotating blade that is separate from the body, as in standard spinners, spinnerbaits, and buzzbaits, but sometimes the whole lure rotates, as is the case in the Devon minnow and similar lures. Spinners attract fish by visual stimulus and by creating vibrations that act on the fish's lateral lines; if used correctly, they will appeal to any predatory fish.

ANTI-KINK DEVICES

The keel effect of an anti-kink vane or weight between main line and leader helps to reduce line twist. An anti-kink weight should be fitted immediately above the swivel for maximum effect, but weights should not be used if they interfere with the action of a lure.

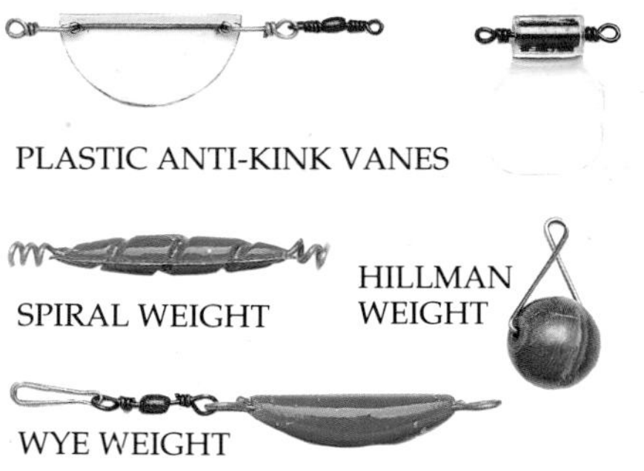
PLASTIC ANTI-KINK VANES
SPIRAL WEIGHT
HILLMAN WEIGHT
WYE WEIGHT

STANDARD SPINNERS

The most common type, the clevis, has a blade mounted on a shaft via a clevis (link). Another type, the sonic, has a blade mounted directly over the shaft. A standard spinner must be retrieved to make the blade rotate in stillwater, but in running water the current works the blade. Fish upstream in fast water, because fishing downstream makes the lure swim too shallow. In slow water, fish downstream because casting upstream allows the lure to sink too quickly.

CLEVIS TYPE
SONIC TYPE

Blade shapes and actions
The shape and thickness of a spinner blade affects the action of the lure. The high water resistance of a broad blade makes it ideal for stillwaters and slow streams, but in fast water it will rise to the surface. A thin blade has less resistance and can be fished in fast water without skating on the surface.

KEY TO BLADES
1 Indiana; **2** French; **3** Colorado; **4** Fluted; **5** In-line; **6** Willowleaf; **7** Ripple; **8** June Bug.

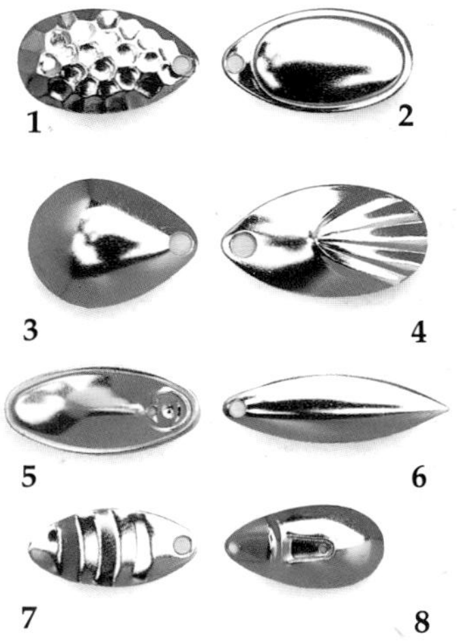
1
2
3
4
5
6
7
8

UPSTREAM SPINNING

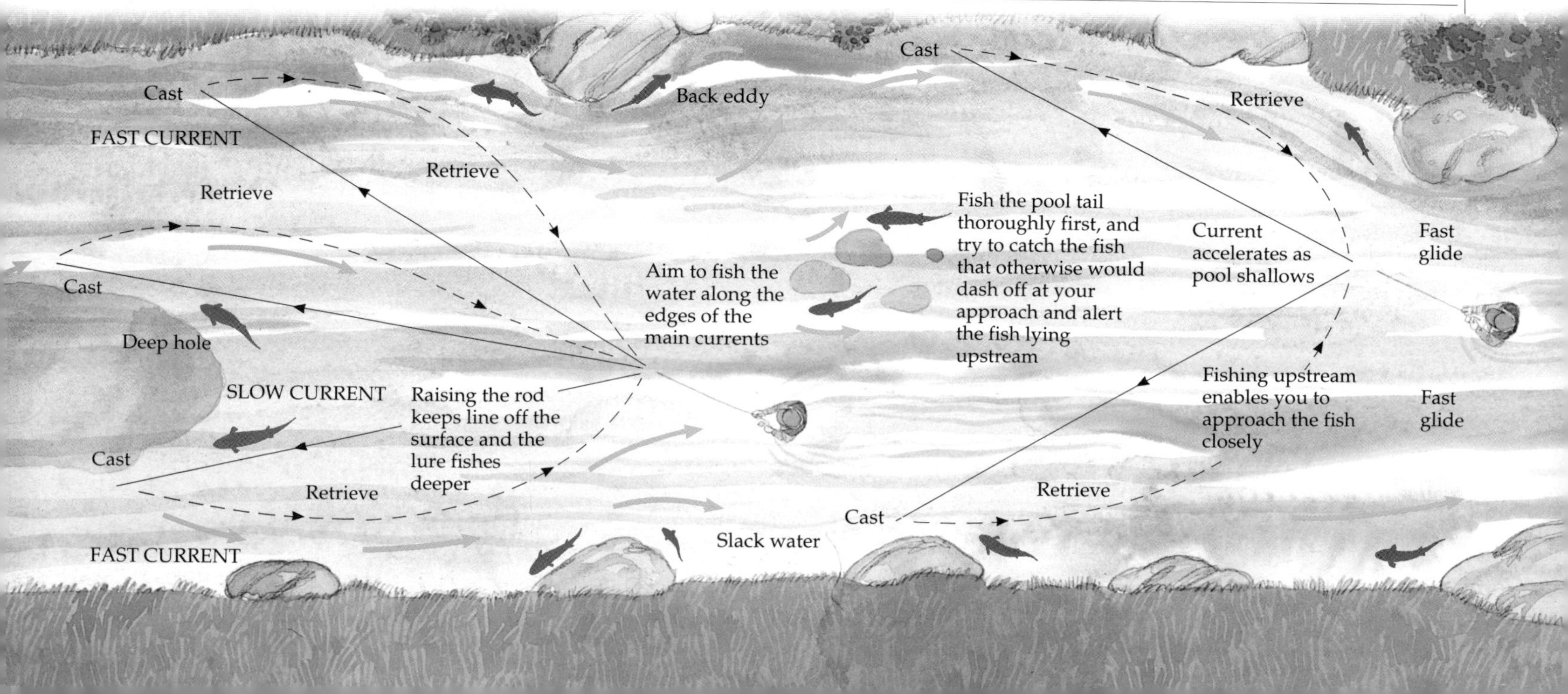
Cast
FAST CURRENT
Retrieve
Back eddy
Cast
Retrieve
Retrieve
Cast
Deep hole
SLOW CURRENT
Aim to fish the water along the edges of the main currents
Fish the pool tail thoroughly first, and try to catch the fish that otherwise would dash off at your approach and alert the fish lying upstream
Current accelerates as pool shallows
Fast glide
Raising the rod keeps line off the surface and the lure fishes deeper
Fishing upstream enables you to approach the fish closely
Fast glide
Cast
Retrieve
Retrieve
Cast
Slack water
FAST CURRENT

Floating Lures

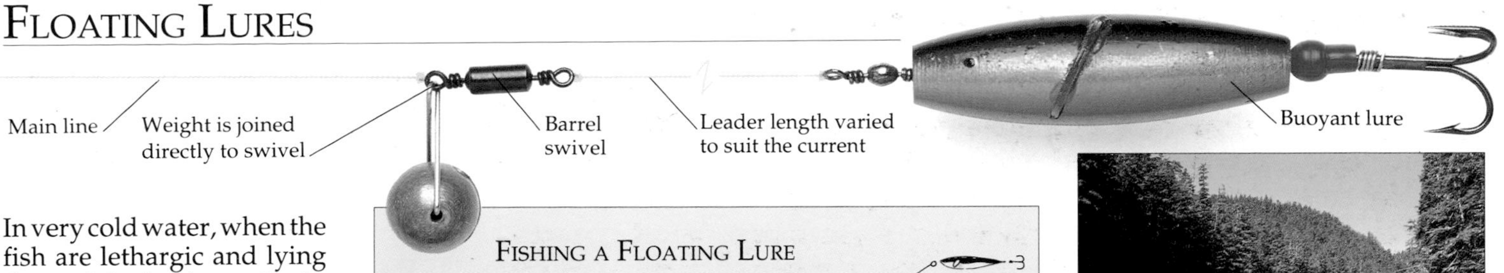

Main line
Weight is joined directly to swivel
Barrel swivel
Leader length varied to suit the current
Buoyant lure

In very cold water, when the fish are lethargic and lying deep, fish the lure slowly and close to the bottom. It is not possible to fish a heavy lure slowly enough without snagging, and the solution is to use a floating lure sunk by a suitable weight. By varying the leader length to suit the current, you can work the lure at the fish's eye level.

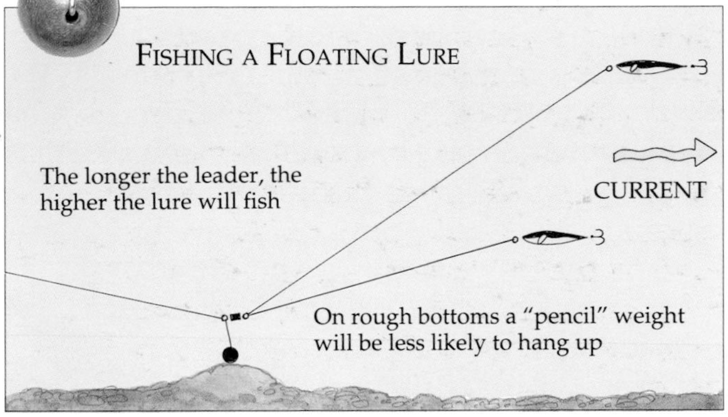

Fishing a Floating Lure
The longer the leader, the higher the lure will fish
CURRENT
On rough bottoms a "pencil" weight will be less likely to hang up

COLDWATER SPINNING
A slow retrieve is vital in cold water, and a sunken floating lure fishes slowly without snagging.

Spinnerbaits & Buzzbaits

The most obvious difference between a spinnerbait and a buzzbait is in the blade. A spinnerbait has a fluttering blade – such as a broad, teardrop-shaped Colorado or Indiana, or a narrow, elliptical willowleaf – while the buzzbait has a single or double buzzblade rotating on a shaft. The buzzbait is designed solely for surface fishing, where its blade causes noisy, splashy disturbance. This makes it an excellent lure for weedy shallows or turbid water; vary the retrieve until successful. Twin-bladed lures, which create even more disturbance, are ideal for slow retrieves. Spinnerbaits are more versatile and can be fished at all speeds and from the surface to the bottom, or even jigged vertically around cover. Tipping the hooks of Indiana and willowleaf spinners with worms, minnows, or strips of pork rind can improve their success rate.

SUMMER SPINNING
In hot, sunny weather, when fish seek the shade of weedbeds and brush, buzzbaits are excellent lures for drawing them from their cover.

Downstream Spinning

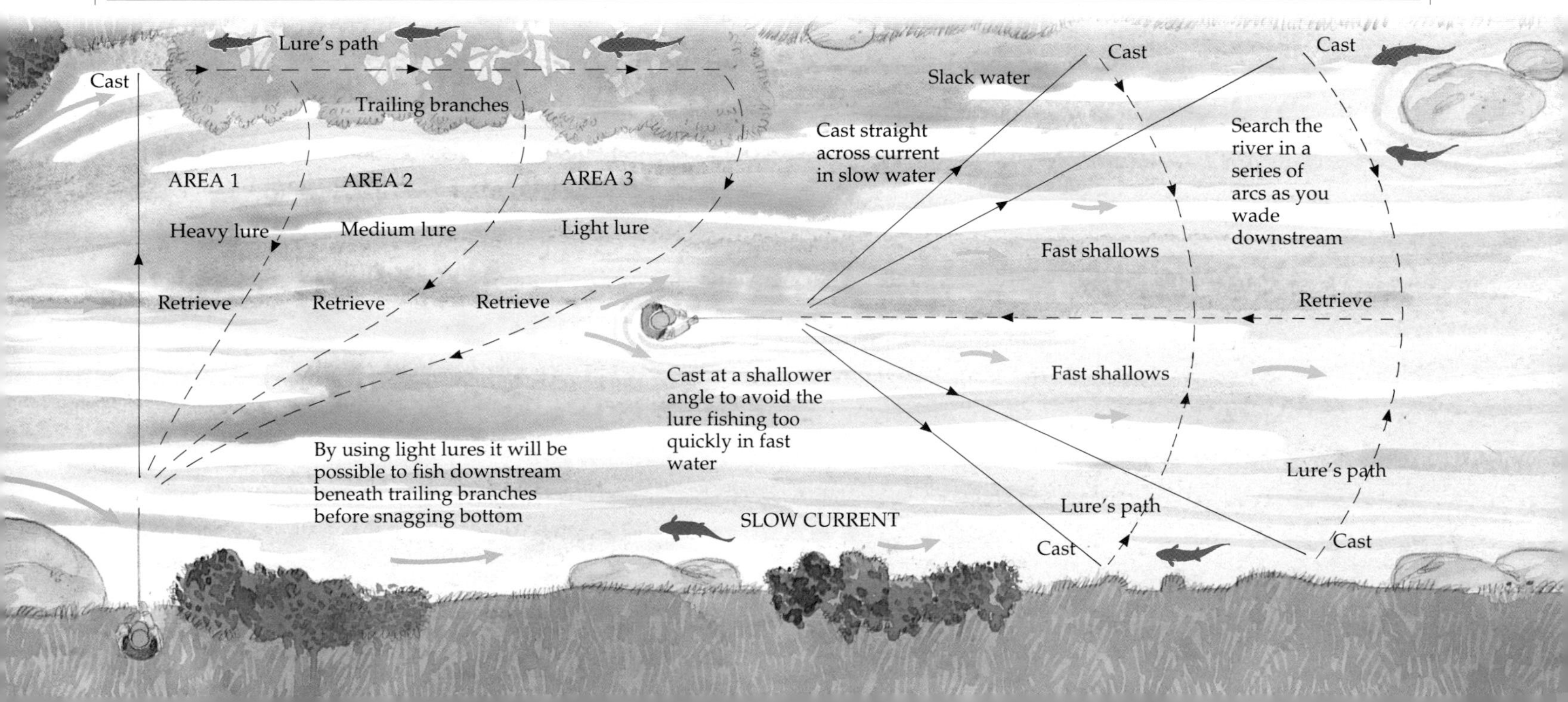

Lure's path
Cast
Trailing branches
AREA 1
AREA 2
AREA 3
Heavy lure
Medium lure
Light lure
Retrieve
Retrieve
Retrieve
By using light lures it will be possible to fish downstream beneath trailing branches before snagging bottom
Slack water
Cast
Cast
Cast straight across current in slow water
Search the river in a series of arcs as you wade downstream
Fast shallows
Retrieve
Fast shallows
Cast at a shallower angle to avoid the lure fishing too quickly in fast water
SLOW CURRENT
Lure's path
Lure's path
Cast
Cast

Lure Fishing – Spoons

Spoons can be divided into the broad categories of trolling spoons and casting spoons. The trolling spoons are generally too thin to be cast far and their use is restricted to trolling from a moving boat. Casting spoons can be either of the weedless or non-weedless types, the former having hooks with nylon or metal weedguards that prevent them from snagging on weeds, submerged brush, or other aquatic debris.

A spoon's action depends on its shape, weight, and the speed of the retrieval. Deeply concave spoons wobble more than shallow ones, while light spoons have more action than heavy ones of similar size. Use light, thin spoons in shallow water or the top layers of a lake, and heavy, thick models in deep water. Each spoon has an optimum retrieve rate that imparts the most enticing action, and this can be found by trial and error.

Spoon-fishing Tackle

The most suitable tackle for spoon fishing is a light spinning outfit, or a medium baitcasting outfit, plus mono line with a short wire leader if necessary. There is no need for a sensitive rod, because bite indication is never a problem when fishing with artificial lures. Always attach the spoon to the line or leader with a good-quality swivel, because tying the line direct to the attachment hole of the spoon can interfere with its action, as can adding weight to the rig. In addition, line twist can be severe with some types of spoon. Fit a rounded snap swivel into the attachment hole and join the line to it.

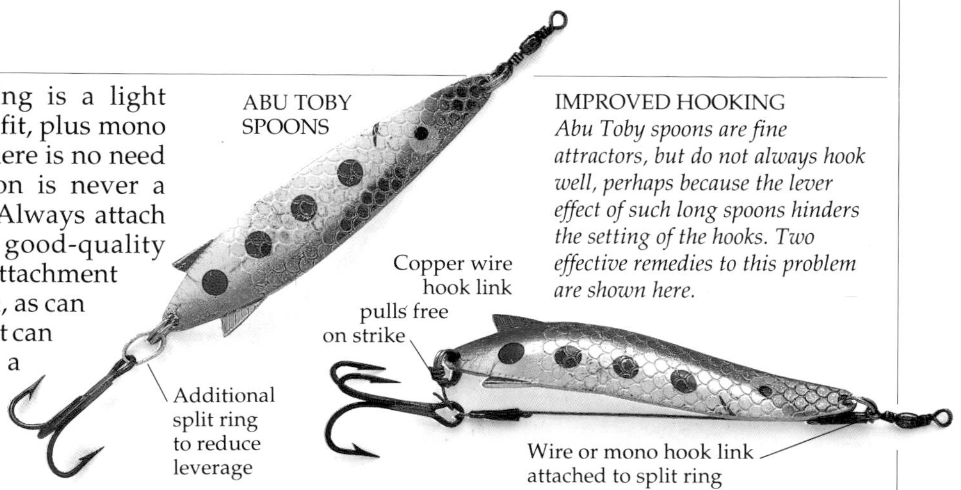

IMPROVED HOOKING
Abu Toby spoons are fine attractors, but do not always hook well, perhaps because the lever effect of such long spoons hinders the setting of the hooks. Two effective remedies to this problem are shown here.

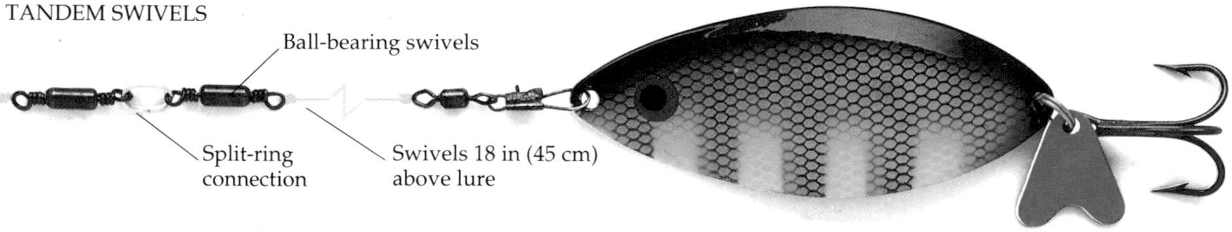

TANDEM SWIVELS
Two ball-bearing swivels joined by a split ring, about 18 in (45 cm) from the spoon, will virtually eliminate line twist.

Casting Patterns

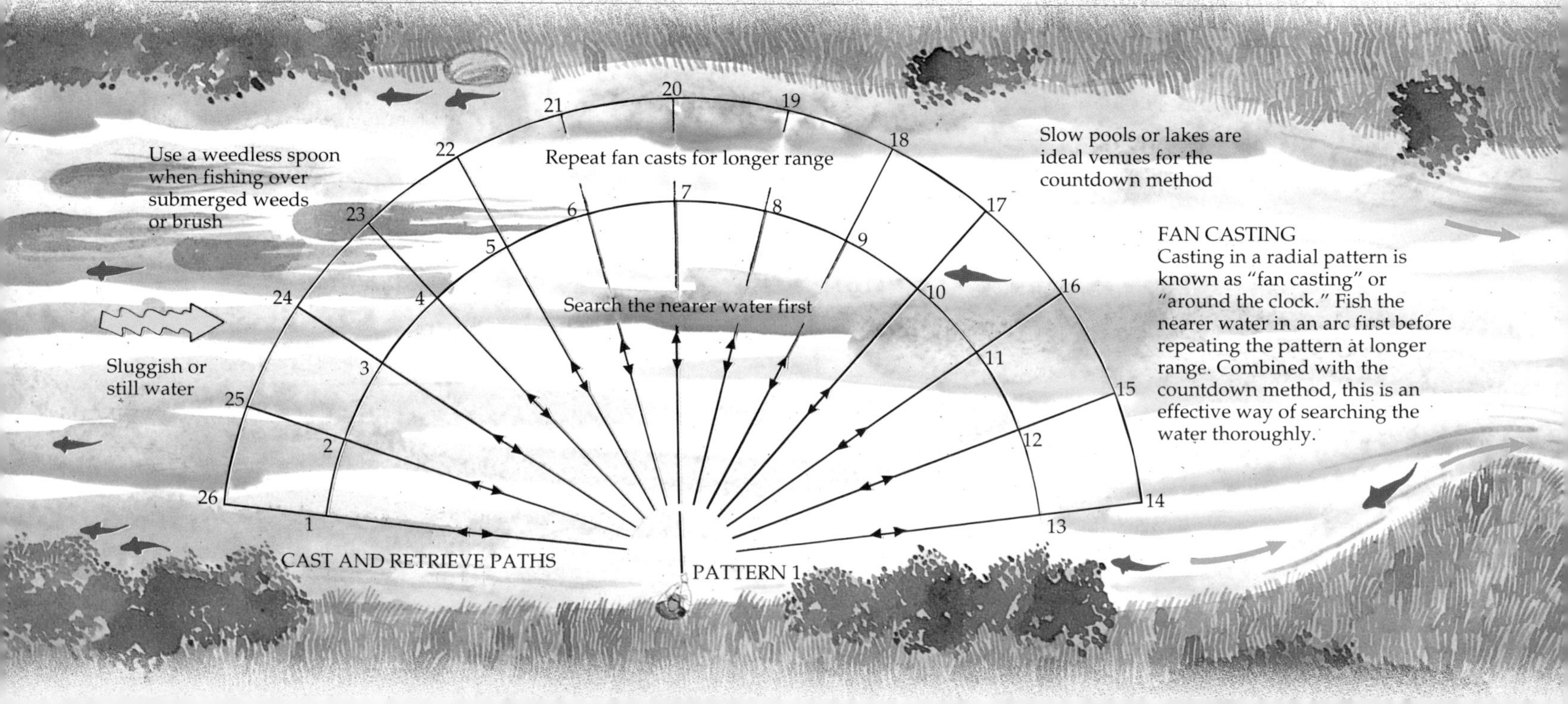

FAN CASTING
Casting in a radial pattern is known as "fan casting" or "around the clock." Fish the nearer water in an arc first before repeating the pattern at longer range. Combined with the countdown method, this is an effective way of searching the water thoroughly.

Spoon-fishing Techniques

In lakes, the countdown method gives consistent fishing depth if the retrieve rate is constant, but rivers currents will affect the spoon's depth. Retrieve a spoon cast upstream quicker than one cast downstream because it will sink deeper, traveling with the flow. Use light spoons for upstream casting and for shallow or slowly retrieved downstream work. Heavy spoons are good when cast downstream in fast water or upstream in slow pools.

The countdown method
This helps you to find, and fish at, the feeding depth of your quarry. Cast the spoon out, allow it to sink, and count the number of seconds that pass until it hits bottom. Then retrieve steadily. If it reaches bottom on a count of, say, 10, and you get no strikes on the retrieve, on the next cast retrieve after a count of 8. Reduce the count by 2 on each subsequent cast until a fish strikes. Repeat the successful count to fish the taking zone.

The Countdown Method

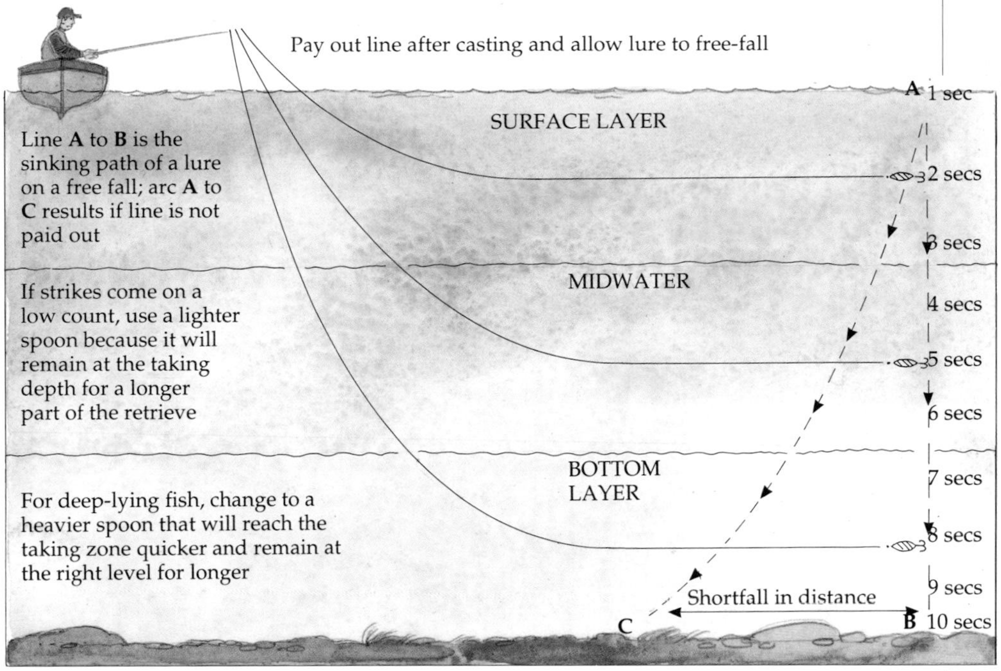

Pay out line after casting and allow lure to free-fall
A 1 sec
SURFACE LAYER
Line **A** to **B** is the sinking path of a lure on a free fall; arc **A** to **C** results if line is not paid out
2 secs
3 secs
MIDWATER
If strikes come on a low count, use a lighter spoon because it will remain at the taking depth for a longer part of the retrieve
4 secs
5 secs
6 secs
BOTTOM LAYER
7 secs
For deep-lying fish, change to a heavier spoon that will reach the taking zone quicker and remain at the right level for longer
8 secs
9 secs
Shortfall in distance
C
B 10 secs

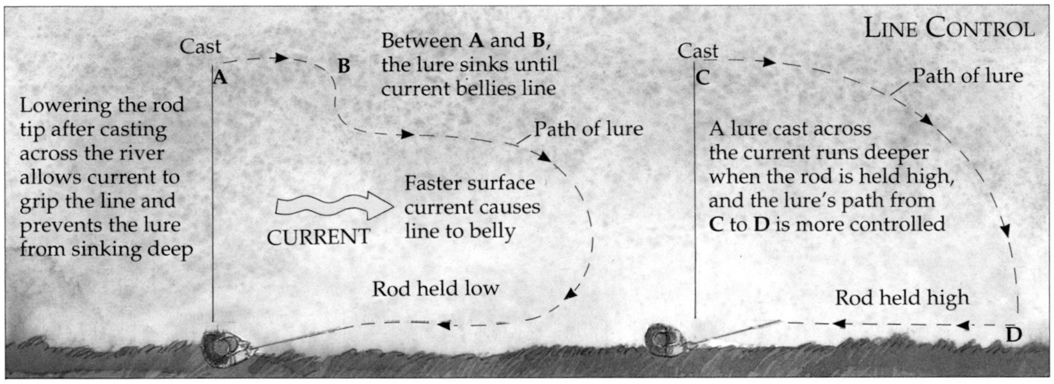

Line Control
Cast
A
B
Between **A** and **B**, the lure sinks until current bellies line
Lowering the rod tip after casting across the river allows current to grip the line and prevents the lure from sinking deep
Path of lure
Faster surface current causes line to belly
CURRENT
Rod held low
Cast
C
Path of lure
A lure cast across the current runs deeper when the rod is held high, and the lure's path from **C** to **D** is more controlled
Rod held high
D

Line control
When fishing upstream, holding the rod tip high lifts the spoon in the water, while keeping it low allows the spoon to sink. This is most obvious with a short line. When casting across the flow, however, current drag on the line holds the spoon up while a high rod allows it to sink. This effect decreases the more downstream you cast, until the upstream rule applies.

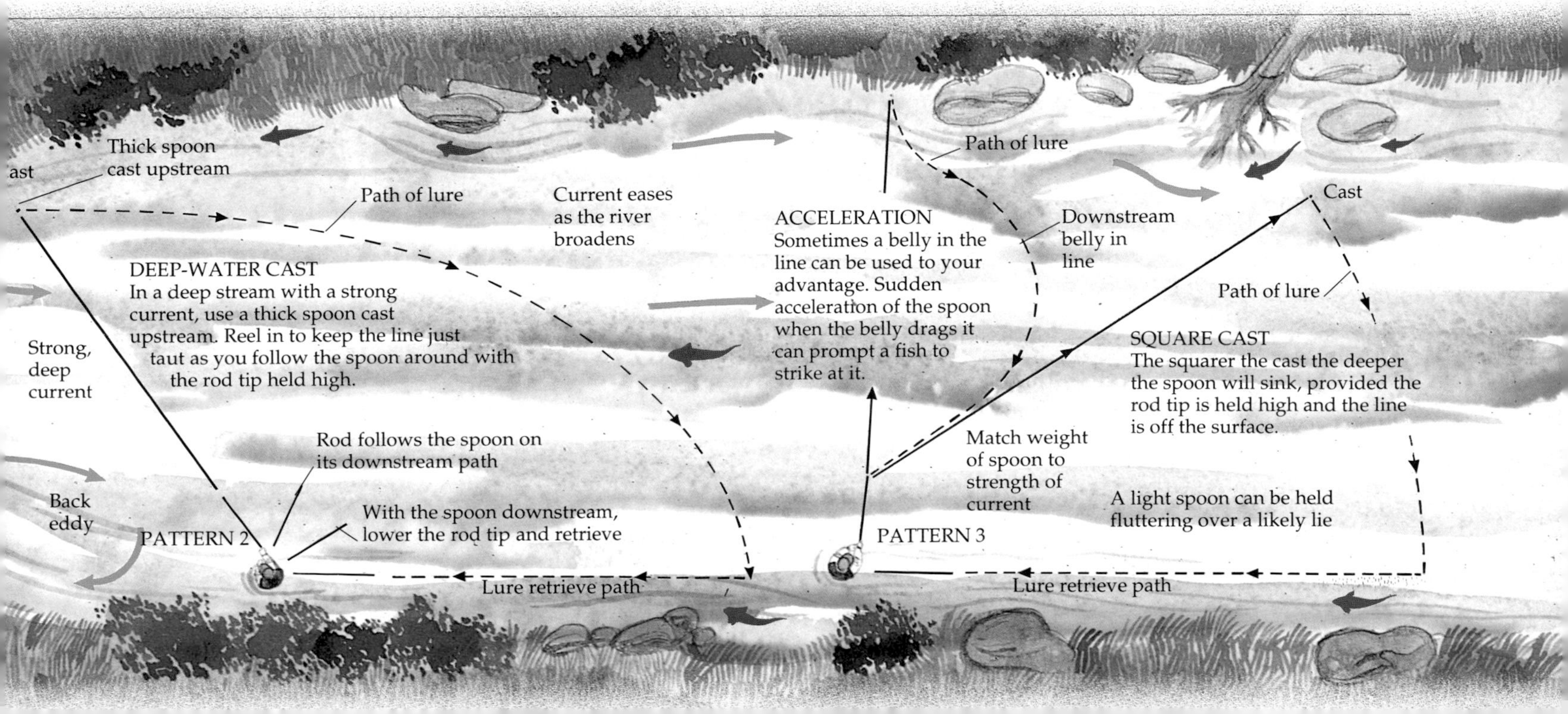

ast
Thick spoon cast upstream
Path of lure
Current eases as the river broadens
DEEP-WATER CAST
In a deep stream with a strong current, use a thick spoon cast upstream. Reel in to keep the line just taut as you follow the spoon around with the rod tip held high.
Strong, deep current
Rod follows the spoon on its downstream path
Back eddy
PATTERN 2
With the spoon downstream, lower the rod tip and retrieve
Lure retrieve path
Path of lure
ACCELERATION
Sometimes a belly in the line can be used to your advantage. Sudden acceleration of the spoon when the belly drags it can prompt a fish to strike at it.
Downstream belly in line
Cast
Path of lure
SQUARE CAST
The squarer the cast the deeper the spoon will sink, provided the rod tip is held high and the line is off the surface.
Match weight of spoon to strength of current
A light spoon can be held fluttering over a likely lie
PATTERN 3
Lure retrieve path

Lure Fishing – Plugs

Within the ranks of what we term "plugs" are lures for fishing at all levels, from the surface to the bottom, and at all speeds. As with all artificial lure fishing, matching the lure to the quarry and the conditions is vital. In general, the smaller the quarry is, the smaller the lure should be: a 12 in (30 cm) lure might be none too large for a pike but it would not be effective for trout. Fishing cold or muddy water necessitates getting the lure down to eyeball level, and in such conditions the first choice of lure would be a vibrating plug or a deep diver, whereas in warmer water, where predatory fish are more alert, a quickly retrieved, shallow-diving crankbait or surface lure is called for.

The Open Loop

Open-looped knot

A split ring, link swivel, or tight knot can adversely affect a lure's action. Tying the lure to the line with an open-looped knot allows it to swing freely.

Surface Lure Techniques

Surface lures are at their most effective in shallow water, where fish lying near the bottom are not too far away to be attracted by them. The water should also be calm, because surface choppiness can affect their action. A propbait can be cast into small gaps in surface weeds and then twitched back on a slack line or retrieved steadily, in which case the action of the propeller will cause more disturbance than is achieved by most surface plugs. To prevent the nose dipping below the surface and spoiling the action, tie the lure direct to the line or leader without a snap or swivel. Crawler-type lures with projecting arms or wide, scooped faceplates fish best over shallow water on a moderate retrieve: vary the retrieve until the best action is achieved. The popper or chugger surface lures have a concave face that makes a popping sound on a short, twitched retrieve, although when fished into small openings in weedbeds they are often taken when stationary. Stickbaits are the best surface lures for bringing fish up from the depths, and the basic method of retrieve for these is known as "walking the dog".

Stickbaits
Cast out a stickbait, jerk the rod tip vertically, then let the line go slack, and the lure will slip to one side. Repeat the action and the lure will dodge to the other side. This is known as "walking the dog". Fast jerks without letting the line go slack result in the lure moving to one side only. A fast, tip-actioned rod is best for this technique, and because stickbaits float it is an ideal method over submerged weeds or brush.

Heddon

STICKBAITS
These are effective lures for most gamefish.

Walking the Dog

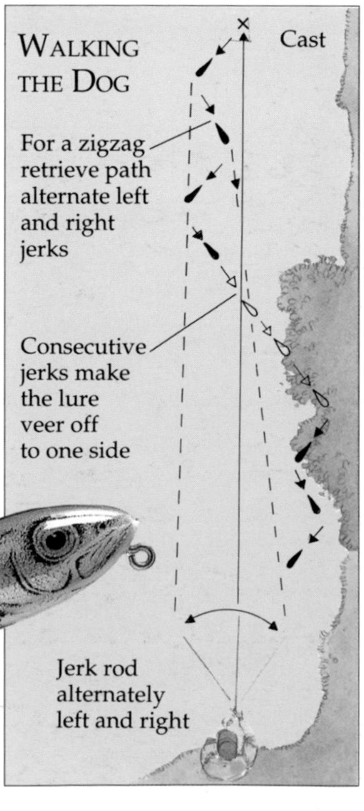
Cast
For a zigzag retrieve path alternate left and right jerks
Consecutive jerks make the lure veer off to one side
Jerk rod alternately left and right

Minnow plugs
Drifting a floating minnow plug downstream allows you to fish at far greater range than you could cast such a light lure. For bankside lies, drift the lure down past the fish. When you stop the line, the lure will dive to about 12 in (30 cm), depending on the speed of the current, and you can then bring it back upstream through the lie. From midriver, fish the lure back in a series of arcs by swinging the rod from side to side during the retrieve.

Fishing a Minnow Plug

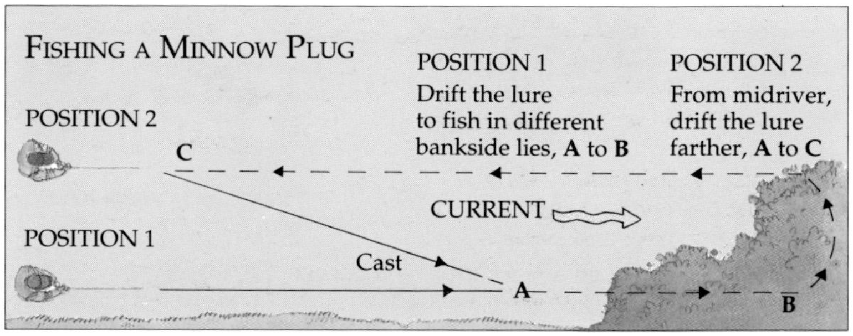
POSITION 1
Drift the lure to fish in different bankside lies, A to B
POSITION 2
From midriver, drift the lure farther, A to C
POSITION 2
POSITION 1
C
CURRENT
Cast
A
B

Plug Fishing Methods

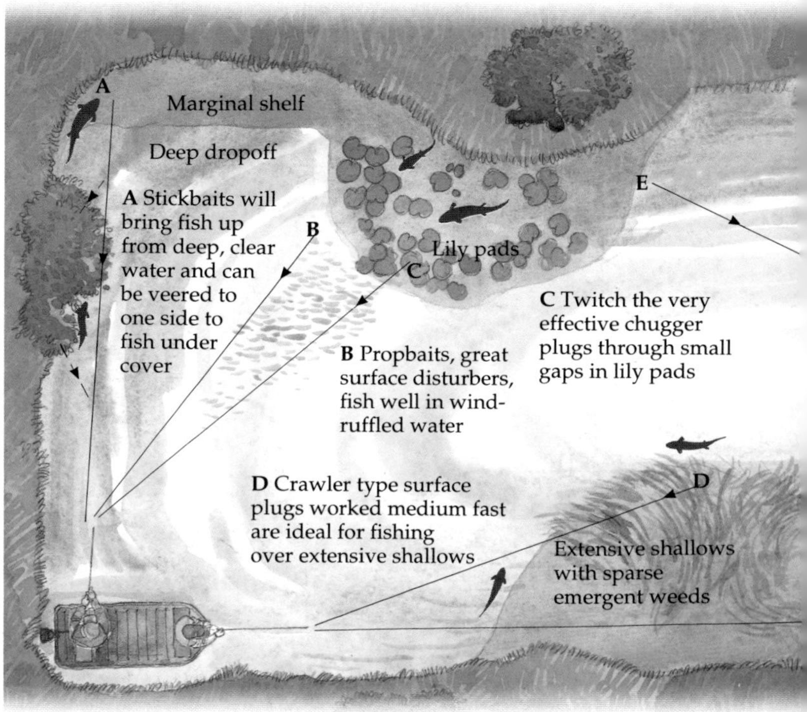
Marginal shelf
Deep dropoff
A Stickbaits will bring fish up from deep, clear water and can be veered to one side to fish under cover
B Propbaits, great surface disturbers, fish well in wind-ruffled water
C Twitch the very effective chugger plugs through small gaps in lily pads
Lily pads
D Crawler type surface plugs worked medium fast are ideal for fishing over extensive shallows
Extensive shallows with sparse emergent weeds
A
B
C
D
E

Crankbait Techniques

Crankbaits, which are plugs with lips that cause them to dive to a greater or lesser degree, are a very useful group of lures. Some are sinking plugs, made in a variety of densities to fish at different depths, while others float at rest and dive when retrieved. Try out your crankbaits in deep, clear water to find their approximate maximum working depths, and use an indelible felt-tip pen to mark each lure with its depth. When fishing, choose the lure to suit the water. Fishing shallow water calls for a shallow-diving lure, while a sinking deep-diver is needed to fish deep holes. To attain maximum depth, make a long cast and keep the rod tip low on the retrieve. Raising the tip lifts the lure in the water, as does using too thick a line. Generally, in water temperatures above about 60°F (16°C), predators are more active and willing to hit a lure fished quickly, while in cold or dirty water they are lethargic and more likely to be tempted by a slowly moving crankbait. In cold water, bumping bottom is a good tactic, and the crankbait's tendency to fish nose-down means that the lip often bounces the lure clear of any potential snags.

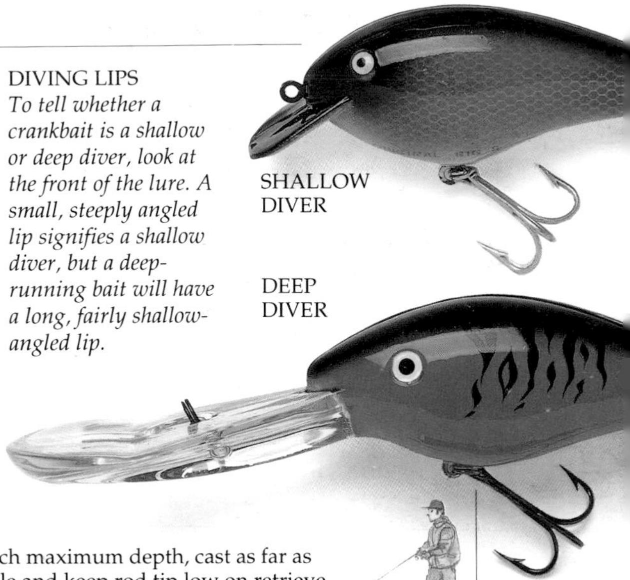
SHALLOW
DIVER
DEEP
DIVER

DIVING LIPS
To tell whether a crankbait is a shallow or deep diver, look at the front of the lure. A small, steeply angled lip signifies a shallow diver, but a deep-running bait will have a long, fairly shallow-angled lip.

Floating divers
For prospecting the water layers with a floating diver, choose one that will dive to a depth of about 12 ft (3.7 m) on a fast retrieve. With this type of lure, it is possible to follow the bottom contours quite closely by varying the speed of retrieve and thus the depth of the lure. However, to fish the surface or deeper holes effectively, choose a lure designed specifically for those purposes. Fishing the lure on the shady side of a bottom feature such as a sunken tree, and parallel to it, keeps it in the likeliest water for the longest period.

The Versatile Floating Diver

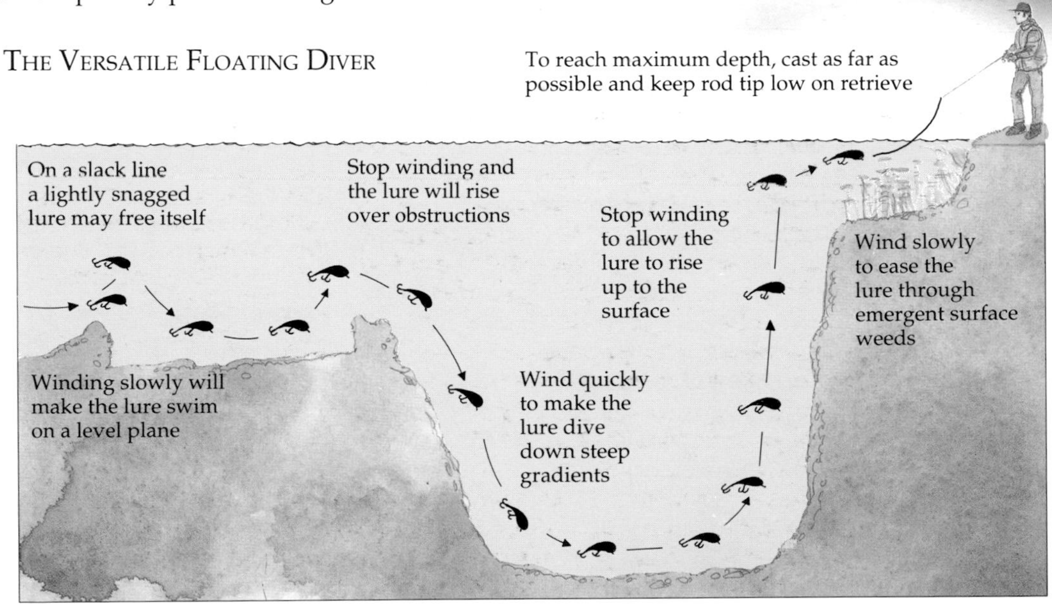
To reach maximum depth, cast as far as possible and keep rod tip low on retrieve
On a slack line a lightly snagged lure may free itself
Stop winding and the lure will rise over obstructions
Stop winding to allow the lure to rise up to the surface
Wind slowly to ease the lure through emergent surface weeds
Winding slowly will make the lure swim on a level plane
Wind quickly to make the lure dive down steep gradients

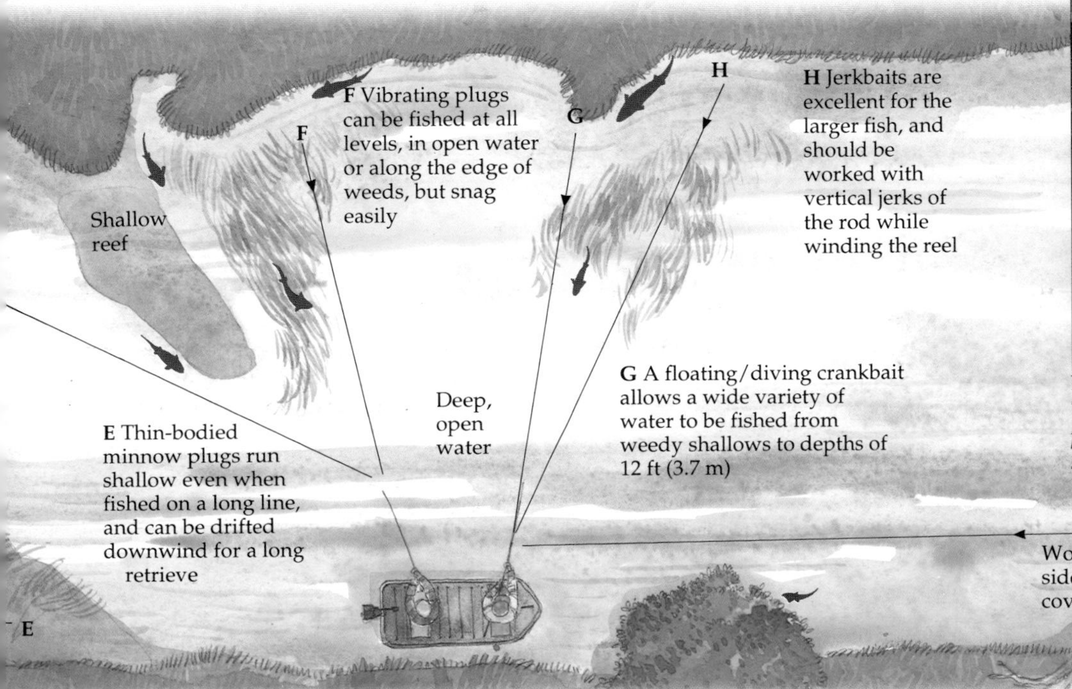
F Vibrating plugs can be fished at all levels, in open water or along the edge of weeds, but snag easily
H Jerkbaits are excellent for the larger fish, and should be worked with vertical jerks of the rod while winding the reel
Shallow reef
Deep, open water
E Thin-bodied minnow plugs run shallow even when fished on a long line, and can be drifted downwind for a long retrieve
G A floating/diving crankbait allows a wide variety of water to be fished from weedy shallows to depths of 12 ft (3.7 m)
Work the shaded side of cover
F
G
H
G
E

DEEP-DIVING PLUGS
This pike was taken on a deep-diving plug. These plugs, which have a lot of water resistance, should be used with baitcaster reels.

Legering

Legering is a versatile technique that allows the bait to be cast a long way and presented at or near the bottom to attract fish that feed there. Although it lacks the finesse of float fishing, it does allow the bait to be presented effectively in situations where a float rig would be working at its limits. These include fishing at long range, on fast rivers, under weed rafts, and in deep water or rough weather on big lakes and pits. Apart from when fishing with a bolt rig, legering generally involves using the minimum practical amount of weight in a given set of circumstances, in order to produce the lowest level of resistance to a taking fish. The lowest possible resistance is achieved by freelining, a variant of legering in which the only weight on the line is that of the baited hook.

ROD RESTS
A legered bait does not need constant manipulation, so the rod can be left on rod rests until the bite indicator shows that it is time to strike.

Bite Indicators

Because there is no float on a leger rig, bites are detected either by touch (holding the line over a finger or between finger and thumb so that the tiniest pull on the line can be felt) or by using a bite indicator. The simplest indicator is the rod tip itself, but other methods are preferable when more sensitivity is required. Quivertips, springtips, and swingtips, fitted into the tip ring, show up taps that would be missed on a rod tip, while a bobbin clipped on the line between reel and butt ring allows some slack line to be taken before the strike is made. Monkey climbers are used either alone or in conjunction with electronic indicators that sound when there is a pull on the line.

SWINGTIP
A swingtip is sensitive, but limits casting distance. Add lead wire in strong winds or undertows.

QUIVERTIP
A quivertip will "soften" close-range bites and is sensitive enough to show bites developing.

MONKEY CLIMBER
This is connected to the line to indicate any pull on it. Add a light stick for night fishing.

TOUCH LEGERING
Point rod at the bait. Crook a finger over the line, or hold it between thumb and finger.

The Running Leger

This is a simple but effective rig for close-range work. If split shot are used for weight and pinched on to the loop of nylon (the link), the rig will not snag since the shot will pull off when put under tension. If the shot on the link are butted up against one another, the rig can be made to roll along the bottom to make the bait run through the swim, which is often a highly effective method of fishing for chub and barbel. Conversely, if the shot is spaced apart, the rig will hold bottom firmly in fast water. The link on the running leger should be stopped about 12 in (30 cm) from the hook by a plastic leger stop or a BB shot. Use thick nylon for the link to ensure that it stands clear of the main line.

RUNNING LEGER IN ACTION

The Fixed Paternoster

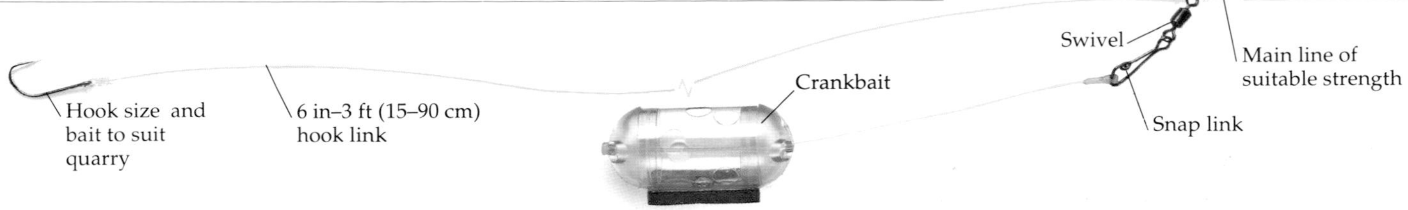

This rig is excellent for fast-flowing waters, and especially effective on stillwaters when fishing over dense weeds, where running leger rigs are prone to snagging. Tie the main line and the hook link to one eye of a swivel, and to the other attach a 12 in (30 cm) mono link carrying the crankbait. A hook link of about 18 in (45 cm) will usually suffice, but for fishing on the drop increase it to 2 or 3 ft (60 or 90 cm), and when tentative bites are being experienced reduce it to about 6 in (15 cm). The crankbait link's breaking strain should be less than that of the main line so that it, and not the main line, will break if the crankbait should snag.

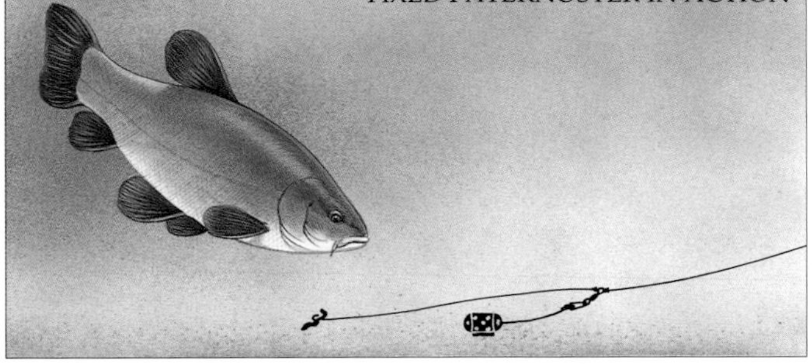
FIXED PATERNOSTER IN ACTION

The Sliding Link Leger

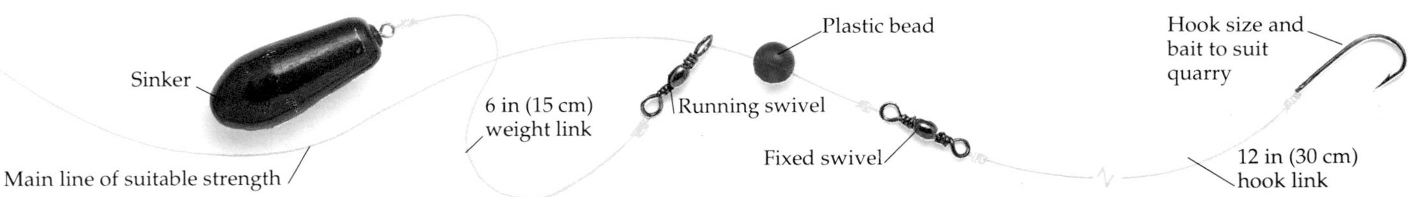

Sometimes it is desirable to allow the fish to take a little line before the strike is made. Predators, for example, often spend a while toying with a bait before taking it properly. In these circumstances, a sliding link is preferable to a fixed paternoster because it offers less resistance to the take. Thread a swivel and then a small bead onto the main line, and tie another swivel to the end of it. Attach the hook link to the other end of this swivel, and the weight link to the free-running swivel. Use lighter line for the weight link than for the main line so that the link can be broken if the sinker snags. The bead prevents the swivels from tangling.

SLIDING LINK LEGER IN ACTION

The Bolt Rig

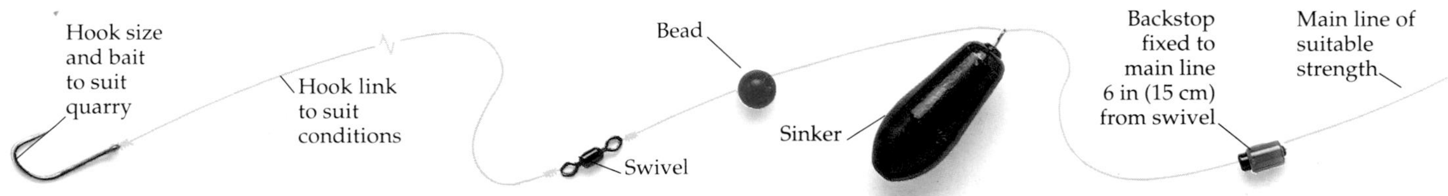

This rig uses a heavy weight, which is free to slide along the line between a swivel and a backstop. It was first developed for carp that had grown wary of conventional rigs, which produced increasing tension as they moved off with the bait; deeply suspicious, they would reject it. A freelined bait might appear to be the logical answer, but the bolt rig works better. When a carp first picks up a bait fished on a bolt rig, it is not aware of the weight due to the short length of slack line. However, as soon as it begins to make off, the backstop on the line pulls up hard against the heavy leger weight. This startles the carp, causing it to bolt and hook itself.

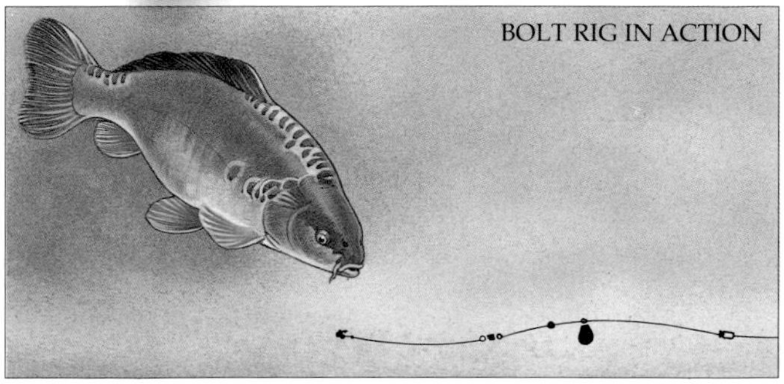
BOLT RIG IN ACTION

Float Fishing – Running Water

Floats attached bottom-end only, such as the jig, come into their own on slow-flowing rivers, and a jig really scores when the wind is blowing. Because it is attached bottom-end only, most of the line between the jig and the rod is under water and thus impervious to the wind or surface movement. On fast-flowing waters, floats attached top and bottom (by a pair of float rubbers) are the order of the day. Loafers, sticks, and Avons all fall into this group.

CASTING A JIG
For fishing at long range, let the float swing smartly behind you when you begin the cast and then push hard forward with the rod to achieve distance. A more relaxed version of this cast will achieve less distance, but with less risk of the hook rig catching in bankside vegetation.

Split Shot

Split shot do more than just add weight to the line. Positioned in particular ways on the line, shot can present a bait in various fashions, ensure that different types of bite register on the float, and prevent tangling of the rig in casting. Split shot are available in a variety of sizes from the biggest, termed SSG or swan shot, down to the so-called dust shot that is often used near to the hook to produce a slow descent of the bait through the water.

Shot size	Weight (grams)
SSG	1.89
AAA	0.81
BB	0.4
No. 1	0.28
No. 4	0.17
No. 6	0.105
No. 8	0.063
No. 10	0.034
No. 12	0.02
No. 13	0.012

Plumbing the Depth

When using a float, it is important to know the depth of the swim you are fishing, and you can find it by using a plummet. Fit the plummet onto the hook and gently lower it to the bottom, then reposition the float so that it just protrudes from the surface. The distance between the float and the hook will be the approximate depth of the water. Plumb various other points around the swim to build up a mental picture of the bottom.

THE PLUMMET
A plummet, a small weight, fits over or clamps onto the hook.

Basic Jig Rigs

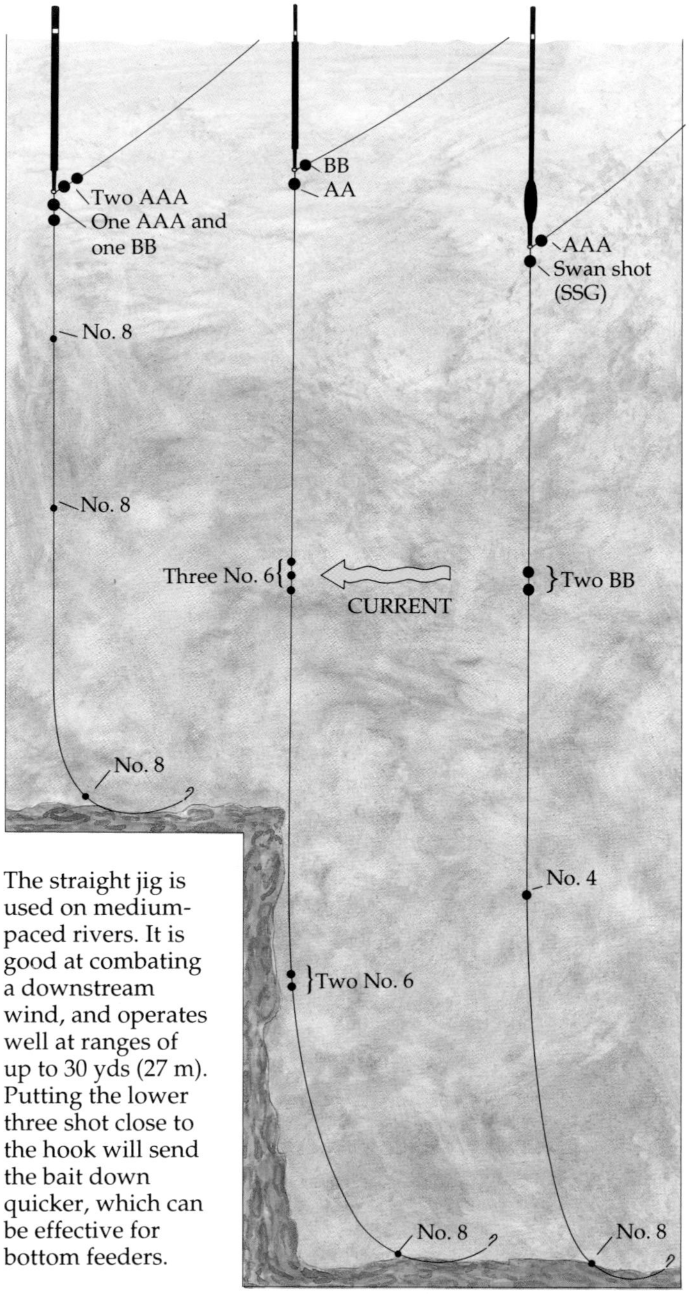

The straight jig is used on medium-paced rivers. It is good at combating a downstream wind, and operates well at ranges of up to 30 yds (27 m). Putting the lower three shot close to the hook will send the bait down quicker, which can be effective for bottom feeders.

The insert jig float is ideal on wide, slow-flowing rivers when fish are feeding on the drop (the thin insert gives good bite indication). This rig can be used in quite deep swims, but because of the sensitivity of the float, it cannot be held back and must be allowed to drift freely.

Use a bodied jig for fishing big, slow rivers at medium to long range. The buoyant bulb enables the rig to be heavily shotted for good casting distance. The shotting pattern can be modified for fish taking on the drop or to get the bait down quickly to bottom feeders.

LOCKING SHOT
These lock a float attached bottom-end only to the required point on the line.

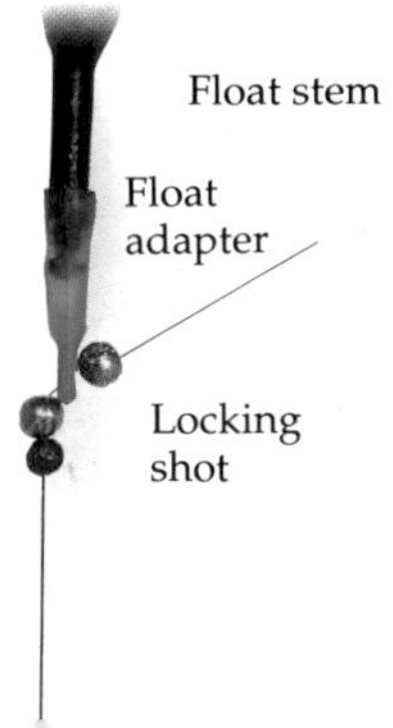

Basic Stick Float Rigs

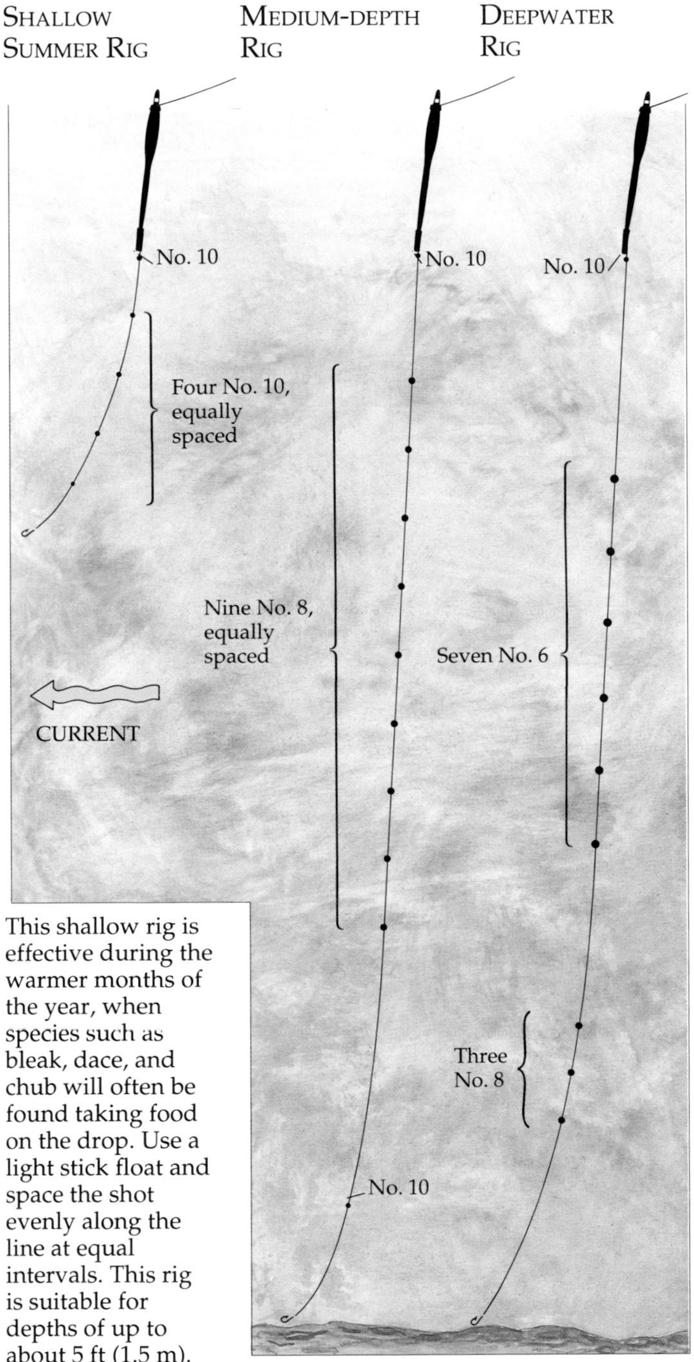

This shallow rig is effective during the warmer months of the year, when species such as bleak, dace, and chub will often be found taking food on the drop. Use a light stick float and space the shot evenly along the line at equal intervals. This rig is suitable for depths of up to about 5 ft (1.5 m).

This is a rig for medium depths and moderate currents. In depths of 3 to 6 ft (1 to 1.8 m), use a float with a wire stem or heavy cane base; use a light float in shallower water. In fast water, group some of the No. 8 shot just above the hook length. This rig is effective for chub and barbel.

This rig works well in depths of up to about 10 ft (3 m). Use a float with a heavy base to ensure that the bait gets down quickly to where the intended quarry is lying. This is a good rig to use for species such as barbel, roach, chub, and bream, when they are feeding on or near the bottom.

DEPTH MARKER
Pinch a shot onto the line to mark the minimum depth you want to fish.

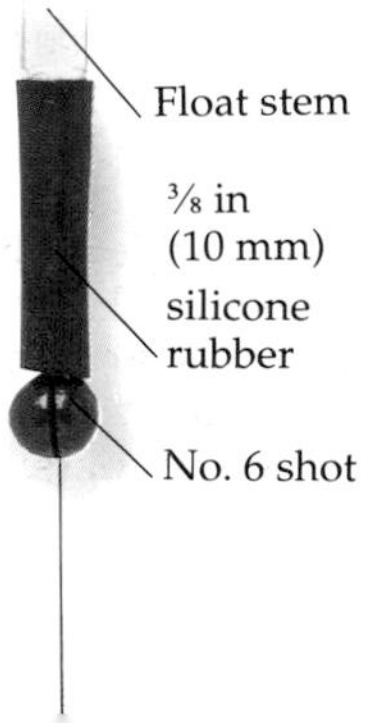

Trotting a Stick Float

Trotting a stick float involves letting it drift downstream with the current and holding back on it at intervals so that the bait swings upward, enticing fish to take it. Set the float slightly overdepth, that is, so that the distance from the float to the hook is slightly greater than the depth of the water. Cast a little downstream of you, leave the bail arm open, and allow the float to "trot" along with the current. Press the tip of your forefinger lightly against the spool rim so that you can control the amount of line pulled from the reel as the float travels downstream. Holding back gently on the drifting float will make the bait trip along just off the bottom; holding back hard on it will swing the bait upward.

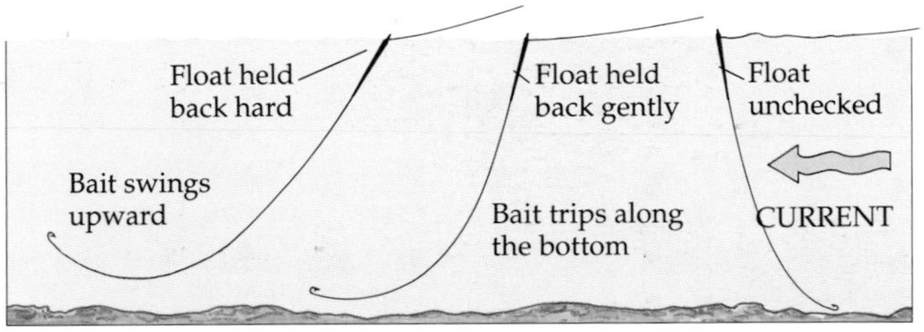

TACKLE CONTROL
When you are trotting a float, you may find it easier to control your tackle if you are standing rather than sitting on the bank.

BACKSHOTTING

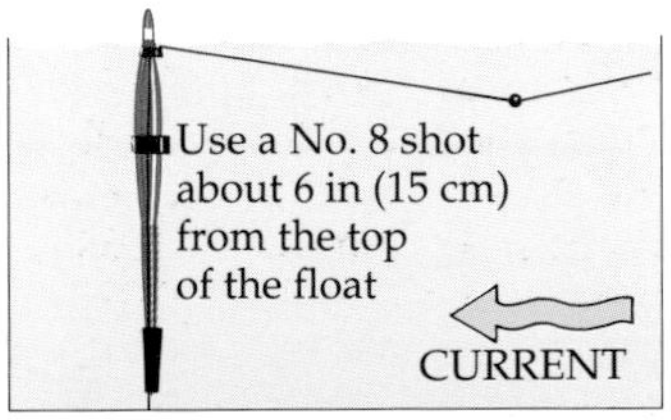

Backshotting
To minimize the effects of the wind on a stick float, sink the line for a short distance behind it by backshotting. In most situations, a single No. 8 shot pinched onto the line between the float and the rod, about 6 in (15 cm) from the float, will be sufficient.

FEEDING
To attract fish and get them feeding, use a catapult to throw small pieces of hookbait into the swim just before you cast. The loose bait will slowly sink or drift with the current, and fish that are feeding on it will not be unduly wary of your hookbait when it arrives.

Float Fishing – Stillwaters

For stillwater fishing, the float is usually attached bottom-end only. The line passes through a ring inserted into the base of the float, and the float is held in position on the line by split shot (known as locking shot) fixed either side of it. During the summer months, stillwater fish will often be found in the upper layers of the water and can be caught by fishing "on the drop" (fishing a bait that sinks slowly through the water). The setup in this situation involves positioning most of the shot around the float with just a few small dust shot down the line. When bites are not expected on the drop, use bulk shot halfway between the float and hook to get the bait down quickly through the upper layers. If bites are not forthcoming, try moving the bottom shot on the rig to anywhere from 4 to 18 in (10 to 45 cm) from the hook.

Casting

For long-range work on large stillwaters, it is best to use an overhead cast. Wind the float to about a yard from the rod tip. Next, open the bail arm with your free hand (or, on a closed-face, reel, press the line release button) and as you do so press the line against the spool with the index or middle finger of your rod hand. With the line still trapped against the side of the spool, bring the rod back smartly over the shoulder of your rod arm. Punch the rod forward over your head, removing your finger from the spool to release the line. Allow the float to shoot out over the water, climbing as it does so. As the float describes an arc through the air, follow its path with the rod tip until the rod is horizontal. As the float nears the water, slow its flight and ensure a gentle touchdown by putting the index or middle finger of your rod hand on the side of the spool to slow the speed of the line as it leaves the reel.

Feathering
Slowing the speed of the line to make the float land gently on the water is known as "feathering" the cast. Feathering also reduces the risk of the terminal tackle becoming tangled. This is because when the line is slowed, the momentum of the terminal tackle pulls the whole rig out straight.

CONTROLLED LANDINGS
Feather the cast to make the float touch down gently on the water, and close the bail arm when it lands.

Basic Techniques

The two basic stillwater techniques are the lift method and fishing on the drop. For the lift method, wind the line in so that only the tip of the float is above the water. If a fish takes the bait, the float will lift.

When fishing on the drop, first count the number of seconds it takes for the shot to cock the float (to pull it upright) after it has hit the water. On subsequent casts, if the float does not cock properly in the usual time, strike immediately: a fish has taken the bait.

The Lift Method

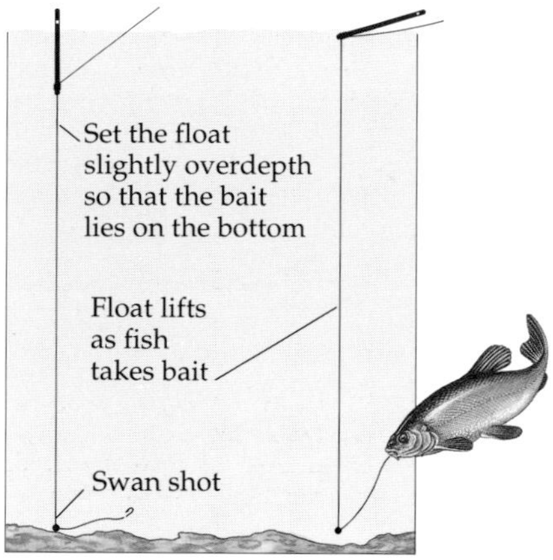

Basic Stillwater Rigs

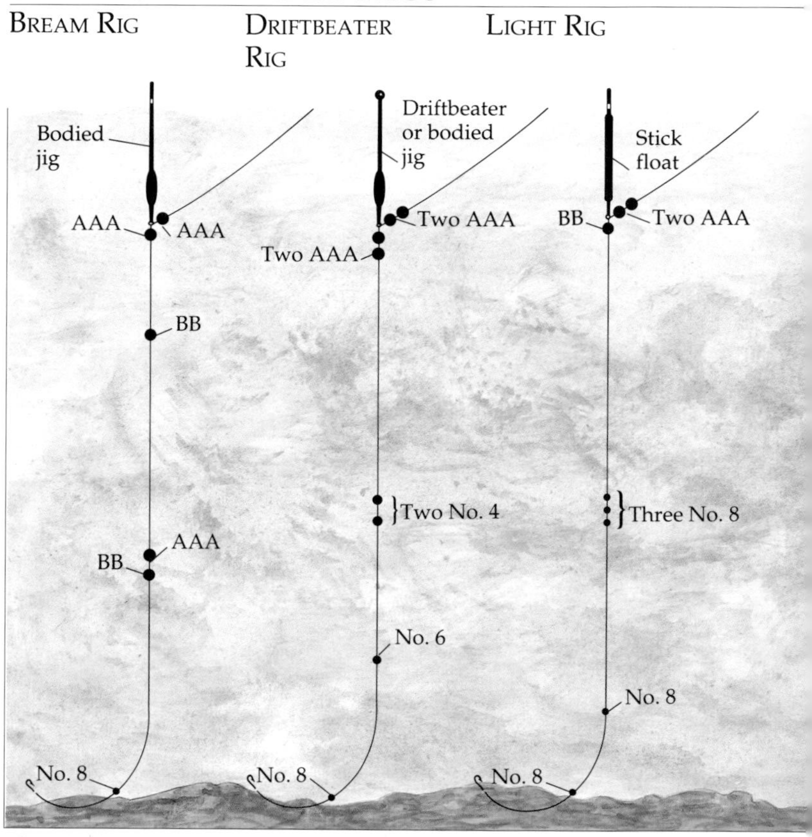

The ideal rig for catching bream. The bodied jig's buoyancy allows it to carry plenty of weight, in the form of locking shot, to eliminate tangling and make distance casting easier. The bulk shotting near the hook takes the bait down quickly.

Driftbeaters fish well in rough, windy conditions and are best fished overdepth. Plenty of weight in the locking shot keeps the float steady, and progressively lighter shot pinched on down the rig allow the bait to be fished on the drop.

This rig is ideal for fishing at a range of about 15 yds (14 m), but can be used at distances up to 25 yds (23 m). It is at its best in light winds when there is minimal surface drift. Always feather the line when casting, to prevent tangling.

Fishing on the drop

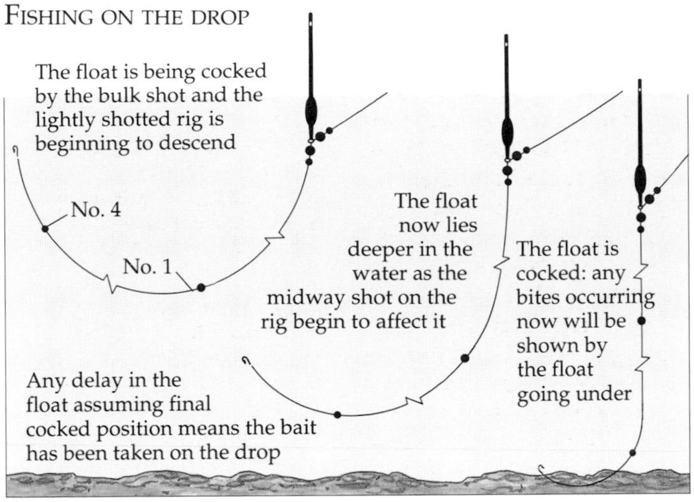
The float is being cocked by the bulk shot and the lightly shotted rig is beginning to descend
No. 4
No. 1
The float now lies deeper in the water as the midway shot on the rig begin to affect it
The float is cocked: any bites occurring now will be shown by the float going under
Any delay in the float assuming final cocked position means the bait has been taken on the drop

Shallow-Water Rig · Long-Range Rig · Canal Rig

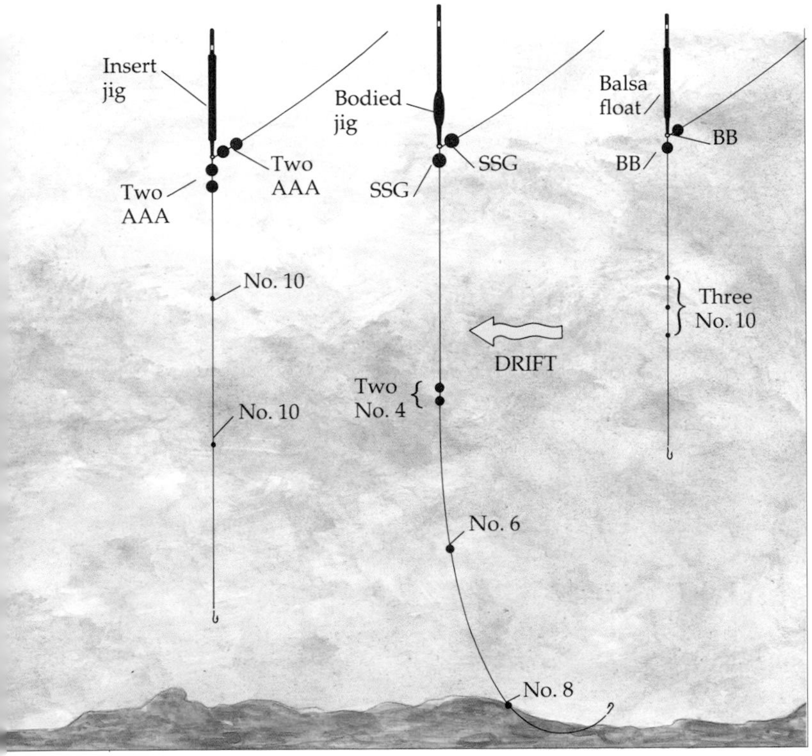
Insert jig
Two AAA
Two AAA
No. 10
No. 10
Bodied jig
SSG
SSG
DRIFT
Two No. 4
No. 6
No. 8
Balsa float
BB
BB
Three No. 10

Insert jig rigs such as this are best used with small shot spaced out between float and hook. They are not designed for use with heavy bulk shotting down the rig. In shallow swims, the shot on the rig need be no bigger than No. 10.

This rig is for use on big lakes and on gravel pits. The basic shotting pattern shown here could be altered for fishing on the drop, in which case slightly heavier shotting, such as a few well-spaced No. 8s, will give better bite registration.

The small balsa float ensures a quiet touchdown on casting, and most of the cocking weight is concentrated around the float. The rest of the shot are small and allow the bait to fall slowly and naturally through the water.

Fishing the Sliding Float

Sliding floats come into their own when swims are significantly deeper than the length of the rod. Bodied jigs, preferably loaded to some degree, are the best floats to use. This loading ensures that the float does not slide up the line during casting, while the buoyant body allows plenty of shot to be used along the rig to get the bait down to the bottom quickly. A stop knot is tied in above the float and its position is adjusted until the correct setting (which is the depth of the swim) has been found. The float runs freely up the line until it reaches the knot, which will not pass through the ring at the base of the float because of the bead.

THE SLIDING STOP KNOT

The sliding stop knot is easy to tie in fine mono. To ensure it does not catch on the rod rings during casting, either leave the ends about ⅜ in (10 mm) long or tie the knot in soft cotton.

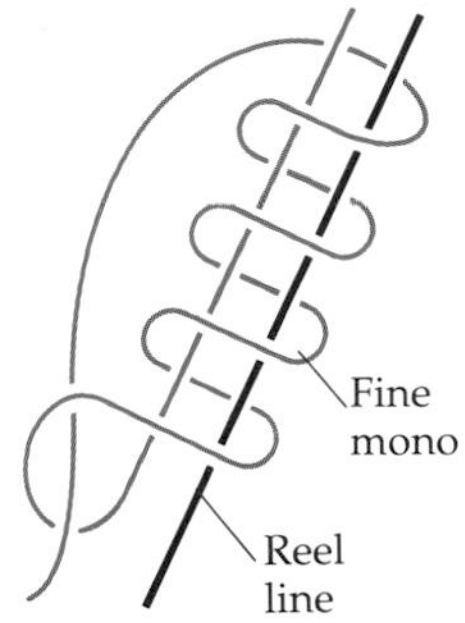
Fine mono
Reel line

BANKSIDE VEGETATION

A sliding rig has only a short length of line beyond the float when casting. This is useful when bankside vegetation limits casting space.

SLIDING FLOAT RIG

Bodied jig (peacock quill or sarcandas reed stem)
Sliding stop knot
Bead
Three AAA
No. 8

Sliding Controller Float Rig

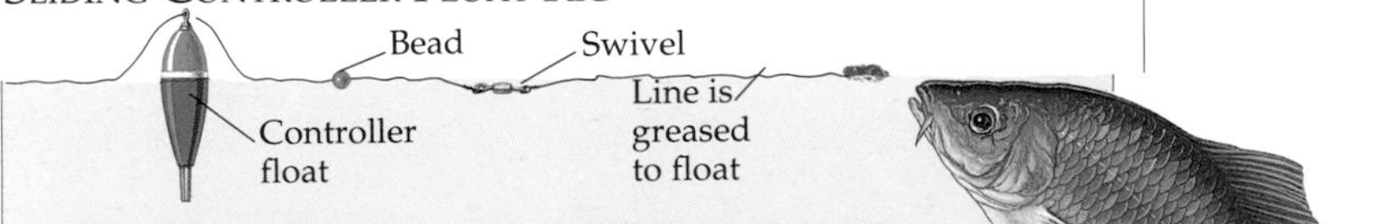
Bead
Swivel
Controller float
Line is greased to float

Sliding controller floats are excellent for presenting surface baits such as crickets and grasshoppers for panfish and bass, or floating casters for roach and rudd. The float acts basically as a casting weight, and when the bait is taken the controller is not pulled under the surface. Instead, the line runs freely through a ring attached to the top of the float. The line between the swivel and the hook should be well greased to reduce resistance to a taking fish. The sliding controller float can also act as a bite indicator: strike when it begins to slide across the surface.

Pole Fishing – Stillwaters & Canals

When fishing a stillwater, the first task is to use a plummet *(see page 222)* to find the shelf or dropoff where fish are likely to be. Start searching at about 16 ft (5 m) out, and shorten or lengthen the pole until it is found. On a canal, start by fishing just off the bank, and if you get no results, fish further out: if the canal is not too wide, fish the middle channel and then along the far bank. Most canals can be fished comfortably with a 33 ft (10 m) pole.

Pole Tips

On waters where big fish are a distinct possibility, it is essential to use a pole with an elasticated tip. The tip elastic *(see page 228)* acts as a shock absorber and helps to prevent the hook from tearing free. You can turn a flick tip into an elasticated tip by using one of the conversion kits on the market. Alternatively, the components (tensioner, bung, elastic, PTFE bush, and line connector) can be bought individually.

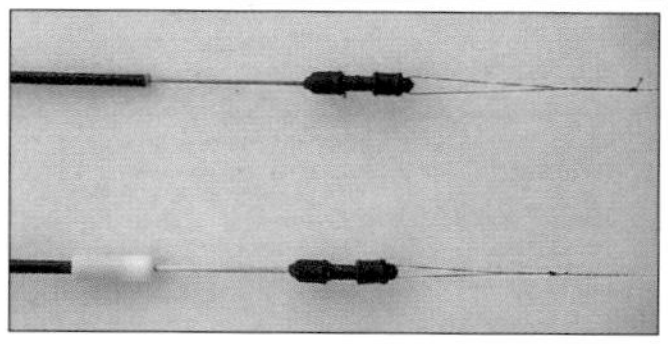

ELASTICATED TIPS

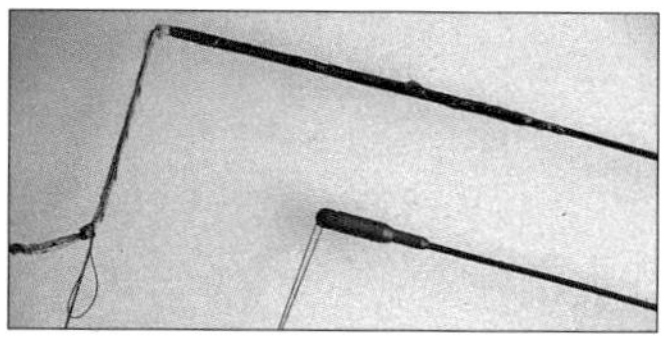

FLICK TIPS

Casting

Set up the top three sections, attach the line and terminal rig, and cast underhand or overhand to get the terminal rig out. Then add more sections to the pole (or extend it, if it is telescopic) until the required length is reached.

Always keep well away from overhead power lines when fishing with a pole, especially if it is made of carbon fiber, and do not use one during a thunderstorm.

UNDERHAND CAST

Hold the pole in one hand and the terminal rig in the other. Swing the pole up and out, and at the same time release the terminal rig.

OVERHAND CAST

This is similar to the underhand cast, but the pole is held and cast vertically, instead of from a nearly horizontal position.

Basic Stillwater Rigs

Balsa Bristle Rig

Bodied Bristle Rig

Small-bodied Bristle Rig

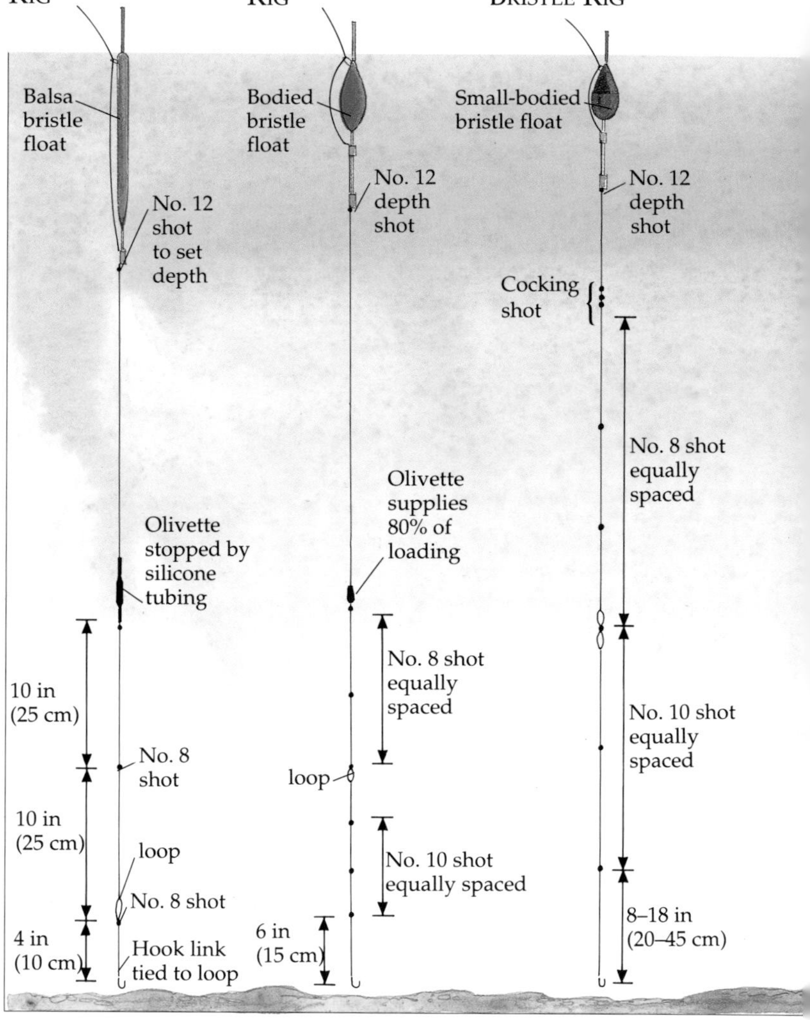

This float is designed for fishing baits near or on the bottom in a flat calm or slight ripple. It is a good float for detecting bites from roach and small bream, and when it is correctly shotted, only the bristle should show above the water. The shotting pattern gets the whole rig quickly down to mid-depth, after which the small shot sink the bait more slowly to the lake bed. This can produce bites on the drop as well as on the bottom.

The bodied bristle float has a cane stem and is used for fishing on the drop. It can be used in conditions from flat calm to choppy, and only the bristle should be visible above the surface, for bite detection. On this rig the shotting is evenly spaced to take the bait down at a steady rate. To get the bait down quickly to fish on the bottom, move the shot nearer the hook, and when fish are near the surface, place the shot directly under the float.

This is a good rig to use in deep water, and it is usually fished about 6 to 12 in (15 to 30 cm) overdepth. It is especially suitable for bottom-feeding species such as bream, because it gets the bait down quickly to them. The rig is set to depth with a No. 12 shot, and cocked by three closely grouped No. 8s. Below these are three equally spaced No. 10s, the lower of which is placed 8 to 18 in (20 to 45 cm) from the hook.

Basic Canal Rigs

Dibber (Flat-top) Rig | **Mini Jig Rig** | **Float Leger Rig**

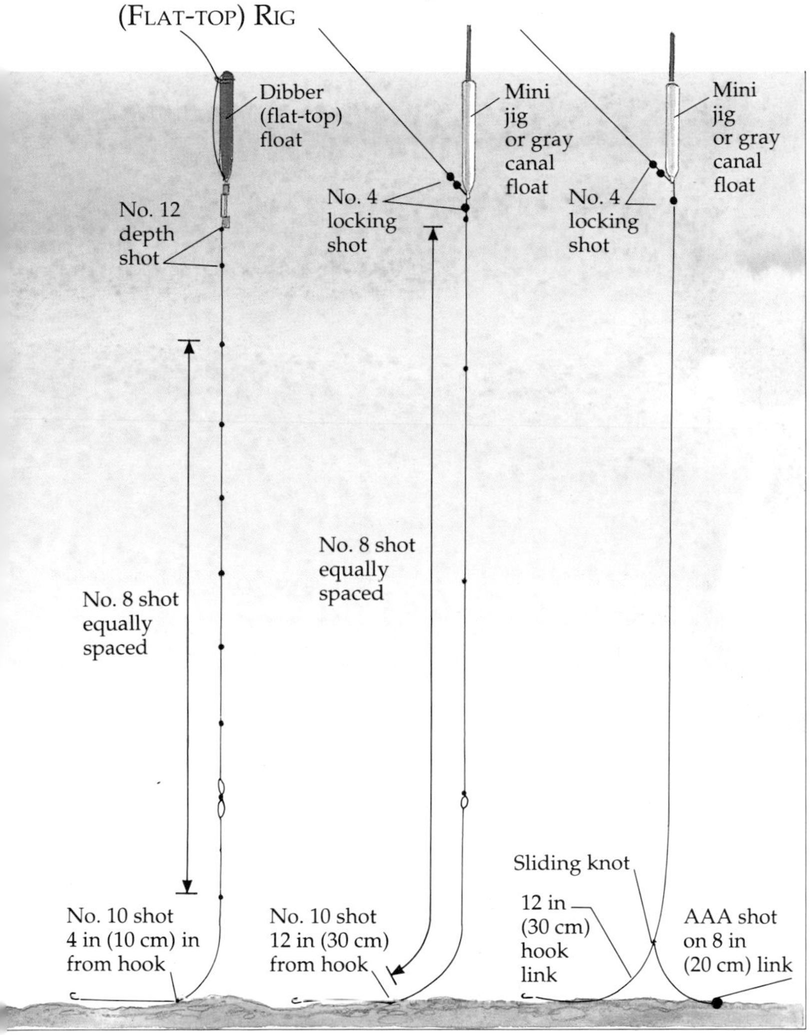

The dibber rig can be used for fishing the far shelf of a canal in very choppy conditions, and it is also useful on a lake when an undertow is occurring. It is designed to take fish on the drop, and is a good rig for bream fishing. The shotting consists of a No. 12 depth shot, with eight No. 8 shot evenly spaced below it. A single No. 10 shot is positioned 4 in (10 cm) from the hook, and the top of the float should only just protrude above the surface, for bite detection.

This rig can be used on lakes and canals, and it is a good choice for bream, tench, or large roach. The float is attached bottom-end only, with locking shot pinched on at either side of the base ring, and the pole tip is usually sunk to keep the line under water. This prevents line drift, which can adversely affect bait presentation. Back shotting might also be required in a wind: pinch on a No. 8 shot about 8 in (20 cm) above the float to sink the line.

This version of the mini jig rig is designed for use in rough conditions, when the bait needs to be firmly anchored on the bottom. A small bottom sinker or an AAA shot is carried on an 8 in (20 cm) length of line attached to the main line by a sliding knot, which should be about 12 in (30 cm) from the hook. Reduce this distance if bites are not registering on the float but the bait is being sucked, and lengthen it if the wind and current increase.

Handling the Pole

Take-apart poles are shipped (lengthened) by adding more sections, and unshipped (shortened) by removing sections. Telescopic poles and whips are shipped by pulling sections out, and unshipped by pushing them back in. Always keep pole sections free of dirt to prevent wear and ensure easy shipping and unshipping.

HOLDING A POLE
Fish from a sitting position. Hold the pole across one thigh or put the butt against your pelvis and hold it with one or both hands.

POLE RESTS
Pole rests keep the pole off the ground while you are changing the terminal tackle, unhooking fish, or chumming.

UNSHIPPING
To land a fish caught on a long pole, unship the pole until it is short enough to allow the fish to be brought to the net or hand.

SWINGING TO HAND
When the pole has been unshipped to about two or three sections long, small or medium-sized fish can be swung to hand.

FISHING DISTANCE
A long pole allows you to place baits with great accuracy into distant swims, and to fish in areas that may be inaccessible with running tackle.

Pole Fishing – Running Water

Pole fishing on fast-flowing water requires small round-bodied floats, such as bung floats, that can be held back or allowed to run at the speed of the current. The bodied bristle float can be used on slow-flowing rivers. There are two basic styles of pole fishing for running water. The first involves using a long pole and a short line for holding back and slowing the bait's passage. The second style employs a long pole and long line – such as a 33 ft (10 m) pole and 30 ft (9 m) of line – for running the float and bait at the speed of the current and fishing the full length of the swim.

Feeding Methods

To attract fish to the swim when you are fishing on the bottom, throw in small balls of bread-based chum (if legal) containing hookbait samples. When fishing on the drop, throw or slingshot loose feed, such as maggots, into the water below the pole tip, or use a pole pot. This is clipped to the top section of the pole and filled with feed, then the pole is extended and swung out over the swim, and the pot is inverted to empty its contents into the water.

USING A SLINGSHOT
A good way to get chum or loose feed out to the vicinity of the hookbait is to use a slingshot. When using one, either put the pole on the bank or on pole rests, or place it across your lap and hold it down with the forearm of the arm holding the slingshot.

Pole Elastic

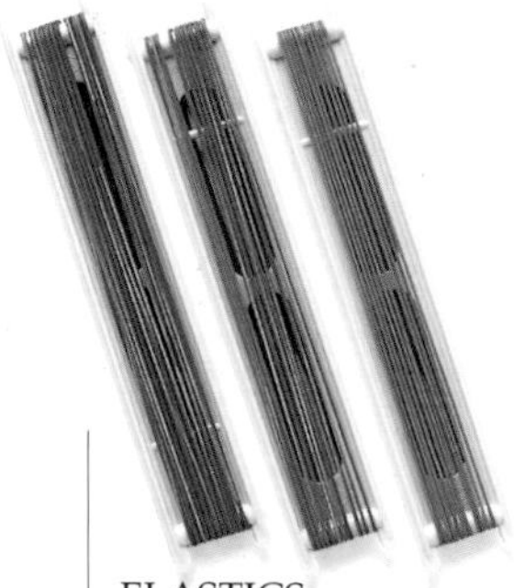

ELASTICS
Three sizes of elastic (No. 4, No. 5, and No. 6) on winders.

Elastic for use on elasticated pole tips *(see page 226)* is available in eight sizes (numbered 1 to 8), each of a different breaking strain. It is supplied on carriers or winders that can be used when empty for holding pre-assembled float rigs. Pole elastic is usually coated with a lubricant to ensure that it runs freely through the PTFE bung in the pole tip, and periodic applications of lubricant are advisable to keep a pole's elastic in good condition. Many anglers carry a number of additional pole top sections rigged up with elastics of various strengths for different species.

Rigs for Running Water

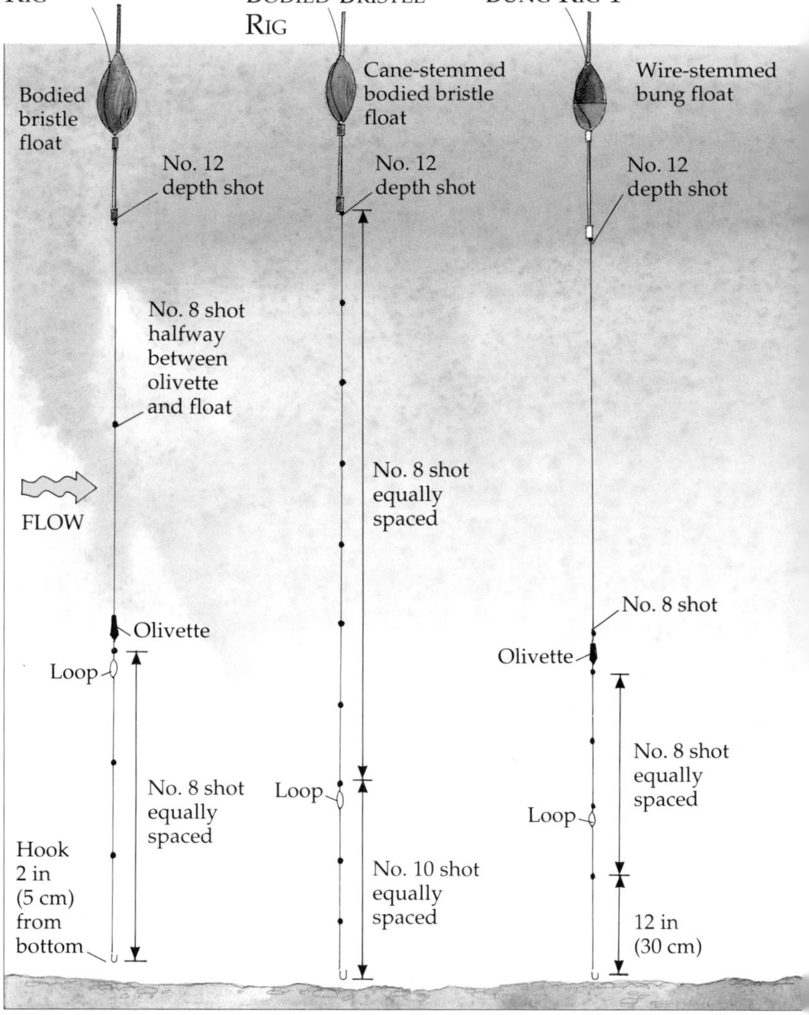

This rig is used for catching fish near the bottom in slow to medium-paced water between 5 and 7 ft (1.5 and 2.1 m) deep. The swim should be chummed and the float, attached top and bottom, run through at the speed of the current. The rig is weighted by an olivette with a single No. 8 shot above it and three No. 8s below it. The baited hook should fish just off bottom, and the bristle of the float should show above the water for bite indication.

A short version of this rig will catch surface and midwater feeders in the top 2 to 3 ft (60 to 90 cm) of medium-paced water, but it can be made longer to fish the full depth of the river, as shown here. It should be run through the swim at the speed of the current, with just the bristle of the float, which is attached top and bottom, showing above the surface. The shotting consists of eight equally spaced No. 8 shot above two equally spaced No. 10s.

With this versatile rig, you can fish a bait on the bottom below the pole tip, hold back in deep, fast water over chum, or run the bait through at the speed of the current. Position the bulk shot or an olivette at about 30 in (75 cm) from the hook, with three No. 8 shot spaced equally below it. Attach the float top and bottom, with the tip of the bristle showing above the water for bite indication. This rig gives excellent bait control, even in fast-flowing rivers.

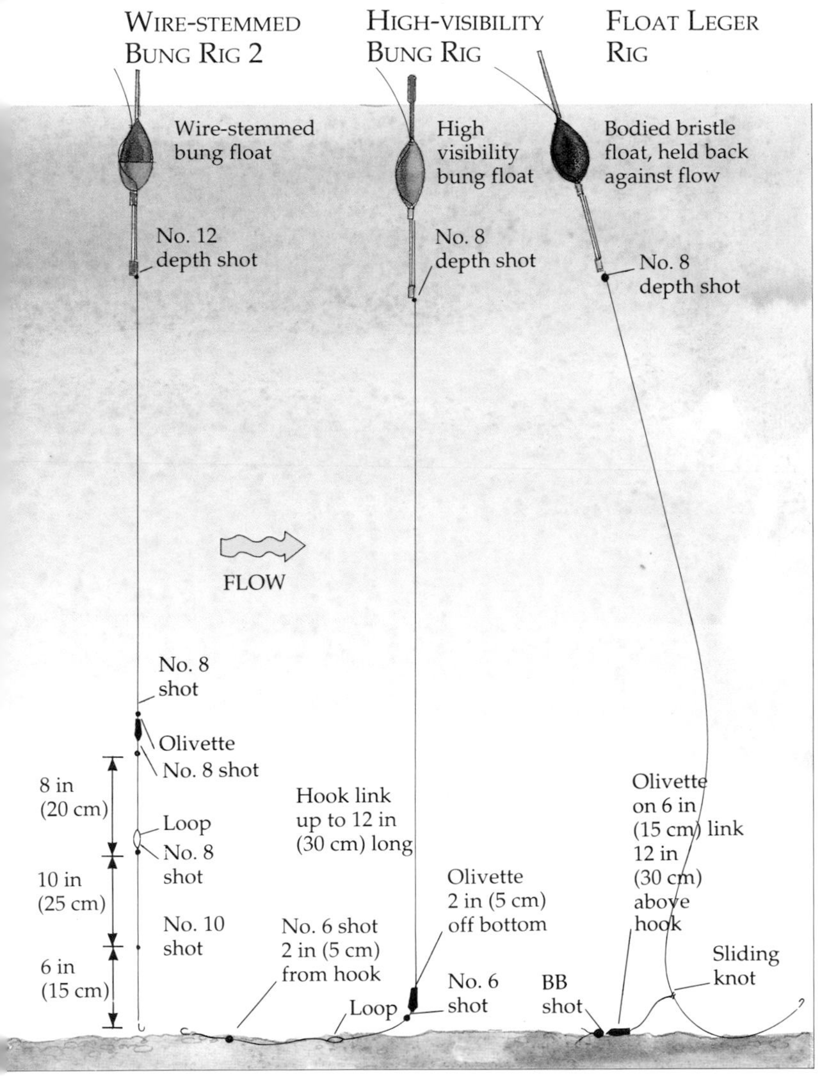

Use this rig to present baits just off the bed for fish that feed in the bottom third of the water, and run it through at the speed of the current. Position bulk shot or an olivette 2 ft (60 cm) from the hook, or at one-third of the distance from the hook to the float. Fix a No. 8 shot just above the bulk shot or olivette, another just below it, with a No. 8 and a No. 10 spaced below that. Set the float so that the bristle just shows above the surface.

This rig is suitable for fishing close-in for small, bottom-feeding fish of up to 8 oz (227 g). Set the float so that the bristle is above the surface, and fish the rig through the margins, no more than about 6 to 10 ft (1.8 to 3 m) out and held back slightly. The simple shotting pattern consists of bulk shot or an olivette set 12 in (30 cm) from the hook, and a No. 6 shot just below it, and another No. 6 near the hook. The olivette takes the bait down quickly through the layers.

This rig can be used for presenting a static bait on the bottom. It will also allow you to make a bait move slowly along the bottom towards the bank, and to hold it back hard to inch the bait slowly through the swim. The float is well overshotted by a small sinker attached to the line 12 in (30 cm) from the hook by a short link of about 6 in (15 cm) of mono. Attach the float top and bottom, and set it so that only the bristle is protruding above the water.

Pole Fishing Weights

The weights most widely used in pole fishing are split shot and olivettes, plus small bomb weights for float leger rigs. Olivettes thread onto the line and are used in place of bulk shot; barrel leads can also be used, but they are more prone to tangling. Lead wire is better than split shot when using seed baits.

BARRELS

OLIVETTES

SPLIT SHOT

LEAD WIRE

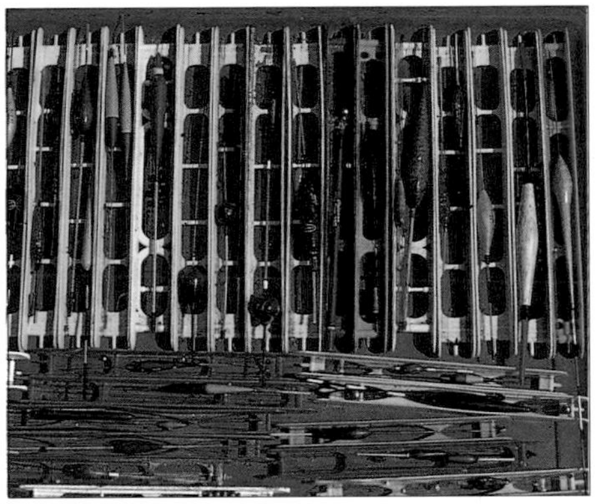
FLOAT RIGS
With pre-assembled float rigs you can change your tackle quickly and easily.

Olivette and Split Shot Sizes

Olivette size (Paquita)	Weight (grams)	Olivette size (Torpille)	Weight (grams)	Shot size	Weight (grams)
12	3.0				
11	2.45	11	2.5		
10	2.1	10	2.0		
				SSG	1.89
9	1.85	9	1.5		
8	1.56	8	1.2		
7	1.36	7	1.0		
6	1.16				
5	0.82				
				AAA	0.81
		6	0.8		
4	0.67				
		5	0.6		
		4	0.5		
3	0.44				
		3	0.4	BB	0.4
2	0.37	2	0.3		
				No. 1	0.28
1	0.25			No. 2	0.24
		1	0.2	No. 3	0.20
0	0.17			No. 4	0.17
2/0	0.13	0	0.13	No. 5	0.13
3/0	0.105			No. 6	0.105
				No. 7	0.083
4/0	0.081				
				No. 8	0.063
				No. 9	0.049
				No. 10	0.034
				No. 11	0.026
				No. 12	0.020
				No. 13	0.012

TROLLING

Trolling is a method by which a bait, either natural or artificial, is pulled along through the water behind a moving boat. It is used on stillwaters and rivers for fish such as trout and walleye, and is also used on saltwater, for example in big-game fishing *(see page 258)*. The boat can be powered either by oars or by a motor, and the trailed bait, which can be fished at practically any depth, is intended to resemble a live fish to any predators it passes. Trolled spoons, plugs, and even flies can be made to fish deep by the addition of weights or by using lead-cored line, while natural baits are often fished below a sliding float, set overdepth, to give an early indication that a predator has taken hold.

READING A LAKE

Deep lakes can be divided into separate layers, the epilimnion, thermocline, and hypolimnion. During summer and autumn the epilimnion will be warmer than the hypolimnion, and the reverse is true in winter. The water temperatures within each of these two layers are fairly uniform, but there is a sharp change in temperature within the thermocline. Strong winds will cause the layers to tilt, resulting in the epilimnion becoming "thicker" on the lee shore. Fish that show a marked preference for cold water, such as lake trout, will move deeper as the summer progresses, and the best way to locate these deep-swimming fish is to use an echo sounder.

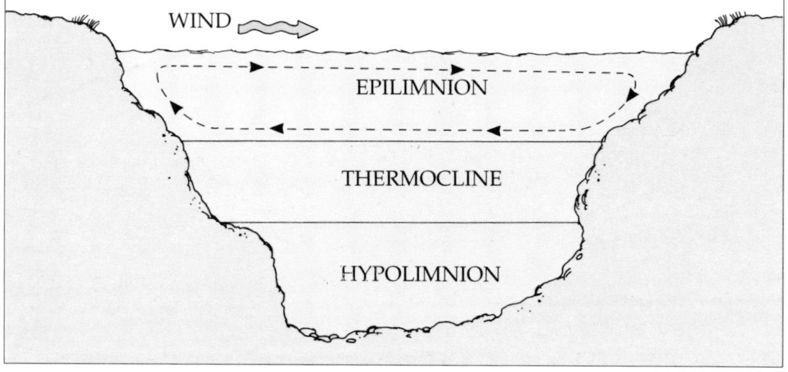

TROLLING THE LAYERS

A wet fly can be trolled just under the surface by using a medium sinking fly line and a standard leader. To fish deeper, the same pattern can be trailed behind the boat on a lead-cored line, or alternatively a heavy tube fly can be employed. Small plugs, too, can be fished relatively deep on a lead-cored line, or on a small-diameter wire line that cuts easily through the water. To fish even deeper, it is necessary to move on to a heavy, vaned trolling weight attached well up the line above the lure. Alternatively, a downrigger can be used for really deep work, its great advantage being that the lure can be fished at a constant, preset depth.

BOATS
Trolling is best done from a motorboat, but a rowboat may also be used.

Trolling with multiple rods
A trio of anglers can fish together, with minimal risk of their lines tangling, by fishing at different depths and distances. The angler in the stern should fish his lure or bait shallow and closest to the boat, so that if a take occurs on one of the other rods he can get his bait in quickly and operate the motor.

TROLLING WITH MULTIPLE RODS

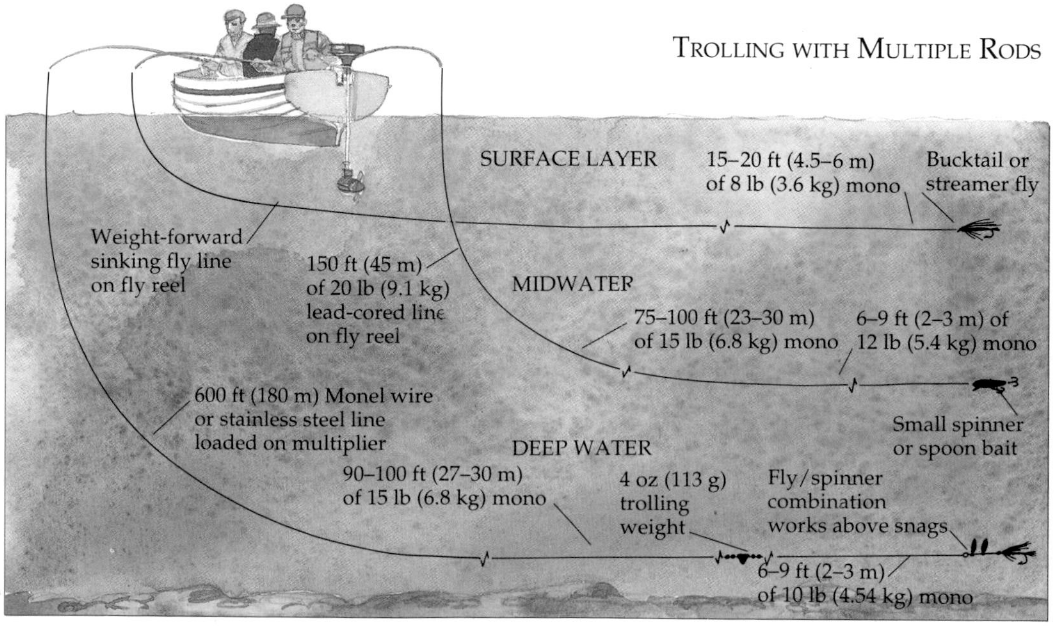

ROD LAYOUT

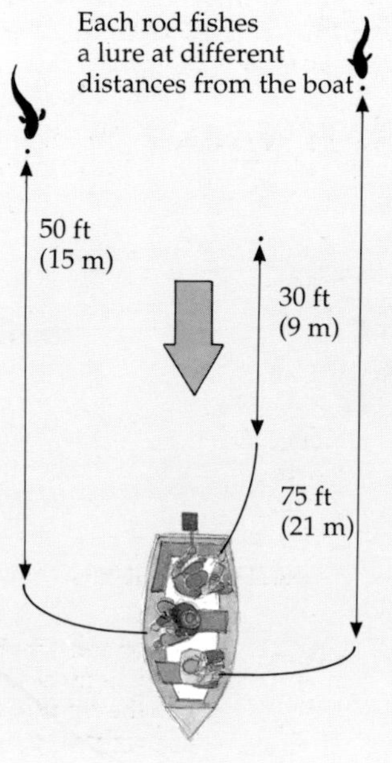

Using a Downrigger

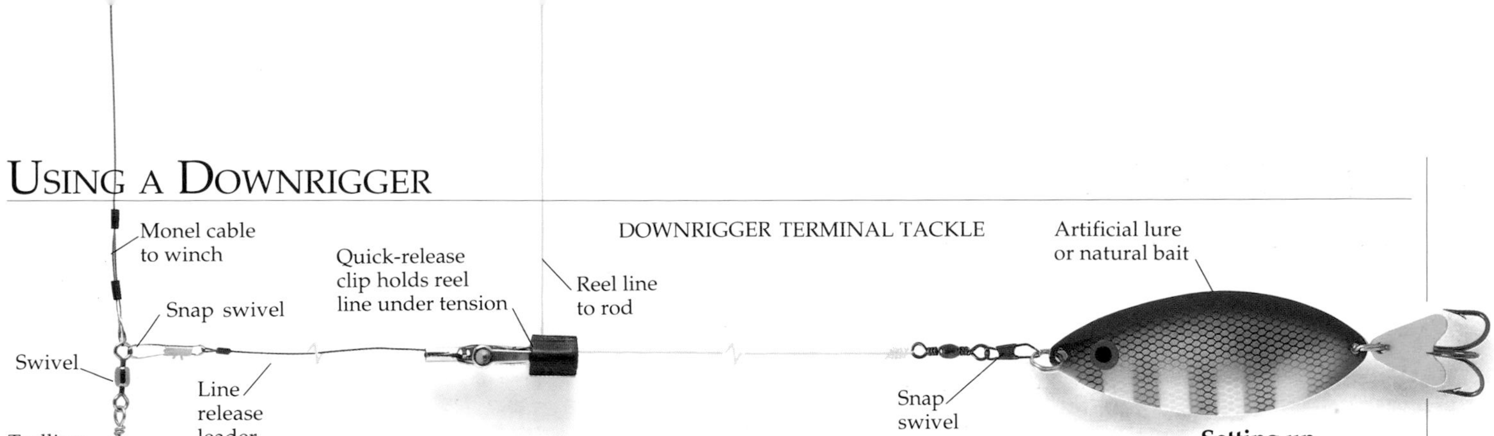

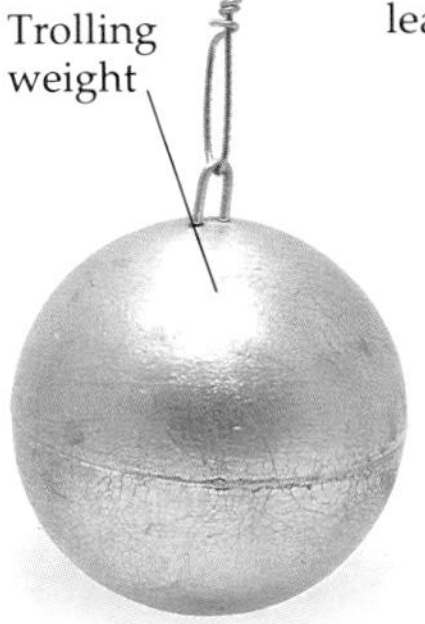

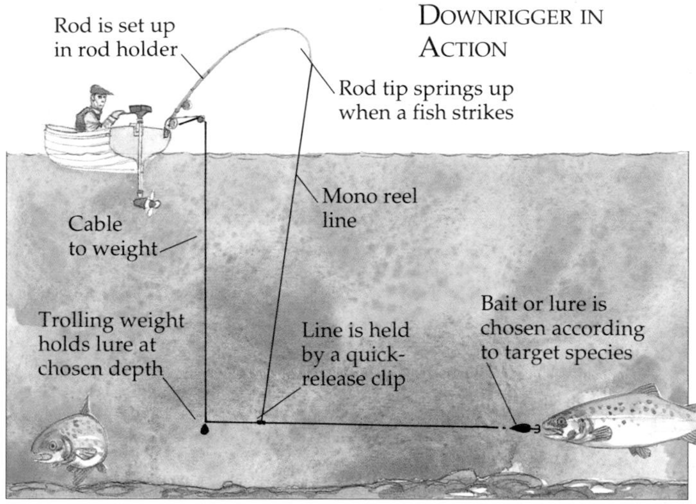

The downrigger not only fishes constantly at a preset depth, it also allows the fish to be played out on a line unencumbered by a heavy weight. This is because a large weight, around 3 lb (1.4 kg), is needed to take the lure down to the required fishing depth; it is attached to a separate, strong line, and is connected to the reel line by a clip that releases the line when a predator strikes.

The downrigger is fished off the stern of the boat. The cable to which the weight is attached is normally run off a winch and marked at intervals with a waterproof marker pen so that the depth the lure is sent down to can be gauged. (Using an echo sounder makes this marking unnecessary.) After the rig has been sent down to the prescribed depth, the reel line is tightened right up to put a good bend in the rod. When a fish grabs hold of the lure, the clip releases the line and the rod tip springs back straight, indicating the take and often also setting the hooks.

Setting up
The leader to which the lure is attached can be anywhere between a yard and tens of yards in length. When lowering the lure and weight, the reel on the rod should have its clutch set but with the anti-reverse off or out of gear with the ratchet on. When the rig is in position and ready to begin working, the reel is set for action.

DOWNRIGGER WINCH
The cable that carries the trolling weight is run off a winch secured near the stern of the boat.

DEEPWATER FISHING
Using a downrigger enables you to fish at depths of 500 ft (150 m) or more.

Baitwalking

Baitwalking is a method of fishing a buoyant deadbait or plug near to the bottom with little risk of fouling. A snag-resistant weight is repeatedly allowed to sink to the bottom and then lifted off again by raising the rod tip and retrieving some line.

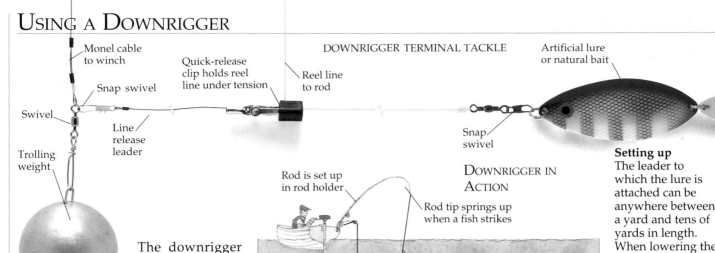

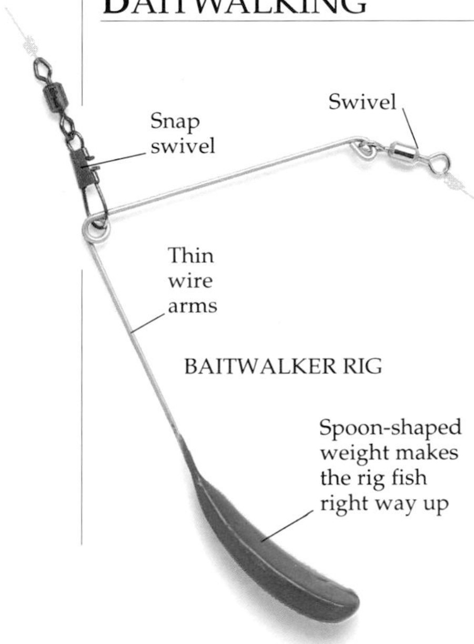

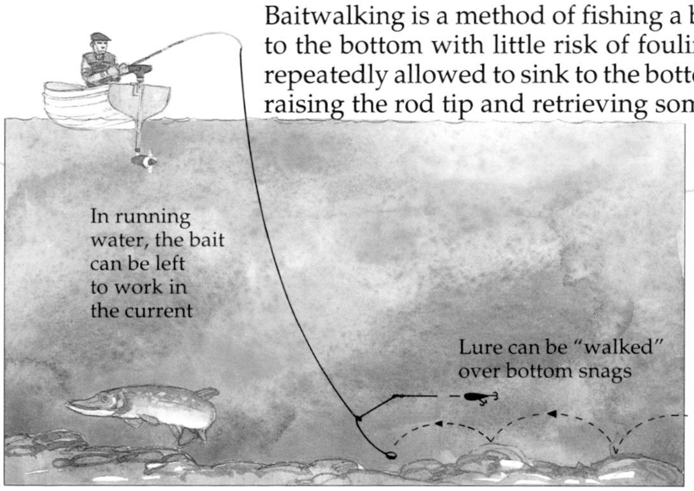

The Overhead Cast

The overhead cast is an important part of all fly fishing. It is essential for those who take up fly fishing to master it, and the better their technique, the more successful anglers they will be. The main elements of the basic overhead cast are the back cast and forward cast, plus the false cast. These are described here together with suggestions on how to improve your technique and correct common casting faults. The way in which you hold the rod for casting is also important, but it depends largely on your personal preference and the distance you wish to cast. Try the grips shown here, then choose the one that most suits your casting requirements.

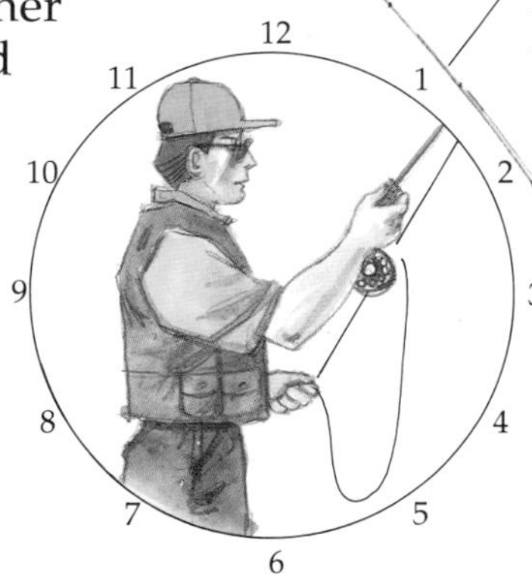

THE CLOCK FACE
These clock face positions are used to describe the rod movements during casting.

The Grip

Continental grip
In this grip, the forefinger points along the rod. This style is best for short, accurate casts with dry flies or nymphs on rivers and small stillwaters.

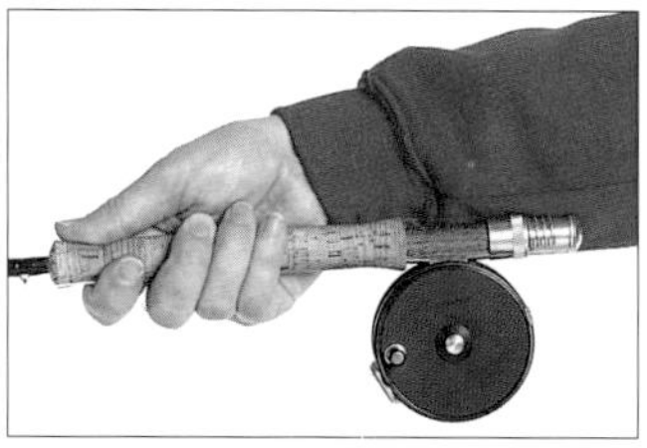

Continental grip

Standard grip
The style preferred by many all-around anglers who fish a variety of different methods and waters. Fine both for short, accurate work and for long-distance casting on large rivers and lakes. With the thumb running along the top of the handle, the strain on the wrist is not too great when a long line is aerialized.

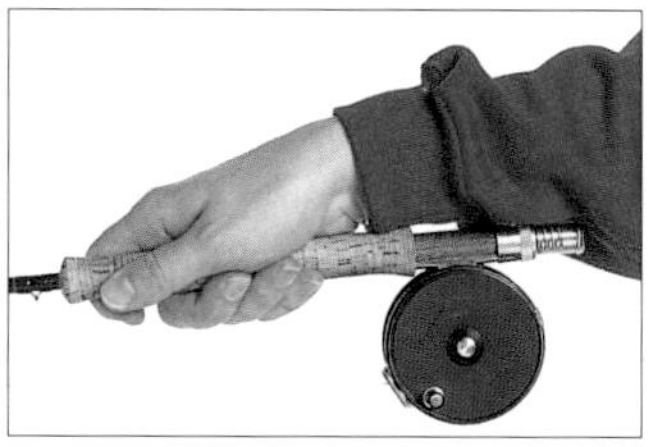

Standard grip

Tournament grip
A strong but relaxed grip, ideal for long-distance work with weight-forward or shooting-head lines. Lacks the fine control needed for short, accurate casting.

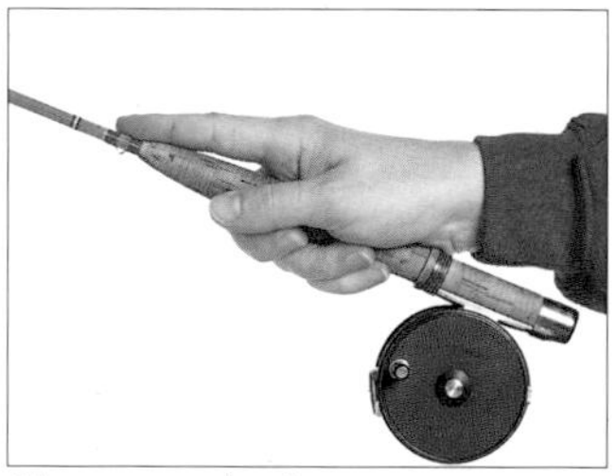

Tournament grip

BACK CAST

The momentum of the line bends the rod back
Stop the rod when it is at the 11:30 position
A
B
C
Begin with the rod pointing down
Bring the rod sharply but smoothly upward
Put your weight on your forward foot

BALANCED TACKLE
Good casting depends on balanced tackle. Fly size, line weight, and rod rating must match.

Back cast
A good back cast is the prerequisite for a good forward delivery, and neglecting this essential movement results in a poor casting technique. Before you begin, stand with the foot on your rod side forward, with the rod tip in the 4:00 position, about 20 ft (6 m) of line extended beyond the rod tip (**A**). Trap the line between your index finger and the rod handle.

To begin the back cast, bend your elbow to raise your forearm (**B**), accelerating the rod smoothly and progressively from the 4:00 position to the 11:30 position and lifting the line from the water **(C)**. Stop the rod at this point and pause briefly, allowing the line to extend fully behind you, before commencing the forward cast; momentum will flex the rod tip back a little to 11:00. This pause is vital, and practice will teach you how long it should be, but if it is too long the line will lose momentum and drop low behind you. If it is too brief it will result in a whiplash effect that can crack and thus weaken the fly line, or even cause the fly to snap off.

Keep your wrist straight during the back cast, because bending it allows the rod to drift too far back. This will make your forward cast more of a throwing action than a smooth, controlled delivery.

False casting
This enables you to get extra line in the air to increase your casting distance, and involves making repeated back and forward casts before allowing the line to land. The rod movements are the same as for an overhead cast, but instead of trapping the line with your rod hand index finger you hold it, between the butt ring and the reel, with your free hand. Pull line from the reel during each back cast and shoot it at the end of each forward cast. Work the rod between 1:00 and 1:30 and when sufficient line is aerialized, make a normal forward cast and release the line.

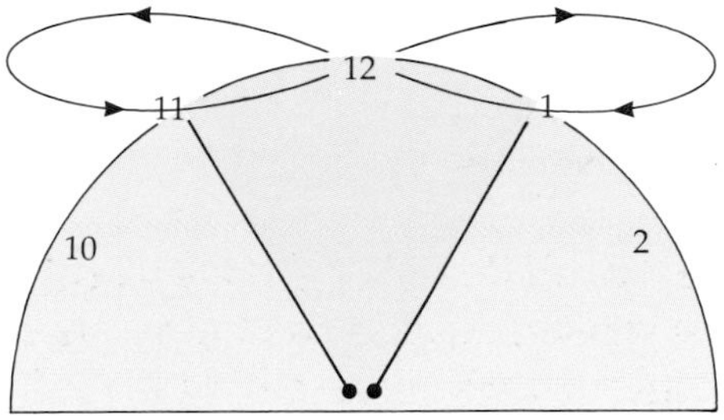

TIGHT LOOP

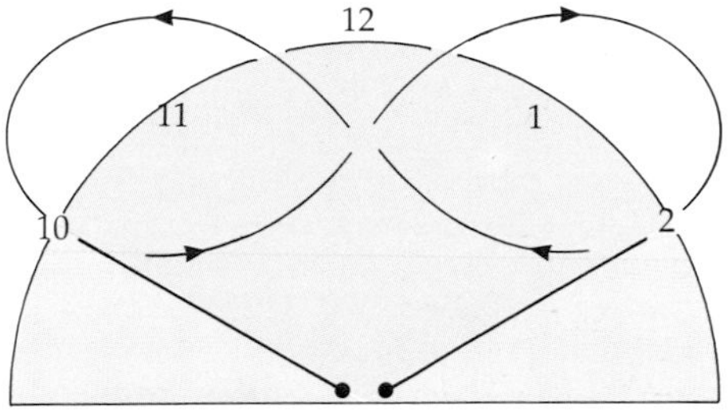

WIDE LOOP

Casting loops
The shape the line makes in the air is governed by the arc through which the rod tip is moved during false casting. A small arc will create a tight loop, a large arc a wide loop.

A tight loop, formed by moving the rod tip through an arc from 11:00 to 1:00, will enable you to cast farther than a large loop will, but a tight loop is not always desirable. For example, when casting a team of flies, the possibility of tangles is reduced by increasing the arc to 10:00 to 2:00 and thus casting a wider loop.

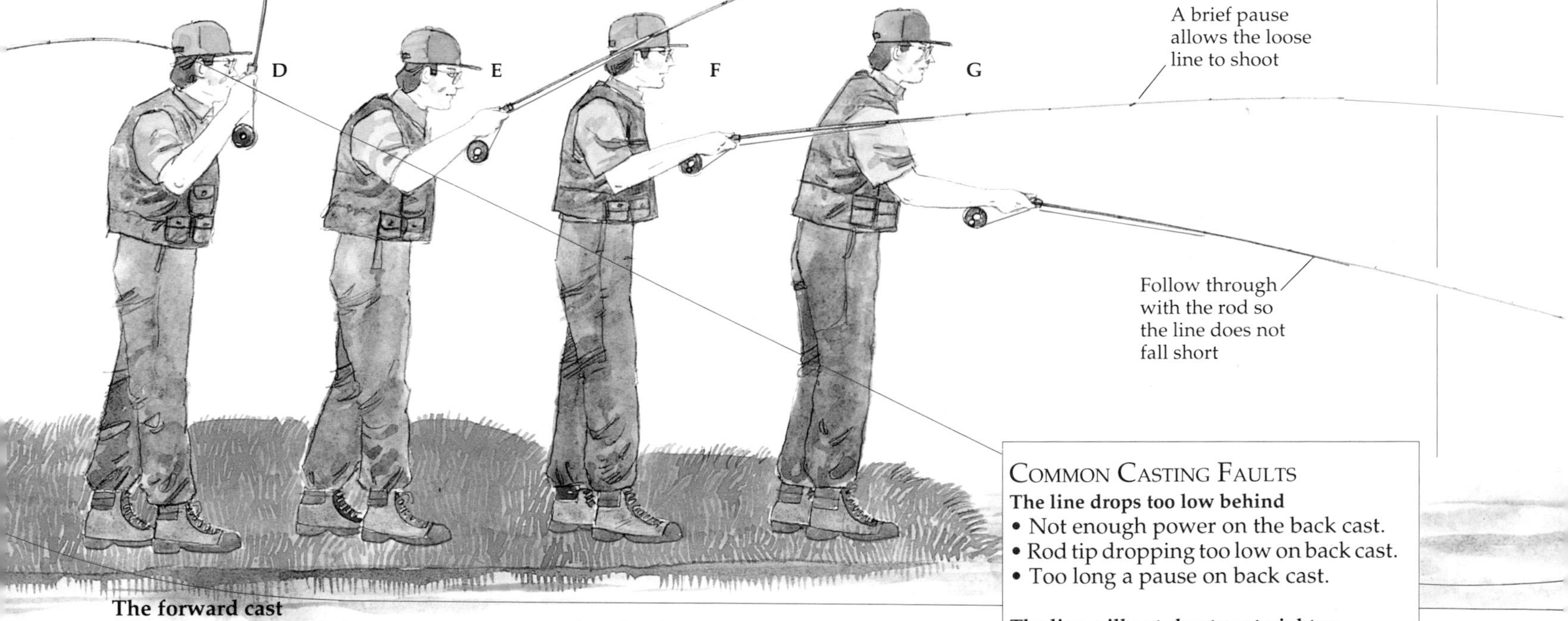

The bending rod acts like a spring, storing power that is released during the forward cast, throwing the line forward
FORWARD CAST
D
E
F
G
The line is released as the rod approaches 1:30 to 2:00
A brief pause allows the loose line to shoot
Follow through with the rod so the line does not fall short

The forward cast
With the rod flexed under compression and the line at full extension, accelerate the rod smoothly forward (**D**) to about the 2:00 position. Stop it there abruptly (**E**) and with a slight forward flick of your wrist. This wrist action is similar to the one you would use when lightly tapping a nail with a hammer, and when you do it you should aim your rod hand at an imaginary point about 3 ft (1 m) above the surface of the water.

Allow the rod to follow through as the line extends fully in front of you and falls gently to the water (**F**, **G**). The tapping motion and follow-through should be made in one continuous action.

Shooting line
There is an optimum length of line that any particular rod can aerialize, and to make a longer cast it is necessary to "shoot" line. This is achieved by pulling extra line from the reel, and allowing it to lie on the ground during the back cast.

When the rod reaches the 2:00 position (**E**) on the forward cast, lift the index finger of your rod hand to release the line. The momentum of the line extending in front of you will pull the loose line through the rings, adding extra distance to the cast. Aim high enough to allow all the extra line to straighten fully before it lands on the water.

Common Casting Faults

The line drops too low behind
- Not enough power on the back cast.
- Rod tip dropping too low on back cast.
- Too long a pause on back cast.

The line will not shoot or straighten
- Line released too early.
- Failure to follow through.
- Insufficient power on forward punch.
- Slack line between false casts.

The line lands in a heap
- Too short a pause on back cast.
- Aiming too low.
- Aiming too high in a facing wind.

The flies snap off
- Too short a pause on back cast.
- Leader point too fine for the size and weight of the fly.

The Roll Cast

To make a roll cast, you lift the line off the water and roll it forward, without first making a back cast, by using a rapid forward punch that swings over and curves downward. It is invaluable where there are obstructions behind you that prevent a normal overhead cast, and in many other situations, for example when you want to lift a sunk line and roll it onto the surface, prior to lifting it off for an overhead cast. The roll cast is a very versatile technique that should be part of every fly fisher's repertoire.

Making a roll cast
Begin by taking up a suitable stance, with one foot slightly in front of the other and the rod pointing down the line (**A**). Then begin a smooth, steady draw (**B**), raising your rod hand to just above shoulder height and lifting the rod to the 10:30 or 11:00 position *(see page 232)*. This steady draw allows a loop of line to form between the rod top and the water. While the line is still moving, raise the rod slightly (**C**), then punch it rapidly forward and down (**D**). The rod is now flexed and under maximum compression, and the line follows its path, bellying out slightly behind you and coming off the water close to your feet. As you power the rod down through the 3:00 position, the belly of line will roll forward (**E**). Follow through smoothly (**F**) so that the line unfolds and straightens above the water.

Stance
With any cast, the starting position is important if you are to achieve controlled turnover and make a smooth delivery, so take up position and stand with your best foot forward. For most right-handed anglers, this will mean the right foot, but it can pay to make the left foot the front foot, since this will open up the cast during the forward roll.

If necessary, take up any loose line with your free hand and hold on to it, as in the overhead cast, until late in the forward movement of the cast.

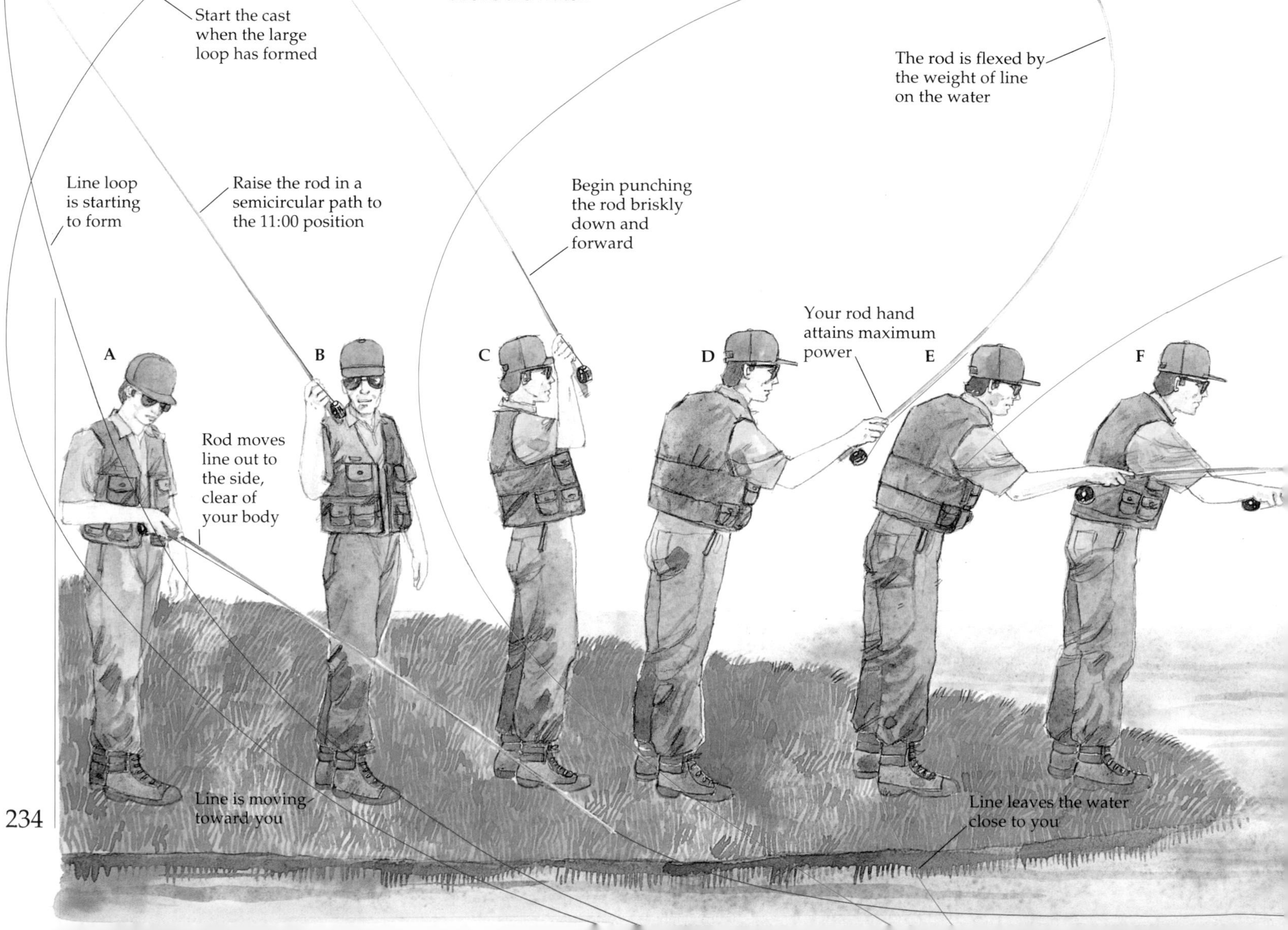

Start the cast when the large loop has formed
The rod is flexed by the weight of line on the water
Line loop is starting to form
Raise the rod in a semicircular path to the 11:00 position
Begin punching the rod briskly down and forward
Your rod hand attains maximum power
A
B
C
D
E
F
Rod moves line out to the side, clear of your body
Line is moving toward you
Line leaves the water close to you

CASTING FROM A BOAT (*left*)
Anglers fishing on the drift use the roll cast when short-lining with a team of three flies, or for lifting off a short line to cover fish that rise close to the boat. The roll cast, being one continuous movement, enables you to cover fish much faster than with an overhead cast, in which there is a delay while you make the back cast.

CASTING ON A RIVER (*right*)
When you are fishing on a river, the roll cast is useful if you want to change direction quickly or where obstructions prevent an overhead cast. Salmon anglers fishing large rivers with long rods find that the roll cast is also invaluable for lifting a sunk line to the surface before making an overhead cast.

Common Roll-casting Faults

Fly gets caught up behind

- When the rod is lifted too quickly, the bow from rod tip to water will not form properly, because the tension on the line is too great. The line will consequently lift and come through low, and then go behind you.
- If you hold your rod hand too low during the lift and roll, the line will come through too low and flat.

The line fails to roll out in front

- A lack of power during the forward movement, which should be a smooth but punchy action.
- The line is not straight or under tension before beginning the cast.
- Poor timing. If the lift and roll are hurried, the rod cannot build up power against the drag of the line as it comes off the water through the bow.

Line tangles on forward roll-down

- The rod has been brought up and over in the same vertical plane, causing the line to hang up. To remedy this, tilt the rod away from your body during the lift and roll.
- The line has not been kept tight by your line hand, causing a loss of power.
- A lack of power during the forward movement of the rod.

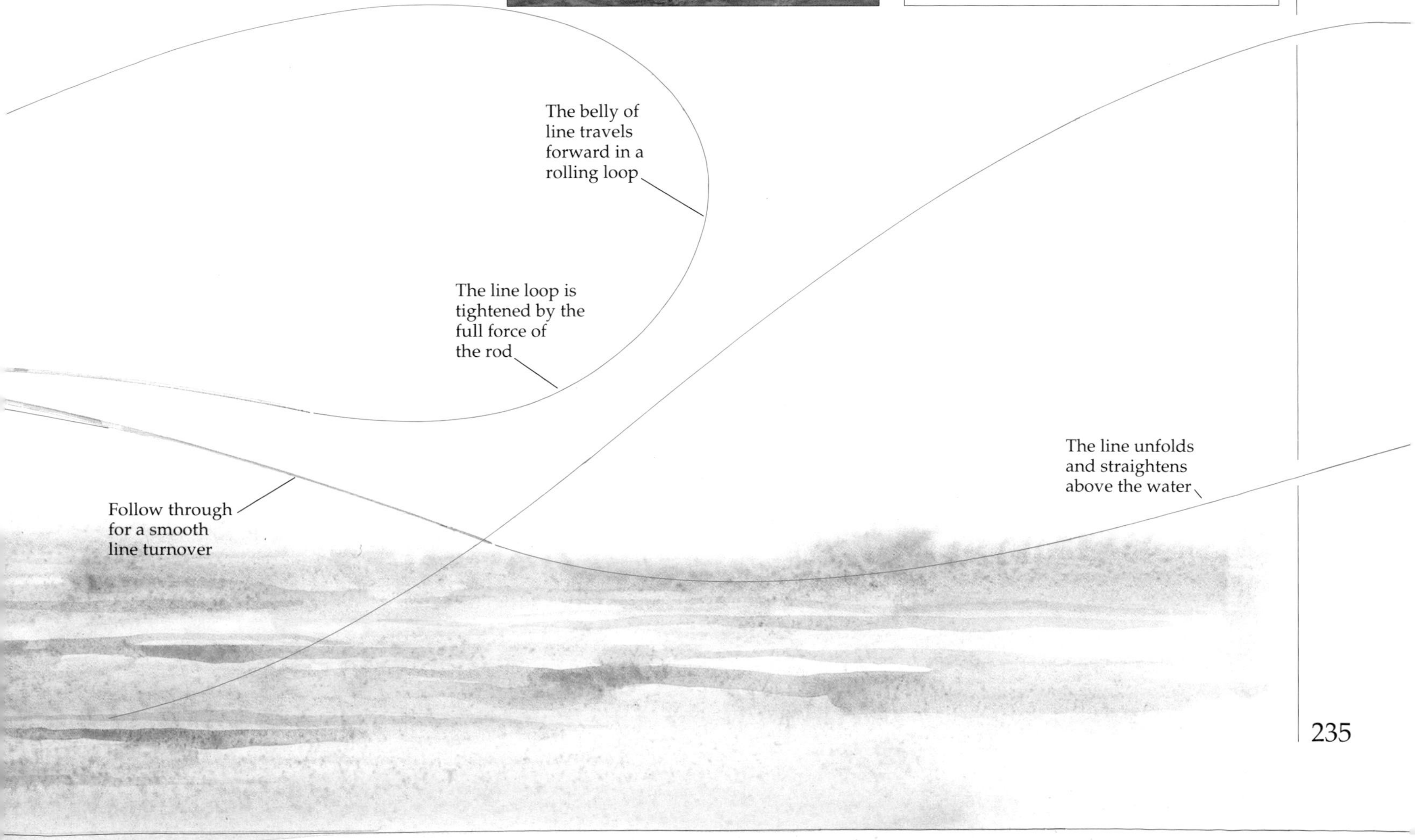
The belly of line travels forward in a rolling loop
The line loop is tightened by the full force of the rod
Follow through for a smooth line turnover
The line unfolds and straightens above the water

Wet-fly Fishing

Wet-fly, because it encompasses so many different styles, is one of the most universal methods of catching gamefish, best suited to streamy water but also effective on slower, canal-like stretches and stillwaters if the fly is worked properly. Styles and tactics have evolved to suit different conditions, seasons, and species of fish. One thing never changes: whether using willowy rods and sparse Clyde-style fly dressings in northern England, or tip-actioned, single-handed wands and bucktail streamers in North America, devotees of wet-fly enjoy their sport in some of the most wild and beautiful areas of the world.

Basic Wet-Fly Leader

Wet flies are fished either singly or, especially for trout, in teams of three equally spaced flies. Slim flies tied on the point and on the middle dropper will fish deeper than the larger pattern on the top dropper, which can be worked either on or just below the surface.

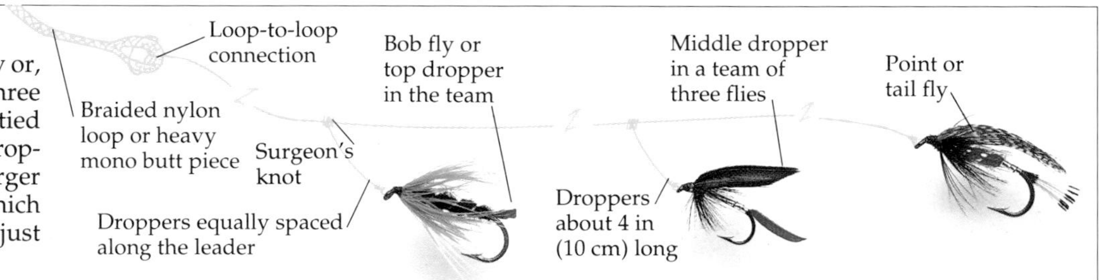
Loop-to-loop connection
Braided nylon loop or heavy mono butt piece
Surgeon's knot
Droppers equally spaced along the leader
Bob fly or top dropper in the team
Middle dropper in a team of three flies
Droppers about 4 in (10 cm) long
Point or tail fly

Upstream Fishing

The upstream method uses the speed of the current to present a fly on smooth glides and steady streams, or on the flat pockets in broken water. Because you approach from downstream there is less chance of being detected by the fish, so takes can be very positive. If the fish can be seen and are on the move looking for food, allow enough lead with the cast for the fly to sink to the correct depth. For trout lying deep, use a leaded fly to get down to the holding depth. Watch for movement of the leader or the fish as the fly passes by.

APPROACHING UNSEEN

Stalking your quarry from behind, so that you are within its blind spot, allows you to approach much closer and to use a shorter cast than if you approached from another angle. A short line is less vulnerable to drag induced by the current, so it allows a faster response to a take.

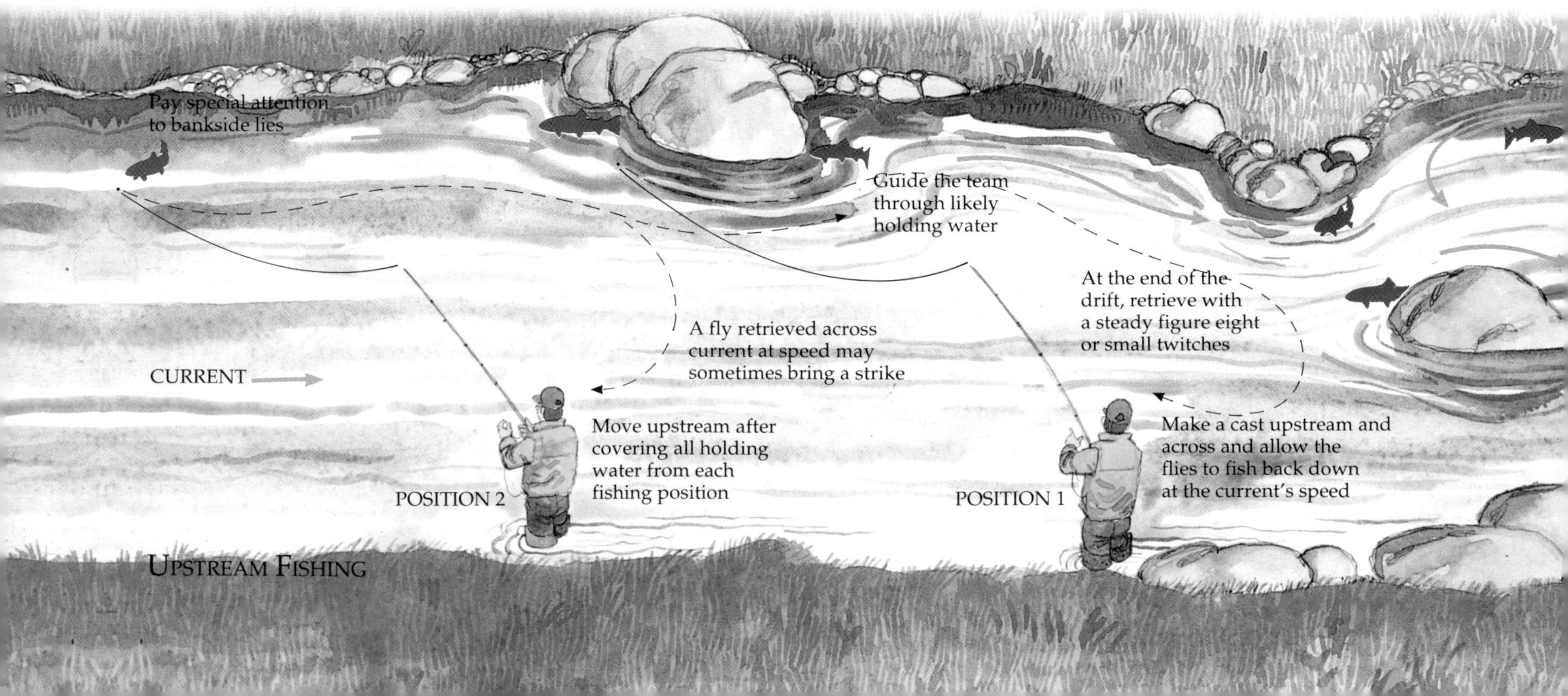
Pay special attention to bankside lies
Guide the team through likely holding water
At the end of the drift, retrieve with a steady figure eight or small twitches
A fly retrieved across current at speed may sometimes bring a strike
CURRENT
Move upstream after covering all holding water from each fishing position
Make a cast upstream and across and allow the flies to fish back down at the current's speed
POSITION 2
POSITION 1

Upstream Fishing

Downstream Fishing

A wet fly fished downstream and across follows the path of the fly line in a sweeping curve, and as the fly swings through this arc, gamefish find its movement irresistible. Controlling the speed of the fly is the key to consistent success. As the fly line sweeps around, keep the rod in line with it, because this produces a more controlled swing and improves take detection. A square cast produces a fast sweep and is a good tactic when using a team of three wet flies for trout. A long cast downstream and across makes a shallower angle and a slower swing, which is more effective for salmon.

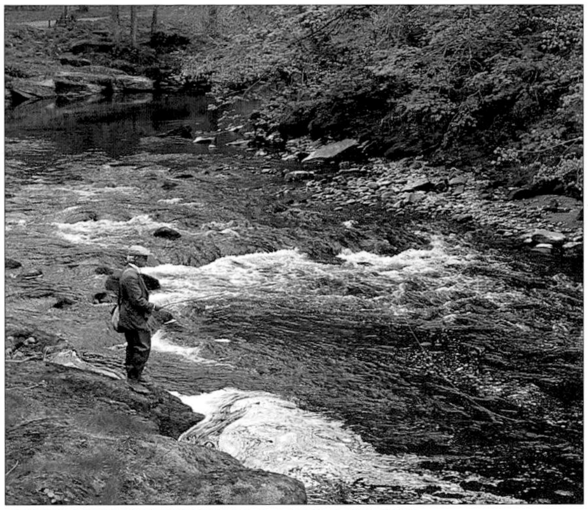

FISHING DOWNSTREAM AND ACROSS
When you are fishing downstream and across, search all the possible fish-holding water, especially the areas between the main current and slack water.

Mending line
When a fish rises in a streamy run but comes short, the reason can often be poor presentation: if the fly is fishing too fast, the fish will miss it. "Mending" the fly line slows the fly as it swings across the fish, and is achieved by throwing an upstream bow into the line immediately after the cast. This gives a slower, more controlled swing over the path **A** to **D**. If a fish is holding at **B** or **C**, but the swing is still too quick, several mends might be needed before the fly passes over it.

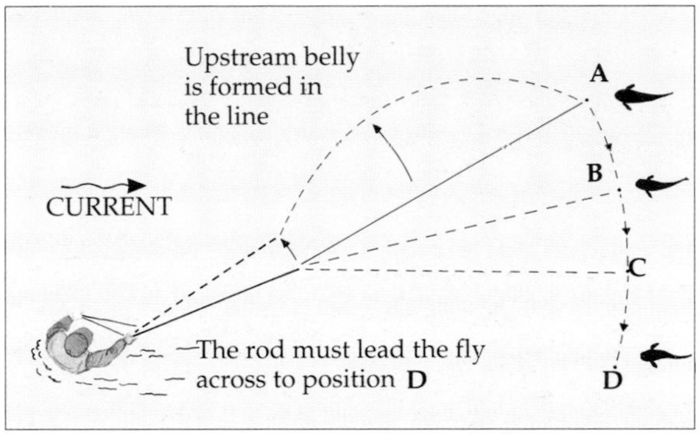
Upstream belly is formed in the line
CURRENT
A
B
C
D
The rod must lead the fly across to position D

Deep wading
Even with upstream mending, the fly will fish too quickly over its path from position 1. Fishing from position 2 eases the problem because the angle is more acute, but the wading angler at 3 can cover the fish at the same speed but with a much shorter cast.

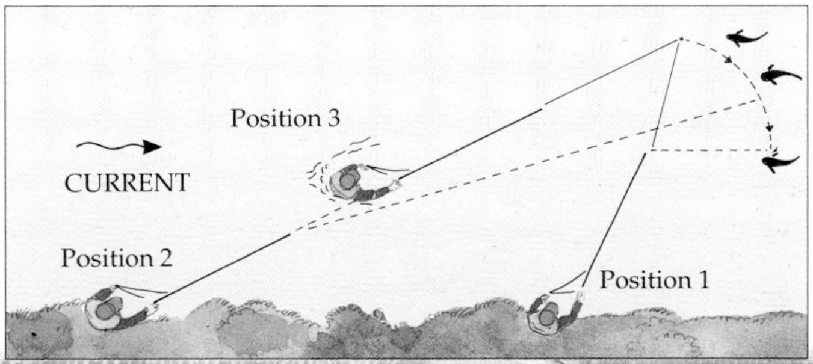
Position 3
CURRENT
Position 2
Position 1

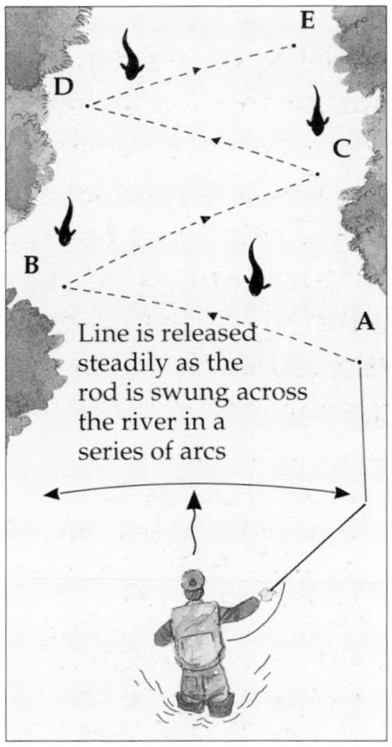
E
D
C
B
A
Line is released steadily as the rod is swung across the river in a series of arcs

Leading the fly
This is a method for fishing down water too deep to wade or where overgrown banks obstruct casting. Cast to **A**, then swing the rod across your body while releasing line to slow the fly. This makes the fly follow the path **A** to **B**. Repeating, by swinging the rod back to the start position and releasing more line, will drop the fly down to **C**. This can be repeated (to **D**, **E**, and beyond) until as long a line as practical has been fished. Takes will usually come on the swing across, so do not feed the line too quickly once the fly begins to move across.

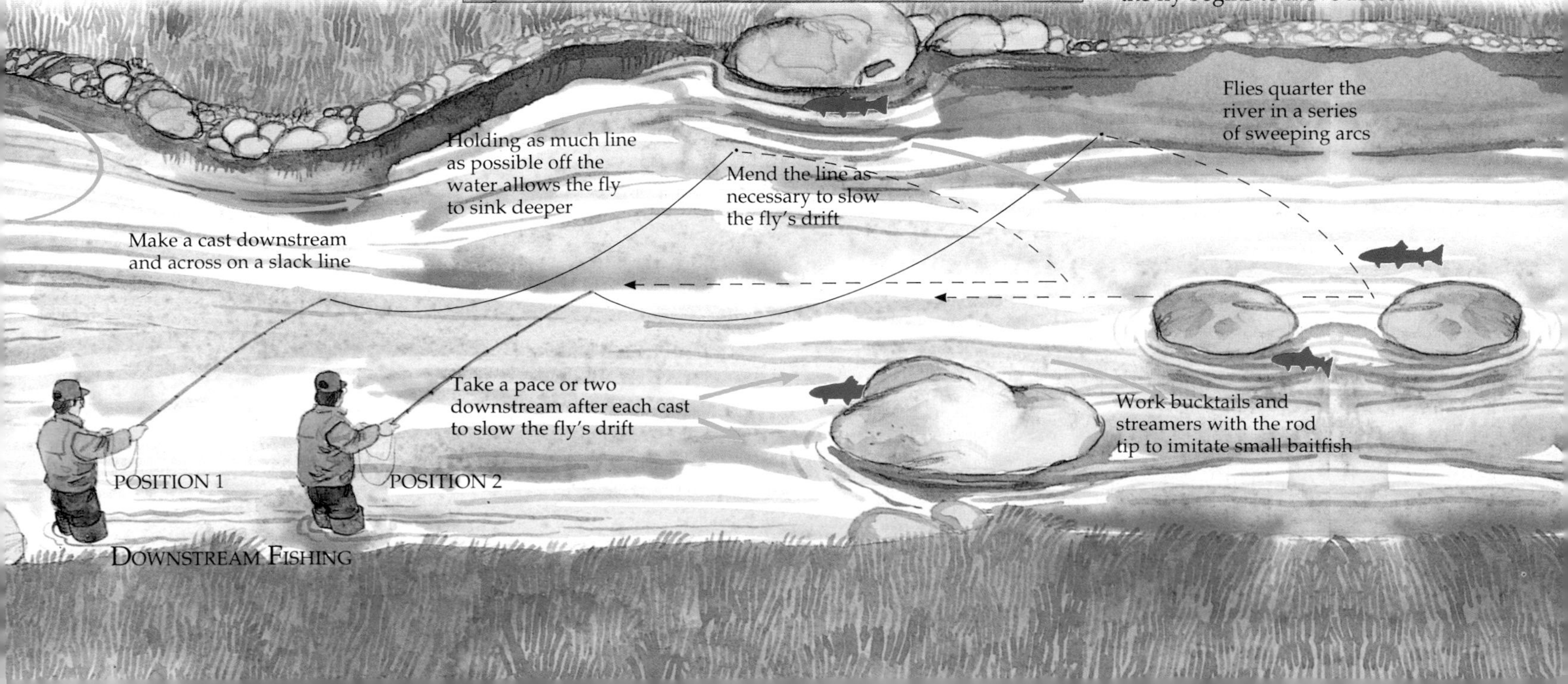
Flies quarter the river in a series of sweeping arcs
Holding as much line as possible off the water allows the fly to sink deeper
Mend the line as necessary to slow the fly's drift
Make a cast downstream and across on a slack line
Take a pace or two downstream after each cast to slow the fly's drift
Work bucktails and streamers with the rod tip to imitate small baitfish
POSITION 1
POSITION 2

DOWNSTREAM FISHING

Dry-fly Fishing

Dry-fly fishing becomes an obvious choice for the angler when trout are feeding on surface flies. Immortalized in the 19th century by experts such as Frederic M. Halford and Theodore Gordon, who placed great emphasis on exact imitation, dry-fly fishing has now become one of the most widely used methods for catching trout. It will also take many other species, including grayling, carp, and pike, and even salmon and sea trout can be caught on dry flies. The dry fly is fished on waters ranging from fast, rocky streams to large stillwaters, but the basic principle is always the same: to catch a fish on an artificial fly worked on or in the surface.

The Trout's Vision

Because light bends when it enters water, a trout can only see objects on the surface that are (from its point of view) within an angle of about 48° each side of the vertical. This gives it a total "window" of vision of surface objects of about 96°, extended by a further 32° each side of the vertical for objects beyond the surface (including nearby anglers). Beyond the boundary of the window, light striking the surface at angles of less than 10° does not penetrate the water; all the trout sees is a reflection of its underwater surroundings.

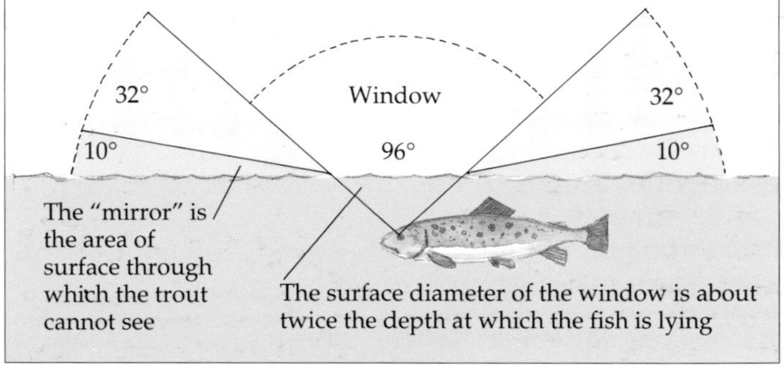

32°
Window
32°
10°
96°
10°
The "mirror" is the area of surface through which the trout cannot see
The surface diameter of the window is about twice the depth at which the fish is lying

Upstream Fishing

In rivers, fish prefer to lie facing the current. By approaching them from downstream you increase your chances of remaining unobserved, and by casting just upstream of your target fish you can get your fly to drift gently downstream into its field of vision. Good watercraft is essential. Keep a low profile, learn how to identify likely lies, and cover the water carefully. Travel light for free mobility, and wear polarized sunglasses and a wide-brimmed hat or visor to cut out the reflected glare that makes it difficult to see into the water.

FISH FINDING
Back eddies and areas behind bridge buttresses are good places to look for feeding trout. Watch out for fish facing downstream into the reverse current of a back eddy: if you approach them from downstream they may spot you. Present the fly downstream of the target fish to avoid the line entering its window of vision.

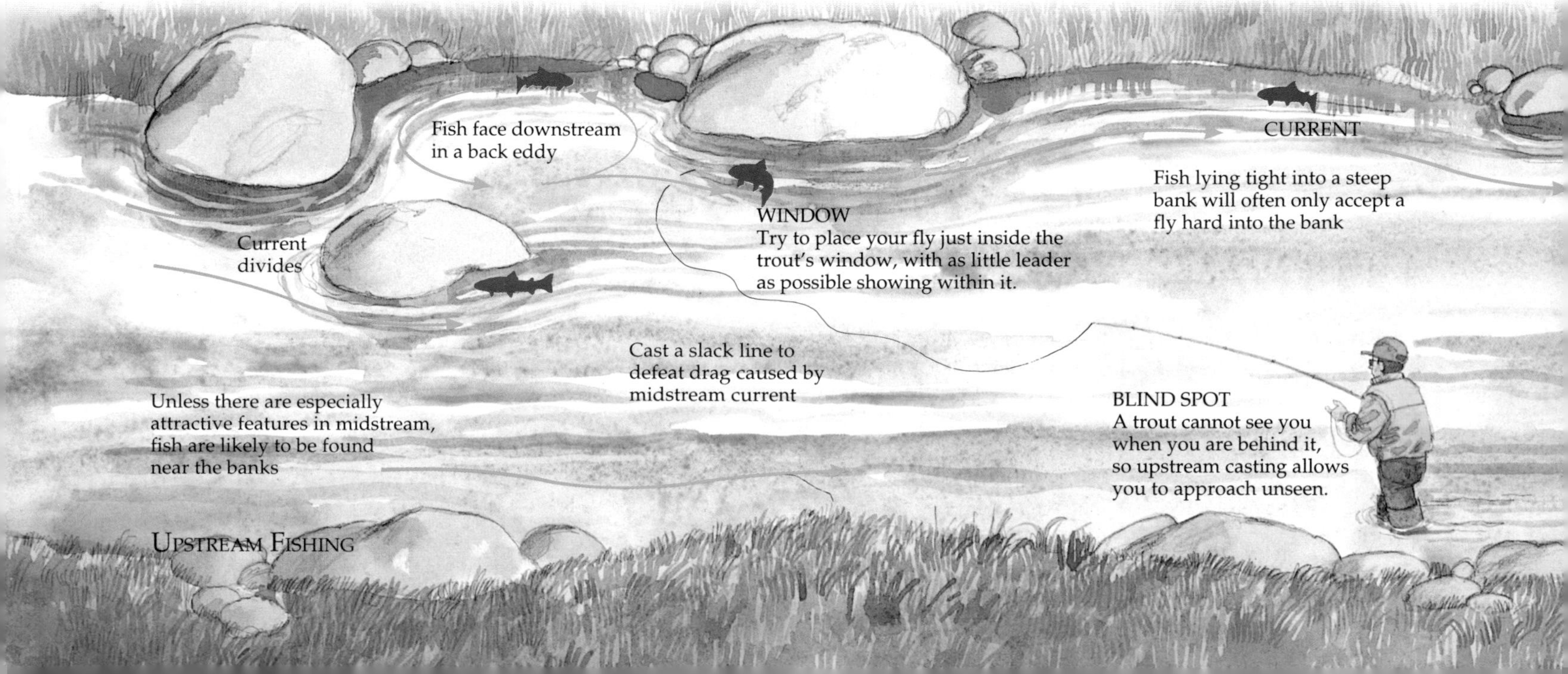

Fish face downstream in a back eddy
CURRENT
Fish lying tight into a steep bank will often only accept a fly hard into the bank
WINDOW
Try to place your fly just inside the trout's window, with as little leader as possible showing within it.
Current divides
Cast a slack line to defeat drag caused by midstream current
Unless there are especially attractive features in midstream, fish are likely to be found near the banks
BLIND SPOT
A trout cannot see you when you are behind it, so upstream casting allows you to approach unseen.

UPSTREAM FISHING

Stillwater Fishing

In stillwaters, trout tend to cruise the water, taking their food in a series of rises. By observing several successive rises you can anticipate the direction of travel of a fish, and cast your fly 3 to 10 ft (1 to 3 m) ahead of it so that there is time for the fly to settle before the fish reaches it. Let the fly drift naturally, and try to avoid drag: if drag occurs, your fly and leader will create a wake that will inevitably spook the fish. Use a fine, pale-colored, double-strength or super-strong monofil for leaders when surface fishing, and avoid the darker sort that tend to scare the fish.

SURFACE FEEDING
Dry flies and emergers come into their own during light winds or flat calms, when fish feed on insects at the surface.

Dealing with a flat calm
Fish are easily spooked by a floating leader when dry flies are fished in a flat calm. Ensure that your leader sinks quickly by degreasing it with a mixture of fuller's earth and detergent or with a commercial degreaser. Keeping the line tight to the fly helps the leader to cut through the surface, as will a small nymph tied on a dropper above the dry fly or, as here, tied New Zealand style. The nymph sinks the leader but not the dry fly.

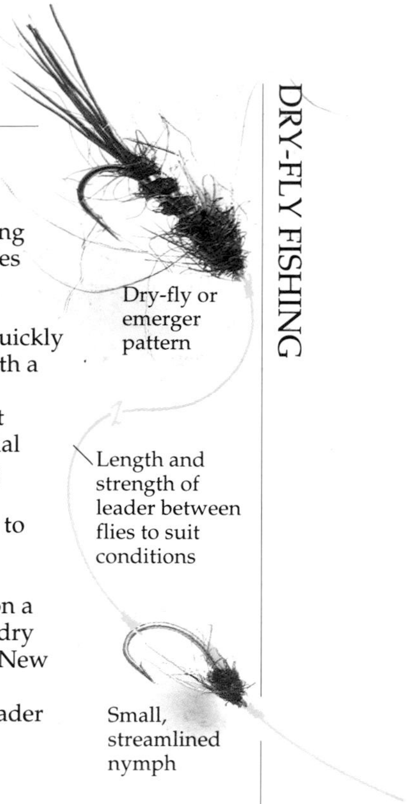
Dry-fly or emerger pattern
Length and strength of leader between flies to suit conditions
Small, streamlined nymph

Downstream Fishing

Fishing downstream is a good way to present a dry fly to fish in lies that are impossible to cover with upstream tactics. If a downstream trout is taking sedges, surface drag can be used to advantage by skating a fly across its nose to induce a take. This is achieved by making the line draw tight as the fly reaches the fish. The drifted fly can also be fished drag-free by feeding out line as it drifts downstream. The disadvantage with this method is that the fish is directly downstream of the angler, and this gives a poor hooking angle.

WADING
Unlike upstream dry-fly anglers, those fishing downstream usually wade. Wading gives you a better angle of presentation, better coverage of the water, and keeps your profile lower. When wading do not lift your feet too high: it can be dangerous in faster flows. Always wear a buoyancy aid.

SKATING THE FLY
To skate the fly across the stream in front of a feeding fish, tighten the line as the fly reaches it. The drag of the current will then pull the fly toward midstream.
The tightened line straightens and the fly begins to skate
Cast a slack line across and downstream
CURRENT
THE DRIFTED FLY
To drift a fly to a fish, pay out line so that the current carries it downstream without drag. The fish will see the fly before the line appears in its window of vision, so there is less chance of spooking the fish and more chance of a take.
Feed out loose line at a speed to match the current

DOWNSTREAM FISHING

Nymph Fishing

Nymph fishing has progressed in many ways since the early 20th century, when G. E. M. Skues wrote his classic books on the subject. It no longer means just the subsurface fishing of an exact imitation of the trout's food, because today there are many different patterns, tied on hooks of various lengths, shapes, and sizes, that are classified as nymphs. For example, the use of fluorescents and bright synthetic fibers has led to a vast range of modern nymph dressings that arguably look more like lures than representations of the trout's food. In addition, there are now many tactics for fishing up to three patterns on a cast for both river and stillwater, so nymph fishing is no longer even restricted to using a single fly.

Sight Indicators

A sight indicator or bob is a visual aid, attached to the leader, that gives early warning of a taking fish. There are several different types available commercially, and most have a fluorescent finish that provides maximum visibility.

The Orvis Never-Miss foam ball can be slid to any position on the leader depending on water depth, and is reusable, unlike the self-adhesive Orvis Stay-On indicator. Moser's Butterfly Loop is an integral part of the leader system, being a length of braided nylon looped at each end for connection between the fly line and the leader butt. Visibility is enhanced by fluorescent wool incorporated into the braid.

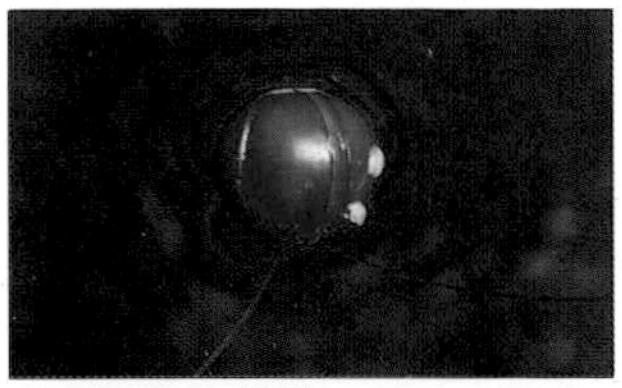

Orvis Never-Miss

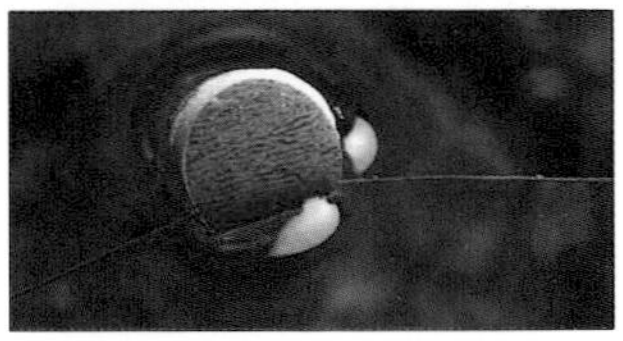

Orvis Stay-On

Moser's Butterfly Loop

River Nymphing

A nymph will often take trout that are on the move, either bulging below the surface or rooting about in the bottom weeds, and refusing to rise to a dry fly. This refusal to take a dry fly is often associated with preoccupied feeding on shrimps or ascending nymphs. It is essential to get the fly down to the feeding fish, so a weighted pattern is often required. Cast with enough lead to allow the fly time to sink to the required depth.

THE INDUCED TAKE
The clear waters of a limestone stream are ideal places to practice the induced take.

Inducing a take
Trout find flies that rise in front of their noses hard to resist. To induce a take in this way, you must be able to see the fish and make the fly rise at the right time. Allow a weighted fly to sink to the trout's holding depth, and then lift it, by raising the rod, as it nears the fish.

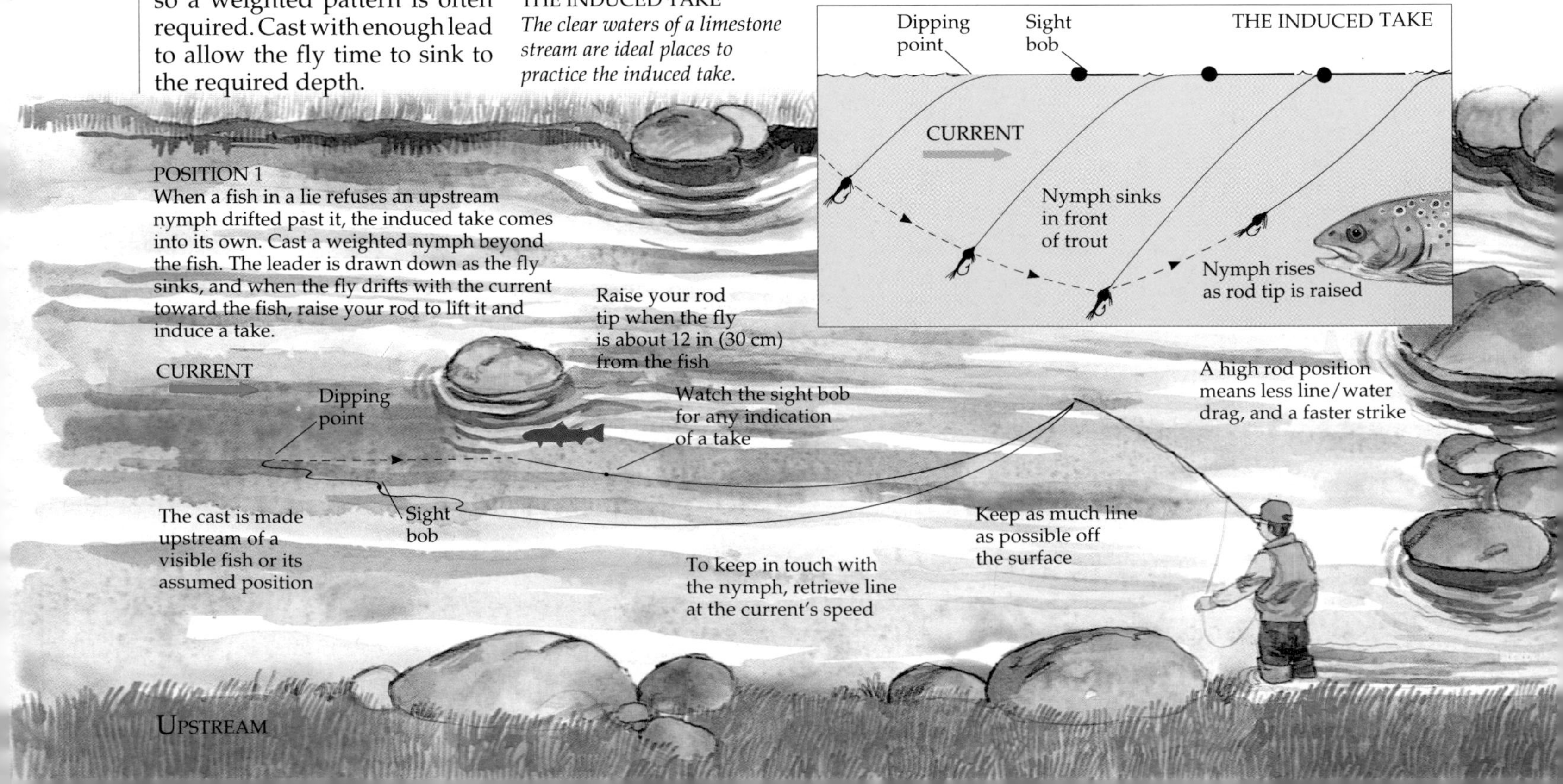

THE INDUCED TAKE
Dipping point
Sight bob
CURRENT
Nymph sinks in front of trout
Nymph rises as rod tip is raised
POSITION 1
When a fish in a lie refuses an upstream nymph drifted past it, the induced take comes into its own. Cast a weighted nymph beyond the fish. The leader is drawn down as the fly sinks, and when the fly drifts with the current toward the fish, raise your rod to lift it and induce a take.
CURRENT
Dipping point
Raise your rod tip when the fly is about 12 in (30 cm) from the fish
Watch the sight bob for any indication of a take
A high rod position means less line/water drag, and a faster strike
The cast is made upstream of a visible fish or its assumed position
Sight bob
Keep as much line as possible off the surface
To keep in touch with the nymph, retrieve line at the current's speed
UPSTREAM

STILLWATER NYMPHING

The larval and pupal stages of many aquatic insects are eaten by trout, as are water lice, tadpoles, snails, shrimps, daphnia, and corixids, to name just a few. Nymph fishers therefore tie flies to represent many such items of the trout's diet, creating either imitative or general patterns, and classify all of these flies as nymphs.

However, it is argued by some fly fishers that the only true nymphs are the nymphs of the Ephemeroptera *(see page 100)*, and that all the other aquatic creatures represented with artificial flies are therefore misrepresentations. This is strictly true, but nymph fishing today is defined not by true imitations but by the methods used.

It is difficult to pinpoint exactly where nymph fishing ends and wet-fly and lure fishing begin, but most stillwater anglers who fish with an artificial fly that represents an aquatic lifelike presentation, consider themselves to be nymph fishers.

Stalking
This is a method for clear waters where the fish can be seen and a specific target selected, and is useful on small stillwaters for catching large, deep-cruising trout. Use a fly that has some weight and a good entry into the water, so that it gets down quickly to the cruising depth, and apply an induced take before the fish has passed by. On large waters, big fish can be ambushed in the margins.

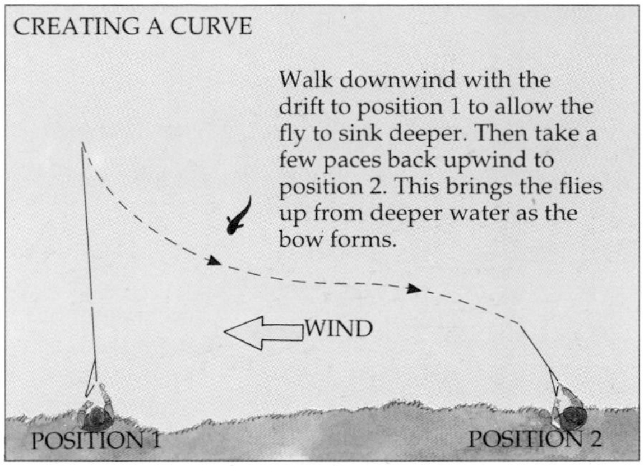
CREATING A CURVE
Walk downwind with the drift to position 1 to allow the fly to sink deeper. Then take a few paces back upwind to position 2. This brings the flies up from deeper water as the bow forms.
WIND
POSITION 1
POSITION 2

Fishing a curve
Flies fished in a curve are always attractive to fish, in streams or in stillwaters. It is the change of speed and direction that deceives them. Wind puts a natural bow in the fly line, but it can pay to walk along the bank to create your own curve.

LINE COLOR
Nymph fishermen find that pale-colored fly lines are a great aid in detecting subtle takes.

THE OPEN LOOP
Attach the fly to the leader with a universal or grinner knot, leaving a small loop when you tighten it. This will allow the fly to move freely and naturally.

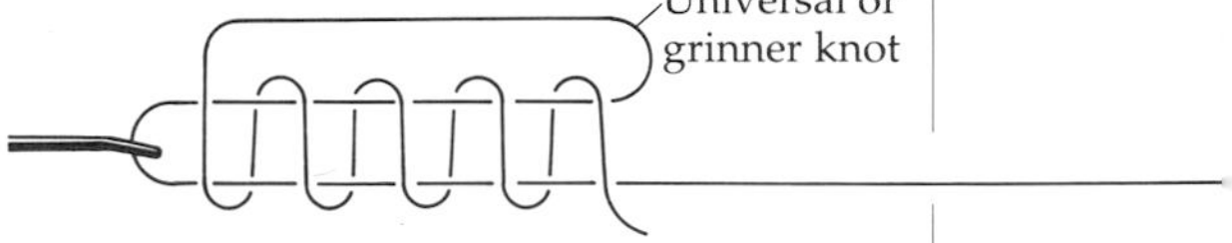
Universal or grinner knot

Open loop allows fly to move more freely

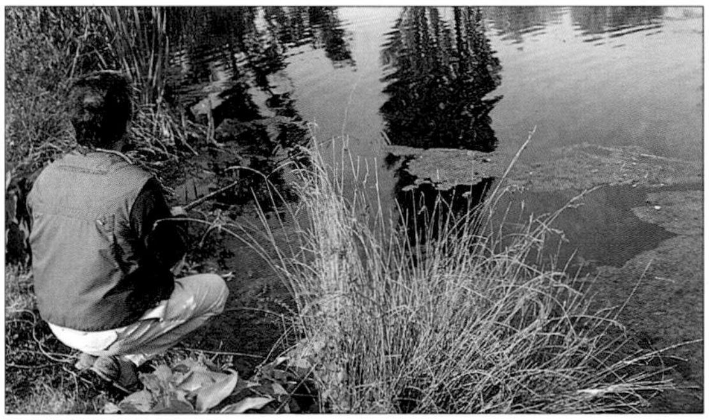
CONCEALMENT
Study the cruising patterns of the fish when stalking, but stay hidden, keep a low profile, and wear somber clothing.

Walker's Mayfly nymph

Lead bug

STALKING FLIES
Walker's Mayfly Nymph is an excellent example of a leaded fly for stalking. Small, weighted bug or midge patterns can be effective with choosy fish on warm days, but these flies can be hard to see, so use a sight bob to make them easier to spot.

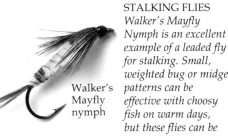

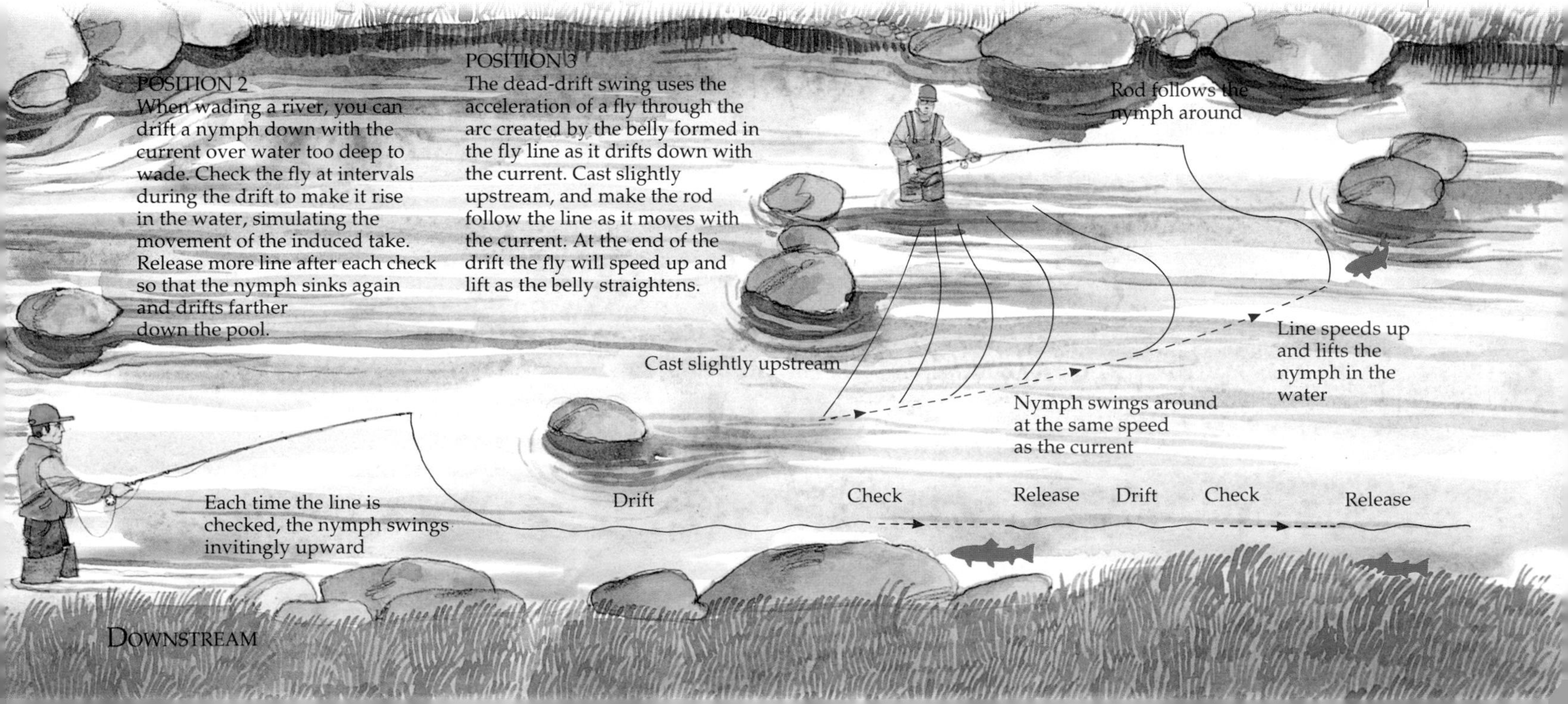
POSITION 2
When wading a river, you can drift a nymph down with the current over water too deep to wade. Check the fly at intervals during the drift to make it rise in the water, simulating the movement of the induced take. Release more line after each check so that the nymph sinks again and drifts farther down the pool.
POSITION 3
The dead-drift swing uses the acceleration of a fly through the arc created by the belly formed in the fly line as it drifts down with the current. Cast slightly upstream, and make the rod follow the line as it moves with the current. At the end of the drift the fly will speed up and lift as the belly straightens.
Rod follows the nymph around
Cast slightly upstream
Line speeds up and lifts the nymph in the water
Nymph swings around at the same speed as the current
Each time the line is checked, the nymph swings invitingly upward
Drift
Check
Release
Drift
Check
Release
DOWNSTREAM

Boat Fly Fishing

The technique of "fishing the drift" is an effective tactic for catching stillwater trout. This style of fishing involves working a team of three or four flies on a short line from a drifting boat, and is especially effective on breezy days and on wild waters. It has now largely been replaced by more modern, longer-line styles that use floating or sinking lines. With all these styles, the top dropper will take a lot of fish if it is worked properly. The secret is a steady lift at the end of the retrieve, holding the fly in the water's surface for as long as possible. Long leaders are now the norm, and the traditional flies have been replaced by newer patterns such as Raiders, Mini Muddlers, and emergers. However, a team of old favorites such as a Wickham's on the top dropper, a Silver Invicta on the middle dropper, and a Gold Ribbed Hare's Ear on the point is still an effective combination, particularly in high summer.

Safe Casting Angles

When two anglers share a boat, each must fish a restricted area to avoid interfering with the other's fishing and, more importantly, to avoid injuries that can arise from careless casting. If both are right-handed, angler A can fish safely in sector 3 and, with allowance for angler B's movements and safety, in sectors 1 and 2. Angler B can fish safely in sector 4. If one angler is left-handed, he or she should take position A and can then fish sectors 1, 2, and 3. If both are left-handed, the sector pattern is the reverse of that for two right-handed anglers.

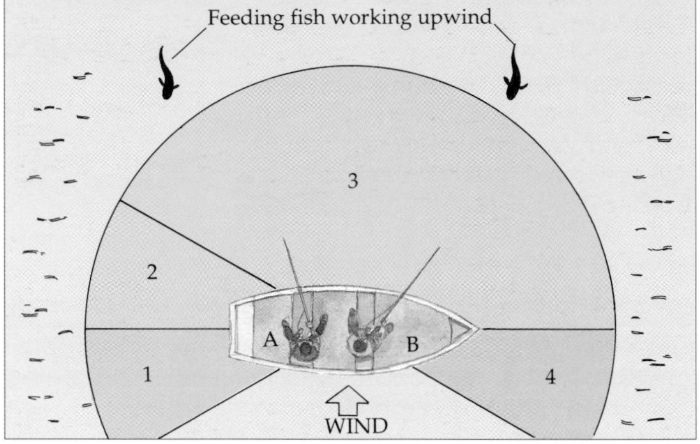
Feeding fish working upwind
3
2
1
4
A
B
WIND

Fishing the Drift

A 10 to 11 ft (3 to 3.4 m) rod gives good control when lifting the flies to the surface, and casts a wide enough loop to avoiding tangling them. Using long droppers improves presentation and allows for several fly changes before a dropper has to be replaced. Always keep in touch with the flies, and strike at the slightest sign of a rise to the team. Look for unusual movements downwind of the boat, and drift windlanes (flat tracts of water that run for considerable distances down the waves) because they usually hold fish.

LOCAL KNOWLEDGE
Lake fish populations are often localized, and without the assistance of a local fisherman or guide on waters that are unfamiliar to you, you could waste much time fishing unproductive areas. Here, a guide is controlling the drift of the boat, allowing the fisherman to retrieve his team of flies through the productive shallows around a rocky outcrop.

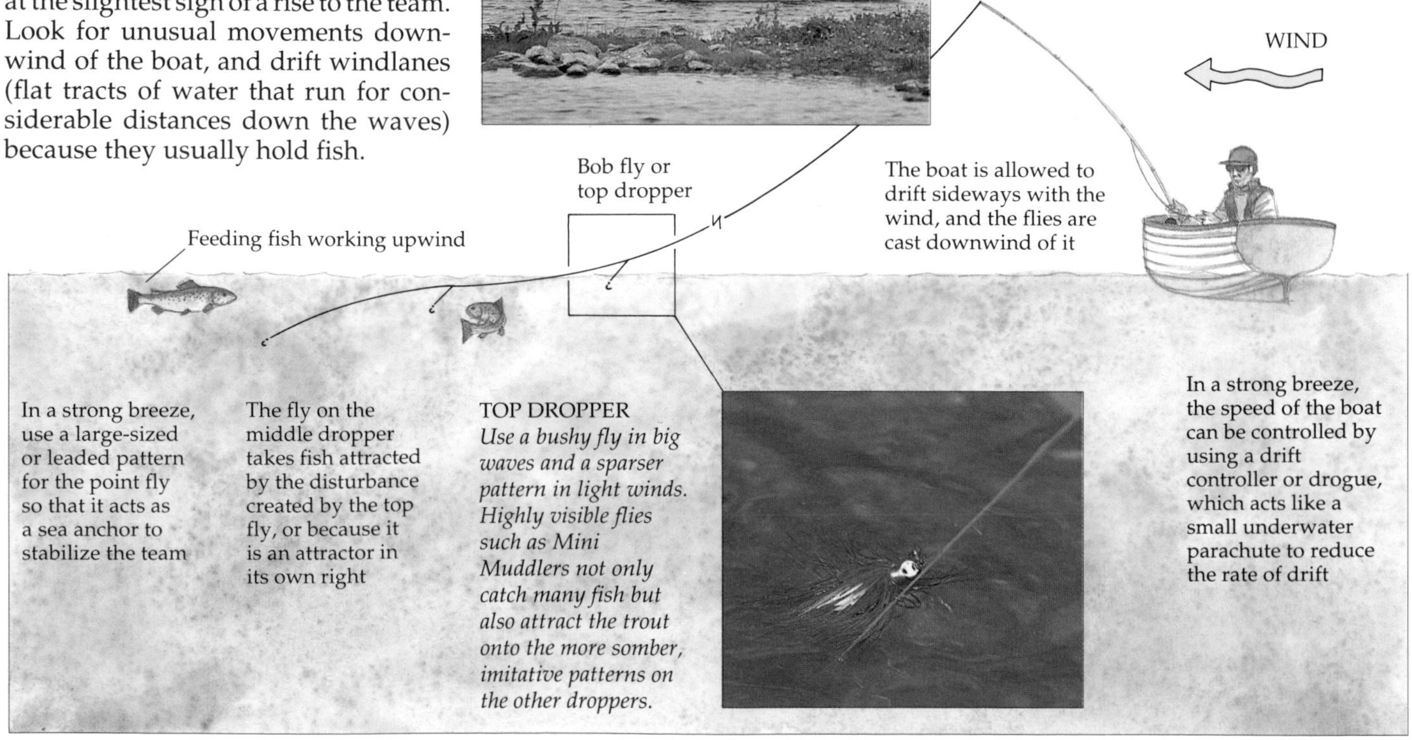
WIND
Bob fly or top dropper
The boat is allowed to drift sideways with the wind, and the flies are cast downwind of it
Feeding fish working upwind
In a strong breeze, use a large-sized or leaded pattern for the point fly so that it acts as a sea anchor to stabilize the team
The fly on the middle dropper takes fish attracted by the disturbance created by the top fly, or because it is an attractor in its own right
TOP DROPPER
Use a bushy fly in big waves and a sparser pattern in light winds. Highly visible flies such as Mini Muddlers not only catch many fish but also attract the trout onto the more somber, imitative patterns on the other droppers.
In a strong breeze, the speed of the boat can be controlled by using a drift controller or drogue, which acts like a small underwater parachute to reduce the rate of drift

Sunk Line Fishing

The tactic of lift and hold with a sunk, high-density (Hi-D) line can be very effective for fish lying deep. As the flies sink through the layers, use a steady retrieve to keep in touch with them and detect takes on the drop. Draw the flies to the surface as the boat drifts down on them, but stop the draw just as the top dropper comes into view or is about to break surface, and hold it there for as long as possible. Bright attractor patterns provoke the fish into taking as the flies are held before being lifted out, and nymphs fished behind a bright top dropper catch well when the trout are feeding on midges.

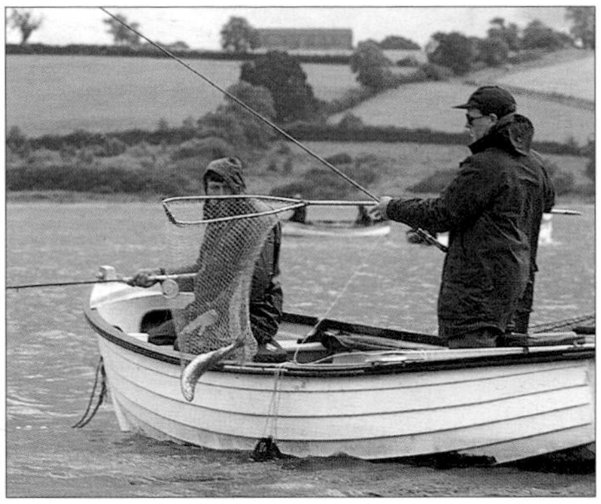

TIME FOR THE HI-D
An early-season bright day, when the fish are lying deep, is just the time for the fast-sinking line and a flashy attractor on the top dropper.

FISHING THE HI-D
Fast-sinking, high-density lines are a necessity when you want to reach trout lying deep; WF #7 to #8 lines with 10 ft (3 m) rods are a popular choice. To find the holding depth of the fish, try the countdown method (*see page 216*). Once the holding depth has been found, vary the retrieve rate until you find the most productive taking speed.

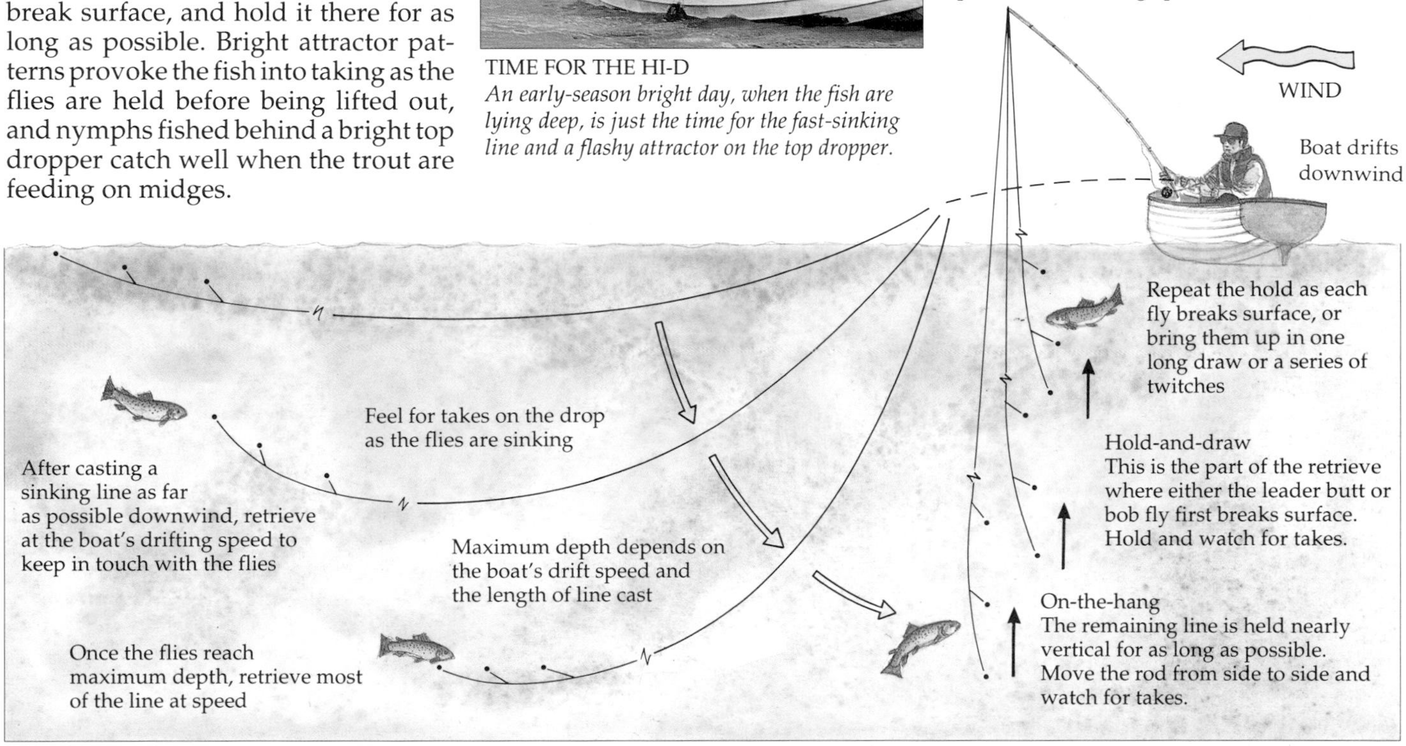
WIND
Boat drifts downwind
Repeat the hold as each fly breaks surface, or bring them up in one long draw or a series of twitches
Feel for takes on the drop as the flies are sinking
After casting a sinking line as far as possible downwind, retrieve at the boat's drifting speed to keep in touch with the flies
Hold-and-draw
This is the part of the retrieve where either the leader butt or bob fly first breaks surface. Hold and watch for takes.
Maximum depth depends on the boat's drift speed and the length of line cast
On-the-hang
The remaining line is held nearly vertical for as long as possible. Move the rod from side to side and watch for takes.
Once the flies reach maximum depth, retrieve most of the line at speed

Dapping

Dapping, the technique of tripping a fly lightly over the surface of the water, has a reputation for producing large trout, salmon, and sea trout from large stillwaters. Long rods 15 to 17 ft (4.6 to 5.2 m) and a floss "blow line" that carries in the wind are essential. The filamentous strands of the blow line fray in use, but a knot tied every 18 in (45 cm) will prevent the line from disintegrating. Dapped natural flies are illegal on some waters.

WORKING THE FLY
The blow line is fed out to work the fly on the surface as far as possible downwind of the boat. The fly is worked by holding it just above the water and dropping it gently onto the surface at intervals, by allowing it to float, and by drawing it lightly across the surface. On windy days, a second fly adds stability.

Boat-Fishing Etiquette

When drifting along a shoreline, keep clear of bank anglers and do not drift too close to the shore. At the end of the drift, motor upwind well away from other boats, do not disturb the "hot spot" area where the fish are, and never cut into another boat's drift too soon. Only stand up if it is absolutely necessary, and always wear eye protection and a life jacket.

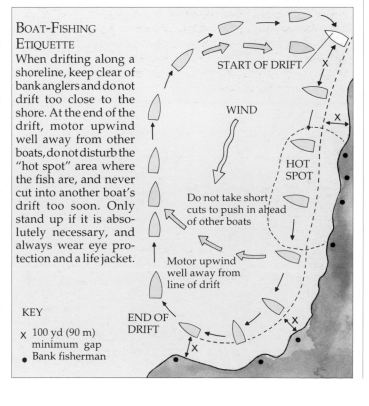

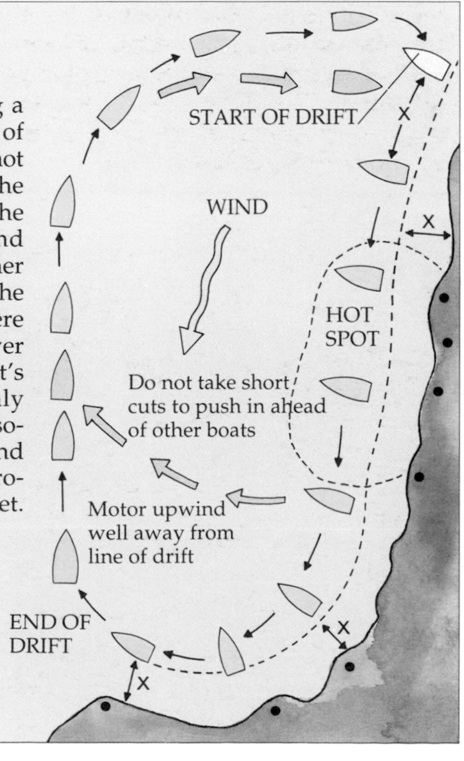
START OF DRIFT
WIND
HOT SPOT
Do not take short cuts to push in ahead of other boats
Motor upwind well away from line of drift
END OF DRIFT
X
X
X
X

KEY
X 100 yd (90 m) minimum gap
● Bank fisherman

Inshore Fishing

By using an outboard-powered dinghy or a small motor cruiser, you can fish waters that are beyond the reach of the shore angler but not far enough offshore to warrant being worked by larger boats. These include not only those close to the shore, but also the quiet bays, estuaries, and saltwater creeks that are often very productive because they are seldom fished.

Safety at Sea

When you are in charge of a boat, of whatever size, it is essential that you are capable of handling it properly and that you and your companions know exactly what to do in an emergency. The boat must be seaworthy and of adequate size, with a reliable motor, a full tank of fuel, and basic emergency equipment including life-jackets, compass, flares, a first-aid kit, and, if possible, a radio. Before setting out, get an up-to-date weather forecast, and let someone know where you are going and when you expect to return.

Boat Fishing

When fishing from an anchored boat in shallow water, the noise from the boat and the anglers can create a "scare area" into which most fish (apart from flatfish) are reluctant to stray. This area extends not only around the boat but also below it. In shallow water, if the fish cannot go deep enough to avoid the sound they may avoid the area of the boat altogether, and then it will not be possible to take them by drop-down fishing, in which the baits are simply lowered over the side.

Uptide fishing, in which the baits are cast upcurrent and well away from the boat, will overcome this problem. It works best in depths to around 40 ft (12 m), but it can be used much deeper. Wired sinkers are used to anchor the baits, and the length of line cast needs to be at least three times the depth of the water being fished.

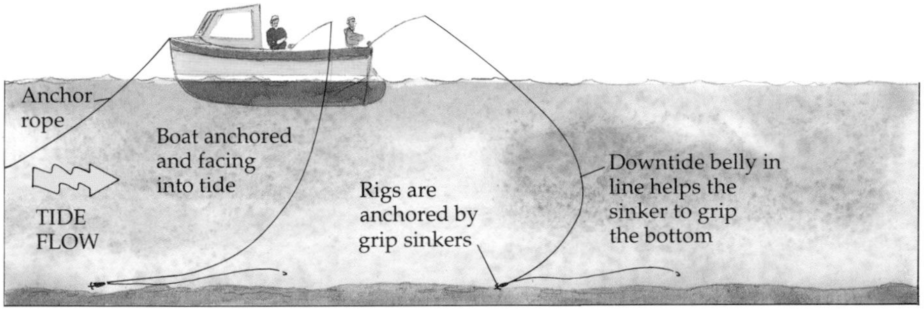

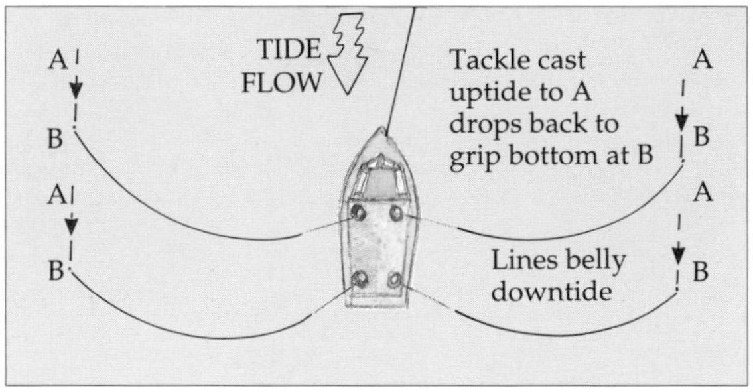

Casting and striking
Use a 9 to 10 ft (2.7 to 3 m) saltwater spinning outfit, and cast uptide and away from the boat. After it hits bottom, the sinker will roll back a short way before taking hold. When you get a bite, wind in quickly until you feel the weight of the fish on the line, and then strike.

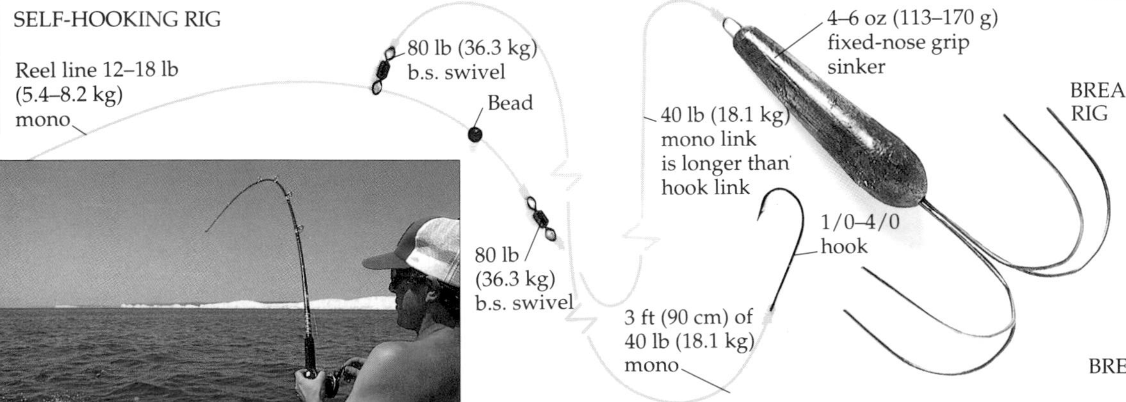

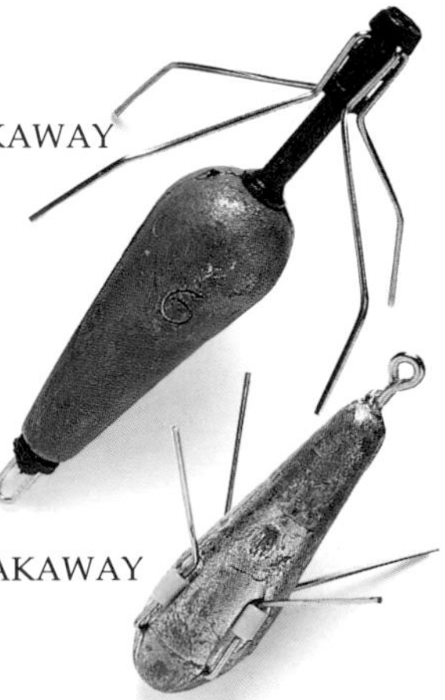

SMALL-BOAT SHARK
Fishing from a dinghy accounts for a small shark. Sharks are not the usual quarry of small-boat anglers, but the technique frequently takes dogfish, tope, and other small inshore shark species.

SELF-HOOKING RIG
This rig is used for species such as cod and flatfish, which start eating the bait almost as soon as they pick it up. As they move off with the bait, they hook themselves by pulling against the grip of the sinker. The sliding rig (see opposite) *is used for fish that run with the bait.*

SINKERS *(above)*
Sinkers for inshore fishing can be of the breakaway type or have fixed wires on the flank or the nose (see pages 60–61). *Those with long nose wires give the best grip; breakaways work best in shallow waters with medium tides.*

Bottom Fishing

Not all boat-angling situations either suit or demand casting long distances, nor do they require specialized rods. Bottom (or downtide or drop-down) fishing in waters that are deeper than about 30 ft (9 m), particularly reef and general drift fishing, can be done perfectly well with standard boat tackle. Rods are generally around 7 ft (2.1 m) long, reels do not need to have good casting ability, and a wide variety of rigs can be used.

The sinkers do not have to hold bottom securely, so need not be wired. They must, however, be able to maintain bottom contact, and so they must be matched to the strength of the tide and of the line – the lower each of these is, the less weight will be required. In addition, the weight of sinker being used should be changed as the strength of the tide increases or decreases.

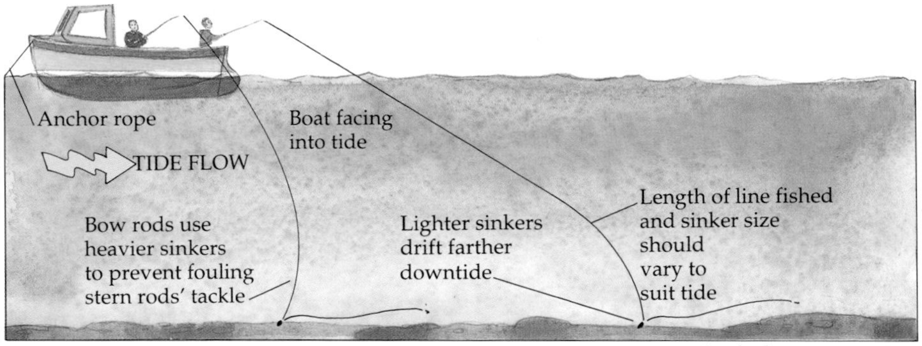

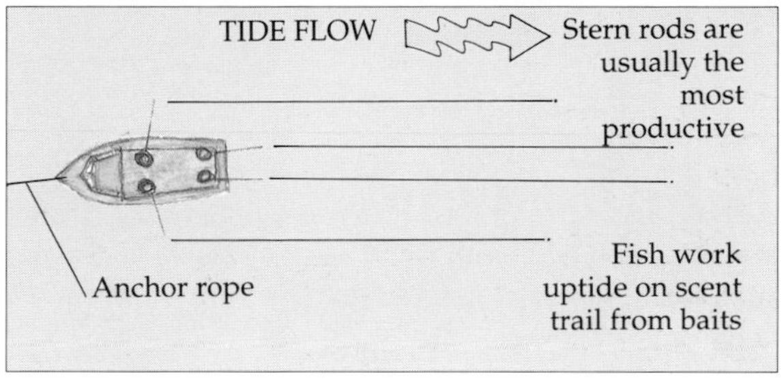

Spacing the baits
In bottom fishing, the baits all lie in line with the rod tips and therefore require careful spacing. If the rods at the front of the boat carry heavy sinkers and the stern rods the lightest that will hold, the current will drag them at different speeds and they will not tangle.

SLIDING RIG
Fish such as bass, which run with a bait before eating it, will drop it if they feel any resistance from the sinker. The sliding rig allows unhindered feeding movement, so that the angler can wait until the fish has the bait inside its mouth before striking. When using a sliding rig, the reel is set on free spool to allow the line to be taken without moving the sinker.

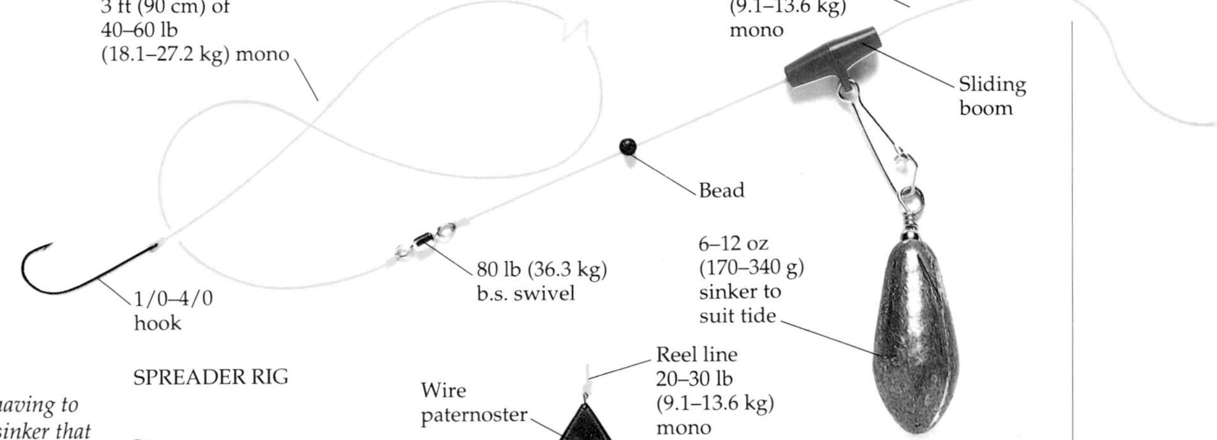

BOTTOM SINKERS *(below)*
To maintain bottom contact without having to pay out an excessive line, you need a sinker that combines adequate weight with a simple, streamlined shape that offers little resistance to the current. The bank sinker meets these requirements and is the shape least likely to snag, making it the best choice for most bottom fishing.

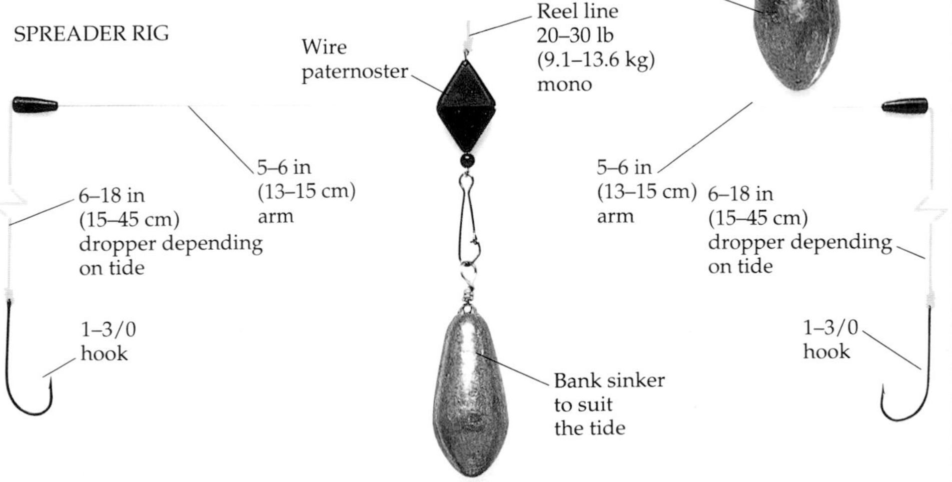

SPREADER RIG
This is a type of paternoster, a rig that presents baits on short lengths of mono, called droppers or snoods, above a sinker. The droppers are attached to the leader or to booms, and spaced so that they do not tangle with each other. This spreader rig has two wire booms, each carrying a short dropper, allowing two baits to be fished at the bottom as a team. The dropper lengths should be varied with changes in the tide: use droppers of 18 in (45 cm) in a fast-flowing tide, but shorten them to about 6 in (15 cm) at slack water to help minimize tangling. Flatfish, whiting, and codling are among the species that are highly susceptible to this type of bait presentation.

OFFSHORE FISHING

Fish tend to increase in numbers, size, and variety of species with greater water depth and distance from shore. But this does not mean that you will always have to sail a long way out to find large fish: they move to wherever their instincts tell them to be at any given time, which may be not far from the shore. For example, the biggest examples of cod, conger, and turbot are usually to be found well offshore at depth, but they could just as easily be within a few minutes' sailing time of port. One of the factors that determines the location of large fish is the availability of food, including sandeels and the mackerel that prey on them. These and other food items are found in large numbers over features such as offshore sandbanks and reefs, regardless of their distance from shore, so these features are often very productive fishing venues for the offshore angler.

DRIFT FISHING
Fishing on the drift over rough ground is not suited to light tackle, because fierce tides demand heavy sinkers to take the terminal tackle down to where the largest fish feed. In addition, big fish have to be bullied to prevent them from gaining the sanctuary that rough ground affords.

FISHING OVER SANDBANKS

Sandbanks are exciting places to fish, because they are one of the few types of offshore feature likely to concentrate clean-ground species of fish in the way that wrecks attract rough-ground species. Moreover, the fish likely to be feeding in good numbers around a large, steep bank include prized angling species such as bass, turbot, brill, and cod. The supporting cast can include numerous species of ray, plus plaice, dab, whiting, and even pollack.

Bank-fishing rigs
Bank-rig design depends on whether you are fishing at anchor or on the drift. For anchored-boat fishing, use a standard sliding rig *(see page 245)*, made of 4 ft (1.2 m) of heavy mono and armed with a 4/0 Aberdeen hook. When drift fishing, increase the leader length to 10 to 20 ft (3 to 6 m) and attach the sinker via a long, tubular boom.

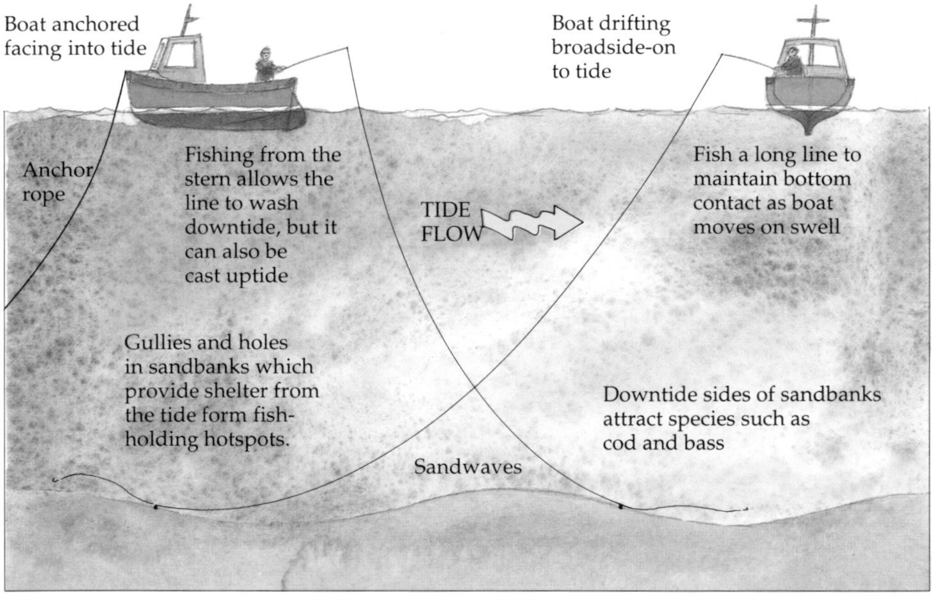
Boat anchored facing into tide
Anchor rope
Fishing from the stern allows the line to wash downtide, but it can also be cast uptide
TIDE FLOW
Boat drifting broadside-on to tide
Fish a long line to maintain bottom contact as boat moves on swell
Gullies and holes in sandbanks which provide shelter from the tide form fish-holding hotspots.
Downtide sides of sandbanks attract species such as cod and bass
Sandwaves

BANK-FISHING SINKERS
Because a sandbank is a maze of ridges and gullies, end tackle often wanders from its intended path and this can lead to tangles. A studded watch weight is less prone to wandering and tangling than other types of sinker.

WATCH WEIGHT

Fishing on the drift
Drifting is by far the easiest way to fish a large bank, because it requires no prior knowledge of where the gullies and sandwaves are. If you start the drift well uptide of the lip of the bank, and pay out enough line to cope with variations in depth, your baits will cover every nook and cranny along the boat's line of travel. Bites show as a slow pulling-over of the rod tip (and of the rod itself, if unattended). Bass, turbot, and cod are typical bank species.

Fishing at anchor
When fishing from an anchored boat, you cannot cover as much ground with your baits as when fishing on the drift. As a result, you need to place your baits in the areas most likely to hold feeding fish, which are gullies and the downtide slopes of sandwaves. Free-swimming fish, such as bass, are usually found near the lip of the bank, skate and rays near the base, and flatfish over the middle section. The most reliable way to find these features is to use an echo sounder.

Fishing Offshore Reefs

A reef attracts a rich variety of marine creatures, including fish, because it offers abundant cover, and the varying bottom topography provides a wide range of habitats. Because of the large number of species likely to be present, the reef angler is often faced with the question of which one to fish for, and having decided, may well find the baits being taken by other species anyway. For example, fishing specifically for conger does not rule out other species taking the bait, although the size of the baits and hooks will have a limiting effect. One of the most effective rigs for general reef fishing is baited mackerel feathers, and this fact is reflected in the alternative rigs shown here. Like feather rigs, they present the baits above the sinker so that they flutter enticingly and are clear of bottom snags. They avoid many of the common problems with store-bought feathers, including short droppers and poor hooks.

Fishing on the Drift

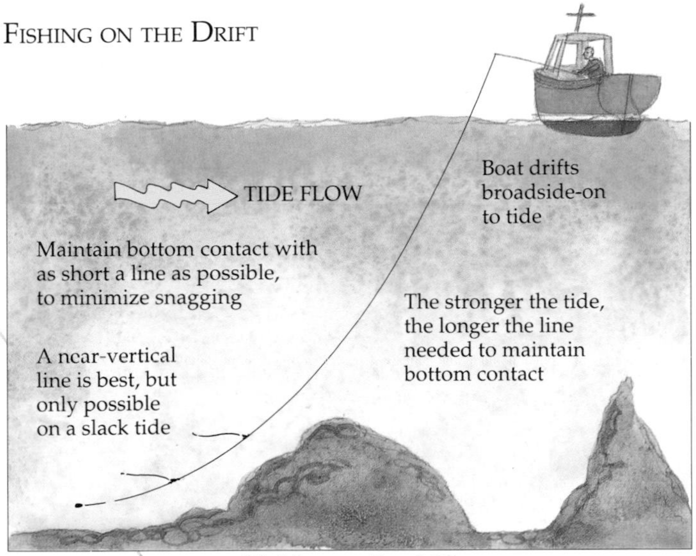

DRIFT RIG

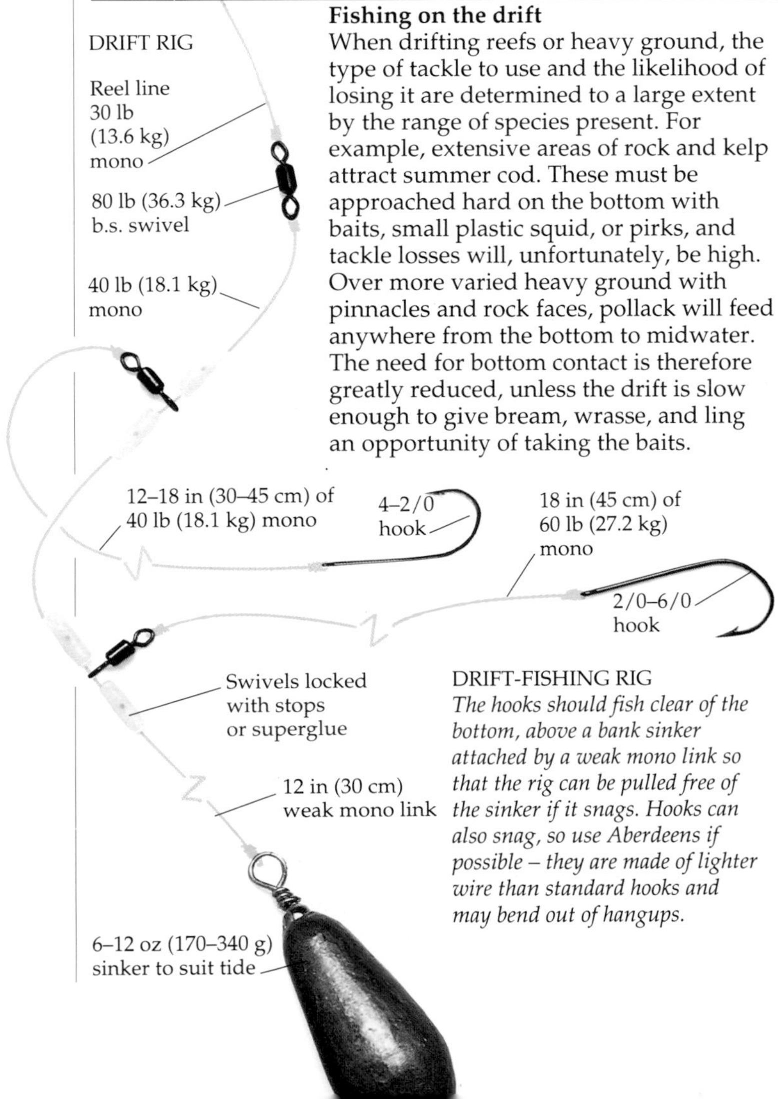

Fishing on the drift
When drifting reefs or heavy ground, the type of tackle to use and the likelihood of losing it are determined to a large extent by the range of species present. For example, extensive areas of rock and kelp attract summer cod. These must be approached hard on the bottom with baits, small plastic squid, or pirks, and tackle losses will, unfortunately, be high. Over more varied heavy ground with pinnacles and rock faces, pollack will feed anywhere from the bottom to midwater. The need for bottom contact is therefore greatly reduced, unless the drift is slow enough to give bream, wrasse, and ling an opportunity of taking the baits.

DRIFT-FISHING RIG
The hooks should fish clear of the bottom, above a bank sinker attached by a weak mono link so that the rig can be pulled free of the sinker if it snags. Hooks can also snag, so use Aberdeens if possible – they are made of lighter wire than standard hooks and may bend out of hangups.

Fishing at anchor
There is less risk of hangups when fishing at anchor than when drift fishing because the terminal tackle is stationary. In addition, the static baits can be fished hard on the bottom, making them accessible to slow-feeding species – such as conger, ling, wrasse, and bream – that might not take a drifted bait. However, a grapnel anchor with a trip release should always be used, to avoid costly anchor loss if hangups do occur, and sinkers should be attached by weak links to minimize tackle losses.

MULTI-COVER RIG

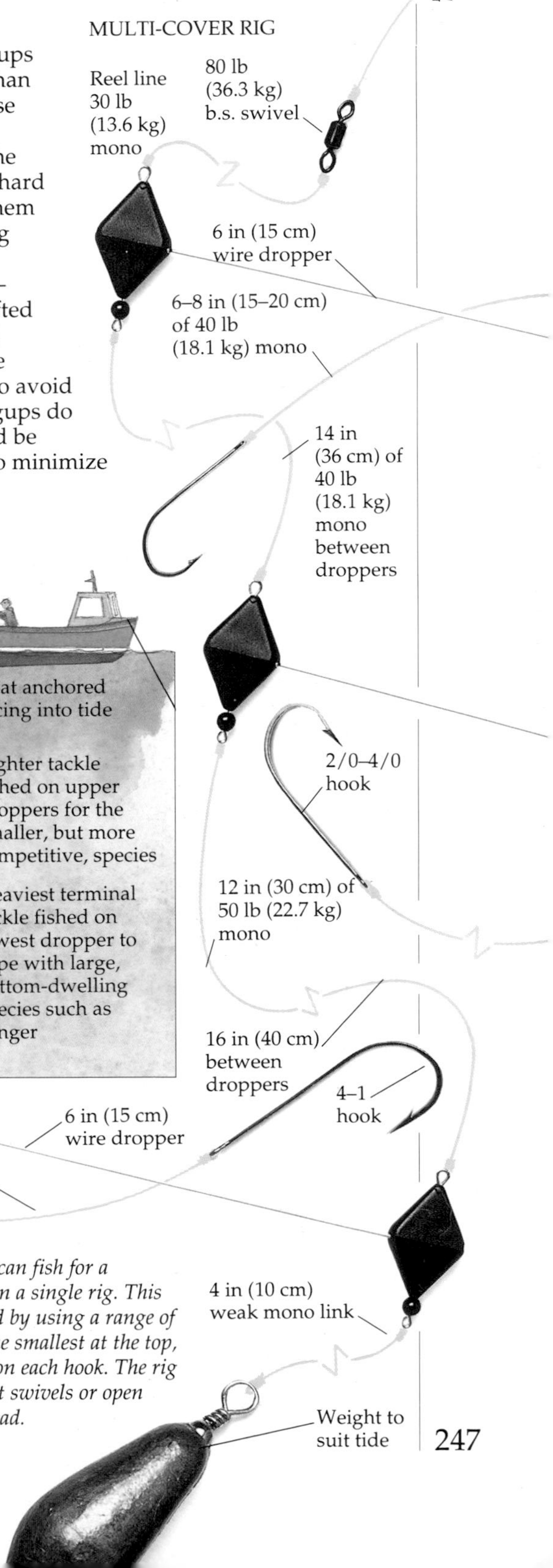

Fishing at Anchor

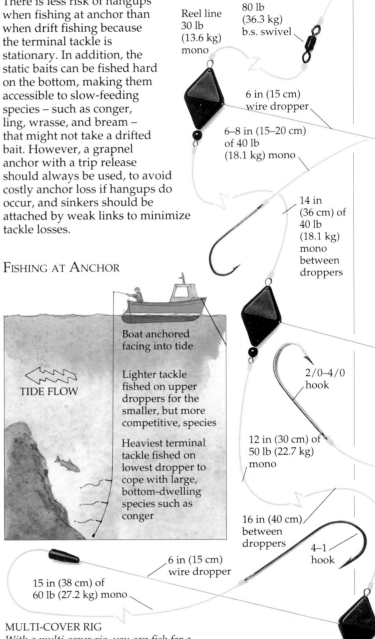

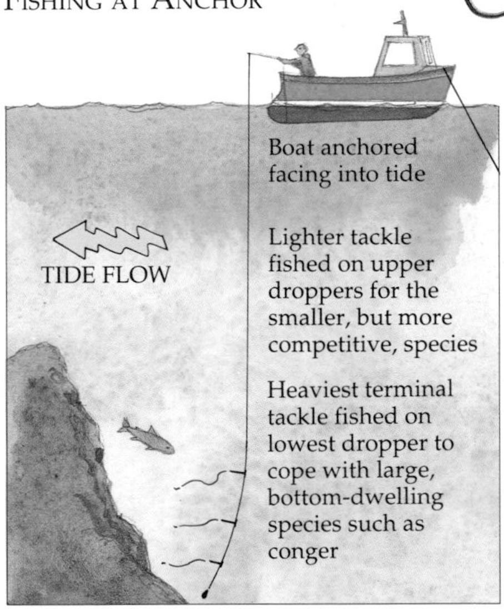

MULTI-COVER RIG
With a multi-cover rig, you can fish for a number of different species on a single rig. This multiple coverage is achieved by using a range of hook sizes on the rig, with the smallest at the top, and perhaps a different bait on each hook. The rig shown here has droppers, but swivels or open blood loops can be used instead.

WRECK FISHING

Ships can be wrecked anywhere from the shore to mid-ocean, but the best angling wrecks will be in water deeper than 200 ft (60 m), and the greatest concentrations are usually found in the vicinity of major ports. Wrecks can end up on virtually any type of ground, and from an angling point of view it does not matter where they settle out. In time, algae begins to grow on a wreck, followed by encrusting animals such as barnacles; eventually, a complete food chain is established. For fish, a wreck on sandy ground is like an oasis in a desert, and in rocky areas it provides more food and even better cover, for both predators and prey, than the surrounding rocks. A broken-up wreck will offer more cover than one that is relatively intact, so it will attract larger numbers of fish. The more broken-up a wreck becomes, the better its angling potential will be.

FISHING AT ANCHOR

Working a wreck from an anchored boat is a very specialized affair that makes great demands on the skills of both skipper and anglers. The skipper must make allowances for wind and tide, both of which can vary greatly over very short periods of time, and make continual fine adjustments to keep the stern of the boat just uptide of the edge of the wreck. Anchoring is always done at the slacker periods of neap tides and requires good sea conditions. At best, anglers will get 2 to 2½ hours of anchored fishing before the new tide starts to swing the boat out of position and it is time to switch to fishing on the drift. However, as the boat starts to swing, baits missing target can land on the sandwaves that build around some wrecks and are caused by the tide. Clean-ground species, including large monkfish and flounder, often frequent these sandwaves and sometimes feed tight up to the hulk.

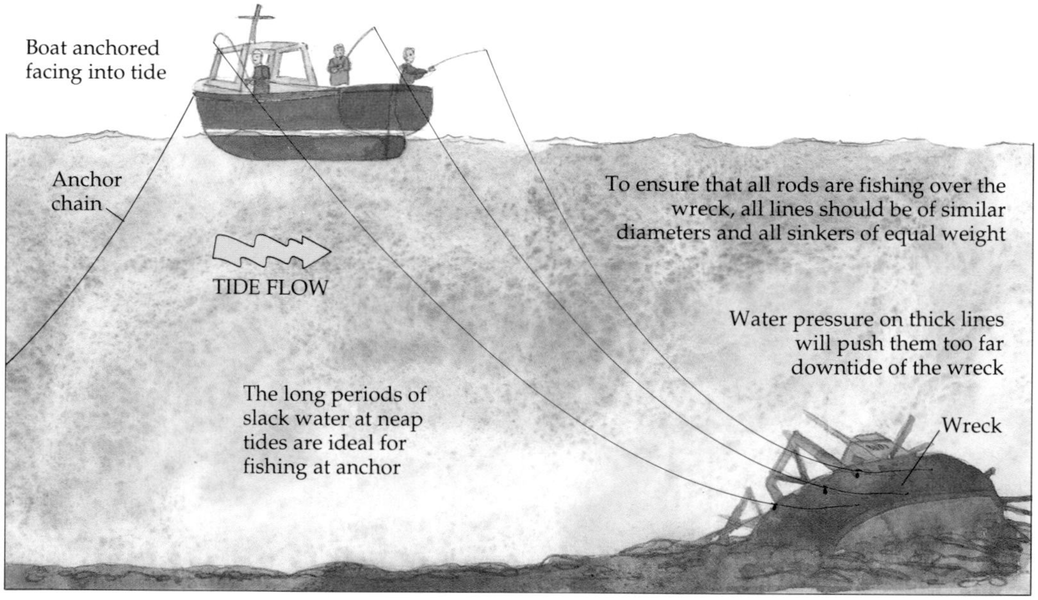

Fishing into the hulk
When fishing into a hulk for fish such as large conger and ling, you need very heavy tackle and wire leaders, and big baits placed right into the main wreckage, where they feed. Conger live in holes, and you need to drop the baits almost onto their heads to get them to show any interest. They take incredibly lightly and must be given time to do so, but they must be dragged quickly from their retreats the instant the hook is driven home, otherwise they will not be moved. Ling are quicker onto the baits than conger, so the best conger wrecks are those where the ling population has been thinned.

RUNNING LEGER FOR CONGER
The strong, simple running leger is the best rig to use for big-fish work over snaggy terrain. Provided you follow the basic design, you can vary the lengths and components to suit your personal preferences, but for conger fishing it is better to use wire rather than mono for the terminal leader.

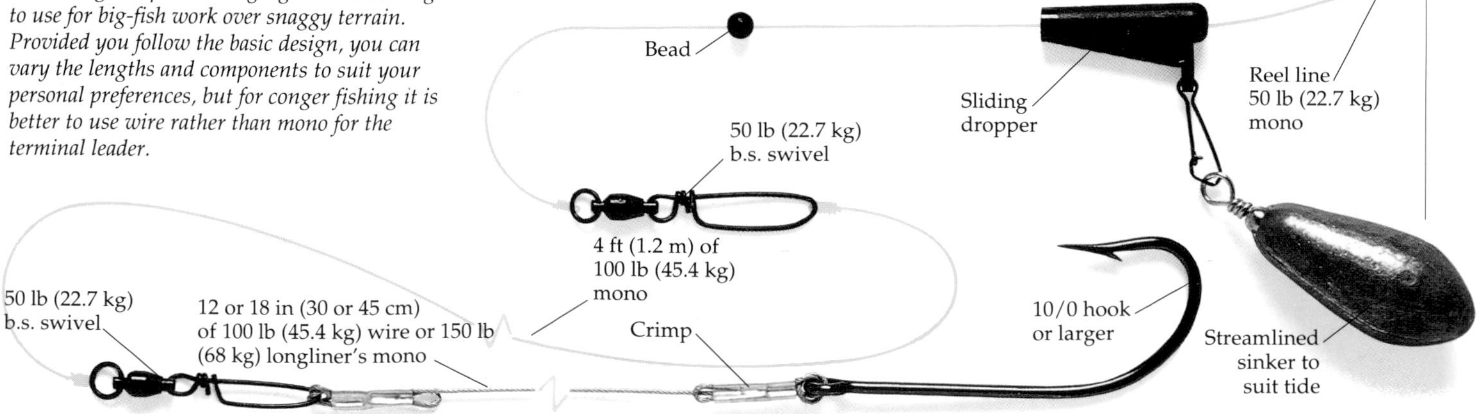

Fishing on the Drift

Drift fishing over wrecks is far easier on both skipper and anglers than fishing at anchor. A buoy is dropped to mark the starting position, and after each drift over the wreck the boat is taken back uptide for another pass.

Fish on most wrecks divide into two main categories: those feeding at or near the bottom, such as conger, ling, and cod, and higher-level feeders, such as pollack and coalfish, which hunt prey fish all around the pressure wave caused by water forced up over the wreck by the tide. Conger, and more particularly ling, can be taken on a slow drift but are better approached at anchor. The rest are best fished for by drifting with rubber eels and pirks.

TACKLE LOSSES

Most wrecks offer excellent fishing, but tackle losses due to snagging can be high, even in calm weather and a placid sea.

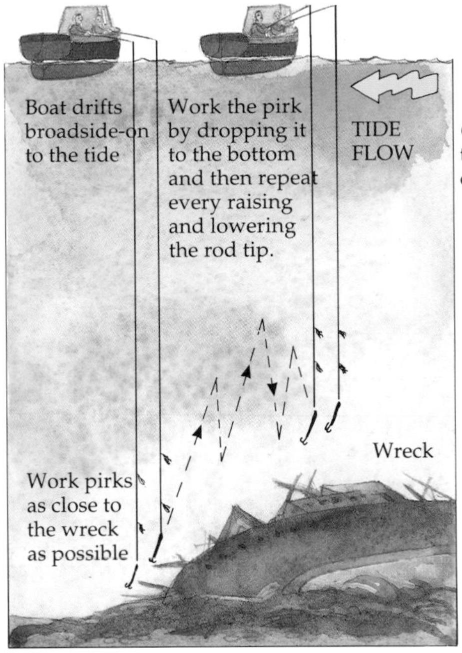

Bottom fishing

Baited pirks, and small plastic squid rigged above a pirk, are excellent lures for cod and ling, and will occasionally take deep-feeding pollack. Both are fished right on the bottom, so tackle losses can be high, and it is essential to use pirks of the correct weight for the stength of tide. Plastic squid should be rigged on short, heavy mono standoff droppers, as close to the pirk as practical.

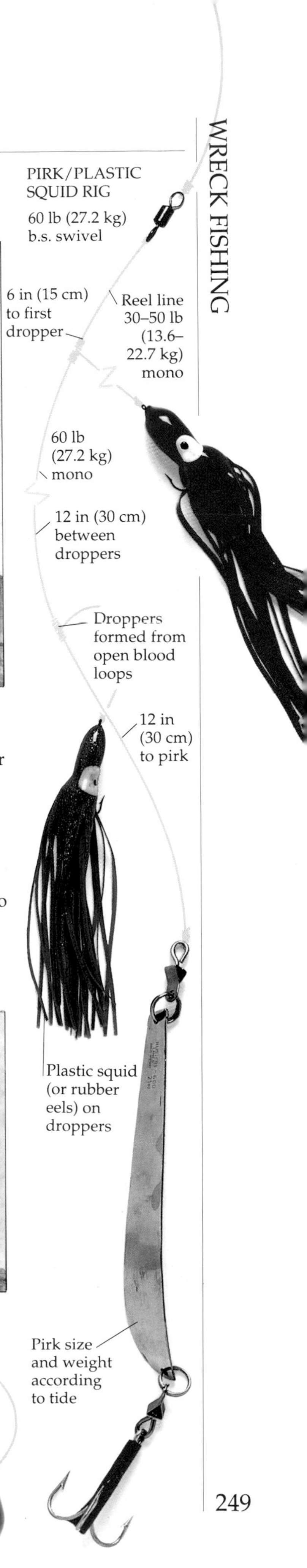

Fishing the flying collar

This rig is effective for pollack and other species feeding above the wreck, but cod and ling might also grab at it in the initial stages of the retrieve. Flick the rig away from the boat to avoid tangles on the drop, and count the number of turns of the reel handle you make on the retrieve to get an idea of where fish might take. Set the drag light, or the hook will tear free as a taking fish kicks for bottom in one continuous, powerful run.

Fishing the Flying Collar

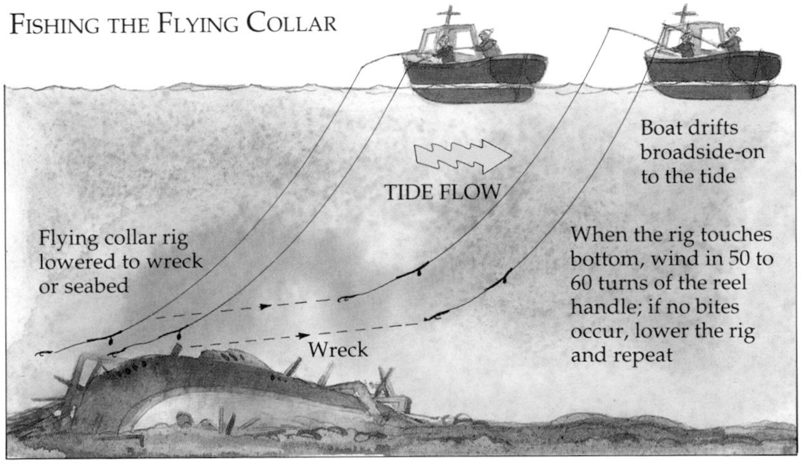

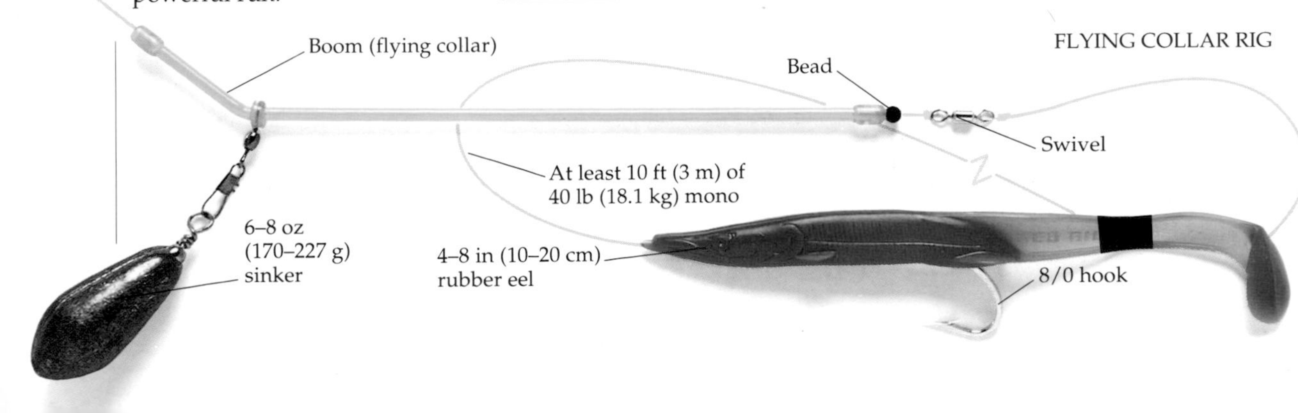

SURFCASTING

Casting a bait from the beach into the surf is one of the most enjoyable styles of shore angling. It is also one of the most physical forms of angling, using more body movement than any other. However, in surf fishing it is not brute force that produces a good cast but correct technique. The first step is to master the basic casting action, which you can do quite quickly, but to develop good casting rhythm and movement, you must practise until they become automatic. Distance will come naturally once the rhythm is perfected. The off-the-ground cast is easy to learn, but it cannot be learned properly from books alone; a few lessons from a skilled surfcaster or a qualified casting coach will amply repay the time invested.

LOADING A SHOCK LEADER

BAITCASTER REEL

To load a shock leader *(see page 253)* onto a baitcaster, start with the knot near the right-hand flange. Lay it in open coils to the left and then to the right, stopping short of the knot. Open coils prevent the leader from biting into the main line, and if the knot is on the right it will not cut your thumb during the cast.

SPINNING REEL

It is not necessary to load the leader manually onto a spinning reel because the reel will cross-lay it automatically. However, starting with the knot at the rear of the spool and winding a minimum of six evenly spaced turns forward reduces the chance of the knot stripping bunches of line on the cast.

The grip
The reel-up position is more commonly used than the reel-down, and feels more natural. The reel-down position is favored by many distance casters because the stronger hand supplies the power, leaving the weaker to control the spool.

REEL-UP POSITION

REEL-DOWN POSITION

THE OFF-THE-GROUND CAST

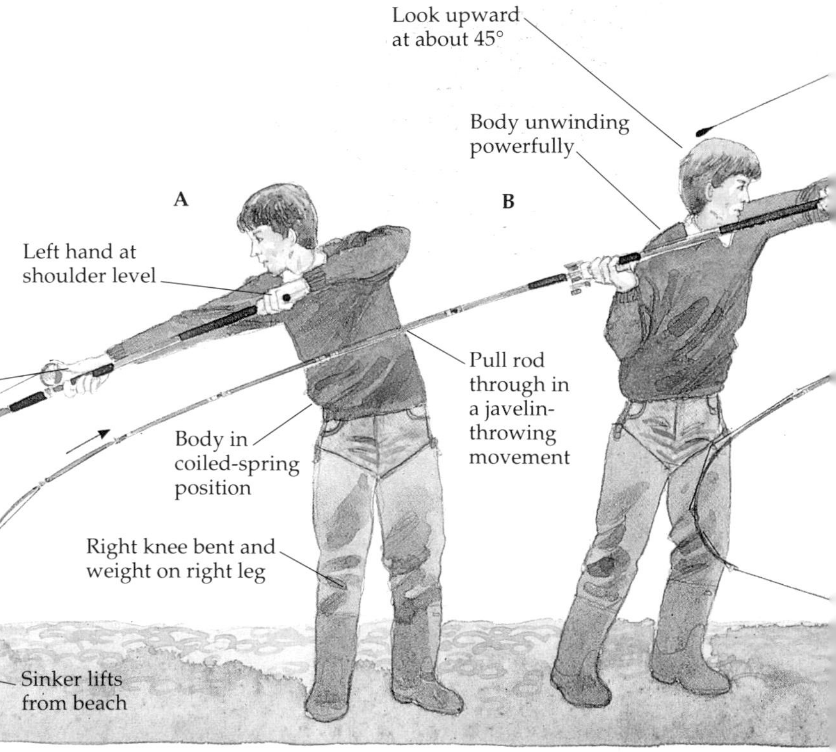

The stance
Scrape a line in the sand or pebbles to mark out the direction of the cast. Then stand with your right foot on the line and your left foot 6 in (15 cm) back, with both feet angled slightly forward. With the reel set ready to cast, swivel your waist and shoulders to position the sinker on the beach with the rod tip just off the ground.

THE STANCE

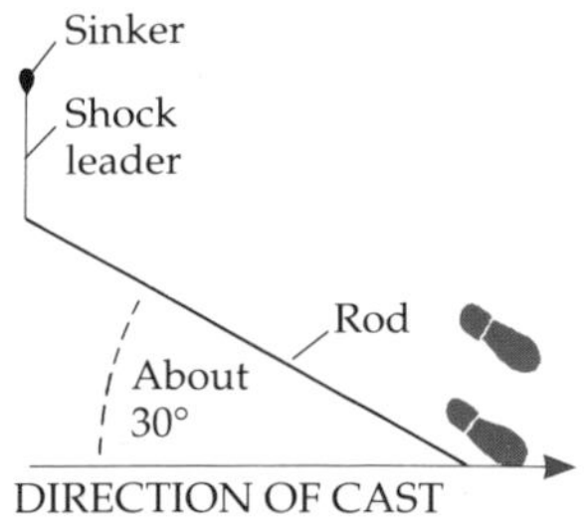

The Cast
Set the reel for casting *(see page 212)*, with the sinker hanging at 3 to 4 ft (90 cm to 1.2 m) from the tip ring. Brake the line with your thumb or finger, depending on the type of reel you are using. Then adopt the correct stance, taking your weight on your right leg **(A)**. Your left hand should be next to your right shoulder, your left elbow raised, and your right arm extended. Turn your head to face the cast direction, looking upward at about 45° **(B)**. Start to uncoil your body powerfully but smoothly to the left, simultaneously pulling the rod forward like a javelin along its own axis, not in a side sweep. Your left hand starts to rise while your right arm moves in close to your chest

Common Casting Faults

Laying out the tackle on the beach before setting your feet in position reduces the "feel" through the muscles of your legs, back, and waist. Set your feet first, then swivel your waist and shoulders to lay out the sinker on the beach.

A second fault is to push the rod too soon in the initial stages of the cast (steps **A** to **C**). The rod should follow you rather than be pushed ahead of you. Concentrate on getting your head turned in the casting direction and "unwinding" your body like a spring, and the arm movement should then follow naturally.

SUITABLE TERRAIN
Off-the-ground casting is a technique for fairly clean, smooth beaches. It cannot be used on very rough ground, or when wading in the surf.

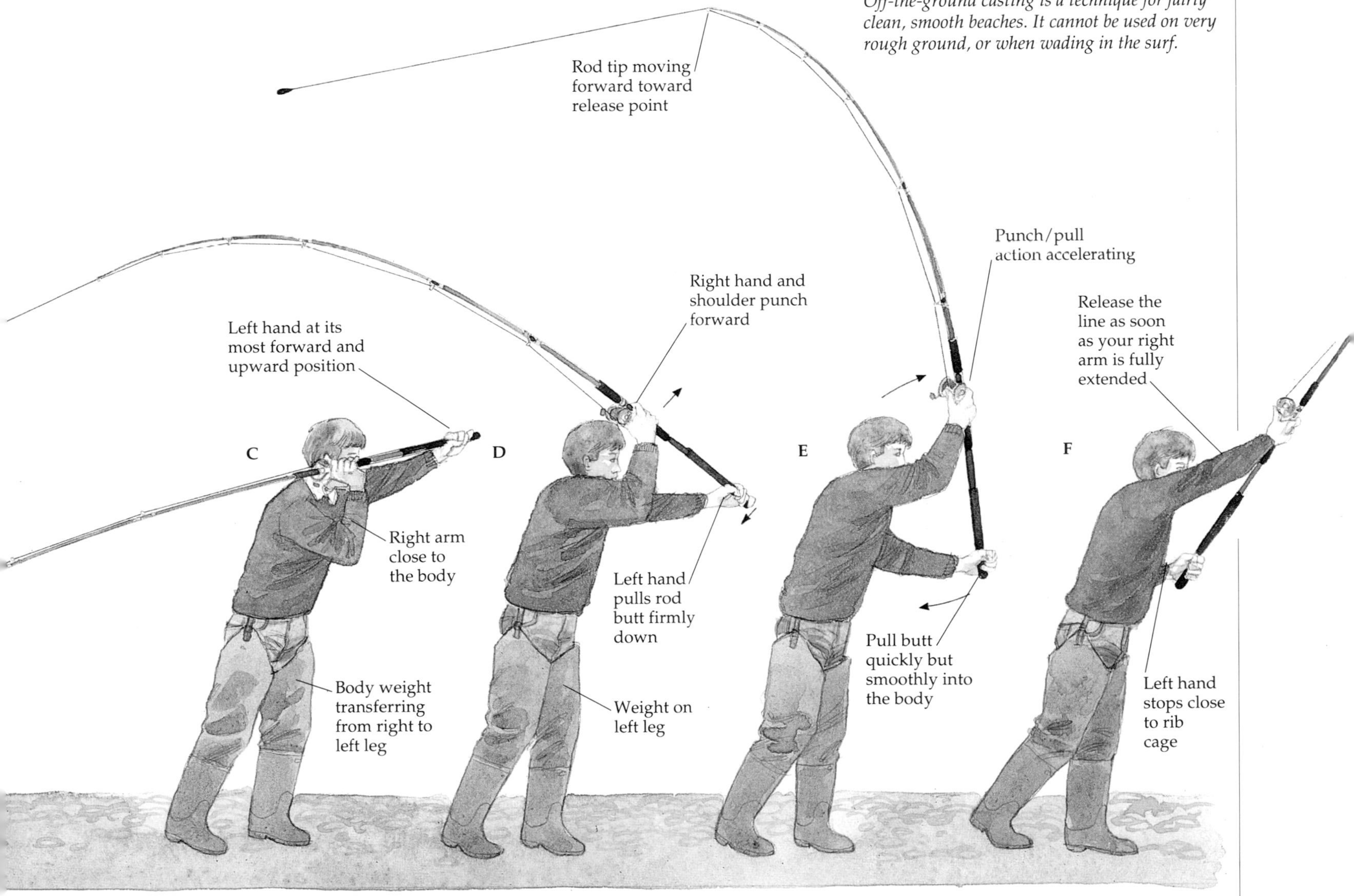
Rod tip moving forward toward release point
Punch/pull action accelerating
Right hand and shoulder punch forward
Release the line as soon as your right arm is fully extended
Left hand at its most forward and upward position
C
D
E
F
Right arm close to the body
Left hand pulls rod butt firmly down
Pull butt quickly but smoothly into the body
Left hand stops close to rib cage
Body weight transferring from right to left leg
Weight on left leg

as its elbow flexes. With your left arm now at its fullest extension, and your right hand at eye level, transfer your body weight to your left leg **(C)**. The extra power that comes into the cast from the transfer of body weight translates into increased casting speed, which can be felt through the rod because the butt seems to tighten up in your hands.

As your left arm reaches maximum extension, start to punch your right hand upward and at the same time pull the rod butt down sharply towards your ribcage with your left hand **(D)**. This casting action should be one smooth, continuous movement, with no break between the initial "javelin throw" and the punch/pull sequence.

Continue the punch/pull sequence, accelerating the rod smoothly toward the release point **(E)**. Your left hand should be pulling the rod butt towards your ribcage and your right arm should begin to straighten from the elbow. Your chest should be pointing in the direction of the cast with most of your body weight transferred to your left leg.

The powerful but smooth punch/pull action results in a fast, smooth turnover of the top tip. Release the line, when your right arm is at full extension and your left hand is tucked in against your ribcage **(F)**. Stop the reel as soon as the sinker hits the water, to prevent the line from overruning under its own momentum and tangling.

SHORE FISHING 1

When fished at distance from a low vantage point, such as a beach, all leaders present baits hard on the bottom regardless of where the sinker (weight) is positioned. Most leaders are variations on the simple themes of the running leger and the paternoster, and the exact type of terminal rig to use at any particular time depends on local geography, sea conditions, and the way in which the target species is known to feed. To perform at their best, terminal rigs need to be as simple and free from self-snagging as possible. Use booms *(see page 60)* to keep sinkers and snoods (short lengths of line that carry the hooks) clear of each other and of the reel line.

LEADER KNOTS

Basic knot

A leader knot must be strong, reliable, and have a slim profile for safe passage through the rings. Tighten the half hitch with pliers before tying the knot in the reel line.

1 Tie a half hitch in leader; thread reel line through it.

2 Pull half hitch tight, then tie a knot in reel line.

3 Tighten reel line knot, pull up to half hitch.

High-performance knot

Tie the reel line through a hole in the leader for a strong but very slim knot. This works best when the reel line is much thinner than the leader.

1 Flatten end of leader with pliers and make a hole with a hot needle.

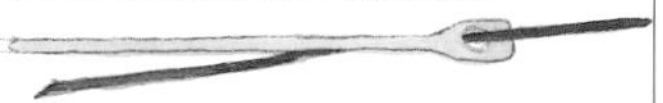

2 Tie a knot in reel line.

3 Tighten knot close to hole; trim and superglue.

BASIC TWO-HOOK PATERNOSTER

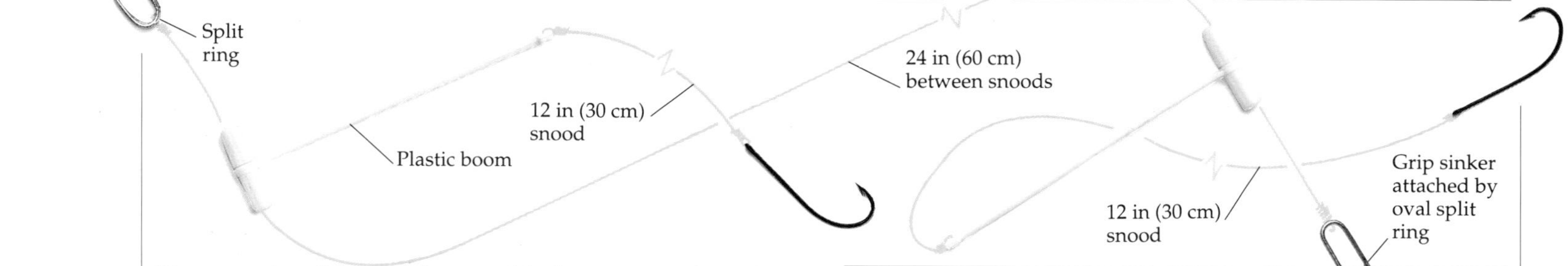

Slow-moving fish, and those unlikely to run with or drop a bait at any hint of resistance, are best approached with a simple two-hook paternoster rig. In this one, each snood is tied to a loop dropper, formed by knotting a loop in the reel line and supported by plastic tubing to reduce tangles, but booms and swivels are effective alternatives to droppers. The wired grip sinker, besides anchoring the bait, will encourage fish to hook themselves as they pull the bait against its resistance. This is without equal as an all-around rig for a wide range of fish including flatfish and codling.

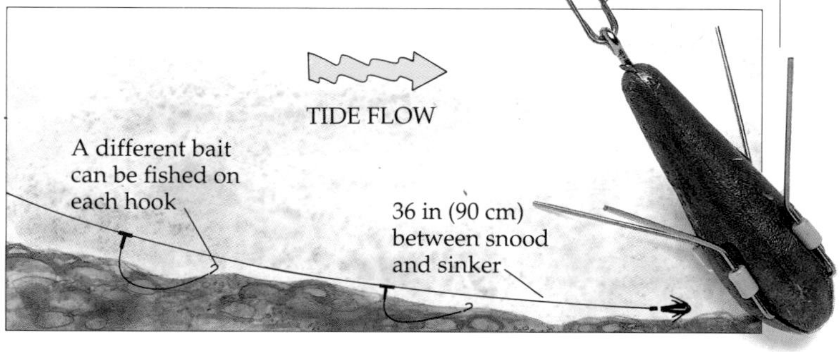

BASIC RUNNING LEGER

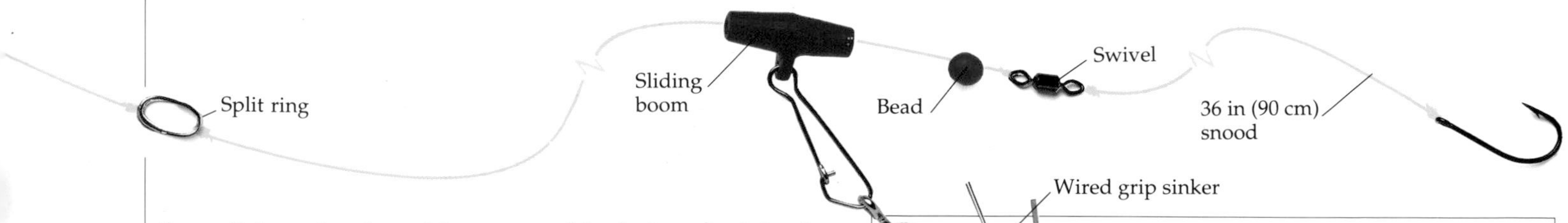

Some fish, such as bass, like to run with a bait and might eject it should they sense something is wrong. Others, such as tope, make long runs before swallowing baits properly. All these fish must be allowed to take line freely before the strike is made, and the basic running leger rig allows them to do so. It is not a rig that lends itself to distance work, but it is excellent for medium-distance casting and for backing up the beach on a flooding tide. It is also a very good big-bait leader for fish such as conger, dogfish, and rays, although no fish will have any qualms about picking it up.

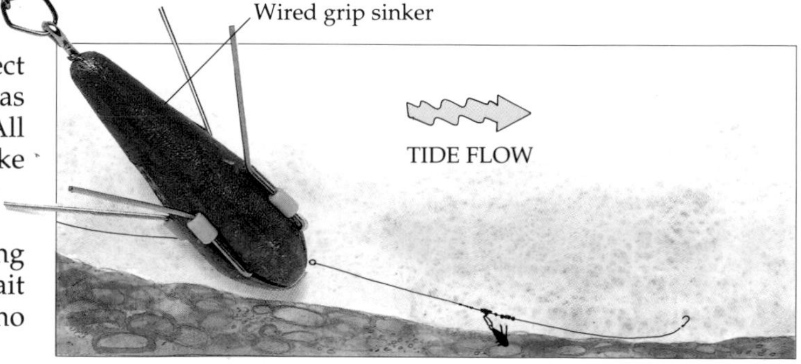

Basic Running Paternoster

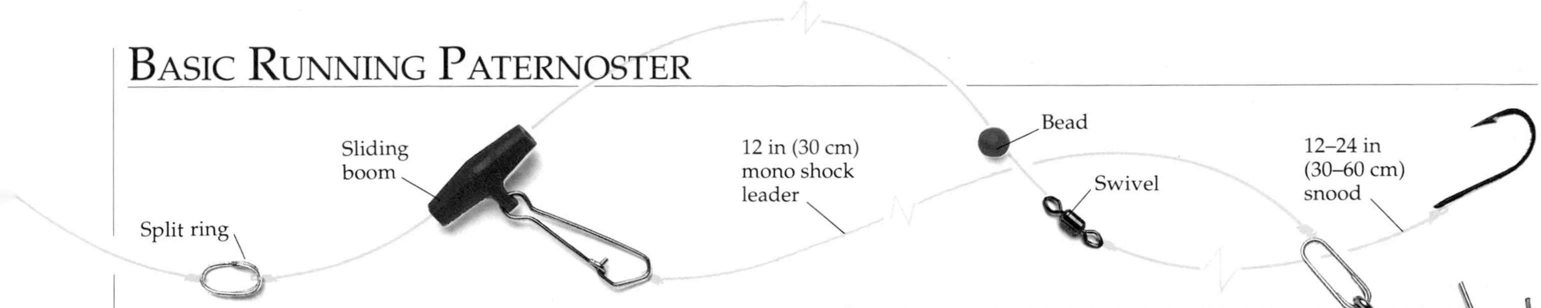
Split ring
Sliding boom
12 in (30 cm) mono shock leader
Bead
Swivel
12–24 in (30–60 cm) snood

The difference between this rig and the running leger is that the sinker is carried on a length of mono shock leader. (A shock leader is one that is made of heavier line than the reel line, to absorb the strain of casting a heavy sinker.) Having this shock leader between the sliding boom and the sinker makes for easier casting, because both sinker and bait hang at about the same point above the ground when you are standing in the casting position. It is a better rig than the running leger for slow or finicky fish that do not have to be allowed lots of line before the strike can be made.

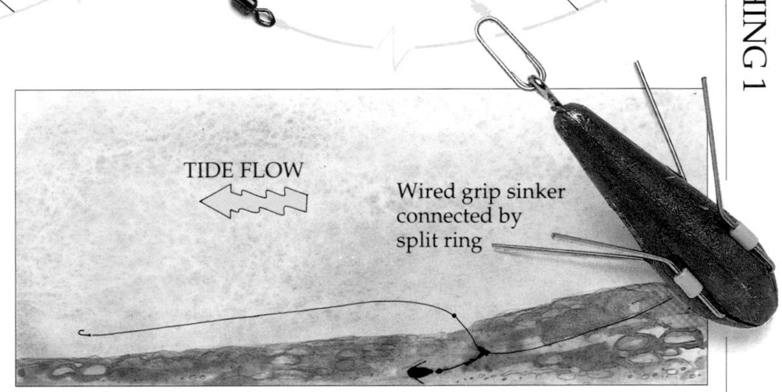
TIDE FLOW
Wired grip sinker connected by split ring

Anchoring the Bait

Uptide casting
Although tides appear to move up and down a beach, the direction of flow is often parallel to the shore. When such lateral currents are strong, bottom-holding and bite-detection problems can make the shore angler's life extremely difficult. The way to get around these problems is to use a wired grip sinker. These are available in a variety of sizes and wiring styles to offer differing degrees of hold to suit a wide range of conditions. When fishing a grip sinker uptide, cast well uptide of your rod rest and allow the sinker to fall freely. Before re-engaging the reel gearing, walk back to the rest, free-spooling line to create a bow. The force of the tide on the bow will help the grip wires to dig in well. A taking fish will dislodge the sinker, and the line will fall slack as the fish drops away downtide.

ROD POSITION
In heavy surf it is not only the strength of the tide that can cause difficulty in anchoring the bait: seaweed brought in by the breakers can foul the line and drag the sinker free. Holding the rod high, while feeling for bites, helps the line to clear the breakers.

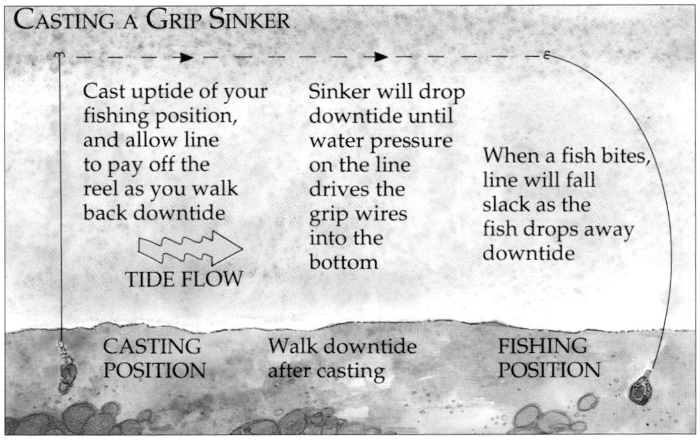
CASTING A GRIP SINKER
Cast uptide of your fishing position, and allow line to pay off the reel as you walk back downtide
TIDE FLOW
Sinker will drop downtide until water pressure on the line drives the grip wires into the bottom
When a fish bites, line will fall slack as the fish drops away downtide
CASTING POSITION
Walk downtide after casting
FISHING POSITION

Avoiding snags
Typical snags that can cause tackle "hangups" include flotsam, weeds, and heavy ground. When fishing heavy ground close in, and when there is heavy ground between you and cleaner, snagfree ground, sinker shape is important. All sinkers can snag, but the bomb-shaped type is less likely to than the rest. Where hangups are inevitable, attach the sinker by means of a sacrificial weak link.

WEIGHT LIFTER
Hangups can be a problem when shore fishing, because it is often difficult to lift the terminal tackle clear of any snags. A vaned device, known as a weight lifter, helps lift the sinker clear of snags when the tackle is retrieved rapidly with the rod held high.

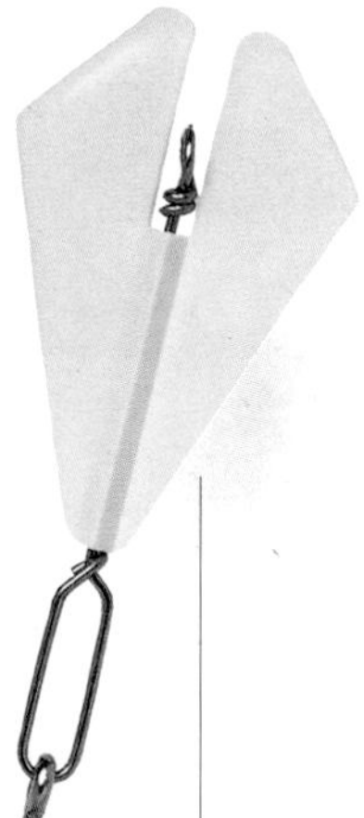

Searching the bottom
There are times when using the rolling leger technique with a plain sinker offers a distinct advantage over using an anchored bait, especially when fish are reluctant to move about or when they gather in isolated pockets, which are not always easy to locate. By casting the sinker well uptide and allowing it to roll slowly back down, you can search and cover large areas of ground with the bait or baits. However, if the tidal currents are strong, the sinker will travel too quickly to present the bait effectively, and it is prone to hangups on snaggy ground.

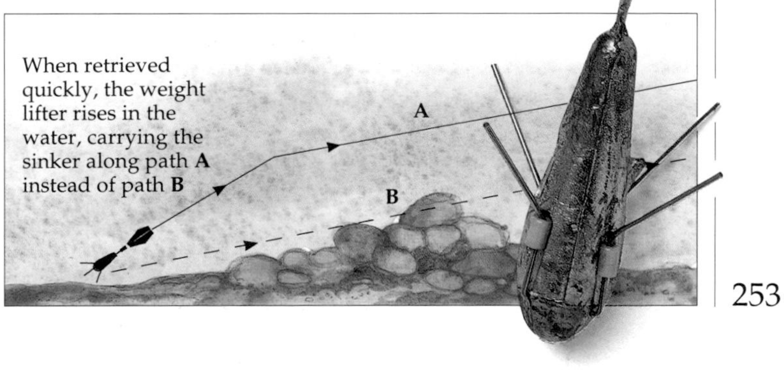
When retrieved quickly, the weight lifter rises in the water, carrying the sinker along path A instead of path B
A
B

SHORE FISHING 2

Not all shore fishing is done from the gradually shelving vantage point of a beach, nor do all coastal species of fish feed on or near to the bottom at all times. The sea is a three-dimensional world, with its unseen downward dimension assuming increasingly greater importance for anglers where deep water touches land. This could be beneath rock ledges, below harbor walls, or alongside piers and breakwaters. To get the best out of shore fishing in deep water, you must position your baits at the most appropriate depth. This could mean, for example, suspending a bloodworm or a strip of fish beneath a float, or working a suitably heavy or weighted lure through the feeding zone. Spinning and float fishing have much to commend them as techniques for shore fishing, but it is important to use suitable tackle. The range of saltwater spinning and float tackle is increasing, but you may have to turn to the heavier end of the freshwater tackle stand to find what you need.

THINK FIRST
A dropnet, which can be lowered on a rope, is the only feasible means of landing fish from such a precarious position. Plan how to land your catch before starting to fish – not after.

FLOAT FISHING

Float fishing is regarded by many sea anglers as a sort of extension of freshwater fishing, and indeed, much of the tackle used is freshwater gear. Its use is limited, however, but not so much by the range of species that can be caught on it as by the conditions often prevailing where those fish live and feed. Fishing for mullet in quiet harbors, for example, presents no problems to standard freshwater tackle, but other situations call for a heavier approach. For instance, heavy tackle is needed when fishing baits just above kelp for wrasse, because these powerful fish will dive for cover the moment they take a bait. Fishing for pollack from rocky headlands, when they are feeding at some distance from the shore, also requires heavy tackle to get the baits out far enough and to control the situation at long range. Freshwater rods suitable for light float fishing include 10 to 13 ft (3 to 4 m) float and leger rods and 7 to 10 ft (2.1 to 3 m) spinning rods. Use a surfcaster for the really heavy work.

HEAVYWEIGHT FLOAT RIG

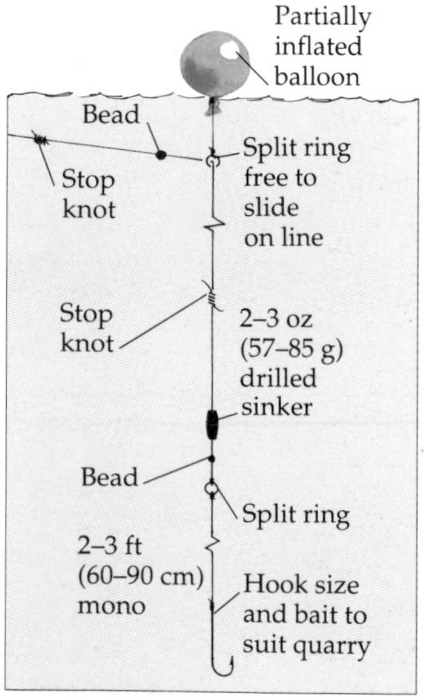

Heavyweight float fishing
This rig is designed for situations where standard sea float tackle cannot cope. These include fishing in a fast current, where as much as 5 oz (142 g) of weight may be required to maintain depth, or when a big bait is to be drifted out to predators such as small sharks *(see page 256)*. It is based on the sliding float principle, and uses a very large float, such as a balloon. This is tied to a swivel or split ring, running freely on the line below a bead and stop knot. Below the swivel or split ring are a slip barrel sinker, a bead, and then a mono or wire hook length.

Sliding float fishing
Always use a sliding rather than a fixed float when fishing at depths greater than the length of the rod. With any float rig, you can wind in line only until the float reaches the top rod ring, and if the float is fixed for fishing at, say, 20 ft (6 m), you will still have 20 ft (6 m) of line paid out. This will make it difficult to retrieve the terminal tackle or to play or land a hooked fish. A sliding float rig is also preferable where casting room is limited, such as on a cramped rock ledge: with only the float and hook length hanging free, casting control and accuracy are much improved. A small sliding stop knot tied on the line above the float controls the depth at which the hook will fish, but winds easily through the rod guides.

HARBOR FISHING
This garfish was taken from the deep water off a harbor wall, an ideal venue for float fishing.

SLIDING FLOAT RIG

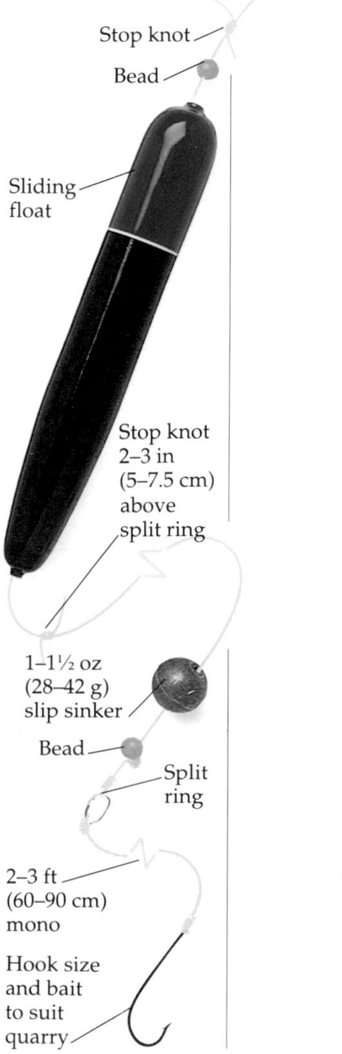

Bottom Fishing

Bottom fishing over heavy ground is always difficult, and losses of both tackle and fish will probably be high. These problems must be accepted as unavoidable if you are to have any reasonable hope of success, but there are ways of minimizing them. The most important of these is to keep your rigs as simple as possible. Basic single-hook terminal tackle is not only less likely to snag than a more complicated rig, but is also cheaper and therefore more expendable. Hangups usually occur either at the hook or the sinker, so these should be attached by weak links so that the rest of the rig can be pulled free of them if they snag (but do not use a weak link for the hook length if you are after sharp-toothed species). Alternatively, you can use a buoyant leger rig to float the bait clear of the bottom and thus of potential snags.

Buoyant leger fishing
Using a buoyant leger rig, it is possible to float a bait at a fixed distance above the bottom. This offers improved bait presentation as well as reducing the risk of snagging. For example, it can help to prevent the bait from becoming "lost" between rocks and therefore inaccessible to fish, and reduces the risk of crab damage that can render a bait worthless within minutes of it touching bottom. The rig is simply a balsa float slipped onto the hook length of a leger rig, and the height to which the bait rises is determined by the position of a stop knot.

BUOYANT LEGER RIG

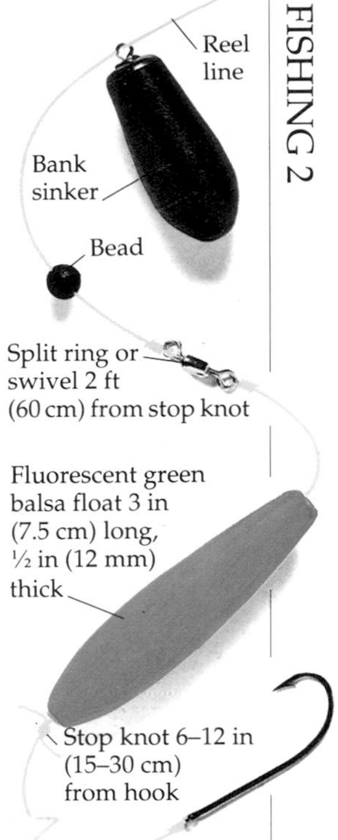

Supported-line fishing
This technique employs a balloon to support the line, so that the terminal tackle rises clear of snags when it is retrieved: it has no effect on bait presentation. Using a supported line, you can cast onto clean ground to the seaward side of snags and be reasonably sure that the tackle will make it back for another throw. You can use whichever bottom-fishing rig you prefer: simply slide a swivel or split ring, attached to a balloon, onto the reel line before attaching the terminal tackle.

SUPPORTED-LINE FISHING

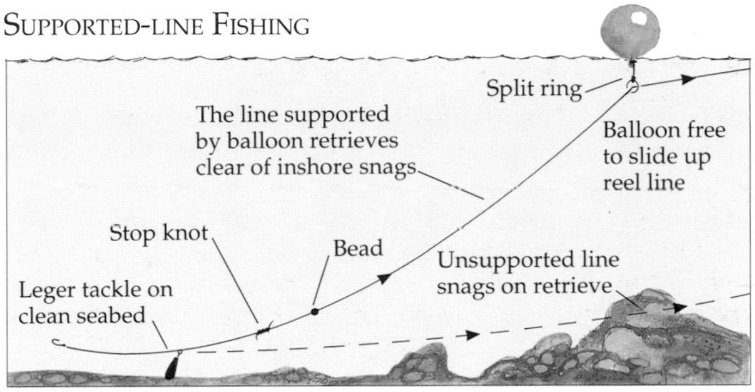

Spinning

SHALLOW SPINNING RIG

SHALLOW SPINNING RIG
Cast this rig with a gentle lobbing action. If you cast too vigorously, the upleader sinker will travel ahead of the lure, causing tangles.

Spinning offers certain advantages over bait fishing, one being that with only a small box of lures and a light rod and reel to carry, you can easily cover long stretches of coastline in a day's fishing. Rocky shores provide some of the best saltwater spinning venues, because they usually attract a wide variety of the predatory species, such as mackerel, bass, and pollack, which strike readily at artificial lures. When spinning, search the water as thoroughly as possible by varying the lure depth and using a radial casting pattern *(see page 216)*. Suitable lures to use include plugs, spinners, wobbling spoons, and jigs, and you should carry a selection of different types so that you can use whichever is most suitable for the species you are seeking and for the prevailing conditions. Fish usually attack from below, so use dark-colored lures when the sky is bright and switch to lures with light or reflective finishes when fishing in poor light conditions.

LANDA LUKKI TURBO SPOON
Use a heavy lure like this for deep spinning.

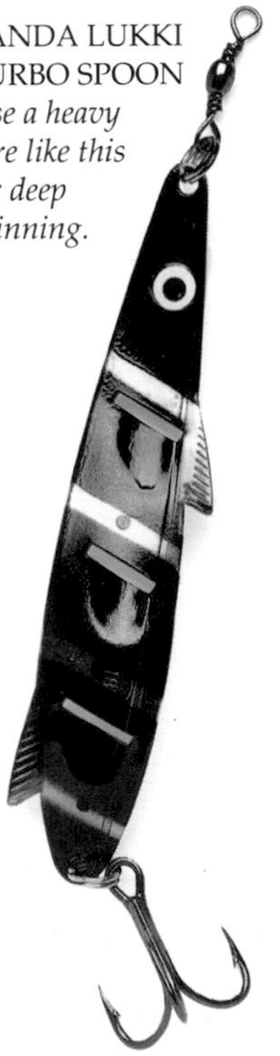

Lure weight
The greater the distance you can cast a lure, the more water you can cover with it. For this reason, and to fish deep in strong tides, a heavy lure (fished on tackle that can handle it) is often preferable to a light one. Ideally, the lure should be self-weighted, but this is not always possible, and you may need to add a streamlined anti-kink weight to the line *(see page 214)*. To minimize the risk of tangling, straighten the line by checking its flow from the reel just before the lure hits the water, or start winding in the moment it touches down.

SAFETY FIRST
Rocky shores usually have deep water close inshore. This makes them suitable venues for spinning, which generally works best in waters more than 6 ft (1.8 m) deep. However, deep water and spray-soaked rocks are a dangerous combination: wear suitable shoes with good grip and always fish with a companion.

Shark Fishing

Sharks can be caught by a number of techniques, including drift fishing, bottom fishing from an anchored boat, shore fishing, and trolling with natural baits, either live or dead *(see page 258)*. They can also be taken on fly tackle. The basic techniques shown here are suitable for sharks that feed in the middle and upper layers, such as blue shark, mako, and porbeagle, and for tope and other small sharks that feed near or at the bottom.

Because sharks have abrasive skins and very sharp, strong teeth, it is essential to use a wire leader at the end of the terminal tackle. One end of this leader is attached to the hook by a crimped loop, and crimped loop at the opposite end joins it to the main line (or an intermediate length of heavy mono leader) via a swivel.

Crimping a Wire Leader

1 Slide the crimp onto the wire. Pass the wire through the hook or swivel eye, then tie a single loop knot and pull it tight with pliers.

2 Slide the crimp over the loose end of wire. Leave a short length of the loose end protruding beyond the crimp.

3 Loop the loose end, and tuck it back inside the crimp. This will prevent the sharp end of the wire from causing any damage.

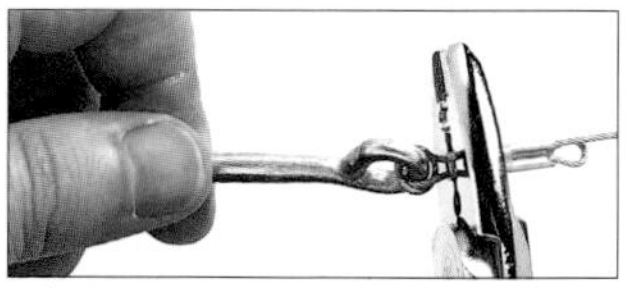

4 Squeeze the crimp tightly closed with the pliers. Squeeze it at as many points as possible along its length.

Drift Fishing

Blue sharks and makos are mainly open-water species, feeding on pelagic school fish such as mackerel and pilchard, while porbeagle hunt closer to the shore over shallow-lying reefs. All can be caught from a drifting boat on 30 to 80 lb (13.6 to 36.3 kg) class boat rods, using baits suspended by floats (balloons) over a chum slick. Sharks have a keen sense of smell and can lock onto very low concentrations of scents, so the slick will attract their attention. Moving their heads from side to side to detect the greatest concentration of scent, they will follow it to its source.

Spacing the Baits

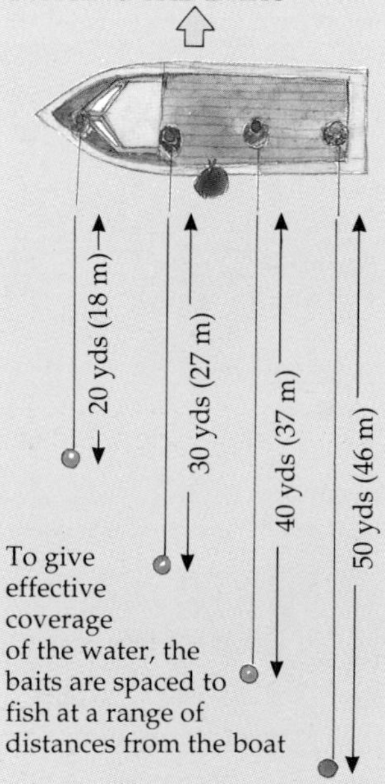

To give effective coverage of the water, the baits are spaced to fish at a range of distances from the boat

Using Chum

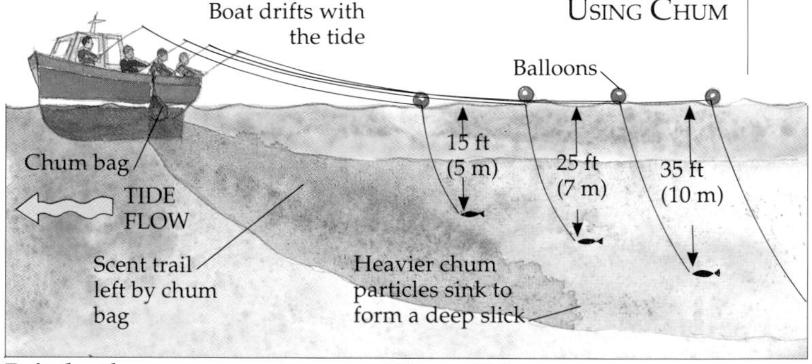

Bait depths
Until you discover at what depth the sharks are feeding, your baits should be set to fish at different depths, as well as at different distances from the boat. The bait fished furthest from the boat should also be the deepest, and that closest to the boat should be the shallowest.

Chum slick
As the boat drifts along, it leaves a widening slick of chum behind it. The heavier pieces of chum sink deeper than the lighter ones, so the slick deepens, as well as widens, the further it is from the boat. This ensures that all the baits are within the slick.

SHARK DRIFT RIG

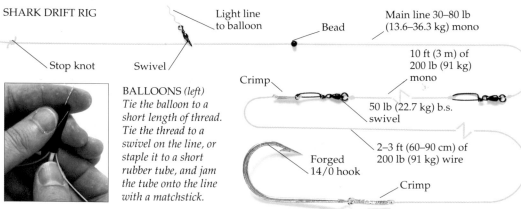

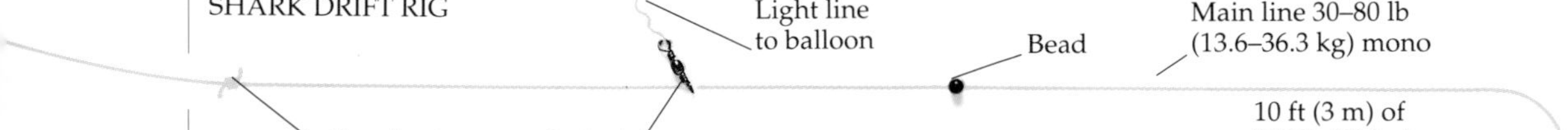

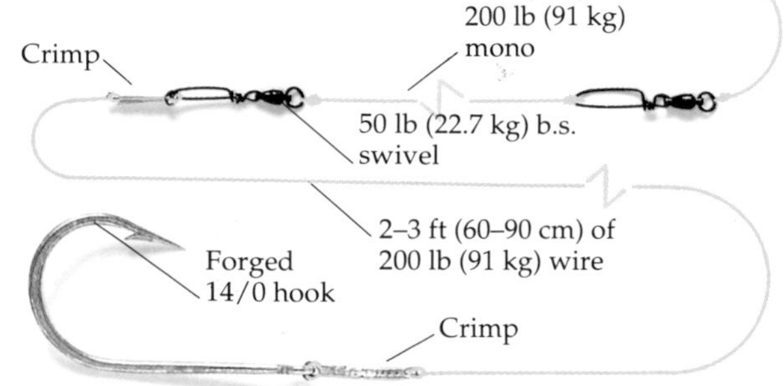

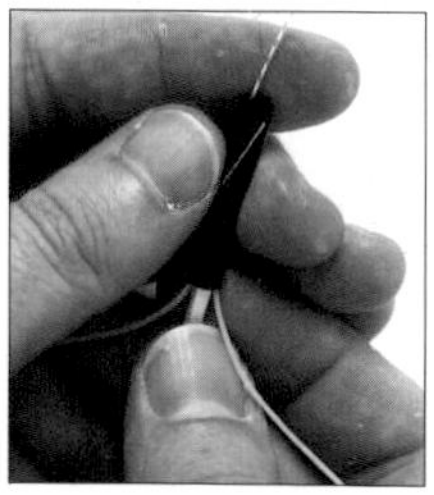

BALLOONS *(left)*
Tie the balloon to a short length of thread. Tie the thread to a swivel on the line, or staple it to a short rubber tube, and jam the tube onto the line with a matchstick.

SHARK RIG
To avoid damage to the main line, the leader of a shark rig should be at least as long as the fish being sought – some say longer, because many sharks roll around when hooked and get wrapped up in the leader. A long wire leader is difficult to handle, so use a relatively short length of braided wire at the hook end and attach it to the main line via an intermediate trace of heavy commercial monofilament.

Boat Fishing for Tope

The tope is one of the many small and medium-sized shark species that hunt near or at the bottom, feeding on fish such as cod, whiting, and flatfish over clean or mixed ground close inshore. Tope seem to hunt either as loners, or in single-sex groups that gather over feeding grounds. They can be caught by bottom fishing from an anchored boat or from the shore, and the best bait is cut or whole fish.

When fishing from an anchored boat, you can use either uptide or downtide casting techniques *(see page 244)*. For uptide fishing, use a soft-tipped uptide rod around 10 ft (3 m) long, and a wired grip sinker that will hold bottom in the prevailing tide. Pay out enough line to allow a belly to form in it when the sinker has taken hold. For downtide work, use a 30 lb (13.6 kg) class boat rod and a suitable plain sinker.

CATCH AND RELEASE
This tope has provided fine sport on suitable tackle and is being returned safely to the sea.

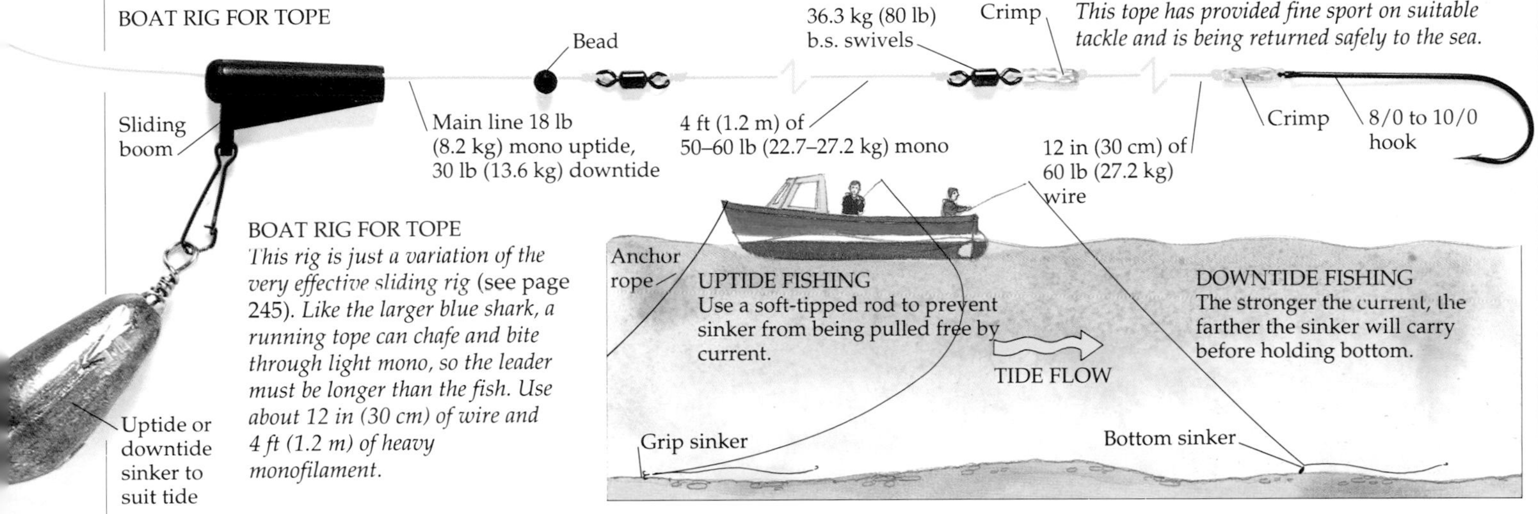

BOAT RIG FOR TOPE
This rig is just a variation of the very effective sliding rig (see page 245). *Like the larger blue shark, a running tope can chafe and bite through light mono, so the leader must be longer than the fish. Use about 12 in (30 cm) of wire and 4 ft (1.2 m) of heavy monofilament.*

Shore Fishing for Tope

Tope are often found within casting range of the shore. Rock ledges and headlands looking out onto sand can attract them, as do steep beaches of sand, pebbles, or mixed ground. Use a good-quality shore rod that can cast weights of up to 6 oz (170 g). The reel should be loaded with about 300 yds (275 m) of 20 to 25 lb (9.1 to 11.3 kg) mono, because a tope can run a long way when hooked.

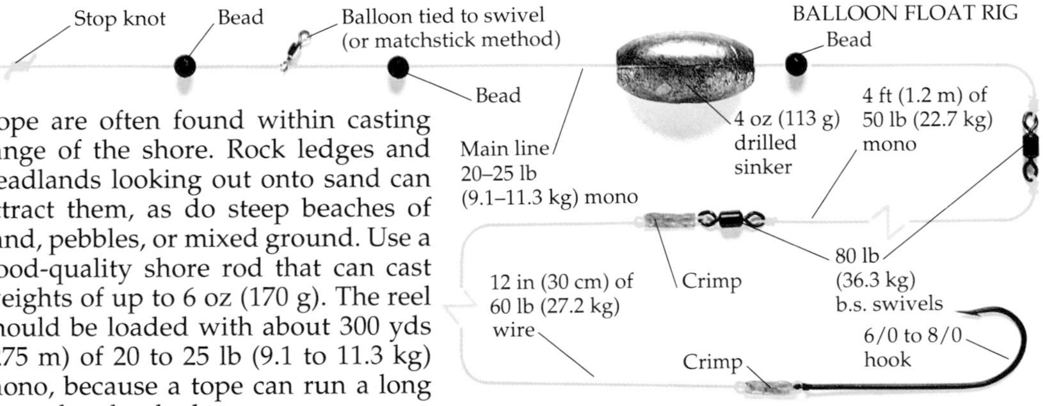

Shore rigs
Use either a simple sliding rig, or one with a balloon float and weighted by a barrel sinker. A long flowing leader prevents damage to the main line, and also allows the fish to pick up the bait and make a run before the hook is set. Casting a long leader with a big bait is difficult, but you should use one made up of at least 4 ft (1.2 m) of heavy monofilament and 12 in (30 cm) of wire.

Fishing for Dogfish

Smoothhounds and most of the small sharks collectively known as dogfish, including the smooth dogfish, are shallow-water species that feed mainly on crabs and mollusks. These sharks have flattened teeth that crush rather than cut, and are commonly caught by casting from the shore and by boat fishing over shallow offshore banks. When hooked they are capable of putting up a hard fight.

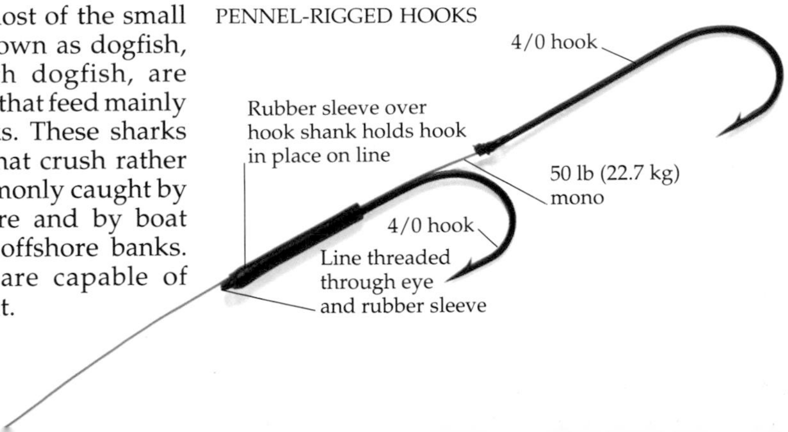

Dogfish rigs
For sharks with crushing rather than cutting teeth, you need a heavy mono sliding rig about 4 ft (1.2 m) long. Use a single hook or a pennel rig, baited with peeler crab portions. The advantage of the pennel rig over a single hook is that you can present a bigger bunch of crab portions, with a hook at each end.

Big-game Fishing

Big-game fishing is the pursuit, with rod-and-line tackle, of a wide range of large fish, including billfish, sailfish, wahoo, tarpon, the larger species of tuna, and large, active sharks, such as the mako and tiger. Most big-game fishing is done from charter boats, many of which provide tackle, bait, and instruction if required. The species sought depends partly on the preferences of the anglers and partly on what is available in the waters being fished, as do the techniques and tackle employed. Some big-game fishers prefer fly tackle, but the majority use boat tackle in the 12 to 130 lb (5.4 to 59 kg) IGFA classes, and methods such as lure trolling, deadbait trolling, and even livebaiting. All have their advantages and drawbacks, all catch plenty of fish, and on its day, each one can outfish the others. It all depends on the circumstances and conditions prevailing at the time, and no technique is good enough to warrant the neglect of the others. An open mind is just as important for success in big-game fishing as it is in any other form of angling.

Lure Trolling

There are a great many species of fish that will take a trolled lure, so it is difficult to predict what you are going to catch when trolling, but there is a hard core of species that will regularly respond to the technique. These include marlin, sailfish, tuna, and similar large pelagic feeders favoring deep, open water, often where the ocean floor is quite literally miles below the surface. Middleweight gamefish such as wahoo, dolphinfish, and bonito will also hit a moving lure in open water. Whether these fish are truly big-game species is arguable, but large specimens occur, and at any size all of them are hard to subdue. Lure trolling is especially useful in open water where the fish are not concentrated in any particular area, because it allows the coverage of a lot of ground. The lures work as a spread at the surface, and are chosen so that each has a slightly different action. Together they create noise and leave a trail of bubbles behind them, which draws large predatory fish up from below. These then attack the lures.

Lure-fishing pattern
Big-game boats typically fish four rods at a time: one from each side, held clear of the boat on outriggers up to 45 ft (14 m) long, and two from the stern. Between them they usually fish a combination of submerged lures and lures that skip the surface. Each rod fishes with a different length of line paid out, for example 120 ft (37 m) and 140 ft (43 m) for the outrigger lines, and 70 ft (21 m) and 90 ft (27 m) for the stern lines. This spread of lures is designed to create the impression of a small school of baitfish, but when a fish gives chase, it will not necessarily go for the outermost lures. The stern lines often produce the most strikes, perhaps because fish are attracted toward them by the wake of the boat.

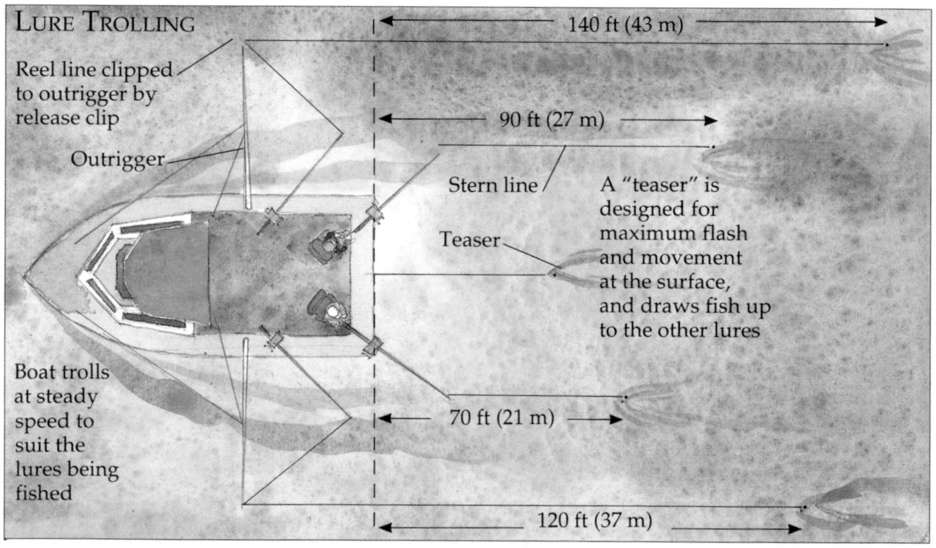

LURE SELECTION
Although manufacturers often label their lures as being for particular species, such as marlin or tuna, the fact is that any lure can take any species in the right circumstances. Select a range of lures, including Kona Heads and plastic squid, that will give you a good choice of colors, sizes, and actions to suit the quarry you happen to be after and the prevailing conditions.

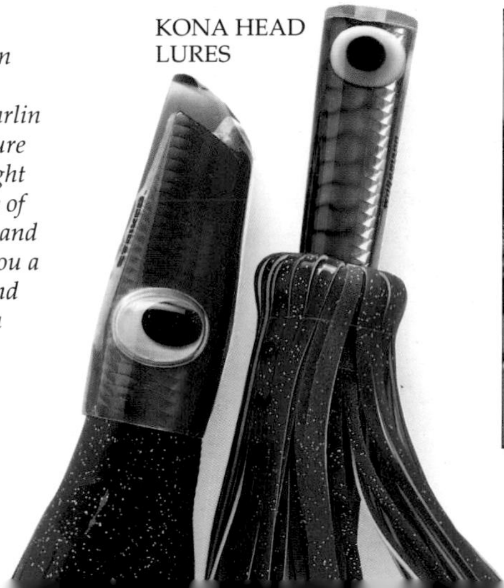
KONA HEAD LURES

BIG-GAME SPECIES
In addition to billfish and other very large species, many smaller fish – such as this barracuda – are often grouped under the general heading of big-game fish. Other such species include dolphinfish, albacore, king mackerel, and amberjack.

Bait Fishing

There is nothing more stimulating to the aggressive instincts of most predatory fish than the natural scent or movement of a prey fish. This makes natural baits generally more effective than artificial lures, but there are some drawbacks to using them. For example, wahoo are very adept at chopping baits off just astern of the hook, and some species take livebaits more readily than others: black marlin are more susceptible to a slowly trolled tuna or dolphinfish than to a lure, but sometimes the reverse is true of blue marlin. Livebaits also attract sharks, which are only rarely willing to strike at a lure. This can be a problem if other species are your quarry, and it does not diminish when dead or cut baits are used, because the sharks home in on the scent instead of the vibration. However, there is more chance of a dead or cut bait being grabbed by one of the highly prized species than by a shark if it is trolled rather than fished static.

Deadbait trolling
The appearance and smell of a deadbait make it potentially more attractive to predators than an artificial lure, but the presentation should allow it to "swim" in a natural manner or this advantage will be lost. With mullet, balao, and other small baitfish, rigging is fairly simple, but larger baits such as bonito and dolphinfish need to have their mouths stitched shut to reduce water resistance, and their pectoral and dorsal fins stitched erect to keep them upright. Large baits should be trolled at a much slower speed than small baits and lures.

Deadbait Rigs

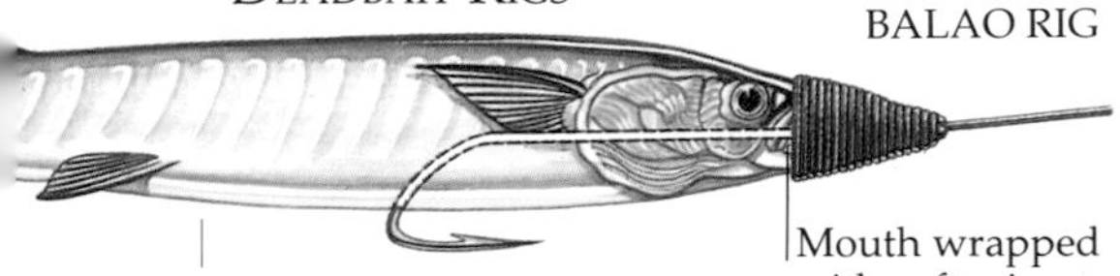

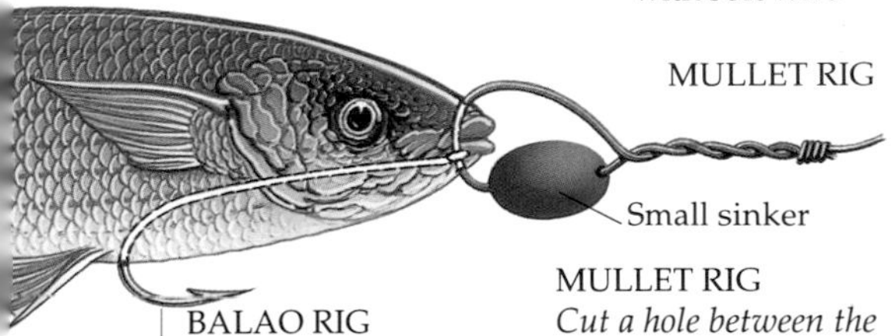

BALAO RIG
Pass the hook into the mouth and out through the body cavity, then close the mouth over it. To close the mouth, bind it with soft wire.

MULLET RIG
Cut a hole between the pelvic fins and remove the entrails. Push the hook shank through the hole into the mouth, and attach it to the line via a wire loop through the lips.

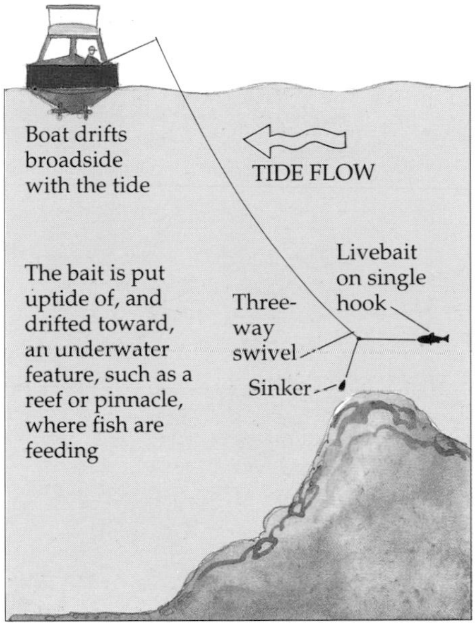

Livebait drifting
This technique is used mainly to catch amberjack and other species when they are feeding over small targets such as pinnacles and reefs. The main drawback with the technique is interference from other species, particularly sharks, although when amberjack are present in large numbers they usually monopolize the feeding. Small baitfish, such as grunts, are hooked through the nostrils or lips, sent down with a heavy sinker uptide of the holding area, and drifted along the bottom toward the target.

Livebait trolling
Livebaits must be treated with care if they are to remain alive, and trolled slowly to prevent them from drowning. Use only those fish that have suffered minimal hook damage during catching, and rig them in the least injurious way possible. The best approach for large baits such as bonito and dolphinfish is to use the bridle rig, which involves tying the bait to the hook instead of impaling it on it, and thus minimizes bleeding. Small baits can also be rigged this way, but are are more effective when put onto a wide-gap livebait hook via their nostrils.

FISHING VENUES
Mid-ocean islands, such as the Azores, offer deepwater fishing for species such as marlin within a short sailing time from harbor.

Trolling and Drifting

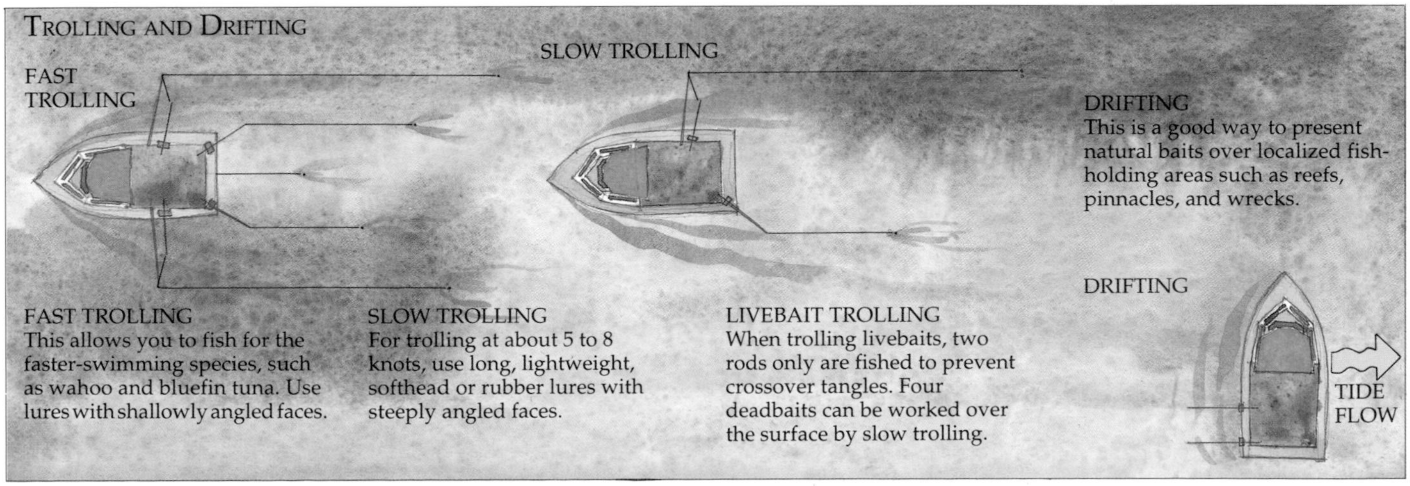

FAST TROLLING
SLOW TROLLING
DRIFTING
This is a good way to present natural baits over localized fish-holding areas such as reefs, pinnacles, and wrecks.
DRIFTING
Boat drifts broadside with the tide
TIDE FLOW
The bait is put uptide of, and drifted toward, an underwater feature, such as a reef or pinnacle, where fish are feeding
Livebait on single hook
FAST TROLLING
This allows you to fish for the faster-swimming species, such as wahoo and bluefin tuna. Use lures with shallowly angled faces.
SLOW TROLLING
For trolling at about 5 to 8 knots, use long, lightweight, softhead or rubber lures with steeply angled faces.
LIVEBAIT TROLLING
When trolling livebaits, two rods only are fished to prevent crossover tangles. Four deadbaits can be worked over the surface by slow trolling.

THE WATER

THE OBSERVANT ANGLER WHO LEARNS how to "read" the water, whether it be a small pond or a stretch of ocean, will be able to deduce what fish might be present, where in the water they are likely to be, what they are feeding on, and where and how to present the lure or bait to catch them. Acquiring and using this knowledge does not guarantee a catch, but it makes a catch much more likely than will guesswork or relying on luck.

If you fish a particular water regularly, spend time studying it at different times of the day and watching the movements and feeding habits of the fish. This will help you to locate and catch fish on that water, and will also provide you with knowledge of fish and their habitat that you can put to good use on other waters.

Binoculars and polarized sunglasses are a great help when you are studying the activities of fish. Binoculars enable you to watch for small, distant clues to fish movements, such as slight surface disturbances. They are especially useful at sea, for spotting changes in water color that might indicate fish-holding areas or for locating schools of baitfish rising to the surface to escape attacking predators.

In this chapter, you will find the signs to look out for on a variety of different waters, including streams, stillwaters, and the open sea.

LOOKING FOR CLUES
Time spent studying the water to find out where the fish are likely to be is never wasted.

Streams & Rivers 1

Streams and rivers can be divided into two basic types: limestone (or chalk) streams, fed by springs and containing high levels of calcium carbonate and other mineral nutrients; and rainfed (or freestone) streams, fed mainly by surface runoff and generally low in minerals. They can be further subdivided into three zones: the rushing upland stream; the moderately paced middle reaches; and the wide, deep, lower reaches.

MOUNTAIN STREAMS
The fast-flowing trout streams of mountainous areas are fed by surface runoff and melting snow. The water provides little in the way of food, so the fish they contain tend to be small.

Characteristics of Streams

Streams generally originate up in the hills or mountains, where rainfall is at its highest. Their tumbling upper reaches tend to be rich in oxygen but cold and rock-strewn, offering little in the way of either comfortable habitats or food for fish. As these young waterways begin to flow through less rugged countryside and are joined by tributaries, they grow in size and slow in pace, allowing vegetation to gain a foothold. Aquatic weeds begin to establish themselves, while earthy, rather than rocky, banks play host to trees, bushes, and plants. When the river becomes old, winding slowly across a wide flood plain, the types of aquatic weed and the species of fish present change, with those able to tolerate lower oxygen levels in the water and greater turbidity (muddiness) becoming dominant.

Types of stream
Some streams have as their source a bubbling spring, created by rainwater that has percolated through a porous rock, such as limestone, until it has reached a material that is less permeable, such as clay. Because the water cannot filter through the clay, it emerges as a spring at the base of the limestone. Other streams result from water seeping out of bogland, which is able to retain water and continue releasing it long into dry spells.

Rivers that begin their lives in rain-soaked hills are much more at the mercy of the weather than those that are springfed. Long dry spells can see a rainfed river reduced to the merest trickle, making life very difficult for the fish that inhabit it; in drought years, some rivers dry up completely. At the other extreme, sudden heavy rain can transform them into boiling torrents, sometimes in a matter of hours.

LIMESTONE STREAMS
The gin-clear water of a limestone stream has a high mineral content, enabling it to support abundant vegetation and thriving fish populations.

Snowfed rivers tend to be at their best in summer. During the spring months, snow on the mountains melts, creating a rise in the levels of the rivers that drain them. Sometimes, the thaw can be rapid, turning these streams and rivers into torrents. This meltwater is freezing cold, and not much good for fishing in. It is better to wait until toward the end of the snow melt, when air and water temperatures are rising, the flow has eased, and water levels are on the decline. A winter of low snowfall followed by a dry spring and summer will see the flow of snowfed rivers drastically reduced.

Streams and rivers emerging from reservoirs and managed lakes tend to enjoy steadier levels of flow, because it is possible to vary the amount of water passing through or over the exit sluice gates or dam. In times of low rainfall, compensation water can be released to keep up river flows, and because a stillwater acts as the source, the river may well never become too muddy, even after very wet weather.

The zones of a river
The species of fish present in a river vary from one zone to another. In the upper reaches, where the water is flowing at its fastest and clearest, and carrying the greatest amount of dissolved oxygen (caused by its being "broken up" by the mass of stones and boulders which make up the riverbed), trout and grayling will be found. Food is normally in limited supply, being restricted to the larvae of a few species of insect and shrimps (plus whatever terrestrials fall in), so the fish tend to remain small.

Farther downstream, where the river becomes deeper and the flow steadier, weedbeds provide cover for fish and attract the animal life on which they feed. This, combined with the less turbulent flow, results in more species being present, including smallmouth bass, pike, and perch. Trout and grayling may also be found, if the water is clean.

In the latter part of most rivers' lives, flow is slow, particularly in summer. The riverbed usually consists of soft mud and silt, and weed growth may be profuse. The mud and silt are often in suspension, which results in reduced visibility and an unsuitable environment for the species found further upstream. Instead, bottom-loving fish, more tolerant of water with lower dissolved oxygen levels, are present. These include catfish and carp.

VEGETATION

Vegetation in and along streams and rivers provides many benefits to both anglers and fish. Trees and other plants growing at the water's edge can help to bind and stabilize the bank, protecting it from erosion, and aquatic weeds can help to filter pollution from the water as well as hold up water levels during times of low rainfall. Weedbeds of all kinds also provide protective cover for fish and a home for the many different species of invertebrate on which they feed, and provide predators, such as pike, with concealment while they lie in wait for their prey. Overhanging trees also give cover, and terrestrials such as beetles and caterpillars often fall from their branches into the water, as do berries (elderberries, for instance, are taken by roach and chub).

WEEDBEDS
Lush beds of weeds are home to large populations of aquatic invertebrates, which attract feeding fish. Weeds protruding above the surface are easy to spot, but submerged weedbeds may not be so obvious: look for the slack water they create.

BANKSIDE VEGETATION
Fish like to lie beneath undercut banks and overhanging bankside trees and plants, which offer them shade from the sun, cover from predators such as herons (and anglers), and a source of insects and other foods.

SURFACE INDICATIONS

An ability to read the water can greatly improve an angler's success rate. Surface flow is rarely uniform, and patches of disturbance or areas of slack can provide clues as to what is happening under the water.

WATER FLOW
By studying the flow patterns of a stream you can learn a lot about its underwater features. For example, rocks and weeds create ripples and patches of slack water, while deep holes, containing slack water that offers fish respite from the current, appear to be slightly darker than the surrounding areas of water.

Underwater obstructions
Swirls and whorls in an otherwise uniform stretch of fast-flowing river reveal the presence of an underwater obstruction, such as a large boulder or an outcrop of rock. It is likely that an area of slacker water will exist behind it, and possibly on either side as the flow is deflected. Many fish, including trout and salmon, like to lie up and rest in such areas of slack water. In winter, a similar surface disturbance, or even a small patch of slack water, may betray the existence of a bed of true bulrush that has died back but is still big enough to obstruct the flow and create an area of sheltered water immediately behind it.

Fallen, sunken trees, often carried down the river on a flood before coming to rest, also create areas of slack water behind them and are much loved by roach, particularly where a sandbank is built up by the deflected flow.

Water flow
Where bends occur on rivers, the main flow is deflected by the outer bank and a visible "crease" develops between it and the slacker inside water. When the stream or river is running at normal level, species such as chub tend to lie right on the crease. They swim slowly or just hold a position in the slacker water, but are always ready to move out into the main flow to inspect items brought down by the main current.

As river levels rise after rain, or temperatures plummet, the fish will move progressively into the slacker water. At such times, slack water and gentle eddies can be full of fish, because they offer a comfortable environment in which to escape the raging current.

Where a river or stream consists of a series of pools and rapids or glides, fish are often to be found right at the necks or tails of the pools. At spawning time, migratory fish frequently rest in these spots while making their way upstream to their spawning grounds.

Streams & Rivers 2

Upland Streams & Rivers

The bed of an upland stream usually consists of rocks, boulders, and stones, over and between which races fast, and generally shallow, water. In the highest reaches, trout are the only gamefish likely to be present, and these never grow to any size on their thin diet of insect larvae, freshwater shrimps, and the occasional worm.

These little trout, often still carrying their parr markings, spend their lives hiding in slacks behind stones and boulders, ever ready to dart out into the current to grab a passing morsel. In these small pockets of slack water they also grub about in the bed for the few invertebrates present.

Lower down, where the water is less turbulent, the trout are often joined by grayling and salmon. The salmon will be both immature parrs (this is where they were born) and adults that have returned to spawn in the headwaters from which they originated.

In this lower part of an upland stream, the water gradually deepens and there will be depressions in the bed gouged out by floodwater. It is in these depressions or holes and behind boulders and rocks that the trout and grayling are found. The returning salmon also rest behind rocks during their upstream journey, before seeking patches of smooth gravel on which to spawn.

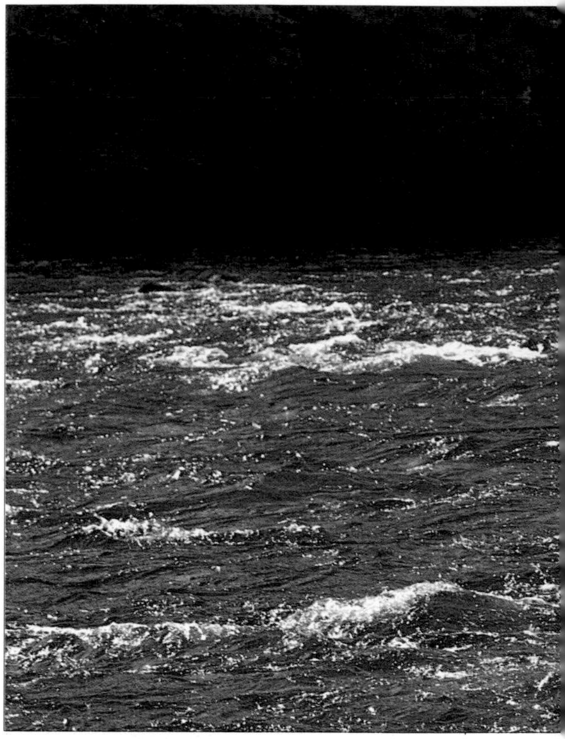

Lowland Streams & Rivers

Lowland streams contrast strongly with their upland counterparts. As the speed of the current slows, deposition of suspended material begins, resulting in a riverbed that changes downstream from rocks and boulders, through beds of gravel and sand, to silt banks. Each attracts its own varieties of fauna and flora and, as a rule, invertebrate life is plentiful. Because of this abundant food supply there are many varieties of fish present, including predators such as pike and perch.

LOWLAND RIVERS
Many lowland rivers are fast flowing, although not as fast as upland streams, and submerged rocks can cause considerable surface turbulence. Stretches that contain submerged rocks are usually best fished from the bank rather than from a boat, especially if you are unfamiliar with them.

Slacks and eddies
The calmer water behind submerged rocks and boulders provides comfortable living quarters for many fish. These underwater obstacles may not be visible in normal conditions, so a visit to a river during a dry spell, when the water level is low and the rocks are exposed, is well worthwhile. Draw a map or make a mental note of the positions of the rocks and the adjacent lies, so that you know where to find them when the stream returns to its normal height.

Other areas likely to hold fish include the slack water around and behind bridge supports, the eddies that often form where a river meets a smaller or slower flowing stream, and deep holes. These holes are scoured into the riverbed by the force of the flow during high water conditions. When the flow returns to normal, they often act as natural larders, collecting many invertebrate food items brought down on the current. Bottom-feeding fish such as carp and catfish find such holes highly appealing.

BRIDGES
A bridge supported on piers built on the riverbed creates a variety of water conditions. Water channeled between the pier bases speeds up, while areas of slack water form behind the piers, and if the bridge is low it will provide the fish with plenty of shade on sunny days. Barbel and bream are among the species that are attracted to this shaded water.

UPLAND STREAMS
(left)
The lower parts of an upland stream are good places to fish for trout, salmon, and grayling. Too fast, shallow, and rocky for boat fishing, they can be fished from the bank or by wading. Wading is especially effective when the river is wide or one bank is inaccessible because of vegetation.

UPLAND TROUT
(right)
The little trout in the high reaches of upland streams often retain their parr markings throughout their lives.

Confluences and islands
At the confluence of two streams of similar size and pace, a "crease", a small area of slack water between the two, is created. Fish like to lie in this slack, since it requires them to expend little energy yet allows them to move quickly into the stream on either side of them to intercept food drifting down with the current.

When two streams flowing at different speeds or of disparate size join up, the secondary (lesser) stream in both cases tends to be "held up". This results in the final length of the secondary stream running more slowly and even a little deeper. Fish are attracted to this steadier water, particularly during times of high water when the speed of the major stream increases to the point where it becomes uncomfortable for them.

Islands also hold great attraction for fish. This is because they deflect the flow, creating numerous areas of slack water, and are often thickly covered with trees and undergrowth. Much of this vegetation overhangs the river, producing cover and a canopy from which terrestrial creatures often fall.

Dam pools and millpools
These turbulent spots, with their oxygen-rich water, are a great attraction to many species. Trout (if the river is clean) are found up in the fastest, white water of a pool, while lower down the pool species such as smallmouth bass and catfish will be in evidence. Species such as perch, bream, and roach, which have a preference for calmer water, lie in the steadier flow at the tail of the pool, and in the slacks and eddies created to the sides. Pike are not far away, either, often tucked in close to the bank and using the marginal weed for camouflage.

In some dam pools, the actual dam sill is quite deeply undercut, and a light leger rig cast into the white water will be caught by the undertow and pulled underneath. Bites tend to be very positive, and sometimes the fish responsible for them can be very surprising. For as well as the expected bass and panfish, fish such as perch and bream will, remarkably, also take up residence below an undercut sill.

DAM POOLS
Dams are built across rivers to raise the upstream water level or to control the downstream flow. The water tumbling over a dam mixes with air as it falls, and so becomes well oxygenated. In hot weather, when oxygen levels in the rest of the river are low, the dissolved oxygen in a dam pool makes it very attractive to fish.

Dams
Dams are built across rivers to create reservoirs for drinking water or for driving hydroelectric turbines. A dam can help to maintain the flow of the river that runs out of the reservoir, keeping the levels topped up in times of low rainfall, but the effect on the fish in the river depends on how the water is released. Water released from spillways at the top of the dam is relatively warm, but water released from the base of the dam is often extremely cold. At hydroelectric dams in regions where the summers are hot, cold water released via the turbines often provides an ideal habitat for trout, but elsewhere a sudden introduction of cold water into a river normally fed from the spillways can have a severe dampening effect on sport, which only picks up again after the effects of the artificial flood have passed through.

Where water is constantly being released from the lake via the spillways in times of normal rainfall, it sometimes falls with such force that deep holes are formed below the dam. Fish are attracted to these and will only move out during times of heavy flow, finding refuge downstream and often behind the structures built to prevent bank erosion.

STILLWATERS 1

The term "stillwaters" covers a broad spectrum of waters. At one end of this spectrum is the tiny, springfed farm pond, either a natural feature or created in a shady corner of a field to provide a source of cool drinking water for livestock on hot summer days. At the other end are enormous man-made and natural expanses of water, some of which (such as the Great Lakes) are much bigger than many of the world's smaller countries.

CHARACTERISTICS OF STILLWATERS

Each type of stillwater presents the angler with a unique set of problems that must be solved if success is to be achieved. Different types also have many features in common, however, and the knowledge and experience gained when fishing one can be used to advantage on others. For example, while lakes may vary enormously in size and topography, all of them will usually have features such as bays, promontories (points), and shallow margins. In addition, the weeds found in the bays and shallows of big lakes and reservoirs are very often the same varieties seen in little ponds and medium-sized lakes, and in many cases the invertebrate life living among the weeds, and the species of fish in close proximity to them, are also the same. Your chances of angling success on any stillwater will be greatly increased if you learn what goes on beneath the surface.

Types of stillwater
The vast majority of stillwaters are natural features, fed by springs, streams, or rivers, and usually with one or more rivers draining them. A great many ponds and lakes are artificial, however, having been formed by the damming of a stream or river or by excavation. Most of those formed by damming are shallow where the watercourse enters and are at their deepest at the dam end.

Many of the small artificial stillwaters were created to form ornamental lakes, but most large waters were dammed to provide reservoirs of drinking or irrigation water, or for hydroelectric power. These waters vary greatly in size, from relatively small reservoirs that you could walk around in a couple of hours or less, to massive and deep expanses of water with shorelines measured in thousands of miles.

Another important group of stillwaters are those created by the flooding of worked-out pits and quarries, such as the gravel and clay pits resulting from the extraction of materials for use in the construction industry. The bottoms of flooded clay and gravel pits are often highly irregular, and the water can be very deep with few shallow areas. The water is also usually very clear, and weed growth is often profuse in less deep areas. The invertebrate life can be prolific, but often there are very few suitable spawning sites for fish. This situation leads to a food-rich environment containing a low population of fish, and because these fish have little competition, their growth rates are usually rapid.

GRAVEL PITS *(above)*
A flooded gravel pit can acquire a fish population naturally by the introduction of fish eggs by birds, but many pits are artificially stocked.

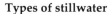

PONDS *(left)*
Small ponds often hold surprisingly large fish, especially when managed as fisheries, but overstocking can result in stunted fish.

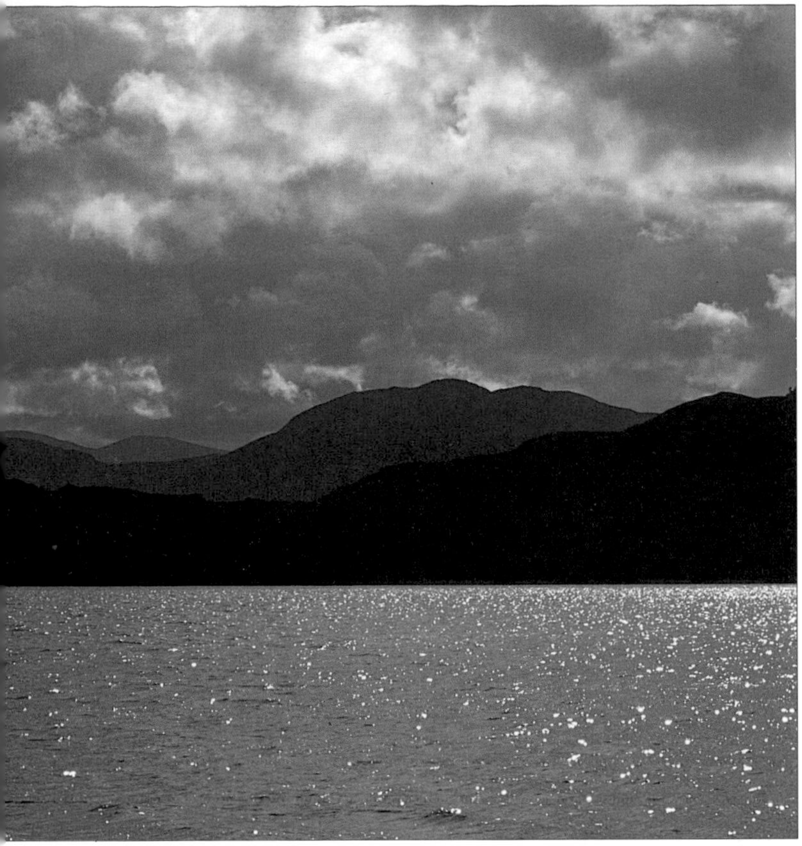

FISHING LARGE WATERS
The shores and shallow margins of large waters are in most respects similar to the edges of small waters, and are fished in much the same way. But if you are going to fish offshore on a really large water, it pays to obtain a chart of it so that you can locate likely fish-holding areas such as bars, underwater plateaus, shallows, and deepwater dropoffs. A sonar will help you to search the bottom and, together with a water temperature probe, to detect the colder layers that may hold species such as arctic char and lake trout.

Water color
As stillwaters begin to warm up each spring, minute plant organisms known as phytoplankton begin to multiply. The extent to which their population expands depends on a number of factors, including the depth and temperature of the water, the amount of weed growth, and the quantity of nitrates and phosphates present in solution (washed in from farmland treated with fertilizer). In hot summers, shallow, fertilizer-polluted stillwaters turn green as the phytoplankton population explodes.

Phytoplankton are eaten by zooplankton, which is the animal constituent of plankton and includes fish larvae and simple animal organisms such as daphnia (water fleas). Great clouds of orange-red daphnia can often be seen in the warmer shallows of clear stillwaters, rising and falling through the water layers and drifting with the wind.

If zooplankton occur in sufficient numbers, they help to keep a water clear of phytoplankton, and this encourages the growth of weeds, which need clear water and sunlight to thrive. As well as helping stillwaters to remain clear, zooplankton are an important food item for many species of freshwater fish, and they are particularly loved by reservoir rainbow trout.

Shallow waters usually warm up more quickly than deeper ones, encouraging the rapid growth of weeds and phytoplankton. Exceptions to this include springfed pools, with their constant supply of cold water, and small pools surrounded by thick tree growth, which reduces the amount of sunlight that can reach the water.

WATER COLOR
Many small stillwaters are turned green in summer by the presence of huge numbers of phytoplankton. A large population of zooplankton, which eat phytoplankton, plus a good growth of aquatic weeds, which consume nutrients that would otherwise be taken up by phytoplankton, can help to keep the water clear.

Underwater Features

When fishing stillwaters, try to locate underwater features that attract fish. Inflowing streams, for example, prove attractive to fish because their water often contains food, and may be cooler and contain more oxygen than the stillwater, particularly during long spells of warm weather.

Fish also gather around rocks and fallen or submerged trees, and feed on the algae, snails, and other invertebrates that take up residence on them. Schools of baitfish feel secure alongside or even among submerged branches, and predators lie in wait for them, close by and well camouflaged in the same branches. Another place to look for predatory fish is near the dropoff line between the marginal shallows and deep water, where they lie in wait for baitfish schools patrolling the dropoff in search of food.

SUBMERGED TREES
Trees that have fallen into the water, for instance when a riverbank is eroded and collapses, become gathering places for fish that find cover and food among the trunks and branches. Submerged trees are often also found in flooded pits and in lakes formed by damming, and may be in deep water a long way from the shore.

STILLWATERS 2

VEGETATION

Vegetation in stillwaters is usually restricted to the margins and shallows, and takes the form of weeds, rushes, beds of sedge, and water lilies. Weeds, rushes, and sedge provide many benefits, from helping to keep the water clear (by taking in nutrients to the detriment of phytoplankton), to giving sanctuary to various species of fish and the creatures on which they feed. Floating plants can also help to keep water clear of excessive phytoplankton. On ponds and small lakes where the surface is almost covered by such plants, the amount of sunlight entering the water is greatly reduced. Phytoplankton, being plants, cannot survive without any sunlight, so the water stays clear.

Reedbeds
Beds of reed line the margins of many stillwaters, and are as common on recently created waters as on well-established lakes. Their stems play host to a wide variety of animal life, including many invertebrates such as snails and the larvae of damselflies and dragonflies. Normally too dense for fish to swim in and out of, they are nonetheless attractive to some species. Pike and perch, for example, lurk alongside reed stems waiting for passing prey, beautifully camouflaged by their markings.

REEDBEDS *(above)*
Reeds are tall grasses that can reach a height of about 10 ft (3 m). When there is no wind, any movement of reed stems may be caused by fish.

WATER LILIES *(right)*
Most species of water lily normally grow in depths of no more than about 6 ft (1.8 m). The presence of these plants in an area of water thus gives a rough indication of its maximum depth.

Water lilies
Fish love to lie under the broad leaves of water lilies on hot days, and can often be heard making distinctive kissing sounds as they suck small animals from the undersides of the pads.

Although the pads themselves are often tightly packed on the surface, sometimes even riding up over one another, the stems below the water never seem to form an impenetrable barrier. Predatory fish lie in ambush among them, and slim fish such as pickerel and perch can swim between lily stems with ease.

Bigger, more rounded species such as carp can make their way through, but they tend to set the stems and pads rocking as they go – a phenomenon well worth looking out for when wandering the banks of a stillwater in search of fish.

Bankside plants

Trees, bushes, and other plants overhanging the banks of stillwaters provide cover for fish and are also a source of food, because terrestrial creatures such as spiders, beetles, and caterpillars frequently fall from their branches and leaves into the water. Fish also find a plentiful supply of food where the roots of marginal plants extend into the water, creating a habitat for insect larvae and snails.

FISHING A SMALL POND *(above)*
On this small pond, good places to seek out fish include the lily beds (where a fish snatching a food item from beneath a pad has created ripples) and the water below the overhanging trees that line the banks.

Brush piles

Fishery managers responsible for lakes and reservoirs with virtually featureless beds often create artificial fish-holding areas. One common way of doing this is by anchoring large piles of tree branches or cut trees to the bottom.

These brush piles, whose positions are usually marked by buoys or indicated by signs on the shore, offer fish the same sort of cover and feeding opportunities that they get from submerged or sunken trees *(see page 267)*.

OVERHANGING PLANTS
The water beneath overhanging vegetation is a good place to fish for the many species, including trout, that feed on terrestrials. Trees and bushes offer concealment for you as well as cover for the fish, but can make casting difficult, so fishing from a boat is often a better option than bank fishing.

Surface Indications

In the flowing water of streams and rivers, underwater obstructions and other features create surface disturbances that can indicate areas likely to hold fish *(see pages 262–65)*. Surface indications of this type seldom occur on stillwaters, but the fish often betray their presence by creating their own surface disturbances.

Bubbles and ripples

Bottom-feeding fish such as catfish and carp send up clouds of silt while searching the bed for food. And, as their noses disturb the silt, pockets of gas that are released from it bubble up to the surface. Patches of bubbles indicate one or more fish foraging in one particular area, and lines of bubbles reveal the presence of fish working along the bottom. Trout and other fish that feed at the surface create ripples that reveal their position, and big fish foraging in shallow water for food often set up bow-waves that can ripple the surface.

Wind lanes and scumlanes

On big waters in windy weather, lines of calm water may appear on the otherwise wind-ruffled surface. These "wind lanes" are often caused by obstructions on the bank, such as trees, that deflect the wind, creating a long, narrow slick of calm water. In strong winds, foam spray caused by breaking waves collects in the smooth water, creating "scumlanes."

During the summer months, hatching insects are blown into wind lanes and become trapped, unable to escape because of the greater surface tension of the unbroken strip of smooth water. Many species of fish, but particularly trout, will take advantage of this harvest and can be seen working their way upwind along the lanes.

SCUMLANES
In addition to the scumlanes formed by foam blown into wind lanes, there are those made up of pollen, leaves, twigs, and other pieces of debris that collect against a shore when the wind blows from the same direction for several days. These scumlanes attract fish because they often include items of food such as insects and daphnia.

Shorelines

Unlike offshore waters, which can usually be read only by studying charts and by echo sounding, it is normally possible to make a direct survey of all the fishable stretches of a shore. Select the lowest spring tide available in daylight and walk the shoreline, making notes about landmarks and other features of the lower, middle, and upper shore, and perhaps using a camera or camcorder to record the scene for later reference.

Types of Shoreline

Shores vary in many ways, the most obvious being in the type of substrate (seabed material), which may be sand, pebbles, rocks, or a mixture of these. Different species of fish often prefer different substrates, but the amount of shelter, the gradient of the shore, the presence of freshwater inflows, and food availability also play a part in determining the numbers and species of fish found along a shore. For the angler, the important thing is to understand what motivates fish movements.

Pebble beaches
Pebble beaches tend to give the impression of being devoid of life, but this is far from true. The pebbles, which may be stacked high by wave action, are often just the visible part of a complex, multi-substrate mix, sometimes including clays and old peat beds, at or beyond the low water mark. Cod, bass, rays, conger, and even flatfish are regularly caught from pebble beaches.

Watch for signs of submerged banks causing variations in the wave pattern beyond the low-water mark. At low water, aim to drop baits on their seaward sides; as they deepen on the flood, drop the baits into the gullies in front. It is also worth putting baits close to boulders, groins, and anything else that breaks the normal pattern of the pebbles.

Sandy shores
The size of the sand particles on a sandy shore influences the types of fish-food organisms, and thus the species of fish, that will be present. Fine particles with high amounts of organic matter are good for lugworms, mollusks, and shrimps, and therefore for the fish that feed on them. They also become stirred up and color the water with the least bit of wave action, and the low light levels in the colored water tempt species such as cod, which normally feed along the shore only at night, to feed during daylight.

Coarser sands, which settle out very quickly, are often associated with surf beaches, where bass, flounders, and small turbot are taken when a surf is running. A gentle gradient assists the wind in bringing good surf conditions, because friction between the seabed and the water slows the bottom of a wave, causing the top to overtake it and turn. This happens more readily in shallow water than in deep, and a line of breaking waves can be a sign of banks and gullies beyond the low-water line.

Any undulation on an otherwise featureless beach will be of interest to fish. They travel along channels, and are attracted to banks, which enhance wave movements, evicting concealed food items from the bed. Fish also gather at scour holes at the ends of breakwaters, picking up food items that have been washed into them.

PEBBLE BEACHES
On a pebble beach, the most productive water is usually out beyond the low-water mark, where the pebbles give way to grit and fine sand.

SANDY SHORES
In temperate waters, sandy shores attract species such as bass and flatfish. These are also found over sand in warmer waters, along with rays (such as this eagle ray), bonefish, and many species of shark, some of them large and dangerous.

Cliffs
The main attractions of cliff-lined shores are almost-permanent water, very often with good depth, and the presence of a wide range of features including kelp jungles for wrasse, broken rock for conger, pinnacles for pollack, and clean ground for rays, tope, and flatfish.

However, cliffs must be fished with care. Every year, anglers are plucked from low ledges by large swells, and spray and rain make rocks dangerously slippery. Good climbing boots, a safety rope, a minimum of tackle, and reliable company are essential, as is a safe retreat route for when the tide floods in.

SURF BEACHES *(left)*
The typical surf beach is a broad expanse of sand, facing the open ocean, where waves whipped up by the wind come crashing ashore. Fishing a gently shelving surf beach requires fairly long casting, but a steep beach should be fished with short- to medium-distance casts. When wading a surf beach, beware of the undertow, which can pull your feet from under you.

ROCKY BEACHES *(below)*
Some of the most productive shores are those with rocky, bouldery ground. Deepwater rock ledges with rough and clean ground within casting range also fish well.

PIER FISHING *(above)*
Long casting is usually unnecessary when fishing from piers, because many species, including bass, pollack, mullet, and conger, feed close to the underwater structure.

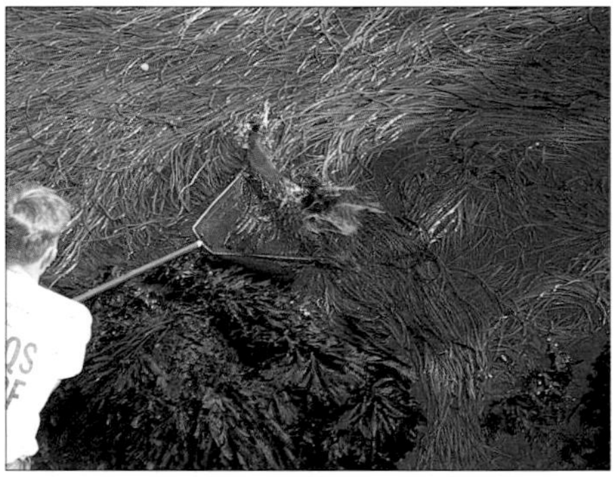

WEEDBEDS *(above)*
Despite the frustrations of snagged tackle, fishing weedbeds can be very productive because many species of fish are attracted to them by the cover and food they find there. Here, an angler is landing a large mullet that was hooked in a dense mat of weeds.

Rocks, gullies, and kelp beds
Variations in shoreline geography, unless pronounced, are less important on rocky shores than on sand. This is because the numerous nooks and crannies offer fish a wide range of sheltered spots and feeding areas. As on sandy shores, however, the larger features such as gullies and holes still provide shelter from the tide, areas into which food might settle, and ambush points for picking off victims passing overhead. Shell-crunching wrasse and night-stalking conger take maximum advantage of the available cover, while pollack, bass, and cod often move in to hunt over patchy, broken ground.

Beds of kelp, a common type of seaweed, tend to show only along the extreme lower shore at the lowest tides. Some anglers curse them because tackle snags in them, but they provide good cover for baitfish, and large kelp "jungles" hold lots of big fish.

Piers, jetties, and sea walls
Man-made structures frequently offer deep water at their bases and the chance for anglers to hit different or even deeper water by casting from them. Casting can, however, place the bait beyond fish that have been attracted to a structure because of the food that is available there. An open-framed pier standing on sand offers fish and their food a degree of shelter in an otherwise featureless world. Food collects in the scour holes, crabs thrive around the supports, and food is dumped in from facilities on the pier.

Most stone piers and harbor arms are built on deposited rock, which attracts a wide range of food types and fish. The bases of walls built on natural rock butting onto sand are usually rich in crabs, prawns, and small fish using the weed fringes for cover. Mullet browse microscopic organisms on the stonework, and predators such as bass may move in on the tide to feed after dusk.

Estuaries

Estuaries are dynamic environments, changing uniformly as the predictable freshwater inflow makes its effect felt, and changing unpredictably when heavy rains, often a long way inland, result in larger than normal amounts of freshwater flowing down the river. Even fish able to tolerate some degree of freshwater need time to acclimatize during sudden spates, which force them to move downstream or out into the sea to a point where they can find the salinity (saltiness) that they are accustomed to.

ESTUARINE FLOUNDER
In temperate waters, most estuaries are home to large numbers of flounder.

Types of Estuary

In a typical estuary, the river creates a plume of freshwater that extends into the saltwater of the sea. An area of brackish water is created where the two meet and mix. The size of this brackish zone at any one time depends on the size of the estuary, the tide, and the amount of freshwater that is entering from the river.

Estuaries vary greatly in size and topography. Some rivers enter the sea through narrow, rocky channels, others carve their way through wide expanses of mudflats or marshland, and others create huge deltas. They also differ in the quality of the freshwater flowing downstream into the sea, but despite all their differences the same basic rules governing species diversity and distribution apply.

Estuarine species
The main factor limiting the species of inshore marine fish that enter a particular part of an estuary is salinity. Fish that can tolerate low salinity, such as mullet, move readily into the brackish water of an estuary, or even into the freshwater zone, in search of food. Other species, such as cod, cannot cope with low salinity and are found only in those parts of an estuary where the level of salinity is relatively high.

Migratory fish, such as salmon and sea trout, travel down estuaries to mature at sea, and return as adults to run upstream to spawn. As they run through estuaries, they adjust their body chemistry to cope with the changes in salinity.

Upper reaches
The species in the upper reaches of an estuary are invariably limited, often to immature flounder, an occasional bass, and mullet where the flow is slack. Channel geography and food availability are the main factors determining where fish are likely to be found. Look for them where bends in channels create slow spots, obstacles create still eddies, and shallow bays onto which a rising tide spills offer quiet areas. Dips and holes within these quiet areas have the added attraction of being gathering points for food carried along by the flow.

Lower reaches
The lower reaches of an estuary often contain the same sort of fish-holding areas as the upper reaches. In addition, larger estuaries may have extensive banks of deposited silt that attract fish because they are rich in food items such as worms, mollusks, and crabs. In small estuaries with fast-flowing, channeled outlets, bars of deposited silt often form where the easing of the flow allows suspended material to fall. Such bars have all the attractive qualities of large banks, but on a very localized scale, making fish very much easier to locate. Wind throws up a telltale surf over a bar, and this rough water also churns food out of hiding. This is carried to the downtide edge of the bar, where fish gather to feed.

Creeks, lagoons, and stream outfalls
Large estuaries can form a number of special geographical features at or near their mouths, of which creeks are perhaps the most common. Mullet and flounder enter these muddy openings on the tide, and sole will push into them if they are adjacent to the open shore.

Lagoons formed by deposited silt trapping large expanses of water can quickly become food-rich because water movement is greatly reduced, allowing the contained area to warm more than adjacent areas. Access for fish may well be restricted, but once they are inside, the attractions of the relatively warm water and abundant food supply ensure continued patronage and, very often, good rates of growth. Mullet and flounder are typical of the species found in lagoons.

Stream outfalls, whether dissecting beaches or discharging over rocks, are themselves usually too small to contain fish. Their importance comes from the very localized changes in salinity that they create, which fish such as bass and flounder are seemingly unable to resist. For anglers, the water around any discharge of freshwater into the sea, however small, is worth investigating.

Mangrove creeks
Coastal creeks lined with mangrove trees are common in the subtropics and tropics in areas of organic enrichment, particularly where shallow banks and flats have been formed by the deposition of organic debris from rivers.

The trees grow on these banks and flats, supported by cagelike root structures that hold their trunks above the water. When submerged at high tide, these root structures offer an ideal sanctuary for small fish and are important nursery areas for a number of estuarine and coastal species.

Wherever small fish gather, they attract larger predators, and barracuda, tarpon, crevalle jack, guitarfish, and stringray are typical of the many predatory species found in mangrove creeks. Look for them in the deep holes scoured out on bends, in the areas of slack water downtide of sharp bends, and lying in ambush among the roots of the mangroves.

MANGROVE CREEKS *(above)*
Tarpon love to explore mangrove creeks and, like this one, are not deterred by shallow water. Channels and creeks in mangrove swamps contain many good places for fish to lie up in. For example, a twisting creek scours deep holes on its bends into which food will settle, and which provide fish with respite from the strong flow. The downtide corner of a sharp bend also provides shelter from the flow, and is a convenient point for a big fish to lie in wait for a passing meal.

ESTUARY MUD *(left)*
Most broad estuaries have large expanses of mud. This mud can support very large populations of the marine creatures, such as mollusks and worms, that many fish species feed on.

Offshore Temperate Waters

To the uninitiated, the sea appears to be a vast and featureless expanse of water, offering no clues as to where within it the fish might be. But, beneath the surface, it contains many features that attract a rich diversity of life, including fish that gather at them for cover and to feed. The location of many features, such as wrecks and outcrops of rock, can be read directly from charts and checked from a boat by echo sounding. At times, fish can also be found by reading surface indications, usually in shallow water or close to the shore. These indications include swirls and eddies created by rocks, and the activities of seabirds.

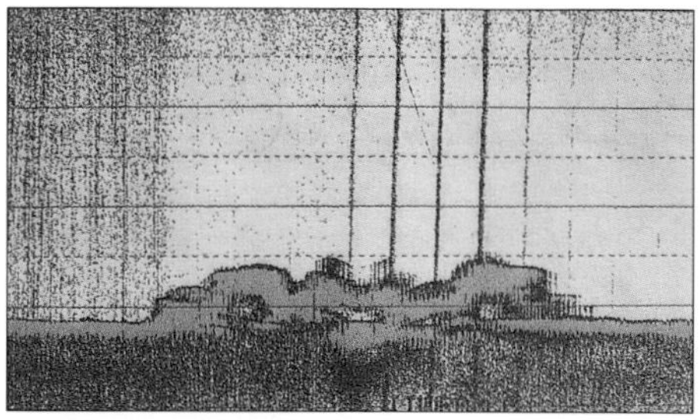

TAKING SOUNDINGS
An echo sounder provides you with a profile of the seabed beneath your boat, enabling you to locate features that might hold fish. This monochrome echo sounder trace shows the outline of a large wreck lying in deep water.

Types of Water

The nature of any stretch of sea plays an important part in determining the numbers and species of fish that are present. For example, a featureless seabed of sand results in low fish diversity and angling productivity, while rocks and wrecks are good places to fish because they attract large numbers of many different species. Deep water has better temperature stability than shallow water, so its fish population remains more stable throughout the year. If it is too deep or too turbid (colored by silt), however, there may be insufficient light penetration for weed growth, which provides fish with cover. Inflowing freshwater reduces salinity *(see page 272)*, and pollution by sewage attracts species that feed on it, such as mackerel, but deters those that need the high levels of dissolved oxygen found in unpolluted water.

Banks and gullies
On otherwise featureless ground, such as sand or mud, banks and gullies are the best places to look for fish. Banks are usually found near islands and headlands, where fierce tidal currents carry sand and silt in suspension. Where the tidal flow eases, material settles out into huge, ever-changing mounds, crisscrossed by gullies and sand waves. Baitfish, especially sandeels, swarm over such areas, attracting bass, turbot, brill, and other predators.

Gullies cut into banks by tidal action provide predatory flatfish with excellent ambush points, and bass hunt sandeels taking refuge there from the tidal flow. Away from banks, gullies accumulate creatures such as crabs, worms, and small fish, which are carried across the shallows by the tide until they drop into the deeper water of the gullies. This abundant food supply attracts many species including flatfish, bass, cod, ray, and shark.

BOAT FISHING *(above)*
Fishing from an anchored or drifting boat over a good fish-holding area, such as a gully, wreck, or reef, is usually very productive.

SANDBANKS *(left)*
The presence of a sandbank, a good place to fish, is often indicated by surface "boils" where the tidal flow is forced up over the bank.

Dropoffs
Large dropoffs, where the depth of the water increases sharply, are invariably areas of intermediate ground linking either fairly featureless areas or more productive ground. Unless they have attractive features of their own, such as fish-holding weedbeds, most of those that link featureless areas hold few fish and thus have little value to the angler. Dropoff edges linking productive areas, however, attract many species of fish.

Predatory flatfish gather along downtide slopes, breaking from cover to intercept sandeels passing overhead, and rays gather there to shelter from the current. Tope and other sharks hunt dropoffs between reefs and banks, picking off fish carried away from the edges by the tide, and reef conger may take refuge in convenient lairs.

Dropoffs should be fished from a drifting boat, starting well uptide of the area where fish are expected to be and going well beyond it.

ISLANDS
Islands tend to attract large numbers of fish because their interaction with the tidal flow creates a variety of different habitats. For example, where two islands are close together, the water rushing between them can scour out a deep hole in the seabed. Big skate often take up residence in such holes, feeding on the large numbers of food items that get swept into them by the tide. Skate will also congregate in the deep water on the downtide sides of islands.

Islands
The value of islands as concentrators of fish depends on a combination of layout and size. Groups of islands are more useful than single islands because they have a far greater effect on the surrounding waters. By deflecting, channeling, increasing, or suppressing the tidal flow, they create a broad range of habitats likely to draw in good numbers of many different fish species.

Areas of disturbed tidal flow aid the formation of banks and sand waves. Fast water attracts sandeels and mackerel, which in turn draw in tope, bass, pollack, and even porbeagle. Wrasse and conger feed in the quieter corners of bays and coves, and slack areas along the edges of strong flows allow sedentary species such as skates and rays to choose the degree of flow that suits them best.

Pinnacles and ledges
Submerged rock pinnacles are often found on deepwater reefs, and their peaks, reaching up towards the surface, may attract species that normally favor shallower water. The pinnacle base will be much the same as any other reef, attracting a wide variety of organisms, small fish, and their predators.

The peaks of submerged pinnacles can present a hazard to boats, and ledges are usually more hospitable places to fish, particularly on the drift. A lack of features can bring a certain uniformity of fish food items, and of the fish themselves, but small reef species are common, and larger predators will be nearby.

Wrecks and reefs
Wrecks are, in effect, man-made reefs, and they attract and hold the same kinds of fish as natural reefs. What these fish are depends on the depth. Shallow wrecks and reefs could have a good number of bass, plus wrasse, conger, and small pollack, which give way to cod, coalfish, ling, better pollack, and bigger conger as the depth increases.

On a wreck or a reef, the fish usually concentrate where cover and food availability are greatest, but some lie just off or along one side. It can take several drifts or some very skilful anchoring to present the bait where feeding fish are holed up.

Surface Indications

Away from the shore, areas likely to hold fish can be located by looking for surface indications, some man-made, others natural. Buoys and isolated danger marks indicate hazards to shipping, and many of these hazards, such as rocks, attract fish. Port and starboard navigation buoys mark channel edges, and sometimes areas of deep-lying, rocky ground – good places to fish – are dotted with crab pot markers.

Man-made markers are generally more reliable than natural surface indications. For instance, the edge of a steep bank is often betrayed by lines of white water, but these will not lie above the lip. The deeper the water, the farther downtide they appear, and in rough weather they may merge with existing waves. Swirls, erupting boils, overfalls, and eddies all denote seabed obstructions, such as reefs and wrecks, that are deflecting water upward in the tidal flow. These signs may also appear at varying distances downtide of the obstructions that cause them.

Diving gannets are good indicators of mackerel near the surface; more general seabird activity may indicate that predators are driving small fish to the surface. The predators will usually be mackerel but could be something more highly prized, such as bass.

CRAB POT MARKERS
Ground that supports a large population of crabs also attracts good numbers of fish. Crab pot markers are a reliable indication of such ground.

Offshore Tropical Waters

Tropical coastal waters support large numbers of many different species of fish, occupying every available niche from the seabed to the surface, and the upper layers of the water remain rich in fish well beyond the continental shelf. This makes tropical waters much more productive for anglers than their temperate counterparts. In addition to wreck, reef, and bank fishing *(see page 274)*, tropical waters offer bottom and midwater fishing from small boats and the shore, fly fishing, inshore trolling, poling the flats, and big-game fishing in the deep, blue water beyond the edge of the shelf.

Types of Water

The upper layers of tropical waters contain more fish than those of cooler seas, and some tropical species are unrestricted in their ability to roam the open ocean in search of food. Most species, however, must stay close to the areas that provide them with suitable food; upwellings, coastal shallows, and the sunlit reaches close to the surface are just such places. Over fishable seabed, much the same rules apply as in temperate waters, with wrecks, pinnacles, banks, gullies, and other features having concentrations of food and fish. In addition, large inshore gamefish like to patrol specific contours along the upper continental slope or the outer edges of fringing reefs.

FEEDING TARPON *(above)*
Tarpon often gather to feed at the surface, where they can be caught by casting to them from a drifting or anchored boat.

REEF FISHING *(left)*
Boats have gathered to fish just outside the reef to the right of this small island.

CORAL FLATS *(below)*
Coral flats, extensive areas of coral sand in very shallow water, are prime areas for bonefish and stingray.

Gullies, dropoffs, and banks
Tropical gullies, like those elsewhere, act as out-of-the-tide resting places and areas into which food carried on the tide can settle. Large predators, such as tarpon, love to hunt in shallow gullies, and the downtide edges of gullies, banks, and dropoffs make excellent ambush points for the slower bottom-living species.

Baitfish feeding over banks always draw predators, and the depth of the water determines just which predators these might be. There are almost invariably stingray and shark, and possibly amberjack, dolphinfish, crevalle jack, and striped marlin. Large sand-loving species, including jack, bass, and roosterfish, move into very shallow water, venturing almost onto the beaches.

Coral flats
Bonefish, small shark, barracuda, and stingray are the principal coral flat species. Stingray happily lie in wait for food, but the more free-swimming species both browse and hunt and so are easily spooked by an approaching boat. For this reason, angers use light, shallow-drafted skiffs that are poled within casting distance of the fish.

Coral reefs
Small to medium-sized fish such as porgies, snappers, and groupers congregate in large numbers over the offshore coral reefs. Their distribution over a reef depends to some degree on its depth, and the biggest groupers are often found on the deepest parts.

Sunken coral heads are important features of the shallow parts of reefs. These huge, mushroom-shaped growths of coral are home to a wide variety of small marine creatures and the fish that feed on them. These fish in turn attract predators, including small sharks.

Gullies sculpted into reefs or between sections of reef present slow-moving predators with good ambush points, while faster-swimming species hunt along the gullies and around the reef slopes. Barracuda patrol the upper edges of the dropoffs, while hammerhead and possibly larger reef shark species are the main predators further down. Where gullies are particularly deep, otherwise offshore species will move into them, even where they are close inshore.

Huge pinnacles lunging skyward from deep water are where the very largest groupers and other reef creatures are to be found. Like the deeper gullies, areas of pinnacle rock and pinnacle coral (where the water is shallow enough for coral to grow) provide some of the best hunting and ambush points on the reef. Efficient predators grow fat on the easy pickings, and this is where the best fishing is likely to be found.

TROLLING *(above)* *The best way to fish for fast-swimming big game species, such as marlin, wahoo, tuna, and sailfish, is by trolling with lures or natural baits.*

TEASERS *(left)* *Trolling a string of brightly colored teasers in addition to lures or baits will tempt marlin, tuna, and sailfish up from the depths.*

Deep water and dropoffs
The blue water of the deep sea is about as featureless as the ocean gets, but variations in the uniformity of the sea are created by upwellings of cold, nutrient-rich water. This water contains multitudes of tiny organisms, which attract baitfish schools; small predators congregate to hunt the baitfish, and are themselves taken by large gamefish. Upwellings are thus good places to fish, and their locations are often revealed by flocks of seabirds that gather to feed on the baitfish.

Fishing dropoffs, which are easily located by means of charts and an echo sounder, is a different matter. Baitfish concentrate more predictably, for example in midwater at the outer edges of deep reefs or deep rock pinnacles. The upper edges of drops are patroled by sharks, particularly hammerhead, and barracuda hunt along the shallowest edges of a reef. Close to the surface and along shallow edges, the higher water temperatures suit fast-swimming game species such as wahoo and sailfish.

All these fish respond to lures and slowly trolled livebaits. Where the water is at its deepest, a spread of lures and additional teasers will tempt fish such as marlin and sailfish up from depth. Other fish may not strike at surface lures and will require baits set perhaps about 30 to 40 ft (10 to 12 m) down on downriggers.

Floating weed rafts
Floating weed rafts are a regular phenomenon in areas touched by major oceanic currents. The North Atlantic Drift, for example, brings attendant circulating clumps of algae known as sargassum. These can combine to form quite large rafts, which make a very important contribution to the biology of an area. They are also extremely valuable from an angling point of view, acting as a surface signpost on an otherwise featureless sea.

Dolphinfish and some smaller species have a habit of taking refuge beneath floating objects. These need not be weed rafts – they could be boxes, oildrums, tree roots, or other flotsam – but sargassum is the most abundant. Alongside any sizable floating object is a good place to stop a boat and start chumming with handfuls of cut fish. Very soon, the dolphinfish schools will gather off the stern where some truly exciting light-tackle sport is virtually assured.

Dolphinfish may well be gamefish in their own right, but they are also a source of food for larger predators such as marlin. Trolling Kona Heads along the outer edges of long sargassum rafts, as opposed to more aimless quartering of areas likely to be patrolled by marlin, can thus be very productive.

Conservation

The origins of all vertebrates, including ourselves, can be traced back to the primitive fish that evolved in the waters and swamps of the late Cambrian period, which ended over 500 million years ago. Some of the descendants of these early fish left the water to colonize the land, while others remained aquatic and evolved into the 22,000 or more species of fish alive today. These fish, like most living creatures, live in harmony with their environment, their numbers rising or falling according to the availability of food.

Some, however, are theatened with extinction. This may be a slow, natural process, caused for instance by changes in weather patterns to which a species cannot adapt, but many immediate and avoidable threats are posed by human activities.

WEED CUTTING

Good fishery management often involves some degree of intervention, such as cutting away excess weed growth, in order to keep the water in prime condition.

Pollution

One of the most visible and widespread threats to fish, particularly freshwater species, is pollution of the water in which they live. This pollution takes many forms, including the discharge of inadequately treated sewage into rivers, lakes, and seas; the poisoning of waters by industrial waste products, agricultural chemicals, and oil spills; acidification of lakes and streams by acid rain; and contamination of the groundwaters that feed springs. Anglers, by the very nature of their sport, are often the first to become aware of changes in water quality caused by pollution. If you suspect that a stretch of water is becoming polluted, report it immediately to the relevant authorities and to local conservation groups.

Another threat to fish comes not from the quality of the water but from its quantity. Increasing demands for water, brought about by population growth, industrialization, and irrigation, have seriously depleted many rivers and lakes.

Eutrophication

The process of eutrophication is something of a paradox, in that it is the enrichment of water by the inflow of nutrients, which might appear beneficial but is actually a serious problem. The nutrients involved are nitrates and phosphates. Nitrates enter rivers, lakes, and the sea when rain washes nitrate-based fertilizers from farmland soil; phosphates also come from fertilizers, but their main sources are industrial and domestic effluents (phosphates are widely used in detergents).

When these nutrients enter water in excessive amounts, they promote the rapid growth of algae. These algae cover the surface of the water, preventing sunlight from reaching submerged plants. This sets up a chain reaction in which the submerged plants die, the bacteria that decompose the remains use up oxygen dissolved in the water, and this reduction in available oxygen causes the death of more plants and subsequently of the animal life inhabiting the water, including the fish.

Acidification

Over the past few decades, thousands of lakes and many rivers in the Northern Hemisphere have become devoid of fish because of the effects of acid rain. Scandinavia and Canada are two of the worst-affected areas. This rain is created when sulfur dioxide, nitrogen dioxide, and nitrogen oxide – released into the air when fossil fuels are burned – react with moisture in the air to form sulfuric and nitric acids.

Acid rain makes the water in rivers and lakes acidic, and also frees large amounts of aluminum from the soil. The acidity of the water kills fish eggs and fry, and the aluminum affects the gills of fish, making them clog up with mucus. The combination of acidity and aluminum also kills off most plant life and the small creatures that fish feed on.

AGROCHEMICALS
Many of the chemicals used in modern intensive farming can prove very harmful if washed into streams, lakes, or the sea. These chemicals include fertilizers, which promote excessive algae growth, and herbicides and pesticides that can damage aquatic plant, insect, and animal life.

Fish Stocks

One of the most serious threats to many species of fish is that of overfishing. This is a particular problem for marine species that are fished for commercially, because of the huge numbers that are caught and the difficulty of enforcing size limits and catch quotas.

Freshwater fish are generally easier to protect from serious overfishing. For example, in most developed countries, freshwater fishing is largely for sport and is successfully regulated by licenses, permits, closed seasons, minimum size limits, and, in some cases, catch limits. In addition, most freshwater fish are relatively easy to breed for stocking depleted waters and for maintaining population levels.

Sea anglers can contribute to the maintenance of fish stocks by imposing personal minimum size limits and releasing, unharmed, any fish they do not intend to eat.

Catch-and-release fishing
Releasing fish after capture is an excellent way to help maintain fish stocks, and on some fisheries it is mandatory. However, fish must always be handled carefully if they are not to die from injury caused by rough treatment.

Use barbless hooks, or flatten barbs with pliers to make hooks easier to remove. If possible, leave the fish in the water and hold it gently while you unhook it, so that you cause as little damage as possible to its scales and its protective coating of slime. If the fish has swallowed the hook, carefully cut the leader as close to the hook as possible and leave the hook in place rather than try to remove it; the fish's digestive juices will soon break it down.

After unhooking, support the fish in the water with both hands and turn it to face into the current, if there is one. If it is exhausted, continue supporting it until it has recovered its strength and is ready to swim away.

SHARK CONSERVATION
Releasing sharks after capture, as this angler is doing, will help to ensure their survival. Many shark species have declined alarmingly in numbers, partly because of angling but also because so many are being taken for their fins. Shark finning is a particularly nasty form of commercial fishing: the sharks' fins are cut off, and the still-alive but fatally maimed fish are dumped back into the sea to die.

Species Under Threat

Several hundred species of fish have been classified by international and national agencies as actually or potentially in danger of extinction. Those listed here are some of the threatened, endangered, or vulnerable species that anglers might encounter. They should not be fished for in the areas named (in most cases it is illegal to do so), and if one is caught by accident it should be carefully unhooked and released.

Acipenseridae	
Shortnose sturgeon (*Acipenser brevirostrum*)	USA, Canada
Lake sturgeon (*Acipenser fulvescens*)	USA, Canada
Adriatic sturgeon (*Acipenser naccarii*)	Italy
Atlantic sturgeon (*Acipenser oxyrhynchus*)	USA, Canada
Common sturgeon (*Acipenser sturio*)	Europe
Pallid sturgeon (*Scaphirhynchus albus*)	USA
Clupeidae	
Allis shad (*Alosa alosa*)	Europe
Lamnidae	
Great white shark (*Carcharodon carcharias*)	South Africa
Percichthyidae	
Eastern freshwater cod (*Maccullochella ikei*)	Australia
Trout cod (*Maccullochella macquariensis*)	Australia
Clarence River cod (*Maccullochella* sp.)	Australia
Mary River cod (*Maccullochella* sp.)	Australia
Retropinnidae	
Australian grayling (*Prototroctes maraena*)	Australia
Salmonidae	
Atlantic whitefish (*Coregonus canadensis*)	Canada
Kiyi (*Coregonus kiyi*)	USA, Canada
Whitefish (*Coregonus lavaretus, C. albula,* and *C. oxyrhynchus*)	Europe
Blackfin cisco (*Coregonus nigripinnis*)	USA, Canada
Shortnose cisco (*Coregonus reighardi*)	USA, Canada
Shortjaw cisco (*Coregonus zenithicus*)	USA, Canada
Huchen (*Hucho hucho*)	Eastern Europe
Apache trout (*Oncorhynchus apache*)	USA
Gila trout (*Oncorhynchus gilae*)	USA
Adriatic trout (*Salmothymus obtusirastris*)	Balkans

Glossary

A

Adipose fin A small, fatty fin between the dorsal fin and the tail fin.
AFTMA The American Fishing Tackle Manufacturers Association. Its activities include setting technical standards for fishing tackle, and its fly tackle specifications have become the world standard.
Alevin A recently hatched salmon or trout (*see also* **Grilse, Kelt, Parr, Smolt**).
Algae Any of a number of groups of simple plants that contain chlorophyll but lack true roots, stems, and leaves. They live in water or moist ground, and include diatoms, seaweeds, and spirogyra.
Amphidromous fish Fish that regularly migrate between freshwater and saltwater for reasons other than spawning, for example to feed or to overwinter (*see also* **Anadromous fish, Catadromous fish, Potamodromous fish**).
Anadromous fish Fish that spend most of their lives in the sea but ascend rivers to spawn (*see also* **Amphidromous fish, Catadromous fish, Potamodromous fish**).
Anal fin The fin behind the anus of a fish.
Aorta The main artery carrying blood from the heart.
Articular The rear bone of the lower jaw of a fish. It is hinged to the upper jaw and the quadrate (*see also* **Dentary, Maxillary, Premaxillary, Quadrate**).

B

Bag limit The maximum permissible number or weight of fish that can be taken from a particular water: always check local regulations before fishing.
Baitfish Any small fish, such as minnows and sandeels, that are preyed on by larger species and commonly used as angling bait.
Baiting needle A long needle used for mounting dead fish and other large baits onto terminal tackle.
Banks The right bank of a river is on your right when you are facing downstream, and the left bank is on your left.
Basin A depression in the Earth's surface; the drainage basin of a river system; a very large depression in the Earth's surface, containing an ocean and the rivers that drain into it, for example the Pacific Basin (*see also* **Drainage basin**).
Benthic A term describing anything living at or near the bottom of a lake or the sea.
Biomass The total mass of all the living organisms in a given area or in a given body of water (aquatic biomass).
Bowfishing Fishing with a bow and arrow. It is permitted on many American waters, and the quarry is usually "trash" fish (such as carp) that are competing with more highly prized species such as bass. The arrow is tied to the end of the line, and the reel is mounted on the bow.
Brackish water Water that is slightly salty (*see also* **Salinity**).
Breaking strain The maximum load or weight that a line, swivel, or other piece of tackle can sustain without breaking.
b.s. The abbreviation for breaking strain.
Bulk shot A number of split shot grouped together on a line to concentrate weight at a particular point.
Butt pad A leather or rubber pad, strapped around the waist, into which the butt of a rod is placed so that greater leverage can be exerted when fighting large, powerful fish. It is also known as a rod socket (*see also* **Fighting chair**).

C

Caeca See **Pyloric caeca**
Catadromous fish Freshwater fish that move to the lower river or sea to spawn (*see also* **Amphidromous fish, Anadromous fish, Potamodromous fish**).
Caudal peduncle The relatively slender part of a fish's body between the last dorsal and anal fins and the base of the tail fin (the caudal fin). It is also known as the "wrist" of the fish.
Cleithrum A bone at the rear of the skull of a fish. It is the main bone supporting the pectoral fin (*see also* **Pectoral fin, Supracleithrum**).
Coarse fish Any freshwater fish of angling interest other than gamefish and panfish (*see also* **Gamefish, Panfish**).

D

Deadbait Dead fish or other creatures used as bait for predators (*see also* **Livebait**).
Dead drift A fly-fishing technique in which the fly (dry or wet) is allowed to drift freely along in the current.
Demersal fish Fish that live in deep water or on the sea floor (*see also* **Pelagic fish**).
Dentary The front bone of the lower jaw of a fish (*see also* **Articular, Maxillary, Premaxillary, Quadrate**).
Deoxygenation Reduction in the dissolved oxygen content of a water, caused by hot weather or the introduction of pollutants such as sewage. Excessive deoxygenation is fatal to fish.
Detritus Accumulated silt and organic debris on the bed of a river or stillwater.
Disturbance pattern A wet- or dry-fly pattern that creates a fish-attracting disturbance when retrieved or worked across the current (*see also* **Wake fly**).
Dorsal fin The fin on the back of a fish, sometimes divided into two or three partly or entirely separate sections.
Drainage A drainage basin or a drainage system; the process of draining.
Drainage basin The catchment area of a river system (*see also* **Basin**).
Drainage system A river and its tributaries.

E

Eddy A patch of water that is less disturbed than the surrounding water, found for instance on the edge of a current or where two streams converge (*see also* **Pool, Riffle, Run, Scour, Slack**).
Electrofishing Passing an electric current through the water to stun the fish, so that they can be collected unharmed for tagging or scientific examination or for relocation to another water.
Esophagus The gullet of a fish.
Euryhaline fish Fish, such as most species of salmon and trout, that can live in both freshwater and saltwater.

F

Fighting chair A swivel chair bolted to the deck of a boat, from which a big-game angler can fight marlin and other large, powerful fish that can take a long time to subdue. The angler is strapped in by a harness, and either the harness or the chair is equipped with a butt pad or rod socket (*see also* **Butt pad**).
Filter feeder A fish that feeds by filtering plankton from the water.
Fingerling A small, immature fish, such as a juvenile trout.
Fish ladder A series of interconnected pools created up the side of a river obstruction, such as a dam, to allow salmon and other fish to pass upstream.
Foul-hook To hook a fish anywhere but in the mouth.
Fresh-run fish A migratory fish, such as a salmon, that has just left the sea and is traveling up a river to spawn.
Freshwater The water of most rivers and stillwaters, containing little or no dissolved salts (*see also* **pH, Salinity**).
Fry Very young fish, especially those that have only recently hatched.

G

Gall bladder A small pouch, on or near the liver of a fish, which stores bile. Bile is a fluid produced by the liver, and aids the absorption of food by the gut.
Gamefish Any fish valued for its sporting qualities (*see also* **Coarse fish, Panfish**).
Gill arch The structure behind the gill covers of a bony fish (or within the gill slits of a cartilaginous fish) that supports the gill filaments and gill rakers.
Gill filaments The parts of a fish's gills that absorb oxygen from the water.
Gill rakers Toothlike projections on the gill arches. They can be used to trap food items, such as plankton, carried in the water flowing through the gills.
Gonads The reproductive organs that are responsible for the production of sperm or eggs (*see also* **Testes, Ovaries**).
Grain A unit of weight, used for instance in

the classification of fly lines. 1 gram = 15.4 grains, 1 oz = 437.6 grains.
Greenheart A tropical American tree, *Ocotea rodiae;* its wood was once used for making fishing rods.
Grilse A young Atlantic salmon making its first spawning run, usually after one and a half to two years in the sea (*see also* **Alevin, Kelt, Parr, Smolt**).

H

Handline A simple tackle rig often used by youngsters fishing from piers and harbor walls. It consists of a sinker and a hook attached to a line that is wound on a wooden or plastic frame.
Hatch The simultaneous surfacing of large numbers of insect nymphs of the same species. At the surface, the adult insects (or duns) emerge from the nymphal cases and usually rest for a while before flying off (*see also* **Rise**).

I

Ice fishing A specialized form of angling, developed in North America, for fishing through holes cut in the ice of frozen-over waters. The species sought include crappies, walleye, northern pike, pickerel, and perch, and the principal techniques are jigging and tilt (or tip-up) fishing. Jigging involves working a natural bait with a short stick, which has a specially shaped handle around which the line is wound. In tilt fishing, the bait is fished static from a rig incorporating an arm or flag that tilts up to signal a bite.
Ichthyology The scientific study of fish and their habits.
IGFA The International Game Fish Association, based in Fort Lauderdale, Florida. It maintains lists of record fish and also sets technical standards for fishing tackle.
Interoperculum In bony fish, the front lower bone of the gill cover (*see also* **Operculum, Preoperculum, Suboperculum**).
Invertebrate A creature that has no backbone, for instance an insect or a worm (*see also* **Vertebrate**).

J

Jig A small artificial lure with a metal head, often dressed with feathers.
Jigging Fishing by jerking a jig or other bait up and down in the water; an ice-fishing technique (*see also* **Ice fishing**).

K

Keeper ring A small ring just above the handle of a fishing rod, to which the lure or hook can be attached when not in use.
Kelt A salmon or trout that has spawned (*see also* **Alevin, Grilse, Parr, Smolt**).
Krill Tiny, shrimplike crustaceans, of the family Euphausiidae, that form an essential part of the marine food chain.

L

Lacustrine A term that describes anything of, relating to, or living in lakes.
Ladder See **Fish ladder**
Left bank See **Banks**
Lie A quiet or sheltered spot in the water where a fish can rest, hide from predators, or wait for food to come by.
Limnology The scientific study of lakes and ponds and the plant and animal organisms that live in them.
Livebait Any natural bait, such as a worm, maggot, or small fish, that is used live (*see also* **Deadbait**).
Low-water fly A sparsely dressed fly on a small hook, used mostly for salmon fishing in shallow water.

M

Mark An area of the sea that offers good fishing, usually one that can be located by taking the bearings of shore features.
Marrow spoon A long, slender spoon that can be passed down the gullet of a dead fish to remove its stomach contents. It is used mainly by trout anglers to find out what the fish are actually feeding on at a given time.
Maxillary The rear bone of the upper jaw of a fish (*see also* **Articular, Dentary, Premaxillary, Quadrate**).
Milt The semen of a male fish; a term for the semen-filled testes and sperm ducts of a male fish, also known as soft roe (*see also* **Ova, Roe, Testes**).

N

Neap tides The tides that occur midway between spring tides. They have smaller rises and falls than those at other times of the month (*see also* **Spring tides**).
Nictitating membrane A thin membrane that can be drawn across the eyeball to protect and clean it. Found on many fish species, including some sharks.

O

Operculum In bony fish, the uppermost and largest of the gill cover bones (*see also* **Interoperculum, Preoperculum, Suboperculum**).
Osmosis The process by which a fish takes in or excretes water through its skin in order to maintain the correct balance of salts and fluids within its body tissues.
Otoliths Oval, stonelike structures within the ears of a fish or other vertebrate, which help it to maintain its balance; they are also known as ear stones.
Ova The eggs of a fish or other creature. The mass of eggs within the ovarian membranes of a female fish is termed hard roe (*see also* **Milt, Roe, Ovaries**).
Ovaries The reproductive glands (gonads) of a female fish, which are responsible for the production of eggs (*see also* **Testes**).
Oviducts The ducts between the ovaries and vent in most female fish, along which the ripe eggs pass during spawning.
Oviparous fish Fish that lay eggs from which the young later hatch. All skates, some sharks and rays, and most bony fish are oviparous (*see also* **Ovoviviparous fish, Viviparous fish**).
Ovoviviparous fish Fish whose eggs are fertilized and hatched within the female's body. The eggs are enclosed in separate membranes and the embryos within them receive no nourishment from the mother. Most sharks and rays are ovoviviparous (*see also* **Oviparous fish, Viviparous fish**).

P

Panfish Any small American freshwater food fish, such as a sunfish or perch, that is fished for by anglers but is too small to be considered a true gamefish (*see also* **Coarse fish, Gamefish**).
Parabolic-action rod Another term for a through-action rod.
Parr Young salmon and trout up to two years old, distinguishable from smolts by the dark bars (parr marks) on their sides (*see also* **Alevin, Grilse, Kelt, Smolt**).
Pectoral fins The pair of fins just behind the head of a fish.
Pelagic fish Fish that live at the surface, in the upper waters, of the open ocean (*see also* **Demersal fish**).
Pelvic fins The pair of fins on the lower body of a fish; also called ventral fins.
pH The pH number of a liquid, such as water, indicates its acidity or alkalinity. Pure water has a pH of 7; water with a pH of less than 7 is acidic, and water with a pH of more than 7 is alkaline. Acid rain typically has a pH of less than 5.
Pharyngeal teeth Teeth at the back of the throat, found in many fish species such as the members of the carp family. These teeth crush food as it is swallowed (*see also* **Vomerine teeth**).
Pisciculture The breeding and rearing of fish, for example in hatcheries and fish farms.
Pool A relatively wide, rounded area of a river, usually found just downstream of fast, narrow run (*see also* **Eddy, Riffle, Run, Scour, Slack**).
Potamodromous fish Fish that migrate regularly within large freshwater systems (*see also* **Amphidromous fish, Anadromous fish, Catadromous fish**).
Predatory fish Any fish that prey on other living creatures, particularly other fish.
Premaxillary The front bone of the upper jaw of a fish (*see also* **Articular, Dentary, Maxillary, Quadrate**).
Preoperculum In bony fish, the bone at the rear of the cheek, just in front of the gill cover (*see also* **Interoperculum, Operculum, Suboperculum**).
Pyloric caeca Fleshy, fingerlike tubes at the junction between the stomach and intestine of a fish. They produce enzymes that play a part in the digestive process.

Q

Quadrate The bone that joins the upper jaw of a fish to its skull (*see also* **Articular, Dentary, Maxillary, Premaxillary**).

R

Rays The soft or spiny supporting elements of fish fins.
Redd A hollow scooped in the sand or gravel of a riverbed by breeding trout or salmon as a spawning area.
Reversed-taper handle A rod handle that tapers toward the butt end.
Riffle A small rapid in a river or stream (*see also* **Eddy, Pool, Run, Scour, Slack**).
Right bank See **Banks**
Riparian A term that describes anything of, inhabiting, or situated on a riverbank; often used in connection with ownership and fishing rights.
Rip-rap Broken rock, deposited loosely on a riverbed or on the banks to help prevent erosion. It is also used to form breakwaters and embankments.
Rise The action of a fish coming to the surface to take an insect; the taking to the air of a large hatch of mayflies or other insects on which trout feed (*see also* **Hatch**).
Rod socket See **Butt pad**
Roe A collective term for fish milt and ova (*see also* **Milt, Ova**).
Run A fast-flowing stretch of river; the movement of fish inshore or upstream for spawning; the flight of a hooked fish trying to escape; a small stream or brook. (*See also* **Eddy, Pool, Riffle, Scour, Slack.**)

S

Salinity The level of dissolved salts in the water. Freshwater normally contains less than 0.2% salts, brackish water contains up to 3% salts, and saltwater (such as seawater) more than 3%. Normal seawater contains 3.433% salts – 2.3% sodium chloride (common salt), 0.5% magnesium chloride, 0.4% sodium sulphate, 0.1% calcium chloride, 0.07% potassium chloride, and 0.063% other salts.
Saltwater Water containing a high level of dissolved salts (*see also* **Salinity**).
Scour Erosion caused by flowing water; a shallow, fast-flowing, gravel-bottomed stretch of river (*see also* **Eddy, Pool, Riffle, Run, Slack**).
Sea anchor A cone-shaped bag, usually made of canvas, which can be trailed behind a drifting boat to slow it.
Seminal vesicle A small gland that adds nutrient fluid to the milt of a male fish during spawning (*see also* **Milt**).
Sink-and-draw A method of fishing in which the lure, fly, or bait is made to rise and fall alternately during the retrieve by raising and lowering the rod tip.
Sink-tip A floating fly line with a sinking tip, used to fish flies just below the surface.
Slack Tidal water where there is little surface movement during the interval between the ebbing and flowing tides; a stretch of river with very little current, for instance above a dam (*see also* **Eddy, Pool, Riffle, Run, Scour**).
Slip A narrow strip of feather. Slips are widely used in fly tying.
Smolt A young salmon or sea trout, silver in color, on its first journey to the sea (*see also* **Alevin, Grilse, Kelt, Parr**).
Spring tides The tides that occur around the time of full and new moons. They have larger rises and falls than those at other times of the month (*see also* **Neap tides**).
Strike To tighten the line to set the hook when a fish bites, usually by raising the rod tip or lifting the rod.
Suboperculum In bony fish, the rear lower bone of the gill cover (*see also* **Interoperculum, Operculum, Preoperculum**).
Supracleithrum A bone at the upper rear of the skull of a fish. It is one of the bones that support the pectoral fin (*see also* **Cleithrum, Pectoral fin**).
Surface film The apparent elastic-like film on the surface of water, which is created by surface tension.
Surface tension The natural tendency of the surface of water (and other liquids) to behave like an elastic sheet. It is caused by forces acting between the water molecules: the molecules at the surface are much more strongly attracted to each other, and to the molecules below them, than they are to the molecules of air above them.
Swim The stretch of a river, or the part of a pond or lake, that is being fished in at a particular time.

T

Take The action of a fish in picking up or grabbing a bait or lure.
Taper The narrowing in diameter, from butt to tip, of a rod, and the narrowing of the end section of a fly line. The rate of taper determines the action of the rod or line.
Terminal tackle The tackle, including the hook or lure, attached to the end of the reel line (main line).
Testes (singular: testis) The reproductive glands (gonads) of a male fish, which are responsible for the production of sperm (*see also* **Ovaries**).
Tilt fishing A technique used in ice fishing; it is also known as tip-up fishing (*see also* **Ice fishing**).
Tippet The thin end section of a fly leader, to which the fly is tied.
Tube fly An artificial fly consisting of a metal or plastic tube, dressed with feathers, hair, or other materials and threaded onto the line. The hook, usually a treble, is then attached to the end of the line.

V

Vas deferens The duct that carries sperm from the testis of a spawning male fish (*see also* **Milt, Testes**).
Vent The anus of a fish. It is also the orifice through which a spawning female fish lays her eggs (or, in the case of a viviparous fish, gives birth) and through which a male fish discharges his milt during spawning (*see also* **Viviparous fish, Milt**).
Vertebra An individual segment of the backbone of a fish.
Vertebrate A creature that has a backbone, for instance a fish or a mammal (*see also* **Invertebrate**).
Viviparous fish Fish whose ripe eggs are fertilized and hatched within the female's body; they give birth to live young. Unlike those of ovoviviparous fish, the developing embryos receive nourishment from the mother. Some sharks and some bony fish, such as surfperch, are viviparous (*see also* **Oviparous fish, Ovoviviparous fish**).
Vomerine teeth Teeth on the vomer, a bone at the front of the roof of the mouth of bony fish (*see also* **Pharyngeal teeth**).

W

Wake fly A dry fly that creates a splashy, fish-attracting wake when pulled across or through the surface of the water (*see also* **Disturbance pattern**).
Wobbling A freshwater spinning technique using a lure, or a small, dead fish mounted on treble hooks, for bait. The bait is cast a long way out, and retrieved in an erratic fashion by making side-to-side movements of the rod tip and at the same time varying the speed of the retrieve.
Wrist See **Caudal peduncle**

Y

Yolk sac The membrane-covered food pouch found on the belly of a newly hatched fish. It nourishes the growing fish until it is able to feed itself.

INDEX

Index of Scientific Names

ACKNOWLEDGMENTS

This book was the work of a dedicated team of authors, photographers, and illustrators, plus a huge network of specialists and suppliers, to whom we would like to express our gratitude.

First, thanks to Martin at Photo Summit, whose coffee and excellent prints helped to get the book started; to John Wilson for his time, hospitality, and advice; to Mike Millman for his help and his willingness to try the impossible at short notice; to Ron Worsfold for the loan of his pole rigs; and to the late and much-missed Trevor Housby for his advice and encouragement.

Of all our suppliers, special mention must be made of Don Neish and Peter Morley at Don's of Edmonton, for supplying tackle at ludicrously short notice. Other individuals and companies whose contributions were especially valuable were Simon Bond (Shimano); Alan Bramley and Fiona Hemus (Partridge of Redditch); Bob Brownsdon (Shakespeare); Peter Drennan and daughter Sally (Drennan International); Sue and Chris Harris (Harris Angling Company); Chris Leibbrandt (Ryobi Masterline); David McGinlay (Daiwa); and John Rawle (Cox & Rawle).

We would also like to thank Richard Banbury (Orvis); Breakaway Tackle; Browning; Paul Burgess (Airflo); Jeremy Buxton (Asset Optics); Pat Byrne (D.A.M); Alan Caulfield (Penn); Darren Cox (DCD); Roy Eskins (HUFFishing); Brendan Fitzgerald (House of Hardy); Michael McManus (Carroll McManus); Nick Page (Nican Enterprises); Graeme Pullen (Blue Water Tackle); Andrew Reade (Keenets); Nicholas Stafford-Deitsch (Edington Sporting Co.); Mike Stratton (Thomas Turner & Sons); B. W. Wright (Nomad); Val and Chris (Vanguard Tackle, Boston); Bruce Vaughan and Dennis Moss (Wychwood Tackle); Clive Young (Young's of Harrow); and Nick Young (Leeda).

Finally, special thanks to Barbara, Hilary, and Jane for their support in difficult times; to the unflappable Janet at Ace; to Steve, Andy, Tim, Nick, Sara, and Gary at the studio; to Krystyna and Derek at Dorling Kindersley for their patience; and to Peter Kindersley, whose confidence allowed it to happen.

CREDITS

Illustrators
Colin Newman *pages 124–203*
Ian Heard *pages 210–219, 226–259*
Lyn Cawley *pages 82–87, 92–93, 208–209*
Alan Suttie *pages 15, 52, 206, 223–225, 259*
Maurice Pledger *pages 220–221*

Photographers
Key: *t* top, *c* center, *b* bottom, *l* left, *r* right.

2 Peter Gathercole
3 Steve Gorton
6 Trevor Housby
7 t Mansell Collection, *c* Tim Heywood, *b* Mike Millman
8 t Trevor Housby, *c, b* Peter Gathercole
9 t, c Mike Millman, *b* John Wilson
10 John Wilson
12 Mike Millman
14–31 Steve Gorton and Andy Crawford
32–33 Steve Gorton; *antique reel by* Rodney Coldron
34–53 Steve Gorton and Andy Crawford
54–57 Peter Gathercole
58–79 Steve Gorton and Andy Crawford

80 John Wilson
82–87 Steve Gorton
88–91 Steve Gorton and Andy Crawford
92–93 Steve Gorton; *worms, sandeel by* Mike Millman
94–95 Mike Millman
96–97 Steve Gorton

98–121 Peter Gathercole, *with additional photos 100 t, 102 b* by Heather Angel

122 Oxford Scientific Films/Richard Davis
123 Oxford Scientific Films/Rudolf Ingo Riepl

204 Peter Gathercole
206–209 Steve Gorton
210 t Andy Crawford, *c* John Wilson, *b* Mike Millman
211 t and b John Wilson, *c* Peter Gathercole
212 Jim Tyree
213 Jim Tyree, *b* John Wilson
214 Steve Gorton
215 t Steve Gorton, *tl and c* John Wilson
216–218 Steve Gorton
219 t Steve Gorton, *b* John Wilson
220–221 Steve Gorton
222 t and b Steve Gorton, *c* Jim Tyree
223 c and br Jim Tyree, *bl* Steve Gorton
224 t Steve Gorton, *b* Jim Tyree
225 t Steve Gorton, *c* Jim Tyree
226–227 Jim Tyree
227 b Rodney Coldron
228 Jim Tyree, Andy Crawford
229 Mike Millman, Andy Crawford
230 John Wilson
231 t and b Steve Gorton, *cl and cr* John Wilson
232 c Steve Gorton, *b* Peter Gathercole
235 tl and tr Peter Gathercole
236 c Steve Gorton, *t and b* Peter Gathercole
237 Peter Gathercole
238–243 Peter Gathercole
244 John Darling
246 Mike Millman
249 Mike Millman
250–251 Jim Tyree
251 tr John Darling
252–253 Steve Gorton
253 c John Darling
254–255 Mike Millman
257 John Darling
258–259 Trevor Housby

261 Heather Angel
262 t Peter Gathercole, *b* John Wilson
263 John Wilson
264 t John Darling, *c* Jim Tyree, *b* John Wilson
265 tr Peter Gathercole, *b* Rodney Coldron
266 t Peter Gathercole, *c* Jim Tyree, *b* John Wilson
267 c John Wilson, *b* Mike Millman
268–269 John Wilson
270 c Jim Tyree, *b* Mike Millman
271–273 Mike Millman
274 t and b Phill Williams, *c* Mike Millman
275 t Mike Millman, *b* Phill Williams
276 Mike Millman
277 c John Wilson, *b* Mike Millman
278 Peter Gathercole
279 t Oxford Scientific Films, *b* Mike Millman

Manufacturers and Suppliers
The tackle was supplied by the manufacturers named in the main body of the book, except the Abu tackle, which was supplied by Don's of Edmonton. The floats, pages 62–63, were supplied by Drennan, and the Milo pole floats by Keenets. The lures, pages 88–91, were provided by Harris Angling Company. The flies were tied by Peter Gathercole. Other suppliers who have provided equipment for this book include:

Airflo, Fly Fishing Technology Ltd., Powys;
Asset Optics, Oxfordshire;
Blue Water Tackle, Hampshire;
Breakaway Tackle, Suffolk;
Browning, Bedfordshire;
Carroll McManus Ltd., East Sussex;
Cox & Rawle, Essex;
Daiwa Sports Ltd., Strathclyde;
D.A.M. (UK) Ltd., Worcestershire;
DCD, Warwickshire;
Don's of Edmonton, London;
Drennan International Ltd., Oxford;
Edington Sporting Co., Wiltshire;
Harris Angling Company, Norfolk;
House of Hardy, London;
HUFFishing, Bedfordshire;
Keenets (UK) Ltd., Wiltshire;
Leeda Group, Worcestershire;
Nican Enterprises, Hampshire;
Nomad UK, Lancashire;
Orvis, Hampshire;
Partridge of Redditch, Worcestershire;
Penn UK, Strathclyde;
Ryobi Masterline Ltd., Gloucestershire;
Shakespeare Company (UK) Ltd., Worcestershire;
Shimano Europe, Swansea;
Thomas Turner & Sons, Berkshire;
Vanguard Tackle, Lincolnshire;
Wychwood Tackle, Oxfordshire;
Youngs of Harrow, Middlesex.

INSIDE BOXING

PARIS
PARIS
PARIS
BUTCH
Bud

INSIDE BOXING

Robert Seltzer

MetroBooks

MetroBooks
An Imprint of Friedman/Fairfax Publishers

Library of Congress Cataloging-in-Publication Data

Seltzer, Robert.
Inside boxing / Robert Seltzer.
p. cm.
Includes index.
ISBN 1-56799-821-6
1. Boxing—United States—History—20th century. 2. Boxers (Sports)—United States—Biography. I. Title.

GV1125 .S45 2000
796.83--dc21

99-059128

Editor: Benjamin Mott
Art Director: Jeff Batzli
Designer: Charles Donahue
Photography Editor: Valerie Kennedy
Production Managers: Camille Lee and Maria Gonzalez

Color separations by Leefung Asco Repro Ltd. Co.
Printed in China by Leefung Asco Printers Ltd.

1 3 5 7 9 10 8 6 4 2

For bulk purchases and special sales, please contact:
Friedman/Fairfax Publishers
Attention: Sales Department
15 West 26th Street
New York, NY 10010
212/685-6610 FAX 212/685-1307

Visit our website:
www.metrobooks.com

19.99

Dedication

To the three most wonderful people in my little corner of the world.

Acknowledgments

Boxing is the most brutal sport in the world, a sport that makes football and hockey look like a Thursday afternoon bridge game. But exploring its history has been a rich, enlightening endeavor, one in which I was assisted by friends and colleagues throughout the country.

I owe a huge debt to Gary Miles, a fine writer and editor at the *Philadelphia Inquirer*. Without his help and recommendation, this book would not have been possible. I also would like to thank all my editors at Barnes & Noble Publishing, especially Nathaniel Marunas, who provided invaluable help as we reached the end of the project.

I began researching this book long before I knew I would write it. And for that, I want to thank my fellow sportswriters, men who shared their wisdom with me in bars and arenas throughout the country, sometimes thoughtfully, sometimes sardonically, but always with a passion and insight that stamped them as experts. They include men like Ed Schuyler, Jr., Pat Putnam, Royce Feour, Joe Maxse, Tom Archdeacon, Tom Loverro, Tim Kawakami, Chris Thorne, Wallace Matthews, Bill Stickney, Ron Borges, Bert Sugar, Michael Katz, and many more.

For every editor who has ever struggled with my prose on deadline, especially Gary Howard, now the sports editor of the *Milwaukee Journal Sentinel*, I would like to extend my hand...and sympathy.

I thank Bill Knight and Robert Holguin, who provided both encouragement and advice throughout this project. I also would like to thank the management of the *El Paso Times*, especially executive editor Dionicio "Don" Flores, who has always encouraged boxing coverage in the sports section of his paper. I am indebted, also, to Nora Salazar and Judy Soles McMillie, both of whom are as efficient as they are patient. And a special thank you to Lulu Ballesteros, whose heart is as broad as her smile.

Finally, I would like to thank three of the finest writers I have known...my Dad, who encouraged my love of books and boxing; my daughter, Katy, who once wrote her own (condensed) version of *Animal Farm* for a grade school English assignment; and my son, Christopher, who once consoled me over an editorial I had written, saying, "Don't worry, Dad. I know there's not much room for poetry in the newspaper business."

—El Paso, Texas, June 2000

PAGE 2: Oscar De La Hoya and Felix Trinidad (both of whom were undefeated welterweight champions at the time thanks to today's infinitely subdivided championship belts) squared off in one of the modern era's most highly anticipated fights on September 18, 1999. ABOVE: Two of the great lightweights of their day shake hands before a fight: powerful left-hander Lew Tendler (left) and ring legend Benny Leonard. These men fought two epic bouts, one in 1922 and the next almost a year later to the day, in 1923. The first fight was ruled a no-decision after 12 rounds, and the second was won by Leonard, by decision, after 15. Born Benjamin Leiner in 1896, Leonard was one of the greatest lightweights ever to step into the ring. He was a near-perfect balance of power, speed, agility, and strategy; moreover, he was a successful Jewish fighter at a time when Jews were discouraged from participating in professional boxing. Leonard defended the lightweight crown for an amazing stretch of 7 years, 7 months. PAGES 6–7: Rocky Marciano folds Jersey Joe Wolcott over with a murderous left to the midsection during the 4th round of their famous title bout on September 23, 1952.

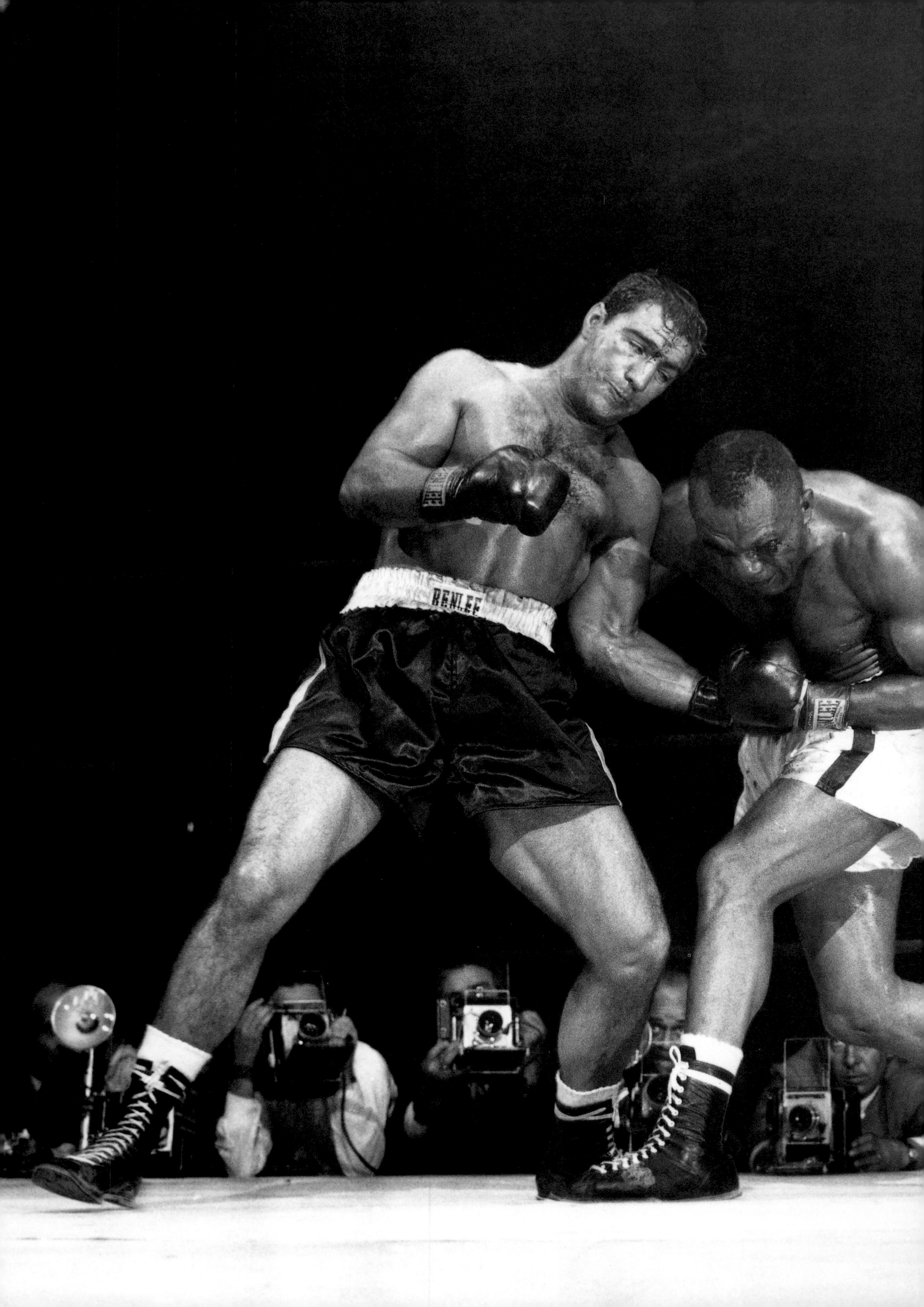
BENLEE

CONTENTS

EV LAST

Introduction

If boxing ever became a kind of fencing with fists, a mere trial of skills, reflexes and agility, and not the test of courage, will and resilience that it is now, then it would lose its appeal for many who are neither sadists nor seekers after the trappings of virility.

—Hugh McIlvanney

Hell is not roped off. The ring is. And that may be the only difference between the two venues. Boxing is a ballistic ballet, a sport that can be lovely one minute, ugly the next. The beauty? Well, it is embodied in wondrous athletes such as Sugar Ray Robinson and Muhammad Ali, both of whom turned the ring into a ballroom, their movements so precise they appeared to be choreographed. But the beauty is everywhere, even in less graceful boxers such as Julio Cesar Chavez. He was not a dancer, but he was a marvel in his prime, his skills as subtle as they were incandescent—a dip of the shoulder here, a twitch of the head there. Poetry in motion? Well, yes, but it was more than that. It was poetry in commotion, because boxing is the most devious sport of all. Great boxers are great con men. They lead their opponents into thinking that they will do one thing, only to turn around and do another. They are pickpockets, not muggers.

Who could forget, for example, Ali performing his rope-a-dope routine against George Foreman in Zaire, Africa, during the legendary "Rumble in the Jungle" on October 30, 1974? Ali leaned against the ropes, a move that invited Foreman to pound his tender ribs. Ah, but there was one thing Foreman did not count on: those ribs, those inviting ribs, were not as vulnerable as his own psyche. Foreman, who would prove to be a wiser man during his comeback years, fell into a trap that night. Yes, Ali looked like a human percussion instrument, daring to get pounded by a bigger, stronger, younger man. But it was Foreman, not Ali, who got thumped. The heavyweight champion, sapped from punching an opponent who refused to wilt, grew fatigued in the middle rounds, his arms so heavy they seemed welded to his sides. And then, in the 8th round, Ali struck, knocking out the champion with a thunderbolt of a right hand. Foreman landed on his back and, struggling to his feet, looked up at the African sky, almost as if he thought the punch had emerged from the heavens. Perhaps it had. The pickpocket had overwhelmed the mugger; the beauty had conquered the brute. "Muhammad outsmarted me," Foreman would say years later. "That's all there is to it."

But if boxing can be as lovely as ballet, it can also be as brutal as a brawl in a back alley. For every Ali, Robinson, and Chavez, there is a pug out there, somewhere, intent on disgracing the sport that the great champions have elevated to

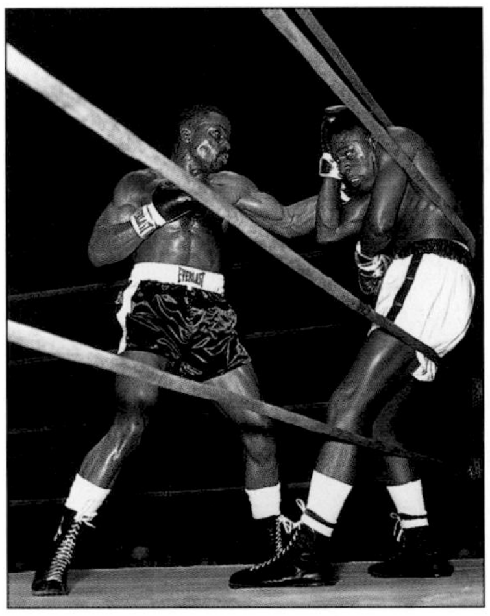

OPPOSITE: **Sugar Ray Robinson, his trunks stained with blood, is declared the winner in his brutal battle for the middleweight crown against Jake La Motta on February 14, 1951. The first and only person to have beaten Robinson up until then? La Motta, who had pulled the feat off way back on February 5, 1943.** ABOVE: **Rubin "Hurricane" Carter drives a cowering George Benton into the ropes during their 10-round bout on May 25, 1963, in New York City. Although Benton was the higher ranked middleweight going into the fight, Carter won the split decision over the Philadelphia native. Both men would go on to become quite famous, Carter as the long-suffering victim of a racist miscarriage of the U.S. judicial system (he was falsely convicted of a triple homicide and sent to prison for nineteen years) and Benton as one of the great trainers of his day.**

LEFT: Muhammad Ali and Joe Frazier, two of the greatest heavyweight fighters in history, beam for the cameras. Though their bouts are the stuff that boxing legends are made of, and though they maintained a heated feud out of the ring (mainly due to the rigors of self-promotion), it is tempting to think that the two men would have been good friends in another life.

EVERLAST

art. Is Mike Tyson, the former heavyweight champion of the world, the greatest pug in boxing history? Perhaps that is too harsh. Yes, he has been guilty of repulsive and illegal behavior, but he has paid for that behavior. Tyson is a lonely, confused, miserable man, his insecurities so profound that he should have a psychiatrist in his corner. But boxing is an unforgiving sport, and nobody knows that better than Tyson, the terror of the heavyweight division from 1986 to 1990. Tyson lost his title, and then he lost his freedom, receiving a three-year prison sentence for raping a teenage beauty contestant on July 19, 1991. When he came back in 1995, he was not the "Iron Mike" who had knocked out 35 opponents and left a trail of prone bodies in his wake.

Opposite: Behold a scene from one of the most fabled fights of modern boxing history, when a resurgent Muhammad Ali rose from the ashes of his banishment from professional boxing and scorched the heavily favored George Foreman to reclaim the heavyweight championship in 1974. In this shot from the 5th round of the so-called "Rumble in the Jungle," Foreman slips a left through Ali's defenses and catches the challenger on the jaw. Above: On September 7, 1996, Mike Tyson mauls Bruce Seldon in the 1st round; a few seconds later, Tyson knocked Seldon out to capture the heavyweight title. The victory recalled Tyson's swift rise through the heavyweight ranks as an up-and-comer; he was so good for a stretch in the mid-1980s that most observers thought he was on the way to becoming one of the best ever.

Evander Holyfield stripped Tyson of his heavyweight title on November 9, 1996, in Las Vegas, and ripped off the cloak of invincibility "Iron Mike" had worn throughout much of his comeback. It was one of the biggest upsets in boxing history, but one man refused to be shocked, and he was the only man who counted—Holyfield. Who could blame him? Holyfield, after all, was no Bruce Seldon, the self-proclaimed "Atlantic City Express." Seldon met Tyson on September 7, 1996, in Las Vegas, but Seldon fought as if he wanted to win an Oscar, not a boxing match. Tyson landed a right to the jaw early in the 1st round, and Seldon performed a rumba, his legs moving independently of his torso. Tyson fired again and again, and the rumba intensified, becoming a rhythmic dance to the beat of the pounding Seldon felt in his head.

There was only one problem: the first blow landed, but the subsequent punches missed—finding air, not flesh. But Seldon did not care; he continued to dance, continued to feign a mild concussion, because he wanted the referee to stop the match. The referee finally obliged. The fight—no, the performance—lasted 109 seconds.

No, Holyfield was no Bruce Seldon. He performed no rumbas against Tyson. The fight was a dance, all right, but it was the ballistic ballet that all boxing fans crave. Holyfield pounded Tyson for 11 rounds, and the last blow was the cruelest of all—a right hand that sent Tyson into the ropes, battered and bloodied, his arms dangling like the sleeves of an empty jacket. The referee stopped the bout 37 seconds into the 11th round. Afterward, Tyson was uncharacteristically gracious. "He's a good fighter," Tyson said, still dazed, at the postfight press conference. "I'd like to fight him again."

The grace and dignity did not last long. Tyson and Holyfield met again on June 28, 1997, in Las Vegas—one of the wildest farces in boxing history. Tyson, unable to subdue Holyfield with his fists, resorted to his teeth. He bit the champion on both ears, took a chunk out of the right one, then spit it out as if it were a piece of gristle. The referee stopped the bout at the end of the 3rd round, when both fouls occurred. "I wanted to kill him," Tyson would say later. Tyson turned Holyfield into steak tartare, and the world recoiled in horror. The Nevada Athletic Commission responded swiftly and decisively, fining the fighter $3 million and revoking his license for one year. "I just snapped," Tyson said.

The great sportswriter Jimmy Cannon called boxing "the red-light district" of sports, and Tyson seemed to reinforce what critics had long suspected—that boxing is a sewer minus the manhole cover. But is it really? If Tyson lowered the sport, Holyfield elevated it. The champion forgave Tyson, confirming that Holyfield is a man of uncommon class and dignity, in clear contrast to his opponent. This act was the only saving grace to the sad, shabby episode of the biting incident—and a clear victory for the sport of boxing.

LEFT: Evander Holyfield, standing up to the man he branded a "bully," lands a right uppercut en route to his 11th-round knockout of Mike Tyson on November 9, 1996. Over the course of the rivalry between these two fighters, the behaviour of the devoutly religious and soft-spoken Holyfield proved to be the perfect antidote to Tyson's disreputable behavior and shrill pronouncements.

The Sport 1

"Cowardice disgusts you, no matter where it happens, no matter what form it takes. Bravery exalts a man. It can be pointless and done for dirty reasons, but the act itself never has demeaned the human race, although it is possible the motives may sicken you."
—Jimmy Cannon, *Nobody Asked Me, But...*

The origins of the sport of boxing are as dark and murky as a cave, which was probably the venue for the first match in boxing history. Think of it, two cave men performing in front of their tribes, their clans—the ancestors of Roberto Duran and Sugar Ray Leonard. If that sounds far-fetched, remember that boxing is the most visceral, brutal and, thus, primitive sport in the world. Every day, in bars and back alleys from Altoona, Pennsylvania, to Waco, Texas, to Lodi, California, men get arrested for doing what it is perfectly legal to do in the ring—beat the hell out of each other. And they have been doing it for centuries, thus continuing a tradition that started when the first pugilists made fists in a cave.

But is that really a sport? Is that really an art, as the great writer A.J. Liebling claimed? Does a guy in a white shirt and a black bow tie, also known as a referee, truly bring civility to an activity that seems so uncivilized? The answer is a resounding "yes." Liebling was right. Boxing is an art. Why? Because of men like Muhammad Ali and Sugar Ray Robinson. If Baryshnikov had been able to hook off the jab—and brag about it afterwards—he, not Ali, would have been "The Greatest." But it was Ali, a ballet artist with attitude, who lifted his sport to the ozone. "Me. We!" Ali once recited in the shortest poem he ever wrote—an ode to his favorite subject, himself.

But there were no Alis, no Robinsons, when the sport originated in those dark, gloomy caves. It was a grim, brutal activity, unrefined by art or humor or round-card girls. There were no million-dollar paychecks, no ring announcers, no promoters whose hair defied gravity. No, there were just two guys fighting for honor or food or territory. It was prehistoric mayhem.

Ancient stone carvings indicate that the Sumerians, who lived in what is now Iraq, boxed at least five thousand years ago. They were the forerunners of Ali and Robinson, and they spread the activity to other parts of the ancient world, including Greece, where the sport became a brutal, ugly spectacle. Two men would sit on flat stones, face to face, mano a mano, with their fists wrapped in strips of leather. There was a signal, the ancient equivalent of the opening bell, and the two men would batter each other until one of them fell to the ground, unconscious,

Opposite: John Sholto Douglas, the Marquess of Queensberry, changed boxing forever by bringing order to the chaos that had reigned in the boxing matches of his day. He lived in England from 1844 to 1900, but his rules became the foundation for the sport as the entire world came to know it.
Above: Light heavyweight Harry Greb, "the Pittsburgh Windmill," was one of the most ferocious fighters of his day, a boxer who rained physical abuse on his opponents in such frightening fashion that one writer described his style as "the Manly Art of Modified Murder." He was the only boxer to beat Gene Tunney, and he beat him severely, winning the light heavyweight crown in the process. Amazingly, Greb (born Edward Henry Berg) fought the last five years of his career blind in one eye, a fact he concealed. Tragically, Greb died at the age of 32 on the operating table.

ABOVE: **The ancient Greeks were avid practitioners of boxing, as this vase, which dates from the 6th century B.C., clearly illustrates. Note the leather wrapping around the contestants' fists; the Romans would later "improve" on this by weighting the leather (the *cesti*) with lead and in some cases even adding spikes.**

as flat as a cardboard cut-out. But that was not always the end of it. The winner would sometimes continue to pound his victim until he died.

In ancient Rome, a brutal sport became even more brutal. The boxers wore *cesti*, leather straps plated with metal, on their hands and forearms. It was an ugly, diabolical game. The contestants did not need swords, spears, or tridents, because their own limbs were the weapons; the slightest movement, the slightest forearm shiver, could blind or kill an opponent. But the brutality would not last; developed as a spectator sport, it eventually outraged the spectators, including the officers who developed it. Approximately 100 years before the birth of Christ, the Romans banned the sport.

The sport re-emerged in the early 1700s, when James Figg, one of the most famous athletes in England, introduced modern boxing to the world. He opened a boxing school in London, a latter-day gladiator camp, teaching his students the style that would become known as bare-knuckle fighting. But how did he arrive at a style that had eluded centuries of pugilists before him? Figg was a wrestler, but in one of those acts of serendipity that bridge the old world to the new, he grew tired of half-nelson this and full-nelson that, and he threw a punch. Yes, a punch. It may have been a jab or a hook or a cross—or, perhaps, a silly, awkward hybrid of all three. We are not sure. What is certain is that Figg started it all, helping to launch the procession of boxers that leads to contemporary champions such as welterweight dynamo Felix Trinidad. It was a modest beginning, but a beginning nonetheless.

In 1743, Jack Broughton yanked the sport one step—one bob and weave—closer to the twentieth century. He introduced rules to a sport that gloried in its lack of rules, and these codes became standards for all boxing matches. They were known as the London Prize Ring Rules, and they helped make the sport more civilized, although they may not seem civilized to contemporary boxing fans. One rule, for example, required that boxers continue to fight, without rest periods, until one man could no longer go on. Brutal? Undoubtedly. But the rules were intended to attract the nobility to this savage sport. Broughton also conducted boxing classes at the Haymarket Academy in London, advertising them as instructions in the mystery of boxing, the wholly British art for gentlemen.

And then it happened. In 1872, John Sholto Douglas—a British sportsman also known as the Marquess of Queensberry—sponsored a new boxing code. It was revolutionary, and the Marquess of Queensberry, building on the modest cornerstone of his compatriot James Figg, launched the modern era in the sport. John Sholto Douglas was to boxing what Elvis Presley was to rock 'n' roll—a dynamic figure who altered, forever, his chosen profession, his chosen world. The rules were so brilliantly simple that they have been taken for granted by every succeeding generation of boxers and fans. They required boxers to wear gloves, a requirement which would cut down on the brutal injuries that made the contestants look like walking hematomas. They called for three-minute rounds, rather than the one long continuous flurry of action under the old rules, with a one-minute rest period between rounds. The rules also stated that a man down on one knee could not be struck, and that a fallen man must be given 10 seconds to get back on his feet.

Pierce Egan, the great historian of what he called "boxiana," coined the term "the sweet science" in 1824. It was a lovely term, lending credibility to a sport filled with loutish brutes. But was it accurate? Egan detected a beauty, an artistry, in the sport, but he saw science and strategy where most fans saw chaos and mayhem. And the reason was simple—the sport was decades away from the revolution that the Marquess of Queensberry would engineer. And, even after the Marquess of Queensberry rules, the sport was slow to enact the code; some fights were waged under the rules, others were not, and that was true for both England and the United States. There was no rhyme or reason, no governing body, to legitimize the sport, to make sense of it. It was as haphazard, as unrefined, as a street fight.

"Sweet science" indeed. The sport was neither sweet nor scientific. Professional bouts were glorified cockfights, with the boxing matches staged on carnival or circus grounds, the "ring" provided by fans who held hands to form a wall of humanity. There were no rest periods, and fights lasted until one of the pugs, battered and exhausted, could no longer continue. Some fighters were so brutish that they frowned on throwing punches. Why be so elegant, so dainty, when tactics such as gouging, biting, and kicking were more effective?

It was out of this brutal environment that the great John L. Sullivan emerged. He was a neighborhood bully, but his neighborhood was the world—an area as vast as his ego. "I can lick any sumbitch in the house," he liked to say, and he was right. He stood 5-feet-11 (180cm) and weighed 180 pounds (82kg), and every ounce seemed to be concentrated in his right hand, which could unleash a lightning bolt of a punch. But the great John L. was not just a sporting figure; he was a social figure, famous for his exploits both inside and outside the ring. And what were those exploits? He was a drunk, a glutton, a bully, and a wife beater—and, yes, the country loved him, making him the first sports superstar of the American landscape, a Babe Ruth in short pants. But why? Why elevate a man so vile and despicable, a man who scorned all the qualities the country seemed to treasure—trust, loyalty, generosity, good will?

An Irish-American from a working class background in Roxbury, Massachusetts, he embodied the raw spirit of the country, a country that seemed without limits as it pushed westward in the late 1800s. The nation was exploding during the Industrial Revolution; according to the U.S. Census of 1880, New York became the first city to top one million. One million. If that was not exhilarating, if that did not fill you with pride, then, dammit, you were not an American. This was the United States of America, big and tough and sprawling, and nobody symbolized that toughness more than the great John L. himself. A scoundrel and a wastrel, he fought for liquor as readily as for cash,

Dapper in a dark suit, John L. Sullivan—"The Boston Strongboy," "The Hercules of the Ring," "The Prizefighting Caesar," "His Fistic Highness"—cuts a remarkably civilized figure for a man who became a legend by striding across the American cultural landscape smashing his bare fists into the faces of his opponents.

The Confusing World of Champions

In an age when fighters collect world titles as if they were postage stamps, the great boxers of yesterday—Jack Dempsey, Joe Louis, Sugar Ray Robinson—would be aghast.

Every last one of them would cringe at what is happening to their sport because they fought in an era in which there were eight weight classes, each division represented by one—count them, one—world champion.

Today, it has come to this: there are seventeen weight classes, and everybody but your cousin Fred is a champion of something or other.

Does that sound like an exaggeration?

Well, consider the number of organizations that sponsor world champions: there is the IBF, the WBA, the WBC, the WBO, the IBO, the IBC, the WBF, the WBU, the...

Is there an Elks Lodge in your area?

An American Legion Post?

A post office?

A bar?

They probably sponsor world champions, too.

And if you multiply the weight classes by the number of sanctioning bodies, that means there are almost as many world champions as there are fans to pay for their fights.

"It's ridiculous," says Eddie Futch, the former trainer, now 88. "The boxing organizations are worthless. I don't know how the public buys all of their shenanigans."

It has become so absurd that Eric Esch, also known as "Butterbean," is a champion—never mind that this "champ" boasts all the mobility of a heavy bag. He weighs more than 300 pounds, qualifying him as a human land mass, but he is not the heavyweight champion. No, he is the heavyweight champion of the four-rounder. Yes, he is an undercard fighter who reigns as a "world titlist," and his championship belt is as impressive as the belly that he cinches it around—you could tow a truck with that belt. Butterbean is sanctioned by the International Boxing Association, a fledgling group that does not boast many quality fighters. Butterbean makes about $50,000 per fight, about as much as strawweight champion Ricardo Lopez, one of the greatest fighters in the world, earns—a travesty to both Lopez and the sport he loves. But that is boxing for you.

"We know Butterbean's not a serious contender," said Dean Chance, a former major league pitcher who won the Cy Young award in 1964 and now runs the IBA. "But he's a great guy, and he's entertaining, and that's what it's all about." Is there anything wrong with that? Certainly not. Boxing has always boasted its share of entertainers: witness Chuck Wepner, the "Bayonne Bleeder," and Randall "Tex" Cobb, who took a brutal beating from then world heavyweight champion Larry Holmes on November 26, 1982, in Houston. Holmes, hugging the beaten fighter after the bout, offered him a rematch. "Sure," Cobb replied, "but next time we fight in a phone booth."

The entertainment is here to stay, and that is good. But the days when there were only eight weight classes are gone, and that is too bad. Not that boxing is devoid of quality champions, not at all. The sport still boasts fighters who could reign in almost any era—Evander Holyfield, Roy Jones, Felix Trinidad, Oscar De La Hoya.

So it is wrong to be bitter and crusty, looking at the old days as if they were the only days. It is just that, well, the world of champions was a lot less complicated when there were only eight weight classes. And only one champion in each class.

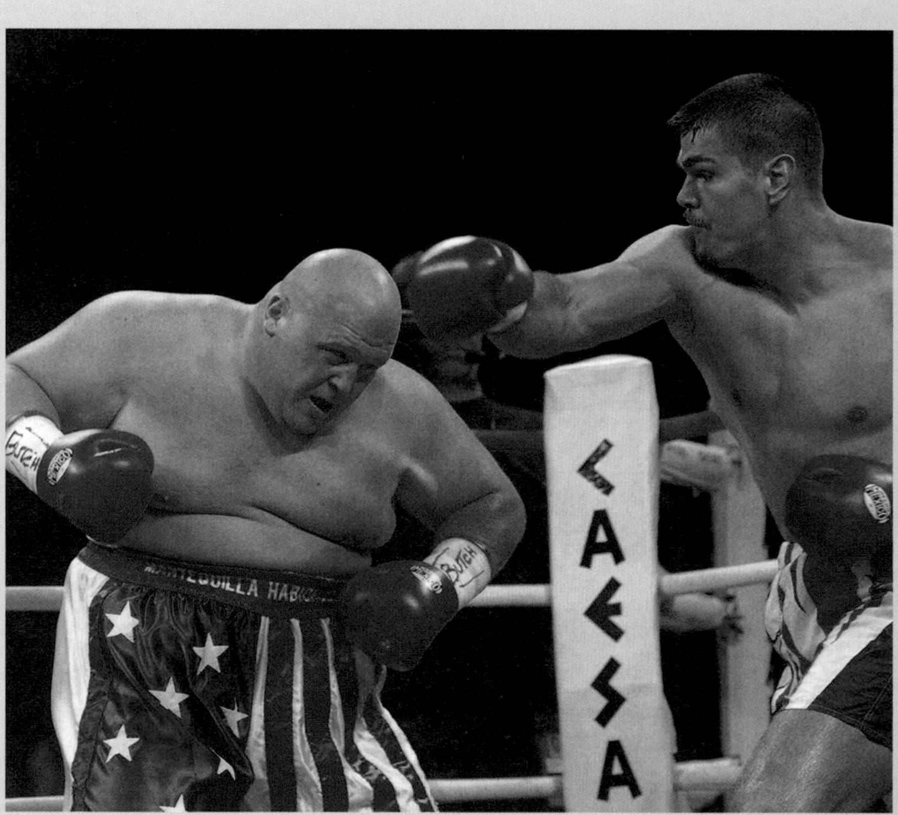

Eric Esch, the overweight boxer better known as Butterbean, blocks a punch with his head during a fight against Troy Roberts on September 18, 1998.

Copyrighted by John Wood N.Y.
John L. Sullivan

and the fans loved him for it. And why not? The citizens were conquering the country, and Sullivan was conquering every man in the house—it was a strange but ideal marriage.

Born decades too early to exploit scientific training regimens, Sullivan knew nothing about aerobics or weight training, not to mention diet and nutrition. Sullivan ingested calories at a pace that would add 30 or 40 pounds to his frame between fights, but he knew nothing about nutrition or metabolism. And what if he had been born in a later generation? What if he had been able to take advantage of modern training methods? Sullivan would have spit on modern training methods, just as he spit on opponents. He would sooner train with a drinking buddy than with a fitness guru. Tough guys drink, right? And Sullivan was a tough guy. He trained by walking mile after mile through the working class neighborhoods of Boston, stopping at every saloon along the way. If his right hand delivered a thunderous punch, and it did, it was from his version of weight lifting—the constant repetitions with a mug of beer, up and down, from the bar to his throat, over and over again. The great John L. could drink as passionately as he could fight. By modern standards, Sullivan was soft and fleshy, his belly bulging over pants so tight that they looked like a second layer of skin. But, belly or no belly, he impressed the sporting public. Fans were blinded by his aura. They looked at a fat guy, but they saw a statue, a man with the hard physique of a coal miner. They saw a legend.

"Look at the Statue," wrote John Boyle O'Reilly. "That is Sullivan, life, body and spirit. See the tremendous chest, filled with capacious lungs and a mighty heart, capable of pumping blood everywhere at once. See the ponderous fist and the massive wrist; and the legs and feet—ah! there you see the limbs of a perfect boxer—light as a dancer, firm as a tower. And then, look up to the buttressed, Samson neck, springing beautifully from the great shoulders; look at the head—large, round as a Greek's, broad-browed, wide-chinned, with a deep dimple, showing the good nature, and a mouth and lips that ought to be cut in granite, so full are they of doomful power and purpose."

Sullivan, already proclaiming himself the heavyweight champion of the world, yearned to prove it—not in the saloons, where he made his boasts, but in the ring, where his fists could make good on those boasts. He challenged Paddy Ryan, the true heavyweight champion of the world, deriding him from the pages of every sports section on the East Coast. Ryan finally relented. He met Sullivan in an outdoor arena on February 7, 1882, in New Orleans, Louisiana, where the *New Orleans Picayune* regretted that there was "no legal remedy to avert the disgusting spectacle," since an anti-boxing bill had been stalled in the legislature.

It may have been a "disgusting spectacle," but at least it was a short one. The fans had no sooner settled into their seats than Ryan was being deposited on his. The great John L. landed a right to the jaw, sending Ryan to the floor a mere 30 seconds after the fight started. Ryan struggled to his feet, but he would go down eight more times. The final knockdown came less than 11 minutes after the fight started, with Ryan sprawled on his back, as flat as an ink blot. His handlers threw in the sponge, the flag of surrender that would be replaced by the towel, and the sport crowned a new heavyweight champion of the world, bare-knuckle style—Sullivan could not only lick any sumbitch in the house, he could lick any sumbitch in the world. He was 23 years old.

OPPOSITE: Heavyweight champion John L. Sullivan, seen in this 1885 photograph striking a pugilistic pose in front of a woodsy backdrop, was a hero thanks to his exploits in and out of the ring. He was the last and greatest of the bare-knuckle champions. RIGHT: "Gentleman" Jim Corbett was the first boxing champion of the new breed: he trained heavily, used strategy to win fights, and fought wearing gloves. This photograph was taken in 1894, two years after his historic defeat of John L. Sullivan in what was the first official heavyweight bout to be fought under the Marquess of Queensberry rules.

RIGHT: This rare photograph (perhaps the only existing one ever taken of such a fight) shows the last official bare-knuckle bout in history, waged between John L. Sullivan and Jake Kilrain in a ring in rural Richburg, Mississippi, on July 8, 1889. Sullivan finally pounded Kilrain badly enough in the 75th round of the heavyweight title fight that Kilrain's trainers threw in the sponge before the next round could begin.

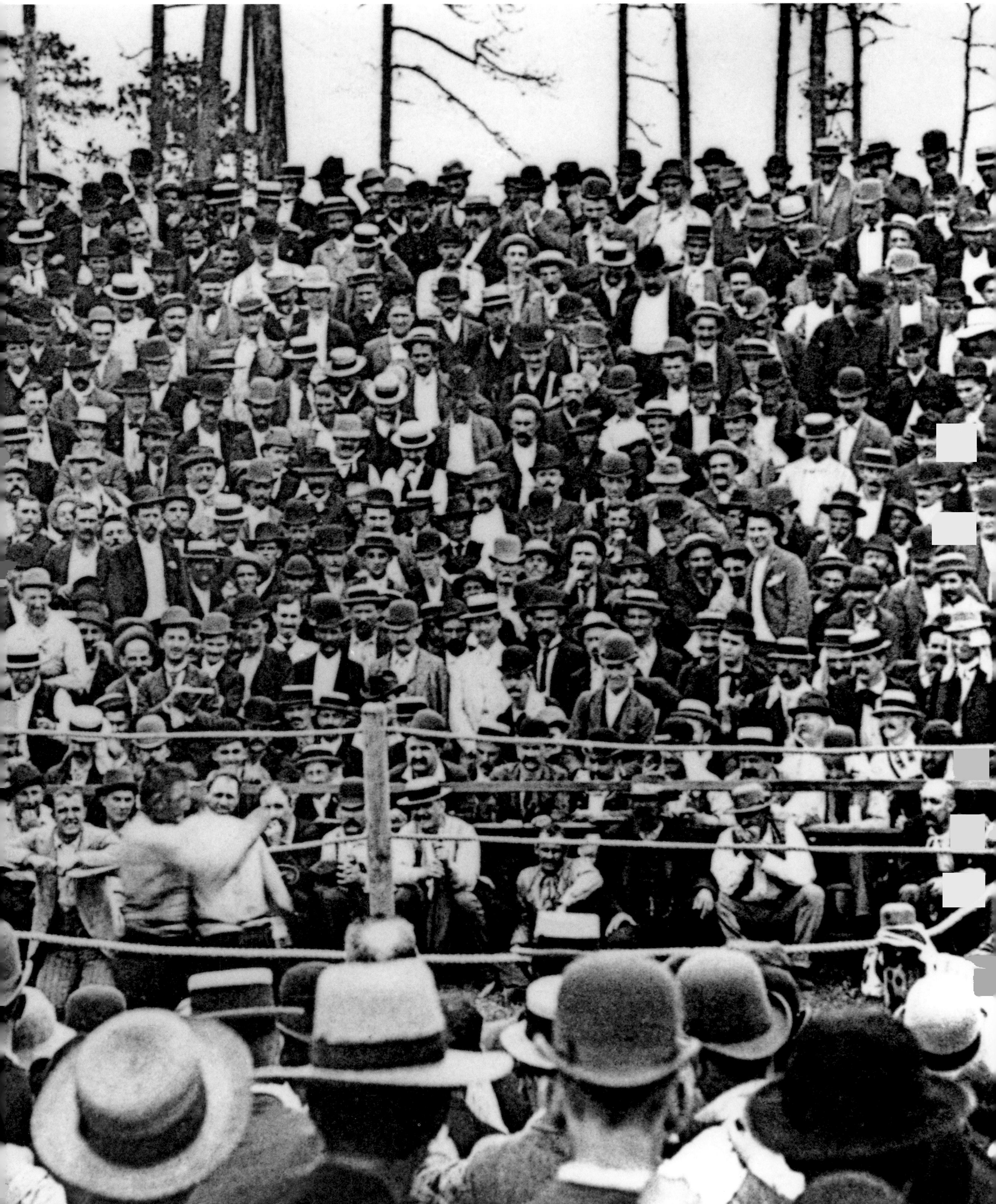

ABOVE: Known as "The Old Master," Joe Gans (right) was one of the slickest boxers of the early twentieth century. Here, Gans poses for the camera with challenger Mike "Twin" Sullivan in 1906. Born Joseph Gaines in 1874, Gans got his early pugilistic education in Baltimore, where he was prize fighting while just a teenager. At the age of 17, Gans won a rematch against lightweight champion Frank Erne with a knockout in the 1st round. By doing so, Gans became only the second fighter in modern history to win a championship in the 1st round and the first African-American ever to win the lightweight crown. Gans was one of the most scientific boxers of his day: he would carefully study his opponents to discover their weaknesses and then mercilessly put his observations to use in the ring. Sadly, this boxing pioneer died of tuberculosis at the tender age of 36. LEFT: Heavyweight Jack Johnson was one of boxing's trailblazers, as much for his talent as for his defiance of the status quo. At a time when integrated fights were frowned upon and popular opinion held that no black man could ever win the heavyweight championship, Johnson arranged to battle Tommy Burns for the crown. The landmark fight took place on December 26, 1908, in Sydney, Australia, and proved to be a mainly one-sided affair. Johnson brutalized Burns for almost 14 rounds before the local police brought the slaughter to a stop. Here, Johnson sizes up Burns during their famous bout.

On July 8, 1889, about seven years after he won the bare-knuckle title, Sullivan waged the last bare-knuckle fight in history. He met Jake Kilrain under a broiling sun near Biloxi, Mississippi, a spot now marked by a historical sign off the Gulf Coast, on Interstate Highway 12. "This is it," Bert Sugar, the boxing historian known for his prose and his cigar, would say 100 years later, standing only a foot from the sign. "This is it."

If Sugar regarded the site as a shrine, it is no wonder. The Sullivan-Kilrain match was one of the most grueling fights in boxing history—a fight in which the two men tried to subdue not just each other, but also their desire to lie down and quit, just flat quit, out of a fatigue so complete it was mind-numbing. And who could have blamed them? The fight lasted 75 rounds—75 rounds—a figure hard to grasp for a generation in which a 12-round bout qualifies as an epic match. It went on for two hours, 16 minutes and 23 seconds—an eternity for the men who endured the savagery on a day fit for the gate-keepers of hell.

In the 44th round, Sullivan began to vomit—the result, no doubt, of his drinking habits. Kilrain, seeing his chance for redemption, asked the champion, "Will you draw the fight?" And Sullivan, his belly still performing a rumba, roared back, "No, you loafer!" And so it went, for 10, 20, 30 more rounds. And then, in the 75th round, Sullivan fired a tremendous combination, his arms spinning like rotary blades, and Kilrain went down—a man beaten by the heat and the champion. Kilrain, slumped in his corner, refused to come out for the 76th round, and his handlers threw in the sponge.

The great John L. would never be so great again, his weaknesses exposed just as his hands were being covered—by gloves. He was 33 years old when he agreed to fight "Gentleman Jim" Corbett, who was as elegant as Sullivan was brutish, in 1892. The fight was waged under the Marquess of Queensberry rules, and Sullivan seemed lost—a pug matched against an artist. Corbett, a quick and clever fighter, outboxed the former bare-knuckle champion, helping to launch the era when boxing would become, once and for all, the "sweet science."

During the early 1900s, boxing remained illegal throughout most of the United States. Then in 1920, New York passed the Walker Law, which permitted public prizefighting—a huge breakthrough, considering that New York had hounded Sullivan less than 40 years earlier, forcing him to fight John Flood on a barge floating along the Hudson River. Those days of backroom brawling were over for good. In 1921, George "Tex" Rickard promoted the first match to draw a $1 million gate, the heavyweight championship bout between challenger Jack Dempsey and Frenchman Georges Carpentier on July 2, 1921, in Jersey City, New Jersey. The sport had arrived, legitimized by both fans and legislators, an astounding turn of events for a spectacle with such brutal origins and so rooted in the human tendency toward violence.

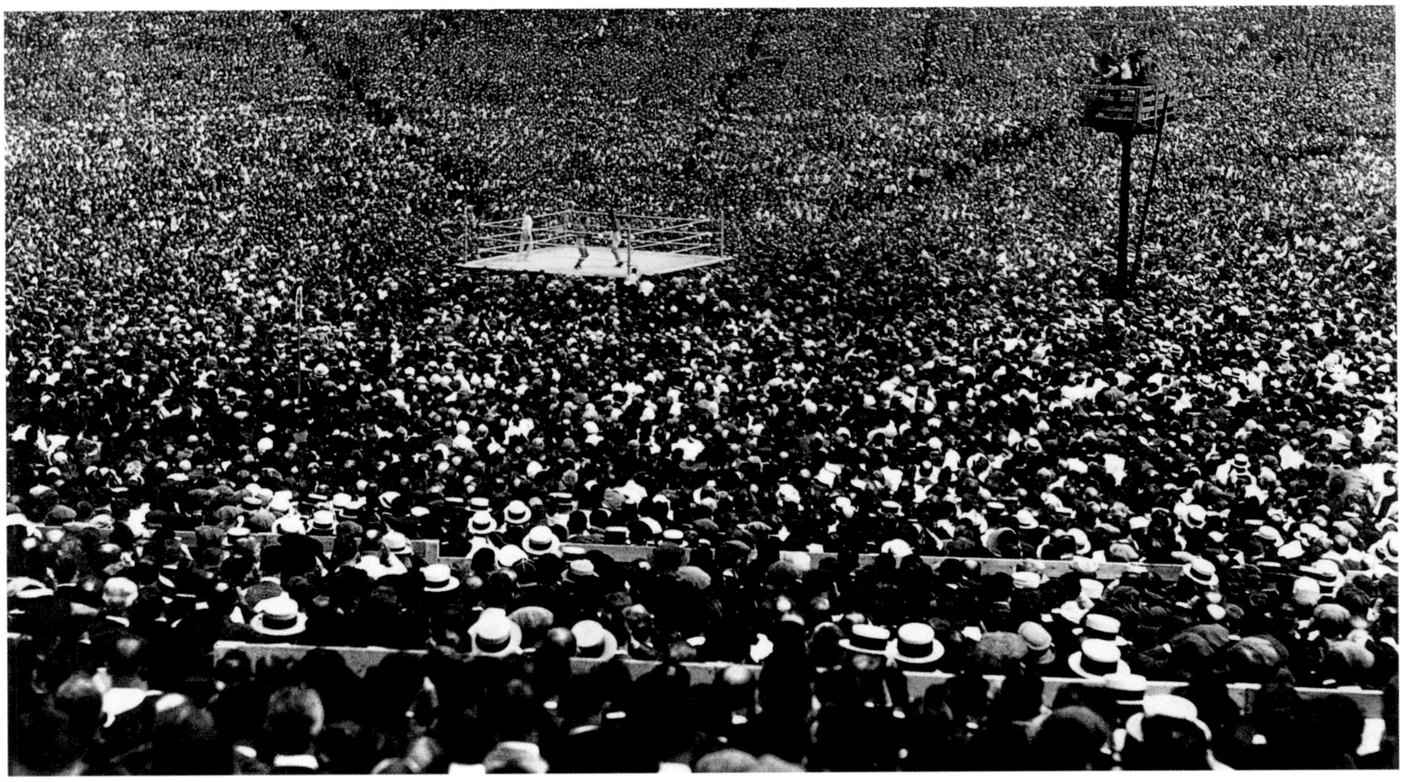

ABOVE: Above: By the early 1920s, professional boxing had become a full-blown sensation, as the impressive crowd for this July 2, 1921, fight between Jack Dempsey and Georges Carpentier shows. The first bout to attract a $1 million gate, it was billed as "The Battle of the Century." Alas, like so many overhyped contests before and since, the fight turned out to be something of a wash: Dempsey crushed his outclassed opponent in just the 4th round.

The Fighters 2

No one looking at his countenance could fail to see that he was a fighting man by profession, and any judge of the fancy, considering his 6 feet in height, his 13 stone of solid muscle, and his beautifully graceful build, would admit that he had started his career with advantages which, if they were only backed by the driving power of a stout heart, must carry him far.

—Sir Arthur Conan Doyle, *The Lord of Falconbridge*

Fighters are prisoners of their bodies, their physiques the stone walls that trap them, that force them to fight in a certain style. Take Joe Frazier, the former heavyweight champion, for example. Frazier was short and squat, with a punch that could travel from his instep to your chin, and he fought with the fury of a scorned lover. He was a great fighter, not a great boxer, because he was not built for boxing; he was built for back-alley brawls. "I'll be a-smokin," he liked to say before his fights, describing his rough-and-tumble style. "Just like always." Frazier rarely threw the jab—one of the few great fighters in history who excluded that punch from his arsenal—but he boasted surprisingly good defense, his head bobbing with the frenetic motion of a speed bag. And he was so intimidating that George Foreman, who ended up defeating him for the heavyweight title, was terrified of him. "I was afraid of him," Foreman said. "I didn't want to fight him. I knew he loved to ride that motorcycle of his, and I was hoping he'd get into a crash and die before the fight. Frazier was mean, man, vicious. He could hit like a mule, but that wasn't the worst of it. You'd hit him, and he'd smile. Scary."

OPPOSITE: Junior welterweight champion Julio Cesar Chavez celebrates his 2nd-round knockout of Scott Walker on February 9, 1996. ABOVE: One of the classic rivalries of boxing was between these two men, Jake LaMotta and Sugar Ray Robinson. Where Robinson was poetry in motion, the very embodiment of coordination and fluid power, LaMotta was stolid and sturdy, an earthbound, muscular fighter who was capable of weathering unbelievable abuse. Together they produced some of boxing's great match-ups.

Muhammad Ali, who met his short, squat counterpart in three epic bouts, was different. Tall and sleek, with a spine that seemed to be made out of cartilage rather than bone, he was remarkably supple, able to bend his back to avoid punches that were all but certain to slam him—crunch—right in the jaw. Like all great boxers, Ali hated to get hit, so he maintained a zone, a distance, between himself and his opponent—a kind of force field that prevented him from getting rapped on the jaw. He did not mind taking shots to the belly—witness his open invitation to George Chuvalo, who hit him at will in the midsection on March 29, 1966, in Toronto—but the chin, well, that was another story. Ali did not want that. So he would dance from side to side, the ultimate moving target, always staying close enough to punch but far enough to keep from getting punched. It was a delicate balance, one that he maintained throughout much of his career. "Can't nobody beat me," Ali would scream. "I'm too pretty." He was a boxer.

Two fighters, two styles—one a raw, unpolished brawler, the other an elegant dancer. Why were they so different? They were limited by their bodies, although their skills—and their hearts—allowed them to overcome whatever limitations their physiques imposed on their styles. And that is true not just of Ali and Frazier, but of every great fighter who has ever stepped into the ring. There is no blueprint, no outline, for greatness in this sport. A great fighter may be as coarse and unrefined as Jake LaMotta, the "Raging Bull," or as subtle and efficient as Julio Cesar Chavez, "el gran campeon Mexicano"—the great Mexican champion. Ultimately, great fighters share only two qualities: a fierce desire to win and the ability to achieve that win, with whatever style they choose—or whatever style their bodies choose for them.

Jack Johnson

Proud and arrogant, a furious puncher, he should have been the hero, the darling, of the United States of America, just as John L. Sullivan had been a generation before. He boasted, after all, many of the traits that endeared the great John L. to the sporting public—he was smug and boastful, with a taste for both liquor and women. This janitor's son was also, throughout most of his career, unbeatable.

Born in Galveston, Texas, in 1878, Jack Johnson also happened to be black, and so, unlike John L. Sullivan, he was vilified, the target of a country that preferred its heroes white. The great John L. had refused to defend his title against black fighters, and the world applauded his decision. But Tommy Burns, then the world heavyweight champion, gave Johnson a shot, and Johnson made history, slamming white America in the gut with his victory.

Johnson proved that power and cunning could elevate a man above narrow thinking and within reach of the heavyweight title. Johnson, who stood 6 feet 1¼ inches (186cm) and weighed 192 pounds (87kg), was not just a great fighter; he was a superb boxer, his hand speed so startling that he seemed to be playing patty-cake with his opponents.

Johnson won the world heavyweight title on December 26, 1908, in Sydney, Australia, stopping Burns in the 14th round, and in the process becoming the first black man to rule the world with his fists—and, some hoped, the last. Johnson floored Burns with a peculiar punch: a right uppercut that he delivered without pivoting, like one of those rock-'em-sock-'em robots that would hit toy stores several generations later. It was a punch that packed both fistic and social significance—Jack Johnson, black heavyweight champion. The racists came out of hiding, storming the fighter like ants attacking a picnic table. One of them was the great American adventure writer Jack London, who apparently reserved his love and sensitivity for wild dogs, not black heavyweight champions.

"The fight, if fight it must be called, was like that between a pigmy and a colossus," London, reporting from ringside for the *New York Herald*, wrote. "A dew drop had more of a chance than Burns with the giant Texan." London called for a former champion, James J. Jeffries, to come out of retirement and challenge the black title holder. "Remove that golden smile from Jack Johnson's face," London exhorted. Jeffries, who emerged from his alfalfa farm in California, challenged Johnson on July 4, 1910, in Reno, Nevada—the first of a procession of Great White Hopes. Johnson stopped him in the 15th round, conquering both his opponent and his racist supporters. But the racists would have their day. Age and fast living caught up to Johnson, and they were more brutal than any opponent he had faced in the ring.

Convicted of violating the Mann Act for transporting a white woman, Belle Schreiber, from Pittsburgh to Chicago for "immoral purposes" (a trumped-up charge using a statute created to stop organized crime), the champion jumped bail and fled to Europe in 1913. He continued to fight, successfully defending his title three times, but he conducted most of his "training" sessions at nightclubs in Paris, and he became slow and awkward.

On April 5, 1915, in Havana, Cuba, he fought Jess Willard, the latest in a series of white challengers. The promoter lured the champion by suggesting that federal authorities would consider a pardon if he lost the fight—a suggestion that would fuel speculation and debate for years to come. Willard floored the heavyweight king in the 26th round. Johnson, then 37, lay on the canvas for several minutes, shielding his eyes from the fierce sun—proof, skeptics suggested, that he

Opposite: Two of the greatest fighters of the early 1900s, middleweight champion Stanley Ketchel (left) and heavyweight champion Jack Johnson (center), pose with boxing official Jim Coffrath before their bout on October 16, 1909, won by Johnson with a 12th-round knockout. Johnson added the middleweight crown to his collection with the win.

CABLE Co

could have risen from the knockdown. Whether or not he took a dive, the former champion never got the pardon that the promoter had waved in his face. Johnson returned to the United States in 1920, serving nine months of his sentence at Leavenworth Penitentiary in Kansas. Johnson died in a car accident on June 10, 1946, in Raleigh, North Carolina. He was 68.

Jack Dempsey and Gene Tunney

They were the Ali and Frazier of their era—the brawler and the boxer, inextricably linked by their two historic meetings. Jack Dempsey was the brawler, Gene Tunney the boxer, and as with all timeless pairings, their fights were great theater, providing so much drama that fans still discuss the matches generations later. And who could blame them? The fights were classics.

Tunney defeated Dempsey in both fights, and the country never forgave him. Dempsey was a hero or, more appropriately, an anti-hero—Babe Ruth with a scowl, a charismatic figure who enchanted the public with his fierce determination. He was the John L. Sullivan of his era, minus some of the vices, and captured the imagination of a country that still treasured toughness and individuality. Dempsey was a legend, and unlike most such figures, he did not have to retire before the status was bestowed upon him; he earned it during his career.

Born and raised in Manassa, Colorado, the ninth of thirteen children born to poor and hard-luck parents, William Harrison Dempsey left home in his teens, hopping freight trains and working in copper mines in Colorado and Utah. He toiled in the pits, and he chewed pine tar, a habit that strengthened his jaw against the assaults he would soon face in the ring. The ring? The world was his ring, at least in the beginning, because he stood up to the bullies and roughnecks in the mining camps, developing the reputation that would lead to his nickname, "the Manassa Mauler." The teenager tired of working for pay and fighting for free, and he hit the freights again, this time stopping not at mining camps but at saloons, where he could fight for small purses. He adopted the name Jack after the great nineteenth-century lightweight—a name that he graced with his exploits in the ring. Dempsey destroyed Jess Willard, the erstwhile "Great White Hope," on July 4, 1919, in Toledo, Ohio, battering him so brutally that the Dempsey camp, according to legend, found a tooth embedded in one of his gloves. The fighting hobo was the new heavyweight champion, a popular but somewhat malignant presence on the boxing landscape. Sportswriters described his "concentrated cruelty," his "will to kill": "His body, muscled like a panther cat's, seems to ignite with malice, to burn and flash; then his fists reach out, savagely, lethally to destroy the weaving shape in front of him and get revenge for something he has just remembered, a wrong done, a score that must be evened, something that happened to him long ago," penned an awed writer in *Time* magazine.

Tunney was different. He was a delicate man in a savage sport—tall and handsome, with unmarked features that he wanted to keep unmarked. He was born in Greenwich Village, New York, the son of respectable working-class parents. Tunney was bright and articulate, often more so than the sportswriters who were forced to thumb through another play by Shakespeare or another novel by William Somerset Maugham to track down another quotation, another pearl of wisdom, from this most unusual of heavyweight prizefighters.

If he was gentle and articulate outside the ring, Tunney was remarkably dainty and composed inside the ring—an ideal foil for his opponent. This was not

ABOVE: A souvenir program proved amazingly prescient in its use of the word "history" to describe the first championship bout between Jack Dempsey and Gene Tunney, on September 23, 1926. It proved to be a fight for the ages, and was another illustration of technique versus determination where technique (that is, Tunney) carried the day. OPPOSITE: Heavyweight champion Jack Dempsey, looking as solid and noble as a Greek statue in this photograph, was feared and admired for his "killer instinct," but it was his incredible hand speed, wicked left hook, and high tolerance for pain that made him a truly lethal opponent.

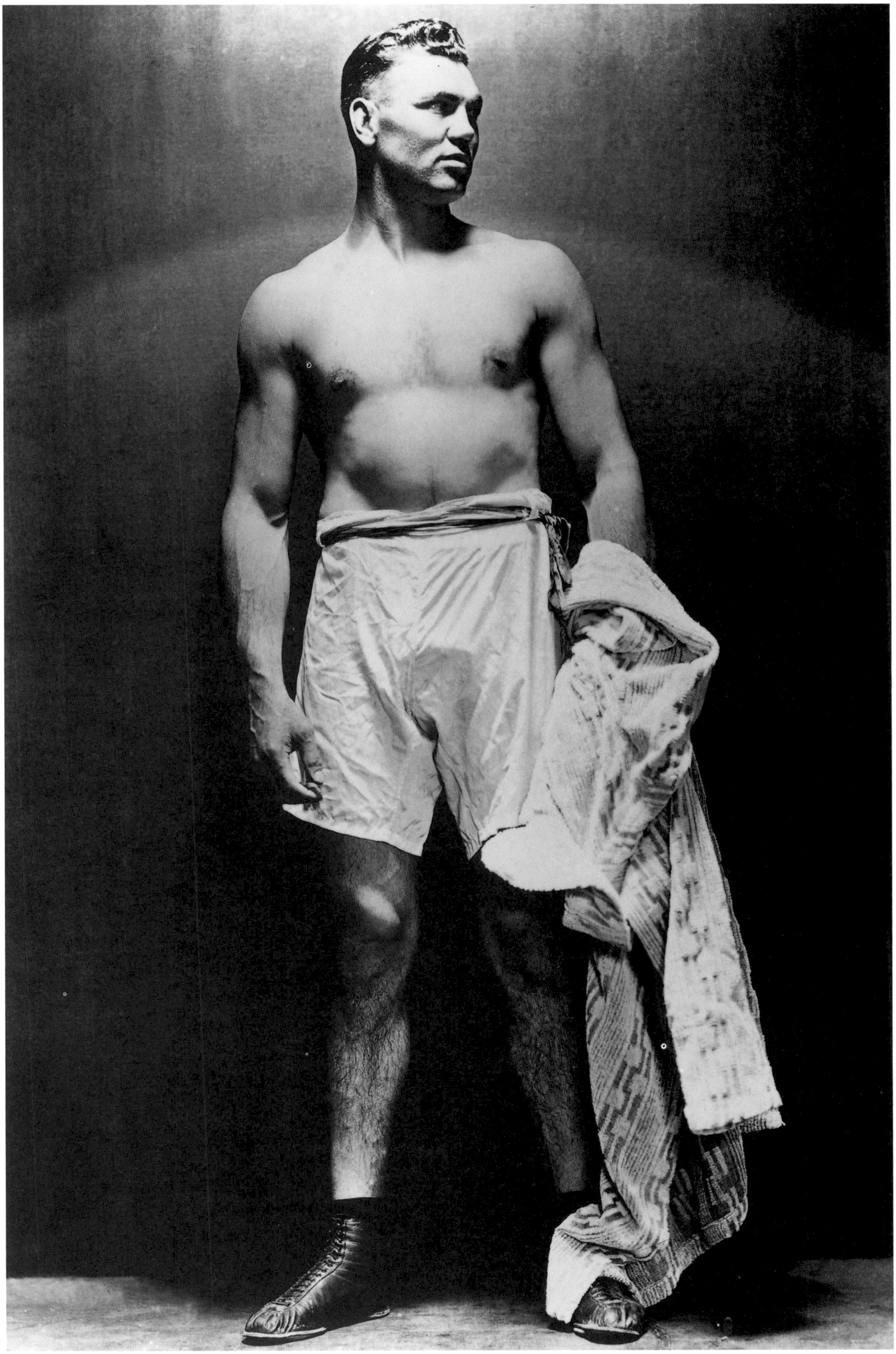

In the infamous "long-count" episode of the rematch between Dempsey and Tunney, the Manassa Mauler stands in his corner as the referee counts over the fallen Tunney. Tunney went on to win this September 22, 1927, bout by decision, but the 4 extra seconds he got on the mat tarnished the victory, adding an asterisk to what otherwise was another tactical masterpiece.

"the Manassa Mauler," a bruiser who would accept five punches for the privilege of delivering one. No, Tunney was a clever and shifty boxer, as elusive as a wisp of smoke—the forerunner of such great heavyweights as Ali and Larry Holmes. He was the perfect challenger for Dempsey.

"Gene Shows He Has No Carbon in Ring Machinery," a *Chicago Tribune* headline trumpeted before the two men faced each other in the ring. They met for the first time on September 23, 1926, in Philadelphia—a long-anticipated match between two of the greatest heavyweights in the world. Tunney won a clear-cut decision, frustrating the champion with his superior boxing skills. But if Dempsey lost in one arena, he won in another, because the public would grow to love him more in defeat than it had in victory. The antihero had become a hero. "Honey," Dempsey explained to his wife, "I forgot to duck."

They fought again almost exactly a year later, on September 22, 1927, in Chicago, marking the first $2 million gate in boxing history. The challenger staggered Tunney with a right hand in the 7th round, following up with a combination that dropped the champion onto the seat of his white silk trunks. There was only one problem: Dempsey failed to retreat to a neutral corner following the knockdown, as the rules of the day clearly stated. The referee shoved Dempsey into a neutral corner, thus giving the champion extra time to recover from the knockdown, although it seems clear that Tunney could have risen before 10 seconds, long count or no long count. Tunney went on to score another 10-round decision, but the long-count controversy persists to this day; right or wrong, it makes Dempsey shine more brightly than the man who defeated him, the gentle man in a savage sport.

Joe Louis

Almost thirty years after Jack Johnson won the heavyweight title, another black champion emerged on the scene—Joe Louis. But this was a different time, a different America, and the nation embraced Louis as passionately as it had scorned Johnson. The warmer response was hardly surprising. Louis was a proud but humble man, more quiet and dignified than his predecessor, who had behaved in a way that was unacceptable to bigoted Americans. "The Brown Bomber," as Louis was called, once said that his opponents "can run, but they can't hide," and that seems as close as he ever came to boasting.

Not that Louis escaped racism. How could he? He was a black man in the 1930s. "The Brown Bomber"? As offensive as that nickname might be to contemporary society, it was one of the milder tags that sportswriters hung on the gifted champion. They also called him "the Shufflin' Shadow," "the Dusky Downer," "the Dark Destroyer," "the Sable Cyclone," and "the Coffee-Colored Kayo King."

"A physician who has observed Louis...compares the bomber to a primordial organism; says in temperament, he is like a one-celled beastie of the mire-and-steaming ooze period," Meyer Berger wrote in *The New York Times Magazine* in 1936. "Fighting, he displays boxing intelligence tantamount to the stalking instinct of the panther....He becomes sheer animal."

Physicians—or sportswriters—rarely described white fighters in such an ugly and offensive manner. But they failed to understand one thing about Louis: he was a powerful man, perhaps the greatest punching machine to ever step into the ring, his combinations short and sweet and solid. He was also ruthless in the ring, exhibiting the coldhearted brutality of a contract killer. But most great fighters are ruthless; it is, after all, an ugly sport, a sport in which inflicting punishment and inflicting it often are the primary goals. Louis was no different in that regard.

ABOVE: As stoic as he was powerful, Joe Louis barely smiles as announcer Hal Totten raises the champ's arm in the aftermath of the Brown Bomber's crushing knockout of James J. Braddock on June 22, 1937. Embracing Louis is his manager, Julius Black. It was a stunning comeback: one year before Louis won the heavyweight championship from Braddock, the Bomber had been delivered his first beating, at the hands of Max Schmeling. OPPOSITE: On June 22, 1938—a year to the day after taking the heavyweight title from James Braddock—champion Joe Louis avenged his demoralizing loss to Max Schmeling by felling the German in the first round of the rematch. Here, Louis daintily steps back as he surveys what 124 seconds of pummeling has done to his opponent.

What truly set Louis apart from other boxers of the day—and what the racists failed to recognize—was that he was perhaps the smartest fighter of his generation, a man who never made the same mistake twice. Never. Louis was not the dancer—or the showman—that Ali would be, but he was a tremendous boxer, a model of economy and precision. He could flatten you with punches that traveled only 5 inches (13cm). Louis an animal? Hardly. He was a gifted, intelligent boxer, a man who, despite the racism of his day, became a national hero as socially significant as Jackie Robinson, who would break the color barrier in major league baseball a generation later. Louis "was a tremendous puncher, with tremendous hand speed, and he never wasted movement," said trainer Eddie Futch, his boyhood friend.

If Louis became "a black hero in white America"—the title of the brilliant biography by Chris Mead—it was because of his two battles with the German fighter Max Schmeling. Schmeling became a symbol of Nazi

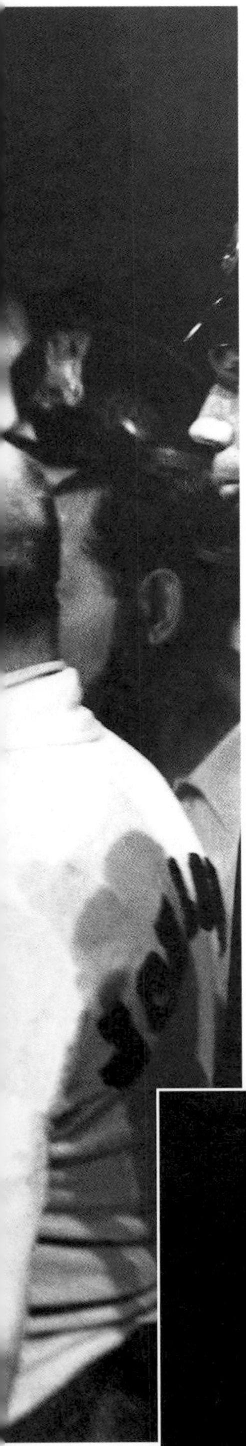

Germany, particularly during the second fight, and while some historians feel the label was unfair, it did not seem to matter. History is an overwhelming force, carrying with it a tidal wave of emotions and sentiments, and to fans in the United States, Schmeling was Nazi Germany.

Schmeling shocked the American, then an up-and-comer, on June 19, 1936, in New York, knocking him out in the 12th round. The German had detected a weakness in Louis, a weakness that the sportswriters, in all their wisdom, had failed to notice. Whenever the American threw the jab, he dropped his left, thus leaving him open to right-hand counters. Schmeling battered Louis throughout the bout, but the final combination was the most brutal of the fight: two right hands to the jaw—the first an uppercut, the second a chopping blow. The American fell into the ropes, both of his arms hanging over the middle strands, where he remained so motionless that he looked like a subject for a still life. The invincible warrior finally crumpled onto the canvas. "All you have to do to beat him is walk into him and bang him with a solid punch," Jack Dempsey, the former champion, said of Louis. "I don't think he'll ever whip another good fighter."

Dempsey was wrong. Louis and Schmeling fought again on January 22, 1938, at Yankee Stadium in New York, but this was a different Louis. He had committed a disastrous error in the first fight, dropping his left after firing the jab, and he had corrected that mistake in training—a mistake he would never repeat. The American also entered the ring as heavyweight champion, having won the title with an 8th-round knockout of Jimmy Braddock less than a year earlier in Chicago. When asked if he was nervous heading into the fight, Louis responded, "Yeah, I'm afraid that I might kill Schmeling tonight."

With all the confidence that comes with winning the title, Louis climbed into the ring against the symbol of Nazi Germany. Louis destroyed him. He pinned Schmeling against the ropes, and the challenger looked like a flounder in a net, writhing helplessly against the assault. Louis pounded him relentlessly, each punch landing on the ribs with a sickening thud. The challenger fell to the canvas, his ribs broken, the vision of Nazi Germany shattered. The fight had lasted 124 seconds. Louis, already a hero to black America, became a hero to all of America. "He's a credit to his race—the human race," Jimmy Cannon wrote. The rest of the nation was just as proud, just as effusive. "Louis has finally come into his full estate as a great world's champion," wrote Dan Parker of the *New York Daily Mirror*. "If anyone doubts his greatness after his masterful job last night, he's plain plumb prejudiced."

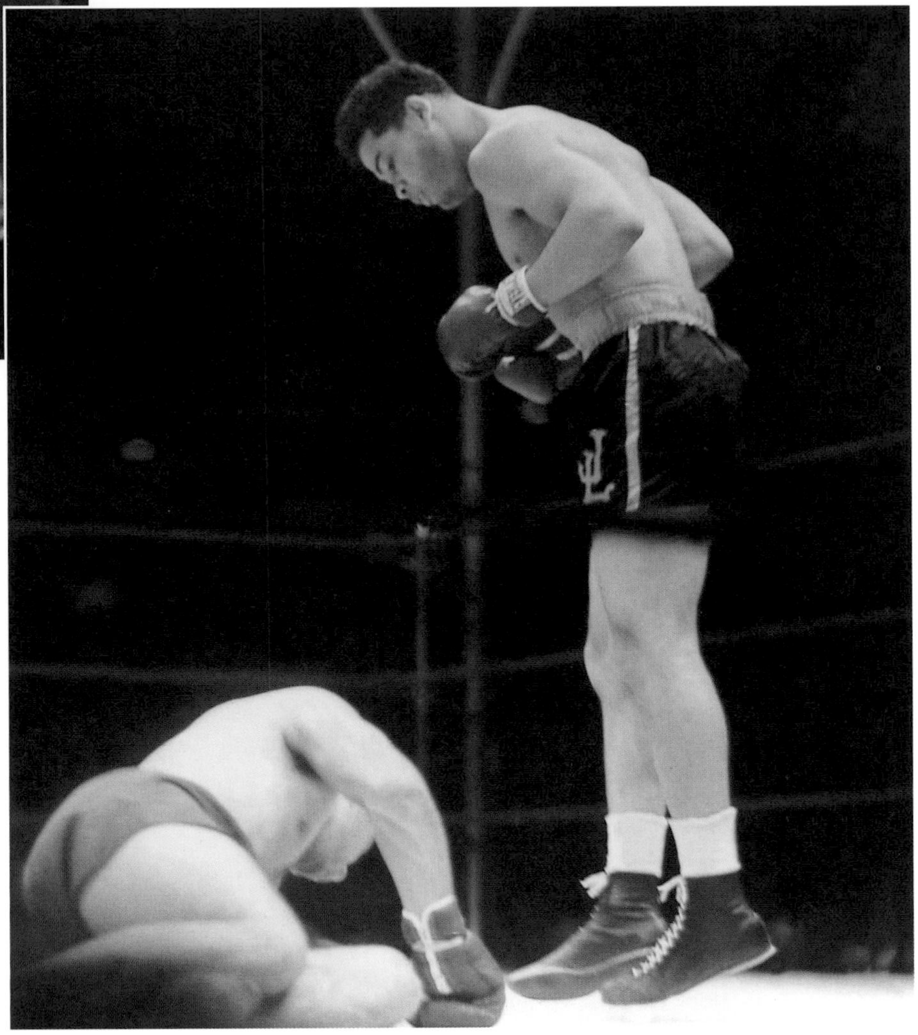

Louis retired after World War II, only to return two years later, but his skills were as faded as his press clippings. He lost a heavyweight title bid to Ezzard Charles, who had won the championship on

September 9, 1950, in New York. Then, in one of the saddest spectacles in boxing history, he fought a young up-and-comer, Rocky Marciano, who knocked out the former champion on October 26, 1951, in New York—the last battle of a great warrior and an even greater human being.

Sugar Ray Robinson

The great boxing historian Pierce Egan may have coined the term "the sweet science" in 1824, but it took Walker Smith to give the phrase substance and credibility more than one hundred years later. Walker Smith? You might know him better as Sugar Ray Robinson, perhaps the greatest fighter who ever lived—a status that *Ring Magazine* bestowed upon him in 1997. Fans still marvel at his artistry. He threw combinations that had never been seen before or since—firing hooks off uppercuts and uppercuts off hooks, usually with a dizzying speed that rendered his superb defense unnecessary. After all, who could counter a hailstorm of punches to the body and head?

"He was the greatest fighter of all time," Ali said. "I styled my dancing moves after him. He had a hard, hard punch and could back up and dance. He was a pretty fighter with excellent rhythm." Great stylists began to emerge after the turn of the century—fighters such as heavyweight champion Jack Johnson, lightweight champion Benny Leonard, and featherweight champion Kid Chocolate. They bobbed and weaved, feinted and counterpunched, jabbed and crossed over with the right—tactics that, though common today, were considered revolutionary in the bare-knuckle days. The stylists pushed boxing, step by step, punch by punch, into the twentieth century.

"There were great fighters before Robinson, but it was Robinson who put everything together in one package—speed, grace, power," said Eddie Futch, the great former trainer who guided more than fifteen fighters to world titles during his career. "If you look at some of the boxers Robinson fought—Jake LaMotta, Gene Fullmer, Carmen Basilio—you see a clear contrast in styles. They were the awkward brawlers. He was the artist."

Ali was not the only boxer who copied that sweet, graceful style. Robinson altered boxing just as surely

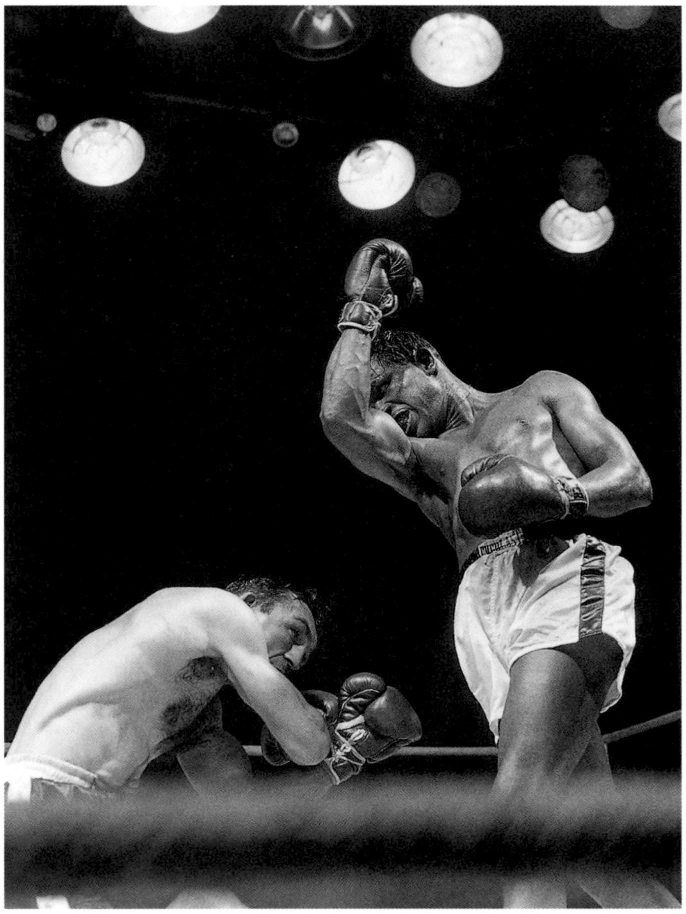

OPPOSITE: Bending so low his head almost touches the canvas, Jake LaMotta barely avoids the dazzlingly quick blows of Sugar Ray Robinson on Valentine's Day, 1951. Robinson won this fight, the last of their classic rivalry, and in the process secured the middleweight crown. ABOVE: Sugar Ray Robinson, heroically ignoring the ill effects of a 103-degree fever caused by a viral infection, scored a 15th-round decision over Carmen Basilio in this middleweight title fight on March 25, 1958.

as he altered the nervous systems of his opponents—perhaps with the same disastrous results. Why? Because there was only one Sugar Ray Robinson, and while Ali and Sugar Ray Leonard were successful imitators, most fighters were pathetic copycats. They showed good taste, not good judgment, in copying a legend. In the end, these clones were miserable failures.

"If anyone has come along since to equal Sugar Ray Robinson, I don't know who it has been," Futch said. "Muhammad Ali was a great boxer—a great boxer—the nearest thing to Sugar Ray Robinson. But Robinson could do things that Ali couldn't. Ali didn't have that one-punch knockout power that Robinson did. Ali went 41 rounds with Joe Frazier and never once put him down.

"Sugar Ray Robinson represented the finest qualities you can find in a boxer—his style, his class, his grace and his consummate artistry. He could box, and he could punch. You wouldn't expect a ballet dancer to be able to kill you with one punch, but Robinson could."

LEFT: Sugar Ray Robinson unleashes a furious combination against Ralph "Tiger" Jones on January 19, 1955, one of the first fights for the ex-champion following his return from retirement on January 5 that year.

One man who discovered that painful truth was Artie Levine, a top contender whom Robinson knocked out in the 10th round on November 6, 1946, in Cleveland. "Robinson caught Levine with a shot to the chin," Futch recalled. "Levine backed into the ropes, and Robinson started raining punches on him. Levine had his arms up, and he was blocking everything Robinson threw. Robinson noticed the body was open. He threw a right to the body, and Levine went down. The referee counted him out." After the fight, Futch went to the dressing room, where one of his boxers was preparing for the walkout bout. "Levine came in, and he was upset," Futch said. "I asked him, 'What's up?' He said, 'That was a fast count. The ref just said 10, and that was it.' I had to explain that 10 was the last number the referee had counted, not the first. The poor man had been out cold."

Robinson was so quick that he could get away with an illegal punch—a left hook that snaked around the body and landed on the small of the back. Imagine a nightstick jammed into the base of your spine. "That punch paralyzed his opponents," said George Benton, a former middleweight contender who trained ten world champions. "Referees never saw it because it came so quickly." Benton, a native of Philadelphia, had firsthand knowledge of that punch. "I remember once, when I was 15 years old. I was an amateur, boxing in New York. I was fighting this older kid who had been training in Sugar Ray's gym. The kid had picked up that left hook from Robinson. He hit me with it, and it took my legs away. I lost the decision. It was an education."

From 1940 to 1964, Robinson compiled a professional record of 175-19-6, including 110 knockouts. Eighteen of those losses came after he was 30. His only loss before that point was to LaMotta on February 5, 1943—the only fight LaMotta won in six meetings with Robinson. "You know why Jake LaMotta did so well against him?" Benton asked. "Because LaMotta had a great chin, and because he was half-nuts. I don't mean insane. But LaMotta had no fear, and a person without fear has to be a little crazy. How else can you explain all those punches he took from Robinson?" How do you explain it? You cannot explain it any more than you can explain how Robinson threw them in the first place, how he threw the most beautiful combinations in boxing history.

Henry Armstrong

Henry Armstrong was a whirlwind, his fists flashing out of a vortex that seemed impossible to defend. Of all his attributes—and he had many—the single most important was his energy. He was like a sprinter in a long-distance race who churned furiously while his opponents loped steadily. There was no feeling-out process for Armstrong, no taking a round off to size up his opponent. No, his feeling-out process came before the fight, in the dressing room, where he would work out feverishly. Not warm up—work out, speed bag and all. Armstrong had to release some of that energy and tension before the fight; otherwise, he would be a maniac, his punches spraying like machine-gun fire, during the fight.

Born Henry Jackson on December 12, 1912, in Columbus, Missouri, he was one of fifteen children whose father worked as a farmer and butcher. As a teenager during the Depression, he worked for the Missouri-Pacific Railroad, but one day he saw a newspaper headline that served as a giant recruitment poster—a recruitment poster for prizefighting. The headline stated, "Kid Chocolate Earns $75,000 For Half-Hour's Work." That was the only vocational guidance the young man needed. He quit his job, telling his buddies, "I'm coming back in a Cadillac."

Changing his name to Armstrong, a tribute to a former fighter named Harry Armstrong, he almost came back in an ambulance, not a Cadillac, because his dream met with disaster in his professional debut on July 27, 1931. He was knocked out in the 3rd round by Al Iovino, a southpaw. But the young man picked himself—and his career—off the canvas, developing the frenetic style that would help offset his short stature. Armstrong stood only 5 feet 5 1/2 inches (166cm), but he punched so furiously that his short reach became an asset, turning a disadvantage into an advantage with his punishing inside fighting. The sportswriters called him "Hammerin' Hank."

Bobbing, weaving, and punching his way through the division, Armstrong won his first world title on October 29, 1937, with a 6th-round knockout over featherweight king Petey Sarron. But the featherweight division was not enough, not for a man as talented and ambitious as Armstrong. Next? He jumped to the wel-

Adding the lightweight title to his welterweight and featherweight crowns with the win, Henry "Hurricane Hank" Armstrong celebrates his 15-round decision over Lou Ambers on August 17, 1938. The campaign to win all three world titles was waged partly out of financial considerations, and partly to get attention: given the boxing world's fixation with heavyweight Joe Louis, there was little notice paid to such chicken-legged lightweights as Armstrong. But the brain trust backing Armstrong—which included Hollywood luminaries George Raft and Al Jolson—decided that "Hammerin' Hank" (as he was also known), with his unbelievable energy and stamina, could pull off the trifecta. They were right. Hank Armstrong won all three world titles in just more than nine months, making good money in the process and proving that he was one of the very best boxers to fight in any weight class ever.

terweight division, a leap of about 20 pounds (9kg) that he executed easily, if not wisely. How did he do it? He trained on beer. Armstrong would not revolutionize training routines with his curious regimen, but it was successful. He pounded welterweight champion Barney Ross on May 31, 1938, in New York, scoring a unanimous decision to win his second world title in less than a year.

With two title belts cinched around his waist, Armstrong yearned to expand his wardrobe—with, yes, another championship belt. This time he went down to the lightweight division—the weight class between featherweight and welterweight—to challenge Lou Ambers, the world champion who was one of the classiest stylists of his era. It would prove one of the toughest bouts in the careers of both men. Fighting with a torn lip that forced him to swallow his own blood for the last 5 rounds, Armstrong faced three opponents—nausea, fatigue, and Ambers. But he hung on; somehow, he hung on, capturing a split decision in a brutal, grueling 15-round match. Armstrong won the lightweight title only ten weeks after defeating Ross, making it three world titles in less than a year—a sensational achievement that no other fighter has ever matched.

After winning the lightweight title, Armstrong relinquished the first crown he won—the featherweight title. Then he made what turned out to be his only lightweight defense: losing a decision to Ambers after being penalized 5 rounds for punching low. Two titles won, two titles gone. Ah, but it was the third division, the welterweight division, in which Armstrong left his mark. He defended the welterweight title an astounding nineteen times, including eleven in one year—1939. The streak ended when Fritzie Zivic outpointed him on January 17, 1941.

Willie Pep

They called him "the Will-o'-the-Wisp," and he turned his matches into exhibitions that boasted all the dread and menace of a pillow fight. This was not prizefighting; this was, well, boxing. And Willie Pep was one of the greatest boxers who ever lived, a guy who could go entire rounds without getting breathed on, much less pounded on. Was his style exciting? It depended on how much artistry you wanted to see in your pugs. If you preferred mayhem over craft, Pep was not your guy, and he was not the guy for some of the sportswriters of his day. He outpointed Chalky Wright for the world featherweight title on November 20, 1942, in New York, and the pundits were not pleased. "Pep retreated faster and more frequently than Rommel's Afrika Corps," wrote Dick McCann of the New York *Daily News.* Columnist Frank Graham was even more brutal: "There is, in short, nothing to distinguish Pep from a dozen other featherweights." Wrong. Pep was special. He could not punch hard, but since he was not getting punched in return, it was not a critical deficit. Pep held the featherweight title for seven years, off and on, and he compiled an amazing record of 229-11-1, with sixty-five knockouts, from 1940 to 1966. The smart sportswriters saw the real thing in Pep. "Pep was the greatest creative artist I ever saw in a ring," wrote the great sportswriter W.C. Heinz in 1979. "Pep was a poet, often implying, with his feints and his footwork, more than he said."

RIGHT: Featherweight great Willie Pep, his face bleeding from 15 rounds of punishment, celebrates a dramatic victory by decision over Sandy Saddler on February 11, 1949, at Madison Square Garden. The Fred Astaire of the ring, Pep was a defensive specialist who more than made up for his lack of power with dazzling footwork and beguiling feints. Making the comeback victory over the taller, stronger Saddler even more remarkable was the fact that this was the second stage of Pep's career; the first had been brought to a close by a January 8, 1947, airplane crash that had left Pep with life-threatening injuries. Five months later, Pep was not only on his feet but in the ring.

FRIDAY NIGHT BOXING

Pep was absurdly dominant—135-1-1, with a five-year unbeaten streak—until he met Sandy Saddler on October 29, 1948, in New York. The champion was short and clever, while the challenger was tall and powerful, one of the most bruising punchers the division had ever seen. Pep was a three-to-one favorite, but the favorite looked like an underdog the moment the bell rang. Saddler crushed Pep in the 4th round, turning "the Will-o'-the-Wisp" into a fencing dummy in short pants, stationary and vulnerable. Pep won the rematch three months later, surviving cuts above both eyes to regain his title with a unanimous decision. The creative genius overcame the puncher, but Pep had lost his defensive mastery against his most worthy opponent, finishing the bout with bruises all over his face. They fought two more times, with Pep losing both of the battles, the most brutal being the third fight in their classic series. Pep and Saddler looked like the ancestors of Roberto Duran—one of the dirtiest fighters of the 1970s, '80s, and '90s—grabbing, pushing, and thumbing each other in the eyes. They locked bodies in the 7th round, becoming one amorphous mass with four arms, four legs, and two fighting hearts. Pep returned to his corner, complaining about a pain that was later diagnosed as a dislocated shoulder. The bell rang for the 8th round, but Pep, ahead on all three cards, remained on his stool, and Saddler won the fight. "He beat me with a double arm-lock," Pep said, moaning after the fight. Saddler disagreed. "I thought a punch to the kidney did it," he said. "But if they say I twisted his arm, okay, I twisted it."

Rocky Marciano

It was a thunderclap of a punch, and it landed where every great punch should land—in our collective consciousness. If you were at the fight, or if you have seen the famous photograph of the punch, you will never forget it. It is not a pretty picture, but it is a classic one: Rocky Marciano catching Jersey Joe Walcott on the jaw—188 pounds (85kg) of force concentrated in one leather glove. Marciano won the heavyweight title with that punch—a right hand that turned Walcott into an ugly caricature of himself, his features suddenly distorted, his ears where his cheeks should have been, his mouth where his nose should have been, his eyes so blank that he looked like a dead fish. It was horrible, and boxing fans will remember it forever.

Marciano delivered that right hand on September 23, 1952, in Philadelphia, and it seemed to cement his status as a legend-in-the-making. Why? Because it was not merely an awesome punch; it was an awesome punch that came when Marciano needed it most. Behind on points, his nose broken from the relentless attack of a man almost eleven years older, Marciano needed a miracle to win the fight—and he got it. Marciano knocked out Walcott in the 13th round and captured the heavyweight title that Walcott had seemed certain to retain.

"The Brockton Blockbuster" went on to win six more fights, including a surprisingly easy rematch over Walcott and two classic battles with Ezzard Charles, a clever boxer and a solid puncher. He also won a fight without having to land a single blow—the computer fight with Muhammad Ali in 1969. Experts fed information on each boxer into the computer, including strengths and weaknesses, and the computer spit out the result. Ali and Marciano acted out the result in a ring in a film studio. Fans, not knowing the outcome of this computer matchup, witnessed the contrived battle as if it were a real fight. It was not, and boxing experts

ABOVE: Rocky Marciano and trainer Charlie Goldman discuss strategy during training camp for the champ's title defense against Roland La Starza on September 24, 1953. As always, Marciano won, on this occasion with an 11th-round knockout at New York's Polo Grounds. Amazingly, Marciano had the shortest reach among all heavyweight champions.

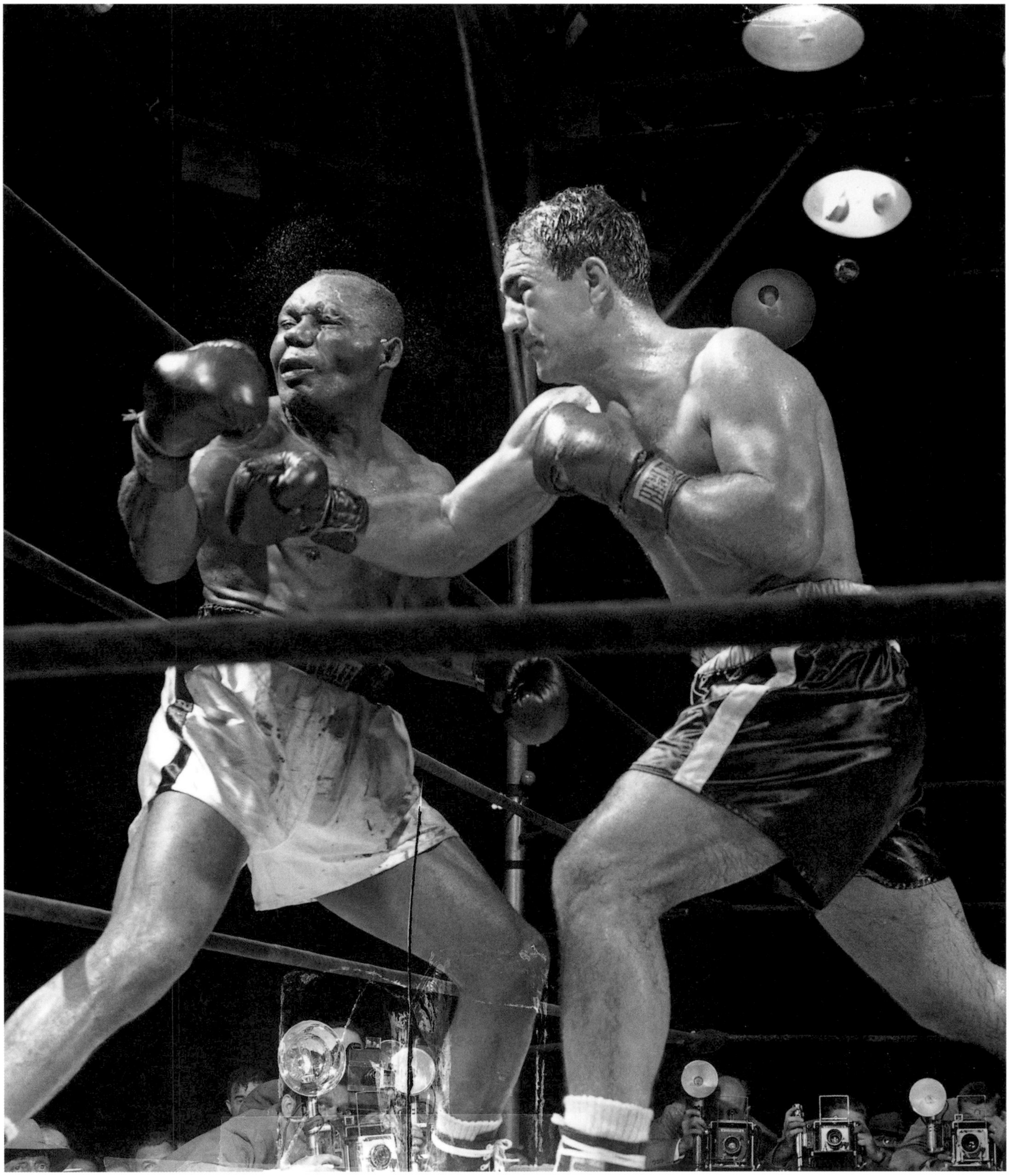

ABOVE: **Rocky Marciano slams his signature right into the jaw of Jersey Joe Walcott on September 23, 1952, one of the most famous punches in boxing history. Born Rocco Francis Marchegiano, Marciano began his pro career in 1947 with a knockout of Lee Epperson. Before his next fight, almost a year and a half later, the raw, awkward Marciano had put in serious time studying the sweet science with legendary trainer Charlie Goldman. Goldman tinkered with everything about Marciano's game except one: his right power punch. Goldman called it the "Suzy-Q" and it sure came in handy throughout Marciano's romp through the heavyweight division.**

will tell you why: because Marciano won. For all of his toughness, for all of his determination and will power, Rocky Marciano was no Muhammad Ali. But it was a testament to his character and his reputation that somebody, even if it was a computer, thought he could beat the great Ali.

Marciano retired in 1956, having won forty-nine fights, forty-three of them by knockout—the only champion in any weight class to retire undefeated. He threw thousands of punches in his career, from Connecticut to California, sometimes landing more blows in a round than some fighters did in entire fights.

But of all the punches he delivered, of all the jabs and hooks and crosses, none was more famous than the one he threw on the night of September 23, 1952.

Archie Moore

They put on a fight, and an antique show broke out. Archie Moore scored a unanimous decision over Joey Maxim on December 17, 1952, in St. Louis, capturing the light heavyweight title with a brilliant display of boxing. It was a special moment—not just because Moore was gifted, but because he was gifted and old. He was 36, or 39, depending on who you asked, and Maxim was only 30. But age did not seem to matter to Moore. He fought with the passion and enthusiasm of a man half his age. Maxim found that out, and so did dozens of other fighters throughout the years. Years? Try decades. Moore fought from 1936 to 1963, compiling an astounding record of 194-26-8, with 141 of the wins coming by knockout.

If Moore fought long past the age when most fighters would have retired, there was a good reason for it. Moore wanted a title, and nobody would give him a shot at one. Moore had fought for sixteen years, ten of them as a contender, before Maxim finally gave him the opportunity he deserved. "I made up in fifteen rounds what I had missed in sixteen years," Moore said.

And it soon became clear why all the other champions had ducked Moore throughout his career. He was a terror, as clever as he was powerful—a man who could befuddle you with his defense and flatten you with his offense. Moore was a boxer-puncher. He may have been a complete fighter, but it was his defense that seemed so remarkable. The aging champion called it "escapology," the art of making your opponent think you are here when you are actually over there. Moore did it with superior upper body movement, his arms crossed in front of him in case a punch strayed too close. He was so clever and shifty that one sportswriter dubbed him "the Mongoose."

"Escapology" failed "the Mongoose" on December 10, 1958, in Montreal. Moore was 44 years old, and for one night at least, he looked every year of it. The contender, Yvon Durelle, a crude and aggressive fighter from Canada, dropped the champion three times in the 1st round and once in the 5th, hammering him so brutally that the old man, dazed and disoriented, stumbled across the ring for much of the fight. Then something remarkable happened. The old man began to rally—the champion floored Durelle in the 7th, the 10th and, for the 10-count, the 11th. "The Mongoose" escaped again, coming back to knock the same man out in the 3rd round less than a year later.

After the Durelle rematch, Moore fought for four more years, including a match against Muhammad Ali, who said he was embarrassed to fight someone on Social Security. Moore retired in 1963, but if boxing missed the old man, it would not miss him forever. The ex-champion returned in 1987, not as a fighter but as a training consultant. And whom did he train but another ageless wonder, George Foreman. Foreman came back from a ten-year retirement to knock out Michael Moorer on November 5, 1994, and become the oldest heavyweight champion in boxing history—45 years old. "He's a wise man, and he can teach me a lot," Foreman said.

And so he did.

ABOVE: Archie Moore, the ageless marvel whose career spanned three decades, backs up challenger Joey Maxim on January 27, 1954. It was Moore's third match with the man from whom he had grabbed the light heavyweight title (on December 17, 1952). Moore won all three fights with Maxim. OPPOSITE: Archie Moore ducks low to avoid the blows of his opponent, Giulio Rinaldi of Italy, during the 12th round of their 15-round June 10, 1961, match-up. Though somewhere in his late forties at the time, Moore successfully defended his light heavyweight championship title, winning the fight by decision. Moore, also known as "the Mongoose," has the best knockout total in history: he sent more than 140 challengers to the mat over the course of his remarkable, and remarkably long, career.

Muhammad Ali

The debate will rage for as long as men lace on a pair of gloves to whack each other in the ring: who was the greatest fighter who ever lived? Sugar Ray Robinson or Muhammad Ali? In the end the question, while intriguing, is pointless. Like van Gogh and Picasso, Ali and Robinson were different artists working in different genres—the former a heavyweight, the latter a welterweight and middleweight. Who was the best? It is impossible to answer that question without losing sleep over it. But one thing is clear. Like van Gogh and Picasso, Ali and Robinson were startling, almost breathtaking originals—showmen who could dazzle you the moment they stepped into the ring, as creative as they were brutal.

Ali was tall and pretty, and in his prime, when his talent matched his audacity, he could fire his combinations faster than the camera crew could shoot them, leaving a trail of opponents sprawled on the canvas with no photographic evidence—punch, punch, punch, click—of what put them there. He was amazing, and he did it all as a heavyweight, a weight class filled with pachyderms, which made his achievement all the more remarkable. Ali weighed about 215 pounds (98kg), at least 60 pounds (27kg) more than Robinson, but he was

ABOVE: The brash, rhyme-slinging Cassius Clay answers questions during a press conference while legendary trainer Angelo Dundee (standing far right) looks on. RIGHT: Muhammad Ali towers defiantly over the fallen Sonny Liston and taunts him, daring him to get up from the mat. Ali won this May 25, 1965, rematch by 1st-round knockout. After their first clash more than a year earlier, which Ali won in the 7th by TKO, Cassius Marcellus Clay was reborn as Muhammad Ali.

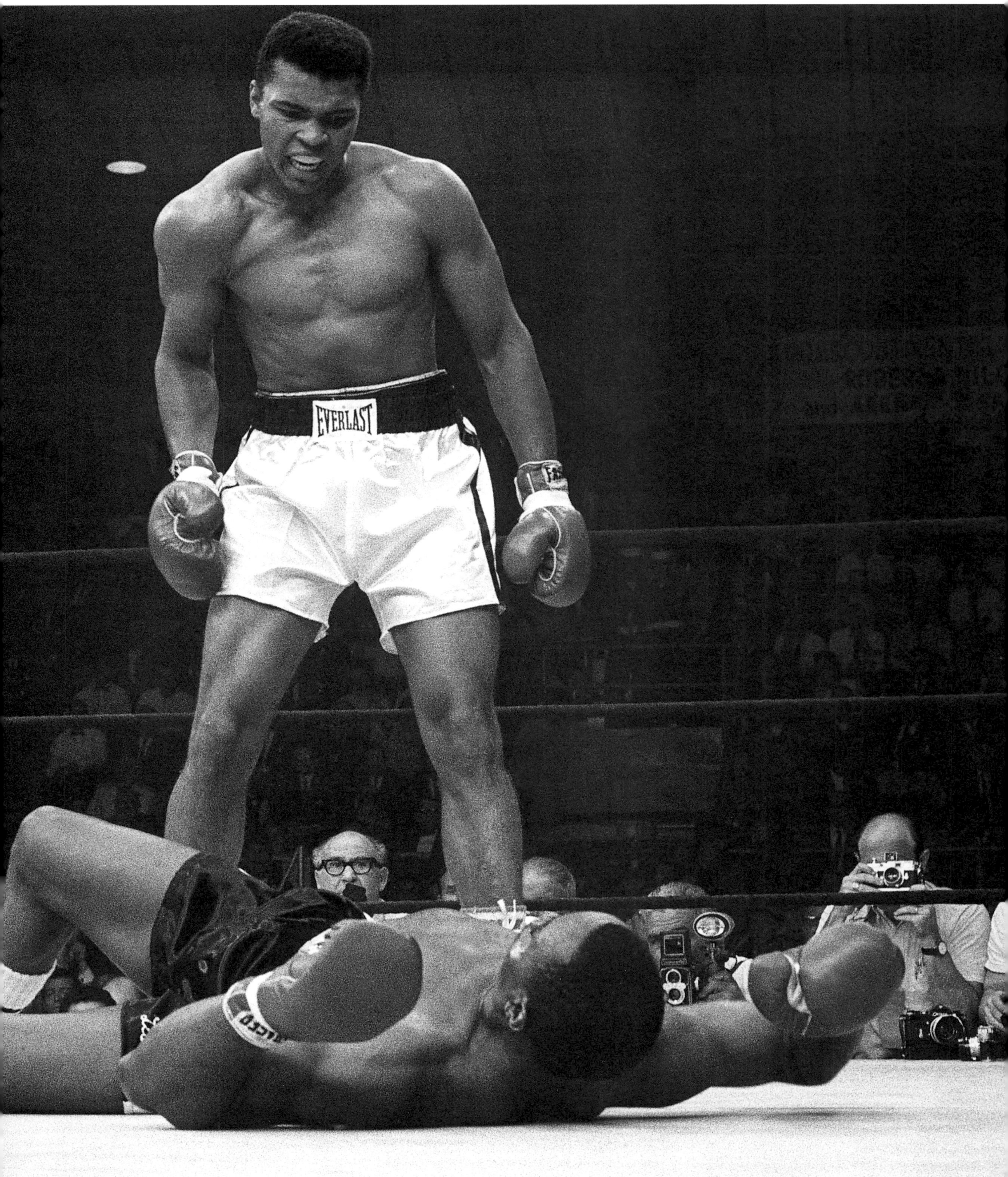
EVERLAST

a featherweight—smooth and fast and graceful—until he stepped on the scale. But he could punch—and boast—like a heavyweight.

This colorful fighter is something to see
And the greatest heavyweight champion
I know he will be
—Muhammad Ali

Unlike Robinson, who was a model of precision, Ali did everything wrong. He never learned how to box—not in the conventional sense, anyway—but he created a unique style, and he had the athletic ability to overcome his mechanical flaws. "He was a very limited fighter," said Eddie Futch, who trained the greatest rival Ali ever faced, Joe Frazier. "But what he did, he did extremely well."

Ali won the heavyweight title on February 25, 1964, in Miami Beach, Florida, scoring a stunning knockout over Sonny Liston in one of the biggest upsets in boxing history. He won it again ten years later, with his reflexes and timing—but not his heart and wit—vastly inferior during his comeback. He defeated George Foreman, again with a stunning knockout, to regain the title. "The Greatest" would not stop there. Ali lost the title and regained it one more time, with both the defeat and the victory coming against Leon Spinks in 1978. At that time, he was the only man to win the heavyweight title three times, a feat since matched by Evander Holyfield. And he did it during perhaps the greatest era for heavyweights in boxing history. He fought Liston, Frazier, Archie Moore, George Foreman, Floyd Patterson, Jerry Quarry, Jimmy Ellis, Ken Norton, Ron Lyle, Earnie Shavers, Larry Holmes, and Bob Foster.

"He is the Prince of Heaven," Norman Mailer wrote in his book *The Fight*, repeating the kind of hyperbole that Ali inspired—and often expressed—throughout his career. But Mailer was not alone in his praise. "He was a great, great, great fighter," said George Benton, an assistant trainer under Futch during the 1970s. "And as vicious as he could be inside the ring, that's how sweet he was outside the ring. He wouldn't hurt a fly." That is something that Frazier never understood.

Ali and Frazier fought in three memorable wars, the final battle being the legendary "Thrilla in Manila" on October 1, 1975. Futch stopped the fight after the 14th round, with Frazier protesting on his stool, his eyes closed by 42 minutes of punishment. Ali collapsed after the bout, his heart having kept him up long after his legs wanted him to go down. "This is the closest thing to death there is," he said after the fight. The two men should have been bonded by those three battles, respect replacing the hostility they felt in the ring. But Ali taunted Frazier in and out of the ring, sometimes mercilessly, and Frazier, a proud man, had a difficult time forgetting and forgiving. "It's sad," Benton said. "Ali never meant the things he said to Frazier. But he was a businessman and a boxer, and he was just trying

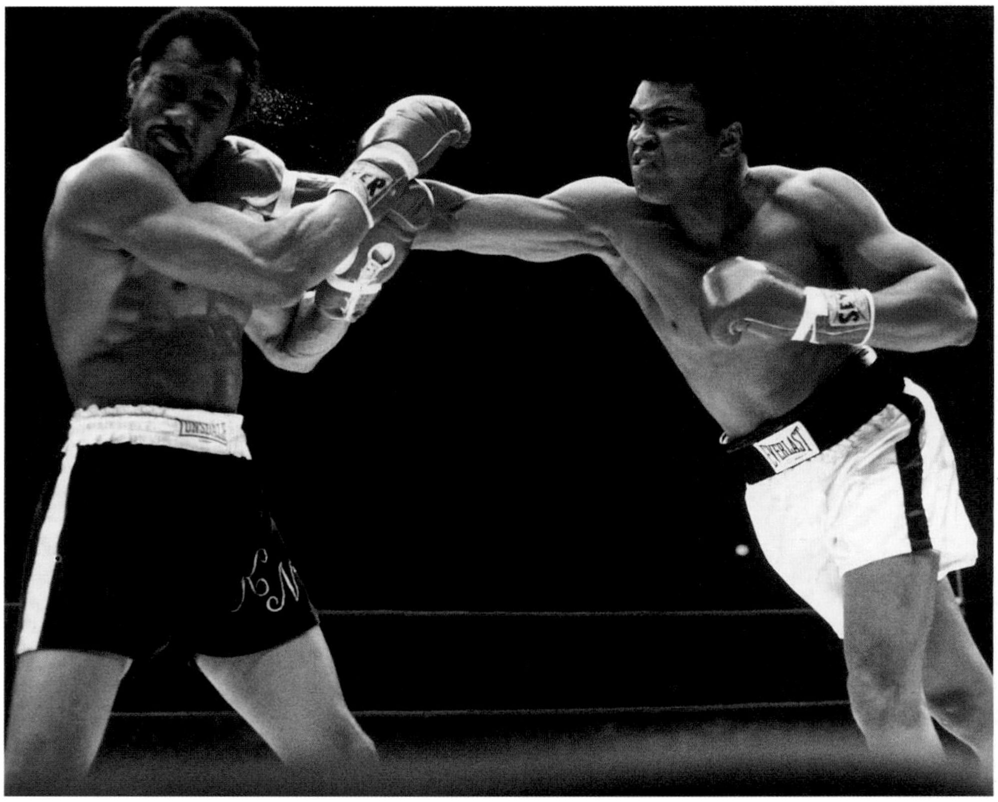

Above: Ali uses his long reach to rocket his right glove into the face of Ken Norton during one of their two fights in 1973. On the comeback trail in 1973, Ali first met Norton in March of that year and got the worst of the encounter: losing the fight and suffering a broken jaw for his efforts. Six months later, however, the glove was on the other fist: Ali stopped Norton, paving the way for the storied match-up against George Foreman in Kinshasa, Zaire, in 1974. Opposite: Muhammad Ali rocks George Foreman with a straight right during their legendary "Rumble in the Jungle" on October 30, 1974.

A Closer Look

Muhammad Ali, a biblical scholar in short pants, grabbed Joe Frazier in the middle of the ring. "I'm God," Ali told him.

Frazier—a fighter, not a scholar—was taken aback, but only momentarily. "What?" Frazier asked.

"I'm God," Ali repeated.

"Well, then, God's gonna get whupped tonight," Frazier said.

Frazier did whup Ali, not God, on March 8, 1971, in Madison Square Garden—the first of their three classic meetings. But if Ali proved mortal in the ring, he was still a titanic figure—loud and brash and talented. Even today, without his trunks, tassels, and gloves, Muhammad Ali could never be like the rest of us; he could never be ordinary. We thought the ring was his stage, but we were wrong; the world was his stage. And he commanded it with a presence that few people—athletes or politicians or entertainers—could match. He once knocked out the Beatles, all four of them, with a single punch. Sure, it was a publicity stunt, in a grimy old gym in Miami, but it seemed appropriate—the five greatest entertainers in the world going toe-to-toe. The Beatles sang "Love Me Do," while Ali recited "Me. We!" but both the Beatles and Ali were about ambition, about attaining heights that most men could not see, much less negotiate.

Who was this man, this enigma? Was he an actor? No, but he generated more drama than a troupe of Broadway stars. Was he a magician? No, but his hands were so fast that slow-motion cameras sometimes failed to pick up his punches. Was he a politician? No, but he could be more eloquent and impassioned than those who were. So who was this man? He was the greatest fighter—some might say the greatest figure—of his generation, and he remains a charismatic individual to this day.

Ali now suffers from Parkinson's disease, a chronic condition of the nervous system. The sickness forces him to walk slowly and speak haltingly, as if he were considering every word and measuring it for its impact upon the listener—a seemingly preposterous notion. After all, Ali never cared what his audience thought. Or did he? Oh, he cared all right, because the more outrageous the comment, the more satisfaction he got out of the reaction to it. The one thing Ali could not stand was indifference, and it was the one response he never got. People either loved him or hated him, although more and more people love Ali today. He has become an almost mythical figure, his stature growing stronger even as his body grows weaker.

It would be easy to pity this man, once so dynamic, now so frail. But it seems wrong to feel sorry for him. Why? It seems wrong to pity a man who refuses to pity himself. Ali never expected pity as a fighter, and he does not expect it as a man.

After losing to Frazier, then the heavyweight champion of the world, in their first fight, Ali sat in a wheelchair in a hospital corridor, his jaw swollen to the size of a grapefruit. A reporter told him that people were saying he did not want a rematch with Frazier. Ali looked at him for a second. "Oh, how wrong they are," he said quietly. "How wrong they are." *Sports Illustrated* later splashed across its cover the headline "End of the Ali Legend." The end? Hardly. It was the beginning, and the legend had as much to do with Ali the man as with Ali the fighter. "What I suffered physically was worth what I've accomplished in life," Ali said at a news conference to discuss his health in 1984. "A man who is not courageous enough to take risks will never accomplish anything in life." *Sports Illusrated* later came to the same conclusion, voting him athelete of the century in 1999.

Today, Ali lives on a farm in Berrien Springs, Michigan, with his fourth wife, Lonnie. He still punches the heavy bag, and he walks several miles every morning when his schedule allows. The ex–heavyweight champion travels widely to preach the religion of Islam, which he embraced more than thirty years ago, when he changed his name from Cassius Clay to Muhammad Ali. "It's the God in me that people connect with," Ali once said, explaining his hold on people.

No, he was not God, despite the assertion to Frazier on that night almost thirty years ago. But he was godlike, a deeply spiritual man who could be as caring outside the ring as he was vicious inside the ring. Ali seemed to rule the world in and out of the ring. What makes this man truly special is that more than any other athlete in history—more than Jack Johnson, more than Joe Louis, even more than Jackie Robinson—he has made the public look upon athletes as human beings, as people who could embody their eras as much as kings and statesmen did. "My name is known in Serbia, Pakistan, Morocco," he once said. "These are countries that don't follow the Kentucky Derby." Ali claimed he was more famous than the Pope. "And I don't have to wear one of those funny hats," he said.

For all his dazzling skills in the ring, however, Ali crossed over from athlete to social phenomenon because of the one battle he refused to wage—in Vietnam. "I got no quarrel with them Viet Cong," he said on February 17, 1966, when he refused induction into the armed services.

When Ali carried the torch for the 1996 Olympics in Atlanta, the world rejoiced. He walked slowly, the once magnificent Ali shuffle reduced to a slow, halting gait, and his hand trembling from the weight of the torch. But one thing remained as bright and vibrant as ever: his smile, sometimes mischievous, sometimes beatific. It was a wonderful moment.

Some fighters remain champions forever. Ali is one of them.

OPPOSITE: One of the most stirring sights in Olympic history occurred at the start of the 1996 Summer Olympics, when former Olympian Muhammad Ali—by then much afflicted by Parkinson's disease—mounted the stage and lit the device that in turn set the Olympic Cauldron aflame.

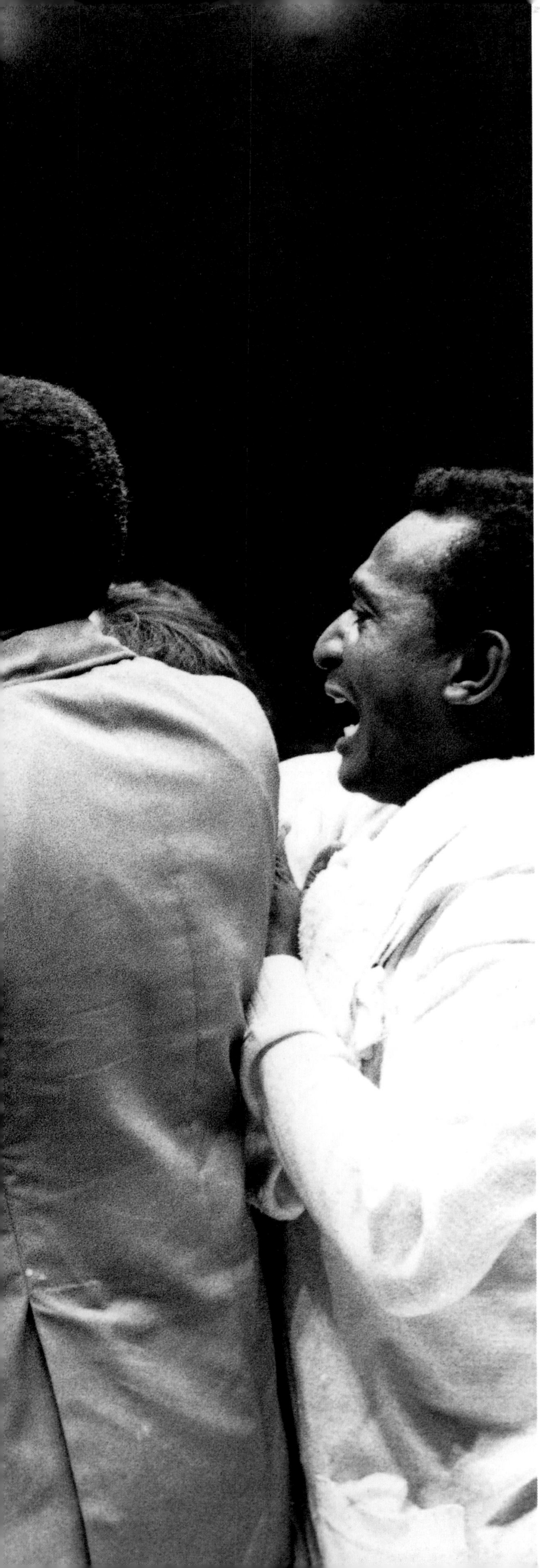

to drum up interest in their fights." Ali succeeded in doing just that: the fights comprised perhaps the greatest trilogy in boxing history. "Ali and Frazier were great fighters, anyway," boxing historian Bert Sugar said. "But they made each other greater."

Roberto Duran

Geography meant nothing to Roberto Duran. No matter where he traveled, no matter where he fought, in New York or Las Vegas or Panama City, the streets were always with him—the streets of his youth, where fighting was more than a pugilistic exercise; it was a way of life. And Duran accepted it, mentally remaining on those streets even when his million-dollar paychecks told him to run, to flee, to get as far away from his past as possible. Not that Duran lived on the streets, mind you; he just took the streets with him wherever he went, especially into the ring, where he was one of the most artfully dirty fighters to ever thumb an opponent in the eye. A dirty fighter artful? Yeah, because his dirty tactics were subtle—or as subtle as dirty tactics can be in this brutal sport. If he missed a punch, for example, it did not matter, because he might catch you with his elbow in his follow-through. And if he landed the punch—well, that was worse, because he might catch you with his elbow anyway just for good measure. And his head was a third fist; he did not bother to glove it, but it was a fist.

Duran grew up in Panama City, Panama, shining shoes, peddling mangoes, and dancing in saloons. He also played the drums, and he might have become an accomplished musician, the star of his high school band, except for one thing—he discovered that he liked pounding people more than percussion instruments. Duran quit school in the third grade, his education moving to a less elegant academic forum—the streets. He was a star pupil, acquiring the only certificate of honor that means anything in the back alley: a reputation. Oh, yes, he had a reputation. Duran once dropped a horse with a single blow, according to legend, and whether the story was true or not, it should have been true. The legend of "Manos de Piedra"—"Hands of Stone"—was born.

Handlers rush to congratulate Roberto Duran, a legend in the making, after his devastating knockout of Scottish lightweight champion Ken Buchanan on June 26, 1972. The hard-hitting street fighter from the barrios of Panama City had come a long way from shining shoes for a pittance.

If Duran was a street fighter, he was a street fighter with class, a man whose punching power overshadowed his remarkable boxing ability. At first he fought for pocket change, the purses only slightly higher than the money he had earned peddling mangoes, but his earning power—and his reputation—grew. The young fighter fulfilled a dream on September 13, 1971, when he fought in the mecca of boxing, Madison Square Garden. The fans saw a nobody, a skinny pug with ribs that threatened to burst through his skin. They derided him, seeing a fraud in short pants—a sensation in Panama, perhaps, but not in the United States. They were wrong. Duran knocked out Benny Huertas that day, leaving him so motionless, so deathly motionless, that in another setting the cops could have drawn a chalk outline around his body and started dusting for glove-prints. Huertas was out for six minutes. The fraud had proven himself.

The fans grew to love him, not just for his boxing ability but for the fierceness and menace with which he displayed it. Here was a man who loved only one thing more than beating people up—humiliating them after he beat them up. He destroyed Carlos Palomino, once a tremendous fighter, on June 22, 1979, in New York, snarling afterward, "Quit. You don't got it no more." But that was kind and generous compared to what he had told Ray Lampkin on March 2, 1975, in Panama City. He flattened Lampkin in the 14th round, and when the ambulance attendants carted the poor guy off to the hospital, Duran shouted, "Next time, I'll kill him."

ABOVE: **Roberto Duran (left) stuns Carlos Palomino in the 4th round with a left hook during this June 22, 1979, welterweight bout at Madison Square Garden. Both fighters went the distance, but Duran won the fight by decision.**

Duran won the world lightweight title on June 22, 1979, in New York when he stopped Ken Buchanan in the 13th round. He defended his crown twelve times, becoming, according to boxing observers, the greatest lightweight champion in history. "He was one of the greatest boxers I've ever seen," said Teddy Atlas, who trained former heavyweight champion Michael Moorer. "And it was because of his reflexes. He had the reflexes of a cat—so quick, with split-second timing that made it difficult to hit him." But his appetite for both food and fun proved bigger than his talent, and "Manos de Piedra" became "Belly of Jelly," eating and partying his way out of the lightweight division.

When Duran challenged Sugar Ray Leonard for the welterweight title in Montreal, he turned back to the tough-talking days of his youth. He taunted Leonard, and then he turned to Juanita, the wife of the welterweight champion, making crude, ugly comments in public—flirtatious remarks that made Leonard, usually calm and composed, seethe with anger. They fought on June 20, 1980, but Duran won the match long before fight night—at the weigh-in and press conferences where he provoked Leonard and his wife. He psyched out the man who usually did the psyching out, forcing him to fight an artless fight. Leonard, abandoning the wondrous legs that had carried him to a record of 25-0, stood toe-to-toe with the legendary "Manos de Piedra," and he paid for his foolishness. Duran pounded out a unanimous decision over the welterweight champion. "Duran did a number on Ray," said Angelo Dundee, who trained Leonard. "He got to him."

ABOVE: **Roberto Duran is considered by many experts to be the greatest lightweight champion in boxing history. Among many other distinctions, he managed over the course of his career to score a knockout in every round from 1 to 15.**

They fought again, but the good life had done what Leonard could not—it conquered Duran, and he was in no condition, mentally or physically, to defend the title he had won in such a brutal and convincing manner. Leonard, returning to the foot movement that had made him the Muhammad Ali of the welterweight division, toyed with Duran and turned the ring into a dance studio. In the 8th round Duran, confused and frustrated, uttered two of the most infamous words in boxing hisory: "No mas"—"No more"—and walked back to his corner, taking a shot in the ribs as he turned away from Leonard. Duran claimed that he was suffering an upset stomach from a steak dinner earlier that day, that it was his belly, not his opponent, who defeated him that night. Critics scoffed. They offered a different theory—that Duran, a proud fighter, could not deal with a fighter who thrived on dainty tactics such as footwork. Footwork. My God, Duran expected a street fight, not a tango, and yet here was Leonard engaged in an activity that required a chaperone, not a referee. No, Duran could not tolerate such strategy, observers said, and so he quit.

The fistic odd couple met a third time, on February 24, 1989, in Las Vegas, and Duran promised both a victory and an explanation—an explanation for his surrender nine years before. The boxing world got neither. Leonard scored a unanimous decision over Duran, although it was the Panamanian who looked like the winner. Duran was fresh and unmarked, while Leonard was bruised and bloodied, with a face that only Lon Chaney could love—the result of the dirty fighting that Duran had raised to an art. So much for the victory Duran promised—and so much for the explanation. Duran, apparently bitter over his defeat, told the sporting world to forget his vow. There would be no revelations, no excavations into the past, to explain an act that remains shrouded in mystery.

DURAN

LEFT: Sugar Ray Leonard lands a right to the jaw of Roberto Duran during their historic Montreal fight, on June 20, 1980. Duran won a unanimous 15-round decision and the welterweight title in what had to be a devastating loss for Leonard, who for years had been the darling of the boxing community and whose incredibly successful career had been launched at the very same arena during the 1976 Olympics.

Sugar Ray Leonard

One of the saddest spectacles in boxing history took place on March 1, 1997, in Atlantic City, New Jersey. One of the players was ex-champion Sugar Ray Leonard, then 40 years old, the greatest fighter of his era. But his era was twenty years earlier, and it showed.

The other player was Hector "Macho" Camacho, then 34, who stopped Leonard in the 5th round, landing about ten unanswered punches to the head before the referee finally stopped the bout. Leonard, who had returned after a six-year retirement, did not look like the fleet-footed, chiseled athelete he had been in his prime. He looked old, weak, and fragile.

ABOVE: Sugar Ray Charles Leonard (named after the R&B giant) battles welterweight champion Wilfred Benitez on November 30, 1979, for the title. In the closing seconds of the final round, Leonard won by knockout. In an era when television was becoming ever more popular, Leonard was the perfect candidate to bring his division popularity: he was good-looking, extremely charismatic, and had all the right moves, from his quick footwork to his patented flurries of punches. OPPOSITE: In the September 16, 1981, fight billed as "the Showdown," Sugar Ray Leonard set out to dispel the idea that his victory against Roberto Duran had somehow been a gift by taking on the supposedly invincible Thomas Hearns, "the Motor City Cobra." It was an exciting, back-and-forth affair; in the 14th round, at a point where Hearns held the upper hand on all three judges' score cards, Leonard dug deep and brought out everything he had, destroying Hearns. With the victory, Leonard unified the welterweight crown.

T.H.

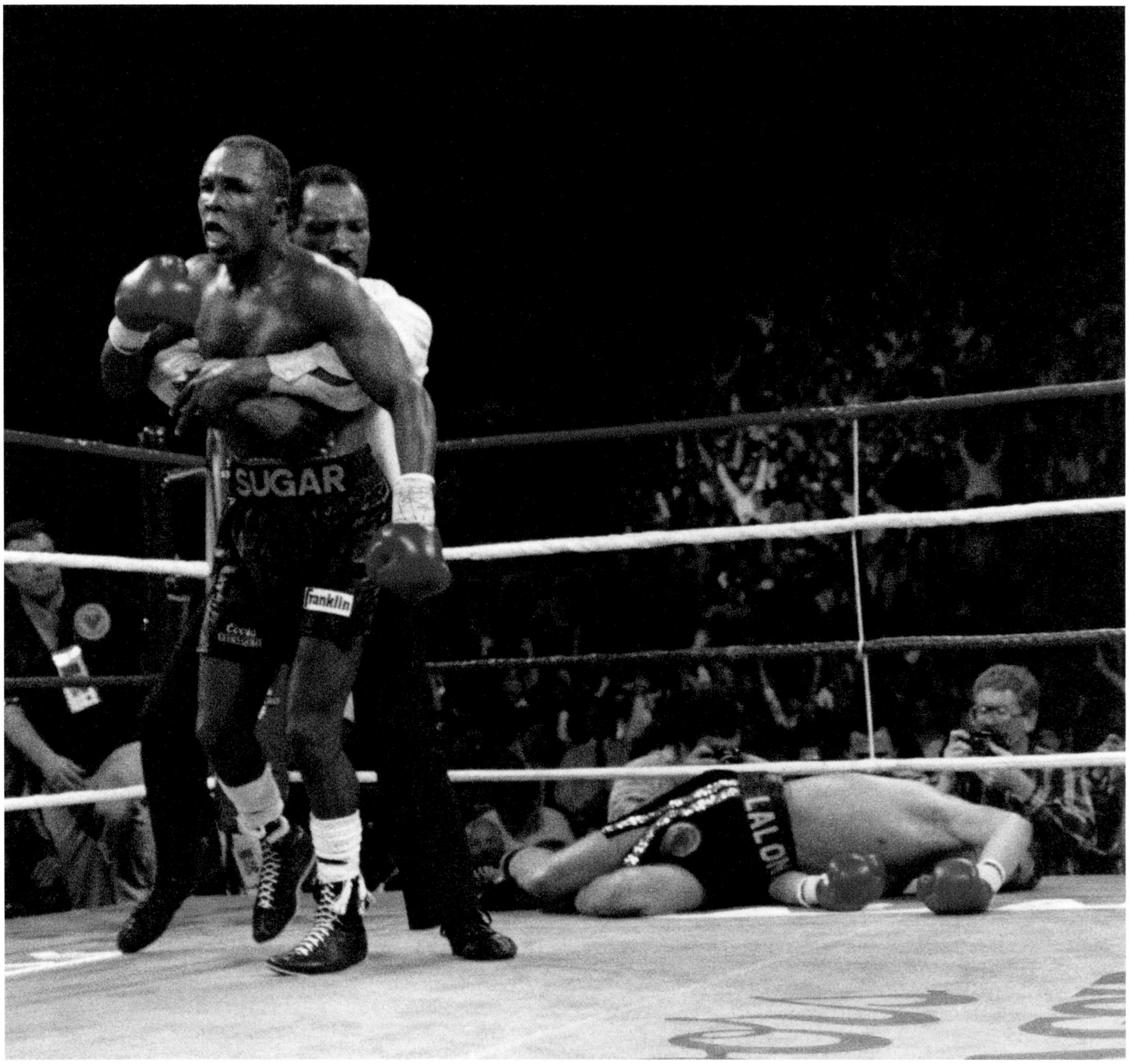

Sometimes great fighters are like unwelcome guests; they do not know when to leave. Ray Charles Leonard was no different. He had come back from retirement before, on February 9, 1991, when he faced Terry Norris, a young fighter eager to make his reputation against an aging legend. Leonard fell to the two most brutal opponents a fighter can face: time and the left hook. Norris battered Leonard, who had returned after a two-year exile from the ring. Before the start of the 12th and final round, Mike Trainer, the lawyer who represented the ex-champion, told him, "Try to stay on your feet, and then we'll get out of Dodge." Leonard did stay on his feet, proving that his heart, it not his talent, was as impressive as ever. But it was time to leave, and he knew it. He grabbed the ring microphone in Madison Square Garden after the bout, addressing the crowd that had come to see a fight and had stayed to see a retirement bash.

"This is my last fight," Leonard said simply. "It took this kind of a fight to prove to me it's time for me to venture away from boxing. If there was anyone I'd like to turn this over to, it's Terry Norris. I had to find out for myself. I've always been a risk-taker." It was a bittersweet victory for Norris. "It's a sad victory," he said. "I beat my idol, and I beat him badly. I didn't want it to be that way. He's still my idol." Leonard got out of Dodge that night, but it did not last; he came

OPPOSITE: Sugar Ray Leonard and Marvelous Marvin Hagler meet in the center of the ring during their April 6, 1987, middleweight title bout, a match Leonard won by a split decision. It was a tremendous comeback victory for the 31-year-old Leonard, who had been retired for five years before the fight. ABOVE: Referee Richard Steele restrains a surging Sugar Ray Leonard during during the 9th round of a fight against Donny Lalonde, November 7, 1988. Leonard won the fight by TKO in the same round.

back, against Camacho. "The Macho Man" beat him—and beat him easily. Why do great fighters subject themselves to such indignities?

Leonard would not learn; great fighters seldom do. After all, he had been an awesome fighter in his prime. And hadn't other, even older fighters defied the ravages of time and triumphed? Unfortunately Leonard had to find out the hard way that old fighters sometimes really do just fade away.

But if those final two fights—against Norris and Camacho—left sad, bitter memories, it is only because they stand out in a career that was as glorious as it was electrifying. Leonard was a great fighter, his achievements amplified because he filled the void that Muhammad Ali created when he retired in 1981. He was the Ali of the lighter weight divisions, a showman who wore short pants and gloves instead of a top hat and tails. Like Sugar Ray Robinson before him, he could dazzle you or flatten you; he was that versatile. And he proved it in fight after fight, defeating the greatest boxers of his generation—Roberto Duran, Thomas Hearns, Wilfred Benitez, and "Marvelous" Marvin Hagler.

In retrospect, it is easy to see why Leonard thought he could beat Norris and Camacho. After all, he had come back before, returning from a five-year absence to defeat one of the greatest fighters of the 1980s—Hagler. Leonard scored a split decision over Hagler on April 6, 1987, in Las Vegas, forcing the middleweight champion into a retirement that he was wise enough to maintain. If only Leonard had been so wise.

Thomas Hearns

It was June 12, 1989, in Las Vegas, and the sportswriters crafted their stories for the obituary sections of their newspapers. Why? Because Thomas Hearns, as a fighter, was dead—or so the sportswriters thought. The only difference between Hearns and a can of tomatoes, the critics said, was in the nutritional value. Or was it? Hearns did not believe it, and he set out to disprove

RIGHT: Thomas Hearns, "the Motor City Cobra," staged a comeback in the late 1980s that included this June 12, 1989, rematch against Sugar Ray Leonard, who had beaten him in dramatic fashion in the 14th round of their September 16, 1981, match-up. The 1989 fight was scored a draw by the judges, though many observers felt Hearns had fought the better bout.

what his recent past seemed to confirm. After all, here was a man who had been clubbed by "Marvelous" Marvin Hagler and Iran Barkley, a knockout victim each time. And now he was facing Sugar Ray Leonard, who had already beaten him on September 16, 1981—a 14th-round knockout in one of the greatest fights of all time.

To Hearns, the rematch was not a fight; it was a revival meeting. He wanted to find out if he could redeem himself. He wanted to find out if he could achieve grace in a 20-foot (6m) ring, where one punch can mean the difference between doom and salvation. He wanted to find out, more than anything, if he could whup Sugar Ray Leonard. Hearns did just that, dropping him twice in a tense and exciting match, but he would not get the decision. The judges scored the fight a draw, a travesty for the man who wanted to prove so much. He accepted the decision gracefully. "I leave it up to the judges," he said. "I'm proud of the draw. I have to be thankful for what I received."

For a fighter who seemed washed up before the Leonard fight, Hearns proved remarkably durable after the bout, going on to defeat Virgil Hill for the light heavyweight title on June 3, 1991, in Las Vegas. Hearns was a tremendous puncher early in his career; his tall, thin frame belied his power. But punching power is not about bulk or muscles; it is about speed and balance, timing and coordination, and Hearns boasted all of these qualities, hammering opponents on the inside or strafing them from the outside.

Hearns retained that power, but he also became a smart fighter in the twilight of his career, his kamikaze style tempered by craft and guile. Witness his bout against the hard-punching James Kinchen on November 4, 1988, in Las Vegas. Kinchen staggered Hearns in the middle rounds, and Hearns grabbed his opponent as if he were a dance partner, holding him so tight that the referee could barely pry the two men apart. "I held onto him like he was my woman," Hearns said. Like Leonard, Hearns fought the greatest fighters of his era—Leonard, Hagler, Roberto Duran, Pepino Cuevas. He did not always win, but when he lost, he lost spectacularly, throwing punches until his chin betrayed him. That will be his ultimate legacy to boxing—the tension

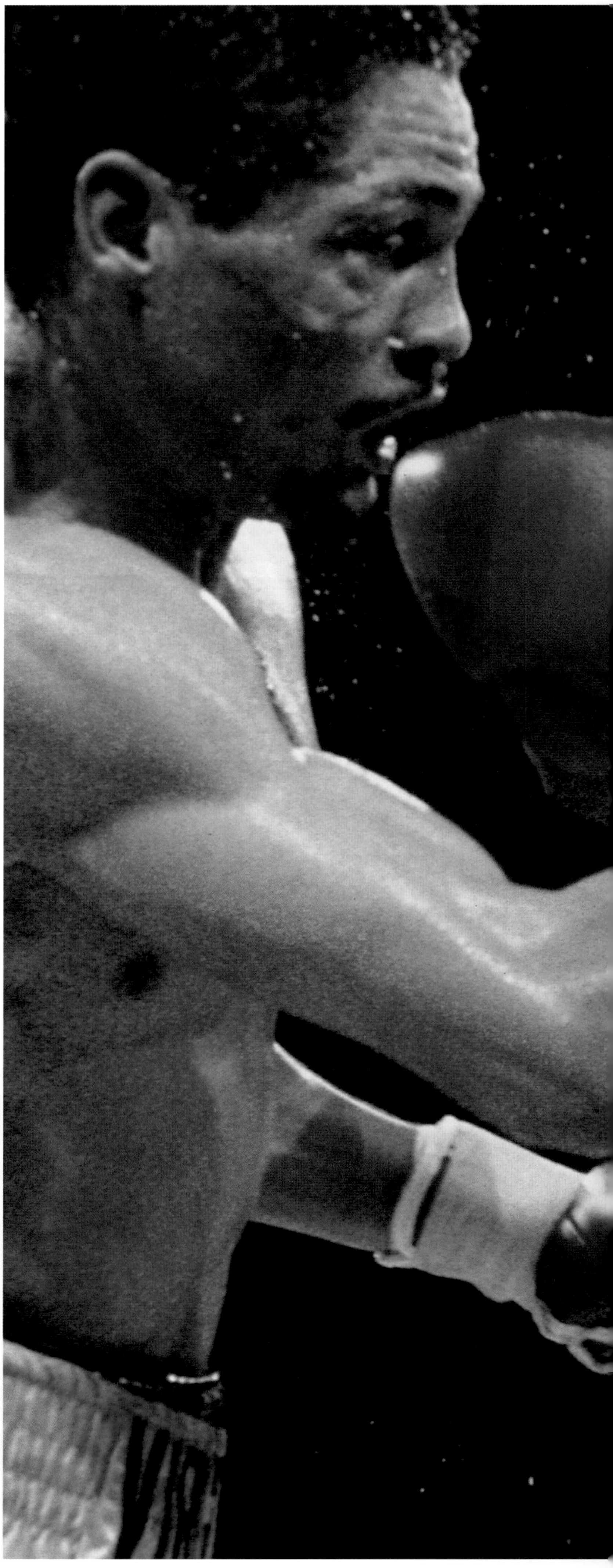

RIGHT: **An extremely determined Hearns outjabs Virgil Hill to reclaim the light heavyweight title on June 3, 1991.**

and excitement he brought to the sport. He was not the showman that Ali and Leonard were, but he was every bit as entertaining, the thrills coming from the heart and fury he displayed in the ring.

"Marvelous" Marvin Hagler

The first name was not a name at all. It was an adjective, but it applied—"Marvelous" Marvin Hagler. Then again, maybe the name should have been "Menacing" Marvin Hagler, because he intimidated opponents long before they stepped into the ring. Maybe it was the scowl, the shaved head, or the pet names he gave his fists, "Knock" and "Out." Or maybe it was his motto, a paean to brutality, if not grammar—"Destruct and destroy."

It must have been all of those things, because it was certainly not his ring presence. Hagler was not a monster in the ring, not in the sense that Roberto Duran or Thomas "the Hit Man" Hearns was. He was a cautious, scientific boxer, a southpaw who could fight as a right-hander, switching stances so smoothly and fluidly, sometimes in the middle of a combination, that opponents were stunned, first by his movement, then by his punches. "Destruct and destroy?" Perhaps, but it seemed more like "Dazzle and destroy." "He's the monster man," trainer Angelo Dundee said, perpetuating an image that seemed inaccurate.

ABOVE: Marvelous Marvin Hagler appears focused in the moments before his September 27, 1980, fight against Alan Minter. After years of frustration, typified by the Antuofermo fight in 1979 that by most accounts had been won by Hagler, "Marvelous" slugged his way to the middleweight championship with a decisive 3rd-round knockout of Minter. OPPOSITE: Marvelous Marvin Hagler and Vito Antuofermo rough each other up on the inside on November 30, 1979, during a title bout that ended in a draw. Since his professional debut in 1973, Hagler created quite a reputation for himself in the middleweight division, proving he could win from both sides and with amazing changes in rhythm. But of course, he wanted more. His first attempt to win the title was here against Antuofermo and many outraged observers thought that Hagler had been robbed of a victory by the decision.

Or was it inaccurate? Hagler could be a monster, but he pressed the attack only if he was pressed in return. And he was pressed on April 15, 1985, in Las Vegas, when he knocked out Hearns in one of the most sensational fights in boxing history. "It was 3 minutes of mayhem, of controlled, educated violence sustained at an almost unendurable level of intensity," wrote Harry Mullan, editor of the British magazine *Boxing News.* "They smashed terrifying hooks at each other, full-blooded blows which were designed to intimidate and destroy."

Like many great fighters before him, Hagler found more obstacles outside the ring than inside. Rather than duck his punches, champions ducked him, refusing to give him a shot at their titles. He lost two matches in Philadelphia, home to some of the greatest middleweights in the world—to Bobby "Boogaloo" Watts and Willie "the Worm" Monroe—but he returned to prove himself in the same town, beating Eugene Hart, Bennie Briscoe, and, in a rematch, Monroe. And it was then that the ducking started. Hagler became bitter and frustrated, a contender for life—or so he thought. Legislators championed his cause, trying to lobby on his behalf. When he finally got his shot against middleweight champion Vito Antuofermo on November 30, 1979, in Las Vegas, the judges scored the fight a draw—an injustice that enraged an already bitter man. The bitterness did not last long. He got another shot, this one against Alan Minter on

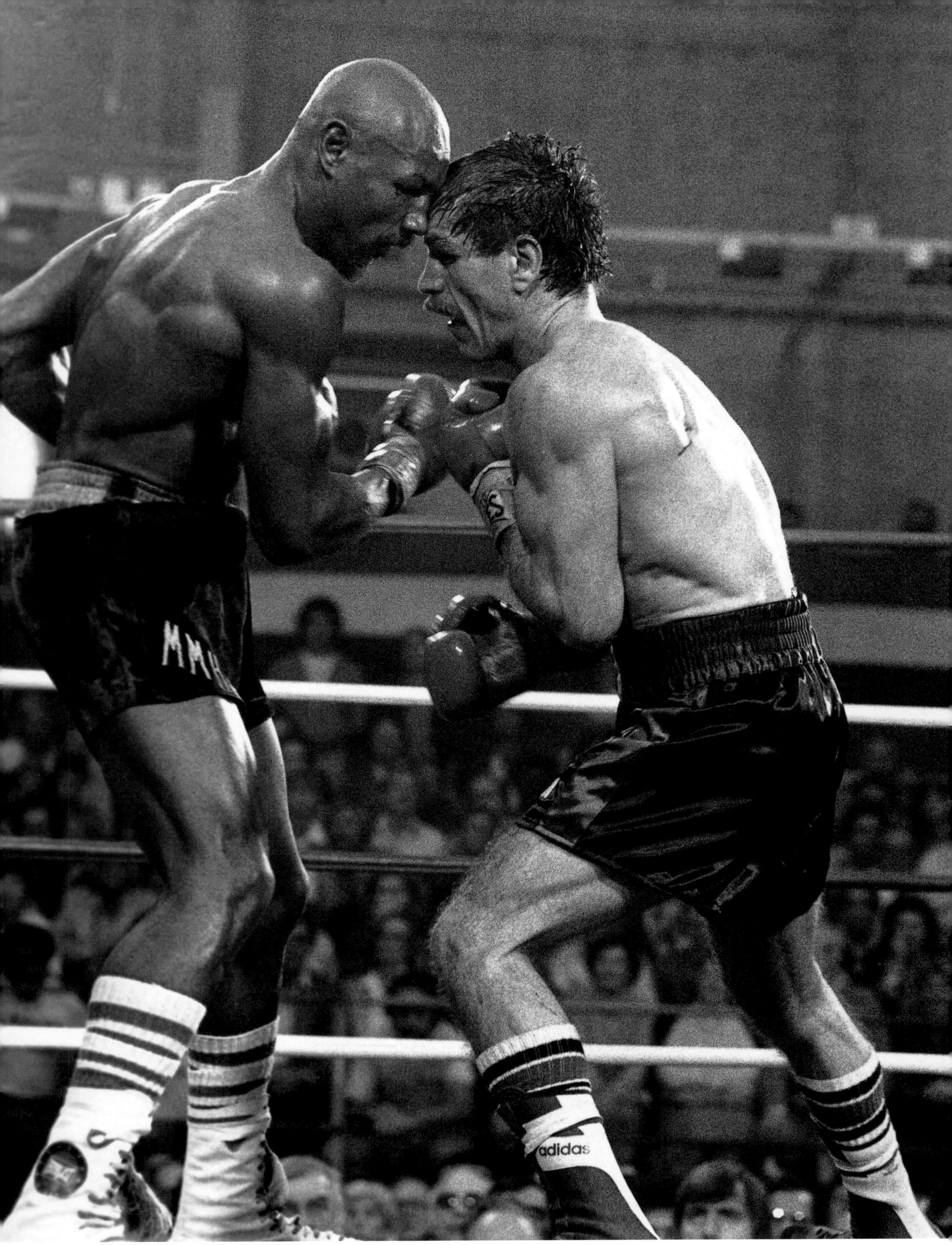
MMH
adidas

September 27, 1980, in London, and he exploited the opportunity by removing the judges from consideration. He knocked out Alan Minter in the 3rd round, sparking a riot that forced the new champion to hide under the ring. "The violence doesn't really bother me," Hagler said afterward, shrugging his shoulders.

Hagler held onto his title for seven years, which included thirteen successful defenses, an astounding streak that ended when Sugar Ray Leonard upset him on April 6, 1987. It was a controversial decision, and Hagler responded with the anger that had fueled him

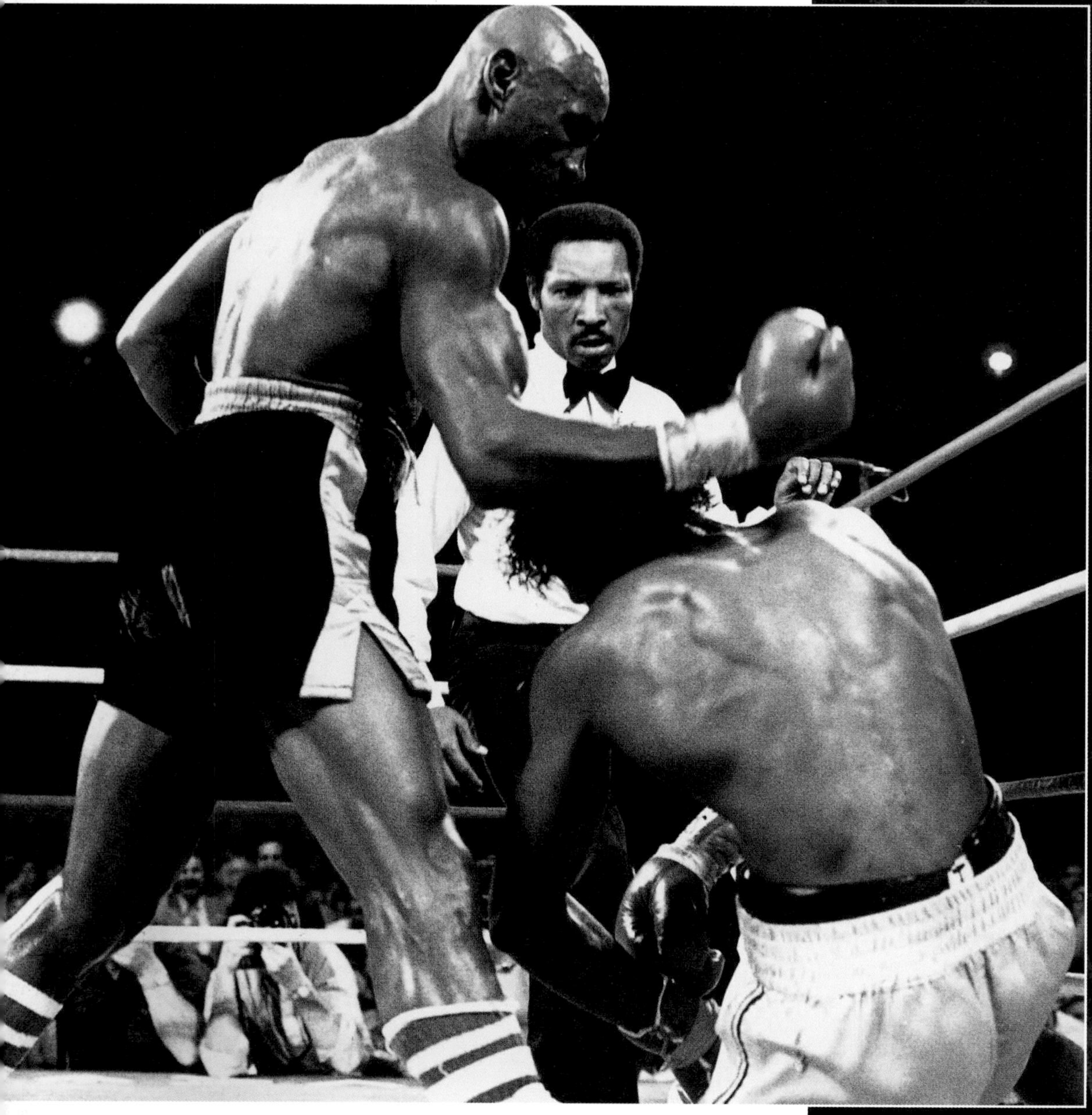

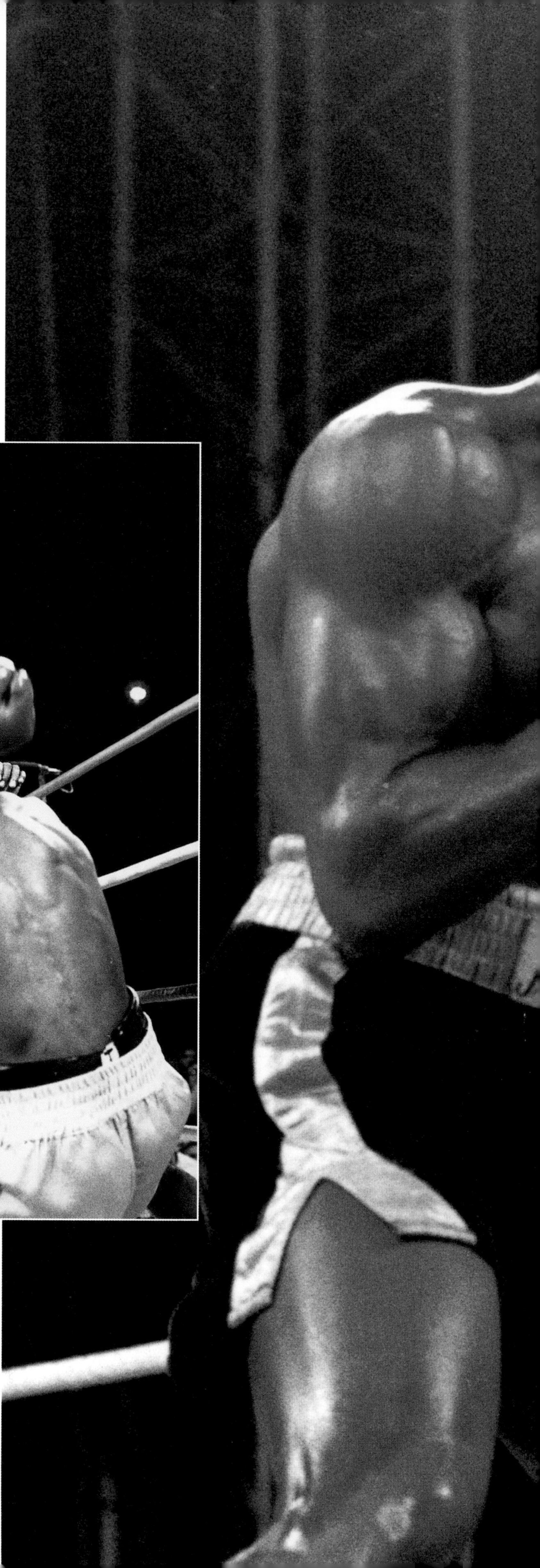

ABOVE: Marvelous Marvin Hagler hammers Thomas Hearns to the floor in their classic middleweight bout, April 15, 1985. RIGHT: Marvin Hagler rocks challenger John Mugabi with a thunderous left during the 2nd round of this title defense on March 10, 1986, in Las Vegas.

earlier in his career, when he could not get the title shot he deserved. He was so bitter that he retired and moved to Italy, where he became a star of action movies—a real-life warrior turned into a celluloid hero, his motto still "Destruct and destroy."

George Foreman

If Muhammad Ali towered above the rest of the world, George Foreman stood with the common man, pleasant and humble and unassuming. But he was not a common man. He was the oldest heavyweight champion to walk the planet. Foreman reached that status with a remarkable performance on November 5, 1994, when he knocked out Michael Moorer in the 11th round. Foreman, the fistic Everyman, was 45 years old, seven years older than Jersey Joe Walcott was when he defeated Ezzard Charles for the heavyweight title on June 5, 1952. "My promoter kept saying that I could make history," Foreman said afterward, wearing a pair of sunglasses to conceal the bruises on his face. "He said, 'History, George, history.' And I knew he was no Barnum and Bailey. I knew he was being sincere."

ABOVE: George Foreman smashes a left to the head of Joe Frazier, flooring the heavyweight champion for the sixth and final time on January 22, 1973. This devastating display of power—Frazier went to the mat three times in the 1st round and three times in the 95 seconds the referee allowed of the subsequent round—gave Foreman the championship. Interestingly, it was the first time in almost sixty years that the heavyweight title had been decided in a locale outside the United States. OPPOSITE: A reborn George Foreman stalks the ring after knocking Gerry Cooney out in the 2nd round of their January 15, 1990, heavyweight bout. Few observers realized it at the time, but the apparently over-the-hill Foreman was just four years away from making boxing history.

Foreman was bigger than boxing, and not just becaust he stood 6 feet 3 inches (191cm) and weighed 250 pounds (114kg). No, he transcended the sport because he could relate to his fans and his fans could relate to him. He was a rarity: a man who delighted in his imperfections. When he strolled toward the ring, his stomach visible several seconds before the rest of his body, he seemed to say, "It's okay to be heavy. Feel good about yourself." And so the boxing world felt good about this benign brawler.

Before his comeback in 1987, Foreman was not sweet, caring, and pleasant. He was moody and self-absorbed, interested more in his pet lions than in the people around him. And, my, could he punch. He owned the heaviest hammers this side of a hardware store, both of them encased in 10-ounce (285g) leather gloves. One shot from either of them—left or right—and the ring would turn into a grotesque roller-coaster ride, with the man who took the punch hanging on for dear life. "I have the cannon effect," Foreman said. "On a battleship, you have these guns that go boom! The gunners know that if one shot hits, that's all it's gonna take. That's what my hands are like."

Foreman learned how to box in the Job Corps, where he acquired a skill that would win him an Olympic gold medal in 1968 and the world heavyweight title five years later. He won the championship with his 2-round demolition of Joe Frazier on January 22, 1973, in Kingston, Jamaica, perhaps the most impressive display of punching power in heavyweight history. Then he lost the crown a year later, when Muhammad Ali stopped him in the 8th

A Closer Look

George Foreman stood in the center of the ring, almost 30 minutes into a horrible beating, his breath gone and his strength about to follow, when something amazing happened. Something miraculous. The George Foreman of 1994 became the George Foreman of 1974—a time warp that shocked the world.

One second the old man was marooned in his own body, conscious but unable to make his arms and legs respond to the messages from his brain. And the next second? Young and vibrant again, he was trying to decapitate Michael Moorer, the heavyweight champion of the world. Moorer kept his head, but he could not keep the crown that sat upon it. The old man, behind on all three cards, knocked him out in the 10th round, flattening him with one of the greatest combinations in boxing history—a left jab followed by a chopping right, both of them short and sweet and punishing. And, oh yes, amazing. Foreman became the oldest heavyweight champion in history, seven years older than the previous oldest champion, Jersey Joe Walcott. It happened on November 5, 1994, in Las Vegas, and boxing fans will remember it forever. "This is the greatest thrill of my athletic career," Foreman said.

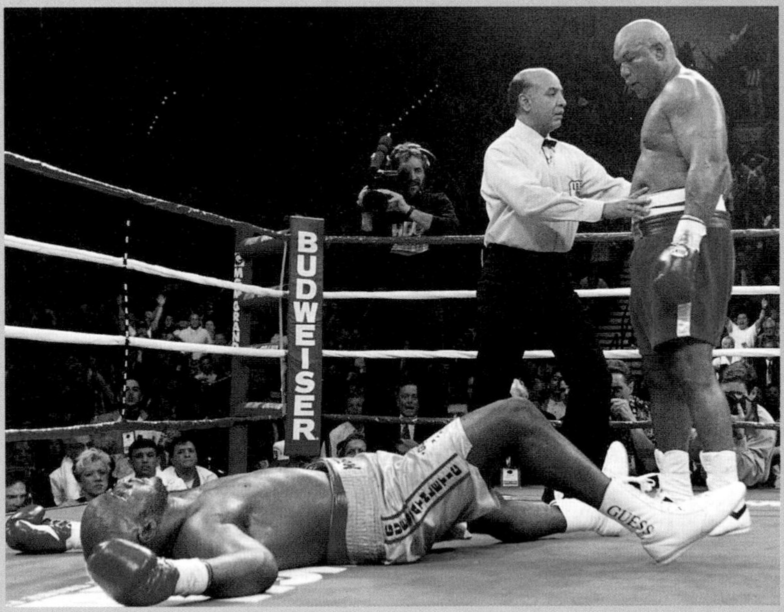

With his victory over Moorer, he regained the title he had lost to Muhammad Ali twenty years before, during the legendary "Rumble in the Jungle" on October 30, 1974. "I've been heavyweight champion of the world before, and I know what it feels like," Foreman said. "But, when I saw Moorer on his back, all I wanted to do was let the Almighty know that I appreciate living this long."

Foreman, who had been retired for ten years, launched his comeback against Steve Zouski on March 9, 1987—a comeback that inspired laughter throughout the boxing world. The old man hit the canvas about six times—not from punches he absorbed, but from punches he threw. He would fire the overhand right, delivering the punch with the follow-through of a baseball pitcher, and fall down when he missed. It was an embarrassing episode, but he won the fight, and it taught him a lesson: he began to shorten his punches—and stay on his feet.

The fans stopped laughing on January 15, 1990, when Foreman crushed Gerry Cooney in the 2nd round. Then he fought Evander Holyfield for the undisputed title a year later, acquiring even more fans and admirers with his courageous, albeit losing, performance against a man twelve years younger. Spectators left the arena as if they had just witnessed a heartwarming musical, not a brutal heavyweight fight. "I had more fun this time than the first time," Foreman said. "I didn't take myself seriously, but every time I stood in front of a microphone, I was very conscious of what I said, because I knew the kids were listening. That's how I want to be remembered—as someone who cared about the kids."

A man who seemed to thrive on intimidation both inside and outside the ring during his first incarnation, Foreman became gentler during his ten years away from the ring, when he discovered that people were nice to him even though they had nothing to gain from their association with him.

"I was a nobody," Foreman said. "People didn't even know I was champ. They just called me the 'Big-un.' I was so spoiled when I was champ. I didn't do anything for myself. Then I retired, and I was lost. I didn't even know how to pump gas at those self-serve stations. People were always ready to help the 'Big-un.' I learned to appreciate human beings. When you've lost a human being, you've lost something special."

And that is exactly what the fans thought of Foreman—they thought he was something special. "George has been so unbelievable for this sport," the late Dan Duva once said. "Without him, there would be no humor in this business. He's done far more for this sport than anyone ever thought he would."

OPPOSITE: George Foreman lands a punishing left en route to a stunning, historic victory over Michael Moorer on November 5, 1994. The win, which gave Foreman both the WBA and the IBF heavyweight crowns, caused the boxing world to reevaluate Foreman's place in the pantheon of boxing deities. ABOVE: Becoming the oldest man to win the heavyweight title, George Foreman stares at the man he clubbed into submission, Michael Moorer.

round in Kinshasa, Zaire—an upset as shocking as the one Foreman had administered against Frazier. "If I had been smart, Ali would never have beaten me," Foreman said. "But Ali was tricking me, making me punch myself out, and I didn't even realize it." Then 29, Foreman announced his retirement after losing a decision to Jimmy Young, a wily but light-hitting boxer, on March 17, 1977, in San Juan, Puerto Rico. It was not the loss that caused Foreman to walk away from boxing. It was what happened after the loss.

"I was back in the dressing room after the fight, and I had this gigantic experience," Foreman said. "For a split second, just a split second, I was dead. I told everyone I was dying. They thought I was going crazy. I was in a deep, dark nothing place, and there was a horrible smell to go along with the nothingness.

"Then a giant hand reached out and saved me. And when I had this vision, I collapsed. I told my doctor, 'Take your hat off, because the thorns on it are making your head bleed.' I started reciting verses from the Bible that I didn't even know."

The doctor called it heat prostration, but Foreman called it a revelation. The ex-champion became a Protestant minister a year later, waging battles that were strictly of the spiritual variety. He built a church in north Houston, the Church of the Lord Jesus Christ, and he began to discard the "material things" he had acquired with his ring earnings, including his seven cars. "I started realizing there was more to this world than George Foreman," he said. Foreman was content to remain a full-time preacher until 1986, when he refused, for what he thought were sound reasons, to help a member of his flock. "One kid was getting into trouble, so his mother came to me for help," Foreman said. "She asked me if I could show her son how to box. She thought boxing would keep him out of trouble, the same way it did for me. I said, 'Now how can I teach a kid how to fight when I'm a preacher?' It wouldn't look right. The kid ended up going to prison." So Foreman experienced another revelation, this one just as vivid, if not as dramatic, as the one in San Juan. "I had no right to refuse to help the kid just because I was afraid of what people would think," Foreman said. "So I thought I could help the church by boxing and raising money. I put on my short pants again. They were tight." Thus began his quest, which ended when he beat Moorer.

Foreman enjoyed his dual life, rhapsodizing in the church one minute, terrorizing in the ring the next. If there was any contradiction between saving souls and putting them to sleep, he did not see it. The fighting preacher was having too much fun doing both. And the boxing world was glad he did.

Larry Holmes

After one of his comeback fights in 1991, Larry Holmes jumped into the air, staying aloft for so long that he looked like a statue mounted on a pedestal of air. Then, quoting another aging entertainer, James Brown, the former heavyweight champion shouted, "I feeeeeeel good!" Feel good? Larry Holmes? The man who once told the world to kiss him on a part of his anatomy concealed by his silk trunks? Yes, that Larry Holmes. Like George Foreman, another former champion who returned to the ring, Holmes was a different man during his comeback—wiser, if not kinder and gentler. "There was real animosity between Larry and me in the old days," said Bob Arum, who promoted Holmes during his comeback. "He was rude, impolite, and he would shout at me in public. I refused to talk to him for years. But he changed. He enjoyed himself more the second time around. He and George became much calmer. They've proved what you can accomplish by being a gentleman."

If Holmes was bitter the first time around, there was good reason for it. He followed the toughest act in sports history: Muhammad Ali. Holmes was a great fighter, but great was not good enough, not for the man who chased Ali. Think of it. Who were the guys that followed Elvis into Sun Studio in Memphis, Tennessee? Jerry Lee Lewis, Carl Perkins, Johnny Cash? They were titanic talents, all of them, but they were not Elvis. And Holmes was not Ali. He tried to be Ali, tried to imitate his magnificent style, according to the critics, and who could blame him? After all, the kid sparred with "the Greatest" in the mid-1970s, and he was so good that Ali called him the future heavy-

OPPOSITE: In one of the greatest heavyweight title fights ever waged—even though the title had been split by now among various organizations and was something of a travesty—Larry Holmes strafes Ken Norton with a right on June 9, 1978. The fight went the distance and was a classic back-and-forth contest, with the two giants trading ground-shaking power punches throughout. In the 15th round, Holmes dug a little deeper and in a closing flurry secured the split decision—by 1 point. Unheralded until then, Holmes had finally won some notoriety—if not exactly respect.

weight champion of the world. The kid, trying to punch his way out of the projects in Easton, Pennsylvania, was mesmerized. "He was the heavyweight champion of the world, and I was a kid," Holmes said. "Shoot, man, you couldn't tell me nothing. I was on cloud nine."

For Holmes, his greatest triumph would prove his greatest downfall. He defeated Ken Norton on June 9, 1978, in Las Vegas, scoring a split decision to win the heavyweight title in one of the greatest bouts in boxing history—a tough, grueling match, with both fighters so tired that they ended up in a sweaty embrace, their bodies draped across each other like shabby overcoats. "I wanted to take him out," Holmes said. "I hurt him a few times, and he hurt me, but because of his determination and my determination, we both finished."

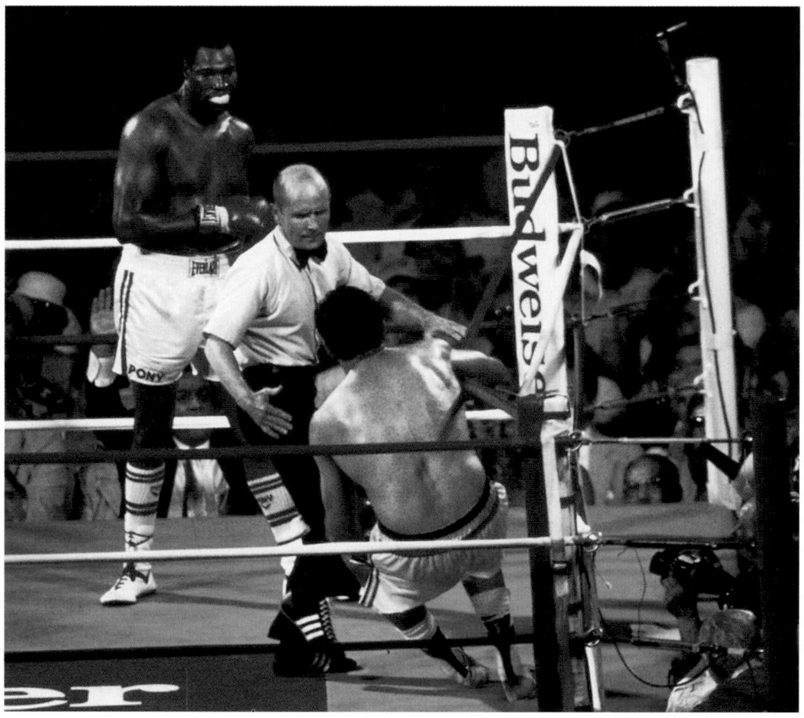

ABOVE: Larry Holmes scored a 13th-round knockout against Gerry Cooney—part of a record eight consecutive knockouts in defense of his title—in this much-ballyhooed match-up on June 11, 1982. OPPOSITE: Larry Holmes and the WBC belt he defended against Cooney in Las Vegas.

The kid became what Ali had predicted, the heavyweight champion of the world, but he was not a champion so much as a successor to the champion, a successor to the man. The critics called him a carbon copy of Ali, and he bristled. Holmes fell from cloud nine, nose-diving through the mists of the ozone, the rarified heights becoming the agonizing lows. And he landed on his butt.

Holmes was arrogant, and he admitted it freely. "I always thought I could get along with people by telling 'em where it's at from the beginning," he said. It was a noble stance, perhaps, but a misguided one. Holmes, hounded by the ghost of Ali, became moody and defensive, detecting slights where none were intended. For Holmes, the idol had become the tormentor, and Holmes tried to squash the anguish in the only forum where he felt comfortable: the ring. He met Ali on October 2, 1980, in Las Vegas—the sparring partner versus the professor—but Holmes did not get the satisfaction he wanted. He beat the old man, all right, beat him badly, with Ali cowering on the ropes like a helpless child, unable to stop the punishment he would have avoided in his prime. But America felt bad about the spectacle, and Holmes felt worse, so when the referee stopped the bout in the 11th round, the anguish continued, and Larry Holmes went on being Larry Holmes, the successor to Muhammad Ali.

When Holmes lost to Michael Spinks on September 21, 1985, becoming the first heavyweight champion to lose his title to a light heavyweight champion, he blamed the defeat on politics. When he lost the rematch seven months later, he went ballistic, telling a national television audience that the cable network HBO could kiss him "where the sun didn't shine." A carbon copy of Ali? Please. Ali was loud and outrageous, but he had an undeniable grace and dignity that his successor seemed to lack.

After retiring in 1986, Holmes returned to challenge Mike Tyson, then the heavyweight champion of the world, on January 22, 1988, in Atlantic City. Tyson stopped the ex-champion in the 4th round, with Holmes falling flat on his back, his legs shooting up awkwardly as he crashed to the canvas. The ex-champ started to gag, and the referee, afraid the fallen fighter was choking on his mouthpiece, tried to yank it out. "I'm going to laugh all the way to the Lafayette Savings and Loan," Holmes said before returning to his home in Easton.

If Holmes had ended his career there, the world would still know him as the carbon copy of Ali—loud

PONY
PONY
PONY

and arrogant and profane. But he came back, and he came back a different man, proud to be Larry Holmes—not a carbon copy, but an original. Holmes began to enjoy himself—perhaps the biggest shock of his career. When he upset Ray Mercer on February 7, 1992, in Atlantic City, the crowd cheered him in the early rounds, chanting, "Larry, Larry, Larry." The ex-champion fed off the energy, but instead of getting pumped up, he became more relaxed; at one point, trapped in the corner, Holmes looked into a television camera, said, "Watch this," and popped Mercer with a straight right to the forehead. It was as close as a fight gets to a lounge act. And the fans loved it. "To tell you the truth, I thought the Mercer fight was going to be the end of Larry," Arum said. "Mercer hits hard and has a great chin. But Larry proved us all wrong."

During his second comeback, Holmes challenged two heavyweight champions, Evander Holyfield and Oliver McCall, losing both fights by decision. But he won something more important during his return to the ring—the respect of the fans who had scorned him for years. And he savored it. "People used to say I was just a carbon copy of Ali," he said. "Now I don't care what they say."

Michael Spinks

Michael Spinks was Gumby in short pants, bending, twisting, and throwing punches—so many punches from so many angles that he looked like a picnicker shooing away a squadron of flies. "If I walked into a gym, and I saw Spinks training for the first time, yes, I would be tempted to change his style," said Eddie Futch, who trained the former light heavyweight and heavyweight champion. But Futch was wise and didn't tamper with an ugly style that produced beautiful results.

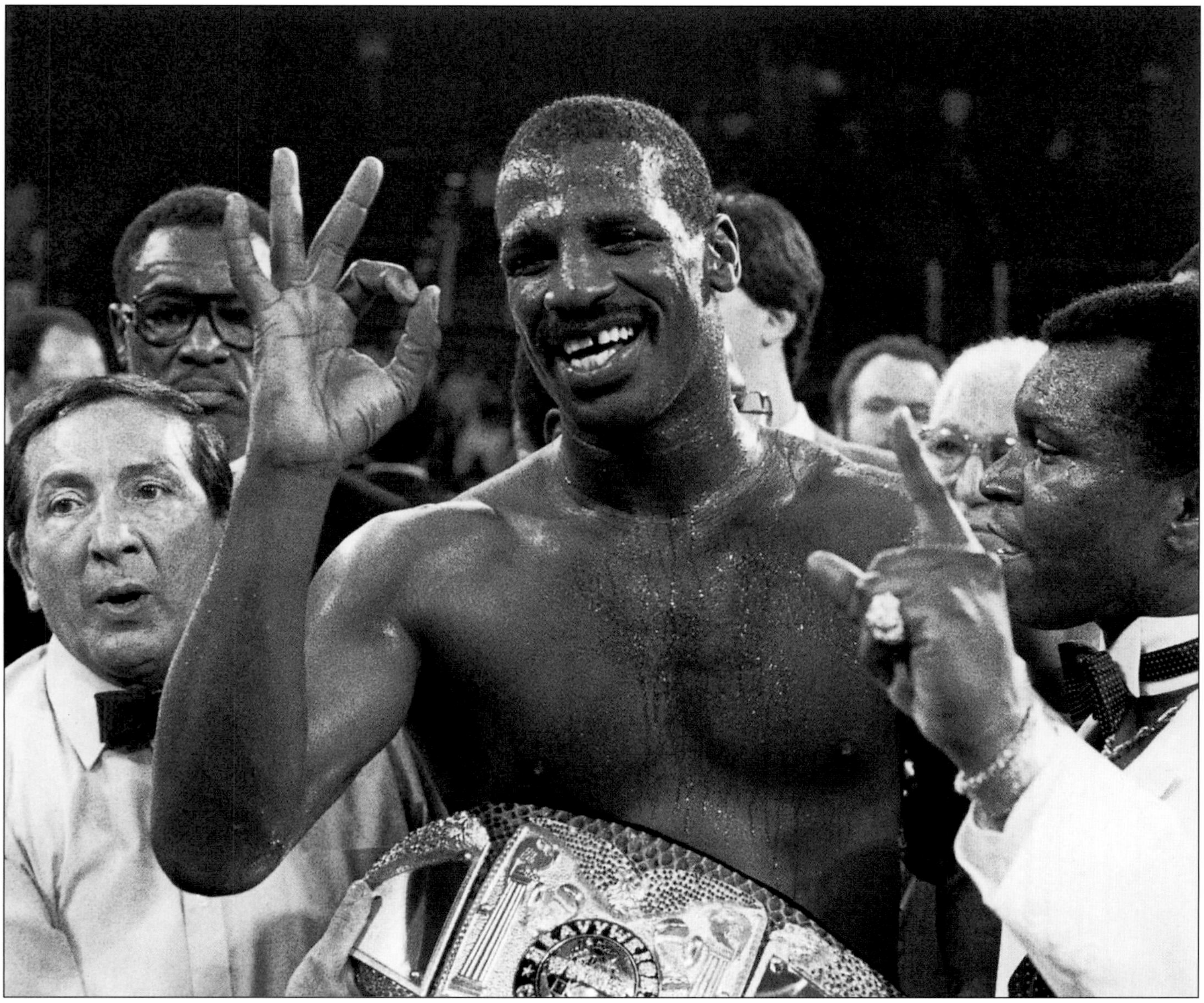

Above: **On September 21, 1985, Michael Spinks avenged his brother Leon's June 2, 1981, loss to Larry Holmes. With the dramatic upset, Michael and Leon became the only brothers to have been world heavyweight champions. Here, Spinks is congratulated by promoter Butch Lewis (right).**

From 1981 to 1985, Spinks dominated the light heavyweight division, dazzling opponents with his movement, then clubbing them with the overhand right that he called "the Spinks Jinx." He won the title on July 18, 1981, in Las Vegas, scoring a unanimous decision over Mustafa Muhammad. The champ remained in the division for four more years, defending his title ten times, before the irony of his situation hit him like a right cross to the temple. Here he was, the undisputed master of his division, but his success was straitjacketing him, leaving him with no more opponents, no more bouts to test his ability, to raise the bar. So he fled.

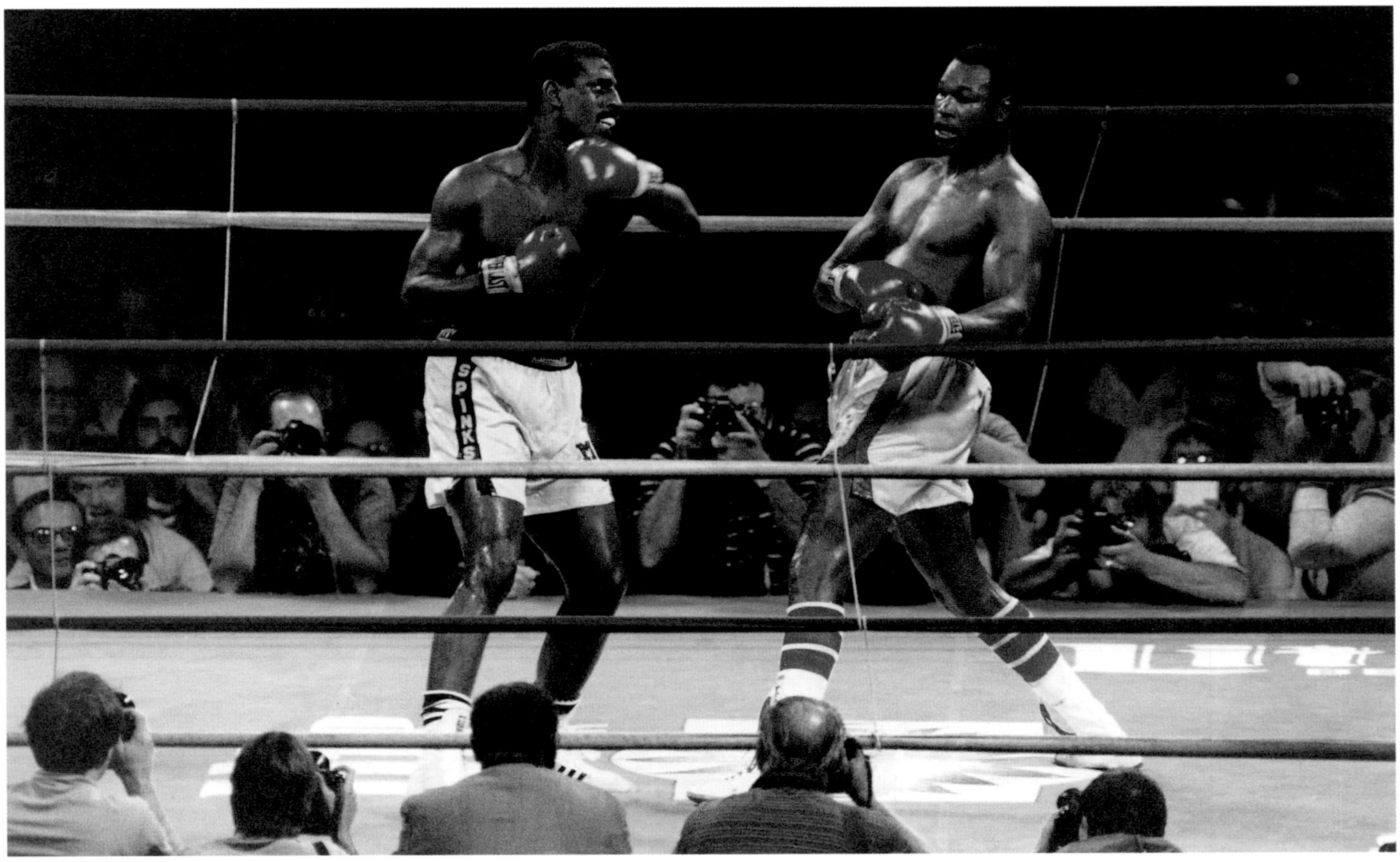

ABOVE: **Normally a light heavyweight, Michael Spinks had bulked up to challenge Larry Holmes for the heavyweight title. In a stunning upset victory, Spinks beat his opponent to win the heavyweight crown on September 21, 1985. Spinks won a unanimous decision over Holmes, who would lose to Spinks again in a 1986 rematch.**

If Spinks escaped, his destination did not exactly look like a sanctuary. He climbed to the heavyweight division, a weight class ruled by the most dominant champion of the era: Larry Holmes. It was a downright crazy idea. Spinks hired fitness guru Mackie Shilstone to give him a new body—the body of a heavyweight. He lifted weights and ran wind sprints, abandoning the long-distance road work that boxers had favored since the turn of the century. The hard work paid off; Spinks became a heavyweight, shocking the boxing world when he stepped on the scale—he weighed 200 pounds (91kg), 21 pounds (10kg) less than Holmes. Okay, the critics said, he looked like a heavyweight, with the thick upper body of his new mates in the division, but could he fight like a heavyweight? The answer was yes. Spinks upset Holmes on September 21, 1985, in Las Vegas, to become the first reigning light heavyweight champion to win the heavyweight title. Then he won the rematch seven months later, when he survived an early battering to score a hotly disputed split decision over the ex-champion.

With his rival now retired, Spinks fought a man who threatened to become as dominant as Holmes: Mike Tyson. They called it "the Fight of the Century," but it is hard for a fight to be considered one for the ages when it lasts only 91 seconds. Tyson destroyed Spinks on June 27, 1988, in Atlantic City by decking him with a right uppercut to the jaw. The ex–light heavyweight, who had never been floored, looked like a light heavyweight again, weak and frail, his head crashing to the canvas, his eyes receding into his skull. It was a sad end to a glorious ride.

The former two-time champion retired a few months later, his latest defeat failing to overshadow what had been a brilliant career. He left the ring with a record of 31-1 with 21 knockouts—not bad for a kid who seemed like a reluctant warrior. Spinks entered boxing for the same reason that his older brother Leon did—to learn how to defend himself. He was 13 when he walked into a gym for the first time, and he cried during his first few sparring sessions. Leon called him a sissy, and Michael, on the verge of abandoning the sport he had just picked up, decided to persevere. "Michael got so good that he would give Leon a pretty hard time in the gym," said Claudell Atkins, a childhood friend. "Their sparring sessions weren't wars or anything. They weren't out to kill each other. But if Leon ever dropped his hands too low—whomp—Michael would nail him."

Both Michael and Leon went on to win the heavyweight title, becoming the only brothers to share that status in boxing history, although Michael was the superior fighter, the man whose ring record marked him as an immortal.

ABOVE: Reigning heavyweight champion Mike Tyson looks on as former champion Larry Holmes topples into the ropes on January 22, 1988. The fight was an ill-advised comeback attempt by Holmes against an opponent who at the time was absolutely lethal in the ring in fight after fight.
OPPOSITE: Mike Tyson and Donovan "Razor" Ruddock first met on March 18, 1991; at the time, Tyson was still on the comeback trail following his stunning loss to Buster Douglas. Tyson won the Ruddock fight by TKO, but many observers felt the refs had stopped the fight prematurely and that Tyson had gotten away with an easy win. The two men met again, on June 28 that year, and Tyson proved that the abbreviated first encounter had been a lucky one for Ruddock. In the second fight, shown here, Tyson sent Ruddock to the mat twice and broke the larger man's jaw en route to winning a 12-round decision. Here, "Iron" Mike smashes "Razor" Ruddock in the face with a piledriver left during the second fight (Tyson's last before going to prison on a rape conviction), dislodging Ruddock's mouth guard in the process.

Mike Tyson

It was 1985, and the kid was sparring at a gym in Catskill, New York, getting ready to launch an attack that could turn a forest into a field of pencil shavings. "I want to be the greatest heavyweight who ever lived," he said. "That's my goal."

The kid was Mike Tyson, and he spoke with the sweet passion of youth, his lisp as disarming as his left hook. This was "Kid Dynamite," the young man whom *Ring Magazine* called "the savior of boxing." The fans loved him, but the love affair would not last. In the end, the savior of boxing could not save himself, much less the fight game. Was it a losing battle? Perhaps, but he kept trying, his reclamation project suddenly downsized in scope from the boxing world to one individual in the boxing world—himself. It will be his biggest challenge.

From 1986 to 1990, Tyson was the terror of the heavyweight division—a reign that started when he defeated Trevor Berbick to become the youngest heavyweight champion in history. The champion went 10-0 with 8 knockouts during that span, including victories over Larry Holmes and Tony Tucker, and he did it with a style that was as efficient as it was brutal, combining superb defense with explosive offense. He taunted opponents before and after fights, once saying that Tyrell Biggs moaned like a woman when he received a shot to the ribs. "Mike has a lot of ability, but I think he's only reached about 30 percent of his potential," Kevin Rooney, his ex-trainer, said during that period. "When he gets older, he's going to be scary. I wouldn't want to say he can become the greatest. I mean when you say the greatest, what's next? Being God? But I will say this: he can become a great, great champion, one of the best that ever lived."

Then he met a journeyman on February 11, 1990, in Tokyo, and the journeyman earned one of the biggest—and quickest—promotions in the history of the working class, going from pug to heavyweight champion in one startling night. James "Buster" Douglas knocked out Tyson in the 10th round with a combination that shocked the world.

Tyson came back, trying to reclaim his position as the "baddest" man on the planet. He won four fights, but he was no longer the baddest man in the world: he had to change his motto or find a new planet, because

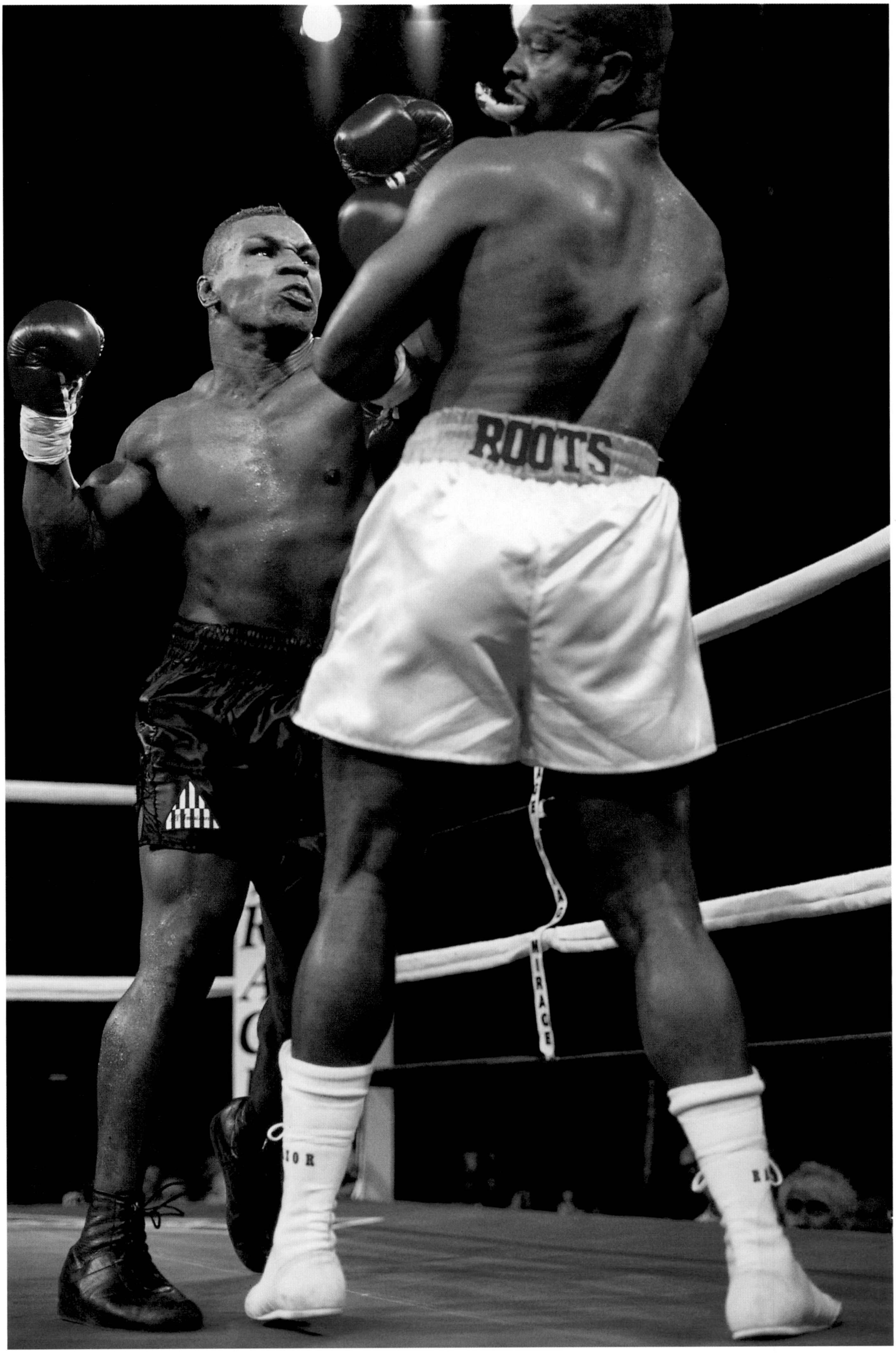
ROOTS
MIRACE

the best heavyweight in the world was Evander Holyfield. Holyfield had dethroned Douglas with a 3rd-round knockout on October 25, 1990, in Las Vegas. If Tyson wanted to regain his status, he had to beat Holyfield, a quiet man with none of the menace—or disturbing charisma—of the erstwhile "Kid Dynamite."

The fight was scheduled for the fall of 1991, but it was postponed for five years. Tyson was convicted of raping a teenage beauty contestant at a posh hotel in Indianapolis, Indiana, on July 19, 1991, a conviction that sent him to prison for three years. He was the biggest draw in boxing—and its most tragic figure—with his once glorious career lost in the rubble of his own excesses, his own paranoia. "The sport will continue with or without Mike Tyson," said Gil Clancy, the color commentator for CBS. "I go back to the time Rocky Marciano retired. They said boxing was going to die, and it didn't. When Muhammad Ali retired, they said boxing was going to die, and it didn't. When Sugar Ray Leonard retired, they said boxing was going to die, and it didn't. Boxing will survive."

Released from prison in the spring of 1995, Tyson won four comeback fights, including a 1st-round knockout of Bruce Seldon to capture the world heavyweight title. He looked like his old self again, but his old rival was still out there: Holyfield, who had lost, regained, and lost the title since defeating Douglas six years before. Tyson met Holyfield on November 9, 1996, in Las Vegas in one of the most anticipated bouts in the history of the division. Holyfield crushed Tyson, landing about fifteen unanswered punches—each one more solid than the last—before the referee finally stopped the bout 37 seconds into the 11th round. Holyfield joined Ali as the only three-time heavyweight champion in boxing history. "I fought each round competitively," Holyfield said. "I fought the fight a round at a time."

When they met again eight months later, Tyson turned the ring into a buffet, biting the champion on both ears before the referee stopped the fight in the 3rd round. It was one of the most bizarre spectacles in ring history, and it shocked the world. The question is, why did he do it? Tyson, after all, was perfect for his sport, a thug whose fists were like blackjacks or tire irons—weapons that he brandished with a savage pride. But "Iron Mike" went too far this time. It is not easy to go too far in this sport, but Tyson did, and the Nevada Athletic Commission revoked his license for the biting incident. "Please don't torture me any longer," he told the commission a year later. "I made a mistake. Other fighters have made more. I'm just a human being trying to live my life."

The commission reinstated his license in 1998, but Tyson received a stern warning from the chairman. "I want to warn you, from my view, this will be your last chance," Elias Ghanem said. "You will either conduct yourself in accordance with our rules and regulations, or you will probably never fight again in Nevada." It was the last chance for a man whose first chance—eighteen years earlier—had begun what had promised to be such a heartwarming story.

The tale of "Kid Dynamite" began in Brooklyn, New York, where Tyson turned the world into his ring by fighting on the streets, robbing people, and finally landing in a juvenile detention facility at the Tryon School in Johnstown, New York. He wandered into a gym one day—the gym above the police station in Catskill, New York—and Cus D'Amato, who managed former heavyweight champion Floyd Patterson, spotted him. He dubbed him the future heavyweight champion of the world. Tyson was thirteen years old. D'Amato, who became his surrogate parent in 1979, died on November 4, 1985. "I think [Tyson] was struggling with who he wanted to be," said Teddy Atlas, a trainer who was himself a protégé of D'Amato. "And you know what? We all do. But all of us don't grow up to be heavyweight champion of the world, and all of us don't have to cope with that kind of attention. He created this image of a villain, and it got stronger and stronger. And he had to keep going through with the act."

Now the commission—and the world—are wondering when the curtain will finally fall on that performance.

James "Buster" Douglas

It was a short reign—just long enough for James "Buster" Douglas to fatten both his bank account and his belly.

Yes, Douglas would live the good life, damaging his career in his pursuit of pleasure. But back in 1990, none of that seemed to matter, because for a few glori-

A Closer Look

When James "Buster" Douglas clubbed Mike Tyson on February 10, 1990, the world tried to embrace him as a folk hero. There was only one problem—how do you get your arms around a guy who goes from heavyweight champion to overweight champion quicker than you can say "Pass the potatoes"? Douglas ate his way out of the title, losing the crown in his first defense, to Evander Holyfield, less than a year later. "He went down like a dog," Don King, who had promoted Tyson, crowed lustily after the fight. "And then he howled at the moon." Subdued by sloth and arrogance, Douglas retired to do what he did best: eat. He earned—stole?—$21 million for the fight, and he invested most of it in his appetite, stuffing his face as if he were stoking a fire in his belly. Douglas began to eat his life away, just as he had once eaten his title away, and it was tragic. He ballooned to 400 pounds (182kg), and he became almost unrecognizable, his eyes disappearing into his face. "It didn't matter what I ate," Douglas said. "As long as it was food, just food. I would eat anything."

ABOVE: Buster Douglas stands over the vanquished Mike Tyson, February 10, 1990.

It was self-destructive, but Douglas kept on eating, his appetite overcoming his common sense. Then, in the summer of 1994, it happened—the former heavyweight champion collapsed in a diabetic coma. He was 33 years old, a man who should have been in the prime of his life, but there he was, in a hospital emergency room, the prime of his life slipping away. "When I got out of the hospital, I got back on my feet," Douglas said. "It hit me. I needed to get a goal, something to get me back where I was."

Douglas may never get back where he was, but only because the destination seemed so unreachable the first time around. After all, how many times can you be on top of the world, the piece of real estate where Douglas resided after defeating Tyson in 1990? Douglas was such a huge underdog that the Las Vegas casinos refused to post odds on the fight, but he did it, knocking out Tyson in the 10th round to win the world heavyweight title—one of the biggest upsets in boxing history. The new champion felt like a kid, hugging his title belt as if it were a teddy bear.

Not bad for a guy who seemed like a reluctant warrior, a guy so lackadaisical that his own father did not believe in him. And who could blame the old man? Billy Douglas was a middleweight contender in the 1970s, and he tried to mold his son into the kind of fighter he had been—a monster who could make a street fight look like a friendly debate. But "Buster" rebelled. He saw himself as a boxer, a Picasso with padded gloves, and the old man got frustrated. "I never knew if 'Buster' really wanted to be a fighter," Billy Douglas said. "I just didn't know if he had the determination."

On one glorious night, Douglas proved his father—and all his other critics—wrong. He battered Tyson, the invincible champion, by flooring him with a combination so sweet and pure that it looked like a shadowboxing routine. Tyson, who landed on his black silk trunks, scrambled around the ring on all fours, searching for the mouthpiece that had tumbled out of his mouth from the final punch. He searched and searched, and the referee counted and counted, but the referee reached 10 before the fighter reached his mouthpiece. And so ended one of the biggest upsets in boxing history.

"I feel excited again," Douglas said after getting out of the hospital. And no wonder: Douglas launched his comeback about two years after collapsing into the diabetic coma. The ex-champion lost more than 150 pounds (68kg), and the glorious boxer he used to be reemerged from layers of fat—and years of abuse. He knocked out Tony LaRosa on June 22, 1996, his first bout since the disastrous loss to Holyfield on October 25, 1990. Then he won five more fights, two of them by knockout, before suffering a setback as critical as the defeat against Holyfield almost ten years before: a shocking loss to Lou Savarese, who knocked out the ex-champion in the 1st round. "I didn't take it seriously enough," Douglas said. "I didn't train the way I should have. I know what I did wrong. I learned my lesson."

Douglas will keep fighting, and while he may never recover from the loss to Savarese, he has recaptured something more significant than his heavyweight crown—his life. And that may represent the single greatest comeback in boxing history. "I'm excited, but it's not just about boxing," Douglas said before fighting Savarese. "It's about living, it's about life, because I almost left it. I didn't feel good about myself back then, but now I feel great about myself. I feel like a very fortunate young man."

ous months, Douglas was a bona fide hero, the man who conquered the "bad guy" of boxing—heavyweight champion Mike Tyson. He knocked out Tyson on February 11 in Tokyo, scoring one of the biggest upsets in boxing history.

If Douglas savored his victory, who could blame him? He was living a dream. When he was growing up in Columbus, Ohio, most of his friends found their heroes in comic books. Not Buster. He found one in real life—his father, Billy Douglas. Buster began boxing when he was 10 years old, following in the footsteps of his dad, a middleweight contender in the 1970s. Billy, who worked at an auto parts factory during his fighting days, never encouraged his son to box; he didn't have to. Watching his father fight, Buster felt so much pride that he wanted to fight, too

"It was exciting," the son recalled. "He took me to some of his fights. I even went to Madison Square Garden to watch him box. It was wild."

Yet, while Buster loved his father, he did not want to be like him—at least not in the ring. The old man was a brawler, and Buster wanted to box. He wanted to win, but he did not want to get hurt on his way to victory.

"I just had that in me—attack, attack, attack," Billy said, "but Buster was completely different. He was a boxer, not a puncher."

They had their rough moments, moments so emotionally draining that Buster considered retiring from boxing. It came to a head on May 30, 1987, when Buster met Tony Tucker, then the International Boxing Federation heavyweight champion. Buster was ahead on points going into the 10th round. Then he walked into a right hand that rendered his brilliant boxing in the nine other rounds irrelevant. He went down—down and out.

"James told me after the fight that he was sitting on the stool after the ninth round and decided he just didn't want to win the fight," said John Johnson, who managed Douglas. "He just gave up. All the distractions with his father had gotten to him."

If Buster gave up on that fight, however, he did not give up on his career. He worked his way up the rankings, earning a shot at Tyson. He won with a spectacular display of boxing and punching, and it made the old man proud.

It would not last. Douglas lost the title in his first defense, to Evander Holyfield, on October 25, 1990, in Las Vegas, Nevada. It was a shocking defeat, as devastating as the Tyson bout had been exhilarating. And it left Douglas with a curious legacy. He was not one of the greatest heavyweights in history—he would be hard pressed to crack the Top 20—but he enjoyed one of the most magical nights a fighter has ever experienced.

Julio Cesar Chavez

For almost twenty years, Julio Cesar Chavez threw left hook after left hook, punches that damaged more livers than all the tequila in Guadalajara. They called him "el gran campeon Mexicano"—the great Mexican champion—but he was more than that. He was the greatest fighter of his generation, a man who won eighty-seven fights, seventy-five of them by knockout, before suffering the first blemish on his record: the controversial draw against Pernell "Sweetpea" Whitaker on September 11, 1993, in San Antonio.

Julio Cesar Chavez was a calm, efficient boxer, a master at wearing opponents down with repeated blows to the body. His strategic method enabled him to put together a tremendous wins record over the course of his career.

How did he do it? He was not flashy or powerful, but he was nonetheless an exciting fighter. Chavez was a model of economy, every punch as short and sweet as a hatchet stroke. And he was smart, too. Chavez maintained the delicate balance that every great fighter must master—the line between fury and tranquillity. He turned his fights into sparring sessions, exercises in methodical destruction.

Like most great fighters, he set up his combinations with a single punch, but it was not the jab. It was the left hook to the liver, a punch that left most of his opponents wondering where he concealed the sledgehammers. The answer? Inside his leather gloves. "If you go downstairs, to the body, you can take away a man's will and desire," Chavez said.

A superb fighter for almost seven years, Chavez became a great one—at least in the eyes of the boxing carried out step by step—first the body, then the head. He was amazingly accurate, and he seemed to know where a punch would inflict the most pain, the most damage. Just ask Rosario, who looked like a gargoyle after the fight, his face bruised and swollen, a man who was beaten long before the referee stopped the punishment. "The guy just knows how to fight," said George Benton, who trained Whitaker. "It's as simple as that. The guy knows how to fight."

Julio Cesar Chavez celebrates after winning the final rounds to defeat David Kamau on September 16, 1995, by decision. At this point in his career, Chavez was just beginning to show signs of being mortal.

world—on November 21, 1987, when he won the lightweight title with an 11th-round knockout of Edwin Rosario. It was a strange, almost remarkable fight, because Chavez took the heavier punches throughout the bout; he just did not take as many as Rosario did. Chavez remained calm and composed throughout the match, as if the demolition had to be

One of ten children born to Rodolfo and Isabelita Chavez, he grew up in Culiacan, Mexico, a working-class town in the state of Sinaloa. The father was a brakeman for the railroad, but the pay was so bad that the children sometimes ate boiled weeds for dinner. He supplemented his income by selling the medicine that the Mexican government supplied to poor families.

"Thank God I became a boxer," Chavez said. "Now I can help my family with money."

Chavez turned pro when he was 18, about eight years after walking into a gym for the first time. He fought his first thirty-three bouts in Mexico, sometimes earning as little as $6 per fight. The young fighter won all of them, thirty-one by knockout. "My older brothers were boxers," Chavez said. "One day, one of my brothers lost a fight. I was so angry, not at my brother, but at the world. I hated losing. I hated the thought of losing. I was 10 years old, and I promised myself that I would never lose." Later in his career, the greatest fighter of his era would lose that status, passing the mantle, stubbornly and grudgingly, to younger, stronger fighters. First was the draw with Whitaker, a fight that most observers felt Whitaker had won. Chavez fought his fight, calmly pursuing his opponent throughout the match, but to no avail. Whitaker was too fast, too elusive. Then came Frankie Randall, who dropped the great fighter en route to a decision on January 29, 1994, in Las Vegas. And then came perhaps the toughest opponent of his career—Oscar De La Hoya, who fought Chavez in 1996 and 1998. De La Hoya stopped him both times, conquering him with speed, power, and youth. The last fight forced Chavez, proud but beaten, to contemplate retirement. "He was a great champion, but his time is past," De La Hoya said. "It's time for him to retire."

Pernell Whitaker

If Julio Cesar Chavez was calm and composed in the ring, Pernell "Sweetpea" Whitaker was loud and brash, a fighter whose style owed more to Abbott and

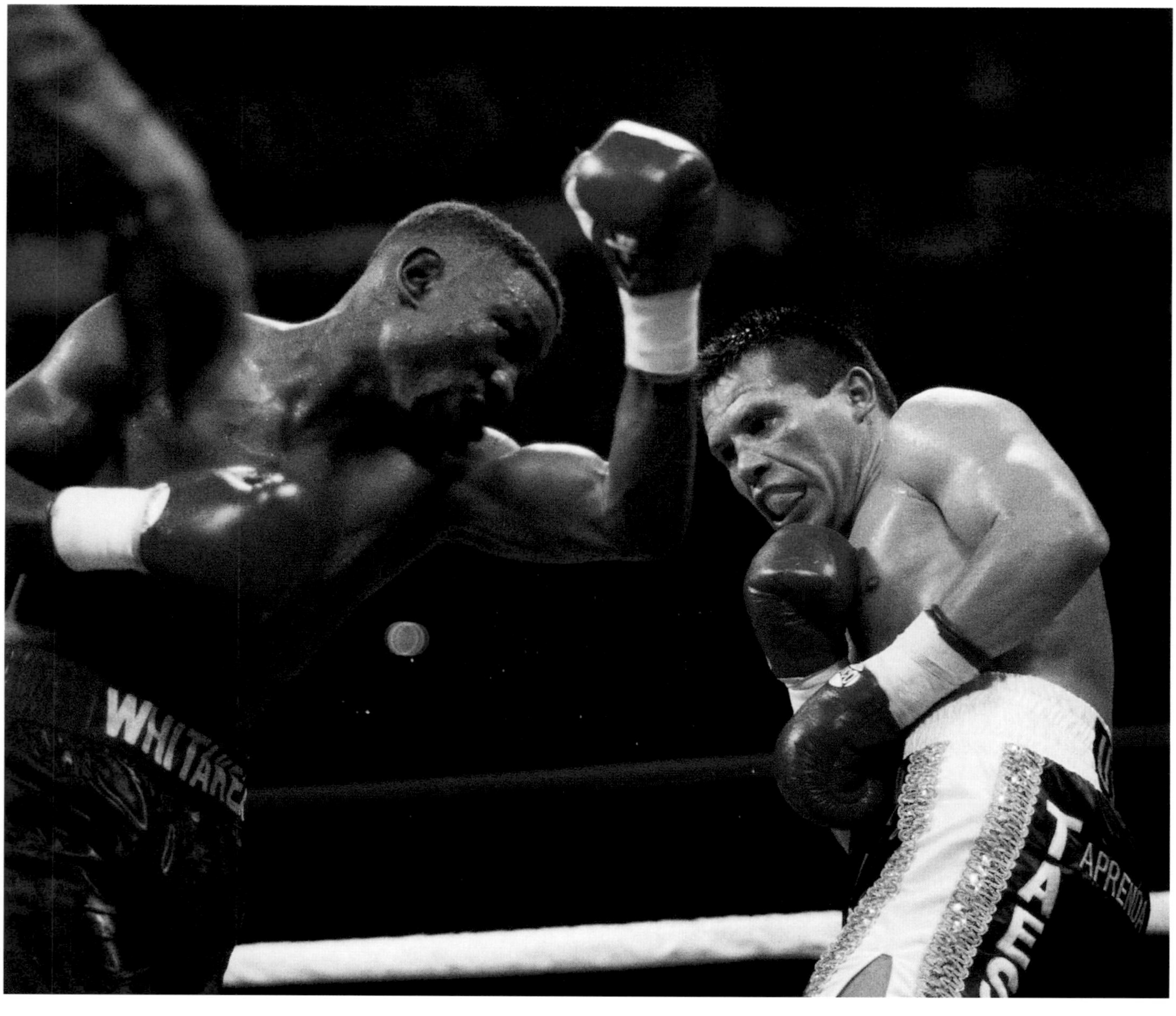

Above: Julio Cesar Chavez ducks a left thrown by Pernell Whitaker during their September 11, 1993, match-up in San Antonio, Texas. The fight was scored a draw, but many observers felt Whitaker had won.

Costello than to Leonard and Hearns. Does that sound crazy? Well, Whitaker looked crazy. He fought like a cartoon character, jumping on the ropes, sticking out his tongue, and clapping at his virtuosity in the ring. "I've screamed at him to remain focused in the ring, but he does what he wants to do," said Lou Duva, who helped guide the champion to world titles in four weight classes: lightweight, junior welterweight, welterweight, and junior middleweight. "It makes me mad. I don't know why he does it. I think he's so dominating in the ring that things get monotonous for him. He gets bored, and he thinks he has to spice things up."

And who could blame him? Whitaker recoiled at the thought of getting hit, but it was not out of fear—or even concern—for his own safety. It was just that Whitaker, who took as much pride in his defense as he did in his offense, was so elusive that he could not even imagine getting hit. He fought entire bouts, punching and retreating, punching and retreating, without losing a single round, sometimes without absorbing a single punch, making his decisions seem as definitive as knockouts.

Whitaker was a smooth, elegant boxer, his footwork so dainty that he looked like a ballerina, but there was still the clownish streak, the one that riled his trainers. Who could forget his battle against Roger Mayweather on March 28, 1987, when he did everything but throw a cream pie at his opponent? He slipped behind Mayweather during one of the clinches, pulling down Mayweather's trunks and running away—an antic that left the referee looking like a schoolteacher trying to discipline the class clown. Whitaker went on to win the fight, but the lapse of concentration caused him to suffer the first knockdown of his career. "Nobody knows if he can take a punch," Chavez said. "We'll find out."

Chavez was wrong. Chavez tried to find out—relentlessly, if not desperately—but, try as he might, he missed punch after punch, punishing the air, not the man in front of him. The two men fought to a draw, a decision that was booed by most of the sixty thousand fans in the Alamodome in San Antonio. "You saw the fight," Whitaker said afterward. "Everybody knows I won."

ABOVE: **Much like Willie Pep, Pernell Whitaker was a defensive specialist. Alas, it was Whitaker's misfortune to arrive at a time of excellent competition in his division, especially in the person of Oscar De La Hoya. Whitaker met his match in De La Hoya, seen here on the mat, who wrested the welterweight title from Whitaker with a decision in this April 12, 1997, fight.**

The public bestowed upon Whitaker what the judges had denied him—a victory. It may have been a symbolic victory, but it did not matter to Whitaker, because the boxing world crowned him with the mythical title that Chavez had held for so long—greatest fighter in the world, pound for pound. And he relished it. "It's the only title that means anything to me," he said.

The welterweight fighter held the mythical title of champion until April 12, 1997, when he met Oscar De La Hoya, the only American athlete to win a gold medal in the 1992 Olympics. Whitaker sneered at his young opponent, calling him "Liberace," a reference to the gaggle of female fans who screamed and shrieked at "the Golden Boy" during the prefight weigh-in at Caesars Palace in Las Vegas. Liberace? Maybe, but if this was Liberace, it was Liberace from hell, a guy who would happily smash you in the face with one of his candelabra.

Whitaker tried to elude the young fighter, bobbing and dipping throughout the bout, but De La Hoya was not Chavez. "The Golden Boy" refused to pursue him calmly and patiently, letting precious rounds slip away in the process, as Chavez had done four years before. No, De La Hoya boxed furiously, forcing a fight that Whitaker tried to avoid. He scored a decision over Whitaker, and this time there was no controversy, although Whitaker tried to create one, saying he had gotten robbed again. Wrong. De La Hoya beat him fair and square, wresting the mythical title of the greatest fighter in the world, pound for pound, from the proud virtual champion. "Whitaker can say all he wants, but I'm the welterweight champion," De La Hoya said, calmly holding up his championship belt.

Evander Holyfield

It was Body Beautiful versus Body Bountiful, and the beauty won. The two men fought on October 25, 1990, in Las Vegas, but they waged their own battles long before that, in the arena where all fights are won or lost—the gym. Punish yourself in the gym, the credo goes, and you will punish your opponent in the ring. Evander Holyfield punished himself; James "Buster" Douglas did not. So Body Beautiful beat Body Bountiful, knocking him out in the 3rd round to capture the heavyweight championship of the world. Score one for dedication and hard work—Holyfield weighed 208 pounds (94kg), 38 pounds (17kg) less than his pudgy opponent.

Who would have guessed that Body Beautiful was once Body Pitiful, a short, scrawny kid who agonized on the bench of his high school football team in Atlanta? It was more than twenty years ago, but the memories seem sharp and vivid because Holyfield cherishes the failures as much as he does the successes; they make him stronger, more determined, reminding him that he was not born the heavyweight champion of the world. So, yes, he treasures the past, and he keeps that little guy—so distant, yet so near—close to his heart. "I know I'm still the little guy," Holyfield said.

RIGHT: Evander Holyfield pounds Dwight Muhammad Qawi to capture the cruiser weight title on June 12, 1986. Holyfield has always been in top physical shape at every stage of his career.

"But, if I were a coach, I'd rather have a big heart than a big man."

A 5-foot-4-inch (163cm), 115-pound (52kg) cornerback, the high school junior abandoned football in 1978, the season on the bench having bruised his ego as well as his butt. He turned to boxing, a sport he would grow to love. Here was a competition where every youngster, no matter how short or light, had an equal chance to succeed—or fail. And as the youngster grew, so did his love for the sport. He compiled an amateur record of 160-14, with 75 knockouts, and won a bronze medal in the light heavyweight division at the 1980 Olympics in Los Angeles. Not bad for the scrawny kid who was overlooked by his high school football coach. "You know, I was picked on so much when I was small that I still have that little-guy mentality," Holyfield said.

Holyfield maintained that attitude as a professional, winning the world cruiser weight title in his twelfth professional fight—a stirring decision over Dwight Muhammad Qawi, formerly Dwight Braxton, "the Camden Buzzsaw." The champion defended his title five times, every time with sensational knockouts, and he became known as the greatest cruiser weight in history. So what? It was like calling Herbert Hoover the greatest president to come out of West Branch, Iowa.

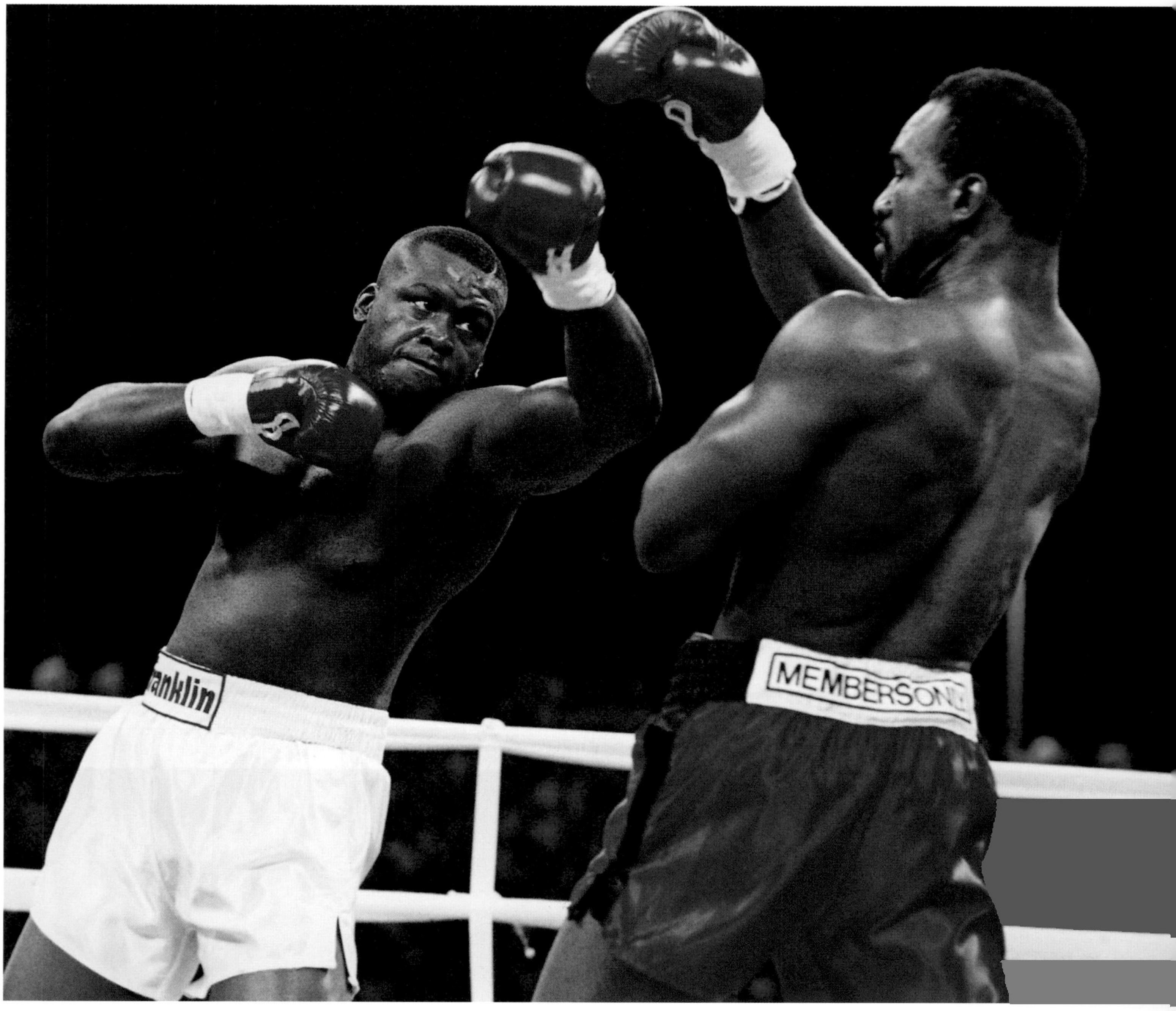

ABOVE: Holyfield dodges a blow by champion Buster Douglas during a title bout on October 25, 1990. Holyfield triumphed, winning the heavyweight title from Douglas scant months after Douglas had stunned the boxing world by knocking out the seemingly invincible Mike Tyson. Holyfield's victory set the stage for one of the more unusual rivalries in boxing history, which would see Tyson try to reclaim the heavyweight crown in a couple of highly publicized bouts.

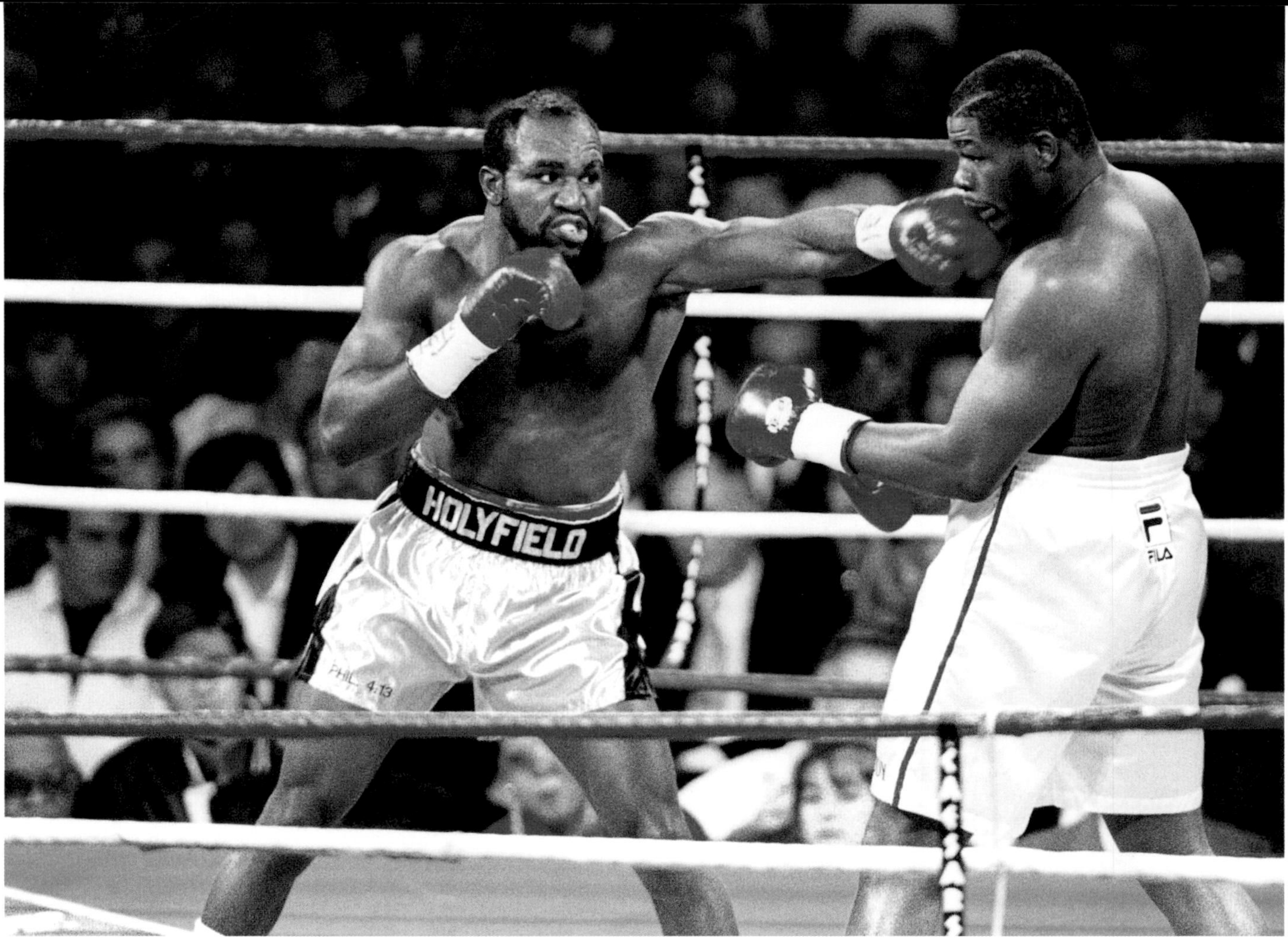

ABOVE: Evander Holyfield and Riddick Bowe had one of the classic rivalries of heavyweight boxing. The gigantic Bowe proved a good match for the athletic (though much smaller) Holyfield, who won one and lost two of their three bouts. Still, Holyfield had the greater overall career, going on to best Mike Tyson and join Ali as the only other three-time heavyweight champion. This fight, their first, took place on November 13, 1992.

Holyfield did not need that kind of praise, so like Michael Spinks before him, he moved on and up—to the heavyweight division. "It's definitely a challenge," said Tim Hallmark, the fitness guru who was hired to turn Holyfield into a heavyweight. "But, then, it's always a challenge when you talk about putting weight on, because you're talking about a major change. You might do it with a person off the street very easily. But with an athlete, you just don't want to put weight on; you want to put weight on and, at the same time, have him perform as well as he possibly can."

While most boxers confine their workouts to jogging and gym sessions, Holyfield ran, swam, sparred, and lifted weights during three workouts a day, six days a week—a brutal pace that he thought would make him a brutal force. He was right. Holyfield knocked out Douglas for the title, a fight he seemed destined to win from the moment he stepped into the ring, when he skipped from corner to corner in what looked like a victory dance.

When he met Riddick Bowe on November 13, 1992, in Las Vegas, he was the little guy again, dwarfed by a man whose size matched his talent. The challenger weighed 235 pounds (107kg), 30 pounds (14kg) more than the champion, and it showed. Bowe towered over Holyfield during the prefight instructions, displaying his enormous advantages before the fight even started—30 pounds (14kg) in weight, 3 inches (8cm) in height, 4 inches (10cm) in reach. He made the title holder look like an urchin sitting on a curb—a vivid reminder of why he referred to Holyfield as "that little guy you all call the champion." They would not call him champion for long; Bowe scored a 12-round decision over his brave but overmatched opponent.

The two men fought two more times, forming the greatest trilogy in the heavyweight division since the Ali-Frazier wars of the 1970s. Holyfield won the second fight and Bowe the third, fights that seemed to define the careers of both fighters, just as the Ali-Frazier fights had done two decades earlier. But Holyfield did not need Bowe, a foil to serve as a measuring stick for his heart and skill, because he emerged as a great fighter against another opponent—Mike Tyson.

They met on November 9, 1996, in Las Vegas, and when the opening bell rang, Tyson displayed the same urgency he had shown throughout most of his career.

He threw the first punch of the fight, a wide, arching right hand that sent his opponent into the ropes. Holyfield backpedaled, his hands shooting up awkwardly, but he did not go down, and Tyson seemed shocked. He became even more shocked, emotionally and physically, because for every punch Tyson threw, Holyfield threw three, sometimes four, not all of them landing, but all of them telling Tyson that finally—finally—here was a man who would stand up to him. Holyfield stopped him in the 11th round. "Holyfield's a good fighter," Tyson said. "And I want a rematch."

The challenger got his wish eight months later but, unable to overcome the new champion with his fists, he resorted to his teeth, biting his opponent on both ears in the 3rd round. Referee Mills Lane disqualified Tyson, and Holyfield emerged with another victory over the man he had branded a bully. "When you try to foul to get out of a fight, it's not showing too much courage," Holyfield said afterward. So Holyfield, the man who had given his heart and soul to boxing since his youth, ended up giving a piece of his ear as well.

Roy Jones

When he is attending a fight rather than engaging in one, Roy Jones swaggers up and down the arena, a proud champion in fancy duds—clothes that look like the subject of a Peter Max painting, bright and vivid and colorful. But if he is gaudy and flashy outside the ring, it is nothing compared to how he looks inside the ring, where he is one of the most dominant fighters of the day. He may not be the greatest fighter in the world—but he is the most outrageously talented, combining so much speed and power that, like Ali before him, he gets away with his mechanical flaws. Or are they mechanical flaws? "Everyone thinks I'm an unorthodox fighter, but I'm not," Jones said. "I'm an orthodox fighter. People just don't know what they're looking at."

Perhaps, but Jones makes the unorthodox look orthodox because he is so smooth and graceful. But

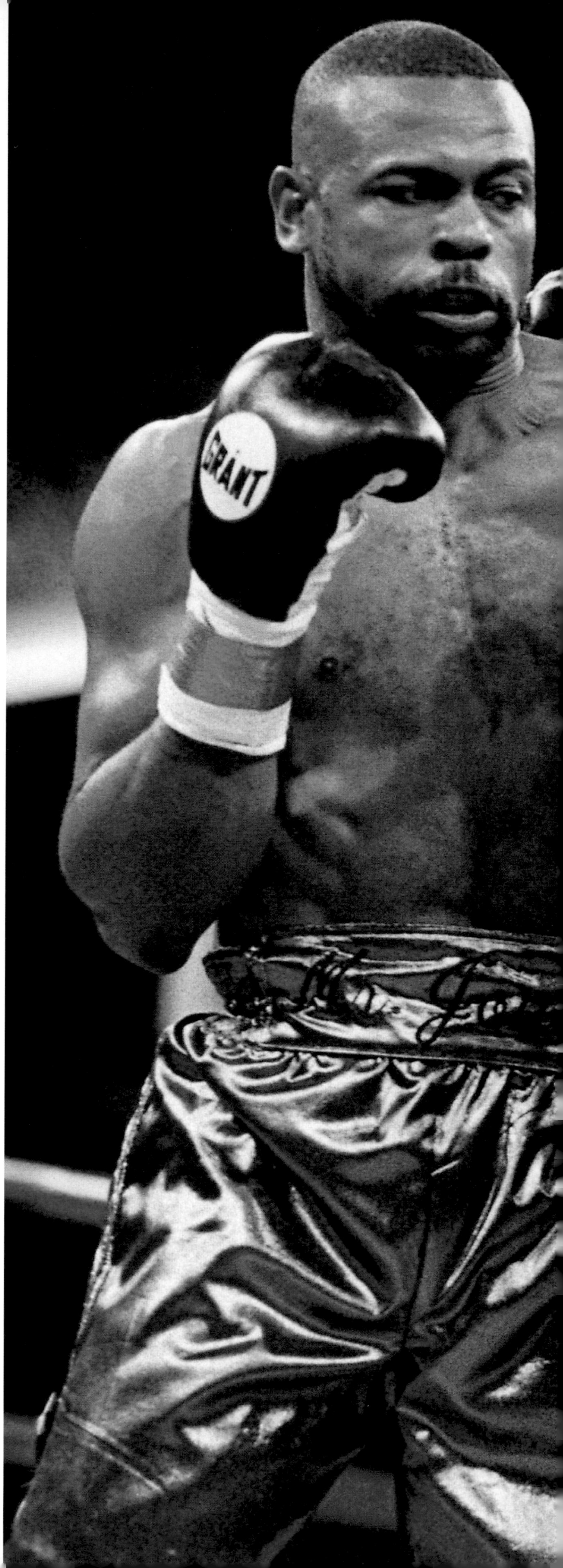

Right: Roy Jones unleashes a left to the body of Otis Grant on November 14, 1998. Jones won this fight by TKO in the 10th. Jones seems to be a boxer for the ages, a combination of blinding speed, incredible athleticism, and awesome power. If he has one flaw, it might be his technique, though some would say it is simply that he has his own style.

WEAR

make no mistake: he does everything wrong; he just gets away with it because of his enormous talent. Jones keeps his hands low, leads with his right, throws punches off the wrong foot—flaws that would send most trainers into therapy. Most trainers, but not Eddie Futch. "He may be the most talented fighter since Sugar Ray Robinson," Futch said.

Jones displayed those skills on November 18, 1994, in Las Vegas, capturing the super middleweight title with a unanimous decision over James Toney, then one of the greatest fighters in the world. It was a fight of contrasts, chin, a target as inviting as a piñata. He seemed out of punching range—at least to everyone but the challenger—but he was not. The left hook came from about 10 inches (25cm) away, a blow as unlikely as it was powerful. Toney crumpled to the floor, near his own corner, as the challenger tried to hit him again on his way down. Toney beat the 10-count, but Jones maintained his peculiar brand of pressure, brutal yet elegant, on his way to a unanimous decision. "God blessed me with a lot of foot speed and hand speed," Jones said. "And I figured that was the way to go. I

Above: Roy Jones pummels the midsection of James Toney, at the time considered one of the most dangerous fighters in his division, en route to capturing the super middleweight title on November 18, 1994. Opposite: Roy Jones celebrates his emphatic 1st-round knockout of Montell Griffin on August 7, 1997, regaining the world light heavyweight title and avenging an earlier loss to Griffin in the process.

and the differences emerged before the opening bell. Toney, the champion, entered the ring with a ski cap and a menacing glare, while Jones chose a more elegant outfit—a white silk tuxedo with gold vest and black bow tie. The champion walked up to the challenger, calmly but defiantly, trying to stare him down before the prefight instructions. Jones refused to be intimidated.

In a stunning 3rd round, Toney committed an error—a stupid and uncharacteristic error. Jones showboated, shuffling his feet and pumping his fists into the air, and the champion responded with his own act of bravado. Toney dropped his hands and stuck out his could feel his power. He's a very strong puncher, and I've been taught to counter strong punchers."

Jones looked unbeatable, and he was—unless the opponent was Jones himself. He lost to Montell Griffin on March 21, 1977, when he was disqualified for an illegal blow. Griffin took a punch to the jaw after dropping to one knee in an attempt to avoid one of those lightning-bolt combinations from the champion. Griffin was awarded the world light heavyweight title, a crown Jones regained with a 1st-round knockout five months later. "The only man who can beat Roy Jones is Roy Jones," said Jones. How true.

GRANT

ER A.C.

The Bosses 3

A boxer solidly constructed, intelligently directed, and soundly motivated is bound to go a long way.

—A.J. Liebling in *The Sweet Science*

They called it Champs Gym, and it was like any gym in the United States—a place with the camaraderie of a tavern, the lighting of a coal mine, and the ambience of a bus station. It was located above an automobile body shop, and it was hard to tell who did the heavier pounding, the mechanics or the boxers. Fight posters lined the walls, and exposed wires snaked out of the sockets, creating a hazard that all the pugs ignored. Champs had class.

When Champs was empty it looked small, but when the fighters started to arrive it looked even smaller, shrinking to the size of a broom closet. Fighters jockeyed for position like basketball players in the paint, keeping a wary eye for unintentional blows from buddies who were shadowboxing. The boxers repeated their routines day after day without bumping into each other—which qualified as a minor miracle. "This is how gyms should be," said Al Fennell, who trained former junior middleweight champion Robert "Bam Bam" Hines.

It was a great place, a kind of hideaway, as long as you were not one of the pugs getting whacked in the ring. The neighborhood men used to go there every day, most of them old guys, as eager and enthusiastic as the young fighters they watched. They sat in chairs lined against the wall, and their discussions were like those common in barber shops—spirited debates about the best fighters in the world, both today and yesterday.

Champs was located in Philadelphia, one of the greatest boxing towns in the world—perhaps the greatest. But there are gyms like Champs everywhere. Oh, the quality of fighters may not be the same at gyms in Tulsa or Canton or Poughkeepsie, but the environments are the same, with a grim charm that only fight people can appreciate. Take the crummy old gym in Secaucus, New Jersey, where Chuck Wepner trained. They called him "the Bayonne Bleeder," and for good reason; every man he fought had razors for fists, leaving him with a face only a plastic surgeon could love. *Screw* magazine once ran a full-page photograph of him; his brows were slashed, his cheeks swollen, his lips split from here to Trenton. The caption stated, "Now THIS is obscene." Wepner bled in the gym, too, and his blood ended up everywhere, on the canvas, on the floors, on the walls—perhaps the most primitive display of splatter art in the world.

ABOVE **Up-and-coming female boxer Lucia Rijker (right) gets some advice from coach Freddie Roach during her March 25, 1998, fight against Marcela Avna at Foxwoods Casino, in Ledyard, Connecticut.** OPPOSITE: **Jack Dempsey was one of the greatest boxers of the first half of the twentieth century; it's amazing to think that he came along just a little more than twenty years after the end of the brawling, bare-knuckle era. Here, Dempsey takes a playful stab at the punching bag in Mac Levy's Gym at Madison Square Garden while legendary promoter and impresario Tex Rickard looks on. Rickard was at least in part responsible for the emergence of boxing from the dark ages of the pre–Marquess of Queensberry era and its rise to immense popularity.**

If gyms are great environments, it is only because they house interesting, colorful people. Interesting people are those who speak their minds, and boxing people are among the most open and genuine in the world. Oh, they will lie to you, all right, but it as honest as lying ever gets. If that sounds crazy, consider the case of promoter Bob Arum who, once trapped in an inconsistency, said, "Yesterday, I was lying. Today, I'm telling the truth." Gyms are full of people like that—not just the fighters, but also the managers, the trainers, and, when they want to check in on their investments, the promoters.

The Trainers

Eddie Futch

It was one of those hot, steamy gyms that turn your pores into water spouts, but one thing made Eddie Futch sweat more than the environment: the thought of sparring with his boyhood friend, Joe Louis, who had just knocked out James J. Braddock to become the heavyweight champion of the world. Scary. It was the summer of 1937, in Detroit, Michigan, and Futch was 27 years old—young enough to be adventurous, but old enough to know that adventurousness could land you in a hospital ward. Smart man, Eddie Futch. Yes, he refused to spar with Louis, and yes, he lived to fight—and, more importantly, train—another day.

The boxing world is grateful. Futch became one of the greatest trainers in boxing history, perhaps the greatest, because he saw fights in slow motion, dissecting them from the corner as if the live action were a fight tape, the drama unfolding slowly, punch by punch, until the keys to victory became clear to the wise, little man at ringside. Then he would climb the steps to the ring, slowly and gingerly in his later years, and discuss the strategy with his fighter. Yes, discuss the strategy. Boxing is a brutal, chaotic sport, but Futch was a calm, gentle man, so there were no theatrics in the corner, no fireworks, no cheerleading. He was emotional, but his emotion came from his inner confidence and his keen intelligence; his fighters knew that and respected him for it. "I've had a lot of trainers," said Marlon Starling, the former welter-

Over the years, trainer Eddie Futch guided many boxers to success, including heavyweight champion Riddick Bowe (to whom Futch is speaking in this photograph).

weight champion of the world. "But Eddie Futch is the only one I've had who knows more about boxing than I do."

When Futch discussed boxing, he was almost professorial. The ring was his classroom, and more than fifteen of his students graduated to world titles, including Marlon Starling, Joe Frazier, Alexis Arguello, Larry Holmes, Michael Spinks, and Riddick Bowe. They were all different, from the elegance of Arguello to the herky-jerky moves of Spinks, but Futch molded all of them into superb fighters, improving their styles with a new move here, a new dip there. He enhanced; he did not dismantle. "No matter how good a fighter is, you can turn his strengths into weaknesses," said Futch, now 88. "Take the fight between Michael Spinks and Gerry Cooney, for example. Cooney had a tremendous left hook, a tremendous left hook, but a straight right beats a left hook every time."

Spinks knocked out Cooney in the 5th round on June 15, 1987, in Atlantic City—the "War at the Shore" that Spinks won with, yes, the straight right. "I don't think there was a better trainer around than my good friend Eddie Futch," said Angelo Dundee, himself one of the greatest trainers in boxing history. Futch was also a compassionate man. "I don't want Marvis hurt," he told Larry Holmes, then the heavyweight champion, before he fought Marvis Frazier on November 25, 1983, in Las Vegas. Marvis Frazier was the son of former heavyweight champion Joe Frazier, whom Futch had also trained. Futch loved both Joe and his son, and he did not want to see either of them get hurt, one physically, the other emotionally. Holmes knocked out the kid in the 1st round. "I want you to get him out of there as fast as you can," Futch had told Holmes.

Futch became a trainer in the 1940s, but his fighters were drawing so little attention that he had to hold down two other jobs, as a hotel busboy and a postal clerk. Then one of his fighters, Lester Felton, won a 10-round decision over the highly regarded Kid Gavilan, who would go on to win the welterweight title, and the boxing world started to take notice of the trainer from Detroit. He stopped moonlighting. "It was a hard road, but that one fight put me on the right path," he said.

One of three children reared in Detroit, Futch preferred basketball over boxing, playing guard in a league sponsored by the YMCA. But one day, he did something that would change his life: he bought a speed bag—one of those big, yellow models that looked more like a heavy bag. "I was punching it one day, and the Y director saw me," Futch recalled. "He was impressed, so he invited me down to the boxing club to work out. I kept saying no, but he kept encouraging me." Futch finally said yes, and when he entered the dark, sweaty gym for the first time, he was fascinated by the fighters, the workouts, even the noise—the rhythmic tapping of the speed bags, the thud of the medicine balls slamming into bellies, the whoosh and whirr of the fighters skipping rope in front of full-length mirrors. The youngster was hooked. He did not realize it, not yet, but he was hooked. "I began to love boxing," he recalled. "One of the boxers in the club was Joe Louis, and I got to know him well."

Futch won city and national tournaments, ultimately capturing the National Amateur Athletic Union championship in 1934. "I loved boxing, but I thought I would make a good teacher of boxing," he said. "I wanted to train other fighters." After Louis won the title, he returned to Detroit, hoping to spar with the boyhood friend who would become one of the greatest trainers in boxing history. "I had sparred with him before he turned professional, but now he was bigger and stronger, and his punches could paralyze you," said Futch, then a junior welterweight. "I said, 'No, I'm not going to work for you, Joe.' He said, 'Eddie, you're going to get paid $10 a round.' That was very good money back then, but I said, 'Yeah, I can use it to pay my doctor's bills.'"

Louis persisted, saying he wanted to spar with his friend to measure his progress as a pro. Futch thought he was the one who would be measured—for a coffin. He said no again, this time more emphatically. "I ended up keeping time for the workouts," Futch said. "He knocked out two of the sparring partners." Afterward, Futch went up to one of the sparring partners and asked, "Are you okay?"

"Yeah, I'm fine," the sparring partner responded. "Why?"

"Well, you got hit pretty hard," Futch said.

"What do you mean?" the guy asked.

"Do you remember stepping into the ring?" Futch asked.

"Yeah," the sparring partner said.

"Do you remember stepping out of the ring?" Futch asked.

"No," the guy said.

"Oh-oh," Futch said. "You got hit harder than I thought."

And to think it could have been Futch. But Futch was too smart to spar with Louis because he exercised the same intelligence he used as a trainer. He retired in 1997, but you can ask his old fighters—and their opponents—about that intelligence.

Angelo Dundee

Leaning across the ropes, close enough to land or absorb a left hook, Angelo Dundee looks like a choreographer, directing his fighters to dip here, bend there. One, two, three, step. Four, five, six, punch. Is this a gym or a dance studio? The answer is both, because like all great trainers, Dundee knows that boxers fight with their legs as well as their hands, their lower bodies putting them in position for their upper bodies to attack—or avoid getting attacked. If boxing is a dance—and it is—Dundee understands the steps as well as anyone, because he trained two of the greatest dancers in history—Muhammad Ali and Sugar Ray Leonard.

"Leonard was a great kid, a great fighter, and nobody's ever had the impact on boxing that Muhammad Ali has," Dundee, 76, said.

While Ali and Leonard were outrageously talented, with fights that captured the attention of the world, Dundee remembers the quiet moments, too: "Ali was still Cassius Clay at the time, and he was going to fight at an arena in Louisville. It was about three hours before the fight, and he asked me if we could go down to the arena. I didn't know what he wanted to do, but I said, 'Sure.'"

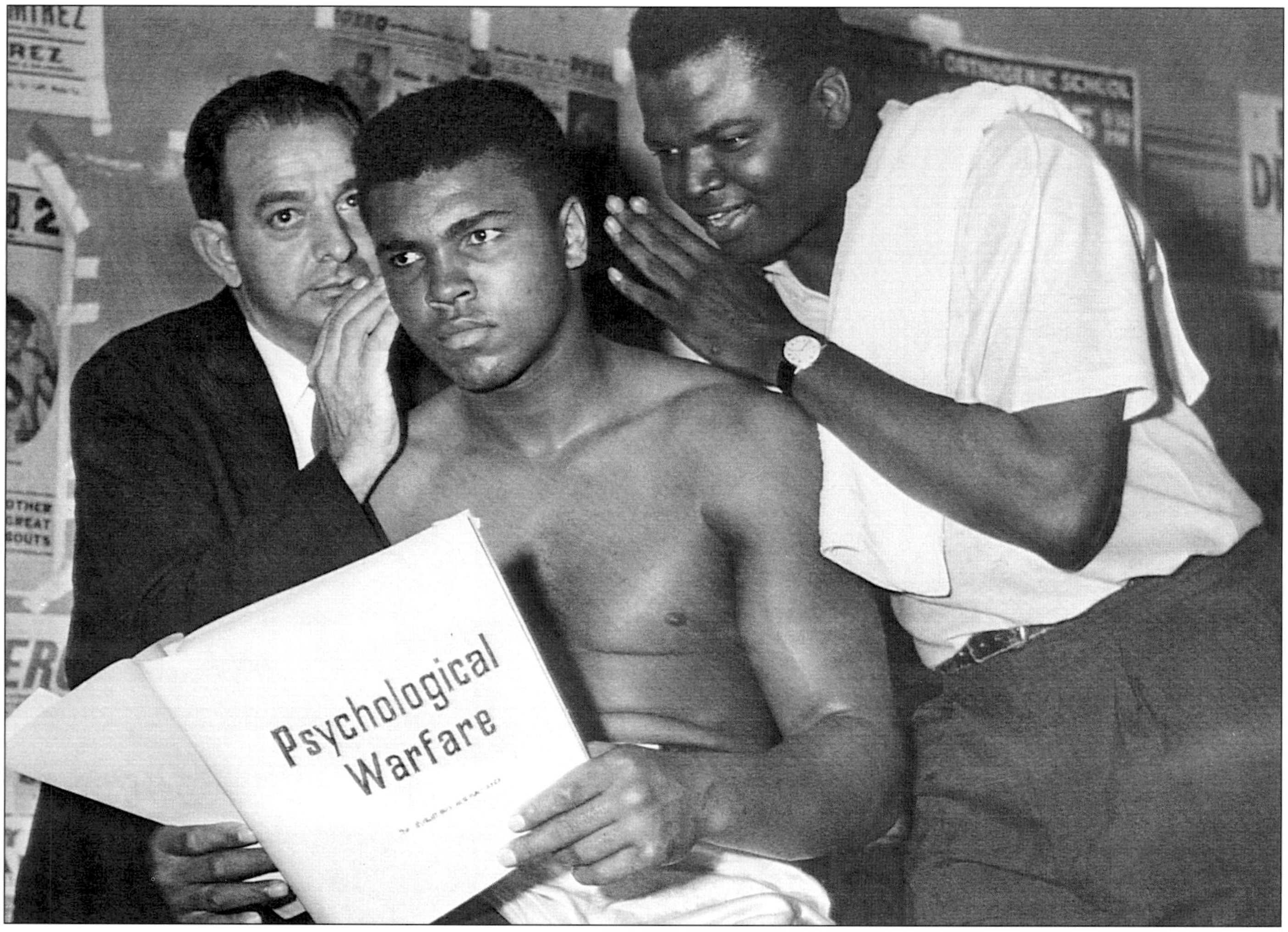

Above: A young Cassius Clay carefully studies a handbook on psychological warfare on February 6, 1964, while trainer Angelo Dundee (left) and motivator Drew Brown refine those principles by whispering into the boxer's ears. As Muhammad Ali, he would go on to add his own chapters to the annals of psychological warfare. **Opposite:** Trainer Angelo Dundee uses a clenched fist to demonstrate a point to Sugar Ray Leonard between rounds in a middleweight title bout against Marvelous Marvin Hagler in 1987. A credit to Dundee's abilities, Leonard won the fight with a split decision.

When trainers and fighters arrived at the dressing room in the arena, Ali started shadowboxing...and shadowboxing...and shadowboxing. Every once in a while, he would stand in front of a full-length mirror, smiling and preening as the sweat slid down his face like thin oil, and then he would resume shadowboxing, his fists punishing the air in the hot, stale dressing room. It went on for three hours. Why? It seemed crazy, but there was a reason for the insanity. Ali, the self-proclaimed greatest of all time, was a master of exploiting fear—not his own, but that of his opponents. But he felt fear, too, felt the dread and anxiety of stepping into the ring, where one left hook can bruise both your jaw and your ego. And on that day, in that dressing room, Ali shadowboxed furiously, and his fear evaporated along with his sweat. "I mean, I've heard of fighters warming up 30 minutes before the fight," Dundee said. "But this sucker warmed up for three hours. He would dance and shout, 'Look at me, ain't I pretty?' For three hours." But the workout relaxed Ali, and Dundee loves fighters who are relaxed. "You've got to have fun," he said. "I like a light situation, because I think you get the best out of that situation. Hey, you've got to be happy."

A native of south Philadelphia, Dundee roamed the streets that Sylvester Stallone would make famous in his *Rocky* films. Dundee was a chubby kid, the constant target of cruel jokes, and he decided to build himself a new body. He began to train as a fighter at the Mason Hall gym in south Philly, overcoming a significant problem in an ingenious manner. His father, a stern but loving Italian immigrant, disapproved of boxing, so the youngster, born Angelo Mirenda, trained under the name of Angelo Dundee, a false surname an older brother had used before him. "Why the name Dundee?" said the trainer, who has since changed his name legally. "Well, there were some Italian fighters who had used the name earlier. There was a Vince Lazarro who changed his name to Dundee, and he became middleweight champ in 1933. Now, kids come up to me and ask, 'Are you related to Crocodile Dundee?'"

After serving in the Air Corps during World War II, Dundee moved to New York, then the boxing capital of the world. He lived in a hotel across the street from Madison Square Garden, a piece of real estate that he regarded as heaven, and he watched the great trainers of his day—Ray Arcel, Whitey Bimstein, and Charlie Goldman. He picked up tricks from each man, learning how to wrap hands, handle cuts, and boost the confidence of a seemingly beaten fighter. Dundee the apprentice became Dundee the master. "All of my fighters have been special," Dundee said. "It takes a special man to climb into the ring." And it takes a special man to train them. Dundee has worked with eleven world champions, either as a trainer or a cut man, including Carmen Basilio, who became his first title holder when he stopped Tony Demarco in the 11th round for the welterweight crown on June 10, 1955, in New York. "Basilio bled easily," Dundee said. "He'd bleed at press conferences. I said that once to some reporters, and he didn't like it. But he got over it."

Unlike his good friend Eddie Futch, who was calm and composed before and after a fight, Dundee was a different man once the bell rang—a man who could make the case of Dr. Jekyll and Mr. Hyde look like a gentle mood swing. He displayed that attitude on May 30, 1987, when he worked the corner for Pinklon Thomas, who was facing Mike Tyson, then the heavyweight champion of the world. The ring doctor tried to examine Thomas, who had absorbed a vicious barrage to the head, between rounds. Dundee bristled, afraid that this intrusion would make his fighter think he was hurt, whether he was or not, and he began screaming at the doctor. "My wife was sitting at ringside, and she got scared for me," Dundee said.

Tyson stopped Thomas in the 6th round, but the trainer-physician bout was almost as exciting. "The chairman of the athletic commission got me by the arm and said, 'That's a $500 fine,'" Dundee recalled. "I kept yelling. Then he said, '$1,000.' I said, 'Amen.' But I gladly paid it."

Dundee gladly paid it because the alternative would have been worse: sitting quietly while his fighter needed his help. "I never know what I'm going to do," he said. "It's always an ad-lib with me. Naturally, I'm looking to win. I'm not a good loser. I don't like to see my fighter lose. The idea is win, win, win."

Opposite: George Benton tapes Evander Holyfield's hands while trainer Lou Duva (second from right) and strength coach Tim Hallmark look on. Having been a fighter of some promise himself, not to mention a gentleman in every sense of the word, Benton easily made the transition to successful trainer.

George Benton

When George Benton fought as a middleweight from 1949 to 1970, compiling a record of 67-12-1, he was the consummate professional—a defensive genius who could punch. Oh yes, he could punch. His right hand was a two-by-four, and whenever he starched a pug, he

would return to his corner slowly and deliberately, as if he had done nothing more strenuous than pick up the mail. Benton was cool; it was part of his code.

Benton was cool in the corner, too. As a middleweight, he never got the opportunity to fight for the title; champions of his day, concerned about their ability to duck his punches, ducked him instead. They turned him into a perennial contender. But Benton does not care, not anymore, because he made up for it as a trainer, a career that represents one of the greatest ironies in boxing. Benton, who could not win a title inside the ring, has won ten outside, in the corner. He trained ten world champions, including heavyweight king Evander Holyfield. "It's a little easier to break through in boxing nowadays," said Benton, 65. "Back then, a champion could pick the guys he wanted to fight. That's not so much the case anymore."

If Benton was elegant as a fighter, he was also elegant as a trainer. He attended training sessions in a suit and tie with a silk handkerchief blossoming from his coat pocket, as if the gym were a fancy restaurant filled with fine ladies. The trainer owned more suits and shoes than he could ever wear, and he knew it, but he kept buying more and more because he remembered "going without" as a kid in the ghettos of north Philadelphia. When Holyfield knocked out James "Buster" Douglas on October 25, 1990, the trainer earned $1 million for the fight, and he was so proud that he kept the check in his wallet for months. "Who would believe that I'd ever make that kind of money?" he asked, shaking his head. "Who would believe it?"

Benton was a hard-nosed kid, and he proved it in the neighborhood gym, developing the style that he would pass on to his fighters. He stayed close to his opponents, moving from side to side, smothering punches with punches of his own. It was not flashy, but it was effective, a style that earned him the nickname "the Professor." "I got to see a lot of great fighters in that gym," he recalled. "Ray Robinson used to come, and people would be lined up on the street, waiting to get in and see him."

A popular boxer in Philadelphia, Benton fought until the summer of 1970, when a gunshot wound ended his ring career—and almost his life. He was standing on a street corner in north Philadelphia, enjoying the night with some buddies, when he was shot in the back by a gunman who had quarreled with his brother, Henry. Police arrested a suspect who, when released on bail, was shot and killed in a gun battle only two weeks later. "I don't even like to talk about that now," said Benton, who was 37 when he was shot. "That incident is done with. But who knows how long I could have gone in boxing?"

With his boxing career over, Benton focused on training, apprenticing under the great Eddie Futch, who was working the corner for Joe Frazier, then the heavyweight champion of the world. "When I'm around anyone in boxing who knows what he's doing, I keep my eyes and ears open," Benton said. "That's what I did with Eddie. He knew his business. He knew how to handle his fighters. He was a good teacher and a good gentleman, and I learned a lot from him."

A great chef as well as a great trainer, Benton loved to cook for his fighters. One day, while preparing a catfish dinner in the kitchen, he peered into the living room, where his fighters were watching old fight tapes. Benton stopped to watch the grainy black-and-white image on the screen, and he was impressed by one of the fighters, who had just scored a vicious knockout. "Hey, that guy's pretty good," Benton said, still holding onto the frying pan. "Who is it?" It was Benton, proving that great trainers are also great judges of talent.

Emanuel Steward

It was a hot, humid night in Wooster, Massachusetts, the site of the 1992 Olympic boxing trials, and Emanuel Steward walked up to the hotel bar, where the sportswriters were downing beers and shots of whiskey. "I'll have a chardonnay," Steward said softly. So there you have it. In a world of beer and whiskey, a rough world in which gentility is measured by how many of your verbs start with the letter F, Steward is a chardonnay kind of guy. Ah, but is he really? Sure,

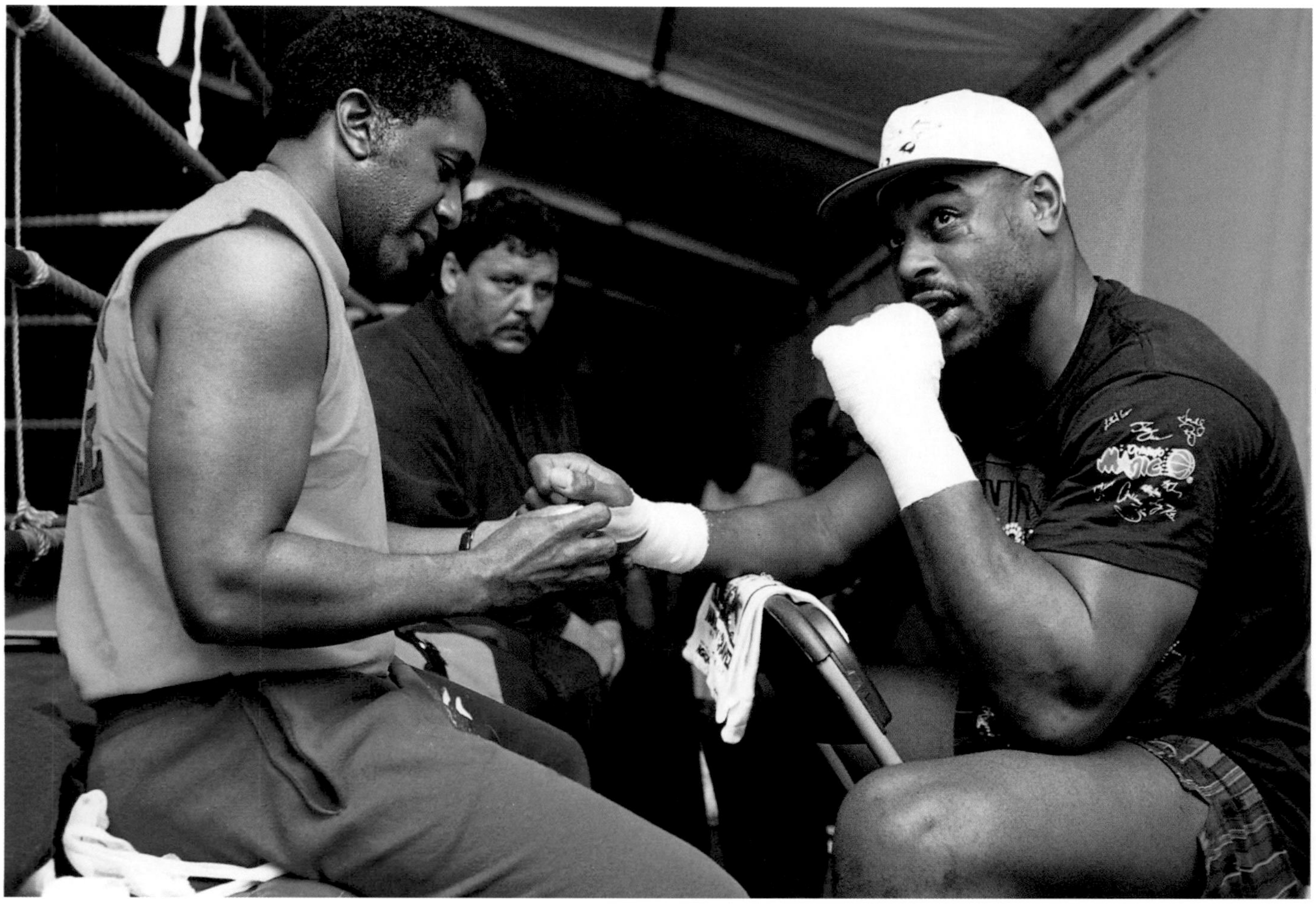

Steward, an impeccable dresser, wears dapper suits with white handkerchiefs neatly tucked in the coat pockets, and sure, he drinks, uh, char-do-nnay. But that is outside the arena. Inside the arena, in the corner, he is one of the toughest men in boxing. He once threatened to walk out on a fighter in the middle of a fight because he felt the man was not trying hard enough. "I want this more than you do," Steward screamed at him.

Steward, the leader of the legendary Kronk Gym in Detroit, saves his gentility for outside the ring. Born on July 7, 1944, in Welch, West Virginia, Steward was 8 years old when he received the greatest Christmas present of his life—boxing gloves. He became fascinated with the basic goal of the sport—to hit and not get hit—and when the family moved to Detroit, he became a national Golden Gloves champion. Then he got a job as the boxing coach for the Kronk Recreation Center. "I love fighters who fight," he said. He advocates a kamikaze style of boxing, a style that has proved remarkably successful. Steward trained the legendary Thomas "the Hit Man" Hearns, the greatest fighter to emerge from that gladiator school in Detroit. Hearns, born in 1958, is still fighting, but he is not the only superb fighter Steward has trained during his career. He has also trained world champions such as Mike McCallum, Dennis Andries, Milt McCrory, Hilmer Kenty, Jimmy Paul, Duane Thomas, Michael Moorer, and John David Jackson—most of them succeeding with the aggressive style that their trainer preaches.

If Hearns is "the Hit Man," then Steward has become the hired gun. He is the "Mr. Fix-it" of boxing, a guy who is called upon to train already successful fighters. Steward turns gyms into repair shops, using tools that he keeps in his head—knowledge and common sense—and the fighters appreciate it. He tinkers with a boxing style, making a suggestion here and there, and then he moves on to his next subject, his next world champion. He is a modern-day paladin—have gloves, will travel. The trainer has worked with Evander Holyfield, Julio Cesar Chavez, and Oscar De La Hoya, each time successfully. "Oscar De La Hoya is already a diamond," Steward said before joining the fighter briefly in 1997. "I just want to polish it."

The Promoters

Tex Rickard

A dapper man in a bow tie and straw hat, George Lewis "Tex" Rickard looked like a refugee from a Broadway musical, his cane more of a prop than a walking aid. But he was no fancy pants—not Tex Rickard. No, he was a man who stubbornly, if elegantly, refused to believe in the calendar. After all, this was the 1900s, but he had one foot in the nineteenth century, and he refused to drag it across the time line. Boxing

loved him for it, because it was this time warp that gave the man his charm, his toughness, his ability to turn lackluster bouts into matches that electrified the world. Rickard could have sold hot chocolate in the Mojave Desert, and the sportswriters loved him for it. They called him "the greatest sports promoter" on the planet.

Rickard worked at a gambling house in the boomtown of Goldfield, Nevada, and he was a man whose job fit his personality perfectly. He mingled among his

OPPOSITE: Seen here on September 24, 1994, trainer Emanuel Steward tapes the hands of Lennox Lewis before a fight against Oliver McCall. Steward consistently lives up to his name, in this case guiding Lewis to victory with his wise stewardship. RIGHT: Tex Rickard (seated, center) was the legendary promoter who brought P.T. Barnum–style showmanship to the art of drawing a fight crowd. Rickard promoted many of the fights featuring Jack Dempsey (seated, left), including the first bout in history to draw a million-dollar gate.

people—the cowboys, the prospectors, the daredevils who would do anything for a buck—and tried to lure them into the house, where the gambling tables and the roulette wheels would do the rest. Rickard was a great host, and the qualities that made him a great host—charm, vision, resourcefulness—would also make him a great promoter.

When his business partners wanted to promote a fight in Goldfield, they picked the right man for the job—Rickard. He staged the lightweight title fight between Joe Gans and Battling Nelson on September 3, 1906, and he proved as entertaining as the fighters themselves. Gans won the fight in 42 rounds, but what Rickard did will last longer. It will last forever, because it became part of history, bringing sports promotions into the twentieth century—a pretty ironic situation for a former gold prospector who loved the rough-and-tumble life of the past. "A showman, that was Tex Rickard," sportswriter Hype Igoe wrote.

Rickard proved it with the Gans-Nelson bout by drawing nationwide publicity when he displayed the $30,000 purse in tall stacks of freshly minted $20 gold pieces. The fight attracted eight thousand fans, and it drew what was then the richest gate in boxing history—$90,000. Not bad for a sport whose contestants once fought on barges to escape the authorities. Yes, no doubt about it, Rickard, the nineteenth-century man, was yanking the sport into the twentieth century.

The promoter also staged the heavyweight title fight between Jack Johnson and Jim Jeffries, "the Great White Hope," in Reno, Nevada—the most significant bout since the Marquess of Queensberry rules. Johnson, who knocked Jeffries out in the 15th round, earned what was the biggest purse in boxing history, $120,000, while Jeffries, a farmer who had come out of retirement, earned $90,000—staggering amounts for a sport that staged, in the beginning, human cockfights.

Rickard did not stop there; he took boxing on a ride that would lead to the multimillion-dollar bouts common today. He promoted the Jack Dempsey–Georges Carpentier heavyweight title bout on July 2, 1921, in Jersey City, New Jersey—the first million-dollar gate in boxing history at $1,789,238. Dempsey clubbed the challenger in the 4th round, a ridiculously easy match, but nobody cared; the spectacle seemed more important than the competition itself. "It will be many, many years...before another Tex Rickard will be seen in action," Igoe wrote.

The Dempsey-Charpentier fight was so huge that *The New York Times* devoted most of its issue, not just the sports section, to coverage of the spectacle on July 3, 1921. "One thing is sure," Irvin S. Cobb reported. "Today, Boyle's Thirty Acres has given to Tex Rickard a richer harvest than any like area of this world's surface has ever yielded."

Don King

There he is, his hair defying gravity, his sentences defying syntax—the greatest promoter in the world, according to a gargantuan, if not objective, source: himself. Don King will promote his sport tirelessly, hyping a fight until his magnificent voice sags to a whisper, his trademark cackle ("Heh, heh, heh") getting fainter and fainter. And a promoter without a voice is like a stripper without a tabletop.

But if there is one thing that King likes to promote more than his sport, it is himself. The man is his own press agent, each outburst representing another release from the publicity machine. He makes a pronouncement and takes an almost childlike joy in his words, laughing as if he were a member of the audience, as enthralled as everybody else—heh, heh, heh—at his remarks, some of which are almost impossible to decipher. His malapropisms make Archie Bunker look like an English professor. Consider these statements:

He once referred to his lawyer as his "banister."

He once said he had a "plutonic" relationship with Ruth Roper, the former mother-in-law of Mike Tyson.

He once said Tyson is like "Manyshnikov."

He once referred to basketball player Sam Bowie as a hero of the Alamo.

And then there is the hair. King says it is an act of God. One day, it was flat; the next day, it was rising toward the heavens, like plants searching for the sunlight. King may be outrageous, but regardless of what people think of him—and he has more detractors than anybody in the fight game—they would have to admit one thing: the man is charming. It is a strange charm, perhaps, the kind a snake oil salesman might employ, but it is a charm nonetheless. "It transcends earthly bounds," King once said.

Don King points a finger at fellow promoter Butch Lewis, standing on the opposite side of real estate tycoon (and casino owner) Donald Trump.

Well, maybe not. But King does transcend boxing. Everybody knows the promoter—everybody, and that includes people who do not know a right cross from a right turn on red after stop. And nothing pleases him more. He is so self-absorbed that after one fight, gripped by an attack of self-pity, he spent more than an hour threatening to resign from the fight game. The poor pugs who were eager to speak at the postfight press conference never got the chance. King was on a roll. The next morning, he forgot what he had said, and the retirement party was off.

And why should he retire, his supporters would ask. He is the most successful promoter in boxing history, a man whose grip on the sport—and hold on the public—has grown since he began staging fights in the Muhammad Ali era. He has promoted some of the greatest fights in history, fights that will be discussed in bars and taverns for as long as men make fists for a living, such as the "Thrilla in Manilla," the "Rumble in the Jungle," and the two fights between Evander Holyfield and Mike Tyson, including the infamous ear-biting incident.

A former numbers runner who spent four years in prison for manslaughter, King began to dominate the boxing scene in 1974, and has promoted more than three hundred world title fights since then. But it has not been easy. The list of fighters who have sued him, usually citing fraud and breach of contract, reads like a who's who: Larry Holmes, Tim Witherspoon, Mike Tyson, Julio Cesar Chavez. Once, trying to make peace with Chavez, King flew to Culiacan, Mexico, the home of the great former champion, where the promoter said he hopped on a burro and yelled to the townspeople, "Donde es Julio? Donde es Julio?"

The FBI has investigated King since the 1980s, usually for the alleged offenses cited by his fighters, but they have never been able to nail him—evidence, he likes to say, of what a great country America is. "If this were Russia," he once said, "I'd be a black ice cube in Siberia." The latest acquittal came in 1998, this one on charges of insurance fraud involving a policy from Lloyd's of London. It was, for King, another example of a wonderful judicial system at work, and he repaid some important members of that system after the trial—the jury that acquitted him. He took them to the Bahamas, all at his own expense—an outrageous show of thanks that he has extended before, to other jurors, at other trials, on other charges. "Only in America," King likes to crow.

When James "Buster" Douglas upset Tyson (then promoted by King) on February 11, 1990, the promoter screamed about an alleged long count that kept his fighter from hanging on to his title. This controversy, regarded as a transparent ploy by most boxing observers, led two U.S. representatives to sponsor bills to create a federal boxing commission. "Don, you've done some good things for boxing," Representative Bill Richard (D-N.M.) told King on *Crossfire*, a cable program. "But you're part of the problem. You have too much power."

"How can you say that?" King responded. "You're a congressman. How can you say that? I work very hard, and I do so in the American way. I'm trying to emulate and imitate what success means in America, and I'm condemned for it. Why? Why?"

Whether you love him or hate him—and most boxing fans fall in one category or the other—King is a born debater, malapropisms and all.

Bob Arum

If promoters were wallflowers, they would not be able to stage a fight between Jimmy and Rocko on the corner of South and Broad in South Philadelphia, much

less a "Thrilla in Manilla" or a "Rumble in the Jungle." But shyness is for the cut men, the guys who carry the spit buckets, not for the promoters. And yet, next to Don King, Bob Arum looks like a mute. But do not be deceived. Arum is one of the most successful promoters in boxing history, and he can talk with the best of them, even if, unlike King, he does not speak as if he has a microphone lodged in his throat. Remember, it was Arum who, caught in an inconsistency, once said, "Yesterday, I was lying. Today, I'm telling the truth."

The promoter is one of the most erudite men in the fight game—and one of the shrewdest. A lawyer who was hired by Robert Kennedy, then the attorney general in the administration of his brother, Arum helped the government win landmark decisions against corporate giants such as Con Edison, Citibank, and Standard Oil. Then, in 1962, he fought to secure the proceeds from the Sonny Liston–Floyd Patterson heavyweight title fight, which were rumored to be heading out of the country. It was his introduction to the world of boxing, a world that fascinated him. "My essential strength as a promoter is that I'm a good administrator," Arum said.

While Don King has virtually monopolized the heavyweight division since the 1970s, Bob Arum has retreated to the lighter weights, promoting some of the biggest fights in history, including the middleweight title fight between "Marvelous" Marvin Hagler and Sugar Ray Leonard on April 6, 1987. He called it the "Fight of the Century"—and the anticipation, if not the competition itself, warranted a tag that had been used countless times before. How many fights of the century can there be? Quite a few, apparently.

The promoter, trying to hype the significance of the bout, arranged for a round table among the great middleweight champions of the past—Jake LaMotta, Rocky Graziano, Carmen Basilio, Joey Giardello, Paul Pender, and Vito Antuofermo. They met at a steak house in Manhattan, some of them threatening to pound the raw meat dangling from the ceiling, and they predicted the outcome of the bout. Most of them picked Hagler, and Graziano, when asked for the strategy he would pursue against Leonard, replied, "I'd try to take his eyes out." Leonard, his eyes intact, upset Hagler.

Arum also tapped a market that the other promoters failed to recognize—the Latino market. Oh, King promoted Chavez for years, but he usually relegated him to undercards on Mike Tyson fights, turning a marquee performer into a warm-up act. Arum was different. He treated Oscar De La Hoya, the latest Latino sensation, like "the Golden Boy," the nickname he had earned when he became the only U.S. boxer to win a gold medal in the 1992 Olympics.

De La Hoya has become a huge star, not just as an attraction on cable TV but also at the grassroots level, in the towns where he fights, the most wondrous example being El Paso, Texas. "The Golden Boy" fought there on June 13, 1998, and the fans followed him everywhere, from the airport to the hotel to the gym—thousands of shrieking females, one of whom tossed her bra at the fighter after his plane landed at the airport. De La Hoya autographed the undergarment, which will probably never get close to a washing machine again. It was phenomenal. "This is unprecedented," said Nigel Collins, the editor of *Ring Magazine*. "The fighter as teen idol." De La Hoya fought Patrick Charpentier, a pug who might have drawn five thousand fans, six thousand tops, in a venue like Las Vegas. But El Paso was not Las Vegas; the fight attracted 45,368 fans, one of the largest crowds to witness a fight in this country since September 15, 1978, when Muhammad Ali fought Leon Spinks before 63,350 fans in the New Orleans Superdome. "The fans [at my fight] were the best I've ever seen in my career," De La Hoya said.

The Duva Family

It was like a mom-and-pop grocery store—without the street corner. No, their street corner was the world. They promoted fights from New York to Paris, from Wales to Germany, and they did it as a family. The patriarch was Lou Duva, born in 1921, a former trucker and bail bondsman who once compared himself to Fred Flintstone. Fred Flintstone? Duva made the caveman seem shy and retiring. Duva once took a pop at junior welterweight Roger Mayweather, who had just defeated one of his fighters, Vinny Pazienza. Duva,

Opposite: Bob Arum, one of the most successful promoters in boxing history, addresses the media.

upset about what he took to be an apparent foul, stormed into the ring after the fight, actually taking a shot at the former champion, who promptly fired back. For his troubles, Duva ended up with a bloody nose—certainly not the first time for this man who got his start in amateur boxing through barroom smokers in Paterson, New Jersey.

In 1984, the family hit the big time, acquiring four world champions—Johnny Bumphus, Rocky Lockridge, Livingstone Bramble, and Mike McCallum. But it would not stop there; with the help of Shelly Finkel, a big-time entertainment manager, the family signed five gold medal winners from the 1984 Olympics: Evander Holyfield, Pernell "Sweetpea" Whitaker, Mark Breland, Meldrick Taylor, and Tyrell Biggs, with Biggs the only one who didn't win a world title. "I think everyone should fight—everyone," said Lou, who boasted a pro record of 15-7. "Everyone should step into the ring to see what it's like."

If Duva was loud and brash, it was just what the family operation needed—a spark of emotion and determination. The family started out small, with Lou, his son Dan, and his daughter-in-law Kathy promoting boxing events at Ice World in Totowa, New Jersey. It was not exactly Madison Square Garden, but their passion made up for the crummy digs. Lou trained the fighters, Kathy handled the publicity, and Dan, a graduate of Seton Hall Law School, handled the nuts and bolts of the promotion. "Those were good days," Lou said.

Dan died of a brain tumor in 1996, and his younger brother, Dino, has assumed the promotional duties with the same grace and dignity.

ABOVE: **Teddy Atlas (left) and Lou Duva (background) counsel heavyweight Michael Moorer.**

Self-Management: the Saga of "Gypsy" Joe

Not all fighters have had the benefit of a good manager or trainer—some have had to do it all for themselves. More than any other boxer in history, Gypsy Joe Harris embodied the traits of a manager, trainer, and promoter. He promoted himself tirelessly, and if he had not been a wily, cunning manager of his own career, he would not have had a career at all. As for training, Harris, who was blind in one eye since childhood, had to devise his own strategy in fight after fight. In the end, unfortunately, Harris did not have the career his skills might have suggested, but his life inside and outside the ring was a compelling one.

Harris, nicknamed "Gypsy" because of his fancy dress and carefree attitude (he was known to change outfits three or four times a day), loved the crowds—in and out of the arena. He worked as a bartender during his fighting days—not because he needed the money, but because he liked the warmth of the fans who frequented the place. They would line up at the bar, and he would regale them with tales of his exploits in the ring, as well as his ambitions: "Be champ of the world. Make a lot of money. That was the dream."

For Harris, the most glorious moment came on March 31, 1967, in Madison Square Garden, when he took a unanimous 10-round decision over welterweight champion Curtis Cokes. More than five hundred Philadelphia fans made the trip to see their hero, and they returned hailing him as the uncrowned champion in the wake of his masterful triumph.

After Cokes, Harris fought eight more times, losing only once, a decision to former champion Emile Griffith on August 6, 1968, in Philadelphia, where a crowd of 13,875 witnessed the fight. He earned the biggest payday of his career—$12,500—for that bout, but it was to be his last.

On the morning of October 11, 1968, Harris was taking a prefight physical for his bout against Manny Gonzalez at the Arena in Philadelphia. Dr. Wilbur H. Strickland, noticing an inflammation of the right eye, took the fighter to University Hospital for a more thorough checkup. It was there that Dr. Harold G. Scheie determined that Harris was blind in one eye.

"My camp knew I was blind," Harris said in a later interview. Alas, the key figures in that camp—promoter Herman Taylor, manager Yank Durham, and trainer Willie Reddish—had since died, so there was no way to confirm or dispute the contention that they knew about the bad eye from the beginning.

In an even more alarming allegation, however, Harris claimed afterward that the athletic commission knew about his bad eye and let him continue fighting because he was such a popular attraction in Philadelphia.

"I told the press that I had been memorizing the eye chart all those years, but I was just trying to protect the commission," Harris said. "They knew about my eye from the beginning. Let me ask you a question. How can a man have a license to examine a person and not realize I was blind?... I turned professional in '65, and they stopped me in '68. Were the doctors sleeping from '65 to '68? Did they just find out?"

In 1972, Harris filed an appeal to have his license reinstated. During a public hearing, Strickland, who died in 1987, acknowledged that the commission realized as early as 1966 that Harris suffered from "defective vision"—but not total blindness—in his right eye. As Harris continued fighting, the doctor said, the eye became more of a concern to the commission, until the organization finally barred him from the ring.

"How much longer would you fight if you got your license?" Zach Clayton, then head of the commission, asked Harris.

"Two or three years," Harris said.

"And what would you do then?"

"Be rich."

Harris lost his appeal.

One of the most popular boxers ever to fight in Philadelphia, Harris had built up a record of 24-1 before the commission "discovered" that he was blind in his right eye. He lost the use of that eye when he was eleven years old, but turned the disability into an asset. In fact, Harris boasted the most creative boxing style since Sugar Ray Robinson, dipping, bending, and twisting to keep his his good eye—his left—on his opponent.

Ironically, the handicap that made him great led to the end of his career, the end of his dream. After his boxing license was taken away, the former No. 1 contender in the world—a man whose fortitude and confidence had given him the strength to overcome so many obstacles in his life—resorted to drugs and liquor. He was trying to kill himself, and when the heroin and whiskey failed to do the trick, he tried something else. One night in 1979, he walked across the Ben Franklin Bridge, intent on diving into the river and drowning himself.

"When your mind is so upset, you're not thinking right, and you'll go and do anything," he recalled. "I was up on that bridge. I told myself I was going to jump off. But then, I thought, 'Hey, I can swim.' I got a little medal for swimming at the recreation center when I was a kid. It seemed kind of funny later. Here I was. I wanted to drown myself, and I could swim."

When his license was revoked, Harris found a job as a street cleaner, then as a construction worker, then as a.... He had forgotten all the jobs he held, but there was one thing he never forgot—the misery he experienced in all of them. Harris was a fighter, and when they took away his right to dance and batter a man in front of a crowd, he lost his heart.

After years of being down and out, Harris suffered three cardiac arrests in 1988—the result, he was certain, of all the time he had spent abusing his body with drugs and alcohol. When it became clear that the on-again, off-again hospitalization wasn't doing the trick, Harris finally kicked the habit on his own. "I said, 'The hell with it.' I went off of it, and I had to stay in the bathroom for days. After three or four days, I didn't need drugs no more. I was cured. I was weak, but I didn't have the urge anymore."

Following his battles with heart disease and addiction, both perhaps the aftereffects of a dream deferred, Harris died on March 6, 1990. His life and career were both a testament to how much a man can accomplish on his own as well as a warning about the fragility of the boxing life.

Great Fights 4

It was not a fight. It was a slaughter, a massacre. Any audience, save a prize-fighting one, would have exhausted its emotions in that first minute.

—Jack London, *The Mexican*

Great boxing matches are massive relocation projects. They bring street fights indoors, creating a sense of excitement—and dread—unlike any other sporting event in the world. They provide controlled mayhem—fury tempered by guile and artistry. And fans remember the bouts long after the fighters have taken off their gloves. Who remembers Super Bowl VI? Or the 1976 NBA finals? Or the 1991 World Series? But a fight, ah, a fight will remain in your memory banks forever, almost as if your mind were a scrapbook. And your memory becomes sharper, more vivid, as the years go on; it recalls details that you may have missed the first time around. Why are fights so exciting? It is the artistry and athleticism, yes, but more than that, it is the sense of danger. The combinations that thrill you one minute can fill you with a sense of dread the next, when the poor pug is unconscious, stretched out on the canvas. "I'm in the hurt business," the great Sugar Ray Robinson once said. Right or wrong, it is that brutality which attracts us to the sport, even though part of us may be disgusted by the ugly spectacle.

ABOVE: **In one of the most sensational bouts of the era, Roberto Duran and Sugar Ray Leonard fight for their lives during their June 20, 1980, middleweight title bout in Montreal.** OPPOSITE: **Playing David to Jess Willard's Goliath on July 4, 1919, challenger Jack Dempsey (left) assesses his much larger opponent across the ring. The far quicker Dempsey didn't take long to figure out how to take down the giant; after 3 rounds of terrible abuse, a broken and battered Jess Willard could not go on.**

If we accept that the attraction to a boxing match is an uneasy combination of the baser and nobler sides of human nature, what is it that makes a particular fight great? Some slugfests go the full 15 rounds and elicit little more than a groan of relief from a bored stadium crowd, while some last only into the first few rounds and are remembered forever. Well, if the initial attraction is a dichotomy, the elements of history's great fights reflect the same dual nature: some achieve legendary status because they showcase incredible feats of bravery and endurance, while others stick in our minds because of their ferocity and violence. For instance, though the contest happened in 1919, no one who is a fan of boxing history will forget the fight between Jack Dempsey and Jess Willard; the spectacular and surprising violence Dempsey unleashed on Willard left the larger man with a shattered face and only lasted 3 rounds. Meanwhile, Willie Pep's remarkable comeback victory over Sandy Saddler in 1949 for the featherweight title was a tribute to man's ability to overcome tragedy (Pep had been in a life-threatening plane crash less than two years earlier), face great odds, and still triumph.

Jack Dempsey vs. Jess Willard
July 4, 1919

They called it "pugilistic murder," a fight so brutal that the referee could have doubled as a coroner. Jack Dempsey, thirteen years younger and almost 70 pounds (32kg) lighter than the heavyweight champion, looked like a toddler challenging the neighborhood bully. He seemed lost and timid in the opening moments of the fight as he cautiously circled his opponent for about a minute. Could this be "the Manassa Mauler," the man who had scored five consecutive 1st-round knockouts? But there was a good reason for this strategy. Dempsey was not timid so much as confused. How could he beat a man so massive? Jess Willard then threw his first punch of the fight, a left that missed. Dempsey countered the punch with a hailstorm of blows, dropping the champion seven times—yes, seven times—in the 1st round. The challenger stood over the fallen fighter each time, ready to pound him again and again.

The fight lasted 3 rounds, with Willard dazed and bloodied on his stool, a man who had entered the ring with a confidence that deserted him with the first left hook to the jaw. The former champion sat in the corner, his eyes vacant; he was as defenseless on the stool as he had been in the ring. Yes, he was a huge man, but Dempsey had countered size with fury, leading sportswriters to coin the term "killer instinct."

ABOVE: Dempsey punches Willard into a corner during their landmark bout on July 4, 1919, while the U.S. flag flaps in the breeze.

They called it the "Massacre at Toledo," and Willard claimed that his opponent had "loaded" his gloves by treating his hand tape with a talcum substance that turned hard as concrete when wet. Perhaps. But Dempsey insisted that his fists did all the damage, enough damage to keep a hospital emergency room busy for weeks—a broken jaw, a split cheekbone, a busted nose, a battered ear, and six broken teeth. Willard never regained proper hearing in his left ear.

Joe Louis vs. Billy Conn
June 18, 1941

Pity the man on the verge of accomplishing the impossible. Why? Because he begins to savor the view from the mountaintop before he has even reached it. He gets cocky and arrogant, and he starts to make the tiny mistakes that great opponents turn into huge mistakes. Billy Conn knew the feeling.

Conn, the light heavyweight champion of the world, met Joe Louis, the heavyweight king, at the Polo Grounds in New York. It was an act of audacity just to face Louis, let alone think you could beat him. But Conn thought he could, even though the heavyweight champion outweighed him by about 30 pounds (14kg). "I beat the main fellows, the contenders, so I figured we'll try Joe Louis, he's just another guy," Conn said. "You don't fight guys like Joe Louis unless you beat all those guys that really knew how to fight, and then you learn how to fight. You're not just some mug coming in off the street corner to fight Joe Louis, because he'd knock you through the middle of next week."

Armed with confidence and ring savvy, Conn outboxed the heavyweight champion through the middle rounds, taking control of the match with his superior

ABOVE: **Light heavyweight Billy Conn was on top of this June 18, 1941, fight against heavyweight Joe Louis, when he became overconfident and tried to knock out the Brown Bomber in the 13th round. It was an ill-advised change in strategy and Louis made the quicker, more agile challenger pay for the mistake with this crushing left hook that sent Conn to the mat for good.**

speed. The light heavyweight king boxed brilliantly, executing a game plan that was an amazing combination of daring and caution. He charged inside to land one, two, three, four blows in a row before darting back outside, almost as if he were both participant and spectator, firing punches one second, admiring his handiwork the next. Conn was in a rhythm, a rhythm he had never experienced before, not against an opponent as talented and menacing as Louis, and he loved it. He stunned the heavyweight champion with a left hook to the jaw in the 12th round, but it was a curious blow, a blow that hurt Conn much more than it did Louis, because it turned a confident man into an overconfident man. "I hurt him in the 12th round, so I figured I'll try and knock him out," Conn said. "I made a mistake. He was waiting for me. He'd have never hit me in the ass if I didn't make a mistake and try to knock him out."

Conn, ahead on two of the three scorecards, rejected the advice of his corner, which was to box cautiously so that he could preserve the win that seemed all but certain. He went for the knockout in the 13th round, charging inside without retreating back outside, as he had done in the earlier rounds, when he built up his lead. Then Louis smashed him with a left hook to the jaw, and just like that, the fight was over. "They told me to stay away from him, that I was beating him all the way," Conn said. "But when I hurt him in the 12th round, he started to hold on. I said, 'I'm going to knock this son of a bitch out. Don't worry about it.'"

So he went out for the 13th round, and he told Louis, "Well, Joe, you're in for a tough fight tonight." Louis flattened him a few seconds later, standing over his opponent to get in the final words. "You're right," Louis said.

Later, Conn found humor in his missed opportunity. "I told my corner, 'Don't worry about it. I'm going to knock him out.' Don't worry about it? And then I made one mistake!"

Muhammad Ali vs. Joe Frazier
March 8, 1971

Forget about Muhammad Ali and Joe Frazier as individuals. They were great fighters, two of the best heavyweights who ever lived, but together, ah, together they reached heights that went beyond greatness. What is the next elevator stop after greatness? It may be too mind-numbing to comprehend, but whatever it is, these two men reached it.

Ali and Frazier were opposites—one tall and pretty, the other short and squat—but the odd couple gave fight fans the most legendary trilogy in boxing history, 123 minutes of fury and elegance, guile and grace, comedy and drama. They also gave us 123 minutes of themselves. Who could have asked for more?

In an age when heavyweights wage their fiercest battles at the negotiating table, demanding more money for less risk, it is worth remembering that Ali and Frazier earned every penny they made. They fought each other three times, but their first battle, on March 8, 1971, in Madison Square Garden, was the best—better than their second meeting, which Ali won by decision on January 28, 1974. The first was even better than their third and final struggle, the fabled "Thrilla in Manilla," won by Ali with a dramatic 14th-round technical knockout on October 1, 1975. "They left a little bit of themselves in the ring," said Eddie Futch, the legendary trainer who worked the corner for Frazier, of the first fight. "They hit their peak that night, and that's saying something."

Ali and Frazier were undefeated, each with a legitimate claim to the heavyweight crown—Frazier because he held the official title, Ali because he lost his outside the ring, where boxing organizations stripped him of his belt for his refusal to be inducted into the armed services. "It was the greatest boxing event I've ever covered," said Ed Schuyler, Jr., the great boxing writer who has covered more than three hundred world title fights for the Associated Press.

The bout attracted 20,455 fans to the Garden, most of them members of the "beautiful people" set. Frank Sinatra took pictures for *Life* magazine, and Burt Lancaster provided the commentary for the closed-circuit telecast. It was like an issue of *People* come to life. "It was packed with celebrities," Schuyler said. "But it was the only fight I've ever witnessed where the celebrities went to see, not to be seen. The stars were the two guys in the ring....By the 9th round, everybody in the arena was standing up."

OPPOSITE: The first installment of what is perhaps the most fabled trilogy of heavyweight match-ups was aired on March 8, 1971, when Muhammad Ali battled Joe Frazier for the world title.

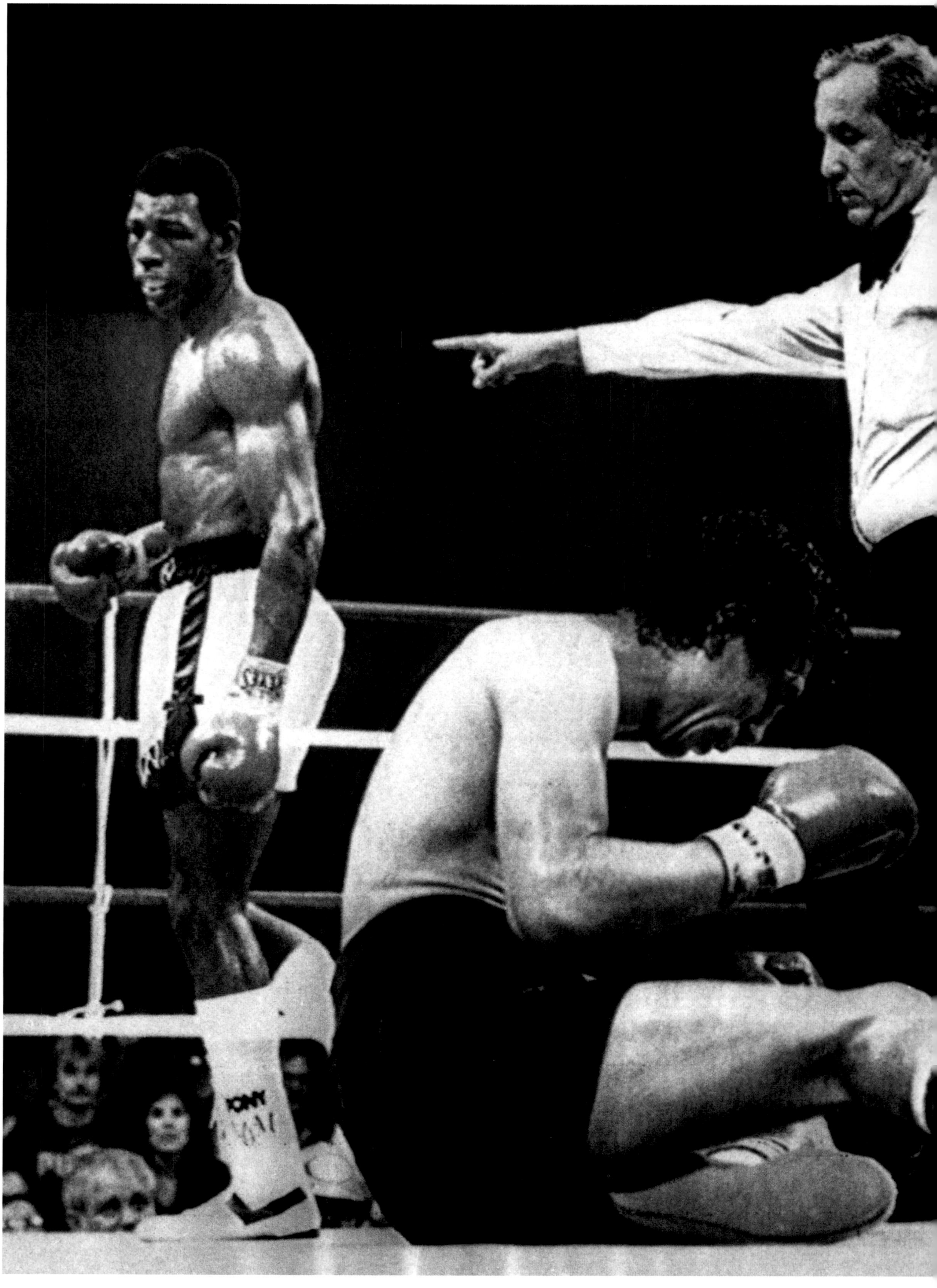
TONY

Ali danced and preened early in the fight, going toe-to-toe in the later rounds when his stamina began to fade. It faded at a bad time, because the longer the fight went on, the fresher the champion seemed. Frazier, stalking his opponent from the start, dropped Ali in the 15th and final round—perhaps the most famous knockdown in boxing history. "I was surprised that Ali got up so quickly," said Arthur Mercante, who refereed the fight. "I had only reached the count of 2. I had never seen anyone recover from a punch like that. It was a tremendous, thunderous left hook. Floyd Patterson hit Ingemar Johannson with a similar shot, but Johannson stayed on the canvas for a long, long time."

Ali almost went down earlier, in the 11th round, but just as his legs were about to cave in, his magnificent heart kept him up. "Ali was out on his feet, and Joe could have knocked him out in that round," Futch said. "But Ali was smart. He started clowning, and he made Joe think he was playing possum. But he wasn't. He was really hurt."

When it was all over, 15 brutal rounds after it started, boxing had an undisputed heavyweight champion. Frazier captured a unanimous decision, and Ali had an easy explanation—"I got hit," he said. The winner flashed a grotesque smile, a stream of blood pouring from a mouth that had been pounded mercilessly for forty-five minutes. "It was a great fight and an unbelievable spectacle, just unbelievable," boxing historian Bert Sugar said. "I haven't seen that kind of passion in the ring since."

Matthew Saad Muhammad vs. Yaqui Lopez
July 13, 1980

If you look at most retired fighters, you will see their records on their faces—the wins and losses stamped on the lumpy ears, the busted noses, the scar tissue that covers their faces like a thick crust. Matthew Saad Muhammad, the former light heavyweight champion, is different. His face is smooth and unmarked, as if he had spent all those years selling insurance, not taking punches. But he did take punches, lots of them, and his face should be designated as one of the wonders of the world because it should be covered with scars—especially when you consider his battle with Yaqui Lopez

LEFT: Light heavyweight champion Matthew Saad Muhammad overcame an early beating and was able to stop challenger Yaqui Lopez in the 14th round of their title bout on June 13, 1980.

on July 13, 1980, at the Playboy Club in McAfee, New Jersey.

Both men took enough punches to deck a gym full of fighters, but Saad Muhammad took more blows early, and Lopez looked like a certain winner. The champion seemed spent by the 5th round; he looked so tired that he resembled one of those marathon dancers, his feet dragging across the floor as he draped himself across his partner, Lopez, who proved to be a partner from hell. The challenger took some shots, too, but he seemed to deliver five for every one he took, and the outcome seemed inevitable to the TV announcers, who thought Saad Muhammad would lose by knockout. "Man, I get a headache every time I see that fight," the champion said years later.

Saad Muhammad took twenty unanswered blows in the 8th round, but the referee did not halt the bout, and the champion recovered, crossing that threshold that seems to separate gifted fighters from oblivion: once they survive the most brutal combinations of their opponents, they are fine; they can take anything from that moment on, and Saad Muhammad did just that. He absorbed the blows and delivered some of his own, coming back so furiously that he floored his opponent four times in the 14th and final round. "I hit him good, but he would not go down," Lopez said. "That's why he's champion."

To this day, the former champion is amazed that he took those shots. "I'm a warrior, and a warrior will not stay down unless he's unconscious," Saad Muhammad said. "But, ooh, how did I take those punches?"

Aaron Pryor vs. Alexis Arguello
November 12, 1982

Alexis Arguello was a smooth, elegant boxer, a man who could inflict more damage with a single punch than most fighters could with dozens of combinations. He was tall and thin, a physique that often led opponents to underestimate him, as did Kevin Rooney, who would go on to train Mike Tyson for five turbulent years in the 1980s. Rooney met Arguello on July 31, 1982, in Atlantic City, and when he spotted his opponent at the

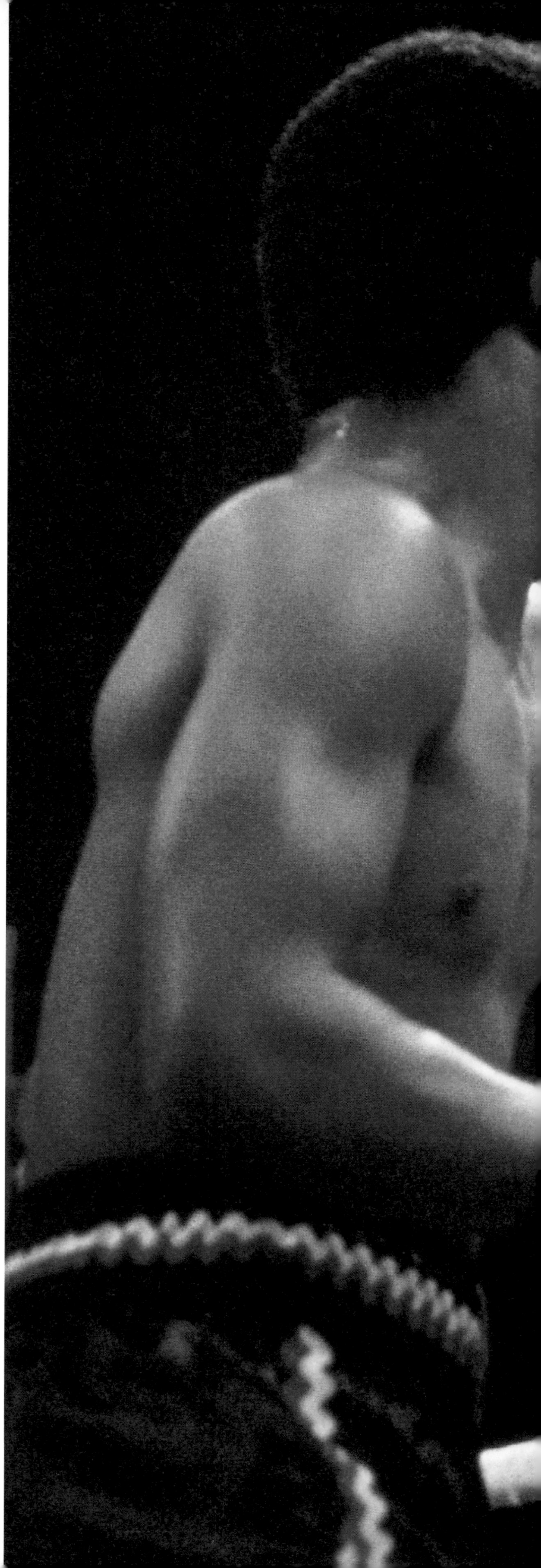

RIGHT: In one of the most exciting boxing contests of the 1980s, Alexis Arguello (right) took on junior welterweight champ Aaron Pryor in a valiant attempt to become the first man to hold titles in four weight classes. Despite a tremendous effort, Arguello was finally knocked out by his equally skilled opponent in the 14th round.

weigh-in, he thought to himself, "This guy's too skinny. I can lick him." The skinny pushover knocked him out in the 2nd round. Rooney was so dazed that a few hours later, he told his wife he had to get ready for the fight that had ended so quickly.

As ambitious as he was efficient, Arguello was attempting to become the first man in history to win world titles in four weight classes. There was only one problem. He was facing Aaron Pryor, the junior welterweight champion, a man who was equally ambitious—and equally talented. He was also the most intimidating man in boxing. Whenever he stepped into the ring, Pryor would point his right arm at his opponent, holding it as if he were staring through the sights of a shotgun. Fans called him "the Hawk."

They met before 23,800 fans at the Orange Bowl in Miami—a crowd that witnessed perhaps the greatest fight of the 1980s. Pryor won the early rounds, throwing punches from all angles, a whirlwind of combinations that seemed impossible to defend against. The champion boxed in the middle rounds, and the challenger began to rally, landing right hands that would have crushed most fighters—most fighters, but not Pryor. Arguello landed an amazing flurry in the 13th round—punch after punch after punch—but he did more damage to himself than to his opponent by tiring himself out with the fusillade. Pryor rallied in the 14th round, throwing the same kind of combinations that his opponent had hurled only moments earlier. Arguello did not weather them as successfully. He retreated to the ropes, taking more punishment before finally crumpling, unconscious, to the canvas.

"Marvelous" Marvin Hagler vs. Thomas Hearns
April 15, 1985

The fight lasted only 7 minutes and 52 seconds, but "Marvelous" Marvin Hagler and Thomas Hearns offered the world a brief history lesson—they took us back in time by showing us how men fought before the discovery of fire. This was no "sweet science." It was furious combat, raw and ugly, and it was no less compelling for its brevity. Hearns knew he had to box, but Hagler, usually a cautious fighter, stormed into the center of the ring, and there went the game plan, as useless as a spit bucket. Hagler, the undisputed middleweight champion, fought like a challenger, but he paid for his aggressiveness, suffering a cut on his forehead with only 30 seconds left in the 1st round. "I started slugging because I had to," Hearns said.

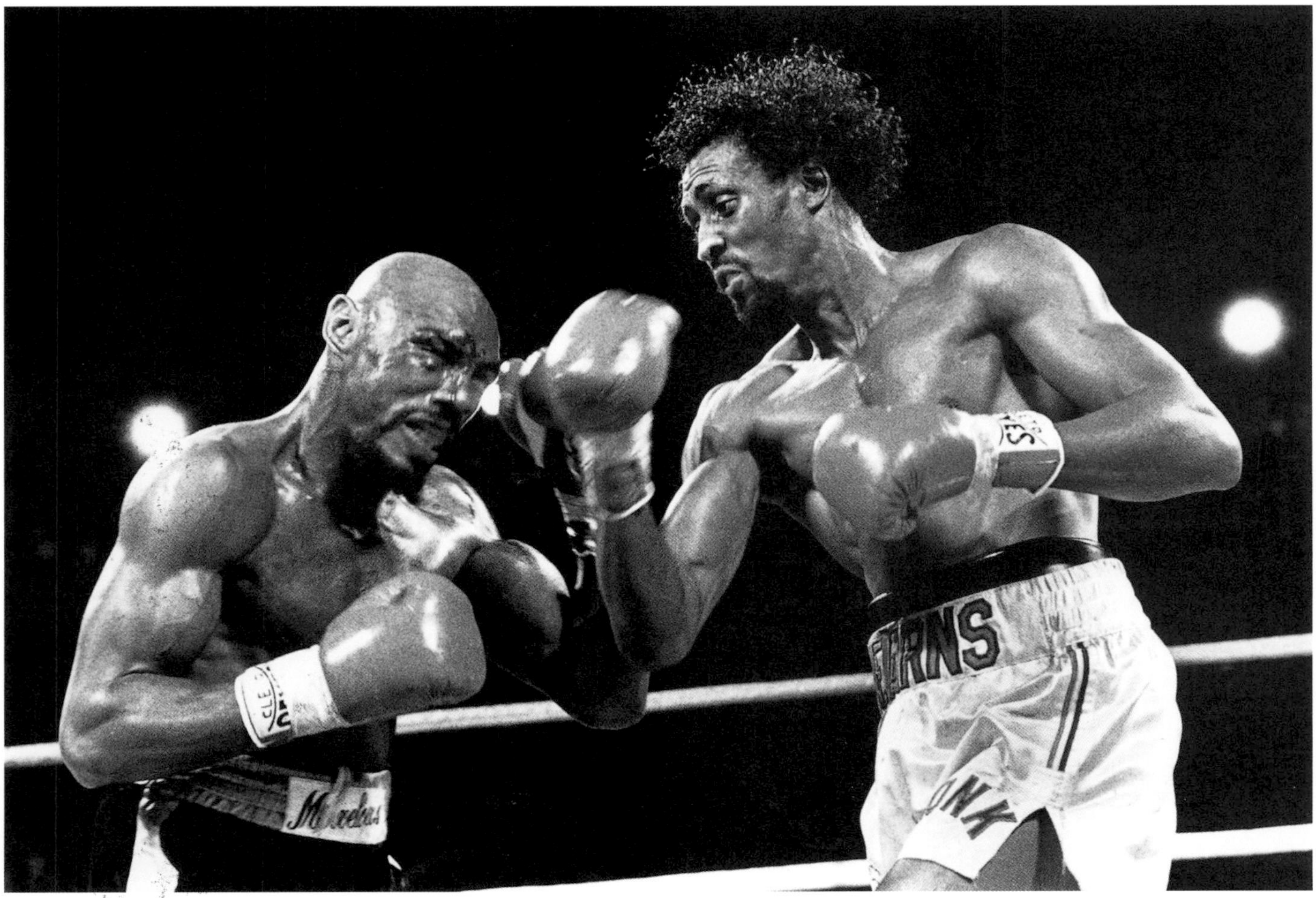

OPPOSITE: In this shot from their classic middleweight title fight, Thomas Hearns (right) crushes Marvelous Marvin Hagler with a right to the head. The passion and fury that both these men brought to this fight made it one of the most exciting ring confrontations ever. ABOVE: In the end, Hagler eventually got the better of his opponent early in the 3rd round, laying Hearns out for good with a devastating flurry of blows punctuated with a thunderous right.

Hearns kept slugging, opening another cut in the 2nd round, this one on the cheek of his opponent. How much more could Hagler take? The champion had been floored only once before, when Juan Roldan nailed him two years earlier, but Hearns was a better puncher, sharper and more accurate, and he was beating Hagler to the punch. But the champion stayed on his feet; somehow he stayed on his feet, and he dared Hearns to stay on his.

The ringside physician examined the champion before the start of the 3rd round and threatened to stop the fight on cuts. Hagler, motivated by the examination, charged at his opponent, who remained in the center of the ring, so flat-footed that he seemed to be wearing ankle weights. The champion hurt the challenger with a combination and followed up with an overhand right that dropped Hearns onto the seat of his gold silk trunks. Hearns beat the 10-count, but he looked like a sleepwalker, his eyes as glazed as a cheap doughnut. Referee Richard Steele stopped the fight and ended perhaps the greatest 3 rounds in boxing history. "Few had witnessed anything like the apocalyptic conflict," British journalist Peter Walsh wrote.

Meldrick Taylor vs. Julio Cesar Chavez
March 17, 1990

They were perfect opponents—one quick and flashy, the other calm and methodical—the two greatest fighters of their era, pound for pound. Meldrick Taylor was the boxer, Julio Cesar Chavez the puncher—but the labels meant nothing, not for these junior welterweights. Why? Because each fighter exhibited traits of the other: Taylor could punch and Chavez could box, each measuring his opponent with the cool intensity of a diamond appraiser. The fight promised great theater, and for once, the match lived up to the hype.

In the 1st round, Taylor seemed nervous, as if he were respectful—perhaps too respectful—of a fighter known for flattening his opponents and then shrugging his shoulders with all the remorse of a hit man. Taylor punched and retreated, darting in and out like a hummingbird, while his opponent calmly chased him. It was still early, but it was a dramatic round, with the two men setting the scene for the battle of attrition that awaited them in the later rounds.

Chavez landed a short, jolting right to the jaw in the 2nd round, a blow that sent his opponent into a Chaplinesque waddle in the middle of the ring. Taylor recovered, but the punch had dramatized the wisdom of his strategy in the 1st round. He began to bleed from the mouth.

The Philadelphian, demonstrating his dazzling hand speed for the first time in the fight, landed a solid combination in the 2nd round, but the Mexican shook his head as if the punches were affectionate pats. Taylor smiled, refusing to get frustrated. He seemed in command. "I fought the best fight I could fight," he said afterward.

In the middle rounds, Taylor abandoned his early caution by fighting on the inside in an attempt to beat his opponent at his own game. He was landing more punches, but he absorbed some in return, and the punches he took were heavier and more punishing; cuts opened in both nostrils and above both eyes. The Philadelphian was winning the fight, but his strategy was risky and dangerous—a game plan that could undermine his success at any moment. "He looked like a monster," Chavez said later.

Then, in the middle of the 12th round, it happened. Chavez landed a straight right to the jaw, which forced his opponent into the corner—a man whose battle plan had suddenly betrayed him. The Mexican pursued him, slowly and calmly, sizing him up for one big punch, one final punch. It was a straight right that cracked Taylor on the jaw, sending him to the floor for the first time in his career. Taylor struggled to his feet, grabbing the ropes as if they were lifelines, but the referee looked into his eyes and waved the bout to an end 2 seconds before the final bell—2 seconds before what would have been a victory for the courageous Philadelphian, who was ahead on two of the three scorecards. Taylor lasted 35 minutes and 58 seconds, but it was not enough. "I asked Taylor if he was okay, and I heard no response," referee Richard Steele said afterward. "I wasn't aware of how close we were to the end of the fight. I thought it was more important to figure out if

OPPOSITE: Emblematic of the respect that the two fighters had for each other, this photograph shows Meldrick Taylor (left) and Julio Cesar Chavez trading blows at the outside limit of their reaches during their dramatic contest on March 17, 1990. The fight was decided by the ref with 2 seconds to go in the final round; if time had wound down without interruption, Taylor would have taken the win by decision, though he had clearly suffered more damage.

the kid could go on. I saw a beaten fighter, a young man who had fought his heart out. He got up, but I was not going to let him take another punch."

After the fight, Taylor was admitted to a hospital in Las Vegas, where he was treated for dehydration, a lacerated tongue, and a small fracture in the bone behind his left eye. "Two seconds," he kept repeating in his hospital room. "Two seconds."

James Toney vs. Michael McCallum
December 13, 1991

For 36 brutal minutes, James Toney and Michael McCallum created an incredibly intense drama in that theater known as the ring. Then, with one brief announcement, the play collapsed with the most unsatisfying of resolutions—a draw. Toney and McCallum fought to a standstill, with Toney retaining his world middleweight title, but while the decision may have been unsatisfactory, the fight was a brilliant display of boxing at its best.

Toney battered his opponent in the 4th round by landing a three-punch combination—overhand right, left hook, overhand right—that sent McCallum into a clumsy rumba. Then McCallum grabbed the champion and tried to spin him around as if he were a dance partner, a tactic that helped McCallum recover. The challenger landed a crunching left hook that seemed to confuse the champion, who looked down and saw his mouthpiece jutting out of his mouth; Toney inhaled and drew it back inside.

The two men pounded each other in the final rounds. The boxers displayed reservoirs of strength, endurance, and will that astounded the crowd at Convention Hall in Atlantic City. Every punch, every flurry, brought "oohs" and "aahs." Toney almost knocked out the challenger in the final round with a left hook to the jaw that was followed by a volley so furious that he finally stepped back in exhaustion. McCallum would not go down. "I had him hurt in the last 2 rounds, but I just couldn't put him away," Toney said.

Opposite: James Toney (left) and Michael McCallum staged a battle for the ages when they met on December 13, 1991. Above: Michael Moorer (bottom) and Bert Cooper (top) unleashed a cascade of violence against each other in their May 16, 1992, match-up at Trump Plaza in Atlantic City. In the 5th round, Cooper was unsteadily wobbling in an eddy of his own blood when the ref ended the fight, awarding the win to Moorer.

Michael Moorer vs. Bert Cooper
May 16, 1992

When Michael Moorer and Bert Cooper make fists, the ringside officials should man an air-raid siren. And when they make fists against each other? Well, they did just that in Atlantic City, and they dropped enough bombs to topple the building in which they were fighting. They fought for something called the World Boxing Organization heavyweight title, but the match was more spectacular than the cheap trinket they were vying for. It was a classic.

It lasted only 15 minutes, but it was 15 minutes of mayhem and brutality. The 1st round compressed 10 rounds of violence into 1, with both fighters landing the kind of punches that would leave most men in body casts. Cooper dropped Moorer early in the round, but when Moorer beat the 10-count, his legs twitching as if from an electrical shock, he rushed at the man who had just pounded him. Moorer landed a two-punch combination to the jaw—chopping left, right hook—and Cooper went down, his head whipping backward like that of a crash-test dummy. It was an incredible display of punching power—2 knockdowns in 3 minutes. But it was not over, not yet.

Cooper dropped his opponent again in the 3rd round, but he returned to his corner with a deep gash over his left eye—the result of an accidental head butt. The two fighters seemed arm-weary in the 4th round, but the shelling was still fearsome, their artillery going from bombs to grenades. In the 5th round, Moorer unloaded about ten straight punches, his final blow a right uppercut that seemed to launch his opponent halfway across the ring. Cooper landed on his black silk trunks, a part of his wardrobe that had become well acquainted with the canvas. When he barely beat the 10-count, his face shooting a geyser of blood, the referee took one look at his eyes and called a halt to a magnificent bout. The end came 2 minutes and 21 seconds into the round.

Riddick Bowe vs. Evander Holyfield
November 13, 1992

They called him "Commander Skylab," a guy who could reach the ozone on the wings of his brash personality. But Riddick Bowe dismissed the criticism—if his head were in the clouds, he said, it was only because his dreams had transported him there. Bowe was right—oh my, was he right—but he had to prove it. Enter Evander Holyfield, the heavyweight champion of the world.

The fighters met in one of the worst eras for heavyweights in history, an era in which the division was filled with fat bellies and fatter paychecks. Ah, but these two fighters took us back to the days of Joe Louis, Rocky Marciano, and Muhammad Ali. Bowe and Holyfield were not legends—not yet, anyway—but they gave boxing fans 36 minutes that would last forever.

Three inches (8cm) shorter and 30 pounds (14kg) lighter than his opponent, Holyfield fought like the bigger man; his spirit overcame his judgment, just as it always did, in fight after fight. He never learned. The champion fought on the inside against the challenger, and he tried—and often succeeded—to jab his way through a minefield of hooks and uppercuts.

In the later rounds, the match became the test of will that most experts had predicted. It was beautiful and ugly, noble and savage, riveting and hard to watch, with both men punching—and taking punches—until most fighters would have collapsed.

Bowe landed a right uppercut to the jaw in the 10th round, a blow that forced the champion into the ropes, where the challenger followed up with about fifteen unanswered punches—hook after hook after hook.

OPPOSITE: Evander Holyfield fends off a crushing right from Riddick Bowe during their legendary first match-up, on November 13, 1992. Though he fought with great courage, Holyfield could not prevail over the larger, stronger Bowe.

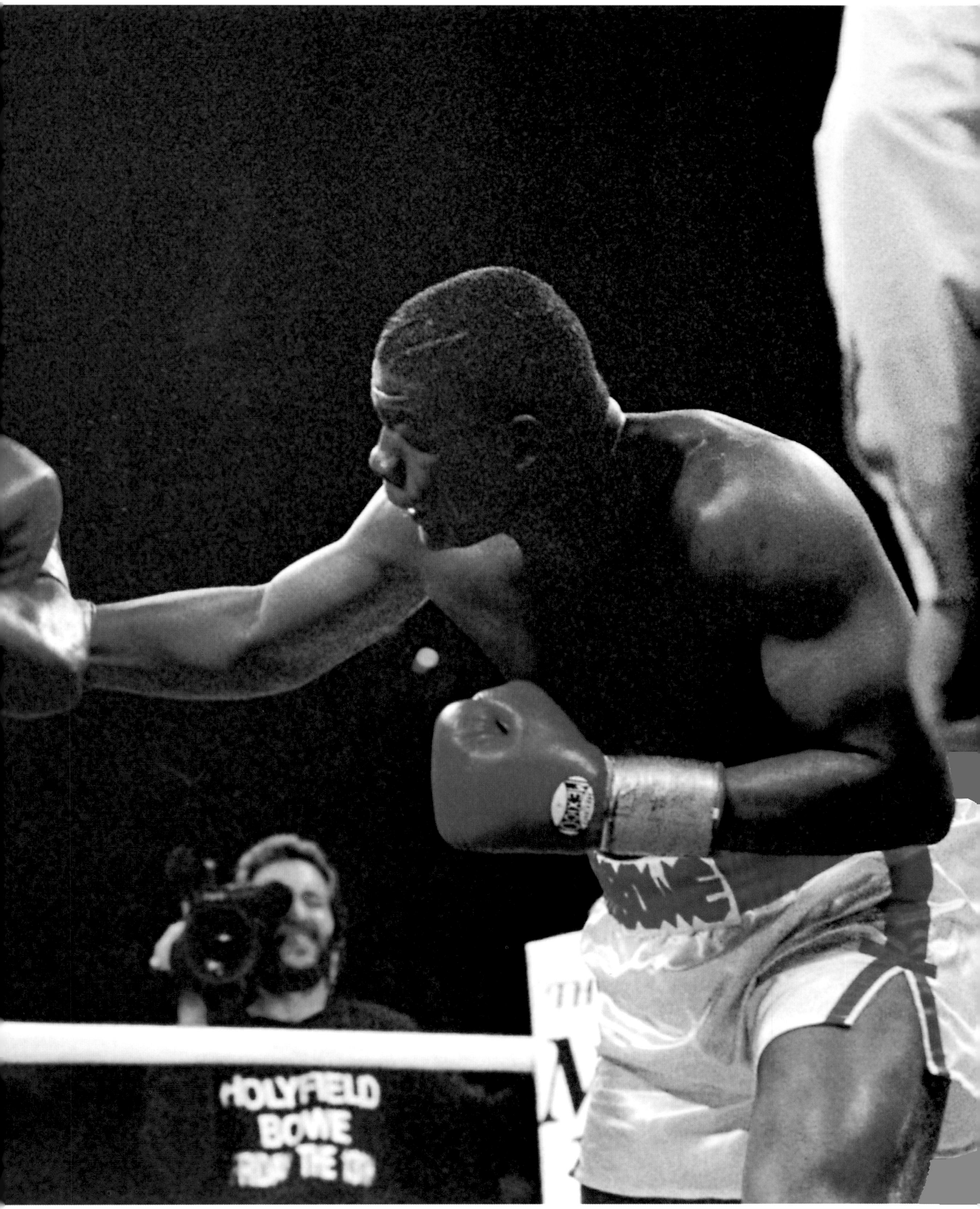
HOLYFIELD
BOWE

The champion refused to go down, his heart keeping him upright just when it seemed his legs would fail him. Then he rallied late in the round by delivering the same brutal punches that he had been absorbing just a few seconds before. It was an incredible exhibition—one of the greatest rounds in heavyweight history. "Suck it up, baby," trainer Lou Duva told the champion between rounds. "And punch like hell."

Bowe dropped the champion with an overhand right in the 11th round, a punch so solid that his opponent crumpled to the canvas, his face frozen in what appeared to be a silent scream. Holyfield scrambled to his feet and grabbed the ropes as the challenger waited in a neutral corner, eager to pound him again. The champion beat the 10-count. "Let's go, Bowe," the crowd roared.

Bowe captured a unanimous decision, jumping wildly when the decision was announced. "Any more questions about his heart?" Rock Newman, who managed Bowe, asked.

Bowe and Holyfield would fight two more times, including the fight with the strangest dive in boxing history—when "Fan Man," a sky diver with a sense of the dramatic, descended from the desert sky into the ring on November 6, 1993, in Las Vegas. Holyfield captured a decision that night, only to get stopped in the 8th round two years later. The fights comprise one of the great trilogies in heavyweight history—right below the Ali-Frazier wars of the 1970s—but it is the first fight that will go down as a classic. "Regardless of how much pressure I put on him, no matter how tired he got, he came back," Holyfield said.

Arturo Gatti vs. Wilson Rodriguez
March 22, 1996

They fought for almost 18 brutal minutes. They turned the ring into a back alley with ropes. And when it was all over, the cheers continued long after the punches had stopped. "I'm just happy I won," Gatti, then the junior lightweight champion, said afterward. Happy? He should have been ecstatic. The fighting was so intense that it looked like a battle of attrition from the start—and it was. Both men started out aggressively, punching with a fury that would have exhausted most fighters. Gatti was careless in the 2nd round, and it was just the opening that Rodriguez wanted—and had anticipated. The champion was a gutsy fighter, and he threw punches without worrying about what he might absorb in return; it made for thrilling—and, for him, dangerous—fighting, because his idea of defense was to smash you with his face before you could smash him with your fists. Exciting? Yes, but the style had cost him his only defeat up to that point—a 6-round loss to King Solomon, a club fighter, four years earlier at the Blue Horizon in Philadelphia.

Gatti displayed the same tendency in fight after fight, recklessly charging at his opponents, his heart and power overcoming his foolishness. But could he withstand the pressure of an opponent who seemed just as tough and strong? Rodriguez seemed to answer that question in the 2nd round, when he dropped the champion onto his yellow silk trunks. The crowd, practically asleep during a miserable undercard at Madison Square Garden, suddenly came to life, cheering wildly as the two warriors threw combination after combination. "When I went down in the 2nd round, I said, 'Oh, my God, I can't believe it,'" Gatti said later.

And the knockdown was just the start of his problems. Gatti absorbed a horrible pounding, his eyes bruised by the end of the 3rd round, his face turning the same shade of red as his gloves. Peering through the slits that his eyes had become, he seemed disoriented, like a man trying to make his way through a dark corridor. But the champion kept punching...and punching...and punching. Then Rodriguez became cocky, wading inside when he could have won the fight by jabbing. Finally, it happened. Gatti landed a left hook to the ribs in the 5th round, a blow that resounded like a drum shot in an empty music studio, and Rodriguez went down, grabbing his side as he fell. The challenger beat the 10-count, but the champion pursued him relentlessly and landed a series of punishing hooks to the body. Gatti finished him in the 6th round with a left hook to the jaw, beating a man who looked like an almost certain winner from the start. "This town will go nuts over Gatti," said Ed Schuyler, Jr., of the Associated Press. "The fans here love fighters with big hearts—like Rocky Marciano."

Opposite: A battered Gatti, who has shown a remarkable ability to weather abuse and still win fights, sits in his corner between rounds.

Canon

The Fight of the Millennium?

They called it "The Fight of the Millennium," a match promised to linger in our memories much longer than the 12 rounds the boxers were scheduled to fight.

In the end, it would be memorable, but more for the disappointment it generated than for the excitement. Blame the hype. Boxing fans crave great fights, great theater, and when they do not get it, they feel bitterness and regret, as if the boxers themselves had let the public down.

It is not the first fight that failed to live up to the hype and it will not be the last. But the Oscar De La Hoya–Felix Trinidad match was supposed to be different. After all, it pitted against each other the two greatest fighters of their era, both undefeated welterweight champions.

Fans expected a brawl, but they saw a tactical match from the beginning, the tension arising not from what was happening as much as from what could happen next. De La Hoya moved from side to side, building up an early lead with a brilliant display of boxing skill. This was not the violent spectacle the fans anticipated; this was a high-priced sparring session. Yes, De La Hoya was boxing beautifully, but his strategy sucked all the drama and excitement out of a match that featured two of the hardest punchers in boxing.

Then De La Hoya, apparently thinking that his lead was comfortable, began to relax in the 10th round, keeping his distance in an effort to preserve what he thought was an easy victory. He should have consulted the judges. As De La Hoya backed up, Trinidad kept moving forward, throwing more punches than he had in the early rounds. It looked like a desperate measure, but would it work?

Despite the shift in momentum during the later rounds, De La Hoya looked like the winner. He boxed well, and he punched sharply and crisply, leaving Trinidad with a bloody nose and a swollen left eye. Nearly 80 percent of the ringside journalists scored the fight for De La Hoya, according to an informal poll by the *Las Vegas Review Journal.*

But if boxing promises anything, it is the unexpected, and this evening was no different. One judge ruled the bout a draw, while the other two scored it for Trinidad—115–113 and 115–114. Trinidad won a majority decision. "I knew he was a great fighter, but I had the will to win," Trinidad said afterward.

De La Hoya was gracious in defeat. "I know I won," he said. "I gave the boxing lesson of my life. People expected me to duke it out, but I was making him miss and making him pay.... I guess it didn't work out."

De La Hoya said he wanted a rematch, and Trinidad said, hmmmm, maybe. "He's a great fighter, and he deserves a rematch, but we'll need to discuss it," Trinidad said.

The fans deserve a rematch, too, but the most brutal battles are often at the negotiating tables, sometimes taking years and years of rancorous wheeling and dealing.

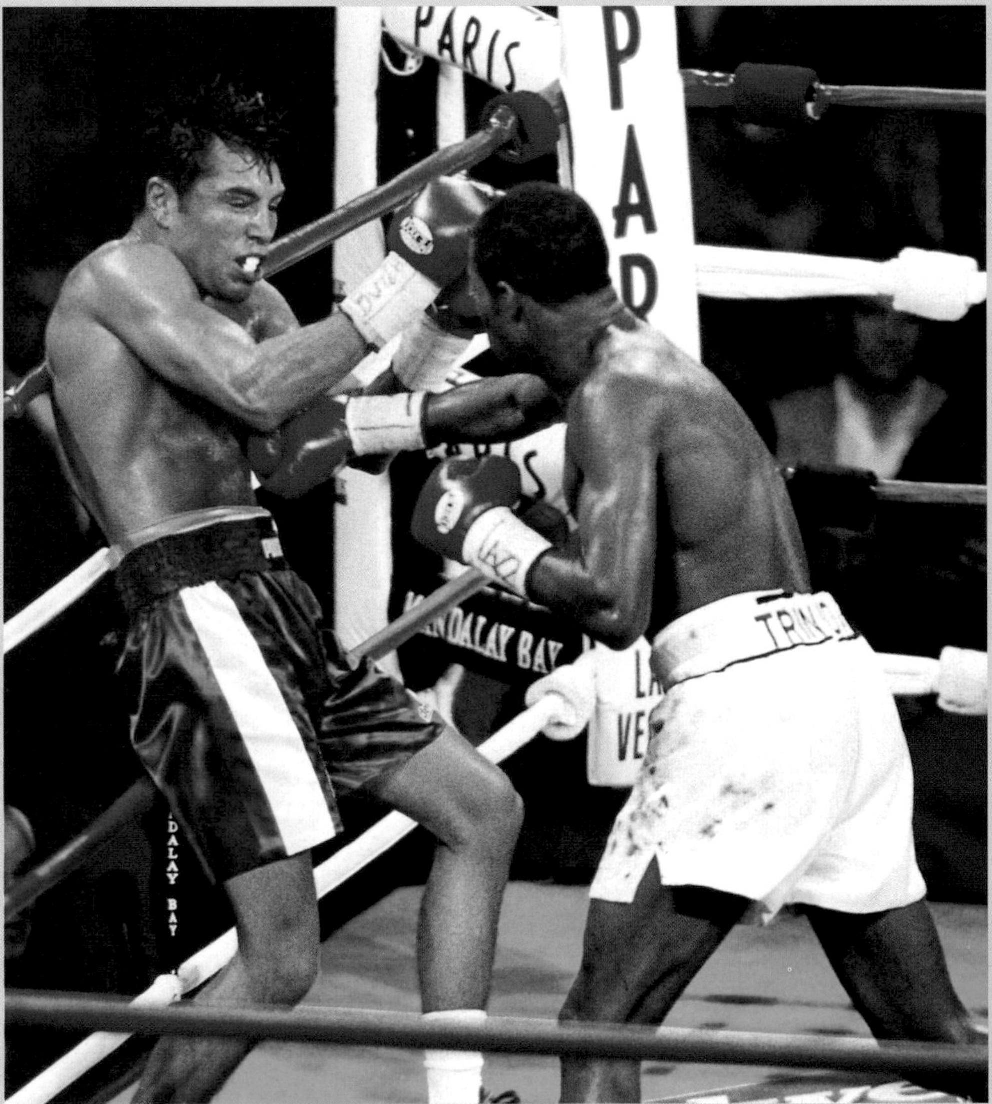

LEFT: Felix Trinidad meets Oscar De La Hoya in their widely anticipated but ultimately disappointing welterweight title bout on September 18, 1999. OPPOSITE: Trinidad celebrates his controversial victory by decision over De La Hoya to win the welterweight crown.

The Future of Boxing

5

As a child, I had no doubt that Joe Louis was a greater man than Franklin D. Roosevelt, and in the tales I heard of great heroes, Corbett, Jeffries, Gans, Ketchel, and Dempsey ranked right along with Perseus and Daniel Boone.

—Leonard Gardner, *Fat City*

It is a dangerous game, but every expert plays it, from the television commentators to the couch potatoes who chug their beer as if it were bottled water. They confer greatness upon fighters before fighters are ready to demonstrate that greatness; one terrific fight, one terrific performance, and they start digging the comparisons out of the footlockers that are their brains. He is the next Sugar Ray Robinson, the next Sugar Ray Leonard, the next Muhammad Ali, the next....

Pity the poor pug who has to wear that label—greatness. Why? Because boxing is not like other sports. It is cruel and unforgiving. Roger Clemens may have a bad game or even a bad year, but if he comes back, the experts will shrug their shoulders and say, "See, I told you he was great." But if a boxer has a bad fight or a bad year, he is probably doomed—exiled to a lifetime of undercards in Altoona, Pennsylvania.

Look at Ken Buchanan, the classy Scotsman. He was the lightweight champion of the world, the next Sugar Ray Robinson, until he met a wild man from Panama on June 26, 1972, in New York. Roberto Duran stopped him in the 13th round, pounding him from here to Edinburgh. He hit the champion below the belt in the final round, smashing him so viciously that the protective cup looked like a crumpled fender. Buchanan fell to his knees, unable to continue.

No, when the experts call you "great," it is no cause for celebration. It is a curse. Oh, most fighters do not realize the danger. They love to hear that word, love to hear the comparisons between themselves and the great boxers of the past. But they are wrong—dead wrong. When they hear that word, they should duck. It is worse than any left hook to the temple.

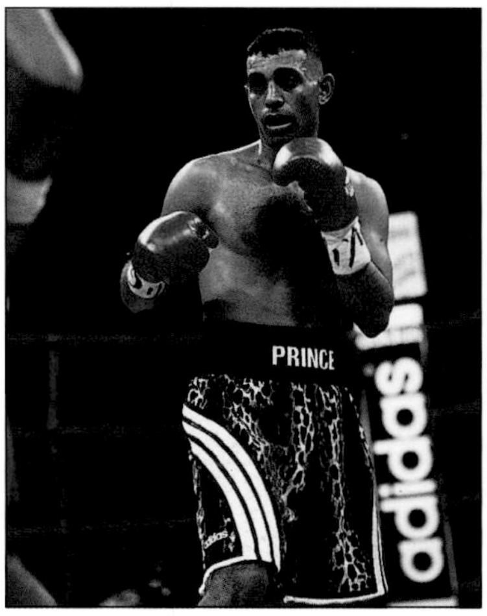

ABOVE: Prince Naseem Hamed of Sheffield, England, boasts extraordinary speed and catlike reflexes—even for a featherweight. If he overcomes his penchant for braggadocio and puts in some serious time with his trainers, he could easily become one of the most spectacular boxers in his generation. OPPOSITE: Floyd Mayweather celebrates his victory over Angel Manfredi on December 13, 1998, in a title bout at the Miccosukee Indian Reservation in Miami, Florida. Mayweather has the potential to become one of the greats of his weight class.

Floyd Mayweather

If Floyd Mayweather wants to avoid the pitfalls of huge expectations, he just has to look in his corner, where his father, Floyd, Sr., is guiding his career. Is there a better man to lead his son along the right road? Probably not, because a man who has made the wrong decisions for himself knows how to make the right decisions

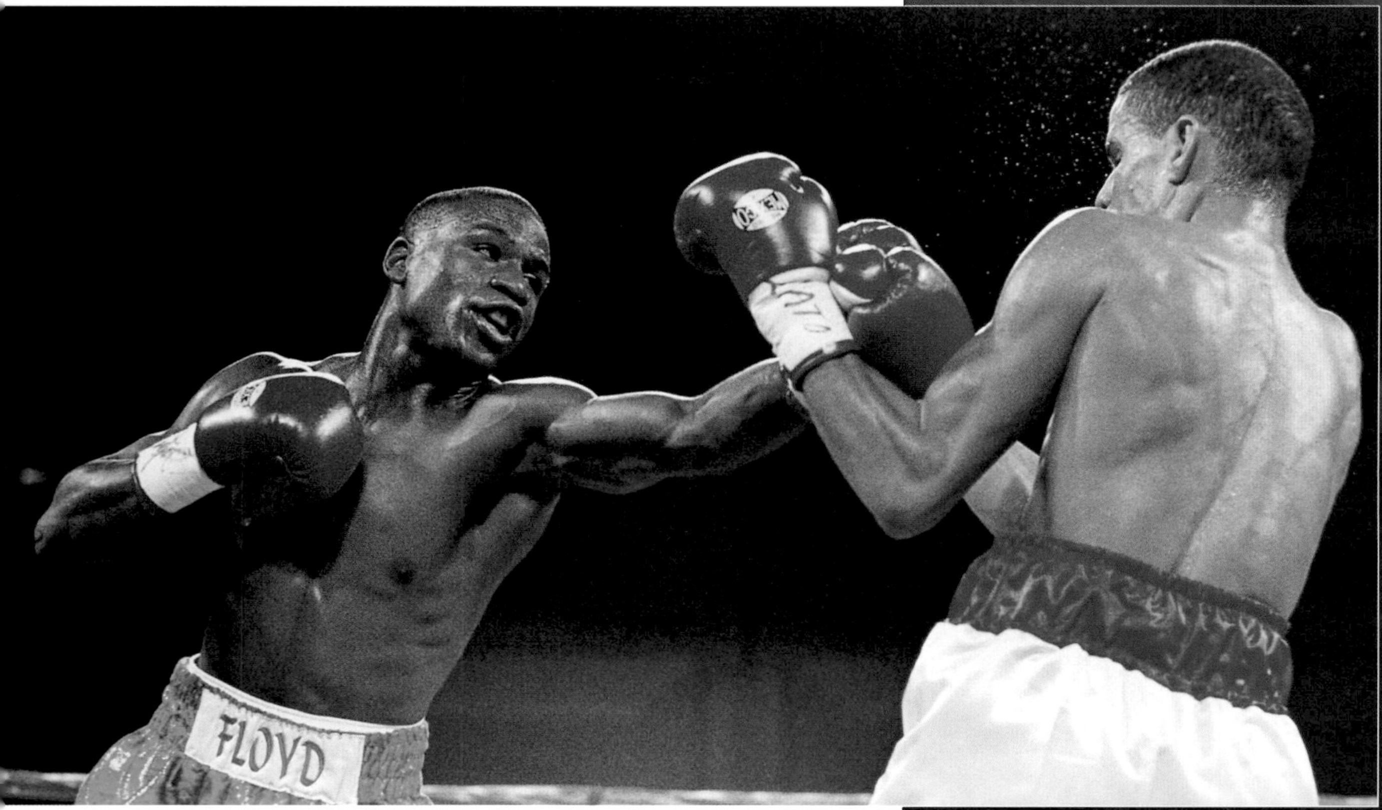

ABOVE: Floyd Mayweather whips a left jab at the head of Carlos Gerena during their September 11, 1999, bout at the Mandalay Bay Resort in Las Vegas, Nevada. Mayweather won the fight by TKO in the 7th round. RIGHT: Angel Manfredi (left) ducks and takes cover during his December 13, 1998, bout against Floyd Mayweather.

for his son. Floyd Sr. served a five-year sentence for drug trafficking, and when his son visited him at the penitentiary in Midland, Michigan, the kid had to fight back his tears. "I was supposed to be a man," the youngster thought. And so he stifled his emotions.

The elder Mayweather, released from prison in 1999, trains his son, and he has done a great job with a great fighter. There is that word again—"great." But father and son are handling it well, refusing to let the praise distract them from their goal, which is, ironically, to achieve greatness. "You never have to make the mistakes I made," the father has told the son. "I made enough for the both of us."

Young but levelheaded, Mayweather comes from a fighting family. His father was a contender, good enough to face Sugar Ray Leonard in 1978, and two of his uncles were talented fighters—one of them, Roger, a two-time world champion. "I taught him to box, and nobody knows or loves him better than me, so nobody's better equipped to take care of him," the elder Mayweather said.

A bronze medalist in the 1996 Olympics in Atlanta, Floyd Mayweather the younger is that rarest of fighters—a flashy boxer with sound technical skills. And power. He is 18-0 as a professional, including an 8th-round knockout of Genaro Hernandez for the world junior lightweight title on October 3, 1998, in Las Vegas. "I'd give myself an eight," Mayweather said of his performance against Hernandez. Hernandez protested. "No one has ever beat me like that,"

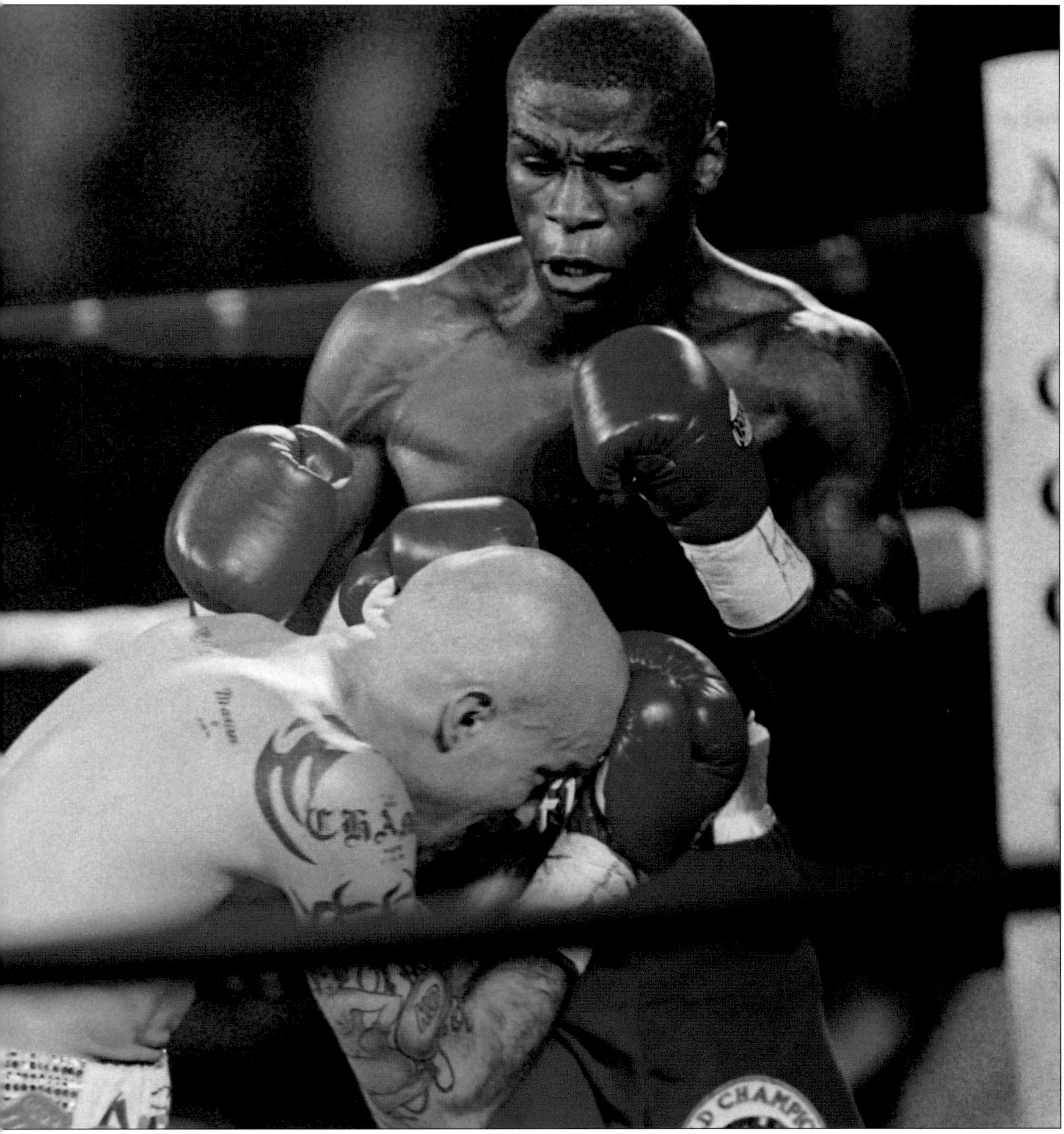

Hernandez said. "So don't you go saying you were an eight, because you were a ten."

A versatile boxer, Mayweather flashed his amazing hand speed throughout the bout, but he also proved that his fists belong in a munitions dump. He pounded his opponent at will by scoring effectively to the body and head. When it was all over, the judges and the referee seemed superfluous, because Hernandez refused to come out for the 9th round, officially ending a fight that was unofficially over from the start. "I got defeated in a real bad way," Hernandez said. "I never thought I would lose a fight like that. No one has ever hit me the way Floyd Mayweather hit me."

As for Mayweather, he did not let the great performance cloud his vision of the future. "Genaro was a great champion," Mayweather said. "He's the best fighter I've fought to this point. I thank him for the opportunity to fight for the championship."

Prince Naseem Hamed

A fighter for the MTV generation, Prince Naseem Hamed is a violent man who makes statements with his fists and his outfits, some of which are louder than his personality. He wears leopard-skin trunks, and he leaps over the ropes to enter the ring amid a burst of smoke, lasers, and fireworks—the kind of spectacle common at rock concerts or wrestling matches. But the entrances are not the most outrageous thing about him. No, Hamed is a gaudy talent as well as a gaudy dresser, and he is not above telling you so.

The featherweight champion is 25-0, and if you have a short attention span, he is the fighter for you—of his 23 knockouts, more than half have come before the end of the 2nd round. He won the title with an 8th-round knockout of Tom Johnson on February 7, 1997, in London, when he floored the champion with a right uppercut that seemed to come from the cheap seats. Johnson had defended the crown eleven times, but he had never faced anyone like the Prince. Who has?

Of all the reigning world champions, Hamed may boast the worst technical skills, but he gets away with it. Sure, he drops his hands, punches off the wrong foot, and sticks out his chin. But he boasts crushing power and tremendous reflexes, his showboating lulling you into the serenity that his fists turn into slumber. Just ask Said Lawal. Hamed knocked out Lawal on March 16, 1996, taking only three punches and 35 seconds to complete the demolition. Punch, punch, punch—goodnight.

Hamed grew up in Sheffield, England, but his parents were from Yemen, where the fighter is treated like royalty. He is not a real prince, but he anointed himself one because he figured all true princes must become kings, and he wants to be the king of boxing. Not the king of the featherweights—the king of boxing, period. "Nobody can stand up to the extraordinary power of my fists," he said after stopping Johnson. "I prefer to flatten my opponent in the 2nd round, but my mother said she wanted a little entertainment."

Talented and cocky, Hamed is the heir to fighters such as Hector "Macho" Camacho and Jorge Paez, guys whose fan base included people who wanted to see them get beaten. Hamed is the same way. Love him or hate him, he is the Fresh Prince of boxing.

ABOVE: In typical fashion, Prince Naseem Hamed prances victoriously around the ring at Madison Square Garden after pounding Kevin Kelley into the mat on December 13, 1997. The knockout came in the 4th round, and Kelley's face tells the brief, brutal story of the fight.

Erik Morales

When he turned 21 on September 1, 1997, Erik Morales refused to celebrate, sacrificing current pleasures for future ecstasies. And oh my, was it ecstasy. The kid waited five days, marking the hours like an inmate awaiting parole, but it was worth it. Morales gave himself the greatest birthday present of his life—a present wrapped in blood, sweat, and grit. He gave himself a world title by stopping Daniel Zaragoza for the junior lightweight crown on September 6 in El Paso. "It was more difficult than I originally thought," Morales said.

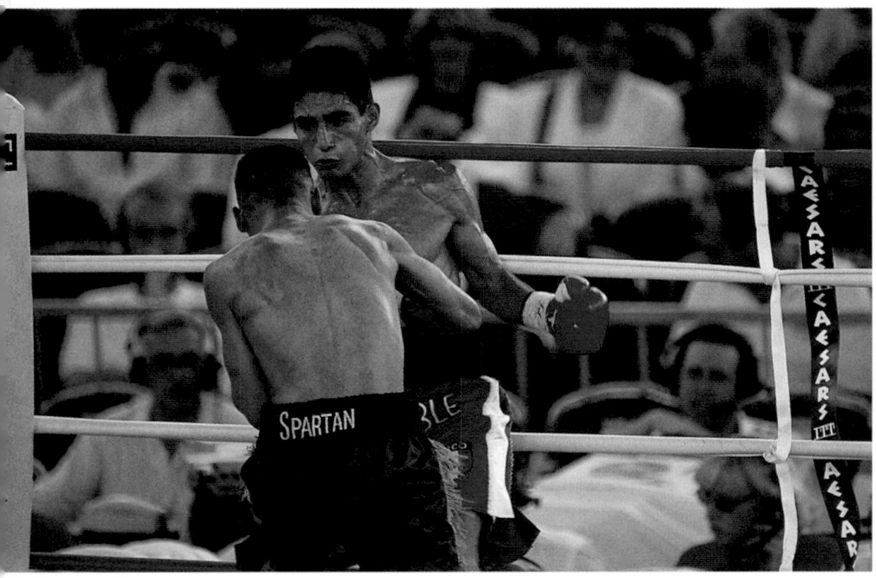

The kid stopped the 40-year-old champion in the 11th round, flooring him with a solid punch to the chest. The old man landed on his butt, sitting on the canvas with his arms wrapped around his knees, in position to perform a sit-up. He sat there for a few seconds, as if contemplating whether to get up and absorb more punishment. Then he shook his head. The old man did not get up; he remained on the canvas, bloody and battered, conceding victory to his young opponent. It was an act of nobility, not cowardice, because the old man fought a tremendous fight, his heart telling him to keep punching long after his body had told him to quit. He finally obeyed his body—his jaw, his ribs, his legs. The crowd of more than six thousand applauded both warriors. "The last punch was a straight right to the solar plexus—and

ABOVE: Erik Morales defends against a stooping, swooping Hector Acero-Sanchez on June 7, 1996, at Caesars Palace. Morales won the fight by decision after 12 tough rounds. The young lightweight promises to become a great fighter in his class. RIGHT: On October 22, 1999, Erik Morales unleashes a sweeping uppercut at the head of Wayne McCullough. The as-yet undefeated Morales won the 12-round unanimous decision over McCullough to successfully defend his WBC super bantamweight crown.

W.B.C.

Christy Martin and the Women of Boxing

Christy Martin burst onto the boxing scene on March 16, 1996, in Las Vegas, shocking the boxing world by fighting like, well, a man. But did she fight like a man? Or have men been fighting—from the moment the first two pugilists made fists in a cave—the way Christy Martin would one day fight? It is not a question that Martin herself ponders. Martin is a boxer, not a feminist. She fights for money and respect, not for equal rights. "I'm just happy to be boxing," she said.

Whether or not she wants the label, Martin is a pioneer—as important to boxing as Jackie Robinson was to major league baseball more than forty years ago. If that seems a little far-fetched, it is only because we do not know the full impact of her trailblazing—not yet. But if a woman knocks out some loutish male for the heavyweight title in the year 2025, we will look back on Martin as a heroic figure.

It may never reach that point, and perhaps it never should. Women fight women, and men fight men, and there is no clamor for intersex matches in the ring. But, then, there was no clamor for female boxing, either. And look at Christy Martin. She is the most famous female boxer in the world, a fighter who is almost universally admired among members of both sexes. When men start talking about female fighters in bars and taverns without snickering, well, you know the women have arrived.

Martin was not an overnight success; it just seems that way. She fought "Dangerous" Deirdre Gogarty on March 16, 1996, in Las Vegas, as part of the undercard for the heavyweight title bout between Mike Tyson and Frank Bruno, which was broadcast throughout the world on pay-per-

OPPOSITE: Christy Martin raises her arms in victory after beating the pulp out of "Dangerous" Deirdre Gogarty on March 16, 1996. Though the fight was an undercard for the heavyweight title bout between Mike Tyson and Frank Bruno, it was much more entertaining to watch. Women's professional boxing may well prove to become a popular facet of the sport, though the final verdict has yet to be handed down. ABOVE: Christy Martin pounds Melinda Robinson into submission during their September 7, 1996, bout in Las Vegas. Martin totally outclassed her opponent and won the fight in the 3rd round by knockout.

ABOVE: Laila Ali (scion of heavyweight great Muhammad Ali) watches as April Fowler crumples to the mat during their October 8, 1999, bout at Turning Stone Casino, in Verona, New York. Ali won by knockout in the 1st round. OPPOSITE: In classic fashion, the aggressive Mia St. John paves the way for a crushing right with a short left jab to the head of Brenda Felter. St. John won this September 18, 1998, fight by TKO in the 4th round. St. John is a promising, undeniably telegenic boxer whose popularity and abilities will no doubt help legitimize the woman's side of the sport.

view. Martin fought spiritedly—much more spiritedly than Tyson or Bruno—and she became a sensation, wowing fans with her heart and technical skills. She survived a bloody nose to win an easy 6-round decision. "She bled like a stuck pig," said her husband, Jim Martin, who also trains her.

In 1992, Christy Salters walked into a gym in Bristol, Tennessee, accompanied by her mother and her puppy, a Pomeranian. It was the strangest entourage in boxing history but trainer Jim Martin, and a former light heavyweight and self-proclaimed "macho guy," saw something in her that his male fighters lacked—spirit and a desire to learn. And, oh yes, she was tough. The trainer thought, hey, maybe she can make some money for me. After all, she was a novelty, a woman in a world dominated by men. So he helped her learn how to box, later becoming her husband as well as her trainer. "This isn't about women's boxing," Martin said. "This is about Christy Martin."

And she is correct. She has a right to be Christy Martin the individual, not Christy Martin the pioneer. Martin stands 5 feet 4 inches (163cm) and weighs 133 pounds (60kg), and she is more exciting than most men. She fires short, crisp combinations, every punch thrown with the "bad intentions" that made Tyson such an awesome fighter in the mid-1980s. And she has made money for both herself and her trainer-husband; she earns about $50,000 per bout, as much as Ricardo Lopez, the great strawweight champion, makes. "I would never promote a women's bout," Bob Arum said in 1996. Arum left that to Don King, who promotes Martin. "I'm sorry, but I think women's boxing is repulsive," Arum said.

A few months later, Arum was promoting women on his fight cards, two of whom are beginning to make names for themselves—Lucia Rijker and Mia St. John. And a couple of prodigal daughters have joined the field, too: Laila Ali and Jacqui Frazier. Alas, Jacqui is too old to have much of a career ahead of her, but Ali the younger is in her early twenties and a fighter of great promise.

Martin may not call herself a pioneer, but that's alright: future boxing historians may well do it for her.

ser.

it took everything out of him," said Morales, a native of Tijuana. Zaragoza, a native of Mexico City, was gracious afterward: "He simply surprised me with his speed. I did the best I could. I'm not as quick as I used to be."

In a fight full of exhilarating moments, the 8th round was the best. Morales landed two solid rights midway through the round, but the champion remained on his feet and retreated to the ropes, where his young opponent turned him into a heavy bag. The challenger landed a series of punishing blows, but he got tired, his arms so heavy that he could barely raise them. He stepped back to rest, and the champion lifted both gloves and shrugged his shoulders, as if to ask, "Is that all you have?" Then he pursued his opponent across the ring, and the crowd responded with a standing ovation. "I decided to do nothing but body work from the 9th round on," Morales said. After he won the fight, Morales looked back to the days leading up to the big event. "Not only was it my dream to finally win a world title," Morales said, "but the dream is even better since I beat Zaragoza."

And he did it for his birthday.

David Reid

Every day, the neighborhood kids trooped to the three-story row house in north Philadelphia to gaze at the display in the windows—forty trophies, most of them gold or silver, gleaming like Cadillacs in a showroom. "This is where the fighter lives," the youngsters would say.

That was four years ago, when "the fighter" was the best amateur boxer in Philadelphia, perhaps the best amateur boxer in the world. David Reid is fast becoming one of the best professional boxers in the world, and his window now features another piece of glowing hardware—a championship belt, the World Boxing Association junior middleweight title. "I do what I want to do in the ring," Reid said. "I think clearly, and I don't get tired."

Like Oscar De La Hoya four years earlier, Reid was the only member of the U.S. boxing team to win a gold medal in the 1996 Olympics. It was an amazing performance. Behind 15-5 after 2 rounds, he crushed Alfredo Duvergel with an overhand right to the temple, a blow that knocked the Cuban to his hands and knees in the

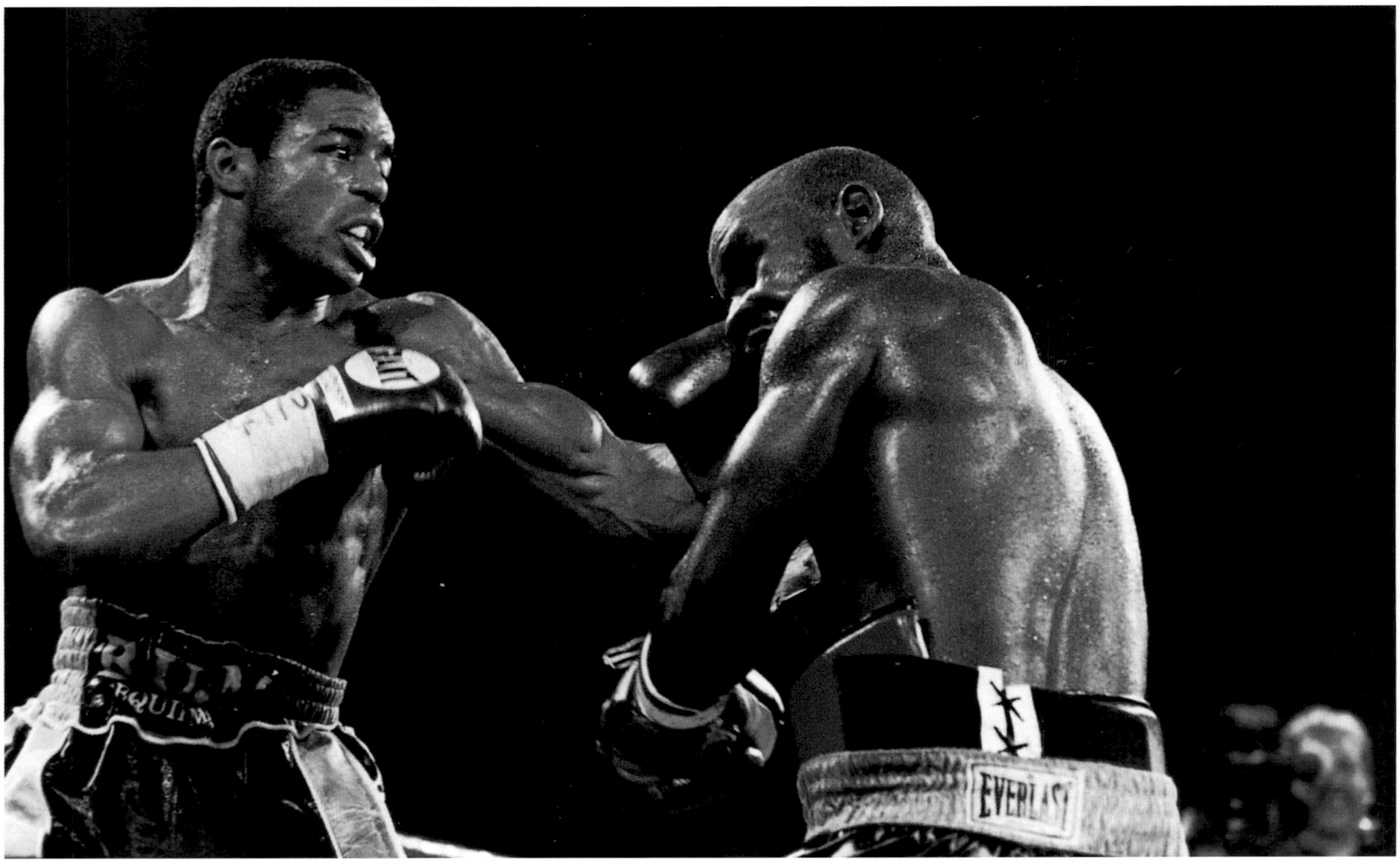

ABOVE: **David Reid unleashes a left cross at the head of Keith Mullings at the Hard Rock Hotel, Las Vegas, on his way to the WBA super welterweight championship, August 28, 1999.**
OPPOSITE: **Junior middleweight David Reid is a smart boxer with awesome physical gifts. And although he is young at this writing, his wisdom—and by extension his promise—is great. Barring the unexpected, Reid should become one of the standout fighters of the era.**

EVERLAST

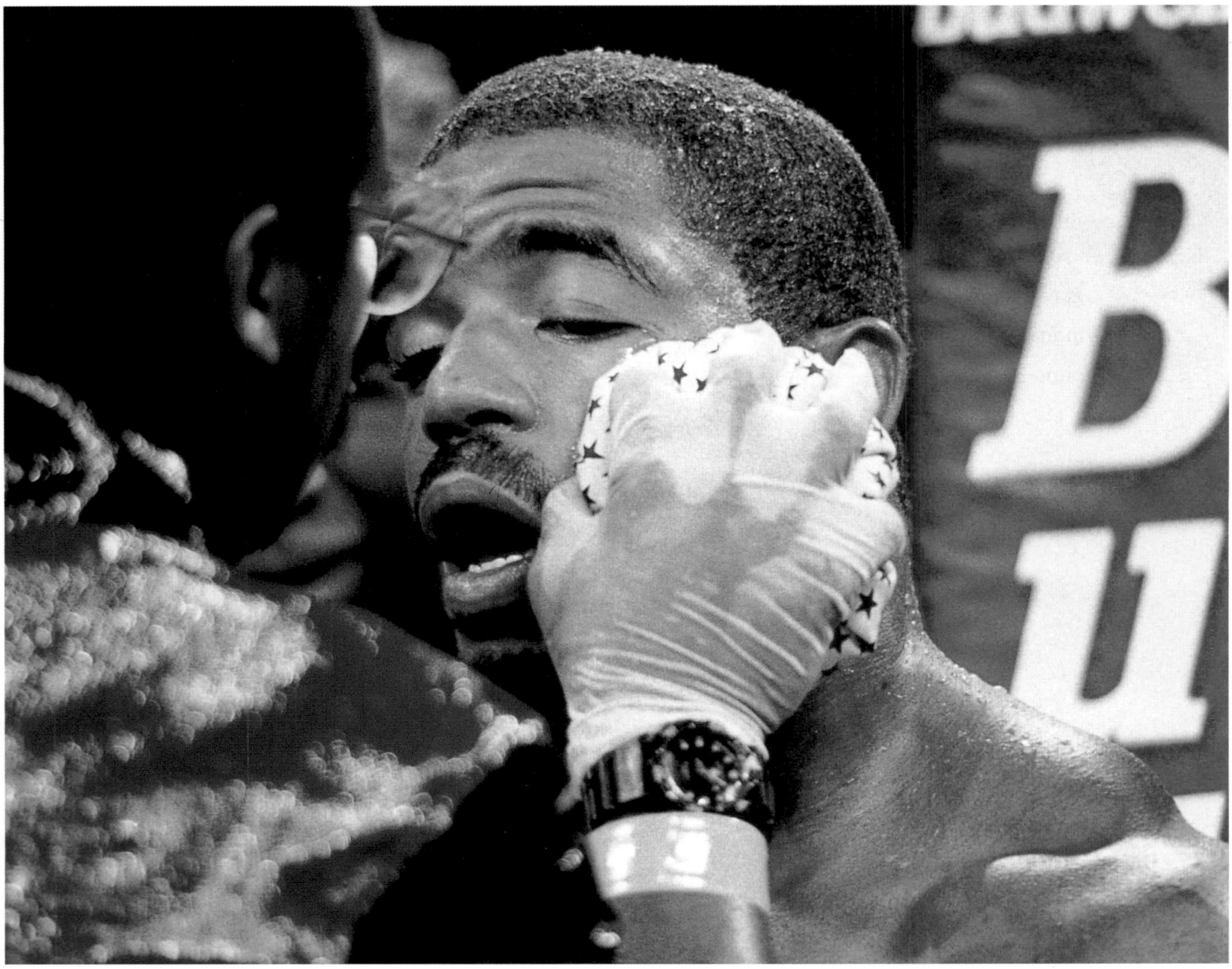

3rd round. Duvergel beat the 10-count, but he lurched across the ring and stumbled into the ropes like a drunk at last call. The referee stopped the fight, and Reid jumped into the air—a young man with the vertical leap of an elevator. "I was going for the home run," Reid said. "He hit me hard a couple of times. I said to myself, 'To win, all you need is to get one in.'"

After the gold medal victory, Reid signed a five-year, $30-million contract, including a $1 million signing bonus, with America Presents. "That's only the first of many millions that young man will earn before he is done," said Mat Tinley, owner of the promotional company.

If the money has corrupted him, Reid is hiding it well. The junior middleweight is one of the most ambitious young boxers in the game, and his handlers are equally ambitious, because they matched him with tough opponents instead of soft touches early in his career, including victories over two former world champions—Simon Brown and Jorge Vaca. "As long as they don't let the other guy come in armed, he doesn't care who he fights," said Al Mitchell, his trainer.

It showed. Through his first eleven fights, a critical phase of his career, his opponents boasted a collective record of 272 wins, 43 losses, 4 draws, and 180 knockouts. Reid is a young man, but his grit and wisdom belie his years. He is becoming a veteran before his time, a smooth boxer with power in both hands. Reid won the World Boxing Association junior middleweight title with a 12-round decision over Laurent Bouduani on March 6, 1999, in Atlantic City. "If this exciting young fighter matures as a professional as expected, and if he wins as we expect him to win, by the year 2001, he could earn $50 million," Tinley said.

ABOVE: Reid receives medical attention for damage to his eye sustained during the March 6, 1999, slugfest against Laurent Boudouani. OPPOSITE: At Bally's Park Place, Atlantic City, Reid hammers Kevin Kelly during their July 16, 1999, match-up.

Reid owes that future to his mother. "He never got into any really bad trouble," said Marie Reid. "But he used to get into fights all the time, and I was afraid he'd get hurt. He was about 10, and I told him to go to the gym. I know most mothers don't like their kids to box, but I wanted him to get off the streets."

Reid did get off the streets, taking his love of mixing it up into a recreation center in north Philadelphia. He enjoyed the indoor fights even more, and there was a good reason: under a policy developed by the boxing coach, Reid could whack his sparring partners, but his sparring partners could not whack him back, which gave the kid the sensation of hitting the heavy bag. That lasted two years. "He loved it," said Fred Jenkins, the coach. "You gotta give young kids a break like that. Boxing is hard enough, and if you make it too hard for the kids, they're gonna sour on it." As good as he is now, if David Reid becomes a great fighter it will be because of what he has yet to overcome. Reid suffered a crushing defeat on March 3, 2000, the first loss of a career that, until then, had looked infinite in its potential. Felix Trinidad dropped the young fighter an astounding four times. "I have to learn from this," Reid said afterward. If he is as good as he seems, he will no doubt profit from the lesson.

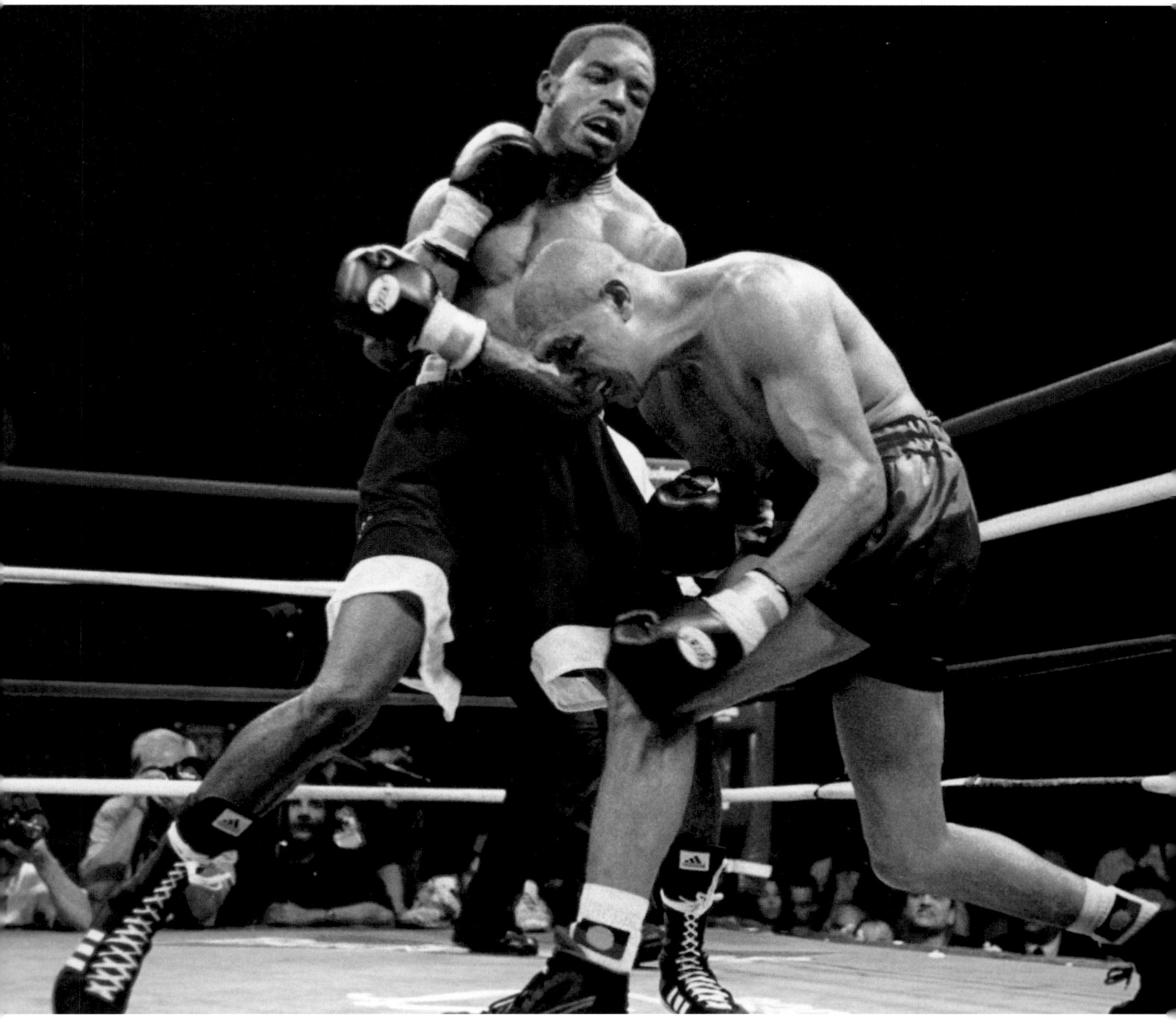

Rankings

Ranking the greatest fighters of all time is a dangerous business, an exercise sure to cause as many fights—or, at least, arguments—as the boxers themselves waged. The following may be such a list. To compile the ratings, we decided to go back in time to an era in which there were only eight weight classes. There are no cruiserweight divisions in these rankings, no junior this and junior that weight categories.

In addition, some fighters were rated in divisions with which they are not normally associated. Gene Tunney, for example, was a tremendous light heavyweight, so we placed him in that category, even though he gained his fame as the world heavyweight champion, the two-time winner over Jack Dempsey. And another heavyweight champ, Ezzard Charles, also excelled as a middleweight and light heavyweight. We rated him in the middleweight category, even though he fought longer in the other divisions.

Finally, because some boxers fought in the junior this and junior that category, you might see them in divisions that seem unfamiliar. We have only one response: we had to put them somewhere.

Again, ranking fighters is a dangerous business. Yet it is somehow irresistible.

HEAVYWEIGHTS

1. Muhammad Ali (1960–1981) 56–5 with 37 knockouts.
2. Joe Louis (1934–1951) 68–3 with 54 knockouts.
3. Larry Holmes (1973–1997) 65–6 with 42 knockouts.
4. Jack Dempsey (1914–1927) 61–6–8 with 50 knockouts.
5. George Foreman (1969–1998) 76–4 with 68 knockouts.
6. Jack Johnson (1897–1938) 78–13–11 with 49 knockouts.
7. Rocky Marciano (1947–1955) 49–0 with 43 knockouts.
8. Evander Holyfield (1984–) 35–5 with 25 knockouts.
9. Joe Frazier (1965–1981) 32–4–1 with 27 knockouts.
10. Jersey Joe Walcott (1930–1953) 53–18–1 with 33 knockouts.

LIGHT HEAVYWEIGHTS

1. Archie Moore (1936–1963) 194–26–8 with 141 knockouts.
2. Michael Spinks (1977–1988) 31–1 with 21 knockouts.
3. Bob Foster (1961–1978) 56–8–1 with 46 knockouts.
4. Tommy Loughran (1919–1937) 96–24–9 with 18 knockouts.
5. Gene Tunney (1915–1928) 65–1–1 with 47 knockouts.
6. Jack O'Brien (1896–1912) 100–7–16 with 46 knockouts.
7. Jack Dillon (1911–1923) 93–6–14 with 61 knockouts.
8. John Henry Lewis (1928–1939) 103–8–6 with 60 knockouts.
9. Maxie Rosenbloom (1923–1939) 208–37–22 with 19 knockouts.
10. Roy Jones (1989–) 42–1 with 34 knockouts.

MIDDLEWEIGHTS

1. Sugar Ray Robinson (1940–1965) 175–19–6 with 110 knockouts.
2. Carlos Monzón (1963–1977) 89–3–8 with 61 knockouts.
3. Charley Burley (1937–1950) 74–11–2 with 43 knockouts.
4. Ezzard Charles (1940–1959) 96–25–1 with 58 knockouts.
5. Harry Greb (1913–1926) 115–8–3 with 51 knockouts.
6. Marvelous Marvin Hagler (1973–1987) 62–3–2 with 52 knockouts.
7. Stanley Ketchel (1904–1910) 53–4–5 with 50 knockouts.
8. Emile Griffith (1958–1977) 85–24–2 with 23 knockouts.
9. Jake LaMotta (1941–1954) 83–19–4 with 30 knockouts.
10. Mickey Walker (1919–1939) 93–19–4 with 60 knockouts.

WELTERWEIGHTS

1. Henry Armstrong (1931–1945) 151–21–9 with 101 knockouts.
2. Sugar Ray Leonard (1977–1997) 36–3–1 with 25 knockouts.
3. Barney Ross (1929–1938) 74–4–3 with 24 knockouts.
4. Julio Cesar Chavez (1980–) 101–3–2 with 85 knockouts.
5. Jimmy McLarnin (1923–1936) 63–11–3 with 20 knockouts.
6. Jose Napoles (1956–1975) 77–7 with 54 knockouts.
7. Aaron Pryor (1976–1990) 39–1 with 35 knockouts.
8. Fritzie Zivic (1931–1949) 157–65–10 with 81 knockouts.
9. Kid Gavilan (1943–1958) 107–30–6 with 28 knockouts.
10. Ted "Kid" Lewis (1909–1929) 169–30–13 with 70 knockouts.

LIGHTWEIGHT

1. Roberto Duran (1967–1999) 102–15 with 69 knockouts.
2. Tony Canzoneri (1925–1939) 138–23–10 with 44 knockouts.
3. Benny Leonard (1911–1932) 89–5–1 with 71 knockouts.
4. Joe Gans (1891–1909) 120–8–10 with 55 knockouts.
5. Ike Williams (1940–1955) 123–25–5 with 60 knockouts.
6. Alexis Arguello (1974–1995) 80–8 with 64 knockouts.
7. Kid Chocolate (1928–1938) 135–9–6 with 51 knockouts.
8. Pernell Whitaker (1984–) 40–3–1 with 17 knockouts.
9. Beau Jack (1940–1955) 83–24–5 with 40 knockouts.
10. Battling Nelson (1896–1917) 60–19–19 with 32 knockouts.

FEATHERWEIGHTS

1. Willie Pep (1940–1966) 230–11–1 with 65 knockouts.
2. Salvador Sanchez (1975–1982) 44–1–1 with 32 knockouts.
3. Sandy Saddler (1944–1956) 144–16–2 with 103 knockouts.
4. Terry McGovern (1887–1908) 59–4–4 with 34 knockouts.
5. Abe Attell (1900–1917) 92–10–16 with 48 knockouts.
6. Wilfredo Gomez (1974–1989) 42–3–1 with 40 knockouts.
7. Azumah Nelson (1985–1996) 39–3–2 with 28 knockouts.
8. Eusebio Pedroza (1973–1992) 42–6–1 with 25 knockouts.
9. Danny Lopez (1971–1992) 42–6 with 39 knockouts.
10. Sergio Palma (1976–1990) 52–5–5 with 21 knockouts.

BANTAMWEIGHTS

1. Ruben Olivares (1965–1988) 88–13–3 with 78 knockouts.
2. Eder Jofre (1957–1976) 72–2–4 with 50 knockouts.
3. Carlos Zarate (1970–1988) 61–4 with 58 knockouts.
4. Manuel Ortiz (1938–1955) 96–28–3 with 49 knockouts.
5. Panama Al Brown (1922–1942) 124–19–10 with 55 knockouts.
6. Khaosai Galaxy (1980–1991) 49–1 with 43 knockouts.
7. Fighting Harada (1960–1970) 55–7 with 22 knockouts.
8. Orlando Canizales (1984–) 50–5–1 with 37 knockouts
9. Lupe Pintor (1974–1995) 56–14–2 with 42 knockouts.
10. Jeff Chandler (1976–1984) 33–2–2 with 18 knockouts.

FLYWEIGHTS

1. Jimmy Wilde (1911–1923) 126–4–2 with 77 knockouts.
2. Miguel Canto (1969–1982) 61–9–4 with 15 knockouts.
3. Frankie Genaro (1920–1934) 82–21–8 with 19 knockouts.
4. Pascual Perez (1952–1964) 84–7–1 with 57 knockouts.
5. Benny Lynch (1931–1938) 82–13–15 with 33 knockouts.
6. Humberto "Chiquita" Gonzalez (1984–1995) 41–3 with 29 knockouts.
7. Hilario Zapata (1977–1993) 43–10–1 with 15 knockouts.
8. Jung-Koo Chang (1980–1991) 38–4 with 17 knockouts.
9. Michael Carbajal (1990–1998) 44–4 with 29 knockouts.
10. Yoko Gushiken (1974–1981) 23–1 with 15 knockouts.

Selected Bibliography

Anderson, Dave. *In the Corner: Great Boxing Trainers Talk About their Art.* New York: William Morrow & Company, Inc., 1991.

Cannon, James J. *Nobody Asked Me, but... The World of Jimmy Cannon.* New York: Holt Rinehart Winston, 1978.

Greenberg. Martin H., ed. *In the Ring: A Treasury of Boxing Stories.* New York: Bonanza Books, 1986.

Heinz, W.C. *Once They Heard the Cheers.* New York: Doubleday, 1979.

Hughes, Bill, and Patrick King, eds. *Come Out Writing: A Boxing Anthology.* London: Macdonald Queen Anne Press, 1991.

Isenberg, Michael T. *John L. Sullivan and His America.* Chicago and Urbana, IL: University of Illinois Press, 1988.

Leibling, A.J. *A Neutral Corner: Boxing Essays.* San Francisco: North Point Press, 1990.

———. *The Sweet Science.* New York: Viking Press, 1956.

McIlvanney, Hugh. *McIlvanney on Boxing.* New York: Beaufort Books, Inc., 1982.

Mead, Chris. *Champion Joe Louis: Black Hero in White America.* New York: Scribner's, 1985.

Miletich, Leo N. *Dan Stuart's Fistic Carnival.* College Station, TX: Texas A&M University Press, 1994.

Oates, Joyce Carol, and Daniel Halpern, eds. *Reading the Fights.* New York: Henry Holt, 1988.

Schulian, John. *Writers' Fighters and Other Sweet Scientists.* Kansas City: Andrews and McMeel, 1983.

Smith, Red. *Press Box: Red Smith's Favorite Sports Stories.* New York: W.W. Norton & Company, 1976.

Sporting News. *Best Sports Stories, 1989 Edition.* St. Louis: The Sporting News Book Publishing, 1989.

Sugar, Bert Randolph. *The 100 Greatest Boxers of All Time*, revised updated edition. New York: Bonanza Books, 1989.

Walsh, Peter. *Men of Steel: The Lives and Times of Boxing's Middleweight Champions.* London: Robson Books, 1993.

Weston, Stanley, and Steven Farhood. *The Ring: Boxing the 20th Century.* New York: BDD Illustrated Books, 1993.

Weston, Stanley, ed. *The Best of the Ring: Recapturing 70 Years of Boxing Classics.* Chicago: Bonus Books, Inc. 1992.

Index

Photo Credits

Allsport: 63, 102; ©Al Bello: 91, 96–97, 101 bottom, 142–143, 146, 148, 152; ©Stephen Dunn: 144; ©John Gichigi: 108; ©Jed Jacobsohn: 136, 137, 140, 149, 150; ©Vincent Laforet: 153; ©Ken Levine: 129; ©Steve Powell: 70; ©Eliot Schechler: 138, 140–141; ©Holly Stein: 68-69, 98, 132-133

AP Wide World Photos: 6–7, 12, 13, 14–15, 21, 34–35, 36–37, 43, 48, 56–57, 58, 60–61, 64, 66–67, 72, 76, 79, 82, 87, 88, 92–93, 94, 105, 119, 122–123, 127, 147

Archive Photos: 17, 116; Reuters: ©Andy Clark: 55; ©Neal Lauron: 9 top, 17 top, 29 top, 95, 101 top, 117 top, 139 top; ©R. Marsh Starks: 28

Brown Brothers: 27

Corbis: Corbis-Bettman: 10–11, 16, 20, 24-25, 29 bottom, 50, 50–51, 59, 62, 65, 71, 72–73, 75, 80, 104, 109, 121, 124–125, Reuters: 77; UPI/Corbis-Bettmann: endpapers, 8, 9 bottom, 37, 38, 39, 47, 53, 74, 83, 84, 107, 117 bottom, 118, 126

FPG International: 100

©Will Hart: 85, 90, 99, 111, 112, 114, 130, 131 top, 131 bottom, 135, 139 bottom, 144-145, 151

Icon Sports Media: ©Robert Beck: 2; ©John McDonough: 81

New York Public Library: 26 bottom; Cranger Collection: 18

Photofest: 5, 22, 23, 26 top, 31, 32, 33, 40–41, 44–45, 46, 49, 52, 89

"WHERE U BOT THE HAT"